Educational Psychology

Educational Psychology

John W. Santrock

UNIVERSITY OF TEXAS AT DALLAS

McGraw Hill

Boston   Burr Ridge, IL   Dubuque, IA   Madison, WI   New York   San Francisco   St. Louis
Bangkok   Bogotá   Caracus   Lisbon   London   Madrid
Mexico City   Milan   New Delhi   Seoul   Singapore   Sydney   Taipei   Toronto

McGraw-Hill Higher Education

A Division of The McGraw-Hill Companies

EDUCATIONAL PSYCHOLOGY

Published by McGraw-Hill, an imprint of The McGraw-Hill Companies, Inc., 1221 Avenue of the Americas, New York, NY 10020. Copyright © 2001 by The McGraw-Hill Companies, Inc. All rights reserved. No part of this publication may be reproduced or distributed in any form or by any means, or stored in a database or retrieval system, without the prior written consent of The McGraw-Hill Companies, Inc., including, but not limited to, in any network or other electronic storage or transmission, or broadcast for distance learning.

Some ancillaries, including electronic and print components, may not be available to customers outside the United States.

This book is printed on acid-free paper.

1 2 3 4 5 6 7 8 9 0 VNH/VNH 0 9 8 7 6 5 4 3 2 1 0

ISBN 0–07–290636–7
ISBN 0–07–118008–7 (ISE)

Vice president and editor-in-chief: *Thalia Dorwick*
Editorial director: *Jane E. Vaicunas*
Executive editor: *Joseph Terry*
Developmental editors: *Mindy De Palma/Susan Kunchandy*
Editorial coordinator: *Barbara Santoro*
Senior marketing manager: *Daniel M. Loch*
Media technology project manager: *Sean Crowley*
Senior project manager: *Marilyn Rothenberger*
Senior production supervisor: *Sandra Hahn*
Coordinator of freelance design: *Michelle D. Whitaker*
Freelance cover/interior designer: *Diane Beasley*
Cover images: Left and right images ©*SuperStock, Inc.;*
Middle image ©*Charles Thatcher/Tony Stone Images*
Senior photo research coordinator: *Carrie K. Burger*
Photo research: *LouAnn K. Wilson*
Senior supplement coordinator: *David A. Welsh*
Compositor: *Electronic Publishing Services, Inc., TN*
Typeface: *10.5/12 Minion*
Printer: *Von Hoffmann Press, Inc.*

The credits section for this book begins on page C–1 and is considered an extension of the copyright page.

Library of Congress Cataloging-in-Publication Data

Santrock, John W.
    Educational psychology / John W. Santrock. — 1st ed.
      p.   cm.
    Includes index.
    ISBN 0–07–290636–7
     1. Educational psychology. 2. Learning, Psychology of. 3. Motivation in education. I. Title.

LB1051 .S262   2001
370.15—dc21
                                                      99–057758
                                                     CIP

International Edition   ISBN 0–07–118008–7
Copyright © 2001. Exclusive rights by McGraw-Hill Companies, Inc., for manufacture and export. This book cannot be re-exported from the country to which it is sold by McGraw-Hill. The International Edition in not available in North America.

www.mhhe.com

To Alan Venable:
For Caring So Much About
This Book and Improving
Children's Education

About the Author

John W. Santrock

John Santrock received his Ph.D. from the College of Education and
Human Development at the University of Minnesota. He taught at the
University of Charleston and the University of Georgia before joining
the faculty at the University of Texas at Dallas. He has worked as a
school psychologist and currently teaches educational psychology at
both the undergraduate and graduate levels. John's grandmother taught
all grades in a one-room school for many years and his father was
superintendent of a large school district. John's research has included
publications in the *Journal of Educational Psychology* that focus on the
contextual aspects of affectively-toned cognition and children's self-
regulatory behavior as well as teachers' perceptions of children from
divorced families. He recently was a member of the editorial board of
Developmental Psychology and his publications include these leading
McGraw-Hill texts: *Child Developmeant (9th Ed.), Adolescence (8th Ed.),
Life-Span Development (7th Ed.), and Psychology (6th Ed.)*

*John Santrock, teaching in his undergraduate educational psychology
class, in which he makes good use of small group discussion.*

Brief Contents

Contents

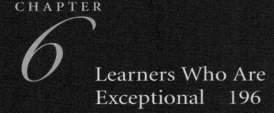

CHAPTER

6

Learners Who Are
Exceptional   196

CHAPTER

7

Behavioral Approaches, Social Cognitive Approaches, and Teaching   236

CHAPTER

8

The Cognitive Information-Processing Approach and Teaching   272

CHAPTER

12 Managing the Classroom   428

CHAPTER

13 Standardized Tests and Teaching   464

CHAPTER

14

Assessing Students,
Learning 494

Epilogue 532

To the Instructor

When McGraw-Hill invited me to write this book, I felt that I was coming home. As the son of a teacher and a school administrator, as a former school psychologist, as a developmental psychologist, and as a parent and grandparent deeply concerned about the education of our nation's children, I was fascinated and awed at the prospect of doing the book. Although I had conducted educational psychology research and written several texts on developmental and general psychology, I had never before been offered the opportunity to explore so comprehensively what psychology can contribute to classroom teaching and children's learning.

But I was cautious in undertaking such a project. I called my former graduate school officemate at Minnesota, Steven Yussen, who is now dean of the School of Education and Human Development at Minnesota, and got his input. I immersed myself in the educational psychology literature for several months, scanning and reading books and research journals. My enthusiasm for the project began to grow as I read about some of the truly innovative efforts that are beginning to take shape in educating children.

But I still was not ready to do the book. I knew that I could not create the educational psychology text I wanted unless I had an outstanding support team of content and teaching experts in the field. I also knew that the book I wanted to create needed an outstanding package of ancillary materials, including the latest technology. With those elements in place, I began to construct the themes of the book, outline the chapters, and write the book's first words.

Why add another educational psychology text to the mix of books already available? My goal was to write a book with a fresh, innovative approach to the field that is engaging to read. The Santrock approach to educational psychology emphasizes important contemporary topics such as diversity, technology, and developmental issues woven together seamlessly with the field's traditional topics in a constructivist theme. The Santrock approach emphasizes the most up-to-date, cutting-edge research and educational programs, which benefited from the extraordinary input from research and teaching expert consultants. The Santrock approach also provides students with an engaging writing style and interactive pedagogical exercises that make the book more enjoyable and interesting. I have extensively explored pedagogical strategies with students. In the process of writing a new college success text (Santrock & Halonen, 1999), I gained new insight about what textbook pedagogy should be in the twenty-first century. *Educational Psychology* has an extremely effective student-friendly pedagogical system that includes self-assessments, concept maps, summary tables, and Adventures for the Mind boxes.

The many expert research and teaching consultants on the project endorsed the need for a new book, and many of them concurred that we accomplished the goal of producing a book that truly is a fresh, innovative approach to the field. Comments by several of these consultants provide insight about what is unique about the Santrock approach in *Educational Psychology:*

"This truly does present a fresh look at educational psychology. I sincerely enjoyed reading these chapters—a statement I rarely have had the opportunity to make about a manuscript! It is well written, concise, and contemporary. John Santrock does an excellent job of organizing and weaving many of the traditional concepts/principles/theories into the text's constructivist theme. Comparing the Santrock text to many other texts would be like comparing apples and oranges. I believe that students and instructors alike will prefer this new author's version of educational psychology. The pedagogical and user-friendly features are excellent strategies."

> Kathryn Linden
> Purdue University

"Compared to other educational psychology books I have read, John Santrock's text is a giant step in the right direction. The text covers cutting-edge topics, such as diversity, constructivism, and technology, clearly, concisely, and comprehensively—far exceeding the competition. The emphasis on constructivist learning and teaching is excellent. The author's use of expert consultants is exceptional. It is exciting to see an author embrace the whole of educational psychology by addressing research, practice, and the interface between them."

> Peter Doolittle
> Virginia Tech University

"John Santrock's text is excellent! The attention to research is most commendable. Certainly it is better than most texts. The style of writing is superb. It flows smoothly and maintains interest with examples blended with research information. Even my husband commented about how many hours I spent reviewing this text. The hours slipped by as the reading was comfortable and the content engaging."

> Jan Hayes
> Memphis State University

"The material in John Santrock's text is relevant, up-to-date, and engaging. The discussion of constructivism text is well done. . . . I also think there is a lot of good practical material in the text (especially the teaching stories and practical tips for teachers)."

> Steven Yussen
> University of Minnesota

The Themes of Successful Learning

Following are some key themes in educating children that are emphasized throughout the text. These themes also appear in the American Psychological Association's learner-centered psychological principles.

- *Successful learners are active, reflective thinkers who construct their understanding.* Children's learning benefits when they actively construct meaning from information and experiences, taking personal responsibility as the architects of their learning. Children's minds are not like empty vessels into which knowledge should be poured. Learning works best when it is active, not passive.
- *Successful learners develop positive learning strategies and effectively monitor their learning.* Children learn best when they can create and effectively use a range of thinking and reasoning strategies. Children's learning outcomes improve when teachers guide them in developing and applying these strategies. Children also learn best when they engage in self-regulatory learning, monitoring their learning and adapting their strategies to fit the learning context.
- *Successful learners are motivated to learn.* Motivation is a critical aspect of learning. Children's learning benefits enormously when they want to learn rather than when they are made to learn. Teachers can help children learn by providing them with environments that stimulate curiosity and effort. Children also are motivated to learn when they perceive that the learning task is relevant.
- *Successful learners are goal directed.* Children's learning benefits when they set appropriate goals, plan how to reach the goals, and monitor their progress toward the goals. Teachers can help children by serving as a resource for setting short-term and long-term goals, developing the best strategies for reaching these goals, and monitoring goal-directed progress.
- *Successful learners have teachers who adapt their instruction to the developmental levels of the learners.* We made a special effort in this book to include examples from children in grades K–12 and where appropriate to address how teaching might need to be adapted depending on the age of the learner.
- *Successful learners have teachers who pay attention to individual differences in learning.* Although children share many commonalities, each child is unique. Outstanding teachers don't just pay lip service in individual variations in learners, they give them serious consideration and incorporate them into effective teaching.
- *Successful learners have teachers who understand the contexts play important roles in learning.* Contexts are the settings in which learning takes place. Learning does not occur in a vacuum, and the diverse contexts in which children live are important to consider in understanding how they learn. Such contexts include the culture in which children live, their ethnic background, poverty, and historical changes such as the technology revolution.

- *Successful learners have teachers who set appropriately challenging standards and recognize that effectively assessing learners is an integral dimension of the learning process.* Learning works best when teachers have appropriately challenging standards and expect children to learn. Effectively assessing learning at all stages of the learning helps teachers evaluate learners' progress toward learning goals.

Content

A comprehensive contemporary educational psychology text cannot be written on the strength of any one author's knowledge and experience. To solve this problem, I asked a number of leading research experts in many areas of educational psychology to serve as expert consultants for the book. I also asked a number of individuals who teach educational psychology on a regular basis to serve as consultants for the book.

Expert Research Consultants   An expert research consultant was assigned to each chapter of the book. In addition, several expert research consultants evaluated themes throughout the book, such as ethnicity/culture, gender, early childhood education, elementary education, and secondary education. They provided me with input about how to shape each of the chapters, reviewed drafts of the chapters, and looked at the final version of the chapters, as well as the book as a whole. A photograph and brief description of each of the expert research consultants is shown in the Expert Review section.

The expert research consultants, many of whom are among the world's leading figures in educational psychology, made *Educational Psychology* a far more accurate, up-to-date portrayal of children's education than I could have by myself.

Expert Teaching Consultants   Some, but not all, of the expert research consultants teach educational psychology on a regular basis in addition to their research agendas. To ensure that *Educational Psychology* has the most desirable research content and qualities for teaching students, a second team of expert consultants was enlisted. The expert teaching consultants was enlisted. The expert teaching consultants are all master teachers who have a successful history of teaching educational psychology. They went over what I wrote with a fine-tooth comb, especially advising me about ways to make the content more student-friendly. A photograph and brief description of each of the expert teaching consultants is shown in the Expert Review section.

Examples of the Research Content   Educational psychology is a changing field with many new exciting projects emerging every year. This book is a very contemporary treatment of the field. For example, more than 400 citations in the book are from 1998, 1999, 2000, and in-press sources.

Following are some of the content highlights in each chapter.

CHAPTER 1 Educational Psychology: A Tool for Effective Teaching

The legacies of William James and John Dewey in contemporary educational psychology

Ethnic minorities and females in the history of educational psychology

The complex, fast-paced nature of teaching

Effective teaching

National Educational Technology Standards (NETS)

Why research is important in educational psychology

Research methods, including the teacher-as-researcher

Research challenges

"I think this is an excellent introductory chapter. The section on research and how to connect it with practice is very good. I especially like the focus on using research to inform teaching."

Dale Schunk
Purdue University

"The section on effective teaching contains a wealth of information and the research section is great."

Rona Dillon
Southern Illinois University–Carbondale

CHAPTER 2 Physical and Cognitive Development

A model school health program: Heart Smart

The vulnerability of early-maturing girls

Components of successful programs for preventing or reducing adolescent problems

Thorough coverage of Piagetian contributions and criticisms

Piagetian and Vyotskian classrooms

A developmental model of reading

Recent recommendations for working with linguistically and culturally diverse children in the classroom

"The treatment of Piaget and Vyotsky is wonderful. The scaffolding, teaching, and educational applications are excellent! The additional focus on adolescence in this chapter is a plus."

Sheryl Cohn
Borough of Manhattan City College

"This is very fine chapter. The author's knowledge of human development clearly comes through. The 'teaching strategies' for Piaget's and Vygotsky's theories are quite good. The language development section offers good information and addresses some practical literacy issues."

James Applefield
University of North Carolina–Wilmington

CHAPTER 3 Social Contexts and Socioemotional Development

Bronfenbrenner's ecological theory and its educational applications

Hetherington's recent research on atmospheres in divorced families and schools

Epstein's latest recommendations for improving school-family linkages

Peer statuses and recent research on rejected children

Strategies for improving students' social skills

Substantial coverage of developmentally appropriate education

The Reggio Emilia approach

Extensive coverage of what makes a successful middle school

Research-based strategies for improving students' self-esteem

Gilligan's most recent ideas focusing on early adolescence as a critical juncture in girls' development

Alice Honig's recent recommendations for improving students' prosocial behavior

Thorough coverage of variations in moral education

The most recent information about service learning, including contemporary research

Emotional intelligence and examples of educational programs that promote it

How to help students cope effectively

"Education students rarely get much developmental work on children's lives and this text should help them in the crucial area of understanding the socioemotional development of children. I loved the section on applying Erikson's theory to the educator's own development! The section on effective schools for adolescents is good. The section on service learning is wonderful. Excellent that Goleman's work on emotional intelligence is presented for the teacher."

Alice Honig
Syracuse University

"This is a strong chapter with lots of good material. There are many good sections in this chapter relevant to adolescence, such as Erikson's stages, Kohlberg's stages, and adolescent problems. This schools section is very nice."

Allan Wigfield
University of Maryland

CHAPTER 4 Individual Variations

Sternberg's most recent applications of his triarchic theory to education

Includes Gardner's eighth type of intelligence (naturalist) and the most recent applications of his view to education, including Project Spectrum and the Key School

A very up-to-date discussion of the nature/nurture issue in intelligence

Extensive coverage of creativity, including Gardner's, Amabile's, and Czikszentmihalyi's ideas

How teachers can be creative role models for students

Extensive information about learning and thinking styles, especially Sternberg's recently developed self-governance framework

Very recent information about trends in temperament (which styles are being researched the most today) and personality (the "big five factors")

Recently developed educational applications involving students' temperament

∞ *"I like the subject matter covered in Chapter 4 and applaud the emphasis on Sternberg's and Gardner's ideas. The applications of their ideas to education is excellent. The self-assessments in this chapter are just superb!"*

O. Suthern Sims
Mercer University

∞ *"I like the discussion of controversial issues in intelligence. I also like the inclusion of personality and temperament, which are not discussed in many educational psychology texts."*

Rita McKenzie
Northern Arizona University

 CHAPTER 5 Sociocultural Diversity

Marian Wright Edelman's ideas

McLoyd's overview of recent trends in antipoverty programs

The Quantum Opportunities program, a mentoring program for students in poverty

Extensive coverage of multicultural education and how to help students improve relations with ethnically diverse others

The Global Lab and other technology connections with students around the world

Very contemporary treatment of gender

Emphasis on gender in context

Discussion of controversy over gender similarities and differences

Extensive information about gender in schools, including up-to-date ideas about teacher-student interaction, curriculum and content, sexual harassment, and reducing gender bias

∞ *"This is a breakthrough chapter in educational psychology texts. For, perhaps, the first time an educational psychology text has addressed the concepts of race, class, culture, and gender adequately and in a manner that will facilitate student learning and understanding."*

Peter Doolittle
Virginia Tech University

∞ *"A strength of the chapters in Santrock's text is the currency of research and authorities cited; such is the case with this chapter. The coverage of culture and diversity is excellent and up-to-date. The section on multicultural education also is excellent and up-to-date. The entire chapter is presented in an interesting, attractive manner. Its content is at the very heart of teaching-learning in our time."*

William Franzen
University of Missouri–St. Louis

 CHAPTER 6 Learners Who Are Exceptional

Recent information about the diversity of children with a disability

Teaching strategies with children who have hearing impairments

Teaching strategies with children who have mental retardation

Teaching strategies with children who have receptive and expressive language disorders

Up-to-date coverage of learning disabilities, including intervention strategies

Contemporary discussion of ADHD, including teaching strategies

Emotional and behavioral disorders, including teaching strategies

Recent ideas from Ellen Winner about children who are gifted and their education

High-potential minority students

Educational issues involving children with disabilities, including very up-to-date coverage of legal aspects, placements and services, parents, and technology

∞ *"This is a terrific chapter. If students only get one chapter of exposure to children who are exceptional, this would be the chapter."*

James Applefield
University of North Carolina–Wilmington

∞ *"This is a well-written chapter. Santrock discusses each disability concisely, then provides sound teaching strategies. I also like the inclusion of gifted education."*

Rita McKenzie
Northern Arizona University

 CHAPTER 7 Behavioral Approaches, Social Cognitive Approaches, and Teaching

Overview of behavioral and cognitive approaches to learning

Educational applications of classical conditioning

Extensive coverage of applied behavior analysis in education

How to use prompts

Alberto and Trautman's hierarchy of strategies for decreasing students' undesirable behaviors

Bandura's most recent reciprocal determinism model

Educational applications of observational learning

Ethnic minority role models and mentors

Cognitive behavior approaches and self-regulation

Using computer simulations to help students learn

Self-instructional methods

Self-regulatory learning, including Winne's and Zimmerman's ideas

∞ *"This is a superb chapter that held my interest from the beginning (and I have read many books on these topics over my many years as a faculty member—and a student myself). John Santrock has added some 'pizazz' to the traditional topics of classical conditioning, operant conditioning, and observational learning. He has interwoven all of the most important personal, cognitive, and cultural factors in learning throughout the chapter. Perhaps that is why I like his presentation so much."*

Kathryn Linden
Purdue University

> "The teaching strategies offer good general suggestions and are well-linked to the chapter's content. The self-assessment, diversity, and technology materials in this chapter are excellent. I especially like the inclusion of social cognitive theory and self-regulation together. The writing style is clear and there was a good selection of topics included."
>
> Dale Schunk
> Purdue University

CHAPTER 8 The Cognitive Information-Processing Approach and Teaching

Overview of the cognitive information-processing approach

Robert Siegler's model of information processing

Emphasis on strategies

Teaching strategies for helping children pay attention

Baddeley's contemporary model of working memory

Extensive coverage of memory and study strategies, including note-taking strategies

How teachers can help students learn concepts

Steps in problem solving, including the final step of rethinking and redefining problems and solutions over time

Obstacles to problem solving, including becoming fixated, having certain biases, not being motivated, and not persisting

Extensive coverage of problem-based learning

In-depth presentation of the Vanderbilt Cognition and Technology Group's Jasper Project

Detailed explanation of how to help students become better problem solvers and thinkers

The Promised Land Learning Community, a technology and education project designed to foster interdisciplinary learning related to diversity

How to teach students for positive transfer of information

Contemporary coverage of metacognition, including strategies for using metacognition in the classroom

> "John Santrock chose great quotes throughout the book, but especially in this chapter. The information on helping students become better thinkers and problem solvers is excellent. The author has done a fine job of encouraging future teachers to provide learning activities that encourage students to investigate and dig for information on their own rather than simply hand over the information on a silver platter."
>
> Karen Paciorek
> Eastern Michigan University

> "This is a strong chapter. I am most impressed with John Santrock's treatment of the information processing approach. This chapter will help to distinguish this book from others in the field."
>
> O. Suthern Sims
> Mercer University

CHAPTER 9 Social Constructivist Approaches, Domain-Specific Approaches, and Teaching

What it means to take a social constructivist approach to teaching, including an overview of constructivist variations

Situated cognition

Rogoff's ideas about scaffolding and cognitive apprenticeship

Extensive coverage of tutoring, including adult-child and child-child tutoring

The Valued Youth Program, a tutoring program that aims to improve the skills of both tutors and students being tutored

Detailed explanations of how to use peer tutoring in the classroom

Up-to-date discussion of cooperative learning variations

Extensive coverage of structuring small-group work, including how to build team skills

In-depth presentation of two innovative social constructivist programs: Brown and Campione's Fostering a Community of Learners and the Schools for Thought program

Bereiter and Scardamalia's Computer Supported Intentional Learning Environments (CSILE)

Cognitive constructivist and social constructivist approaches to reading and writing

Technology programs for improving students' phonological awareness and decoding skills

The social context of writing

Numerous writing exercises teachers can have students engage in

Innovative math curriculum projects at the elementary, middle school, and secondary school levels

Technology and math instruction

Contemporary approaches to teaching science, including Stanford University's middle school life sciences curriculum (HUMBIO)

> "This chapter is a definite strength. The types of programs presented are especially appropriate because they have a definite history. I found this chapter mirrored the way I teach this content with little exception. The text refers back nicely to previous chapters' information. This chapter is a true asset to the text. Much better presentation than comparable texts."
>
> Rayne Dennison
> Penn State University

> "The sections on constructivism are excellent. The number of examples make the material student friendly. The entire section on teachers and peers as joint contributors to students' learning is excellent. The section on cooperative learning is very good. The section on domain specific constructivist approaches is wonderfully constructed and would benefit any reader. The section on evaluating constructivist approaches is great. This is an excellent chapter."
>
> Peter Doolittle
> Virginia Tech University

CHAPTER 10 Planning, Instruction, and Technology

Ideas for organized instructional and lesson planning

Teacher-centered lesson planning and instruction

Stevenson and Stigler's recent research on cross-cultural comparisions in learning mathematics

Teaching strategies for lecturing

Teaching strategies for effective use of questions

Very recent research on the effectiveness of homework at different grade levels

The APA's most recent learner-centered planning and instruction principles

Essential questions

Discovery learning

Integrating the curriculum

The technology revolution

Different types of technology

Educational Internet sites and using the Internet in the classroom

Technology and sociocultural diversity

Teaching strategies for choosing and using technology in the classroom

∽ *"This chapter is definitely a winner (especially compared to other texts on this topic). I like the discussion of technology and education, providing excellent guidelines for using educational technology in the classroom. The sections on games, simulations, CD-ROMS, and Internet use as teaching tools will be of great value to students."*

Tony Williams
Marshall University

∽ *"The topics are well organized and right on target. Santrock's discussion of Learner-Centered Planning and Instruction is simply great! I like the inclusion of problem-based learning and discovery learning in this section. The Technology and Education section is perfect! The author's handling of technology throughout this book is major strength compared to other educational psychology texts. Santrock has included the best technology approaches for helping students learn."*

Kathryn Linden
Purdue University

CHAPTER 11 Motivating Students to Learn

Terry Fox's poignant story of motivation

Teaching strategies for self-determination and choice

Csikszentmihalyi's ideas on achievement and teaching strategies for helping students achieve flow

Developmental changes in achievement motivation

Strategies for helping students change their attributions

Mastery motivation versus helpless and performance orientations

Bandura and Schunk's ideas on self-efficacy

Goal setting, planning, and self-monitoring

Teaching strategies for helping students manage their time

Social motives and social relationships

Sociocultural contexts and motivation

Motivating hard-to-reach, low-achieving students

∽ *"Excellent presentation! This chapter includes all the major perspectives concerning motivation, its definition, and principal components. The research documentation associated with various aspects of motivation is impressively current. The manner in which the content of this chapter is presented should lead students to experience what Csikszentmihalyi calls 'flow.'"*

William Franzen
University of Missouri–St. Louis

∽ *"I think John Santrock's choice of topics in this chapter is excellent. Good work! The content is accurate. The pedagogical aids definitely will be appreciated by students and should foster their learning. I like this text's inclusions of self-assessments. The references are current and the research topics timely."*

Dale Schunk
Purdue University

CHAPTER 12 Managing the Classroom

Management issues in elementary and secondary schools

Getting off to the right start

Emphasis on instruction and creating a positive classroom environment

Teaching strategies for designing the classroom's physical environment

Baumrind's strategies adapted to classroom management

Teaching strategies for establishing classroom rules

How to get students to cooperate without having to resort to discipline to maintain order

Extensive coverage of how to deal with various problem behaviors

Up-to-date discussion of handling aggression

Teaching strategies for reducing bullying

The latest classroom and school-based programs for dealing with problem behaviors (such as programs developed by Weissburg, the Johnsons, and Evertson and Harris)

Teaching strategies for conflict resolution

Developing good speaking and listening skills

How to be assertive and help you students be assertive

∽ *"The material is presented clearly and succinctly, has a proactive stance toward classroom management, and is up to date. I like the inclusion of information about elementary and secondary classrooms. John Santrock has made a concerted effort to address students' needs in his book. The Teaching Strategies sections provide concrete applications of principles presented in the chapter and allow for elaboration of various concepts."*

Mary Burbank
University of Utah

∽ *"This is an outstanding chapter. Very sound sections on Creating a Positive Environment for Learning and on Dealing with Problem Behaviors. The sections on Designing the Physical Environment of the Classroom and on Being a Good Communicator are especially good and thorough, far better than what other texts do on these topics."*

James Applefield
University of North Carolina–Wilmington

CHAPTER 13 Standardized Tests and Teaching

Solid, basic coverage of the nature of standardized tests

Criteria for evaluating a standardized test

Comparison of aptitude and achievement tests

Types of standardized tests

District-, state-, and nationally mandated tests

The teacher's role in standardized testing, including how to prepare students, how to administer tests, and how to communicate test results to parents

Issues in standardized testing, including a comparison of standardized tests and alternate assessments

> *"This chapter offers clear and concise descriptions about the nature of standardized aptitude and achievement tests. Crisp, straightforward suggestions and cautions about standardized tests are presented as are the conflicting issues surrounding these instruments."*
>
> **William Franzen**
> **University of Missouri–St. Louis**

> *"I like the overall discussion of tests. There is good balance of information about elementary and secondary schools. Excellent discussion of the teacher's role in testing. The presentation of statistics is good."*
>
> **Alan Wigfield**
> **University of Maryland**

CHAPTER 14 Assessing Students' Learning

Emphasis on assessment as an integral part of teaching and learning

Discussion of assessment in terms of preinstruction, during instruction, and postinstruction

How to create high-quality assessments

Culturally responsive strategies for assessing students

Current trends in assessment

How to construct different types of test items, including true/false, multiple-choice, matching, short-answer, and essay

Alternative assessments, including authentic assessment, performance-based assessment, and portfolio assessment

Grading, including its purposes and some contemporary issues

The role of computers in assessment

> *"An outstanding chapter! It is a totally 'withit' chapter. The sections on Alternative Assessments, Grading and Reporting Performance, and Computers and Assessment contain material that is absolutely first-rate in presentation of the state-of-the-art information on such topics as authentic assessment, portfolio- and performance-based assessments, electronic portfolios, and so on. The tone of the freshness of the material is set early in the chapter with the attractively presented content within the framework of The Classroom as an Assessment Context and the inclusion of such inserts as Diversity and Education. In sum, first-rate content and presentation of that content!"*
>
> **William Franzen**
> **University of Missouri–St. Louis**

> *"This chapter does a much better job of stressing integration of assessment and instruction than I have seen in other texts. John Santrock has done a good job of covering recent trends in classroom assessment. The teaching strategies for different types of selected-response items are very good. The material on electronic portfolios goes beyond what is found in other texts."*
>
> **James McMillan**
> **Virginia Commonwealth University**

Epilogue   I believe that at the end of a book it is helpful for students to be encouraged to look back and reflect on what they have read and learned. Too often a class or a book ends with the last topic of a main content chapter, in this case Assessing Students' Learning. I believe students benefit from a synthesis of the book's main themes and a take-home message when they have completed the main chapters. To that end, I wrote an epilogue titled "Looking Back, Looking Forward" that summarizes the book's main ideas and motivates teachers to look forward to the extremely important task of educating the nation's children.

Pedagogy and Student-Friendliness

It simply is not enough for an educational psychology text to have solid content. It also has to be pedagogically sound and student-friendly. I have explored alternative ways of presenting ideas and continue to ask college students of varying ages and ability levels to give me feedback on which strategies are the most effective. As a result of these efforts, I developed the following pedagogical and student-friendly features for *Educational Psychology*.

Clear, Logical Writing with Abundant Examples of Concepts   In writing this book, I always tried to keep one main theme in mind: write more to the *student* than to the *instructor*. I strived to communicate complex ideas clearly without stripping them of their meaning. When I introduced a concept, I tried to provide a clear, interesting example of it.

> *"In my opinion, John Santrock is the most effective textbook writer in the field of psychology in the country. He is a master textbook craftsman. My students rave about his books. Reviewing his proposed book,* Educational Psychology, *has been a pleasure. Specifically, the chapter features are outstanding."*
>
> **O. Suthern Sims**
> **Mercer University**

> *"I am extremely impressed with the author's manner of expression and clarity, and with the teaching possibilities for this text. John Santrock has done a fantastic job with the concept presentations."*
>
> **Judith Stechly**
> **West Liberty State College**

> *"This book is fantastic in how it presents information to the student. John Santrock provides clear examples of specific strategies that teachers can implement."*
>
> **Karen Paciorek**
> **Eastern Michigan University**

Preview, Organizational, and Summary Features An educational psychology text needs to be well organized and must include helpful summaries of what has been written. Each chapter begins with a *Preview* and *chapter outline* in cognitive map form. They provide information about the chapter's main topics and themes. Three to six times in each chapter, main sections of the text are introduced with *mini cognitive maps*, advance organizers that visually present the organization of forthcoming material. Each chapter also has three to six *Summary Tables*, which have been a highly popular feature in my texts. They provide students with another form of hierarchical review before they get to the end-of-chapter review. To ensure continuity, the headings in the summary tables match the heading in the corresponding mini cognitive map. The *Overview* at the end of the chapter includes a further brief summary and a cognitive map to help students visualize the chapter's main topics. Also at the end of each chapter, the *Educational Psychology Checklist* asks students to review their understanding of the chapter's contents.

Key Terms The *key terms* are boldfaced in the text, and their definition follows in italic. They also are listed and page-referenced at the end of each chapter, and defined once again in the *Glossary*.

Cross-Linkages This system, unique to this educational psychology text, refers students to the primary discussion of key concepts. A specific page reference appears with a backward-pointing arrow each time a key concept appears in a chapter subsequent to its initial coverage. Cross-linkages provide students with connections between chapters and a more integrated view of educational psychology.

The Real Worlds of Teachers and Students An educational psychology text needs to include many real-world examples of life in the classroom. To this end, we asked a large panel of expert classroom teachers from a wide geographical mix that is representative of urban, suburban, and rural schools, and a wide range of grades, to provide observations, comments, and stories. Many of these contributors are award-winning teachers, and they have greatly enriched the book with their expertise. Their material is included in the following features:

- *Teaching Stories.* These are high-interest, chapter-opening vignettes about effective teaching related to the chapter's content.
- *Through the Eyes of Teachers.* At various places in every chapter, these boxes profile teachers' observations on a relevant topic.
- *Through the Eyes of Children.* These boxes, which appear throughout each of the chapters, provide insights into students' worlds and how they view themselves, their teachers, and the educational process.

"The Teaching Stories add an important quality of authenticity to the text, as do the Through the Eyes of Teachers and Through the Eyes of Children inserts."

James Applefield
University of North Carolina–Wilmington

Self-Assessments Good teachers are self-aware and competent at evaluating themselves. To encourage this self-awareness and self-evaluation, each chapter has one or more *Self-Assessment* boxes. For example, in chapter 3, "Social Contexts and Socioemotional Development," future teachers examine their emotional intelligence, and in chapter 4, "Individual Variations," they explore their effectiveness at inspiring students' creativity. The self-assessments can be powerful tools for helping teachers understand themselves and become better teachers.

"The Summary Tables and Self-Assessments are superb pedagogical features."

Peter Doolittle
Virginia Tech University

Quotations and Adventures for the Mind At the beginning of each chapter, as well as throughout each chapter, quotations also are inserted to stimulate students' thinking. For example, consider Christa McAuliffe's "I touch the future. I teach" (opening chapter 1) and William James' "Knit each new thing onto some acquisition already there" (chapter 8 in the discussion of memory strategies). At the end of each chapter, a section called *Adventures for the Mind* has four critical thinking exercises that are designed to stretch students' thinking about chapter topics.

"I very much like the quotations throughout the book."

James Applefield
University of North Carolina–Wilmington

Diversity and Education Helping future teachers understand diversity and transmit this understanding to students is an important educational agenda. To this end, chapter 5, "Sociocultural Diversity" focuses on this topic. Diversity discussions also are woven throughout the text. In addition, each chapter includes one or more *Diversity and Education* boxes. For example, in chapter 3, "Social Contexts and Socioemotional Development," one of these boxes focuses on Madeline Cartwright, a principal who made a difference in North Philadelphia, and in chapter 5, another box describes the Quantum Opportunities Program, which provides support in technology and science for ethnic minority girls.

"The coverage of topics has depth and has excellent features such as Self-Assessments, Technology boxes, Diversity boxes, and concept maps."

Peggy Perkins
University of Nevada–Las Vegas

Technology Another major challenge is to educate students for the technological world in which they will live and work. To this end, like diversity, information about technology is woven throughout the book, is extensively focused on in a single chapter (chapter 10, "Planning, Instruction, and Technology"), and is presented in one or more boxes in each chapter. *Technology and Education* boxes include "Creative Experiences with Computers: Picasso, Edison, da Vinci, Art, Music, and Spatial Ability" (in chapter 4, "Individual Variations") and "Scientists in Action and Young Children's Literacy," a discussion of the Jasper Project (in chapter 8, "The Cognitive Information-Processing Approach and Teaching").

The topic of technology also is extensively interwoven with content in every chapter through connections to the Santrock *Educational Psychology* website. Approximately 15 to 30 times in each chapter, Internet icons in the margins signal students that they can extend their knowledge and thinking about a topic by going to the Santrock website, which will then connect them to other websites with relevant information about the topic.

> *"The inclusion of diversity and technology is excellent. It is clear that John Santrock really thought through the writing of this text. As I reviewed the book, I made a summary sheet to include its strengths and weaknesses. Guess what? The list to include weaknesses does not exist."*
>
> **Judith Stechly**
> **West Liberty State College**

The Visual Program   An educational psychology textbook needs to be visually appealing to students. I spent considerable time working with the designer and artist in selecting the layout, presentation, and color palette for this book. I carefully selected each artpiece and photograph. As I wrote each photograph legend, I kept in mind how it could expand the student's learning. Each chapter also has a number of cartoons, because we know that students learn best when they are in a good mood.

> *"John Santrock's text compares favorably with other educational psychology texts. This is true of content, layout of materials, and readability. It is especially true in the area of technology."*
>
> **Tony Williams**
> **Marshall University**

Case Studies   A number of case studies that focus on educational psychology issues involving teaching and learning appear on a CD-ROM that is shrinkwrapped with the book. These case studies enable students to think critically about how to solve problems and issues that emerge in educational settings. The topics of the case studies include dealing with individual variations in students, identifying children with learning disabilities, collaborative learning, reaching poorly motivated students, a new teacher who struggles with managing the classroom, dealing with angry parents, and many more.

Class-Testing and Student Focus Groups

This book was class-tested by two instructors in different educational psychology classes before it was published, and a student focus group was convened to provide feedback about the book. Author John Santrock class-tested the book in his undergraduate educational psychology at the University of Texas at Dallas, and Peter Doolittle class-tested the book in his educational psychology class at Virginia Tech. Students were overwhelmingly supportive of the book and provided helpful ideas about improving the content and pedagogy. John Santrock taught the educational psychology class during the summer to 35 students; approximately half of these were experienced classroom teachers coming back to college for recertification, and the other half were prospective teachers. Several of their comments reveal their enthusiasm for our efforts:

> *"I teach in the inner city and this book is a great resource for me. I loved the book. The activities are great and the focus on technology and diversity was extremely useful. Honestly, this course and book by John Santrock are about all I need to learn to be an effective teacher. I am really enriched by the course."*
>
> **Greg Hill**
> **History Teacher and Football Coach**
> **Carter High School**

> *"John Santrock's book and course provided tremendous insight into 'how to be a very effective teacher.' I had been in the business world but decided I wanted to contribute more to children's lives. I'm now in my first year of teaching eighth-grade math. I am using many of the ideas in the educational psychology text in my teaching and they are working great!"*
>
> **Richard Harvell**
> **Eighth-Grade Math Teacher**
> **Renner Middle School**

> *"The book provides a good overview for beginning and practicing teachers. I loved the teaching stories. I took this class after teaching for one year, a year that was not a good experience. John Santrock's book and course have changed my approach to teaching and I am now incredibly enthusiastic about teaching once again."*
>
> **Marcie Welch**
> **Science Teacher**
> **Sarah Zumwalt Middle School**

> *"I thought the book was great. It was very understandable and readable. I was impressed by the way that the information was given in ways that I could understand."*
>
> **Beth Pumpelly**
> **Ninth-/Tenth-Grade English Instructor**
> **Adamson High School**

> *"I loved the book! Its layout was well organized and structured. Its style was clear, precise. and understandable. The web sites were well selected and very helpful."*
>
> **Jennifer Holliman-McCarthy**
> **English Literature Teacher**
> **St. Thomas Acquinas High School**

Acknowledgments

I am deeply indebted to many people who helped to create this extensive project. My editor Joseph Terry shared my vision for doing everything possible to make this book special. Alan Venable virtually became a co-author on this book, so extensive was his involvement in the development of the book and its ancillary materials. Mindy DePalma competently orchestrated many other aspects of the project. I also want to thank Marilyn Rothenberger (Project Manager), Michelle Whittaker (Design Coordinator), and Wendy Nelson (Copy Editor) for their outstanding production work.

On the pages xxv–xxviii, the numerous expert consultants for the book are profiled. They clearly made this book's content far superior to what it would have been without their input. Likewise, the following individuals who teach educational psychology gave me extensive feedback before the first word of the book was written, on different drafts, and when the project was completed. Their efforts are sincerely appreciated and they immensely improved this book.

College Professors
Randy Brown, *University of Central Oklahoma*
Gordon Eisenmann, *Augusta State University*
Vicky Farrow, *Lamar University*
Rita McKenzie, *Northern Arizona University*
Ann Pace, *University of Missouri*
Judith Stechly, *West Liberty State, WV*

In addition, a large panel of individuals who teach at the early childhood, elementary school, middle school, and high school levels provided me with material about special teaching moments they have experienced. These are outstanding teachers, many of whom have received local, regional, or national teaching awards. I owe them a great deal of thanks for sharing the real worlds of their teaching experiences.

Santrock: Educational Psychology Panel of Early Childhood, Elementary, Middle, and High School Teachers
Karen Abra, *School of the Sacred Heart,* San Francisco, CA
Mrs. Lou Aronson, *Devils Lake High School,* Devils Lake, ND
Daniel Arnoux, *Lauderhill Middle Community School,* Broward, FL
Lynn Ayres, *East Middle School,* Ypsilanti, MI
Fay Bartley, *Bright Horizon Children Center,* Bronx, NY
Barbara M. Berry, *Ypsilanti High School,* Ypsilanti, MI
Kristin Blackenship, *Salem Church Elementary,* Midlothian, VA
Andrea Fenton, *Cortez High School,* Glendale Union, AZ
Kathy Fuchser, *Sr. Francis High School,* Humphrey, NE
Lawren Giles, *Baechtel Grove Middle School,* Willits, CA
Jerri Hall, *Miller Magnet Middle School,* Bibb County, GA
Anita Marie Hitchcock, *Holley Navarre Primary,* Santa Rosa Schools, FL
Laura Johnson-Brickford, *Nordhoff High School,* Ojai, CA
Juanita Kerton, *Gramercy School/New York League for Early Learning:* New York, NY
Robynne Kirkpatrick, *Northwest Middle School,* Salt Lake City, UT
Chaille Lazar, *Hedgcoxe Elementary,* Plano, TX

Adriane Lonzarich, *Heartwood,* San Mateo, CA
Margaret Longworth, *St. Lucie West Middle School,* St. Lucie, FL
Chuck Rawls, *Appling Middle School,* Bibb County, GA
Verna Brown Rollins, *West Middle School,* Ypsilanti, MI
Donna L. Shelhorse, *Short Pump Middle School,* Henrico County, VA
Jason Stanley, *Syracuse Dunbar Avoca,* Syracuse, NE
Vicky Stone, *Cammack Middle School,* Huntington, WV
Tamela Varney, *Central City Elementary,* Cabell County, WV
Marlene Wendler, *St. Paul's Lutheran School,* New Ulm, MN
William Willford, *Perry Middle School,* Perry, GA
Susan Youngblood, *Weaver Middle School,* Bibb County, GA

Special thanks also go to Ronna Dillon, for her excellent work in developing the instructor's manual, to Edward Wolfe and Carol Annette Liguori Wolfe for writing superb items for the test bank, and to Peter Doolittle, Virginia Tech, for his creative and technical skills in constructing the items for the Taking It to the Net feature at the end of each chapter and for class-testing the book in his educational psychology class.

Ancillaries

Instructor's Manual by Ronna Dillon
For each chapter, this flexible planner features teaching suggestions, learning objectives, extended chapter outline, lecture/discussion suggestions, video and film recommendations, classroom activity tips, and handout forms. It also includes lecture and activity ideas on technology and diversity issues as well as a Controversy section that highlights a provocative perspective on the chapter topic.

Test Bank by Edward Wolfe and Carol Annette Liguori Wolfe
This test bank includes almost 1000 questions, specifically related to the main text, consisting of multiple choice, stem questions, short answer questions, critical thinking questions, essay questions, and assessments.

Computerized Test Bank (for both Windows and Mac)
This computerized test bank contains all of the questions in the print version and is available in both Macintosh and Windows platforms.

Overhead Transparencies
Hundreds of full-color acetates packaged in a three-ring binder serve as a wonderful teaching tool.

Case Studies CD-ROM
Includes over 30 cases, 2-4 per chapter, of varying grade levels from preschool to high school, followed by critical thinking exercises that tie together the content of the CD and the text. Packaged *free* with each copy of the text.

Presentation Manager CD-ROM
Includes the contents of the Instructor's Manual, Test Bank, and PowerPoint® slides. The Presentation Manager provides an easy-to-use interface for the design and delivery of multimedia classroom presentations.

Student Study Guide by Ronna Dillon

An excellent resource for student review and self-testing with questions, learning objectives, chapter outlines, a Linking "Theory to Practice" section that focuses on technology, diversity issues, and critical thinking for each chapter.

The Educational Psychology Video

This video consists of over 90 minutes of a wide range of diverse classroom footage, interviews, and discussions that dramatically illustrate teaching techniques and principles of educational psychology at all levels, as well as innovative programs and projects in the field of educational psychology.

Website and Online Learning Center

Coming soon! The *Educational Psychology* Website will feature a variety of instructor and student resources including an Online Learning Center with key terms, quizzes, chapter overviews, learning objectives, PowerPoint® Slides, Internet connections, and more.

PageOut™

In just a few minutes, even the most novice computer user can have a professionally designed course website. Simply fill in a series of templates with your information or with content from the Santrock, *Educational Psychology* websitee and Online Learning Center, click on a design, and you've got the perfect website for your course.

Dr. James Applefield is a Professor of Education at the University of North Carolina at Wilmington, where he teaches courses in educational psychology, instructional design, and human development. He is actively involved in promoting the development of preservice teachers through field observations and by stimulating reflective practices. His interests include teacher thinking, student motivation, and the application of instructional design to teacher planning. He earned his Ph.D. in educational psychology at Georgia State University.

Dr. Elizabeth C. Arch is Coordinator of the Undergraduate/Post-Baccalaureate Teacher Education Program in the School of Education at Pacific University, Forest Grove, Oregon. She earned a B.S. in biology from Stanford University, an M.A.T. from the University of Chicago, and a Ph.D. in foundations of education from the University of Southern California. Her areas of special interest are self-efficacy, assessment, and the application of psychological theories to the classroom.

Dr. Mary D. Burbank is a Clinical Instructor in the Department of Education Studies at the University of Utah. Her primary responsibilities include teacher of education for those certifying in secondary education and Director of Program Evaluation. Her teaching and research interests include teacher research, professional development for inservice teachers, and theory-to-practice linkages.

Dr. Sheryl Needle Cohn was formerly an Assistant Professor in the Department of Social Science at the Borough of Manhattan Community College, City University of New York, where she served as Faculty Consultant to the College Board of New York and ETS of New Jersey. She is currently living in Orlando and teaching at the University of Central Florida. Dr. Cohn holds dual degrees in psychology and education, specializing in early childhood development and education, and educational psychology. While completing her doctorate, she taught undergraduate and graduate courses in psychology at Montclair State University in New Jersey. Dr. Cohn has written a book and several articles on a variety of educational topics and serves on a panel for the National Association for the Education of Young Children in Washington, D.C.

Dr. Carlos F. Diaz is a Professor of Education at Florida Atlantic University, Boca Raton, Florida, where he received his Ed.D., Ed.S. and M.Ed. in curriculum and instruction. He was formerly an Associate Professor of Education in the Department of Educational Foundations and Technology, and currently he is Project Director for the Master of Education in Cultural Foundations with E.S.O.L. Endorsement program. He has also been a Visiting Professor at the Center for Multicultural Education, University of Washington, Seattle. Dr. Diaz has authored several books, chapters, and articles, and he has received numerous honors and awards, such as the Teaching Incentive Program Award (1996), the University Award for Excellence in Undergraduate Teaching (1996), Professor of the Year (1993), the 2000 Notable American Men award (1992), and recognition in *Who's Who Among Hispanic Americans, Rising Young Americans, and American Education.*

Dr. Peter Doolittle is an Assistant Professor in the Department of Teaching and Learning at Virginia Polytechnic Institute and State University in Blacksburg, Virginia. His vocational background includes 12 years teaching students from 4th grade through graduate school, in public schools and private schools, across several subject areas including mathematics, computer science, statistics, and educational psychology. He is the recipient of the Phi Delta Kappa Innovative Teacher Award for his work in constructing interactive educational psychology web sites and has been nominated for a Certificate of Teaching Excellence at Virginia Tech. Currently, his professional focus involves synthesizing cognitivism, constructivism, and complexity theory within a framework that integrates educational theory and practice.

Dr. William L. Franzen received his Ph.D. from the University of Wisconsin and has taught at New York University and the University of Toledo. He currently is Professor of Educational Psychology and Dean Emeritus in the College of Education, University of Missouri-St. Louis. His areas of interest include: learning, motivation, development, and cognition. He has provided numerous presentations and consultations to professional and lay groups, teachers, administrators in local and regional communities on innovative educational practices, and on recurring challenges and issues in education. He has served on local school boards of education for more than a decade and as Director on the Missouri School Boards Association.

Dr. Susan Goldman is a professor of psychology at Vanderbilt University, where she also is Co-Director of the Learning Technology Center. She obtained her Ph.D. at the University of Pittsburgh. Dr. Goldman currently is Vice-President of the AERA division (C) on Learning and Instruction and is President of the Society for Text and Discourse. She has published numerous articles and chapters on technology and learning. Her research interests focus on the psychological processes involved in understanding and learning from text, discourse, and integrated media. This work examines learning from single and multiple sources, including electronic environments such as hypertext and communal electronic forums. She is especially interested in the strategies necessary for flexible and adaptive learning. She explores these strategies in individuals who work alone or in small groups in various content areas such as literature, science, social sciences and mathematics. Recently, this research has been situated in the naturally occurring learning contexts of classrooms. Dr. Goldman currently serves on the editorial boards of five educational psychology research journals, including *Educational Psychology Review* and *Learning and Instruction.*

Dr. Algea Harrison is a leading expert in the area of ethnic minority children and families and Professor of Psychology at Oakland University, Rochester, Michigan. She received her Ph.D. from the University of Michigan and has been a visiting professor and scholar at the University of Zimbabwe, the Free University of Amsterdam, and Nanjing University in the People's Republic of China. Dr. Harrison's research interests center on perceptions and behaviors of adolescents and working women that emerge from cultural contexts of development. The conceptual framework for her work is to illustrate the interaction between ethnicity and environment and its impact on social cognition, which subsequently has implications for developmental outcomes. She has been collaborating with international colleagues in a series of cross-cultural studies of adolescents' perceptions of support from their social networks. Dr. Harrison has published in leading journals and authored numerous book chapters.

Dr. Jan Hayes is a Professor in the Department of Educational Leadership in the School of Education at Middle Tennessee State University, Murfreesboro, Tennessee. Professor Hayes holds the Doctorate of Arts in teaching from Middle Tennessee State University. She is interested in effective delivery in teaching and has three times won the Outstanding Teacher Award along with the Distinguished Higher Education Teacher Award in Tennessee. She has published three books on building positive attitudes in school-age students, the most recent being *Attitude, Attitude, Attitude: A Notebook of Activities for Improving Student Attitudes Toward Learning for Grades K–3* (Millennium III Learning, 1997).

Dr. Alice S. Honig is an Emerita Professor in the Department of Child and Family Studies in the College for Human Development. She attended Cornell University and received a B.A. (magna cum laude) from Barnard College, an M.A. from Columbia University, and a Ph.D. at Syracuse University. For 12 years, Professor Honig was on the research staff of the Syracuse University Children's Center and Family Development Research Program. As Program Director, Dr. Honig trained testers to assess the children's progress, worked actively with teachers and with paraprofessional home visitors to program living and learning experiences for young children, and helped in the selection of evaluation measures and design. Dr. Honig has published a number of books, articles, and selected chapters.

Dr. Kathryn W. Linden earned her Ph.D. from Purdue University, where she was Professor of Educational Psychology until her retirement in 1998, when she was named Professor Emerita. For many years she was in charge of the large multidivisional undergraduate educational psychology course that was based on a cooperative learning model she developed in 1972 with two colleagues. She also taught graduate courses in assessment and research methodology. Her special interest in classroom assessment procedures is reflected in the design of two personal computer programs that she has used for reporting group and individual test results in all of her courses. She has authored and co-authored several books, including, most recently, *Cooperative Learning and Problem Solving, 2nd edition* (Waveland Press, 1996). She also published numerous research articles and presented many papers at national and international professional meetings.

Dr. Richard E. Mayer is a Professor of Psychology at the University of California, Santa Barbara (UCSB), where he has served since 1975. He received a Ph.D. in psychology from the University of Michigan in 1973 and served as a Visiting Assistant Professor of Psychology at Indiana University from 1973 to 1975. His research interests are in educational and cognitive psychology. His current research involves the intersection of cognition, instruction, and technology, with a special focus on multimedia learning, involving how people learn from visual and verbal presentations. In the past he has been president of the Division of Educational Psychology of the American Psychological Association, editor of the *Education Psychologist* and *Instructional Science,* and chair of the UCSB Department of Psychology, and he is the year 2000 recipient of the E. L. Thorndike Award for career achievement in educational psychology. Dr. Mayer is on the editorial boards of 12 journals, mainly in educational psychology, and is the author of 12 books and more than 200 articles and chapters, including *The Promise of Educational Psychology* (1999) and *Multimedia Learning* (forthcoming).

Dr. James H. McMillan is Professor of Educational Studies at Virginia Commonwealth University in Richmond, and Director of the Metropolitan Educational Research Consortium. He is author of *Classroom Assessment: Principles and Practice for Effective Teaching, 2nd Edition, Basic Assessment Concepts for Teachers and Principles,* and has also written books in educational psychology and educational research. Some of his publications include articles in *Educational* *Measurement: Issues and Practice, Educational Horizons, Educational and Psychological Measurement,* the *Journal of Educational Psychology,* and the *American Educational Research Journal.* Dr. McMillan currently is investigating the relationship between classroom assessment and grading practices, and teacher decision-making about assessment. For the past several years he has been active in Virginia's new state testing and accountability program, as well as service-learning opportunities for public school students.

Dr. Karen Menke Paciorek has a Ph.D. in early childhood education from Peabody College of Vanderbilt University. She is a Professor of Early Childhood Education at Eastern Michigan University in Ypsilanti, and she has served as president of the Michigan Association for the Education of Young Children. Dr. Paciorek is the editor of *Annual Editions: Early Childhood Education* and *Sources: Notable Selections in Early Childhood Education* published by Dushkin/McGraw-Hill.

Dr. Nan Bernstein Ratner received her Ed.D. from Boston University in applied psycholinguistics in 1982 and is an Associate Professor and Chairman, Department of Hearing and Speech Sciences at the University of Maryland, College Park. With Jean Berko Gleason, she is the co-author of *Psycholinguistics, 2nd Edition.* Professor Ratner's research has focused on normal language acquisition and communicative disorders in young children. Her inter- ests lie primarily in language acquisition, the role of input in language learning, stuttering, and parent-child interaction. She has taught courses in introductory psycholinguistics, fluency disorders, and articulation and phonological disorders, and seminars in speech-language pathology including readings in fluency disturbance, readings in language acquisition, and cross-linguistic analysis of children's language development. Professor Ratner has also worked on numerous books, volumes, and selected book chapters and articles.

Dr. Gilbert Sax received his B.A. and M.A. degrees from the University of California at Los Angeles and his Ph.D. in educational psychology from the University of Southern California in 1958. He taught at the University of Hawaii from 1958 to 1966 and at the University of Washington from 1966 to 1994. He is the author of two textbooks, one in educational research methods and one in educational and psychological measurement.

Dr. Dale Schunk received his Ph.D. from Stanford University and has been head of the Department of Educational Studies at Purdue University since 1993. He is one of the world's leading researchers in the applications of social cognitive theory and motivation to educational settings. He is the author of numerous books and research articles in these areas and recently was President of Division 15 (Educational Psychology) of the American Psychological Association.

Dr. O. Suthern Sims, Jr., has been Professor of Developmental and Educational Psychology in the School of Education at Mercer University since 1986. He was President and Professor of Psychology and Education at Tift College from 1984 to 1986. Dr. Sims was Vice President for Academic Affairs and Dean and Professor of Psychology, Education and Human Services at Wingate University prior to his tenure at Tift. He also served in administrative and faculty positions at the University of Georgia. Dr. Sims is listed in numerous *Who's Who* publications and is a member of several social, civic, and academic organizations, including the American Psychological Association and Phi Kappa Phi. In the past 36 years, he has presented more than 25 papers at professional meetings and authored or co-authored more than 60 monographs and articles.

Dr. David Wendler earned his Ph.D. in educational psychology from the University of Minnesota and is a professor of Education at Martin Luther College, New Ulm, Minnesota. Dr. Wendler has contributed articles to journals such as *Reading Research Quarterly, Lutheran* *Educator,* and *The Whole Idea.* His interests include reading comprehension, intelligence, and memory. He is currently serving as Vice President of the Southwest Minnesota Reading Association and as Chair of the Education Division at Martin Luther College.

Dr. Allan Wigfield is Professor of Human Development at the University of Maryland, College Park. He received his Ph.D. from the University of Illinois. His research focuses on the development and socialization of children's motivation and self-concepts. He also is interested in gender difference in motivation and self-concept. He holds several honors and awards, including the 1992 American Educational Research Association Human Development Research Award, for his work on how the transition to junior high school influences adolescents' motivation. Dr. Wigfield has published numerous journal articles and book chapters on his research, and has co-edited one book and four special issues of journals. He serves on the editorial board of 8 leading journals in developmental and educational psychology.

Dr. Tony L. Williams is Professor of Education and Chair of the Division of Education and Leadership at Marshall University, Huntington, West Virginia. Dr. Williams holds a doctorate in education and educational psychology from West Virginia University. He is a veteran educator, having taught in the public schools of New Jersey, Virginia, and West Virginia as well as having served as a professor at Marshall University for over 20 years. His research and publication interests are in the areas of health and physical development.

Dr. Steven Yussen is currently the Dean of the College of Education and Human Development at the University of Minnesota in the Twin Cities, where he is also a Professor in the Institute of Child Development. Previously, he served as Dean of the College of Education at the University of Iowa (1991–1998), where he was also a Professor of Educational Psychology and Psychology. From 1972–1991, he was a faculty member in the Department of Educational Psychology at the University of Wisconsin and served as chairperson there. His Ph.D. is from the University of Minnesota. Steve's research has focused on cognitive development, memory development, metacognition, and reading. It has led to more than 50 scholarly research articles, book chapters, and edited books, and has earned him such recognition as a Spencer Fellowship, a Guggenheim Fellowship, Fellow status in two divisions of the American Psychological Association (divisions 7-developmental and 13-educational), and service on a number of journal editorial boards including a term as associate editor of Child Development. He is especially proud of the 19 doctoral students he trained at Wisconsin and Iowa, and the more than 60 faculty he had a hand in appointing and promoting at the three universities where he has worked.

Dr. Frank Adams, *Wayne State College*
Dr. Robert R. Ayres, *Western Oregon University*
Professor Roger Briscoe, *Indiana University of Pennsylvania*
Professor Kay Bull, *Oklahoma State University*
Dr. Rayne Sperling Dennison, *Penn State*
Professor Ronna Dillon, *Southern Illinois University*
Dr. David Dungan, *Emporia State University*
Professor Sharon McNeely, *Northeastern Illinois University*
Dr. Peggy Perkins, *University of Nevada, Las Vegas*
Professor Ann K. Wilson, *Buena Vista University*
Dr. Peter Young, *Southern Oregon University*

To the Student

At the beginning of each chapter, you will read a preview and examine an overall cognitive map of the chapter's contents, and read a section called "Teaching Stories."

BEGINNING OF CHAPTER

Preview
A brief look at what the chapter is about, including a series of questions that will explored.

Teaching Stories
This features compelling, high-interest descriptions of teacher-student interaction, classrooms, and educational issues related to the chapter content.

Chapter Outlines
Shows the organization of topics by heading levels.

Mini-Cognitive Map
These mini-maps appear three to five times per chapter and provide students with a more detailed, visual look at the organization of the chapter.

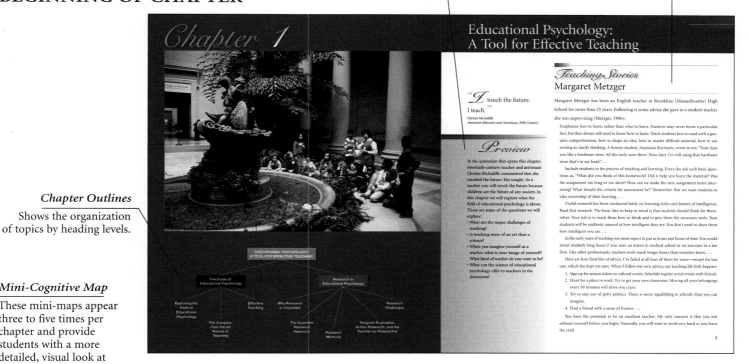

WITHIN CHAPTER

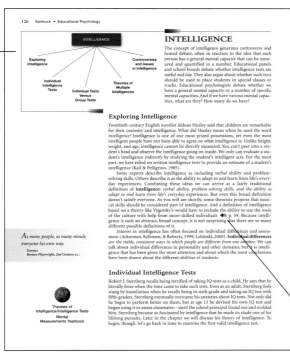

Diversity and Education
This feature appears throughout the chapters to help students understand important issues related to culture, gender, and ethnicity in today's classroom.

Cross-Linkage
This is a system exclusive to this text that refers students back to the main discussion of all key concepts each time they are later introduced in the text. This provides a more integrated learning experience and serves as an excellent study aid.

The within-chapter features include mini-cognitive maps, key terms, Internet icons, cross-linkages, and summary tables, as well as Self-Assessment, Through the Eyes of Teachers, Through the Eyes of Students, Teaching Strategies, quotations, Diversity and Education, and Technology and Education.

Summary Tables

These within-the-chapter reviews are coordinated with, and have the same headings as, the within-the-chapter cognitive maps. They give students a handle on information before they reach the end of the chapter.

Teaching Strategies

This feature provides clear, practical examples of specific strategies that teachers can use in the classroom.

Through the Eyes of Children

This feature provides stimulating student observations into real student's lives and how they view themselves, their teachers, and the educational process.

Through the Eyes of Teachers

This feature presents motivating, revealing comments on relevant topics from expert classroom teachers and award-winning educators.

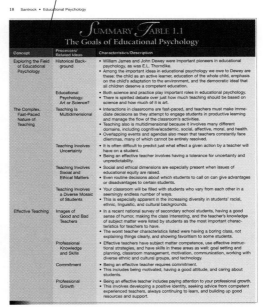

Self-Assessment

This is a powerful tool that helps future teachers evaluate and understand themselves in the effort of becoming better, more self-aware teachers. It appears several times a chapter and includes a series of key reflective questions related to the topics under discussion.

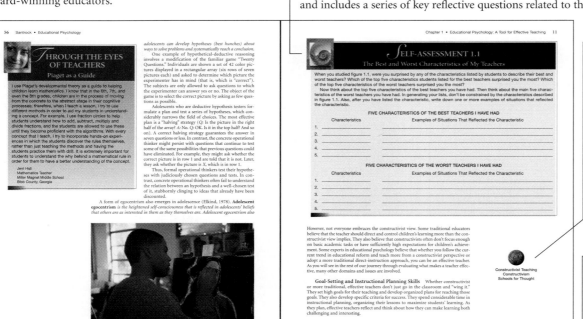

Chapter Web Links

A website icon appearing in the margin next to content guides students to the *Educational Psychology* Website where they will find connecting internet links that provide them with additional information. The label for each Web icon corresponds to the same label on the Santrock Educational Psychology website.

Critical Thinking Questions

Many of the photos are now accompanied by critical thinking questions, designed to encourage students to think more thoroughly about topics and apply the material to their own lives.

At the end of each chapter you will find a chapter review, a list of key terms, an Educational Psychology Checklist, Adventures for the Mind, Taking It to the Net, and Case Studies.

Chapter Reviews

This is featured at the end of each chapter providing a brief summary and a cognitive map of the chapter's contents.

END OF CHAPTER

Technology and Education

This boxed feature found in every chapter highlights important issues related to the impact of technology and how it can be used as a creative teaching tool. Topics related to technology are also featured in a special chapter (chapter 10) and discussed throughout the text.

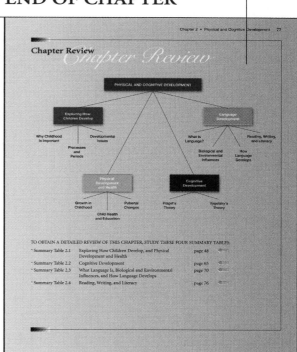

Key Terms

These terms appear boldfaced and defined in the text, as well as in the page-referenced glossary.

Educational Psychology Checklist

This feature provides students with a brief list of key concepts to check off at the end of each chapter.

Adventures for the Mind

This features a series of critical thinking exercises in educational psychology designed to help students set goals, carry out plans, and think creatively and reflectively about each chapter's content.

Taking It to the Net

Students are presented with questions to explore on the internet, related to the chapter. From the *Educational Psychology* Website under Taking it to the Net, students will find links to other websites providing information that will help them to think more deeply about the questions posed.

Case Studies

This free CD-ROM is wrapped with each copy of the text and contains critical thinking exercises that tie together each chapter's content with two to four cases.

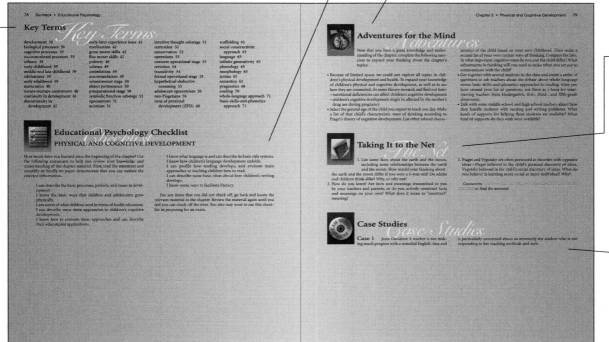

Online Learning Center

MULTIMEDIA

ABOUT THE BOOK

- **Table of Contents**
  Lists the entire TOC.

- **Overview**
  Provides a quick synopsis of the edition and the material covered.

- **Supplements**
  Includes title and ISBN information for all accompanying student and instructor supplements.

- **Meet the Author**
  Have questions or comments concerning the text? Email the author John Santrock.

Welcome to the Santrock:
Educational Psychology
Website!

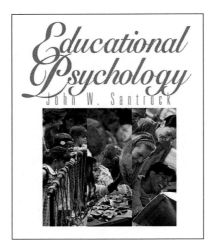

INSTRUCTOR'S RESOURCES

- **Instructor's Manual**
  Click here to see a web version of the IM

- **PageOut Image Bank**
  The McGraw-Hill Introductory Psychology Image Bank provides instructors with over 150 images form which to choose.

STUDENT'S RESOURCES

- **Online Learning Center**
  Links to every text chapter containing learning objectives, quizzes, crossword puzzles, and more!

- **Internet Primer**
  Links to McGraw-Hill Internet Guide providing students with valuable information on Internet navigation.

- **Careers Appendix**
  Links to a list of resources for students interested in a career in psychology.

- **Statistics Primer**
  Provides a quick overview of statistics.

- **Web Resources**
  Links to an extensive range of interesting and useful psychology sites that are keyed to web icons and labels in the text.

Educational Psychology

Chapter 1

EDUCATIONAL PSYCHOLOGY:
A TOOL FOR EFFECTIVE TEACHING

The Goals of
Educational Psychology

Research in
Educational Psychology

Exploring the
Field of
Educational
Psychology

Effective
Teaching

Why Research
is Important

Research
Challenges

The Complex,
Fast-Paced
Nature of
Teaching

The Scientific
Research
Approach

Research
Methods

Program Evaluation,
Action Research, and the
Teacher-as-Researcher

Educational Psychology: A Tool for Effective Teaching

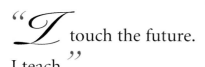

> "*I* touch the future.
> I teach."

Christa McAuliffe
American Educator and Astronaut, 20th Century

Preview

In the quotation that opens this chapter, twentieth-century teacher and astronaut Christa McAuliffe commented that she touched the future. She taught. As a teacher you will touch the future because children are the future of any society. In this chapter we will explore what the field of educational psychology is about. These are some of the questions we will explore:

- What are the major challenges of teaching?
- Is teaching more of an art than a science?
- When you imagine yourself as a teacher, what is your image of yourself? What kind of teacher do you want to be?
- What can the science of educational psychology offer to teachers in the classroom?

Teaching Stories

Margaret Metzger

Margaret Metzger has been an English teacher at Brookline (Massachusetts) High School for more than 25 years. Following is some advice she gave to a student teacher she was supervising (Metzger, 1996):

Emphasize *how* to learn, rather than *what* to learn. Students may never know a particular fact, but they always will need to know how to learn. Teach students how to read with a genuine comprehension, how to shape an idea, how to master difficult material, how to use writing to clarify thinking. A former student, Anastasia Korniaris, wrote to me, "Your class was like a hardware store. All the tools were there. Years later I'm still using that hardware store that's in my head.". . .

Include students in the process of teaching and learning. Every day ask such basic questions as, "What did you think of this homework? Did it help you learn the material? Was the assignment too long or too short? How can we make the next assignment more interesting? What should the criteria for assessment be?" Remember that we want students to take ownership of their learning. . . .

Useful research has been conducted lately on learning styles and frames of intelligence. Read that research. The basic idea to keep in mind is that students should think for themselves. Your job is to teach them how to think and to give them the necessary tools. Your students will be endlessly amazed at how intelligent they are. You don't need to show them how intelligent you are. . . .

In the early years of teaching you must expect to put in hours and hours of time. You would invest similarly long hours if you were an intern in medical school or an associate in a law firm. Like other professionals, teachers work much longer hours than outsiders know. . . .

Here are four final bits of advice. I've failed at all four of them for years—except the last one, which has kept me sane. When I follow my own advice, my teaching life feels happier:

1. Sign up for season tickets to cultural events. Schedule regular social events with friends.
2. Hunt for a place to work. Try to get your own classroom. Moving all your belongings every 50 minutes will drive you crazy.
3. Try to stay out of petty politics. There is more squabbling in schools than you can imagine.
4. Find a friend with a sense of humor. . . .

You have the potential to be an excellent teacher. My only concern is that you not exhaust yourself before you begin. Naturally, you will want to work very hard as you learn the craft.

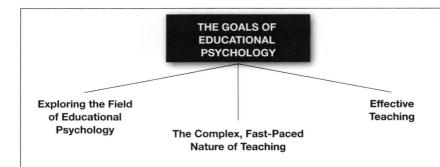

THE GOALS OF
EDUCATIONAL
PSYCHOLOGY

Exploring the Field
of Educational
Psychology

The Complex, Fast-Paced
Nature of Teaching

Effective
Teaching

The Goals of Educational Psychology

Educational psychology is a vast landscape that will take us an entire book to describe. In this introduction we will explore what the field of educational psychology is about, examine the complex, fast-paced nature of teaching, and consider what is involved in being an effective teacher.

Exploring the Field of Educational Psychology

First, let's examine the historical background of educational psychology and discuss whether it is an art or a science.

Historical Background   The field of educational psychology was founded by several pioneers in psychology just before the start of the twentieth century. One of those pioneers was William James (1842–1910). Soon after launching the first psychology textbook, *Principles of Psychology* (1890), he gave a series of lectures called *Talks to Teachers* (James, 1899/1993) in which he discussed the applications of psychology to educating children. James argued that laboratory psychology experiments often can't tell us how to effectively teach children. He argued for the importance of observing teaching and learning in classrooms for improving education. One of his recommendations was to start lessons at a point just beyond the child's level of knowledge and understanding, in order to stretch the child's mind.

A second major figure in shaping the field of educational psychology was John Dewey (1859–1952), who became a driving force in the practical application of psychology. Dewey established the first major educational psychology laboratory in the United States, at the University of Chicago in 1894. Later, at Columbia University, his innovative ideas continued.

**William James
John Dewey**

We owe many important ideas to John Dewey. First, we owe to him the view of the child as an active learner. Before Dewey it was believed that children should sit quietly in their seats and passively learn in a rote manner. In contrast, Dewey believed that children learn best by doing. Second, we owe to Dewey the idea that education should focus on the whole child and emphasize the child's adaptation to the environment. Dewey believed that children should not be just narrowly educated in academic topics but should learn how to think and adapt to a world outside school. He especially thought that children should learn how to be reflective problem solvers. Third, we owe to Dewey the belief that all children deserve to have a competent education. This democratic ideal was not in place at the beginning of Dewey's career in the latter part of the nineteenth century, when education was reserved for a small portion of children, many of whom were boys from wealthy families. Dewey was one of the influential psychologist-educators who pushed for a competent education for all children—girls and boys, as well as children from different socioeconomic and ethnic groups.

Another pioneer was E. L. Thorndike (1874–1949), who initiated an emphasis on assessment and measurement and promoted the scientific underpinnings of learning.

William James   *John Dewey*

James and Dewey created and shaped the field of educational psychology. Many of their ideas are still embodied in current views of how children should be educated.

DIVERSITY AND EDUCATION
Ethnic Minorities and Females in the Early History of Educational Psychology

The most prominent figures in the early history of educational psychology, like in most disciplines, were mainly White males, individuals like William James, John Dewey, and E. L. Thorndike. Prior to changes in civil rights laws and policies in the 1960s, only a few dedicated non-White individuals managed to obtain the necessary degrees and break through the barriers of racial exclusion to take up academic research in the field (Banks, 1998).

Two pioneering African American psychologists were Mamie and Kenneth Clark, who conducted research on African American children's self-conceptions and identity (Clark & Clark, 1939). In 1971, Kenneth Clark became the first African American president of the American Psychological Association. In 1932, Latino psychologist George Sanchez conducted research showing that intelligence tests were culturally biased against ethnic minority children.

In recent decades, there has been growing recognition of the rights and needs of ethnic minorities in higher education. The civil rights movement stimulated educational psychologists—especially those from ethnic minority groups—to reexamine the existing body of knowledge and understanding about children's learning and education, questioning its relevance for ethnic minority children. This questioning has formed the basis for new areas of inquiry, focusing on populations who previously were omitted from subject pools of educational psychology research and from the theoretical ideas of mainstream educational psychology.

We need more qualified educational psychologists from ethnic minority backgrounds. We also need more qualified ethnic minority teachers. Currently less than 15 percent of teachers are from African American and Latino backgrounds, for example, yet in some school districts, especially large urban districts, over 80 percent of students are from ethnic minority backgrounds.

As we mentioned earlier, the most prominently mentioned figures in shaping the field of educational psychology were both White and male. Like ethnic minorities, women also faced barriers in higher education. One often-overlooked person in the history of educational psychology is Leta Hollingworth. She was the first individual to use the term *gifted* to describe children who scored exceptionally high on intelligence tests (Hollingworth, 1916). She also played an early important role in criticizing theories that promoted the idea that males were superior to females (Hollingworth, 1914). For example, she conducted a research study refuting the myth that phases of the menstrual cycle are associated with a decline in females' academic performance.

George Sanchez   *Mamie and Kenneth Clark*   *Leta Hollingworth*

Thorndike argued that one of schooling's most important tasks is to hone children's reasoning skills, and he excelled at doing exacting scientific studies of teaching and learning (Beatty, 1998).

To read further about the history of educational psychology, see the Diversity and Education box, where you can read about ethnic minorities and females in the early history of educational psychology. Thorndike especially promoted the idea that educational psychology must have a scientific base. Next, we will explore the extent to which educational psychology is an art or a science.

Educational Psychology: Art or Science?

Educational psychology is the branch of psychology that specializes in understanding teaching and learning in educational settings. Both science and practice play important roles in educational psychology (Calfee, 1999; Shuell, 1996). The field draws its knowledge from theory and research in psychology, from theory and research more directly created and conducted by educational psychologists, and from the practical experiences of teachers. For example, the theories of Jean Piaget and Lev Vygotsky were not created in an effort to inform teachers about ways to educate children. Yet in chapter 2, "Physical and Cognitive Development," you will see that both of these theories have many applications that can guide your teaching. Other theorists and researchers in educational psychology have tied their activities more directly to learning and teaching in schools. For example, in chapter 11, "Motivating Students to Learn," you will read about Dale Schunk's (1999; Schunk & Ertmer, 2000) classroom-oriented research on self-efficacy (the belief that one can master a situation and produce positive outcomes). Educational psychologists also recognize that teaching sometimes must depart from scientific recipes, requiring improvisation and spontaneity (Gage, 1978).

There is spirited debate about how much teaching can be based on science versus how much of it is art. As a science, educational psychology's aim is to provide you with research knowledge that you can effectively apply to teaching situations. But scientific knowledge alone cannot inform you about all of the teaching situations that you will encounter, and this is where educational psychology is an art. You will need to make some important judgments in the classroom based on your personal skills and experiences as well as the accumulated wisdom of other teachers. As we see next, those judgments often take place in a classroom that is complex and fast-paced.

The Complex, Fast-Paced Nature of Teaching

Many new teachers report that teaching is more difficult than they envisioned. As one elementary school teacher reflected (Efron & Joseph, 1994):

> I didn't think it would be nearly as difficult as it was. I didn't realize the amount of preparation that was needed nor did I realize the amount of emotional stress that is involved in teaching. Never did I realize how emotionally involved you become with students.

Much of the difficulty of being a beginning teacher involves the complexity and fast pace of the classroom. Linda Anderson and her colleagues (1996) described three facets of this complex, fast-paced life of teaching: its multidimensionality, uncertainty, and social/ethical nature. Another complexity in teaching is the increasing diversity of students.

Teaching Is Multidimensional

One reality of teaching is that many events occur simultaneously and in rapid-fire succession (McMillan, 1997). Things happen quickly in the classroom. Researchers have found that a teacher can be involved in as many as 1,000 to 1,500 interactions with students each day (Billips & Rauth, 1987; Jackson, 1968). Amid these interactions, teachers must make immediate decisions to manage the flow of events and keep the time productive (Doyle, 1986).

Teaching also is multidimensional in that it involves many different domains. We often think of teaching in terms of academic or cognitive domains (emphasizing thinking and learning in subject

American Psychological
Association (APA)

The role of the teacher remains the highest calling of a free people. To the teacher, America trusts its most important resource: children.

Shirley Hufstedler,
American Government Official, 20th Century

"My mom told me to tell you that I am the educational challenge you were told about in college."

areas such as English, math, and science). However, teaching also involves social, affective, moral, and health domains, as well as many other aspects of students' lives. In school, students gain understanding and skills in academic subject areas. Also in school, they are socialized by and socialize others, learn or do not learn how to control their emotions, gain or do not gain a positive sense of moral values, and do or do not develop good health knowledge and skills. Thus, a teacher's agenda might consist of not only teaching academic subjects but also promoting socialization and personal development. Teaching involves helping students learn how to be self-reliant and monitor their own work, as well as learn to work cooperatively and productively with others.

Overlapping events and agendas mean that teachers constantly face dilemmas, not all of which can be resolved. And sometimes a decision that resolves one problem fails to address or even intensifies another problem. For example, teachers often must balance what is good for the individual against what is good for the group. A common challenge in the elementary school grades is the need to help one student develop better self-control while at the same time maintaining order and activity in the class as a whole.

Teaching Involves Uncertainty   In the hectic world of the classroom it is difficult to predict what effect a given action by the teacher will have on any particular student. Often teachers must make quick decisions that have uncertain outcomes and hope that they have made the best move for that moment. In this book we will extensively examine the best general principles you can use to instruct and motivate students, assess their learning, and manage the classroom. Although these principles will help you make classroom decisions, every situation you will encounter will in some way be new. Even the students in the same class change from day to day as the result of additional experiences together and intervening events.

Uncertainty and unpredictability also include the need to teach students in ways that teachers might not have been taught themselves. Current educational reform emphasizes the social contexts of learning, the use of portfolios, and conducting long-term projects (Arends, Winitzky, & Tannenbaum, 1998). Increasingly, the teacher's role is seen as being more like that of a guide who helps students construct their knowledge and understanding than that of a director who pours knowledge into students' minds and controls their behavior (Brown, 1997; Brown & Campione, 1996). In these respects many prospective teachers are being asked to teach in ways that are unfamiliar to them.

Teaching Involves Social and Ethical Matters   Earlier we mentioned that schools are settings in which considerable socialization takes place. The social and ethical dimensions of teaching include the question of educational equity. When teachers make decisions about routine matters such as which students to call on, how to call on them, what kinds of assignments to make, or how to group students for instruction, they can create advantages for some students and disadvantages for others. In some cases, they might unintentionally and unconsciously perpetuate injustices toward students from particular backgrounds. For example, in chapter 5, "Sociocultural Diversity," you will discover that, in general, teachers give boys more instruction, more time to answer a question, more hints at the correct answer, and

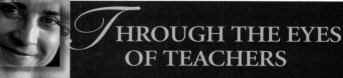

THROUGH THE EYES OF TEACHERS

Knowing About Infinity but Not Rocks

Try to imagine that your years of schooling with all of its theories are like a backpack that you carry, always at hand when needed. However, don't let it get so heavy that you can't be spontaneous and go where children want to take you.

I remember one occasion early in my teaching days when I overheard a 5-year-old say to his friends, "I understand about God, the universe, and infinity. What I don't understand is rocks!" Unfortunately, I was busy with the day's planned activities. I only smiled to myself and didn't ask him what he knew about God, the universe, and infinity, and what he did not know about rocks. Since then, I've learned that some of your best opportunities are spontaneous and can be enlightening to children and adults."

Adriane Lonzarich
Heartwood Preschool
San Mateo, California

more second attempts if they give the wrong answer, than they give to girls (Crawford & Unger, 2000; Sadker, Sadker, & Long, 1997). Why does this happen? How can it be countered? These are important practical questions.

Through the Eyes of Teachers
A Gift to Teach

It is up to each of us to find out what our talents are and to use them to the greatest extent possible to benefit others. My gift is to teach. I try as hard as possible to make a difference in the lives of children. One very important person in my life was Bea Walton, my fourth-grade teacher. She was one of those teachers who comes along once in a lifetime, grabs your heart and mind and hangs on. If we were studying the Battle of Horshoebend, then we were making whole armies of men, cannons, horses and acting it out. To us, we were there! Our days in her room seemed to end before they really got started. I was challenged to become that kind of teacher.

Anita Marie Hitchcock
Kindergarten Teacher
Holley Navarre Primary
Santa Rosa County, Florida

Teaching Involves a Diverse Mosaic of Students   Your classroom will be filled with students who differ in many ways. They will have different levels of intellectual ability, different personality profiles, different interests, varying motivation to learn, and different family, economic, religious, and cultural backgrounds. Students with disabilities and disorders are increasingly being taught in the regular classroom rather than in a separate, self-contained special education room (Walther-Thomas & others, 2000). How can you effectively teach this incredible mosaic of students?

You will want to reach all of your students and teach them in individualized ways that effectively meet their learning needs. Students' vast individual variations and diversity increase the classroom's complexity and contribute to the challenge of teaching. This diversity is especially apparent in the increasing number of students whose racial, ethnic, linguistic, and cultural backgrounds are quite different from those of Anglo students, to whom most American educational systems originally were addressed (Banks & Banks, 1997; Marshall, 1996; Morrison, 2000).

Effective Teaching

Because of the complexity of teaching and the individual variation among students, effective teaching is not like the "one-size-fits-all" sock (Diaz, 1997). Teachers must master a variety of perspectives and strategies, and be flexible in their application. This requires three key ingredients: (1) professional knowledge and skills, (2) commitment, and (3) professional growth. We will evaluate these three needs shortly, but to begin thinking about effective teaching let's explore students' images of good and bad teachers.

No one can be given an education. All you can give is the opportunity to learn.

Carolyn Warner
American Author, 20th Century

ERIC
Clearinghouse on Teaching and
Teacher Education
National Library of Education

Images of Good and Bad Teachers   You have had many teachers in your life, and soon you will be a teacher yourself. Spend a few moments thinking about the teachers you have had and your image of the teacher you want to be. Some of your teachers likely were outstanding and left you with a very positive image. Others probably were not so great. For example, at the beginning of the school year, one teacher makes it a practice to ask his ninth-grade students about their most memorable moments in school so far (Wigginton, 1985). One student wrote about a teacher who came to her house to see her project on birds and said that the teacher treated her like she was somebody special. Another student wrote about his fourth-grade teacher, who always screamed at him to be quiet; this child became so nervous he couldn't concentrate.

In a national survey of almost a thousand students 13 to 17 years of age, having a good sense of humor, making the class interesting, and the teacher's knowledge of the subject matter were the three characteristics students listed as the most important for teachers to have (NASSP, 1997). The characteristics that secondary school students most frequently attributed to their worst teachers were having a boring class, not explaining things clearly, and showing favoritism. These characteristics and others that reflect students' images of their best and the worst teachers are shown in figure 1.1.

TEACHING STRATEGIES
For the Complex, Fast-Paced Classroom

Some strategies for effective teaching in the complex, fast-paced classroom include:

1. *Recognize the importance of your expectations as a beginning teacher.* If you expect things to be simple and easy in the classroom, your expectations will be violated. Expect the classroom to be complex and fast-paced; expect to be challenged to think, adapt, and come up with effective solutions to problems you have not anticipated. With these more realistic expectations in mind, your early experiences as a teacher can be less stressful.
2. *Don't get too frustrated if you can't solve on the spot every problem or dilemma that crops up.* Sometimes it is necessary to move on. The problem might not be as major as you think and might even fix itself, or you can think about it after the school day or on the weekend when you have more time to evaluate how to solve it or adapt to it.
3. *Understand that teaching involves not only academic but also social and ethical worlds.* Good teachers recognize that children are multidimensional beings.
4. *Continually you will be reminded of how truly individual children are.* Do your best to meet their individual needs. Make it a major goal to know the individual, personal characteristics of your students.

Throughout this book we will provide you with many other strategies for effective teaching in your complex, fast-paced classroom. For example, in chapter 10, "Planning, Instruction, and Technology," we will discuss lesson planning, and in chapter 12, "Managing the Classroom," we will explore how to keep things moving smoothly and handle discipline problems when they arise.

These results clearly support the belief that it is a good strategy to have a sense of humor when you teach. Beginning teachers have many opportunities to demonstrate this. Consider this humorous incident (Hess, Machosky, & Deal, 1997):

> A first-grade teacher was writing on the chalkboard just after recess on one hot day. Her back was to the class and she assumed that the students were writing their names on their math papers. When she turned around, one boy was sitting in his seat in his fleece pajamas and tube socks. She asked him what he was doing in his PJs. He responded that he dressed himself today and put his clothes on over his pajamas. He said he took off his clothes because he got hot!

Our childhood images of teachers continue to influence us as adults. One of the expert consultants for this book, Carlos Diaz (1997), now a professor of education at Florida Atlantic University, had this image of Mrs. Oppel, his high school English teacher:

*T*he art of teaching is the art of awakening the natural curiosity of young minds.

Anatole France
French Novelist and Poet, 20th Century

Used by permission of the estate of Glen Dines

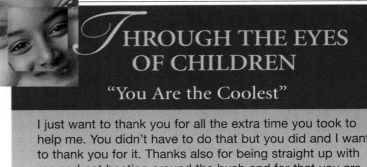

THROUGH THE EYES OF CHILDREN
"You Are the Coolest"

I just want to thank you for all the extra time you took to help me. You didn't have to do that but you did and I want to thank you for it. Thanks also for being straight up with me and not beating around the bush and for that you are the coolest. I'm sorry for the hard times I gave you. You take so much junk but through all that you stay calm and you are a great teacher.

Jessica, Seventh-Grade Student
Macon, Georgia
Letter to Chuck Rawls, her teacher, at the end of the school year

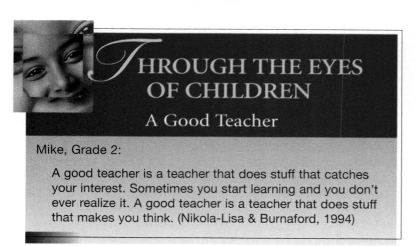

THROUGH THE EYES OF CHILDREN

A Good Teacher

Mike, Grade 2:

A good teacher is a teacher that does stuff that catches your interest. Sometimes you start learning and you don't ever realize it. A good teacher is a teacher that does stuff that makes you think. (Nikola-Lisa & Burnaford, 1994)

CHARACTERISTICS OF BEST TEACHERS	
Characteristics	**% Total**
1. Have a sense of humor	79.2
2. Make the class interesting	73.7
3. Have knowledge of their subjects	70.1
4. Explain things clearly	66.2
5. Spend time to help students	65.8
6. Are fair to their students	61.8
7. Treat students like adults	54.4
8. Relate well to students	54.2
9. Are considerate of students' feelings	51.9
10. Don't show favoritism toward students	46.6

CHARACTERISTICS OF WORST TEACHERS	
Characteristics	**% Total**
1. Are dull/have a boring class	79.6
2. Don't explain things clearly	63.2
3. Show favoritism toward students	52.7
4. Have a poor attitude	49.8
5. Expect too much from students	49.1
6. Don't relate to students	46.2
7. Give too much homework	44.2
8. Are too strict	40.6
9. Don't give help/individual attention	40.5
10. Lack control	39.9

Figure 1.1
Students' Images of Their Best and Worst Teachers

To this day, whenever I see certain words *(dearth, slake)* I recognize them fondly as some of Mrs. Oppel's vocabulary words. As a teacher, she was very calm and focused. She also was *passionate* about the power of language and the beauty of literature. I credit her, at least partially, for my determination to try to master the English language and become a professor and writer. I wish I could bottle these characteristics and implant them in all of my students.

To think about the best and worst characteristics of the teachers you have had, complete Self-Assessment 1.1.

Professional Knowledge and Skills

Effective teachers have good command of their subject matter and a solid core of teaching skills. They have excellent instructional strategies supported by methods of goal setting, instructional planning, and classroom management. They know how to motivate, communicate, and work effectively with students from culturally diverse backgrounds. They also understand how to use appropriate levels of technology in the classroom.

Subject Matter Competence In the last decade, in their wish lists of teacher characteristics, secondary school students have increasingly mentioned "teacher knowledge of their subjects" (NASSP, 1997). Having a thoughtful, flexible, conceptual understanding of subject matter is indispensable for being an effective teacher (Borko & Putnam, 1996). Of course, knowledge of subject matter includes a lot more than just facts, terms, and general concepts. It also includes knowledge about organizing ideas, connections among ideas, ways of thinking and arguing, patterns of change within a discipline, beliefs about a discipline, and the ability to carry ideas from one discipline to another.

Instructional Strategies The principle of constructivism was at the center of William James' and John Dewey's philosophies of education. **Constructivism** *emphasizes that individuals actively construct knowledge and understanding. In the constructivist view, information is not directly poured into children's minds. Rather, children are encouraged to explore their world, discover knowledge, reflect, and think critically.* Today, constructivism includes an emphasis on collaboration—children working with each other in their efforts to know and understand (Oldfather & others, 1999). Thus, a teacher with a constructivist instructional philosophy would not have children memorize information rotely but would give them opportunities to meaningfully construct the knowledge and understanding themselves (Kahn, 1999).

Increasingly, the trend in educational reform is to teach from a constructivist perspective (Bransford, Brown, & Cocking, 1999; Kuhn, 1999; Perkins, 1999). The constructivist belief is that for too long in American education children have been required to sit still, be passive learners, and rotely memorize irrelevant as well as relevant information.

∫ELF-ASSESSMENT 1.1
The Best and Worst Characteristics of My Teachers

When you studied figure 1.1, were you surprised by any of the characteristics listed by students to describe their best and worst teachers? Which of the top five characteristics students listed for the best teachers surprised you the most? Which of the top five characteristics of the worst teachers surprised you the most?

Now think about the top five characteristics of the best teachers you have had. Then think about the main five characteristics of the worst teachers you have had. In generating your lists, don't be constrained by the characteristics described in figure 1.1. Also, after you have listed the characteristic, write down one or more examples of situations that reflected the characteristic.

FIVE CHARACTERISTICS OF THE BEST TEACHERS I HAVE HAD

Characteristics   Examples of Situations That Reflected the Characteristic

1. _____   _____
2. _____   _____
3. _____   _____
4. _____   _____
5. _____   _____

FIVE CHARACTERISTICS OF THE WORST TEACHERS I HAVE HAD

Characteristics   Examples of Situations That Reflected the Characteristic

1. _____   _____
2. _____   _____
3. _____   _____
4. _____   _____
5. _____   _____

However, not everyone embraces the constructivist view. Some traditional educators believe that the teacher should direct and control children's learning more than the constructivist view implies. They also believe that constructivists often don't focus enough on basic academic tasks or have sufficiently high expectations for children's achievement. Some experts in educational psychology believe that whether you follow the current trend in educational reform and teach more from a constructivist perspective or adopt a more traditional direct-instruction approach, you can be an effective teacher. As you will see in the rest of our journey through evaluating what makes a teacher effective, many other domains and issues are involved.

**Constructivist Teaching
Constructivism
Schools for Thought**

Goal-Setting and Instructional Planning Skills   Whether constructivist or more traditional, effective teachers don't just go in the classroom and "wing it." They set high goals for their teaching and develop organized plans for reaching those goals. They also develop specific criteria for success. They spend considerable time in instructional planning, organizing their lessons to maximize students' learning. As they plan, effective teachers reflect and think about how they can make learning both challenging and interesting.

Classroom Management Skills   An important aspect of being an effective teacher is being able to keep the class as a whole working together and oriented toward classroom tasks (Borko & Putnam, 1996). Effective teachers establish and maintain an

THROUGH THE EYES OF TEACHERS
The "Turtle Lady"

Susan Bradburn teaches grades 4 to 6 at West Marian Elementary School in North Carolina. She created a school museum in which students conduct research and create exhibitions. She has put her school museum concept "on wheels" by having students take carts to other classes and into the community, and she has used award money to spread the use of mobile museums to other North Carolina schools.

Nicknamed "the turtle lady" because of her interest in turtles and other animals, Susan takes students on 3-day field trips to Edisto Island, South Carolina, to search for fossils and study coastal ecology. Her students sell calendars that contain their original poetry and art, and they use the proceeds to buy portions of a rain forest so it won't be destroyed.

Susan Bradburn (left) with several students at West Marian Elementary School

environment in which learning can occur. To create this optimal learning environment, teachers need a repertoire of strategies for establishing rules and procedures, organizing groups, monitoring and pacing classroom activities, and handling misbehavior (Evertson, Emmer, & Worsham, 2000; Freiberg, 1999; Weinstein, 1997).

Motivational Skills   Effective teachers have good strategies for helping students become self-motivated to learn (Boekaerts, Pintrich, & Zeidner, 2000). Educational psychologists increasingly believe that this is best accomplished by providing real-world learning opportunities that are of optimal difficulty and novelty for each student (Brophy, 1998). Effective teachers know that students are motivated when they can make choices that are in line with their personal interests. Such teachers give them the opportunity to think creatively and deeply about projects (Runco, 1999).

Communication Skills   Also indispensible to teaching are skills in speaking, listening, overcoming barriers to verbal communication, tuning in to students' nonverbal communication, and constructively resolving conflicts. Communication skills are critical not only in teaching students, but also in interacting effectively with parents. Effective teachers use good communication skills when they talk "with" rather than "to" students, parents, administrators, and others, keep criticism at a minimum, and have an assertive rather than aggressive,

What are some important aspects of professional knowledge and skills that make up effective teaching?

manipulative, or passive communication style (Alberti & Emmons, 1995; Evertson & others, 2000). And effective teachers work to improve students' communication skills as well. This is especially important because communication skills have been rated as the skills most sought after by today's employers (Collins, 1996).

Working Effectively with Students from Culturally Diverse Backgrounds

In today's world of increasing intercultural contact, effective teachers are knowledgeable about people from different cultural backgrounds and are sensitive to their needs (Sadker & Sadker, 2000; Spring, 2000; Wilson, 1999). Effective teachers encourage students to have positive personal contact with diverse other students and think of ways to create such settings. They guide students in thinking critically about cultural and ethnic issues, and they forestall or reduce bias, cultivate acceptance, and serve as cultural mediators (Banks & Banks, 1997). An effective teacher also needs to be a broker or middle person between the culture of the school and the culture of certain students, especially those who are unsuccessful academically (Diaz, 1997).

Technological Skills

Technology itself does not necessarily improve students' ability to learn. A combination of essential conditions is necessary to create learning environments that adequately support students' learning. These conditions include (International Society for Technology in Education, 1999): vision and support from educational leaders; educators who are skilled in the use of technology for learning; content standards and curriculum resources; assessment of the effectiveness of technology for learning; access to contemporary technologies, software, and telecommunication networks; and an emphasis on the child as an active, constructive learner. To read about technology, schools, and communities, see the Technology and Education Box.

Effective teachers develop their technological skills and integrate computers appropriately into classroom learning (Poole, 1998; Roblyer, Edwards, & Havriluk, 1997). This integration should match up with students' learning needs, including the need to prepare for tomorrow's jobs, many of which will require technological expertise and computer-based skills (Maney, 1999).

Effective teachers know how to use and teach students to use computers for discovery and writing, can evaluate the effectiveness of instructional games and computer simulations, know how to use and teach students to use computer-mediated communication resources such as the Internet, and are knowledgeable about various assistive devices to support the learning of students with disabilities.

National Educational Technology Standards (NETS) are being established by the International Society for Technology in Education (ISTE) (1999). NETS standards under development include these:

- *Technology foundation standards for students,* which describe what students should know about technology and be able to do with technology
- *Standards for using technology in learning and teaching,* which describe how technology should be used throughout the curriculum for teaching, learning, and instructional management
- *Educational technology support standards,* which describe systems, access, staff development, and support services that are needed to provide effective use of technology
- *Standards for student assessment and evaluation of technology use,* which describe various means of assessing student progress and evaluating the use of technology in learning and teaching

An example of the effective use of technology involves students in a Chicago elementary school who are exploring the history of Ice Age animals in Illinois (ISTE, 1999). Using

Accomplishments have no color.

Leontyne Price
American Opera Star, 20th Century

Just a step away is the creation of a global, interactive, multimedia database to make the most current information available to all teachers anywhere in the world.

Dee Dickinson
Contemporary American Teacher and Author

**Technology Standards
in Education**
Learning Technology Center

THROUGH THE EYES OF TEACHERS

Friends with the Staff

Make friends with the cook, secretary, and custodian.

Tamela Varney
Third-Grade Teacher
Jefferson Elementary School
Cabell County, West Virginia

TECHNOLOGY AND EDUCATION
Schools and Communities

Not only is technology helping children learn more effectively in school, it also is increasingly opening up schools to communities. In many districts, students and parents can communicate with teachers and administrators through e-mail. Teachers can post students' work on Web pages. Some schools provide students with take-home laptop computers.

Better communication between parents and teachers is one goal of a state-funded Indiana program called the Buddy System. In this program, computers and modems are placed in the homes of 7,000 elementary school students, most of them in grades 4 and 5, for 1 or 2 years. The students' parents, many of whom had never been to their children's schools before, had to go to the schools to pick up the computer equipment and get training on how to use the computers. Many of the parents and teachers report that the computer connection has resulted in increased communication with each other.

A special concern is to enable students from low-income backgrounds to have adequate access to computers. The Foshay Learning Center, a K–12 public school in Los Angeles, has created eight satellite learning centers in low-income apartment complexes. Without leaving their buildings, students in this school can use the computers to get help with homework, learn about technology, and participate in active learning experiences. Such programs are especially important because, according to one survey, only 38 percent of students from families with an income of $20,000 or less had a computer at home, compared to 83 percent of those whose family income was $50,000 or more (*Gallup and National Science Foundation Poll,* 1997).

IBM recently created a Team Tech Volunteer program that will provide technology services to more than 2,500 health and human service agencies. The Team Tech program gives students opportunities to become volunteers in their community and provide technological services that can improve the education and learning of students. Do a thorough assessment of the businesses in your community. Like IBM, some might be willing to provide technological services and expertise for your classroom.

the Internet, they "travel" to the Illinois State Museum (200 miles away) and to the Brookfield Zoo (10 miles away) to gather information and talk with experts via two-way video. Then they construct an electronic database and organize and analyze their findings. They share their findings in multimedia reports posted on a website called "Mastadons in Our Own Back Yard."

Commitment   Being an effective teacher also requires commitment. This includes being motivated, having a good attitude, and caring about students.

Beginning teachers often report that the investment of time and effort needed to be an effective teacher is huge. Some teachers, even experienced ones, report that they have "no life" from September to June. Even putting in hours on evenings and weekends, in addition to all of the hours spent in the classroom, might still not be enough to get things done.

In the face of these demands, it is easy to become frustrated. Commitment and motivation help get effective teachers through the tough and frustrating moments of teaching. Effective teachers also have confidence in their own self-efficacy and don't let negative emotions diminish their motivation.

In any job it is easy to get into a rut and develop a negative attitude. Initial enthusiasm can turn into boredom. Each day, effective teachers bring a positive attitude and enthusiasm to the classroom. These qualities are contagious and help make the classroom a place where students want to be.

Effective teachers also have a caring concern for their students, often referring to them as "my students." They really want to be with the students and are dedicated to helping them learn. Effective teachers do what they have to do to meaningfully engage students in learning, even if it means spending extra time or resources. Although effective teachers are caring, they keep their role as a teacher distinct from student roles. Finally, besides having a caring concern for their students, effective teachers look for ways to help their students consider each other's feelings and care about each other.

Professional Growth   Effective teachers develop a positive identity, seek advice from experienced teachers, maintain their own learning, and build up good resources and supports.

Developing a Positive Identity

Your identity is the whole of you, a composite of many pieces. One of life's most important tasks is to integrate the pieces into a meaningful and positive self-portrait (Deaux, 1999). One of the most important components of your identity will be your vocational identity as a teacher. Fortunately, teaching as a career is gaining more respect. In 1984, only 45 percent of teachers said they would advise young people to pursue a career in teaching, but by 1995 that figure had risen to 67 percent (Louis Harris & Associates, 1995). Today most teachers see a positive identity in their profession (Albert, 1997).

At the same time, your identity includes more than your role as a teacher. It also includes your personal life, lifestyle, relationships, physical health, mental health, and personal interests. Seek to integrate these various pieces of your life into a positive, meaningful identity of who you are. Also keep in mind that although your identity will stay with you the rest of your life, it won't be cast in stone. Through the rest of your college years and in your career as a teacher, you will change and your world will change, especially if you explore new opportunities and challenges.

THROUGH THE EYES OF TEACHERS
A Quiet Supper

Lower your voice when you come home. My husband had to tell me in my first teaching years, over dinner, "Laura, you're not in school anymore." There is a metaphor here. We have a teaching self, and a personal self. These two blend, certainly, and they are aspects of the same being, but they also have their separate places. We should not be COMPLETELY "personal" in school, with students, nor should we be completely our teaching selves at home. It's a dance. It sounds simple, but it's actually quite complicated. Teaching is a lot like performing. Be a performer, but not all the time.

Laura Johnson-Bickford
English Teacher
Norhoff High School
Ojai, California

Seek Advice from Competent Experienced Teachers

Competent experienced teachers can be an especially valuable resource for beginning teachers—and for other experienced teachers as well. Increasingly, teachers engage in collaborative consultation in which people with diverse areas of expertise interact to promote competent instruction and provide effective services for students (Hewitt & Whittier, 1997).

A number of research studies have compared beginning teachers and experienced teachers (Berliner, 1988; Borko & Putnam, 1996; Calderhead, 1996; Leinhardt & Greeno, 1986). In general, experienced teachers are more likely than beginning teachers to:

- Have expertise in managing their classrooms
- Orchestrate smoothly running classrooms
- Engage in well-practiced, virtually automatic routines
- Have extensive knowledge of instructional strategies
- Make deep interpretations of events

However, researchers have found that too often both experienced and beginning teachers lack the rich and flexible understanding of subject matter that is required to teach in ways that are responsive to students' learning needs (Borko & Putnam, 1996). Indeed, it is important to recognize that not every experienced teacher is a good teacher. Some experienced teachers will say, "Forget everything you learned in school and watch what I do instead." This might or might not be a good idea for you. Many new strategies of teaching have been developed in recent years, especially from a constructivist perspective, so it is important to keep an open mind about whether an experienced teacher is giving you the best advice.

Never Stop Learning

Your learning won't stop when you get your college degree—learning is ongoing and lifelong. Currently, there is much educational reform taking place, and reform is likely to continue into the foreseeable future. It is

It is no small thing
To have enjoyed the sun
To have lived light in the spring
To have loved, to have thought, to have done.

  Matthew Arnold
  English Poet and Essayist, 19th Century

**National Center for
Research on Teacher Learning**

TEACHING STRATEGIES
For Effective Teaching

Some general strategies for effective teaching include:

1. *Effective teaching requires teachers to wear many different hats.* It's easy to fall into the trap of thinking that if you have good subject matter knowledge, excellent teaching will follow. As the list of 15 effective teaching characteristics in Self-Assessment 1.2 suggests, being an effective teacher requires many diverse skills.
2. *Engage often in perspective taking.* You want to be the very best teacher you can possibly be. Put yourself in your students' shoes and think about how they perceive you. Think about what they need from you to improve their academic and life skills. Put your heart and mind into helping them construct these skills.
3. *Keep the list of 15 characteristics of effective teachers we have discussed in this chapter with you through your teaching career.* Looking at the list and thinking about the different areas of effective teaching can benefit you as you go through your student teaching, your days, weeks, and months as a beginning teacher, and even your years as an experienced teacher. By consulting it from time to time, you might realize that you have let one or two areas slip and need to spend time improving yourself in those areas.

an exciting time to become a teacher because of the many new developments. Make a commitment to keep up-to-date about research and knowledge on effective teaching. This will include taking advantage of workshops, taking courses beyond your initial degree, reading educational journals and books, and seeking information from experts in various educational domains.

You rarely achieve more than you expect.

Carol Grosse
American Educator, 20th Century

Build Up Good Resources and Supports   Don't think that you have to educate your students by yourself. It is especially important to develop good relationships with your students' parents or guardians and encourage them to be partners with you in educating their child. Throughout this book, we will highlight effective ways for you to do this. Developing good working relationships with your administrator and other teachers also can benefit your teaching. Consulting with experienced teachers can be especially effective. One good strategy is to ask a competent experienced teacher to serve as your mentor, someone you can go to for advice and guidance to help you become a more effective teacher.

Also examine other resources of the school system or community you might call on in teaching your students. A school system might have funds available for a teacher's aide or technology equipment. Get to know educated people in your community who might be willing to serve as mentors for students or come to your class to share their expertise with you and your students. Some businesses have mentoring programs for students. For example, AT&T recently committed to providing 100,000 hours of mentoring, and Pillsbury committed to providing 50,000 hours of mentoring, to students throughout the United States.

We have discussed many different characteristics of effective teaching. To evaluate the extent to which each of the dimensions will characterize your teaching, complete Self-Assessment 1.2.

At this point we have explored many goals of educational psychology. A review of these ideas is presented in summary table 1.1.

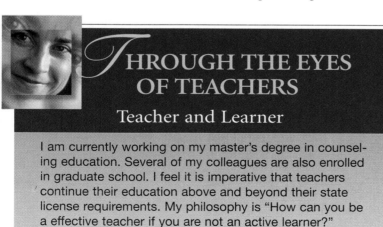

THROUGH THE EYES OF TEACHERS
Teacher and Learner

I am currently working on my master's degree in counseling education. Several of my colleagues are also enrolled in graduate school. I feel it is imperative that teachers continue their education above and beyond their state license requirements. My philosophy is "How can you be a effective teacher if you are not an active learner?"

Donna Shelhorse
Social Studies Teacher, Grade 7
Short Pump Middle School
Henrico County, Virginia

SELF-ASSESSMENT 1.2
Evaluating and Predicting My Effective Teaching Skills

Evaluate yourself on the 15 characteristics in the three main dimensions of effective teaching. Rate yourself on how much you think each will characterize your teaching on a scale from 1 (Not like me at all) to 5 (Very much like me).

Characteristics

Professional Knowledge and Skills	1	2	3	4	5
1. I will have excellent subject matter knowledge and understanding.					
2. I will use effective instructional strategies.					
3. I will have superb goal-setting and planning skills.					
4. I will have outstanding classroom management skills.					
5. I will be able to successfully help students become motivated.					
6. I will have excellent communication skills.					
7. I will work effectively with children from culturally diverse backgrounds.					
8. I will have excellent technological skills.					
Commitment					
9. I will be extremely motivated myself.					
10. I will have a great attitude.					
11. I will have exceptional caring skills.					
Professional Growth					
12. I will develop a very positive, well-integrated identity.					
13. I will extensively seek advice from competent experienced teachers.					
14. I will never stop learning.					
15. I will build up outstanding resources and supports.					

   If you evaluated yourself at the level of 3 or lower on any of these characteristics, spend some time thinking about what you can do to improve your knowledge and skills in these areas. Even if you rated yourself at the levels of 4 or 5 on all of these characteristics, make a serious commitment to learn more about these dimensions of effective teaching. As you study the remainder of this book, you will come across many ideas that will benefit these aspects of effective teaching. And in every chapter, you will complete other self-assessments that give you the opportunity to examine more specific dimensions of your own effective teaching.

Research in Educational Psychology

Research can be a valuable source of information about teaching. We will explore why research is important and how it is done, including how you can be a teacher-researcher.

Why Research Is Important

It sometimes is said that experience is the most important teacher. Your own experiences and those experiences that other teachers, administrators, and experts share with you will make you a

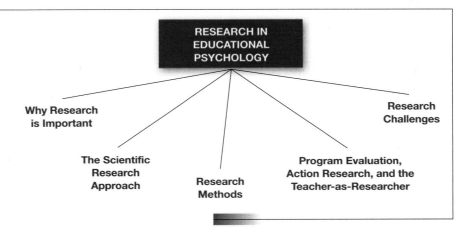

SUMMARY TABLE 1.1
The Goals of Educational Psychology

Concept	Processes/ Related Ideas	Characteristics/Description
Exploring the Field of Educational Psychology	Historical Background	• William James and John Dewey were important pioneers in educational psychology, as was E.L. Thorndike. • Among the important ideas in educational psychology we owe to Dewey are these: the child as an active learner, education of the whole child, emphasis on the child's adaptation to the environment, and the democratic ideal that all children deserve a competent education.
	Educational Psychology: Art or Science?	• Both science and practice play important roles in educational psychology. • There is spirited debate over just how much teaching should be based on science and how much of it is art.
The Complex, Fast-Paced Nature of Teaching	Teaching Is Multidimensional	• Interactions in classrooms are fast-paced, and teachers must make immediate decisions as they attempt to engage students in productive learning and manage the flow of the classroom's activities. • Teaching also is multidimensional because it involves many different domains, including cognitive/academic, social, affective, moral, and health. • Overlapping events and agendas also mean that teachers constantly face dilemmas, many of which cannot be entirely resolved.
	Teaching Involves Uncertainty	• It is often difficult to predict just what effect a given action by a teacher will have on a student. • Being an effective teacher involves having a tolerance for uncertainty and unpredictability.
	Teaching Involves Social and Ethical Matters	• Social and ethical dimensions are especially present when issues of educational equity are raised. • Even routine decisions about which students to call on can give advantages or disadvantages to certain students.
	Teaching Involves a Diverse Mosaic of Students	• Your classroom will be filled with students who vary from each other in a seemingly endless number of ways. • This is especially apparent in the increasing diversity in students' racial, ethnic, linguistic, and cultural backgrounds.
Effective Teaching	Images of Good and Bad Teachers	• In a recent national survey of secondary school students, having a good sense of humor, making the class interesting, and the teacher's knowledge of subject matter were listed by students as the most important characteristics for teachers to have. • The worst teacher characteristics listed were having a boring class, not explaining things clearly, and showing favoritism to some students.
	Professional Knowledge and Skills	• Effective teachers have subject matter competence, use effective instructional strategies, and have skills in these areas as well: goal setting and planning, classroom management, motivation, communication, working with diverse ethnic and cultural groups, and technology.
	Commitment	• Being an effective teacher requires commitment. • This includes being motivated, having a good attitude, and caring about students.
	Professional Growth	• Being an effective teacher includes paying attention to your professional growth. • This involves developing a positive identity, seeking advice from competent experienced teachers, always continuing to learn, and building up good resources and support.

better teacher. However, research also can make you a better teacher (Charles, 1997; Fraenkel & Wallen, 2000).

We all get a great deal of knowledge from personal experience. We generalize from what we observe and frequently turn memorable encounters into lifetime "truths." But how valid are these conclusions? Sometimes we err in making these personal observations or misinterpret what we see and hear. Chances are, you can think of many situations in which you thought other people read you the wrong way, just as they might have felt that you misread them. And when we base information only on personal experiences, we also aren't always totally objective because we sometimes make judgments that protect our ego and self-esteem (McMillan, 2000).

We get information not only from personal experiences, but also from authorities or experts. In your teaching career, you will hear many authorities and experts spell out a "best way" to educate students. But the authorities and experts don't always agree, do they? You might hear one expert one week tell you about a reading method that is absolutely the best, yet the next week hear another expert tout a different method. One experienced teacher might tell you to do one thing with your students, another experienced teacher might tell you to do the opposite. How can you tell which one to believe? One way to clarify the situation is to look at research that has been conducted on the topic.

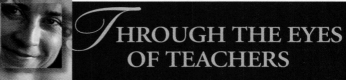

THROUGH THE EYES OF TEACHERS
Never Stop Learning

I am dedicated to teaching and learning. I believe that it is through learning that we grow and mature as persons. Because of my beliefs, I frequently attend workshops and professional conferences, and seek higher degrees. I also read professional literature to expand my knowledge. I constantly seek new and exciting ways to engage my students in learning. If I ever stop learning or become stagnant in my teaching, it will be time for me to retire from the teaching profession.

Jerri Hall
Mathematics Teacher
Miller Magnet School
Bibb County, Georgia

The Scientific Research Approach

Some people have difficulty thinking of educational psychology as being a science in the same way that physics or biology is a science. Can a discipline that studies the best way to help children learn or the ways poverty affects their behavior in the classroom be equated with disciplines that examine how gravity works or how blood flows through the body?

Science is defined not by *what* it investigates but by *how* it investigates. Whether you investigate photosynthesis, butterflies, Saturn's moons, or why some students think creatively and others don't, it is the way you investigate that makes the approach scientific or not.

Educational psychologists take a skeptical, scientific attitude toward knowledge. When they hear a claim that a particular method is effective in helping students learn, they want to know if the claim is based on *good* research. The science part of educational psychology seeks to sort fact from fancy by using particular strategies for obtaining information (Johnson & Christensen, 2000; Kennedy, 1999).

Scientific research *is objective, systematic, and testable. It reduces the likelihood that information will be based on personal beliefs, opinions, and feelings* . Scientific research is based on the **scientific method,** *an approach that can be used to discover accurate information. It includes these steps: Conceptualize the problem, collect data, draw conclusions, and revise research conclusions and theory.*

Conceptualizing a problem involves identifying the problem, theorizing, and developing one or more hypotheses. For example, a team of researchers decides that it wants to study ways to improve the achievement of students from impoverished backgrounds. The researchers have *identified a problem*, which at a general level might not seem like a difficult task. However, as part of the first step, they also must go beyond the general description of the problem by isolating, analyzing, narrowing, and focusing more specifically on what aspect of it they hope to study. Perhaps the researchers decide to discover whether mentoring that involves sustained support,

*R*esearch is formalized curiosity. It is poking and searching with a purpose.

Zora Neale Hurston
American Anthropologist and Author, 20th Century

*S*cience refines everyday thinking.

Albert Einstein
German-Born American Physicist, 20th Century

guidance, and concrete assistance to students from impoverished backgrounds can improve their academic performance. At this point, even more narrowing and focusing needs to take place. What specific strategies do they want the mentors to use? How often will the mentors see the students? How long will the mentoring program last? What aspects of the students' achievement do they want to assess?

As researchers formulate a problem to study, they often *draw on theories and develop hypotheses.* A **theory** *is an interrelated, coherent set of ideas that helps to explain and make predictions.* A theory contains **hypotheses,** *which are specific assumptions and predictions that can be tested to determine their accuracy.* For example, a theory about mentoring might attempt to explain and predict why sustained support, guidance, and concrete experience should make a difference in the lives of children from impoverished backgrounds. The theory might focus on children's opportunities to model the behavior and strategies of mentors, or it might focus on the effects of nurturing, which might be missing in the children's own lives.

The next step is to *collect information (data).* In the study of mentoring, the researchers might decide to conduct the mentoring program for 6 months. Their data might consist of classroom observations, teachers' ratings, and achievement tests given to the mentored students before the mentoring began and at the end of 6 months of mentoring.

Once data have been collected, educational psychologists use *statistical procedures* to understand the meaning of their quantitative data. Then they try to draw *conclusions.* In the study of mentoring, statistics would help the researchers determine whether their observations are due to chance. After data have been collected, educational psychologists compare their findings with what others have discovered about the same issue.

The final step in the scientific method is *revising research conclusions and theory.* Educational psychologists have generated a number of theories about the best ways for children to learn. Over time, some theories have been discarded and others have been revised. This text presents a number of theories related to educational psychology, along with their support and implications. Figure 1.2 illustrates the steps in the scientific method applied to our study of mentoring.

Research Methods

When educational psychology researchers want to find out, for example, whether watching a lot of MTV detracts from student learning, eating a nutritional breakfast improves alertness in class, or getting more recess decreases absenteeism, they can choose from many methods. We will discuss these methods separately, but recognize that in many instances more than one is used in a single study.

Observation   Sherlock Holmes chided his assistant, Watson, "You see but you do not observe." We look at things all the time. However, casually watching two students interacting is not the same as the type of observation used in scientific studies. Scientific observation is highly systematic. It requires knowing what you are looking for, conducting observations in an unbiased manner, accurately recording and categorizing what you see, and effectively communicating your observations (Cone, 1999).

A common way to record observations is to write them down, often using shorthand or symbols. In addition, tape recorders, video cameras, special coding sheets, one-way mirrors, and computers increasingly are being used to make observations more efficient.

Observations can be made in laboratories or in naturalistic settings. A **laboratory** *is a controlled setting from which many of the complex factors of the real world have been removed.* Some educational psychologists conduct research in laboratories at the colleges or universities where they work and teach. Although laboratories often help researchers gain more control in their studies, they have been criticized as being artificial. In **naturalistic observation,** *behavior is observed out in the real world.*

**Generating
Research Ideas**

Step 1
Conceptualize the Problem

A researcher identifies this problem: Many children from impoverished backgrounds have lower achievement than children from higher socioeconomic backgrounds. The researcher develops the hypothesis that mentoring will improve the achievement of children from impoverished backgrounds.

Step 2
Collect Information (Data)

The researcher conducts the mentoring program for 6 months and collects data before the program begins and after its conclusion, using classroom observations, teachers' ratings of children's achievement, and achievement test scores.

Step 3
Draw Conclusions

The researcher statistically analyzes the data and finds that the children's achievement improved over the 6 months of the study. The researcher concludes that mentoring is likely an important reason for the increase in the children's achievement.

Step 4
Revise Research Conclusions and Theory

This research on mentoring, along with other research that obtains similar results, increases the likelihood that mentoring will be considered as an important component of theorizing about how to improve the achievement of children from low-income backgrounds.

Figure **1.2**
The Scientific Method Applied to a Study of Mentoring

Educational psychologists conduct naturalistic observations of children in classrooms, at museums, on playgrounds, in homes, in neighborhoods, and in other settings.

Interviews and Questionnaires   Sometimes the quickest and best way to get information about students and teachers is to ask them for it. Educational psychologists use interviews and questionnaires (surveys) to find out about children's and teachers' experiences, beliefs, and feelings. Most interviews take place face-to-face, although they can be done in other ways, such as over the phone or the

Brandi Binder is evidence of the brain's hemispheric flexibility and resilience. Despite having the right side of her cortex removed because of a severe case of epilepsy, Brandi engages in many activities often portrayed as only "right-brain" activities. She loves music and art, and is shown here working on one of her paintings.

Internet. Questionnaires are usually given to individuals in printed form. They can be filled out in many ways, such as in person, by mail, or via the Internet.

Good interviews and surveys involve concrete, specific, and unambiguous questions and some means of checking the authenticity of the respondents' replies. However, interviews and surveys are not without problems. One crucial limitation is that many individuals give socially desirable answers, responding in a way they think is most socially acceptable and desirable rather than how they truly think or feel. For example, some teachers, when interviewed or asked to fill out a questionnaire about their teaching practices, hesitate to admit honestly how frequently they chide or criticize their students. Skilled interviewing techniques and questions that increase forthright responses are crucial to obtaining accurate information. Another problem with interviews and surveys is that the respondents sometimes simply lie.

Standardized Tests **Standardized tests** *are commercially prepared tests that assess students' performance in different domains.* Many standardized tests allow a student's performance to be compared with the performance of other students at the same age or grade level, in many cases on a national basis (Aiken, 2000). Students might take a number of standardized tests, including tests that assess their intelligence, achievement, personality, career interests, and other skills. These tests could be for a variety of purposes, including providing outcome measures for research studies, information that helps psychologists and educators make decisions about an individual student, and comparisons of students' performance across schools, states, and countries. Chapter 13 discusses standardized testing in detail.

Case Studies A **case study** *is an in-depth look at an individual.* Case studies often are used when unique circumstances in a person's life cannot be duplicated, for either practical or ethical reasons. For example, consider the case study of Brandi Binder (Nash, 1997). She developed such severe epilepsy that surgeons had to remove the right side of her brain's cerebral cortex when she was 6 years old. Brandi lost virtually all control over muscles on the left side of her body, the side controlled by the right side of her brain. Yet at age 17, after years of therapy ranging from leg lifts to mathematics and music training, Brandi is an A student. She loves music and art, which usually are associated with the right side of the brain. Her recuperation is not 100 percent—for example, she has not regained the use of her left arm—but her case study shows that if there is a way to compensate, the human brain will find it. Brandi's remarkable recovery also provides evidence against the stereotype that the left side (hemisphere) of the brain is solely the source of logical thinking and the right hemisphere exclusively the source of creativity. Brains are not that neatly split in terms of most functioning, as Brandi's case illustrated.

Although case studies provide dramatic, in-depth portrayals of people's lives, we need to exercise caution when interpreting them. The subject of a case study is unique, with a genetic makeup and set of experiences that no one else shares. For these reasons, the findings might not generalize to other people.

Correlational Research In **correlational research,** *the goal is to describe the strength of the relation between two or more events or characteristics.* Correlational research is useful because the more strongly two events are correlated

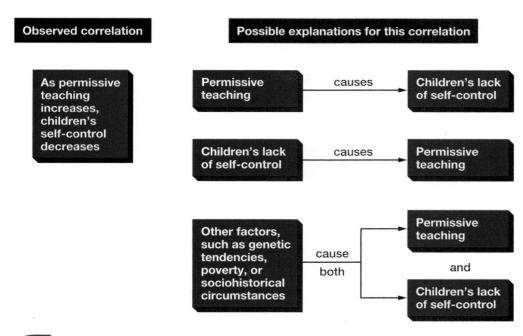

| Observed correlation | Possible explanations for this correlation |

As permissive teaching increases, children's self-control decreases

Permissive teaching → causes → Children's lack of self-control

Children's lack of self-control → causes → Permissive teaching

Other factors, such as genetic tendencies, poverty, or sociohistorical circumstances → cause both → Permissive teaching and Children's lack of self-control

Figure 1.3
Possible Explanations of Correlational Data

An observed correlation between two events does not justify the conclusion that the first event caused the second event. Other possibilities are that the second event caused the first event or that a third, undetermined event causes the correlation between the first two events.

(related or associated), the more effectively we can predict one from the other. For example, if researchers find that low-involved, permissive teaching is correlated with a student's lack of self-control, it suggests that low-involved, permissive teaching might be one source of the lack of self-control.

However, a caution is in order. *Correlation by itself does not equal causation.* The correlational finding just mentioned does not mean that permissive teaching necessarily causes low student self-control. It could mean that, but it also could mean that the student's lack of self-control caused the teachers to throw up their arms in despair and give up trying to control the out-of-control class. It also could be that other factors, such as heredity, poverty, or inadequate parenting, caused the correlation between permissive teaching and low student self-control. Figure 1.3 illustrates these possible interpretations of correlational data.

Experimental Research   Experimental research *allows educational psychologists to determine the causes of behavior.* Educational psychologists accomplish this task by performing an **experiment,** *a carefully regulated procedure in which one or more of the factors believed to influence the behavior being studied is manipulated and all other factors are held constant.* If the behavior under study changes when a factor is manipulated, we say that the manipulated factor causes the behavior to change. *Cause* is the event being manipulated. *Effect* is the behavior that changes because of the manipulation. Experimental research is the only truly reliable method of establishing cause and effect. Because correlational research does not involve manipulation of factors, it is not a dependable way to isolate cause.

Experiments involve at least one independent variable and one dependent variable. The **independent variable** *is the manipulated, influential, experimental factor.* The label *independent* indicates that this variable can be changed independently of any other factors. For example, suppose we want to design an experiment to study the

Correlational Research

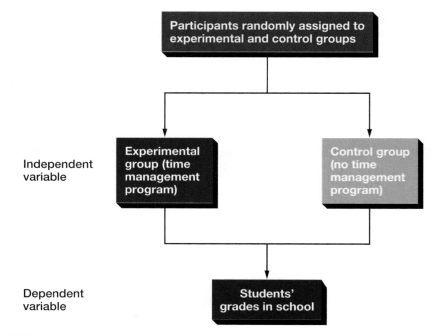

Figure 1.4
The Experimental Strategy Applied to a Study of the Effects of Time Management on Students' Grades

**Experimental
Research**

effects of peer tutoring on student achievement. In this example, the amount and type of peer tutoring could be an independent variable. The **dependent variable** *is the factor that is measured in an experiment.* It can change as the independent variable is manipulated. The label *dependent* is used because the values of this variable depend on what happens to the participants in the experiment as the independent variable is manipulated. In the peer tutoring study, achievement is the dependent variable. This might be assessed in a number of ways. Let's say in this study it is measured by scores on a nationally standardized achievement test.

In experiments, the independent variable consists of differing experiences that are given to one or more experimental groups and one or more control groups. An **experimental group** *is a group whose experience is manipulated.* A **control group** *is a comparison group that is treated in every way like the experimental group except for the manipulated factor.* The control group serves as the baseline against which the effects of the manipulated condition can be compared. In the peer tutoring study, we need to have one group of students who get peer tutoring (experimental group) and one group of students who don't (control group).

Another important principle of experimental research is **random assignment:** *researchers assign participants to experimental and control groups by chance.* This practice reduces the likelihood that the experiment's results will be due to any preexisting differences between the groups. In our study of peer tutoring, random assignment greatly reduces the probability that the two groups will differ on such factors as age, family status, initial achievement, intelligence, personality, health, alertness, and so on.

To summarize the experimental study of peer tutoring and student achievement, each student is randomly assigned to one of two groups: one group (the experimental group) is given peer tutoring; the other (the control group) is not. The independent variable consists of the differing experiences that the experimental and control groups receive. After the peer tutoring is completed, the students are given a nationally standardized achievement test (dependent variable). For an illustration of the experimental research method applied to a different problem—whether a time management program can improve students' grades—see figure 1.4.

Time Span of Research   Another research decision involves the time span of the research. We have several options—we can study groups of individuals all at one time or study the same individuals over time.

Cross-sectional research *involves studying groups of people all at one time.* For example, a researcher might be interested in studying the self-esteem of students in grades 4, 6, and 8. In a cross-sectional study, the students' self-esteem would be assessed at one time, using groups of children in grades 4, 6, and 8. The cross-sectional study's main advantage is that the researcher does not have to wait for the students to grow older. However, this approach provides no information about the stability of individual students' self-esteem, or how it might change over time.

Longitudinal research *involves studying the same individuals over a period of time, usually several years or more.* In a longitudinal research study of self-esteem, the researcher might examine the self-esteem of a group of fourth-grade students, then assess the same students' self-esteem again in sixth grade, and then again in eighth grade. One of the great values of longitudinal research is that we can evaluate how individual children change as they get older. However, because longitudinal research is time consuming and costly, most research is cross-sectional.

At this point we have discussed a number of ideas about why research is important, the scientific research approach, and research methods. A review of these ideas is presented in summary table 1.2.

Program Evaluation, Action Research, and the Teacher-as-Researcher

In discussing research methods so far, we have referred mainly to methods that are used to improve our knowledge and understanding of general educational practices. The same methods also can be applied to research whose aim is more specific, such as determining how well a particular educational strategy or program is working (Graziano & Raulin, 2000). This more narrowly targeted work often includes program evaluation research, action research, and the teacher-as-researcher.

Program Evaluation Research   **Program evaluation research** *is research that is designed to make decisions about the effectiveness of a particular program* (McMillan, 1996). Program evaluation research often focuses on a specific location or type of program. Because it often is directed at answering a question about a specific school or school system, the results of program evaluation research are not intended to be generalized to other settings (Charles, 1997). A program evaluation researcher might ask questions like these:

- Has a gifted program that was instituted 2 years ago had positive effects on students' creative thinking and academic achievement?
- Has a technology program that has been in place for 1 year improved students' attitudes toward school?
- Which of two reading programs being used in this school system has improved students' reading skills the most?

Action Research   **Action research** *is used to solve a specific classroom or school problem, improve teaching and other educational strategies, or make a decision at a specific location* (McMillan, 2000). The goal of action research is to improve educational practices immediately in one or two classrooms, at one school, or at several schools. Action research is carried out by teachers and administrators rather than

Summary Table 1.2

Why Research Is Important, the Scientific Research Approach, and Research Methods

Concept	Processes/ Related Ideas	Characteristics/Description
Why Research Is Important	Its Nature	• Personal experiences and information from experts can help you be an effective teacher. • The information you obtain from research also is extremely important. • It will help you sort through various strategies and determine which are most and least effective. • Research helps to eliminate errors in judgment that are based only on personal experiences.
The Scientific Research Approach	The Nature of Science and the Scientific Method	• Science is defined not by what it investigates but by how it investigates. Scientific research is objective, systematic, and testable, reducing the probability that information will be based on personal beliefs, opinions, and feelings. • Scientific research is based on the scientific method, which includes these steps: conceptualize the problem, collect data, draw conclusions, and revise research conclusions and theory. • A theory is a coherent set of ideas that help explain and make predictions. A theory contains hypotheses.
Research Methods	Observation	• Observations need to be conducted systematically. • Observations can be made in a laboratory or in naturalistic settings.
	Interviews and Questionnaires	• Most interviews take place face-to-face, and most questionnaires (surveys) are given to individuals in printed form to be filled out. • Social desirability and lying can be problematic in interviews and questionnaires.
	Standardized Tests	• They are commercially prepared tests that assess students' performance in different domains.
	Case Studies	• These are studies that give an in-depth look at an individual. • One should be cautious about generalizing from a case study to other individuals.
	Correlational Research	• The goal is to describe the strength of the relation between two or more events or characteristics. • An important research principle is that correlation does not equal causation. • When there is a correlation between two events, the first could cause the second, the second could cause the first, or a third, unknown factor could cause the correlation between the first two events.
	Experimental Research	• This is the only kind of research that can discover behavior's causes. • Conducting an experiment involves examining the influence of at least one independent variable (the manipulated, influential, experimental factor) on one or more dependent variables (the measured factor). • Experiments involve the random assignment of participants to one or more experimental groups (the groups whose experience is being manipulated) and one or more control groups (comparison groups treated in every way like the experimental group except for the manipulated factor).
	Time Span of Research	• Cross-sectional research involves studying groups of people all at one time. • Longitudinal research consists of studying the same people over time.

TEACHING STRATEGIES
For Being a Skillful Teacher-Researcher

Some strategies that can help you be a skillful teacher-researcher include:

1. *As you plan each week's lessons, think about your students and which ones might benefit from your role as a teacher-researcher.* As you reflect on the past week's classes, you might notice that one student seemed to be sliding farther downhill in her performance and that another student seemed to be especially depressed. As you think about such students, you might consider using your observer participation and/or clinical interview skills in the following week in an effort to find out why they are having problems.
2. *Take a course in educational research methods to improve your understanding of how research is conducted.*
3. *Use library or Internet resources to learn more about teacher-researcher skills.* This might include locating information about how to be a skilled clinical interviewer and a systematic, unbiased observer. A good book on improving your observation skills is *A Guide to Observation and Participation in the Classroom* (Reed, Bergemann, & Olson, 1998).
4. *Ask someone else (such as another teacher) to observe your class and help you develop some strategies for the particular research problem you want to solve.*

educational psychology researchers. However, the practitioners might follow many of the guidelines of scientific research that we described earlier, such as trying to make the research and observations as systematic as possible to avoid bias and misinterpretation (Mills, 2000). Action research can be carried out schoolwide or in more limited settings by a smaller group of teachers and administrators; it can even be accomplished in a single classroom by an individual teacher (Calhoun, 1994).

Teacher-as-Researcher   The concept of **teacher-as-researcher** *(also called "teacher-researcher") is the idea that classroom teachers can conduct their own studies to improve their teaching practices.* This is an important outgrowth of action research. Some educational experts believe that the increasing emphasis on the teacher-as-researcher reinvents the teacher's role, fuels school renewal, and improves teaching and student learning (Cochran-Smith & Lytle, 1990; Flake & others, 1995; Gill, 1997). It is increasingly thought that the most effective teachers routinely ask questions and monitor problems to be solved, then collect data, interpret it, and share their conclusions with other teachers (Cochran-Smith, 1995).

To obtain information, the teacher-researcher uses methods such as systematic observation, interviews, and case studies. One good, widely used technique is the *clinical interview,* in which the teacher makes the student feel comfortable, shares beliefs and expectations, and asks questions in a nonthreatening manner. Before conducting a clinical interview with a student, the teacher usually will put together a targeted set of questions to ask. Clinical interviews not only can help you obtain information about a particular issue or problem, but also can provide you with a sense of how children think and feel.

Another popular teacher-as-researcher method is **participant observation,** *in which the observer-researcher is actively involved as a participant in the activity or setting* (McMillan, 2000). The participant observer often will observe for a while and then take notes on what he or she has seen. The observer usually makes these observations and writes down notes over a period of days, weeks, or months and looks for patterns in

What methods can a teacher-as-researcher use to obtain information about students?

**American Education
Research Association (AERA)**

Ethical Principles

the observations. For example, to study a student who is doing poorly in the class without apparent reason, the teacher might develop a plan to observe the student from time to time and record observations of the student's behavior and what is going on in the classroom at the time.

In addition to participant observation, the teacher might conduct several clinical interviews with the student, discuss the child's situation with the child's parents, and consult with a school psychologist about the child's behavior. Based on this work as teacher-researcher, the teacher will be able to create an intervention strategy that considerably improves the student's behavior.

Thus, learning about educational research methods not only can help you understand the research that educational psychologists conduct, but also has another practical benefit. The more knowledge you have about research in educational psychology, the more effective you will be in the increasingly popular teacher-researcher role (Gay & Airasian, 2000).

Research Challenges

Research in educational psychology poses a number of challenges. Some of the challenges involve the pursuit of knowledge itself. Others involve the effects of research on participants. Still others relate to better understanding of the information derived from research studies.

Ethics   Educational psychologists must exercise considerable caution to ensure the well-being of children participating in a research study. Most colleges and school systems have review boards that evaluate whether the research is ethical. Before research is conducted in a school system, an administrator or administrative committee evaluates the research plan and decides whether the research can potentially benefit the system.

The code of ethics adopted by the American Psychological Association (APA) instructs researchers to protect participants from mental and physical harm. The best interests of the participants must always be kept foremost in the researcher's mind (Kimmel, 1996). All participants who are old enough to do so must give their informed consent to participate. If they are not old enough, parental or guardian consent must be obtained. When children and adolescents are studied, parental or guardian consent is almost always obtained. Informed consent means that the participants (and/or their parents or legal guardians) have been told what their participation will entail and any risks that might be involved. For example, if researchers want to study the effects of conflict in divorced families on learning and achievement, the participants should be informed that in some instances discussion of a family's experiences might improve family relationships, but in other cases might raise unwanted family stress. After informed consent is given, participants retain the right to withdraw at any time (Bersoff, 1999).

Because children are vulnerable and usually lack power and control when facing adults, educators always should strive to make their research encounters positive and supportive experiences for each child. Even if the family gives permission for a child to participate in a research study, if the child doesn't want to participate, that desire should be respected.

Gender   Traditionally, science has been presented as nonbiased and value free. However, many experts on gender believe that much educational and other research has been gender-biased (Anselmi, 1998; Doyle & Paludi, 1998). Educational researchers argue that for too long the female experience was subsumed under the male experience (Tetreault, 1997). For example, conclusions about females have been routinely drawn based on research done only with males. Similarly, with regard to socioeconomic bias, conclusions have been drawn about all males and all females from studies that do not include participants from all income backgrounds.

Following are three broad questions that female scholars have raised regarding gender bias in educational research (Tetreault, 1997):

- *How might gender be a bias that influences the choice of theory, questions, hypotheses, participants, and research design?* For example, the most widely known theory of moral development (Kohlberg's) was proposed by a male in a male-dominant society, and for many years males were the main participants in research conducted to support the theory (Gilligan, 1982, 1998; Kohlberg, 1976).
- *How might research on topics of primary interest to females, such as relationships, feelings, and empathy, challenge existing theory and research?* For example, in studies of moral development, it has often been said that the highest level of moral development involves this question, which reflects common male preoccupations: "What is justice for the individual?" (Kohlberg, 1976). However, recent theorizing has shifted away from the typically male emphasis on the individual and autonomy to incorporate a more commonly female "care" perspective, which focuses on relationships and connections with others (Gilligan, 1982, 1998). We will explore these aspects of moral development further in chapter 3, "Socioemotional Development."
- *How has research that has heretofore exaggerated gender differences between females and males influenced the way teachers think about and teach female and male students?* For example, gender differences in mathematics often have been exaggerated and fueled by societal bias.

In chapter 5, "Sociocultural Diversity," we will explore many aspects of gender and education.

Ethnicity and Culture   We need to include more children from ethnic minority backgrounds in our research on educational psychology (Graham, 1992; Lee, 1992). Historically, ethnic minority children essentially have been ignored in research or simply viewed as variations from the norm or average. Their developmental and educational problems have been viewed as "confounds" or "noise" in data, and researchers have deliberately excluded these children from the samples they have selected to study (Ryan-Finn, Cauce, & Grove, 1995). Because ethnic minority children have been excluded from research for so long, there likely is more variation in children's real lives than research studies have indicated in the past (Stevenson, 1995).

One research challenge involves ensuring that educational research does not involve gender bias. What are some of the questions female scholars have raised about gender bias in educational research?

Another research challenge focuses on children from ethnic minority backgrounds. What are some of the ways research has been characterized by ethnic bias? How can this bias be reduced or eliminated?

Researchers also have tended to practice "ethnic gloss" when they select and describe ethnic minority groups (Trimble, 1989). **Ethnic gloss** *means using an ethnic label such as* African American, Latino, Asian American, *or* Native American *in a superficial way that makes an ethnic group seem more homogeneous than it really is.* For example, a researcher might describe a sample as "20 African Americans, 20 Latinos, and 20 Anglo-Americans" when a more precise description of the Latino group would need to specify: "The 20 Latino participants were Mexican Americans from low-income neighborhoods in the southwestern area of Los Angeles. Twelve were from homes in which Spanish is the dominant spoken language, 8 from homes in which English is the main spoken language. Ten were born in the United States, 10 in Mexico. Ten described themselves as Mexican American, 5 as Mexican, 3 as American, 2 as Chicano, and 1 as Latino." Ethnic gloss can cause researchers to obtain samples of ethnic groups that either are not representative or conceal the group's diversity, which can lead to overgeneralization and stereotyping.

Also, historically, when researchers have studied individuals from ethnic minority groups, they have focused on their problems. It is important to study the problems such as poverty that ethnic minority groups face, but it also is important to examine their strengths, such as their pride, self-esteem, problem-solving skills, and extended-family support systems. Fortunately, now, as a more pluralistic view of our society is emerging, researchers are increasingly studying the positive dimensions of ethnic minority groups (Swanson, 1997).

Being a Wise Consumer of Information About Educational Psychology
We live in a society that generates a vast amount of information about children's education in various media, ranging from research journals to newspapers and television. The information varies greatly in quality. How can you evaluate the credibility of this information?

Be Cautious of What Is Reported in the Popular Media
Children's education is increasingly talked about in the news. Television, radio, newspapers, and magazines all frequently report on educational research. Many professional educators and researchers regularly supply the media with information. In some cases, this research has been published in professional journals or presented at national meetings and then picked up by the popular media. And most major colleges and universities have a media relations department that contacts the press about current faculty research.

However, not all information about education that appears in the media comes from professionals with excellent credentials and reputations. Most journalists, television reporters, and other media personnel are not scientifically trained and do not have the skills to sort through the avalanche of material they receive and make sound decisions about which information to report.

Unfortunately, the media focus on sensational, dramatic findings. They want you to stay tuned or buy their publication. When the information they gather from educational journals is not sensational, they might embellish it and sensationalize it, going beyond what the researcher intended.

Another problem with media reports about research is that the media often do not have the luxury of time and space to go into important details about a study. They often only get a few lines or a few minutes to summarize as best they can what can be very complex findings. Too often this means that what is reported is overgeneralized and stereotyped.

Know How to Avoid Drawing Conclusions About Individual Needs on the Basis of Group Research
Nomothetic research *is research conducted at the level of the group.* Most educational psychology research is nomothetic. Individual variations in how students respond is not a common focus. For example, if researchers are interested in the effects of divorce on children's school achievement, they might conduct a study with 50 children from divorced families and 50 children

from intact, never-divorced families. They might find that the children from divorced families, as a group, had lower achievement in school than did the children from intact families. That is a nomothetic finding that applies to children of divorce as a group. And that is what is commonly reported in the media and in research journals as well. In this particular study, it likely was the case that some of the children from divorced families had higher school achievement than children from intact families—not as many, but some. Indeed, it is entirely possible that, of the 100 children in the study, the 2 or 3 children who had the highest school achievement were from divorced families—and that this fact was never reported in the popular media.

Nomothetic research can give teachers good information about the characteristics of a group of children, revealing strengths and weaknesses of the group. However, in many instances, teachers, as well as the child's parents, want to know about how to help one particular child cope and learn more effectively. **Idiographic needs** *are needs of the individual, not the group.* Unfortunately, although nomothetic research can point up problems for certain groups of children, it does not always hold for an individual child.

Recognize How Easy It Is to Overgeneralize About a Small or Clinical Sample   There often isn't space or time in media presentations to go into details about the nature of the sample of children on which the study is based. In many cases, samples are too small to let us generalize readily to a larger population. For example, if a study of children from divorced families is based on only 10 to 20 children, what is found in the study cannot be generalized to all children from divorced families. Perhaps the sample was drawn from families who have substantial economic resources, are Anglo-American, live in a small southern town, and are undergoing therapy. From this study, we clearly would be making unwarranted generalizations if we thought the findings also characterize children who are from low- to moderate-income families, are from other ethnic backgrounds, live in a different geographical location, and are not undergoing therapy.

Be Aware That a Single Study Usually Is Not the Defining Word   The media might identify an interesting research study and claim that it is something phenomenal with far-reaching implications. As a competent consumer of information, be aware that it is extremely rare for a single study to have earth-shattering, conclusive answers that apply to all students and teachers. In fact, where there are large numbers of studies that focus on a particular issue, it is not unusual to find conflicting results from one study to the next. Reliable answers about teaching and learning usually emerge only after many researchers have conducted similar studies and drawn similar conclusions. In our example of divorce, if one study reports that a school counseling program for students from divorced families improved their school achievement, we cannot conclude that the counseling will work as effectively with all students from divorced families until many more studies are conducted.

Remember That Causal Conclusions Cannot Be Drawn from Correlational Studies   Drawing causal conclusions from correlational studies is one of the most common mistakes made by the media. In nonexperimental studies (remember that in an experiment, participants are randomly assigned to treatments or experiences), two variables or factors might be related to each other. However, causal interpretations cannot be made when two or more factors simply are correlated. We cannot say that one causes the other. In the case of divorce, the headline might read, "Divorce causes students to have problems in school." We read the story and find out that the information is based on the results of a research study. Because we obviously cannot, for ethical and practical reasons, randomly assign students to families that will become divorced or remain intact, this headline is based on a correlational study, and the causal statements are unproved. It could well be, for example, that some other factor, such as family conflict or economic problems, is responsible for both children's poor school performance and parents' divorce.

SUMMARY TABLE 1.3
Program Evaluation, Action Research, the Teacher-as-Researcher, and Research Challenges

Concept	Processes/ Related Ideas	Characteristics/Description
Program Evaluation, Action Research, and Teacher-as-Researcher	Their Nature	• Program evaluation research is research designed to make decisions about the effectiveness of a particular program. • Action research is used to solve a specific classroom or social problem, improve teaching strategies, or make a decision about a specific location. • The teacher-as-researcher (teacher-researcher) conducts classroom studies to improve her or his educational practices. • Two popular teacher-researcher methods are clinical interviews and participant observation.
Research Challenges	Ethics	• Educational psychology researchers recognize that a number of ethical concerns have to be met when conducting research. • The interests of the participants always have to be kept in mind.
	Gender	• Every effort should be made to make research equitable for both females and males. • In the past, research too often has been biased against females.
	Ethnicity and Culture	• We need to include more children from ethnic minority backgrounds in educational psychology research. • A special concern is ethnic gloss.
	Being a Wise Consumer of Information About Educational Psychology	• Be cautious about what is reported in the media, avoid drawing conclusions about individual needs on the basis of group research, recognize how easy it is to overgeneralize about a small or clinical sample, be aware that a single study usually is not the defining word, remember that causal conclusions cannot be drawn from correlational studies, and always consider the source of the information and evaluate its credibility.

Always Consider the Source of the Information and Evaluate Its Credibility   Studies are not automatically accepted by the research community. Researchers usually must submit their findings to a research journal, where it is reviewed by their colleagues, who make a decision about whether or not to publish the paper. Although the quality of research in journals is far from uniform, in most cases the research has undergone far more scrutiny and careful consideration of the work's quality than is the case for research or any other information that has not gone through the journal process. And within the media, we can distinguish between what is presented in respected newspapers, such as the *New York Times* and *Washington Post,* as well as credible magazines such as *Time* and *Newsweek,* and what is presented in the tabloids, such as the *National Inquirer* and *Star.*

At this point we have studied many ideas about program evaluation, action research, teacher-as-researcher, and research challenges. A review of these ideas is presented in summary table 1.3. In the next chapter, we will explore the physical and cognitive aspects of children's development.

Chapter Review

Chapter Review

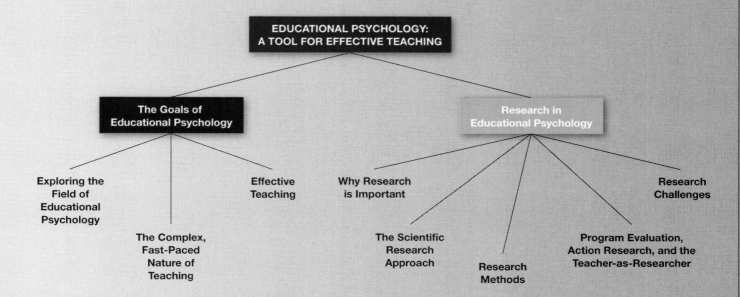

TO OBTAIN A DETAILED REVIEW OF THIS CHAPTER, STUDY THESE THREE SUMMARY TABLES:

Key Terms

educational
   psychology 6
constructivism 10
scientific research 19
scientific method 19
theory 20
hypotheses 20
laboratory 20

naturalistic
   observation 20
standardized tests 22
case study 22
correlational research 22
experimental research 23
experiment 23
independent variable 23

dependent variable 24
experimental group 24
control group 24
random assignment 24
cross-sectional research 25
longitudinal research 25
program evaluation
   research 25

action research 25
teacher-as-researcher 27
participant
   observation 27
ethnic gloss 30
nomothetic research 30
idiographic needs 31

Educational Psychology Checklist
EDUCATIONAL PSYCHOLOGY: A TOOL FOR EFFECTIVE TEACHING

How much have you learned since the beginning of the chapter? Use the following statements to help you review your knowledge and understanding of the chapter material. First, read the statement and mentally or briefly on paper demonstrate that you can outline the relevant information.

_____ I can sketch the historical background of educational psychology.
_____ I can discuss educational psychology as an art and as a science.
_____ I can explain the complex, fast-paced nature of teaching.
_____ I can discuss the challenges of becoming an effective teacher.

_____ I know why research is important and can describe the scientific research approach.
_____ I can compare a number of research methods.
_____ I can discuss program evaluation research, action research, and the teacher-as-researcher.
_____ I can describe a number of research challenges.

For any items that you did not check off, go back and locate the relevant material in the chapter. Review the material until you feel you can check off the item. You also might want to use this checklist later in preparing for an exam.

Adventures for the Mind

Now that you have a good knowledge and understanding of the chapter, complete the following exercises to expand your thinking about the chapter's topics.

• What kind of teacher do you want to become? What strengths do you want to have? What kinds of potential weaknesses might you need to overcome? Take some time to think about these questions. Then you might want to write down your responses and seal them in an envelope that you will open after your first month or two of teaching.
• At the beginning of the chapter, you read teacher-astronaut Christa McAuliffe's quote: "I touch the future. I teach." Don your creative

thinking hat and come up with a brief quote that describes a positive aspect of teaching.
• Think about the grade level you are planning to teach. Consider at least one way that your classroom at that grade level is likely to be complex and fast-paced. How will you cope with this?
• Information about educational psychology appears in research journals and in magazines and newspapers. Find an article in a research or professional journal (such as *Contemporary Educational Psychology, Educational Psychologist, Educational Psychology Review, Journal of Educational Psychology,* or *Phi Delta Kappan*) and an article in a newspaper or magazine on the same topic. How does the research/professional article differ from the newspaper or magazine account? What can you learn from this comparison?

Taking It to the Net

1. What is it about educational psychology that arouses your interest? What topics came to mind when you were considering taking this class?
2. Imagine that you are about to begin teaching in a few weeks. What goals will drive your teaching? Do you want your students to be "higher-order" thinkers? proficient in basic skills? successful in personal growth?

3. You have been asked by another teacher to come to her class and evaluate her teaching. What types of research skills will you employ to complete this evaluation, and how might these different research/evaluation styles lead to different conclusions?

 Connect to http://www.mhhe.com/socscience/psychology/santedu/ttnet.htm to find the answers!

Case Studies

Case 1: *Anita Underwood*: An experienced and enthusiastic third-grade teacher describes in detail her plans and her activities for the first day of class for the new school year and shares her sense of excitement and her fears.

Case 2: *Christie Raymond*: A mature woman in the first month of her first full-time position teaching music in an elementary school loves the work as long as the children are singing, but dislikes the school's emphasis on and her part in disciplining the students. The case describes Christie's classroom teaching in detail as well as her after-school bus duty.

Chapter 2

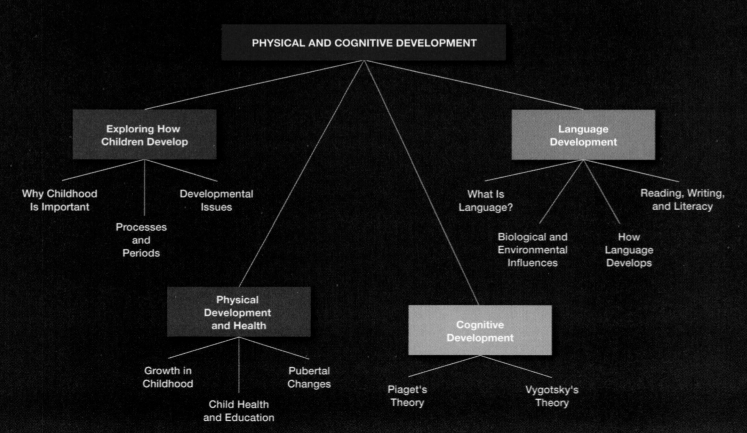

PHYSICAL AND COGNITIVE DEVELOPMENT

Exploring How Children Develop
- Why Childhood Is Important
- Processes and Periods
- Developmental Issues

Physical Development and Health
- Growth in Childhood
- Child Health and Education
- Pubertal Changes

Cognitive Development
- Piaget's Theory
- Vygotsky's Theory

Language Development
- What Is Language?
- Biological and Environmental Influences
- How Language Develops
- Reading, Writing, and Literacy

> "Ah! What would the world be to us If the children were no more? We should dread the desert behind us Worse than the dark before."

Henry Wadsworth Longfellow
American Poet, 19th Century

Preview

Examining the shape of children's development allows us to understand it better. Every childhood is distinct, the first chapter in a new biography. This chapter is about children's physical and cognitive development. These are some of the questions we will explore:

- Do children develop in distinct stages, or is their development smoother and more continuous?
- How do children develop physically, and how does this affect their behavior and learning?
- What is the best way to characterize children's cognitive development? How might knowledge of children's cognitive development influence the way you teach your students?
- How does language develop? What is the best way to teach children to read?

Teaching Stories
Betty Teuful

Betty Teuful teaches language arts to first-grade students in Plano, Texas. She was the school district's teacher of the year in 1998. Literacy is her passion, and she is a strong advocate of literacy not only in her school but throughout the nation. She envisions a literacy revival in which a corps of volunteers become reading tutors in schools, community centers, and hospitals. Betty is working with nonprofit organizations to solicit publishers and businesses to contribute to a national "Read While You Wait" campaign that will saturate clinics, restaurants, airports, and other public facilities with good literature.

She believes that if children don't know how to read, if they don't understand language, and they don't communicate with each other, it won't matter if they are computer literate. In her view, if children are helped to become competent at reading early in their schooling, their motivation to read should last a lifetime. In her words, "We ought to get them hooked on reading."

At Saigling Elementary school, Betty conducts literacy workshops for parents and places book baskets in locations where parents can read while they wait for conferences, meetings, and carpool groups. Enlisting the musical talents of another Saigling teacher, Betty orchestrated the creation of Sing to Read, a program in which students observe patterns, rhymes, and rhythms in songs to help develop their reading skills. Every day after recess, first-grade classes gather to sing songs written on flip charts.

"My students know that every time we have a holiday, I'm going to buy a book and share it with the class," she says. They will say, "What did you find?" Then they all sit down together to read.

Teuful wants to guide children to a sense of self-worth, self-discipline, tolerance, humor, and an attitude of lifelong learning. One of the ways she encourages such traits is by having "Joke Day" every Friday. Students get to write out jokes or riddles and leave them in a basket to be read during the day. They delight in trying to stump the teacher.

Teuful says, "Anything that makes a teacher grow or stretch and think how he or she is instructing is good for children. The worst thing for a teacher is stagnation. I think you have to be willing to try out new ideas and explore new ways for children to learn."

The day after Teufel received her Teacher of the Year award, Saigling first-graders honored her with a flower parade. They brought many varieties of flowers to school, some from their gardens at home, others made with construction or tissue paper. When asked about their teacher, Ryan and Jordan chimed in "She's nice and she's fair."

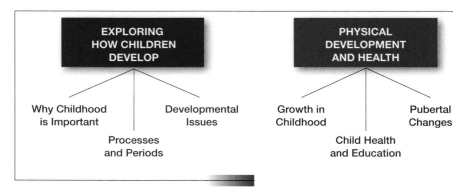

Exploring How Children Develop

Twentieth-century Spanish-born American philosopher George Santayana once reflected, "Children are on a different plane. They belong to a generation and way of feeling properly their own." Let's explore what that plane is like.

Why Childhood Is Important

Why study children's development? As a teacher, you will be responsible for a new wave of children each year in your classroom. The more you learn about children's development, the more you can understand at what level it is appropriate to teach them.

Childhood has become such a distinct phase of the human life span that it is hard to imagine that it was not always thought of in that way. However, in medieval times, laws generally did not distinguish between child and adult offenses and children were often treated like miniature adults.

Today we view children quite differently than was the case in medieval times. We conceive of childhood as a highly eventful and unique time of life that lays an important foundation for the adult years and is highly differentiated from them. We identify distinct periods within childhood in which children master special skills and confront new life tasks. We value childhood as a special time of growth and change, and we invest great resources in caring for and educating our children. We protect them from the excesses of adult work through tough child labor laws, treat their crimes against society under a special system of juvenile justice, and have government provisions for helping children when ordinary family support systems fail or when a family seriously threatens a child's well-being.

Each child develops partly like all other children, partly like some other children, and partly like no other children. We often direct our attention to a child's uniqueness. But psychologists who study development often are drawn to children's shared characteristics—as are teachers who must manage and educate groups of same- or similar-age children. As humans, every person travels some common paths—Leonardo da Vinci, Joan of Arc, Martin Luther King, Jr., Madonna, and most likely you yourself all walked at about 1 year, engaged in fantasy play as a child, developed an expanded vocabulary in the elementary school years, and became more independent as a youth.

Just what do psychologists mean when they speak of a person's "development"? **Development** *is the pattern of biological, cognitive, and socioemotional changes that begins at conception and continues through the life span.* Most development involves growth, although it also eventually involves decay (dying).

An important concept in education related to development is that education should be age-appropriate. That is, teaching should take place at a level that is neither too difficult and stressful nor too easy and boring. As we discuss development in this chapter and the next, keep in mind how the developmental changes we describe can help you understand the optimal level for teaching and learning. For example, it is not a good strategy to try to push children to read before they are developmentally ready; but when they are ready, reading materials should be presented at the appropriate level.

Processes and Periods

Children are the legacy we leave for a time we will not live to see.

Aristotle
Greek Philosopher, 4th Century B.C.

The pattern of development is complex because it is the product of several processes: biological, cognitive, and socioemotional. Development also can be described in terms of periods.

Biological, Cognitive, and Socioemotional Processes

Biological processes *involve changes in the child's body. Genetic inheritance plays a large part.* Biological processes underlie the development of the brain, height, and weight gains, changes in motor skills, and puberty's hormonal changes.

Cognitive processes *involve changes in the child's thinking, intelligence, and language.* Cognitive developmental processes enable a growing child to memorize a poem, imagine how to solve a math problem, come up with a creative strategy, or string together meaningfully connected sentences.

Socioemotional processes *involve changes in the child's relationships with other people, changes in emotion, and changes in personality.* Parents' nurturance toward their child, a boy's aggressive attack on a peer, a girl's development of assertiveness, and an adolescent's feelings of joy after getting good grades all reflect socioemotional processes in development.

In this chapter, we will focus on physical (biological) and cognitive processes. In the next chapter, we will explore socioemotional processes. Remember as you read about biological, cognitive, and socioemotional processes that they are interwoven. Socioemotional processes can shape cognitive processes, cognitive processes can promote or restrict socioemotional processes, biological processes can influence cognitive processes, and so on.

Periods of Development

For the purposes of organization and understanding, we commonly describe development in terms of periods. In the most widely used system of classification, the developmental periods are infancy, early childhood, middle and late childhood, adolescence, early adulthood, middle adulthood, and late adulthood.

Infancy *extends from birth to 18–24 months.* It is a time of extreme dependence on adults. Many activities, such as language development, symbolic thought, sensorimotor coordination, and social learning, are just beginning.

Early childhood *(sometimes called the "preschool years") extends from the end of infancy to about 5 or 6 years.* During this period, children become more self-sufficient, develop school readiness skills (such as learning to follow instructions and identify letters), and spend many hours with peers. First grade typically marks the end of early childhood.

Middle and late childhood *(sometimes called the "elementary school years") extends from about 6 to 11 years of age.* Children master the fundamental skills of reading, writing, and math at this time. Achievement becomes a more central theme of children's lives and they increase their self-control. In this period, they interact more with the wider social world beyond their family.

Adolescence *involves the transition from childhood to adulthood.* It begins around ages 10 to 12 and ends around 18 to 22. Adolescence starts with rapid physical changes, including gains in height and weight and the development of sexual functions. In adolescence, individuals more intensely pursue independence and seek their own identity. Their thought becomes more abstract, logical, and idealistic.

Early adulthood *begins in the late teens or early twenties and stretches into the thirties.* It is a time when work and love become main themes in life. Individuals make important career decisions and usually seek to have an intimate relationship through marriage or a relationship with a significant other. Other developmental periods have been described for older adults, but we will confine our discussion to the periods most relevant for children's education.

The periods of human development are shown in figure 2.1 along with the processes of development (biological, cognitive, and socioemotional). The interplay of these processes produces the periods of human development.

Developmental Issues

Three broad theoretical questions repeatedly come up when we study children's development:

- Is a child's development due more to maturation (nature, heredity) or more to experience (nurture, environment)?
- Is a child's development more continuous and smooth or more discontinuous and stagelike?
- Is a child's development due more to early experiences or more to later experiences?

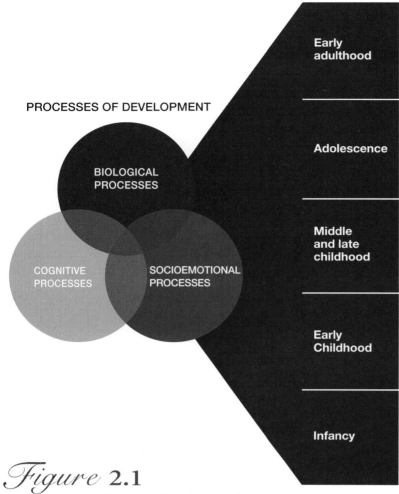

PROCESSES OF DEVELOPMENT

BIOLOGICAL PROCESSES

COGNITIVE PROCESSES

SOCIOEMOTIONAL PROCESSES

Early adulthood

Adolescence

Middle and late childhood

Early Childhood

Infancy

Figure **2.1**
Processes and Periods of Development
Biological, cognitive, and socioemotional processes interact to produce the periods of development.

Maturation and Experience (Nature and Nurture)   We can think of development as produced not only by the interplay of biological, cognitive, and socioemotional processes, but also by the interaction of maturation and experience. **Maturation** *is the orderly sequence of changes dictated by the child's genetic blueprint.* Just as a sunflower grows in an orderly way (unless defeated by an unfriendly environment), so does a child grow in an orderly way, according to the maturational view. We walk before we talk, speak one word before two words, grow rapidly in infancy and less so in childhood, and experience a rush of sexual hormones in puberty after a lull in childhood. The maturationists acknowledge that extreme environments (those that are physically or psychologically barren and hostile) can harm development. However, they believe that basic growth tendencies are genetically wired into the child's makeup.

In contrast, other psychologists emphasize the importance of experiences in children's development. Experiences run the gamut of inputs from the biological environment (nutrition, medical care, drugs, physical accidents) to the social environment (family, peers, schools, communities, media, culture).

The debate about whether development is influenced primarily by maturation or by experience, which is often called the **nature-nurture controversy,** has been a part of psychology since its beginning. *Nature* refers to the child's biological inheritance, *nurture* to environmental experiences. The "nature" proponents claim that biological inheritance is what mainly determines development. The "nurture" proponents argue that environmental experiences are more important.

Continuity and Discontinuity   Think about your development for a moment. Did you gradually grow to become the person you are, in the slow cumulative way a seedling grows into a giant oak? Or did you experience sudden, distinct changes as you grew, like the change of a caterpillar into a butterfly? (See figure 2.2.)

Continuity in development *refers to gradual, cumulative change.* For example, consider the continuity in development when children gradually become better at math or come to understand the importance of treating others fairly. For the most part, psychologists who emphasize experience describe development as gradual and continuous. **Discontinuity in development** *refers to more distinctive, stagelike change.* In this view, each of us passes through a sequence of stages in which change is qualitative rather than quantitative. That is, development does not just produce more of something, it produces something different. As a caterpillar changes into a butterfly, it becomes a different kind of organism. Its development is discontinuous. Similarly, at some point in development a child becomes capable of writing a meaningful sentence, which the child could not have done before, or becomes interested in dating after previously showing no interest in it. This is qualitative, discontinuous change.

Figure 2.2
Continuity and Discontinuity in Development
Is human development like a seedling gradually growing into a giant oak? Or is it more like a caterpillar suddenly becoming a butterfly?

Early and Later Experience
The **early-later experience issue** *focuses on the degree to which early experiences (especially in infancy and/or early childhood) or later experiences are the key determinants of development.* For example, if infants and young children experience highly stressful circumstances, can those experiences be overcome by later, more positive experiences?

The early-later experience issue has a long history and continues to be hotly debated. Some developmentalists believe that unless infants experience warm, nurturant caregiving in the first year or so of life, their development will never be optimal (Bowlby, 1989). Plato was sure that infants who are rocked become better athletes. Nineteenth-century New England ministers told parents in Sunday sermons that the way they handled their infants determined their children's future character. The emphasis on early experience rests on the belief that each life is an unbroken trail on which a psychological quality can be traced back to a specific origin early in development (Kagan, 1992; 1998).

In contrast, proponents of the influence of later experience argue that development ebbs and flows like an ocean. They say that children are capable of change and that later competent caregiving is just as important as, or more important than, early competent caregiving.

People in Western cultures tend to support the early-experience side of this issue. Many of them have been influenced by the views of famous psychoanalytic theorist Sigmund Freud, who believed that virtually all of a person's important life experiences occur in the first 5 years of life, especially in relationships with parents. Many people in Eastern cultures, on the other hand, believe that experiences in the elementary school years are more important than earlier experiences. This stance stems from their view that the key changes in children's cognitive skills, especially their ability to reason, occur after the infant and early childhood years.

Evaluating the Developmental Issues
Most developmentalists believe it is unwise to take an extreme position on these three developmental questions. Development is not all nature, not all nurture (Plomin, 2000; Wahlsteni, 2000). It is not all continuous, not all discontinuous. And it is not all early experience or all later experience. Yet how you lean regarding these questions has a bearing on issues that will affect your teaching. For example, are girls less likely than boys to do well in math and science? And if they are, is this because of their "feminine" nature

or because of society's masculine bias? Depending on how you answer this question, you will find different ways to resolve the teaching problem it implies. For children who grew up with poverty, parental neglect, and poor schooling, can enriched experiences in adolescence remove the "deficits"? Your stance on such issues as nature versus nurture also will influence your answer to that question.

Physical Development and Health

As twentieth-century Welsh poet Dylan Thomas artfully observed, children "run all the sun long." And as their physical development advances, their small worlds widen. In this section, we will focus mainly on the normal aspects of physical development. In chapter 6, "Learners Who Are Exceptional," we will explore strategies for teaching with children who have a physical disability.

Growth in Childhood

The infant's growth is extremely rapid. The young child's growth is slower. This slower rate continues through middle and late childhood. Otherwise, we would be giants.

An important aspect of physical growth is the development of the brain and nervous system. The number and size of the brain's nerve endings continue to grow at least until adolescence. Some of the brain's increase in size also is due to **myelination,** *a process in which many cells of the brain and nervous system are covered with an insulating layer of fat cells. This increases the speed at which information travels through the nervous system.* Myelination in the areas of the brain related to hand-eye coordination is not complete until about 4 years of age. Myelination in brain areas that are important in focusing attention is not complete until the end of the elementary school years (Tanner, 1978). The implications for teaching are that children will have more difficulty focusing their attention and maintaining it for very long in early childhood but their attention will improve as they move through the elementary school years. Even in elementary school and later, many educators believe occasional short breaks sustain children's energy and motivation to learn.

Gross motor and fine motor skills develop extensively during childhood. **Gross motor skills** *involve large-muscle activities, such as running and playing basketball.* **Fine motor skills** *involve finely tuned movements, such as the finger dexterity required for writing and drawing.* Children become increasingly venturesome as their gross motor skills improve.

Preschool and kindergarten teachers should implement developmentally appropriate activities for the exercise of gross motor skills. In early childhood, these include exercises that involve fundamental movement, daily fitness, and perceptual-motor activities (Poest & others, 1990). Walking on a beam is one example of an exercise that promotes fundamental movement skills. Daily fitness activities can include a daily run accompanied by music. Combining fitness with creative movement, music, and children's imagination is a good strategy. Children enjoy moving like snakes, cats, kangaroos, and airplanes.

Avoid recordings and activities that "program" children or involve group calisthenics that are not appropriate for young children. To develop young children's gross

THROUGH THE EYES OF TEACHERS

Doing is Learning

For the very young children we teach in preschool, modeling is the most effective way to teach health. Routine trips to the bathroom become a lesson in proper hand-washing techniques. Before and after lunch are times to teach appropriate hygiene skills. I also incorporate correct ways to brush teeth. These skills are not taught in isolation, but are part of a young child's daily living skills. Learning these skills also fosters children's independence. Our school has a full-time nurse. The nurse's office becomes another classroom, where she reinforces what the teacher already is doing.

Juanita Kirton
Assistant Principal
YAI/NYL Gramercy Preschool
New York City

motor skills, also include perceptual-motor activities. Teachers can ask children to copy their movements, tap and march to the tune of nursery rhymes, and complete safe obstacle courses.

The development of young children's fine motor skills allows them to draw with more control and skill. Art provides considerable insight into children's perceptual worlds. These insights include what children are attending to, how they view space and distance, and how they experience patterns and forms. Teachers can give children a positive context for artistic expression by providing them a work space where they don't have to be worried about being messy or damaging things.

During the elementary school years, children's motor development becomes much smoother and more coordinated. Children gain greater control over their bodies and can sit and attend for longer periods of time. However, classes should still be active and activity oriented. Throughout childhood, boys tend to be better at gross motor skills, girls tend to be better at fine motor skills.

Child Health and Education

Although we have become a health-conscious nation, many children as well as adults do not practice good health habits. All too many children eat too much junk food and spend too much time as couch potatoes.

Physical Education Classes   For too long, exercise was relegated to a back seat in children's education. Even today, only 36 percent of schoolchildren are required to participate in physical education. Too little attention is given to the quality of physical education classes, whether children are getting adequate exercise, and whether they eat properly. Recall our earlier discussion of how physical, cognitive, and socioemotional development are interrelated. Children who come to school hungry and do not exercise regularly (physical development) often do not attend as efficiently in school and are less motivated to study (cognitive development) than their healthier counterparts.

Even when children take a physical education class, they do not always actively participate. Observations of physical education classes at four elementary schools

We are underexercised as a nation. We look instead of play. We ride instead of walk. Our existence deprives us of the minimum of physical activity essential for healthy living.

John F. Kennedy
U.S. President, 20th Century

**Child Health Guide
Physical Education**

As children move through the elementary school years, they gain greater control over their bodies. Physical action is essential for them to refine their developing skills.

TEACHING STRATEGIES
For Physical Development and Health

Some strategies you can use to promote your students' physical development and health are:

1. *If you are involved in children's physical education, systematically observe the extent to which all children are participating.* Work on some strategies for getting nonathletic children to actively engage in physical activities.
2. *If your school does not have a comprehensive program like Heart Smart, get together with some other teachers and investigate the possibilities for instituting such a program.*
3. *Be a good model for healthy behavior yourself.*
4. *Recognize the dramatic changes that puberty brings to students' lives.* Be sensitive to early and late maturational changes, as well as to how puberty is coming earlier. Recognize the vulnerability that early-maturing girls especially face.

found that children moved through space only 50 percent of the time they were in class and moved continuously only an average of 2.2 minutes (Parcel & others, 1987).

Does it make a difference if children are encouraged to exercise vigorously in elementary school? One study says yes (Tuckman & Hinkle, 1988). Children were randomly assigned either to three 30-minute running programs per week or to regular attendance in physical education classes. In cardiovascular fitness and creative thinking, the children in the running program were superior to the children who regularly attended traditional physical education classes.

Is Television the Culprit?
Some experts argue that television might be partly to blame for the poor physical fitness of our nation's children. In one study, children who watched little television were physically more fit than their counterparts who watched a lot of television (Tucker, 1987). The more children watched, the more overweight they were. Whether this was because children spent their leisure time watching television instead of exercising, or whether they ate more junk food that they saw advertised on television, was not investigated. In either case, reducing television viewing is a wise strategy, not only for improved physical fitness but also for spending more time on homework and school-related activities. The amount of time the child spends watching television may be a topic you will want to explore with parents of children who are having difficulty in school.

**Bogalusa
Heart Study**

A Model School-Health Program: Heart Smart
Exercise is an important component in the Bogalusa Heart Study, a large-scale study of children's health that involves ongoing evaluation of 8,000 students in Bogalusa, Louisiana (Freedman & others, in press; Nicklas & others, 1995). Many children in the program already have one or more health risk factors such as obesity or hypertension. The intervention strategy to improve students' health in Bogalusa is called "Heart Smart."

The school is the focus of the intervention. Special attention is given to teachers, who serve as health role models. Teachers who value the role of health in life and engage in health-enhancing behaviors present children with positive models for health. Teacher in-service education is conducted by an interdisciplinary team of specialists that includes physicians, nutritionists, physical educators, and exercise physiologists.

The physical education component of Heart Smart involves two to four class periods each week. It consists of a "Superkids-Superfit" exercise program. The instructor has students participate in aerobic activities that include jogging, race walking, interval workouts, skipping rope, circuit training, aerobic dance, and games. Gym classes begin and end with 5 minutes of walking and stretching.

ᒡELF-ASSESSMENT 2.1
Being a Physically and Mentally Healthy Teacher

Use the following brief assessment to evaluate your health in four areas: exercise/fitness, eating habits, alcohol/drugs and cigarette smoking, and stress control. For each item, respond A = almost always, S = sometimes, or N = almost never.

	A	S	N

Exercise/Fitness
1. I maintain a desired weight and avoid being overweight or underweight.
2. I do vigorous exercises (such as running, swimming, walking briskly) for 15 to 30 minutes at least 3 times a week.
3. I do exercises that improve my muscle tone (such as yoga, calisthenics, and lifting weights) for 15 to 30 minutes at least 3 times a week.
4. I use part of my leisure time to participate in individual, family, or team activities that increase my fitness level (such as gardening, bowling, golf, and baseball).

Eating Habits
5. I eat a variety of foods each day, such as fruits and vegetables, whole-grain breads and cereals, lean meats, dairy products, dry peas and beans, and nuts and seeds.
6. I limit the amount of fat, saturated fat, and cholesterol I eat.
7. I limit the amount of salt I eat.
8. I avoid eating too much sugar (especially frequent candy snacks or soft drinks).

Alcohol/Drugs, Smoking
9. I avoid drinking alcoholic beverages or I drink no more than one or two drinks a day.
10. I avoid using alcohol or other drugs as a way of handling stressful situations or problems in my life.
11. I avoid smoking cigarettes or using other nicotine substances.

Stress Control
12. I have a job or do other work that I enjoy.
13. I find it easy to relax and I express my feelings freely.
14. I have good resources, such as close friends or relatives, whom I can call on in times of stress.
15. I participate in group activities (such as church and community organizations) or hobbies that I enjoy.

Scoring and Interpretation
Give yourself 3 points for each item you answered A (always), 2 points for each S (sometimes) answer, and 1 point for each N (never) answer. Total the points here: _____. If you scored 40–45, your physical and mental health should be excellent. You will be a good health role model for your students. If you scored 35–39, your physical and mental health should be good and you also are likely to be a good health role model for your students. However, there probably are some areas you can improve on. Look at the items you scored 2 or 1 on to determine the areas in which you need to improve. If you scored 30–34, your physical and mental health need some work. There are too many aspects of your physical and mental health that you only practice some of the time or don't practice at all. Work on improving these habits to be a good health role model for students. If you scored below 30, you likely will be a poor health role model for students. Give some serious thought to getting yourself in better physical and mental shape. Your students will benefit from your efforts. Regardless of your total score, examine the pattern of your scores. For example, you might have excellent physical health habits and weak mental health habits. Or you might fall down just in one area of physical health, such as exercise/fitness.

The school lunch program is also part of Heart Smart's intervention. The foods used in the program are low in sodium, fat, and sugar. Instructors explain why students should eat healthy foods, such as a tuna sandwich, and not eat unhealthy foods, such as a hot dog with chili. The school lunch program includes a salad bar. The amount and type of snack foods sold on the school grounds are monitored.

THROUGH THE EYES OF TEACHERS

Transitions

At the middle school level:

- Big 13-year-olds, no matter how big they look, are only 13.
- Small 12-year-olds, no matter how small they look, will be driving cars in 4 years.
- Many students have self-esteem issues related to physical development—height, weight, deformities (real or imagined), breast size, anything that sets them apart as somewhat different.

Lawren Giles
Mathematics Teacher, Grades 7 and 8
Baechtel Grove Middle School
Willits, California

Transition to high school:

- Don't assume students know what is expected of them. This is especially critical in classes that have a mixture of 9th graders and upperclass students. Don't assume you know what they experienced in middle school, but try to acquire some idea. Remember some students may come from different schools. It's worth finding out. I always have my students fill out a basic information sheet with this information.
- Don't hesitate to talk to individual students privately about inappropriate behavior. Removing the audience can help them regain control.

Barbara Berry
French and Humanities Teacher
Ypsilanti High School
Ypsilanti, Michigan

Puberty Change

In no order of things is adolescence the simple time of life.

Jean Erskine Stewart
American Writer, 20th Century

The Heart Smart program includes identifying high-risk children (those with elevated blood pressure, cholesterol, and weight). A multidisciplinary team of physicians, nutritionists, nurses, and counselors works with the high-risk students and their parents to improve the students' diet and level of exercise. Other school health programs that are currently being implemented include the Minnesota Heart Health Program (Kelder & others, 1995) and the Southwest Cardiovascular Curriculum Project (Davis & others, 1995).

Not only is it important for teachers to help students develop good health habits, it also is important for teachers to have positive physical and mental health habits so that they will be more alert, think more clearly, and teach more effectively in the classroom. To evaluate some of the characteristics of being a physically and mentally healthy teacher, see Self-Assessment 2.1.

Pubertal Changes

Puberty *is a phase of maturation that occurs mainly in early adolescence. The changes involve a height and weight spurt and sexual maturation.* The changes start on the average at about 10½ years in females and 12½ years in males (see figure 2.3). One of the most remarkable normal variations is that, of two boys (or two girls) of the same chronological age, one might complete the pubertal sequence before the other has begun it. For example, the onset of puberty can occur as early as 8 years of age in girls and 9½ years in boys, or as late as 13 in girls and 13½ in boys, and still be considered within the normal range.

Puberty is coming earlier and has been doing so since the beginning of the twentieth century, as a result of improved health and nutrition, although the changes in pubertal timing have begun to taper off. Menstruation is a very late pubertal event, with the height/weight spurt usually appearing about 2 years earlier. In 1900, the girl's first menstruation (called menarche) occurred at an average of 14 years of age, whereas today it occurs at about 12 years of age.

Because puberty is coming so much earlier, elementary school teachers are seeing far more students in the late elementary school grades who have entered puberty, especially girls. Today, an increasing number of 9-year-old girls are entering puberty. The increasingly early appearance of puberty calls attention to the importance of including competent instruction in health and sex education in the elementary school years.

Think back to when you were in sixth or seventh grade. Some of your classmates had not yet entered puberty, others were just starting, and yet others were far along the pubertal path. Boys and girls who enter puberty earlier or later than their peers might perceive themselves differently. Today, there is a special concern about early maturation in girls. A host of studies in the last decade have documented that early-maturing girls are vulnerable to developing a number of problems (Brooks-Gunn, 1996; Brooks-Gunn & Paikoff, in press; Petersen, 2000). Early-maturing girls are more likely to smoke, drink, be depressed, have an eating disorder, request earlier independence from their parents, have older friends, and date earlier. Apparently as a result of their socioemotional and cognitive immaturity, combined with their early

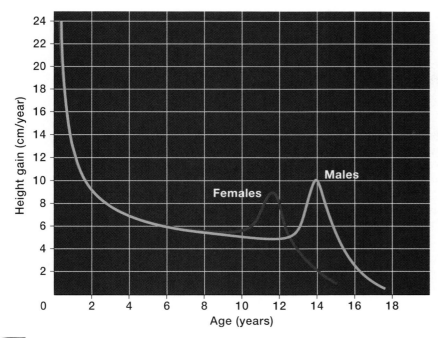

Figure **2.3**
Pubertal Growth Spurt
On the average, the growth spurt that characterizes pubertal change occurs 2 years earlier for girls (10½) than for boys (12½).

physical development, early-maturing girls are easily lured into problem behaviors. The effects of early maturation are not as bleak for boys as for girls, although men who were early-maturing as boys are less advanced in their career development during adulthood (Peskin, 1967). This presumably occurs because early-maturing boys get more positive feedback for their physical development, whereas late-maturing boys get more accolades for their academic achievement.

At this point we have discussed a number of ideas about exploring how children develop and children's physical development and health. A review of these ideas is presented in summary table 2.1.

From Penguin creams and Stranger Things by Berke D. Breathed. Copyright © 1985 by The Washington Post Company. By permission of Little, Brown, and Company.

SUMMARY TABLE 2.1
Exploring How Children Develop, and Physical Development and Health

Concept	Processes/ Related Ideas	Characteristics/Description
Exploring How Children Develop	Why Childhood Is Important	• The more you learn about children's development, the more you can understand the level at which to appropriately teach them. • Today we value childhood as a special time of growth and change and see it as building a foundation for the adult years. • Development is the pattern of biological, cognitive, and socioemotional changes that begins at conception and continues through the life span.
	Processes and Periods	• Development is the product of biological, cognitive, and socioemotional processes, which often are intertwined. • Periods of development include infancy, early childhood, middle and late childhood, adolescence, early adulthood, and late adulthood.
	Developmental Issues	• Three main dichotomies that characterize virtually all facets of development are maturation versus experience (nature and nurture), continuity versus discontinuity, and early versus later experience. • Maturation is the orderly sequence of changes dictated by the child's genetic blueprint. Experience includes the biological and the social environment. • Continuity refers to smooth, gradual growth. Discontinuity involves distinct, stagelike change. • The early-later experience issue focuses on the degree to which early experiences or later experiences determine development. • Most developmentalists do not take extreme stances on these issues.
Physical Development and Health	Childhood Growth	• The infant's growth is extremely rapid, but growth slows in childhood. • An especially important part of physical growth is the development of the brain and nervous system. Myelination involving hand-eye coordination is not complete until about 4 years of age, and myelination involving focusing attention is not finished until about 10. • Children's gross and fine motor skills develop extensively in the childhood years. Positive exercises for gross motor skills in early childhood include fundamental movement, daily fitness, and perceptual-motor activities. Boys are often better at gross motor skills, girls at fine motor skills. • Children's lives should be active and activity oriented.
	Child Health and Education	• For too long, exercise was relegated to a back seat in children's education. Even today, it does not get the attention it deserves. • Researchers have found that when children exercise vigorously in the elementary school years, their cardiovascular fitness increases and their thinking skills improve. • Heavy TV viewing is related to poor physical fitness in children. • One model school-health program is Heart Smart in Bogalusa, Louisiana. The school is the focus of the program, which emphasizes teachers as health role models, exercise activities, nutrition monitoring, and special attention for children at high risk for health problems.
	Pubertal Changes	• Puberty is a phase of maturation that occurs mainly in early adolescence and involves height, weight, and sexual changes. • Females enter puberty about 2 years earlier than males (10½ vs. 12½) and puberty is coming much earlier than a century ago. • Early-maturing girls are vulnerable to a number of problems.

Cognitive Development

Twentieth-century American poet Marianne Moore said that the mind is "an enchanting thing." How this enchanting thing called mind develops has intrigued many psychologists. We will explore two main approaches to how children's thoughts develop: Piaget's theory and Vygotsky's theory. Piaget's and Vygotsky's theories are constructivist. Recall from chapter 1 that this means that they believe that children actively construct their knowledge and understanding.

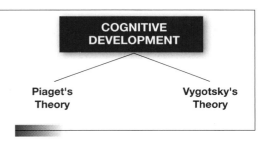

Piaget's Theory

Poet Noah Perry once asked, "Who knows the thoughts of a child?" More than anyone, the famous Swiss psychologist Jean Piaget (1896–1980) knew.

Piaget's Theory

Cognitive Processes   In actively constructing their world, children use schemas. A **schema** *is a concept or framework that exists in an individual's mind to organize and interpret information.* Piaget's interest in schemas focused on how children organize and make sense out of their current experiences.

Piaget (1952) said that two processes are responsible for how children use and adapt their schemas: assimilation and accommodation. **Assimilation** *occurs when a child incorporates new knowledge into existing knowledge.* That is, in assimilation children assimilate the environment into a schema. **Accommodation** *occurs when a child adjusts to new information.* That is, children adjust their schemas to the environment.

Consider an 8-year-old girl who is given a hammer and nail to hang a picture on the wall. She has never used a hammer, but from observing others do this she realizes that a hammer is an object to be held, that it is swung by the handle to hit the nail, and that it usually is swung a number of times. Recognizing each of these things, she fits her behavior into this schema she already has (assimilation). But the hammer is heavy, so she holds it near the top. She swings too hard and the nail bends, so she adjusts the pressure of her strikes. These adjustments reflect her ability to slightly alter her conception of the world (accommodation). Just as both assimilation and accommodation are required in this example, so are they required in many of the child's thinking challenges (see figure 2.4).

Piaget is shown here with his family. Piaget's careful observations of his three children—Lucienne, Laurent, and Jacqueline—contributed to the development of his cognitive theory.

Assimilation occurs when people incorporate new information into their existing knowledge. How might assimilation be involved in the 7-year-old girl's attempt to hang a picture with a hammer and nails?

Accommodation occurs when people adjust to new information. How might accommodation be involved in this 7-year-old girl's successful efforts at hanging the picture with a hammer and nails?

Figure 2.4
Assimilation and Accommodation

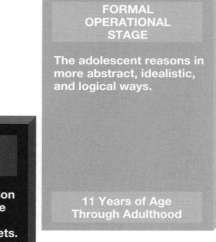

SENSORIMOTOR STAGE

The infant constructs an understanding of the world by coordinating sensory experiences with physical actions. An infant progresses from reflexive, instinctual action at birth to the beginning of symbolic thought toward the end of the stage.

Birth to 2 Years of Age

PREOPERATIONAL STAGE

The child begins to represent the world with words and images. These words and images reflect increased symbolic thinking and go beyond the connection of sensory information and physical action.

2 to 7 Years of Age

CONCRETE OPERATIONAL STAGE

The child can now reason logically about concrete events and classify objects into different sets.

7 to 11 Years of Age

FORMAL OPERATIONAL STAGE

The adolescent reasons in more abstract, idealistic, and logical ways.

11 Years of Age Through Adulthood

Figure **2.5**
Piaget's Four Stages of Cognitive Development

Piagetian Stages   Piaget also believed that cognitive development unfolds in a sequence of four stages. Each of the stages is age-related and consists of distinctive ways of thinking. It is the *different* way of thinking that makes one stage discontinuous from and more advanced than another. Knowing *more* information does not make the child's thinking more advanced, according to Piaget. The advance is *qualitatively* different. Piaget's stages are called sensorimotor, preoperational, concrete operational, and formal operational (see figure 2.5).

The Sensorimotor Stage   The **sensorimotor stage,** *which lasts from birth to about 2 years of age, is the first Piagetian stage. In this stage, infants construct an understanding of the world by coordinating their sensory experiences (such as seeing and hearing) with their motor actions (reaching, touching)* —hence the term *sensorimotor.* At the beginning of this stage, infants show little more than reflexive patterns to adapt to the world. By the end of the stage, they display far more complex sensorimotor patterns.

Piaget believed that *an especially important cognitive accomplishment in infancy is* **object permanence.** *This involves understanding that objects and events continue to exist even when they cannot be seen, heard, or touched.* A second accomplishment is the gradual realization that there is a difference or boundary between oneself and the surrounding environment. Imagine what your thought would be like if you could not distinguish between yourself and your world. Your thought would be chaotic, disorganized, and unpredictable. This is what the mental life of a newborn is like, according to Piaget. The child does not differentiate between self and world and has no sense of object permanence. By the end of the sensorimotor period, the child has both abilities.

The Preoperational Stage   The **preoperational stage** *is the second Piagetian stage. Lasting approximately from 2 to 7 years of age, it is more symbolic than sensorimotor thought but does not involve operational thought (mental representations that are* *reversible—this will be discussed later when we cover the concrete operational stage). It is egocentric, and intuitive rather than logical.*

Preoperational thought can be subdivided into two substages: symbolic function and intuitive thought. The **symbolic function substage** *occurs roughly between 2 and 4 years of age. In this substage, the young child gains the ability to represent mentally an object that is not present.* This stretches the child's mental world to new dimensions. Expanded use of language and the emergence of pretend play are other examples of an increase in symbolic thought during this early childhood substage. Young children begin to use scribbled designs to represent people, houses, cars, clouds, and many other aspects of the world. Possibly because young children are not very concerned about reality, their drawings are fanciful and inventive. Suns are blue, skies are green, and cars float on clouds in their imaginative world. The symbolism is simple but strong, not unlike abstractions found in some modern art. As the famous twentieth-century Spanish artist Pablo Picasso once remarked, "I used to draw like Raphael but it has taken me a lifetime to draw like young children." One 3 ½-year-old looked at the scribble he had just drawn and described it as a pelican kissing a seal (see figure 2.6a). In the elementary school years, children's drawings become more realistic, neat, and precise (see figure 2.6b). Suns are yellow, skies are blue, and cars travel on roads.

Even though young children make distinctive progress in this substage, their preoperational thought still has two important limitations: egocentrism and animism. **Egocentrism** *is the inability to distinguish between one's own perspective and someone else's perspective.* The following telephone interaction between 4-year-old Mary, who is at home, and her father, who is at work, typifies egocentric thought:

Father: Mary, is Mommy there?
Mary: (Silently nods)
Father: Mary, can I speak to Mommy?
Mary: (Nods again silently)

Mary's response is egocentric in that she fails to consider her father's perspective; she does not realize that he cannot see her nod.

Piaget and Barbel Inhelder (1969) initially studied young children's egocentrism by devising the three mountains task (see figure 2.7). The child walks around the model of the mountains and becomes familiar with what the mountains look like from different perspectives. The child also can see that there are different objects on the mountains. The child then is seated on one side of the table on which the mountains are placed. The experimenter moves a doll to different locations around the table. At each location the child is asked to select from a series of photos the one that most accurately reflects the view the doll is seeing. Children in the preoperational stage often pick the view that reflects where they are sitting rather than the doll's view.

Animism *also characterizes preoperational thought. It is the belief that inanimate objects have "lifelike" qualities and are capable of action.* A young child might show animism by saying, "That tree pushed the leaf off and it fell down" or "The sidewalk made me mad. It made me fall down."

What further cognitive changes take place in the preoperational stage? The **intuitive thought substage** *is the second substage of preoperational thought, starting at about 4 years of age and lasting until about 7 years of age. At this substage, children begin to use primitive reasoning and want to know the answers to all sorts of questions. Piaget called this substage "intuitive" because the children seem so sure about their knowledge and understanding, yet are unaware of how they know what they know.* That is, they say they know something but know it without the use of rational thinking.

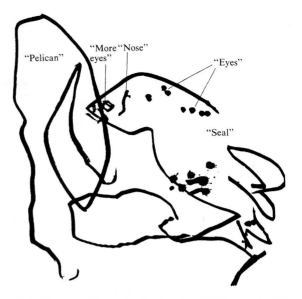

(*a*) A 3½-year-old's symbolic drawing. Halfway into this drawing, the 3½-year-old said it was "a pelican kissing a seal."

(*b*)This 11-year-old's drawing is neater and more realistic but also less inventive.

Figure 2.6
Developmental Changes in Children's Drawings

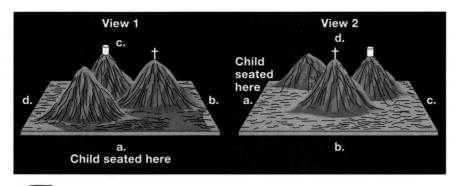

Figure 2.7
The Three Mountains Task

View 1 shows the child's perspective from where he or she is sitting. View 2 is an example of the photograph the child would be shown, mixed in with others from different perspectives. To correctly identify this view, the child has to take the perspective of a person sitting at spot *b*. Invariably, a preschool child who thinks in a preoperational way cannot perform this task. When asked what a view of the mountains looks like from position *b*, the child selects a photograph taken from location *a*, the child's view at the time.

An example of young children's limitation in reasoning ability is the difficulty they have putting things into correct categories. Faced with a collection of objects that can be sorted on the basis of two or more properties, preoperational children seldom are capable of using these properties consistently to sort the objects into appropriate groupings. Look at the collection of objects in figure 2.8a. You would probably respond to the direction "Put the things together that you believe belong together" by grouping the objects by size and shape. Your sorting might look something like that shown in figure 2.8b. In the social realm, if a 4-year-old girl is given the task of dividing her peers into groups according to whether they are friends and whether they are boys or girls, she is unlikely to arrive at a classification of friendly boys, friendly girls, unfriendly boys, unfriendly girls.

Many of these examples show a characteristic of preoperational thought called **centration.** *It involves focusing (or centering) attention on one characteristic to the exclusion of all others.* Centration is most clearly present in young children's lack of **conservation,** *the idea that some characteristic of an object stays the same even though the object might change in appearance.* For example, to adults it is obvious that a certain amount of liquid stays the same regardless of a container's shape. But this is not obvious at all to young children. Rather, they are struck by the height of the liquid in the container. In this type of conservation task (Piaget's most famous), a child is presented with two identical beakers, each filled to the same level with liquid (see figure 2.9). The child is asked if the beakers have the same amount of liquid. The child usually says yes. Then the liquid from one beaker is poured into a third beaker, which is taller and thinner. The child now is asked

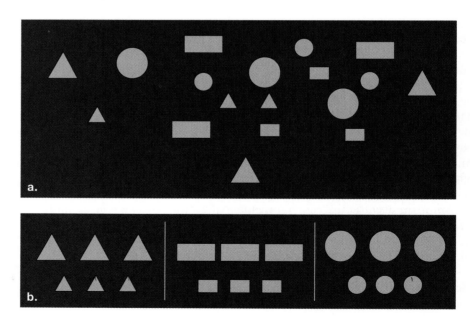

Figure 2.8
Arrays

(a) A random array of objects. *(b)* An ordered array of objects

if the amount of liquid in the tall, thin beaker is equal to the liquid that remains in the second original beaker. Children younger than 7 or 8 usually say no. They justify their answer by referring to the differing height or width of the beakers. Older children usually answer yes. They justify their answers appropriately: If you poured the liquid back, the amount would still be the same.

In Piaget's view, failing the conservation of liquid task indicates that the child is at the preoperational stage of thinking. Passing the test suggests the child is at the concrete operational stage of thinking.

In our definition of the preoperational stage we indicated that preschool children cannot perform operations. In Piaget's theory, **operations** *are mental representations that are reversible.* As in the beaker task, preschool children have difficulty understanding that reversing an action brings about the original conditions from which the action began. The following two examples should further help you understand Piaget's concepts of operations. A young child might know that 4 + 2 = 6 but not understand that the reverse, 6 − 2 = 4, is true. Or let's say a preschooler walks to his friend's house each day but always gets a ride home. If asked to walk home from his friend's house, he probably would reply that he didn't know the way because he never had walked home before.

Some developmentalists do not believe Piaget was entirely correct in his estimate of when conservation skills emerge. For example, Rochel Gelman (1969) trained preschool children to attend to relevant aspects of the conservation task. This improved their conservation skills. Gelman also has shown that attentional training on one type of conservation task, such as number, improves young children's performance on another type of conservation task, such as mass. She believes that young children develop conservation skills earlier than Piaget envisioned and that such skills can be improved with attentional training.

Yet another characteristic of preoperational children is that they ask a lot of questions. The barrage begins around age 3. By about 5, they have just about exhausted the adults around them with "Why?" "Why" questions signal the emergence of the child's interest in figuring out why things are the way they are. Following is a sampling of 4- to 6-year olds' questions (Elkind, 1976):

"What makes you grow up?"
"What makes you stop growing?"
"Who was the mother when everybody was a baby?"
"Why do leaves fall?"
"Why does the sun shine?"

The Concrete Operational Stage   The **concrete operational stage,** *the third Piagetian stage of cognitive development, lasts from about 7 to about 11 years of age. Concrete operational thought involves using operations. Logical reasoning replaces intuitive reasoning, but only in concrete situations. Classification skills are present, but abstract problems are problematic.*

Many of the concrete operations identified by Piaget focus on the way children reason about the properties of objects. At the concrete operational level, children can do mentally what they previously could do only physically, and they can reverse concrete operations. For example, to test conservation of matter, the child is presented with two identical balls of clay. The experimenter rolls one ball into a long, thin shape. The child is asked if there is more clay in the ball or in the long, thin piece of clay. By the time children are 7 or 8 years old, most answer that the amount of clay is the same. To answer this

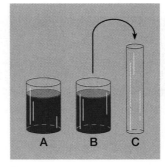
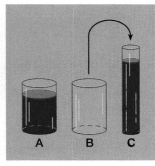

a.   b.

Figure 2.9
Piaget's Conservation Task
The beaker test is a well-known Piagetian test to determine whether a child can think operationally—that is, can mentally reverse actions and show conservation of the substance. (*a*) Two identical beakers are presented to the child. Then, the liquid is poured from B into C, which is taller and thinner than A or B. (*b*) The child is asked if these beakers (A and C) have the same amount of liquid. The preoperational child says no. When asked to point to the beaker that has more liquid, the preoperational child points to the tall, thin beaker.

"I still don't have all the answers, but I'm beginning to ask the right questions."

Drawing by Lorenz; © 1989 The New Yorker Magazine, Inc.

𝒯EACHING STRATEGIES
With Children Who Are Preoperational Thinkers

Following are some strategies for teaching children who are preoperational thinkers (Sund, 1976):

1. *Have children manipulate groups of objects.*
2. *To reduce egocentrism, involve children in social interactions.*
3. *Ask children to make comparisons, such as bigger, taller, wider, heavier, and longer.*
4. *Give children experience in ordering operations.* For example, have children line up in rows from tall to short and vice versa. Bring in various examples of animal and plant life cycles, such as several photographs of butterfly development or the sprouting of beans or kernels of corn. Examples of these natural stages help children's ordering ability.
5. *Have children draw scenes with perspective.* Encourage them to make the objects in their drawings appear to be at the same location as in the scene they are viewing. For example, if they see a horse at the end of a field, they should place the horse in the same location in the drawing.
6. *Construct an inclined plane or hill.* Let children roll marbles of various sizes down the plane. Ask them to compare how quickly the different-size marbles reach the bottom. This should help them understand the concept of speed.
7. *Ask children to justify their answers when they draw conclusions.* For example, when they say that pouring a liquid from a short, wide container into a tall, thin container makes the liquid change in volume, ask "Why do you think so?" or "How could you prove this to one of your friends?"

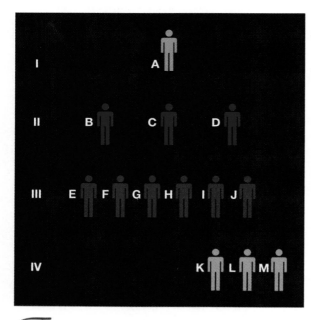

𝒯igure 2.10
Classification

Classification is an important ability in concrete operational thought. When shown a family tree of four generations (I to IV), the preoperational child has trouble classifying the members of the four generations; the concrete operational child can classify the members vertically, horizontally, and obliquely (up and down and across).

problem correctly, children have to imagine that the clay ball can be rolled out into a long, thin strip and then returned to its original round shape. This type of imagination involves a reversible mental action.

A concrete operation is a reversible mental action on real, concrete objects. Concrete operations allow the child to coordinate several characteristics rather than focus on a single property of an object. In the clay example, the preoperational child focuses on height *or* width. The concrete operational child coordinates information about both dimensions.

An important concrete operation is classifying or dividing things into different sets or subsets and considering their interrelationships. Reasoning about a family tree of four generations reveals a child's concrete operational skills (Furth & Wachs, 1975). The family tree shown in figure 2.10 suggests that the grandfather (A) has three children (B, C, and D), each of whom has two children (E through J), and that one of these children (J) has three children (K, L, and M). Concrete operational thinkers understand the classification. For example, they can reason that person J can at the same time be father, brother, and grandson. A preoperational thinker cannot.

Some Piagetian tasks require children to reason about relations between classes. One such task is **seriation,** *the concrete operation that involves ordering stimuli along some quantitative dimension (such as length).* To see if students can serialize, a teacher might place eight sticks of different lengths in a haphazard way on a table. The teacher then asks the student to order the sticks by length. Many young children end up with two or three small groups of "big" sticks or "little" sticks rather than a correct ordering of all eight sticks. Another mistaken strategy they use is to evenly line up the tops of the sticks but ignore the bottoms. The concrete operational thinker simultaneously understands that each stick must be longer than the one that precedes it and shorter than the one that follows it.

Another aspect of reasoning about the relations between classes is **transitivity.** *This involves the ability to logically combine relations to understand certain conclusions.* In this case, consider three sticks (A, B, and C)

TEACHING STRATEGIES
With Children Who Are Concrete Operational Thinkers

Following are some strategies for teaching children who are concrete operational thinkers (Labinowicz, 1980; Sund, 1976):

1. *Encourage students to discover concepts and principles.* Ask revelant questions about what is being studied to help them focus on some aspect of their learning. Refrain from telling students the answers to their questions outright. Try to get them to reach the answers through their own thinking.
2. *Involve children in operational tasks.* These include adding, subtracting, multiplying, dividing, ordering, seriating, and reversing. Use concrete materials for these tasks, possibly introducing math symbols later.
3. *Plan activities in which students practice the concept of ascending and descending classification hierarchies.* Have students list the following in order of size (such as largest to smallest): city of Atlanta, state of Georgia, country of United States, Western Hemisphere, and planet Earth.
4. *Include activities that require conservation of area, weight, and displaced volume.*
5. *Create activities in which children order and reverse order.* Many third-graders have difficulty in reversing order, such as going from tall to short rather than short to tall. And they have trouble, after listing the cities they will pass through in taking a trip, reversing the order for coming home.
6. *Continue to ask students to justify their answers when they solve problems.* Help them to check the validity and accuracy of their conclusions.
7. *Encourage children to work in groups and exchange thoughts with each other.* For example, ask a group of children to create a play, sharing their viewpoints with each other.
8. *Make sure that the materials in the classroom are rich enough to stimulate students' questions.* A versatile insect for classroom discussion is a mealworm. Have students observe it and describe it. An overnight appearance of a more mature mealworm may take place, which can surprise students and encourage them to think about why this occurred.
9. *When trying to teach anything that is complex, create props and visual aids.* For example, in teaching a social science lesson on what a democracy is, show a video that illustrates the concept.
10. *In science, have students manipulate and experiment; in math, use concrete materials; in language arts, encourage children to create and act out; and in social studies, have students discuss their perspectives with each other and take field trips.*

of differing lengths. A is the longest, B is intermediate in length, and C is the shortest. Does the child understand that if A > B, and B > C, then A > C? In Piaget's theory, concrete operational thinkers do, preoperational thinkers do not.

The Formal Operational Stage   The **formal operational stage,** *which emerges at about 11 to 15 years of age, is Piaget's fourth and final cognitive stage. At this stage, individuals move beyond reasoning only about concrete experiences and think in more abstract, idealistic, and logical ways.*

The abstract quality of formal operational thinking is evident in verbal problem-solving. The concrete operational thinker needs to see the concrete elements A, B, and C to make the logical inference that if A = B and B = C, then A = C. In contrast, the formal operational thinker can solve this problem when it is verbally presented.

Accompanying the abstract nature of formal operational thought are the abilities to idealize and imagine possibilities. At this stage, adolescents engage in extended speculation about the ideal qualities they desire in themselves and others. These idealistic thoughts can merge into fantasy. Many adolescents become impatient with their newfound ideals and the problems of how to live them out.

At the same time as adolescents are thinking more abstractly and idealistically, they also are beginning to think more logically. As formal operational thinkers, they think more like scientists. They devise plans to solve problems and systematically test solutions. Piaget's term **hypothetical-deductive reasoning** *embodies the concept that*

THROUGH THE EYES OF TEACHERS

Piaget as a Guide

I use Piaget's developmental theory as a guide to helping children learn mathematics. I know that in the 6th, 7th, and even the 8th grades, children are in the process of moving from the concrete to the abstract stage in their cognitive processes; therefore, when I teach a lesson, I try to use different methods in order to aid my students in understanding a concept. For example, I use fraction circles to help students understand how to add, subtract, multiply and divide fractions, and the students are allowed to use these until they become proficient with the algorithms. With every concept that I teach, I try to incorporate hands-on experiences in which the students discover the rules themselves, rather than just teaching the methods and having the students practice them with drill. It is extremely important for students to understand the why behind a mathematical rule in order for them to have a better understanding of the concept.

Jerri Hall
Mathematics Teacher
Miller Magnet Middle School
Bibb County, Georgia

adolescents can develop hypotheses (best hunches) about ways to solve problems and systematically reach a conclusion.

One example of hypothetical-deductive reasoning involves a modification of the familiar game "Twenty Questions." Individuals are shown a set of 42 color pictures displayed in a rectangular array (six rows of seven pictures each) and asked to determine which picture the experimenter has in mind (that is, which is "correct"). The subjects are only allowed to ask questions to which the experimenter can answer yes or no. The object of the game is to select the correct picture by asking as few questions as possible.

Adolescents who are deductive hypothesis testers formulate a plan and test a series of hypotheses, which considerably narrows the field of choices. The most effective plan is a "halving" strategy (*Q:* Is the picture in the right half of the array? *A:* No. *Q:* OK. Is it in the top half? And so on). A correct halving strategy guarantees the answer in seven questions or less. In contrast, the concrete operational thinker might persist with questions that continue to test some of the same possibilities that previous questions could have eliminated. For example, they might ask whether the correct picture is in row 1 and are told that it is not. Later, they ask whether the picture is *X*, which is in row 1.

Thus, formal operational thinkers test their hypotheses with judiciously chosen questions and tests. In contrast, concrete operational thinkers often fail to understand the relation between an hypothesis and a well-chosen test of it, stubbornly clinging to ideas that already have been discounted.

A form of egocentrism also emerges in adolescence (Elkind, 1978). **Adolescent egocentrism** *is the heightened self-consciousness that is reflected in adolescents' beliefs that others are as interested in them as they themselves are. Adolescent egocentrism also*

What kind of cognitive changes take place in adolescence, according to Piaget?

TEACHING STRATEGIES
With Adolescents Who Are Formal Operational Thinkers

Following are some strategies for teaching students who are formal operational thinkers (Santrock, 1998):

1. *Realize that although Piaget believed formal operational thought emerges between 11 to 15 years of age, many students in this age range actually are concrete operational thinkers or are just beginning to use formal operational thought.* Thus, many of the teaching strategies discussed earlier regarding the education of concrete operational thinkers still apply to many young adolescents. A curriculum that is too formal and too abstract will go over their heads.
2. *Propose a problem and invite students to form hypotheses about how to solve it.* For example, a teacher might say, "Imagine that a girl has no friends. What should she do?"
3. *Present a problem and suggest several ways it might be approached. Then ask questions that stimulate students to evaluate the approaches.* For example, describe several ways to investigate a robbery and ask students to evaluate which is best.
4. *Select a particular problem that is familiar to the class and ask questions related to it.* For example, the teacher asks, "What factors should be considered if we are going to be able to get the economy back on track?"
5. *Ask students to discuss their prior conclusions.* For example, ask, "What steps did you go through in solving this problem?"
6. *Develop projects and investigations for students to carry out.* Periodically ask them how they are going about collecting and interpreting the data.
7. *Encourage students to create hierarchical outlines when you ask them to write papers.* Make sure they understand how to organize their writing in terms of general and specific points. The abstractness of formal operational thinking also means that teachers with students at this level can encourage them to use metaphors.
8. *Also recognize that adolescents are likely to use formal operational thinking in the areas in which they have the most expertise and experience.* For example, a student who loves English and reads and writes a lot might use formal operational thinking in that area. However, the same student might not like math and might show concrete operational thinking in that area.

includes a sense of personal uniqueness. It involves the desire to be noticed, visible, and "on stage." Consider 12-year-old Tracy who says, "Oh my gosh! I can't believe it. Help! I can't stand it!" Her mother asks, "What is the matter?" Tracy responds, "Everyone in here is looking at me." The mother queries, "Why?" Tracy says, "This one hair won't stay in place," as she rushes to the restroom to plaster it with hair spray. Perceived uniqueness also is evident in 16-year-old Margaret's feelings after her boyfriend has broken up with her. She tells her mother, "You have no idea how I feel. You have never experienced this kind of pain."

Egocentrism is a normal adolescent occurrence, more common in the middle school than in high school years. However, for some individuals, adolescent egocentrism can contribute to reckless behavior, including suicidal thoughts, drug use, and failure to use contraceptives during sexual intercourse. Egocentricity leads some adolescents to think that they are invulnerable.

In youth we clothe ourselves with rainbows and go brave as the zodiac.

Ralph Waldo Emerson
American Poet and Essayist, 19th Century

Evaluating Piaget's Theory
What were Piaget's main contributions? Has his theory withstood the test of time?

Contributions   Piaget is a giant in the field of developmental psychology. We owe to him the present field of children's cognitive development. We owe to him a long list of masterful concepts of enduring power and fascination, including the concepts of assimilation, accommodation, object permanence, egocentrism, conservation, and hypothetical-deductive reasoning. We also owe to him the current vision of children as active, constructive thinkers.

Piaget also was a genius when it came to observing children. His careful observations showed us inventive ways to discover how children act on and adapt to their world (Vidal, 2000). Piaget showed us some important things to look for in cognitive development, such as the shift from preoperational to concrete operational thinking. He also showed us how children need to make their experiences fit their schemas (cognitive frameworks), yet simultaneously adapt their schemas to experience. Piaget also revealed how cognitive change is likely to occur if the context is structured to allow gradual movement to the next higher level. And we owe to him the current belief that concepts do not emerge all of a sudden, full-blown, but instead emerge through a series of partial accomplishments that lead to increasingly comprehensive understanding (Haith & Benson, 1998).

Criticisms   Piaget's theory has not gone unchallenged. Questions have been raised about these areas: estimates of children's competence at different developmental levels; stages; training children to reason at higher levels; and culture and education.

- *Estimates of children's competence.* Some cognitive abilities emerge earlier than Piaget thought. For example, as noted above, some aspects of object permanence emerge earlier than he believed. Even 2-year-olds are nonegocentric in some contexts. When they realize that another person will not see an object, they investigate whether the person is blindfolded or looking in a different direction. Conservation of number has been demonstrated as early as age 3, although Piaget did not think it emerged until 7. Young children are not as uniformly "pre-" this and "pre-" that (precausal, preoperational) as Piaget thought.

  Other cognitive abilities can emerge later than Piaget thought. Many adolescents still think in concrete operational ways or are just beginning to master formal operations. Even many adults are not formal operational thinkers. In sum, recent theoretical revisions highlight more cognitive competencies of infants and young children and more cognitive shortcomings of adolescents and adults (Flavell, Miller, & Miller, 1993; Wertsch, 2000).

- *Stages.* Piaget conceived of stages as unitary structures of thought. Thus, his theory assumes developmental synchrony; that is, various aspects of a stage should emerge at the same time. However, some concrete operational concepts do not appear in synchrony. For example, children do not learn to conserve at the same time as they learn to cross-classify. Thus, most contemporary developmentalists agree that children's cognitive development is not as stagelike as Piaget thought (Bjorklund, 2000; Case, 1998, 1999, 2000).

- *Training children to reason at a higher level.* Some children who are at one cognitive stage (such as preoperational) can be trained to reason at a higher cognitive stage (such as concrete operational). This poses a problem for Piaget. He argued that such training is only superficial and ineffective, unless the child is at a maturational transition point between the stages (Gelman & Williams, 1998).

- *Culture and education.* Culture and education exert stronger influences on children's development than Piaget believed (Gelman & Brenneman, 1994; Greenfield, 2000). The age at which children acquire conservation skills is related to the extent to which their culture provides relevant practice (Cole, 1999). An outstanding teacher and educator in the logic of math and science can promote concrete and formal operational thought.

Still, some developmental psychologists believe we should not throw out Piaget altogether. These **neo-Piagetians** *argue that Piaget got some things right, but that his theory needs considerable revision. In their revision of Piaget, more emphasis is given to how children process information through attention, memory, and using strategies* (Case, 1987, 1997, 1998). They especially believe that a more accurate vision of children's thinking requires more knowledge of strategies, how fast and how automatically children process information, the particular cognitive task involved, and dividing cognitive problems into smaller, more precise steps.

TEACHING STRATEGIES
For Applying Piagetian Ideas to Children's Education

Piaget was not an educator and never pretended to be. However, he provided a sound conceptual framework from which to view learning and education. Earlier we provided some specific suggestions for classroom activities based on Piaget's stages. Following are some more general principles in Piaget's theory that can be applied to teaching (Elkind, 1976; Heuwinkel, 1996).

1. *Take a constructivist approach.* In a constructivist vein, Piaget emphasized that children learn best when they are active and seek solutions for themselves. Piaget opposed teaching methods that treat children as passive receptacles. The educational implication of Piaget's view is that in all subjects students learn best by making discoveries, reflecting on them, and discussing them, rather than blindly imitating the teacher or doing things by rote.

2. *Facilitate rather than direct learning.* Effective teachers design situations that allow students to learn by doing. These situations promote students' thinking and discovery. Teachers listen, watch, and question students to help them gain better understanding. Don't just examine *what* students think and the product of their learning. Rather, carefully observe them as they find out *how* they think. Ask relevant questions to stimulate their thinking and ask them to explain their answers.

3. *Consider the child's knowledge and level of thinking.* Students do not come to class with empty heads. They have many ideas about the physical and natural world. They have concepts of space, time, quantity, and causality. These ideas differ from the ideas of adults. Teachers need to interpret what a student is saying and respond in a mode of discourse that is not too far from the student's level.

4. *Use ongoing assessment.* Individually constructed meanings cannot be measured by standardized tests. Math and language portfolios (which contain work in progress as well as finished products), individual conferences in which students discuss their thinking strategies, and written and verbal explanations by students of their reasoning can be used to evaluate progress.

5. *Promote the student's intellectual health.* When Piaget came to lecture in the United States, he was asked, "What can I do to get my child to a higher cognitive stage sooner?" He was asked this question so often here compared to other countries that he called it the American question. For Piaget, children's learning should occur naturally. Children should not be pushed and pressured into achieving too much too early in their development, before they are maturationally ready. Some parents spend long hours every day holding up large flash cards with words on them to improve their baby's vocabulary. In the Piagetian view, this is not the best way for infants to learn. It places too much emphasis on speeding up intellectual development, involves passive learning, and will not work.

6. *Turn the classroom into a setting of exploration and discovery.* What do actual classrooms look like when the teachers adopt Piaget's views? Several first- and second-grade math classrooms provide some good examples (Kamii, 1985, 1989). The teachers emphasize students' own exploration and discovery. The classrooms are less structured than what we think of as a typical classroom. Workbooks and predetermined assignments are not used. Rather, the teachers observe the students' interests and natural participation in activities to determine what the course of learning will be. For example, a math lesson might be constructed around counting the day's lunch money or dividing supplies among students. Often games are prominently used in the classroom to stimulate mathematical thinking. For example, a version of dominoes teaches children about even-numbered combinations. A variation on tic-tac-toe involves replacing Xs and Os with numbers. Teachers encourage peer interaction during the lessons and games because students' different viewpoints can contribute to advances in thinking.

Piaget's is not the only theory of children's cognitive development. Another that has received increased attention in recent years was proposed by Lev Vygotsky.

Vygotsky's Theory

Like Piaget, the Russian Lev Vygotsky (1896–1934) also believed that children actively construct their knowledge. Vygotsky was born in Russia in the same year as Piaget was born, but died much younger than Piaget did, at the young age of 37. Both Piaget's and Vygotsky's ideas remained virtually unknown to American scholars for many

Vygotsky's Theory

years, not being introduced to American audiences through English translations until the 1960s. In the last several decades, American psychologists and educators have shown increased interest in Vygotsky's (1962) views.

Vygotsky's Assumptions

Three claims capture the heart of Vygotsky's view (Tappan, 1998): (1) The child's cognitive skills can be understood only when they are developmentally analyzed and interpreted; (2) cognitive skills are mediated by words, language, and forms of discourse, which serve as psychological tools for facilitating and transforming mental activity; and (3) cognitive skills have their origins in social relations and are embedded in a sociocultural backdrop.

For Vygotsky, taking a developmental approach means that in order to understand any aspect of the child's cognitive functioning, one must examine its origins and transformations from earlier to later forms. Thus, a particular mental act such as using inner speech (see below) cannot be viewed accurately in isolation but should be evaluated as a step in a gradual developmental process.

Vygotsky's second claim, that to understand cognitive functioning it is necessary to examine the tools that mediate and shape it, led him to believe that language is the most important of these tools. Vygotsky argued that in early childhood, language begins to be used as a tool that helps the child plan activities and solve problems.

Vygotsky's third claim was that cognitive skills originate in social relations and culture. Vygotsky portrayed the child's development as inseparable from social and cultural activities. He believed that the development of memory, attention, and reasoning involves learning to use the inventions of society, such as language, mathematical systems, and memory strategies. In one culture this could consist of learning to count with the help of a computer; in another it could consist of counting on one's fingers or using beads.

Vygotsky's theory has stimulated considerable interest in the view that knowledge is *situated* and *collaborative* (Greeno, Collins, & Resnick, 1996; Rogoff, 1998). That is, knowledge is distributed among people and environments, which include objects, artifacts, tools, books, and the communities in which people live. This suggests that knowing can best be advanced through interaction with others in cooperative activities.

Within these basic claims, Vygotsky articulated unique and influential ideas about the relation between learning and development. These ideas especially reflect his view that cognitive functioning has social origins. One of Vygotsky's unique ideas was his concept of the zone of proximal development.

The Zone of Proximal Development

Zone of proximal development (ZPD) is *Vygotsky's term for the range of tasks that are too difficult for children to master alone but that can be learned with guidance and assistance from adults or more-skilled children.* Thus, the lower limit of the ZPD is the level of problem solving reached by the child working independently. The upper limit is the level of additional responsibility the child can accept with the assistance of an able instructor (see figure 2.11). Vygotsky's emphasis on the ZPD underscores his belief in the importance of social influences, especially instruction, on children's cognitive development.

Vygotsky (1987) gave this example of how to assess a child's ZPD: Suppose that, by an intelligence test, the mental age of two children is determined to be 8 years. With Vygotsky in mind, we can't stop there. To go on, we seek to determine how each of these children will attempt to solve problems meant for older children. We assist each child by demonstrating, asking leading questions, and introducing the initial elements of the solution. With this help or collaboration with the adult, one of these children solves problems at the level of a 12-year-old child and the other solves problems at the level of a 9-year-old child. This difference between the children's mental ages and the level of performance they achieve in collaboration with an adult defines the zone of proximal development. Thus, the ZPD involves the child's cognitive skills that are in the process of maturing and their performance level with the assistance of a more skilled person (Panofsky, 1999). Vygotsky (1978) called these the "buds" or "flowers" of development, to distinguish them from the "fruits" of development, which the child already can accomplish independently. An application of Vygotsky's concept of the zone of proximal development is the one-on-one tutoring provided by New Zealand teachers in the Reading Recovery program. Tutoring begins with familiar work, gradually introducing unfamiliar aspects of reading strategies, and then passing increasing control of the activity to the child (Clay & Cazden, 1990).

Scaffolding   Closely linked to the idea of zone of the proximal development is the concept of **scaffolding.** *Scaffolding is a technique of changing the level of support. Over the course of a teaching session, a more-skilled person (teacher or more-advanced peer of the child) adjusts the amount of guidance to fit the student's current performance level.* When the task the student is learning is new, the more-skilled person might use direct instruction. As the student's competence increases, less guidance is given.

Dialogue is an important tool of scaffolding in the zone of proximal development (John-Steiner & Mahn, 1996; Tappan, 1998). Vygotsky viewed children as having rich but unsystematic, disorganized, and spontaneous concepts. These meet with the skilled helper's more systematic, logical, and rational concepts. As a result of the meeting and dialogue between the child and the skilled helper, the child's concepts become more systematic, logical, and rational. We will have much more to say about scaffolding and other social interactive aspects of learning in chapter 9, "Social Constructivist Approaches, Domain-Specific Approaches, and Teaching."

Language and Thought   Vygotsky (1962) believed that young children use language not only for social communication but also to plan, guide, and monitor their behavior in a self-regulatory fashion. The use of language for self-regulation is called inner speech or private speech. For Piaget, private speech was egocentric and immature, but for Vygotsky it was an important tool of thought during the early childhood years.

Vygotsky believed that language and thought initially develop independently of each other and then merge. He said that all mental functions have external or social origins. Children must use language to communicate with others before they can focus inward on their own thoughts. Children also must communicate externally and use language for a long period of time before the transition from external to internal speech takes place. This transition period occurs between the ages of 3 and 7 and involves talking to oneself. After a while, the self-talk becomes second nature to children and they can act without verbalizing. When this occurs, children have internalized their egocentric speech in the form of inner speech, which becomes their thoughts. Vygotsky believed that children who use a lot of private speech are more socially competent than those who don't. He argued that private speech represents an early transition in becoming more socially communicative.

Vygotsky's view challenged Piaget's ideas on language and thought. Vygotsky said that language, even in its earliest forms, is socially based, whereas Piaget emphasized young children's egocentric and nonsocial speech. For Vygotsky, when young children talk to themselves they are using language to govern their behavior and guide themselves, whereas, Piaget believed that such self-talk reflects immaturity. Researchers have found support for Vygotsky's view of the positive role of private speech in children's development (Winsler, Diaz, & Montero, 1997).

Upper limit — Level of additional responsibility child can accept with assistance of an able instructor

Lower limit — Level of problem solving reached on these tasks by child working alone

Zone of proximal development (ZPD)

Figure **2.11**

Vygotsky's Zone of Proximal Development

Vygotsky's zone of proximal development has a lower limit and an upper limit. Tasks in the ZPD are too difficult for the child to perform alone. They require assistance from an adult or a more-skilled child. As children experience the verbal instruction or demonstration, they organize the information in their existing mental structures, so they can eventually perform the skill or task alone.

Vygotsky on Language and Thought

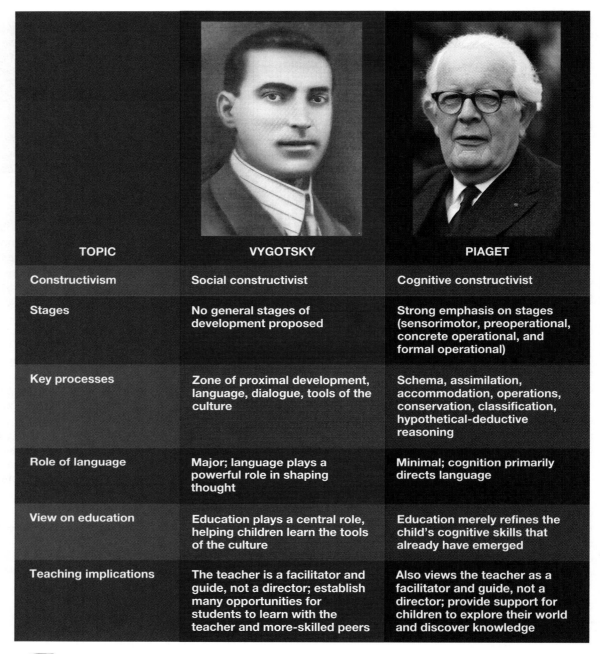

TOPIC	VYGOTSKY	PIAGET
Constructivism	Social constructivist	Cognitive constructivist
Stages	No general stages of development proposed	Strong emphasis on stages (sensorimotor, preoperational, concrete operational, and formal operational)
Key processes	Zone of proximal development, language, dialogue, tools of the culture	Schema, assimilation, accommodation, operations, conservation, classification, hypothetical-deductive reasoning
Role of language	Major; language plays a powerful role in shaping thought	Minimal; cognition primarily directs language
View on education	Education plays a central role, helping children learn the tools of the culture	Education merely refines the child's cognitive skills that already have emerged
Teaching implications	The teacher is a facilitator and guide, not a director; establish many opportunities for students to learn with the teacher and more-skilled peers	Also views the teacher as a facilitator and guide, not a director; provide support for children to explore their world and discover knowledge

Figure **2.12**
Comparing Vygotsky's and Piaget's Theories

Evaluating and Comparing Vygotsky's and Piaget's Theories   Awareness of Vygotsky's theory came later than for Piaget's theory, so Vygotsky's theory has not yet been evaluated as thoroughly. However, it already has been embraced by many teachers and been successfully applied to education (Doolittle, 1997). Vygotsky's view of the importance of sociocultural influences on children's development fits with the current belief that it is important to evaluate the contextual factors in learning. However, criticisms of his theory also have emerged. For example, some critics say he overemphasizes the role of language in thinking.

TEACHING STRATEGIES
Based on Vygotsky's Theory

Following are some ways Vygotsky's theory can be incorporated in the classroom:

1. *Use the student's zone of proximal development in teaching.* Teaching should begin toward the zone's upper limit, where the student is able to reach the goal only through close collaboration with the instructor. With adequate continuing instruction and practice, the student organizes and masters the behavioral sequences required to perform the target skill. As the instruction continues, the performance transfers from the teacher to the student. The teacher gradually reduces the explanations, hints, and demonstrations until the student is able to perform the skill alone. Once the goal is achieved, it can become the foundation for the development of a new ZPD.

2. *Use scaffolding.* Look for opportunities to use scaffolding when students need help with self-initiated learning activities (Elicker, 1996). Also use scaffolding to help students move to a higher level of skill and knowledge. Offer just enough assistance. You might ask, "What can I do to help you?" Or simply observe the student's intentions and attempts, smoothly providing support when needed. When the student hesitates, offer encouragement. And encourage the student to practice the skill. You may watch and appreciate the student's practice or offer support when the student forgets what to do.

3. *Use more-skilled peers as teachers.* Remember that it is not just adults that Vygotsky believed are important in helping students learn important skills. Students also benefit from the support and guidance of more-skilled students. We will say more about the role of peers in teaching in chapter 9, "Social Constructivist Approaches, Domain-Specific Approaches, and Teaching," including peer as tutors.

4. *Monitor and Encourage Children's Use of Private Speech.* Be aware of the developmental change from externally talking to oneself when solving a problem during the preschool years to privately talking to oneself in the early elementary school years. In the elementary school years, encourage students to internalize and self-regulate their talk to themselves.

5. *Assess the student's ZPD, not IQ.* Like Piaget, Vygotsky did not believe that formal, standardized tests are the best way to assess children's learning. Rather, Vygotsky argues that assessment should focus on determining the student's zone of proximal development. The skilled helper presents the child with tasks of varying difficulty to determine the best level at which to begin instruction. The ZPD is a measure of learning potential. IQ, also a measure of learning potential, emphasizes that intelligence is a property of the child. By contrast, ZPD emphasizes that learning is interpersonal. It is inappropriate to say that the child *has* a ZPD.

We already have mentioned several comparisons of Vygotsky's and Piaget's theories, such as Vygotsky's emphasis on the importance of inner speech in development and Piaget's view that such speech is immature. We also said earlier that both Vygotsky's and Piaget's theories are constructivist, emphasizing that children actively construct knowledge and understanding rather than being passive receptacles.

Although both theories are constructivist, *Vygotsky's is a* **social constructivist approach,** *which emphasizes the social contexts of learning and that knowledge is mutually built and constructed.* Piaget's theory does not have this strong social emphasis (Hogan & Tudge, 1999). Moving from Piaget to Vygotsky, the conceptual shift is from the individual to collaboration, social interaction, and sociocultural activity (Rogoff, 1998). For Piaget, children construct knowledge by transforming, organizing, and reorganizing previous knowledge. For Vygotsky, children construct knowledge through social interaction with others (Kozulin, 2000). The implications of Piaget's theory provide support for teaching strategies that encourage children to explore their world and discover knowledge. The main implication of Vygotsky's theory for teaching is that we should establish many opportunities for students to learn with the teacher and more-skilled peers. In both Piaget's and Vygotsky's theories, teachers serve as facilitators and guides rather than directors and molders of learning. Figure 2.12 compares Vygotsky's and Piaget's theories.

In our coverage of cognitive development, we have focused on the views of two giants in the field: Piaget and Vygotsky. However, information processing also has

**Vygotsky Analyzes
Piaget's Theory**

emerged as an important perspective in understanding children's cognitive development. It emphasizes how information enters the mind, how it is stored and transformed, and how it is retrieved to perform mental activities like problem solving and reasoning. It also focuses on how automatically and quickly children process information. Because information processing will be covered extensively in chapter 8, "The Cognitive Information-Processing Approach and Teaching," we mentioned it only briefly here.

At this point we have studied a number of ideas about children's cognitive development. A review of these ideas is presented in summary table 2.2. Next, we will explore another key aspect of children's development—language.

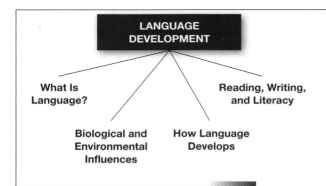

Language Development

Think about how important language is in teachers' and children's lives. They need language to speak to others, listen to others, read, and write. They need language to describe past events in detail and to plan for the future.

What Is Language?

Language *is a form of communication, whether spoken, written, or signed, that is based on a system of symbols.* All human languages are generative. **Infinite generativity** *is the ability to produce an endless number of meaningful sentences using a finite set of words and rules.* This quality makes language a highly creative enterprise. All human language also follows the organizational rules of phonology, morphology, syntax, semantics, and pragmatics.

Language is made up of basic sounds, or phonemes. An example of a phoneme in the English language is /k/, the sound represented by the letter *k* in the word *ski,* the letter *c* in the word *cat,* and the letters *ch* in *Christmas.* **Phonology** *is a language's sound system.* Phonological rules allow some sound sequences to occur (such as *sp, ba,* or *ar*) and prohibit others (such as *zx* or *qp*). To learn the phonology of a language, children must learn its sound inventory and permissible sequences of sounds, which are important later for reading.

Morphology *refers to the rules for combining morphemes, which are meaningful strings of sounds that contain no smaller meaningful parts.* Every word in the English language is made up of one or more morphemes. Some words consist of a single morpheme (such as *help*). Others are made up of more than one morpheme (such as *helper,* which has two morphemes, *help + er;* though not a word itself, the morpheme *-er* means "one who"—in this case, "one who helps"). Just as the rules that govern phonemes ensure that certain sound sequences occur, the rules that govern morphemes ensure that certain strings of sounds occur in particular sequences and conform with other rules. For example, we cannot reorder *helper* to *erhelp* and we cannot talk about an *un*dog or about *desking.*

Syntax *involves the way words are combined to form acceptable phrases and sentences.* If someone says to you, "Bob was slugged by Tom," you know who did the slugging and who was slugged because you understand the sentence structure. This concept of "who does what to whom" is an important type of syntactic information. You also understand that the sentence *You didn't stay, did you?* is a grammatical sentence but *You didn't stay, didn't you?* is not.

Semantics *refers to the meaning of words and sentences.* Every word has a set of semantic features. For example, *girl* and *woman* share the same semantic denotations of *female* and *human* but differ in their meanings regarding age. Words have semantic restrictions on how they can be used with each other in sentences. The sentence *The bicycle talked the boy into buying it candy* is syntactically correct but semantically incorrect. The sentence violates our semantic knowledge that bicycles do not talk!

SUMMARY TABLE 2.2
Cognitive Development

Concept	Processes/ Related Ideas	Characteristics/Description
Piaget's Theory	Cognitive Processes	• Piaget focused on two main processes in children's cognitive development: assimilation and accommodation, both of which involve schemas.
	Piagetian Stages	• Cognitive development unfolds in a sequence of 4 stages: sensorimotor (ages 0–2), preoperational (ages 3–7), concrete operational (ages 7–11), and formal operational (ages 11–15). Each stage is a qualitative advance. • In the sensorimotor stage, infants construct an understanding of the world by coordinating sensory experiences with motor actions and accomplish object permanence. • Thought is more symbolic at the preoperational stage, although the child has not yet mastered some important mental operations. Preoperational thought includes symbolic function and intuitive thought substages. Egocentrism, animism, and centration are constraints. • At the concrete operational stage, children can perform operations, and logical thought replaces intuitive thought when reasoning can be applied to specific or concrete examples. Classification, seriation, and transitivity are important concrete operational skills. • At the formal operational stage, thinking is more abstract, idealistic, and logical. Hypothetical-deductive reasoning becomes important. Adolescent egocentrism characterizes many young adolescents.
	Evaluating Piaget	• We owe to Piaget a long list of masterful concepts as well as the current vision of the child as an active, constructivist thinker. • Piaget was a genius at observing children. • Criticisms of his view focus on estimates of children's competence, stages, training children to reason at a higher cognitive level, and the neo-Piagetian criticism of not being precise enough about how children learn. • Many applications of Piaget's ideas for teaching were presented.
Vygotsky's Theory	Vygotsky's Assumptions	• (1) Cognitive skills need to be interpreted developmentally; (2) cognitive skills are mediated by language; and (3) cognitive skills have their origins in social relations and culture.
	Zone of Proximal Development	• This is Vygotsky's term for the range of tasks that are too difficult for children to master alone but that can be learned with the guidance and assistance of adults and more-skilled children.
	Scaffolding	• A teaching strategy that involves changing the level of support over the course of a teaching session, with the more-skilled person adjusting their guidance to fit the student's current performance level. • Dialogue is an important tool of scaffolding.
	Language and Thought	• Vygotsky believed that language plays a key role in guiding cognition. • Vygotsky's view contrasts with Piaget's view that young children's speech is immature and egocentric.
	Evaluating and Comparing Vygotsky's and Piaget's Theories	• Vygotsky's theory has increasingly been applied to education. • Especially important are his ideas related to sociocultural influences on children's development and learning. • Some critics say he overestimated the importance of language. • Comparisons of Vygotsky's and Piaget's theories involve constructivism, metaphors for learning, stages, key processes, role of language, views on education, and teaching implications. • Vygotsky's theory is social constructivist, Piaget's cognitive constructivist.

*"No, Timmy, not 'I sawed the chair'; it's 'I saw the chair'
or 'I have seen the chair.'"*

© *Glenn Bernhardt.*

Pragmatics *involves the use of appropriate conversation.* This involves knowledge about context in which to say what to whom and how to say it. For example, pragmatics is involved when children learn the difference between polite and rude language, as well as when they learn to tell a joke in such a way that it comes across as funny.

Biological and Environmental Influences

Famous linguist Noam Chomsky (1957) argued that humans are prewired to learn language at a certain time and in a certain way. The strongest evidence for the biological basis of language is that children all over the world acquire language milestones at about the same time developmentally and in about the same order, despite vast variations in the language input they receive. For example, in some cultures adults never talk to their infants under 1 year of age, yet these infants still acquire language.

Children vary in their acquisition of language in ways that cannot be explained by environmental input alone (deVilliers & deVilliers, 1999; Maratsos, 1998). For example, pioneering language researcher Roger Brown (1973) searched for evidence that parents reinforce their children for speaking grammatically. He found that they sometimes smiled and praised their children for sentences they liked but they also reinforced sentences that were ungrammatical.

However, children do not learn language in a social vacuum (Snow, 1999). Enough variation occurs in language development when children's caregivers differ substantially in input styles to know that the environment plays a significant role in language development, especially in the acquisition of vocabulary. Even before they go to school, most children have already been steeped in language. In or out of school, encouragement of language development, not drill and practice, is the key (de Villiers, 1996; de Villiers & de Villiers, 1999). Language development is not simply a matter of being rewarded for saying things correctly and imitating a speaker. Children benefit when their parents and teachers actively engage them in conversation, ask them questions, and emphasize interactive rather than directive language. To read about how urban poverty conditions can restrict the language development of African American children, see the Diversity and Education box.

In sum, children are neither exclusively biological linguists nor exclusively social architects of language (Gleason & Ratner, 1998; MacWhinney, 1999). No matter how long you converse with a dog, it won't learn to talk, because it doesn't have the human child's biological capacity for language; but unfortunately some children fail to develop good language skills even in the presence of very good role models and interaction. An interactionist view emphasizes the contributions of both biology and experience in language development. That is, children are biologically prepared to learn language as they and their teachers interact.

How Language Develops

Language acquisition advances through a number of milestones (Bloom, 1998). Babbling begins at about 3 to 6 months. Infants usually utter their first word at about 10 to 13 months. By 18 to 24 months, infants usually have begun to string two words together. In this two-word stage, they quickly grasp the importance of language in communication, creating phrases such as "Book there," "My candy," "Mama walk," and "Give Papa."

As they move beyond two-word utterances, children clearly show that they know some morphological rules (the rules of language that tell how sounds must be combined). Children begin using the plural and possessive forms of nouns (*dogs* and *dog's*); put appropriate endings on verbs (*-s* when the subject is third-person singular), *-ed* for the past tense; use prepositions (*in* and *on*), articles (*a* and *the*), and various

DIVERSITY AND EDUCATION

African American Language Traditions and Urban Poverty

Shirley Heath (1989) examined the language traditions of African Americans from low-income backgrounds. She traced some aspects of African American English to the time of slavery. Heath also examined how those speech patterns have carried over into African American English today. She found that agricultural areas in the southern United States have an especially rich oral tradition.

Specifically she found that adults do not simplify or edit their talk for children, in essence challenging the children to be highly active listeners. Also, adults ask only "real questions" of children—that is, questions for which the adult does not already know the answer. Adults also engage in a type of teasing with children, encouraging them to use their wits in communication. For example, a grandmother might pretend that she wants to take a child's hat and then starts a lively exchange in which the child must understand many subtleties of argument, mood, and humor—Does Grandma really want my hat? Is she mad at me? Is she making a joke? Can I persuade her to give it back to me? Finally, there is an appreciation of wit and flexibility in how language is used, as well as an acknowledgment of individual differences—one person might be respected for recounting stories, another for negotiating and peacemaking skills.

Heath argues that the language tradition she describes is richly varied, cognitively demanding, and well suited to many real-life situations. She says that the oral and literary traditions among poor African Americans in the cities are well suited for many job situations. Years ago many inner-city jobs required only that a person follow directions in order to perform repetitious tasks. Today many positions require continuous interactions involving considerable flexibility in language, such as the ability to persuade co-workers or to express dissatisfaction, in a subtle way, for example.

Despite its utility in many job situations, the rich language tradition possessed by low-income African Americans does not meet with the educational priorities of our nation's schools. Too often schools stress rote memorization, minimizing group interaction and discouraging individual variations in communicative style. Also, the language tradition of African American culture is rapidly dying in the face of current life among poor African Americans, where the structure of low-income, frequently single-parent families often provides little verbal stimulation for children.

One mother agreed to let researcher Heath tape-record her interactions with her children over a 2-year period and to write notes about her activities with them. Within 500 hours of tape and more than a thousand lines of notes, the mother initiated talk with her three preschool children on only 18 occasions (other than giving them a brief directive or asking a quick question). Few of the mother's conversations involved either planning or executing actions with or for her children.

Heath (1989) points out that the lack of family and community supports is widespread in urban housing projects, especially among African Americans. The deteriorating, impoverished conditions of these inner-city areas severely impede the ability of young children to develop the cognitive and social skills they need to function competently.

---

forms of the verb *to be* ("I *was going* to the store"). Some of the best evidence that children develop morphological rules rather than memorize individual words was demonstrated in a classic experiment by Jean Berko-Gleason (1958). Preschool and first-grade children were presented with cards like the one shown in figure 2.13. The children were asked to look at the card while the experimenter read the words on it aloud. Then the children were asked to supply the missing word. The children showed they knew the morphological rules involved by generating the plural forms of the fictional words.

Similar evidence that children learn and actively apply rules occurs at the level of syntax. After advancing beyond two-word utterances, children speak word sequences that reflect a growing mastery of complex rules for how words should be ordered. Consider *wh-* questions, such as "Where is Daddy going?" Children typically learn by age 3 where to put the *wh-* word but might continue for another year learning to put the question as "Where Daddy is going?"

As children move into the elementary school years, they become skilled at using syntactical rules (the rules about how to combine words to form acceptable phrases

Figure **2.13**

Stimuli in Berko-Gleason's Study of Young Children's Understanding of Morphological Rules

In Jean Berko-Gleason's (1958) study, young children were presented cards such as this one with a "wug" on it. Then the children were asked to supply the missing word and say it correctly. "Wugs" is the correct response here.

Reading

Children pick up words as pigeons pick up peas.

John Ray
English Author, 17th Century

and sentences) to construct lengthy and complex sentences (Goldin-Meadow, 2000). They might say something like, "After the man cut the grass, he left and went home." By the end of elementary school, most children can apply appropriate rules of grammar.

Regarding semantics (the rules about the meaning of words and sentences), as children move beyond the two-word stage, their knowledge of meanings also rapidly advances (Sanford, 2000). The speaking vocabulary of an American 6-year-old child ranges from 6,000 to 14,000 words. Some children are moving along at the awe-inspiring rate of learning more than 20 words a day. By the time children reach the end of elementary school, many have added another 5,000 to 7,000 words to their vocabulary.

Changes in pragmatics (the rules about appropriate conversation) also characterize children's language development. A 6-year-old is a much better conversationalist than a 3-year-old. For example, elementary school children are more sensitive to the needs of others in conversation than preschool children are. They aren't perfect conversationalists (and neither are most adults), but they are better at talking *with* rather than just *to* someone.

In adolescence, vocabulary increases with the addition of more abstract words. More complex grammar forms are better understood, as is the function a word plays in a sentence. Adolescents also show an increased understanding of metaphor and satire. In late adolescence, individuals can better appreciate adult literary works. Figure 2.14 summarizes some of the main milestones in language.

At this point we have discussed a number of ideas about the nature of language, biological and environmental influences, and language development. A review of these ideas is presented in summary table 2.3 on page 70. Next, we will explore an especially important aspect of language in schools—reading.

Reading, Writing, and Literacy

In the twenty-first century, literacy (the ability to read and write) will play an even more powerful role in people's lives than today. The biggest increase in jobs and the best jobs will be in the professional and technical sectors. These jobs require good reading, writing, and communication skills. Schools and teachers assume the most responsibility in our society for providing these skills.

A Developmental Model of Reading

In one view, reading skills develop in five stages (Chall, 1979). The age boundaries are approximate and do not apply to every child. For example, some children learn to read before they enter first grade. Nonetheless, the stages convey a general sense of the developmental changes involved in learning to read:

- *Stage 0.* From birth to first grade, children master several prerequisites for reading. Many learn the left-to-right progression and order of reading, how to identify the letters of the alphabet, and how to write their names. Some learn to read some words that appear on signs. As a result of TV shows like "Sesame Street" and attending preschool and kindergarten programs, many young children today develop greater knowledge about reading earlier than in the past.
- *Stage 1.* In first and second grade, many children learn to read. In doing so, they acquire the ability to sound out words (that is, translate letters into sounds and blend sounds into words). They also complete their learning of letter names and sounds during this stage.
- *Stage 2.* In second and third grade, children become more fluent at retrieving individual words and other reading skills. However, at this stage, reading is still not

AGE PERIOD	CHILD'S DEVELOPMENT/BEHAVIOR
0–6 Months	Cooing Discrimination of vowels Babbling present by end of period
6–12 Months	Babbling expands to include sounds of spoken language Gestures used to communicate about objects
12–18 Months	First words spoken Understand vocabulary 50+ words on the average
18–24 Months	Vocabulary increases to an average of 200 words Two-word combinations
2 Years	Vocabulary rapidly increases Correct use of plurals Use of past tense Use of some prepositions
3–4 Years	Mean length of utterances increases to 3–4 morphemes a sentence Use of "yes" "no" questions, wh- questions Use of negatives and imperatives Increasd awareness of pragmatics
5–6 Years	Vocabulary reaches an average of about 10,000 words Coordination of simple sentences
6–8 Years	Vocabulary continues to increase rapidly More skilled use of syntactical rules Conversational skills improve
9–11 Years	Word definitions include synonyms Conversational strategies continue to improve

11–14 Years	Vocabulary increases with addition of more
	    abstract words
	Understanding of complex grammar forms
	Increased understanding of function a word
	    plays in a sentence
	Understands metaphor and satire

15–20 Years	Can understand adult literary works

Note: This list is meant not to be exhaustive but rather to highlight some of the main language milestones. Also keep in mind that there is a great deal of variation in the ages at which children can reach these milestones and still be considered within the normal range of language development.

Figure **2.14**
Language Milestones

used much for learning. The mechanical demands of learning to read are so taxing at this point that children have few resources left over to process the content.
• *Stage 3.* In fourth through eighth grade, children become increasingly able to obtain new information from print. In other words, they read to learn. They still have difficulty understanding information presented from multiple perspectives

SUMMARY TABLE 2.3
What Language Is, Biological and Environmental Influences, and How Language Develops

Concept	Processes/ Related Ideas	Characteristics/Description
What Is Language?	Its Nature	• Language is a form of communication, whether spoken, written, or signed, that is based on a system of symbols. • Human languages are infinitely generative. All human languages also have organizational rules of phonology (a language's sound system), morphology (rules for combining morphemes, the meaningful strings of sounds that contain no smaller meaningful parts), syntax (rules for combining words to form acceptable phrases and sentences), semantics (meanings of words and sentences), and pragmatics (use of appropriate conversation).
Biological and Environmental Influences	Their Nature	• The strongest evidence for the biological basis of language is that children all over the world reach language milestones at about the same age despite vast differences in their environmental experiences. • However, children do not learn language in a social vacuum. • Most children are bathed in language even before they go to school. • Children benefit when parents and teachers actively engage them in conversation, ask them questions, and talk *with,* not just *to,* them. • In sum, biology and experience interact to produce language development. Children are biologically prepared to learn language as they and their caregivers interact.
How Language Develops	Changes and Milestones	• Language acquisition advances through stages. • Babbling occurs at about 3 to 6 months, the first word at 10 to 13 months, and two-word utterances at 18 to 24 months. • As children move beyond two-word utterances, they can demonstrate that they know some morphological rules, as documented in Berko-Gleason's study. • Children also advance in their understanding of syntax, semantics, and pragmatics. • By the end of elementary school, most children can apply appropriate rules of grammar. • In adolescence, vocabulary increases with the addition of more abstract words. In late adolescence individuals can better appreciate adult literary works.

within the same story. For children who don't learn to read, a downward spiral unfolds that leads to serious difficulties in many academic subjects.

- *Stage 4.* In the high school years, many students become fully competent readers. They develop the ability to understand material told from many different perspectives. This allows them to engage in sometimes more sophisticated discussions of literature, history, economics, and politics. It is no accident that great novels are not presented to students until high school, because understanding the novels requires advanced reading comprehension.

Approaches to Reading   As the previous discussion has implied, **reading** *is the ability to understand written discourse.* Children cannot be said to read if all they can do is respond to flash cards, as in some early child-training programs.

Early reading requires mastering the basic language rules of phonology, morphology, syntax, and semantics. A child who has poor grammatical skills for speech and listening and does not understand what is meant by "The car was pushed by a truck" when it is spoken and cannot understand its meaning in print either. Likewise, a child who cannot determine what pronouns refer to (as in *John went to the store with his dog. It was closed.*) will not do well in reading comprehension.

What are some approaches to teaching children how to read? Education and language experts continue to debate how children should be taught to read (Rayner, 2000). The debate focuses on the whole-language approach versus the basic-skills-and-phonetics approach. The **whole-language approach** *stresses that reading instruction should parallel children's natural language learning. Reading materials should be whole and meaningful.* That is, in early reading instruction, children should be presented with materials in their complete form, such as stories and poems. In this way, say the whole-language advocates, children learn to understand language's communicative function.

In the whole-language approach, reading is integrated with other skills and subjects. Reading should be connected with listening and writing skills. Although there are variations in whole-language programs, most share the premise that reading should be integrated with other skills and subjects, such as science and social studies, and that it should focus on real-world, relevant material. Thus, a class might read newspapers, magazines, or books, then write about them and discuss them.

By contrast, the **basic-skills-and-phonetics approach** *emphasizes that reading instruction should teach phonetics and its basic rules for translating written symbols into sounds. Early reading instruction should involve simple materials.* Only after they have learned phonological rules should children be given complex reading materials such as books and poems.

Advocates of the basic-skills-and-phonetics approach often point to low reading achievement scores occurring as an outgrowth of the recent emphasis on holistic, literature-based instruction and the consequent lack of attention to basic skills and phonetics (Baumann & others, 1998). In California, a task force recently recommended that children's reading skills be improved by pursuing a balanced approach that includes teaching phonemic awareness (sounds in words), phonics, and other decoding skills. To read about some resources for improving children's phonological awareness and decoding skills, see the Technology and Education box.

The term *balanced instruction* is now being used to describe combinations of reading approaches (Au, Carroll, & Scheu, in press; Freppon & Dahl, 1998; Pressley, in press; Tompkins, 1997; Weaver, in press). However, "balance" often means different things to different researchers and teachers. For some, "balanced" means a primary emphasis on phonics instruction with minimal whole-language emphasis; for others it means the reverse.

Which approach is best? Researchers have not been able to document consistently that one approach is better than the other. There is very strong evidence that the decoding skills involved in recognizing sounds and words are important in becoming a good reader. A good strategy is to work with kindergarten and first-grade students on developing phonemic awareness, which involves recognizing that separate sounds make up words and that combining these sounds can make words. For students who do not develop this phonemic awareness early in school, their literacy will still benefit if it is taught to them later in school (Pressley, 1996). Some critics believe that because of the prominence of the whole-language approach, some teacher training programs have not adequately instructed future teachers in phonics and other structural rules of language.

There is also good evidence that students in the early years of school benefit from the whole-language approach of being immersed in a natural world of print (Graham & Harris, 1994). This approach helps them understand the purpose of learning to read and builds on their early home experiences with books and language.

Some language experts believe that a combination of the two approaches should be followed (Freppon & Dahl, 1998; Spear-Swerling & Sternberg, 1994). In sum, there

Whatever the process, the result is wonderful. Gradually from naming an object we advance step-by-step until we have traversed the vast difference between our first stammered syllable and the sweep of thought in a line of Shakespeare.

Helen Keller
American Essayist, 20th Century

Phonetics

TECHNOLOGY AND EDUCATION

Technology Resources for Improving Phonological Awareness and Decoding Skills

Two resources that can be used to improve students' phonological awareness and decoding skills are Read-Along Books and Word Picker (Cognition and Technology Group at Vanderbilt, 1997).

Read-Along Books are easy-to-read books written with short, decodable words that combine with rhythm and rhyme patterns to improve students' skills in associating sounds with letters. Computer versions of the books include tools that pronounce sentences and words as needed. After students become competent in these skills, they can record the stories in their own voice.

Word Picker is a software tool that helps students build on their letter-sound knowledge to discover conventional spellings for words that they want to write. As the children work on creating their own books in a multimedia format, they can click on Word Picker. Scrolling through a list of words, they search for words that start with the same letter as the word they want to write. Then they click on different words to hear them pronounced and to observe how they are divided into syllables. When they find the word they want, they type it out.

After students write their own books, they can read the printed versions of their books in class to others. Read-Along Books and Word Picker are part of the Young Children's Literacy Project at Vanderbilt University. The current versions are most appropriate for grade 1. Future projects are planned for preschool to grade 3.

Reading and writing also are combined in IBM's Writing to Read program for kindergarten and first-grade students. Five learning stations are coordinated to provide an active learning environment: computer, work journal, writing/typing, listening library, and making words.

These students are participating in IBM's Writing to Read *program, which uses a variety of learning stations to improve students' literacy.*

**A Guide to
Children's Reading Success**

is every reason to believe that students learn to read best when they are exposed to both whole-language experiences and decoding skills. Indeed, a combination of whole-language and phonics approaches also recently was recommended by a national panel of experts after reviewing the research evidence on the effectiveness of reading approaches (Snow, 1998).

In a recent national survey of K–5 elementary school teachers' attitudes toward and experiences with different reading approaches, these findings emerged (Baumann & others, 1998):

- 89 percent of teachers believed in using a balanced approach of combining skills with literature and language-rich activities.
- 63 percent thought that phonics should be taught directly to help readers become skillful and fluent.
- 71 percent believed that children need to be immersed in literature and literacy to achieve fluency.
- When asked which reading skills were essential or important, the vast majority of K–2 teachers said "instruction in phonics" (99 percent), "meaning vocabulary" (99 percent), and "sight words" (96 percent).

• Teachers also used whole-language strategies. For example, K–2 teachers regularly read aloud (97 percent) and engaged children in oral language (83 percent) and journal writing (78 percent).

In sum, balance, eclecticism, and common sense characterize the reading and language arts instructional practices of many elementary school teachers. As educational psychologist David Berliner (1997) commented, teachers often are not extremist on the issue of whole language versus phonics. They tend to be pragmatists, using what works. This seems to be a reasonable strategy, given the vast individual variations in children's abilities.

Teaching Delayed Readers   Based on experiences with more than 3,000 delayed readers over more than 25 years, Irene Gaskins (1998) believes the following strategies can improve outcomes for delayed readers: (1) staff development, (2) instruction and support services to address roadblocks, (3) congruence between the remedial program and regular classroom programs, and (4) enough time to prepare students to be successful.

Staff Development   Staff development must be ongoing, collaborative, and in-depth as it engages teachers and support staff in exploring and understanding research-based principles of instruction and curriculum. This might involve weekly team meetings, including discussion of the latest research on reading in professional journals.

Instruction and Support Services   Unlike their more successful classmates, delayed readers often don't figure out on their own how to learn a word or make an inference. For them, learning these skills might develop only when they receive quality instruction that includes explanations, modeling, and scaffolded practice that is engaging and meaningful. They often need this instruction not only in reading but across the curriculum. Some delayed readers have both academic and nonacademic problems. Thus, support services that include mentors, psychologists, counselors, and social workers could be needed to help the delayed reader overcome roadblocks to success.

THROUGH THE EYES OF TEACHERS

Challenges in Teaching Reading

Following are some selected responses (from the recently conducted national survey of reading instruction approaches) of teachers who were asked to describe their greatest challenges in improving the quality of classroom reading instruction (Baumann & others, 1998):

• *Range of Reading Levels*
  "Providing for the wide range of abilities."
  "My range this year is first-grade level to 10th-grade level."
• *Lack of Time:*
  "Finding enough time to devote to reading instruction."
  "*Time* to plan with colleagues and set up reading programs."
• *Not Enough Money or Materials:*
  "I need more materials."
  "Money! My school system can't/won't fund literature-based classrooms, so I spend my own money (when I can afford it)."
• *Teaching Struggling Readers*
  "When children enter the third grade as non-readers or emergent readers, it is virtually impossible to bring them up to grade level in a year's time."
  "Slow readers! The slow reader is always a challenge to me."
• *Parent Support and Involvement*
  "Getting the parents to reinforce what I teach in the classroom."
• *Class Size*
  "Sheer numbers! I have 32 students for reading."
  "Next year I'm told I will have inclusion students in addition to 39 first-grade students."
• *Diverse Students*
  "Accommodating the needs of *all different* kinds of kids."
  "Accommodating linguistically diverse children."

Congruence Between the Remedial Program and Regular Classroom Programs   Although there is a trend toward including specialists in regular classrooms, many programs continue to pull students out of their regular classroom for remedial instruction. Too often the remedial instruction is poorly coordinated with the curriculum and instruction in the regular classroom. Thus, it is important for remedial teachers to prepare delayed readers with the skills and strategies that are needed in the regular classroom.

Time   Most initiatives for delayed readers envision support for 1 or 2 years. However, helping delayed readers become successful readers often takes longer than this. Thus, programs for delayed readers should begin as early as possible and in many cases need to continue throughout the elementary and middle school years.

Children's Writing

Writing   Children's writing emerges out of their early scribbles, which appear at around 2 to 3 years of age. In early childhood, children's motor skills usually become well enough developed for them to begin printing letters and their name. Most 4-year-olds can print their first name. Five-year-olds can reproduce letters and copy several short words. As they develop their printing skills, they gradually learn to distinguish between the distinctive characteristics of letters, such as whether the lines are curved or straight, open or closed, and so on. Through the early elementary grades, many children still continue to reverse letters such as *b* and *d* and *p* and *q* (Temple & others, 1993). At this point in development, if other aspects of the child's development are normal, these letter reversals are not a predictor of literacy problems.

As they begin to write, children often invent spellings of words. They usually do this by relying on the sounds of words they hear and using those as the basis of forming the words they write.

Teachers and parents should encourage children's early writing without being overly concerned about the proper formation of letters or correct conventional spelling. I (your author) once had a conference with my youngest daughter's first-grade teacher when she brought home a series of papers with her printing of words all marked up and sad faces drawn on the paper. Fortunately, the teacher agreed to reduce her criticism of Jennifer's print skills. Such printing errors should be viewed as a natural part of the child's growth. Spelling and printing corrections can be made in a positive ways and in the context of maintaining early writing and spontaneity.

Like becoming a good reader, becoming a good writer takes many years and lots of practice. Children should be given many writing opportunities in the elementary and secondary school years. As their language and cognitive skills improve with good instruction, so will their writing skills. For example, developing a more sophisticated understanding of syntax and grammar serves as an underpinning for better writing.

So do such cognitive skills as organization and logical reasoning. Through the course of elementary, middle, and high school, students develop increasingly sophisticated methods of organizing their ideas. In early elementary school, they narrate and describe or write short poems. In late elementary and middle school, they move to projects such as book reports that combine narration with more reflection and analysis. In high school, they become more skilled at forms of exposition that do not depend on narrative structure. In chapter 9, "Social Constructivist Approaches, Domain-Specific Approaches, and Teaching," we will examine many strategies for helping children become better writers.

Literacy   As an ongoing goal, learning to read and write should occur in a supportive environment in which children can generate a positive perception of themselves and develop a positive attitude toward both skills (Olson, 2000). Unfortunately, the National Association for the Education of Young Children (NAEYC, the leading organization of early childhood educators)

THROUGH THE EYES OF CHILDREN

The Devl and the Babe Goste

Anna Mudd is the 6-year-old author of "The Devl and the Babe Goste." Anna has been writing stories for at least 2 years. Her story includes poetic images, sophisticated syntax, and vocabulary that reflect advances in language development.

believes, in the push to develop a nation of literate people, too many preschool children are being subjected to rigid, formal prereading programs with expectations and experiences that are too advanced (Bredekamp & Rosegrant, 1996). Learning to read and write and continuing to read and write should be enjoyable experiences for children, not stressful ones.

Teachers and parents should take time to read to children from a wide variety of poetry, fiction, and nonfiction. They should present models for children to emulate by using language appropriately, listening and responding to children's talk, and engaging in their own reading and writing.

For children who have participated extensively in print-related interactions in their homes and communities, literacy often comes quickly in school. However, many children who have not participated extensively in lap reading and similar literacy experiences in preschool will take longer to develop literacy skills (Hiebert & Raphael, 1996). A positive partnership between home and school provides teachers with opportunities to involve parents in helping children improve their literacy skills.

Developing better literacy skills should be an important goal of secondary school teachers as well (Feirson, 1997; Mizelle, Irvin, & Ivey, 1997). Especially important is communication with adolescents about the value of reading and writing skills for success in the adult work world.

Most adolescents are asked to read and write far more than when they were children, and they are assigned reading and writing tasks that increase in complexity. As we indicated earlier in our developmental description of reading, in middle school the focus shifts from "learning to read" to "reading to learn." For many students, this shift can be difficult because teachers often do not provide for a deliberate transition and most students are not given systematic reading instruction past grade 5 (Irvin & Conners, 1989).

Following are some good recommendations for an effective literacy program (Irvin, 1997):

- Take into consideration the nature of adolescent development when encouraging literacy skills. Take advantage of the social proclivity of adolescents by having them do some reading and writing assignments in pairs or as a small-group project. Digital chat rooms, posting writing on the Internet, or producing a radio play can provide students with meaningful literacy tasks and take advantage of their natural inclinations for interacting with peers.
- Help students develop their reading strategies. Work with them to monitor their reading progress, understanding, and purpose. We will have much more to say about such strategies in chapter 8, "The Cognitive Information-Processing Approach and Teaching."
- Integrate the language arts by getting students to connect reading and writing projects. Also teach and reinforce literacy across the curriculum, using literature, social studies, science, math, and other content.

Literacy

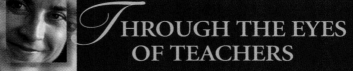

THROUGH THE EYES OF TEACHERS

Observing Young Children's Literacy

Kindergarten teacher Karen West (1998) describes how she notices and responds to situations that involve children's literacy:

I look closely to find out what kids know in a variety of contexts. I work to see and hear what the children notice about literacy each day. For example, when I look at students' written work, miscues often signal that children are reaching out to some new facet of written expressions and they need help towards some new learning. . . .

Students get daily routines going, such as the pledge of allegiance, calendar, and other responsibilities. During the calendar discussion, I notice things about our calendar leader. Does she have one-to-one voice-print match? Does she move from left to right and from the top down on a calendar? I also look at the whole group and notice who is actively engaged and who appears to need some guidance or redirection. As I notice these specific details, I jot down a few notes on my lesson plan clipboard or sticky notes. I rewrite and expand these notes at the end of the day. . . .

The next activity on a typical morning is a read-aloud session. When I read literature to my class, kids are actively involved in the story. Many students have ideas and questions they want to share. For example, through their comments and questions some students connect a story to their lives, connect a book to another book, notice specific details in illustrations, question the author as to "why" a character did or said something, laugh and enjoy the story (evidence that they are comprehending), share their knowledge to increase others' understanding of the story, or spontaneously dramatize a part of the story. . . .

When we go to the library, and the librarian reads aloud, or when a parent visits our class to read, I have a greater opportunity to observe students. I focus on the students and record my observations on paper immediately. It is much easier to record data when someone else is reading a book aloud.

SUMMARY TABLE 2.4
Reading, Writing, and Literacy

Concept	Processes/ Related Ideas	Characteristics/Description
A Developmental Model of Reading	Chall's Five Stages of Reading	• Chall's model proposes 5 stages in reading: (0) From birth to first grade, identify letters of the alphabet and learn to write one's name. (1) In first and second grade, learn to sound out words and complete learning of letter names and sounds. (2) In second and third grade, learn to retrieve individual words and complete learning of letter names and sounds. (3) In fourth through eighth grade, increasingly obtain new information from print. Read to learn. (4) In high school, become a fully competent reader and understand material from different perspectives.
Approaches to Reading	Whole-Language and Basic-Skills-and-Phonetics Approaches	• Current debate focuses on the whole-language approach versus the basic-skills-and-phonetics approach. • The whole-language approach stresses that reading instruction should parallel children's natural language learning and give children whole language materials, such as books and poems. • The basic-skills-and-phonetics approach advocates phonetics instruction and giving children simplified materials. • Today, many experts recommend a balanced approach that combines the two approaches, although "balanced" often means different things to different people. • There is good evidence that beginning readers benefit from an approach using both whole-language experiences and instruction in phonetics and decoding.
Teaching Delayed Readers	Strategies	• This involves effective staff development, instruction and support, congruence between the remedial program and regular classroom programs, and time.
Writing	Developmental Changes	• Children's writing also follows a developmental timetable, emerging out of scribbling. • Most 4-year-olds can print their name. • Most 5-year-olds can reproduce letters and copy several short words. • Advances in children's language and cognitive development provide the underpinnings for improved writing.
Literacy	Its Nature	• Literacy involves learning to read and write. • This should occur in a supportive environment and be an enjoyable experience. • An emphasis on literacy should begin early in children's lives and continue in the secondary school grades.

Children's Literature

• Motivate students to engage in recreational reading. A school reading committee usually can provide leadership book fairs, book exchanges, and schoolwide activities. Recommend to students books that you think they especially would be motivated to read. Remember that you are competing with such activities as watching TV when you are asking for adolescents' leisure time, so motivating them to read is a special challenge (Wigfield & Gutherie, 1997).

At this point we have discussed a number of ideas about reading, writing, and literacy. A review of these ideas is presented in summary table 2.4. In the next chapter, we will continue our exploration of children's development by focusing on their socioemotional development.

Chapter Review

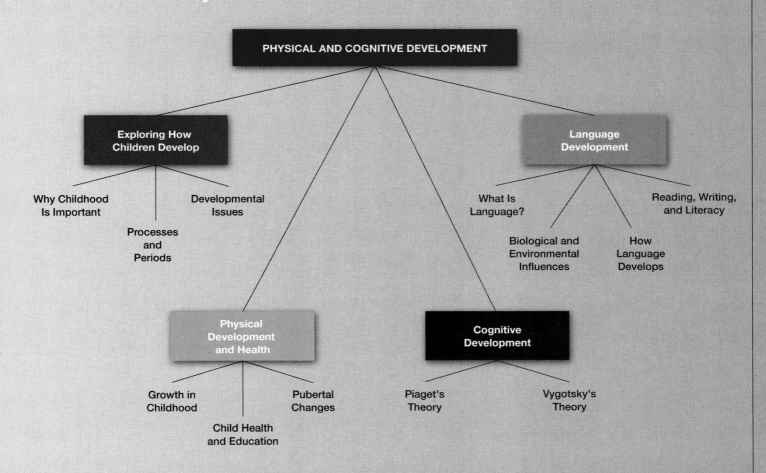

TO OBTAIN A DETAILED REVIEW OF THIS CHAPTER, STUDY THESE FOUR SUMMARY TABLES:

Key Terms

development 38
biological processes 39
cognitive processes 39
socioemotional processes 39
infancy 39
early childhood 39
middle and late childhood 39
adolescence 39
early adulthood 39
maturation 40
nature-nurture controversy 40
continuity in development 41
discontinuity in
   development 41

early-later experience issue 41
myelination 42
gross motor skills 42
fine motor skills 42
puberty 46
schema 49
assimilation 49
accommodation 49
sensorimotor stage 50
object permanence 50
preoperational stage 50
symbolic function substage 51
egocentrism 51
animism 51

intuitive thought substage 51
centration 52
conservation 52
operations 53
concrete operational stage 53
seriation 54
transitivity 54
formal operational stage 55
hypothetical-deductive
   reasoning 55
adolescent egocentrism 56
neo-Piagetians 58
zone of proximal
   development (ZPD) 60

scaffolding 61
social constructivist
   approach 63
language 65
infinite generativity 65
phonology 65
morphology 65
syntax 65
semantics 65
pragmatics 66
reading 70
whole-language approach 71
basic-skills-and-phonetics
   approach 71

Educational Psychology Checklist
PHYSICAL AND COGNITIVE DEVELOPMENT

How much have you learned since the beginning of the chapter? Use the following statements to help you review your knowledge and understanding of the chapter material. First, read the statement and mentally or briefly on paper demonstrate that you can outline the relevant information.

_____ I can describe the basic processes, periods, and issues in development.
_____ I know the basic ways that children and adolescents grow physically.
_____ I am aware of what children need in terms of health education.
_____ I can describe some main approaches to children's cognitive development.
_____ I know how to evaluate these approaches and can describe their educational applications.

_____ I know what language is and can describe its basic rule systems.
_____ I know how children's language development unfolds.
_____ I can profile how reading develops, and evaluate main approaches to teaching children how to read.
_____ I can describe some basic ideas about how children's writing develops.
_____ I know some ways to facilitate literacy.

For any items that you did not check off, go back and locate the relevant material in the chapter. Review the material again until you feel you can check off the item. You also may want to use this checklist in preparing for an exam.

Adventures for the Mind

Now that you have a good knowledge and understanding of the chapter, complete the following exercises to expand your thinking about the chapter's topics:

- Because of limited space, we could not explore all topics in children's physical development and health. To expand your knowledge of children's physical and cognitive development, as well as to see how they are connected, do some library research and find out how:
  –nutritional deficiencies can affect children's cognitive development
  –children's cognitive development might be affected by the mother's drug use during pregnancy
- Select the general age of the child you expect to teach one day. Make a list of that child's characteristic ways of thinking according to Piaget's theory of cognitive development. List other related characteristics of the child based on your own childhood. Then make a second list of your own current ways of thinking. Compare the lists. In what important cognitive ways do you and the child differ? What adjustments in thinking will you need to make when you set out to communicate with the child?
- Get together with several students in the class and create a series of questions to ask teachers about the debate about whole-language versus basic-skills-and-phonetics approaches to reading. After you have created your list of questions, use them as a basis for interviewing teachers from kindergarten, first-, third-, and fifth-grade classrooms.
- Talk with some middle school and high school teachers about how they handle students with reading and writing problems. What kinds of supports for helping these students are available? What kind of supports do they wish were available?

Taking It to the Net

1. List some facts about the earth and the moon, including some relationships between the earth and the moon. How would your thinking about the earth and the moon differ if you were a 6-year-old? Do adults and children think alike? Why, or why not?
2. How do you learn? Are facts and meanings transmitted to you by your teachers and parents, or do you actively construct facts and meanings on your own? What does it mean to "construct" meaning?
3. Piaget and Vygotsky are often portrayed as theorists with opposite ideas—Piaget believed in the child's personal discovery of ideas, Vygotsky believed in the child's social discovery of ideas. What do you believe? Is learning more social or more individual? Why?

Connect to http://www.mhhe.com/socscience/psychology/santedu/ttnet.htm to find the answers!

Case Studies

Case 1 *Joyce Davidson*: A teacher is not making much progress with a remedial English class and is particularly concerned about an extremely shy student who is not responding to her teaching methods and style.

Chapter 3

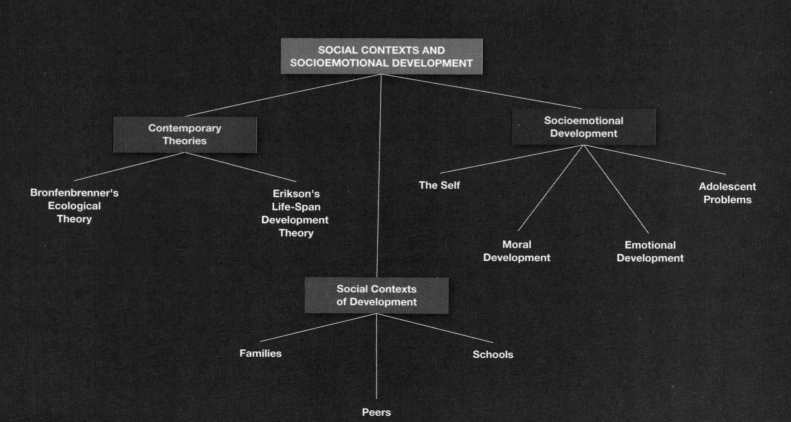

SOCIAL CONTEXTS AND SOCIOEMOTIONAL DEVELOPMENT

Contemporary Theories

Bronfenbrenner's Ecological Theory

Erikson's Life-Span Development Theory

Social Contexts of Development

Families

Schools

Peers

Socioemotional Development

The Self

Moral Development

Emotional Development

Adolescent Problems

Social Contexts and Socioemotional Development

Preview

Parents cradle children's lives, but children's development is also shaped by successive choirs of peers, friends, and teachers. Children's small worlds widen as they become students and develop relationships with many new people. In this chapter, we will explore these social worlds and examine children's socioemotional development. These are some of the questions we will address:

- What are some good and bad parenting strategies? How can teachers foster partnerships between school and family?
- How can teachers improve students' social skills?
- What is the best way to provide a developmentally appropriate education for children?
- What does it take for teachers and children to be emotionally intelligent?
- What are the best strategies for helping adolescents who have problems?

Teaching Stories
Keren Abra

Keren Abra teaches fifth grade in San Francisco. She believes the transition to middle/junior high school involves new responsibilities for students and increased seriousness about studying and achieving. She thinks that an effective teacher pays attention to children's socioemotional lives, not just their academic skills. The following example shows her sensitivity to students' socioemotional development.

Eleven-year-old Julie was very quiet, so quiet that in classroom discussions she whispered her responses. When Keren Abra asked Julie to repeat a comment the first morning of class, students told her that Julie couldn't speak louder. Her writing was so light and tiny that Keren had to hold the paper up close in a strong light to read it. Julie was smart, but her parents had gone through a bitter divorce and her father wandered in and out of her life. Julie needed a good therapist. Both parents agreed, but it had not yet happened.

Julie was significantly underachieving; she had low test scores and did minimal work. A crisis of low grades and incomplete work brought her mother to school one evening to meet with Keren, and her father arrived at school the next morning to talk about Julie's problems.

Later Keren spoke with Julie, who looked terrified. Keren said that, in talking with Julie,

"I kept some objectives in mind. This child needed to know that she was a good student, that she was loved, that adults could be consistent and responsible, and that she didn't have to hide and keep secrets. I told her that her parents had come in because we all were concerned about her and knew we needed to help her. I told her that both her parents loved her very much and asked if she knew this (she and I agreed that nobody's perfect, least of all adults with their own problems). I explained that a tutor was going to help her with her work, especially with developing her ideas. I talked with Julie about how much I liked her and about coming forward more in class.

Change did not happen overnight with Julie, but she did begin to increasingly look me in the eye with a more confident smile. She spoke out more in class, and improved her writing efforts. Her best months were when she was seeing both a therapist and a tutor, although her grades remained a roller coaster. At the end of the school year, she commented that she and her mother both noticed that her best work was when she felt supported and confident. For an 11-year-old, that is a valuable insight."

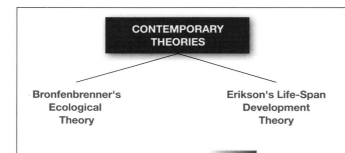

Bronfenbrenner's Theory

CONTEMPORARY THEORIES

A number of theories address children's socioemotional development. We will discuss the relevant behavioral and social cognitive theories in chapter 7. In this chapter we will focus on two main theories: Bronfenbrenner's ecological theory and Erikson's life-span development theory. These two theories were chosen because they are the most comprehensive theories to address the social contexts in which children develop (Bronfenbrenner) and major changes in children's socioemotional development (Erikson).

Bronfenbrenner's Ecological Theory

The ecological theory developed by Urie Bronfenbrenner (1917–) primarily focuses on the social contexts in which children live and the people who influence their development.

Five Environmental Systems
Bronfenbrenner's **ecological theory** *consists of five environmental systems that range from close interpersonal interactions to broad-based influences of culture. Bronfenbrenner (1986, 1997; Bronfenbrenner & Morris, 1998) calls the five systems the microsystem, mesosytem, exosystem, macrosystem, and chronosystem* (see figure 3.1).

A **microsystem** *is a setting in which the individual spends considerable time. Some of these contexts are the student's family, peers, school, and neighborhood.* Within these microsystems, the individual has direct interactions with parents, teachers, peers, and others. For Bronfenbrenner, the student is not a passive recipient of experiences in these settings, but is someone who reciprocally interacts with others and helps to construct the settings.

The **mesosystem** *involves linkages between microsystems.* Examples are the connections between family experiences and school experiences, and between family and peers. Experience in one microsystem can affect experience in another microsystem. For example, children whose parents have rejected them might have difficulty developing positive relationships with teachers.

The **exosystem** *is at work when experiences in another setting (in which the student does not have an active role) influence what students and teachers experience in the immediate context.* For example, consider the school and park supervisory boards in a community. They have strong roles in determining the quality of schools, parks, recreation facilities, and libraries. Their decisions can help or hinder a child's development.

The **macrosystem** *involves the broader culture in which students and teachers live, including the society's values and customs.* For example, some cultures (such as Islamic countries like Egypt or Iran) emphasize traditional gender roles. In other cultures (such as the United States), more varied gender roles are acceptable. In most Islamic countries, educational systems promote male dominance. In the United States, schools increasingly have become sensitive to endorsing the value of equal opportunities for females and males. *Culture* is a very broad term. Culture includes the roles of ethnicity and socioeconomic factors in children's development. We will explore these issues in more detail in chapter 5, "Sociocultural Diversity."

The **chronosystem** *refers to sociohistorical conditions of students' development.* For example, students today are living a childhood of many firsts (Louv, 1990). They are the first day-care generation, the first generation to grow up in the electronic bubble

Urie Bronfenbrenner developed ecological theory, a perspective that is receiving increased attention. His theory emphasizes the importance of both micro and macro dimensions of the environment in which the child lives.

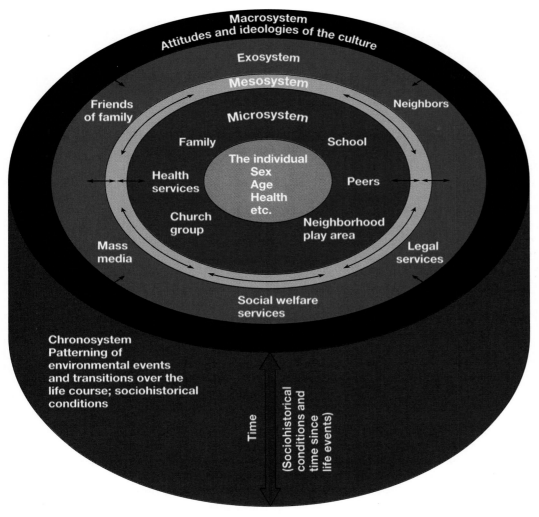

Figure 3.1
Bronfenbrenner's Ecological Theory of Development
Bronfenbrenner's ecological theory consists of five environmental systems: microsystem, mesosystem, exosystem, macrosystem, and chronosystem.

of an environment defined by computers and new forms of media, the first post-sexual-revolution generation, and the first generation to grow up in new kinds of dispersed, deconcentrated cities that are not quire urban, rural, or suburban.

Evaluating Bronfenbrenner's Theory   Bronfenbrenner's theory has gained popularity in recent years. It provides one of the few theoretical frameworks for systematically examining social contexts on both micro and macro levels, bridging the gap between behavioral theories that focus on small settings and anthropological theories that analyze larger settings. His theory has been instrumental in calling attention to the importance of looking at children's lives in more than one setting. As we just saw, a good strategy is to consider not just what goes on in the classroom, but also what happens in students' families, neighborhoods, and peer groups.

Critics of Bronfenbrenner's theory say that it gives too little attention to biological and cognitive factors in children's development. They also point out that the theory does not address the step-by-step developmental changes that are the focus of theories like Piaget's and Erikson's.

Bronfenbrenner and a Multicultural Framework

*T*EACHING STRATEGIES
Based on Bronfenbrenner's Theory

Some strategies that can help you apply Bronfenbrenner's theory in your classroom include:

1. *Think about the child as embedded in a number of environmental systems.* Bronfenbrenner's theory suggests that teachers can benefit by paying attention to the influences of different environmental systems on the child. These include schools and teachers, parents and siblings, the community and neighborhood, peers and friends, the media, religion, and culture (Goncu, 1999; Huitt, 1997).

2. *Pay attention to the connection between schools and families.* Educators are becoming aware that this is an especially important link (Coleman, 1997). In one study of a thousand eighth-graders, the joint impact of family and classroom experiences on students' attitudes and achievement were studied as the students made the transition from the last year of middle school to the first year of high school (Epstein, 1983). Students who were given greater opportunities for communication and decision making, whether at home or in the classroom, showed more initiative and got better grades. In another study that linked contexts, middle school and high school students participated in a program that was designed to connect their families, peers, schools, and parents' work (Cooper, 1995). This outreach program (administered by a university) targeted Latino and African American students in low-income areas. The students commented that the outreach program helped them to bridge the gaps across their different social worlds. Many of the students saw their schools and neighborhoods as contexts in which people expected them to fail, become pregnant and leave school, or behave delinquently. The outreach program provided students with expectations and moral goals to do "something good for your people," such as working in the community and encouraging siblings to go to college.

3. *Recognize the importance of the community, socioeconomic status, and culture in the child's development.* These broader social contexts can have powerful influences on the child's development (Valsiner, 2000). Poverty can overwhelm children's development and impair their ability to learn, although some children in impoverished circumstances are remarkably resilient. We will say much more about poverty and education in chapter 5, "Sociocultural Diversity." In one study of the impact of unemployment on 8,000 families, increases in child abuse were often preceded by job loss (Steinberg, Catalano, & Dooley, 1981). Clearly, many aspects of environmental systems outside of the school can impact children's development and their learning in school.

4. *We live in a changing society, and it is important to understand these sociohistorical changes.* Bronfenbrenner has increasingly given attention to the chronosystem as an important environmental system. He recently has called attention to two alarming problems: (1) the large number of children in America who live in poverty, especially in single-parent families; and (2) a decline in values (Bronfenbrenner & others, 1996). Later in this chapter we will address the topics of moral development and moral education.

Erikson's Theory

Erikson's Life-Span Development Theory

Complementing Bronfenbrenner's analysis of the social contexts in which children develop and the people who are important in their lives, the theory of Erik Erikson (1902–1994) presents a developmental unfolding of people's lives in stages. Let's take Erikson's journey through the human life span.

Eight Stages of Human Development
In Erikson's (1968) theory, eight stages of development unfold as people go through the human life span (see figure 3.2). Each stage consists of a developmental task that confronts individuals with a crisis. For Erikson, each crisis is not catastrophic but a turning point of increased vulnerability and enhanced potential. The more successfully an individual resolves each crisis, the more psychologically healthy the individual will be. Each stage has both positive and negative sides.

Trust versus mistrust *is Erikson's first psychosocial stage.* It occurs in the first year of life. The development of trust requires warm, nurturant caregiving. The positive outcome is a feeling of comfort and minimal fear. Mistrust develops when infants are treated too negatively or are ignored.

Autonomy versus shame and doubt *is Erikson's second psychosocial stage.* It occurs in late infancy and the toddler years. After gaining trust in their caregivers, infants begin to discover that their behavior is their own. They assert their independence and realize their will. If infants are restrained too much or punished too harshly, they develop a sense of shame and doubt.

Initiative versus guilt *is Erikson's third psychosocial stage.* It corresponds to early childhood, about 3 to 5 years of age. As young children experience a widening social world, they are challenged more than they were as infants. To cope with these challenges, they need to engage in active, purposeful behavior. In this stage, adults expect children to become more responsible and require them to assume some responsibilities for taking care of their bodies and belongings. Developing a sense of responsibility increases initiative. Children develop uncomfortable guilt feelings if they are irresponsible or are made to feel too anxious.

Industry versus inferiority *is Erikson's fourth psychosocial stage.* It corresponds approximately with the elementary school years, from 6 years of age until puberty or early adolescence. Children's initiative brings them into contact with a wealth of new experiences. As they move into the elementary school years, they direct their energy toward mastering knowledge and intellectual skills. At no time are children more enthusiastic about learning than at the end of early childhood, when their imagination is expansive. The danger in the elementary school years is developing a sense of inferiority, unproductiveness, and incompetence.

Identity versus identity confusion *is Erikson's fifth psychosocial stage.* It corresponds to the adolescent years. Adolescents try to find out who they are, what they are all about, and where they are going in life. They are confronted with many new roles and adult statuses (such as vocational and romantic). Adolescents need to be allowed to explore different paths to attain a healthy identity. If adolescents do not adequately explore different roles and don't carve out a positive future path, they can remain confused about their identity.

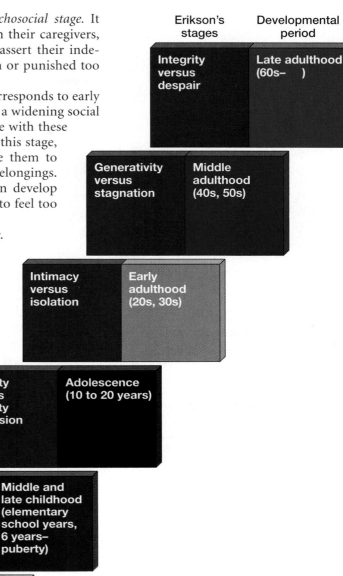

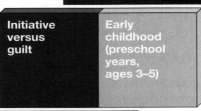

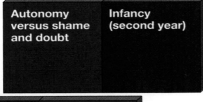

Figure **3.2**
Erikson's Eight Life-Span Stages

Erik Erikson with his wife, Joan, who is an artist. Erikson generated one of the most important developmental theories of the twentieth century.

Intimacy versus isolation *is Erikson's sixth psychosocial stage.* It corresponds to the early adult years, the twenties and thirties. The developmental task is to form positive close relationships with others. Erikson describes intimacy as finding oneself but losing oneself in another person. The hazard of this stage is that one will fail to form an intimate relationship with a romantic partner or friend and become socially isolated. For such individuals, loneliness can become a dark cloud over their lives.

Generativity versus stagnation *is Erikson's seventh psychosocial stage.* It corresponds to the middle adulthood years, the forties and fifties. Generativity means transmitting something positive to the next generation. This can involve such roles as parenting and teaching, through which adults assist the next generation in developing useful lives. Erikson described stagnation as the feeling of having done nothing to help the next generation.

Integrity versus despair *is Erikson's eighth and final psychosocial stage.* It corresponds to the late adulthood years, the sixties until death. Older adults review their lives, reflecting on what they have done. If the retrospective evaluations are positive, they develop a sense of integrity. That is, they view their life as positively integrated and worth living. In contrast, older adults become despairing if their backward glances are mainly negative.

Evaluating Erikson's Theory   Erikson's theory captures some of life's key socioemotional tasks and places them in a developmental framework. His concept of identity is especially helpful in understanding older adolescents and college students. His overall theory was a critical force in forging our current view of human development as lifelong rather than being restricted only to childhood (Kroger, 2000).

Erikson's theory is not without criticism. Some experts believe that his stages are too rigid. Bernice Neugarten (1988) says that identity, intimacy, independence, and many other aspects of socioemotional development are not like beads on a string that appear in neatly packaged age intervals. Rather, they are important issues throughout most of our lives. Although much research has been done on some of Erikson's stages (such as identity), the overall scope of his theory (such as whether the eight stages always occur in the order he proposed) has not been scientifically documented. For example, for some individuals (especially females), intimacy concerns precede identity or develop simultaneously.

At this point we have discussed a number of ideas about Bronfenbrenner's and Erikson's theories. A review of these ideas is presented in summary table 3.1.

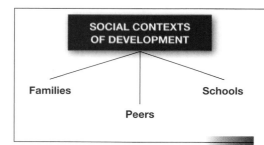

SOCIAL CONTEXTS OF DEVELOPMENT

In Bronfenbrenner's theory, the social contexts in which children live are important influences on their development. Let's explore three of the contexts in which children spend much of their time: families, peers, and schools.

Families

Parenting is a very important profession, but no test of its fitness is ever imposed in the interest of children.

George Bernard Shaw
Irish Playwright, 20th Century

Children grow up in diverse families. Some parents nurture and support their children. Others treat them harshly or ignore them. Some children have experienced their parents' divorce. Others live their entire childhood in a never-divorced family. Others live in a stepfamily. Some children's mothers work full-time and place them in after-school programs. Other children's mothers are present when they come home from school. Some children grow up in an ethnically uniform neighborhood, others in a neighborhood that is more mixed. Some children's families live in poverty, others are economically advantaged. Some children have siblings, others don't. All of these varying circumstances affect children's development and influence students in and beyond the classroom.

TEACHING STRATEGIES
Based on Erikson's Theory

Some strategies that can help you apply Erikson's theory in your classroom are:

1. *Encourage initiative in young children.* Children in preschool and early childhood education programs should be given a great deal of freedom to explore their world. They should be allowed to choose some of the activities they engage in. If their requests for doing certain activities are reasonable, the requests should be honored. Provide exciting materials that will stimulate their imagination. Children at this stage love to play. It not only benefits their socioemotional development but also is an important medium for their cognitive growth. Especially encourage social play with peers and fantasy play. Help children assume responsibility for putting toys and materials back in place after they have used them. Children can be given a plant or flower to care for and be assisted in caring for it. Criticism should be kept to a minimum so that children will not develop high levels of guilt and anxiety. Young children are going to make lots of mistakes and have lots of spills. They need good models far more than harsh critics. Structure their activities and environment for successes rather than failures by giving them developmentally appropriate tasks. For example, don't frustrate young children by having them sit for long periods of time doing academic paper-and-pencil tasks.

2. *Promote industry in elementary school children.* Teachers have a special responsibility for children's development of industry. It was Erikson's hope that teachers could provide an atmosphere in which children become passionate about learning. In Erikson's words, teachers should mildly but firmly coerce children into the adventure of finding out that they can learn to accomplish things that they themselves would never have thought they could do. In elementary school, children thirst to know. Most arrive at elementary school steeped in curiosity and a motivation to master tasks. In Erikson's view, it is important for teachers to nourish this motivation for mastery and curiosity. Challenge students, but don't overwhelm them. Be firm in requiring students to be productive, but don't be overly critical. Especially be tolerant of honest mistakes and make sure that every student has opportunities for many successes.

3. *Stimulate identity exploration in adolescents.* Recognize that the student's identity is multidimensional. Aspects include vocational goals, intellectual achievement, interests in hobbies, sports, music, and other areas. Ask adolescents to write essays about such dimensions, exploring who they are and what they want to do with their lives. Encourage adolescents to think independently and to freely express their views. This stimulates self-exploration. Also encourage adolescents to listen to debates on religious, political, and ideological issues. This will stimulate them to examine different perspectives.

   Recognize that some of the roles adolescents adopt are not permanent. They try on many different faces as they search for a face of their own. Also recognize that a successful identity is attained in bits and pieces over many years. Many adolescents in middle schools are just beginning to explore their identity, but even at this time exposing them to various careers and life options can benefit their identity development. Encourage adolescents to talk with a school counselor about career options as well as other aspects of their identity. Have people from different careers come and talk with your students about their work regardless of the grade you teach.

4. *Examine your life as a teacher through the lens of Erikson's eight stages* (Gratz & Boulton, 1996). For example, you might be at the age at which Erikson says the most important issue is identity versus identity confusion or intimacy versus isolation. Erikson believed that one of identity's most important dimensions is vocational. Your successful career as a teacher could be key in your overall identity. Another important aspect of development for young adults is to have positive close relationships with others. Your identity will benefit from having a positive relationship with a partner and with one or more friends. Many teachers develop strong camaraderie with other teachers or their mentors, which can be very rewarding.

   The characteristics of some of Erikson's other stages can benefit your teaching. Competent teachers trust, show initiative, are industrious and model a sense of mastery, and are motivated to contribute something meaningful to the next generation. In your role as a teacher, you will actively meet the criteria for Erikson's concept of generativity.

Parenting Styles   There can be times when you as a teacher will be asked to give parents advice. There also might be times when it is helpful for you to understand how parents are rearing their children and the effects this has on the children.

Is there a best way to parent? Diana Baumrind (1971, 1996), a leading authority on parenting, thinks so. She believes that parents should be neither punitive nor

Parenting Styles

Summary Table 3.1
Contemporary Theories

Concept	Processes/ Related Ideas	Characteristics/Description
Bronfenbrenner's Ecological Theory	Five Environmental Systems	• Bronfenbrenner's ecological theory consists of five environmental systems that include both micro and macro inputs: microsystem, mesosystem, exosystem, macrosystem, and chronosystem.
	Evaluating the Theory	• Bronfenbrenner's theory is one of the few systematic analyses that includes both micro and macro environments. • Critics say the theory lacks attention to biological and cognitive factors. They also point out that it does not address step-by-step developmental changes.
Erikson's Life-Span Development Theory	Eight Stages of Human Development	• Erikson's stages are trust vs. mistrust, autonomy vs. shame and doubt, initiative versus guilt, industry versus inferiority, identity versus identity confusion, intimacy versus isolation, generativity versus stagnation, and integrity versus despair.
	Evaluating the Theory	• Erikson's theory has made important contributions to understanding socioemotional development, although some critics say the stages are too rigid and that their sequencing lacks research support.

aloof. Rather, they should develop rules for children while at the same time being supportive and nurturant. Hundreds of research studies, including her own, support her view (Bornstein, 1995; Grotevant, 1998). Baumrind says that parenting styles come in four main forms:

- **Authoritarian parenting** *is restrictive and punitive.* Authoritarian parents exhort children to follow their directions and respect them. They place firm limits and controls on their children and allow little verbal exchange. For example, an authoritarian parent might say, "Do it my way or else. There will be no discussion!" Children of authoritarian parents often behave in socially incompetent ways. They tend to be anxious about social comparison, fail to initiate activity, and have poor communication skills.

- **Authoritative parenting** *encourages children to be independent but still places limits and controls on their actions. Extensive verbal give-and-take is allowed and parents are nurturant and supportive.* An authoritative parent might put his arm on the child's shoulder in a comforting way and say, "You know you should not have done that. Let's talk about how you can handle the situation differently the next time." Children whose parents are authoritative often behave in socially competent ways. They tend to be self-reliant, delay gratification, get along with their peers, and show high self-esteem. Because of these positive outcomes, Baumrind strongly endorses authoritative parenting.
- **Neglectful parenting** *is a permissive form of parenting in which parents are uninvolved in their children's lives.* When their offspring are adolescents or perhaps even young children, these parents cannot answer the question "It is 10 P.M. Do you know where your child is?" Children of neglectful parents develop the sense that other aspects of their parents' lives are more important than they are. Children of neglectful parents often behave in socially incompetent ways. They tend to have poor self-control, don't handle independence well, and aren't achievement motivated.
- **Indulgent parenting** *is a parenting style in which parents are highly involved with their children but place few limits or restrictions on their behaviors.* These parents often let their children do what they want and get their way because they believe the combination of nurturant support and lack of restraints will produce a creative, confident child. The result is that these children usually don't learn to control their own behavior. These parents do not take into account the development of the whole child.

The Changing Family in a Changing Society

Increasing numbers of children are being raised in divorced families, stepparent families, and families in which the mother works outside the home. As divorce has become epidemic, a staggering number of children have been growing up in single-parent families. The United States has a higher percentage of single-parent families than virtually any other industrialized country (see figure 3.3). Today, about one in every four children in the United States have lived a portion of their lives in a stepfamily by the time they are 18. Also, more than two of every three mothers with a child from 6 to 17 years of age are in the labor force.

If I had my child to raise all over again,
I'd finger paint more, and point the
finger less.
I'd do less correcting, and more connecting.
I'd take my eyes off my watch, and watch
with my eyes.
I would care to know less, and know to
care more.
I'd take more hikes and fly more kites.
I'd stop playing serious, and seriously
play.
I would run through more fields, and gaze
at more stars.
I'd do more hugging, and less tugging.
I would be firm less often, and affirm
much more.
I'd build self-esteem first, and the house
later.
I'd teach less about the love of power,
and more about the power of love.

Diane Loomans
Contemporary American Poet

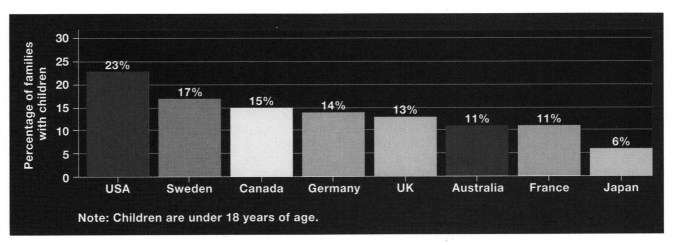

Figure 3.3
Single-Parent Families in Various Countries

Children and Divorce

Children of Divorce The effects of divorce on children are complex, depending on such factors as the age of the child, strengths and weaknesses of the child at the time of the divorce, the type of custody involved, socioeconomic status, and postdivorce family functioning (Hetherington, 1999; Hetherington, Bridges, & Isabella, 1998). The use of support systems (relatives, friends, housekeepers), an ongoing positive relationship between the custodial parent and the ex-spouse, being able to meet financial needs, and quality schooling help children adjust to the stressful circumstances of divorce (Emery, 1999; Parke & Buriel, 1998).

E. Mavis Hetherington's (1995, 1999) research documents the importance of schools when children grow up in a divorced family. Throughout elementary school, children in divorced families had the highest achievement and fewest problems when both the parenting environment and the school environment were authoritative (according to Baumrind's categorization). In the divorced families, when only one parent was authoritative, an authoritative school improved the child's adjustment. The most negative parenting environment occurred when neither parent was authoritative. The most negative school environment was chaotic and neglecting.

In response to the high divorce rate, the state of Florida recently passed a law requiring that all high school students be taught marital and relationship skills (Peterson, 1998). Many schools teach some form of family life course, but marriage and family experts believe such courses need upgrading to include the latest research on communication skills, the factors most likely to cause divorce, strategies for conflict resolution, and family problem-solving techniques (Gottman, 1996).

Ethnic and Socioeconomic Variations in Families Families in different ethnic groups differ in their size, structure, and composition, their reliance on kinships networks, and their levels of income and education (Parke & Buriel, 1998). Large and extended families are more common among minority groups than among the White majority. For example, 19 percent of Latino families have 3 or more children, compared to 14 percent of African American and 10 percent of non-Latino White families. African American and Latino children interact more with grandparents, aunts, uncles, cousins, and more-distant relatives than do non-Latino White children.

Single-parent families are more common among African Americans and Latinos than among non-Latino White Americans. Single parents often have less time, money, and energy than do two-parent households. Ethnic minority parents are less educated and more likely to be low-income than their White counterparts. Still, many impoverished ethnic minority families manage to find ways to raise competent children.

Some aspects of home life can help to protect ethnic minority children from injustice. The community and the family can filter out destructive racist messages, and parents can present alternative frames of reference to counter those presented by the majority. The extended family also can serve as an important buffer to stress (Wakschlag, Chase-Lansdale, & Brooks-Gunn, 1996). It is especially important for teachers to guard against having biased expectations about parents based on their ethnicity. We will say more about ethnicity and children's schooling in chapter 5, "Sociocultural Diversity."

In the United States and most Western cultures, child-rearing practices have been found to differ among different socioeconomic groups. Low-income parents often place a high value on external characteristics such as obedience and neatness. In contrast, middle-class families frequently place a high value on internal characteristics, such as self-control and delay of gratification. Middle-class parents are more likely to explain, praise, accompany their discipline with reasoning, and ask their children questions. Low-income parents are more likely to use physical punishment and criticize their children (Hoff-Ginsberg & Tardif, 1995).

There also are socioeconomic differences in the way that parents think about education (Lareau, 1996). Middle-class parents more often think of education as something that should be mutually encouraged by parents and teachers. Low-income

This mother is working with her son at a Saturday math workshop in Oakland, California, sponsored by Family Math.

parents are more likely to view education as the teacher's job. Thus, the linkages between school and family that we describe next can especially benefit students from low-income families.

School–Family Linkages

In Bronfenbrenner's theory, linkages between the family and the school are an important mesosystem. And in Hetherington's study that we just discussed, an authoritative school environment benefited children from divorced families.

Today's teachers think it is extremely important to get parents involved in children's education. In one survey, teachers listed parental involvement as the number one priority in improving education (Chira, 1993).

What stands in the way of parental involvement? For one thing, education expert Joyce Epstein (1997) says, most parents know so little about their children's education that they can't even ask questions about it. That is why so many conversations begin with a parent asking, "How was school today?" and end with the child responding, "Fine." This low level of parental involvement concerns educators because it is linked with students' low achievement (Eccles & Harold, 1996). For example, in a recent study of more than 16,000 students, the students were more likely to get A's and less likely to repeat a grade or be expelled if both parents were highly involved in their schooling (National Center for Education Statistics, 1997). In this study, high involvement was defined as the parent participating in three or four of the following: school meetings, a teacher conference, a class meeting, or volunteering. A goal of family inclusion and community involvement was made part of the Goals 2000: Educate America Act. This was a welcome official endorsement of the critical role that families play in children's education. Students of all ages report that they want their parents to be more involved in their education (Connors & Epstein, 1995).

One problem that can interfere with building partnerships between school and family is negative perceptions of families (Workman & Gage, 1997). Some children come to school poorly clothed, on drugs, with knives or guns, and without their homework. They might not be motivated to learn and might show little respect for the teacher. In such circumstances, it can be hard to get past blaming parents for the problems you have inherited as a teacher. However, to get parents more positively involved in their children's education, you have to get past the blaming. Think of parents as having potential strengths that, if adequately tapped, can help you educate the child more effectively.

Let's examine several examples of successful partnerships between schools and families. In Lima, Ohio, the goal is for each school to establish a personal relationship with every parent. At an initial parent/teacher conference, parents are given a packet that discusses how they can participate in the child's learning activities at home. Conferences, regular phone calls, and home visits strengthen the school-family connection. These make other kinds of communication (such as progress reports, report

THROUGH THE EYES OF TEACHERS
Parents and the Community

Parents are a primary ingredient of the classroom team at Gramercy School. Many parents of preschool children who are developmentally delayed have no idea as to how or if their child will develop. It becomes the job of the educators and other professionals to assist that parent in the development of their child. We then become partners. There are ongoing parent training groups, support groups, and time can be spent in school with a therapist at any time that the parent wishes. Gramercy School has an open-door policy. Teachers have access to telephones throughout the building and daily communication books and notes are sent home. There are times when some families face a very challenging situation. At these times, I might meet with this parent or I might call in the psychologist to assist with specific issues. We have on occasion asked parents to assist other parents or to be a resource for others. This is powerful and gives support from family to family.

Use of the community is very important. New York City is full of opportunities. I have been able to work closely with the Disabled Library in the neighborhood. They have been great at supplying the school with audio books for the children and lending special equipment for their use. The local fire department has been used for numerous trips. The firemen have been especially attentive to the students because of their various disabilities. The fire department has also come to visit the school, which was very exciting for the children. It was amazing to see how patient they were with the students. I am also encouraged to see that many of the area colleges and universities send interns and student teachers to visit the school. Donations from Hasbro toy company during the holidays makes a big difference in the way some students and families get to spend their holiday vacation. Our students are very visible in the New York City community, where we are located. This helps our neighbors to get to know the staff and children and creates a safer environment.

Juanita Kirton
Assistant Principal
YAI/NYL Gramercy School
New York City

School-Family
Linkages

TECHNOLOGY AND EDUCATION
Communicating with Parents About
Television and Children's Development

Many children spend more time in front of the television set than they do with their parents. In the 1990s, children averaged 26 hours a week watching television. In chapter 2 we indicated that watching lots of television is related to poor physical fitness in children. It also can diminish the amount of time children spend doing homework and in school-related activities. Amazingly, the 20,000 hours of television, on the average, that children watch by the time they graduate from high school represents more hours than they have spent in the classroom!

Following are some recommendations that you can communicate to parents about reducing TV's negative impact and increasing its positive impact on their children's development (Singer & Singer, 1987):

• Help children develop good viewing habits early in life.
• Monitor your children's viewing habits and plan what they will watch, instead of letting them view TV randomly. Be active with young children between planned programs.

• Look for children's programs that feature children in the child's age group.
• Make sure that television is not a substitute for other activities.
• Develop discussions about sensitive television themes with children. Give them the opportunity to ask questions about the programs.
• Balance reading and television activities. Children can "follow up" on interesting television programs by checking out the library books from which some programs have been adapted and by pursuing additional stories by the authors of those books.
• Help children develop a balanced viewing schedule of education, action, comedy, fine arts, fantasy, sports, and so on. Make sure that children are not primarily watching television shows filled with sex and violence.
• Point out positive examples that show how various ethnic and cultural groups contribute to a better society.
• Point out positive examples of females performing competently both in professions and at home.

cards, activity calendars, or discussion of problems that arise during the year) more welcome and successful. To read further about effective communication with parents, see the Technology and Education box.

In a joint effort of the New York City School System and the Children's Aid Society, community organizations have been invited to provide school-based programs for 1,200 adolescents and their families since 1992 (Carnegie Council on Adolescent Development, 1995). The participating school's family resource center is open from 8:30 A.M. to 8:30 P.M. Staffed by social workers, parents, and other volunteers, the center houses adult education, drug-abuse prevention, and other activities. Because many of the families who send adolescents to the school are of Dominican origin, the school offers English-as-a-second-language classes for parents, 400 of whom are currently enrolled. To read about one person who made a difference in improving school-family partnerships at her elementary school, see the Diversity and Education box.

Peers

In addition to families and teachers, peers also play powerful roles in children's development. Just what are peers?

Exploring Peer Relations   In the context of child development, **peers** *are children of about the same age or maturity level.* Same-age peer interaction plays a unique role. Age grading would occur even if schools were not age graded and children were left alone to determine the composition of their own societies. One of the most important functions of the peer group is to provide a source of information and comparison about the world outside of the family.

DIVERSITY AND EDUCATION
Making a Difference in North Philadelphia:
Madeline Cartwright

Madeline Cartwright was formerly the principal of the James G. Blaine public school in a neighborhood enshrouded in poverty and rocked by violence. Cartwright became the principal of Blaine school in 1979. She grew up in Pittsburgh's poor Hill District, and she was determined to make a difference in North Philadelphia, one of America's most drug-ridden, devastated inner-city areas.

One of the first things Cartwright did when she became principal was to install a washer and dryer in the school's kitchen, where each morning she and her staff personally washed much of the children's clothing. A Philadelphia chemical company provided her with free soap powder. Cartwright said this is the only way many of the children in her school will know what it is like to have clean clothes. She is proud that the kids in her school "looked good and had clean clothes," and she knows it made them feel better about themselves.

The most important thing Cartwright did when she became the principal was to, as she said, "browbeat" parents into getting involved in the school. She told them that she came from the same circumstances they did and that, here at Blaine school, the children were going to get a better education and have a better life than most children who attended her elementary school when she was growing up. But she told the parents that this was only going to happen if they worked with her and became partners with the school in educating and socializing the children.

When she came to Blaine school, she told the parents, "This place is dirty! How can your kids go to school in a place like this!" One of the parents commented, "You must think you are in the suburbs." The parent expected the neighborhood and the school to be dirty. Cartwright told the parent, "The dirt in the suburbs is the same as the dirt in North Philadelphia—if you don't *move* it. And the same detergents work here." Cartwright rounded up 18 parents and scrubbed the building until it was clean.

Blaine's school auditorium overflowed with parents when parent meetings were scheduled. Cartwright made children bring their parents to the meetings. She told the children, "Your parents need to know what we are doing in school." She gave the children a doughnut or a pretzel the next day if one of their parents came. She told the parents they could come to her if they had problems—that she could direct them to places and people who would help them solve their problems. Because of Cartwright's efforts, parents now feel comfortable at Blaine school (Louv, 1990).

Madeline Cartwright is an elementary school principal who has made a powerful difference in many impoverished children's lives. Especially important is Cartwright's persistence in getting parents more involved in their children's education.

Good peer relations might be necessary for normal development (Howes & Tonyan, 2000; Ryan & Patrick, 1996; Rubin, 2000). Social isolation, or the inability to "plug in" to a social network, is linked with many problems and disorders, ranging from delinquency and problem drinking to depression (Kupersmidt & Coie, 1990). In one study, poor peer relations in childhood was associated with dropping out of school and delinquent behavior in adolescence (Roff, Sells, & Golden, 1972). In another study, harmonious peer relations in adolescence was related to positive mental health at midlife (Hightower, 1990).

TEACHING STRATEGIES
For Forging School-Family Linkages

Joyce Epstein (1996) described six areas in which school-family linkages can be forged:

1. *Provide assistance to families.* Schools can provide parents with information about child-rearing skills, the importance of family support, child and adolescent development, and home contexts that enhance learning at each grade level. Teachers are an important contact point between schools and families. Teachers can become aware of whether the family is meeting the basic physical and health needs of the child.

2. *Communicate effectively with families about school programs and their child's progress.* This involves both school-to-home and home-to-school communication. Encourage parents to attend parent-teacher conferences and other school functions. Their attendance conveys to their children that they are interested in their children's school performance. Set up times for parent meetings that are convenient for them to attend. Most parents cannot come to meetings during the school day because of other obligations. One option is "work nights" for parents and children to come to school and work on various projects to improve the school's physical appearance, mount artwork, and so on. Teachers can monitor the percentage of parents who come to functions. If the turnout is low, brainstorm with parents, other teachers, and administrators to come up with strategies that will increase participation. Also, work on developing activities in which parents can get to know each other, not just know the teacher.

   Some specific strategies for improving communication are (Rosenthal & Sawyers, 1997):

   - Invite parents to meet you before the school year begins at an orientation, or invite parents to a potluck dinner.
   - Send home children's work each week accompanied by a note or a letter. The letter might review the week's activities and include suggestions for helping children with their homework. Send the letter in the parents' primary language.
   - In schools with computerized telephone systems, record messages about study units and homework assignments so that parents can call at their convenience. In McAllen, Texas, the school district has developed a community partnership with local radio stations. The district sponsors "Discusiones Escolares," a weekly program in Spanish that encourages parents to become more involved in their children's education. Parents can check out copies of the script or a cassette tape of each program from the parent coordinators at their schools.
   - Encourage principals to set up lunch meetings with parents to find out their concerns and ask for suggestions.
   - Use PTA/PTO meetings effectively. Sometimes the parent-teacher conference is the only contact teachers have with parents. Schedule the first conference in the first two weeks of school so that parents can raise concerns, ask questions, and make suggestions. This can avoid potential problems from the outset. At this first meeting, try to find out about the family's structure (intact, divorced, stepfamily), rules, roles, and learning style. Practice active listening skills and say something positive about their child to establish yourself as someone who can be approached.
   - Another way of making a school family-friendly is to create a parent room or parent center at the school (Johnson, 1994). Here parents can help each other, help the school, and receive information or assistance from the school or community.

3. *Encourage parents to be volunteers.* Improve training, work, and schedules to involve parents as volunteers at school or attendance at school meetings. Try to match the skills of volunteers to classroom needs.

4. *Involve families with their children in learning activities at home.* This includes homework and other curriculum-linked activities and decisions. Parents are the most effective when they learn good tutoring strategies and support the work of schools. Epstein (1998; Epstein, Salinas, & Jackson, 1995) coined the term *interactive homework* and designed a program that encourages students to go to their parents for help. In one elementary school that uses Epstein's approach, a weekly teacher's letter informs parents about the objective of each assignment, gives directions, and asks for comments. One interactive homework assignment had parents accompany their children to neighbors' houses to discuss the local citrus industry. Epstein and her colleagues (1995) have developed manuals for teachers that provides hundreds of examples of interactive homework exercises in elementary schools. These can be obtained from the Center on Families, Communities, Schools, and Children's Learning at Johns Hopkins University in Baltimore.

5. *Include families as participants in school decisions.* Parents can be invited to be on PTA/PTO boards, various committees, councils, and other parent organizations.

6. *Coordinate community collaboration.* Help interconnect the work and resources of community businesses, agencies, colleges and universities, and other groups to strengthen school programs, family practices, and student learning. Schools can alert families to community programs and services that will benefit them.

Children spend considerable time with peers and friends. What peer statuses can children have? How do peer relations change developmentally?

Peer Statuses   Developmentalists have pinpointed four types of peer status: popular children, neglected children, rejected children, and controversial children (Rubin, Bukowski, & Parker, 1998; Wentzal & Asher, 1995).

Many children worry about whether they are popular or not. **Popular children** *are frequently nominated as a best friend and are rarely disliked by their peers.* Popular children give out reinforcements, listen carefully, maintain open lines of communication with peers, are happy, act like themselves, show enthusiasm and concern for others, and are self-confident without being conceited (Hartup, 1983).

Neglected children *are infrequently nominated as a best friend but are not disliked by their peers.* **Rejected children** *are infrequently nominated as someone's best friend and are often actively disliked by their peers.* **Controversial children** *are frequently nominated both as someone's best friend and as being disliked.*

Rejected children often have more serious adjustment problems than do neglected children (Dishion & Spracklen, 1996; Rubin's others, 2000). In one study, more than a hundred fifth-grade boys were evaluated over a period of 7 years until the end of high school (Kupersmidt & Coie, 1990). The most important factor in predicting whether rejected children would engage in delinquent behavior or drop out of secondary school was aggression toward peers in elementary school. Aggression, impulsiveness, and disruptiveness characterize the majority of rejected children, although 10 to 20 percent of rejected children are actually shy.

A special peer relations concern involves bullying. We will discuss bullying in chapter 12, "Managing the Classroom," where we will provide strategies for dealing with bullies.

Friendship   Friendships contribute to peer status and provide other benefits:

- *Companionship.* Friendship gives children a familiar partner, someone who is willing to spend time with them and join in collaborative activities.
- *Physical support.* Friendship provides resources and assistance in times of need.
- *Ego support.* Friendship helps children feel they are competent, worthy individuals. Especially important in this regard is social approval from friends (Berndt & Keefe, 1996).

Friendships

• *Intimacy/affection.* Friendship provides children with a warm, trusting, close relationship with others. In this relationship, children often feel comfortable about disclosing private, personal information.

Having friends can be a developmental advantage, but friendships are not all alike (Hartup, 2000; Hartup & Stevens, 1997). There are developmental advantages for children in having friends who are socially skilled and supportive. However, it is not developmentally advantageous to have coercive and conflict-ridden friendships. And it sometimes is disadvantageous to a child or adolescent to be friends with someone who is several years older. Students with older friends engage in more deviant behaviors than their counterparts who have same-age friends (Berndt, 1996). Early-maturing adolescents are especially vulnerable in this regard (Magnusson, 1988).

Developmental Changes in Peer Relations

During the elementary school years, children's peer groups increasingly consist of same-sex peers (Maccoby, 1995). After extensive observations of elementary school playgrounds, two researchers characterized the settings as "gender school" (Luria & Herzog, 1985). They said that boys teach one another the required masculine behavior and strictly reinforce it, and that girls often pass on the female culture and mainly congregate with each other.

In early adolescence, participation in coed groups increases (Dunphy, 1963). Also in adolescence, many students become members of cliques, and allegiance to the clique can exert a powerful influence over their lives. Group identity with the clique can override the adolescent's personal identity. In any secondary school there will be three to six well-formed cliques. Some typical cliques are jocks, populars, brains, druggies, and toughs. Although many adolescents want to be in a clique, some are fiercely independent and have no desire to be in one.

Friendship likely plays a more important developmental role in secondary school than in elementary school (Sullivan, 1953). Adolescents disclose more personal information to their friends than younger children do (Buhrmester & Furman, 1987). And adolescents say that they depend more on their friends than on their parents to satisfy their needs for companionship, reassurance of worth, and intimacy (Furman & Buhrmester, in press).

Schools

In school, children spend many years as members of a small society that exerts a tremendous influence on their socioemotional development.

Schools' Changing Social Developmental Contexts

Social contexts vary through the early childhood, elementary school, and adolescent years (Minuchin & Shapiro, 1983). The early childhood setting is a protected environment whose boundary is the classroom. In this limited social setting, young children interact with one or two teachers, usually female, who are powerful figures in their lives. Young children also interact with peers in dyads or small groups.

The classroom still is the main context in elementary school, although it is more likely to be experienced as a social unit than is the early childhood classroom. The teacher symbolizes authority, which establishes the climate of the classroom, the conditions of social interaction,

I didn't belong as a kid, and that always bothered me. If only I'd known that one day my differences would have been an asset, then my early years would have been a lot better.

Bette Midler
Contemporary Movie Actress and Singer

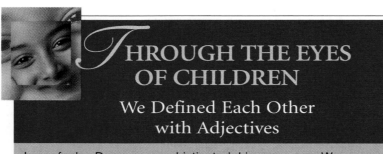

THROUGH THE EYES OF CHILDREN

We Defined Each Other with Adjectives

I was funky. Dana was sophisticated. Liz was crazy. We walked to school together, went for bike rides, cut school, got stoned, talked on the phone, smoked cigarettes, slept over, discussed boys and sex, went to church together, and got angry at each other. We defined each other with adjectives and each other's presence. As high school friends, we simultaneously resisted and anticipated adulthood and womanhood.

What was possible when I was 15 and 16? We still had to tell our parents where we were going! We wanted to do excitedly forbidden activities like going out to dance clubs and drinking whiskey sours. Liz, Dana, and I wanted to do these forbidden things in order to feel: to have intense emotional and sensual experiences that removed us from the suburban sameness we shared with each other and everyone else we knew. We were tired of the repetitive experiences that our town, our siblings, our parents, and our school offered to us. . . .

The friendship between Dana, Liz, and myself was born out of another emotional need: the need for trust. The three of us had reached a point in our lives when we realized how unstable relationships can be, and we all craved safety and acceptance. Friendships all around us were often uncertain. We wanted and needed to be able to like and trust each other. (Garrod & others, 1992, pp. 199–200)

TEACHING STRATEGIES
For Improving Children's Social Skills

In every class you teach, some children will likely have weak social skills. One or two might be rejected children. Several others might be neglected. Are there things you can do to help these children improve their social skills? As you think about this, keep in mind that improving social skills is easier when children are 10 years of age or younger (Malik & Furman, 1993). In adolescence, peer reputations become more fixed as cliques and peer groups take on more importance. Following are some good strategies for improving children's social skills:

1. *Help rejected children learn to listen to peers and "hear what they say" instead of trying to dominate peer relations.* In one study, socially rejected young adolescents were coached on the importance of showing behaviors (such as having better empathy, listening carefully, and improving communication skills) that would improve their chance of being liked by others (Murphy & Schneider, 1994). The intervention helped the rejected youth develop better friendships.

2. *Help neglected children attract attention from peers in positive ways and hold their attention.* They can do this by asking questions, listening in a warm and friendly way, and saying things about themselves that relate to the peers' interests. Also work with neglected children on entering groups more effectively.

3. *Provide children low in social skills with knowledge about how to improve these skills.* In one study of sixth- and seventh-graders, knowledge of both appropriate and inappropriate strategies for making friends was related positively to peer acceptance (Wentzel & Erdley, 1993). Knowledge of appropriate strategies included knowing:

   - how to initiate interaction, such as asking someone about their favorite activities and asking the other child to do things together
   - that it is important to be nice, kind, and considerate
   - that it is necessary to show respect for others by being courteous and listening to what others have to say
   - that providing social support helps a friendship, that you need to show that you care, and that it is a good idea to compliment others

   Knowledge of inappropriate strategies included knowing:

   - that it is not a good idea to be aggressive, show disrespect, be inconsiderate, hurt others' feelings, gossip, spread rumors, embarrass others, or criticize others
   - not to present yourself negatively, be self-centered, care only about yourself, or be jealous, grouchy, or angry all the time
   - not to engage in antisocial behavior, such as fighting, yelling at others, picking on others, making fun of others, being dishonest, breaking school rules, or taking drugs

4. *Read and discuss appropriate books on peer relations with students and devise supportive games and activities* (Bhavnagri & Samuels, 1996). Include these as thematic units in your curriculum for young children. Make books on peer relations and friendship available to older children and adolescents.

and the nature of group functioning. Peer groups are more important now and students have an increased interest in friendship.

As children move into middle and junior high school, the school environment increases in scope and complexity. The social field is now the whole school rather than the classroom. Adolescents interact with teachers and peers from a broader range of cultural backgrounds on a broader range of interests. More of the teachers are male. Adolescents' social behavior becomes weighted more strongly toward peers, extracurricular activities, clubs, and the community. Secondary school students are more aware of the school as a social system and might be motivated to conform to it or challenge it.

Early Childhood and Elementary School Education

There are many variations in how young children are educated. Some are educated in academically oriented programs, others in child-centered kindergartens that emphasize play and careful nurturing. A special interest focuses on developmentally appropriate education.

Early Childhood Education

Developmentally Appropriate Education   It is time for a numbers game in an early childhood class at the Greenbrook School in South Brunswick, New Jersey. With little prodding from the teacher, twenty-three 5- and 6-year-olds fetch geometric puzzles, playing cards, and counting equipment from the shelves that line the room. At one round table, some young children fit together brightly colored shapes. One girl forms a hexagon out of triangles. Other children gather around her to count how many parts were needed to make the whole. After about 30 minutes, the children prepare for storytime. They put away the counting equipment and sit in a circle around one young girl. She holds up a giant book about a character named Mrs. Wishywashy, who insists on giving the farm animals a bath. The children recite the whimsical lines, clearly enjoying one of their favorite stories. The hallway outside the kindergarten is lined with drawings that depict the children's own interpretations of the book. After the first reading, volunteers act out various parts of the book. There is not one bored face in the room.

This is not reading, writing, and arithmetic the way most adults remember it. A growing number of educators believe that young children learn best through active, hands-on teaching methods that involve such activities as games and dramatic play. They know that children develop at varying rates and that schools need to allow for these individual differences. They also believe that schools should focus on improving children's socioemotional development as well as their cognitive development. **Developmentally appropriate education** *is based on knowledge of the typical development of children within an age span (age appropriateness) as well as the uniqueness of the child (individual appropriateness).* Developmentally appropriate education contrasts with developmentally inappropriate practice, which ignores concrete, hands-on teaching methods. Direct teaching largely through abstract, paper-and-pencil activities presented to large groups of young children is believed to be developmentally inappropriate. Although we are discussing developmentally appropriate education in this chapter on socioemotional development, the concept applies to children's physical and cognitive development as well.

The National Association for the Education of Young Children (NAEYC) has been instrumental in increasing the number of schools that adopt developmentally appropriate practices (Bredekamp & Copple, 1997; NAEYC, 1996). Their recommendations hold for the education of children through 8 years of age. In figure 3.4 on pages 100–101, you can examine NAEYC's recommended educational practices.

Do developmentally appropriate educational practices improve young children's development? Yes. Young children in developmentally appropriate classrooms are likely to have less stress, be more motivated, be more skilled socially, have better work habits, be more creative, have better language skills, and demonstrate better math skills than children in developmentally inappropriate classrooms (Hart & others, 1996; Sherman & Mueller, 1996; Stipek & others, 1995).

How common are programs that use developmentally appropriate practice? Unfortunately, as few as one-third to one-fifth of early childhood programs follow this educational strategy. Even fewer elementary schools do.

THROUGH THE EYES OF CHILDREN

Learning About Bugs and Books

Dear State Committee:

We think Mrs. Hitchcock is the best teacher in the state because she was very nice to us on the very first day of school. She always has a smile on her face and she never frowns. She is kind and pretty. Mrs. Hitchcock teaches us good manners and how to help each other. We get to play with toys, learn about bugs, and have fun centers. She reads books to us and is a good storyteller.

At the end of the day, Mrs. Hitchcock gives us hugs and tells us goodbye when we go home. She loves us and we love her.

Mrs. Hitchcock's Happy Herd
(Letter dictated to Mrs. Hitchcock's teacher assistant by her kindergarten class at Holley Navarre Primary School, Florida)

Mrs. Hitchcock (left) and some members of the "Happy Herd."

Child-initiated activities and small-group instruction are the exception rather than the rule (Dunn & Kontos, 1997).

An increasingly popular approach to young children's education in the United States is the developmentally appropriate education practiced in Reggio Emilia, a small town in Northern Italy. There children are encouraged to learn by investigating and exploring topics that interest them. A wide range of stimulating media and materials are available for children to use as they learn. Children often explore topics in a group. Two co-teachers serve as guides. The Reggio Emilia teachers view a project as an adventure. The project might start from a teacher's suggestion, a child's idea, or an event such as a snowfall or something else unexpected. Children are given ample time to think about and plan the project. Cooperation is a major theme in the Reggio Emilia approach (Firlik, 1996). Reggio Emilia reflects the constructivist approach to education that initially was described in chapters 1 and 2 and will be explored in greater depth in later chapters, especially chapter 9, "Social Constructivist Approaches, Domain-Specific Approaches, and Teaching."

NAEYC
Reggio Emilia

Early Childhood Education for Disadvantaged Children   For many years, many children from low-income families did not receive any education before they entered first grade. In the 1960s, an effort was made to break the cycle of poverty and inadequate education for young children in the United States. **Project Head Start** *was designed to provide young children from low-income families opportunities to acquire the skills and experiences that are important for success in school.* Funded by the federal government, Project Head Start began in 1965 and continues to serve disadvantaged children today.

Intervening educationally in impoverished children's lives is a good strategy. In high-quality Head Start programs, parents and communities are involved in positive ways. The teachers are knowledgeable about children's development and use developmentally appropriate practices. Researchers have found that when young children from low-income families experience a quality Head Start program, there are substantial long-term benefits. These include being less likely to drop out of school, be in a special education class, or be on welfare than their low-income counterparts who did not attend a Head Start program (Lazar & others, 1982; Schweinhart, 1999). However, Head Start programs are not all created equal. One estimate is that 40 percent of the 1,400 Head Start programs are inadequate (Zigler & Finn-Stevenson, 1999; Zigler & Styfco, 1994). More attention needs to be given to developing high-quality Head Start programs (Raver & Zigler, 1997).

The Transition to Elementary School   As children make the transition to elementary school, they interact and develop relationships with new and significant others. School provides them with a rich source of ideas to shape their sense of self.

A special concern about early elementary school classrooms is that they not proceed primarily on the basis of negative feedback. I (your author) vividly remember my first-grade teacher. Unfortunately, she never smiled; she ran the classroom in a dictatorial manner, and learning (or lack of learning) progressed more on the basis of fear than of enjoyment and passion. Fortunately, I experienced some warmer, more student-friendly teachers later on.

Elementary Education

Children's self-esteem is higher when they begin elementary school than when they complete it (Blumenfeld & others, 1981). Is that because they experienced so much negative feedback and were criticized so much along the way? We will say more about the roles of reinforcement and punishment in children's learning in chapter 7, and about managing the classroom in chapter 12.

For now, though, consider the following two elementary school classrooms and what effect they might have on children's learning and self-esteem (Katz & Chard, 1989). In one, students spend the entire morning making identical pictures of traffic

Componen	Appropriate practice	Inappropriate practice
Curriculum goals	Experiences are provided in all developmental areas—physical, cognitive, social, and emotional.	Experiences are narrowly focused on cognitive development without recognition that all areas of the child's development are interrelated.
	Individual differences are expected, accepted, and used to design appropriate activities.	Children are evaluated only against group norms, and all are expected to perform the same tasks and achieve the same narrowly defined skills.
	Interactions and activities are designed to develop children's self-esteem and positive feelings toward learning.	Children's worth is measured by how well they conform to rigid expectations and perform on standardized tests.
Teaching strategies	Teachers prepare the environment for children to learn through active exploration and interaction with adults, other children, and materials.	Teachers use highly structured, teacher-directed lessons almost exclusively.
	Children select many of their own activities from among a variety the teacher prepares.	The teacher directs all activity deciding what children will do and when.
	Children are expected to be mentally and physically active.	Children are expected to sit down, be quiet, and listen or do paper-and-pencil tasks for long periods of time. A major portion of time is spent passively sitting, watching, and listening.
Guidance of socioemotional development	Teachers enhance children's self-control by using positive guidance techniques, such as modeling and encouraging expected behavior, redirecting children to a more acceptable activity, and setting clear limits.	Teachers spend considerable time enforcing rules, punishing unacceptable behavior, demeaning children who misbehave, making children sit and be quiet, and refereeing disagreements.
	Children are provided many opportunities to develop social skills, such as cooperating, helping, negotiating, and talking with the person involved to solve interpersonal problems.	Children work individually at desks and tables most of the time and listen to the teacher's directions to the total group.

Figure **3.4**   Developmentally Appropriate and Inappropriate Practice in

Componen	Appropriate practice	Inappropriate practice
Language development, literacy, and cognitive development	Children are provided many opportunities to see how reading and writing are useful before they are instructed in letter names, sounds, and word identification. Basic skills develop when they are meaningful to children. An abundance of these activities is provided to develop language and literacy: listening to and reading stories and poems; taking field trips; dictating stories; participating in dramatic play; talking informally with other children and adults; and experimenting with writing.	Reading and writing instruction stresses isolated skill development, such as recognizing single letters, reading the alphabet, singing the alphabet song, coloring within predefined lines, and being instructed in correct formation of letters on a printed line.
	Children develop an understanding of concepts about themselves, others, and the world around them through observation, interaction with people and real objects, and the seeking of solutions to concrete problems. Learning about math, science, social studies, health, and other content areas is integrated through meaningful activities.	Instruction stresses isolated skill development through memorization. Children's cognitive development is seen as fragmented in content areas, such as math or science, and times are set aside for each of these.
Physical development	Children have daily opportunities to use large muscles, including running, jumping, and balancing. Outdoor activity is planned daily so children can freely express themselves.	Opportunity for large muscle activity is limited. Outdoor time is limited because it is viewed as interfering with instructional time, rather than as an integral part of the children's learning environment.
	Children have daily opportunities to develop small muscle skills through play activities, such as puzzles, painting, and cutting.	Small motor activity is limited to writing with pencils, coloring predrawn forms, and engaging in similar structured lessons.
Aesthetic development and motivation	Children have daily opportunities for aesthetic expression and appreciation through art and music. A variety of art media are available.	Art and music are given limited attention. Art consists of coloring predrawn forms or following adult-prescribed directions.
	Children's natural curiosity and desire to make sense of their world are used to motivate them to become involved in learning.	Children are required to participate in all activities to obtain the teacher's approval; to obtain extrinsic rewards, such as stickers or privileges; or to avoid punishment.

Early Childhood—NAEYC Recommendations

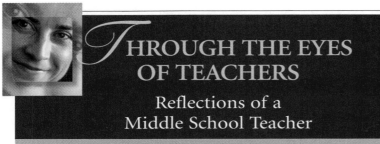

I believe that a good teacher should passionately be on the side of her students. That does not mean I support them in everything they do. It means I demand the best of them and am willing to help them be their best selves. It means I listen, explain, support, and allow without judgment, sarcasm, or the need to impose the truth from the outside in. The passage from childhood to adulthood we call adolescence is a very vulnerable journey. It is often a difficult time for students and for their families. It is an adolescent's "job" to rebel at times and to question the family environment that was such a comfortable cocoon during childhood. No matter how wonderful the parents, how loving the family, each adolescent needs to have other adults in whom to confide. . . .

Sarah Lawrence Lightfoot, a professor of education at Harvard, says that we teachers need to see ourselves reflected in our students—we need to see them as our destiny, and the students need to see themselves in us. The faces of my students have changed since my mother's generation. The immigrants now are more likely to come from the Philippines, Hong Kong, Guatemala, Mexico, or El Salvador than from Italy, Germany, Norway, or France. But the journey is similar, the experiences echo each other, and the welcome need be just as tender. When I look at them I see my past, and I hope that they are able to see in me something of their future.

Judy Logan
Middle School Teacher
San Francisco

lights as they sit glued to their chairs. The teacher seems uninterested in their work, except when she occasionally comes around and informs them of their mistakes. The teacher makes no attempt to get the students to relate the pictures to anything else the class is doing.

In the other class, students are investigating a school bus. They write to the district's school superintendent and ask if they can have a bus parked at their school for a few days. They study the bus, discover how it functions, and discuss traffic rules. Then, in the classroom, they build their own bus out of cardboard. The students are having fun, but they also are practicing writing, reading, and even some arithmetic. When the class has parents' night, the teacher is ready to report on how each child is doing. But the main thing the parents want to do is to see the bus, because their children have been coming home and talking about the bus for weeks. Which class would you say reflects developmentally appropriate education?

The Schooling of Adolescents   Two special concerns about adolescent schooling are the transition to middle or junior high school and the keys to an effective school for young adolescents.

The Transition to Middle or Junior High School This transition can be stressful because it coincides with many other developmental changes (Eccles, 2000; Seidman, 2000). Students are beginning puberty and have increased concerns about their body image. The hormonal changes of puberty stimulate increased interest in sexual matters. Students are becoming more independent from their parents and want to spend more time with peers. They are changing from learning in a small, more personalized classroom to learning in a larger, more impersonal school. Achievement becomes more serious business and getting good grades becomes more competitive.

As students move from elementary to middle or junior high school, they experience the **top-dog phenomenon.** *This refers to moving from the top position (in elementary school, to being the oldest, biggest, and most powerful students in the school) to the lowest position (in middle or junior high school, being the youngest, smallest, and least powerful students in the school).* Schools that provide more support, less anonymity, more stability, and less complexity improve student adjustment during this transition (Fenzel, Blyth, & Simmons, 1991). Also, one recent study found that when parents were attuned to their young adolescents' developmental needs and supported their autonomy in decision making, the students were better adjusted during the school transition (Eccles, Lord, & Buchanan, 1996).

Effective Schools for Adolescents   When Joan Lipsitz (1984) was director of the Center for Early Adolescence at the University of North Carolina, she searched for the nation's best middle schools. Based on the recommendations of education experts and observations in schools across the nation, four middle schools were chosen for their excellence. Three main themes characterized these truly outstanding schools:

1. They were willing and able to adapt virtually all school practices to the individual variations in their students' physical, cognitive, and socioemotional development. One effective middle school developed an advisory scheme so that each

student had daily contact with an adult who was willing to listen, explain, comfort, and prod the student.

2. They took seriously what is known about the development of young adolescence. Too many middle and junior high schools are simply downward extensions of high schools. But younger and older adolescents differ in many ways. For example, the intense changes of puberty that envelop young adolescents are largely completed by the time high school is reached. One effective middle school fought to keep its schedule of minicourses on Friday so that every student could be with friends and pursue personal interests. Two other effective middle schools made sure that small groups of students worked with small groups of teachers who could vary the tone and pace of the school day, depending on the students' needs.

3. They gave as much emphasis to students' socioemotional development as to their cognitive development. Young adolescents are often emotionally fragile as they widen their social worlds and have more responsibility on their own shoulders. In our achievement-oriented society, it is easy to lose sight of just how important students' socioemotional needs are. These effective middle schools did not.

Middle School Education
Middle School Teachers and Students
Middle School Resources

Recognizing that the vast majority of middle schools do not approach the excellence of the schools described by Lipsitz, in 1989 the Carnegie Council on Adolescent Development issued a very negative evaluation of America's middle schools. The report, *Turning Points: Preparing Youth for the 21st Century*, concluded that most young adolescents attended massive, impersonal schools, learn irrelevant curricula, trust few adults in school, and lack access to health care and counseling. To improve middle schools, the Carnegie report recommended the following:

- Developing smaller "communities" or "houses" to lessen the impersonal nature of large middle schools
- Lowering the student-to-counselor ratios from several hundred-to-1 to 10-to-1.
- Involving parents and community leaders in schools
- Developing curricula that produce students who are literate, understand the sciences, and have a sense of health, ethics, and citizenship
- Having teachers team-teach in more flexibly designed curriculum blocks that integrate several disciplines, rather than presenting students with disconnected, rigidly separated 50-minute segments
- Boosting students' health and fitness with more in-school programs and helping students who need health care to get it

At this point we have studied many ideas about the roles of social contexts (families, peers, and schools) in children's development. A review of these ideas is presented in summary table 3.2.

SOCIOEMOTIONAL DEVELOPMENT

So far we have discussed some of the most important *social contexts* that influence students' socioemotional development: families, peers, and schools. In this section, we will focus more on the *individual students* themselves, as we explore their self, moral development, and emotional development.

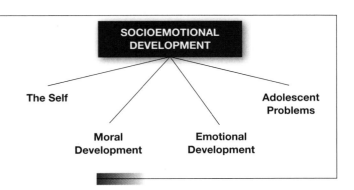

The Self

According to twentieth-century Italian playwright Ugo Betti, when children say "I," they mean something unique, not to be confused with any other. Psychologists often refer to that "I" as the self. Two important aspects of the self are self-esteem and identity.

SUMMARY TABLE 3.2
Social Contexts of Development

Concept	Processes/ Related Ideas	Characteristics/Description
Families	Parenting Styles	• Baumrind proposed four parenting styles: authoritarian, authoritative, neglectful, and indulgent. • Authoritative parenting is associated with children's social competence.
	The Changing Family in a Changing Society	• Greater numbers of children are growing up in diverse family structures than at any other point in history. • A special concern is the number of children of divorce. • Other special concerns are ethnic and socioeconomic variations in families. • Middle-income families are more likely to use discipline that encourages internalization, low-income families discipline that focuses on external characteristics.
	School-Family Linkages	• Fostering school-family partnerships involves providing assistance to families, communicating effectively with families about school programs and student progress, encouraging parents to be volunteers, involving families with their children in learning activities at home, including families in school decisions, and coordinating community collaboration.
Peers	Exploring Peer Relations	• Peers are children of about the same age or maturity level. • Social isolation, or the inability to "plug in" to a social network, is linked with many problems.
	Peer Statuses	• Children can have one of four peer statuses: popular, rejected, neglected, or controversial. Rejected children often have adjustment problems.
	Friendship	• Friendship is an important aspect of students' social relations.
	Developmental Changes in Peer Relations	• Peer relations begin to consume more of children's time in elementary and secondary schools. Same-sex peer groups predominate in elementary school. • In early adolescence, participation in coed groups increases.
Schools	Changing Social Developmental Contexts	• Schools involve changing social developmental contexts. • The early childhood setting is a protected environment with one or two teachers, usually female. • Peer groups are more important in elementary school. • In middle school, the social field enlarges to include the whole school, and the social system becomes more complex.
	Early Childhood and Elementary School	• Quality early-childhood education involves developmentally appropriate education that is age-appropriate and individual-appropriate. • Reggio Emilia is an increasingly popular developmentally appropriate program. • Head Start has provided early childhood education for children from low-income families. High-quality Head Start programs are effective educational interventions, but up to 40 percent of these programs may be ineffective. • A special concern is that early elementary school classrooms proceed primarily on the basis of negative feedback.
	Schooling for Adolescents	• The transition to middle or junior high is stressful for many students because it coincides with so many physical, cognitive, and socioemotional changes. It involves going from the top-dog position to the lowest position in a school hierarchy. • Effective schools for young adolescents adapt to individual variations in students, take seriously what is known about the development of young adolescents, and give as much emphasis to socioemotional as to cognitive development.

TEACHING STRATEGIES
With Students Who Have Low Self-Esteem

When students have low self-esteem, what can schools and teachers do to improve their self-evaluations? Research on this question suggests that there are four keys to improving students' self-esteem (Bednar, Wells, & Peterson, 1995; Harter, 1990, 1998):

1. *Identify the causes of the low self-esteem and the areas of competence important to the self.* This is critical. Is the child's low self-esteem due to poor school achievement? family conflict? weak social skills? Students have the highest self-esteem when they perform competently in areas that they themselves feel are important. Thus, find out from low-self-esteem students what areas of competence they value. In Susan Harter's (1990, 1996, 1999) research, physical appearance and social approval from classmates were especially important contributors to self-esteem. Social approval from classmates was more important to young adolescents' self-esteem than approval from teachers. Nonetheless, teacher approval was still important. And teacher approval played a more powerful role in the self-esteem of young adolescents whose parents showed them little approval.

2. *Provide emotional support and social approval.* Interest in self-esteem arose from the work of the psychotherapist Carl Rogers (1961). Rogers said that the main reason individuals have low self-esteem is that they have not been given adequate emotional support and social approval. He especially thought that as children grow up, they too often get told "You didn't do that right," "Don't do that," "You should have done that better," or "How could you be so dumb?" Virtually every class has children who have gotten too much negative evaluation. These children might come from an abusive and demeaning family that constantly puts them down, or they might have been in prior classrooms that delivered too much negative feedback. Your emotional support and social approval can make a big difference in helping them value themselves more. A school counselor also likely will benefit these children. For children in single-parent families, a Big Brother or Big Sister program can provide another significant adult who can give the child emotional support and social approval. Keep in mind that peer approval becomes especially important in the secondary school years. In one recent study, both parental and peer support were related to adolescents' general feelings of self-worth (Robinson, 1995). Thus, the recommendations made earlier in the chapter for improving children's social skills might improve adolescents' self-esteem as well.

3. *Help children achieve.* Achieving can improve children's self-esteem. Straightforward teaching of real academic skills often improves children's achievement, and subsequently their self-esteem. Often it is not enough to tell children they can achieve something; you also have to help them develop their academic skills.

   Henry Gaskins is a volunteer who began an after-school tutorial program for students in Washington, D.C. For 4 hours a night and all day Saturday, 80 students receive one-on-one assistance from Gaskins, his wife, two adult volunteers, and academically talented peers. In addition to being tutored in specific subjects, students set personal goals and develop a plan to reach these goals. Many of the parents of these students are high school dropouts and either can't or are not motivated to provide academic support for their children. Gaskins improves children's self-esteem by improving their academic skills.

4. *Develop children's coping skills.* When children face a problem and cope with it rather than avoid it, their self-esteem often improves. Students who cope rather than avoid are likely to face problems realistically, honestly, and nondefensively. This produces in them favorable thoughts about themselves that raise their self-esteem. On the other hand, for students with low self-esteem, their unfavorable self-evaluations trigger denial, deception, and avoidance. This type of self-generated disapproval makes a student feel personally inadequate. Much more about improving students' coping skills appears later in this chapter.

Self-Esteem   **Self-esteem** *is the global evaluative dimension of the self. Self-esteem also is referred to as self-worth or self-image and reflects an individual's overall confidence and satisfaction themselves.* For example, a child might perceive that she is not just a person but a *good* person.

For many students, low self-esteem is temporary. But in some students, low self-esteem can translate into other, more serious problems. Persistent low self-esteem is linked with low achievement, depression, eating disorders, and delinquency (Harter & Marold, 1992). The seriousness of the problem depends not only on the nature of

"Who are you?" said the caterpillar. "I—I hardly knew, Sir, just at present— at least I knew who I was when I got up this morning, but I think I've changed several times since then."

Lewis Carroll
English Writer, 19th Century

Identity Development

the student's low self-esteem but on other conditions as well. When low self-esteem is compounded by difficult school transitions (such as the transition to middle school) or family problems (such as divorce), the student's problems can intensify.

Identity Development   Another important aspect of the self is identity. Earlier in the chapter we indicated that Erik Erikson (1968) believed that the most important issue in adolescence involves identity development—searching for answers to questions like these: Who am I? What am I all about? What am I going to do with my life? How can I make it my own? Not usually considered during childhood, these questions surface as common, virtually universal, concerns during the high school and college years.

Canadian researcher James Marcia (1980, 1998) analyzed Erikson's concept of identity and concluded that it contains four statuses of identity: identity diffusion, identity foreclosure, identity moratorium, and identity achievement. The extent of an adolescent's exploration and commitment determine the adolescent's identity status. *Exploration* involves examining meaningful alternative identities. *Commitment* means showing a personal investment in an identity and staying with whatever that identity implies.

In **identity diffusion,** *adolescents have not yet explored meaningful alternatives or made commitments.* Not only are they undecided about occupational and ideological paths, they don't show much interest in such matters. Many young adolescents are identity diffused. In **identity foreclosure,** *adolescents have made a commitment but have not adequately explored alternative avenues.* This most often occurs when parents hand down commitments in an authoritarian manner. In **identity moratorium,** *adolescents are in the midst of exploring alternative courses of action but their commitments either are absent or only vaguely defined.* In **identity achievement,** adolescents have adequately explored alternative paths and made a commitment. Marcia's four statuses of identity are shown in figure 3.5.

Many high school students will be exploring different areas of their identity, although some will be identity diffused and others will be foreclosed because of the authoritarian ways of their parents. Adolescents can be exploring alternative identities in numerous areas, such as vocational, religious, intellectual, political, sexual, gender, ethnic, and interests (the kinds of things people like to do, such as sports, art, music, reading, and so on). An adolescent can be farther along the path to identity in some of these areas than in others.

Moral Development

Few people are neutral about moral development. Many parents worry that their children are growing up without traditional values. Teachers complain that their students don't consider others' feelings.

Domains of Moral Development   **Moral development** *concerns rules and conventions about just interactions between people.* These rules can be studied in three domains: cognitive, behavioral, and emotional.

In the cognitive domain, the key issue is how students *reason* or *think* about rules for ethical conduct. In the behavioral domain, the focus is on how students actually *behave* rather than on the morality of their thinking. And in the emotional domain, the emphasis is on how students morally *feel*. For instance, do they associate strong enough guilt feelings with an immoral action to resist performing that action? Do they show empathy toward others? (Damon, 2000)

"While we're at supper, Billy, you'd make Daddy and Mommy very happy if you'd remove your hat, your sunglasses, and your earring."

Drawing by Ziegler; © 1985 The New Yorker Magazine, Inc.

Identity status				
Position on occupation and ideology	**Identity moratorium**	**Identity foreclosure**	**Identity diffusion**	**Identity achievement**
Crisis	Present	Absent	Absent	Present
Commitment	Absent	Present	Absent	Present

Figure **3.5**
Marcia's Four Statuses of Identity

Piaget's Theory   Interest in how students think about moral issues was stimulated by Piaget (1932). He extensively observed and interviewed 4- to 12-year-old children. He watched them play marbles, seeking to learn how they used and thought about the game's rules. He also asked children about ethical rules, quizzing them about theft, lies, punishment, and justice. From this he derived a stage theory of moral development.

Heteronomous morality *is Piaget's first stage of moral development. It lasts from approximately 4 to 7 years of age. Justice and rules are conceived of as unchangeable properties of the world, removed from the control of people.* **Autonomous morality** *is Piaget's second stage of moral development, reached at about 10 years of age or older. At this point, the child becomes aware that rules and laws are created by people and that, in judging an action, the actor's intentions as well as the consequences should be considered.* Children 7 to 10 years of age are in a transition between the two stages, showing some features of both.

The heteronomous thinker also believes in **immanent justice,** *the concept that if a rule is broken, punishment will be meted out immediately.* Young children believe that a violation is in some way automatically connected to punishment. They often look around in a worried fashion after committing a transgression, expecting inevitable punishment. Older children, being moral autonomists, recognize that punishment is socially mediated and occurs only if a relevant person witnesses the wrongdoing, and that even then punishment is not inevitable.

Piaget said that moral development is mainly advanced through the mutual give-and-take of peer relations. In the peer group, where all members have similar power and status, rules are negotiated and disagreements reasoned about and eventually settled. In Piaget's view, parents play a less important role in children's moral development because they have so much more power than children and hand down rules in an authoritarian way.

Kohlberg's Theory   Lawrence Kohlberg (1976, 1986), like Piaget, stressed that moral development primarily involves moral reasoning and unfolds in stages. Kohlberg arrived at his theory after interviewing children, adolescents, and adults (primarily males) about their views on a series of moral dilemmas. Following is an example of the type of dilemma he presented:

Lawrence Kohlberg, the architect of a provocative cognitive developmental theory of moral development.

A woman is near death and is suffering from a special kind of cancer. There is only one drug that doctors think might save her. It was recently discovered by a druggist living in the same town as the woman. The drug was expensive to make, but the druggist is charging 10 times what the drug cost him to make. The sick woman's husband, Heinz, tries to borrow the money to buy the drug from every place he can think of but he can't raise enough money. He tells the druggist that his wife is dying and asks him to sell it to him cheaper or let him pay later. But the druggist says, "No, I discovered it and I deserve to make money from it." Later, Heinz gets desperate, breaks into the druggist's store, and steals the drug for his wife.

After reading the story (or, in the case of young children, hearing it read to them), individuals are asked a series of questions, such as these: Was Heinz right to steal the drug? Is it a husband's duty to steal the drug? Would a good husband steal? Did the druggist have the right to charge so much for the drug? Why or why not?

LEVEL 3
Postconventional Level
Full Internalization

Stage 5
Community Rights Versus Individual Rights

The person understands that values and laws are relative and that standards can vary from one person to another. The person recognizes that laws are important for society but knows that laws can be changed. The person believes that some values, such as freedom, are more important than the law.

Stage 6
Universal Ethical Principles

The person has developed moral judgments that are based on universal human rights. When faced with a dilemma between law and conscience, a personal, individualized conscience is followed.

LEVEL 2
Conventional Level
Intermediate Internalization

Stage 3
Interpersonal Norms

The person values trust, caring, and loyalty to others as the basis of moral judgments. Children often adopt their parents' moral standards at this stage, seeking to be thought of as a "good girl" or "good boy."

Stage 4
Social System Morality

Moral judgments are based on understanding and the social order, law, justice, and duty.

LEVEL 1
Preconventional Level
No Internalization

Stage 1
Punishment and Obedience Orientation

Children obey because adults tell them to obey. People base their moral decisions on fear of punishment.

Stage 2
Individualism and Purpose

Moral thinking is based on rewards and self-interest. Children obey when it is in their best interest to obey. What is right is what feels good and what is rewarding.

Figure **3.6**
Kohlberg's Levels and Stages of Moral Development

Kohlberg's Levels and Stages of Moral Development   Based on the reasons individuals gave in response to the above dilemma and ten others like it, Kohlberg constructed a theory of moral development that has three main levels with two stages at each of the levels. A key concept in understanding Kohlberg's theory is **internalization.** *This refers to the developmental change from behavior that is externally controlled to behavior that is internally controlled.*

Preconventional reasoning *is the lowest level of moral development in Kohlberg's theory. At this level, the child shows no internalization of moral values. Moral reasoning is controlled by external rewards and punishment.* **Conventional reasoning** *is the second or intermediate level in Kohlberg's theory. At this level, the child's internalization is intermediate. The child abides internally by certain standards, but they are essentially the standards imposed by other people, such as parents, or by society's laws.* **Postconventional reasoning** *is the highest level in Kohlberg's theory. At this level, morality is completely internalized and not based on external standards.* The student recognizes alternative moral courses, explores options, and then decides on the moral code that is best for him or her. A summary of Kohlberg's three levels and six stages, along with examples of each of the stages, is presented in figure 3.6.

In studies of Kohlberg's theory, longitudinal data show a relation of the stages to age, although the two highest stages, especially stage 6, rarely appear (Colby & others, 1983). Before age 9, most children reason about moral dilemmas at a preconventional level. By early adolescence, they are more likely to reason at the conventional level.

Kohlberg believed that underlying changes in cognitive development promote more advanced moral thinking. He also said that children construct their moral thoughts as they pass through the stages—that they do not just passively accept a cultural norm for morality. Kohlberg argued that a child's moral thinking can be advanced through discussions with others who reason at the next higher stage. Like Piaget, Kohlberg thought that the mutual give-and-take of peer relations promotes more advanced moral thinking because of the role-taking opportunities they provide children.

Kohlberg's Critics   Kohlberg's provocative theory has not gone unchallenged (Turiel, 1997). One powerful criticism centers on the idea that moral thoughts don't always predict moral behavior. The criticism is that Kohlberg's theory places too much emphasis on moral thinking and not enough on moral behavior. Moral reasons sometimes can be a shelter for immoral behavior. Bank embezzlers and U.S. presidents endorse the loftiest of moral virtues, but their own behavior can prove to be immoral. No one wants a nation of stage-6 Kohlberg thinkers who know what is right yet do what is wrong.

Another line of criticism is that Kohlberg's theory is too individualistic. Carol Gilligan (1982, 1998) distinguishes between the justice perspective and the care perspective. Kohlberg's is a **justice perspective** *that focuses on the rights of the individual, who stands alone and makes moral decisions.* The **care perspective** *views people in terms of their connectedness. Emphasis is placed on relationships and concern for others.* According to Gilligan, Kohlberg greatly underplayed the care perspective, possibly because he was a male, most of his research was on males, and he lived in a male-dominant society.

In extensive interviews with girls from 6 to 18 years of age, Gilligan found that they consistently interpret moral dilemmas in terms of human relationships, not in terms of individual rights. Gilligan (1990, 1996) also recently argued that girls reach a critical juncture in their development in early adolescence. At about 11 or 12 years of age, they become aware of how much they prize relationships, yet they also come to realize that this interest is not shared by the male-dominant society. The solution, says Gilligan, is to give relationships and concern for others a higher priority in our society. Gilligan does not recommend totally throwing out Kohlberg's theory. She believes the highest level of moral development occurs when individuals combine the care and justice perspectives in positive ways.

Carol Gilligan (right in maroon dress) with some of the females she has interviewed about their relationships with others. According to Gilligan, girls experience life differently than boys do; in Gilligan's words, girls have a "different voice." She believes that relationships color every aspect of a female's life.

THROUGH THE EYES OF CHILDREN

Life on the Make-Believe Planet of Pax

Elementary-school-age children were asked to pretend that they had taken a long ride on a spaceship to a make-believe planet called Pax (Katz, 1987). The children were asked their opinions about various situations in which they found themselves.

Regarding wages on their make-believe planet, all but two children said that janitors should earn as much as teachers. The holdouts said teachers should make less because they stay in one room or because cleaning toilets is more disgusting and therefore deserves higher wages. All but one thought that not giving a job to a qualified applicant who had different characteristics (a striped rather than a dotted nose) was unfair.

In one situation, the mayor of a city on Pax was criticized by the press. Several children argued that the reporters should be jailed. One child said that if she were the mayor and was getting criticized, she would worry, make speeches, and say, "I didn't do anything wrong," as a lot of earthly politicians do. Another child said that the mayor should not put the newspaper people out of work because that might make them print more bad things. Instead, the child recommended having them write comics instead.

As a teacher, might you find an educational purpose for this exercise of getting students to pretend they are on a make-believe planet?

Moral Education

Character Education

Moral Education

Moral education is hotly debated in educational circles. We will study one of the earliest analyses of moral education, then turn to some contemporary views.

The Hidden Curriculum   More than 60 years ago, educator John Dewey (1933) recognized that even when schools do not have specific programs in moral education, they provide moral education through a "hidden curriculum." The **hidden curriculum** *is conveyed by the moral atmosphere that is a part of every school.* The moral atmosphere is created by school and classroom rules, the moral orientation of teachers and school administrators, and text materials. Teachers serve as models of ethical or unethical behavior. Classroom rules and peer relations at school transmit attitudes about cheating, lying, stealing, and consideration for others. And through its rules and regulations, the school administration infuses the school with a value system.

Character Education   **Character education** *is a direct approach to moral education that involves teaching students basic moral literacy to prevent them from engaging in immoral behavior and doing harm to themselves or others.* The argument is that behaviors such as lying, stealing, and cheating are wrong and that students should be taught this throughout their education. Every school should have an explicit moral code that is clearly communicated to students. Any violations of the code should be met with sanctions (Bennett, 1993). Instruction in moral concepts with respect to specific behaviors, like cheating, can take the form of example and definition, class discussions and role-playing, or rewarding students for proper behavior.

Some character education movements are the Character Education Partnership, the Character Education Network, the Aspen Declaration on Character Education, and the publicity campaign "Character Counts." Among the books that promote character education are William Bennett's (1993) *The Book of Virtues* and William Damon's (1995) *Greater Expectations.*

Values Clarification   **Values clarification** *means helping people to clarify what their lives are for and what is worth working for. In this approach, students are encouraged to define their own values and to understand the values of others.* Values clarification differs from character education in not telling students what their values should be.

In the following values clarification example, students are asked to select, from among ten people, the six who will be admitted to a safe shelter because a third world war has broken out (Johnson, 1990):

> You work for a government agency in Washington and your group has to decide which six of the following ten people will be admitted to a small fallout shelter. Your group has only 20 minutes to make the decision. These are your choices:
> • A 30-year-old male bookkeeper
> • The bookkeeper's wife, who is 6 months pregnant
> • A second-year African American male medical student who is a political activist
> • A 42-year-old male who is a famous historian-author
> • A Hollywood actress who is a singer and dancer
> • A female biochemist

- A 54-year-old male Rabbi
- A male Olympic athlete who is good in all sports
- A female college student
- A policeman with a gun

In this type of values clarification exercise, there are no right or wrong answers. The clarification of values is left up to the individual student. Advocates of values clarification say it is value-free. However, critics argue that its controversial content offends community standards. They also say that because of its relativistic nature, values clarification undermines accepted values and fails to stress right behavior.

Cognitive Moral Education   **Cognitive moral education** *is an approach based on the belief that students should learn to value things like democracy and justice as their moral reasoning develops. Kohlberg's theory has been the basis for a number of cognitive moral education programs.* In a typical program, high school students meet in a semester-long course to discuss a number of moral issues. The instructor acts as a facilitator rather than as a director of the class. The hope is that students will develop more advanced notions

This adolescent volunteered to work in the National Helpers Network, which gives students an opportunity to participate in service learning. Among the services provided are helping with environmental concerns, improving neighborhoods, and tutoring. Students also participate in weekly seminars that encourage them to reflect on their active involvement in the community. For more information about the National Helpers Network, call 212-679-7461.

of such concepts as cooperation, trust, responsibility, and community. Toward the end of his career, Kohlberg (1986) recognized that the moral atmosphere of the school is more important than he initially envisioned. For example, in one study, a semester-long moral education class based on Kohlberg's theory was successful in advancing moral thinking in three democratic schools but not in three authoritarian schools (Higgins, Power, & Kohlberg, 1983).

Service Learning   **Service learning** *is a form of education that promotes social responsibility and service to the community.* In service learning, students might engage in tutoring, help the elderly, work in a hospital, assist at a day-care center, or clean up a vacant lot to make a play area. An important goal of service learning is for students to become less self-centered and more motivated to help others (Waterman, 1997).

Service learning takes education out into the community (Levesque & Prosser, 1996). One eleventh-grade student worked as a reading tutor for students from low-income homes with reading skills well below their grade levels. She commented that until she did the tutoring she didn't realize how many students had not experienced the same opportunities that she had when she was growing up. An especially rewarding moment was when one young girl told her, "I want to learn to read like you do so I can go to college when I grow up." Thus, service learning can benefit not only students but also the recipients of their help.

Researchers have found that service learning benefits students in a number of ways:

- Their grades improve, they become more motivated, and they set more goals (Johnson & others, 1998; Serow, Ciechalski, & Daye, 1990).
- Their self-esteem improves (Hamburg, 1997).
- They become less alienated (Calabrese & Schumer, 1986).
- They increasingly reflect on society's political organization and moral order (Yates, 1995).

Moral Development and Education
Service Learning

*I*t *is one of the beautiful compensations of life that no one can sincerely try to help another without helping himself.*

Charles Warner
American Novelist, 19th Century

TEACHING STRATEGIES
For Improving Children's Prosocial Behavior

Prosocial behavior involves the positive side of moral development (in contrast to antisocial behavior like cheating, lying, and stealing). Prosocial behavior is behavior that is regarded as being altruistic, fair, sharing, or generally empathetic (Eisenberg & Fabes, 1998). What are some strategies that teachers can adopt to improve students' prosocial behavior? They include these (Honig & Wittmer, 1996: Wittmer & Honig, 1994):

1. *Value and emphasize consideration of others' needs.* This encourages students to engage in more helping activities. Nel Noddings (1992) explains the morality of caring as one of teaching students to feel for others, which leads to empathy and concern.
2. *Model prosocial behaviors.* Students imitate what teachers do. For example, a teacher who comforts a student in times of stress is likely to observe students imitating her comforting behavior. When teachers yell at students, they likely will observe more incidents of students yelling at others, too.
3. *Label and identify prosocial and antisocial behaviors.* Often go beyond just saying, "That's good" or "That's nice" to a student. Be specific in identifying prosocial behaviors. Say, "You are being helpful" or "You gave him a tissue. That was very nice of you because he needed to wipe his nose." Or regarding antisocial behavior, to a young child you might say something like, "That's not being nice. How would you feel if he messed up your papers like that?"
4. *Attribute positive behaviors to each student.* Attribute positive intentions to a positive act, such as "You shared because you like to help others."
5. *Notice and positively encourage prosocial behaviors but don't overuse external rewards.* Commenting on positive behaviors and attributing positive characteristics to students rather than using external rewards helps students to internalize prosocial attitudes.
6. *Facilitate perspective taking and understanding others' feelings.* Helping students notice and respond to others' feelings can increase their consideration of others.
7. *Use positive discipline strategies.* Reason with students when they do something wrong. If a student is too aggressive and harms another student, point out the consequences of the student's behavior for the victim. Avoid harsh, punitive behavior with students. We will more extensively explore discipline strategies in chapter 12, "Managing the Classroom."
8. *Lead discussions on prosocial interactions.* Set up discussion sessions and let children evaluate how goods and benefits are distributed justly among people with varying needs, temperaments, talents, and troubles.
9. *Develop class and school projects that foster altruism.* Let children come up with examples of projects they can engage in that will help others. These projects might include cleaning up the schoolyard, writing as pen pals to children in troubled lands, collecting toys or food for individuals in need, and making friends with older adults during visits to a nursing home.
10. *Use technology to promote prosocial behavior.* Make a videotape of children behaving prosocially and show it to the class to increase sharing.
11. *Invite moral mentors to visit the class.* Recruit and involve moral mentors in the classroom. Invite people who have contributed altruistically to the lives of others in the community. In one classroom, a teacher invited a high school swimming star who spends time helping children with a disability to come talk with her class.

Required community service has increased in high schools. In one survey, 15 percent of the nation's largest school districts had such a requirement (National Community Service Coalition, 1995). Even though required community service has increased in high schools, in another survey of 40,000 adolescents, two-thirds said they had never done any volunteer work to help other people (Benson, 1993). The benefits of service learning, for both the volunteer and the recipient, suggest that more adolescents should be required to participate in such programs.

At this point, we have discussed a number of ideas about the self and moral development. A review of these ideas is presented in summary table 3.3. Next, we will explore the nature of children's emotional development and adolescent problems.

SUMMARY TABLE 3.3
The Self and Moral Development

Concept	Processes/ Related Ideas	Characteristics/Description
The Self	Self-Esteem	• Self-esteem is the global, evaluative dimension of the self. It also is referred to as self-worth or self-image. • Four keys to increasing students' self-esteem are to (1) identify the causes of low self-esteem and the domains of competence important to the student, (2) provide emotional support and social approval, (3) help students achieve, and (4) develop students' coping skills.
	Identity Development	• Marcia proposed that adolescents have one of four identity statuses (based on the extent to which they have explored or are exploring alternative paths and whether they have made a commitment): identity diffused, identity foreclosed, identity moratorium, identity achieved.
Moral Development	Domains of Moral Development	• Moral development concerns rules and conventions about just interactions between people. • These rules can be studied in three domains: cognitive, behavioral, and emotional.
	Piaget's Theory	• Piaget proposed two stages of moral thought. In heteronomous morality (ages 4–7 years), justice and rules are thought of as unchangeable. • The heteronomous thinker believes in immanent justice. • In autonomous morality (10 years and older), children become aware that rules and laws are created by people and can be changed. • In this second stage, children also consider the intentions of the actor. • Piaget believed that the mutual give-and-take of peer relations advances moral development.
	Kohlberg's Theory	• Kohlberg, like Piaget, stressed that the key to understanding moral development is moral reasoning and that it unfolds in stages. • Kohlberg identified three levels of moral development (preconventional, conventional, and postconventional), with two stages at each level. As individuals go through the three levels, their moral thinking becomes more internalized. • Kohlberg argued that cognitive changes, discussions with others who are at the next-higher stage, and role-taking opportunities can advance moral development. • Two main criticisms of Kohlberg's theory: (1) Kohlberg did not give enough attention to moral behavior. (2) Kohlberg's theory gives too much power to the individual and not enough to relationships with others. In this regard, Gilligan argued that Kohlberg's theory is a male-oriented justice perspective. She believes that what is needed in moral development is a female-oriented care perspective.
	Moral Education	• The hidden curriculum is the moral atmosphere that every school has. • Character education is a direct education approach that advocates teaching students basic moral literacy. • Values clarification emphasizes helping students clarify what their lives are for and what is worth working for. • Cognitive moral education encourages students to develop such values as democracy and justice as their moral reasoning develops. Kohlberg's theory has been the basis for a number of cognitive moral education programs.
	Service Learning	• This involves educational experiences that promote social responsibility and service to the community.

THROUGH THE EYES OF CHILDREN

Amos Bear Gets Hurt

Amos is a large, squishy plush bear that resides in a kindergarten class. Each weekend he travels home with a different child, returning on Monday morning to relate his "adventures." He often is the first object children head to when they are tired, ill, or upset.

The teacher noticed that the children recently had been using Amos as a punching bag. So she arrived early the next day and bandaged Amos' arm with surgical gauze. When the children arrived, they wanted to know what was wrong with Amos. The teacher replied that he must have gotten hurt last night.

The children's response in caring for Amos was intense. One child wanted to fetch drugs, another to make coffee; still another went to search for money to pay Amos' doctor bills. Amos got shots, was rebandaged, and was given medicine. Once he survived this ordeal, the children's consensus was that Amos needed a rest and some food. This led Amanda to remark, "Could we give him a diet cola. I think he is a vegetarian. He has no pulse."

Throughout the ordeal, the children treated Amos in a caring, tender way. He was cradled in someone's arms most of the time, was not allowed to bump into anything, and was passed from one child to the next with great delicacy.

Amos' situation stimulated the children's empathy (Read, 1995). The Amos Bear situation took place at the Helen Turner School in Hayword, California, where Laurie Read taught until her death in 1992.

Amos Bear getting assistance from his young caregivers.

Emotional Development

Students experience emotions—the joy of accomplishing something for the first time, sadness on learning about a friend's illness, anger during an argument with a peer. Students like or dislike teachers, feel happy when they have been accepted by their classmates, feel guilty when they don't study hard enough (Graham, 1996).

Exploring Emotion

Emotions (also called feelings or affect) can be classified as either positive or negative. **Positive affectivity (PA)** *refers to the range of positive emotions, whether high energy (enthusiasm and excitement) or low energy (calm and peacefulness). Joy and happiness are examples of positive affectivity.* **Negative affectivity (NA)** *refers to negative emotions such as anxiety, anger, guilt, and sadness.* It is possible to be high on both PA and NA dimensions at the same time. For example, a student might be in a high-energy state and enthusiastic yet also be angry.

Emotional Intelligence

In his book *Emotional Intelligence*, Daniel Goleman (1995) argues that when it comes to predicting a student's competence, IQ as measured by standardized intelligence tests can matter less than emotional intelligence. What is emotional intelligence? **Emotional intelligence** *consists of emotional self-awareness* (such as separating feelings from actions), *managing emotions* (such as controlling anger), *reading emotions* (such as taking the perspective of others), and *handling relationships* (such as solving relationship problems). Goleman believes that self-awareness is especially important in emotional intelligence because it enables students to exercise some self-control. The idea is to encourage students to not repress their feelings but instead become aware of them so they can cope more effectively.

Working with students to help them use anxiety wisely is another aspect of improving their emotional intelligence. Anxiety can serve a useful function as long as it does not spin out of control. Worrying is a rehearsal for danger and can motivate students to search for a solution to a problem. For example, although it is usually a good idea for students to think positively when a test looms on the horizon, if they have not yet adequately prepared for the test a little dose of worry can energize them to do so. Anxiety becomes a problem when worrying becomes an end in itself and blocks thinking.

Perhaps the most visible aspects of emotional intelligence are the "people skills" of empathy, graciousness, and being able to read a social situation. These skills help students get along with others and improve their social interactions.

It is important for teachers to evaluate both the student's emotional and intellectual skills, when considering the student's competence. By responding to the items in Self-Assessment 3.1, you can get a sense of how emotionally intelligent you are.

An example of a school that promotes emotional intelligence is the Nueva Day School in Hillsborough, California. It has a class called "self science" in which the subject matter is feelings, both the student's own and those involved in relationships. Teachers speak to emotional issues such as hurt feelings over being left out, envy, and disagreements that could erupt into a physical conflict. The topics in the school's self science class include these:

- Self-awareness. Teachers help students recognize feelings and build a vocabulary for them. They also help students see links among thoughts, feelings, and reactions.
- Detecting whether thoughts or feelings are ruling a decision.
- Seeing the consequences of alternative choices.
- Applying insights about feelings to decisions about drinking, smoking, and sex.
- Recognizing strengths and weaknesses: seeing oneself in a positive but realistic light.
- Managing emotions. Teachers help students recognize what is behind a feeling, such as the hurt that triggers anger or depression. Students also learn how to cope with anxiety and sadness.
- Taking responsibility for decisions and actions, as well as following through on commitments.
- Understanding that empathy, understanding others' feelings, and respecting differences in how people feel about things are key dimensions of getting along in the social world.
- Recognizing the importance of relationships and learning how to be a good listener and asker of questions; being assertive rather than passive or aggressive; and learning how to cooperate, resolve conflicts, and negotiate.

Names for these classes range from "Social Development" to "Life Skills" to "Social and Emotional Learning." Their common goal is to improve every student's emotional competence as part of regular education. This contrasts with emotional skills being taught only in remedial classes for students who are faltering or have been identified as "troubled."

Adolescent Problems

Too many of today's adolescents are not getting an adequate opportunity to make the transition from childhood to adulthood in a competent way. As many as 25 percent of adolescents have more than one developmental problem. The problems that harm the most adolescents have been called the "Big Four" adolescent problems: (1) drug abuse, (2) juvenile delinquency, (3) adolescent pregnancy, and (4) school-related problems, such as low achievement and dropping out (Dryfoos, 1990). Increasingly, at-risk adolescents have more than one of these problems. The highest-risk youth—as many as 10 percent—do it all.

Drug Abuse   What roles can schools and teachers play in preventing and intervening in drug abuse? They can do the following:

- Take a K–12 approach with age-appropriate components.
- Include teacher training in their drug-abuse curriculum. The best-designed drug-abuse curriculum is ineffective in the hands of an inadequately prepared teacher.

THROUGH THE EYES OF CHILDREN
Rescuing a Rain Forest

The children in Ena Kern's class in a tiny school in the Swedish countryside learned that with the destruction of rain forests in the Southern Hemisphere, many small animals were dying. A boy in her class made a simple suggestion: "Why don't we save the rain forest by buying it?"

So the children began raising money. They organized country fairs. They wrote songs about the rain forests and performed them in public:

Oh, you beautiful rain forest   *We must prevent it!*
Why do you have to die?   *You cannot be cut down!*
All species need you.   *We all need you.*

Soon schoolchildren across Sweden heard about the project and thousands of them took up the effort—and the song. Even the king of Sweden came to the school and backed the project. The money was sent to an area in Costa Rica called Monte Verde, where a project had been established to raise money to save Costa Rica's rain forests. Their teacher, Mrs. Kern, said that if you have a problem, ask children for a solution and try it. They can change the world. (Goleman, Kaufman, & Ray, 1993)

Emotional Intelligence

Childhood innocence

$\mathcal{S}$ELF-ASSESSMENT 3.1

How Emotionally Intelligent Am I?

Good teachers are emotionally intelligent. By responding to the following items, you can get a sense of your emotional intelligence. Score each of the items from 1 (very much unlike me) to 5 (very much like me):

	1	2	3	4	5

Emotional Self-Awareness
1. I am good at recognizing my emotions.
2. I am good at understanding the causes of my feelings.
3. I am good at separating my feelings from my actions.

Managing Emotions
4. I am good at tolerating frustration.
5. I am good at managing my anger.
6. I have positive feelings about myself.
7. I am good at coping with stress.
8. My emotions don't interfere with my ability to focus and accomplish my goals.
9. I have good self-control and am not impulsive.

Reading Emotions
10. I am good at taking the perspectives of others (such as students and parents).
11. I show empathy and sensitivity to others' feelings.
12. I am good at listening to what other people say.

Handling Relationships
13. I am good at analyzing and understanding relationships.
14. I am good at solving problems in relationships.
15. I am assertive (rather than passive, manipulative, or aggressive) in relationships.
16. I have one or more close friendships.
17. I am good at sharing and cooperating.

Scoring and Interpretation

Add up your scores for all 17 items. My Total Emotional Intelligence Score Is: _____. If you scored 75–85, you probably are very emotionally intelligent and your students will benefit considerably from this. You likely will be an emotionally intelligent model for your students, one who is emotionally self-aware, manages emotions effectively, knows how to read emotions, and has positive relationships with others. If you scored 65–74, you probably have good emotional intelligence, but there probably are some areas that you still need to work on. Look at the items on which you scored 3 or below to see where you need to improve. If you scored 45–64, you likely have average emotional intelligence. Give some serious thought to working on your emotional life. Examine your emotional weaknesses and strive to improve them. If you scored 44 or below, you likely have below-average emotional intelligence. This likely will interfere with your competence as a teacher. If your scores are in the average or below-average range, examine the resources available for improving your emotional intelligence. You might contact the counseling service at your college for some recommendations. It is a sign of strength, not a weakness, when you recognize the importance of calling on resources for improving your life skills.

- Include social skills training that focuses on helping children to develop coping skills and resist peer pressure.
- Use peer-led programs, which often are more effective than teacher-led or counselor-led programs, especially when senior high students are the leaders for middle school students.
- Make the school-based program part of community-wide prevention that involves parents, peers, role models, media, police, businesses, and youth agencies.

TEACHING STRATEGIES
For Helping Students Cope Effectively

One aspect of emotional intelligence is being able to cope effectively with stressful circumstances. What are some good strategies teachers can use to help students cope more effectively? They include these:

1. *Don't avoid students' stress, especially when it impinges on the classroom.* Students' stress can provide excellent learning opportunities. Work with students so they look at stress as a challenge rather than a threat.
2. *Work cooperatively with the student's other teachers and with his or her parents.* You might notice stress in a child whose parents aren't aware of it. If you do, talk with the parents about the stress, evaluate what is causing it, and develop a cooperative plan to deal with it.
3. *Help remove at least one stressor from the student's life.* For example, Lisa had been coming to school hungry each morning. Her teacher arranged for Lisa to have a hot breakfast at school each morning, which improved her concentration in class. This in turn helped Lisa take her attention away from her anxiety about her parents' impending divorce.
4. *Work with students to help them discard ineffective coping strategies and learn new ones that are more effective.* Monitor students under stress to see if they are using ineffective coping strategies such as taking the stress out on others, keeping feelings to themselves, refusing to believe what is happening, and or trying to reduce tension by acting out. Encourage students to develop new ways to cope, such as establishing an optimistic outlook. This can be accomplished by helping students challenge their self-defeating thoughts and keep themselves from wallowing in self-pity.
5. *Evaluate the resources available to help students cope with stress.* These might include parents, extended family, friends, a mentor, a school counselor, or various agencies. Contact the resources you believe can help students cope more effectively.

Juvenile Delinquency   Policies of detention, expulsion, security guards, and corporal punishment have not been effective in reducing delinquency (Dryfoos, 1990). Yet schools can play an important role in preventing and intervening in delinquency (Farrington, 2000). Schools with strong governance, fair discipline, student participation in decision making, and high investment in school outcomes by both students and staff have a better chance of curbing delinquency. Especially important is upgrading the education of youth from impoverished backgrounds. Programs should focus more broadly than on delinquency alone. For example, it is virtually impossible to prevent delinquency without also considering the quality of education available for high-risk youth.

An increasing concern is the high rate of violence among adolescents. Sixteen percent of seniors say they have been threatened by a weapon at school; 7 percent say they have been injured by a weapon (U.S. Department of Education, 1993). One of every five high school students routinely carries a firearm, knife, or club to school. Many teachers say they have been verbally abused, physically threatened, or physically attacked by students.

In the late 1990's, a series of school shootings gained national attention. In April, 1999, two Columbine High School (in Littleton, Colorado) students, Eric Harris (18) and Dylan Klebold (17) shot and killed 12 students and a teacher, wounded 23 others, and then killed themselves. In May, 1998, slightly-built Kip Kinkel strided into a cafeteria at Thurston High school in Springfield, Oregon, and opened fire on his fellow students, murdering two and injuring many others. Later that day, police went to Kip's home and found his parents lying dead on the floor, also victims of Kip's violence. In 1997, three students were killed and five others wounded in a hallway at Heath High School in West Paducah, Kentucky, by a 14-year-old student. These are but three of many school shooting incidents that have occurred in recent years.

**Great
Transitions**

A sign at the entrance of the high school where the shooting spree took place asks Kip "why?" What are some possible reasons Kip Kinkel committed these brutal acts of violence?

Students from Columbine High School in Littleton, Colorado, leave the school after two classmates went on a shooting rampage in April, 1999.

Is there any way that psychologists can predict whether a youth will turn violent? It's a complex task but they have pieced together some clues (Cowley, 1998). The violent youth are overwhelmingly male and many are driven by feelings of powerlessness. Violence seems to infuse these youth with a sense of power. Sixteen-year-old Luke Woodham was known as a chubby nerd at his school in Pearl, Mississippi. But in the fall of 1997, he shed that image by stabbing his mother to death and shooting nine of his classmates, killing two of them. Woodham wrote in a letter, "I killed because people like me are mistreated every day. Murder is not weak and slow-witted. Murder is gutsy and daring."

Small town shooting sprees attract attention but youth violence is far greater in poverty-infested areas of inner cities. Urban poverty fosters powerlessness and the rage that goes with it. Living in poverty is frustrating and many inner city neighborhoods provide almost daily opportunities to observe violence. Many urban youth who live in poverty also lack adequate parent involvement and supervision.

University of Virginia psychologist Dewey Cornell (1998) says that many youth give clear indications of their future violence but aren't taken seriously. Cornell University psychologist, James Garbarino (1999, 2000) says there is a lot of ignoring that goes on in these kinds of situations. Parents often don't want to acknowledge what might be a very upsetting reality. Harris and Klebold were members of the Trenchcoat Mafia clique of Columbine outcasts. The two even had made a video for a school video class the previous fall that depicted them walking down the halls at the school and shooting other students. Allegations were made that a year earlier the Sheriff's Department had been given information that Harris had bragged openly on the Internet that he and Klebold had built four bombs.

Kip Kinkel had an obsession with guns and explosives, a history of abusing animals, and a nasty temper when crossed. When police examined his room, they found two pipe bombs, three larger bombs, and bomb-making recipes that Kip had downloaded from the Internet. Clearly, some signs were presented in these students' lives to suggest some serious problems but it is still very difficult to predict whether youth like these will actually act on their anger and sense of powerlessness to commit murder.

Garbarino (1999, 2000) has interviewed a number of youth killers. He concludes that nobody really knows precisely why a tiny minority of youth kill but that it might be a lack of a spiritual center. In the youth killers he interviewed, Garbarino often found a spiritual or emotional emptiness in which the youth sought meaning in the dark side of life. We will discuss a number of ideas about teaching strategies for reducing violence and effectively dealing with it when it occurs in chapter 12, "Managing the Classroom."

Adolescent Pregnancy   The United States has the highest adolescent pregnancy rate of any country in the industrialized world. Each year nearly a million American teenage girls become pregnant, and more than 70 percent of them are unmarried (Child Trends, 1997). As one 17-year-old Los Angeles mother commented, "We are children having children." Adolescent mothers often drop out of school, fail to gain employment, and become dependent on welfare. In adulthood, the mean family income of females who gave birth before age 17 is one half that of families in which the mother delays birth until her middle or late twenties.

How can we reduce the high adolescent pregnancy rate? We can do the following:

- *Encourage abstinence in middle school students.* Adolescents are not ready to cope with sexuality's intense, varied feelings or to understand sexuality's complex meanings. For older adolescents, a good strategy is to restrict behavior to sexual exploration short of sexual intercourse.
- *Improve and expand sex education.* More than three-fourths of U.S. parents today want schools to teach sex education, including information about birth control. In Sweden, sex does not have the mystery and conflict it has in American society. Swedish adolescents are sexually active at a younger age and are exposed to more explicit sex on television than their American counterparts. Yet the U.S. adolescent pregnancy rate is three times that of Sweden and seven times that of Holland. In Sweden, beginning at age 7 each child experiences a thorough grounding in reproductive biology. By age 10 to 12, the Swedish child has learned about different forms of contraception. Swedish teachers are expected to discuss sex-related questions with students regardless of the subject they are teaching.
- *Motivate adolescents to reduce their pregnancy risk.* Adolescents need to look to the future and see that they have an opportunity to become successful. This means providing adolescents with opportunities to improve their academic and career-related skills.

Adolescent Problems
and Education

School-Related Problems   The fourth main area that keeps adolescents from successfully negotiating the path from childhood to adulthood involves school-related problems. Low school achievement and low grades can lead to dropping out of school. And students who drop out are more likely than high school graduates to:

- have fewer job prospects and lower salaries, be unemployed, and be on welfare
- have more problem behaviors, such as drug abuse, delinquency, and early sexual intercourse
- become divorced and have unstable marriages

The good news is that since the middle of the twentieth century, the high school dropout rate has gone down dramatically. In 1950, more than half of individuals in their twenties had not completed high school. The corresponding figure today is less than 15 percent. However, the dropout rate for Native Americans and Latinos is still precariously high. More than 80 percent of Native Americans do not graduate from high school, and more than one-third of Latinos do not. The dropout rate for African Americans, once very high, now approaches the dropout rate of non-Latino Whites— about 10 percent. Still, in some low-income urban areas, the dropout rate for African Americans is over 50 percent.

One innovative program for reducing high school drop out rates is the I Have a Dream (IHAD) program. It was created in 1981 by philanthropist Eugene Lang, who made an impromptu offer to a class of sixth-graders at P.S. 121 in East Harlem to pay

SUMMARY TABLE 3.4
Emotional Development and Adolescent Problems

Concept	Processes/ Related Ideas	Characteristics/Description
Emotional Development	Exploring Emotion	• Emotions (also called feelings or affect) can be classified as positive (positive affectivity) or negative (negative affectivity).
	Emotional Intelligence	• This consists of developing emotional self-awareness, managing emotions, reading emotions, and handling relationships.
Adolescent Problems	Their Nature	• As many as 25 percent of adolescents have more than one developmental problem. • The "Big Four" adolescent problems are drug abuse, delinquency, adolescent pregnancy, and school-related problems. • An analysis of successful programs for intervening in adolescent problems revealed that two main factors were at work: individualized attention and community-wide multiagency collaboration.

their college tuition. Seventy-five percent of these students were projected to be high school dropouts. Yet 90 percent graduated and 60 percent went on to college. Today, IHAD programs are conducted in more than 50 cities in 28 states. Usually an entire grade is selected for inclusion in the program, most often the third or fourth grade. These children (called "dreamers") are provided with academic, social, cultural, and recreational activities until they graduate from high school.

Common Components of Successful Programs

Joy Dryfoos (1990) analyzed the programs that have been successful in preventing or reducing adolescent problems. The two most important components were (1) intensive individualized attention and (2) community-wide multiagency collaboration.

In the IHAD program, sponsors and staff attempt to give individualized attention to and develop a long-term relationship with a child. Many children develop problems because they have not had someone to care for them, someone who is there when they need help and support (Price, 2000). In a successful substance-abuse program, a student assistance counselor might be available for individual counseling and referral for treatment. In a delinquency program, a family worker might provide support and guidance to a predelinquent and ask the family to make changes in their lives to help prevent delinquent acts.

The basic philosophy of community-wide programs is that a number of different programs and services need to be in place (Perry, 1999; Phillips, 1997). One successful substance-abuse program implemented a community-wide health-promotion campaign that used local media and community education in concert with a substance-abuse curriculum in the schools. In a successful delinquency program, a neighborhood development approach involved local residents in neighborhood councils. They worked with schools, police, courts, gang leaders, and the media to reduce delinquency.

At this point we have discussed many ideas about children's emotional development and adolescent problems. A review of these ideas is presented in summary table 3.4. In the last two chapters we have examined how students develop, focusing mainly on the general pattern. In the next chapter, we give more attention to individual variations in students.

The Search
Institute

Chapter Review

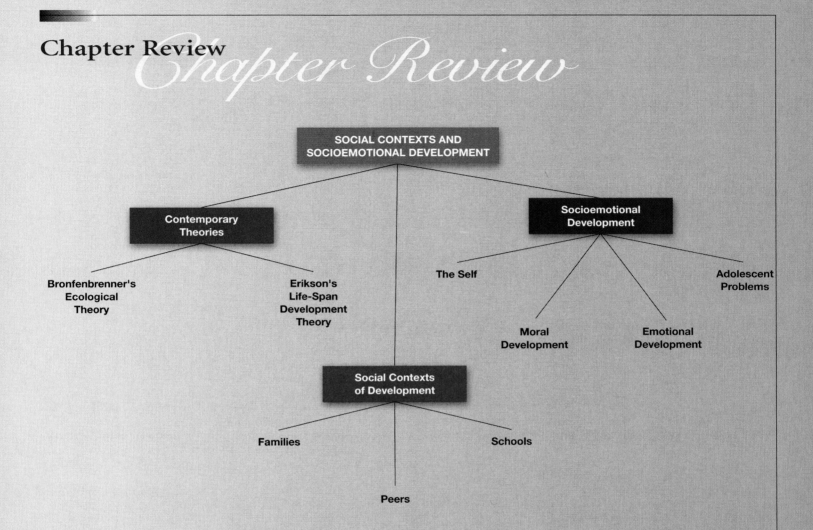

TO OBTAIN A DETAILED REVIEW OF THIS CHAPTER, STUDY THESE FOUR SUMMARY TABLES:

Key Terms

ecological theory 82
microsystem 82
mesosystem 82
exosystem 82
macrosystem 82
chronosystem 82
trust versus mistrust 84
autonomy versus shame
   and doubt 85
initiative versus guilt 85
industry versus inferiority 85
identity versus identity
   confusion 85
intimacy versus isolation 86

generativity versus
   stagnation 86
integrity versus despair 86
authoritarian parenting 88
authoritative parenting 89
neglectful parenting 89
indulgent parenting 89
peers 92
popular children 95
neglected children 95
rejected children 95
controversial children 95
developmentally appropriate
   education 98

Project Head Start 99
top-dog phenomenon 102
self-esteem 105
identity diffusion 106
identity foreclosure 106
identity moratorium 106
identity achievement 106
moral development 106
heteronomous morality 107
autonomous morality 107
immanent justice 107
internalization 108
preconventional
   reasoning 108

conventional reasoning 108
postconventional
   reasoning 108
justice perspective 109
care perspective 109
hidden curriculum 110
character education 110
values clarification 110
cognitive moral
   education 111
service learning 111
positive affectivity (PA) 114
negative affectivity (NA) 114
emotional intelligence 114

Educational Psychology Checklist

SOCIAL CONTEXTS AND SOCIOEMOTIONAL DEVELOPMENT

How much have you learned since the beginning of the chapter? Use the following statements to review your knowledge and understanding of the chapter material. First, read the statement and mentally or briefly on paper demonstrate that you can outline and discuss the relevant information.

_____ I can describe some important contemporary theories of socioemotional development.
_____ I know which parenting techniques are positively linked with children's socioemotional development.
_____ I am aware of how to foster school-family partnerships.
_____ I can describe the most effective ways to improve students' social skills.
_____ I can discuss the nature of developmentally appropriate education and give examples of it.
_____ I know the main ways that middle schools need to be improved.

_____ I can describe the best ways to improve students' self-esteem.
_____ I know what moral development is and can discuss some theories of moral development.
_____ I can distinguish between different approaches to moral education, and I understand what service learning is.
_____ I can describe the nature of emotion and know what it takes to be emotionally intelligent.
_____ I can discuss the "Big Four" adolescent problems and the components of successful programs designed to intervene in adolescent problems.

For any items that you did not check off, go back and locate the relevant material in the chapter. Review the material until you feel you can check off the item. You also may want to use this checklist later in preparing for an exam.

Adventures for the Mind

Now that you have a good knowledge and understanding of the chapter, complete the following exercises to expand your thinking about the chapter's topics.

- Think about the age of students you intend to teach. Which of Erikson's stages is likely to be central for them? What, if anything, does Bronfenbrenner's theory suggest about important resources for students at that age? Does his system suggest particular challenges to students or ways that you as a teacher might facilitate their success?
- Interview several teachers from local schools about how they foster family-school linkages. Try to talk with a kindergarten teacher, an elementary teacher, a middle school teacher, and a high school teacher.

- Which approach to moral education (character education, values clarification, or cognitive moral education) do you like the best? Why? Should schools be in the business of having specific moral education programs? Get together with several other students in this class and discuss your perspectives.
- In a parent-teacher conference, a parent tells you that the emotional intelligence "self-science" exercises you have been doing lately with students are a lot of fluff, nor serious academic subject matter, and that you shouldn't be wasting students' time on such things. How would you respond?

Taking It to the Net

1. According to Bronfenbrenner, you are a member of several different "systems," or interrelated groups. Name at least five groups of which you are a member. Do you think it is more beneficial to study students as individuals or as members of groups? Why?
2. Think back to how you were raised. Were your parents generally democratic in their dealings with you? Or were they over-Indulgent? perfectionist? How do you think their style of parenting has affected you? Is there a relationship between parenting style and the child's subsequent adult attitudes?

3. You are preparing to teach a unit on World War II, and a colleague has suggested that you show clips from a few documentaries and war movies in your class to gain your students' interest. How might these violent images affect your students?

Connect to http://www.mhhe.com/socscience/psychology/santedu/ttnet.htm to find the answers!

Case Studies

Case 1: *Carol Brown:* A teacher, after socially integrating a diverse class, sees her efforts threatened when a child's pencil case disappears and is thought to have been stolen. Her students' reactions are not what she had expected. (First grade—topic: Diversity, Moral Development)

Case 2: *Scott Donovan:* A teacher discovers that four of his students plagiarized parts of a lengthy writing assignment. He is not sure if he contributed to the problem because of the nature of the assignment and the students' inability to work independently. (10th grade—topics: Cheating, English Teaching, Instruction, Moral Development)

Chapter 4

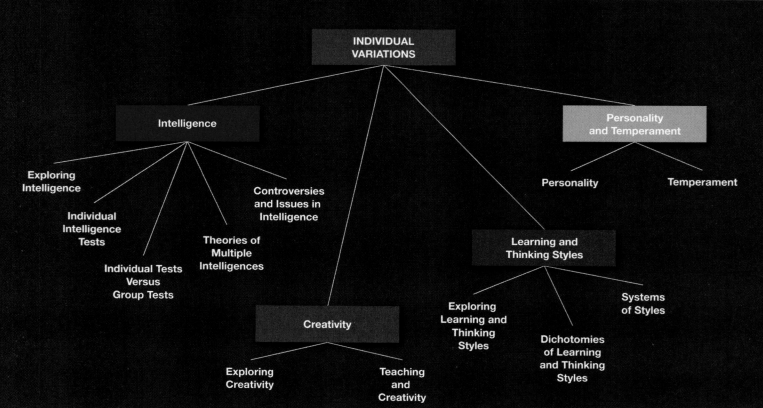

INDIVIDUAL VARIATIONS

Intelligence

- Exploring Intelligence
- Individual Intelligence Tests
- Individual Tests Versus Group Tests
- Theories of Multiple Intelligences
- Controversies and Issues in Intelligence

Creativity

- Exploring Creativity
- Teaching and Creativity

Learning and Thinking Styles

- Exploring Learning and Thinking Styles
- Dichotomies of Learning and Thinking Styles
- Systems of Styles

Personality and Temperament

- Personality
- Temperament

Individual Variations

"*Individuals play out their lives in different ways.*"

Thomas Huxley
English Biologist, 19th Century

Preview

No two students are exactly alike. An important educational task is to provide an education that allows students to competently play out their lives in individual ways. This chapter focuses on students' individual variations. These are some of the questions we will explore:

• What does it mean to be intelligent? Is it more than "book smarts"? Can you teach students to be intelligent?

• What are the best strategies for helping your students become more creative?

• What kind of learning styles are your students likely to have? What kind of learning style do you have? Are some learning styles better than others?

• What kind of temperament and personality traits are you likely to encounter in your students? How might these affect their behavior in the classroom?

Teaching Stories
Anita Marie Hitchcock

Anita Marie Hitchcock was the 1998 Teacher of the Year in Santa Rosa, Florida. She teaches kindergarten. Following are some of her recommendations for beginning teachers:

Our children need "cheerleaders." As teachers we hold the key to how children are going to feel about their experiences in school. We have to find that "something special" in each child and let the child know that he or she is terrific in some way. If children lack self-confidence, they will not have what they need to try over and over as many times as it takes to succeed.

In my classroom of 28 kindergartners, I have one legally blind child, two with learning disabilities (one of whom has auditory and visual difficulties), one child with only one ear, nine children with missing teeth, one child who reads above the fourth-grade level, one who says he is "allergic to nasty stuff," four with skinned knees or elbows, and children with lots of other differences. An important message is that we are not all the same.

My students are not unaware of their differences, whether they involve strengths or weaknesses. I just make sure they don't become concerned about them. I encourage them to look for positive aspects in others as well as themselves. I help them to understand that if they tell another student he or she is doing well (even though it may not match what they can do themselves), it not only helps the other student to work harder but makes them feel good about themselves.

Don't ever give up working with a difficult child or a situation that seems hopeless. If you look at the glass as half empty you won't see the possibilities that exist for helping a child. However, if you look at the glass as half full, not only will you know that the possibilities are there but you can begin trying as hard as it takes and as many times as it takes to get the job done.

Ms. Hitchcock's students say very positive things about her. The legally blind student commented, "I like to play with computers and she lets us play. She's a good teacher. She lets me work a whole bunch." Another student said, "She's nice because she teaches us how to make stuff. Sometimes, she lets us read books by ourselves."

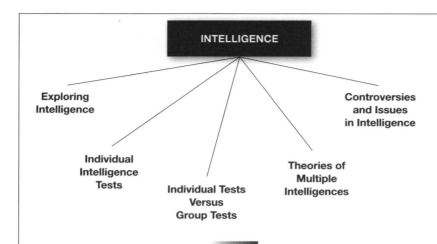

INTELLIGENCE

The concept of intelligence generates controversy and heated debate, often in reaction to the idea that each person has a general mental capacity that can be measured and quantified in a number. Educational panels and school boards debate whether intelligence tests are useful and fair. They also argue about whether such tests should be used to place students in special classes or tracks. Educational psychologists debate whether we have a general mental capacity or a number of specific mental capacities. And if we have various mental capacities, what are they? How many do we have?

Exploring Intelligence

Twentieth-century English novelist Aldous Huxley said that children are remarkable for their curiosity and intelligence. What did Huxley mean when he used the word *intelligence?* Intelligence is one of our most prized possessions, yet even the most intelligent people have not been able to agree on what intelligence is. Unlike height, weight, and age, intelligence cannot be directly measured. You can't peer into a student's head and observe the intelligence going on inside. We only can evaluate a student's intelligence *indirectly* by studying the student's intelligent acts. For the most part, we have relied on written intelligence tests to provide an estimate of a student's intelligence (Kail & Pelligrino, 1985).

Some experts describe intelligence as including verbal ability and problem-solving skills. Others describe it as the ability to adapt to and learn from life's everyday experiences. Combining these ideas we can arrive at a fairly traditional definition of **intelligence:** *verbal ability, problem-solving skills, and the ability to adapt to and learn from life's everyday experiences.* But even this broad definition doesn't satisfy everyone. As you will see shortly, some theorists propose that musical skills should be considered part of intelligence. And a definition of intelligence based on a theory like Vygotsky's would have to include the ability to use the tools of the culture with help from more-skilled individuals ◀▥ p. 59. Because intelligence is such an abstract, broad concept, it is not surprising that there are so many different possible definitions of it.

Interest in intelligence has often focused on individual differences and assessment (Ackerman, Kyllonen, & Roberts, 1999; Lubinski, 2000). **Individual differences** *are the stable, consistent ways in which people are different from one another.* We can talk about individual differences in personality and other domains, but it is intelligence that has been given the most attention and about which the most conclusions have been drawn about the different abilities of students.

Individual Intelligence Tests

Robert J. Sternberg recalls being terrified of taking IQ tests as a child. He says that he literally froze when the time came to take such tests. Even as an adult, Sternberg feels stung by humiliation when he recalls being in sixth grade and taking an IQ test with fifth-graders. Sternberg eventually overcame his anxieties about IQ tests. Not only did he begin to perform better on them, but at age 13 he devised his own IQ test and began using it to assess classmates—until the school principal found out and scolded him. Sternberg became so fascinated by intelligence that he made its study one of his lifelong pursuits. Later in the chapter we will discuss his theory of intelligence. To begin, though, let's go back in time to examine the first valid intelligence test.

*A*s many people, as many minds; everyone his own way.

Terence
Roman Playwright, 2nd Century B.C.

Theories of Intelligence/Intelligence Tests
Mental
Measurements Yearbook

The Binet Tests   In 1904 the French Ministry of Education asked psychologist Alfred Binet to devise a method of identifying children who were unable to learn in school. School officials wanted to reduce crowding by placing in special schools students who did not benefit from regular classroom teaching. Binet and his student Theophile Simon developed an intelligence test to meet this request. The test is called the 1905 Scale. It consisted of 30 questions, ranging from the ability to touch one's ear to the abilities to draw designs from memory and define abstract concepts.

Alfred Binet

Binet developed the concept of **mental age (MA),** *an individual's level of mental development relative to others.* Not much later, in 1912, William Stern created the concept of **intelligence quotient (IQ),** *which refers to a person's mental age divided by chronological age (CA), multiplied by 100.* That is, IQ = MA/CA × 100.

If mental age is the same as chronological age, then the person's IQ is 100. If mental age is above chronological age, then IQ is more than 100. For example, a 6-year-old with a mental age of 8 would have an IQ of 133. If mental age is below chronological age, then IQ is less than 100. For example, a 6-year-old with a mental age of 5 would have an IQ of 83.

The Binet test has been revised many times to incorporate advances in the understanding of intelligence and intelligence testing. These revisions are called the Stanford-Binet tests (because the revisions were made at Stanford University). By administering the test to large numbers of people of different ages from different backgrounds, researchers have found that scores on a Stanford-Binet test approximate a normal distribution (see figure 4.1). As described more fully in chapter 13, "Standardized Tests and Teaching," a **normal distribution** *is symmetrical, with a majority of the scores falling in the middle of the possible range of scores and few scores appearing toward the extremes of the range.*

The current Stanford-Binet is administered individually to people aged 2 through adult. It includes a variety of items, some of which require verbal responses, others nonverbal responses. For example, items that reflect a typical 6-year-old's level of performance on the test include the verbal ability to define at least six words, such as *orange* and *envelope,* as well as the nonverbal ability to trace a path through a maze.

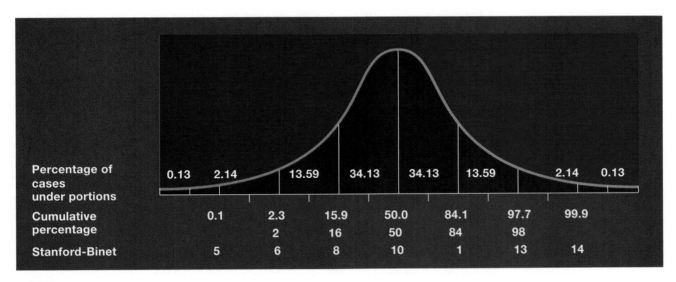

Percentage of cases under portions	0.13	2.14	13.59	34.13	34.13	13.59	2.14	0.13
Cumulative percentage		0.1	2.3	15.9	50.0	84.1	97.7	99.9
			2	16	50	84	98	
Stanford-Binet		5	6	8	10	1	13	14

Figure **4.1**

The Normal Curve and the Stanford-Binet IQ Scores
The distribution of IQ scores approximates a normal curve. Most of the population falls in the middle range of scores. Notice that extremely high and extremely low scores are very rare. Slightly more than two-thirds of the scores fall between 84 and 116. Only about 1 in 50 individuals has an IQ of more than 132 and only about 1 in 50 individuals has an IQ of less than 68.

Items that reflect an average adult's level of performance include defining such words as *disproportionate* and *regard,* explaining a proverb, and comparing idleness and laziness.

The fourth edition of the Stanford-Binet was published in 1985. One important addition to this version was the analysis of the individual's responses in terms of four functions: verbal reasoning, quantitative reasoning, abstract visual reasoning, and short-term memory. A general composite score is still obtained to reflect overall intelligence. The Stanford-Binet continues to be one of the most widely used tests to assess students' intelligence (Aiken, 2000).

**David
Wechsler**

The Wechsler Scales   Another set of tests widely used to assess students' intelligence is called the Wechsler scales, developed by David Wechsler. They include the Wechsler Preschool and Primary Scale of Intelligence–Revised (WPPSI-R) to test children 4 to 6½ years of age; the Wechsler Intelligence Scale for Children–Revised (WISC-R) for children and adolescents 6 to 16 years of age; and the Wechsler Adult Intelligence Scale–Revised (WAIS-R).

In addition to an overall IQ, the Wechsler scales also yield verbal and performance IQs. Verbal IQ is based on 6 verbal subscales, performance IQ on 5 performance subscales. This allows the examiner to quickly see patterns of strengths and weaknesses in different areas of the student's intelligence. Examples of Wechsler subscales are shown in figure 4.2.

Individual Tests Versus Group Tests

Intelligence tests like the Stanford-Binet and Wechsler are given on an individual basis, as is done with the Stanford-Binet and the Wechsler. A psychologist approaches an individual assessment of intelligence as a structured interaction between the examiner and the student. This provides the psychologist with an opportunity to sample the student's behavior. During the testing, the examiner observes the ease with

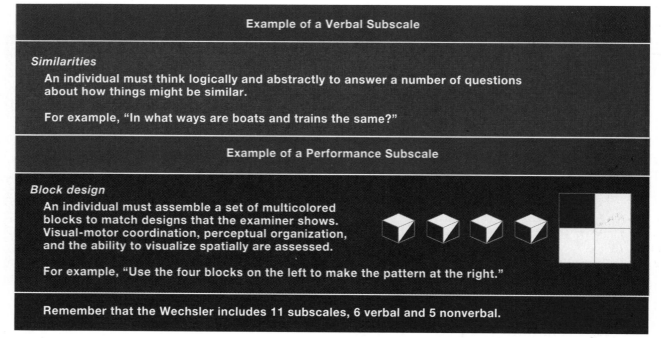

Figure **4.2**

Sample Subscales of the Wechsler Adult Intelligence Scale for Children–Revised

which rapport is established, the student's enthusiasm and interest, whether anxiety interferes with the student's performance, and the student's degree of tolerance for frustration.

Students also often are given an intelligence test in a group all at the same time (Drummond, 2000). Group intelligence tests include the Lorge-Thorndike Intelligence Tests, the Kuhlman-Anderson Intelligence Tests, and the Otis-Lennon School Mental Abilities Tests. Group intelligence tests are more convenient and economical than individual tests, but they do have their drawbacks. When a test is given to a large group, the examiner cannot establish rapport, determine the student's level of anxiety, and so on. In a large-group testing situation, students might not understand the instructions or might be distracted by other students.

Because of such limitations, when important decisions are made about students, a group intelligence test should always be supplemented with other information about the student's abilities. For that matter, the same strategy holds for an individual intelligence test, although it usually is wise to have less confidence in the accuracy of group intelligence test scores. Many students take tests in large groups at school. A decision to place a student in a class for students who have mental retardation, a special education class, or a class for students who are gifted should not be based on a group test alone. In such instances, an extensive amount of relevant information about the student's abilities outside the testing situation should be obtained (Domino, 2000).

Theories of Multiple Intelligences

Is it more appropriate to think of a student's intelligence as a general ability or as a number of specific abilities?

Early Views   Binet and Stern both focused on a concept of general intelligence, which Stern called IQ. Wechsler believed it is possible and important to describe both a person's general intelligence and more specific verbal and performance intelligences. He was building on the ideas of Charles Spearman (1927), who said that people have both a general intelligence, which he called *g*, and specific types of intelligence, which he called *s*. As early as the 1930s, L. L. Thurstone (1938) said people have seven of these specific abilities, which he called primary abilities: verbal comprehension, number ability, word fluency, spatial visualization, associative memory, reasoning, and perceptual speed. More recently, the search for specific types of intelligence has heated up (Gregory, 2000; Torff, 2000).

Sternberg's Triarchic Theory   According to Robert J. Sternberg's (1986) **triarchic theory of intelligence,** *intelligence comes in three forms: analytical, creative, and practical.*

Analytical intelligence involves the ability to analyze, judge, evaluate, compare, and contrast. Creative intelligence consists of the ability to create, design, invent, originate, and imagine. Practical intelligence focuses on the ability to use, apply, implement, and put into practice. Consider these three students:

- Ann scores high on traditional intelligence tests, such as the Stanford-Binet, and is a star analytical thinker.
- Todd does not have the best test scores but has an insightful and creative mind.
- Art is street-smart and has learned to deal in practical ways with his world although his scores on traditional intelligence tests are low.

Some students are equally high in all three areas; others do well in one or two. Sternberg (1997a, 1999, 2000; Sternberg, Torff, & Grigorenko, 1998) says that students with different triarchic patterns "look different" in school. Students with high analytic ability tend to be favored in conventional schooling. They often do well in direct instruction classes in which the teacher lectures and students are given objec-

Robert J. Sternberg, who developed the triarchic theory of intelligence.

Sternberg's Theory
Robert J. Sternberg

"You're wise, but you lack tree smarts."

tive tests. They often are considered to be "smart" students who get good grades, show up in high-level tracks, do well on traditional tests of intelligence and the SAT, and later get admitted to competitive colleges.

Students who are high in creative intelligence often are not on the top rung of their class. Sternberg says that creatively intelligent students might not conform to teachers' expectations about how assignments should be done. Instead of giving conformist answers, they give unique answers, for which they sometimes get reprimanded or marked down. No good teacher wants to discourage creativity, but Sternberg believes that too often a teacher's desire to improve students' knowledge depresses creative thinking.

Like students high in creative intelligence, students with high practical intelligence often do not relate well to the demands of school. However, these students often do well outside the classroom. They might have excellent social skills and good common sense. As adults, they sometimes become successful managers, entrepreneurs, or politicians, despite undistinguished school records.

Sternberg believes that few tasks are purely analytic, creative, or practical. Most require some combination of these skills. For example, when students write a book report, they might (1) analyze the book's main themes, (2) generate new ideas about how the book might have been written better, and (3) think about how the book's themes can be applied to people's lives.

Sternberg believes it is important in teaching to balance instruction related to the three types of intelligence. That is, students should be given opportunities to learn through analytical, creative, and practical thinking, in addition to conventional strategies that focus on simply "learning" and remembering a body of information. You might be wondering whether there is a Sternberg triarchic intelligence test available. As yet, there isn't.

Gardner's Eight Frames of Mind

Howard Gardner (1983, 1993) believes there are eight types if intelligence. They are described below along with examples of the occupations in which they are reflected as strengths (Campbell, Campbell, & Dickinson, 1999):

Howard Gardner, here working with a young child, developed the view that intelligence comes in the forms of these eight kinds of skills: verbal, mathematical, spatial, bodily kinesthetic, musical, interpersonal, intrapersonal, and naturalist.

- *Verbal skills:* the ability to think in words and to use language to express meaning (authors, journalists, speakers)
- *Mathematical skills:* the ability to carry out mathematical operations (scientists, engineers, accountants)
- *Spatial skills:* the ability to think three-dimensionally (architects, artists, sailors)
- *Bodily-kinesthetic skills:* the ability to manipulate objects and be physically adept (surgeons, craftspeople, dancers, athletes)
- *Musical skills:* a sensitivity to pitch, melody, rhythm, and tone (composers, musicians, and sensitive listeners)
- *Interpersonal skills:* the ability to understand and effectively interact with others (successful teachers, mental health professionals)
- *Intrapersonal skills:* the ability to understand oneself and effectively direct one's life (theologians, psychologists)
- *Naturalist skills:* the ability to observe patterns in nature and understand natural and human-made systems (farmers, botanists, ecologists, landscapers)

Gardner says that the different forms of intelligence can be destroyed by brain damage, that each involves unique cognitive skills, and that each shows up in unique ways in both the gifted and idiot savants (individuals who have mental retardation but have an exceptional talent in a particular domain, such as drawing, music, or numerical computation). Self-Assessment 4.1 gives you an opportunity to evaluate your strengths and weaknesses in Gardner's eight areas.

**Multiple
Intelligences Links**

SELF-ASSESSMENT 4.1
Evaluating Myself on Gardner's Eight Types of Intelligence

Read the following items and rate yourself on a 4-point scale. Each rating corresponds to how well a statement describes you: 1 = Not like me at all, 2 = Somewhat like me, 3 = Somewhat unlike me, and 4 = A lot like me.

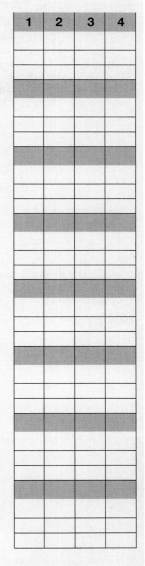

	1	2	3	4

Verbal Thinking
1. I do well on verbal tests, such as the verbal part of the SAT.
2. I am a skilled reader and read prolifically.
3. I love the challenge of solving verbal problems.

Logical/Mathematical Thinking
4. I am a very logical thinker.
5. I like to think like a scientist.
6. Math is one of my favorite subjects.

Spatial Skills
7. I am good visualizing objects and layouts from different angles.
8. I have the ability to create maps of spaces and locations in my mind.
9. If I had wanted to be, I think I could have been an architect.

Bodily-Kinesthetic Skills
10. I have great hand-eye coordination.
11. I excel at sports.
12. I am good at using my body to carry out an expression, as in dance.

Musical Skills
13. I play one or more musical instruments well.
14. I have a good "ear" for music.
15. I am good at making up songs.

Insightful Skills for Self-Understanding
16. I know myself well and have a positive view of myself.
17. I am in tune with my thoughts and feelings.
18. I have good coping skills.

Insightful Skills for Analyzing Others
19. I am very good at "reading" people.
20. I am good at collaborating with other people.
21. I am a good listener.

Naturalist Skills
22. I am good at observing patterns in nature.
23. I excel at identifying and classifying objects in the natural environment.
24. I understand natural and human-made systems.

Scoring and Interpretation

Total your scores for each of the eight types of intelligence and place the totals in the blank that follows label for each kind of intelligence. Which areas of intelligence are your strengths? In which are you the least proficient? It is highly unlikely that you will be strong in all eight areas or weak in all eight areas. By being aware of your strengths and weaknesses in different areas of intelligence, you can get a sense of which areas of teaching students will be the easiest and most difficult for you. If I (your author) had to teach musical skills, I would be in big trouble because I just don't have the talent. However, I do have reasonably good movement skills and spent part of my younger life playing and coaching tennis. If you are not proficient in some of Gardner's areas and you have to teach students in those areas, consider getting volunteers from the community to help you. For example, Gardner says that schools need to do a better job of calling on retired people, most of whom likely would be delighted to help students improve their skills in the domain or domains in which they are competent. This strategy also helps to link communities and schools with a sort of "intergenerational glue."

THROUGH THE EYES OF TEACHERS

Accommodating Differences

Another teacher introduced me to her way of accommodating differences in her English classroom. Each student has his/her own daily folder. Inside each folder, she will write instructions to each student about what is expected of him/her during the work that will generally be assigned to the class that week. One student may be told to only do five of the 20 spelling words that week. Another may be told that he only has to write one page on the writing assignment that is generally a 3 page assignment. Another may be told to find a story to read on the same topic that the rest of the class is doing. Another may be asked to also write a poem with a metaphor that pertains to that topic and which abides by the general guidelines for a poetry writing contest. She explains that each of us has differences. Some of us play basketball better than others. Some of us run faster than others. So, it is not fair to expect everyone in the classroom to accomplish the same things.

Lynn Ayres
English and Drama Teacher
East Middle School
Ypsilanti, Michigan

Project Spectrum   Project Spectrum is an innovative attempt by Gardner (1993; Gardner, Feldman, & Krechevsky, 1998) to examine the proposed eight intelligences in young children. Project Spectrum begins with the basic idea that every student has the potential to develop strengths in one or more areas. It provides a context in which to more clearly see the strengths and weaknesses of individual children.

What is a Spectrum classroom like? The classroom has rich and engaging materials that can stimulate the range of intelligences. Teachers do not try to evoke an intelligence directly by using materials that are labeled "spatial," "verbal," and so on. Rather, they use materials that relate to a combination of intelligence domains. For example, a naturalist corner houses biological specimens that students can explore and compare. This area elicits students' sensory capacities and logical analytic skills. In a story-telling area, students create imaginative tales with stimulating props and design their own storyboards. This area encourages students to use their linguistic, dramatic, and imaginative skills. In a building corner, students can construct a model of their classroom and arrange small-scale photographs of the students and teachers in their class. This area stimulates the use of spatial and personal skills. In all, the Spectrum classroom has twelve such areas that are designed to improve students' multiple intelligences.

The Spectrum classroom can identify skills that are typically missed in a regular classroom. In one first-grade Spectrum classroom was a boy who was the product of a highly conflicted home and had been at risk for school failure. When Project Spectrum was introduced, the boy was identified as being the best student in the class at taking apart and putting together common objects, like a food grinder and a doorknob. His teacher became encouraged when she found that he possessed this skill, and his overall school performance began to improve.

In addition to identifying unexpected strengths in students, Project Spectrum also can locate undetected weaknesses. Gregory was doing very well in first grade, especially in skills in math computation and conceptual knowledge. However, he performed poorly in a number of other Spectrum areas. He did well only in the areas in which he needed to give the correct answer and a person in authority gave it to him. As a result of the Spectrum program, Gregory's teacher began to search for ways to encourage him to take risks on more open-ended tasks, to try things out in innovative ways, and to realize that it's okay to make mistakes.

Project Spectrum has developed theme-related kits that tap the range of intelligences. Two such themes are "Night and Day" and "About Me." Students experience the basics of reading, writing, and calculating in the context of themes and materials with which they are motivated to work.

These children attend the Key School, which has "pods" where they can pursue activities of special interest to them. Every day, each child can choose from activities that draw on Gardner's eight frames of mind. The school's pods include gardening, architecture, gliding, and dancing.

The Key School   The Key School, a K–6 elementary school in Indianapolis, immerses students in activities that involve a range of skills that closely correlate with Gardner's eight frames of mind (Goleman, Kaufman, & Ray, 1993). Each

TEACHING STRATEGIES
Related to Gardner's Eight Frames of Mind

Following are some further strategies that teachers can use with children that are related to Gardner's eight types of intelligence (Berger & Pollman, 1996; Campbell, Campbell, & Dickinson, 1999):

1. *Verbal skills*
   - Read to children and let them read to you.
   - Discuss authors of books with children.
   - Visit libraries and bookstores with children.
   - Have children keep journals of significant events.
   - Have children summarize and retell a story they have read.

2. *Mathematical skills*
   - Play games of logic with children.
   - Be on the lookout for situations that can inspire children to think about and construct an understanding of numbers.
   - Take children on field trips to computer labs, science museums, and electronics exhibits.
   - Do math activities with children, such as counting objects and experimenting with numbers.

3. *Spatial skills*
   - Have a variety of creative materials for children to use.
   - Have children navigate mazes and create charts.
   - Take children to art museums and hands-on children's museums.
   - Go on walks with children. When they get back, ask them to visualize where they have been and then draw a map of their experiences.

4. *Bodily-kinesthetic skills*
   - Provide children with opportunities for physical activity and encourage them to participate.
   - Provide areas where children can play indoors and outdoors. If this is not possible, take them to a park.
   - Take children to sporting events and the ballet.
   - Encourage children to participate in dance activities.

5. *Musical skills*
   - Provide children with a tape recorder or record player they can use.
   - Give children an opportunity to play musical instruments.
   - Create opportunities for children to make music and rhythms together using voices and simple instruments.
   - Take children to concerts.
   - Encourage children to make up their own songs.

6. *Insightful skills for self-understanding*
   - Encourage children to have hobbies and interests.
   - Listen to children's feelings and give them sensitive feedback.
   - Encourage children to use their imagination.
   - Have children keep a journal or scrapbook of their ideas and experiences.

7. *Insightful skills for understanding others*
   - Encourage children to work in groups.
   - Help children to develop communication skills.
   - Provide group games for children to play.
   - Encourage children to join clubs.

8. *Naturalist skills*
   - Take children to natural science museums.
   - Create a naturalist learning center in the classroom.
   - Engage children in outdoor naturalist activities, such as taking a nature walk or adopting a tree.
   - Have children make collections of flora or fauna and classify them.

Multiple intelligence
and Education

day every student is exposed to materials that are designed to stimulate a whole range of human abilities. These include art, music, language skills, math skills, and physical games. In addition, attention is given to understanding oneself and others.

Like other public schools, the Key School is open to any child in Indianapolis, but it is so popular that its students have to be chosen by lottery. The teachers are selected with an eye toward their special abilities in certain domains. For example, one teacher is competent at signing for the deaf, a skill in both linguistic and kinesthetic domains.

The Key School's goal is to allow students to discover where they have natural curiosity and talent, then let them explore these domains. Gardner says that if teachers give students the opportunity to use their bodies, imaginations, and different senses, almost every student will find that she or he is good at something. Even students who are not outstanding in some area will find that they have relative strengths.

Every 9 weeks, the school emphasizes different themes, such as the Renaissance in sixteenth-century Italy and "Renaissance Now" in Indianapolis. Students develop projects related to the theme. The projects are not graded. Instead, students present them to their classmates, explain them, and answer questions. Collaboration and teamwork are emphasized in the theme projects and in all areas of learning.

Evaluating the Multiple-Intelligence Approaches Many educators believe that Sternberg's and Gardner's approaches have much to offer. These approaches have stimulated teachers to think more broadly about what makes up a student's competencies, and they have motivated educators to develop programs that instruct students in multiple domains. They also have contributed to the interest in assessing intelligence and classroom learning in innovative ways that go beyond conventional standardized paper-and-pencil memory tasks. We will discuss these innovative strategies for classroom assessment in chapter 13.

Some critics say that classifying musical skills as a main type of intelligence is off base, because it seems to imply that many other skill domains also should be classified that way. For example, there are outstanding chess players, prizefighters, writers, politicians, physicians, lawyers, ministers, and poets—yet we do not refer to chess intelligence, prizefighter intelligence, and so on. Other critics say that research has not yet been done to support the thesis that Sternberg's three intelligences and Gardner's eight intelligences are the best ways to categorize intelligence.

Controversies and Issues in Intelligence

As we mentioned, the topic of intelligence is surrounded by controversy. Controversies include whether nature or nurture is more important in determining intelligence, how much intelligence tests are culturally biased, and whether IQ tests should be used to place children in particular schooling tracks.

The Bell-Curve
Controversy

Nature and Nurture In chapter 2, we introduced the question of how extensively nature (heredity) and nurture (environment) influence children's development ◀ p. 40. Some scientists proclaim that intelligence is primarily inherited and that environmental experiences play only a minimal role in its manifestation (Herrnstein & Murray, 1994; Jensen, 1969). Heredity is an important part of the intelligence equation (Scarr, 1996). However, the emerging view of the nature-nurture issue is that many complicated qualities, such as intelligence, probably have some

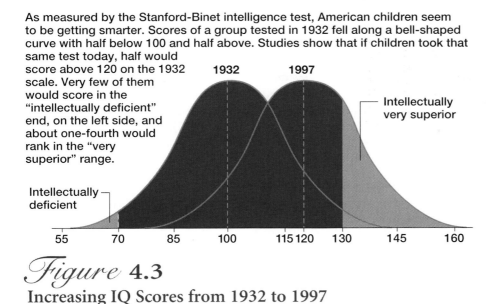

As measured by the Stanford-Binet intelligence test, American children seem to be getting smarter. Scores of a group tested in 1932 fell along a bell-shaped curve with half below 100 and half above. Studies show that if children took that same test today, half would score above 120 on the 1932 scale. Very few of them would score in the "intellectually deficient" end, on the left side, and about one-fourth would rank in the "very superior" range.

Intellectually deficient

1932   1997

Intellectually very superior

55   70   85   100   115 120   130   145   160

Figure 4.3
Increasing IQ Scores from 1932 to 1997

genetic loading that gives them a propensity for a particular developmental trajectory, such as low, average, or high intelligence. But the actual development of intelligence requires more than just heredity.

Most experts today agree that the environment also plays an important role (Ceci & others, 1997). This means that improving childrens' environments can raise their intelligence. It also means that enriching childrens' environments can improve their school achievement and the acquisition of skills needed for employment. Craig Ramey and his associates (1988) found that high-quality early educational day care (through 5 years of age) significantly raised the tested intelligence of young children from impoverished backgrounds. Positive effects of this early intervention were still evident in the intelligence and achievement of these students when they were in middle school (Campbell & Ramey, 1994).

Another argument for the importance of environment in intelligence involves the increasing scores on IQ tests around the world. Scores on these tests have been increasing so fast that a high percentage of people regarded as having average intelligence at the turn of the century would be considered below average in intelligence today (Hall, 1998) (see figure 4.3). If a representative sample of today's children took the Stanford-Binet test used in 1932, about one-fourth would be defined as very superior, a label usually accorded to fewer than 3 percent of the population. Because the increase has taken place in a relatively short period of time, it can't be due to heredity but rather might be due to such environmental factors as the explosion in information people are exposed to and the much higher percentage of the population receiving education.

The interaction of heredity and environment are so complex and dynamic that psychologist William Greenough (1997, 2000) says that to ask what's more important, nature or nurture, is like asking what's more important to a rectangle, its length or its width. We still do not know what, if any, specific genes actually promote or restrict a general level of intelligence. If such genes exist, they certainly are found both in children whose families and environments appear to promote the development of children's abilities and in children whose families and environments do not appear to be as supportive. Regardless of one's genetic background, growing up "with all the advantages" does not guarantee high intelligence or success, especially if those advantages are taken for granted. Nor does the absence of such advantages guarantee low intelligence or failure, especially if the family and child can make the most of whatever opportunities are accessible to them.

Ethnicity and Culture　　Are there ethnic differences in intelligence? Are conventional tests of intelligence biased, and if so, can we develop culture-fair tests?

Ethnic Comparisons　　On average in the United States, children from African American and Latino families score below children from non-Latino White families on standardized intelligence tests. Most comparisons have focused on African Americans and Whites. African American schoolchildren score 10 to 15 points lower than White American schoolchildren (Neisser & others, 1996). Keep in mind that this is an average difference. Many African American children score higher than many White children. Estimates are that 15 to 25 percent of African American schoolchildren score higher than half of all White schoolchildren.

Are these differences based on heredity or environment? The consensus answer is environment (Brooks-Gunn, Klebanov, & Duncan, 1996). One reason to think so is that in recent decades, as African Americans have experienced improved social, economic, and educational opportunities, the gap between White and African American children on conventional intelligence tests has declined (Jones, 1984). Between 1977 and 1996, as educational opportunities for African Americans increased, the gap between their SAT scores and those of their White counterparts also shrank 23 percent (College Board, 1996). And when children from disadvantaged African American families are adopted by more advantaged middle-class families, their scores on intelligence tests are closer to the national average for middle-class children than to the national average for children from low-income families (Scarr & Weinberg, 1983).

Cultural Bias and Tests

Cultural Bias and Culture-Fair Tests　　Many of the early tests of intelligence were culturally biased, favoring urban children over rural children, children from middle-class families over children from low-income families, and White children over minority children (Miller-Jones, 1989). The standards for the early tests were almost exclusively based on White middle-socioeconomic-status children. And some of the items were obviously culturally biased. For example, one item on an early test asked what you should do if you find a 3-year-old in the street. The "correct" answer was "Call the police." However, children from impoverished inner-city families might not choose this answer if they had had bad experiences with the police, and children living in rural areas might not have had police nearby. The contemporary versions of intelligence tests attempt to reduce such cultural bias.

Another problem is that even if the content of test items is appropriate, the language in which they appear might not be (Serpell, 2000). Some children from ethnic minority groups will have trouble understanding the written language of the test. Consider Gregory Ochoa. When he was in high school, he and his classmates were given an IQ test. Gregory looked at the test questions and didn't understand many of the words. Spanish was spoken at his home, and his English was not very good. Several weeks later Gregory was placed in a "special" class in which many of the other students had names like Ramirez and Gonzales. The class was for students who were mentally retarded. Gregory lost interest in school and eventually dropped out. He joined the Navy, where he took high school courses and earned enough credits to attend college. He graduated from San Jose City College as an honor student, continued his education, and eventually became a professor of social work at the University of Washington in Seattle. To read further about possible IQ test bias, see the Diversity and Education box.

"YOU CAN'T BUILD A HUT, YOU DON'T KNOW HOW TO FIND EDIBLE ROOTS AND YOU KNOW NOTHING ABOUT PREDICTING THE WEATHER. IN OTHER WORDS, YOU DO TERRIBLY ON OUR I.Q. TEST."

© 1991 by Sydney Harris—"You Want Proof? . . ." W.H. Freeman and Company.

DIVERSITY AND EDUCATION
Larry P. and the Controversy over
Cultural Bias in IQ Tests

Larry P. is African American and poor. When he was 6 years old, he was placed in a class for the "educable mentally retarded" (EMR), which is supposed to mean that Larry learns much more slowly than average students. The primary reason Larry was placed in the EMR class was his very low score of 64 on an intelligence test.

Is there a possibility that the intelligence test Larry took was culturally biased? This question continues to be debated. The controversy has been the target of various lawsuits that challenge the use of standardized IQ tests to place African American students in EMR classes. The initial lawsuit, filed on Larry P.'s behalf in California, claimed that the IQ test underestimated his true learning ability. His lawyers argued that IQ tests place too much emphasis on verbal skills and fail to account for the backgrounds of African American students from low-income families, and that Larry P. was incorrectly labeled as mentally retarded and might be burdened with that stigma forever.

As part of the lengthy court battle involving Larry P., six African American EMR students were independently retested by psychologists. The psychologists made sure that they established good rapport with the students and made special efforts to overcome the students' defeatism and distraction. For example, items were reworded in terms more consistent with the students' social background and recognition was given to nonstandard answers that showed a logical, intelligent approach to problems. This modified testing approach produced scores of 79 to 104—17 to 38 points higher than the students received when initially tested. In every case, the scores were above the ceiling for placement in an EMR class.

In Larry's case, the judge ruled that IQ test are culturally biased and should not be used in decisions about placing students in EMR classes. However, in subsequent rulings, such as *Pase v. Hannon* in Illinois, judges have ruled that IQ tests are not culturally biased. And a task force established by the American Psychological Association recently concluded that IQ tests are not culturally biased (Neisser & others, 1996). The controversy continues.

Culture-fair tests *are tests of intelligence that are intended to be free of cultural bias.* Two types of culture-fair tests have been devised. The first includes items that are believed to be familiar to children from all socioeconomic and ethnic backgrounds, or items that at least are familiar to the children taking the test. For example, a child might be asked how a bird and a dog are different, on the assumption that all children have been exposed to birds and dogs. The second type of culture-fair test has all of the verbal items removed. Figure 4.4 shows a sample from the Raven Progressive Matrices Test, which exemplifies this approach. Even though such tests are designed to be culture-fair, students with more education score higher on them than their less-educated counterparts.

These attempts to produce culture-fair tests remind us that conventional intelligence tests probably are culturally biased, yet the effort to create a truly culture-fair test has not yet succeeded. It is important to consider also that what is viewed as intelligent in one culture might not be thought of as intelligent in another culture (Lonner, 1990). In most Western cultures, students are considered intelligent if they are both smart (have considerable knowledge and can solve verbal problems) and fast (can process information quickly). In contrast, in the Buganda culture in Uganda, students who are wise, slow in thought, and say the socially correct thing are considered intelligent. And in the widely dispersed Caroline Islands, one of the most important dimensions of intelligence is the ability to navigate by the stars.

Ability Grouping and Tracking
Another controversial issue is whether it is beneficial to use students' scores on an intelligence test to place them in ability groups. Two types of ability grouping have been used in education: between-class and within-class.

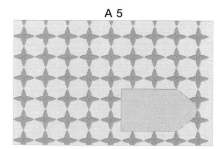

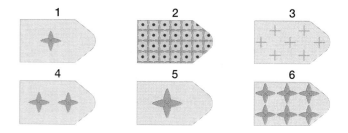

Figure 4.4
Sample Item from the Raven Progressive Matrices Test

Individuals are presented with a matrix arrangement of symbols, such as the one at the top of this figure and must then complete the matrix by selecting the appropriate missing symbol from a group of symbols.

Between-Class Ability Grouping (Tracking) **Between-class ability grouping (tracking)** *consists of grouping students based on their ability or achievement.* Tracking has long been used in schools as a way to organize students, especially at the secondary level (Slavin, 1990, 1995). The positive view of tracking is that it narrows the range of skill in a group of students, making it easier to teach them. Tracking is said to prevent less able students from "holding back" more talented students.

A typical between-class grouping in schools involves dividing students into a college preparatory track and a general track. Within the two tracks, further ability groupings might be made, such as two levels of math instruction for college preparatory students. Another form of tracking takes place when a student's abilities in different subject areas are taken into account. For example, the same student might be in a high-track math class and a middle-track English class.

Critics of tracking argue that it stigmatizes students who are consigned to low-track classes (Smith-Maddox & Wheelock, 1995). For example, students can get labeled as "low-track" or "the dummy group." Critics also say that low-track classrooms often have less-experienced teachers, fewer resources, and lower expectations (Wheelock, 1992). Further, critics stress that tracking is used to segregate students according to ethnicity and socioeconomic status because higher tracks have fewer students from ethnic minority and impoverished backgrounds. In this way, tracking can actually replay segregation within schools. The detractors also argue that average and above-average students do not get substantial benefits from being grouped together.

Does research support the critics' contention that tracking is harmful to students? Researchers have found that tracking harms the achievement of low-track students (Brewer, Rees, & Argys, 1995; Slavin, 1990). However, tracking seems to benefit high-track students (such as those in a gifted program).

$\mathscr{T}$EACHING STRATEGIES
Related to Intelligence Tests

Psychological tests are tools. Like all tools, their effectiveness depends on the knowledge, skill, and integrity of the user. A hammer can be used to build a beautiful kitchen cabinet and it can be used as a weapon of assault. Similarly, psychological tests can be well used or badly abused. Following are some cautions about IQ that can help teachers avoid using information about a student's intelligence in negative ways:

1. *Scores on IQ tests easily can lead to unwarranted stereotypes and negative expectations about students.* Too often, sweeping generalizations are made on the basis of an IQ score. Imagine that you are in the teacher's lounge on the second day of school in the fall. You mention one of your students, and another teacher remarks that she had him in her class last year. She says that he was a real dunce and that he scored 83 on an IQ test. How hard is it to ignore this information as you go about teaching your class? Probably difficult. But it is important that you not develop the expectation that because Johnny scored low on an IQ test it is useless to spend much time teaching him. An IQ test should always be considered a measure of current performance. It is not a measure of fixed potential. Maturational changes and enriched environmental experiences can advance a student's intelligence.
2. *IQ tests are misused when they are looked upon as the main or sole characteristic of competence.* A high IQ is not the ultimate human value. As we have seen in this chapter, it is important for teachers to consider not only students' intellectual competence in areas such as verbal skills, but also their creative and practical skills.
3. *Especially be cautious in interpreting the meaningfulness of an overall IQ score.* It is wiser to think of intelligence as consisting of a number domains. Keep in mind the different types of intelligence described by Sternberg and Gardner. By considering the different domains of intelligence, you can find that every student has at least one strength. If the intellectual areas in which the student is performing poorly are important for the student's competence and future success, develop a plan to help the student improve in those areas.

One variation of between-class ability grouping is the **nongraded (cross-age) program,** *in which students are grouped by their ability in particular subjects regardless of their age or grade level* (Fogarty, 1993). This type of program is used far more in elementary than in secondary schools, especially in the first three grades. For example, a math class might be composed of first-, second-, and third-graders grouped together because of their similar math ability. The **Joplin plan** *is a standard nongraded program for instruction in reading.* In the Joplin plan, students from second, third, and fourth grade might be placed together because of their similar reading level.

We mentioned that tracking has negative effects on low-track students. When tracks are present, it is especially important to give low-achieving students an opportunity to improve their academic performance and thus change tracks. In the San Diego County Public Schools, the Achieving Via Individual Determination (AVID) program provides support for underachieving students. Instead of being placed in a low track, they are enrolled in rigorous courses but are not left to achieve on their own. A comprehensive system of support services helps them succeed. For example, a critical aspect of the program is a series of workshops that teach students note-taking skills, question-asking skills, thinking skills, and communication skills. The students also are clustered into study groups and urged to help each other clarify questions about assignments. College students, many of them AVID graduates, serve as role models, coaches, and motivators for the students. At each AVID school, a lead teacher oversees a team of school counselors and teachers from every academic discipline. In the summer, these teams attend a weeklong professional development institute at which experienced AVID teachers give workshops on effective teaching strategies. In recent years, the dropout rate in AVID schools declined by more than one-third, and an amazing 99 percent of the AVID graduates have enrolled in college.

Tracking

In sum, tracking is a controversial issue especially because of the restrictions it places on low-track students. Too often, scores on a single group IQ test are used to place students in a particular track. Researchers have found that group IQ tests are not good predictors of how well students will do in a particular subject area (Garmon & others, 1995).

In chapter 6, "Learners Who Are Exceptional," we will discuss issues that are closely related to ability grouping in our coverage of children with various disabilities and gifted children.

Within-Class Ability Grouping **Within-class ability grouping** *involves placing students in two to three groups within a class to take into account differences in students' abilities.* A typical within-class ability grouping occurs when elementary school teachers place students in several reading groups based on their reading skills. A second-grade teacher might have one group using a third-grade, first-semester reading program; another using a second-grade, first-semester program; and a third group using a first-grade, second-semester program. Such within-class grouping is far more common in elementary than in secondary schools. The subject area most often involved is reading, followed by math. Although many elementary school teachers use some form of within-class ability grouping, there is no clear research support for this strategy.

At this point we have studied a number of ideas about intelligence. A review of these ideas is presented in summary table 4.1. Just as psychologists have sought to discover what makes a child intelligent, as we will see next, they also have explored what makes children creative.

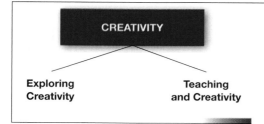

Creativity

Teresa Amabile remembers that when she was in kindergarten, she rushed into class every day, excited about getting to the easel and playing will all of those bright colors and big paintbrushes. She and her classmates also had free access to a table with all kinds of art materials on it. Teresa remembers telling her mother every day when she got home that she wanted to play with crayons and draw and paint.

Teresa's kindergarten experience unfortunately was the high point of her artistic interest. The next year she entered a conventional elementary school and things began to change. She no longer had free access to art materials every day, and art became just another subject for Teresa, something she had to do for an hour and a half on Friday afternoon.

Week after week, all through elementary school, it was the same art class. For Teresa, the class was restrictive and demoralizing. She recalls being given small reprints of painting masterpieces, a different one each week; one week in second grade, students were presented with pictures of Leonardo da Vinci's *Adoration of the Magi* and told to take out their art materials and try to copy the masterpiece. For Teresa and the other students, it was an exercise in frustration. Teresa says that elementary school students do not have the skill development even to make all those horses and angels fit on the page, let alone make them look like the masterpiece. Teresa and the other students could tell that they were not doing well what the teacher asked them to do. And they were not getting any help in developing their artistic skills. Needless to say, Teresa's desire to go home and paint after school each day diminished rapidly.

Teresa Amabile eventually obtained her Ph.D. in psychology and went on to become one of the leading researchers in the field of creativity. Her hope is that teachers will not crush students' enthusiasm for creativity like hers did (Conti & Amabile, 1999; Goleman, Kaufman, & Ray, 1993).

What do you mean, "What is it?" It's the spontaneous, unfettered expression of a young mind not yet bound by the restraints of narrative or pictorial representation.

by Sidney Harris

SUMMARY TABLE 4.1
Intelligence

Concept	Processes/Related Ideas	Characteristics/Description
Exploring Intelligence	What Is Intelligence?	• Intelligence consists of verbal ability, problem-solving skills, and the ability to adapt to and learn from life's everyday experiences. • Interest in intelligence often focuses on individual differences and assessment.
Individual Intelligence Tests	The Binet Tests	• Binet and Simon developed the first intelligence test. • Binet developed the concept of mental age, and Stern created the concept of IQ as = MA/CA $\times$ 100. • The Stanford-Binet score distribution approximates a normal curve.
	The Wechsler Scales	• The Wechsler scales also are widely used to assess intelligence. • They yield an overall IQ, as well as verbal and performance IQs.
Individual Tests Versus Group Tests	Strengths and Weaknesses	• Group tests are more convenient and economical, but they have a number of drawbacks (lack of opportunities to establish rapport; distraction from other students). • A group intelligence test should always be supplemented with other relevant information when decisions are made about students. This also holds for an individual intelligence test.
Theories of Multiple Intelligences	Spearman's Theory	• Spearman proposed that people have a general intelligence (g) and specific types of intelligence (s).
	Sternberg's Triarchic Theory	• According to Sternberg's triarchic theory of intelligence, intelligence comes in three forms: analytical, creative, and practical.
	Gardner's Eight Frames of Mind	• Gardner believes there are eight types of intelligence: verbal, math, spatial, bodily-kinesthetic, musical, insight about others, insight about self, and naturalist. • Project Spectrum and the Key School involve educational applications of Gardner's theory of multiple intelligences.
	Evaluating the Multiple-Intelligences Approach	• These approaches have much to offer, stimulating teachers to think more broadly about what makes up a student's competencies.
Controversies and Issues in Intelligence	Their Nature	• Three such issues are (1) the nature-nurture question of how heredity and environment interact to produce intelligence, (2) how fairly intelligence testing applies across cultural and ethnic groups, (3) whether students should be grouped according to ability (tracking). • It is especially important to recognize that intelligence tests are an indicator of current performance, not fixed potential.

Exploring Creativity

Creativity *is the ability to think about something in novel and unusual ways and come up with unique solutions to problems.* J. P. Guilford (1967) distinguished between **convergent thinking,** *which produces one correct answer and is characteristic of the kind of thinking required on conventional intelligence tests,* and **divergent thinking,** *which produces many answers to the same question and is more characteristic of creativity* (Michael, 1999). For example, a typical convergent item on a conventional intelligence test is, "How many quarters will you get in return for 60 dimes?" The question has only

Teresa Ambile's Research
Csikszentmihalyi's Ideas

TECHNOLOGY AND EDUCATION

Creative Experiences with Computers: Picasso, Edison, da Vinci, Art, Music, and Spatial Ability

For three decades, filmmaker Robert Abel made the screen come alive with special-effects films like *2001: A Space Odyssey*. Today, Abel is working on creative ways to use computers to educate students. Using a desktop mouse or a touch screen, students explore on their computer monitors as their curiosity beckons. They can follow a lead from text to photos or music and back again. In an application to art, students view some of Picasso's paintings, then, by clicking the mouse, they choose various interpretations of the paintings. Abel's use of computers is being tried out in some Los Angeles schools. His goal is to use the computers to turn on students to discover ideas.

The software programs The Genius of Edison and Leonardo the Inventor can be used to expose students to the thinking of two creative geniuses (Holzberg, 1997). The Genius of Edison is a multimedia presentation, that lets students ages 10 and older explore thirteen of Edison's inventions. Leonardo the Inventor also stimulates this same age range of students to think more creatively. Both programs are published by The Learning Company, Cambridge, Massachusetts.

Another effort to encourage students' creativity is Picture It! software by Microsoft for grades 5 to 12 (Pogue, 1997). It lets students and teachers create sophisticated images with only a few mouse clicks. Students initially scan pictures into the computer, then recolor, crop, move, and resize them. They can cut images, place them on another background, or create a collage.

Two other pieces of software relate to Howard Gardner's musical and spatial aspects of intelligence. The Julliard Musical Adventure, software created by the staff of the Julliard School of Music, is designed to introduce students 9 years and older to the vocabulary of music and the elements of musical composition (Goldberg, 1997). It is built around an adventure game in which students explore a castle to solve musical puzzles. The Julliard musical software is published by Theatrix Interactive, Emeryville, California.

The Neighborhood Map Machine is software that helps students to improve their spatial skills by exploring maps (Rothstein, 1997). Kindergarten to 6th-grade students can create maps, then attach photographs and narratives to go along with the map. A teaching guide provides tips for using the program in social studies (place recognition, compass reading, transportation, and the environment) and cross-curricular instruction (connections with math and science). This program is published by Tom Snyder Products, Watertown, Massachusetts.

Filmmaker Robert Abel (center) talks with a group of middle-school students about expanding their creative thinking by exploring computer displays of art and music.

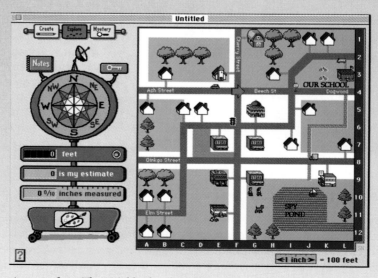

A screen from The Neighborhood Map Machine software, which guides children in developing their spatial skills.

SELF-ASSESSMENT 4.2
How Good Am I at Fostering Creativity?

Rate each of the following activities as they apply to you in terms of how often you engage in them. 1 = Never, 2 = rarely, 3 = sometimes, and 4 = a lot.

	1	2	3	4
1. I come up with new and unique ideas.				
2. I brainstorm with others to creatively find solutions to problems.				
3. I am internally motivated.				
4. I'm flexible about things and like to play with my thinking.				
5. I read about creative projects and creative people.				
6. I'm surprised by something and surprise others every day.				
7. I wake up in the morning with a mission.				
8. I search for alternative solutions to problems rather than giving a pat answer.				
9. I spend time around creative people.				
10. I spend time in settings and activities that stimulate me to be creative.				

Examine your overall pattern of responses. What are your strengths and weaknesses in creativity? Keep practicing your strengths and work on improving your weaknesses to provide students with a creative role model.

one right answer. In contrast, divergent questions have many possible answers. For example, what image comes to mind when you hear the phrase "sitting alone in a dark room" or the question "What are some unique uses for a paper clip?"

Are intelligence and creativity related? Although most creative students are quite intelligent, in other respects the reverse is not necessarily true. Many highly intelligent students (as measured by high scores on conventional intelligence tests) are not very creative. If Sternberg had his way, creative thinking would become part of a broader definition of intelligence.

Teaching and Creativity

An important teaching goal is to help students become more creative. Strategies that can inspire children's creativity include brainstorming, providing students with environments that stimulate creativity, not overcontrolling students, encouraging internal motivation, fostering flexible and playful thinking, introducing students to creative people, and being a creative role model for students.

To evaluate how good you are at fostering creativity, complete Self-Assessment 4.2. Also, to read about the use of technology to stimulate creativity, see the Technology and Education box. At this point, we have studied a number of ideas about creativity. A review of these ideas is presented in summary table 4.2. Just as there are individual differences in children's intelligence and creativity, as we see next children also vary in their learning and thinking styles.

THROUGH THE EYES OF CHILDREN
The 8-Year-Old Filmmaker and Oozy Red Goop

Steven was 8 years old and wanted to get a scout badge in filmmaking. His father bought him a super-8 movie camera. Steven got the inspiration to make a horror movie.

He started imagining what he needed to do to make a movie. Needing some red, bloody-looking goop to ooze from the kitchen cabinets, he got his mother to buy thirty cans of cherries. Steven dumped the cherries into the pressure cooker and produced an oozy red goop.

His mother gave him free rein in the house, letting him virtually convert it into a child's movie studio. Steven told his mother he needed to make some costumes, which she obligingly made.

The son's name: Steven Spielberg, whose mother supported his imagination and passion for film making. Of course, Spielberg went on to become one of Hollywood's greatest producers with such films as *E.T.* and *Jurassic Park.* (Goleman, Kaufman, & Ray, 1993)

TEACHING STRATEGIES

For Encouraging Students' Creativity

Some strategies you can use to inspire creativity in your students are:

1. *Have students engage in brainstorming and come up with as many ideas as possible.* **Brainstorming** *is a technique in which students are encouraged to come up with creative ideas in a group, play off each other's ideas, and say practically whatever comes to mind that seems relevant to a particular issue* (Rickards, 1999; Sternberg & Lubart, 1995). Students are usually told to hold off from criticizing others' ideas at least until the end of the brainstorming session.

   Whether in a group or on an individual basis, a good creativity strategy is to come up with as many new ideas as possible. Famous twentieth-century Spanish artist Pablo Picasso produced more than 20,000 works of art. Not all of them were masterpieces. The more ideas students produce, the better their chance of creating something unique.

   Creative people are not afraid of failing or getting something wrong. They might go down 20 dead-end streets before they come up with an innovative idea. They recognize that it's okay to win some and lose some. Like Picasso, they are willing to take risks.

2. *Provide students with environments that stimulate creativity.* Some classrooms nourish creativity, others inhibit it. Teachers who encourage creativity often rely on students' natural curiosity. They provide exercises and activities that stimulate students to find insightful solutions to problems, rather than ask a lot of questions that require rote answers. Teachers also encourage creativity by taking students on field trips to locations where creativity is valued. Howard Gardner (1993) believes that science, discovery, and children's museums offer rich opportunities to stimulate creativity. For a description of some computer programs that can be used to encourage students' creativity, read Technology and Education.

3. *Don't overcontrol.* Teresa Amabile (1993 (Csikszentmihalyi, 2000; Runko & Pritzker, 1999) says that telling students exactly how to do things leaves them feeling that originality is a mistake and exploration is a waste of time. If, instead of dictating which activities they should engage in, you let your students select their interests and you support their inclinations, you will be less likely to destroy their natural curiosity. Amabile also believes that when teachers hover over students all of the time, they make them feel that they are constantly being watched while they are working. When students are under constant surveillance, their creative risk-taking and adventurous spirit diminish. Students' creativity also is diminished when teachers have grandiose expectations for their performance and expect perfection from them, according to Amabile.

   Chuck Jones (1993), the creator of Wile E. Coyote, Road Runner, and many other cartoon characters, says that the child's job is to play and to experiment, but too often he or she gets criticized by parents and teachers for playing, experimenting, and trying out different things. Jones offers several examples of how adults criticize children's art. A child makes a drawing of a flower and the teacher says, "That's not a bad drawing but why is the flower bigger than you?" Jones says that's enough to kill the child's enthusiasm. When you discover something you have never seen, it appears huge, much bigger than you are. About another child's drawing, a parent asks, "What's this stuff?" The child replies, "That's me. I'm dancing." The parent says, "Yeah, but you only have one knee. You don't have all of those knees." Jones says this is nonsense. All you have to do is think about what you feel like when you are dancing. You feel like you have fourteen knees and ankles all over the place!

4. *Encourage internal motivation.* Excessive use of prizes, such as gold stars, money, or toys, can stifle creativity by undermining the intrinsic pleasure students derive from creative activities. Creative students' motivation is the satisfaction generated by the work itself. Competition for prizes and formal evaluations often undermine intrinsic motivation and creativity (Amabile & Hennessey, 1992). However, this is not to rule out material rewards altogether. We will say more about internal and external motivation in chapter 11, "Motivating Students to Learn."

5. *Foster flexible and playful thinking.* Creative thinkers are flexible and play with problems—which gives rise to a paradox. Although creativity takes effort, the effort goes more smoothly if students take it lightly. Humor can grease the wheels of creativity (Goleman, Kaufman, & Ray, 1993). When students are joking around, they are more likely to consider unusual solutions to problems. Having fun helps to disarm the inner censor that can condemn a student's ideas as being off-base. As one clown named Wavy Gravy put it, "If you can't laugh about it, it just isn't funny anymore."

6. *Introduce students to creative people.* You might not have Wavy Gravy nearby to invite to your classroom, but it is a good strategy to identify the most creative people in your community whom you can invite. Ask them to come to your class and describe what helps them become creative or to demonstrate their creative skills. A writer, a poet, a craftsperson, a musician, a scientist, and many others can bring their props and productions to your class.

$\mathcal{S}$UMMARY $\mathcal{T}$ABLE 4.2
Creativity

Concept	Processes/ Related Ideas	Characteristics/Description
Exploring Creativity	Its Nature	• Creativity is the ability to think about something in novel and interesting ways and come up with unique solutions to problems. • Guilford distinguished between convergent thinking (which produces one correct answer and is characteristic of the type of thinking required on conventional intelligence tests) and divergent thinking (which produces many answers to the same question and is characteristic of creativity). • Although most creative students are quite intelligent, the reverse is not necessarily true.
Teaching and Creativity	Its Nature	• Following are some ways teachers can foster creativity in students: develop brainstorming sessions, provide environments that stimulate creativity, don't overcontrol students, encourage internal motivation, foster flexible and playful thinking, and introduce students to creative people.

Learning and Thinking Styles

Teachers will tell you that children approach learning and thinking in an amazing variety of ways. And teachers themselves vary in their styles of learning and thinking.

Exploring Learning and Thinking Styles

The two main topics we have discussed so far—intelligence and creativity—are abilities. A *style* is a preferred way of using one's abilities (Sternberg, 1994, 1997b). **Learning and thinking styles** *are not abilities; rather, they are preferences in how people use their abilities.* None of us has just a single learning and thinking style; each of us has a profile of many styles. Individuals vary so much that literally hundreds of learning and thinking styles have been proposed by educators and psychologists. The following coverage of learning and thinking styles is not meant to be exhaustive, but introduces widely discussed styles. In the next sections, we will describe several dichotomies of learning styles, then examine two ways to profile students' styles.

Dichotomies of Learning and Thinking Styles

Three of the most widely discussed style dichotomies in approaches to learning are field dependent/independent, impulsive/reflective, and deep/surface.

Field Dependent/Independent Styles   The **field dependent/independent styles** *involve the extent to which the surrounding field (environment) dominates the student's perception* (Witkin & Goodenough, 1976). Students for whom the surrounding field dominates perception are said to have a field-dependent style. A student for whom the surrounding environment does not dominate perceptions is described as field independent (Bertini, 2000). Students with a field-dependent style have trouble locating the information they are searching for because they can't distinguish it from other information. In contrast, field-independent students are better at disentangling the information they are seeking from other information in the

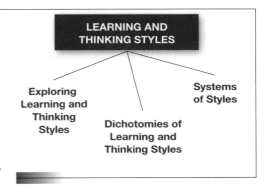

Learning Styles

TEACHING STRATEGIES
With Field-Dependent and Field-Independent Children

Following are some strategies that teachers can use in working with students who are field dependent or field independent (Jonassen & Grabowski, 1993).

1. *When working with field-dependent students:*
   - Understand that they have a tendency to learn by following a prescribed pattern of performance. Thus, they like instructional support and benefit from organizational cues, such as advance organizers.
   - Know that they like feedback, especially informative feedback, about how their learning is progressing.
   - Realize that they often like to work on group projects and collaborate with other students.
   - If you want to help the field-dependent student become more field-independent, you will need to begin exercises with clear structure, numerous cues, and consistent feedback. As the student progresses, scaffold by removing structure, then cues, then finally reducing feedback. Also help field-dependent students begin to set their own goals and evaluate the meaningfulness of information. If cross-age peer tutoring is available, pair the field-dependent student with an older field-independent student. In addition, the following strategies for working with field-independent students also can help a field-dependent student to become more field-independent. However, remember that you will have to be more patient and provide more support to get the field-dependent student to succeed at these tasks.
2. *When working with field-independent students:*
   - Ask them to solve problems and figure out the underlying organization of ideas. For example, encourage them to outline ideas or draw concept maps.
   - Give them some opportunities to generate projects both independently and collaboratively.
   - Encourage them to pose questions.
   - When they do projects, urge them to gather extensive content resources and reference materials.

field. For example, a field-independent student can look at a complex drawing that contains an embedded figure and detect the figure, whereas a field-dependent student struggles with this. In a way, field-independent students are good at "finding a needle in a haystack." Field-dependent students tend to place information in their memory as it appears in the environment, while field-independent students are more likely to reorganize and restructure the information. Researchers have found that field-independent individuals have better analytical skills, while their field-dependent counterparts often do better at interpersonal relations (Witkin, 1976). Thus, not surprisingly, females are more likely to be field dependent and males to be field independent. Field-dependent teachers are more likely to use discussion methods and field-independent teachers are more likely to lecture (Witkin, 1976).

Impulsive/Reflective Styles
The **impulsive/reflective styles,** *also referred to as conceptual tempo, involves a student's tendency either to act quickly and impulsively or to take more time to respond and reflect on the accuracy of an answer* (Kagan, 1965). Impulsive students often make more mistakes than reflective students.

Research on impulsivity/reflection has implications for education (Jonassen & Grabowski, 1993). Reflective students are more likely than impulsive students to do well at these tasks:

- Remembering structured information
- Reading comprehension and text interpretation
- Problem solving and decision making

Reflective students also are more likely than impulsive students to set their own learning goals and concentrate on relevant information. And reflective students usually

TEACHING STRATEGIES
With Impulsive Children

Some ways teachers can help impulsive children become more reflective include:

1. *Monitor students in the class to determine which ones are impulsive.*
2. *Talk with them about taking their time to think through an answer before they respond.*
3. *Encourage them to label new information as they work with it.*
4. *Model the reflective style as a teacher.*
5. *Help students set higher standards for their performance.*
6. *Recognize when impulsive students start to take more time to reflect and compliment them on their improvement.*

have higher standards for performance. The evidence is strong that reflective students learn more effectively and do better in school than impulsive students.

In thinking about impulsive and reflective styles, keep in mind that although most children learn better when they are reflective rather than impulsive, some children are simply fast, accurate learners and decision makers. Reacting quickly is a bad strategy only if you come up with wrong answers. Also, some reflective children might ruminate forever about a problem and have difficulty getting closure. Teachers can encourage these children to retain their reflective orientation but arrive at more timely solutions. In chapter 7, "Behavioral Approaches, Social Cognitive Approaches, and Teaching," we will discuss a number of other strategies for helping students self-regulate their behavior.

Deep/Surface Styles   The **deep/surface styles** *involves the extent to which students approach learning materials in a way that helps them understand the meaning of the materials (deep style) or as simply what needs to be learned (surface style)* (Marton, Hounsell, & Entwistle, 1984). Students who approach learning with a surface style fail to tie what they are learning into a larger conceptual framework. They tend to learn in a passive way, often rotely memorizing information. Deep learners are more likely to actively construct what they learn and give meaning to what they need to remember. Thus, deep learners take a constructivist approach to learning. Deep learners also are more likely to be self-motivated to learn, whereas surface learners are more likely to be motivated to learn because of external rewards, such as grades and positive feedback from the teacher (Snow, Corno, & Jackson, 1996).

Systems of Styles

Some conceptualizations of learning and thinking styles have been directed not at a single dichotomy, such as deep or surface learning, but at revealing where a child stands on a system of styles. We will examine two of these systems, one that has been used for many years (the Myers-Briggs Type Indicator) and one that has only recently been proposed (Sternberg's system of self-government).

THROUGH THE EYES OF TEACHERS
Learning Styles and Different Forms of Reading

In teaching, I have long been aware of learning styles and realized that children learn in various ways. What is right for one may not be right for another. Sometimes a student will need to read a passage aloud to grasp and retain its meaning while the student next to her may need to have someone else read it. Still another student may need to block out all sound and read it silently several times, allowing the sight of the words to push the knowledge into her memory. Then there are those who may need to read it or have it read to them after which they must make something or draw something. For this reason, I try to provide a variety of activities for students to choose so several methods of learning will be covered.

Verna Rollins
Language Arts Teacher
West Middle School
Ypsilanti, Michigan

TEACHING STRATEGIES
To Help Surface Learners Think More Deeply

Some strategies that teachers can use to help surface learners process information more deeply include:

1. *Monitor students to determine which ones are surface learners.*
2. *Discuss with them the importance of not just rotely memorizing material. Encourage them to connect what they are learning now with what they have learned in the past.*
3. *Ask questions and give assignments that require students to fit information into a larger framework.* For example, instead of just asking students to name the capital of a particular state, ask them if they have visited the capital and what their experiences were, what other cities are located in that section of the United States, or how large or small the city is.
4. *Be a model who processes information deeply rather than just scratching the surface.* Explore topics in depth and talk about how the information you are discussing fits within a larger network of ideas.
5. *Avoid using questions that require pat answers.* Instead, ask questions that require students to deeply process information. Connect lessons more effectively with children's existing interests.

Myers-Briggs Type Indicator The Myers-Briggs Type Indicator provides scores for each child on four dichotomies (Myers, 1962):

- *Extraversion/introversion (EI).* This involves whether children focus on the outer world of people or the inner life of ideas. Extraverts enjoy spending time interacting with others while introverts prefer more solitary activities like studying alone in a library. We will have more to say about extraversion/introversion later in the chapter when we discuss personality traits.
- *Sensing/intuiting (SN).* Sensing students like to gather extensive information through their senses before they take action. By contrast, intuiting students rely on their intuition in making up their mind about something.
- *Thinking/feeling (TF).* Thinkers use systematic reasoning and logically analyze problems. They avoid letting their emotions become involved in making decisions. By contrast, feelers trust their emotions.
- *Judging/perceiving (JP).* Judgers evaluate and criticize. They enjoy debating and arguing about an issue. By contrast, perceivers use their perceptual skills to develop aesthetic appreciation. Perceivers especially enjoy art and craft activities.

When students take the Myers-Briggs inventory, they are given scores on these pairs of characteristics and are provided feedback about which ones they prefer (Cohen & Swerdlik, 1999). A four-letter code designation (*ISFP* stands for introverted, sensing, feeling, and perceiving, for example) corresponds to an academic style with its own strengths and weaknesses. Some teachers believe that knowing students' Myers-Briggs profiles can help them improve their instructional strategies.

Sternberg's System of Styles Another broad system of learning styles has recently been proposed by Robert J. Sternberg (O'Hara & Sternberg, 1999; 1997b). His triarchic theory of intelligence was presented earlier in the chapter. Sternberg also proposed a system of learning and thinking styles that involves mental self-government. The main theme of his system is that students organize and govern themselves in different ways and that these variations correspond to the different forms of government that exist around the world. As shown in figure 4.5, Sternberg's system consists of thirteen learning and thinking styles under five categories: functions, forms, levels, scope, and leaning.

Sternberg believes that each student tends to adopt one style in each of the five categories, although the student's style might vary with the task or situation. For

Thinking Styles

Style	Characterization	Example
Functions		
Legislative	Likes to create, invent, design, do things his or her own way, have little assigned structure.	Likes doing science projects, writing poetry, stories, or music, and creating original artworks.
Executive	Likes to follow directions, do what he or she is told, be given structure.	Likes to solve problems, write papers on assigned topics, do artwork from models, build from designs, learn assigned information.
Judicial	Likes to judge and evaluate people and things.	Likes to critique work of others, write critical essays, give feedback and advice.
Forms		
Monarchic	Likes to do one thing at a time, devoting to it almost all energy and resources.	Likes to immerse self in a single project, whether art, science, history, business.
Hierarchic	Likes to do many things at once, setting priorities for which to do when and how much time and energy to devote to each.	Likes to budget time for doing homework so that more time and energy are devoted to important assignments.
Oligarchic	Likes to do many things at once, but has trouble setting priorities.	Likes to devote sufficient time to reading comprehension items, so might not finish standardized verbal-ability test.
Anarchic	Likes to take a random approach to problems; dislikes systems, guidelines, and practically all constraints.	Writes an essay in stream-of-consciousness form; in conversations, jumps from one point to another; starts things but doesn't finish them.
Levels		
Global	Likes to deal with big picture, generalities, abstractions.	Writes an essay on the global message and meaning of a work of art.
Local	Likes to deal with details, specifics, concrete examples.	Writes an essay describing the details of a work of art and how they interact.
Scope		
Internal	Likes to work alone, focus inward, be self-sufficient.	Prefers to do science or social studies project on his or her own.
External	Likes to work with others, focus outward, be interdependent.	Prefers to do science or social studies project with other members of a group.
Leaning		
Liberal	Likes to do things in new ways, defy conventions.	Prefers to figure out how to operate new equipment even if it is not the recommended way, prefers open-classroom setting.
Conservative	Likes to do things in tried-and-true ways, follow conventions.	Prefers to operate new equipment in traditional way; prefers traditional classroom setting.

Figure 4.5
Sternberg's System of Learning and Thinking Styles

instance, a student who likes to work independently in a biology class (internal scope) might prefer to do social studies projects with others (external scope).

Sternberg stresses that teachers benefit students when they vary their teaching styles to match up with individual students. This works best when teachers have a full range of styles they can call on when interacting with students. Figure 4.6 shows which

TEACHING STRATEGIES
For Students with Diverse Learning and Thinking Styles

Some strategies for teaching students with diverse learning and thinking styles are:

1. *Your classroom will have students with diverse learning and thinking styles. And these styles matter.* Be sure not to confuse these styles with abilities, such as intelligence. Styles involve how students use their abilities. Keep in mind that every student will have a combination of learning and thinking styles.
2. *As a teacher, profile the system of styles that each student uses to learn and think.* Evaluate which ones are benefiting the student's learning, which ones are harming it. Being reflective and processing information deeply usually benefit students more than being impulsive and processing information in a shallow way. Regarding other categories, such as Sternberg's global and local styles, one style is not necessarily preferred over the other, and students often learn best when their preferred style matches their teacher's style. Accordingly, be aware of which styles dominate the way you learn and think. Consider ways to expand the range of positive learning and thinking styles you present to students, so that you are not just reaching only those students whose particular styles are most compatible with your tendencies.
3. *Remember that styles can vary with context and across schools, grades, and subjects.* Howard Gardner (1993) says that a student might have an impulsive style in the musical realm but a reflective style when working on a jigsaw puzzle.

teaching methods link up best with students' styles. Notice that the oligarchic and anarchic learning styles have been omitted from figure 4.6 because they are incompatible with just about any method of instruction. However, teachers who have students with an oligarchic style need to help them set priorities because these students try to do too many things at once. And teachers with students who have an anarchic style need to help the students learn to engage in self-regulation because they tend to approach problems in a random way and don't like guidelines.

In Sternberg's research, teachers tend to overestimate how compatible their own styles are with those of their students. Also, teachers' styles differ not only across schools, but across grades and subjects as well. This suggests that the learning context often places demands on teachers that require them to adapt their style to the environment. Sternberg says that teachers of younger students need to be more legislative and less executive than teachers with older students. Groups of students also differ. Students from low-income backgrounds tend to be more judicial, oligarchic, local, and conservative than middle-socioeconomic-status students.

At this point we have studied a number of ideas about learning and thinking styles. A review of these ideas is presented in summary table 4.3. Next, we will turn our attention to personality and temperament, which also need to be considered when individual differences and children's education are evaluated.

Method of Instruction	Most Compatible Styles
Lecture	Executive/hierarchical
Thought-based questioning	Judicial/legislative
Cooperative learning	External
Problem solving of given problems	Executive
Projects	Legislative
Small-group recitation	External/executive
Small-group discussion	External/judicial
Reading	Internal/hierarchical
For details	Local/executive
For main ideas	Global/executive
For analysis	Judicial
Memorization	Executive/local/conservative

Figure **4.6**
Linking Sternberg's Styles with Teaching Methods

SUMMARY TABLE 4.3
Learning and Thinking Styles

Concept	Processes/Related Ideas	Characteristics/Description
Exploring Learning and Thinking Styles	Their Nature	• Styles are not abilities but rather preferred ways of using abilities. • Each individual has a number of learning and thinking styles.
Dichotomies of Learning and Thinking Styles	Field Dependent/Independent Styles	• This dichotomy involves the extent to which the surrounding field (environment) dominates the student's perception. When it dominates, the student is said to be field dependent; when it doesn't, the student is called field independent.
	Impulsive/Reflective Styles	• Also referred to as conceptual tempo, this dichotomy involves a student's tendency to act quickly and impulsively or to take more time to respond and reflect on the accuracy of an answer. • Impulsive students typically make more mistakes than reflective students.
	Deep/Surface Styles	• This dichotomy involves the extent to which students approach learning in a way that helps them understand the meaning of materials (deep style) or as simply what needs to be learned (surface style).
Systems of Styles	The Myers-Briggs Type Indicator	• This system has been used for many years and provides scores for each child on four dichotomies: Extraversion/introversion, sensing/intuiting, thinking/feeling, and judging/perceiving. • Students are given a four-letter code designation that corresponds to an academic style with its own strengths and weaknesses.
	Sternberg's System of Styles	• This system of styles involves self-government. It consists of thirteen styles under five categories: functions (legislative, executive, judicial), forms (monarchic, hierarchic, oligarchic, anarchic), levels (global, local), scope (internal/external), and leaning (conservative, liberal). • Sternberg believes that students benefit when teachers vary their teaching styles to match students' styles. • Styles can vary across schools, grades, and subjects.

Personality and Temperament

Not only is it important to be aware of individual variations in children's cognition, it also is important to understand individual variations in their personality and temperament.

Personality

We make statements about personality all the time and prefer to be around people with certain types of personality. Let's examine just what the term *personality* means.

Exploring Personality   **Personality** *refers to distinctive thoughts, emotions, and behaviors that characterize the way an individual adapts to the world.* Think about yourself for a moment. What is your personality like? Are you outgoing or shy? considerate or caring? friendly or hostile? These are some of the characteristics involved in personality. As we see next, one view stresses that there are five main factors that make up personality.

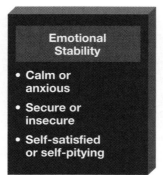

Emotional Stability

- Calm or anxious
- Secure or insecure
- Self-satisfied or self-pitying

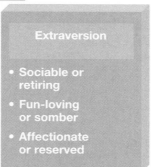

Extraversion

- Sociable or retiring
- Fun-loving or somber
- Affectionate or reserved

The "Big Five" Personality Factors   As with intelligence, psychologists are interested in identifying the main dimensions of personality (Ryckman, 2000). Some personality researchers believe they have identified the **"big five" personality factors:** *emotional stability, extraversion, openness to experience, agreeableness, and conscientiousness* (see figure 4.7). *A number of research studies point toward these factors as important dimensions of personality* (Costa, 2000; Costa & McRae, 1995, 1998; Hogan, 1987; McNulty, 2000).

Thinking about personality in terms of the "big five" factors can give you a framework for thinking about the personalities of your students. Your students will differ in their emotional stability, how extraverted or introverted they are, how open to experience they are, how agreeable they are, and how conscientious they are. However, some experts believe that the "big five" don't capture all of personality. They say that the range of personality also should include such factors as how positive (joyous, happy) or negative (angry, sad) students are, as well as how self-assertive they are.

Person-Situation Interaction   In discussing learning and thinking styles, we indicated that a student's style can vary according to the subject matter the student is learning or thinking about. The same is true for personality characteristics. According to the concept of **person-situation interaction,** *the best way to characterize an individual's personality is not in terms of personal traits or characteristics alone, but also in terms of the situation involved.* Researchers have found that students choose to be in some situations and avoid others (Ickes, Snyder, & Garcia, 1997).

Openness

- Imaginative or practical
- Interested in variety or routine
- Independent or conforming

Figure **4.7**
The Big Five Factors of Personality

The "Big Five"

Suppose you have an extravert and an introvert in your class. According to the theory of person-situation interaction, you can't predict which one will show the best adaptation unless you consider the situation they are in. The theory of person-situation interaction predicts that the extravert will adapt best when he is asked to collaborate with others, and that the introvert will adapt best when he is asked to carry out tasks independently. Similarly, the extravert likely will be happier when socializing with lots of people at a party, the introvert when in a more private setting alone or with a friend.

In sum, don't think of personality traits as always dooming a student to behave in a particular way across all situations. The context or situation matters (Burger, 2000; Derlega, Winstead, & Jones, 1999). Monitor

Agreeableness

- Softhearted or ruthless
- Trusting or suspicious
- Helpful or uncooperative

Conscientiousness

- Organized or disorganized
- Careful or careless
- Disciplined or impulsive

TEACHING STRATEGIES
Involving Students' Temperaments

These are some teaching strategies related to students' temperaments (Sanson & Rothbart, 1995):

1. *Show attention to and respect for individuality.* Teachers need to be sensitive to the student's signals and needs. The goal of good teaching might be accomplished in one way with one student, in another way with another student, depending on the students' temperaments. Some temperament characteristics pose more teaching challenges than others. For example, a student's proneness to distress, as exhibited by frequent irritability, might contribute to avoidant or coercive interchanges with teachers.

2. *Consider the structure of the student's environment.* Crowded, noisy classrooms often pose greater problems for a "difficult" child than for an "easy" child. Fearful, withdrawn students often benefit from slower entry into new contexts.

3. *Be aware of problems that can emerge because of labeling a child "difficult" and packaged programs for "difficult children."* Some books and programs for parents and teachers focus specifically on the child's temperament (Cameron, Hansen, & Rosen, 1989; Turecki & Tonner, 1989). Most of these focus on the difficult child. Acknowledging that some children are harder to teach than others is often helpful, and advice on how to handle a particular temperament also can be useful. However, whether a particular characteristic is truly "difficult" depends on its fit with the environment, so the problem does not necessarily rest with the child. As with labeling a child as more or less intelligent, labeling the child as "difficult" has the danger of becoming a self-fulfilling prophecy. Also keep in mind that temperament can be modified to some degree.

situations in which students with varying personality characteristics seem to feel most comfortable and provide them with opportunities to learn in those situations. If a particular personality trait is detrimental to the student's school performance (perhaps one student is so introverted that he fears working in a group), think of ways you can support the student's efforts to change.

Temperament

Temperament is closely related to personality and to learning and thinking styles. **Temperament** *is a person's behavioral style and characteristic ways of responding.* Some students are active, others are calm. Some respond warmly to people, others fuss and fret. Such descriptions involve variations in students' temperaments.

Scientists who study temperament seek to find the best ways to classify temperaments. The most well known classification was proposed by Alexander Chess and Stella Thomas (Chess & Thomas, 1977; Thomas & Chess, 1991). They believe that there are three basic styles or clusters of temperament:

- An **easy child** *is generally in a positive mood, quickly establishes regular routines, and easily adapts to new experiences.*
- A **difficult child** *tends to react negatively, has aggressive tendencies, lacks self-control, and is slow to accept new experiences.*
- A **slow-to-warm-up child** *has a low activity level, is somewhat negative, shows low adaptability, and displays a low intensity of mood.*

A difficult temperament or a temperament that reflects a lack of control can place a student at risk for problems. In one study, adolescents with a difficult temperament had unusually high incidences of drug abuse and stressful events (Tubman & Windle, 1995). In another study, a temperament factor labeled "out of control" (being irritable and distractible) assessed when children were 3 to 5 years of age was related to acting out and behavioral problems at 13 to 15 years of age (Caspi & others, 1995).

SUMMARY TABLE 4.4
Personality and Temperament

Concept	Processes/Related Ideas	Characteristics/Description
Personality	Exploring Personality	• Personality refers to distinctive thoughts, emotions, and behaviors that characterize the way an individual adapts to the world.
	The "Big Five" Personality	• Psychologists recently have identified the "big five" personality factors: emotional stability, extraversion, openness to intellect, agreeableness, and conscientiousness. • The "big five" give teachers a framework for thinking about a student's personality characteristics.
Temperament	Person-Situation Interaction	• The concept of person-situation interaction states that the best way to characterize an individual's personality is not in terms of traits alone, but in terms of both the traits and the situations involved.
	Its Nature	• Temperament refers to a person's behavioral style and characteristic way of responding. • Chess and Thomas believe there are three basic temperament styles or clusters: easy, difficult, and slow-to-warm-up. A difficult temperament places a child at risk for problems. • In education involving students' temperaments, teachers can show attention to and respect for individuality, consider the structure of a student's environment, and be aware of the problems involved when labeling a student as "difficult" and packaged programs for "difficult children."

Temperament

Everyone must form himself as a particular human being.

Johann Wolfgang von Goethe
German Poet, 19th Century

Across the same age span, a temperament factor labeled "approach" (friendliness, eagerness to explore new situations) was associated with a low incidence of anxiety and depression.

New classifications of temperament continue to be forged (Kagan, 2000). In a recent review of temperament, Mary Rothbart and John Bates (1998) concluded that, based on current research, the best framework for classifying temperament involves a revision of Chess and Thomas' categories (easy, difficult, and slow-to-warm-up). The classification of temperament now focuses more on (1) positive affect and approach, (2) negative affect, and (3) effortful control (self-regulation).

At this point, we have discussed a number of ideas about personality and temperament. A review of these ideas is presented in summary table 4.4

This chapter has been about individual variations. Because individual variations are so important in effectively teaching children, we will address them throughout the book. For example, in chapter 6 we will focus on teaching exceptional students, including those with a learning disability and those who are gifted. And in chapter 5 we will explore individual variations in students' culture, ethnicity, socioeconomic status, and gender.

Chapter Review

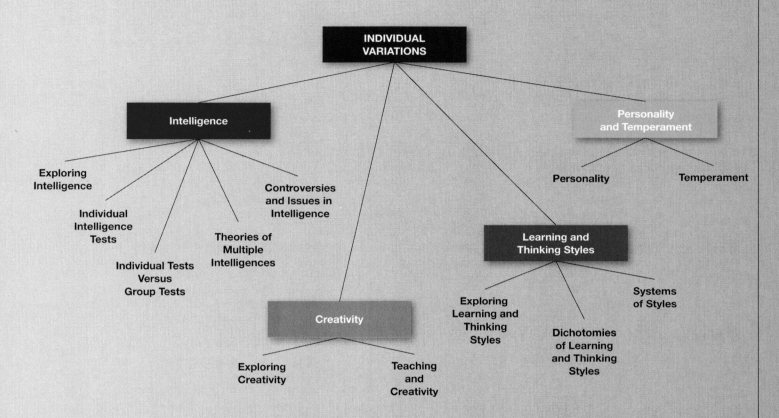

TO OBTAIN A DETAILED REVIEW OF THIS CHAPTER, STUDY THESE FOUR SUMMARY TABLES:

Key Terms

intelligence 126
individual differences 126
mental age (MA) 127
intelligence quotient
  (IQ) 127
normal distribution 127
triarchic theory of
  intelligence 129
culture-fair tests 137

between-class ability grouping
  (tracking) 138
nongraded (cross-age)
  program 139
Joplin plan 139
within-class ability
  grouping 140
creativity 141
convergent thinking 141

divergent thinking 141
brainstorming 144
learning and thinking
  styles 145
field dependent/independent
  styles 145
impulsive/reflective styles 146
deep/surface styles 147
personality 151

"big five" personality
  factors 152
person-situation
  interaction 152
temperament 153
easy child 153
difficult child 153
slow-to-warm-up child 153

Educational Psychology Checklist
INDIVIDUAL VARIATIONS

How much have you learned since the beginning of the chapter? Use the following statements to help you review your knowledge and understanding of the chapter material. First, read the statement and mentally or briefly on paper demonstrate that you can outline the relevant information.

_____ I can define intelligence and describe the main individual intelligence tests.
_____ I can discuss strengths and weaknesses of group intelligence tests.
_____ I can describe different approaches to multiple intelligences.
_____ I am aware of the issues and controversies that are involved in the concept of intelligence.

_____ I can define what creativity is and describe some important aspects of teaching and creativity.
_____ I know what learning and thinking styles are.
_____ I can discuss some important types of students' and teachers' learning and thinking styles.
_____ I am aware of what personality and temperament are, as well as some of the most important personality characteristics and temperament styles.

For any items that you did not check off, go back and locate the relevant material in the chapter. Review the material until you feel that you can check off the item. You also may want to use this checklist later in preparing for an exam.

Adventures for the Mind

Now that you have a good knowledge and understanding of the chapter, complete the following exercises to expand your thinking about the chapter's topics.

• Examine the results of Self-Assessment 4.1 or other evidence of your own intelligence profile according to Gardner. In what frames of mind do you come out strongest? In which of Sternberg's three areas do you feel you are the strongest?

• Together with four or five other students in the class, practice the technique of brainstorming. Use your brainstorming session to come up with a list of settings in your community that are most likely to stimulate students' creativity at the following educational levels: kindergarten, elementary school, middle school, and high school.

• Interview several teachers about students' different learning and thinking styles. Ask them what teaching strategies they use to accommodate these differences in students.

• Form a small group of five or six students from your class and have one person identify his or her personality and temperament traits. Have other members do the same, in turn. After all have presented, discuss how the individuals in your group are similar or different.

Taking It to the Net

1. A student is intentionally defying your repeated requests to be quiet. How well do you control your emotions in this situation? Are you adept at managing your emotions in various situations?

2. How would you classify your learning style? Active or Reflective? Sensing or Intuitive? Visual or Verbal? Sequential or Global? Does it matter? Is so, how?

3. How would you classify your personality/temperament? Introverted or Extroverted? Sensing or Intuitive? Thinking or Feeling? Judging or Perceiving? How do these characteristics affect your behavior?

Connect to http://www.mhhe.com/socscience/psychology/santedu/ttnet.htm to find the answers!

Case Studies

Case 1: *Alice Peterson*: A teacher is having problems with a class into which every student brings unique and difficult problems into the classroom, leading her to wonder if she is reaching anyone. Her instruction does not seem to match her students' needs. (Pre-first grade—topic: Behavior Management, Cognitive Development, Diversity, Instruction, Motivation)

Case 2: *Laura Conway*: A resource room teacher is surprised and saddened to discover that one of her favorite sixth-grade students hates the resource room and wants to stop coming.

Chapter 5

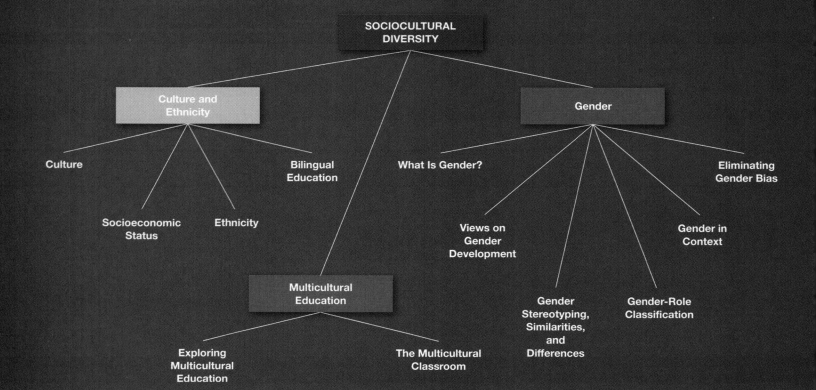

SOCIOCULTURAL DIVERSITY

Culture and Ethnicity

Culture

Socioeconomic Status

Ethnicity

Bilingual Education

Multicultural Education

Exploring Multicultural Education

The Multicultural Classroom

Gender

What Is Gender?

Views on Gender Development

Gender Stereotyping, Similarities, and Differences

Gender-Role Classification

Gender in Context

Eliminating Gender Bias

Preview

Ours is a diverse, multicultural world that teems with a multitude of ethnic groups, customs, and values. Our sociocultural world also involves gender. How best to educate children from such diverse cultural backgrounds, as well as girls and boys, are topics of considerable interest today. These are some of the questions we will explore in this chapter:

- Why is it so difficult to get people from different cultural and ethnic groups to respect each other?
- What is the best way to help impoverished children learn and cope?
- What controversies are involved in multicultural education?
- How extensive are ethnic and gender biases in schools? What can be done about these biases?

Teaching Stories
Margaret Longworth

Margaret Longworth taught high school for a number of years and was a teacher of the year. She recently moved to the middle school level and currently teaches language arts at West Middle School in St. Lucie, Florida. When considering the sociocultural diversity of students, she believes it is important for teachers to make schools "user friendly" for parents. In her words:

Many parents—especially ethnic minority parents of color—are very intimidated by schools. They think teachers know everything. Principals know everything. And God forbid that they ever would need to approach the school board. To combat this intimidation, I became "user friendly." Many students and parents center their lives around the church in my community. So, to break the barriers between school and home, my Haitian paraprofessional began setting up meetings for me at the Haitian churches. The churches gave me their Sunday evening services. After they completed their preliminaries, they turned the service over to me. Through the assistance of an interpreter, I presented opportunities to help them develop academic and life skills through education. I talked with them about special education classes, gifted classes, language programs, and scholarships, and encouraged them to keep their children in school. In turn, they felt confident enough to ask me about different happenings at school. Because of the parent school church connections that I was able to build up, I rarely had a discipline problem. If I did have to call parents, they would leave work or whatever they were doing and show up in my classroom. Many of these parents developed a relationship with the principal and guidance counselor and felt free to talk with school officials.

Margaret Longworth believes that in the classroom the key to improving children's interethnic relations is understanding. She comments:

Understanding other persons' points of view requires spending time with them and getting to know them—how they think and feel. As students talk with each other and begin to appreciate each other, they soon learn that in many ways they aren't that different after all.

An indication of Margaret Longworth's success as teacher is the note Marie Belvillius, a Haitian American high school student, recently sent to her:

When I looked out the window I'd see darkness. When I looked at the sky I would see shadows of sadness. All the crazy things in this world make me wonder about the madness. Since you came into our lives you have given us happiness. You showed us how to turn our back on sadness and madness. A lot of us have done some stupid or crazy things. But you didn't give up on us. You showed us what we are capable of. You never let us down. I'd like to say: THANK YOU.

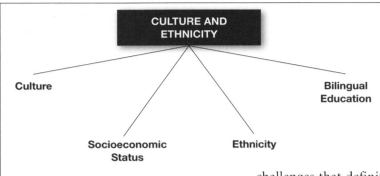

Culture and Ethnicity

The students in the schools of Fairfax County, Virginia, near Washington, D.C., come from 182 countries and speak more than a hundred languages. Although the Fairfax county schools are a somewhat extreme example, they are harbingers of what is to come in America's schools in the not-too-distant future. We can predict that by the year 2025, 50 percent of all public school students will be from backgrounds that are currently classified as "minority." This challenges that definition of what is minority and what is nonminority. Clearly, an important educational goal is to help students develop respect for people from different cultural and ethnic backgrounds (Valsiner, 2000).

Culture

Culture *refers to the behavior patterns, beliefs, and all other products of a particular group of people that are passed on from generation to generation.* These products result from the interactions among groups of people and their environments over many years (Thomas, 2000). A cultural group can be as large as the United States or as small as an isolated Amazon tribe. Whatever its size, the group's culture influences the behavior of its members (Berry, 2000; Matsumoto, 1996).

Psychologist Donald Campbell and his colleagues (Brewer & Campbell, 1976; Campbell & LeVine, 1968) found that people in all cultures tend to

- believe that what happens in their culture is "natural" and "correct" and what happens in other cultures is "unnatural" and "incorrect,"
- perceive their cultural customs as universally valid,
- behave in ways that favor their cultural group,
- feel proud of their cultural group, and
- feel hostile toward other cultural groups.

Psychologists and educators who study culture are often interested in comparing what happens in one culture with what happens in one or more other cultures. **Cross-cultural studies** *involve such comparisons, providing information about the degree to which people are similar and to what degree certain behaviors are specific to certain cultures.*

Comparisons of American students with Chinese, Japanese, and Taiwanese students revealed that American students tended to go about their work more independently, whereas Asian students were more likely to work in groups (Stevenson, 1995). These differences in cultures have been described with two terms: *individualism* and *collectivism* (Triandis, 1997, 2000). **Individualism** *refers to a set of values that give priority to personal goals rather than to group goals.* Individualist values include feeling good, personal distinction, and independence. **Collectivism** *consists of a set of values that support the group. Personal goals are subordinated to preserve group integrity, interdependence of the group's members, and harmonious relationships.* Many Western cultures such as the United States, Canada, Great Britain, and the Netherlands are described as individualistic. Many Eastern cultures such as China, Japan, India, and Thailand are labeled collectivistic. Mexican culture also has stronger collectivistic characteristics than United States culture. However, the United States has many collectivistic subcultures, such as Chinese American and Mexican American.

Cross-Cultural Comparisons
World Wide Classroom

TEACHING STRATEGIES
For Working with Students from Individualistic and Collectivistic Backgrounds

You yourself come from a cultural background that has individualistic or collectivistic leanings, or in some cases possibly both. As a teacher, you will need to interact effectively with students, parents, teachers, and school personnel who come from individualistic *and* collectivistic backgrounds.

If you are an individualist, these strategies will help you interact more effectively with students, parents, and school personnel from collectivistic cultures (Triandis, Brislin, & Hui, 1988):

1. *Pay more attention to group memberships.*
2. *Place more emphasis on cooperation than on competition.*
3. *If you have to criticize, do so carefully and only in private.* Criticizing someone from a collectivistic culture in public places causes them to "lose face."
4. *Cultivate long-term relationships.* Be patient. People in collectivistic cultures like dealing with "old friends."

If you are a collectivist, these strategies will help you interact more effectively with students, parents, and school personnel from individualistic cultures (Triandis, Brislin, & Hui, 1988):

1. *Compliment the person more than you are used to doing in your culture.*
2. *Avoid feeling threatened if the individualist acts competitively.*
3. *It is okay to talk about your accomplishments and be less modest than you are used to being, but don't boast.*
4. *Recognize that individualists don't value allegiance to the group as much as you do.*

Many of psychology's basic concepts have developed in individualistic cultures like the United States. Consider the flurry of *self*-terms in psychology that have an individualistic focus: *self-actualization, self-esteem, self-concept, self-efficacy, self-reinforcement, self-criticism, self-serving bias, self-doubt,* and so on. These *self*- terms all were created by American psychologists, leading some critics to argue that American psychology is strongly tilted toward individualistic rather than collectivist values (Lonner, 1990).

Humans always have lived in groups, whether large or small. They always have needed one another for survival. Critics argue that the Western emphasis on individualism undermines the human species' need for relatedness (Kagitcibasi, 1996). Some social scientists believe that many problems in Western cultures have intensified because of the cultural emphasis on individualism. Compared to collectivistic cultures, individualistic cultures tend to have higher rates of suicide, drug abuse, crime, adolescent pregnancy, divorce, child abuse, and mental disorders (Triandis, 1994, 2000). However, regardless of their cultural background, people need a positive sense of *self* and *connectedness to others* to develop fully as human beings.

Socioeconomic Status

Most countries have many subcultures. One of the most common ways of categorizing subcultures involves socioeconomic status.

What Is Socioeconomic Status?
Andrea and Brian come from families of differing socioeconomic status. What does this mean? **Socioeconomic status (SES)** *refers to the categorization of people according to their economic, educational, and occupational characteristics.* The most emphasis is given to distinctions between individuals of low and middle socioeconomic status. Socioeconomic status carries certain inequities. Low-SES individuals often have less education, less power to influence a community's institutions (such as schools), and fewer economic resources.

Children's
Defense Fund

THROUGH THE EYES OF TEACHERS

Viewing Public School Teaching as a Calling

Michael Terrell, who teaches first and second grades at Gavin H. Cochran Elementary School in Louisville, Kentucky, created "ParentShare," a literacy program that is now being used in five states. The program provides parents with popular magazines. Terrell also has obtained more than $2 million in toys and money for a holiday project for needy children.

The elementary school where he teaches is in a low-income neighborhood in which 96 percent of the students receive subsidized lunches. Michael Terrell sees public school teaching as a calling, believing that it serves an important role in integrating students from diverse social, cultural, and economic backgrounds. One of his former students, Jill Mayer, said that "once you are one of Michael Terrell's students, you are his student for life."

Michael Terrill, teaching at Gavin H. Cochran Elementary School in Louisville, Kentucky

*W*hat happens to a dream deferred?
Does it dry up
like a raisin in the sun?

Langton Hughes
American Poet and Author, 20th Century

Poverty and Learning
Urban Education
and Children in Poverty

Poverty   In a report on the state of America's children, the Children's Defense Fund (1992) described what life is like for all too many children. When sixth-graders in a poverty-stricken area of St. Louis were asked to describe a perfect day, one boy said that he would erase the world, then sit and think. Asked if he wouldn't rather go outside and play, the boy responded, "Are you kidding, out there?"

Currently, more than 20 percent of U.S. children live in poverty. In 1998, the poverty line for a family of four was an income of $16,450. The poverty rate for U.S. children is almost twice as high as in other industrialized nations. For example, Canada has a child poverty rate of 9 percent; Sweden, 2 percent. The U.S. child poverty rate is especially high for female-headed families—just short of 50 percent. More than 40 percent of African American and almost 40 percent of Latino children currently live below the poverty line. Compared to non-Latino White children, children of color are more likely to experience persistent poverty over many years. Nonetheless, in terms of actual numbers, there are more non-Latino White children (almost 9 million) living below the poverty line, than African American children (almost 4 million) or Latino children (also almost 4 million) living in poverty, because there are far more non-Latino White children overall in the United States.

Educating Students from Low-SES Backgrounds

Children in poverty often face problems at home and at school that present barriers to their learning (Webb, Metha, & Jordan, 2000). At home, they might have parents who don't set high educational standards for them, who are incapable of reading to them, and who don't have enough money to pay for educational materials and experiences such as books and trips to zoos and museums. They might be malnourished and live in areas where crime and violence are a way of life.

One recent study compared the home language environments of 3-year-old children from professional and welfare families (Hart & Risley, 1995). All of the children developed normally in terms of learning to talk and acquiring all of the forms of English and basic vocabulary. However, there were enormous differences in the sheer amount of language to which the children were exposed and the level of language development the children eventually attained. For example, in a typical hour, parents in professional careers spent almost twice as much time interacting with their children as welfare parents did with their children. The children of professional parents heard about 2,100 words per hour, the children in the welfare families heard only about 600 words an hour. Somewhat amazingly, the researchers found that the average 3-year-old *child* from a professional family had a recorded vocabulary that exceeded the recorded vocabulary size of the average welfare *parent!*

The schools that children from impoverished backgrounds attend often have fewer resources than schools in higher-income neighborhoods (Shade, Kelly, & Oberg, 1997). Schools in low-income areas are more likely to have more students with lower achievement test scores, lower graduation rates, and lower percentages of students going to college. And they are more likely to have young teachers with less experience than schools in higher-income neighborhoods, although federal aid has helped improve learning in some schools located in low-income areas. Schools in low-income areas also are more likely to encourage rote learning, whereas schools in higher-income

In his book Savage Inequalities, *Jonathan Kozol* (above) *vividly portrayed the problems that children of poverty face in their neighborhood and at school. What are some of these problems?*

areas are more likely to work with children to improve their thinking skills (Spring, 1998). In sum, far too many schools in low-income neighborhoods provide students with environments that are not conducive to effective learning, and the schools' buildings and classrooms often are old, crumbling, and poorly maintained.

In *Savage Inequalities,* Jonathan Kozol (1991) vividly described some of these problems that children of poverty face in their neighborhood and at school. Following are some of Kozol's observations in one inner-city area. East St. Louis, Illinois, which is 98 percent African American, has no obstetric services, no regular trash collection, and few jobs. Nearly one-third of the families live on less than $7,500 a year, and 75 percent of its population lives on welfare of some form. Blocks upon blocks of housing consist of dilapidated, skeletal buildings. Residents breathe the chemical pollution of nearby Monsanto Chemical Company. Raw sewage repeatedly backs up into homes. Lead from nearby smelters poisons the soil. Child malnutrition is common. Fear of violence is real. The problems of the streets spill over into the schools, where sewage also backs up from time to time. Classrooms and hallways are old and unattractive, athletic facilities inadequate. Teachers run out of chalk and paper, the science labs are 30 to 50 years out of date, and the school's heating system has never worked right. A history teacher has 110 students but only 26 books.

Kozol says that anyone who visits places like East St. Louis, even for a brief time, comes away profoundly shaken. After all, these are innocent children who have done nothing to deserve such terrible conditions. Kozol's interest was in describing what life is like in the nation's inner-city neighborhoods and schools, which are predominantly African American and Latino. However, as we indicated earlier, there are many non-Latino White children who live in poverty, although many of these are in suburban or rural areas. Kozol argues that many inner-city schools are still segregated, are grossly underfunded, and do not provide anywhere near adequate opportunities for children to learn effectively.

One recent trend in antipoverty programs is to conduct two-generation intervention (McLoyd, 1998, 2000). This involves providing both services for children (such as educational day care or preschool education) and services for parents (such

**Interview with
Jonathan Kozol**

THROUGH THE EYES OF CHILDREN
Lafayette and Pharoah

Ten-year-old Lafayette lives in an impoverished housing project in Chicago. His father has a drug habit and has trouble holding down a job. Lafayette lives with his mother.

The housing project where Lafayette lives is not safe. Lafayette told his friend, "You grow up 'round it. There are a lot of people in the projects who say they're not gonna do drugs, that they're not gonna drop out of school, that they won't be on the streets. But they're doing it now. Never say never. But I say never. My older brother didn't set a good example for me, but I'll set a good example for my younger brother."

A few days later, the police came to get his 17-year-old brother, Terrence, because he had been identified as a robbery suspect. The police came into the apartment and handcuffed Terrence in front of Lafayette and his younger brother, 7-year-old Pharoah, who told his mother, "I'm just too young to understand how life really is."

Several months later, their mother herded Lafayette and Pharoah into the hallway, where they crouched against the walls to avoid stray bullets. Lafayette told his mother, "If we don't get away, someone's gonna end up dead. I feel it." Shortly thereafter, a 9-year-old friend of the boys was shot in the back of the head as he was walking into the building where he lived. The bullet was meant for someone else (Kotlowitz, 1991).

Clearly, Lafayette and Pharoah face a lot of hurdles in being able to make the transition from childhood to adulthood competently. They live in a violent, decaying neighborhood, have older siblings who already have dropped out of school and who are engaging in delinquency, don't have a quiet place to do homework or have anyone in their family who can help them with it, and are growing up in a family in which education has not had a high priority. If you were a teacher in the inner-city school they attend, what would you do to help Lafayette and Pharoah overcome such challenging obstacles to their educational success?

Diversity
Diversity Resources

as adult education, literacy training, and job skill training). Recent evaluations of the two-generation programs suggest that they have more positive effects on parents than they do on children (St. Pierre, Layzer, & Barnes, 1996). Also discouraging for the education of these children is that when the two-generational programs show benefits, they are more likely to be health benefits than cognitive gains. To read about one effective program for intervening in the lives of children living in poverty, see the Diversity and Education box.

At this point we have studied a number of ideas about culture and socioeconomic status. A review of these ideas is presented in summary table 5.1 on page 167. Next we will explore ethnicity.

Ethnicity

Relations between people from different ethnic backgrounds, not just in the United States but in virtually every corner of the world, are often charged with bias and conflict. What do we mean by the term *ethnicity*?

Exploring Ethnicity The word *ethnic* comes from the Greek word that means "nation." **Ethnicity** *refers to a shared pattern of characteristics such as cultural heritage, nationality, race, religion, and language.* Everyone is a member of one or more ethnic groups.

How does ethnicity differ from race? The term *race*, now discredited as a biological concept, refers to the classification of people or other living things according to specific physiological characteristics. The term has never worked well in describing people in any scientific sense because humans are so diverse that they don't fit into neatly packaged racial categories. Thus, race no longer is recognized as an authentic scientific concept. Popularly, the word *race* has loosely been used to refer to everything from a person's mannerisms to religion to skin color. Social psychologist James Jones (1994, 1997) points out that thinking in racial terms has become embedded in most cultures. He says that people often stereotype other people because of their supposed race and inappropriately classify them as being more or less intelligent, competent, responsible, or socially acceptable on this basis. Although the term *race* won't go away from the American vocabulary, we will mainly use the term *ethnicity* in this book.

Nowhere is the changing tapestry of American culture more apparent than in the changing ethnic balances among America's citizens. At the onset of the twenty-first century, one-third of all school-age children fall into the category now loosely referred to as "children of color" (African Americans, Latinos, Asian Americans, and Native Americans). By the year 2025 that figure will reach one-half. This changing demographic promises not only the richness that diversity produces but also difficult challenges in extending the American dream to individuals of all ethnic groups. Historically, people of color have found themselves at the bottom of the American economic and social order. They have been disproportionately represented among the poor and the inadequately educated (Edelman, 1997).

TEACHING STRATEGIES
With Children in Poverty

Following are some strategies for teaching children who are living in poverty:

1. *If you teach in a school in a low-income neighborhood, make sure that helping children improve their thinking skills is an important goal for you.*
2. *Where poverty and other factors make it difficult to maintain safety and discipline, recognize the right, workable tradeoff between discipline and children's freedom.* We will say more about classroom discipline in chapter 12, "Managing the Classroom."
3. *Because many children from low-income backgrounds might come to your class not having experienced high parental standards for achievement and thus might lack the motivation to learn, pay special attention to motivating these children to learn.* We will address this topic further in chapter 11, "Motivating Students to Learn."
4. *Recognize that many parents in poor areas are not able to provide much academic supervision or assistance to their children.* Look for ways to support the parents who can be trained and helped to do so. Find ways that parents can contribute to their children's education even if they can't read themselves, can't afford to donate money, or have trouble making it to a PTA meeting because the bus is unsafe.
5. *Recognize that parents in poor areas can be quite talented, caring, responsive people in ways that teachers might not expect without getting to know them.* Most impoverished communities have people whose wisdom and experience defy stereotypes. Find these people and ask them to volunteer their services to help support children's learning in your classroom, accompany children on field trips, and make the school more attractive.
6. *Avoid creating tension between poorer and richer children who share the same classroom or school by favoring the products or performances of children who have greater opportunities, such as dance lessons, acting classes, and money for special projects.*
7. *Many children from low-income backgrounds benefit from having a mentor, a positive role model who agrees to be responsible for spending time with the child and helping to improve the child's learning and coping.* Look around the community for possible mentors whose contributions you believe would benefit low-income students. We will have much more to say about mentoring in chapter 7, "Behavioral Approaches, Social Cognitive Approaches, and Teaching" and chapter 11, "Motivating Students to Learn." Diversity and Education describes a mentoring program that worked for children from low-income backgrounds.

What are some positive teaching strategies with children in schools in low-income neighborhoods?

An important point about any ethnic group is that it is diverse. There are many ready examples: Mexican Americans and Cuban Americans are Latinos, but they had different reasons for migrating to the United States, come from varying socioeconomic backgrounds, and experience different rates and types of employment in the United States. Individuals born in Puerto Rico are distinguished from Latino individuals who have immigrated to the United States in that they are born U.S. citizens and are therefore not immigrants regardless of where they live in the United States. The U.S. government currently recognizes 511 *different* Native American tribes, each having a unique ancestral background with differing values and characteristics. Asian Americans include individuals of Chinese, Japanese, Filipinos, Koreans, and Southeast Asian origin, each group having distinct ancestries and languages. The diversity of Asian Americans is reflected in their educational attainment. Some

DIVERSITY AND EDUCATION
The Quantum Opportunities Program

A downward trajectory is not inevitable for students living in poverty. One potential path for these students is to become involved with a caring mentor. The Quantum Opportunities Program, funded by the Ford Foundation, was a 4-year, year-round mentoring effort (Carnegie Council on Adolescent Development, 1995). The ninth-grade students in the program were from ethnic minority, poverty backgrounds. Each day for 4 years, mentors provided sustained support, guidance, and concrete assistance to the students.

The Quantum program required students to participate in these kinds of activities:

- Academic-related activities outside school hours, including reading, writing, math, science, social studies, peer tutoring, and computer skills training
- Community service projects, including tutoring elementary school students, cleaning up the neighborhood, and volunteering in hospitals, nursing homes, and libraries
- Cultural enrichment and personal development activities, including life skills training and planning for college or a job

In exchange for their commitment to the program, students were offered financial incentives that encouraged their participation, completion, and long-range planning. A stipend of $1.33 was given to students for each hour they participated in these activities. For every 100 hours of education, service, or development activities completed, a student received a $100 bonus. The average cost per participant was $10,600 for all 4 years, which is one-half the cost of only 1 year in prison.

An evaluation of the Quantum project compared the mentored students with a nonmentored control group. Follow-up studies found that 63 percent of the mentored students graduated from high school but only 42 percent of the control group did; 42 percent of the mentored students are currently enrolled in college, but only 16 percent of the control group are; and compared to the mentored group, the control-group students were twice as likely to receive food stamps or welfare and had more arrests.

THROUGH THE EYES OF TEACHERS
Learning in Context

Maria Garcia-Rameau, a Spanish teacher at Scarborough High School in Houston, Texas, believes it is important for students to learn in context. She teaches Spanish by immersion and works with the home economics and language arts departments to celebrate Spanish holidays and to teach *The Old Man and the Sea* and *Bless Me, Ultima* across the curriculum. She organizes Cinco de Mayo celebrations, outings to museums, and trips to Mexico for students.

Maria Garcia-Rameau

achieve a high level of education, many others have little education. For example, 90 percent of Korean Americans graduate from high school, but only 71 percent of Vietnamese males do.

Ethnicity and Schools   School segregation is still a factor in the education of children of color in the United States (Simons, Finlay, & Yang, 1991). Almost one-third of African American and Latino students attend schools in which 90 percent or more of the students are from minority groups, typically their *own* minority group.

The school experiences of students from different ethnic groups vary considerably. African American and Latino students are much less likely than non-Latino White or Asian American students to be enrolled in academic, college preparatory programs, and much more likely to be enrolled in remedial and special education programs. Asian American students are far more likely than students from other ethnic minority groups to take advanced math and science courses in high school. African American students are twice as likely as Latinos, Native Americans, or Whites to be suspended from school. Ethnic minorities of color constitute the majority

SUMMARY TABLE 5.1
Culture and Socioeconomic Status

Concept	Processes/ Related Ideas	Characteristics/Description
Culture	Its Nature	• *Culture* refers to the behavior patterns, beliefs, and all other products of a particular group of people that are passed on from generation to generation. • The products result from the interaction between groups of people and their environment over many years. • Cross-cultural studies compare what happens in one culture with what happens in one or more other cultures, providing information about the degree to which people are similar and the degree to which certain behaviors are specific to certain cultures. • Cultures have been classified as individualistic (having a set of values that give priority to personal goals rather than group goals) and collectivistic (having a set of values that support the group). • Many Western cultures are individualistic, many Eastern cultures collectivistic.
Socioeconomic Status	What Is Socioeconomic Status?	• Socioeconomic status (SES) is the categorization of people according to economic, educational, and occupational characteristics. • The most emphasis is given to distinctions between individuals with low and middle socioeconomic status. • Low-SES individuals usually have less education, less power to influence schools and other community institutions, and fewer economic resources than higher-SES individuals.
	Poverty	• Currently more than 20 percent of America's children live in poverty.
	Educating Children from Low-SES Backgrounds	• Children in poverty face problems at home and at school that present barriers to their learning. • Schools in low-income neighborhoods often have fewer resources and less-experienced teachers, and are more likely to encourage rote learning rather than thinking skills.

in 23 of the 25 largest school districts in the United States, a trend that is increasing (Banks, 1995). However, 90 percent of the teachers in America's schools are non-Latino White, and the percentage of minority teachers is projected to be even lower in coming years.

Prejudice, Discrimination, and Bias   **Prejudice** *is an unjustified negative attitude toward an individual because of the individual's membership in a group.* The group toward which the prejudice is directed might be defined by ethnicity, sex, age, or virtually any other detectable difference (Monteith, 2000). Our focus here is prejudice against ethnic groups of color.

People who oppose prejudice and discrimination often have contrasting views about it. On the one side are individuals who value and praise the strides made in civil rights in recent years. On the other side are individuals who criticize American schools and other institutions because they believe that many forms of discrimination and prejudice still exist there (Jackson, 1997; Murrell, 2000).

American anthropologist John Ogbu (1989) proposed the view that ethnic minority students are placed in a position of subordination and exploitation in the American educational system. He believes that students of color, especially African

Prejudice

THROUGH THE EYES OF TEACHERS

Pride and Prejudice

Ypsilanti is a very interesting school district. It's about 50% black and 50% white, now. When I came here, 30 years ago, we were having frequent racial incidents, riots, and demonstrations. I heard about my (future) school while I was still teaching in another state because it was on the national t.v. news as a result of racial protests. There was not a week that went by, my first few years of teaching in Ypsilanti, that I was not accused of being prejudiced against blacks. I took it personally until I realized that the color of *every*one's skin was a daily issue in this town at that time. In the cafeteria and in the gym, when the kids were permitted to select their own seats, all the black kids would be on one side and all the whites would be on the other. There was one racially mixed kid that I had my 3rd year of teaching, and I could always pick him out of any crowd because he'd be the darkest kid on the white side or the whitest kid on the black side of the gym. Of course, I arrived in Ypsilanti a few months after Dr. King's assassination, so mine was not a unique experience for that era. What *was* unusual was the way Ypsilanti dealt with the problem.

The Ypsilanti School District is now a national model for race relations. Our Perry Pre-School and kindergarten program has been written up in national teaching textbooks. I'm always amazed at how much we take it for granted here in Ypsi. What our school district has done to change the racial climate in our school district is a source of tremendous pride to me.

What we did was really quite simple. We bussed all of our kindergarten kids to one school which we then made into an exemplary pre-school and kindergarten program. We then equally distributed our first through sixth graders among our other 6 elementary schools. Now, by the time I get our kids in 7th grade, whenever I tell my kids to select their own groups to do a project, they almost always self-select into male groups and female groups, but I almost never see a self-selected all black or all white group.

These days, if the kids accuse me of being prejudiced, it's because they think I favor the girls over the boys. They have no idea how happy that accusation makes me.

Lynn Ayres
English and Drama Teacher
East Middle School
Ypsilanti, Michigan

American and Latino students, have inferior educational opportunities, are exposed to teachers and school administrators who have low academic expectations for them, and encounter negative stereotypes of ethnic minority groups. In one study of middle schools in predominantly Latino areas of Miami, Latino and White teachers rated African American students as having more behavior problems than African American teachers rated the same students as having (Zimmerman & others, 1995).

Like Ogbu, educational psychologist Margaret Beale Spencer (Spencer & Dornbusch, 1990) says that a form of institutional racism permeates many American schools. That is, well-meaning teachers, acting out of misguided liberalism, fail to challenge children of color to achieve. Such teachers prematurely accept a low level of performance from these children, substituting warmth and affection for high standards of academic success.

Diversity and Differences   Historical, economic, and social experiences produce both prejudicial and legitimate differences between various ethnic groups ◀▌ page 13. Individuals who live in a particular ethnic or cultural group adapt to the values, attitudes, and stresses of that culture. Their behavior might be different from one's own, yet be functional for them. Recognizing and respecting these differences is an important aspect of getting along in a diverse, multicultural world (Spencer, 2000).

Unfortunately, the emphasis often placed on differences between ethnic minority groups and the White majority has been damaging to ethnic minority individuals. For too long, virtually all differences were thought of as *deficits* or inferior characteristics on the part of the ethnic minority group.

Another important dimension of every ethnic group is its diversity ◀▌ page 29. Not only is U.S. culture diverse—so is every ethnic group within the U.S. culture, as we underscored earlier in the chapter. As we will see next, the language of children from various ethnic groups is also diverse.

Bilingual Education

In Chapter 2, we discussed how children's language development takes place ◀▌ page 66. Here we will examine the best ways to teach children whose native language is not English.

Octavio's parents moved to the United States a year before he was born. They do not speak English fluently and always have spoken to Octavio in Spanish. At age 6, Octavio has just entered first grade in San Antonio. He speaks no English. What is the best way to teach Octavio?

As many as 10 million children in the United States come from homes in which English is not the primary language. Many, like Octavio, live in a community in which English is the main form of communication. To be successful, they have to master the English language.

Bilingual Education

Bilingual education *aims to teach academic subjects to immigrant children in their native languages (most often Spanish) while gradually adding English instruction.* Most bilingual programs are transitional programs developed to support students until they can understand English well enough to learn in the regular classroom (Ovando & McLaren, 2000). A typical program changes to English-only classes at the end of second or third grade, although some programs continue instruction in the child's primary language until sixth grade. In most programs, at least half of instruction will be in English from the beginning (Garcia, 1992).

Proponents of bilingual education argue that teaching immigrants in their native language shows respect for their family and community culture and increases the students' self-esteem, making their academic success more likely. Critics argue that bilingual education harms immigrant children by failing to adequately instruct them in English, which will leave them unprepared for the workplace. In rebuttal, supporters of bilingual education say that it aims to teach English. Some states have recently passed laws declaring English to be their official language, creating conditions in which schools are not obligated to teach minority children in languages other than English (Rothstein, 1998). In 1998, California voters repealed bilingual education altogether. Supporters of the repeal claimed that most Spanish-speaking voters opposed bilingual education, though polling after the election did not bear out this contention. Ironically, test scores released shortly after the election revealed that the scores of children in bilingual programs in several large school districts were higher, on average, than scores of native English-speaking children.

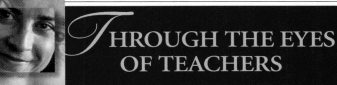

THROUGH THE EYES OF TEACHERS

Helping a Romanian Student Develop Proficiency in English

Cristina, a 12-year-old Romanian student, has been in America for about 15 months and is developing proficiency in English. Knowing she needs to learn to speak, read, and write standard English to be a successful, contributing member of American society, I looked for strengths that she brought to our community. She was fortunate in being able to attend school in Romania and was able to read and write in her first language at an appropriate level for her age. I have altered many assignments I give to her to take into account the context of her language learning. Once, when the class was engaging in a writing exercise, I had to use gestures and my knowledge of other Romance languages to help her understand the writing task. I also had her accompany her writing with drawings that were unhampered by language deficiencies.

Verna Rollins
Language Arts Teacher
West Middle School
Ypsilanti, Michigan

Researchers have found that bilingualism is not detrimental to the child's performance in either language (Hakuta, 2000; Hakuta & Garcia, 1989). Indeed, researchers have found that bilingualism has a positive effect on children's cognitive development. Children who are fluent in two languages perform better than their single-language counterparts on tests of analytical reasoning, concept formation, and cognitive flexibility (Hakuta, Ferdman, & Diaz, 1987). They also are more conscious of the structure of spoken and written language and better at noticing errors of grammar and meaning, skills that benefit their reading abilities (Bialystock, 1997).

The United States is one of the few countries in the world in which most students graduate from high school knowing only their own language. For example, in Russia, schools have 10 grades, called forms, that roughly correspond to the 12 grades in American schools. Children begin school at age 7 in Russia. Russian students begin learning English in the third form. Because of the emphasis on teaching English in Russian schools, most Russian citizens under the age of 40 today are bilingual, able to speak at least some English in addition to their native language.

Is it better to learn a second language as a child or as an adolescent? Adolescents make faster initial progress, but their eventual success in the second language is not as great as children's. For example, in one study, adults who had immigrated to the United States from China and Korea at various ages were given a test of grammatical knowledge (Johnson & Newport, 1989). Those who had begun learning English at 3 to 7 years of age scored as well as native speakers of English on the test, but as age of arrival to the United States (and onset of learning English) increased into later childhood and then adolescence, test scores gradually declined. Children's ability to learn to pronounce a second language with an accent also decreases with age, with an

TEACHING STRATEGIES
For Working with Linguistically and Culturally Diverse Children

Following are some classroom recommendations for working with linguistically and culturally diverse children (NAEYC, 1996):

1. *Recognize that all children are cognitively, linguistically, and emotionally connected to the language and culture of their home.*
2. *Acknowledge that children can demonstrate their knowledge and capacity in many ways.* Whatever language children speak, they should be able to show their capabilities and also feel appreciated and valued.
3. *Understand that without comprehensible input, second-language learning can be difficult.* It takes time to be linguistically competent in any language. Although verbal proficiency in a second language can be attained in 2 to 3 years, the skills needed to understand academic content through reading and writing can take 4 or more years. Children who do not become proficient in their second language after 2 or 3 years usually are not proficient in their first language either.
4. *Model appropriate use of English and provide the child with opportunities to use newly acquired vocabulary and language.* Learn at least a few words in the child's first language to demonstrate respect for the child's culture.
5. *Actively involve parents and families in the child's learning.* Encourage and assist parents in becoming knowledgable about the value for children of knowing more than one language. Provide parents with strategies to support and maintain home-language learning.
6. *Recognize that children can and will acquire the use of English even when their home language is used and respected.*
7. *To learn more about working with linguistically and culturally diverse children, collaborate with other teachers and children.*

A first- and second-grade bilingual English-Cantonese teacher instructing students in Chinese in Oakland, California.

especially sharp decline occurring after the age of about 10 or 12 (Asher & Garcia, 1969). Adolescents can become competent in a second language, but they have a more difficult time of it than younger children do.

At this point we have discussed many ideas about ethnicity and bilingual education. A review of these ideas is presented in summary table 5.2. Next, we continue our exploration of cultural and ethnic aspects of children's education by examining multicultural education.

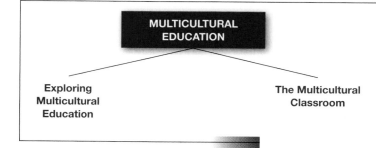

MULTICULTURAL EDUCATION

Exploring Multicultural Education

The Multicultural Classroom

Multicultural Education

In 1963, President John Kennedy said, "Peace is a daily, a weekly, a monthly process, of gradually changing opinions, slowly eroding old barriers, quietly building new structures." Cultural and ethnic tensions regularly threaten this fragile peace. The hope is that multicultural education can contribute to making our nation more like what the late civil rights leader Martin Luther King dreamed of: a nation where children will be judged not by the

SUMMARY TABLE 5.2
Ethnicity and Bilingual Education

Concept	Processes/Related Ideas	Characteristics/Description
Ethnicity	Exploring Ethnicity	• *Ethnic* comes from the Greek word meaning "nation." *Ethnicity* refers to a shared pattern of characteristics such as cultural heritage, nationality, race, religion, and language. • Everyone is a member of one or more ethnic groups. • The term *race* is now discredited as a biological term but unfortunately continues to be used in stereotyping people. • The school population increasingly consists of children of color, predicted to reach 50 percent by 2025.
	Ethnicity and Schools	• School segregation is still a factor in the education of children of color. • African American and Latino students are less likely than non-Latino White and Asian American students to be enrolled in college preparatory courses.
	Prejudice, Discrimination, and Bias	• Prejudice is an unjustified negative attitude toward an individual because of the individual's membership in a group. • Ogbu believes there continues to be considerable prejudice against children of color in American education.
	Diversity and Differences	• Historical, economic, and social experiences produce legitimate differences between ethnic groups, and it is important to recognize these differences. • However, too often the differences are viewed as deficits on the part of the minority group when compared to the mainstream non-Latino White group. • It is important to recognize the extensive diversity that exists within each cultural group.
Bilingual Education	Its Nature and Controversies	• Bilingual education aims to teach academic subjects to immigrant children in their native languages (most often in Spanish) while gradually adding English instruction. • Proponents of bilingual education argue that it helps immigrants to value their family and culture, as well as increase their self-esteem, thus making academic success more likely. • Critics say it harms immigrant children by failing to adequately instruct them in English and leaving them unprepared for the workplace. • However, researchers have found that bilingualism does not interfere with performance in either language. • Second-language learning is more successful in childhood than in adolescence.

color of their skin but by the quality of their character. An important goal of multicultural education is to promote equality and fair treatment for all groups (Barber, 2000; Banks, 1997a).

Exploring Multicultural Education

Let's explore some of the dimensions of multicultural education.

What Is Multicultural Education?   **Multicultural education** *is education that values diversity and includes the perspectives of a variety of cultural groups on a regular basis.* Multicultural education is controversial. Its enthusiasts believe that children of color should be empowered and that multicultural education

Multicultural Education Resources

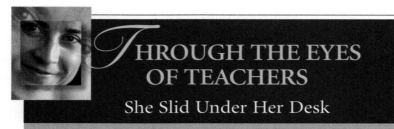

THROUGH THE EYES OF TEACHERS

She Slid Under Her Desk

After moving from Haiti to New York City in 1969, I graduated from Hunter College with a B.S. in accounting and worked in that field from 1974 to 1991. When I moved to Florida in that year I was immediately approached by some Haitian educators who asked me to join their field because of a dire need for Haitian educators there.

I told them I was not a teacher, but at their insistence I accepted work as a substitute teacher at an elementary school in Fort Lauderdale. As I was looking at the student roster in class, I noticed the last name Louis. I called out the child's name and asked her if she was Haitian, unaware at that time of the stigma attached to my nationality in South Florida. She became so embarrassed by my question that she literally slid under her desk and disappeared. Later she told me one-on-one, "You're not supposed to say that you are Haitian around here."

That is when I understood the immensity of the problem, and that is why I became a teacher. For the past seven years I have been teaching ESOL (English for Speakers of Other Languages) in addition to other middle school subjects. I believe that I've made a difference in the lives of my students by giving them a sense of pride in their heritage and by providing a learning environment in which they can grow.

I believe that to achieve equality, the educational system must recognize the ethnic background and gender of the student. The student's home culture isn't to be discarded, but used instead as a teaching tool. What works best in improving children's inter-ethnic problems is to confront the problems head-on. I create actual lessons teaching empathy and tolerance towards others. I have used my free time to go to mainstreamed teachers' rooms to talk to American students about human rights and prejudice toward students of different nationalities and cultures, in particular the Haitian students who are continually harassed and sometimes beaten in school.

Try always to know your students as human beings, and they will surely open up to you and learn. Tell them that you believe in them. If you believe they can achieve, they will.

Daniel Arnoux
ESOL Teacher
Lauderhill Middle Community School
Broward, Florida

benefits all students. Its critics argue that all children should be taught a common core of cultural values, especially White Anglo-Protestant values (Spring, 1998). Advocates of multicultural education don't oppose teaching a core of such values as long as it does not make up the entire curriculum.

Empowering Students   The term **empowerment** *refers to providing people with the intellectual and coping skills to succeed and make this a more just world.* In the 1960s to 1980s, multicultural education was concerned with empowering students and better representing minority and cultural groups in curricula and textbooks. Empowerment continues to be an important theme of multicultural education today. In this view, schools should give students the opportunity to learn about the experiences, struggles, and visions of many different ethnic and cultural groups (Banks, 1997a). The hope is that this will raise minority students' self-esteem, reduce prejudice, and provide more-equal educational opportunities. The hope also is that it will help White students become more tolerant toward minority groups and that both White students and students of color will develop multiple perspectives within their curricula.

Sonia Nieto (1992), a Puerto Rican who grew up in New York City, says that her education made her feel that her cultural background was somehow deficient. She provides the following recommendations:

- *The school curriculum should be openly antiracist and antidiscriminatory.* Students should feel free to discuss issues of ethnicity and discrimination.
- *Multicultural education should be a part of every student's education.* This includes having all students become bilingual and study different cultural perspectives. Multicultural education should be reflected everywhere in the school, including bulletin boards, lunch rooms, and assemblies.
- *Students should be trained to be more conscious of culture.* This involves getting students to be more skillful at analyzing culture and more aware of the historical, political, and social factors that shape their views of culture and ethnicity. The hope is that such critical examination will motivate students to work for political and economic justice.

Teaching a Core of White Anglo-Protestant Values   In the 1980s and 1990s, some educators opposed the emphasis on including information about diverse ethnic groups in the curriculum. They also opposed ethnocentric education that emphasized a particular non-White minority group. In one proposal, Arthur Schlesinger (1991) argued that all students should be taught a set of core values that, he claimed, are derived from the White Anglo-Protestant tradition. These core values include mutual respect, individual rights, and tolerance of differences. Critics of Schlesinger's view point out that these are not peculiarly White Anglo-Protestant values but values that most ethnic and religious groups in America endorse. Indeed, multicultural education includes the Western tradition.

In another proposal, E. D. Hirsch (1987) stressed that all students should be taught a common core of cultural knowledge to ensure that they become "culturally literate." He listed a number of names, phrases, dates, and concepts that he believes students at different grade levels should know. Hirsch claims that a program of cultural literacy based on his terms and concepts will help students from impoverished backgrounds and immigrants adapt to mainstream American culture. Although Hirsch's early presentation of his ideas did not address cultural differences or social injustice, he recently updated his work to make it more multicultural.

Exploring
Multicultural Education

The Multicultural Classroom

A number of strategies and programs are available to improve relations among children from different ethnic groups. To begin, we will discuss one of the most powerful strategies.

The Jigsaw Classroom

When social psychologist Eliot Aronson was a professor at the University of Texas at Austin, the school system contacted him for ideas to reduce the increasing racial tension in classrooms. Aronson (1986) developed the concept of the **jigsaw classroom,** *which involves having students from different cultural backgrounds cooperate by doing different parts of a project to reach a common goal.* Aronson used the term *jigsaw* because he saw the technique as much like a group of students cooperating to put different pieces together to complete a jigsaw puzzle.

How might this work? Consider a class of students, some White, some African American, some Latino, some Native American, and some Asian American. The lesson concerns the life of Joseph Pulitzer. The class might be broken up into groups of six students each, with the groups being as equally mixed as possible in terms of ethnic composition and achievement level. The lesson about Pulitzer's life is divided into six parts, and one part is assigned to each member of each six-person group. The parts might be passages from Pulitzer's biography, such as how the Pulitzer family came to the United States, Pulitzer's childhood, his early work, and so on. All students in each group are given an allotted time to study their parts. Then the groups meet, and each member works to teach her or his part to the group. Learning depends on the students' interdependence and cooperation in reaching the same goal. We will say much more about cooperative learning in chapter 9.

Sometimes the jigsaw classroom strategy is described as creating a superordinate goal or common task for students. Team sports, drama productions, and music performances are additional examples of contexts in which students cooperatively and often very enthusiastically participate to reach a superordinate goal.

Positive Personal Contact with Others from Different Cultural Backgrounds

Contact by itself does not do the job of improving relationships. For example, busing ethnic minority students to predominantly White schools, or vice versa, has not reduced prejudice or improved interethnic relations (Minuchin & Shapiro, 1983). What matters is what happens after students arrive at a school. In one comprehensive study of more than 5,000 fifth-graders and 4,000 tenth-graders, multiethnic curricula projects that focused on ethnic issues, mixed work groups, and supportive teachers and principals all helped improve students' interethnic relations (Forehand, Ragosta, & Rock, 1976).

Positive personal contact that involves sharing doubts, hopes, ambitions, and much more is one way to improve interethnic relations.

TECHNOLOGY AND EDUCATION
The Global Lab and Other Technology Connections with Students Around the World

Traditionally, students have learned within the walls of their classroom and interacted with their teacher and other students in the class. With advances in telecommunications, students can learn from and with teachers and students around the world. The teachers and students might be from schools in such diverse locations as Warsaw, Tokyo, Istanbul, and a small village in Israel.

The Global Laboratory Project is one example that has capitalized on advances in telecommunications (Schrum & Berenfeld, 1997). It consists of science investigations that involve environmental monitoring, sharing data via telecommunication hookups, and placing local findings in a global context. In an initial telecommunications meeting, students introduced themselves and described their schools, communities, and study locations. The locations included Moscow, Russia; Warsaw, Poland; Kenosha, Wisconsin; San Antonio, Texas; Pueblo, Colorado; and Aiken, South Carolina. This initial phase was designed to help students develop a sense of community and become familiar with their collaborators from around the world. As their data collection and evaluation evolved, students continued to communicate with their peers worldwide and to learn more not only about science but also about the global community.

Classrooms or schools also can use fax machines to link students from around the country and world (Cushner, McClelland, & Safford, 1996). Fax machines transfer artwork, poetry, essays, and other materials to other students in locations as diverse as Europe, Asia, Africa, and South America. Students also can communicate the same day with pen pals through e-mail, where once it took weeks for a letter to reach someone in a faraway place. An increasing number of schools also use videotelephone technology in foreign language instruction. Instead of simulating a French café in a typical French language class, American students might talk with French students who have placed a videotelephone in a French café in their country.

Such global technology projects can go a long way toward reducing American students' ethnocentric beliefs. The active building of connections around the world through telecommunications gives students the opportunity to experience others' perspectives, better understand other cultures, and reduce prejudice.

Global technology projects can help students become less ethnocentric.

Relations improve when students talk with each other about their personal worries, successes, failures, coping strategies, interests, and so on. When students reveal personal information about themselves, they are more likely to be perceived as individuals than simply as members of a group. Sharing personal information frequently produces this discovery: People from different backgrounds share many of the same hopes, worries, and feelings. Sharing personal information can help break down in-group/out-group and we/they barriers.

Perspective Taking Exercises and activities that help students see other people's perspectives can improve interethnic relations. In one exercise, students learn certain proper behaviors of two distinct cultural groups (Shirts, 1977). Subsequently, the two groups interact with each other in accordance with those behaviors. As a result, they experience feelings of anxiety and apprehension. The exercise is designed to help students understand the culture shock that comes from being in a cultural setting with people who behave in ways that are very different from what one is used to. Students also can be encouraged to write stories or act out plays that involve prejudice or discrimination. In this way, students "step into the shoes" of students who are culturally different from themselves and feel what it is like to not be treated as an equal (Cushner, McClelland, & Safford, 1996).

In language arts, students can study familiar stories and be asked to take the perspective of different characters (Prutzman & Johnson, 1997). A retelling of the familiar story "Little Red Riding Hood" from the perspective of the wolf is *The Maligned Wolf* (Fearn, 1972). As students read the story, they become aware of biases against various groups, such as wolves, and the perspectives of different characters within the same story. Students also can be asked to rewrite the story from the perspectives of other characters, such as the grandmother. They also can be asked to retell other stories from different points of view, such as the story of "Cinderella" from the stepmother's view.

Studying people from different parts of the world also encourages students to understand different perspectives (Mazurek, Winzer, & Majorek, 2000). In social studies, students can be asked why people in certain cultures have customs different from their own. Teachers can also encourage students to read books on many different cultures. To read further about bringing the global community into American students' classrooms, see Technology and Education.

An increasing number of Internet websites allow students to communicate with students in other parts of the United States and around the world. Among these projects are the Global Lab Project (discussed in the Technology and Education box), the Global Schoolhouse Project, the Jason Project, and Global Show-n-Tell. You can access these student global communication projects by visiting the Santrock *Educational Psychology* website and clicking on the Global Internet Communication entry for chapter 5.

**The Global Lab Project
Global Internet Communication**

Critical Thinking and Emotional Intelligence   Students who learn to think deeply and critically about interethnic relations are likely to decrease their prejudice and stereotyping of others (Cushner, McClelland, & Safford, 2000). Students who think in narrow ways are often prejudiced. However, when students learn to ask questions, think first about issues rather than respond automatically, and delay judgment until more complete information is available, they become less prejudiced.

Emotional intelligence benefits interethnic relations. Recall from chapter 3 that being emotionally intelligent means having emotional self-awareness, managing your emotions, reading emotions, and handling relationships ◀▥ page 112. Consider how the following emotionally intelligent skills can help students to improve their relations with diverse others: understanding the causes of one's feelings, being good at managing one's own anger, being good at listening to what other people are saying, and being motivated to share and cooperate.

Reducing Bias   Louise Derman-Sparks and the Anti-Bias Curriculum Task Force (1989) created a number of tools to help young children reduce, handle, or even eliminate their biases. The anti-bias curriculum argues that although differences are good, discriminating against someone is not. It encourages teachers to confront troublesome bias issues rather than covering them up.

These are some of the anti-bias strategies recommended for teachers:

- Create an anti-bias classroom environment by displaying images of children from various ethnic and cultural groups. The books you select for students also should reflect this diversity.
- Select play materials, art materials, and classroom activities that encourage ethnic and cultural understanding. Use dramatic play to illustrate nonstereotypic roles and families from diverse backgrounds.
- Use the "persona" dolls. The 16 dolls represent diverse ethnic and cultural backgrounds. Each doll is given a life story designed to reduce bias.

THROUGH THE EYES OF TEACHERS

Finding Parallels

The meatpacking industry of Nebraska has brought many Latinos to our area. I find my students have a definite negative attitude toward them, usually as a result of their parents' influence. My effort at helping them realize their prejudice is to teach David Guterson's *Snow Falling on Cedars* to senior level students. Though the fictional novel takes place off Puget Sound and deals with Japanese immigrants during World War II, I take students through discussion questions that provide striking similarity to their prejudice against Latinos. I have no way to measure the degree of their prejudice, but I feel that education and awareness are key steps in decreasing the problem.

Kathy Fuchser
English and Journalism Teacher
St. Francis High School
Humphrey, Nebraska

- Help students resist stereotyping and discriminating against others. Make it a firm rule that no aspect of a child's or an adult's identity is an acceptable target of teasing or exclusion.
- Participate in consciousness-raising activities to better understand your cultural views and deal with any stereotypes or biases you might have.
- Establish genuine parent/teacher dialogue that opens up discussion of each other's views; exchange information on how children develop prejudices; and inform parents about the anti-bias curriculum.

Increasing Tolerance The "Teaching Tolerance Project" provides schools with resources and materials to improve intercultural understanding and relationships between White children and children of color (Heller & Hawkins, 1994). The biannual magazine *Teaching Tolerance* is distributed to every public and private school in the United States (you can obtain a free copy by contacting: Teaching Tolerance, 400 Washington Ave., Birmingham, AL 36104). The magazine's purpose is to share views on and provide resources for teaching tolerance. For elementary school teachers, the "Different and Same" videos and materials can help children become more tolerant (they are available from Family Communications, Pittsburgh, Pennsylvania).

The Comer School
Development Program
Multicultural Pavilion

James Comer (left) *is shown with some inner-city African American students who attend a school where Comer has implemented his community team approach.*

TEACHING STRATEGIES
For Multicultural Education

We already have discussed many ideas that will benefit children's relations with people who are from ethnic and cultural backgrounds different from their own. Further guidelines for multicultural teaching include these recommendations from leading multicultural education expert James Banks (1997a):

1. *Become more sensitive to racist content in materials and classroom interactions.* A good source for learning more about racism is Paul Kivel's (1995) book *Uprooting Racism.*
2. *Learn more about different ethnic groups.* Read at least one major book on the history and culture of American ethnic groups. One book that includes historical descriptions of these groups is Banks' (1997b) *Teaching Strategies for Ethnic Studies.*
3. *Be sensitive to your students' ethnic attitudes and don't accept the belief that "kids do not see colors."* Respond to students' cultural views in sensitive ways.
4. *Use trade books, films, videotapes, and recordings to portray ethnic perspectives.* Banks' (1997b) book *Teaching Strategies for Ethnic Studies* describes a number of these.
5. *Be sensitive to the developmental needs of your students when you select various cultural materials.* In early childhood and elementary school classrooms, make the learning experience specific and concrete. Banks believes that fiction and biographies are especially good choices for introducing cultural concepts to these students. Banks recommends that students at these levels can study such concepts as similarities, differences, prejudice, and discrimination but are not developmentally ready to study concepts like racism and oppression.
6. *View students positively regardless of their ethnicity.* All students learn best when their teachers have high achievement expectations for them and support their learning efforts.
7. *Recognize that most parents, regardless of their ethnicity, are interested in their children's education and want them to succeed in school.* However, understand that many parents of color have mixed feelings about schools because of their own experiences with discrimination. Think of positive ways to get parents of color more involved in their children's education and view them as partners in their children's learning.

The School and Community as a Team   Yale psychiatrist James Comer (1988; Comer & others, 1996) believes that a community team approach is the best way to educate children. Three important aspects of the Comer Project for Change are (1) a governance and management team that develops a comprehensive school plan, assessment strategy, and staff development program; (2) a mental health or school support team; and (3) a parents' program (Goldberg, 1997). The Comer program emphasizes no-fault (the focus should be on solving problems, not blaming), no decisions except by consensus, and no paralysis (that is, no naysayer can stand in the way of a strong majority decision). Comer believes the entire school community should have a cooperative rather than an adversarial attitude. The Comer program is currently operating in more than 600 schools in 82 school districts in 26 states.

One of the first schools to implement the Comer approach was the Martin Luther King, Jr., Elementary School in New Haven, Connecticut. When the Comer program began there, its students were an average of 19 months below grade level in language arts and 18 months below grade level in math. After 10 years of the Comer program,

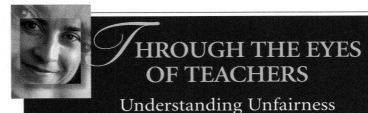

THROUGH THE EYES OF TEACHERS
Understanding Unfairness

I use literature to help students understand other people and how they have sometimes been treated unfairly. During January I focus on the southeastern United States in our social studies class and integrate language arts by having the whole class read *Meet Addy* and *Mississippi Bridge.* On Martin Luther King Day we read his biography. . . . We get a little overview of how the Jews were treated in World War II through *Number the Stars.* We also get interested in learning more about Anne Frank. When the children read how these minorities were treated, they understand more fully that all people are more similar to them than different.

Marlene Wendler
Fourth-Grade Teacher
St. Paul's Lutheran School
New Ulm, Minnesota

the students' national achievement test scores were at grade level, and after 15 years they were 12 months above grade level. Even though no socioeconomic changes had taken place in this predominantly African American, low-income, inner-city area over this period, school absenteeism dropped dramatically, serious behavior problems decreased, parent participation increased substantially, and staff turnover was almost nil.

At this point, we have studied many ideas about multicultural education. A review of these ideas is presented in summary table 5.3.

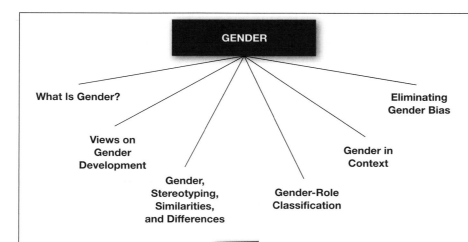

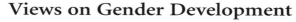

Gender

A well-known nineteenth-century nursery rhyme by J. O. Halliwell goes like this:

> What are little boys made of?
>   Frogs and snails and puppy dogs' tails.
> What are little girls made of?
>   Sugar and spice and all that's nice.

What differences does the rhyme imply exist between boys and girls? Are any of them valid? Issues of real and perceived gender differences can be vital to effective teaching.

What Is Gender?

Gender *refers to the sociocultural dimensions of being female or male.* Gender is distinguished from **sex,** *which involves the biological dimensions of being female or male.* **Gender roles** *are the social expectations that prescribe how males and females should think, act, and feel.*

Views on Gender Development

There are various ways to view gender development. Some stress biological factors in the behavior of males and females, others emphasize social influences, others emphasize cognitive factors.

Gender Resources

Biological Views   In humans the 23rd pair of chromosomes (the sex chromosomes) determine whether the fetus is a female (XX) or a male (XY). No one denies the presence of genetic, biochemical, and anatomical differences between the sexes. Even gender experts with a strong environmental orientation acknowledge that girls and boys are treated differently because of their physical differences and their different roles in reproduction. What is at issue is the directness or indirectness of biological and environmental influences. For example, androgen is the predominant sex hormone in males. If a high androgen level directly influences brain functioning, which in turn increases some behavior like aggression or activity level, then the biological effect is direct. If a child's high androgen level produces strong muscle development, which in turn causes others to expect the child to be a good athlete and, in turn, leads the child to participate in sports, then the biological effect on behavior is more indirect.

Some biological approaches address differences in the brains of females and males (Eisenberg, Martin, & Fabes, 1996). One approach focuses on differences between females and males in the corpus callosum, the massive band of fibers that connects the brain's two hemispheres. Other approaches emphasize variations in the

$\mathcal{S}$UMMARY $\mathcal{T}$ABLE 5.3
Multicultural Education

Concept	Processes/ Related Ideas	Characteristics/Description
Exploring Multicultural Education	Its Nature and Controversy	• Multicultural education is education that values diversity and includes the perspectives of various cultural groups on a regular basis. • Multicultural education is controversial. On the one side of the debate are enthusiasts who believe that children of color should be empowered. • On the other side are people who argue that all children should be taught a common core of cultural values, especially White Anglo-Protestant values.
	Empowering Students	• *Empowerment* refers to providing people with the intellectual and coping skills to succeed and make this a more just world. • Empowerment is an important aspect of multicultural education today. It involves giving students the opportunity to learn about the experiences, struggles, and visions of many different ethnic and cultural groups. • The hope is that empowerment will raise minority students' self esteem, reduce prejudice, and provide more-equal educational opportunities.
	Teaching a Core of White Anglo-Protestant Values	• Proponents of this strategy argue that such values as mutual respect, individual rights, and tolerance of differences are White Anglo-Protestant values and should be taught to all children. • Critics argue that these are not peculiarly White Anglo-Protestant values but simply Western tradition. • Hirsch argued that students should be taught a common core of cultural knowledge to ensure that they become "culturally literate."
The Multicultural Classroom	The Jigsaw Classroom	• This involves having students from different cultural backgrounds cooperate by doing different parts of a project to reach a common goal.
	Positive Contact with Others from Different Cultural Backgrounds	• Mere contact alone between ethnic groups does not improve interethnic relations. Relations improve when students talk with each other about their worries, successes, failures, coping strategies, interests, and so on.
	Perspective Taking	• Exercises and activities that help students see other people's perspectives can improve interethnic relations.
	Critical Thinking and Emotional Intelligence	• Students who think deeply and critically about interethnic relations are likely to decrease their prejudice and stereotyping of others. • Interethnic relations can be improved by helping students be emotionally intelligent (which involves understanding the causes of their feelings, managing their anger, being good at listening to what others say, and being motivated to share and cooperate).
	Reducing Bias	• An anti-bias curriculum encourages teachers to confront troublesome bias issues rather than cover them up.
	Increasing Tolerance	• Resources and materials are available to improve students' tolerance.
	The School and Community as a Team	• Comer's program is especially good at uniting the school and community to improve interethnic relations.

left and right hemispheres of the brains of males and females. At present, these are controversial views. What we do know is that the brains of females and males are far more similar than they are different. We also know that the brain has considerable plasticity and that experiences can modify its growth.

In sum, biology is not destiny when gender attitudes and behavior are at issue. Children's socialization experiences matter a great deal ◀▥ page 40.

Fathers and Sons

Socialization Views   Both identification and social learning theories describe social experiences that influence children's gender development. **Identification theory** *stems from Freud's view that the preschool child develops a sexual attraction to the opposite-sex parent. Then, by about 5 or 6 years of age, the child renounces this attraction because of anxious feelings. Subsequently the child identifies with the same-sex parent, unconsciously adopting the same-sex parent's characteristics.* Today, most gender experts do not believe gender development proceeds in this way. Children become gender-typed much earlier than 5 or 6 years of age. Males typically become masculine and females feminine even when the same-sex parent is not around.

The **social learning theory of gender** *emphasizes that children's gender development occurs through observation and imitation of gender behavior, as well as through reinforcement and punishment of gender behavior.* Parents often use rewards and punishments to teach their daughters to be feminine ("Karen, you are being a good girl when you play gently with your doll") and masculine ("Keith, a big boy like you is not supposed to cry").

Many parents encourage boys and girls to engage in different types of play and activities. Girls are more likely to be given dolls and, when old enough, are more likely to be assigned babysitting duties. Girls are encouraged to be more nurturant than boys. Fathers are more likely to engage in aggressive play with their sons than with their daughters. Parents allow their adolescent sons to have more freedom than their adolescent daughters.

Peers also extensively reward and punish gender-related behavior. After extensive observations of elementary school classrooms, two researchers characterized the play settings as "gender school" (Luria & Herzog, 1985). In elementary school, boys usually hang out with boys and girls with girls. It is easier for "tomboy" girls to join boys' groups than for "feminine" boys to join girls' groups, because of our society's greater sex-typing pressure on boys. Developmental psychologist Eleanor Maccoby (1997), who has studied gender for a number of decades, believes that peers play an especially important gender-socializing role, teaching each other what is acceptable and unacceptable gender behavior.

Television also has a gender-socializing role, portraying females and males in particular gender roles. Even with the onset of more diverse programming in recent years, researchers still find that television presents males as more competent than females (Wroblewski & Huston, 1987). In one analysis of rap videos on TV, teenage girls were primarily shown as concerned with dating, shopping, and their appearance (Campbell, 1988). They were rarely depicted as interested in school or career plans. Attractive girls were mainly pictured as "airheads," unattractive girls as intelligent. Schools and teachers also have gender-socializing influences on boys and girls. We will discuss these influences later in the chapter.

Cognitive Views   Two cognitive views on gender are (1) cognitive developmental theory and (2) gender schema theory. According to the **cognitive developmental theory of gender,** *children's gender typing occurs after they have developed a concept of gender.* Once they consistently conceive of themselves as female or male, children organize their world on the basis of gender. Initially developed by Lawrence Kohlberg (1966) (whose theory of moral development you read about in chapter 3), this theory argues that gender development proceeds this way: "I am a girl. I want to do girl things. Therefore, the opportunity to do girl things is rewarding." Kohlberg believes it is not until children reach Piaget's concrete operational stage of

As reflected in this tug-of-war battle between boys and girls, the playground in elementary school is like going to "gender school." Elementary school children show a clear preference for being with and liking same-sex peers. Eleanor Maccoby has studied children's gender development for many years. She believes peers play especially strong roles in socializing each other about gender roles.

thinking at about 6 or 7 years of age that they understand gender constancy—that a male is still a male regardless of whether he wears pants or a skirt or whether his hair is long or short (Tavris & Wade, 1984).

Gender schema theory *states that an individual's attention and behavior are guided by an internal motivation to conform to gender-based sociocultural standards and stereotypes.* A gender schema is a cognitive structure, or network of associations, that organizes and guides an individual's perceptions along gender lines. Gender schema theory suggests that "gender-typing" occurs when children are ready to encode and organize information along the lines of what is considered appropriate or typical for females and males in a society (Rodgers, 2000).

At this point we have discussed a number of ideas about what gender is and views on gender development. A review of these ideas is presented in summary table 5.4. Next, we will continue our exploration of gender, starting with gender stereotyping, similarities, and differences.

Gender Stereotyping, Similarities, and Differences

How pervasive is gender stereotyping? What are the real differences between boys and girls?

Gender Stereotyping   **Gender stereotypes** *are broad categories that reflect impressions and beliefs about what behavior is appropriate for females and males.* All stereotypes, whether they relate to gender, ethnicity, or other categories, refer to an image of what the typical member of a category is like. Many stereotypes are so general they are ambiguous. Consider the categories of "masculine" and "feminine." Diverse behaviors can be assigned to each category, such as scoring a touchdown or growing facial hair for "masculine," playing with dolls or wearing lipstick for "feminine." And the behaviors that make up a category can be modified in the face

SUMMARY TABLE 5.4
What Gender Is, and Views on Gender Development

Concept	Processes/ Related Ideas	Characteristics/Description
What Is Gender?	Its Nature	• *Gender* refers to the sociocultural dimension of being female or male, as distinguished from sex, which is the biological dimension of being female or male. • Gender roles are expectations that prescribe how males and females should think, feel, and act.
Views on Gender Development	Biological	• The 23rd pair of chromosomes (the sex chromosomes) determine whether a fetus is female (XX) or male (XY). • At issue is the directness or indirectness of biological effects. • The brains of females and males are far more similar than different. • When students' gender behavior is at issue, biology is not destiny. Socialization matters.
	Socialization	• Two socialization views are identification theory and social learning theory. • Identification theory stems from Freud's view that the family is a crucible for the young child's identification with a same-sex parent. Today, gender experts do not believe that Freud's psychosexual view is the best way to explain children's gender development. • Social learning theory argues that children's gender development occurs through observation of gender models and rewards and punishments for gender-appropriate and gender-inappropriate behavior. • Parents, peers, television, and teachers all are involved in this social learning framework. • Peers especially play a powerful role in rewarding gender-appropriate behavior and punishing gender-inappropriate behavior.
	Cognitive	• Two cognitive views on gender are cognitive developmental theory and gender schema theory. Kohlberg's cognitive developmental theory states that gender-typing occurs after children have developed a concept of gender. • Gender schema theory emphasizes that children develop a cognitive gender schema, a network of associations, that organizes and guides their perceptions along gender lines. These associations are influenced by what is culturally considered appropriate gender behavior.

If you are going to generalize about women, you will find yourself up to here in exceptions.

Dolores Hitchens
American Mystery Writer, 20th Century

of cultural change. At one point in history, muscular development might be thought of as masculine, at another time a more lithe, slender physique might be the paradigm masculine body. Earlier in the twentieth century, being dependent was thought to be an important dimension of femininity, whereas today a much greater emphasis is placed on females' sensitivity to others in relationships. Which behaviors are popularly held to reflect a category also can fluctuate according to socioeconomic circumstances. For example, more low-income than middle-class individuals have a rough-and-tough image of masculinity.

Stereotyping students as "masculine" or "feminine" can have significant consequences. Labeling a male "feminine" or a female "masculine" can diminish their social status and acceptance in groups.

Gender stereotyping changes developmentally. Stereotypic gender beliefs begin to take root during the early childhood years, increase in the early elementary school years, and then decline somewhat in the middle and late elementary school years (Bigler, Liben, & Yekel, 1992). In early adolescence, gender stereotyping might increase again. As their bodies change dramatically during puberty, boys and girls are often confused and concerned about what is happening to them. The safe strategy for boys is to become the very best male possible (that is, "masculine"), and the safe strategy for girls is to become the very best female possible (that is, "feminine"). Thus, gender intensification created by pubertal change can produce greater stereotyping in young adolescents (Galambos & others, 1985).

Stereotypes are often negative and can be wrapped in prejudice and discrimination. **Sexism** *is prejudice and discrimination against an individual because of the person's sex.* A person who says that a woman cannot be a competent engineer is expressing sexism. So is a person who says that a man cannot be a competent early childhood teacher. Later in this chapter, when we discuss gender in the schools, we will describe some strategies for creating a nonsexist classroom.

Exploring Gender Similarities and Differences in Academically Relevant Domains

Many aspects of students' lives can be examined to determine how similar or different girls and boys are (Crawford & Unger, 2000).

Physical Performance   Because physical education is an integral part of U.S. educational systems, it is important to address gender similarities and differences in physical performance (Eisenberg, Martin, & Fabes, 1996). In general, boys outperform girls in athletic skills such as running, throwing, and jumping. In the elementary school years the differences often are not large; they become more dramatic in the middle school years (Smoll & Schutz, 1990). The hormonal changes of puberty result in increased muscle mass for boys and increased body fat for girls. This leads to an advantage for boys in activities related to strength, size, and power. Nonetheless, environmental factors are involved in physical performance even after puberty. Girls are less likely to participate in activities that promote the motor skills necessary to do well in sports (Thomas & Thomas, 1988).

Activity level is another area of physical performance in which gender differences occur. From very early in life, boys are more active than girls are (Eaton & Enns, 1986). In the classroom, this means that boys are more likely than girls to fidget and move around the room, and are less likely to be paying attention. In physical education classes, boys expend more energy through movement than girls do.

Math Skills   On the average, boys perform better at math and this has long been a source of concern (Eisenberg, Martin, & Fabes, 1996). However, the gender difference in math is not uniform across contexts and ages. Boys do better at math related to measurement, science, and sports; girls do better at math that involves such traditional female tasks as cooking and sewing (Linn & Hyde, 1989). And in one study, girls in third grade were better in almost every area of math evaluated (counting, computation, and measurement, for example) (Marshall & Smith, 1987); however, by sixth grade, girls' superior math performance declined and girls had fallen behind boys on verbal math problems and measurement. In a recent study of eighth- and tenth-graders, boys

THROUGH THE EYES OF TEACHERS

Providing Girls with Positive Math Experiences

As a math teacher, I hope I do everything in my power to encourage girls to have more confidence in math. Of course, I want every girl *and* boy in my class to see that they can succeed in math. I do not allow boys to monopolize the answering of questions in my classroom. I call on girls and boys equally and I don't let any student get off the hook by saying "I don't know" or by shrugging their shoulders. I will guide students to a solution.

In one project I assign to my 8th grade algebra students, they have to research a math concept and report about it to the class. I encourage as many students as possible, boys and girls, to research some of the famous female mathematicians. When the girls see how much women had to sacrifice in the name of mathematics years ago, it helps them to see how fortunate their opportunities are today.

Jeri Hall
Mathematics Teacher
Miller Magnet Middle School
Bibb County, Georgia

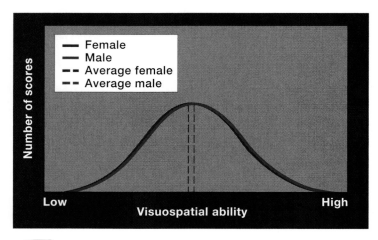

Figure 5.1
Visuospatial Ability of Males and Females

Notice that, although an average male's visuospatial ability is higher than an average female's, the overlap between the sexes is substantial. Not all males have better visuospatial ability than all females—the substantial overlap indicates that, although the average score of males is higher, many females outperform most males on such tasks.

Telementors for Girls

scored higher than girls on science tests, especially among average- and high-ability students (Burkham, Lee, & Smedon, 1997). In science classes that emphasized "hands-on" lab activities, girls, science test scores improved considerably. This suggests the importance of active involvement of students in the science classrooms to promote gender equity.

Another area of math that has been examined for possible gender differences is visuospatial skills, which include being able to mentally rotate objects and determine what they would look like when rotated. These types of skills are important in courses like plane and solid geometry. Some experts argue that if there is a gender difference in visuospatial skills, it is very small. For example, figure 5.1 shows that although the average score on visuospatial skills is higher for males than for females, male and female scores substantially overlap— and many females have higher scores on visuospatial tasks than most males do.

Overall, gender differences in math skills tend to be small. Statements like "Males outperform females in math" should not be read as a claim that all males outperform all females in math. Rather, such statements refer to averages (Hyde & Plant, 1995). And in some recent studies no differences have been found. For example, in the National Assessment of Educational Progress (1996, 1997) study, there were no differences in the average scores of eighth- and twelfth-grade females and males, although in fourth grade the average math score for boys was higher than the average math score for girls.

Many gender experts believe the gender differences in math and science that do exist are due to the experiences that boys and girls have. There are far more male than female math and science models in the culture. Boys take more math and science courses than girls do. And parents have higher expectations for boys' math and science skills. In one study of 1,500 families, parents bought more math and science books and games for their sons than for their daughters, said that boys have more math talent than girls, and commented that boys are better suited to a career in math (Eccles & others, 1991).

"So according to the stereotype, you can put two and two together, but I can read the handwriting on the wall."

Verbal Skills   A major review of gender similarities and differences conducted in the 1970s concluded that girls have better verbal skills than boys do (Maccoby & Jacklin, 1974). However, more recent analyses suggest that there are no differences in girls' and boys' verbal skills. That is, today males score as high as females on the verbal portion of the SAT test. And boys and girls show similar vocabulary, reading skills, and writing achievement.

Relationship Skills   Sociolinguist Deborah Tannen (1990) distinguishes between rapport talk and report talk. **Rapport talk** *is the language of conversation and a way of establishing connections and negotiating relationships.* **Report talk** *is talk that gives information.* Making a speech is an example of report talk. Males hold center stage through such verbal performances as storytelling, joking, and lecturing with information. Females enjoy private talk more and conversation that is relationship-oriented.

Tannen says that boys and girls grow up in different worlds of talk. Parents, siblings, peers, teachers, and others talk to girls and boys differently. The play of boys and girls is different. Boys tend to play in large groups that are hierarchically structured, and their groups usually have a leader who tells the others what to do and how to do it. Boys' games have winners and losers, and boys often argue about who won. Boys often boast of their skill and argue about who is best at what. In contrast, girls are more likely to play in small groups or pairs, and the center of a girl's world is often a best friend. In girls' friendships and peer groups, intimacy is pervasive. Turn-taking is more characteristic of girls' games than boys' games. And much of the time, girls simply like to sit and talk with each other, concerned more about being liked by others than jockeying for status in some obvious way.

In sum, Tannen and other gender experts, such as Carol Gilligan (1982, 1998), whose ideas you read about in chapter 3, believe that girls are more relationship-oriented than boys are. They also believe that this relationship orientation should be prized as being more important than our culture currently takes it to be. The clear implication is for teachers to value and support children's relationship skills in the classroom.

Aggression and Self-Regulation   One of the most consistent gender differences is that boys are more physically aggressive than girls. The difference is especially pronounced when children are provoked, and this difference occurs across all cultures and appears very early in children's development. Both biological and environmental factors have been proposed to account for gender differences in physical aggression. Biological factors include heredity and hormones; environmental factors include cultural expectations, adult and peer models, and the rewarding of physical aggression in boys. When verbal aggression is examined, gender differences often disappear (Eagly & Steffen, 1986).

An important skill is to be able to regulate and control one's emotions and behavior. Males usually show less self-regulation than females (Eisenberg, Martin, & Fabes, 1996). And this low self-control can translate into behavioral problems. In one study, children's low self-regulation was linked with greater aggression, teasing others, overreaction to frustration, low cooperation, and inability to delay gratification (Block & Block, 1980).

Gender Controversy   The previous sections revealed some substantial differences in physical abilities, aggression and self-regulation, and relationship skills, but small or nonexistent differences in areas such as math and verbal skills. Controversy swirls about such similarities and differences. Alice Eagly (1996, 2000) argues that the belief that gender differences are small or nonexistent is rooted in the feminist commitment to gender similarity and seen as a route to political equality. Many feminists fear that gender differences will be interpreted as deficiencies on the part of females and be seen as biologically based. They argue that such conclusions could revive traditional stereotypes that females are innately inferior to males (Unger & Crawford, 1996). Eagly responds that a large body of research on gender now exists and reveals stronger gender differences than feminists acknowledge. This controversy is evidence that negotiating the science and politics of gender is not an easy task.

Gender-Role Classification

Let's explore what gender-role classification is and then examine some contextual influences on it.

What Is Gender-Role Classification?
The concept of gender-role classification involves categorization of persons in terms of personality traits. In the past, a well-adjusted boy was supposed to be independent, aggressive, and powerful. A well-adjusted female was supposed to be dependent, nurturant, and uninterested in power. Masculine characteristics were considered to be healthy and good by society, feminine characteristics were considered undesirable.

In the 1970s, as more females and males began to express open dissatisfaction with the burdens imposed by rigid gender expectations, alternatives to femininity and masculinity were proposed. Instead of restricting masculinity to male competency and femininity to female competency, it was proposed that individuals could have both "masculine" and "feminine" traits. This thinking led to the development of the concept of **androgyny,** *which refers to the presence of desirable masculine and feminine characteristics in the same person* (Bem, 1977; Spence & Helmreich, 1978). The androgynous boy might be assertive ("masculine") and nurturant ("feminine"). The androgynous girl might be powerful ("masculine") and sensitive to others' feelings ("feminine").

Measures have been developed to assess androgyny. One of the most widely used measures is the Bem Sex-Role Inventory. To see whether your gender-role classification is masculine, feminine, or androgynous, complete Self-Assessment 5.1.

Gender experts such as Sandra Bem argue that androgynous individuals are more flexible, competent, and mentally healthy than their masculine or feminine counterparts. To some degree, though, which gender-role classification is "best" depends on the context. For example, feminine orientations might be more desirable in close relationships because of the expressive nature of close relationships, and masculine orientations might be more desirable in traditional academic and work settings because of the achievement demands in these contexts.

Male Issues

Of special concern are adolescent boys who adopt a strong masculine role. Researchers have found that high-masculinity adolescent boys often engage in problem behaviors, such as delinquency, drug abuse, and unprotected sexual intercourse (Pleck, 1995). They present themselves as virile, macho, and aggressive, and often do poorly in school. Too many adolescent males base their manhood on the caliber of gun they carry or the number of children they have fathered (Sullivan, 1991).

Androgyny and Education
Can and should androgyny be taught to students? In general, it is easier to teach androgyny to girls than to boys, and it is easier to teach it before the middle school grades. For example, in one study a gender curriculum was put in place for one year in the kindergarten, fifth, and ninth grades (Guttentag & Bray, 1976). It involved books, discussion materials, and classroom exercises with an androgynous bent. The program was most successful with the fifth-graders, least successful with the ninth-graders. The ninth-graders, especially the boys, showed a boomerang effect—more traditional gender-role attitudes after the year of androgynous instruction than before it.

Despite such mixed findings, the advocates of androgyny programs believe that traditional sex-typing is harmful for all students and especially has prevented many girls from experiencing equal opportunity. The detractors argue that androgynous educational programs are too value-laden and ignore the diversity of gender roles in our society.

SELF-ASSESSMENT 5.1
What Gender-Role Orientation Will I Present to My Students?

The items to the right are from the Bem Sex-Role Inventory. To find out whether your gender-role classification is masculine, feminine, or androgynous, rate yourself on each item from 1 (never or almost never true) to 7 (always or almost always true).

1. self-reliant	1	2	3	4	5	6	7	31. makes decisions easily	1	2	3	4	5	6	7
2. yielding	1	2	3	4	5	6	7	32. compassionate	1	2	3	4	5	6	7
3. helpful	1	2	3	4	5	6	7	33. sincere	1	2	3	4	5	6	7
4. defends own beliefs	1	2	3	4	5	6	7	34. self-sufficient	1	2	3	4	5	6	7
5. cheerful	1	2	3	4	5	6	7	35. eager to soothe hurt feelings	1	2	3	4	5	6	7
6. moody	1	2	3	4	5	6	7	36. conceited	1	2	3	4	5	6	7
7. independent	1	2	3	4	5	6	7	37. dominant	1	2	3	4	5	6	7
8. shy	1	2	3	4	5	6	7	38. soft spoken	1	2	3	4	5	6	7
9. conscientious	1	2	3	4	5	6	7	39. likable	1	2	3	4	5	6	7
10. athletic	1	2	3	4	5	6	7	40. masculine	1	2	3	4	5	6	7
11. affectionate	1	2	3	4	5	6	7	41. warm	1	2	3	4	5	6	7
12. theatrical	1	2	3	4	5	6	7	42. solemn	1	2	3	4	5	6	7
13. assertive	1	2	3	4	5	6	7	43. willing to take a stand	1	2	3	4	5	6	7
14. flatterable	1	2	3	4	5	6	7	44. tender	1	2	3	4	5	6	7
15. happy	1	2	3	4	5	6	7	45. friendly	1	2	3	4	5	6	7
16. strong personality	1	2	3	4	5	6	7	46. aggressive	1	2	3	4	5	6	7
17. loyal	1	2	3	4	5	6	7	47. gullible	1	2	3	4	5	6	7
18. unpredictable	1	2	3	4	5	6	7	48. inefficient	1	2	3	4	5	6	7
19. forceful	1	2	3	4	5	6	7	49. acts as a leader	1	2	3	4	5	6	7
20. feminine	1	2	3	4	5	6	7	50. childlike	1	2	3	4	5	6	7
21. reliable	1	2	3	4	5	6	7	51. adaptable	1	2	3	4	5	6	7
22. analytical	1	2	3	4	5	6	7	52. individualistic	1	2	3	4	5	6	7
23. sympathetic	1	2	3	4	5	6	7	53. does not use harsh language	1	2	3	4	5	6	7
24. jealous	1	2	3	4	5	6	7	54. unsystematic	1	2	3	4	5	6	7
25. has leadership abilities	1	2	3	4	5	6	7	55. competitive	1	2	3	4	5	6	7
26. sensitive to the needs of others	1	2	3	4	5	6	7	56. loves children	1	2	3	4	5	6	7
27. truthful	1	2	3	4	5	6	7	57. tactful	1	2	3	4	5	6	7
28. willing to take risks	1	2	3	4	5	6	7	58. ambitious	1	2	3	4	5	6	7
29. understanding	1	2	3	4	5	6	7	59. gentle	1	2	3	4	5	6	7
30. secretive	1	2	3	4	5	6	7	60. conventional	1	2	3	4	5	6	7

Scoring

Add up your ratings for items 1, 4, 7, 10, 13, 16, 19, 22, 25, 28, 31, 34, 37, 40, 43, 46, 49, 55, and 58. Divide the total by 20. That is your masculinity score.

Add up your ratings for items 2, 5, 8, 11, 14, 17, 20, 23, 26, 29, 32, 35, 38, 41, 44, 47, 50, 53, 56, and 59. Divide the total by 20. That is your femininity score.

Interpretation

If your masculinity score is above 4.9 (the approximate median for the masculinity scale) and your femininity score is above 4.9 (the approximate femininity median), than you would be classified as androgynous on Bem's scale.

Gender-Role Transcendence Some critics of androgyny say enough is enough and that there is too much talk about gender this and gender that. They believe that androgyny is less of a panacea than originally envisioned (Doyle & Paludi, 1997). An alternative is **gender-role transcendence,** *the view that people's competence should be conceptualized in terms of them as persons rather than in terms of their masculinity, femininity, or androgyny* (Pleck, 1983). That is, we should think about ourselves and our students as people, not as masculine, feminine, or androgynous.

To be meek, patient, tactful, modest, honorable, brave, is not to be either manly or womanly, it is to be humane.

Jane Harrison
English Writer, 20th Century

Parents should rear their children to be competent individuals, not masculine, feminine, or androgynous, say the gender-role critics. They believe such gender-role classification leads to too much stereotyping.

Gender In Context

Earlier we said that the concept of gender-role classification involves categorizing people in terms of personality traits. However, recall from our discussion of personality in chapter 4, "Individual Variations," that it is beneficial to think of personality in terms of person-situation interaction rather than personality traits alone.

Helping Behavior and Emotion

To see the importance of also considering gender in context, let's examine helping behavior and emotion. The stereotype is that females are better than males at helping. But it depends on the situation. Females are more likely than males to volunteer their time to help children with personal problems and engage in caregiving behavior. However, in situations where males feel a sense of competence or that involve danger, males are more likely to help (Eagly & Crowley, 1986). For example, a male is more likely than a female to stop and help a person stranded by the roadside with a flat tire.

She is emotional, he is not. That's the master emotional stereotype. However, like helping behavior, emotional differences in males and females depend on the particular emotion involved and the context in which it is displayed (Shields, 1991). Males are more likely to show anger toward strangers, especially male strangers, when they feel they have been challenged. Males also are more likely to turn their anger into aggressive action. Emotional differences between females and males often show up in contexts that highlight social roles and relationships. For example, females are more likely to discuss emotions in terms of relationships. And they are more likely to express fear and sadness.

Culture

The importance of considering gender in context is most apparent when examining what is culturally prescribed behavior for females and males in different countries around the world (Greene, 2000). In the United States there is now more acceptance of androgyny and similarities in male and female behavior, but in many other countries roles have remained gender-specific. For example, in Egypt the division of labor between Egyptian males and females is dramatic. Egyptian males are socialized and schooled to work in the public sphere; females are socialized to remain in the private world of home and child rearing. The Islamic religion that predominates in Egypt dictates that the man's duty is to provide for his family and the woman's is to care for her family and household. Any deviations from this traditional masculine and feminine behavior is severely disapproved of. Likewise, in China, although women have made some strides, the male role is still dominant. Androgynous behavior and gender equity are not what most males in China want to see happen.

Eliminating Gender Bias

How gendered are social interactions between teachers and students? What can teachers do to reduce or eliminate gender bias in their classrooms? ◀▥ page 28.

Gender Equity

Teacher-Student Interaction

Following are some of the ways that teachers and students interact with each other on the basis of gender (Beal, 1994; Sadker & Sadker, 2000; Sadker, Sadker, & Long, 1997):

- In a typical classroom, girls are more compliant, boys more rambunctious. Boys demand more attention, girls are more likely to quietly wait their turn. Teachers are more likely to scold and reprimand boys, as well as send boys to school authorities for disciplinary action. Educators worry that girls' tendency to be compliant and quiet comes at a cost: diminished assertiveness.

- In many classrooms, teachers spend more time watching and interacting with boys while girls work and play quietly on their own. Most teachers don't intentionally favor boys by spending more time with them, yet somehow the classroom frequently ends up with this type of gendered profile.

- Boys get more instruction than girls and more help when they have trouble with a question. Teachers often give boys more time to answer a question, more hints at the correct answer, and further tries if they give the wrong answer.

- Boys are more likely than girls to get lower grades and to be grade repeaters, yet girls are less likely to believe that they will be successful in college work.

What are some of the ways that teachers interact with students on the basis of gender?

- Girls and boys enter first grade with roughly equal levels of self-esteem. Yet by the middle school years, girls' self-esteem is significantly lower than boys' (American Association of University Women, 1992).

- When elementary school children are asked to list what they want to do when they grow up, boys describe more career options than girls do.

Curriculum and Athletics Content

Schools have made considerable progress in reducing sexism and sex stereotyping in books and curriculum materials (Eisenberg, Martin, & Fabes, 1996)—largely in response to Title IX of the Educational Amendment Act of 1972, which states that schools are obligated to ensure equal treatment of females and males. As a result, textbooks and class materials are available that are free of gender bias. Also, schools now offer girls far more opportunities to take vocational educational courses and participate in athletics than was the case when their parents and grandparents went to school. In 1972, 7 percent of high school athletes were girls. Today, that figure has risen to nearly 40 percent. Schools no longer can expel or eliminate services for pregnant adolescents.

Nonetheless, bias still remains at the curricular level. For example, school text adoptions occur infrequently, and therefore many students still are studying gender-biased books.

Sexual Harassment

Sexual harassment occurs in many schools (Bracey, 1997). In a study of eighth- to eleventh-graders by the American Association of University Women (1993), 83 percent of the girls and 60 percent of the boys said that they had been sexually harassed. Girls reported being more severely harassed than boys. Sixteen percent of the students said they had been sexually harassed by a teacher. Examples of harassment by students and teachers in this study included

Sexual Harassment

- sexual comments, jokes, gestures, or looks
- sexual messages about a student on bathroom walls and other places, or sexual rumors spread about the student
- spying on a student who was dressing or showering at school
- flashing or mooning
- comments that a student was a gay or lesbian
- touching, grabbing, or pinching in a sexual manner

*T*EACHING STRATEGIES
For Eliminating Gender Bias

Every student, female or male, deserves an education that is free of gender bias. Here are some strategies for attaining this desirable educational climate (Derman-Sparks & Anti-Bias Curriculum Task Force, 1989; Sadker & Sadker, 1994):

1. *If you are given biased textbooks to use with students, discuss this with your students.* By talking with your students about stereotyping and bias in the texts, you can help them think critically about such important social issues. If these textbooks are not gender-fair, supplement them with other materials that are. Many schools, libraries, and colleges have gender-fair materials that you can use.

2. *Make sure that school activities and exercises are not gender biased.* Assign students projects in which they find articles about nonstereotypical males and females, such as a female engineer or a male early childhood education teacher. Have students create a display of photographs and pictures of women and men performing the same kind of tasks at home and at work. Use the display to talk with students about the tasks that adults do and what the students will be doing when they grow up. Invite people from the community who have nonstereotypical jobs (such as a male flight attendant or a female construction worker) to come to your class and talk with your students.

3. *Be a nonsexist role model as a teacher.* Help students learn new skills and share tasks in a nonsexist manner.

4. *Analyze the seating chart in your classroom and determine whether there are pockets of gender (or ethnicity) segregation.* When your students work in groups, monitor whether the groups are balanced by gender and ethnicity.

5. *Enlist someone to track your questioning and reinforcement patterns with students.* Do this on several occasions to ensure that you are giving equal attention and support to girls and boys.

6. *Use nonbiased language.* Don't use the pronoun *he* to refer to inanimate objects or unspecified persons. Replace words like *fireman, policeman,* and *mailman* with words like *firefighter, police officer,* and *letter carrier.* To improve your use of nonsexist language, consult *The Non-Sexist Word Finder: A dictionary of gender-free usage* (Maggio, 1987). Also ask students to suggest fair terminology (Wellhousen, 1996).

7. *Keep up-to-date on sex equity in education.* Read professional journals on this topic. Be aware of your own rights as a female or male, and don't stand for sexual inequity and discrimination.

- intentionally brushing up against a student in a sexual way
- pulling a student's clothing off or down
- blocking way or cornering a student in a sexual way
- being forced to kiss someone, or do something sexual other than kissing

The Office for Civil Rights of the U.S. Department of Education recently published a 40-page policy guide on sexual harassment. In this guide, a distinction is made between quid pro quo and hostile environment sexual harassment (Chmielewski, 1997). **Quid pro quo sexual harassment** *occurs when a school employee threatens to base an educational decision (such as a grade) on a student's submission to unwelcome sexual conduct.* For example, a teacher gives a student an A for allowing the teacher's sexual advances, or the teacher gives the student an F for resisting the teacher's approaches. **Hostile environment sexual harassment** *occurs when students are subjected to unwelcome sexual conduct that is so severe, persistent, or pervasive that it limits the students' ability to benefit from their education.* Such a hostile environment is usually created by a series of incidents, such as repeated sexual overtures.

Sexual harassment is a form of power and dominance of one person over another, which can result in harmful consequences for the victim. Sexual harassment can be especially damaging when the perpetrators are teachers and other adults who have considerable power and authority over students (Lee & others, 1995). As a society, we need to be less tolerant of sexual harassment (Firpo-Triplett, 1997).

At this point we have discussed many further ideas about gender. A review of these ideas is presented in summary table 5.5. In the next chapter, we will continue our exploration of individual variations by studying learners who are exceptional.

THROUGH THE EYES OF TEACHERS
The Inclusive Quilt

Judy Logan has taught language arts and social studies for many years in San Francisco. Following is her description of the inclusive quilt project.

In my 25 years of teaching middle school, one of my goals has been for my classroom to be a blend of some of the things I know and some of the things my students know. The quilt experience serves as an example. . . . My idea was to have the students feel connected not only to women in the fields of science, politics, art, social reform, music, sports, literature, journalism, space, law, civil rights, education, humor, etc., but also to the women in their own families.

I put a big piece of butcher paper on the blackboard, with the word *Inclusive* at the top, and asked the students to develop a list of what was needed to make our quilt truly inclusive. Hands popped up, and students volunteered categories first. We should have women in medicine. Sports. Civil Rights. The list grew.

What else? How else can we make this quilt inclusive? What else do we know about diversity? Hands popped up again to create a second list. We should have Native American women. European American women. Latino women. Asian American women. Lesbian women. Again, our list grew. . . . We began to brainstorm a third list of individual women who were potential subjects for quilt squares. We created a long list of possibilities like Nancy Reagan, Jackie Kennedy, and Martha Washington, who did not end up on the final quilt itself, because the students decided they didn't want to have a lot of presidents' wives on the quilt. They ended up honoring Eleanor

Roosevelt and Abigail Adams, who fit other categories on our list, such as social reform. . . .

Seventh and eighth graders, who are not officially part of this sixth grade core assignment, began to hear about the quilt and volunteer to join us. They come in at lunch time. "Can we do a patch, too?" Yes . . . "Mrs. Logan, can I do you?" Yes, I would be honored. Frankie, an eighth grader, asks if she can do herself as a Future Woman. What a good idea I reply, and give her a blank patch. . . .

I give some thought to whom I want to honor on my patch. I decide to honor Brenda Collins, who is also named Eagle Woman. She is a member of the Bird Clan of the Cherokee Nation. She is a medicine woman, the first woman of her clan to get a Ph.D. and a teacher at Santa Rosa Junior College. She is also a friend and mentor. I have heard her speak several times, and I remember her saying that to be an educated Indian woman is like having a foot in each of two canoes, in rapid waters, always balancing two cultures. I decide to put two canoes and rapid water on her patch, with an eagle's wing by one canoe, and her doctoral degree by the other canoe. . . .

The finished quilt is colorful and diverse. No two patches are the same. I have provided the outline, the framework for the assignment, but each participant has created something uniquely their own. . . . A good curriculum is like a poem that follows a particular pattern, but that allows the audience to bring their own experiences to the construction of its meaning. It leaves a corner open for the reader to enter (Logan, 1997, pp. 1–23).

Judy Logan, in front of the inclusive quilt in her classroom.

SUMMARY TABLE 5.5
Exploring Gender

Concept	Processes/ Related Ideas	Characteristics/Description
Gender Stereotyping, Similarities, and Differences	Gender Stereotyping	• Gender stereotypes are broad categories that reflect impressions and beliefs about what behavior is appropriate for females and males. • All stereotypes involve an image of what the typical member of a category is like. • Some gender stereotypes can be harmful for children, especially those that involve sexism (prejudice and discrimination against a person because of the person's sex).
	Exploring Gender Similarities and Differences in Academically Relevant Domains	• We explored gender similarities and differences in physical performance, math skills, verbal skills, relationship skills (rapport and report talk), and aggression/self-regulation. • In some cases, gender differences are substantial (as in physical performance, aggression, and relationship skills); in others they are small or nonexistent (as in math and verbal skills). • Today, controversy still swirls about how common or rare such physical differences really are.
Gender-Role Classification	What Is It?	• This focuses on how masculine, feminine, or androgynous an individual is. In the past, competent males were supposed to be masculine (powerful, for example), females feminine (nurturant, for example). • The 1970s brought the concept of androgyny, the idea that the most competent individuals have both masculine and feminine positive characteristics. • A special concern involves adolescents who adopt a strong masculine role.
	Androgyny and Education	• Programs that have tried to teach androgyny to students have had mixed results.
	Gender-Role Transcendence	• Some experts believe too much attention is given to gender in our society and that we should instead pursue gender-role transcendence.
Gender in Context	Helping Behavior and Emotion	• Evaluation of gender-role categories and gender similarities and differences in different areas like helping behavior and emotion suggest that the best way to think about gender is not in terms of personality traits but instead in terms of person-situation interaction (gender in context).
	Culture	• Although androgyny and multiple gender roles are often available for American children to choose from, many countries around the world still enforce rigid, traditional gender roles. In these countries, such as Egypt and China, the male role is dominant.
Eliminating Gender Bias	Teacher-Student Interaction	• Girls are more compliant, boys more rambunctious. • Teachers give boys more attention and more instruction than girls. • Boys get lower grades. • By middle school, girls have lower self-esteem. • Boys list more career options than girls do.
	Curriculum and Athletics Content	• Schools have made considerable progress in reducing sexism and sex stereotyping in books and curriculum materials, but some bias still exists.
	Sexual Harassment	• This is a special concern in schools and is more pervasive than once believed. • Recently, a distinction was made between quid pro quo and hostile environment sexual harassment.

Chapter Review

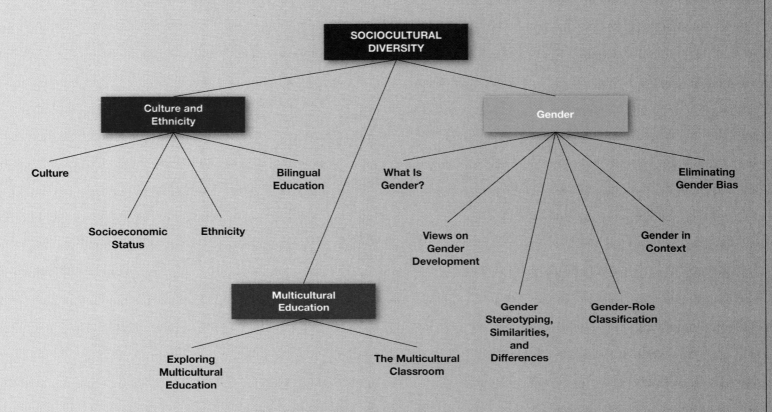

TO OBTAIN A DETAILED REVIEW OF THIS CHAPTER, STUDY THESE FIVE SUMMARY TABLES:

Key Terms

culture 160
cross-cultural studies 160
individualism 160
collectivism 160
socioeconomic status
   (SES) 161
ethnicity 164
prejudice 167

bilingual education 169
multicultural education 171
empowerment 172
jigsaw classroom 173
gender 178
sex 178
gender roles 178
identification theory 180

social learning theory of
   gender 180
cognitive developmental
   theory of gender 180
gender schema theory 181
gender stereotypes 181
sexism 183
rapport talk 185

report talk 185
androgyny 186
gender-role
   transcendence 187
quid pro quo sexual
   harassment 190
hostile environment sexual
   harassment 190

Educational Psychology Checklist
SOCIOCULTURAL DIVERSITY

Use the following statements to help you review your knowledge and understanding of the chapter material. First, read the statement and mentally or briefly on paper demonstrate that you can outline and discuss the relevant information.

_____ I have some good ideas about how to interact more effectively with people from diverse cultures, such as individualistic and collectivistic cultures.

_____ I can describe socioeconomic status and ways to support impoverished children's learning and coping.

_____ I can discuss what ethnicity is, the schooling experiences of children of color, and the nature of differences and diversity.

_____ I know what bilingual education is, the controversy surrounding it, and some good teaching strategies for working with linguistically and culturally diverse children.

_____ I can describe multicultural education, the debate involved, and some effective teaching strategies and programs in the multicultural classroom.

_____ I can discuss gender development, how gender stereotyping works, and similarities and differences in gender behavior in a number of areas.

_____ I can describe what gender-role classification is and possible problems with it.

_____ I understand what it means to talk about the importance of gender in context.

_____ I can discuss reducing bias in schools.

For any items that you did not check off, go back and locate the relevant material in the chapter. Review the material until you feel you can check off the item. You also may want to use this checklist later in preparing for an exam.

Adventures for the Mind

Now that you have a good knowledge and understanding of the chapter, complete the following exercises to expand your thinking about the chapter's topics.

• No matter how well intentioned we are, life circumstances produce some negative attitudes toward people who are different from us. Think about people from cultural and ethnic backgrounds different from yours and people of the other sex. Do you have any negative attitudes toward these people? If so, which ones? Did the negative attitude come from one bad encounter with someone you decided was representative of the group? Have you learned any prejudices by modeling the attitudes of others you admire? What will it take for you to eliminate your negative attitudes toward this group or person? What can you do in your future classroom to help children reduce their prejudices?

• With three or four other students in the class, come up with a list of specific diversity goals for your future classrooms. Also brainstorm and come up with some innovative activities to help students gain positive diversity experiences, such as the inclusive quilt discussed in this chapter.

• Imagine that you are teaching a social studies lesson about the westward movement in U.S. history and a student makes a racist, stereotyped statement about Native Americans, such as, "The Indians were hot-tempered and showed their hostility toward the White settlers." How would you handle this situation? (Banks, 1997b).

• Observe lessons being taught in several classrooms that include boys and girls and students from different ethnic groups. Did the teachers interact with females and males differently? If so, how? Did the teachers interact with students from different ethnic groups in different ways? If so, how?

Taking It to the Net

1. Imagine yourself at the front of your classroom. Imagine that you have twenty pairs of eyes looking at you, and that these twenty pairs come from five different countries, four distinct ethnic backgrounds, three different religions, and two sexes. How might this level of diversity affect your teaching?

2. A colleague of yours is continually placing offensive pictures of sex acts on your car window. You ask the person to stop, but the pictures continue. Is this sexual harassment? If only you and the other person know about it, is it worth reporting? Why, or why not?

3. It was just announced that Lebiere has the highest GPA in school, is the recipient of more awards than any other student in school, and has accepted a full scholarship to a prestigious university. Picture Lebiere in your mind. Is Lebiere male or female? Why did you picture him or her that way?

Connect to http://www.mhhe.com/socscience/psychology/santedu/ttnet.htm to find the answers!

Case Studies

Case 1 *Anyssa*: Gifted program placement of African-American child.

Case 2 *Esperanza*: Placement issue for migrant Hispanic child.

Case 3 *James Colbert:* A third-grade teacher in an inner-city school is trying his best to teach language arts using basal readers and a district-required curriculum. He is especially concerned about one Spanish-speaking child who appears to want to learn but who speaks English only at school.

Chapter 6

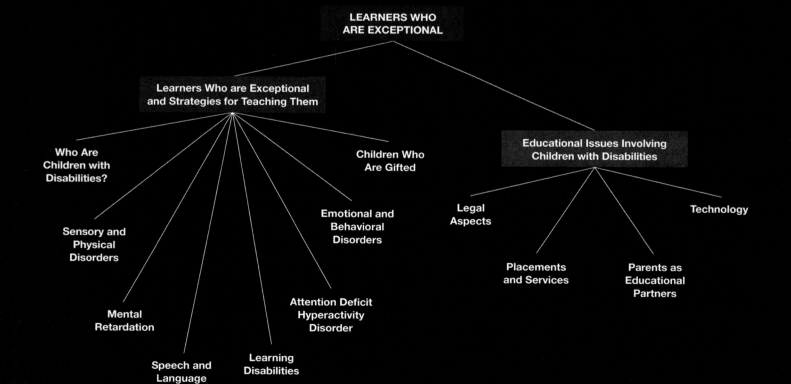

LEARNERS WHO ARE EXCEPTIONAL

Learners Who are Exceptional and Strategies for Teaching Them

Who Are Children with Disabilities?

Sensory and Physical Disorders

Mental Retardation

Speech and Language Disorders

Learning Disabilities

Attention Deficit Hyperactivity Disorder

Emotional and Behavioral Disorders

Children Who Are Gifted

Educational Issues Involving Children with Disabilities

Legal Aspects

Placements and Services

Parents as Educational Partners

Technology

Preview

For many years, public schools did little to educate children with disabilities. However, in the last several decades, federal legislation has mandated that children with disabilities receive a free, appropriate education. And increasingly, children with disabilities are being educated in the regular classroom. These are some of the questions we will explore in this chapter:

- What are the challenges of educating children with various disabilities and the best strategies for teaching them?
- Should children who are gifted be provided with special educational opportunities?
- What are the legal aspects of working with children who have disabilities?
- Should children with disabilities be taught mainly in the regular classroom or in a specialized setting?
- What challenges are involved in educating children with disabilities in the regular classroom?
- What technologies are available for educating children with disabilities?

Teaching Stories
Verna Rollins

Verna Rollins teaches language arts at West Middle School in Ypsilanti, Michigan, and has developed a reputation for effectively dealing with so-called "hard to teach" or "difficult" students. She has found that the best strategy to use with these students is to find out what they need, decide how to provide it, provide it, and constantly evaluate whether it is working. She tells the story of one such student who was mainstreamed into her regular education classroom at the insistence of his mother but against the wishes of the special education staff. Following is Verna Rollins' description of how this went:

> Jack was in a special education classroom for children with physical disabilities. He has twisted legs, cerebral palsy, seizures, and some other brain damage from birth. He also has a comparatively short attention span. Since he drools, speaks in a loud monotone, stutters when he is excited, and has so little motor control that his penmanship is unreadable, people often think he is mentally retarded. He was not challenged to read or to write in his special classroom, essentially being made to think that he couldn't really do well at either one. Actually, he is quite bright.
>
> My strategies included making sure that he had all the equipment he needed to succeed. I gave him tissues for the drooling and mutually agreed-upon reminders to wipe his mouth. I found that he could speak softly and without stuttering if he calmed down. We developed a signaling plan in which I would clear my throat when he talked too loudly and I would prompt him with the phrase "slow speech" when he was too excited to speak in a smooth voice.
>
> He used a computer to take quizzes and needed a little more time to complete any task, but he was so excited about being "out in the real world" that his attention span improved, as did his self-worth. In fact, his mother wrote a letter to me expressing her gratitude for the "most positive influence you have been on him! You have reinstilled and greatly increased his love of reading and writing. You have given my child a wonderful gift."

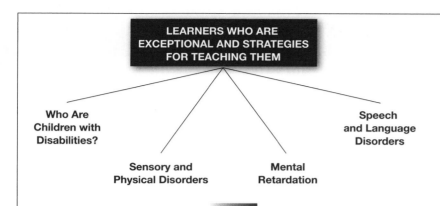

Learners Who Are Exceptional and Strategies for Teaching Them

Learners who are exceptional include both children with some type of disability and children who are classified as gifted. We will discuss both types of exceptionalities but focus mainly on the former. We begin our discussion of the diversity of children who are exceptional by identifying who they are.

Who Are Children with Disabilities?

Approximately 10 percent of all children receive special education or related services (Reschly, 1996). Figure 6.1 shows the approximate percentages of children with various disabilities who receive special education services (U.S. Department of Education, 1996). Within this group, a little more than half have a learning disability. Substantial percentages of students also have speech or language impairments (21 percent of those with disabilities), mental retardation (12 percent), or serious emotional disturbance (9 percent).

The concepts of *disability* and *handicap* can be differentiated. A **disability** *involves a limitation on a person's functioning that restricts the individual's abilities. A* **handicap** *is a condition imposed on a person who has a disability. This condition could be imposed by society, the physical environment, or the person's own attitudes.*

Educators increasingly speak of "children with disabilities" rather than "disabled children" to emphasize the person, not the disability. Children with disabilities also are no longer referred to as "handicapped"; the term *handicapping conditions* is still used to describe the impediments to the learning and functioning of individuals with a disability that have been imposed by society. For example, when children who use a wheelchair do not have adequate access to a bathroom, transportation, and so on, this is referred to as a handicapping condition.

Sensory and Physical Disorders

You might have students in your class who have sensory or physical disorders.

Sensory Disorders   Sensory disorders include visual and hearing impairments. Sometimes these impairments are described as part of a larger category called "communication disorders" along with the speech and language disorders, which we will discuss later in the chapter.

Visual Impairments   Some students might have mild vision problems that have not been corrected. If you notice students squinting a lot, holding books close to their face to read them, rubbing their eyes frequently, and complaining that things appear blurred or that words move about on the page, refer them to the appropriate

Exploring Disabilities

Disability	Total	Percent of total
Specific learning disabilities	2,513,977	51.1
Speech or language impairments	1,023,665	20.8
Mental retardation	570,855	11.6
Serious emotional disturbance	428,168	8.7
Multiple disabilities	89,646	1.8
Hearing impairments	65,568	1.3
Orthopedic impairments	60,604	1.2
Other health impairments	106,509	2.2
Visual impairments	24,877	0.5
Autism	22,780	0.5
Deaf-blindness	1,331	0.0
Traumatic brain injury	7,188	0.1
All disabilities	4,915,168	100.0

Note: The figures represent children with a disability who received special education services in the 1994–1995 school year. Children with multiple disabilities also have been counted under various single disabilities.

Figure **6.1**
The Diversity of Children Who Have a Disability

The currently accepted description is "children with disabilities" rather than "disabled children" or "handicapped children." Why the changes in terminology?

Whatever the process, the result is wonderful. Gradually from naming an object we advance step by step until we have traversed the vast distances between our first stammered syllable and the sweep of thought in a line of Shakespeare.

Helen Keller
American Essayist, 20th Century

school professionals to have their vision checked (Boyles & Contadino, 1997). Many will only need corrective lenses. However, a small portion of students (about 1 in every 1,000 students) have more serious visual problems and are classified as visually impaired. This includes students who have low vision and students who are blind.

Children with **low vision** *have a visual acuity of between 20/70 and 20/200 (on the familiar Snellen scale in which 20/20 vision is normal) with corrective lenses.* Children with low vision can read large-print books or with the aid of a magnifying glass. Children who are **educationally blind** *cannot use their vision in learning and must use their hearing and touch to learn.* Approximately 1 in every 3,000 children is educationally blind. Almost one-half of these children were born blind, and another one-third lost their vision in the first year of life. Many children who are educationally blind have normal intelligence and function very well academically with appropriate supports and learning aids. However, multiple disabilities are not uncommon in educationally blind students. Students who have multiple disabilities often require a range of support services to meet their educational needs.

An important task in working with a child who has visual impairments is to determine the modality (such as touch or hearing) through which the child learns best (Bowe, 2000). Preferential seating in the front of the class often benefits the child with a visual impairment.

For half a century, recorded textbooks from Recording for the Blind and Dyslexic have contributed to the educational progress of students with visual, perceptual, or other disabilities. More than 77,000 volumes of these audio and computerized books are available at no charge (phone: 1-800-803-7201).

Hearing Impairments   A hearing impairment can make learning very difficult for children. Children who are born deaf or experience a significant hearing loss in the first several years of life usually do not develop normal speech and language. You also might have some children in your

Visual Impairments

THROUGH THE EYES OF CHILDREN
Eyes Closed

In kindergarten, children truly begin to appreciate, not fear or think strange, each other's differences. A few years ago a child in my kindergarten class was walking down the hall with his eyes closed and ran into the wall. When I asked him what he was doing, he said, "I was just trying to do like Darrick. How come he does it so much better?" Darrick is his classmate who is legally blind. He wanted to experience what it was like to be blind. In this case, imitation truly was the greatest form of flattery."

Anita Marie Hitchcock
Kindergarten Teacher
Holle Navarre Primary
Santa Rosa County, Florida

*T*EACHING STRATEGIES
With Children Who Have Hearing Impairments

The following strategies can help you communicate with a student who has a hearing impairment (Himber, 1989):

1. *Be patient.*
2. *Speak slowly and give the child time to process information.*
3. *Don't shout, because this doesn't help. Speaking distinctly is more helpful.*
4. *Reduce distractions and background noises when talking with students who have hearing impairments.*
5. *Face the student to whom you are speaking, because the student needs to read your lips and see your gestures.*

Hearing Impairments

class who have hearing impairments that have not yet been detected. If you have students who turn one ear toward a speaker, frequently ask to have something repeated, don't follow directions, or frequently complain of earaches, colds, and allergies, consider having the student's hearing evaluated by a specialist, such as an audiologist (Patterson & Wright, 1990).

Many children with hearing impairments receive supplementary instruction beyond the regular classroom. Educational approaches to help students with hearing impairments learn fall into two categories: oral and manual. **Oral approaches** *include using lip reading, speech reading (a reliance on visual cues to teach reading), and whatever hearing the student has.* **Manual approaches** *involve sign language and finger spelling.* Sign language is a system of hand movements that symbolize words. Finger spelling consists of "spelling out" each word by signing each letter of each word. A total communication approach that includes both oral and manual approaches is increasingly being used with students who are hearing impaired (Hallahan & Kaufmann, 2000; Heward, 1996).

A number of medical and technological advances, including the following, also have improved the learning of children with hearing impairments (Boyles & Contadino, 1997):

- Cochlear implants (a surgical procedure)
- Placing tubes in the ears (a surgical procedure for middle-ear dysfunction)
- Hearing aids and FM amplification systems
- Telecommunication devices, the teletypewriter-telephone, and RadioMail (using the Internet)

Physical Disorders   Physical disorders in children can include orthopedic impairments, such as cerebral palsy and seizure disorders. Many children with physical disorders require special education as well as related services, such as transportation, physical therapy, school health services, and psychological services.

Orthopedic Impairments   **Orthopedic impairments** *involve restrictions in movement because of muscle, bone, or joint problems.* Depending on the severity of the restriction, some children might have only limited restriction, others might not be able to move at all. Other children cannot control the movement of their muscles. Orthopedic impairments can be caused by prenatal or perinatal problems, or they can be due to disease or accident during the childhood years. With the help of adaptive devices and medical technology, many children with orthopedic impairments function well in the classroom (Boyles & Contadino, 1997).

Cerebral palsy *is a disorder that involves a lack of muscular coordination, shaking, or unclear speech.* The most common cause of cerebral palsy is lack of oxygen at birth. In the most common type of cerebral palsy, which is called *spastic,* children's muscles

Cerebral Palsy

are stiff and difficult to move. The rigid muscles often pull the limbs into contorted positions. In a less common type, *ataxia,* the child's muscles are rigid one moment and floppy the next moment, making movements clumsy and jerky.

Computers especially can help children with cerebral palsy learn. If they have the coordination to use the keyboard, they can do their written work on the computer. A pen with a light can be added to a computer and used by the student as a pointer. Many children with cerebral palsy have unclear speech. For these children, speech and voice synthesizers, communication boards, talking notes, and page turners can improve their communication.

Seizure Disorders   The most common seizure disorder is **epilepsy,** *a nervous disorder characterized by recurring sensorimotor attacks or movement convulsions.* Epilepsy comes in different forms (Barr, 2000). In one common form called *absent seizures,* a child's seizures are brief in duration (often less than 30 seconds) and they might occur anywhere from several to a hundred times a day. Often they occur as brief staring spells, although motor movements such as twitching of the eyelids might appear. In another common form of epilepsy labeled *tonic-clonic,* the child loses consciousness and becomes rigid, shakes, and displays jerking motions. The most severe portion of tonic-clonic seizure lasts for about 3 to 4 minutes. Children who experience seizures are usually treated with one or more anticonvulsant medications, which often are effective in reducing the seizures but do not always eliminate them. When they are not having a seizure, students with epilepsy show normal behavior. If you have a child in your class who has a seizure disorder, become well acquainted with the procedures for monitoring and helping the child during a seizure. Also, if a child seems to space out a lot in your class, especially under stress, it might be worthwhile to explore whether the problem is boredom, drugs, or potentially a neurological condition. One individual was diagnosed with mild epilepsy late in high school after he had several accidents while learning to drive. The only prior indication was that he did poorly on some of his tests in school and said that he seemed to just space out on them. His teachers thought he was malingering, but the spacing out likely represented the beginning signs of mild epilepsy.

THROUGH THE EYES OF CHILDREN
It's Okay to Be Different

Why me? I often ask myself, why did I have to be the one? Why did I get picked to be different? It took more than 10 years for me to find answers and to realize that I'm not *more* different than anyone else. My twin sister was born with no birth defects but I was born with cerebral palsy.

People thought I was stupid because it was hard for me to write my own name. So when I was the only one in the class to use a typewriter, I began to feel I was different. It got worse when the third-graders moved on to the fourth grade and I had to stay behind. I got held back because the teachers thought I'd be unable to type fast enough to keep up. Kids told me that was a lie and the reason I got held back was because I was a retard. It really hurt to be teased by those I thought were my friends. . . .

I have learned that no one was to blame for my disability. I realize that I can do things and that I can do them very well. Some things I can't do, like taking my own notes in class or running in a race, but I will have to live with that. . . .

There are times when I wish I had not been born with cerebral palsy, but crying isn't going to do me any good. I can only live once, so I want to live the best I can. . . . Nobody else can be the Angela Marie Erickson who is writing this. I could never be, or ever want to be, anyone else.

Angie Erickson
Ninth-Grade Student
Wayzata, Minnesota

Mental Retardation

Increasingly, children with milder forms of mental retardation are being taught in the regular classroom.

Characteristics   The most distinctive feature of mental retardation is inadequate intellectual functioning. Long before formal tests were developed to assess intelligence, individuals with mental retardation were identified by a lack of age-appropriate skills in learning and in caring for themselves. Once intelligence tests were created, numbers were assigned to indicate how mild or severe the retardation was ◀▥ p. 127. A child might be only mildly retarded and able to learn in the regular classroom, or severely retarded and unable to learn in that setting.

Epilepsy
Mental Retardation

TYPE OF MENTAL RETARDATION	IQ RANGE	PERCENTAGE
Mild	55–70	89
Moderate	40–54	6
Severe	25–39	4
Profound	Below 25	1

Figure **6.2**

Classification of Mental Retardation Based on IQ

In addition to low intelligence, deficits in adaptive behavior and developmental onset also are included in the definition of mental retardation. Adaptive skills include skills needed for self-care and social responsibility such as dressing, toileting, feeding, self-control, and peer interaction. Thus, **mental retardation** *is a condition with an onset before age 18 that involves low intelligence (usually below 70 on a traditional individually administered intelligence test) and difficulty in adapting to everyday life.* The low IQ and low adaptiveness should be evident in childhood, not following a long period of normal functioning that is interrupted by an accident or other type of assault on the brain.

Classification and Types of Mental Retardation   As indicated in figure 6.2, mental retardation is classified as mild, moderate, severe, or profound. Approximately 75 to 85 percent of students with mental retardation fall into the mild category (Shonkoff, 1996). By late adolescence, individuals with mild mental retardation can be expected to develop academic skills at approximately the sixth-grade level (Terman & others, 1996). In their adult years, many can hold jobs and live on their own with some supportive supervision or in group homes. Individuals with more severe mental retardation require more support.

If you have a student with mental retardation in your classroom, the degree of retardation is likely to be mild. Children with severe mental retardation are more likely to also show signs of other neurological complications, such as cerebral palsy, epilepsy, hearing impairment, visual impairment, or other metabolic birth defects that affect the central nervous system (Terman & others, 1996).

Most school systems still use the classifications mild, moderate, severe, and profound. However, because these categorizations based on IQ ranges aren't perfect predictors of functioning, the American Association on Mental Retardation (1992) developed a new classification system based on the degree of support required for the child with mental retardation to function at their highest level (Hallahan & Kaufmann, 2000). As shown in figure 6.3, these are the new categories: intermittent, limited, extensive, and pervasive.

Intermittent	Supports are provided "as needed." The individual may need episodic or short-term support during life-span transitions (such as job loss or acute medical crisis). Intermittent supports may be low or high intensity when provided.
Limited	Supports are intense and relatively consistent over time. They are time-limited but not intermittent. Require fewer staff members and cost less than more intense supports. These supports likely will be needed for adaptation to the changes involved in the school–to–adult period.
Extensive	Supports are characterized by regular involvement (e.g., daily) in at least some setting (such as home or work) and are not time-limited (for example, extended home-living support).
Pervasive	Supports are constant, very intense, and are provided across settings. They may be of a life-sustaining nature. These supports typically involve more staff members and intrusiveness than the other support categories.

Figure **6.3**

Classification of Mental Retardation Based on Levels of Support

Causes   Mental retardation is caused by genetic factors and brain damage.

Genetic Factors   The most commonly identified form of mental retardation is **Down syndrome,** *which is genetically transmitted. Children with Down syndrome have an extra (47th) chromosome.* They have a round face, a flattened skull, an extra fold of skin over the eyelids, a protruding tongue, short limbs, and retardation of motor and mental abilities (see figure 6.4). It is not known why the extra chromosome is present, but the health of the male sperm or female ovum might be involved (MacLean, 2000; Vining, 1992). Women between the ages of 18 and 38 are far less likely than younger or older women to give birth to a child with Down syndrome. Down syndrome appears in about 1 in every 700 live births. African American children are rarely born with Down syndrome.

With early intervention and extensive support from the child's family and professionals, many children with Down syndrome can grow into independent adults (Boyles & Contadino, 1997). Children with Down syndrome can fall into the mild to severe retardation categories (Terman & others, 1996).

Fragile X syndrome *is the second most commonly identified form of mental retardation. It is genetically transmitted by an abnormality on the X chromosome, resulting in severe retardation in males and less severe retardation in females.* Characteristics of fragile X children include an elongated face, prominent jaws, elongated ears, a flattened bridge of the nose, and poor coordination. About 7 percent of mild mental retardation in females is a result of fragile X syndrome.

Brain Damage   Brain damage can result from many different infections and environmental hazards (Das, 2000; Hallahan & Kaufmann, 2000). Infections in the pregnant mother-to-be, such as rubella (German measles), syphilis, herpes, and AIDS, can cause retardation in the child. Meningitis and encephalitis are infections that can develop in childhood. They cause inflammation in the brain and can produce mental retardation.

Environmental hazards that can result in mental retardation include blows to the head, malnutrition, poisoning, birth injury, and alcoholism or heavy drinking on the part of the pregnant woman. **Fetal alcohol syndrome (FAS)** *involves a cluster of abnormalities, including mental retardation and facial abnormalities, that appear in the offspring of mothers who drink alcohol heavily during pregnancy. FAS appears in approximately one-third of the offspring of pregnant alcoholic women.*

Figure **6.4**
A Child with Down Syndrome
What causes a child to develop Down syndrome?

Speech and Language Disorders

There are many types of speech and language disorders.

The Nature of Speech and Language Disorders   **Speech and language disorders** *include a number of speech problems (such as articulation disorders, voice disorders, and fluency disorders) and language problems (difficulties in receiving information and expressing language).* As you saw earlier in figure 6.1, slightly more than one-fifth of all children who receive special education services have a speech or language impairment.

Exploring Specific Speech and Language Disorders
Articulation disorders *are problems in pronouncing sounds correctly.* A child's articulation at 6 or 7 years is still not always error-free, but it should be by age 8. A child

Speech and Language Disorders

TEACHING STRATEGIES
With Children Who Have Mental Retardation

During the school years, the main goals often are to teach children with mental retardation basic educational skills such as reading and mathematics, as well as vocational skills (Boyles & Contadino, 1997). Following are some positive teaching strategies for interacting with children who have mental retardation:

1. *Always keep in mind the child's level of mental functioning when teaching a child who has mental retardation.* Children who have mental retardation will be at a considerably lower level of mental functioning than most other students in your class. If you start at one level of instruction, and the child is not responding effectively, move to a lower level.
2. *Individualize your instruction to meet the child's needs.*
3. *As with other children with a disability, make sure that you give concrete examples of concepts.* Make your instructions clear and simple.
4. *Children with mental retardation often need to practice what they have learned, repeat steps a number of times, and overlearn a concept to retain it.*
5. *Be sensitive to the child's self-esteem. Especially avoid comparisons with children who do not have mental retardation.*
6. *Have positive expectations for the child's learning.* It is easy to fall into the trap of thinking that the child with mental retardation cannot achieve academically. Set a goal to maximize his or her learning.
7. *Recognize that many children with mental retardation not only have academic needs, but also require help in improving their self-maintenance and social skills.*
8. *Use teacher aides and recruit volunteers to help you educate children with mental retardation.* Many well-educated, sensitive older adults who are retired might be especially interested in helping. They can assist you in increasing the amount of one-on-one instruction the child receives.
9. *Some teachers who use applied behavior analysis strategies report success in improving children's self-maintenance, social, and academic skills.* If you are interested in using these strategies, consult a resource like *Applied Behavior Analysis for Teachers* by Paul Alberto and Anne Troutman (1995). All children need to be positively reinforced. The precise steps involved in applied behavior analysis can especially help you use positive reinforcement effectively with children who have mental retardation.
10. *If you teach in secondary school, give consideration to the types of vocational skills students with mental retardation will need in order to obtain a job.*
11. *Involve the parents of the child who has mental retardation as equal partners in the child's education.*

with an articulation problem might find communication with peers and the teacher difficult or embarrassing. As a result, the child might avoid asking questions, participating in discussions, or communicating with peers. Articulation problems can usually be improved or resolved with speech therapy, though it might take months or years.

Voice disorders *are reflected in speech that is hoarse, harsh, too loud, too high-pitched, or too low-pitched.* Children with cleft palate often have a voice disorder that makes their speech difficult to understand. If a child speaks in a way that is consistently difficult to understand, refer the child to a speech therapist.

Fluency disorders *often involve what is commonly called "stuttering."* Stuttering occurs when a child's speech has a spasmodic hesitation, prolongation, or repetition. The anxiety many children feel because they stutter often just makes their stuttering worse. Speech therapy is recommended.

Language disorders *involve significant impairments in children's receptive and expressive language* (Boyles & Contadino, 1997). Language disorders can result in significant learning problems. Treatment by a language therapist generally produces improvement in the child with a language disorder, but the problem usually is not

TEACHING STRATEGIES

With Children Who Have Receptive and Expressive Language Disorders

Here are some strategies to support students with a receptive language disorder:

1. *Use a multisensory approach to learning rather than an oral approach alone. Supplement oral information with written materials or directions.*
2. *Monitor the speed with which you present information. Slow down or go back and and check with the children for understanding.*
3. *Give them some time to respond, as much as 10 to 15 seconds.*
4. *Provide concrete, specific examples of abstract concepts.*

Here are some strategies to support a child with an oral expressive language disorder:

1. *Give the child plenty of time to respond.*
2. *Recognize that the child has trouble responding orally, so consider asking the child to do written work rather than an oral report.*
3. *Provide choices or give the initial sound in word-finding problems.*
4. *Let the child know ahead of time what question might be asked so that the child can prepare the answer and thus appear more competent among peers.*

eradicated (Goldstein & Hockenberger, 1991). Language disorders include difficulties in these areas:

- Phrasing questions properly to get the desired information
- Understanding and following oral directions
- Following conversation, especially when it is rapid and complex

These difficulties involve both receptive and expressive language.

Receptive language *consists of linguistic information that is received by the brain.* Children with a receptive language disorder have a glitch in the way they receive information. Information comes in, but the child's brain has difficulty responding to it quickly, which can cause the child to appear disinterested or aloof.

Once a message is received and interpreted, the brain needs to form a response. **Expressive language** *involves the ability to express one's thoughts.* Some children can easily understand what is said to them, but they have difficulties when they try to form a response and express themselves.

There are several observable characteristics of children who have an oral expressive language disorder (Boyles & Contadino, 1997):

- They might appear shy and withdrawn, and have problems interacting socially.
- They might give delayed responses to questions.
- They might have a problem finding the correct words.
- Their thoughts might be disorganized and disjointed, frustrating the listener.
- They might omit integral parts of the sentence or information needed for understanding.

At this point we have discussed many ideas regarding who children with disabilities are, sensory and physical disorders, mental retardation, and speech and language disorders. A review of these ideas is presented in summary table 6.1. Next, we evaluate learning disabilities, which can be closely linked with language disorders because many children with learning disabilities have deficient reading and writing skills.

It is a luxury to be understood.

Ralph Waldo Emerson
American Poet and Essayist, 19th Century

SUMMARY TABLE 6.1
Children with Disabilities, Sensory and Physical Disorders, Mental Retardation, and Speech and Language Disorders

Concept	Processes/ Related Ideas	Characteristics/Description
Who Are Children with Disabilities?	Their Identity	• As estimated 10 percent of U.S. children with a disability receive special education services. • Slightly more than 50 percent of these students are classified as having a learning disability (in the federal classification, this includes attention deficit hyperactivity disorder (ADHD). • Substantial percentages of children with a disability have mental retardation, speech and language disorders, or a serious emotional disturbance. • The term *children with disabilities* is now used rather than *disabled children,* and children with disabilities are no longer referred to as "handicapped children."
Sensory and Physical Disorders	Sensory Disorders	• These include visual and hearing impairments. Sometimes they are described as part of a larger category called "communication disorders" along with speech and language disorders. • Visual impairments include low vision and being educationally blind. An important task is to determine which modality (such as touch or hearing) the student who is visually impaired learns best in. • A number of technological devices help these students learn. • Educational strategies for students with hearing impairments fall into two main categories: oral and manual. Increasingly, both approaches are used with the same student in a total-communication approach.
	Physical Disorders	• Among the physical disorders that students might have are orthopedic impairments (such as cerebral palsy) and seizure disorders (such as epilepsy).
Mental Retardation	Characteristics	• Mental retardation is a condition with an onset before age 18 that involves low intelligence (usually below 70 on an individually administered intelligence test) and difficulty in adapting to everyday life.
	Classification and Types	• Mental retardation has been classified in terms of four categories based mainly on IQ scores: mild, moderate, severe, and profound. • More recently, a classification system based on degree of support required has been advocated.
	Causes	• These include genetic factors (as in Down syndrome and fragile X syndrome) and brain damage (which can result from many different infections, such as AIDS) and environmental hazards such as blows to the head and heavy drinking by the mother when she was pregnant.
Speech and Language Disorders	Their Nature	• These disorders include a number of speech problems (such as articulation disorders, voice disorders, and fluency disorders) and language problems (difficulties in receiving and expressing language).
	Exploring Specific Disorders	• Articulation disorders are problems in pronouncing words correctly. • Voice disorders are reflected in speech that is too hoarse, loud, high-pitched, or low-pitched. Children with cleft palate often have a voice disorder. • Fluency disorders often involve what we commonly call "stuttering." • Language disorders involve significant impairments in children's receptive and expressive language. Receptive language is linguistic information that is received by the brain. Expressive language involves the ability to express one's thoughts.

Learning Disabilities

Paula doesn't like kindergarten and can't seem to remember the names of her teacher and classmates. Bobby's third-grade teacher complains that his spelling is awful. Eleven-year-old Tim says reading is really hard for him and a lot of times the words don't make much sense. Each of these students has a learning disability.

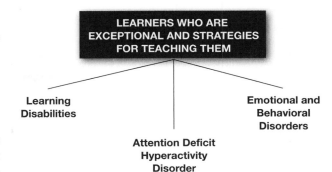

LEARNERS WHO ARE EXCEPTIONAL AND STRATEGIES FOR TEACHING THEM

Learning Disabilities

Attention Deficit Hyperactivity Disorder

Emotional and Behavioral Disorders

Characteristics Children with a **learning disability** *(1) are of normal intelligence or above, (2) have difficulty in at least one academic area and usually several, and (3) have no other diagnosed problem or disorder, such as mental retardation, that is causing the difficulty.* The global concept of learning disabilities includes problems in listening, concentrating, speaking, thinking, memory, reading, writing, and spelling, and social skills (Kamphaus, 2000; Keogh & MacMillan, 1996; Spear-Swerling & Sternberg, 1994). About 5 percent of the total population of all school-age children receive special education or related services because of a learning disability. In the federal classification of children receiving special education and related services, attention deficit hyperactivity disorder (ADHD) is included in the learning disabilities category. Because of the significant interest in ADHD today, we will discuss it by itself following learning disabilities.

The percentage of children classified as having learning disability has increased substantially—from less than 30 percent of all children receiving special education and related services in 1977–1978 to a little more than 50 percent today. Some experts say that the dramatic increase in children classified as having a learning disability reflects poor diagnostic practices and overidentification. They believe that teachers sometimes are too quick to label children with the slightest learning problem as having a learning disability instead of recognizing that the problem might rest in their ineffective teaching. Other experts say the increase in children being classified as having a learning disability is justified (Hallahan, Kaufmann, & Lloyd, 1999).

Learning Disabilities

Diagnosing whether a child has a learning disability is a difficult task. A learning disability often encompasses co-occurring conditions that can include problems in listening, concentrating, speaking, reading, writing, reasoning, math, or social interaction. Thus, individual children with a learning disability can have very different profiles (Henley, Ramsey, & Algozzine, 1999). Learning disabilities often appear in association with such medical conditions as lead poisoning and fetal alcohol syndrome (American Psychiatric Association, 1994). And learning disabilities can occur with other disabilities such as communication disorders and emotional behavioral disorders (Polloway & others, 1997; Rock, Fessler, & Church, 1997; Schoenbrodt, Kumin, & Sloan, 1997).

About three times as many boys as girls are classified as having a learning disability (U.S. Department of Education, 1996). This gender difference has been given various explanations, such as greater biological vulnerability of boys and referral bias (boys more likely to be referred by teachers because of their disruptive, hyperactive behavior).

By definition, children do not have a learning disability unless they have an academic problem. Some of the most common academic areas in which children with a learning disability have problems are reading, written language, and math (Hallahan & Kaufmann, 2000; Lerner, 2000).

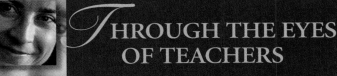

THROUGH THE EYES OF TEACHERS

Creating the Character
Uey Long

Nancy Downing, a second-grade teacher at McDermott Elementary School in Little Rock, Arkansas, takes a multisensory approach to education, which she developed while working with her own child who has learning difficulties. She created Downfeld Phonics using phonics, sign language, and lively jingles to make learning fun for students. She developed the character Uey Long (a uey is the sign over a short vowel) to demonstrate vowel rules. Nancy makes sure that every child has a coat, even if she has to donate one, and gives each student a hug and a final compliment or piece of advice at the end of the school day.

Nancy Downing

The most common problem for children with a learning disability involves reading, especially phonological skills (recall from chapter 2, "Physical and Cognitive Development," that these involve being able to understand how sounds and letters match up to make words) ◀▥ p. 65. **Dyslexia** *is a severe impairment in the ability to read.*

Children with a learning disability often have difficulties in handwriting, spelling, or composition. They might write extremely slowly, their writing products might be virtually illegible, and they might make numerous spelling errors because of their inability to match up sounds and letters.

Early in the history of diagnosing learning disabilities, difficulties in math were given little attention. Increasingly, though, math is being recognized as an academic area in which learning disabilities can occur. Students with a learning disability in math might make an abundance of computational errors or use inefficient strategies in solving math problems.

Current classification of learning disabilities involves an "either/or" determination: A child either has a learning disability or does not. Yet in reality, learning disabilities vary in their intensity (Reschly, 1996; Terman & others, 1996). Severe learning disabilities, such as dyslexia, have been recognized for more than a century and are relatively easy to diagnose. However, most children with a learning disability have a milder form, which often makes them hard to distinguish from children without a learning disability. In the absence of nationally accepted criteria for classification, there continues to be considerable variability in the identification of students with a learning disability from one state to the next and even one teacher to the next (Lyon, 1996).

Despite variations in degree, the impact of having a learning disability is real and persistent (Bender, 1998; Raymond, 2000). Most learning disabilities are lifelong. Compared to children without a learning disability, children with a learning disability are more likely to show poor academic performance, high dropout rates, and poor employment and postsecondary education records (Wagner & Blackorby, 1996). Children with a learning disability who are taught in the regular classroom without extensive support rarely achieve the level of competence of even children who are low-achieving and do not have a disability (Hocutt, 1996). Still, despite the problems they encounter, many children with a learning disability grow up to lead normal lives and engage in productive work (Pueschel & others, 1995).

Improving outcomes for children with a learning disability is a challenging task and generally has required intensive intervention for even modest improvement in outcomes. No model program has proven to be effective for all children with learning disabilities (Terman & others, 1996).

Identification   As we said earlier, diagnosing a child with a learning disability, especially in a mild form, is very difficult. A child with a learning disability typically does not look disabled, can communicate verbally, and does not stand out in a crowd (Larsen, 1997).

Initial identification of a child with a possible learning disability is usually made by the classroom teacher. If a learning disability is suspected, the teacher calls on specialists. An interdisciplinary team of professionals is best

THROUGH THE EYES OF TEACHERS

Some Learning Disabilities Show Up Later

For some children, it's not until third or fourth grade that teachers become aware that children are having problems with reading. This may occur because the number of words that children are called upon to read expands at such a phenomenal rate. Children can't just learn them by sight anymore. Most children begin to infer the relationships between sounds and symbols by fourth grade or earlier; by fourth grade they have made those inferences even if they haven't explicitly been taught to them. By contrast, children with learning disabilities often don't figure out those links for themselves or during the course of normal classroom learning. Thus, they need to be explicitly taught about them to a greater degree than other students.

Later, students start having more trouble with the complex vocabulary that is being introduced to them and they may not be able to remember as many words. As the pace of learning accelerates in later grades, more and more information has to be gained through reading. In the earlier grades students get a lot of information orally; they are not expected to get all or even most of their information from reading. When the switch takes place from learning-to-read to reading-to-learn, children with learning disabilities may have trouble because they don't read competently. What also shows up in elementary school is that many children with learning disabilities have difficulty with spelling.

Gail Venable,
Language Arts/Special Education
Teacher/Consultant, San Francisco

suited to verify whether a student has a learning disability (Pueschel & others, 1995; Venn, 2000). Individual psychological evaluations (of intelligence) and educational assessments are needed in this regard (Overton, 2000).

In the early childhood years, disabilities are often identified in receptive and expressive language. Input from parents and teachers is considered before making a final diagnosis. For many school systems, the trigger for assessing students with learning disabilities is a two-grade-level lag in reading (Purcell-Gates, 1997). This can be a major impediment to identifying disabilities at the age when help can be the most effective—during the first 2 years of elementary school. If the two-grade lag is rigidly interpreted, many children can't get help even if they are showing clear signs of a learning disability. For the school-age child, level of intelligence needs to be determined along with the student's current level of achievement. In addition, tests of visual-motor skills, language, and memory may be used.

Intervention Strategies   Many interventions have focused on improving the student's reading ability (Lyon & Moats, 1997). For example, in one study, instruction in phonological awareness at the kindergarten level had positive effects on reading development when these children reached first grade (Blachman & others, 1994).

Unfortunately, not all children who have a learning disability that involves reading problems have the benefit of appropriate early intervention. Most children whose reading disability is not diagnosed until third grade or later and receive standard interventions fail to show noticeable improvement (Lyon, 1996). However, intensive instruction over a period of time by a competent teacher can remediate the deficient reading skills of many students. For example, in one study, 65 severely dyslexic students were given 65 hours of individual instruction in addition to group instruction in phonemic awareness and thinking skills (Alexander & others, 1991). The intensive intervention significantly improved the dyslexic children's reading skills.

Children with severe phonological deficits that lead to poor decoding and word recognition skills respond to intervention more slowly than children with mild to moderate reading problems (Torgesen, 1995). Also, the success of even the best-designed reading intervention depends on the training and skills of the teacher.

Disability in basic reading skills has been the most common target of intervention studies because it is the most common form of learning disability, is identifiable, and represents the area of learning disabilities about which we have the most knowledge (Lyon, 1996). Interventions for other types of learning disabilities have been created, but they have not been as extensively researched.

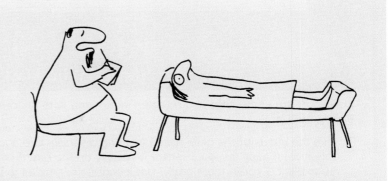

"*Your feelings of insecurity seem to have started when Mary Lou Gurnblatt said, 'Maybe I don't have a learning disability—maybe you have a teaching disability.'*"

© 1975 Tony Saltzman. Phi Delta Kappan.

THROUGH THE EYES OF TEACHERS
Teaching Children with Learning Disabilities

Throughout the last several years, up to one-half of the 24 students in my third-grade class have been diagnosed with learning disabilities. The majority of these students have difficulties with reading; therefore, modifications are often made in the other subject areas where reading is involved. For example, in math, I often have my students pair up to work on word problems. They take turns reading the problems and thinking through the solutions together. Both students seem to benefit from each other in these situations.

In social studies and science, I often have teams work on discussing related problems, such as planning a fund-raiser as a part of an economics unit. Within the team, leaders and recorders are assigned to read the directions and write the answers for their team, which takes some pressure off of having to spell and read independently. Tests and quizzes are also read aloud in these subject areas. Another strategy that is helpful when teaching students with learning disabilities is to give directions in short pieces, often demonstrating what you want them to do.

These children especially seem to benefit from hands-on experiences as well as art activities. After making salt dough maps one year, my students developed an understanding of the landforms and three regions of Virginia. They may not have been able to grasp these concepts just from reading the textbook and listening to discussions. I have found that many of the strategies that are useful when teaching students with learning disabilities actually benefit the whole class.

Kristin Blankenship
Salem Church Elementary
Chesterfield County, Virginia

*T*EACHING STRATEGIES
With Children Who Have Learning Disabilities

Following are some helpful strategies in working with children who have learning disabilities (Wadlington, Jacob, & Bailey, 1996):

1. *Take the needs of the child with a learning disability into account during instructional time.* Clearly state the objective of each lesson. Present it visually on the board or with an overhead projector as well. Be sure directions are explicit. Explain them orally. Use concrete examples to illustrate abstract concepts.

2. *Provide accommodations for testing and assignments.* This refers to changing the academic environment so that these children can demonstrate what they know. An accommodation usually does not involve altering the amount of learning the child has to demonstrate. Common accommodations include reading instructions to children, highlighting important words (such as *underline,* and *answer two of the three questions*), untimed tests, and extra time on assignments.

3. *Make modifications.* This strategy changes the work itself, making it different from other children's work in an effort to encourage children's confidence and success. Asking a child with dyslexia to give an oral report while other children give written reports is an example of a modification.

4. *Improve organizational and study skills.* As we mentioned earlier, many children with a learning disability do not have good organizational skills. Teachers and parents can encourage them to keep long-term and short-term calendars and create "to-do" lists each day. Projects should be broken down into their elements, with steps and due dates for each part.

5. *Work with reading and writing skills.* As we indicated earlier, the most common type of learning disability involves reading problems. Make sure that expert diagnosis of the child's reading problems has been made, including the particular deficits in reading skills involved. Children with a reading problem often read slowly, so they need more advance notice of outside reading assignments and more time for in-class reading. Many children with a learning disability that involves writing deficits find that a word processor helps them compose their writing projects more quickly and competently. Compensatory tools that can be used include handheld talking electronic dictionaries (like the Franklin Language Master, which gives students alternate spellings for phonetic attempts—*nummonia* for *pneumonia,* for example—where spellcheckers might fail them, and provides definitions for easily confused words such as *there* and *their*), talking word processors that give valuable auditory feedback, and taped books. Some agencies will record textbooks for students for a minimal fee.

Using such teaching strategies is not meant to give children with a learning disability an unfair advantage, just an equal chance to learn. Balancing the needs of children with learning disabilities and those of other children is a challenging task.

**Parent's and Educators'
Resources**

One recent analysis of intervention studies with children with learning disabilities found that a combined model of strategy instruction and direct instruction had the most positive effects (Swanson & Hoskyn, 1998). These types of instruction especially had positive effects on reading comprehension, vocabulary, and creativity. Among the instructional components that worked the best with children with learning disabilities were small interactive groups, technology, augmentation of teacher instruction (such as homework), directed questioning, and strategy cueing.

Attention Deficit Hyperactivity Disorder

Matthew has attention deficit hyperactivity disorder, and the outward signs are fairly typical. He has trouble attending to the teacher's instructions and is easily distracted. He can't sit still for more than a few minutes at a time, and his handwriting is messy. His mother describes him as very fidgety.

Characteristics   **Attention deficit hyperactivity disorder (ADHD)** *is a disability in which children consistently show one or more of the following characteristics over a period of time: (1) inattention, (2) hyperactivity, and (3) impulsivity.* Children who are inattentive have difficulty focusing on any one thing and might become bored with a task after only a few minutes. Children who are hyperactive show high levels of physical activity, almost always seeming to be in motion. Children who are impulsive have difficulty curbing their reactions and don't do a good job of thinking before they act. Depending on the characteristics children with ADHD display, they can be diagnosed as having (1) ADHD with predominantly inattention, (2) ADHD with predominantly hyperactivity/impulsivity, or (3) ADHD with both inattention and hyperactivity impulsivity.

The U.S. Department of Education figures on children with a disability shown in figure 6.1 include children with ADHD in the category of children with specific learning disabilities, an overall category that comprises slightly more than one-half of all children who receive special education services. The number of children diagnosed and treated for ADHD has increased substantially, by some estimates doubling in the 1990s. The disorder occurs as much as 4 to 9 times more in boys than in girls. There is controversy about the increased diagnosis of ADHD (Terman & others, 1996). Some experts attribute the increase mainly to heightened awareness of the disorder. Others are concerned that many children are being misdiagnosed without undergoing extensive professional evaluation based on input from multiple sources.

Signs of ADHD can be present in the preschool years. Parents and preschool or kindergarten teachers might notice that the child has an extremely high activity level

ADHD

Many children with ADHD show impulsive behavior, such as this child who is jumping out of his seat and throwing a paper airplane at other children. How would you handle this situation if this were to happen in your classroom?

TEACHING STRATEGIES

With Children Who Have ADHD

Here are some strategies for teaching children with attention deficit hyperactivity disorder:

1. *Academic-oriented strategies.* These include the following (Davila, Williams, & MacDonald, 1991):

   - Repeat and simplify instructions about in-class and homework assignments.
   - Supplement verbal instructions with visual instructions.
   - Modify testing if necessary.
   - Use peer and adult tutoring.
   - Involve a special education resource teacher.
   - State clear expectations and give the child immediate feedback.
   - Use behavior management techniques; especially provide positive feedback for children's progress. In chapter 7, "Behavioral Approaches, Social Cognitive Approaches, and Teaching," we will discuss these approaches in considerable detail.
   - Connect learning to real-life experiences.
   - Give children choices and allow them to engage in self-determination.
   - Use computer instruction, especially learning that involves a gamelike format.

2. *Medication-related strategies.* It is estimated that about 85 to 90 percent of children with ADHD are taking stimulant medication such as Ritalin to control their behavior (Tousignant, 1995). A child should be given medication only after a complete assessment that includes a physical examination. Typically a small dose is administered as a trial to examine its effects. If the child adequately tolerates the small dose, the dosage might be increased.

   The problem behaviors of children with ADHD can be temporarily controlled with prescriptive stimulants (Swanson & others, 1993). For many other children with ADHD, a combination of medication, behavior management, effective teaching, and parental monitoring improves their behavior. However, not all children with ADHD respond positively to prescription stimulants, and some critics believe that physicians are too quick to prescribe stimulants for children with milder forms of ADHD (Clay, 1997). The teacher plays an important role in observing whether the medication is at too high a level, making the child dazed and lethargic. Sometimes, especially for elementary school students, teachers administer medication when a dosage is required during the school day. It is important for teachers and parents not to convey a message to the child that medication is the answer to all of their academic difficulties (Hallahan & Kaufmann, 2000). Children with ADHD should be encouraged to take responsibility for their behavior in addition to any help that medication may provide them.

and limited attention span. They might say the child is "always on the go," "can't sit still even for a second," or "never seems to listen." Many children with ADHD are difficult to discipline, have little tolerance for frustration, and have problems in peer relations. Other common characteristics of children with ADHD include general immaturity and clumsiness.

Although signs of ADHD are often present in the preschool years, their classification often doesn't take place until the elementary school years (Guyer, 2000; Pueschel & others, 1995). The increased academic and social demands of formal schooling, as well as stricter standards for behavioral control, often illuminate the problems of the child with ADHD (Whalen, 2000). Elementary school teachers typically report that this type of child has difficulty in working independently, completing seatwork, and organizing work. Restlessness and distractibility also are often noted. These problems are more likely to be observed in repetitive or taxing tasks, or tasks the child perceives to be boring (such as completing worksheets or doing homework).

It used to be thought that ADHD decreased in adolescence, but now it is believed that this often is not the case. Estimates suggest that ADHD decreases in only about one-third of adolescents. Increasingly it is recognized that these problems also can continue into adulthood.

Definitive causes of ADHD have not been found. For example, scientists have not been able to identify causal sites in the brain. However, a number of causes have been proposed, such as low levels of certain neurotransmitters (chemical messengers in the brain), prenatal and postnatal abnormalities, and environmental toxins such as lead. Heredity might play a role, as 30 to 50 percent of children with ADHD have a sibling or parent who has the disorder (Woodrich, 1994).

Emotional and Behavioral Disorders

Most children have emotional problems at some time during their school years. A small percentage have problems that are so serious and persistent that they are classified as having an emotional or behavioral disorder. **Emotional and behavioral disorders** *consist of serious, persistent problems that involve relationships, aggression, depression, fears associated with personal or school matters, as well as other inappropriate socioemotional characteristics.* Approximately 9 percent of children who have a disability and require an individualized education plan fall into this classification. Boys are three times as likely as girls to have the disorder (U.S. Department of Education, 1996).

Various terms have been used to describe emotional and behavioral disorders, including *emotional disturbances, behavior disorders,* and *maladjusted children.* The term *serious emotional disturbance* (SED) recently has been used to describe children with these types of problems for whom it has been necessary to create individualized learning. However, critics argue that this category has not been clearly defined (Council for Exceptional Children, 1998).

Behavioral Disorders
Autism
Conduct Disorders

Autism   **Autism,** *an often severe developmental disorder, has its onset in infancy. It includes deficiencies in social relationships, abnormalities in communication, and restricted, repetitive, and stereotyped patterns of behavior.* Like other disorders, autism has a range of severity. Some children with autism never learn to speak, others show communication and social irregularities (Mesibov, 2000). Some display autistic behaviors many times a day, others more sporadically. Social deficiencies include a failure to make eye contact when communicating and rarely seeking others for interaction or affection. Communication deficiencies include poor synchrony and lack of reciprocity in conversation, as well as stereotyped, repetitive use of language. Stereotyped patterns can include compulsive rituals and self-stimulatory actions such as rocking, spinning, and finger flicking. Autistic individuals also can become distressed over small changes in the environment. Rearrangement of events or even furniture in the course of a day can cause children who are autistic to get extremely upset, reflecting their inflexibility in adapting to new routines.

What causes autism? The current consensus is that autism involves an organic brain dysfunction. There is no evidence that family socialization causes autism (Rutter & Schopler, 1987). Some children with autism have mental retardation, and others show average or above-average intelligence.

Children with autism benefit from a well-structured classroom, individualized instruction, or small-group instruction (Pueschel & others, 1995). As with children who have mental retardation, applied behavior analysis procedures sometimes have been effective in helping autistic children learn more effectively (Alberto & Troutman, 1995). If you have a child with autism in your class, consult with a special education professional to further your understanding and education of this type of learner.

Aggressive, Out-of-Control Behaviors   Some children who are classified as having a serious emotional disturbance and engage in disruptive, aggressive, defiant, or dangerous behaviors are removed from the classroom (Terman & others, 1996). These children are much more likely to be boys than girls and more likely to come from low-income than from middle- or high-income families (Achenbach & others, 1991). Children with a serious emotional disturbance are more likely than any other children with a disability to initially be classified as having a disability-related problem during the secondary school years. However, the majority of these children began to show signs of their emotional problem in the elementary school years (Wagner, 1995).

Experts on behavioral and emotional disorders say that when these children are returned to the regular classroom, both the regular classroom teacher and a special education teacher or consultant must spend a great deal of time helping them adapt and learn effectively (Hocutt, 1996). This means devoting several hours per week for several weeks for one or two students to help them make an effective transition back into the classroom. The more severe the problem, the less likely it is that a return to the classroom will work (Wagner, 1995).

In chapter 3, we discussed juvenile delinquency, school violence, rejected students, and improving students' social skills ◀◀ p. 114. Many of the comments and recommendations we made there apply to children with a serious emotional disturbance. In chapter 7, "Behavioral Approaches, Social Cognitive Approaches, and Teaching," and chapter 12, "Managing the Classroom," we will say more about strategies and plans for effectively dealing with children who show emotional and behavioral problems.

Depression
Anxiety

Depression, Anxiety, and Fears   Some children turn their emotional problems inward. Their depression, anxiety, or fears become so intense and persistent that their ability to learn is significantly compromised. All children feel depressed from time to time, but most get over their despondent, down mood in a few hours or a few days. However, for some children the negative mood is more serious and longer-lasting. **Depression** *is a type of mood disorder in which the individual feels worthless, believes that things are not likely to get better, and behaves lethargically for a prolonged period of time.* When children show these signs for 2 weeks or longer, they likely are experiencing depression. Poor appetite and not being able to sleep well also can be associated with depression.

Depression is much more likely to appear in adolescence than in childhood and has a much higher incidence in girls than in boys (Culbertson, 1997). Experts on depression say that this gender difference is likely due to a number of factors. Females tend to ruminate on their depressed mood and amplify it, whereas males tend to distract themselves from the negative mood; girls' self-images are often more negative than those of boys during adolescence; and societal bias against female achievement might be involved (Nolen-Hoeksema, 1990).

Be vigilant in recognizing the signs of depression in children. Because it is turned inward, depression is far more likely to go unnoticed than aggressive, acting-out behaviors. If you think that a child has become depressed, talk with the child's parents and discuss the possibility of obtaining professional counseling. Cognitive therapy has been especially effective in helping individuals become less depressed, as have some drug therapies (Beckham, 2000; Coyne, 2000; Mahoney, 1991).

Anxiety involves a vague, highly unpleasant feeling of fear and apprehension (Kowalski, 200). It is normal for children to be concerned or worried when they face life's challenges, but some children have such intense and prolonged anxiety that it substantially impairs their school performance. Some children also have personal or school-related fears that interfere with their learning. If a child shows marked or substantial fears that persist, discuss the

THROUGH THE EYES OF TEACHERS

Teaching Children with an Emotional Disorder

At the YAI/NYL schools, we developed our own behavior manual for the early childhood program. The manual stresses the need for teachers, professionals, and families to work together, when addressing the behavior needs of students with disabilities. Simple techniques, such as low lights, deep breathing exercise, more open space in the classroom, less visual distraction in the room, soft music, stretching exercises, observation techniques, building trust and respect, predictable patterns (daily schedule), flexibility of staff and clear communication, are just a few of the many strategies for working with children with an emotional disorder. These strategies also can be very effective for working with children with many different types of disabilities.

Juanita Kirton
Assistant Principal
YAI/NYL Garmecy School
New York City

SELF-ASSESSMENT 6.1
Evaluating My Experiences with People Who Have Various Disabilities and Disorders

Read each of the following statements and place a checkmark next to the ones that apply to you.

1. SENSORY DISORDERS

_____ I know someone with a sensory disorder and have talked with them about their disability.

_____ I have observed students with sensory disorders in the classroom and talked with their teachers about their strategies for educating them.

2. PHYSICAL DISORDERS

_____ I know someone with a physical disorder and have talked with them about their disability.

_____ I have observed students with physical disorders in the classroom and talked with their teachers about strategies for educating them.

3. MENTAL RETARDATION

_____ I know someone who has mental retardation and have talked with their parents about their child's disability.

_____ I have observed in the classroom students with mental retardation and talked with their teachers about their strategies for educating them.

4. SPEECH AND LANGUAGE DISORDERS

_____ I know someone with a speech and language disorder and have talked with them about their disability.

_____ I have observed students with a speech and language disorder in the classroom and talked with their teacher about strategies for educating them.

5. LEARNING DISABILITIES

_____ I know someone who has a learning disability and have talked with them about their disability.

_____ I have observed students with learning disabilities in the classroom and talked with teachers about their strategies for educating them.

6. ATTENTION DEFICIT HYPERACTIVITY DISORDER

_____ I know someone with ADHD and have talked with them about their disability.

_____ I have observed students with ADHD in the classroom and talked with teachers about their strategies for educating them.

7. EMOTIONAL AND BEHAVIORAL DISORDERS

_____ I know someone with an emotional and behavioral disorder and have talked with them about their disorder.

_____ I have observed students with emotional and behavioral disorders and talked with their teachers about strategies for educating them.

For those disabilities that you did not place a checkmark beside, make it a point to get to know and talk with someone who has the disability and observe students with the disability in the classroom. Then talk with their teachers about their strategies for educating them.

matter with the parents and recommend professional counseling or clinical help. Some behavioral therapies have been especially effective in reducing excessive or inaccurate anxiety and fear (Baldwin & Baldwin, 1998). More information about anxiety appears in chapter 11, "Motivating Students to Learn."

At this point we have discussed a number of different disabilities and disorders. To evaluate your experiences with individuals who have these disabilities, complete Self-Assessment 6.1. In this last section, we explored a number of ideas about learning disabilities, attention deficit hyperactivity disorder, and emotional and behavioral disorders. A review of these ideas is presented in summary table 6.2. Next we will study children who are gifted.

Summary Table 6.2

Learning Disabilities, Attention Deficit Hyperactivity Disorder, and Emotional and Behavioral Disorders

Concept	Processes/ Related Ideas	Characteristics/Description
Learning Disabilities	Characteristics	• Children with a learning disability are of normal intelligence or above, they have difficulties in at least one academic area and usually several, and their difficulty is not attributable to some other diagnosed problem or disorder, such as mental retardation. • Diagnosing whether a child has a learning disability is difficult. • About three times as many boys as girls have a learning disability. • The most common problem for children with a learning disability is reading. Dyslexia is a severe impairment in the ability to read and spell. • Children with a learning disability often have difficulties in handwriting, spelling, or composition, and increasingly are diagnosed with difficulties in math. • Controversy surrounds the "learning disability" category; some critics believe it is overdiagnosed; others argue that it is not.
	Identification	• Diagnosis is difficult, especially for mild forms. • Initial identification of children with a possible learning disability often is made by the classroom teacher, who then asks specialists to evaluate the child.
	Intervention Strategies	• Many interventions targeted for learning disabilities focus on reading ability and include such strategies as improving decoding skills. • The success of even the best-designed interventions depends on the training and skills of the teacher.
Attention Deficit Hyperactivity Disorder	Characteristics	• ADHD is a disability in which children consistently show problems in one or more of these areas: inattention, hyperactivity, and impulsivity. • Although signs of ADHD may be present in early childhood, diagnosis of ADHD often doesn't occur until the elementary school years. • Many experts recommend a combination of academic, behavioral, and medical interventions to help students with ADHD learn and adapt.
Emotional and Behavioral Disorders	Exploring Emotional and Behavioral Disorders	• They consist of serious, persistent problems that involve relationships, aggression, depression, fears associated with personal or school matters, as well as other inappropriate socioemotional characteristics. • The term *serious emotional disturbances* recently has been used to describe this category of disorders although it is not without criticism.
	Autism	• Autism includes deficiencies in social relationships, abnormalities in communication, and restricted, repetitive, and stereotyped patterns of behavior. • The current consensus is that autism involves an organic brain dysfunction. There is no evidence that it is caused by family socialization. • Children with autism benefit from a well-structured classroom, individualized instruction, or small-group instruction.
	Aggressive, Out-of-Control Behaviors	• In severe instances of this, students are removed from the classroom. • The problems are far more characteristic of boys than of girls.
	Depression, Anxiety, and Fears	• These students turn their problems inward. • Their depression, anxiety, or fears become so intense and persistent that their ability to learn is significantly compromised.

Children Who Are Gifted

The final type of exceptionality we will discuss is quite different from the disabilities and disorders that we have described so far. **Children who are gifted** *have above-average intelligence (usually defined as an IQ of 120 or higher) and/or superior talent in some domain such as art, music, or mathematics.* Programs for gifted children in schools typically base admission to the programs on intelligence and academic aptitude, although there is increasing call to widen the criteria to include such factors as creativity and commitment (Renzulli & Reis, 1997) ◀▥ p. 141. Some critics argue that too many children in "gifted programs" aren't really gifted in a particular area but are just somewhat bright, usually cooperative, and, usually, White. They believe the mantle of brilliance is cast on many children who are not that far from simply being "smart normal." Although general intelligence as defined by an overall IQ score still remains as a key component of many states' criteria for placing a child in a gifted program, changing conceptions of intelligence increasingly include ideas such as Gardner's multiple intelligences and placement criteria are likely to move away from a specific IQ score (Davidson, 2000) ◀▥ p. 130.

Characteristics   Ellen Winner (1996), an expert on creativity and giftedness, recently described three criteria that characterize children who are gifted:

1. *Precocity.* Children who are gifted are precocious when given the opportunity to use their gift or talent. They begin to master an area earlier than their peers. Learning in their domain is more effortless for them than for children who are not gifted. In most instances, children who are gifted are precocious because they have an inborn high ability in a particular domain or domains, although this inborn precocity has to be identified and nourished.
2. *Marching to their own drummer.* Children who are gifted learn in a qualitatively different way than children who are not gifted. One way they march to a different drummer is that they require less support, or scaffolding, from adults to learn than their nongifted peers do. Often they resist explicit instruction. They also often make discoveries on their own and solve problems in unique ways within their area of giftedness. They can be normal or below normal in other areas.
3. *A passion to master.* Children who are gifted are driven to understand the domain in which they have high ability. They display an intense, obsessive interest and an ability to focus. They are not children who need to be pushed by their parents. They frequently have a high degree of internal motivation.

Alexandra Nechita recently burst onto the child prodigy scene. She paints quickly and impulsively on large canvases, some as large as 5 feet by 9 feet, and often completes several of these large paintings in a week. Her paintings—in the modernist tradition—sell for up to $80,000 apiece. When she was only 2 years old, Alexandra colored in coloring books for hours. She had no interest in dolls or friends. Once she started school, she couldn't wait to get home to paint. And she continues to paint, relentlessly and passionately. It is, as she says, what she loves to do.

In addition to the three characteristics of gifted children that we have just mentioned (precocity, marching to a different drummer, and a passion to master), a fourth area in which they excel involves *information-processing skills.* Researchers have found that children who are gifted learn at a faster pace, process information

LEARNERS WHO ARE EXCEPTIONAL AND STRATEGIES FOR TEACHING THEM

Children Who Are Gifted

Children Who are Gifted
Gifted Education

Alexandra Nechita, pictured here when she was 10 years old, is a student who is gifted in the domain of art. She is precocious, marches to the tune of a different drummer, and has a passion to master her domain.

more rapidly, are better at reasoning, use better strategies, and monitor their understanding better than their nongifted counterparts (Jackson & Butterfield, 1986; Sternberg & Clickenbeard, 1995).

The Classic Terman Studies

Lewis Terman (1925) followed the lives of approximately 1,500 children whose Stanford-Binet IQs averaged 150 into the adult years. Their developmental outcomes were impressive. For the 800 men, 78 obtained doctorates (they include two past presidents of the American Psychological Association), 48 earned M.D.s, and 85 earned law degrees. These figures are 10 to 30 times greater than the educational achievements of the 800 men of the same age chosen randomly as a comparison control group.

Of the 672 women studied, two-thirds graduated from college in the 1930s and one-fourth attended graduate school (Terman & Oden, 1959). Despite their impressive educational achievements for their time, when asked to order life's priorities they often placed family first, friendship second, and career third, even though 25 of the 30 most successful women did not have children. The gifted women in Terman's study represented a cohort whose childhood, and most of their adulthood, was lived prior to the women's movement and the prevalence of the dual-career couple and the single-parent family (Tomlinson-Keasey, 1993). Studies of gifted girls and women today suggest that they have a stronger confidence in their cognitive abilities than did their gifted counterparts in Terman's study (Tomlinson-Keasey, 1997).

As a group, Terman's gifted were intellectually precocious but they were not emotionally disordered or maladjusted. This finding also has appeared in a number of studies of children who are gifted—namely, that they are as well adjusted as, or are better adjusted than, children who are not gifted (Winner, 1996). However, children who are extremely precocious (such as those having an IQ of 180 or higher) often show more adjustment problems than children who are not gifted (Keogh & MacMillan, 1996).

Steven Ceci (1990) has argued that an analysis of the Terman group's development brings up an important point. It was not just their high IQs that gained them success. Many of Terman's gifted came from upper-income families, and their parents had high achievement expectations for them and played a guiding role in their success. However, a few of the most successful gifted individuals in Terman's study did come from low-income families. Thus, success in life for individuals who are gifted doesn't require being born into material wealth.

Educating Children Who Are Gifted

Underchallenged gifted children can become disruptive, skip classes, and lose interest in achieving. Sometimes these children just disappear into the woodwork, becoming passive and apathetic toward school (Rosselli, 1996).

Four program options for gifted children are these (Hertzog, 1998):

- Special classes. Historically, this has been the common way to educate children who are gifted. The special classes during the regular school day are called "pull-out" programs (Schiever & Maker, 1997). Some special classes also are held after school, on Saturdays, or in the summer.
- Acceleration and enrichment in the regular classroom setting.
- Mentor and apprenticeship programs. Some experts believe these are important, underutilized ways to motivate, challenge, and effectively educate children who are gifted (Pleiss & Feldhusen, 1995).
- Work/study and/or community service programs.

The wave of educational reform has brought into the regular classroom many strategies that once were the domain of separate gifted programs. These include an emphasis on problem-based learning, having children do projects, creating portfolios, and critical thinking. Combined with the increasing emphasis on educating all children in the regular classroom, many schools now try to challenge and motivate children who are gifted in the regular classroom (Hertzog, 1998). Some schools also include after-school or Saturday programs or develop mentor apprenticeship, work/study, or community service programs. Thus, an array of in-school and out-of-school opportunities is provided.

An ongoing debate focuses on whether children who are gifted should be placed in acceleration or enrichment programs (Feldhusen, 1997). An **acceleration program** *moves children through the curriculum as quickly as they are able to progress.* Acceleration programs include early entrance (to kindergarten, first grade, middle school, high school, or college), skipping grades, taking extra courses or honors courses, and taking advanced placement classes. **Curriculum compacting** *is a variation of acceleration in which teachers skip over aspects of the curriculum that they believe children who are gifted do not need.*

An **enrichment program** *provides children with opportunities for learning that are usually not present in the curriculum.* Enrichment opportunities can be made available in the regular classroom, through "pullout" to a special class; through a gifted education resource teacher who consults with the regular classroom teacher; through independent study, in after-school, Saturday, or summer sessions, and in apprenticeship and mentoring programs; and through work/study arrangements. One type of enrichment program, the *schoolwide enrichment model,* includes developing children's critical and creative thinking skills, and giving them opportunities to select areas of study (Renzulli & Reis, 1997). Children are identified for this type of program by multiple criteria that include creativity and commitment.

Research evaluation of acceleration and enrichment programs has not revealed which approach is best (Winner, 1997). Some researchers have found support for acceleration programs (Kulik, 1992), although critics say a potential problem of grade skipping is that it places children with others who are physically more advanced and socioemotionally different (Gross, 1993). Other researchers have found support for enrichment programs (Delcourt & others, 1994; Renzulli & Reis, 1997).

Ellen Winner (1997) argues that too often children who are gifted are socially isolated and underchallenged in the classroom. It is not unusual for them to be ostracized and labeled "nerds" or "geeks" (Silverman, 1993). A gifted child who is the only such child in the room does not have the opportunity to learn with students of like ability. Many eminent adults report that school was a negative experience for them, that they were bored and sometimes knew more than their teachers (Bloom, 1985). Winner believes that American education will benefit when standards are raised for all children. When some children are still underchallenged, she recommends that they be allowed to attend advanced classes in their domain of exceptional ability. For example, some especially precocious middle school students are allowed to take college classes in their area of expertise.

THROUGH THE EYES OF CHILDREN

Children Who Are Gifted Speak

James Delisle (1984) interviewed hundreds of elementary school children who are gifted. Following are some of their comments.

In response to: Describe Your Typical School Day

> Oh what a bore to sit and listen,
> To stuff we already know.
> Do everything we've done and done again,
> But we must still sit and listen.
> Over and over read one more page
> Oh bore, oh bore, oh bore.

Girl, Age 9, New York

> I sit there pretending to be reading along when I'm really six pages ahead. When I understand something and half the class doesn't, I have to sit there and listen.

Girl, Age 11, New York

In response to: Describe a Perfect Day

> If I learned to understand something new in most subjects.

Boy, Age 12, New York

In response to: What Activities and Methods Do Teachers Use That Make Learning Worthwhile?

> My fifth grade teacher makes learning fun by doing an activity to help you learn. We have math sales and that helps us with money while it's also fun to learn. In studying the Constitution we made bills and voted on them."

Girl, Age 10, Connecticut

In response to: What Makes a Teacher a Gifted Teacher?

> She is capable of handling our problems and has a good imagination to help us learn.

Girl, 10, Louisiana

> Will challenge you and let the sky be your limit.

Boy, 11, Michigan

> Opens your mind to help you with your life.

Boy, 11, New Jersey

DIVERSITY AND EDUCATION
High-Potential Minority Students

Children of color, especially those who come from low-income backgrounds, are underrepresented in programs for children who are gifted (Frasier & Passaw, 1995). Once identified, these children might still fare poorly if their programs do not take sociocultural dimensions into account (Ford, 1996).

In one recent study, Project START, a collaboration between a university and a school district, identified and served high-potential, low-income children, most of whom were from ethnic minority backgrounds (Tomlinson, Callahan, & Lelli, 1997). Among the components of the program were an emphasis on Howard Gardner's multiple-intelligences view (see chapter 4, "Individual Variations"), language immersion, mentoring by community members, and a family outreach program.

One child who benefited from Project START was Charelle, a third-grade African American. She was often late for school because of her family's circumstances, but when she arrived she quickly became absorbed in her schoolwork. Her second-grade teacher had recognized that Charelle had especially good writing skills and had let her engage in many writing activities. Her third-grade teacher also had a flexible approach that allowed Charelle to choose a number of the activities.

Another child who was helped by Project START was an African American girl named Belinda. The mentoring portion of the program was what sparked her development. She was paired for 2 years with a female TV meteorologist who worked with her every Tuesday. Unlike other days, she was never late or absent on Tuesdays. The mentor helped her to not become so frustrated with her academic work and to be more persistent and patient in completing assignments. The mentor also improved Belinda's curiosity to learn about new things. Prior to the mentor relationship, Belinda had refused to participate in physical education. With her mentor's encouragement, she began to exercise regularly and her motor coordination improved.

Belinda's mother, a single mother with four children, also became very responsive to the family outreach aspect of the project. She learned which agencies she could call when she needed help for her children, learned how to control her anger, and improved her parenting skills.

A special concern is the education of high-potential students from low-income, ethnic minority backgrounds. To read about these students, see Diversity and Education.

At this point we have studied a number of ideas about children who are gifted. A review of these ideas is presented in summary table 6.3. Next, we will continue our exploration of learners who have disabilities by examining the many changes that are taking place in their education.

Educational Issues Involving Children with Disabilities

The legal requirement that schools serve all children with a disability is fairly recent. We will explore the legal aspects of working with children who have a disability, profile the placements and services available for children with disabilities, discuss factors that affect the outcomes for children receiving special education services, as well as examine the roles of parents and technology in educating these children.

Legal Aspects

Let's first examine the historical background.

The Council for Exceptional Children

Historical Background   Beginning in the mid 1960s to mid 1970s, legislatures, the federal courts, and the United States Congress laid down special educational rights for children with disabilities. Prior to that time, most children with a

SUMMARY TABLE 6.3
Children Who Are Gifted

Concept	Processes/ Related Ideas	Characteristics/Description
Characteristics	What Makes a Child Gifted	• Children who are gifted have above-average intelligence (usually defined as an IQ of 120 or higher) and/or superior talent in some domain, such as art, music, or mathematics. Some critics argue that gifted programs include too many children who are just somewhat bright, usually cooperative, and, usually, White. Winner described children who are gifted as having three main characteristics: precocity, marching to the tune of a different drummer, a passion to master.
The Classic Terman Studies	Backgrounds and Success of Gifted Children	• These studies revealed the successful lives of many children who are gifted. Many of the Terman gifted not only had superior IQs but also came from high-income families in which their parents guided and monitored their achievement. Many children who are gifted do not have emotional disorders.
Educating Children Who Are Gifted	Creating Challenges	• Underchallenged gifted students can show school-related problems. Educational programs available for children who are gifted include special classes ("pullout" programs), acceleration, enrichment, mentor and apprenticeship programs, as well as work/study or community service programs. Debate focuses on whether acceleration or enrichment programs benefit children who are gifted the most. Children who are gifted increasingly are being educated in the regular classroom. Some experts recommend that increasing the standards in the regular classroom will help children who are gifted, although some of the programs just discussed (such as mentoring and additional instruction) might be needed for children who still remain underchallenged.

disability were either refused enrollment or inadequately served by schools. In 1975, Congress enacted **Public Law 94-142,** *the Education for All Handicapped Children Act, which required that all students with disabilities be given a free, appropriate public education and which provided the funding to help implement this education.*

In 1983, Public Law 94-142 was renamed the **Individuals with Disabilities Education Act (IDEA).** *The IDEA spells out broad mandates for services to all children with disabilities. These include evaluation and eligibility determination, appropriate education and an individualized education plan (IEP), and education in the least restrictive environment (LRE)* (Martin, Martin, & Sherman, 1996).

Legal Aspects

Evaluation and Eligibility Determination   Children who are thought to have a disability are evaluated to determine their eligibility for services under the IDEA. Schools are prohibited from planning special education programs in advance and offering them on a space-available basis.

Children must be evaluated before a school can begin providing special services (Wolery, 2000). Parents should be involved in the evaluation process. Reevaluation is required at least every 3 years (sometimes every year), when requested by parents, or when conditions suggest a reevaluation is needed. A parent who disagrees with the school's evaluation can obtain an independent evaluation, which the school is required to consider in providing special education services. If the evaluation finds that child has a disability and requires special services, the school must provide the child with appropriate services.

In giving rights to others that belong to them, we give rights to ourselves.

John F. Kennedy
U.S. President, 20th Century

INDIVIDUALIZED EDUCATION PROGRAM

NAME _____ DATE OF BIRTH _____/_____/_____ GRADE LEVEL _____ ❑ MALE ❑ FEMALE

CHILD/STUDENT ADDRESS _____ PARENT/GUARDIAN _____

PARENT ADDRESS _____ HOME TELEPHONE _____ WORK TELEPHONE _____

EFFECTIVE DATES From: _____ To: _____ MEETING DATE _____ ❑ INITIAL IEP ❑ PERIODIC REVIEW

ADDITIONAL CONSIDERATIONS

Considerations for the IEP team as they complete the IEP process, steps 1–5. Refer to State of Ohio Model Policies and Procedures for the Education of Children with Disabilities and IEP *Tour Book* for specific information on procedures/process. If needed, use space provided or attach additional sheet.

	Discussed and Not Applicable for This Child/Student	Discussed and Incorporated into IEP
1. Testing and assessment programs, including proficiency tests [See IEEE Addendum 608a]	❑	❑
2. Transition from early childhood ages 3-5 to school-age programs	❑	❑
3. Transition services statement no later than age 16 [See IEP Addendum 608b]	❑	❑
4. A plan to address behavior if the IEP and MFE team have determined this to be a concern	❑	❑
5. Physical education must be addressed for ALL children and incorporated into the IEP	(MUST BE INCORPORATED)	❑
6. Extended school year services	❑	❑
7. Children/students with visual impairments [See IEP Addendum 608c]	❑	❑

Relevant Information/Suggestions (e.g., medical information, other information)

Present Levels of Development/ Functioning/Performance	Annual Goals	Objectives
[Refer to State of Ohio Model Policies and Procedures for the Education of Children with Disabilities or IEP Tour book for specific information on procedures/process] **Step 1** Review the results of the evaluation team report or intervention-based multifactored evaluation or current IEP. In a narrative form, explain the child's/student's present levels of performance. Include progress, strengths, capabilities, interests, and needs displayed in school, at home, and in the community. **Step 2** Determine the area(s) of the child's/student's needs.	**Step 3** Write goals and objectives in area of need (What will the child/student be able to do in one year?)	What are the intermediate/sequential steps leading to the goal?

Figure 6.5
An Example of An Individualized Education Plan (IEP) Form

(continued om next page)

Evaluation of Each Objective					Services	Initation/ Duration	LRE
Procedures	Criteria	Schedule	Who	Review of Progress			
How?	*What? How much?*	*When will we review?*	*Who is responsible?*	*Results?*	**Step 4** Determine special education services, including related services, needed to implement each goal, as well as the amount of services. *(e.g., modifications, supplemental aids, assistive technology providers)*		**Step 5** Determine setting in which to deliver the service. *(Where will services be provided?)*

IEP SUMMARY FOR EFFECTIVE DATES

Name _____

EXTENT OF PARTICIPATION IN REGULAR EDUCATIONAL ENVIRONMENT OR, FOR PRESCHOOL, PARTICIPATION WITH TYPICALLY DEVELOPING PEERS

Additional modifications:

REASON FOR PLACEMENT IN SEPARATE FACILITY (if applicable)

Having considered each of the separate delivery options, this IEP team has decided that placement in a separate facility is appropriate because:

School district of residence: _____

School district of service: _____

Building: _____

Date of Next IEP Review: _____

Date of Last MFE: _____

Next MFE to be Completed By: _____

CHILD/STUDENT ID#: _____

AGE AS OF NEXT DECEMBER 1

Specify age in years: _____

IEP Meeting Participants' Signatures

1. Parent(s): _____
2. Child's/Student's Teacher: _____
3. District Representative: _____
4. Child/Student: _____
5. Other Titles: _____
6. _____
7. _____
8. _____
9. _____
Chairperson of IEP Team: _____

Consent

(For initial placement or charge in special education services and placement only)

❏ I give consent to initiate special education and related services specified in this IEP.

❏ I waive my right to notification of special education and related services by certified mail.

❏ I give consent to initiate special education and related services specified in this IEP except for _____.

❏ I do not give consent for special education services a this time.

Parent Signature: _____ **Date:** _____

PARENT NOTICE OF PROCEDURAL SAFEGUARDS:

❏ I have received a copy of the parent notice of procedural safeguards, or

❏ I have a current copy of the parent notice of procedural safeguards.

Parent Signature: _____ **Date:** _____

State and federal rules and regulations mandate that every child/student with a disability be reevaluated at least every three years. THIS IS TO NOTIFY YOU that your child will be provided that mandated reevaluation prior to his/her next periodic review. Applicable if this box is checked ❏

Summary of Services for EMIS Purposes

Disability (circle the child's/student's primary disability)							LRE:	Related Services: (list all services to be received)
MH	DB	HI	VI	SH	OH	OHI		
SBH	DH	SLD	P/D	AU	TBI		Attendance option for Preschool/kindergarden:	

Figure 6.5
An Example of An Individualized Education Plan (IEP) Form *(concluded)*

THROUGH THE EYES OF TEACHERS

Subsiding Whispers of Fear

When schools in my county began to hear that they would be inclusion schools, the rumors began to fly and the fears began to escalate. The whispers were that classroom teachers would have a deaf child in their room and would receive no prior training to help the child, or be left alone to deal with a child who has an emotional disorder who throws chairs around the room.

What we found was completely the opposite. The more help and facts we were given, the more the whispers of fear went away. At one of the meetings, one of our kindergarten teachers pointed out that this was no different from what kindergarten teachers have been doing all along. She was right.

Anita Marie Hitchcock
Kindergarten Teacher
Holley Navarre Primary
Santa Rosa County, Florida

Inclusion

The IDEA has many specific provisions that relate to the parents of a child with a disability (Hardman, Drew, & Egan, 1999). These include requirements that schools send notices to parents of proposed actions, that parents be allowed to attend meetings regarding the child's placement or individualized education plan, and the right to appeal school decisions to an impartial evaluator.

Appropriate Education and the Individualized Education Plan (IEP)

The IDEA requires that students with disabilities have an **individualized education plan (IEP).** *The IEP is a written statement that spells out a program specifically tailored for the student with a disability. In general, the IEP should be (1) related to the child's learning capacity, (2) specially constructed to meet the child's individual needs and not merely copy what is offered to other children, and (3) designed to provide educational benefits.* Figure 6.5 on pages 222–223 shows one state's IEP form.

Least Restrictive Environment (LRE)

Under the IDEA, the child with a disability must be educated in the **least restrictive environment (LRE).** *This means a setting that is as similar as possible to the one in which children who do not have a disability are educated.* This provision of the IDEA has given a legal basis to making an effort to educate children with a disability in the regular classroom. The education of children with a disability in the regular classroom used to be called "mainstreaming." However, that term has been replaced by the term **inclusion,** *which means educating a child with special educational needs full-time in the regular classroom* (Idol, 1997). Today, **mainstreaming** *means educating a student with special educational needs partially in a special education classroom and partially in a regular classroom* (Idol, 1997).

Not long ago it was considered appropriate to educate children with disabilities outside the regular classroom. However, today schools must make every effort to provide inclusion for children with disabilities (Friend & Bursuck, 1999; Siegel, 1997). These efforts can be very costly financially and very time consuming in terms of faculty effort.

The principle of "least restrictive environment" compels schools to examine possible modifications of the regular classroom before moving the child with a disability to a more restrictive placement (Smith & others, 1998). Also, regular classroom teachers often need specialized training to help some children with a disability, and state educational agencies are required to provide such training (Heward, 2000).

Many legal changes regarding children with disabilities have been extremely positive. Compared to even several decades ago, far more children today are receiving competent, specialized services. For many children, inclusion in the regular classroom, with modifications or supplemental services, is appropriate. However, some experts believe that separate programs can be more effective and appropriate for other children with disabilities (Martin, Martin, & Terman, 1996).

Research studies that have focused on outcomes for children related to inclusion suggest these conclusions (Hocutt, 1996):

- *Children's academic and social success:* These outcomes are affected more by the quality of the instruction given than by where the child is placed (such as regular classroom, resource room, or special education classroom). When inclusion is used, it works best when regular classroom teachers are given lengthy, often

Increasingly, children with disabilities are being taught in the regular classroom, as is this child with mild mental retardation.

multiyear training, planning time, administrative support, and sometimes additional instructional staff.

- *Children with severe emotional disturbance:* Children with this disorder are more likely to succeed if they participate in vocational education and are integrated into the school through activities like sports. However, children who have a long history of course failures are more likely to drop out of school if they are placed in the regular classroom.

- *Children with hearing impairments:* Children with these disorders gain some academic advantages but have lower self-esteem when they are in the regular classroom. The strength of the child's auditory and oral skills is crucial to success in the regular classroom.

- *Children with educable mental retardation* (usually defined as having an IQ from 50 to 70 along with adaptive behavior problems): These children are sensitive to the regular classroom environment. A supportive teacher, competent instruction, and supportive classmates seem to have an even greater impact on these children than on children without disabilities.

- *Children with severe mental retardation* (IQ below 50): Programs that provide supportive transitional services have been successful in avoiding placements of these children in residential settings.

- *Nondisabled children:* Nondisabled children do not appear to be negatively affected by the inclusion of children with a disability in the regular classroom as long as supportive services are provided. This research finding is especially important because many parents of nondisabled students worry that teachers will not have adequate time to help their child learn because they will be spending so much time with children who have disabilities. When the inclusion program brings a lower overall teacher–child ratio, children who do not have a disability actually are likely to benefit academically from inclusion.

Let's now explore the range of placements and services for children with disabilities.

Placements and Services

Children with disabilities can be placed in a variety of settings, and a range of services can be used to improve their education.

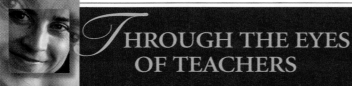

Placements   The following range of placements of children with disabilities is ordered from least restrictive to most restrictive (Deno, 1970):

- Regular classroom with supplementary instructional support and with or without medical support
- Regular classroom with supplementary instructional support provided in the regular classroom
- Part of time spent in a resource room
- Full-time placement in a special education class
- Special schools
- Homebound instruction
- Instruction in a hospital or other institution

As indicated in figure 6.6, of children receiving special education, slightly more than one-third receive it in the regular classroom; approximately the same percentage get services in a resource room; and slightly less than 25 percent receive services in a separate class. About one-third of children who receive special education in a separate class spend 80 percent or more of their school day in the regular classroom. Another one-third spend 40 to 79 percent of their school day in the regular classroom, and the final one-third spend 0 to 39 percent there (Hocutt, 1996).

Services   Services for children can be provided by the regular classroom teacher, a resource teacher, a special education teacher, a collaborative consultant, other professionals, or an interactive team.

Special Education Resources

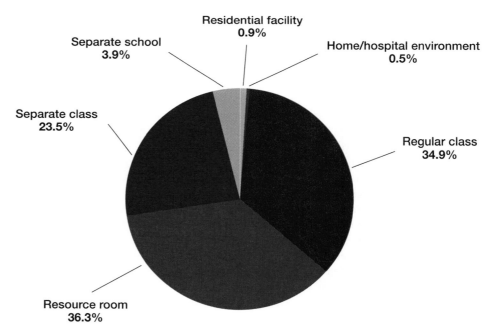

Figure 6.6

Percentage of Special Education Services Provided in Various Settings

Source: Office of Special Education Programs, *Implementation of the Individuals with Disabilities Education Act.* Washington, DC: U.S. Department of Education, 1994

The Regular Classroom Teacher   With the increase in inclusion, the regular classroom teacher is responsible for providing more of the education of children with disabilities than in the past. The following strategies can help you provide a more effective education for these children:

- Carry out each child's individualized educational plan (IEP).
- Encourage your school to provide increased support and training in how to teach children with disabilities.
- Use the support that is available and seek other support. Many well-educated, conscientious people in the community might be willing to volunteer some of their time to help you provide more individualized instruction for students with disabilities. This in turn provides a lower teacher–student ratio that benefits all of your students.
- Become more knowledgeable about the types of children with disabilities in your classroom. Read education journals, such as *Exceptional Children, Teaching Exceptional Children,* and *Journal of Learning Disabilities,* and to keep up-to-date on the latest information about these children. Look into taking a class at a college or university or a continuing education course on topics like exceptional children, mental retardation, learning disabilities, or emotional and behavioral disorders.
- Be cautious about labeling children with a disability. It is easy to fall into the trap of using the label as an explanation of the child's learning difficulties. For example, a teacher might say, "Well, Larry has trouble with reading because he has a learning disability," when in fact the teacher really knows only that for some unknown reason Larry is having trouble with reading. Also, labels have a way of remaining after the child has improved considerably. Remember that terms like *mental retardation* and *learning disability* are descriptive labels for disorders. Always think of children with disabilities in terms of what the best conditions are for improving their learning and how they can be helped to make progress rather than in terms of unchanging labels.
- Remember that children with disabilities benefit from many of the same teaching strategies that benefit children without disabilities:

Be caring, accepting, and patient.
Have positive expectations for learning.
Help children with their social and communication skills as well as academic skills.
Plan and organize the classroom effectively.
Be enthusiastic and help children become motivated to learn.
Monitor children's learning and provide effective feedback.

- Help children without a disability to understand and accept children with a disability. Give children without a disability information about children with a disability and create opportunities for them to interact with each other in positive ways. Peer tutoring and cooperative learning activities can be used to encourage positive interaction between children without a disability and children with a disability (Fuchs & others, 1994; Slavin, 1995). We will discuss these activities further

THROUGH THE EYES OF TEACHERS

Take Responsibility

It is really important for general education teachers to take responsibility for students with special needs. These children are part of their classroom. The teacher should not think of his/her classroom roster as 20 students plus the child in the wheelchair. Always make sure that children with special needs are not left behind. This happens more than you think. The class may go to the library with the teacher leading the line. The students follow in a single file, but no one thinks to push the child sitting in the wheelchair into the line. And special education teachers and assistants may not always be around to perform routine tasks; they service many children throughout the school.

Read and review the Individual Education Plan (I.E.P.) for each child in your class and preferably your entire grade level to ensure that all goals and objectives as well as any classroom modifications are being met. Is the child supposed to be seated near the teacher? Is the student hearing impaired and should not sit near a fan or air conditioning unit? Is the student supposed to take tests in small groups, one-on-one, or read aloud? Don't presume the special education teacher will tell you everything in a child's I.E.P.

Chaille Lazar
Special Education Teacher
Hedgrove Elementary School
Plano, Texas

*O*nly with the winter-patience can we bring
The deep-desired, long-awaited spring.

Anne Morrow Lindbergh
American Poet and Writer, 20th Century

in chapter 9, "Social Constructivist Approaches, Domain-Specific Approaches, and Teaching." In one recent study, peer-assisted learning strategies benefited the reading skills of children with disabilities (Fuchs & others, 1997).

• Keep up-to-date on the technology that is available for educating children with a disability. We will discuss this topic shortly.

Special Education Projects

The Resource Teacher   A resource teacher can provide valuable services for many children who have a disability. Many children with disabilities spend most of their school day in a regular classroom and a small portion of their day in a resource room where a resource teacher works with them. In a typical arrangement, a child might spend 1 or 2 hours a day in the resource room and the remainder of time in the regular classroom. In many situations, resource teachers work with these children to improve their reading, writing, or mathematical skills.

It is important for the regular classroom teacher and the resource teacher to collaborate and coordinate their efforts. In some cases, the resource teacher will work with the child in the regular classroom setting rather than seeing the child in a resource room.

The Special Education Teacher   Some teachers have extensive training in special education and teach children with disabilities in a separate "special education classroom." Some children will spend time with the special education teacher part of the school day and be mainstreamed the rest of the day, as happens with a resource teacher. However, the special education teacher typically assumes greater responsibility for the child's overall program than the resource teacher, who usually works in support of the regular classroom teacher. A child might learn reading, writing, mathematics, or science with the special education teacher and be mainstreamed for physical education, art, or music. The most frequent area in which the special education teacher works with the child who has a disability is reading, and the most frequent classification of a special education teacher is as a teacher of children who have specific learning disabilities (U.S. Department of Education, 1996).

In some school systems, if more than a set percentage (say, 60 percent) of the child's time is spent with a special education teacher, the child's program is called *self-contained special education*. Self-contained special education also is in effect when children are educated in separate schools for children with disabilities.

Related Services   In addition to regular classroom teachers, resource teachers, and special education teachers, a number of other special education personnel provide services for children with disabilities (U.S. Department of Education, 1996). These include teacher aides, psychologists, counselors, school social workers, nurses, physicians, occupational therapists, and physical therapists, as well as speech and hearing specialists, such as audiologists. In addition, transportation services also might be provided if needed by the children.

Teacher aids especially can help the regular classroom teacher provide individualized instruction for children with disabilities. Some teacher aides are certified to work with children who have disabilities. Psychologists might be involved in assessing whether a child has a disability and might be part of the team that creates the IEP. They and counselors might also work with some children who have a disability. My (your author's) first job was as a school psychologist assigned to a reading clinic to evaluate the cognitive and socioemotional skills of children with reading problems. School psychologists might make recommendations to teachers about ways that children with a disability can learn more effectively. School social workers often help to coordinate family and community services for children with a disability. Nurses and physicians might conduct medical assessments and/or prescribe medication for children with disabilities. Physical therapists and occupational therapists might be

TEACHING STRATEGIES
For Communicating with Parents
of Children with Disabilities

Following are some strategies for effectively communicating with parents of students with disabilities (Felber, 1997):

1. *Let parents know that you understand and appreciate their child's individuality.* Make it a point to talk about their child's strengths rather than focusing only on their child's problems. Especially focus on positive aspects of their child at the beginning and the end of the conversation.
2. *Place yourself in the shoes of parents of a child with a disability.* It is important to realize the frustration that many parents with a student who has a disability often feel. They may be struggling with a new diagnosis of their child or be confronting the complexities of an education plan for their child for the first time. Relay a diagnosis with compassion and an appropriate degree of hope for the child.
3. *Provide parents with information about their child's disability.* Once a child has been diagnosed with a disability, teachers should engage parents in an ongoing conversation about what this diagnosis means for the child. It is important for teachers and parents to work cooperatively in establishing and meeting realistic learning goals for the child. Know what resources can be used to help the child and discuss these with parents.
4. *Talk with parents, not to them.* View each meeting with the child's parents as an opportunity to learn more about the child. It is easy to fall into the trap of acting like an authority and talking "to" rather than "with" parents. View parents as being an equal partner with you and other professionals in educating the child with a disability. Encourage parents to ask questions and express their emotions. If you don't know the answer to a parent's question, tell them that you will try to find out the information for them.
5. *Avoid stereotyping children.* Educate yourself about childrens' diversity and the range of backgrounds they come from. Avoid making stereotypical judgments about children and their parents based on their socioeconomic status, ethnicity, family structure, religion, or gender. Good relationships and effective communication are undermined by biased assumptions.
6. *Reach out to parents to establish and maintain effective communication with them.* Tell them how important they are in helping you and other school professionals to understand and educate their child. Be sure to support their attendance at individualized education plan (IEP) meetings.
7. *Talk with parents about how the media can provide erroneous portrayals of children with disabilities.* Popular magazines, newspapers, movies, television, and radio at times provide inaccurate information about children with disabilities. Caution parents about this and tell them that they are always welcome to discuss anything they read about or hear pertaining to their child's disability with you or other school personnel.

involved in helping children recover from remediable physical or cognitive impairments. Speech and hearing specialists may be included when their skills will help improve children's skills in their area of expertise.

Collaborative Consultation and Interactive Teaming   In the last two decades, experts on educating children with disabilities have increasingly advocated more collaborative consultation (Idol, 1997; O'Shea & O'Shea, 1997). In **collaborative consultation,** *people with diverse expertise interact to provide services for children.* Researchers have found that collaborative consultation often results in gains for children, as well as improved skills and attitudes for teachers (Idol, Nevin, & Paolucci-Whitcomb, 1994).

Ideally, collaborative consultation encourages shared responsibility in planning and decision making. It also enables educators with diverse expertise to construct effective alternatives to traditional educational approaches (Pugach & Johnson, 1995). When collaborative consultation is used, many children remain in the regular classroom and the regular classroom teacher is actively involved in planning the child's education (Bryant & Bryant, 1998).

Only from the alliance of one person working with another are great things born.

Antoine de St. Exupéry
French Essayist and Novelist, 20th Century

Increasingly, the term *interactive teaming* is being used (Thomas, Correa, & Morsink, 1995). Interactive team members are professionals and parents who collaborate to provide direct or indirect services to children (Coben & others, 1997). They share knowledge and skills, teaching other members their expertise when appropriate. Actual team sizes vary, and teams change in composition depending on the complexity of the child's needs. Persons involved can include educational, medical, administrative, vocational, and allied health specialists, social services personnel, and parents.

Parents as Educational Partners

Educators and researchers increasingly recognize how important it is for teachers and parents to jointly guide the learning of children with disabilities (Williams & Cartledge, 1997). The Individuals with Disabilities Education Act (IDEA) mandates parent participation in developing educational programs for all children with disabilities.

Technology

Technology Resources
Assistive Technology

The Individuals with Disabilities Education Act (IDEA), including its 1997 amendments, requires that technology devices and services be provided to students with disabilities if they are necessary to ensure a free, appropriate education (Behrmann, 1994; Bryant & Seay, 1998; Lewis, 1998). Earlier in this chapter, we briefly mentioned technology devices that can be used to help students with disabilities (such as students with a visual impairment, a hearing impairment, or cerebral palsy). Here we will provide a more comprehensive look at using technology in the education of students with disabilities. In chapter 10, "Planning, Instruction, and Technology," we will explore technology and learning in more detail.

Two types of technology that can be used to improve the education of students with disabilities are instructional technology and assistance technology (Blackhurst, 1997). **Instructional technology** *includes various types of hardware and software, combined with innovative teaching methods, to accommodate students' learning needs in the classroom.* This technology can include videotapes, computer-assisted instruction, or complex hypermedia programs in which computers are used to control the display of audio and visual images stored on videodisc. The use of telecommunication systems, especially the Internet and its World Wide Web, hold considerable promise for improving the education of students with or without a disability.

Assistive technology *consists of various services and devices to help students with disabilities function within their environment.* Examples include communication aids, alternative computer keyboards, and adaptive switches. To locate such services, educators can use computer databases such as the Device Locator System (Academic Software, 1996).

Teams of educators and other professionals often combine these technologies to improve the learning of students with disabilities (Elkind, 2000). For example, students who are unable to use their hands to operate a computer keyboard might use a voice-operated computer (assistive technology) that provides instruction from a software program that was designed to provide spelling instruction (instructional technology). To read further about instructional and assistive technologies, see Technology and Education.

At this point we have studied many ideas about educational issues involving children with disabilities. An overview of these ideas is presented in summary table 6.4. In the next chapter we will turn our attention to behavioral approaches, social cognitive approaches, and teaching.

TECHNOLOGY AND EDUCATION
Exploring Instructive and Assistive Technologies

Instructive and assistive technologies include traditional applications, constructivist applications, word processing, and other assistive technologies (Roblyer, Edwards, & Hariluk, 1997).

Traditional Applications

Traditional applications involve the use of computer-based tutorials, drill and practice, and games. For example, these applications have been used to improve the decoding and vocabulary skills of children with a learning disability, especially those who have reading problems. Game-type software is often used to motivate children with a disability.

Constructivist Applications

An increasing trend is to use computer-based applications that are constructivist rather than based on tutorial or drill-and-practice methods. Constructivist applications focus on students' understanding and thinking skills. More and more computer-based learning programs include simulation of real-world problems (Cognition and Technology Group at Vanderbilt, 1997).

Among the constructivist technology applications that can be used effectively with children with disabilities are cognitive organizers like Idea Fisher and Inspiration. Both can be used with children who have a learning disability. Word prediction software can be used to help children with physical disabilities write on a computer.

Word Processing

Word processing has helped many children with disabilities make progress in their written language skills (Holzberg, 1995). Talking word processors such as Write Out Loud, Intellitalk, Kids Works 2, and The Amazing Writing Machine can be especially helpful in the education of children with speech problems. On request, these programs read text aloud.

Other Assistive Technologies

Many children with physical disabilities (such as cerebral palsy) cannot use traditional devices like a keyboard and a mouse. Touch screens, touch tablets, optical pointers, alternative keyboards, and voice-controlled devices are alternatives that allow them to use a computer (see figure 6.7).

Software or special hardware such as closed-circuit television can enlarge computer images and text for children with a visual impairment. Printers can produce large print or Braille. Tactile devices that scan a page and translate the text into vibrating, tactile displays also can be used with children who are visually impaired. Captioned video provides subtitles for television and other video presentations so that children who are hearing impaired can read what others are saying.

Telecommunication technologies for the deaf allow children with hearing impairments to communicate with people over the phone. The Internet allows children with a disability who are homebound to access educational opportunities.

(a)

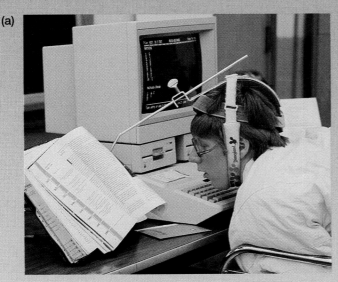

(b)

Figure 6.7   Special Input Devices

These special input devices can help students with physical disabilities use computers more effectively. *(a)* A student uses a special input device attached to the student's head to send signals to the computer. *(b)* Many students with physical disabilities such as cerebral palsy cannot use a conventional keyboard and mouse. Many can use alternative keyboards effectively.

$\mathcal{S}$UMMARY $\mathcal{T}$ABLE 6.4
Educational Issues Involving
Children with Disabilities

Concept	Processes/Related Ideas	Characteristics/Description
Legal Aspects	Historical Background	• Beginning in the mid 1960s to mid 1970s, the educational rights for children with disabilities were laid down. In 1975, Congress enacted Public Law 94-14, the Education All Handicapped Children Act, which mandated that all children be given a free, appropriate public education. In 1983, Public Law 94-142 was renamed the Individuals with Disabilities Education Act (IDEA), which spells out broad mandates for services to all children with disabilities.
	Evaluation and Eligibility Determination	• Children who are thought to have a disability are evaluated to determine their eligibility for services. The IDEA has many provisions that relate to the parents of children with disabilities.
	Appropriate Education and the Individualized Education Plan (IEP)	• The IEP consists of a written plan that spells out a program specifically tailored for the child with a disability. The plan should (1) relate to the child's capacity, (2) be individualized and not a copy of a plan that is offered to other children, and (3) be designed to provide educational benefits.
	Least Restrictive Environment (LRE)	• This concept, which is contained in the IDEA, states that children with disabilities must be educated in a setting that is as similar as possible to the one in which children without disabilities are educated. This provison of the IDEA has given a legal basis to making an effort to educate children with disabilities in the regular classroom. The term *inclusion* means educating children with disabilities full-time in the regular classroom. The term *mainstreaming* means educating children with disabilities partially in the regular classroom and partially in a special education class. The trend is toward using inclusion more. Children's academic and social success are affected more by the quality of instruction than by where the child is placed.
Placements and Services	Placements	• The range of placements include regular classroom without supplementary support and with or without medical support; regular classroom with supplementary instructional support provided in the regular classroom; part of the time spent in a resource room; full-time placement in a special education class; special schools; homebound instruction; and instruction in a hospital or other institution.
	Services	• Services include those provided by the classroom teacher in the regular classroom, those provided by a resource teacher (either in a separate resource room or in the regular classroom), those provided by a special education teacher, and other services provided by teacher aides, psychologists, collaborative consultants, and interactive teams.
Parents as Educational Partners	Communication Strategies	• Some good communication strategies include letting parents know that you understand and appreciate their child's individuality; placing yourself in the parents' shoes; providing them with information about their child's disability; talking *with,* not *to,* parents; avoiding stereotypes; reaching out to establish and maintain contact with them; and talking with them about how the media sometimes provide erroneous portrayals of children with disabilities.
Technology	Instructional and Assistive Technology	• Instructional technology includes various types of hardware and software, combined with innovative teaching methods, to accommodate children's needs in the classroom. Assistive technology consists of various services and devices to help children with disabilities function within their environment.

Chapter Review

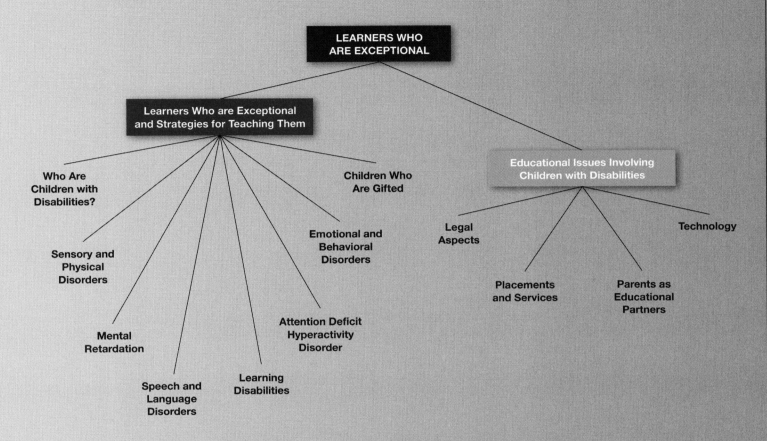

TO OBTAIN A DETAILED REVIEW OF THIS CHAPTER, STUDY THESE FOUR SUMMARY TABLES:

Key Terms

disability 198
handicap 198
low vision 199
educationally blind 199
oral approaches 200
manual approaches 200
orthopedic impairments 200
cerebral palsy 200
epilepsy 201
mental retardation 202
Down syndrome 203
fragile X syndrome 203

fetal alcohol syndrome 203
speech and language
 disorders 203
articulation disorders 203
voice disorders 204
fluency disorders 204
language disorders 204
receptive language 205
expressive language 205
learning disability 207
dyslexia 208

attention deficit hyperactivity
 disorder (ADHD) 211
emotional and behavioral
 disorders 213
autism 213
depression 214
children who are gifted 217
acceleration program 219
curriculum compacting 219
enrichment program 219
Public Law 94-142 221

Individuals with Disabilities
 Education Act (IDEA) 221
individualized education
 plan (IEP) 224
least restrictive
 environment (LRE) 224
inclusion 224
mainstreaming 224
collaborative consultation 229
instructional technology 230
assistive technology 230

Educational Psychology Checklist
LEARNERS WHO ARE EXCEPTIONAL

How much have you learned since the beginning of the chapter? Use the following statements to help you review your knowledge and understanding of the chapter material. First, read the statement and mentally or briefly on paper demonstrate that you can outline and discuss the relevant information.

_____ I am aware of the variety of exceptional learners.
_____ I can describe students with sensory or physical disorders and educational strategies for helping them.
_____ I know about the different categories and causes of mental retardation and can discuss some educational strategies for working with these children.
_____ I am aware of the nature of speech and language disorders, as well as educational strategies related to these disorders.
_____ I understand the nature of learning disabilities and strategies for educating children who have these disabilities.
_____ I can describe attention deficit hyperactivity disorder and strategies for helping students with this disorder.

_____ I know what emotional and behavioral disorders are and can describe some educational strategies for working with children who have these disorders.
_____ I understand the nature of children who are gifted, including educational strategies for working with them.
_____ I can discuss the basic legal aspects of working with children who have disabilities.
_____ I am aware of the placements and services for children with disabilities.
_____ I can describe some positive strategies for communicating with the parents of children with disabilities.
_____ I know some types of technology that can be used to educate children with a disability.

For any items that you did not check off, go back and study the related material in the chapter. Review the material until you feel you can check off the item. You also may want to use this checklist later in preparing for an exam.

Adventures for the Mind

Now that you have a good knowledge and understanding of this chapter, complete the following exercises to expand your thinking.

- Place yourself in the role of a parent with a child in your class. Imagine that you have just been notified by the school that your child has a learning disability. Write down answers to these questions:
- What feelings are you likely to be having as a parent?
- As a parent, what questions do you want to ask the teacher? Now write down how you, as the teacher, will respond to these questions.
- In Self-Assessment 6.1, you were encouraged to evaluate your experiences with people who have different disabilities. Select one of these disabilities (such as mental retardation or a learning disabil-

ity) and read in depth about it. After you have extensively studied this disability, make up a list of recommendations for working with children who have this disability.
- Together with 3 or 4 other students in your class, come up with a list and description of software programs that you think would benefit children who are gifted. One good source of information on such software is the journal *Electronic Learning*.
- Interview an elementary school, middle school, and high school teacher about their impressions of the recent changes regarding inclusion and other aspects of educating children with disabilities. Ask them what their most successful strategies are in working with children who have disabilities. Also ask what the biggest challenges are.

Taking It to the Net

1. You ask Jeremy to spell *car* and he writes *h-a-r*, but when asked to read the word *car* he reads it perfectly. What's happening in Jeremy's mind? Could it be dyslexia? Why, or why not?
2. You recommend that Jasmine be assessed for possible entry into your school's gifted program, but the school psychologist informs you that Jasmine is a C student. Is it possible to be a "gifted underachiever"?

3. Many children with disabilities have difficulties accessing information they need because their movement is restricted, due to either their own physical limitations or limitations in buildings and equipment. How might you reduce these limits on access to information? Could wireless laptop computers help? How?

Connect to http://www.mhhe.com/socscience/psychology/santedu/ttnet.htm to find the answers!

Case Studies

Case 1 *Gabrielle:* This case study explores how Gabrielle was identified as a child with learning disabilities.

Case 2 *Angie:* This case study explores the social problems Angie experiences because of her speech impediment.

Case 3 *Kathryn Carlson:* Kathryn is a resource room teacher. She has been unsuccessful with a student whose classification might

not be warranted and whose social behaviors threaten the success of a mainstreaming program.

Case 4 *Diane News:* Diane's school district is starting a gifted and talented program. Diane must recommend four students from her class for the program, but she has five potential candidates. The parent of one of the students has threatened Diane, telling her that she must recommend his daughter.

Chapter 7

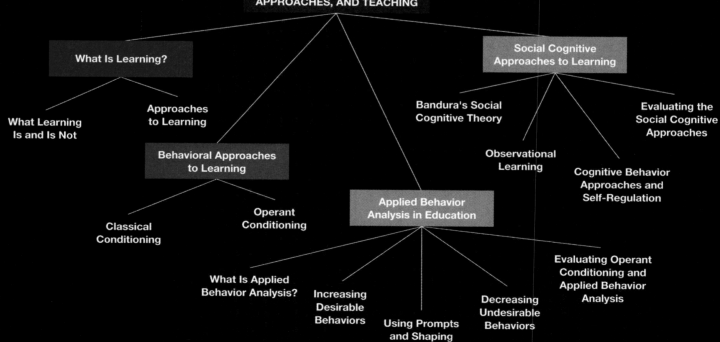

BEHAVIORAL APPROACHES, SOCIAL COGNITIVE APPROACHES, AND TEACHING

What Is Learning?

What Learning Is and Is Not

Approaches to Learning

Behavioral Approaches to Learning

Classical Conditioning

Operant Conditioning

Applied Behavior Analysis in Education

What Is Applied Behavior Analysis?

Increasing Desirable Behaviors

Using Prompts and Shaping

Decreasing Undesirable Behaviors

Evaluating Operant Conditioning and Applied Behavior Analysis

Social Cognitive Approaches to Learning

Bandura's Social Cognitive Theory

Observational Learning

Cognitive Behavior Approaches and Self-Regulation

Evaluating the Social Cognitive Approaches

Behavioral Approaches, Social Cognitive Approaches, and Teaching

Preview

Virtually everyone agrees that helping students learn is an important function of schools. However, not everyone agrees on the best way to learn. In this chapter we will explore the behavioral and social cognitive approaches to learning. These are some of the questions we will examine:

- What are some different ways that children learn?
- What are some alternatives to punishing students when you want them to behave?
- How can you use observational learning to improve a student's behavior?
- What strategies can be used to improve children's self-regulatory skills?

> "To learn is a natural pleasure."

Aristotle
Greek Philosopher, 4th Century B.C.

Teaching Stories
Garnetta Chan

Garnetta Chan teaches third grade at Mckinley School in the outskirts of New Brunswick, New Jersey, amid low-income housing projects and deteriorating factories. She has been teaching for more than 25 years. One of her main goals is for her students to enjoy learning. She also strives to provide them with a safe and secure environment. Class rules are clearly posted in her room. Garnetta believes that the children in her class have so much uncertainty in their lives that they need to know the classroom is a place where things are consistent. She says, "They have to have limits. There need to be consequences for their behaviors so that they will develop responsibility for their actions."

Along with limits, Garnetta provides praise for her students. She calms an angry child with a soft word and prevents disruption with a hand on a shoulder. She offers many of the relationship qualities they lack in their personal lives. It is not unusual for students to return to her classroom years after they have moved on, just to chat or to discuss a problem.

Garnetta's caring extends beyond the classroom walls. For example, one day a little boy appeared outside her classroom windows, his face pressed against the glass. He had been in Garnetta's class but a social service agency had removed him from his foster home and placed him with his father, which meant he had to go to another school. Although Garnetta was opposed to the move, she had not been able to convince the authorities that he was better off where he was. Garnetta invited him in. He found his old chair and the sweatshirt he had left behind. The children accepted him, and you could tell by the smile on his face that he felt at home. Garnetta had heard that the boy was not attending school regularly and was seen out late at night unsupervised. She immediately got on the phone and called his caseworker, recommending that he be allowed to return to her school. Garnetta even volunteered to pick him up at his new address and drive him each day to her school. Although his return to the school was not allowed, that day Garnetta gave him all the support she could and in a caring way tried to help him understand why he had to return to the other school.

Garnetta hopes that her efforts pay off and that potential high school dropouts will become high school graduates. She strives to be a positive model for her students, wanting them to see the pride she has in herself and her career. She says, "I want them to see that teaching is as great as being a doctor or a lawyer."

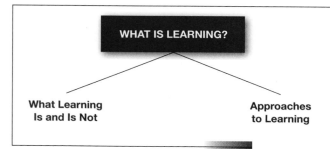

What Is Learning?

Learning is a central focus of educational psychology. When people are asked what schools are for, a common reply is: "To help children learn."

What Learning Is and Is Not

When children learn how to use a computer, they might make some mistakes along the way, but at a certain point they will get the knack of the behaviors required to use the computer effectively. The children will *change* from being individuals who cannot operate a computer into being individuals who can. Once they have learned how to use a computer, they don't lose those skills. It's like learning to drive a car. Once you have learned how, you don't have to learn all over again. Thus, learning involves a *relatively permanent* influence on behavior, which comes about through *experience*. Putting these pieces together, we arrive at a definition: **Learning** *is a relatively permanent change in behavior that occurs through experience.*

Not everything we know is learned. Recall our discussion of heredity and experience, or nature and nurture, in chapter 2. We inherit some capacities—they are inborn or innate, not learned. For example, we don't have to be taught to swallow, to flinch at loud noises, or to blink when an object comes too close to our eyes. However, most human behaviors do not involve heredity alone. When children use a computer in a new way, work harder at solving problems, ask better questions, explain an answer in a more logical way, or listen more attentively, the experience of learning is at work.

The scope of learning is broad (Domjan, 2000). It involves academic behaviors and nonacademic behaviors. It occurs in schools and everywhere else that children experience their world.

Approaches to Learning

A number of approaches to learning have been proposed, including behavioral and cognitive approaches.

Behavioral   The learning approaches that we discuss in the first part of this chapter are called *behavioral*. **Behaviorism** *is the view that behavior should be explained by observable experiences, not by mental processes.* For the behaviorist, behavior is everything that we do that can be directly observed: a child creating a poster, a teacher smiling at a child, one student picking on another student, and so on. **Mental processes** *are defined by psychologists as the thoughts, feelings, and motives that each of us experiences but that cannot be observed by others.* Although we cannot directly see thoughts, feelings, and motives, they are no less real. They include children *thinking* about ways to create the best poster, a teacher *feeling* good about children's efforts, and children's inner *motivation* to control their behavior.

For the behaviorist, these thoughts, feelings, and motives are not appropriate subject matter for a science of behavior because they cannot be directly observed. Classical conditioning and operant conditioning, two behavioral views that we will

Experience is a great teacher.

Aristotle
Greek Philosopher, 4th Century B.C.

**Behavioral
Approaches**

discuss shortly, adopt this stance. Both of these views emphasize **associative learn-ing,** *which consists of learning that two events are connected (associated).* For example, associative learning occurs when a student associates a pleasant event with learning something in school, such as the teacher smiling when the student asks a good ques-tion. The discussion of applied behavior analysis later in the chapter also reflects the behavioral view of focusing on observable behavior and associative learning.

Cognitive   Psychology has become more *cognitive* in the last part of the twentieth century. This cognitive emphasis has become the basis for numerous ap-proaches to learning (Driscoll, 2000; Roeddiger, 2000). We discuss four main cognitive approaches to learning in this book: social cognitive; cognitive information processing; cognitive constructivist; and social constructivist. The *social cognitive* approaches, which emphasize how behavior, environment, and person (cognitive) factors interact to influence learning, will be covered later in this chapter. The second set of approaches, *cognitive information processing,* focuses on how children process information through attention, memory, thinking, and other cognitive processes. They will be explored in chapter 8. The third set of approaches, *cognitive constructivist,* emphasizes the child's cognitive construction of knowledge and understanding. They initially were presented in the form of Piaget's theory in chapter 2 and will be further examined in chapters 8 and 9 ◀▥ p. 49. The fourth set of cognitive approaches, *social constructivist,* focuses on collaboration with others to produce knowledge and understanding. The social con-structivist approaches initially were introduced in the form of Vygotsky's theory in chapter 2 and they will be further evaluated in chapter 9 ◀▥ p. 60.

Adding these four cognitive approaches to the behavioral approaches, we arrive at five main approaches to learning that we discuss in this book: behavioral, social cognitive, cognitive information processing, cognitive constructivist, and social con-structivist. All contribute to our understanding of how children learn. A summary of the five approaches is presented in figure 7.1.

At this point we have discussed a number of ideas about what learning is and var-ious approaches to learning. A review of these ideas is presented in summary table 7.1. Let's now explore the behavioral approaches in greater detail.

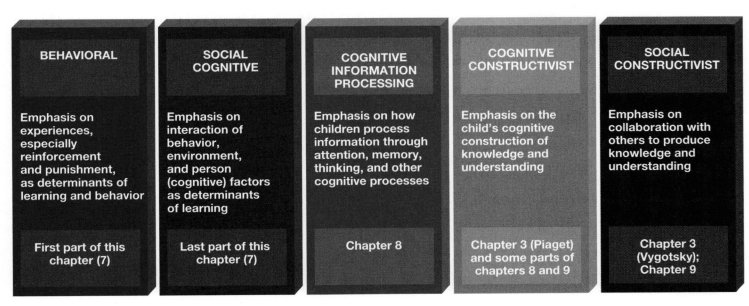

Figure **7.1**
Approaches to Learning

SUMMARY TABLE 7.1
What Is Learning?

Concept	Processes/ Related Ideas	Characteristics/Description
What Learning Is and Is Not	Defining Learning	• Learning is a relatively permanent change in behavior that occurs through experience. Experience is a great teacher. Learning is not involved in inborn, innate behaviors such as reflexes.
Approaches to Learning	Behavioral	• The approaches discussed in the first part of this chapter are called *behavioral*. Behaviorism is the view that behavior should be explained by experiences that can be directly observed, not by mental processes. Classical conditioning and operant conditioning, both of which are behavioral views, emphasize associative learning.
	Cognitive	• Psychology has become more *cognitive* in the last part of the twentieth century. This cognitive emphasis is reflected in four cognitive approaches to learning we discuss in this book. The first set of approaches, *social cognitive*, emphasizes the interaction of behavior, environment, and person (cognition), in explaining learning. The second set of approaches, *cognitive information processing*, focuses on how children process information through attention, memory, thinking, and other cognitive processes. The third set of approaches, *cognitive constructivist*, emphasizes the child's construction of knowledge and understanding. The fourth set, *social cognitive*, focuses on collaboration with others to produce knowledge and understanding. Adding these four cognitive approaches to the behavioral approaches, these are the five main approaches to learning we discuss in this book.

Classical Conditioning   Operant Conditioning

Behavioral Approaches to Learning

The behavioral approaches emphasize the importance of children making connections between experiences and behavior (Greeno, Collins, & Resnick, 1996). The first behaviorist approach we will examine is classical conditioning.

Classical Conditioning

Ivan Pavlov

In the early 1900s, Russian physiologist Ivan Pavlov was curious to know how the body digests food. In his experiments, he routinely placed meat powder in a dog's mouth, which caused the dog to salivate. Pavlov began to observe that the meat powder was not the only stimulus that caused the dog to salivate. The dog salivated in response to a number of stimuli associated with the food: the sight of the food dish, the sight of the person who brought the food into the room, and the sound of the door closing when the food arrived.

Exploring Classical Conditioning **Classical conditioning** *is a type of learning in which an organism learns to connect or associate stimuli. In classical conditioning, a neutral stimulus (such as the sight of a person) becomes associated with a meaningful stimulus (such as food) and acquires the capacity to elicit a similar response.* To fully understand Pavlov's (1927) theory of classical conditioning, one must understand two types of stimuli and two types of responses: unconditioned stimulus (US), unconditioned response (UR), conditioned stimulus (CS), and conditioned response (CR).

Figure 7.2 summarizes the way classical conditioning works. An **unconditioned stimulus (US)** *is a stimulus that automatically produces a response without any prior learning.* Food was the US in Pavlov's experiments. An **unconditioned response (UR)** *is an unlearned response that is automatically elicited by the US.* In Pavlov's experiments, the dog's salivation in response to food was the UR. A **conditioned stimulus (CS)** *is a previously neutral stimulus that eventually elicits a conditioned response after*

Ivan Pavlov (1849–1936), the Russian who developed the concept of classical conditioning.

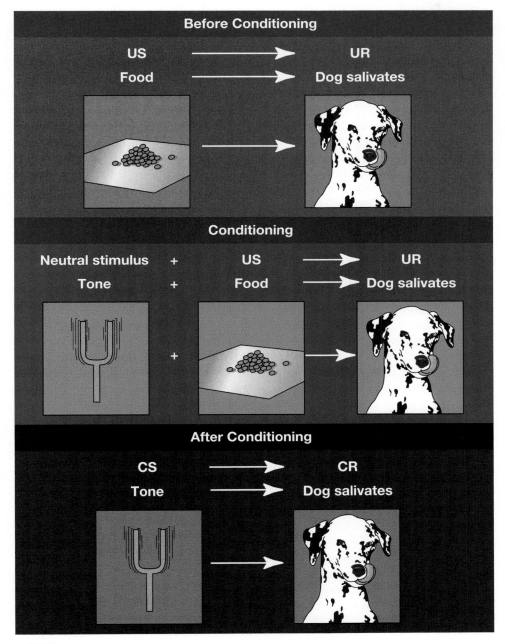

Pavlov's Classical Conditioning

In one experiment, Pavlov presented a neutral stimulus (tone) just before an unconditioned stimulus (food). The neutral stimulus became a conditioned stimulus by being paired with the unconditioned stimulus. Subsequently, the conditioned stimulus (tone) by itself was able to elicit the dog's salivation.

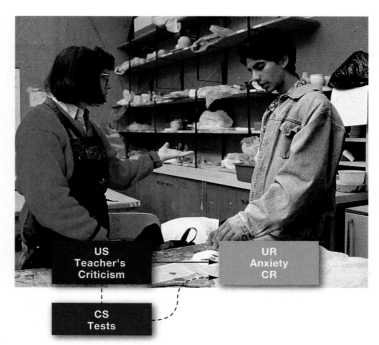

US
Teacher's
Criticism

UR
Anxiety
CR

CS
Tests

Figure **7.3**

**Classical Conditioning Involved in Teachers'
Criticism of Children and Tests**

Classical Conditioning

being associated with the US. Among the conditioned stimuli in Pavlov's experiments were various sights and sounds that occurred prior to the dog's actually eating the food, such as the sound of the door closing before the food was placed in the dog's dish. A **conditioned response (CR)** *is a learned response to the conditioned stimulus that occurs after US-CS pairing.*

Classical conditioning can be involved in both positive and negative experiences of children in the classroom. Among the things in the child's schooling that produce pleasure because they have become classically conditioned are a favorite song, feelings that the classroom is a safe and fun place to be, and a teacher's warmth and nurturing. For example, a song could be neutral for the child until the child joins in with other classmates to sing it with accompanying positive feelings.

Children can develop fear of the classroom if they associate the classroom with criticism, so the criticism becomes a CS for fear, as figure 7.2 suggests. Classical conditioning also can be involved in test anxiety. For example, a child fails and is criticized, which produces anxiety; thereafter, the child associates tests with anxiety, so they then can become a CS for anxiety (see figure 7.3).

Some children's health problems also might involve classical conditioning. Certain physical complaints—asthma, headaches, ulcers, high blood pressure—might be partly due to classical conditioning. We usually say that such health problems are caused by stress. Often what happens, though, is that certain stimuli, such as a parent's or teacher's heavy criticism, are conditioned stimuli for physiological responses. Over time, the frequency of the physiological responses can produce a health problem. A teacher's persistent criticism of a student can cause the student to develop headaches, muscle tension, and so on. Anything associated with the teacher, such as classroom learning exercises and homework, might trigger the student's stress and subsequently be linked with ulcers or other physiological responses.

Generalization, Discrimination, and Extinction In studying a dog's responses to various stimuli, Pavlov rang a bell before giving meat powder to the dog. By being paired with the US (meat), the bell became a CS and elicited the dog's salivation. After a time, Pavlov found that the dog also responded to other sounds, such as a whistle. The more bell-like the noise, the stronger the dog's response. **Generalization** *in classical conditioning involves the tendency of a new stimulus similar to the original conditioned stimulus to produce a similar response.* Let's assume that the test on which the student was criticized on was a biology test. When the student begins to prepare for a chemistry test, she also becomes very nervous because these two subjects are closely related in the sciences. Thus, the student's anxiety generalizes from taking a test in one subject to taking a test in another.

Discrimination *in classical conditioning occurs when the organism responds to certain stimuli but not others.* To produce discrimination, Pavlov gave food to the dog only after ringing the bell and not after any other sounds. Subsequently, the dog responded only to the bell. In the case of the student taking tests in different classes, she doesn't become nearly as nervous about taking an English test or a history test because they are very different subject areas.

Extinction *in classical conditioning involves the weakening of the conditioned response (CR) in the absence of the unconditioned stimulus (US).* In one session, Pavlov rang the bell repeatedly but did not give the dog any food. Eventually the dog quit salivating. Similarly, if the student who gets nervous while taking tests begins to do much better on tests, her anxiety will fade.

Systematic Desensitization   Sometimes the anxiety and stress associated with negative events can be eliminated by classical conditioning. **Systematic desensitization** *is a method based on classical conditioning that reduces anxiety by getting the individual to associate deep relaxation with successive visualizations of increasingly anxiety-producing situations.* Imagine that you have a student in your class who is extremely nervous about talking in front of the class. The goal of systematic desensitization is to get the student to associate public speaking with relaxation rather than anxiety. Using successive visualizations, the student might practice systematic desensitization 2 weeks before the talk, then a week before, 4 days before, 2 days before, the day before, the morning of the talk, on entering the room where the talk is to be given, on the way to the podium, and during the talk.

Desensitization involves a type of counterconditioning (McNeil, 2000); Schunk, 1996). The relaxing feelings that the student imagines (US) produce relaxation (UR). The student then associates anxiety-producing cues (CS) with the relaxing feelings. Such relaxation is incompatible with anxiety. By initially pairing a weak anxiety-producing cue with relaxation and gradually working up the hierarchy (from 2 weeks before the talk to walking up to the podium to give the talk), all of the anxiety-producing cues should generate relaxation (CR).

Chances are, you will have students who fear speaking in front of the class, or have other anxieties, and there may be circumstances in your own life where you might benefit from replacing anxiety with relaxation. For example, it is not unusual for some teachers to feel very comfortable when talking in front of their students but to get very nervous if asked to give a presentation at a teaching conference. Counselors and mental health professionals have been very successful at getting individuals to overcome their fear of public speaking using systematic desensitization. Should you be interested in adopting this strategy, do it with the help of school psychologist rather than on your own.

Evaluating Classical Conditioning   Classical conditioning helps us understand some aspects of learning better than others. It excels in explaining how neutral stimuli become associated with unlearned, involuntary responses (LoLordo, 2000). It is especially helpful in understanding students' anxieties and fears. However, it is not as effective in explaining voluntary behaviors, such as why a student studies hard for a test or likes history better than geography. For these areas, operant conditioning is more relevant.

Operant Conditioning

Our examination of operant conditioning begins with a general definition, then turns to the views of Thorndike and Skinner.

What is Operant Conditioning?   **Operant conditioning** *(also called instrumental conditioning) is a form of learning in which the consequences of behavior produce changes in the probability that the behavior will occur.* Operant conditioning's main architect was B. F. Skinner, whose views built on the connectionist views of E. L. Thorndike.

Thorndike's Law of Effect   At about the same time that Ivan Pavlov was conducting classical conditioning experiments with dogs, American psychologist E. L. Thorndike (1906) was studying cats in puzzle boxes ◀ p. 4. Thorndike placed a hungry cat inside a box and put a piece of fish outside. To escape from the box, the cat had to learn how to open the latch inside the box. At first the cat made a number of ineffective responses. It clawed or bit at the bars and thrust its paw through the openings. Eventually the cat accidentally stepped on the treadle that released the door bolt. When the cat was returned to the box, it went through the same random activity until it stepped on the treadle once more. On subsequent trials, the cat made fewer

Thorndike Connections

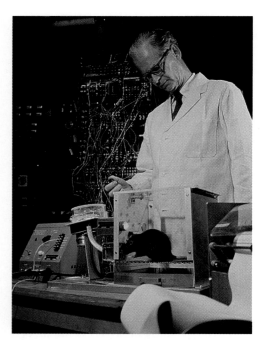

B. F. Skinner (1904–1990), the American who was the main architect of the concept of operant conditioning.

Skinner's Operant Conditioning Positive Reinforcement

*R*eward and punishment . . . these are the spur and reins whereby people are set on work and guided.

John Locke
English Philosopher, 17th Century

and fewer random movements, until it immediately clawed the treadle to open the door. Thorndike's **law of effect** *states that behaviors followed by positive outcomes are strengthened and that behaviors followed by negative outcomes are weakened.*

The key question for Thorndike was how the correct stimulus-response (S-R) bond strengthens and eventually dominates incorrect stimulus-response bonds. According to Thorndike, the correct S-R association strengthens, and the incorrect association weakens, because of the *consequences* of the organism's actions. Thorndike's view is called *S-R theory* because the organism's behavior is due to a connection between a stimulus and a response. As we see next, Skinner's approach significantly expanded on Thorndike's basic ideas.

Skinner's Operant Conditioning   Operant conditioning, in which the consequences of behavior lead to changes in the probability that the behavior will occur, is at the heart of B. F. Skinner's (1938) behaviorism. Consequences—rewards or punishments—are contingent on the organism's behavior. More needs to be said about reward and punishment.

Reinforcement and Punishment   **Reinforcement (reward)** *is a consequence that increases the probability that a behavior will occur.* In contrast, **punishment** *is a consequence that decreases the probability a behavior will occur.* For example, you might tell one of your students, "Congratulations. I'm really proud of how good the story is that you wrote." If the student works harder and writes an even better story the next time, your positive comments are said to reinforce or reward the student's writing behavior. If you frown at a student for talking in class and the student's talking decreases, your frown is said to punish the student's talking.

Reinforcement can be complex. *Reinforcement* means to strengthen. In **positive reinforcement,** *the frequency of a response increases because it is followed by a stimulus,* as in the example in which the teacher's positive comments increased the student's writing behavior. Similarly, complimenting parents on being at a parent-teacher conference might encourage them to come back again. Positive reinforcement is usually pleasant (as when a teacher praises a student's work), but it also can be unpleasant (as when students do work they don't want to in order to get a good grade).

"Once it became clear to me that, by responding correctly to certain stimuli, I could get all the bananas I wanted, getting this job was a pushover."

Conversely, in **negative reinforcement,** *the frequency of a response increases because the response either removes a stimulus or involves avoiding a stimulus.* For example, a father nags at his son to do his homework. He keeps nagging. Finally, the son gets tired of hearing the nagging and does his homework. The son's response (doing his homework) removed the unpleasant stimulus (nagging). Consider your own behavior after a stressful day of teaching. You have a headache, take some aspirin, and the headache goes away. Taking aspirin is reinforced when this behavior is followed by a reduction of pain.

One way to remember the distinction between positive and negative reinforcement is that in positive reinforcement something is added or obtained. In negative reinforcement, something is subtracted, avoided, or escaped. It is easy to confuse negative reinforcement and punishment. To keep these terms straight, remember that negative reinforcement increases the probability a response will occur, while punishment decreases the likelihood it will occur. Figure 7.4 summarizes the concepts of positive reinforcement, negative reinforcement, and punishment and presents examples of each.

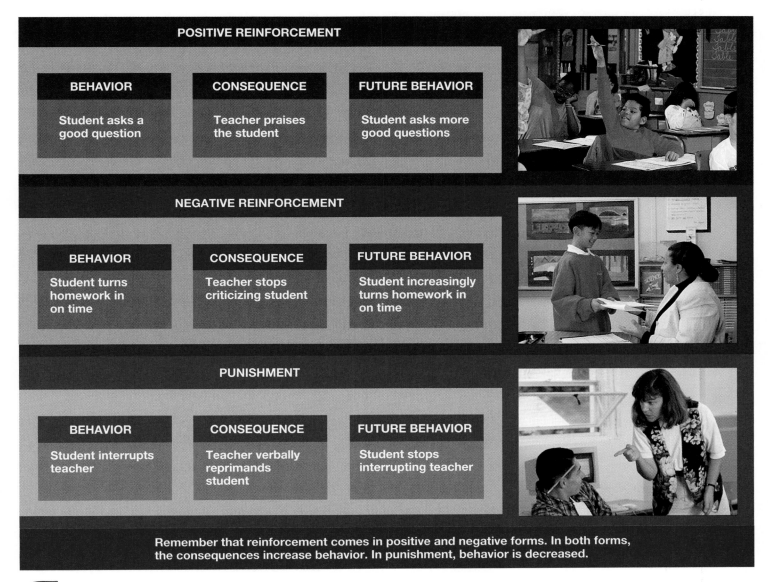

POSITIVE REINFORCEMENT

BEHAVIOR	CONSEQUENCE	FUTURE BEHAVIOR
Student asks a good question	Teacher praises the student	Student asks more good questions

NEGATIVE REINFORCEMENT

BEHAVIOR	CONSEQUENCE	FUTURE BEHAVIOR
Student turns homework in on time	Teacher stops criticizing student	Student increasingly turns homework in on time

PUNISHMENT

BEHAVIOR	CONSEQUENCE	FUTURE BEHAVIOR
Student interrupts teacher	Teacher verbally reprimands student	Student stops interrupting teacher

Remember that reinforcement comes in positive and negative forms. In both forms, the consequences increase behavior. In punishment, behavior is decreased.

Figure **7.4**
Reinforcement and Punishment

THROUGH THE EYES OF CHILDREN

"Watch Her Mom"

One year a third-grade teacher at Salem Church Elementary School in Chesterfield County, Virginia, had an especially loud, active group of third-graders. The teacher, Kristen Blankenship, used a combination of individual and group positive reinforcement as a management strategy.

Not having a cafeteria, students ate their lunches in the classroom. While joining her son, Daniel, for lunch one day, his mother pulled Kristen aside, smiled, and said that Daniel had just whispered to her, "Watch her Mom. She never yells, but she sure knows how to keep them in line."

Generalization, Discrimination, and Extinction

In our coverage of classical conditioning, we discussed generalization, discrimination, and extinction. These processes also are important dimensions of operant conditioning. Remember that in classical conditioning, generalization is the tendency of a stimulus similar to the conditioned stimulus to produce a response similar to the conditioned response. **Generalization** *in operant conditioning means giving the same response to similar stimuli.* Especially of interest is the extent to which behavior generalizes from one situation to another. For example, if a teacher's praise gets a student to work harder in class, will this generalize to the student working harder out of class on homework assignments? Or if the teacher praises the student for asking good questions related to English, will this generalize to history, math, and other subjects?

Remember that in classical conditioning, discrimination means responding to certain stimuli but not others. **Discrimination** *in operant conditioning involves differentiating among stimuli or environmental events.* For example, a student knows that the tray on the teacher's desk labeled "Math" is where she is supposed to place today's math work, while another tray labeled "English" is where today's English assignments are to be put. This might sound overly simple, but it is important because students' worlds are filled with such discriminative stimuli. Around school these discriminative stimuli might include signs that say, "Stay Out," "Form a Line Here," and so on. We will have more to say about discriminative stimuli later in the section on applied behavior analysis.

In operant conditioning, **extinction** *occurs when a previously reinforced response is no longer reinforced and the response decreases.* In the classroom, the most common use of extinction is for the teacher to withdraw attention from a behavior that the attention is maintaining. For example, in some cases a teacher's attention inadvertently reinforces a student's disruptive behavior, as when a student pinches another student and the teacher immediately talks with the perpetrator. If this happens on a regular basis, the student might learn that pinching other students is a good way to get the teacher's attention. If the teacher withdraws his attention, the pinching might extinguish. We will have more to say about extinction in our discussion of applied behavior analysis.

At this point we have discussed a number of ideas about the behavioral approaches of classical and operant conditioning. A review of these ideas is presented in summary table 7.2.

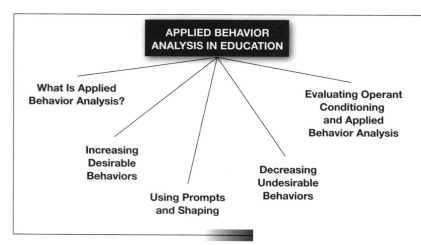

Applied Behavior Analysis in Education

Many applications of operant conditioning have been made outside of research laboratories in the wider worlds of classrooms, homes, business settings, hospitals, and other real-world settings.

What Is Applied Behavior Analysis?

Applied behavior analysis *involves applying the principles of operant conditioning to change human behavior.* Three uses of applied behavior analysis are especially important

SUMMARY TABLE 7.2
Behavioral Approaches to Learning

Concept	Processes/ Related Ideas	Characteristics/Description
Classical Conditioning	Exploring Classical Conditioning	• In classical conditioning, the organism learns to connect or associate stimuli. A neutral stimulus (such as the sight of a person) becomes associated with a meaningful stimulus (such as food) and acquires the capacity to elicit a similar response. • Classical conditioning involves these factors: Unconditioned stimulus (US), conditioned stimulus (CS), unconditioned response (UR), and conditioned response (CR).
	Generalization, Discrimination, and Extinction	• Classical conditioning also involves generalization, discrimination, and extinction. • Generalization is the tendency of a new stimulus similar to the original conditioned stimulus to produce a similar response. • Discrimination occurs when the organism responds to certain stimuli and not to others. • Extinction involves the weakening of the CR in the absence of the US.
	Systematic Desensitization	• This is a method based on classical conditioning that reduces anxiety by getting the individual to associate deep relaxation with successive visualizations of increasingly anxiety-producing situations.
	Evaluating Classical Conditioning	• Classical conditioning is better at explaining involuntary behavior than voluntary behavior.
Operant Conditioning	What Is Operant Conditioning?	• In this type of learning (also called instrumental conditioning), the consequences of behavior produce changes in the probability that the behavior will occur. • Operant conditioning's main architect was B. F. Skinner, who built on the connectionist view of E. L. Thorndike.
	Thorndike's Law of Effect	• Thorndike's law of effect states that behaviors followed by positive outcomes are strengthened, those followed by negative behaviors are weakened. • His view was called S-R theory.
	Skinner's Operant Conditioning	• Skinner greatly expanded on Thorndike's ideas. Reinforcement (reward) is a consequence (either positive or negative) that increases the probability that a behavior will occur; punishment is a consequence that decreases the probability that a behavior will occur. • In positive reinforcement, a behavior increases because it is followed by a rewarding stimulus (such as praise). • In negative reinforcement, a behavior increases because the response removes an aversive (unpleasant) stimulus. • Generalization, discrimination, and extinction also are involved in operant conditioning. Generalization means giving the same response to similar stimuli. Discrimination refers to differentiating among stimuli or environmental events. Extinction occurs when a previously reinforced response is no longer reinforced and the response decreases.

in education: increasing desirable behavior, using prompts and shaping, and decreasing undesirable behavior (Alberto & Troutman, 1995). Applications of applied behavior analysis often use a series of steps (Hayes, 2000). These often begin with some general observations and then turn to determining the specific target behavior that

Behavior Analysis Resources

**Stimulus Control
of Operant Behavior**

needs to be changed, as well as observing its antecedent conditions. Behavioral goals are then set, particular reinforcers or punishers are selected, a behavior management program is carried out, and the success or failure of the program is evaluated.

Increasing Desirable Behaviors

Five operant conditioning strategies can be used to increase a child's desirable behaviors: choose effective reinforcers; make reinforcers contingent and timely; select the best schedule of reinforcement; consider contracting; and use negative reinforcement effectively.

Choose Effective Reinforcers

Not all reinforcers are the same for every child. Applied behavior analysts recommend that teachers find out what reinforcers work best with which children—that is, individualize the use of particular reinforcers. For one student it might be praise, for another it might be getting to spend more time participating in a favorite activity, for another it might involve being a hall monitor for a week, and for yet another it could be getting to surf the Internet. To find out the most effective reinforcers for a child, you can examine what has motivated the child in the past (reinforcement history), what the student wants but can't easily or frequently get, and the child's perception of the reinforcer's value. Some applied behavior analysts recommend asking children which reinforcers they like best (Raschke, 1981). Another recommendation is to consider novel reinforcers to reduce the child's boredom. Natural reinforcers like praise and privileges are generally recommended over material rewards like candy, stars, and money (Hall & Hall, 1998).

Activities are some of the most common reinforcers used by teachers. Named after psychologist David Premack, the **Premack principle** *states that a high-probability activity can serve as a reinforcer for a low-probability activity.* The Premack principle is at work when an elementary school teacher tells a child, "When you complete your writing assignment, you can play a game on the computer" or an early education teacher says to a child, "If you pick up the blocks, then you may help Mrs. Manson prepare the snacks." The use of the Premack principle is not restricted to a single child. It also can be used with the entire class. A teacher might tell the class, "If all of the class gets their homework done by Friday, we will take a field trip next week."

Make the Reinforcer Contingent and Timely

For a reinforcer to be effective, the teacher must give it only after the child performs the particular behavior. Applied behavior analysts often recommend that teachers make "If . . . then" statements to children. For example, "Tony, *if* you finish ten math problems, *then* you can go out to play." This makes it clear to Tony what he has to do to get the reinforcer. Applied behavior analysts say that it is important to make the reinforcer *contingent* on the child's behavior. That is, the child has to perform the behavior to get the reward. If Tony did not complete ten math problems and the teacher still lets him go out to play, the contingency has not been established.

Reinforcers are more effective when they are given in a timely way, as soon as possible after the child performs the target behavior. This helps children see the contingency connection between the reward and their behavior. If the child completes the target behavior (such as doing the ten math problems by midmorning) and the teacher doesn't give the child playtime until late afternoon, the child might have trouble making the contingency connection.

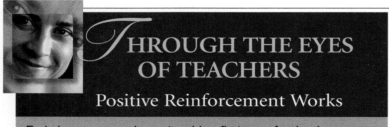

THROUGH THE EYES OF TEACHERS

Positive Reinforcement Works

Early in my career, I was teaching first-year foreign language classes (French, Latin and Spanish) to ninth graders in a junior high school. Collaborating with a colleague, a guidance counselor, I experimented with positive verbal reinforcement as a way of focusing students on the task at hand and engaging them in learning. I consciously tried to offer positive reinforcement whenever possible and kept track of the number of times per class I did. I and the counselor observed the effects on the amount of participation and behavior of the students. Participation increased and behavior improved.

Barbara Berry
French and Humanities Teacher
Ypsilanti High School
Ypsilanti, Michigan

Use the Best Schedule of Reinforcement   Most of the examples given so far assume *continuous reinforcement;* that is, the child is reinforced every time she or he makes a response. In continuous reinforcement, children learn very rapidly, but when the reinforcement stops (the teacher stops praising), extinction also occurs rapidly. In the classroom, continuous reinforcement is rare. A teacher with a classroom of 25 or 30 students can't praise a child every time the student makes an appropriate response.

Partial reinforcement involves reinforcing a response only part of the time. Skinner (1953) developed the concept of **schedules of reinforcement,** *which are partial reinforcement timetables that determine when a response will be reinforced.* The four main schedules of reinforcement are fixed-ratio, variable-ratio, fixed-interval, and variable-interval.

On a **fixed-ratio schedule,** *a behavior is reinforced after a set number of responses.* For example, a teacher might praise the child only after every fourth correct response, not after every response. On a **variable-ratio schedule,** *a behavior is reinforced after an average number of times, but on an unpredictable basis.* For example, a teacher's praise might average out to being given every fifth response but be given after the 2nd correct response, after 8 more correct responses, after the next 7 correct responses, and after the next 3 correct responses.

Interval schedules are determined by time elapsed since the last behavior was reinforced. On a **fixed-interval schedule,** *the first appropriate response after a fixed amount of time is reinforced.* For example, a teacher might praise a child for the first good question the child asks after 2 minutes have elapsed or give a quiz every week. On a **variable-interval schedule,** *a response is reinforced after a variable amount of time has elapsed.* On this schedule, the teacher might praise the child's question-asking after 3 minutes have gone by, then after 15 minutes have gone by, after 7 minutes have gone by, and so on. Giving a pop quiz at uneven intervals also reflects a variable-interval schedule.

What is the effect of using these schedules of reinforcement with children?

- Initial learning is usually faster with continuous rather than partial reinforcement, which means that when a behavior is first being learned, continuous reinforcement works better. However, partial reinforcement produces greater persistence and greater resistance to extinction than continuous reinforcement does (Hackenberg, 2000). Thus, once a response is mastered, partial reinforcement works better than continuous reinforcement.
- Children on fixed schedules show less persistence and faster response extinction than children on variable schedules. The most persistence is shown by children on a variable-interval schedule. This schedule produces slow, steady responding because children don't know when the wait is going to be over. As we mentioned earlier, a pop quiz is a good example of the variable-interval schedule. If the teacher starts making the pop quiz more predictable (giving it once a week, on Fridays), children will begin to show the stop-start work pattern that characterizes the fixed-interval schedule. That is, they won't work hard for most of the week, then toward the end of the week they will start cramming for the quiz. Thus, if your goal as a teacher is to increase children's persistence after the behavior has been established, variable schedules work best, especially the variable-interval schedule (Lee & Belfiore, 1997). Figure 7.5 shows the different response patterns associated with the different schedules of reinforcement.

Schedules of
Reinforcement

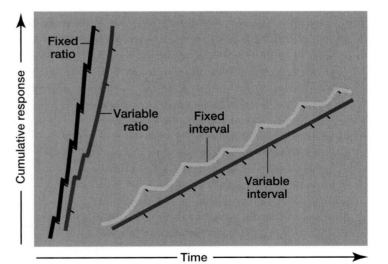

Figure **7.5**

Schedules of Reinforcement and Different Patterns of Responding

In this figure, each hash mark indicates the delivery of reinforcement. Notice on the fixed-interval schedule the drop-off in responding after each response, on the variable-interval schedule the high, steady rate of responding, on the fixed-interval schedule the immediate drop-off in responding after reinforcement and the increase in responding just before reinforcement (which results in a scallop-shaped curve), and on the variable-interval schedule the slow, steady rate of responding.

Consider Contracting   **Contracting** *involves putting reinforcement contingencies in writing.* If problems arise and children don't uphold their end of the bargain, the teacher can refer the children to the contract they agreed to. Applied behavior analysts suggest that a classroom contract should be the result of input from both the teacher and the student. Classroom contracts have "If . . . then" statements and are signed by the teacher and child, then dated. A teacher and child might agree on a contract that states that the child agrees to be a good citizen by doing _____, _____, and _____. As part of the contract, the teacher agrees to _____ if the student behaves in this manner. In some instances, the teacher asks another child to sign the contract as a witness to the agreement.

Use Negative Reinforcement Effectively   Remember that in negative reinforcement, the frequency of response increases because the response removes an aversive (unpleasant) stimulus (Alberto & Troutman, 1995). A teacher who says, "Thomas, you have to stay in your seat and finish writing your story before you join the other students in making a poster," is using negative reinforcement. The negative condition of being left in his seat while the other children are doing something enjoyable will be removed if Thomas finishes the story he should have completed earlier. In another example of negative reinforcement, Maria stops her disruptive behavior in order to avoid being ridiculed by her peers.

Using negative reinforcement has some drawbacks. Sometimes when teachers try to use this behavioral strategy, children throw a tantrum, run out of the room, or destroy materials. These negative outcomes happen most often when children don't have the skills or capabilities to do what the teacher asks of them. We will discuss such self-regulatory skills later in this chapter.

Using Prompts and Shaping

Earlier in our discussion of operant conditioning, we indicated that discrimination involves differentiating among stimuli or environmental events. Students can learn to discriminate among stimuli or events through differential reinforcement. Two differential reinforcement strategies available to teachers are prompts and shaping (Alberto & Troutman, 1995).

Prompts   A **prompt** *is an added stimulus or cue that is given just before a response and increases the likelihood that the response will occur.* A reading teacher who holds up a card with the letters *w-e-r-e* and says, "Not was, but . . ." is using a verbal prompt. An art teacher who places the label *watercolors* on one group of paints and *oils* on another also is using prompts. Prompts help get behavior going. Once the students consistently show the correct responses, the prompts are no longer needed.

Instructions can be used as prompts. For example, as the art period is drawing to a close, the teacher says, "Let's get ready for reading." If the students keep doing art, the teacher adds the prompt, "Okay, put away your art materials and come with me over to the reading area." Some prompts come in the form of hints, as when the teacher tells students to line up "quietly." Bulletin boards are common locations for prompts, frequently displaying reminders of class rules, due dates for projects, the location of a meeting, and so on. Some prompts are presented visually, as when the teacher places her hand on her ear when a student is not speaking loudly enough.

Shaping   When teachers use prompts, they assume that students can perform the desired behaviors. But sometimes students do not have the ability to perform them. In this case, shaping is required. **Shaping** *involves teaching new behaviors by reinforcing successive approximations to a specified target behavior.* Initially, you reinforce any response that in some way resembles the target behavior. Subsequently, you reinforce a response that more closely resembles the target, and so on until the student performs the target behavior, and then you reinforce it.

Suppose you have a student who has never completed 50 percent or more of her math assignments. You set the target behavior at 100 percent, but you reinforce her for successive approximations to the target. You initially might provide a reinforcer (some type of privilege, for example) when she completes 60 percent, then the next time only when she completes 70 percent, then 80, then 90, and finally 100 percent.

Consider also a boy's shy behavior. The target behavior is to get him to approach a group of peers and talk with them. Initially you might need to reinforce him for simply smiling at a classmate. Next, you might reinforce him only if he says something to a classmate. Next, you might reinforce him only if he engages in a prolonged conversation with a classmate. And finally, you should reward him only if he engages in the target behavior, joining in with a group of peers and talking with them.

Shaping can be an important tool for the classroom teacher because most students need reinforcement along the way to reaching a learning goal. Shaping can be especially helpful for learning tasks that require time and persistence to complete. However, when using shaping, remember to implement it only if the other types of positive reinforcement and prompts are not working. Also remember to be patient. Shaping can require the reinforcement of a number of small steps en route to a target behavior, and these might take place only over an extended period of time.

Decreasing Undesirable Behaviors

When teachers want to decrease children's undesirable behaviors (such as teasing, hogging a class discussion, or smarting off to the teacher), what are their options? Applied behavior analysts Paul Alberto and Anne Troutman (1995) recommend that when teachers want to decrease a child's undesirable behavior, they should consider using these steps in this order:

1. Use differential reinforcement.
2. Terminate reinforcement (extinction).
3. Remove desirable stimuli.
4. Present aversive stimuli (punishment).

Thus, the teacher's first option should be differential reinforcement. Punishment should be used only as a last resort and always in conjunction with providing the child information about appropriate behavior.

Use Differential Reinforcement   In differential reinforcement, the teacher reinforces behavior that is more appropriate or that is incompatible with what the child is doing. For example, the teacher might reinforce a child for doing learning activities on a computer rather than playing games with it, for being courteous rather than interrupting, for being seated rather than running around the classroom, or for doing homework on time rather than late.

Terminate Reinforcement (Extinction)   The strategy of terminating reinforcement involves withdrawing positive reinforcement from a child's inappropriate behavior. Many inappropriate behaviors are maintained by positive reinforcement, especially the teacher's attention. Applied behavior analysts point out that this can occur even when the teacher gives attention to an inappropriate behavior by criticizing, threatening, or yelling at the student. Many teachers find it difficult to determine whether they are giving too much attention to inappropriate behavior. A good strategy is to get someone to observe your classroom on several occasions and chart the patterns of reinforcement you use with your students. If you become aware that you are giving too much attention to a student's inappropriate behavior, ignore that behavior and give attention to the student's appropriate behavior. Always combine taking attention away from inappropriate behavior with giving attention to appropriate behavior. For instance, when a student stops monopolizing the conversation in a group discussion after you withdraw your attention, compliment the student on her improved behavior.

TEACHING STRATEGIES
For Using Time-Out

In using time-out, you have several options:

1. *Keep the student in the classroom, but deny the student access to positive reinforcement.* This strategy is most often used when a student does something minor. The teacher might ask the student to put his head down on the desk for a few minutes or might move the student to the periphery of an activity so the student can still observe other students experiencing positive reinforcement.
2. *For time-out to be effective, the setting from which the student is removed has to be positively reinforcing and the setting in which the student is placed has to not be positively reinforcing.* For example, if you seat a student in the hall outside your classroom and students from other classes come down the hall and talk with the student, the time-out is clearly not going to serve its intended purpose.
3. *If you use time-out, be sure to identify the students' behaviors that resulted in time-out.* For example, say to the student, "You tore up Corey's paper, so go to time-out right now for 5 minutes." Don't get into an argument with the student or accept lame excuses as to why the student should not get a time-out. If necessary, take the student to the time-out location. If the misbehavior occurs again, reidentify it and place the student in a time-out again. If the student starts yelling, knocking over furniture, and so on when you assess time-out, add time to time-out. Be sure to let the student out of time-out when the designated time away from positive reinforcement is up. Don't comment on how well the student behaved during time-out, just return the student to the prior activity.
4. *Keep records of each time-out session, especially if a time-out room is used.* This will help you monitor effective and ethical use of time-outs.

Remove Desirable Stimuli   Suppose you have tried the first two options, and they haven't worked. A third option is to remove desirable stimuli from the student. Two strategies for accomplishing this are "time-out" and "response cost."

This second-grade student has been placed in "time-out" for misbehaving. What are some guidelines for using "time-out"?

Time-Out   The most widely used strategy that teachers use to remove desirable stimuli is **time-out.** *In other words, take the student away from positive reinforcement.*

Response Cost   A second strategy for removing desirable stimuli involves **response cost,** *which refers to taking a positive reinforcer away from a student, as when the student loses certain privileges.* For example, after a student misbehaves, the teacher might take away 10 minutes of recess time or the privilege of being a class monitor. Response cost typically involves some type of penalty or fine. As with the time-out, response cost should always be used in conjunction with strategies for increasing the student's positive behaviors.

Present Aversive Stimuli (Punishment)   Most people associate the presentation of aversive (unpleasant) stimuli with punishment, as when a teacher yells at a student or a parent spanks a child. However, in accordance with the definition of

Punishment

punishment given earlier in the chapter, the consequence has to decrease the undesirable behavior (Branch, 2000). All too often, though, aversive stimuli are not effective punishments, in that they do not decrease the unwanted behavior. Applied behavior analysts say that some teachers turn too quickly to aversive stimuli when trying to get a student's behavior in line. This might occur because the teacher was harshly disciplined at home when growing up, has developed a style of handling stress by yelling or screaming, feels that he or she can effectively exercise such power over smaller charges, or is unaware of how positive reinforcement can be used to reduce unwanted student behaviors.

The most common types of aversive stimuli that teachers use are verbal reprimands. These are more effectively used when the teacher is near the student rather than across the room and when used together with a nonverbal reprimand such as a frown or eye contact (Van Houten & others, 1982). Reprimands are more effective when they are given immediately after unwanted behavior rather than later, and when they are quick and to the point. Such reprimands do not have to involve yelling and shouting, which often just raise the noise level of the classroom and present the teacher as an uncontrolled model for students. Instead, a firmly stated "stop doing that" with eye contact is often sufficient to stop unwanted behavior. Another strategy is to take the student aside and reprimand the student in private rather than in front of the entire class.

Many countries, such as Sweden, have banned the physical punishment of schoolchildren by principals and teachers. However, in America, 24 states still allow it (Hyman, 1994). Male minority students from low-income backgrounds are the most frequent recipients of physical punishment in schools. Physical punishment of students is not recommended in any circumstance. It can be abusive and magnifies all of the problems associated with punishment.

Numerous problems are associated with using aversive stimuli as intended punishment:

- Especially when you use intense punishment like yelling or screaming, you are presenting students with an out-of-control model for handling stressful situations.
- Punishment can instill fear, rage, or avoidance in students. Skinner's biggest concern was this: What punishment teaches is how to avoid something. For example, a student who experiences a punitive teacher might show a dislike for the teacher and not want to come to school.
- When students are punished, they might become so aroused and anxious that they can't concentrate clearly on their work for a long time after the punishment has been given.
- Punishment tells students what not to do rather than what to do. If you make a punishing statement such as "No, that's not right," always accompany it with positive feedback, such as "but why don't you try this."
- What is intended as punishment can turn out to be reinforcing. A student might learn that misbehaving will not only get the teacher's attention but put the student in the limelight with classmates as well.

A final lesson in all of this is to spend a lot more class time monitoring what students do right rather than what they do wrong. Too often it is disruptive behavior, not competent behavior, that grabs a teacher's attention. Every day make it a point to scan your classroom for positive student behaviors that you ordinarily would not notice and give students attention for them.

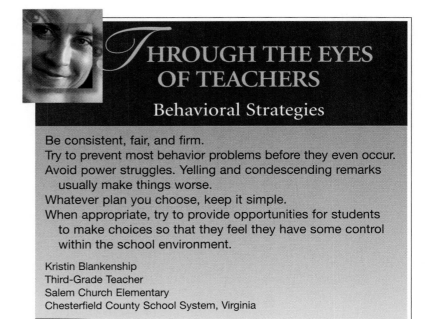

THROUGH THE EYES OF TEACHERS

Behavioral Strategies

Be consistent, fair, and firm.
Try to prevent most behavior problems before they even occur.
Avoid power struggles. Yelling and condescending remarks usually make things worse.
Whatever plan you choose, keep it simple.
When appropriate, try to provide opportunities for students to make choices so that they feel they have some control within the school environment.

Kristin Blankenship
Third-Grade Teacher
Salem Church Elementary
Chesterfield County School System, Virginia

Evaluating Operant Conditioning and Applied Behavior Analysis

Operant conditioning and applied behavior analysis have made contributions to teaching practice (Axelrod, 1996). Reinforcing and punishing consequences are part of teachers' and students' lives. Teachers give grades, praise and reprimand, smile and frown. Learning about how such consequences affect students' behavior improves your capabilities as a teacher. Used effectively, behavioral techniques can help you manage your classroom. Reinforcing certain behaviors can improve some students' conduct and, used in conjunction with the time-out, can increase desired behaviors in some incorrigible students.

Critics of operant conditioning and applied behavior analysis argue that the whole approach places too much emphasis on external control of students' behavior. They say that a better strategy is to help students learn to control their own behavior and become internally motivated. Critics also point to potential ethical problems when operant conditioning is used inappropriately, as when a teacher immediately resorts to punishing students instead of first considering reinforcement strategies, or punishes a student without also giving the student information about appropriate behavior. Another criticism is that when teachers spend a lot of time using applied behavior analysis, they might focus too much on student conduct and not enough on academic learning. We will have much more to say about student conduct in chapter 12, "Managing the Classroom."

At this point we have discussed many ideas about applied behavior analysis in education. A review of these ideas is presented in summary table 7.3. Critics of operant conditioning believe that denying the importance of cognitive factors ignores the richest aspects of the student's existence—their thoughts. Next, we will explore some of these cognitive factors.

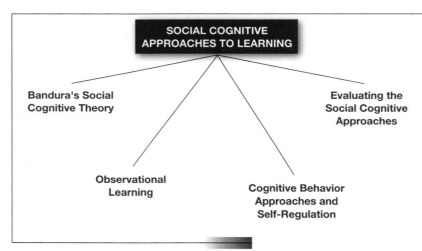

Albert Bandura

Social Cognitive Approaches to Learning

Students' thoughts affect their behavior and learning. In this section, we will explore several variations on this theme, beginning with social cognitive theory.

Bandura's Social Cognitive Theory

Social cognitive theory *states that social and cognitive factors, as well as behavior, play important roles in learning.* Cognitive factors might involve the student's expectations for success; social factors might include students' observing their parents' achievement behavior.

Albert Bandura (1986, 1997, 1998, 2000) is one of the main architects of social cognitive theory. He says that when students learn, they can cognitively represent or transform their experiences. Recall that in operant conditioning, connections occur only between environmental experiences and behavior.

Bandura developed a **reciprocal determinism model** *that consists of three main factors: behavior, person (cognitive), and environment. As shown in figure 7.6, these factors can interact to influence learning:* Environmental factors influence behavior, behavior affects the environment, person (cognitive) factors influence behavior, and so on. Bandura uses the term *person,* but we have modified it to *person (cognitive)* because so many of the person factors he describes are cognitive. The person factors Bandura describes that do not have a cognitive bent are mainly personality traits and temperament. Recall from chapter 4, "Individual Variations," that such factors might

Summary Table 7.3
Applied Behavior Analysis in Education

Concept	Processes/ Related Ideas	Characteristics/Description
What Is Applied Behavior Analysis?	Its Nature	• It involves applying the principles of operant conditioning to change human behavior.
Increasing Desirable Behaviors	Choose Effective Reinforcers	• Find out which reinforcers work best with which students. • The Premack principle states that a high-probability activity can be used to reinforce a low-probability activity.
	Make the Reinforcer Contingent and Timely	• "If . . . then" statements can be used to make it clear to students what they have to do to get a reward. • Applied behavior analysts recommend that a reinforcement be *contingent*— that is, be given only if the student performs the behavior and timely.
	Use the Best Schedule of Reinforcement	• Skinner described a number of schedules of reinforcement. • Most reinforcement is partial. Skinner described four schedules of partial reinforcement: fixed-ratio, variable-ratio, fixed-interval, and variable-interval.
	Consider Contracting	• This involves putting reinforcement contingencies in writing.
	Use Negative Reinforcement Effectively	• Although this can increase some students' desirable behavior, exercise caution with students who don't have good self-regulatory skills.
Using Prompts and Shaping	Prompts	• A prompt is an added stimulus or cue that increases the likelihood that a discriminative stimulus will produce a desired response.
	Shaping	• This involves teaching new behaviors by reinforcing successive approximations to a specified target behavior.
Decreasing Undesirable Behaviors	Use Differential Reinforcement	• The teacher might reinforce behavior that is more appropriate or that is incompatible with what the student is doing.
	Terminate Reinforcement (Extinction)	• This involves taking reinforcement away from a behavior. • Many inappropriate behaviors are maintained by teacher attention, so taking away the attention can decrease the behavior.
	Remove Desirable Stimuli	• The most widely used strategy that this involves is the time-out, which consists of taking the student away from positive reinforcement. We discussed several variations of time-out procedures. • A second strategy is response cost. This occurs when a positive reinforcer, such as a privilege, is taken away from the student.
	Present Aversive Stimuli (Punishment)	• An aversive stimulus becomes a punisher only when it decreases behavior. The most common form of punisher in the classroom is verbal reprimand. • Punishment should be used only as the last option. • Remember that when punishment is used, it should be enacted in conjunction with reinforcement of desired responses. • Physical punishment should not be used in the classroom.
Evaluating Operant Conditioning and Applied Behavior Analysis	Contributions and Criticism	• Used effectively, behavioral techniques can help you manage your classroom. • Critics say that these approaches place too much emphasis on external control and not enough on internal control. They also argue that ignoring cognitive factors leaves out much of the richness of students' lives. Critics warn about potential ethical problems when operant conditioning is used inappropriately. And some critics say that teachers who focus too much on managing the classroom with operant techniques may place too much emphasis on conduct and not enough on academic learning.

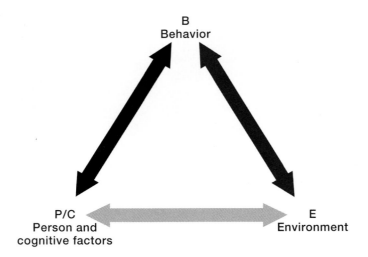

Figure 7.6
Bandura's Reciprocal Determinism Model of Learning

In Bandura's model, cognitive/person factors, environmental factors, and behavior reciprocally influence each other. What are some examples of person (cognitive) factors in learning?

Self-Efficacy

Albert Bandura has been one of the leading architects of social cognitive theory.

include being introverted or extraverted, active or inactive, calm or anxious, and friendly or hostile. Cognitive factors include expectations, beliefs, attitudes, strategies, thinking, and intelligence.

Consider how Bandura's model might work in the case of the achievement behavior of a high school student we will call Sondra:

- *Cognition influences behavior.* Sondra develops cognitive strategies to think more deeply and logically about how to solve problems. The cognitive strategies improve her achievement behavior.
- *Behavior influences cognition.* Sondra's good grades lead her to have positive expectancies about her abilities and give her self-confidence.
- *Environment influences behavior.* The school Sondra attends recently developed a pilot study-skills program to help students learn how to take notes, manage their time, and take tests more effectively. The study-skills program improves Sondra's achievement behavior.
- *Behavior influences environment.* The study-skills program is successful in improving the achievement behavior of many students in Sondra's class. The students' improved achievement behavior stimulates the school to expand the program so that all students in the high school participate in it.
- *Cognition influences environment.* The expectations and planning of the school's principal and teachers made the study-skills program possible in the first place.
- *Environment influences cognition.* The school establishes a resource center where students and parents can go to check out books and materials on improving study skills. The resource center also makes study-skills tutoring services available to students. Sondra and her parents take advantage of the center's resources and tutoring. These resources and services improve Sondra's thinking skills.

In Bandura's learning model, person (cognitive) factors play important roles. The person (cognitive) factor that Bandura (1997, 1998, 2000) has emphasized the most in recent years is **self-efficacy,** *the belief that one can master a situation and produce positive outcomes.* Bandura says that self-efficacy has a powerful influence over behavior. For example, a student who has low self-efficacy might not even try to study for a test because he doesn't believe it will do him any good. We will have much more to say about self-efficacy in chapter 11, "Motivating Students to Learn."

Next, we discuss an important learning process the exploration of which is another of Bandura's main contributions. As you read about observational learning, note how person (cognitive) factors are involved.

Observational Learning

Our exploration of observational learning focuses on the nature of observational learning, Bandura's classic Bobo doll study, and Bandura's contemporary model.

What is Observational Learning?
Observational learning, *also called imitation or modeling, is learning that occurs when a person observes and imitates someone else's behavior.* The capacity to learn behavior patterns by observation eliminates tedious trial-and-error learning. In many instances, observational learning takes less time than operant conditioning.

The Classic Bobo Doll Study
The following experiment by Bandura (1965) illustrates how observational learning can occur even by watching a model who is not reinforced or punished. The experiment also illustrates a distinction between learning and performance.

Figure 7.7

Bandura's Classic Bobo Doll Study: The Effects of Observational Learning on Children's Aggression

In the left frame, an adult model aggressively attacks the Bobo doll. In the right frame, a kindergarten-age girl who has observed the model's aggressive actions follows suit. In Bandura's experiment, under what conditions did the children reproduce the model's aggressive actions?

Equal numbers of kindergarten children watched one or another of three films in which a model beat up an adult-size plastic toy called a Bobo doll (see figure 7.7). In the first film, the aggressor was rewarded with candy, soft drinks, and praise for aggressive behavior. In the second film, the aggressor was criticized and spanked for the aggressive behavior. And in the third film, there were no consequences for the aggressor's behavior.

Subsequently, each child was left alone in a room filled with toys, including a Bobo doll. The child's behavior was observed through a one-way mirror. Children who watched the films in which the aggressor's behavior either was reinforced or went unpunished imitated the aggressor's behavior more than did the children who saw the aggressor be punished. As you might expect, boys were more aggressive than girls. An important point in this study is that observational learning occurred just as extensively when modeled aggressive behavior was not reinforced as when it was reinforced.

A second important point in this study focuses on the distinction between *learning* and *performance*. Just because students don't perform a response doesn't mean they didn't learn it. In Bandura's study, when children were rewarded (with stickers or fruit juice) for imitating the model, differences in the children's imitative behavior in the three conditions were eliminated. Bandura believes that when a child observes behavior but makes no observable response, the child may still have acquired the modeled response in cognitive form.

Bandura's Contemporary Model of Observational Learning

Since his early experiments, Bandura (1986) has focused on the specific processes that are involved in observational learning. These include attention, retention, motor reproduction, and reinforcement or incentive conditions (see figure 7.8):

> *We are in truth more than half what we are by imitation.*
>
> **Lord Chesterfield**
> *English Statesman, 18th Century*

Figure 7.8

Bandura's Model of Observational Learning

In Bandura's model of observational learning, four processes need to be considered: attention, retention, motor reproduction, and reinforcement or incentive conditions. How might these processes be involved in this classroom situation in which a teacher is demonstrating how to tell time?

- *Attention.* Before students can imitate a model's actions, they must attend to what the model is doing or saying. A student who is distracted by two other students who are talking might not hear what a teacher is saying. Attention to the model is influenced by a host of characteristics. For example, warm, powerful, atypical people command more attention than do cold, weak, typical people. Students are more likely to be attentive to high-status models than to low-status models. In most cases, teachers are high-status models for students.
- *Retention.* To reproduce a model's actions, students must code the information and keep it in memory so that it can be retrieved. A simple verbal description or a vivid image of what the model did assists students' retention. For example, the teacher might say, "I'm showing the correct way to do this. You have to do this step first, this step second, and this step third" as she models how to solve a math problem. A video with a colorful character demonstrating the importance of considering other students' feelings might be remembered better than if the teacher just tells the students to do this. Such colorful characters are at the heart of the popularity of "Sesame Street" with children. Students' retention will be improved when teachers give logical and clear demonstrations. In the next chapter, we will further examine the role of memory in children's learning.
- *Motor reproduction.* Children might attend to a model and code in memory what they have seen but, because of limitations in their motor ability, not be able to reproduce the model's behavior. A 13-year-old might watch basketball player David Robinson and golfer Nancy Lopez execute their athletic skills to perfection, or observe a famous pianist or artist perform their skills, but not be able to reproduce their motor actions. Teaching, coaching, and practice can help children improve their motor performances.
- *Reinforcement or incentive conditions.* Often children attend to what a model says or does, retain the information in memory, and possess the motor skills to perform the action, but are not motivated to perform the modeled behavior. This was demonstrated in Bandura's classic Bobo doll study when children who saw the model being punished did not reproduce the punished model's aggressive actions. However, when they subsequently were given a reinforcement or incentive (stickers or fruit juice), they did imitate the model's behavior.

Bandura believes that reinforcement is not always necessary for observational learning to take place. But if the child does not reproduce the desired behaviors, three types of reinforcement can help do the trick: (1) Reward the model, (2) reward the child, or (3) instruct the child to make self-reinforcing statements such as "Good, I did it!" or "Okay, I've done a good job of getting most of this right, now if I keep trying I will get the rest." We will have much more to say about such self-management strategies shortly.

As you can see, you will be an important model in students' lives and you have many options for providing students with an array of competent models. To evaluate the roles that models and mentors have played in your own life and can play in your students' lives, complete Self-Assessment 7.1. In the next section, we continue our exploration of approaches that have ties to behaviorism but believe that cognitive factors are important aspects of students' learning.

Children need models more than critics.

Joseph Joubert
French Essayist, 19th Century

Cognitive Behavior Approaches and Self-Regulation

Operant conditioning spawned applications to education and other real-world settings, and the interest in cognitive behavioral approaches has also produced such applications.

Cognitive Behavior Approaches   In the **cognitive behavior approaches,** *the emphasis is on getting students to monitor, manage, and regulate their own behavior rather than let it be controlled by external factors.* In some circles, this has been called *cognitive behavior modification.* Cognitive behavior approaches stem from both cognitive psychology, with its emphasis on the effects of thoughts on behavior,

TEACHING STRATEGIES
Involving Observational Learning

Observational learning is a powerful learning process in classrooms. Following are some good strategies involve observational learning.

1. *Think about what type of model you will present to students.* Every day, hour after hour, students will watch and listen to what you say and do. Just by being around you, students will absorb a great deal of information. They will pick up your good or bad habits, your expectations for their high or low achievement, your enthusiastic or bored attitude, your controlled or uncontrolled manner of dealing with stress, your learning style, your gender attitudes, and many other aspects of your behavior.

2. *Demonstrate and teach new behaviors.* Demonstrating means that you, the teacher, are a model for your students' observational learning. Demonstrating how to do something, like solve a math problem, read, write, think, control anger, and perform physical skills, is a common teacher behavior in classrooms. For example, a teacher might model how to diagram a sentence, develop a strategy for solving algebraic equations, or shoot a basketball. When demonstrating how to do something, you need to call students' attention to the relevant details of the learning situation. Your demonstrations also should be clear and follow a logical sequence.

   Observational learning can especially be effective in teaching new behaviors (Schunk, 1996). The first time students are required to learn how to multiply, to solve an algebraic equation, to write a paragraph with a topical sentence, or to give an effective talk, they benefit from watching and listening to a competent model.

3. *Think about ways to use peers as effective models.* The teacher is not the only model in the classroom. As with teachers, children can pick up their peers' good and bad habits, high or low achievement orientations, and so on, through observational learning. Remember that students are often motivated to imitate high-status models. Older peers usually have higher status than same-age peers. Thus, a good strategy is to have older peers from a higher grade model how to engage in the behaviors you want your students to perform. For students with low abilities or who are not performing well, a low-achieving student who struggles but puts considerable effort into learning and ultimately performs the behaviors can be a good model (Schunk, 1996). More about the role of peers appears in chapter 9, "Social Constructivist Approaches, Domain-Specific Approaches, and Teaching," where we will discuss peer collaboration and peers as tutors.

4. *Think about ways that mentors can be used as models.* Students and teachers benefit from having a mentor—someone they look up to and respect, someone who serves as a competent model, someone who is willing to work with them and help them achieve their goals (Rhodes, 2000). As a teacher, a potential mentor for you is a more experienced teacher, possibly someone who teaches down the hall and has had a number of years of experience in dealing with some of the same problems and issues you will have to cope with.

   In the Quantum Opportunities program, students from low-income backgrounds significantly benefited from meeting with a mentor over a 4-year-period (Carnegie Council on Adolescent Development, 1995). These mentors modeled appropriate behavior and strategies, gave sustained support, and provided guidance. Just spending a few hours a week with a mentor can make a difference in a student's life, especially if the student's parents have not been good role models. To read further about male and ethnic minority role models and mentors in children's education, see Diversity and Education.

5. *Evaluate which classroom guests will provide good models for students.* Who else would be beneficial models for your students? For a change the pace of classroom life for you and your students, invite guests who have something meaningful to talk about or demonstrate. Recall what we said in chapter 4 about Gardner's theory of multiple intelligences: There likely are some domains (physical, musical, artistic, or other) in which you don't have the skills to serve as a competent model for your students. When you need to have such skills demonstrated to your students, spend some time locating competent models in the community. Invite them to come to your classroom to demonstrate and discuss their skills. If this can't be arranged, set up field trips in which you take students to see them where they are working or performing.

6. *Consider the models children observe on television, videos, and computers.* Students observe models when they watch television programs, videos, films, or computer screens in your classroom. The principles of observational learning we described earlier apply to these media. For example, the extent to which the students perceive the media models as high or low in status, intriguing or boring, and so on, will influence the extent of their observational learning. And as we indicated in chapter 3, "Social contexts and Socioemotional Development," it is important to monitor children's TV watching to ensure that they are not being exposed to too many negative models, especially violent ones. To read further about television and children's education see Technology and Education.

DIVERSITY AND EDUCATION
Where Are the Male and Ethnic Minority Role Models and Mentors in Children's Education?

There are far more White than ethnic minority role models in students' classrooms. In 1997, of the 2.6 million public school teachers in the United States, only 346,000 were minorities. Less than 700,000 of the 2.6 million teachers are men, and most of them teach in secondary schools where they are lured by additional incentives for coaching athletic teams.

The absence of male African American teachers is especially noticeable. In our country, 12 percent of the population and 16.5 percent of public school children are African American, but only 7.4 percent of our schoolteachers are African American—and only a small percentage of those are men. This situation is likely to get even worse. In a survey by the Higher Education Institute at UCLA in 1996, only 4 percent of the male college freshmen planned on entering the teaching profession, down from 10 percent in 1966 (Sax & others, 1996).

Most education experts believe students benefit from having role models from both sexes and diverse cultural groups (Henry, 1997). The education program at Livingstone College in Salisbury, North Carolina, is trying to do something about the shortage of male ethnic minority teachers. They developed a special program to recruit ethnic minority men into the teaching profession. One of the program's graduates, Nakia Douglas, teaches kindergarten. He says he wants to eliminate all of the negative stereotypes about African American males—that they are poor role models, aren't responsible, and shouldn't be teaching young children. Another graduate, Mistor Williams, teaches history to eighth-graders in a school with a large percentage of ethnic minority students. He says that he feels the responsibility to provide a role model and support to many students who do not have a positive male influence in their lives.

If you are a white female, think about ways you can bring women and men of color into your classroom to talk with students and demonstrate their work skills. This is especially important when you have a number of students of color in your class.

Regardless of your ethnic background, look around the community for possible mentors for students, especially students who come from low-income backgrounds and who lack positive role models. For example, the aim of the 3-to-1 mentoring program is to surround each ethnic minority male student with three positive ethnic minority role models (Everbach, 1997). The program began when several African American men were challenged by a sermon delivered by Zach Holmes at the St. Lukes Methodist Church in Dallas. In the sermon, Reverend Holmes urged his congregation to become more involved with children, both their own and children in the community who don't have good role models. The 3-to-1 mentoring program has signed up more than 200 men and 100 boys (ages 4 to 18). That's far short of the goal of 3 mentors for each boy, but the men are working on increasing the number of mentors in the program. Some of the men in the mentoring program have their own children, like Dr. Leonard Berry, a physician, who has two sons and a daughter. He heeded the minister's challenge and regularly participates in the mentoring program, which involves academic tutoring as well as outings to activities such as sporting and cultural events. Last year the mentors took the students to visit the Johnson Space Center in Houston.

As a teacher you do not have to wait for someone in the community to bring mentors to your students. Look around the community in which you teach and evaluate who would be good candidates for mentoring your students or starting a mentoring program. Contact them and get the program started. Clearly, mentoring programs can benefit all students, male or female, of any ethnic background.

Dr. Leonard Berry is a mentor in the 3-to-1 program in Dallas. He is shown here with Brandon Scarbough, 13 (front), and his own son, Leonard, 12 (back). Brandon not only has benefited from Dr. Berry's mentoring but also has become friends with his son.

TECHNOLOGY AND EDUCATION
Educational Lessons from "Sesame Street"

One of television's major programming attempts to educate young children is "Sesame Street," which is designed to teach both cognitive and social skills. The program began in 1969 and is still going strong. A fundamental message of "Sesame Street" is that education and entertainment work well together (Lesser, 1972). On "Sesame Street," learning is exciting and entertaining.

"Sesame Street" also illustrates the point that teaching can be done in both direct and indirect ways. Using the direct way, a teacher tells children exactly what they are going to be taught and then actually teaches it to them. This method is often used on "Sesame Street" to teach cognitive skills. But social skills usually are communicated in indirect ways on the show. Thus, rather than telling children "You should cooperate with people," a sequence of events is shown to help children figure out what it means to be cooperative and what the advantages are.

Should the world be shown to children as it is, or as it ought to be? The "Sesame Street" advisory board of educators and psychologists decided that the real world should be shown, but with an emphasis on what the world would be like if everyone treated each other with decency and kindness. To show the world as it really is, the program might show an adult doing something unjustifiably inconsiderate to another adult, with alternative ways of coping with this acted out. Finally, the program would portray the happy outcomes when people stop acting inconsiderately.

Some of the attentional techniques used on "Sesame Street" are worthwhile to consider in the classroom. These involve first *catching* the child's attention, then *directing* it, and finally *sustaining* it. Music and sound are very effective in eliciting children's attention. For example, in teaching children to discriminate sounds, an automobile horn might be sounded or a computer's keyboard repeatedly pressed. Music is especially useful because it

leads children to become actively involved in what they are watching or listening. It is not unusual for children watching "Sesame Street" to get up out of their seats and start dancing and singing along with the jingles.

Once the child's attention has been captured, it should be directed to something. Surprise and novelty are especially helpful in this regard. They make children work hard to figure out what is going to happen. Their attention is directed because they begin to anticipate what is going to happen next.

Once attention is directed, it then needs to be maintained. "Sesame Street" especially uses humor to accomplish this. Humor is judiciously placed: Ernie outsmarts Bert; the Cookie Monster annoyingly interrupts a lecture given by Kermit the Frog. For young children, physical gags often are funnier than verbal ones, and much of the humor that is effective involves physical acts that are surprising and incongruous.

What educational lessons can be learned from "Sesame Street"?

and behaviorism, with its emphasis on techniques for changing behavior. Cognitive behavior approaches try to change students' misconceptions, strengthen their coping skills, increase their self-control, and encourage constructive self-reflection (Kendall, 2000; Meichenbaum, 1993).

Self-instructional methods *are cognitive behavior techniques aimed at teaching individuals to modify their own behavior.* Self-instructional methods help people alter what they say to themselves.

Imagine a situation in which a high school student is extremely nervous about taking standardized tests, such as the SAT. The student can be encouraged to talk to himself in more positive ways. Following are some self-talk strategies that students and teachers can use to cope more effectively with such stressful situations (Meichenbaum, Turk, & Burstein, 1975):

$\mathcal{S}$ELF-ASSESSMENT 7.1
Models and Mentors in My Life and My Students' Lives

Having positive role models and mentors can make an important difference in whether individuals develop optimally and reach their full potential. First, evaluate the role models and mentors who have played an important part in your life. Second, think about the type of role model you want to be for your students. Third, give some thought to how you will incorporate other models and mentors in your students' lives. Fourth, explore who your education mentor might be.

My Models and Mentors
List the most important role models and mentors in your life. Then describe what their positive modeling and mentoring have meant to your development.

Role Models and Mentors	Their Contributions
1. _____	_____
2. _____	_____
3. _____	_____
4. _____	_____
5. _____	_____

The Type of Role Model I Want to Be for My Students
Describe which characteristics and behaviors you believe are the most important for you to model for your students.
1. _____
2. _____
3. _____
4. _____
5. _____

How I Will Incorporate Models and Mentors in My Classroom
Describe a systematic plan for bringing models and mentors into your students' lives in one or more domain(s) you plan to teach, such as math, English, science, music, and so on.
_____
_____
_____
_____

Who Will Be My Education Mentor? What Would My Ideal Education Mentor Be Like?
Do you have someone in mind who might serve as an education mentor when you become a teacher? If so, describe the person.
_____
_____

What would your ideal education mentor be like?
_____
_____
_____
_____

• *Prepare for anxiety or stress*
  "What do I have to do?"
  "I'm going to develop a plan to deal with it."
  "I'll just think about what I have to do."
  "I won't worry. Worry doesn't help anything."
  "I have a lot of different strategies I can use."

• *Confront and handle the anxiety or stress*
  "I can meet the challenge."
  "I'll keep on taking just one step at a time."
  "I can handle it. I'll just relax, breathe deeply, and use one of the strategies."
  "I won't think about my stress. I'll just think about what I have to do."

• *Cope with feelings at critical moments*
  "What is it I have to do?"
  "I knew my anxiety might increase. I just have to keep myself in control."
  "When the anxiety comes, I'll just pause and keep focusing on what I have to do."

• *Use reinforcing self-statements*
  "Good, I did it."
  "I handled it well."
  "I knew I could do it."
  "Wait until I tell other people how I did it!"

In many instances, the strategy is to replace negative self-statements with positive ones. For example, a student might say to herself, "I'll never get this work done by tomorrow." This can be replaced with positive self-statements like these: "This is going to be tough but I think I can do it." "I'm going to look at this as a challenge rather than a stressor." "If I work really hard, I might be able to get it done." Or in having to participate in a class discussion, a student might replace the negative thought "Everyone else knows more than I do so what's the use of saying anything" with positive self-statements like these: "I have as much to say as anyone else." "My ideas may be different, but they are still good." "It's okay to be a little nervous; I'll relax and start talking." Figure 7.9 shows posters that students in one fifth-grade class developed to help them remember how to talk to themselves while listening, planning, working, and checking.

Talking positively to oneself can help teachers and students reach their full potential. Uncountered negative thinking has a way of becoming a self-fulfilling prophecy. You think you can't do it, and so you don't. If negative self-talk is a problem for you, at random times during the day ask yourself, "What am I saying to myself right now?" Moments that you expect will be potentially stressful are excellent times to examine your self-talk. Also monitor your students' self-talk. If you hear students saying, "I can't do this" or "I'm so slow I'll never get this done," spend some time getting them to replace their negative self-talk with positive self-talk.

Cognitive behaviorists recommend that students improve their performance by monitoring their own behavior. This can involve getting students to keep charts or records of their behavior. When I wrote this book, I (your author) had a chart on my wall with each of the chapters listed. I planned how long it would take me to do each of the chapters, and then as I completed each one I checked it off and wrote down the date of completion. Teachers can get students to do some similar monitoring of their own progress by getting them to keep records of how many assignments they have finished, how many books they have read, how many homework papers they have turned in on time, how many days in a row they have not interrupted the teacher, and so

POSTER 1
While Listening

1. Does this make sense?
2. Am I getting this?
3. I need to ask a question before I forget.
4. Pay attention.
5. Can I do what the teacher is saying to do?

POSTER 2
While Planning

1. Do I have everything together?
2. Do I have my friends tuned out so I can get this done?
3. I need to get organized first.
4. What order can I do this in?
5. I know this stuff.

POSTER 3
While Working

1. Am I working fast enough?
2. Stop staring at my girlfriend (boyfriend) and get back to work.
3. How much time is left?
4. Do I need to stop and start all over?
5. This is hard for me but I can manage it.

POSTER 4
While Checking

1. Did I finish everything?
2. What do I need to recheck?
3. Am I proud of this work?
4. Did I write all of the words?
5. I think I'm finished. I organized myself. Did I daydream too much, though?

Figure **7.9**
Some Posters Developed by a Fifth-Grade Class to Help Them Remember How to Effectively Talk to Themselves

$\mathcal{S}$ELF-ASSESSMENT 7.2

Self-Monitoring

Self-monitoring can benefit you as well as your students. Many successful learners regularly self-monitor their progress to see how they are doing in their effort to complete a project, develop a skill, or perform well on a test or other assessment. For the next month, self-monitor your study time for this course you are taking in educational psychology. To achieve high grades, most experts recommend that students spend 2 or 3 hours out of class studying, doing homework, and working on projects for every hour they are in class in college. The experience of self-monitoring your own study time should give you a sense of how important such skills are for your students to develop. You might adapt this form for students' homework, for example. Remember from our discussion of Bandura's cognitive social learning theory that self-efficacy involves your belief that you can master a situation and produce positive outcomes. One way to evaluate self-efficacy is your expectancy for attaining a particular score on an upcoming quiz or test. Determine what score or grade you want to achieve on your next quiz or test. Then each day you study, rate your self-efficacy for achieving the score you desire on a 3 point scale: 1=not very confident, 2=moderately confident, and 3=very confident.

FORM FOR SELF-MONITORING STUDY TIME

DATE	ASSIGNMENT	TIME STARTED	TIME FINISHED	STUDY CONTEXT			SELF-EFFICACY
				WHERE?	WITH WHOM?	DISTRACTIONS	

on. In some cases, teachers place these self-monitoring charts on the walls of the classroom. Alternatively, if the teacher thinks that negative social comparison with other students will be highly stressful for some students, then keeping private records (in a notebook, for example) that are periodically checked by the teacher is probably the better strategy.

Self-monitoring is an excellent strategy for improving learning, and one that you can help students learn to do effectively. By completing Self-Assessment 7.2, you should get a sense of the benefits of self-monitoring for your students.

Self-Regulatory Learning   **Self-regulatory learning** *consists of the self-generation and self-monitoring of thoughts, feelings, and behaviors in order to reach a goal.* These goals might be academic (improving comprehension while reading, becoming a more organized writer, learning how to do multiplication, asking relevant questions) or they might be socioemotional (controlling one's anger, getting along better with peers). What are some of the characteristics of self-regulated learners? Self-regulatory learners (Winne, 1995, 1997)

- set goals for extending their knowledge and sustaining their motivation
- are aware of their emotional makeup and have strategies for managing their emotions
- periodically monitor their progress toward a goal
- fine-tune or revise their strategies based on the progress they are making
- evaluate obstacles that may arise and make the necessary adaptations

Researchers have found that high-achieving students are often self-regulatory learners (Pintrich, 2000; Pressley, 1995; Schunk & Zimmerman, 1994; Zimmerman, 1998, 2000). For example, compared with low-achieving students, high-achieving students set more specific learning goals, use more strategies to learn, self-monitor their learning more, and more systematically evaluate their progress toward a goal.

A Model of Self-Regulatory Learning   Teachers, tutors, mentors, counselors, and parents can help students become self-regulatory learners (Randi & Corno, 2000; Weinstein, Husman, & Dierking, 2000). Barry Zimmerman, Sebastian Bonner, and Robert Kovach (1996) developed a model for turning low-self-regulatory students into students who engage in these multistep strategies: (1) self-evaluation and monitoring, (2) goal-setting and strategic planning, (3) putting a plan into action and monitoring it, and (4) monitoring outcomes and refining strategies (see figure 7.10).

Self-Regulatory
Learning

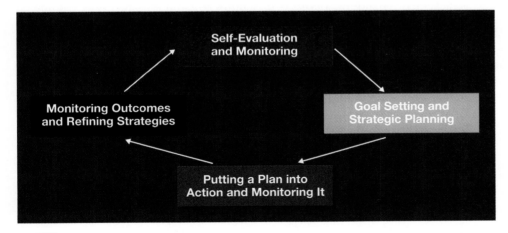

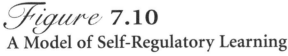

Figure **7.10**
A Model of Self-Regulatory Learning

Zimmerman and colleagues describe a seventh-grade student who is doing poorly in history and apply their self-regulatory model to her situation. In step 1, she self-evaluates her studying and test-preparation by keeping a detailed record of them. The teacher gives her some guidelines for keeping these records. After several weeks, the student turns the records in and traces her poor test performance to low comprehension of difficult reading material.

In step 2, the student sets a goal, in this case of improving reading comprehension, and plans how to achieve the goal. The teacher assists her in breaking the goal into components, such as locating main ideas and setting specific goals for understanding a series of paragraphs in her textbook. The teacher also provides the student with strategies, such as focusing initially on the first sentence of each paragraph and then scanning the others as a means of identifying main ideas. Another support the teacher might offer the student is adult or peer tutoring in reading comprehension if it is available.

In step 3, the student puts the plan into action and begins to monitor her progress. Initially, she may need help from the teacher or tutor in identifying main ideas in the reading. This feedback can help her monitor her reading comprehension more effectively on her own.

In step 4, the student monitors her improvement in reading comprehension by evaluating whether it has had any impact on her learning outcomes. Most importantly: Has her improvement in reading comprehension led to better performance on history tests?

Self-evaluations reveal that the strategy of finding main ideas has only partly improved her comprehension, and only when the first sentence contained the paragraph's main idea. So, the teacher recommends further strategies. Figure 7.11 describes how teachers can apply the self-regulatory model to homework.

Social Origins of Self-Regulation   The development of self-regulation is influenced by many factors, among them modeling and self-efficacy (Schunk & Zimmerman, 1997).

Models are important sources for conveying self-regulatory skills. Among the self-regulatory skills that models can engage in are planning and managing time effectively, attending to and concentrating, organizing and coding information strategically, establishing a productive work environment, and using social resources. For example, students might observe a teacher engage in an effective time management strategy and verbalize appropriate principles. By observing such models, students can come to believe that they also can plan and manage time effectively, which creates a sense of self-efficacy for academic self-regulation and motivates students to engage in those activities.

Self-efficacy can influence a student's choice of tasks, effort expended, persistence, and achievement (Bandura, 1997, 2000; Schunk & Zimmerman, 1997). Compared with students who doubt their learning capabilities, those with high self-efficacy for acquiring a skill or performing a task participate more readily, work harder, persist longer in the face of difficulty, and achieve at a higher level. Self-efficacy can have a strong effect on achievement, but it is not the only influence. High self-efficacy will not result in competent performance when requisite knowledge and skills are lacking. We will further explore self-efficacy, setting goals, planning, and self-regulation in chapter 11, "Motivating Students to Learn."

Teachers who encourage students to be self-regulatory learners convey the message that students are responsible for their own behavior, for becoming educated, and for becoming contributing citizens to society. Another message conveyed by self-regulatory learning is that learning is a personal experience that requires active and dedicated participation by the student (Zimmerman, Bonner, & Kovach, 1996).

Evaluating the Social Cognitive Approaches

The social cognitive approaches have made important contributions to educating children. While keeping the behaviorists' scientific flavor and emphasis on careful observation, they significantly expanded the emphasis of learning to include social and

1. Self-Evaluation and Monitoring

- The teacher distributes forms so that students can monitor specific aspects of their studying.
- The teacher gives students daily assignments to develop their self-monitoring skills and a weekly quiz to assess how well they have learned the methods.
- After several days, the teacher begins to have students exchange their homework with their peers. The peers are asked to evaluate the accuracy of the homework and how effectively the student engaged in self-monitoring. Then the teacher collects the homework for grading and reviews the peers' suggestions.

2. Goal Setting and Strategic Planning

- After a week of monitoring and the first graded exercise, the teacher asks students to give their perceptions of the strengths and weaknesses of their study strategies. The teacher emphasizes the link between learning strategies and learning outcomes.
- The teacher and peers recommend specific strategies that students might use to improve their learning. Students may use the recommendations or devise new ones. The teacher asks students to set specific goals at this point.

3. Putting a Plan into Action and Monitoring It

- The students monitor the extent to which they actually enact the new strategies.
- The teacher's role is to make sure that the new learning strategies are openly discussed.

4. Monitoring Outcomes and Refining Strategies

- The teacher continues to give students opportunities to gauge how effectively they are using their new strategies.
- The teacher helps students summarize their self-regulatory methods by reviewing each step of the self-regulatory learning cycle. She also discusses with students the hurdles the students had to overcome and the self-confidence they have achieved.

Figure **7.11**

Applying the Self-Regulatory Model to Homework

cognitive factors. Considerable learning occurs through watching and listening to competent models and then imitating what they do. The emphasis in the cognitive behavior approach on self-instruction, self-talk, and self-regulatory learning provides an important shift from learning controlled by others to taking responsibility for one's own learning (Higgins, 2000). These self-enacted strategies can significantly improve students' learning.

Critics of the social cognitive approaches come from several camps. Some cognitive theorists believe the approaches still focus too much on overt behavior and external factors and not enough on the details of how cognitive processes such as thinking, memory, problem solving, and the like actually take place. Some developmentalists criticize them for being nondevelopmental, in the sense that they don't specify age-related, sequential changes in learning. And humanistic theorists fault them for not placing enough attention on self-esteem and caring, supportive relationships. All of these criticisms also can be, and have been, leveled at the behavioral approaches, such as Skinner's operant conditioning, discussed earlier in the chapter.

At this point, we have discussed many aspects of the social cognitive approaches. A review of these ideas is presented in summary table 7.4. This chapter focused on the cognitive approaches to learning that still retain some behavioral leanings. In the next chapter, we will examine approaches with a purely cognitive bent.

SUMMARY TABLE 7.4
Social Cognitive Approaches to Learning

Concept	Processes/ Related Ideas	Characteristics/Description
Bandura's Social Cognitive Theory	Its Nature	• Albert Bandura is the main architect of social cognitive theory. His reciprocal determinism model of learning includes three main factors: person (cognition), behavior, and environment.
		• The person (cognitive) factor given the most emphasis by Bandura in recent years is self-efficacy, the belief that one can master a situation and produce positive outcomes.
Observational Learning	What Is Observational Learning?	• Also called imitation or modeling, it is learning that occurs when a person observes and imitates someone else's behavior.
	The Classic Bobo Doll Study	• In this experiment, Bandura illustrated how observational learning can occur even by watching a model who is not reinforced or punished. The experiment also demonstrates a distinction between learning and performance.
	Bandura's Contemporary Model of Observational Learning	• Since his early experiments, Bandura has focused on the specific processes that are involved in observational learning.
		• These include attention, retention, motor reproduction, and reinforcement or incentive conditions.
Cognitive Behavior Approaches and Self-Regulation	Cognitive Behavior Approaches	• These approaches emphasize getting students to monitor, manage, and regulate their own behavior rather than let it be externally controlled. In some circles, this is called cognitive behavior modification.
		• Cognitive behavior approaches try to change students' misconceptions, strengthen their coping skills, increase their self-control, and encourage their constructive self-reflection.
		• Self-instructional methods are cognitive behavior techniques aimed at teaching individuals to modify their own behavior.
		• In many cases, it is recommended that students replace negative self-statements with positive ones.
		• Cognitive behaviorists believe that students can improve their performance by monitoring their behavior.
	Self-Regulatory Learning	• Self-regulatory learning consists of the self-generation and self-monitoring of thoughts, feelings, and behaviors to reach a goal. High-achieving students are often self-regulatory learners.
		• One model of self-regulatory learning involves these components: self-evaluation and monitoring, goal setting and strategic planning, putting a plan into action, and monitoring outcomes and refining strategies.
		• Self-regulatory learning gives students responsibility for their learning.
		• The theory of self-regulatory learning are influenced derives from many influences, including modeling and self-efficacy.
Evaluating the Cognitive Social Approaches		• These approaches have significantly expanded the scope of learning to include cognitive and social factors, in addition to behavior.
		• The concept of observational learning is an important one, and a considerable amount of learning in classrooms takes place in this manner.
		• The cognitive behavior emphasis on self-instruction, self-talk, and self-regulatory learning provides an important shift from learning controlled by others to self-management of learning.
		• Critics of the cognitive and social learning approaches say that they still place too much emphasis on behavior and external factors and not enough on the details of cognitive processes. They also are criticized for being non-developmental and not giving enough attention to self-esteem and warmth.

Chapter Review

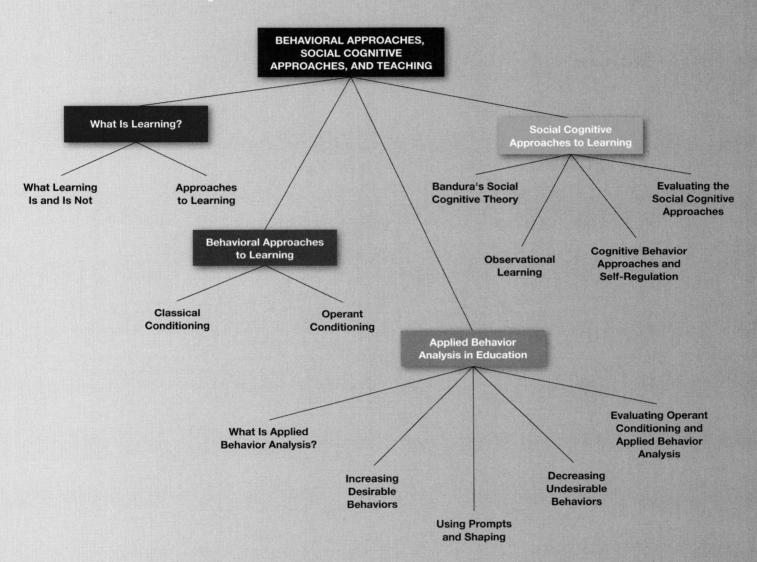

TO OBTAIN A DETAILED REVIEW OF THIS CHAPTER, STUDY THESE FOUR SUMMARY TABLES:

Key Terms

learning 238
behaviorism 238
mental processes 238
associative learning 239
classical conditioning 240
unconditioned stimulus
  (US) 241
unconditioned response
  (UR) 241
conditioned stimulus
  (CS) 241
conditioned response
  (CR) 242

generalization (classical
  conditioning) 242
discrimination (classical
  conditioning) 242
extinction (classical
  conditioning) 242
systematic
  desensitization 243
operant conditioning 243
law of effect 244
reinforcement (reward) 244
punishment 244
positive reinforcement 244
negative reinforcement 245

generalization (operant
  conditioning) 246
discrimination (operant
  conditioning) 246
extinction (operant
  conditioning) 246
applied behavior analysis 246
Premack principle 248
schedules of
  reinforcement 249
fixed-ratio schedule 249
variable-ratio schedule 249
fixed-interval schedule 249
variable-interval schedule 249

contracting 250
prompt 250
shaping 250
time out 252
response cost 252
social cognitive theory 254
reciprocal determinism
  model 254
self-efficacy 256
observational learning 256
cognitive behavior
  approaches 258
self-instructional methods 261
self-regulatory learning 265

Educational Psychology Checklist

BEHAVIORAL APPROACHES, SOCIAL COGNITIVE APPROACHES, AND TEACHING

How much have you learned since the beginning of the chapter? Use the following statements to help you review your knowledge and understanding of the chapter material. First, read the statement and mentally or briefly on paper demonstrate that you can outline and discuss the relevant information.

_____ I know what learning is and is not.
_____ I can describe a number of different approaches to learning.
_____ I am aware of what classical conditioning is.
_____ I can discuss what operant conditioning is.
_____ I know some good strategies for increasing desirable behaviors, using prompts and shaping, and decreasing undesirable behaviors.
_____ I am aware of some of the alternatives to using punishment.

_____ I can list some strengths, as well as criticisms, of operant conditioning and applied behavior analysis.
_____ I can describe Bandura's social cognitive theory.
_____ I know how observational learning works.
_____ I understand what the cognitive behavior approach is.
_____ I am aware of what constitutes self-regulatory learning.
_____ I can evaluate the strengths of the social cognitive approaches, as well as criticisms of them.

For any items that you did not check off, go back and locate the relevant material in the chapter. Review the material until you feel you can check off the item. You also may want to use this checklist later in preparing for an exam.

Adventures for the Mind

Now that you have a good knowledge and understanding of the chapter, complete the following exercises to expand your thinking about the chapter's topics.

- These are some of the behavioral concepts you studied in this chapter that can be used to increase desirable behavior: positive reinforcement, the Premack principle, and negative reinforcement. Match these concepts to the following situations:
- Sarah sits at the front of the auditorium where a speech is being given to get away from the talking that is going on in the back.
- Thomas puts his toys away more frequently now because he earns colored stickers when he does.
- Nickie is finishing more of her homework now because she is allowed to listen to CDs when she is done.
- Consider the following students' undesirable behaviors. You want to decrease the behaviors. What is the best strategy for each?

- Andrew, who likes to utter profanities every now and then
- Sandy, who tells you to quit bugging her when you ask her questions
- Matt, who likes to mess up other students' papers
- Rebecca, who frequently talks with other students around her while you are explaining or demonstrating something
- In the Technology and Education box, we described some of the effective techniques used on "Sesame Street" to increase children's attention and help them learn. Watch an episode. How were these strategies used on the show you watched? Describe any additional techniques used on the show that you might be able to use in your classroom.
- Letitia is a high school student who doesn't have adequate self-regulatory skills, and this is causing her to have serious academic problems. She doesn't plan or organize, has poor study strategies, and uses ineffective time management. Using Zimmerman's four-step strategy, design an effective self-regulation program for Letitia.

Taking It to the Net

1. You have a student who curses a lot in class. How might you change your student's behavior? Could it be as easy as A-B-C?
2. When you approach a task, do you generally feel confident? Do you believe in your ability to succeed? Why, or why not?

3. You are about to be evaluated by either your principal, who is supportive, or your vice principal, who is adversarial. Which observer's evaluation is more likely to result in improvements in your performance?

Connect to http://www.mhhe.com/socscience/psychology/santedu/titnet.htm to find the answers!

Case Studies

Case 1   *Melissa Reid:* Melissa, an enthusiastic young student teacher, struggles to gain the respect of her senior-level composition class and improve their behavior. She is devastated when she finds that one of her student's papers is full of vindictiveness and hatred toward her.

Case 2   *Linda Pierce:* Linda is concerned that her students are not responding well to the research and writing assignment that she and her fellow teachers have created. This study explores her attempts to help the students meet the demands of the assignment.

Chapter 8

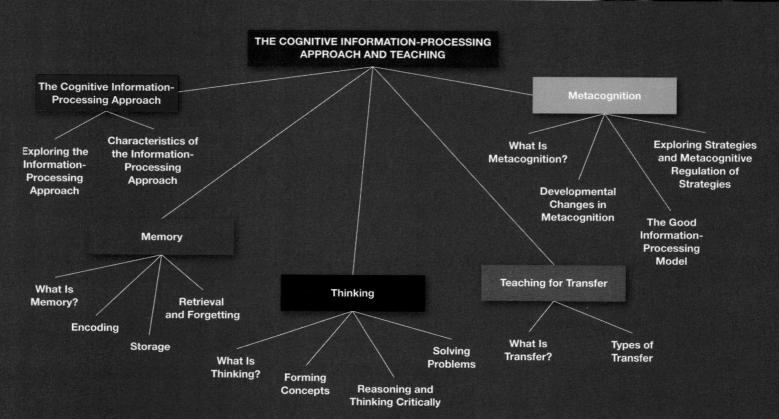

THE COGNITIVE INFORMATION-PROCESSING APPROACH AND TEACHING

- **The Cognitive Information-Processing Approach**
  - Exploring the Information-Processing Approach
  - Characteristics of the Information-Processing Approach
  - Memory
    - What Is Memory?
    - Encoding
    - Storage
    - Retrieval and Forgetting
- **Thinking**
  - What Is Thinking?
  - Forming Concepts
  - Reasoning and Thinking Critically
  - Solving Problems
- **Metacognition**
  - What Is Metacognition?
  - Developmental Changes in Metacognition
  - Exploring Strategies and Metacognitive Regulation of Strategies
  - The Good Information-Processing Model
- **Teaching for Transfer**
  - What Is Transfer?
  - Types of Transfer

The Cognitive Information-Processing Approach and Teaching

"The mind is an enchanting thing."

Marianne Moore
American Poet, 20th Century

Preview

Children thirst to know and understand. In their effort to know and understand, they process information. These statements reflect a cognitive information-processing approach, the focus of this chapter. These are some of the questions we will explore:

- What are the key features of the information-processing approach?
- How do children construct their memory?
- How do children think, and what are the best ways to guide their thinking?
- How can you effectively teach so that children will transfer their learning from the classroom to other contexts?
- What is metacognition? How can you help children use better strategies in remembering and solving problems?

Teaching Stories
Laura Bickford

Laura Bickford chairs the English Department at Nordoff High School in Ojai, California. She recently spoke about how she encourages students to think:

I believe the call to teach is a call to teach students how to think. In encouraging critical thinking, literature itself does a good bit of work for us but we still have to be guides. We have to ask good questions. We have to show students the value in asking their own questions, in having discussions and conversations. In addition to reading and discussing literature, the best way to move students to think critically is to have them write. We write all the time in a variety of modes: journals, formal essays, letters, factual reports, news articles, speeches, or other formal oral presentations. We have to show students where they merely scratch the surface in their thinking and writing. I call these moments "hits and runs." When I see this "hit and run" effort, I draw a window on the paper. I tell them it is a "window of opportunity" to go deeper, elaborate, and clarify. Many students don't do this kind of thinking until they are prodded to do so.

I also use metacognitive strategies all the time—that is, helping students know about knowing. These include: asking students to comment on their learning after we have finished particular pieces of projects and asking them to discuss in advance what we might be seeking to learn as we *begin* a new project or activity. I also ask them to keep reading logs so they can observe their own thinking as it happens. For example, they might copy a passage from a reading selection and comment on it. Studying a passage from J. D. Salinger's *A Catcher in the Rye,* a student might write: "I've never thought about life the way that Holden Caulfield does. Maybe I see the world differently than he does. He always is so depressed. I'm not depressed. Salinger is good at showing us someone who is usually depressed. How does he manage to do that?" In addition, I ask students to comment on their own learning by way of grading themselves. This year a student gave me one of the most insightful lines about her growth as a reader I have ever seen from a student. She wrote, "I no longer think in a monotone when I'm reading." I don't know if she grasps the magnitude of that thought or how it came to be that she made that change. It is magic when students see themselves growing like this."

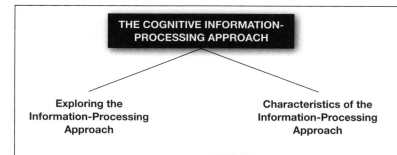

The Cognitive Information-Processing Approach

How capable are children? Proponents of the information-processing approach believe they are highly capable. Children attend to information being presented and tinker with it. They develop strategies for remembering. They form concepts. They reason and solve problems.

Exploring the Information-Processing Approach

The **information-processing approach** *emphasizes that children manipulate information, monitor it, and strategize about it. Central to this approach are the processes of memory and thinking.* According to the information-processing approach, children develop a gradually increasing capacity for processing information, which allows them to acquire increasingly complex knowledge and skills (Stevenson, Hofer, & Randel, 1999).

Some information-processing approaches have stronger constructivist leanings than others. Those that do have a constructivist bent see teachers as cognitive guides for academic tasks and children as learners who are trying to make sense of these tasks (Mayer, 1996, 1999). Piaget's cognitive developmental theory, described in chapter 2, exemplifies the cognitive constructivist approach ◀▥ p. 49. So do some information-processing approaches in this chapter (Ceci, 2000). Information-processing approaches that emphasize a more passive child who simply memorizes information provided by the environment are not constructivist.

Behaviorism and its associative model of learning was a dominant force in psychology until the 1950s and 1960s, when many psychologists began to acknowledge that they could not explain children's learning without referring to mental processes such as memory and thinking (Gardner, 1985). The term *cognitive psychology* became a label for approaches that sought to explain behavior by examining mental processes. Although a number of factors stimulated the growth of cognitive psychology, none was more important than the development of computers. The first modern computer, developed by John von Neumann in the late 1940s, showed that inanimate machines could perform logical operations. This suggested that some mental operations might be carried out by computers, possibly telling us something about the way human cognition works. Cognitive psychologists often draw analogies to computers to help explain the relation between cognition and the brain. The physical brain is described as the computer's hardware, cognition as its software. And although computers and software aren't perfect analogies for brains and cognitive activities, nonetheless, the comparison contributed to our thinking about the child's mind as an active information-processing system.

Our life is what our thoughts make it.

Marcus Aurelius
Roman Emperor and Philosopher, 2nd Century A.D.

Characteristics of the Information-Processing Approach

Robert Siegler (1998) described three main characteristics of the information-processing approach:

- *Thinking.* In Siegler's view, thinking is information processing. In this regard, Siegler provides a broad perspective on thinking. He says that when children perceive, encode, represent, and store information from the world, they are engaging in thinking. Siegler believes that thinking is highly flexible, which allows individuals to adapt and adjust to many changes in circumstances, task requirements, and goals. However, there are some limits on the human's remarkable thinking abilities. Individuals can attend to only a limited amount of information at any point in time, and there are limits on how fast we can process information. Later in the chapter we will explore children's attention in more depth.

• *Change mechanisms.* Siegler argues that in information processing the main focus should be on the role of mechanisms of change in development. He believes that four main mechanisms work together to create changes in children's cognitive skills: encoding, automatization, strategy construction, and generalization. **Encoding** *is the process by which information gets into memory.* Siegler states that a key aspect of solving problems is to encode the relevant information and ignore the irrelevant parts. Because it often takes time and effort to construct new strategies, children must practice them in order to eventually execute them automatically and maximize their effectiveness. The term **automaticity** *refers to the ability to process information with little or no effort.* With age and experience, information processing becomes increasingly automatic on many tasks, allowing children to detect connections among ideas and events that they otherwise would miss. The third and fourth change mechanisms are strategy construction and generalization. **Strategy construction** *involves the discovery of a new procedure for processing information.* Siegler says that children need to encode key information about a problem and coordinate the information with relevant prior knowledge to solve the problem. To fully benefit from a newly constructed strategy, children need to *generalize,* or apply, it to other problems. Later in the chapter, we will discuss generalization under the topic of transfer of learning. **Transfer** *occurs when the child applies previous experiences and knowledge to learning or problem solving in a new situation.*

Strategies

• *Self-modification.* The contemporary information-processing approach argues that, like in Piaget's theory of cognitive development, children play an active role in their development. They use knowledge and strategies that they have learned in previous circumstances to adapt their responses to a new learning situation. In this manner, children build newer and more sophisticated responses from prior knowledge and strategies. The importance of self-modification in processing information is exemplified in **metacognition,** *which means cognition about cognition, or "knowing about knowing"* (Flavell, 1999; Flavell & Miller, 1998). We will study metacognition in the final section of this chapter and especially will emphasize how students' self-awareness can enable them to adapt and manage their strategies during problem solving and thinking.

Now that we have studied some general properties of the information-processing approach, let's examine some of its main cognitive processes in greater detail. We will begin with memory. Some of the aspects of memory that we will explore are encoding, automatization, and strategies, which are critical change mechanisms according to Siegler's view of information processing.

Memory

Twentieth-century playwright Tennessee Williams once commented that life is all memory except for that one present moment that goes by so quickly that you can hardly catch it going. But just what is memory?

What Is Memory?

Memory *is the retention of information over time.* Educational psychologists study how information is initially placed or encoded into memory, how it is retained or stored after being encoded, and how it is found or retrieved for a certain purpose later. Memory anchors the self in continuity. Without memory you would not be able to connect what happened to you yesterday with what

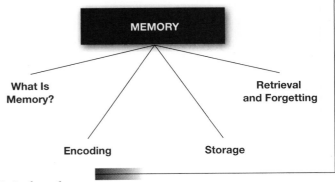

Memory Links

As I used to say to my clients, memory is life.

Saul Bellow
American Author, 20th Century

is going on in your life today. Today, educational psychologists emphasize that it is important not to view memory in terms of how children add something to it but rather to underscore how children actively construct their memory (Schneider & Bjorklund, 1998).

The main body of our discussion of memory will focus on encoding, storage, and retrieval. Thinking about memory in terms of these processes should help you to understand it better (see figure 8.1). For memory to work, children have to take information in, store it or represent it, and then retrieve it for some purpose later.

As you learned earlier, *encoding* is the process by which information gets into memory. **Storage** *is the retention of information over time.* **Retrieval** *means taking information out of storage.* Let's now explore each of these three important memory activities in greater detail.

Encoding

In everyday language, encoding has much in common with attention and learning. When a student is listening to a teacher, watching a movie, listening to music, or talking with a friend, she or he is encoding information into memory. Although children can perform some activities automatically, to perform many others they must pay **attention,** *which refers to concentrating and focusing mental resources.* One critical skill in paying attention is doing it *selectively* (Pashler, 1998). As the teacher gives instructions for completing a task, students need to attend to what she is saying and not be distracted by other students who are talking. As students study for a test, they need to focus selectively on the book they are reading and tune out or eliminate other stimuli such as the sound of a television. In one research study, 8-year-old children tended to use exhaustive attentional searches to find information, whereas 11-year-olds used more selective attentional strategies in searching for information (Davidson, 1996).

Being able to *shift* from one activity to another when appropriate is another challenge related to attention. For example, learning to write good stories requires shifting among the competing tasks of forming letters, composing grammar, structuring paragraphs, and conveying the story as a whole. Older children and adolescents are better than younger children at making appropriate shifts of attention.

Another problem for many young children is that they focus too much on the attention-grabbing aspects of a task or situation rather than on what is important. They focus on *salient* aspects of a situation rather than on its *relevant* aspects. For example, when preschoolers watch a video on which a clown is giving directions for solving a problem, they often focus more on the clown's attention-grabbing appearance than on the instructions he is giving. By the middle of elementary school, children are better at focusing their attention on the relevant dimensions of a task (Paris & Lindauer, 1982). This change often signals greater reflection and less impulsiveness. Of course, there are individual differences in attention, and some elementary school children need help in attending to the relevant dimensions of a task rather than the salient dimensions.

One reason older children are better at deploying attention than younger children is that they are more likely to construct a plan of action to guide their attentional efforts when they are trying to solve a problem. However, younger children often can effectively use attention-focusing strategies when these are provided to them. Possibly school experiences help children become more aware of their own attentional capabilities, or perhaps as they develop, they come to understand that their mind works best when it is active and constructive (Lovett & Pillow, 1996). Attending to something relevant is an active, effortful process that draws on mental resources, rather than a passive process of receiving the available information.

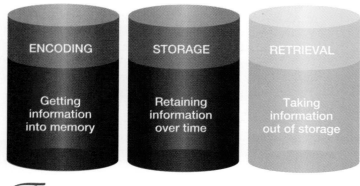

Figure **8.1**

Processing Information in Memory

As you read about the many aspects of memory in this chapter, it should help you to think about the organization of memory in terms of these three main activities.

TEACHING STRATEGIES
For Helping Children Pay Attention

Some strategies to get your students to pay attention include:

1. *Encourage students to pay close attention and minimize distraction.* Talk with children about how important it is to pay attention when they need to remember something. Give them exercises in which they get opportunities to give their undivided attention to something.
2. *Use cues or gestures to signal that something is important.* This might involve raising your voice, repeating something with emphasis, and writing the concept on the board or on a transparency.
3. *Help students generate their own cue or catch phrase for when they need to pay attention.* Possibly vary this from month to month. Give them a menu of options to select from, such as "Alert," "Focus," or "Zero in." Get them to say their word or pet phrase quietly but firmly to themselves when they catch their minds wandering.
4. *Use instructional comments.* These might include "Okay, we are ready to start discussing . . . Now, pay attention" or "I'm going to ask you a question about this next topic on the test next week."
5. *Make learning interesting.* Boredom can set in quickly for students, and when it does their attention wanes. Relating ideas to students' interests increases their attention. So does infusing the classroom with novel, unusual, or surprising exercises. Just starting off a biology exercise on heredity and aging with a question like "Can you live to be 100?" or "Might someone be able to live to be even 400 some day?" is sure to capture students' attention. Think of dramatic questions like these to introduce various topics.
6. *Use media and technology effectively as part of your effort to vary the pace of the classroom.* Video and television programs have built-in attention-getting formats, such as zooming in on an image, flashing a vivid, colorful image on the screen, and switching from one setting to another. Look for relevant videos and television programs that can help you vary the classroom's pace and increase students' attention. Also, the next time you watch a video or a TV program, think about the way your attention is being captured and reflect on how you might use variations of this in your own classroom. However, too many teachers show videos because it keeps students quiet, even though they are passively watching and not actively viewing; this practice does not promote learning. Also, if the curriculum is dull, it doesn't matter what kinds of "tricks" or "splashes" the teacher uses—students will not effectively learn. Make sure that the media and technology you use captures students' attention in meaningful ways that promote effective learning (Goldman, 1998).
7. *Focus on active learning to make learning enjoyable.* Using media and technology effectively is not the only way to do this. A different exercise, a guest, a field trip, and many other activities can be used to make learning more enjoyable, reduce student boredom, and increase attention.
8. *Don't overload students with too much information.* We live in an information society where sometimes the tendency is to feel like you have to get students to learn everything. But students who are given too much information too fast might not attend to anything.
9. *Be aware of individual differences in students' attentional skills.* As we saw in chapter 6, "Learners Who Are Exceptional," some students have severe problems in paying attention. You will need to take this into account when presenting material. Before you begin an exercise, look around the room for potential distractions, such as an open window to a playground where students are being noisy. Close the window and draw the shade to eliminate the distraction.
10. *Once you get students' attention, another important task is to maintain it.* Many of the strategies recommended so far can also help you in this area as well, such as making the class interesting, surprising your students every now and then, and so on. Another strategy for maintaining attention is to avoid a particular pattern of focusing on and calling on particular students. For example, a common tendency is to call on high-achieving rather than low-achieving students, or to give boys more attention than girls. Avoid such predictable patterns and spread your attention and requests around the class in a more random way. The word *random* as used here means that each student has an equal chance of being called on.

Rehearsal   Rehearsal *is the conscious repetition of information over time to increase the length of time information stays in memory.* Rehearsal does not hold more information in memory, it just keeps the same information in memory longer. Rehearsal works best when individuals need to remember a list of items for a brief period of time. When they must retain information over long periods of time, as when they are studying for a test they won't take until next week, other strategies usually work better than rehearsal. A main reason that rehearsal does not work well for retaining information over the long term is that rehearsal often involves just rotely repeating information without imparting any meaning to it. When students construct their memory in meaningful ways, they remember better. As we will see next, they also remember better when they process material deeply and elaborate it.

Levels of Processing

Deep Processing   Following the discovery that rehearsal is not an efficient way to remember information over the long term, Fergus Craik and Robert Lockhart (1972) proposed that we can process information at a variety of levels. Their theory, **levels of processing theory,** *states that the processing of memory occurs on a continuum from shallow to deep, with deeper processing producing better memory.* The sensory or physical features of stimuli are analyzed first at a *shallow* level. This might involve detecting the lines, angles, and contours of a printed word's letters or a spoken word's frequency, duration, and loudness. At an *intermediate* level of processing, the stimulus is recognized and given a label. For example, a four-legged, barking object is identified as a dog. Then, at the *deepest* level, information is processed semantically, in terms of its meaning. For example, if a child sees the word *boat,* at the shallow level she might notice the shapes of the letters, at the intermediate level she might think of the characteristics of the word (for instance, that it rhymes with *coat*), and at the deepest level she might think about the last time she went fishing with her dad on a boat and the kind of boat it was. Researchers have found that individuals remember information better when they process it at a deeper level (Craik, 2000; Hunt & Ellis, 1999).

Elaboration   Cognitive psychologists soon recognized, however, that there is more to good memory than just depth of processing. They discovered that when individuals use elaboration in their encoding of information, their memory benefits. **Elaboration** *is the extensiveness of information processing involved in memory.* Thus, when you present the concept of democracy to students, they likely will remember it better if they come up with good examples of it. Thinking of examples is a good way to elaborate information. For instance, self-reference is an effective way to elaborate information. If you are trying to get students to remember the concept of fairness, the more they can generate personal examples of inequities and equities they have personally experienced, the more likely it is that they will remember the concept. Likewise, students will likely remember the concept of a symphony if they associate it with the last time their parents took them to the symphony rather than just rehearse the words that define what a symphony is. Thinking about personal associations with information makes the information more meaningful and helps students remember it.

One reason elaboration works so well in producing good memory is that it adds to the *distinctiveness* of memory code (Ellis, 1987). To remember a piece of information, such as a name, an experience, or a fact about geography, students need to search for the code that contains this information among the mass of codes in their long-term memory. The search process is easier if the memory code is unique (Hunt & Kelly, 1996). The situation is not unlike searching for a friend at a crowded airport—if your friend

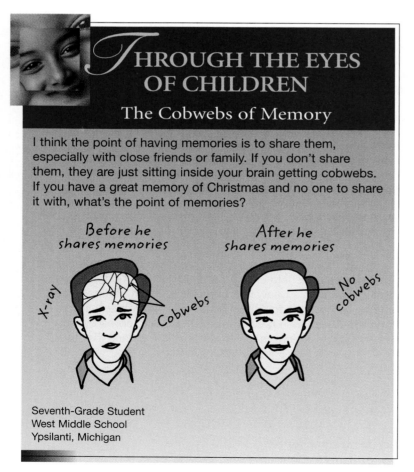

THROUGH THE EYES OF CHILDREN

The Cobwebs of Memory

I think the point of having memories is to share them, especially with close friends or family. If you don't share them, they are just sitting inside your brain getting cobwebs. If you have a great memory of Christmas and no one to share it with, what's the point of memories?

Before he shares memories

After he shares memories

X-ray

Cobwebs

No cobwebs

Seventh-Grade Student
West Middle School
Ypsilanti, Michigan

is 6 feet 3 inches tall and has flaming red hair, it will be easier to find him in the crowd than if he has more common features. Also, as a person elaborates information, more information is stored. And as more information is stored, it becomes easier to differentiate the memory from others. For example, if a student witnesses another student being hit by a car that speeds away, the student's memory of the car will be far better if she deliberately encodes her observations that the car is a red 1995 Pontiac with tinted windows and spinners on the wheels than if she only observes that it is a red car.

FRANK & ERNEST reprinted by permission of Newspaper Enterprise Association, Inc.

Constructing Images

When we construct an image of something, we are elaborating the information. For example, how many windows are there in the apartment or house where your family has lived for a substantial part of your life? Few of us ever memorize this information, but you probably can come up with a good answer, especially if you reconstruct a mental image of each room. Take a "mental walk" through the house, counting the windows as you go.

Allan Paivio (1971, 1986) believes that memories are stored in one of two ways: as a verbal code or as an image code. For example, you can remember a picture by a label (*The Last Supper*, a verbal code) or by a mental image. Paivio says that the more detailed and distinctive the image code, the better your memory of the information will be. We will have more to say about imagery later in the chapter when we discuss memory strategies.

Organization

When students organize information when they are encoding it, their memory benefits. To understand the importance of organization in encoding, complete the following exercise: Recall the 12 months of the year as quickly as you can. How long did it take you? What was the order of your recall? Your answers are probably: a few seconds and in natural order (January, February, March, and so on). Now try to remember the months in alphabetical order. Did you make any errors? How long did it take you? There is a clear distinction between recalling the months in natural order and alphabetically. This exercise is a good one to use with your students to help them understand the importance of organizing their memories in *meaningful* ways.

The more you present information in an organized way, the easier your students will remember it. This is especially true if you organize information hierarchically or outline it. Also, if you simply encourage students to organize information, they often will remember it better than if you give them no instructions about organizing (Mandler, 1980).

Chunking *is a beneficial organizational memory strategy that involves grouping or "packing" information into "higher-order" units that can be remembered as single units.* Chunking works by making large amounts of information more manageable and more meaningful. For example, consider this simple list of words: *hot, city, book, forget, tomorrow, smile.* Try to hold these in memory for a moment, then write them down. If you recalled all seven words, you succeeded in holding 34 letters in your memory.

THROUGH THE EYES OF TEACHERS

Imagination as a Form of Transportation

Second-grade teacher Beth Belcher transforms a lesson about transportation into the game of "Scattergories." After her students settle on a description of transportation as "a way of getting from one place to another," she divides them into teams and asks them to list as many types of transportation they can think of. Belcher says she wants students to engage in deep thinking. If more than one team comes up with the same answer, like "car," "train," or "plane," they don't get any points. "Elevator" is a winner. And then a 6-year-old girl says that "imagination" is a form of transportation, a way of getting from one place to another. Belcher says that moments like that are incredibly rewarding. (Briggs, 1998)

Storage

After children encode information, they need to retain or store the information. Among the most prominent aspects of memory storage are the three main stores, which vary according to time: sensory memory, working (or short-term) memory, and long-term memory.

Memory's Time Frames Children remember some information for less than a second, some for about half a minute, and other information for minutes, hours, years, even a lifetime. The three types of memory that vary according to their time frames are *sensory memory* (which lasts a fraction of a second to several seconds); *short-term memory* (also called *working memory;* lasts about 30 seconds), and *long-term memory* (which lasts up to a lifetime).

Sensory Memory **Sensory memory** *holds information from the world in its original sensory form for only an instant,* not much longer than the brief time a student is exposed to the visual, auditory, and other sensations. Its information is quickly lost unless students engage in mental processes like rehearsal to transfer it into short-term or long-term memory.

Students have a sensory memory for sounds for up to several seconds, sort of like a brief echo. However, their sensory memory for visual images lasts only for about one-fourth of a second. Because sensory information lasts for only a fleeting moment, an important task for the student is attend to the sensory information that is important for learning.

Short-Term Memory

Short-Term (Working) Memory **Short-term memory (also called working memory)** *is a limited-capacity memory system in which information is retained for as long as 30 seconds, unless the information is rehearsed or otherwise processed further, in which case it can be retained longer.* Compared to sensory memory, short-term memory is limited in capacity but relatively longer in duration. Its limited capacity intrigued George Miller (1956), who described this in a paper with a catchy title: "The Magical Number Seven, Plus or Minus Two." Miller pointed out that on many tasks, students are limited in how much information they can keep track of without external aids. Usually the limit is in the range of 7±2 items.

The most widely cited example of the 7±2 phenomenon involves **memory span,** *the number of digits an individual can report back without error in a single presentation.* How many digits individuals can repeat back depends on how old they are. In one study, memory span increased from 2 digits in 2- to 3-year-olds, to 5 digits in 7-year-olds, to 6 or 7 digits in 13-year-olds (Dempster, 1981). Many college students can handle lists of 8 or 9 digits. Keep in mind that these are averages and individuals differ. For example, many 7-year-olds have a memory span of fewer than 6 or 7 digits, others have a memory span of 8 or more digits.

Long-Term Memory **Long-term memory** *is a type of memory that holds enormous amounts of information for a long period of time in a relatively permanent fashion.* A typical human's long-term memory capacity is staggering. The distinguished computer scientist John von Neumann put the size at 2.8 × 10 (280 quintillion) bits, which in practical terms means that long-term memory storage is virtually unlimited. Even more impressive is the efficiency with which individuals can retrieve information. It often takes only a moment to search through this vast storehouse to find the information we want. Think

"Can we hurry up and get to the test? My short-term memory is better than my long-term memory."

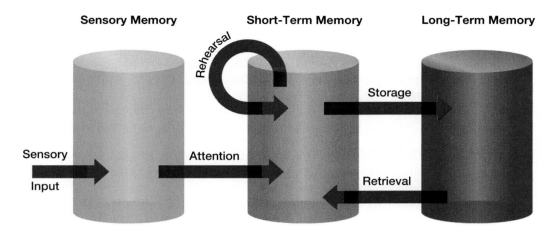

Figure **8.2**

Atkinson and Shiffrin's Theory of Memory

In this model, sensory input goes into sensory memory. Through the process of attention, information moves into short-term memory, where it remains for 30 seconds or less, unless it is rehearsed. Then, the information goes into long-term memory storage; from here it can be retrieved for some purpose later.

about your own long-term memory. Who wrote the Gettysburg Address? Who was your first-grade teacher? When were you born? Where do you live? You can answer thousands of such questions instantly. Of course, not all information is retrieved so easily from long-term memory. Later in this chapter we will examine ways that students can retrieve hard-to-recall information.

A Model of the Three Memory Stores   The three-stage concept of memory we have been describing was developed by Richard Atkinson and Richard Shiffrin (1968). According to the **Atkinson-Shiffrin model,** *memory involves a sequence of these three stages: sensory memory, short-term (working) memory, and long-term memory* (see figure 8.2). As we have seen, much information makes it no farther than the sensory memories of sounds and sights. This information is retained only for a brief instant. However, some information, especially that to which we pay attention, is transferred to short-term memory, where it can be retained for about 30 seconds (or longer with the aid of rehearsal). Atkinson and Shiffrin claimed that the longer information is retained in short-term memory through the use of rehearsal, the greater its chance is of getting into long-term memory. Notice in figure 8.2 that information in long-term memory also can be retrieved back into short-term memory.

Some contemporary experts on memory believe that the Atkinson-Shiffrin model is too simple (Baddeley, 1998; Bartlett, 1998). They argue that memory doesn't always work in a neatly packaged three-stage sequence as Atkinson and Shiffrin proposed. For example, these contemporary experts stress that working memory uses long-term memory's contents in more flexible ways than simply retrieving information from it.

Baddeley's Model   The **working-memory model** *was proposed by British psychologist Alan Baddeley (1993, 1995, 1998, 1999). Working memory is a kind of mental "workbench" that lets individuals manipulate, assemble, and construct information when they make decisions, solve problems, and comprehend written and spoken language. In Baddeley's model, working memory consists of a general "executive" and two subsystems that help the executive do its job* (see figure 8.3). One of the subsystems is the articulatory loop, which is specialized to process language information. The other subsystem is the visuospatial scratchpad, which includes imagery skills, such as visualizing an object or a scene.

I come into the fields and spacious palaces of my memory, which house treasures of countless images of things of every manner.

St. Augustine
Christian Church Father, 5th Century

Exploring Memory Models

Figure 8.3
A Theory of Working Memory
In Baddeley's theory of working memory the
two subsystems—the visuospatial scratchpad
and the articulatory loop—help the executive
do its job. The visuospatial scratchpad involves
our spatial imagery skills, the articulatory loop
our language skills.

Many contemporary psychologists believe that the terms *short-term memory* and *working memory* should not be used interchangeably. In most instances they prefer the concept of working memory because of its active, constructive emphasis. They believe that the Atkinson-Shiffrin model places too much emphasis on rehearsal and that the concept of working memory provides a more accurate picture of research results on memory.

Now that we have studied memory's time frames and several models of memory that focus on these, let's examine the contents of long-term memory in more depth.

Long-Term Memory's Contents   Just as different types of memory can be distinguished by how long they last, memory can be differentiated on the basis of its *contents*. For long-term memory, many contemporary psychologists accept the hierarchy of contents described in figure 8.4 (Squire, 1987). In this hierarchy, long-term memory is divided into the subtypes of declarative and procedural memory. Declarative memory is subdivided into episodic memory and semantic memory.

Declarative and Procedural Memory   **Declarative memory** *is the conscious recollection of information, such as specific facts or events that can be verbally communicated.* Declarative memory has been called "knowing that," and more recently has been labeled "explicit memory." Demonstrations of students' declarative memory could include recounting an event they have witnessed or describing a basic principle of math. However, students do not need to be talking to be using declarative memory. If students simply sit and reflect on an experience, their declarative memory is involved.

Procedural memory *is knowledge in the form of skills and cognitive operations. Procedural memory cannot be consciously recollected, at least not in the form of specific events or facts.* This makes procedural memory difficult, if not impossible, to communicate verbally. Procedural memory is sometimes called "knowing how," and recently it also has been described as "implicit memory" (Schacter, 2000). When students apply their abilities to perform a dance, ride a bicycle, or type on a computer keyboard, their procedural memory is at work. It also is at work when they speak grammatically correct sentences without having to think about how to do it.

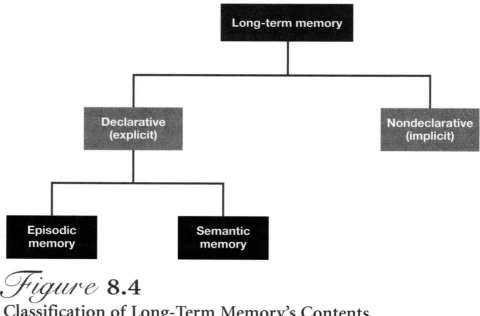

Figure 8.4
Classification of Long-Term Memory's Contents

Knowledge in different fields of experience, such as knowledge of chess, involves semantic memory.

Episodic and Semantic Memory   Cognitive psychologist Endel Tulving (1972, 2000) distinguishes between two subtypes of declarative memory: episodic and semantic. **Episodic memory** *is the retention of information about the where and when of life's happenings.* Students' memories of the first day of school, who they had lunch with, or the guest who came to talk with their class last week are all episodic.

Semantic memory *is a student's general knowledge about the world.* It includes:

• Knowledge of the sort learned in school (such as knowledge of geometry)
• Knowledge in different fields of expertise (such as knowledge of chess, for a skilled 15-year-old chess player)
• "Everyday" knowledge about meanings of words, famous people, important places, and common things (such as what being "street smart" means or who Nelson Mandela or Alan Greenspan is)

Semantic memory is independent of the person's identity with the past. For example, students might access a fact—such as "Lima is the capital of Peru"—and not have the foggiest idea when and where they learned it.

Content Knowledge and How It Is Represented in Long-Term Memory

Does what students already know about a subject affect their ability to remember new information about that subject? How do students represent information in their memory?

Content Knowledge   Our ability to remember new information about a subject does depend considerably on what we already know about it (Keil, 1999). For example, a student's ability to recount what she saw when she was at the library is largely governed by what she already knows about libraries, such as where books on certain topics are located, how to check books out, and so on. If she knew little about libraries, the student would have a much harder time recounting what was there.

The contribution of content knowledge to memory is especially evident when we compare the memory of experts and novices in a particular knowledge domain. An expert is the opposite of a novice (someone who is just beginning to learn a content area). Experts demonstrate especially impressive memory in their areas of expertise. One reason why children remember less than adults is that they are far less expert in most areas.

"Knowledge is power."

Francis Bacon
English Philosopher, 17th Century

In areas where children are experts, their memory is often extremely good. In fact, it often exceeds that of adults who are novices in that content area. This was documented in a study of 10-year-old chess experts (Chi, 1978). These children were excellent chess players, but not especially brilliant in other ways. Like for most 10-year-olds, their memory spans for digits were shorter than an adult's. However, when they were presented chess boards, they remembered the configurations far better than did the adults who were novices at chess.

How do students acquire such a rich knowledge base? Their expertise is developed over a long period of time in which they show considerable motivation to learn more about a topic. Expert knowledge in areas like chess, music, tennis, and many other domains often requires considerable amounts of practice over many years (Schneider & Bjorklund, 1998).

Network Theories **Network theories** *describe how information in memory is organized and connected. They emphasize nodes in the memory network.* The nodes stand for labels or concepts. Consider the concept "bird." One of the earliest network theories described memory representation as hierarchically arranged with more concrete concepts ("canary," for example) nestled under more abstract concepts (like "bird"). However, it soon was realized that such hierarchical networks are too neat to accurately portray how memory representation really works. For example, students take longer to answer the question "Is an ostrich a bird?" than to answer the question "Is a canary a bird?" Thus, today memory researchers envision the memory network as more irregular and distorted. A *typical* bird, such as a canary, is closer to the node or center of the category "bird" than is the atypical *ostrich*.

Experts in a particular area usually have far more elaborate networks of information about that area than novices do (see figure 8.5). The information they represent in memory has more nodes, more interconnections, and better hierarchical organization. It's not that experts have a better memory than novices in general; their memory is superior in a particular domain.

Schema Theories Long-term memory has been compared to a library of books. The idea is that our memory stores information just as a library stores books. In this analogy, the way students retrieve information said to be similar to the process they use to locate and check out a book. However, the process of retrieving information from long-term memory is not as precise as the library analogy suggests. When we search through our long-term memory storehouse, we don't always find the *exact* "book" we want, or we might find the "book" we want but discover that only "several pages" are intact—we have to *reconstruct* the rest.

Schema theories *state that when we reconstruct information, we fit it into information that already exists in our mind.* A **schema** *is information—concepts, knowledge, information about events—that already exists in a person's mind.* You might recall our description of schemas in Piaget's theory (in chapter 2, "Physical and Cognitive Development"). Schemas from prior experiences influence the way we encode, make inferences about, and retrieve information. Unlike network theories, which assume that retrieval involves specific facts, schema theory claims that long-term memory searches are not very exact. We often don't find precisely what we want, and we have to reconstruct the rest. Often when asked to retrieve information, we fill in the gaps between our fragmented memories with a variety of accuracies and inaccuracies.

We have schemas for all sorts of information. If you tell a story to your class and then ask the students to write down what the story was about, you likely will get many different versions. That is, your students won't remember every detail of the story you told and will reconstruct the story with their own particular stamp on it. Suppose you tell your class a story about two men and two women who were involved in a train crash in France. One student might reconstruct the story by saying they died in a plane crash, another might describe three men and three women, another might say the crash was in Germany, and so on. The reconstruction and distortion of memory

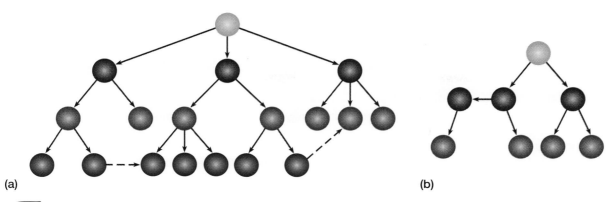

Figure 8.5

An Example of How Information is Organized in the Mind of an Expert and a Novice

(a) An expert's knowledge is based on years of experience in which small bits of information have been linked with many other small pieces, which together are placed in a more general category. This category is in turn placed in an even more general category of knowledge. The dotted lines are used as pointers, associations between specific elements of knowledge that connect the lower branches and provide mental shortcuts in the expert's mind. *(b)* The novice's knowledge shows far fewer connections, shortcuts, and levels than an expert's knowledge.

is nowhere more apparent than in the memories given by people involved in a trial. In criminal court trials like that of O. J. Simpson, the variations in people's memories of what happened underscores how we reconstruct the past rather than take an exact photograph of it.

A **script** *is a schema for an event.* Scripts often have information about physical features, people, and typical occurrences. This kind of information is helpful when teachers and students need to figure out what is happening around them. In a script for an art activity, students likely will remember that you will instruct them on what to draw, that they are supposed to put on smocks over their clothes, that they must get the art paper and paints from the cupboard, that they are to clean the brushes when they are finished, and so on. For example, a student who comes in late to the art activity likely knows much of what to do because he has an art activity script.

**Mneumonics
Study Strategies**

Retrieval and Forgetting

After students have encoded information and then represented it in memory, they might be able to retrieve some of it but might also forget some of it.

Retrieval   When we retrieve something from our mental "data bank," we search our store of memory to find the relevant information. Just as with encoding, this search can be automatic or it can require effort. For example, if you ask your students what month it is, the answer might immediately spring to their lips. That is, the retrieval may be automatic. But if you ask your students to name the guest speaker who came to the class two months earlier, the retrieval process likely will require more effort.

An item's position on a list also affects how easy or difficult it will be to remember it. The **serial position effect** *is that recall is better for items at the beginning and end of a list than for items in the middle.* Suppose that, when you give a student directions about where to go to get tutoring help, you say: "Left on Mockingbird, right on Central, left on Balboa, left on Sandstone, and right on Parkside." The student likely will remember "Left on Mockingbird" and "Right on Parkside" better than "Left on Balboa." The **primacy effect** *is that items at the beginning of a list tend to be remembered.* The **recency effect** *is that items at the end of the list also tend to be remembered.*

TEACHING STRATEGIES
For Helping Students Remember and Study Effectively

We have already described a number of strategies for remembering things better. Here we summarize and expand on them, and add a few more for good measure. Barbara Moely and her colleagues (Moely, Santulli, & Obach, 1995) found considerable variation in the teaching of memory and study strategies in school. Some teachers did try to help students with their memory and study strategies, but overall there was little instruction in strategy, across a broad range of activities. Strategies were most likely to be taught in math and problem solving. An important educational goal for the teacher is to incorporate more strategy instruction in the classroom. It is not enough just to teach students content knowledge. Following are some good ideas for helping children improve their memory and study strategies:

1. *Motivate children to remember material by understanding it rather than rotely memorizing it.* Children will remember information better over the long term if they understand the information rather than just rotely rehearse and memorize it. Rehearsal works well for encoding information into short-term memory, but when children need to retrieve the information from long-term memory it is much less efficient. So, for most information, encourage children to understand it, give it meaning, elaborate on it, and personalize it. Give children concepts and ideas to remember and then ask them how they can relate the concepts and ideas to their own personal experiences and meanings. Give them practice on elaborating a concept so they will process the information more deeply.
2. *Assist students in organizing what they put into their memory.* Children will remember information better if they organize it hierarchically. Give them some practice on arranging and reworking material that requires some structuring.
3. *Give children some mnemonic strategies.* **Mnemonics** *are memory aids for remembering information.* Mnemonic strategies can involve imagery and words. Following are some different types of mnemonics:

   • *Method of loci.* In the **method of loci,** *children develop images of items to be remembered and mentally store them in familiar locations.* Rooms of a house or stores on a street are common locations used in this memory strategy. For example, if children need to remember a list of concepts, they can mentally place them in the rooms of their house, such as entry foyer, living room, dining room, kitchen, and so on. Then when they need to retrieve the information, they can imagine the house, mentally go through the rooms, and retrieve the concepts.
   • *Rhymes.* Examples of mnemonic rhymes are the spelling rule *"i before e except after c,"* the month rule "Thirty days hath September, April, June, and November," the bolt-turning rule "Right is tight, left is loose," and the alphabet song.
   • *Acronyms.* This strategy involves creating a word from the first letters of items to be remembered. For example, *HOMES* can be used as a cue for remembering the five original Great Lakes: *H*uron, *O*ntario, *M*ichigan, *E*rie, and *S*uperior.
   • *Keyword method.* Another mnemonic strategy that involves imagery is the **keyword method,** *in which vivid imagery is attached to important words.* This method has been used to practical advantage in teaching students how to rapidly master new information such as foreign vocabulary words, the states and capitals of the United States, and the names of U.S. presidents. For example, in teaching children that Annapolis is the capital of Maryland, you could ask them to connect vivid images of Annapolis and Maryland, such as two apples getting married (Levin, 1980) (see figure 8.6).

   Some educators argue against teaching children to use mnemonics because they involve rote memorization. Clearly, as we said earlier, remembering for understanding is preferred over rote memorization. However, if children need to learn lists of concepts, mnemonic devices can do the trick. Think of mnemonic devices as a way for children to learn some specific facts that they might need to know to solve problems.
4. *Encourage children to spread out and consolidate their learning.* Talk with children about the importance of regularly reviewing what they learn. Children who have to prepare for

Figure 8.6
The Keyword Method

To help children remember the state capitals, the keyword method was used. A special component of the keyword method is the use of mental imagery, which was stimulated by presenting the children with a vivid visual image, such as two apples being married. The strategy is to help the children associate *apple* with Annapolis and *marry* with Maryland.

(continued)

a test will benefit from distributing their learning over a longer period rather than cramming for the test at the last minute. Cramming tends to produce short-term memory that is processed in a shallow rather than deep manner. A final, concentrated tune-up before the test is better than trying to learn everything at the last minute.

5. *Get children to ask themselves questions.* When children ask themselves questions about what they have read or an activity, they expand the number of associations they make with the information they need to retrieve. At least as early as the middle of elementary school, the self-questioning strategy can help children to remember. For example, as children read, they can be encouraged to periodically stop and ask themselves questions, such as "What is the meaning of what I just read?" "Why is this important?" and "What is an example of the concept I just read?" Students can use the same self-questioning strategy when they listen to you conduct a lesson, hear a guest give a talk, or watch a video. If you periodically remind children to generate questions about their experiences, they are more likely to remember the experiences.

6. *Help children learn how to take good notes.* Taking good notes either from a lecture or a text benefits memory (Kiewra, 1989). When children are left to take notes without being given any strategies, they tend to take notes that are brief and disorganized. When they do write something down, it often is a verbatim record of what they just heard. Give children some practice in taking notes and then evaluate their note taking. Encourage children not to write down everything they hear when they take notes. It is impossible to do this anyway, and it can prevent them from getting the big picture of what the speaker is saying. Following are some good note-taking strategies:

- *Summarizing.* One note-taking strategy that you can help children practice is the summary method of listening for a few minutes and then writing down the main idea that a speaker is trying to get across in that time frame. Then the child listens for several more minutes and writes down another idea, and so on.
- *Outlining.* Another note-taking strategy you can get children to practice is to outline what the speaker is saying. An outline would be similar to the organization of the chapters in this book, with first-level heads being the main topics, second-level heads as subtopics under the first-level heads, and third-level heads under the second-level heads. Keep in mind that it is not enough to just tell children to "outline"—you will have to show them how.
- *Concept maps.* Yet another strategy is to get children to practice drawing concept maps, much like the cognitive maps you have studied several times in each chapter of this book. The concept maps are similar to outlines but visually portray information in a more spiderlike format. All three note-taking strategies described so far— summarizing, outlining, and creating concept maps—help children evaluate which ideas are the most important to remember. The latter two strategies—outlining and concept maps—also help children hierarchically arrange the material, which underscores an important theme of memory: It works best when it is organized.

7. *Give children opportunities to practice the PQ4R method for reading and studying.* Various systems have been developed to help people to remember information that they are studying. One of the earliest systems was called *SQ3R,* which stands for *Survey, Question, Read, Recite,* and *Review.* A more recently developed system is called *PQ4R,* which stands for *Preview, Question, Read, Reflect, Recite,* and *Review.* Thus, the PQ4R system adds an additional step, "Reflect," to the SQ3R system. Students from the later elementary school years on will benefit from practicing the PQ4R system (Adams, Carnine, & Gersten, 1982). The system benefits students by getting them to meaningfully organize information, ask questions about it, reflect on it, and review it. Following are more details about the steps in the PQ4R system:

- *Preview.* Tell your students to briefly survey the material to get a sense of the overall organization of ideas. Tell them to be sure to look at the headings to see the main topics and subtopics that will be covered.
- *Question.* Encourage the children to ask themselves questions about the material as they read it. Earlier in our description of memory and study strategies we highlighted the importance of readers generating questions for themselves.
- *Read.* Now tell the children to read the material. Encourage your students to be *active* readers. This involves getting them to immerse themselves in what they are reading and striving to understand what the author is saying. This helps students to avoid being *empty* readers whose eyes just track the lines of text but whose minds fail to register anything important.
- *Reflect.* By occasionally stopping and reflecting on the material, students increase its meaningfulness. Encourage the children to be *analytic* at this point in studying. After they have read something, challenge them to break open the ideas and scratch beneath their surface. This is a good time for them to think out applications and interpretations of the information, as well as connecting it with other information already in their long-term memory.
- *Recite.* This involves children self-testing themselves to see if they can remember the material and reconstruct it. At this point, encourage the children to make up a series of questions about the material and then try to answer them.
- *Review.* Tell your students to go over the material and evaluate what they know and don't know. At this point they should reread and study the material they don't remember or understand well.

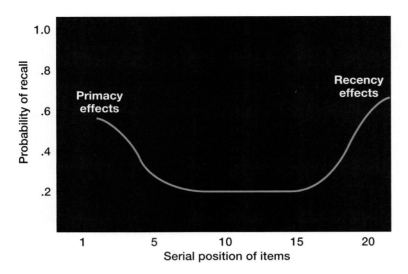

Figure **8.7**
Serial Position Effect
When a person is asked to memorize a list of words, the words memorized last usually are recalled best, those at the beginning next best, and those in the middle least efficiently.

Figure 8.7 shows a typical serial position effect with a slightly stronger recency effect than primacy effect. The serial position effect applies not only to lists, but also to events. If you spread out a lesson on history over a week and then ask students about it the following Monday, they likely will have the best memory for what you told them on Friday of last week and the worst memory for what you told them on Wednesday of last week.

Another factor that affects retrieval is the nature of the cues people use to prompt their memory. Students can learn to create effective cues. For example, if a student has a "block" about remembering the name of the guest who came to class two months ago, she might go through the alphabet, generating names with each letter. If she manages to stumble across the right name, she likely will recognize it.

Another consideration in understanding retrieval is the **encoding specificity principle:** *that associations formed at the time of encoding or learning tend to be effective retrieval cues.* For example, imagine that a 13-year-old child has encoded this information about Mother Teresa: She was born in Albania, lived most of her life in India, became a Roman Catholic nun, was saddened by seeing people sick and dying in Calcutta's streets, and won a Nobel Prize for her humanitarian efforts to help the poor and suffering. Words such as *Nobel Prize, Calcutta,* and *humanitarian* then can be used as retrieval cues when the child tries to remember her name, what country she lived in, and her religion. The concept of encoding specificity is compatible with our earlier discussion of elaboration: the more elaboration children use in encoding information, the better their memory of the information will be. Encoding specificity and elaboration reveal how interdependent encoding and retrieval are.

Yet another aspect of retrieval is the nature of the retrieval task itself. **Recall** *is a memory task in which individuals must retrieve previously learned information, as students must do for fill-in-the-blank or essay questions.* **Recognition** *is a memory task in which individuals only have to identify ("recognize") learned information, as is often the case on multiple-choice tests.* Many students prefer multiple-choice items because they provide good retrieval cues, which fill-in-the-blank and essay items don't do.

Forgetting   One form of forgetting involves the cues we just discussed. **Cue-dependent forgetting** *is retrieval failure caused by a lack of effective retrieval cues* (Nairne, 2000). The notion of cue-dependent forgetting can explain why a student might fail to retrieve a needed fact for an exam even when he is sure he "knows" the information. For example, if you are studying for a test in this course and are asked a question about a distinction between recall and recognition in retrieval, you likely will remember the distinction better if you possess the cues "fill-in-the-blank" and "multiple-choice," respectively.

The principle of cue-dependent forgetting is consistent with **interference theory,** *which states that we forget, not because we actually lose memories from storage, but rather because other information gets in the way of what we are trying to remember.* For a student who studies for a biology test, then studies for a history test, and then takes the biology test, the information about history will interfere with remembering the information about biology. Thus, interference theory implies that a good study strategy is to study last what you are going to be tested on next if you have multiple courses to study for. That is, the student taking the biology test would have benefited from studying history first and studying biology afterward. This strategy also fits with the recency effect we described earlier. Take a moment and think about how your

SELF-ASSESSMENT 8.1
How Effective Are My Memory and Study Strategies?

Teachers who themselves practice using good memory and study strategies are more likely to model and communicate these to their students than teachers who don't use such strategies. Candidly respond to the following items about your own memory and study strategies. Rate yourself on this scale: 1 = Never, 2 = some, 3 = moderate, 4 = almost always, and 5 = always. Then total your points.

	1	2	3	4	5
1. I study for understanding rather than memorize material in a rote fashion.					
2. I organize information hierarchically as part of my memory strategies.					
3. I use mnemonic strategies.					
4. I spread out my studying to consolidate my learning.					
5. I ask myself questions about what I have read or about class activities.					
6. I have a good note-taking system.					
7. I use the PQ4R method or a similar study method.					

TOTAL _____

Scoring and Interpretation

If you scored 31–35 total points, you likely use solid memory and study strategies. If you scored 26–30 points, you likely have reasonably good memory and study strategies. If you scored 25 points or less, you might need to improve your current strategies. In doing so, you will likely prepare yourself better to guide children to becoming more effective learners.

If you would like to learn more about effective memory and study strategies, one resource is a book I have co-authored called *Your Guide to College Success* (Santrock & Halonen, 1999). Also, to gain more experience in developing good memory and study strategies, contact the study skills center at your college or university; specialists there likely will be able to help you.

knowledge of interference theory can help you when you review for students what you plan to test next.

Another source of forgetting is memory decay. According to **decay theory,** *new learning involves the creation of a neurochemical "memory trace," which will eventually disintegrate. Thus, decay theory suggests that the passage of time is responsible for forgetting.* Memories decay at different speeds. Some memories are vivid and last for long periods of time, especially when they have emotional ties. We can often remember these "flashbulb" memories with considerable accuracy and vivid imagery. For example, consider a car accident you were in or witnessed, the night of your high school graduation, an early romantic experience, and where you were when you heard about Princess Diana's death. Chances are, you can retrieve this information even though the events happened a long time ago.

To evaluate your own memory and study strategies, complete Self-Assessment 8.1. At this point we have studied many ideas about cognitive information-processing approaches and memory. A review of these ideas is presented in summary table 8.1.

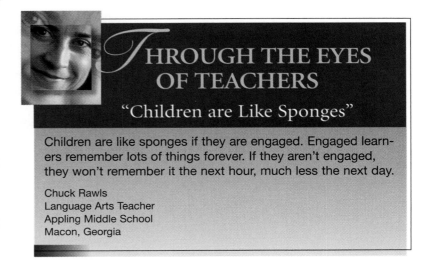

THROUGH THE EYES OF TEACHERS
"Children are Like Sponges"

Children are like sponges if they are engaged. Engaged learners remember lots of things forever. If they aren't engaged, they won't remember it the next hour, much less the next day.

Chuck Rawls
Language Arts Teacher
Appling Middle School
Macon, Georgia

*S*UMMARY *T*ABLE 8.1
The Cognitive Information-Processing Approach and Memory

Concept	Processes/ Related Ideas	Characteristics/Description
Exploring the Information-Processing Approach	Its Nature	• This approach emphasizes that children manipulate information, monitor it, and strategize about it. Central to this approach are the processes of memory and thinking. • The development of computers stimulated interest in cognitive psychology.
	Characteristics of the Information-Processing Approach	• These include thinking, change mechanisms (encoding, automatization, strategy construction, and generalization), and self-modification (which includes metacognition).
Memory	What Is Memory?	• Memory is the retention of information over time and involves encoding, storage, and retrieval.
	Encoding	• In everyday language, encoding has much to do with attention and learning. • Rehearsal, deep processing, elaboration, constructing images, and organization are other processes involved in encoding.
	Memory Storage	• One way that memory varies involves its time frames: sensory memory, short-term memory (or working memory), and long-term memory. • The Atkinson-Shiffrin model states that memory involves a sequence of three stages: sensory, short-term (working), and long-term memory. • Baddeley's model of working memory describes working memory as a kind of mental "workbench." Working memory consists of a general "executive" and two subsystems (phonological loop and visuospatial scratchpad). Many contemporary psychologists prefer the term *working memory* to *short-term memory* because of its active, constructivist nature. • Memory can be differentiated on the basis of its content. Many cognitive psychologists accept this hierarchy of long-term memory's contents: Division into declarative and procedural memory subtypes, with declarative memory further subdivided into episodic and semantic memory. Declarative memory is the conscious recollection of information, such as specific facts or events. It has been called explicit memory. Procedural memory is knowledge of skills and cognitive operations about how to do something. It is hard to communicate verbally and has been called implicit memory. Episodic memory is the retention of information about the where and when of life's happenings; semantic memory is a student's general knowledge about the world. • Two major approaches to how information is represented are network theories (which focus on how information is organized and connected, with emphasis on nodes) and schema theories (which stress that students often reconstruct information and fit it into an existing schema). A script is a schema for an event.
	Retrieval and Forgetting	• Retrieval is influenced by the serial position effect (memory is better for items at the beginning and end of lists than in the middle), how effective retrieval cues are, encoding specificity, and the memory task (such as recall versus recognition). • Forgetting can be explained in terms of cue-dependent forgetting (failure to use effective retrieval cues), interference theory (because information gets in the way of what we are trying to remember), and decay (losing information over time).

Thinking

What does it mean to think? How can teachers help students to become better thinkers?

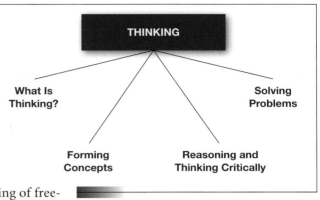

What Is Thinking?

Thinking *involves manipulating and transforming information in memory. This often is done to form concepts, reason, think critically, and solve problems.* Students can think about the concrete, such as a vacation at the beach or how to win at a video game, or if they are in middle or high school, they can think in more abstract ways, such as pondering the meaning of freedom or identity. They can think about the past (what happened to them last month) and the future (what will their life be like in the year 2020). They can think about reality (such as how to do better on the next test) and fantasy (what it would be like to meet Elvis Presley or land a spacecraft on Mars).

One of the most important types of thinking is creative thinking, which we discussed in chapter 4, "Individual Variations" ◄▐▐▐ p. 141. Another important type is collaborative thinking, which we will evaluate in chapter 9, "Social Constructivist Approaches, Domain-Specific Approaches, and Teaching." The next sections explore forming concepts, reasoning, thinking critically, and solving problems.

I think, therefore I am.

Rene Descartes
French Philosopher and Mathematician, 17th Century

Forming Concepts

Forming concepts is an important aspect of constructing information.

What Are Concepts?
Concepts *are categories used to group objects, events, and characteristics on the basis of common properties.* Concepts are elements of cognition that help to simplify and summarize information (Medin, 2000). Imagine a world in which we had no concepts: we would see each object as unique and would not be able to make any generalizations. If we had no concepts, we would find the most trivial problems to be time-consuming and even impossible to solve. Consider the concept of book. If a student were not aware that a book is sheets of paper of uniform sizes, all bound together along one edge, and full of printed words and pictures in some meaningful order, each time the student encountered a new book she would have to figure out what it was. In a way, then, concepts keep us from "reinventing the wheel" each time we come across a new piece of information.

Concepts also aid the process of remembering, making it more efficient. When students group objects to form a concept, they can remember the concept, then retrieve the concept's characteristics. Thus, when you assign math homework, you probably won't have to go through the details of what math is or what homework is. Students will have embedded in their memory a number of associations with math and homework. In ways such as this, concepts not only help to jog memory, they also make communication more efficient. If you say, "It's time for art," students know what this means because they have the relevant concepts. You don't have to go into a lengthy explanation of what art is. Thus, concepts help students to simplify and summarize information, as well as improve the efficiency of their memory, communication, and time use.

Students form concepts through direct experiences with objects and events in their world. For example, in forming a concept of cartoons, children might initially

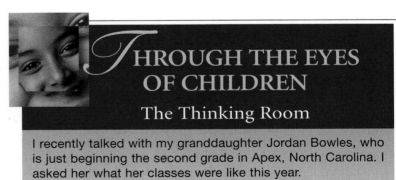

THROUGH THE EYES OF CHILDREN
The Thinking Room

I recently talked with my granddaughter Jordan Bowles, who is just beginning the second grade in Apex, North Carolina. I asked her what her classes were like this year.

She responded, "The usual stuff. Well, there is this one new class that I go to once a week. It's in the thinking room."

I then asked her what she was supposed to learn there.

Jordan said, "They are going to teach me not to jump to conclusions and my mom is happy about that."

experience TV cartoon shows, then read comic strips, and eventually look at some political caricatures. Students also form concepts through experience with *symbols* (things that stand for or represent something else). For example, words are symbols. So are math formulas, graphs, and pictures.

Some concepts are relatively simple, clear, and concrete, whereas others are more complex, fuzzy, and abstract (Barsalou, 2000). The former are easier to agree on. For example, most people can agree on the meaning of "baby." But we have a harder time agreeing on what is meant by "young" or "old." We agree on whether something is an apple more readily than on whether something is a fruit. Some concepts are especially complex, fuzzy, and abstract, like the concepts involved in theories of economic collapse or string theory in physics.

Forming Concepts

Exploring Concept Formation   Further understanding of concept formation involves the features of concepts, definitions and examples of concepts, concept maps and hierarchical organization, hypothesis testing, and prototype matching.

Features   An important aspect of concept formation is learning the key features, attributes, or characteristics of the concept. These are the defining elements of a concept, the dimensions that make it different from another concept. For example, in our earlier example of the concept of book, they key features include sheets of paper, being bound together along one edge, and being full of printed words and pictures in some meaningful order. Other characteristics such as size, color, and length are not key features that define the concept of book. Consider also these critical features of the concept of dinosaur: extinct, gigantic, and reptile. Thus, in the case of the concept of dinosaur, the feature "size" is important.

Definitions and Examples of Concepts   An important aspect of teaching concepts is to clearly define them and give carefully chosen examples of them. The *rule-example* strategy is an effective strategy for teaching concept that involves defining a concept and giving examples of it (Tennyson & Cocchiarella, 1986). This strategy consists of four steps:

1. *Define the concept.* As part of defining it, link it to a superordinate concept and identify its key features or characteristics. A *superordinate* concept is a larger class into which it fits. Thus, in specifying the key features of the concept of dinosaur, you might want to mention the larger class into which it fits: reptiles.
2. *Clarify terms in the definition.* Make sure that the key features or characteristics are well understood. Thus, in describing the key features of the concept of dinosaur, it is important for students to know what a reptile is: a cold-blooded, usually egg-laying vertebrate with an external covering of scales or horny plates that breathes by means of lungs.
3. *Give examples to illustrate the key features or characteristics.* With regard to dinosaurs, one might give examples and descriptions of different types of dinosaurs, such as triceratops, brontosaur, and stegosaur. The concept can be further clarified by giving examples of other reptiles that are not dinosaurs, such as snakes, lizards, crocodiles, and turtles. Indeed, giving non-examples of a concept as well as examples is often a good strategy for teaching concept formation. More examples are required when you teach complex concepts and when you work with less sophisticated learners (Moore, 1998).
4. *Provide additional examples. Ask students to categorize these, explain their categorization, or have them generate their own examples of the concept.* Other dinosaur types might be given, such as pterodactyl, ornitholestes, and dimetrodon, or students could be asked to generate these examples. They also might be asked to think up other non-examples of dinosaurs, such as dogs, cats, and whales.

Concept Maps   A **concept map** *is a visual presentation of a concept's connections and hierarchical organization.* Getting students to create a map of a concept's features or characteristics can help them to learn the concept. The concept map also might embed the concept in a superordinate category and include examples and non-examples of the concept. The visual aspects of the concept map relate to our earlier discussion of the use of imagery in memory. You might create a concept map with the assistance of students, or let them try to develop it individually or in small groups. Figure 8.8 shows an example of a concept map for the concept of dinosaur. You have already seen that we use concept maps extensively in this book—several times within each chapter at the beginning of major sections, and at the end of each chapter in the Chapter Review. We also sometimes call concept maps "cognitive maps."

Concept Maps

Hypothesis Testing   Recall from our discussion of the scientific approach to research, in chapter 1, that *hypotheses* are specific assumptions and predictions that can be tested to determine their accuracy ◀▥ p. 20. Students benefit from the practice of developing hypotheses about what a concept is and is not (Ross, 2000). One way this is done is to come up with a rule about why some objects fall within a concept and others do not. Here is an example of how you can give your students practice in developing such hypotheses: Present your students with the picture of geometric forms shown in figure 8.9. Then silently select the concept of one of those geometric forms (such as "circle" or "green circle") and ask your students to develop hypotheses about what concept you have selected. They zero in on your concept by asking you questions

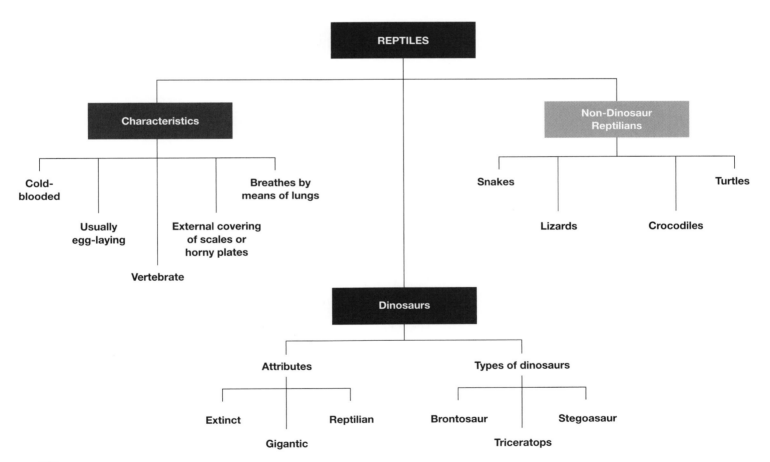

Figure **8.8**

Example of a Concept Map for the Concept of Dinosaur

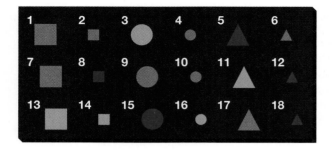

Figure **8.9**
Getting Students to Generate Hypotheses About a Concept

You can use arrangements like the one shown here to help students generate hypotheses about what concept you have in mind. This encourages students to develop the most efficient strategies for understanding what a concept is. For example, you might select the concept "squares and purple triangles" or "purple triangles and purple squares" and ask students to figure out what concept you're thinking of. You also can let students take turns selecting the concept.

related to the geometric forms and eliminating nonexamples. You might also let the students take turns "being the teacher"—they select a concept and answer questions from the other students as they generate hypotheses about what the concept is. Work with your students on developing the most efficient strategies for identifying the correct concept.

Prototype Matching   In **prototype matching,** *individuals decide whether an item is a member of a category by comparing it with the most typical item(s) of the category* (Rosch, 1973). The more similar the item is to the prototype, the more likely it is that the individual will say the item belongs to the category; the less similar, the more likely the person will judge that it doesn't belong in the category. For example, a student's concept of a football player might include being big and muscular like an offensive lineman. But some football players, such as many field goal kickers, are not so big and muscular. An offensive lineman is a more prototypical example of a football player than a field goal kicker. When students consider whether someone belongs in the category "football player," they are more likely to think of someone who looks like an offensive lineman than to think of someone who looks like a field goal kicker. Similarly, robins are viewed as being more typical birds than ostriches or penguins. Nonetheless, members of a category can vary greatly and still have qualities that make them a member of that category (see figure 8.10).

Knit each new thing onto to some acquisition already there.

William James
American Psychologist, 19th–20th Centuries

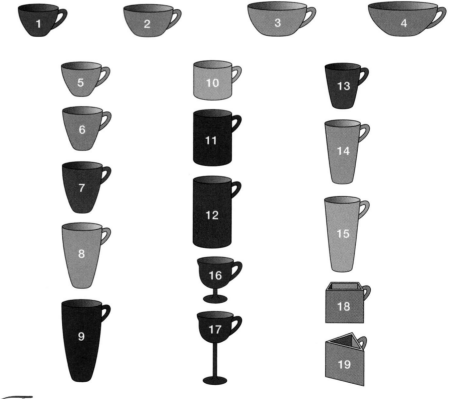

Figure **8.10**
When Is a Cup a "Cup?"

Which of these would you describe as the prototype for the concept "cup"? In one study, participants were most likely to choose number 5 (Labov, 1973). Some participants called number 4 a bowl and number 9 a vase because they were so different from the prototype.

$\mathcal{T}$EACHING STRATEGIES
For Helping Students Form Concepts

Following are strategies teachers can use in helping students form concepts:

1. *Use the rule-example strategy.* Remember that this involves four steps: (1) Define the concept, (2) clarify the terms in the definition, (3) give examples to illustrate the key features or characteristics, and (4) provide additional examples, ask students to categorize these, explain their categorization, or have them generate their own examples of the concepts.

2. *Help students learn not only what a concept is but also what it is not.* Let's return to the concept "cartoon." Students can learn that even though they are humorous, jokes, clowns, and funny poems are not cartoons. Their concept formation benefits from learning that North America is not a "nation" but rather is a "continent" and that touching someone is a behavior, not a thought. If you are teaching the concept of triangle, ask students to list the characteristics of "triangle" such as "three-sided," "geometric shape," "can be of any size," "can be of any color," "sides can vary in length," "angles can be different," and so on; also ask them to list examples of things that are not triangles, such as circles, squares, and rectangles.

3. *Make concepts as clear as possible and give concrete examples.* Spend some time thinking about the best way to present a new concept, especially an abstract one. Make it as clear as possible. If you want students to understand the concept "vehicle," ask them to come up with examples of it. They probably will say "car" and maybe "truck" or "bus." Show them photographs of other vehicles, such as a sled and a boat, to illustrate the breadth of the concept.

4. *Help students relate new concepts to concepts they already know.* Earlier in the chapter, we discussed the strategy of outlining for taking notes. Once students have learned this procedure, it is easier for them to learn how to construct concept maps, because you can show them how concept maps are linked with outlining in terms of hierarchical organization. As another example of helping students to relate a new concept to concepts they already know, they might know what gold and silver are but not be aware of what platinum and plutonium are. In this case, build on their knowledge of gold and silver to teach the concepts of platinum and plutonium.

5. *Encourage students to create concept maps.* Getting students to visually map out the hierarchical organization of a concept can help them learn it. The hierarchical arranging can be used to help students understand the concept's characteristics from more general to more specific. Hierarchical organization benefits memory. In one study, when students were presented with the concept "minerals" in the hierarchical concept map shown in figure 8.11, they remembered the information far better than when it was presented in a random, nonorganized way (Bower & others, 1969).

6. *Ask students to generate hypotheses about a concept.* Generating hypotheses encourages students to think and develop strategies. Work with students on developing the most efficient strategies for determining what a concept is.

7. *Give students some experience in prototype matching.* Think of different concepts and then ask students what the prototypes of the concepts are. Then ask them for nonprototypical examples of the concept.

8. *Check for students' understanding of a concept and motivate them to apply the concept to other contexts.* Make sure that students don't just rotely memorize a concept. Get them to expand their knowledge of the concept and elaborate on it by assigning further reading about the concept. Ask students how the concept can be applied in different contexts. For example, in learning the concept of fairness, ask students how fairness can make life smoother not only at school, but also at play, at home, and at work.

Reasoning and Thinking Critically

Let's explore some different types of reasoning, beginning with the distinction between inductive and deductive reasoning.

Inductive Versus Deductive Reasoning   Inductive reasoning
involves reasoning from the specific to the general. That is, it consists of drawing conclusions about all members of a category based on observing only some members. When a student in a literature class reads only a few of Emily Dickinson's poems and is asked to draw conclusions from them about the general nature of Dickinson's

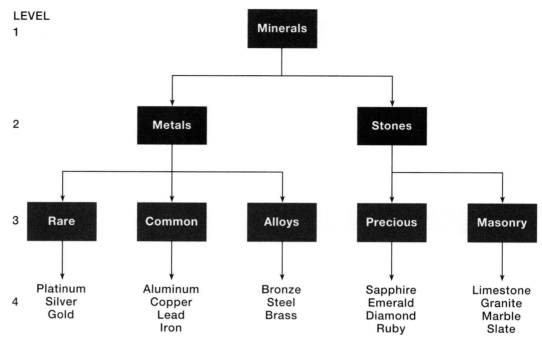

LEVEL
1

2

3

4

Figure 8.11

The Power of Organization in Memory

Memory works best when it is organized. In a 1969 study of Gordon Bower and his colleagues, participants remembered the words better when they were presented in a hierarchical format from general to specific (like the format shown above) than when the words were presented in a random arrangement.

poetry, inductive reasoning is being tapped. When a student is asked whether a concept learned in math class applies to other domains, such as business or science, inductive reasoning also is being called for.

Deductive reasoning *is reasoning from the general to the specific.* It consists of working with general statements and deriving a specific conclusion (Johnson-Laird, 2000). Many puzzles and riddles call on students to engage in deductive reasoning. In some educational domains, such as math and science, students typically learn about a general rule and then are asked to decide whether the rule applies or does not apply to various specific situations. This also involves deductive reasoning.

Reasoning About Analogies   An **analogy** *is a type of formal reasoning that involves four parts, with the relation between the last two parts being the same as the relation between the first two.* For example, a student might be given this analogy to solve: Beethoven is to music as Picasso is to _____. To answer correctly ("art"), the student must induce the relation between Beethoven and music (the former created the latter) and apply this to Picasso (what did he create?).

Critical Thinking   Currently, there is considerable interest in critical thinking among psychologists and educators, although it is not an entirely new idea (Gardner, 1999; Runco, 1999; Moldoveanu & Langer, 1999; Sternberg, 2000). The famous educator John Dewey (1933) proposed a similar idea when he talked about the importance of getting students to think reflectively. The

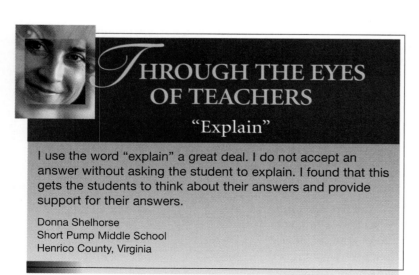

THROUGH THE EYES OF TEACHERS

"Explain"

I use the word "explain" a great deal. I do not accept an answer without asking the student to explain. I found that this gets the students to think about their answers and provide support for their answers.

Donna Shelhorse
Short Pump Middle School
Henrico County, Virginia

well-known psychologist Max Wertheimer (1945) talked about the importance of thinking productively rather than just guessing at a correct answer. **Critical thinking** *involves thinking reflectively and productively, and evaluating the evidence.* At the end of each chapter in this book, activities entitled "Adventures for the Mind" challenge you to think critically about a topic or issue related to the chapter's discussion. Here are some ways teachers can consciously build critical thinking into their lesson plans:

- Ask not only what happened but "how" and "why."
- Examine supposed "facts" to determine whether there is evidence to support them.
- Argue in a reasoned way rather than through emotions.
- Recognize that there is sometimes more than one good answer or explanation.
- Compare various answers to a question and judge which is really the best answer.
- Evaluate and possibly question what other people say rather than to immediately accept it as the truth.
- Ask questions and speculate beyond what we already know to create new ideas and new information.

Jacqueline and Martin Brooks (1993) lament that so few schools really teach students to think critically. In their view, schools spend too much time on getting students to give a single correct answer in an imitative way rather than encouraging students to expand their thinking by coming up with new ideas and rethinking earlier conclusions. They believe that too often teachers ask students to recite, define, describe, state, and list rather than to analyze, infer, connect, synthesize, criticize, create, evaluate, think, and rethink.

Brooks and Brooks point out that many successful students complete their assignments, do well on tests, and get good grades, yet don't ever learn to think critically and deeply. They believe our schools turn out students who think too superficially, staying on the surface of problems rather than stretching their minds and becoming deeply engaged in meaningful thinking.

Daniel Perkins and Sarah Tishman (1997) work with teachers to incorporate critical thinking into classrooms. The following are some of the critical thinking skills they encourage teachers to help their students develop:

- *Open-mindedness.* Get your students to avoid narrow thinking and to explore options. For example, when teaching American literature, teachers might ask students to generate multiple critiques of Aldous Huxley's *Brave New World.*
- *Intellectual curiosity.* Encourage your students to wonder, probe, question, and inquire. Getting students to recognize problems and inconsistencies also is an aspect of intellectual curiosity. In history class, this might mean looking beyond culturally biased views of American history by reading British or Native American views on the American Revolution.
- *Planning and strategy.* Work with your students to help them develop plans, set goals, find direction, and seek outcomes. In physical education, this might involve determining the best strategy to win a basketball or softball game.
- *Intellectual carefulness.* Encourage your students to check for inaccuracies and errors, to be precise, and to be organized. For example, when students write a paper, they learn to structure the content and check the facts that they include.

What are some good strategies for nurturing children's critical thinking?

Exploring Critical Thinking
Critical Thinking Resources

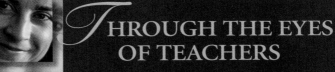

THROUGH THE EYES OF TEACHERS

Encouraging Students to Be Intellectual Risk-Takers

Alan Haskvitz, who teaches social studies at Suzanne Middle School in Walnut, California, believes in learning by doing and the importance of motivating students to improve the community. His students have rewritten voting instructions adopted by Los Angeles County, lobbied for a law requiring state government buildings to have rough-resistant landscaping, and created measures to reduce the city's graffiti. Alan has compiled thousands of teacher resources on this website: http://www. reacheverychild.com. He challenges students to be independent thinkers and intellectual risk-takers. He has students create an ideal island and discuss what everything from government to geography would be like on the island.

Alan Haskvitz with middle school students Simon Alarcon, Tracy Blozis, examining bones and trying to figure out where in the animal kingdom they belong.

Solving Problems

Let's examine what problem solving means and some steps involved in problem solving.

Exploring Problem Solving   **Problem solving** *involves finding an appropriate way to attain a goal.* Consider these tasks that require students to engage in problem solving: creating a project for a science fair, writing a paper for an English class, getting a community to be more environmentally responsive, or giving a talk on the factors that cause people to be prejudiced.

Efforts have been made to specify the steps that individuals go through in effectively solving problems (Bransford & Stein, 1993). Following are four such steps.

1. Find and Frame Problems   Before a problem can be solved, it has to be recognized. In the past, most problem-solving exercises given to students involved well-defined problems with well-defined solutions and operations for attaining the solutions. Schools need to place more emphasis on encouraging students to identify problems instead of just trying to solve well-defined textbook problems. Many real-life problems are ill-defined: They are vague and don't have clearly defined ways of being solved. Consider a student's problem of having to get to a club meeting that is being held at a new location in town an hour soon after the last class at school. First, the student needs to identify the existence of a problem to be solved, such as what time to leave in order to make the club meeting on time. To solve this general problem, the student has to solve several subproblems: Where is the new location? How far away is it? Can I get there in time by riding my bike? Will I have to take a bus? And so on.

Consider also the student faced with creating a science fair project. The student has identified a general problem but needs to zero in on a specific area for the project, such as biology, physics, computer science, psychology, and so on. Exploring such alternatives and then making a decision on which problem area to pursue is an important aspect of problem solving. Then the student must narrow the problem even more. If the student decides to do a project on psychology, she will need to specify the area, such as perception, memory, thinking, or personality. Then the student will have to find a problem within that domain. For example, the student might choose the area of memory and focus on this problem: How reliable are people's memories of traumatic events they have experienced? After considerable exploring and refining, the student has narrowed the topic to a point at which strategies for solving it can be generated.

In sum, an important educational agenda is to give students opportunities to find problems and generate the problems they think need to be solved. Serve as a guide and consultant in helping them frame a meaningful problem and define it clearly.

2. Develop Good Problem-Solving Strategies   Once students find a problem and clearly define it, they need to develop strategies for solving it. Among the effective strategies are setting subgoals, using algorithms, and calling on heuristics.

Subgoaling *involves setting intermediate goals that put students in a better position to reach the final goal or solution.* Students might do poorly in solving problems because they don't generate subproblems or subgoals. Let's return to the science fair project on the reliability of people's memory for traumatic events they have experienced. What might be some subgoaling strategies? One might be locating the right books and research journals on thinking; another might be interviewing teachers about the strategies they use to encourage deep thinking. At the same time as the student is working on this subgoaling strategy, the student likely will benefit from establishing further subgoals in terms of what she needs to accomplish along the way to her final goal of a finished science project. If the science project is due in 3 months, she might set the following subgoals: finishing the first draft of the project 2 weeks before the project is due; having the research completed a month before the project is due; being halfway through the research 2 months before the project is due; having three teacher interviews done 2 weeks from today; and starting library research tomorrow.

Notice that in establishing the subgoals, we worked backward in time. This is often a good strategy (Reed, 2000). Students first create a subgoal that is closest to the final goal and then work backward to the subgoal that is closest to the beginning of the problem-solving effort.

Algorithms *are strategies that guarantee a solution to a problem.* When students solve a multiplication problem by a set procedure, they are using an algorithm. When they follow the directions for diagramming a sentence, they are using an algorithm. Life would be easy if all its problems could be solved by algorithms. But many real-world problems are not so straightforward. They require the use of heuristics.

Heuristics *are strategies or rules of thumb that can suggest a solution to a problem but don't guarantee a solution.* Consider a student who has just gotten his driver's license. He is going to drive over to a friend's house he has never been to before. He drives through an unfamiliar part of town and soon realizes that he is lost. If he knows that the correct direction to turn is north, he might use the heuristic of turning onto the next road that goes in that direction. This strategy might work, but it also might fail. The road might end or it might veer east.

A **means-end analysis** *is a heuristic in which one identifies the goal (end) of a problem, assesses the current situation, and evaluates what needs to be done (means) to decrease the difference between the two conditions.* Another name for means-end analysis is *difference reduction.* Means-end analysis also can involve the use of subgoaling, which we described earlier (Anderson, 1993). Means-end analysis is commonly used in solving problems. Consider a 14-year-old girl who has to do a science project (the end). She assesses her current situation, in which she is just starting to think about the project. Then she maps out a plan to reduce the difference between her current state and the goal (end). Her "means" include talking to several scientists in the community about potential projects, going to library to study about the topic she chooses, and exploring the Internet for potential projects and ways to carry them out.

3. Evaluate Solutions   Once we think we have solved a problem, we might not know whether our solution is effective unless we evaluate it. It helps to have in mind a clear criterion for the effectiveness of the solution. For example, what will be the student's criterion for effectively solving the problem of doing a science fair project? Will it be simply getting it completed? receiving positive feedback about the project? winning an award? winning first place? the self-satisfaction of having set a goal, planned for it, and reached it?

4. Rethink and Redefine Problems and Solutions over Time   An important final step in problem solving is to continually rethink and redefine problems and solutions over time (Bereiter & Scardamalia, 1993). People who are good at problem solving are motivated to improve on their past performances and to make original contributions. Thus, the student who completed the science fair project can look back at the project and think about ways the project can be improved. The student might use feedback from judges or information from others who talked with the student about the project to tinker with and fine-tune it.

Obstacles to Solving Problems   Some common obstacles to solving problems are these: fixation, confirmation bias, lack of motivation, and lack of persistence.

Fixation   It is easy to fall into the trap of becoming fixated on a particular strategy for solving a problem. **Fixation** *involves using a prior strategy and failing to look at a*

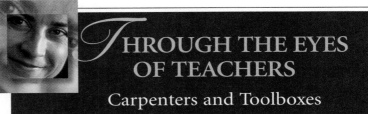

*T*HROUGH THE EYES OF TEACHERS

Carpenters and Toolboxes

In teaching math, I use such problem-solving strategies as working backwards, making a similar but simpler problem, drawing a diagram, making a table, and looking for patterns. We talk about what strategies make the most sense with different types of problems. When students successfully solve a problem, we look to see what methods were used, often finding more than one. I talk about multiple strategies in terms of carpenters having more than one kind of hammer in their toolboxes.

Lawren Giles
Mathematics Teacher
Baechtel Grove Middle School
Willits, California

problem from a fresh, new perspective. **Functional fixedness** *is a type of fixation in which an individual fails to solve a problem because she or he views the elements involved solely in terms of their usual functions.* A student who uses a shoe to hammer a nail has overcome functional fixedness to solve a problem.

A **mental set** *is a type of fixation in which an individual tries to solve a problem in a particular way that has worked in the past.* I (your author) had a mental set about using a typewriter rather than a computer to write my books. I felt comfortable with a typewriter and had never lost any sections I had written. It took a long time for me to break out of this mental set. Once I did, the problem goal of finishing a book became much easier. You might have a similar mental set against using the new computer and video technology available for classroom use. A good strategy is keep an open mind about such changes and monitor whether your mental set is keeping you from trying out new technologies that can make the classroom a more exciting learning atmosphere for students.

Confirmation Bias   **Confirmation bias** *is the tendency to search for and use information that supports our ideas rather than refutes them.* Thus, in solving a problem, a student might have an initial hypothesis that a certain approach is going to work. He tests out the hypothesis and finds out that it is right some of the time. He concludes that his hypothesis was right rather than further exploring the fact that it didn't work some of the time.

We tend to seek out and listen to people whose views confirm our own rather than listen to dissenting views. Thus, you might have a particular teaching style, such as lecturing, that you like to use. If so, you probably will have a tendency to listen more to other teachers who use that style than to teachers who prefer other styles, such as collaborative problem solving by students. Be aware of how easy it is for you and your students to fall into the trap of using confirmation bias to support your ideas and problem-solving efforts.

Lack of Motivation and Persistence   Even if your students already have great problem-solving abilities, that hardly matters if they are not motivated to use them (Pintrich, 2000; Sternberg & Spear-Swerling, 1996). It is especially important for students to be internally motivated to tackle a problem and persist at finding a solution to it. Some students avoid problems or give up too easily.

An important task for teachers is to devise or steer students toward problems that are meaningful to them and to encourage and support them in finding solutions. Students are far more motivated to solve problems that they can relate to their personal lives than textbook problems that have no personal meaning for them. Problem-based learning takes this real-world personal focus.

Problem-Based Learning   **Problem-based learning** *emphasizes solving authentic problems like those that occur in daily life* (Jones, Rasmussen, & Moffit, 1997). An example of problem-based learning involves the program called YouthALIVE! at the Children's Museum of Indianapolis (Schauble & others, 1996). Students solve problems related to conceiving, planning, and installing exhibits; designing videos; creating programs to help visitors understand and interpret museum exhibits; and brainstorming about strategies for building bridges into the community.

The Cognition and Technology Group at Vanderbilt (1997) developed a program of problem-based learning called *The Jasper Project. Jasper* consists of twelve videodisc-based adventures that are designed to improve the mathematical thinking of students in grades 5 and up, as well as help students to make connections with other disciplines, including science, history, and social studies. *Jasper's* creators argue that too often math and other subjects are taught as isolated skills. One of the *Jasper* adventures, *The Right Angle,* can be used not only in geometry classes but also in geography (topography) and history (Native American cultures).

The adventures focus on a character named Jasper Woodbury and others, who encounter a number of real-life problems that need to be solved. Figure 8.12 profiles two of the *Jasper* problem-solving adventures.

As we saw earlier, finding and framing a problem is an important aspect of problem solving. The *Jasper* adventures end with challenges that motivate students to generate new problems to solve. Also, *Jasper* stimulates students to identify a number of subproblems or subgoals on their own.

The Jasper Project

The *Jasper* series also encourages collaborative problem solving among students. As students work together over a number of class periods, they have numerous opportunities to communicate about math, share their problem-solving strategies, and get feedback that helps them refine their thinking. Groups of students present their ideas to the class, discussing the strengths and weaknesses of their strategies and solutions. The collaborative aspect of *Jasper* is at the heart of social constructivist approaches to learning, which we will explore in depth in the next chapter.

Each videodisc adventure includes extension problems. This helps students engage in "what if" thinking by revisiting the original adventures from new points of view. Thus, after finding a way to rescue a wounded eagle in *Rescue at Boone's Meadow* (most students solve the problem with an ultralight airplane that is featured in this adventure), students are presented with a revised problem in which they must rethink how the presence of headwinds or tailwinds might affect their original solution.

The *Jasper* project also encourages teachers to develop actual problem-solving projects after students have worked with a *Jasper* adventure. For example, in one school, after creating a business plan for the adventure *The Big Splash,* students were given the opportunity to gather relevant data to create a business plan to present to the principal. In this instance, the creation of a business plan led to a fun fair being held for the entire school (Barron & others, 1996). In another school, students who had spent time solving problems in the adventure *Blueprints for Success* were given the opportunity to design a playhouse for preschools. Well-designed playhouses were actually built and donated to the preschools in the students' names.

An optional feature of the *Jasper* series is the video-based SMART Challenge series. Its goal is to connect classes of students to form a community of learners that tries to solve *Jasper*-related challenges. SMART stands for Special Multimedia Arenas for Refining Thinking. These arenas use telecommunications, television technology, and Internet technology to give students feedback about the problem-solving efforts of other groups. For example, students who are working on *Blueprint for Success* can

"Blueprint for Success"

Christina and Marcus, two students from Trenton, visit an architectural firm on Career Day. While learning about the work of architects, Christina and Marcus hear about a vacant lot being donated in their neighborhood for a playground. This is exciting news because there is no place in their downtown neighborhood for children to play. Recently, several students have been hurt playing in the street. The challenge is for students to help Christina and Marcus design a playground and ballfield for the lot.

"The Big Splash"

Jasper's young friend Chris wants to help his school raise money to buy a new camera for the school TV station. His idea is to have a dunking booth in which teachers would be dunked when students hit a target. He must develop a business plan for the school principal in order to obtain a loan for his project. The overall problem centers on developing this business plan, including the use of a statistical survey to help him decide if this idea would be profitable.

Figure **8.12**
Problem-Solving Adventures in the *Jasper* Series

TEACHING STRATEGIES
To Help Students Become Better Thinkers

Twentieth-century German dictator Adolph Hitler once remarked that it was such good fortune for people in power that most people do not think. Education should help students become better thinkers. Every teacher would agree with that goal, but the means for reaching it are not always in place in schools. Following are some guidelines for helping students to become better thinkers.

1. *Give students extensive opportunities to solve real-world problems.* Make this a part of your teaching. Develop problems that are relevant to your students' lives. Such real-world problems are often referred to as "authentic," in contrast to textbook problems that too often do not have much meaning for students.

2. *Use thinking-based questions.* One way to analyze your teaching strategies is to see whether you use a lecture-based approach, fact-based questioning, or thinking-based questioning (Sternberg & Spear-Swirling, 1996). In the lecture-based approach, the teacher presents information in the form of a lecture. This is a helpful approach for presenting new information, such as "Today, I'm going to describe the main aspects of the French Revolution." In fact-based questioning, the teacher asks questions primarily designed to get students to describe factual information. This is best used for reinforcing newly acquired information or testing students' content knowledge. For example, the teacher might ask, "When did the French Revolution occur? Who were the king and queen of France at that time?" In thinking-based questioning, the teacher asks questions that stimulate thinking and discussion. For example, the teacher might ask, "Compare the French and American revolutions. How were they similar? How were they different?"

   Make a point to include thinking-based questions in your teaching. They will help your students develop a deeper understanding of a topic.

3. *Monitor students' effective and ineffective thinking and problem-solving strategies.* Keep the four problem-solving steps in mind when you give students opportunities to solve problems. Also keep in mind such obstacles to good problem-solving as becoming fixated, harboring biases, not being motivated, and not persisting.

4. *Be a guide in helping students construct their own thinking.* You can't and shouldn't do students' thinking for them. However, you can and should be an effective guide in helping students construct their own thinking. Teachers who help students construct their own thinking (Brooks & Brooks, 1993):

   Do

   • highly value students' questions
   • view students as thinkers with emerging theories about the world
   • seek students' points of view
   • seek elaboration of students' initial responses
   • nurture students' intellectual curiosity

   Don't

   • view students' minds as empty or see their role as a teacher as simply pouring information into students' minds
   • rely too heavily on textbooks and workbooks
   • simply seek the correct answer to validate student learning

5. *Use technology effectively.* Be motivated to incorporate multimedia programs into your classroom. *The Jasper Project* contains many of the themes of effective thinking and problem solving that we have described in this chapter. Such programs can significantly improve your students' thinking and problem-solving skills.

   Some popular television presentations can be used to foster students' problem-solving and thinking skills (Schauble & others, 1996). For example, *3-2-1 Contact* focuses on 8- to 12-year-olds' appreciation of science; *Square One TV* gives students a better understanding of math and problem solving; and *Ghostwriter* supports the literacy of 7- to 10-year-olds. Kits for these TV programs include videotapes, leader guides, games, puzzles, and magazines. To read about an innovative use of technology, see the Diversity and Education box. Throughout this book, we highlight technology that you can use to help students solve problems more effectively and think more deeply.

6. *Provide positive role models for thinking.* Look around your community for positive role models who can demonstrate effective problem solving and thinking, and invite them to come to your classroom and talk with your students. Also think about contexts in the community, such as museums, colleges and universities, hospitals, and businesses, where you can take students and they can see, observe, and interact with competent problem solvers and thinkers.

(continued)

And have an active and inquiring mind yourself. Every day you are in the classroom, your students will pick up on how you solve problems and think. Examine what we have said about problem solving and thinking in this chapter. Work on being a positive problem-solving and thinking model for students by practicing these strategies. To evaluate your thinking and problem-solving strategies, complete Self-Assessment 8.2.

7. *Involve parents.* A program of parental involvement has been developed at the University of California at Berkeley (Schauble & others, 1996). It is called Family Math (Matematica Para la Familia, in Spanish) and helps parents experience math with their children in a positive, supportive way. In the program, Family Math classes are usually taught by grade levels (K–2, 3–5, and 6–8). Many of the math activities require teamwork and communication between parents and children, who come to better understand not only the math but also each other. Family Math programs have served more than 400,000 parents and children in the United States.

8. *Keep up-to-date on the latest developments in thinking and problem solving.* Continue to actively learn about new developments in teaching students to become more effective problem solvers and thinkers after you have become a teacher. Over the next decade there will especially be new technology programs through which you can improve students' problem-solving and thinking skills. Go to libraries now and then to read educational journals, and attend professional conferences that include information about problem-solving and thinking.

DIVERSITY AND EDUCATION
The Promised Land Learning Community

In 1995, the Discovery Channel presented a series called *The Promised Land,* based on a novel by Nicholas Lemann about the migration of African Americans from Mississippi to Chicago in the 1930s and 1940s. Educators can tape the commercial-free version and show it to students.

The *Promised Land* Learning Community involves a World Wide Web site (http://www.discovery.com/school) and e-mail. The website includes discussion groups, student-produced materials, exchanges of information, and communications among students, artists, and others who have experienced group migration.

The *Promised Land* Learning Community was created to help students and others use Discovery Channel programming to foster interdisciplinary learning related to migration, African American history, race relations, language arts, economics, artistic expression, and cultural awareness (Jones, Rasmussen, & Moffit, 1997). Among the subject areas targeted for interdisciplinary connections are history, geography, and social studies.

Many projects can be generated using the Learning Community, such as exploring family histories, using technology to map migration patterns, comparing and contrasting how blues and spirituals evolved, using oral histories in English-as-a-second-language classes, and connecting themes in the *Promised Land* to other works of literature and U.S. history.

Facilitators are available to help classroom teachers use Learning Community resources effectively. For example, an English teacher might be assisted in using some of the resources for art and music. Mentors, who include accomplished artists, business people, community leaders, and scholars, are available to work with students on the Web or locally if practical. Some community projects are open-ended and invite student contributions. For instance, students can help construct an African American timeline. Participants also can access special projects such as discussions on leadership in which African Americans of all ages participate.

One of the most popular projects for elementary schools involving the Learning Community has been the New Places Project. It attempts to help students from diverse ethnic backgrounds who have just arrived at a new school to adapt and cope effectively with their new experience.

see data from 60 other students about the length of legs for A-frame swing sets and the desired height of the swing sets.

Jasper projects have recently been developed for areas other than math. To read about these, see Technology and Education. To obtain more information about the *Jasper*-related projects, contact the Cognition and Technology Group at Vanderbilt University, Nashville, Tennessee.

At this point, we have discussed many ideas about thinking. A review of these ideas is presented in summary table 8.2.

The Discovery Channel

TECHNOLOGY AND EDUCATION
Scientists in Action and Young Children's Literacy

Two new video projects related to *The Jasper Project* are *Scientists in Action* and the Young Children's Literacy Series (Cognition & Technology Group at Vanderbilt, 1997). Whereas *Jasper* focuses on math problem solving, *Scientists in Action (SIA)* emphasizes problem solving in science (Goldman & others, 1996). One of the SIA stories, *Mystery of Stones River,* lets students explore issues related to water quality. They become familiar with ecosystems and the complex factors involved in developing healthy streams and rivers.

In another *SIA* adventure, *Return to Rochester,* emergency room physicians in Rochester, New York, begin to detect that an increasing number of children are being admitted who share some severe symptoms. A community effort organized by a chemist leads to solving the problem: lead poisoning resulting from children eating paint chips. Students get opportunities to explore such issues as the effects of metals on bodily functioning, experimental techniques for isolating the causes of various disorders, and the importance of community efforts in solving real-world problems.

As with *Jasper,* the *SIA* adventures are being integrated with Internet-based contacts that let students compare their answers with those of other students.

A second *Jasper*-related project is the Young Children's Literacy Series, a multimedia language and literacy program for beginning readers. It is learner-centered and structured around video stories that anchor a series of activities for improving students' deep comprehension, composition, and oral communication.

In one story, the animal characters on a small planet are visited by a stranger named Wongo, who convinces the animals that they need to purchase his magic hats if they want to have imaginative minds and be able to tell good stories (see figure 8.13). All of the animals but Ribbit are enamored of his pitch. As the story unfolds, Ribbit learns to use the components of the scientific method to test whether the hats really are magical. After all of these tests have been completed, the other animals realize that they have been duped. This leaves them with the challenge of how they can keep others from being tricked like they were. The answer: write a book.

The activities involved in the video stories provide students opportunities for rich discussions and communication with other students, both in their classroom and on the Internet. A Web page created by Little Planet Publishing features *The Little Planet Times,* which includes literacy-based challenges that end with a dilemma. Students are invited to write their own responses, which are then published. The address is *http.//www.Little Planet.com.*

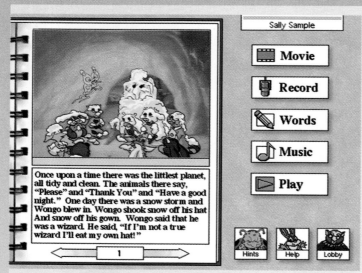

- Pictures from the sequencing activity are used to construct a book in childrens' own words.
- The "Picture" button turns the still picture into a dynamic but silent clip from the story. (This provides dynamic retrieval prompts.)
- The "Record" button is used to orally record what the students want to write for this page. (The recording phase is collaborative; all children from the group add at least one sentence per page.)
- The "Write" button helps students sound out words and select candidates from a list. Alternatively, children or teachers can use the keyboard to write.
- The "Music" button allows children to select from a variety of musical clips ranging from "fast-happy" music to "slow-sad" music. (As children select clips, teachers guide discussions regarding which musical clips are best suited for the emotional tone of the page.)
- The "Play" button lets children see the dynamic visual clip, hear their voices, see the text, and listen to the music they have chosen.
- When all of the pages are completed, the book is printed out in a traditional format, and the children read along in their books as they listen to the integrated-media version on the computer. The children also take the books home to share with their families.

Figure 8.13
Sample Screen and Features from the Story About Wongo

SELF-ASSESSMENT 8.2
How Effective Are My Thinking Strategies?

Teachers who practice good thinking strategies themselves are more likely to model and communicate these to their students than teachers who don't use such strategies. Candidly respond to the following items about your own problem-solving and thinking strategies. Rate yourself 1 = Very much unlike me, 2 = Somewhat unlike me, 3 = Somewhat like me, and 4 = Very much like me, then total your points.

	1	2	3	4
1. I am aware of effective and ineffective thinking strategies.				
2. I periodically monitor the thinking strategies I use.				
3. I am good at reasoning.				
4. I use good strategies for forming concepts.				
5. I am good at thinking critically and deeply about problems and issues.				
6. I construct my own thinking rather than just passively accept what others think.				
7. I like to use technology as part of my effort to think effectively.				
8. I have good role models for thinking.				
9. I keep up-to-date on the latest educational developments in thinking.				
10. I use a system for solving problems like the four-step system described in the text.				
11. I'm good at finding and framing problems.				
12. When solving problems, I use strategies like subgoaling and working backward.				
13. I don't fall into problem-solving traps like fixating, having a confirmation bias, not being motivated, and lacking persistence.				
14. When solving problems, I set criteria for my success and evaluate how well I have met my problem-solving goals.				
15. I make a practice of rethinking and redefining problems over an extended period of time.				
16. I love to work on problem-solving projects.				

TOTAL _____

Scoring and Interpretation

If you scored 60–68 points, your thinking strategies likely are very good. If you scored 50–59 points, you likely have moderately good thinking strategies. If you scored below 50 points, you likely would benefit from working on your thinking strategies.

Several good books that possibly could help you improve your problem-solving and thinking strategies are *Teaching for Thinking* (Sternberg & Spear-Swerling, 1996), *Becoming Reflective Students and Teachers with Portfolios and Authentic Assessment* (Paris & Ayres, 1994), and *Real-Life Problem Solving* (Jones, Rasmussen, & Moffit, 1997).

Teaching for Transfer

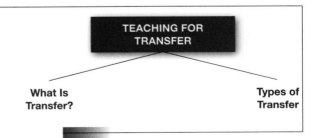

An important educational goal is for students to be able to take what they learn in one situation and apply it to new situations. An important goal of schooling is that students will learn something in school and be able to apply it outside of the classroom. Schools are not functioning effectively if students do well on tests in language arts but can't write a competent letter as part of a job application. Schools also are not effectively educating students if the students do well on math tests in the classroom but can't solve math problems on a job, such as effectively performing accounting procedures. Teaching for transfer helps students make the connection between what they learned in school and applying it outside of the classroom in new contexts.

SUMMARY TABLE 8.2
Thinking

Concept	Processes/ Related Ideas	Characteristics/Description
What Is Thinking?	Its Nature	• Thinking involves manipulating and transforming information in memory. • Thinking often is done to form concepts, reason, think critically, and solve problems.
Forming Concepts	What Are Concepts?	• Concepts are categories used to group objects, events, and characteristics on the basis of common properties. • Concepts are elements of cognition that help to simplify and summarize information. • They also improve memory, communication, and time use.
	Exploring Concept Formation	• To understand concept formation, it is important to know about the features of concepts, definitions and examples of concepts (including the rule-example strategy), concept maps and hierarchical organization, hypothesis testing, and prototype matching.
Reasoning and Thinking Critically	Inductive Versus Deductive Reasoning	• Inductive reasoning involves reasoning from the specific to the general. • Deductive reasoning is reasoning from the general to the specific.
	Reasoning About Analogies	• An analogy is a type of formal reasoning that involves two pairs, where the relationship between the two items in the second pair is the same as the relationship between the two items in the first pair.
	Critical Thinking	• This involves thinking reflectively and productively, and evaluating evidence. • Brooks and Brooks argue that too few schools teach students to think critically and deeply. • Perkins says there are four important critical thinking skills teachers should encourage in students: open-mindedness, intellectual curiosity, planning and strategy, and intellectual carefulness.
Solving Problems	Exploring Problem Solving	• Problem solving involves finding an appropriate way to attain a goal. Four steps in problem solving are (1) finding and framing problems, (2) developing good problem-solving strategies (such as using subgoaling, heuristics, and algorithms), (3) evaluating solutions, and (4) rethinking and redefining problems over time.
	Obstacles to Solving Problems	• These include fixedness (functional fixedness and mental set), confirmation bias, and lacking motivation and persistence.
	Problem-Based Learning	• This emphasizes solving authentic problems like those that occur in daily life. • *The Jasper Project,* a multimedia set of 12 math problem-solving adventures, is an example of problem-based learning. *Jasper*-related projects also have been created for science and literacy.

What Is Transfer?

Transfer

As you learned at the beginning of this chapter, *transfer* occurs when a person applies previous experiences and knowledge to learning or problem solving in a new situation (Gentile, 2000; Mayer & Wittrock, 1996). Thus, if a student learns a concept in math and then uses this concept to solve a problem in science, transfer has occurred. It also has occurred if a student reads and studies about the concept of fairness in school and subsequently treats others more fairly outside the classroom.

Types of Transfer

Transfer can be characterized as either near or far and also as either low-road or high-road (Schunk, 2000).

Near or Far Transfer

Near transfer *occurs when situations are very similar. If the classroom learning situation is similar to the transfer situation, near transfer is at work.* For example, if a geometry teacher instructs students in how to logically prove a concept, and then tests the students on this logic in the same room in which they learned the concept, near transfer is involved. Another example of near transfer occurs when students who have learned to type on a typewriter transfer this skill to typing on a computer keyboard.

Far transfer *means the transfer of learning to a situation that is very different from the one in which the initial learning took place.* For instance, if a student gets a part-time job in an architect's office and applies what was learned in geometry class to helping the architect analyze a spatial problem that is quite different than any problem the student encountered in geometry class, far transfer has occurred.

Low-Road or High-Road Transfer

Gavriel Salomon and David Perkins (1989) distinguished between low-road and high-road transfer. **Low-road transfer** *occurs when previous learning automatically, often unconsciously, transfers to another situation.* This occurs most often with highly practiced skills in which there is little need for reflective thinking. For example, when competent readers encounter new sentences in their native language, they read them automatically.

By contrast, **high-road transfer** *is conscious and effortful.* Students consciously establish connections between what they learned in a previous situation and the new situation they now face. High-road transfer is *mindful*—that is, students have to be aware of what they are doing and think about the connection between contexts. High-road transfer implies abstracting a general rule or principle from previous experience and then applying it to the new problem in the new context. For example, students might learn about the concept of subgoaling (setting intermediate goals) in math class. Several months later, one of the students thinks about how subgoaling might benefit him in completing a lengthy homework assignment in history. This is high-road transfer.

Salomon and Perkins (1989) subdivide high-road transfer into forward-reaching and backward-reaching transfer. **Forward-reaching transfer** *occurs when students think about how they can apply what they have learned to new situations* (from their current situation, they look "forward" to apply information to a new situation ahead). For forward-reaching transfer to take place, students have to know something about the situations to which they will transfer learning. **Backward-reaching transfer** *occurs when students look back to a previous ("old") situation for information that will help them solve a problem in a new context.*

To better understand these two types of high-road transfer, imagine a student sitting in English class who has just learned some writing strategies for making sentences and paragraphs come alive and "sing." The student

"I don't get it! They make us learn reading, writing and arithmetic to prepare us for a world of videotapes, computer terminals and calculators!"

Harley Schwadron—Phi Delta Kappan

THROUGH THE EYES OF TEACHERS

Connecting Students to the Community to Give Context to What They Are Learning

Myron Blosser is an honors and AP biology teacher at Harrisonburg (Virginia) High School. He was the leader in establishing Coast to Coast '98, a science department effort in which 22 students and 8 teachers spent 31 days touring national parks in a motor coach laboratory studying the natural history of water. He is working on the development of Coast to Coast 2000. He coordinates an annual biotechnology symposium that includes renowned scientists and high school students throughout the Shenandoah Valley region of Virginia. Myron sees his role as connecting students to the community to give context to what they are learning.

Myron Blosser, teaching at Harrisonburg High School

TEACHING STRATEGIES
For Helping Students Transfer Information

You want your students to be able to transfer information in positive ways, but this is often difficult to achieve. However, the following teaching strategies will help guide your students to better transfer:

1. *Think about what your students need to know for success in life.* We don't want students to finish high school with a huge data bank of content knowledge but no idea how to apply it to the real world. One strategy for thinking about what students need to know is to use the "working backward" problem-solving strategy we discussed earlier in this chapter. For example, what do employers want high school and college graduates to be able to do? In a national survey of employers of college students, the three skills that employers most wanted graduates to have were (1) oral communication skills, (2) interpersonal skills, and (3) teamwork skills (Collins, 1996). Thus, the three most desired skills for students to have involve communication skills. The employers also wanted students to be proficient in their field, have leadership abilities, have analytical skills, be flexible, and have computer skills. By thinking about and practicing the competencies that your students will need in the future and working with them to improve these skills, you will be guiding them for positive transfer. We will discuss communication skills in chapter 12, "Managing the Classroom," and we will examine teamwork skills in chapter 9, "Social Constructivist Approaches, Domain-Specific Approaches, and Teaching."

2. *Give students many opportunities for real-world learning.* Too often, learning in schools has been artificial, with little consideration for transfer beyond the classroom or textbook. This will be less true for your students if you give them as many real-world problem-solving and thinking challenges as possible. In general, the more similar two situations are, the easier it will be for students to transfer information learned in one to the other. You can bring the real world into your classroom by inviting people from varying walks of life to come and talk with your students. Or you can take your students to the real world by incorporating visits to museums, businesses, colleges, and so on in the curriculum. Such learning opportunities should increase transfer.

3. *Root concepts in applications.* The more you attempt to pour information into students' minds, the less likely it is that transfer will occur. When you present a concept, also define it (or get students to help you define it), and then ask students to generate examples. Challenge them to apply the concept to their personal lives or to other contexts.

4. *Teach for depth of understanding and meaning.* Teaching for understanding and meaning benefits transfer more than does teaching for the retention of facts. And students' understanding improves when they actively construct meaning and try to make sense out of material.

5. *Teach strategies that will generalize.* Transfer involves not only skills and knowledge, but also strategies (Schunk, 1996). Too often students learn strategies but don't understand how to apply them in other contexts. They might not understand that the strategy is appropriate for other situations, or might not know how to modify it for use in another context, or might not have the opportunity to apply it (Pressley & others, 1989).

   One model for teaching strategies that will generalize was developed by Gary Phye (1990; Phye & Sanders, 1994). He described three phases for improving transfer. In an initial *acquisition phase,* students not only are given information about the importance of the strategy and how to use it, but also are given opportunities to rehearse and practice using it. In the second phase, called *retention,* students get more practice in using the strategy, and their recall of how to use the strategy is checked out. In the third phase, *transfer,* students are given new problems to solve. These problems require them to use the same strategy, but on the surface the new problems appear to be different. Phye also believes that motivation is an important aspect of transfer. He recommends that teachers increase students' motivation for transfer by showing them examples of how to use knowledge in their real lives.

begins to reflect on how she could use those strategies to engage readers next year, when she plans to become a writer for the school newspaper. That is forward-reaching transfer. Now consider a student who is at his first day on the job as editor of the school newspaper. He is trying to figure out how to construct the layout of the pages. He reflects for a few moments and thinks about some geography and geometry classes he has previously taken. He draws on those past experiences for insights into constructing the layout of the student newspaper. That is backward-reaching transfer.

Metacognition

We just discussed the importance of teaching in ways that help students transfer knowledge and strategies to new situations. Some cognitive psychologists believe that what is called a metacognitive strategy improves transfer.

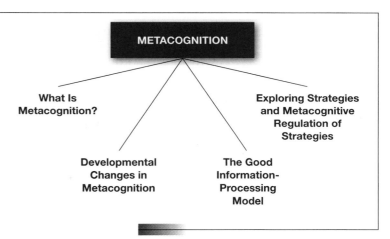

What Is Metacognition?

As you read at the beginning of this chapter, *metacognition* is cognition about cognition, or "knowing about knowing" (Ferrari & Sternberg, 1998; Flavell, 1999; Flavell & Miller, 1998). A distinction can be made between metacognitive knowledge and metacognitive activity (Ferrari & Sternberg, 1998). **Metacognitive knowledge** *involves monitoring and reflecting on one's current or recent thoughts* (Flavell, Miller, & Miller, 1993). This includes both *factual knowledge,* such as knowledge about the task, one's goals, or one's self, and *strategic knowledge,* such as how and when to use specific procedures to solve problems. **Metacognitive activity** *occurs when students consciously adapt and manage their thinking strategies during problem solving and purposeful thinking* (Ferrari & Sternberg, 1998; Kuhn & others, 1995). Thus, a student's awareness and use of the self-regulatory learning strategies discussed in chapter 7, "Behavioral Approaches, Social Cognitive Approaches, and Teaching," involve metacognition ◀▥ p. 265.

Metacognition

Metacognitive skills have been taught to students to help them solve math problems (Cardelle-Elawar, 1992). In each of thirty daily lessons involving math story problems, a teacher guided low-achieving students in learning to recognize when they did not know the meaning of a word, did not have all of the information necessary to solve a problem, did not know how to subdivide the problem into specific steps, or did not know how to carry out a computation. After the thirty daily lessons, the students who were given this metacognitive training had better math achievement and attitudes toward math.

One expert on children's thinking, Deanna Kuhn (1999a, 1999b), believes that metacognition should be a stronger focus of efforts to help children become better critical thinkers, especially at the middle school and high school levels. She distinguishes between first-order cognitive skills, which enable children to know about the world (and have been the main focus of critical thinking programs), and second-order cognitive skills—*meta-knowing skills*—which involve knowing about one's own (and others') knowing.

Developmental Changes in Metacognition

The majority of developmental studies classified as "metacognitive" have focused on metamemory, or knowledge about memory. This includes general knowledge about memory, such as knowing that recognition tests are easier than recall tests. It also encompasses knowledge about one's own memory, such as a student's ability to monitor whether she has studied enough for a test that is coming up next week.

By 5 or 6 years of age, children usually know that familiar items are easier to learn than unfamiliar ones, that short lists are easier than long ones, that recognition is easier than recall, and that forgetting is more likely to occur over time (Lyon & Flavell, 1993). However, in other ways young children's metamemory is limited. They don't understand that related items are easier to remember than unrelated ones and that remembering the gist of a story is easier than remembering information verbatim (Kreutzer, Leonard, & Flavell, 1975). By fifth grade, students understand that gist recall is easier than verbatim recall. Young children also have an inflated opinion of their memory abilities. For example, in one study, a majority of young children predicted that they would be able to recall all ten items of a list of ten items. When tested for this, none of the young children managed this feat (Flavell, Friedrichs, & Hoyt, 1970). As they move through the elementary school years, children give more realistic evaluations of their memory skills (Schneider & Pressley, 1997).

Young children also have little appreciation for the importance of "cognitive cueing" for memory. Cognitive cueing involves being reminded of something by an external cue or phrase, such as "Don't you remember, it helps you to learn a concept when you can think of an example of it." By 7 or 8 years of age, children better appreciate the importance of such cognitive cueing for memory.

The Good Information-Processing Model

Michael Pressley and his colleagues (Pressley, Borkowski, & Schneider, 1989; Schneider & Pressley, 1997) have developed a metacognitive model called the Good Information-Processing Model. It emphasizes that competent cognition results from a number of interacting factors. These include strategies, content knowledge, motivation, and metacognition. They believe that children become good at cognition in three main steps:

1. Children are taught by parents or teachers to use a particular strategy. With practice, they learn about its characteristics and advantages for learning *specific knowledge*. The more intellectually stimulating children's homes and schools are, the more specific strategies they will encounter and learn to use.
2. Teachers may demonstrate similarities and differences in multiple strategies in a particular domain, such as math, which motivates students to see shared features of different strategies. This leads to better *relational knowledge*.
3. At this point, students recognize the general benefits of using strategies, which produces *general strategy knowledge*. They learn to attribute successful learning outcomes to the efforts they make in evaluating, selecting, and monitoring strategy use *(metacognitive knowledge and activity)*.

Exploring Strategies and Metacognitive Regulation of Strategies

In Pressley's (Pressley, 1983; McCormick & Pressley, 1997) view, the key to education is helping students learn a rich repertoire of strategies that result in solutions of problems. Good thinkers routinely use strategies and effective planning to solve problems. Good thinkers also know when and where to use strategies (metacognitive knowledge about strategies). Understanding when and where to use strategies often results from the learner's monitoring of the learning situation.

Pressley argues that when students are given instruction about effective strategies, they often can apply these strategies that they previously have not used on their own. However, some strategies are not effective for young children. For example, young children cannot competently use mental imagery. Pressley emphasizes that students benefit when the teacher models the appropriate strategy and overtly verbalizes the steps in the strategy. Then, students subsequently practice the strategy. Their practice of the strategy is guided and supported by the teacher's feedback until the students can effectively execute the strategy autonomously. When instructing students about employing a strategy, it also is a good idea to explain to them how using the strategy will benefit them.

Just having students practice the new strategy is usually not enough for them to continue to use the strategy and transfer it to new situations. For effective maintenance and transfer, encourage students to monitor the effectiveness of the new strategy relative to their use of old strategies by comparing their performance on tests and other assessments. Pressley says that it is not enough to say, "Try it, you will like it"; you need to say, "Try it and compare."

TEACHING STRATEGIES
For Using Metacognition in the Classroom

Here are some strategies you can use to help your students use metacognition:

1. *Recognize that strategies are a key aspect of solving problems.* Monitor students' knowledge and awareness of strategies for effective learning outcomes. Many students do not use good strategies and are unaware that strategies can help them learn.
2. *Model effective strategies for students.* While doing this, verbalize the steps in the strategy.
3. *Give students many opportunities to practice the strategy.* As students practice the strategies, provide guidance and support to the students. Give them feedback until they can use the strategies independently. As part of your feedback, inform them about where and when the strategies are most useful.
4. *Encourage students to monitor the effectiveness of their new strategy in comparison to the effectiveness of old strategies.* This helps students to see the utility of using the new strategy.
5. *Remember that it takes students a considerable amount of time to learn how to use an effective strategy independently.* Be patient and give students continued support during this tedious learning experience. Keep encouraging students to use the strategy over and over again until they can use it automatically.
6. *Understand that students need to be motivated to use the strategies.* Students are not always going to be motivated to use the strategies. Especially important to students' motivation is their expectations that the strategies will lead to successful learning outcomes. It can also help if students set goals for learning effective strategies. And when students attribute their learning outcomes to the effort they put forth, their learning benefits. We will have much more to say about motivation in chapter 11, "Motivating Students to Learn."
7. *Encourage children to use multiple strategies.* Most children benefit from experimenting with multiple strategies, finding out what works well, when, and where.
8. *Read more about strategy instruction.* A good place to start is the text *Educational Psychology* by Christine McCormick and Michael Pressley (1997), which includes extensive ideas about how to improve children's use of strategies.

Learning how to use strategies effectively often takes time. Initially, it takes time to learn to execute the strategies, and it requires guidance and support from the teacher. With practice, students learn to execute strategies faster and more competently. "Practice" means that students use the effective strategy over and over again until they perform it automatically. To execute the strategies effectively, they need to have the strategies in long-term memory, and extensive practice makes this possible. Learners also need to be motivated to use the strategies.

Let's examine an example of how strategy instruction can be effective. Good readers extract the main ideas from text and summarize them. In contrast, novice readers (for example, most children) usually don't store the main ideas of what they read. One intervention based on what is known about the summarization strategies of good readers consisted of instructing children to (1) skim over trivial information, (2) spend time on redundant information, (3) replace less inclusive terms with more inclusive ones, (4) combine a series of events with a more inclusive action term, (5) choose a topic sentence, and (6) create a topic sentence if there is none present (Brown & Day, 1983). Researchers have found that instructing elementary school students to use these summarization strategies benefits their reading performance (Rinehart, Stahl, & Erickson, 1986).

How can teachers help children improve their metacognitive regulation of strategies?

Summary Table 8.3
Teaching for Transfer and Metacognition

Concept	Processes/Related Ideas	Characteristics/Description
Teaching for Transfer	What Is Transfer?	• Transfer occurs when a person applies previous experiences and knowledge to learning or problem-solving in a new situation.
	Types of Transfer	• Types of transfer include near and far and low-road and high-road. • Near transfer occurs when situations are similar; far transfer occurs when situations are very different. • Low-road transfer occurs when previous learning automatically transfers to another situation. • High-road transfer is conscious and effortful. High-road transfer can be subdivided into forward-reaching and backward-reaching.
Metacognition	What Is It?	• Metacognition is cognition about cognition, or knowing about knowing. • Metacognition involves both metacognitive knowledge and metacognitive activity.
	Developmental Changes	• The majority of metacognitive studies focus on metamemory or what students know about how memory works. • Children's metamemory improves considerably through the elementary school years.
	The Good Information-Processing Model	• Pressley and his colleagues developed a three-part "Good Information-Processing Model": (1) Children develop specific knowledge about a particular strategy, (2) Then they develop relational knowledge by examining similarities and differences in multiple strategies, and (3) Then they recognize the benefits of using strategies, which produces general strategy knowledge, and they learn to attribute successful learning outcomes to their strategy use (metacognition).
	Exploring Strategies and Metacognitive Regulation of Strategies	• In Pressley's view, the key to education is helping students learn a rich repertoire of strategies that result in solutions to problems. • Students benefit when teachers model effective strategies for students, give them opportunities to practice the strategies, encourage them to monitor the effectiveness of their new strategies, and motivate them to use the strategies. • It takes considerable time to learn a new strategy and come to use it independently. • Most children benefit from using multiple strategies, exploring which ones work well, when, and where.

Do children use one strategy or multiple strategies in memory and problem solving? They often use more than one strategy (Schneider & Bjorklund, 1998; Siegler, 1998). Most children benefit from generating a variety of alternative strategies and experimenting with different approaches to a problem, discovering what works well, when, and where (Schneider & Bjorklund, 1998). This is especially true for children from the middle elementary school grades on, although some cognitive psychologists believe that even young children should be encouraged to practice varying strategies (Siegler, 1998).

At this point, we have examined a number of ideas about teaching for transfer and metacognition. A review of these ideas is presented in summary table 8.3. In the next chapter, we will continue our exploration of children's learning, especially focusing on collaborative learning and learning in groups, as well as a number of strategies for teaching children in specific areas such as reading, writing, math, and science.

Chapter Review

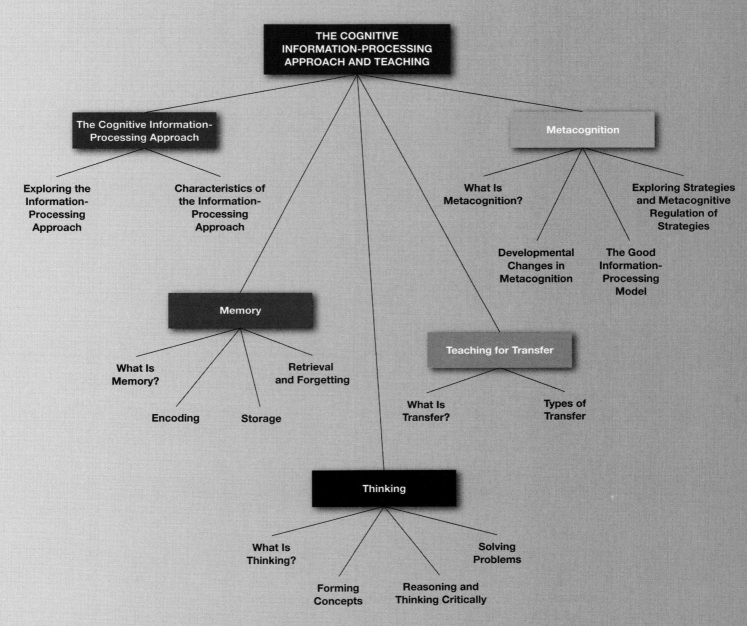

TO OBTAIN A DETAILED REVIEW OF THIS CHAPTER, STUDY THESE THREE SUMMARY TABLES:

Key Terms

Information-processing
    approach 274
encoding 275
automaticity 275
strategy construction 275
transfer 275
metacognition 275
memory 275
storage 276
retrieval 276
attention 276
rehearsal 277
levels of processing theory 278
elaboration 278
chunking 279
sensory memory 280
short-term (working)
    memory 280

memory span 280
long-term memory 280
Atkinson-Shriffrin model 281
working-memory model 281
declarative memory 282
procedural memory 282
episodic memory 283
semantic memory 283
network theories 284
schema theories 284
schema 284
script 285
serial position effect 285
primacy effect 285
recency effect 285
mnemonics 286
method of loci 286
keyword method 286

encoding specificity
    principle 288
recall 288
recognition 288
cue-dependent forgetting 288
interference theory 288
decay theory 289
thinking 291
concepts 291
concept map 293
prototype matching 294
inductive reasoning 295
deductive reasoning 296
analogy 296
critical thinking 297
problem solving 298
subgoaling 298
algorithms 299

heuristics 299
means-end analysis 299
fixation 299
functional fixedness 300
mental set 300
confirmation bias 300
problem-based learning 300
near transfer 307
far transfer 307
low-road transfer 307
high-road transfer 307
forward-reaching
    transfer 307
backward-reaching
    transfer 307
metacognitive
    knowledge 309
metacognitive activity 309

Educational Psychology Checklist

THE COGNITIVE INFORMATION-PROCESSING APPROACH AND TEACHING

How much have you learned since the beginning of this chapter? Use the following statements to help you review your knowledge and understanding of the chapter material. First, read the statement and mentally or on paper briefly show that you understand and can discuss the relevant information.

_____ I know what the information-processing approach emphasizes.
_____ I am aware of the main characteristics of the information-processing approach.
_____ I know what memory is.
_____ I can describe the main ideas involved in the three main areas of memory: encoding, storage, and retrieval.
_____ I can discuss memory and study strategies.
_____ I know what thinking involves.

_____ I can describe the main ideas in forming concepts, reasoning and critical thinking, and solving problems.
_____ I am aware of what teaching for transfer means, including different types of transfer.
_____ I can discuss these aspects of metacognition: what it is, developmental changes, the Good Information-Processing Model, and exploring strategies and metacognitive regulation of strategies.

For any items that you did not check off, go back and locate the relevant material in the chapter. Review the material until you feel that you can check off the item. You may want to use the checklist later in preparing for an exam.

Adventures for the Mind

Now that you have a good knowledge and understanding of the chapter, complete the following exercises to expand your thinking about several topics.

For each of the first three topics, get together with three other students in the class and divide up the work. Have an initial planning meeting, go do the interviews and observations, then reconvene to discuss what you found.

• Select a topic, construct some questions about the topic, and then talk with a 5-year-old, 9-year-old, 13-year-old, and 17-year-old about it. What kind of developmental changes can you detect in how the children and adolescents of different ages processed information in the course of your conversations? Did the adolescents process information more automatically and faster than the children? Did the adolescents seem to have more information-processing capacity?

• Observe a kindergarten, elementary, middle school, and high school classroom and focus on how the teacher maintains students' attention. How effective are the teacher's strategies? Would you do things differently to capture students' attention?

• Interview a kindergarten, elementary, middle school, or high school teacher about how they incorporate critical thinking into their everyday teaching activities.

• Get together with two or three other students in the class and brainstorm about the best ways to guide students in developing better memory and study strategies. Discuss how you might do this differently for children and adolescents at different grade levels. For example, at what age should students start learning effective note-taking strategies? For children too young to be taking elaborate notes, are there gamelike activities that might help them begin to learn the concept and value of taking notes or keeping running records of some event?

Taking It to the Net

1. A small child walks up to you and asks, "Where's my memory?" How do you respond? Where is memory?
2. How might a student's prior knowledge affect their learning of new, related material? Can factual knowledge transfer to a new situation and facilitate learning?

3. There is a large emphasis on using technology in the classroom. Find three good websites that integrate technology into instruction. Here's a good starting point: http://www.mcli.dist.maricopa.edu/tl/.

Connect to http://www.mhhe.com/socscience/psychology/santedu/ttnet.htm to find the answers!

Case Studies

Case 1   *Ken Kelly:* Ken, a ninth-grade teacher, watches a fourth-grade teacher use Socratic method.

Case 2   *Therese Carman:* A second-year teacher is presented with a new district-wide science curriculum that she finds difficult to teach because she relies on the objectives found in the teacher's manual.

Chapter 9

SOCIAL CONSTRUCTIVIST APPROACHES, DOMAIN-SPECIFIC APPROACHES, AND TEACHING

Social Constructivist Approaches to Learning

Constructivist Variations

Situated Cognition

Teachers and Peers as Joint Contibutors to Students' Learning

Scaffolding

Cognitive Apprenticeship

Tutoring

Cooperative Learning

Structuring Small-Group Work

Examples of Social Constructivist Programs

Fostering a Community of Learners

Schools for Thought

Evaluating the Constructivist Approaches

Domain-Specific Constructionist Approaches

Reading

Writing

Mathematics

Science

Social Constructivist Approaches, Domain-Specific Approaches, and Teaching

Preview

Children do some of their thinking by themselves, but as social beings their cognition is often collaborative. Because of our American emphasis on the individual rather than the group, collaborative thinking only recently emerged as an important theme in education. Much of this chapter focuses on the collaborative thinking advocated by social constructivist approaches. In the last part of the chapter, we will examine some domain-specific constructivist approaches. The questions we will explore in this chapter include these:

- What does it mean to take a social constructivist approach in teaching?
- What are some good strategies for including peers in children's learning?
- What is the best way to structure small-group work?
- What are some educational approaches that emphasize collaborative learning?
- What are some specific cognitive and social constructivist approaches to teaching reading, writing, math, and science?

> "The human being is by nature a social animal."
>
> Aristotle
> *Greek Philosopher, 4th Century* B.C

Teaching Stories
Chuck Rawls

Chuck Rawls teaches language arts at Appling Middle School in Macon, Georgia. He provides the following teaching story about peer tutoring:

I was tricked into trying something different my first year of teaching. It was peer teaching in the guise of a school-wide activity known as "Switch Day." This consists of having selected students switch places with members of the faculty and staff. Each student who wants to switch is required to choose a faculty or staff member and then write an essay explaining why he or she wants to switch with that particular person. To my surprise, Chris wrote a very good essay and was selected to switch with me.

It worked wonderfully. Chris delivered the lesson very professionally, and the students were engaged because it was something new and different. It was a riot to watch because Chris, both intentionally and unintentionally, used many of my pet phrases and mannerisms. He really did know his stuff, though, and demonstrated this as he helped students with their seat work.

As the saying goes, "I didn't know he had it in him." Chris became my resident expert on subject-verb agreement, as that was the topic of the lesson and the students remembered what he taught them.

I learned two lessons that day: (1) Don't be afraid to try something different. (2) Peer tutoring works. However, it has to be the right student teaching the right material in the right setting.

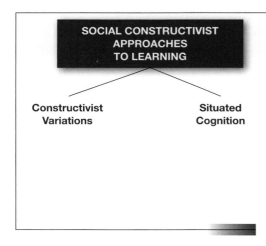

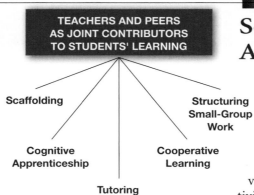

Social Constructivist Approaches to Learning

The social constructivist approaches involve a number of innovations in classroom learning. Before we study these innovations, let us first consolidate our knowledge about constructivist variations and where the social constructivist approaches fit in the overall constructivist framework.

Constructivist Variations

Recall from chapter 1 that **constructivism** *emphasizes that individuals learn best when they actively construct knowledge and understanding.* In the last chapter, our main focus was on the cognitive information-processing approaches to learning, which included some ideas about how the individual child uses information-processing skills to think in constructivist ways. Earlier in this book (in chapter 2, "Physical and Cognitive Development"), we described Piaget's and Vygotsky's theories of development, both of which are constructivist ◀▥ p. 49, 59. According to all of these constructivist approaches, students author their own knowledge. In this chapter, the focus is on social constructivist approaches.

In general, **social constructivist approaches** *emphasize the social contexts of learning and that knowledge is mutually built and constructed.* Vygotsky's social constructivist theory is especially relevant for the current chapter. Vygotsky's model is a social child embedded in a sociohistorical backdrop. Moving from Piaget to Vygotsky, the conceptual shift is from the individual to collaboration, social interaction, and sociocultural activity (Rogoff, 1998). Piaget believed that students construct knowledge by transforming, organizing, and reorganizing previous knowledge and information. Vygotsky believed that students construct knowledge through social interactions with others. The content of this knowledge is influenced by the culture in which the student lives, which includes language, beliefs, and skills.

The implication of Piaget's model is that teachers should provide support for students to explore their world and develop understanding. The implication of Vygotsky's model is that teachers should create many opportunities for students to learn with the teacher and with peers in coconstructing knowledge (Kozulni, 2000). In both Piaget's and Vygotsky's models, teachers serve as facilitators and guides rather than directors and molders of children's learning.

Sometimes the distinctions among constructivist approaches are not clear-cut (Marshall, 1996). For example, when teachers serve as guides for students in discovering knowledge, there are social dimensions to the construction. And the same is true for processing information. If a teacher creates a brainstorming session for students to come up with good memory strategies, social interaction is clearly involved.

Some sociocultural approaches, like Vygotsky's, emphasize the importance of culture in learning; for example, culture can determine what skills are important (such as computer skills, communication skills, teamwork skills). Others focus more exclusively on the immediate social circumstances of the classroom, as when students collaborate to solve a problem.

In one recent analysis of the social constructivist approach, the teacher was described as being drawn to look at learning through the eyes of children (Oldfather

Constructivist Teaching
Vygotsky: Revolutionary Scientist
Vygotsky Links

*K*nowledge that is acquired under compulsion obtains no hold on the mind.

Plato
Greek Philosopher, 4th Century B.C.

& others, 1999). These are some of the characteristics of social constructivist classrooms that were noted in this analysis (Oldfather & others, 1999):

- An important goal orientation of the classroom is the construction of collaborative meaning.
- Teachers closely monitor students' perspectives, thinking, and feeling.
- The teacher and the students are learning and teaching.
- Social interaction permeates the classroom.
- The curriculum and the physical contents of the classroom reflect students' interests and are infused with their cultures.

An isolated individual does not exist.

Antoine de Saint-Exupéry
French Essayist and Novelist, 20th Century

Situated Cognition

Situated cognition *is an important assumption in the social constructivist approaches. It refers to the idea that thinking is located (situated) in social and physical contexts, not within an individual's mind.* Situated cognition conveys the idea that knowledge is embedded in and connected to the context in which the knowledge developed (King, 2000). If this is so, it makes sense to create learning situations that are as close to real-world circumstances as possible. Our discussion of problem-based learning in chapter 8 demonstrated a similar emphasis ◀꜀꜀ p. 302.

Situated
Cognition

Later in this chapter we will explore constructivist approaches in a number of specific domains or situations, such as reading, writing, math, and science. How much instructional practices can be generalized across different domains, such as reading and science, versus how situation-specific they are, is an important issue in educational psychology that we will revisit from time to time in the remaining chapters. Let's now explore some important aspects of social constructivist approaches.

What is the nature of the social constructivist approach to education?

THROUGH THE EYES OF TEACHERS
Teaching Science at the Zoo and Cross-Age Peer Teaching

In Lincoln, Nebraska, several high school science teachers use the Folsum Zoo and Botanical Gardens as a context for guiding students' learning. The science classes are taught in two trailers at the zoo. The teachers emphasize the partnership of students, teachers, zoo, and community. One highlight of the program is the "Bug Bash," when the high school students teach fourth-grade students about insects.

Lincoln zoo crew: Clockwise from back left, teachers Beth Briney, Amy Vanderslice, De Tonack, Sara LeRoy-Toren, and James Barstow.

Teachers and Peers as Joint Contributors to Students' Learning

The idea that teachers and peers can be joint contributors to students' learning involves the concepts of scaffolding, cognitive apprenticeship, tutoring, and cooperative learning (Rogoff, 1998).

Scaffolding

Scaffolding
Cognitive Apprenticeship

In chapter 2, we described **scaffolding** *as a technique of changing the level of support over the course of a teaching session; a more skilled person (teacher or more-advanced peer of the child) adjusts the amount of guidance to fit the student's current performance level* ◀||| p. 61. When the task the student is learning is new, the teacher might use direct instruction. As the student's competence increases, less guidance is provided. Think of scaffolding in learning like the scaffolding used to build a bridge. The scaffolding provides support when needed, but it is adjusted or removed as a project unfolds (Soderman, Gregory, & O'Neill, 1999).

Good tutoring involves scaffolding, as we will see shortly. Look for situations to use scaffolding in the classroom. Work on giving just the right amount of assistance. Don't do for students what they can do for themselves. But do monitor their efforts and smoothly give support and assistance when needed.

Cognitive Apprenticeship

Developmental psychologist Barbara Rogoff (1990) believes that an important aspect of education is **cognitive apprenticeship,** *in which an expert stretches and supports a novice's understanding of and use of the culture's skills.* (Recall our discussion of experts and novices in chapter 8.) The term *apprenticeship* underscores the importance of activity in learning and highlights the situated nature of learning. In a cognitive apprenticeship, teachers often model strategies for students. Then, teachers or skilled peers support students' efforts at doing the task. Finally, they encourage students to continue their work independently.

To illustrate the importance of cognitive apprenticeships in learning, Rogoff (1990) describes the different experiences of students from middle-income and poverty backgrounds. Many middle-income American parents involve their children in cognitive apprenticeships long before they go to kindergarten or elementary school. They read picture books with young children and bathe their children in verbal communication. In contrast, American parents living in poverty are less likely to engage their children in a cognitive apprenticeship that involves books, extensive verbal communication, and scaffolding (Heath, 1989).

A key aspect of a cognitive apprenticeship is the expert's evaluation of when the learner is ready to take the next step with support from the expert (Rogoff, 1998). In one study of science and math students, experts used the timing of the students' participation in discourse to infer understanding of the points of the lesson, providing pauses to allow students to take the responsibility for an idea by anticipating or completing the expert's ideas (Fox, 1993). Experts also used information regarding the length of each response opportunity that students passed up and what the students were doing during the passed-up opportunity (such as calculating or expressing a blank stare). When students passed up two or three opportunities, experts continued with an explanation. If no evidence of understanding appeared during the explanation, the expert repeated or reformulated it. Experts also used collaborative completion of statements as a way to find out what the student understood. A common strategy employed by the experts was to use a "hint" question to get the student unstuck. Experts often attempt to discern students' level of understanding by observing the looks on their faces and how they respond to questions.

Such cognitive apprenticeships continue to be important in classrooms. Students' learning benefits from teachers who think of their relationship with a student as a cognitive apprenticeship, using scaffolding and guided participation to help the student learn.

Tutoring

Tutoring also involves a cognitive apprenticeship between an expert and a novice. Tutoring can take place between an adult and a child, or between a more-skilled child and a less-skilled child.

Classroom Aides, Volunteers, and Mentors   Individual tutoring is an effective strategy that benefits many students, especially those who are not doing well in a particular subject. Classroom aides, volunteers, and mentors can often be effective tutors.

It is frustrating to find that some students need more individual help than you can give them as their teacher because of the needs of the class as a whole. Classroom aides, volunteers, and mentors can help reduce some of this frustration. Monitor and evaluate your class for students you believe could benefit from one-on-one tutoring. Scour the community for individuals with skills in the areas in which certain students need more individual attention. Some parents, college students, and retirees might be interested in filling your classroom tutoring needs.

Several individual tutoring programs have been developed. In the Reading Recovery program, highly skilled teachers tutor first-grade students at risk for reading problems. Evaluations of the Reading Recovery program have found that students who participated in the program in first grade were still performing better in reading in third grade than their counterparts who did not participate in it during first grade (Pinnell & others, 1994).

Developed by Robert Slavin and his colleagues (1995), the comprehensive Success for All program includes one-on-one tutoring, as well as individualized instruction and family support services, for first- through fifth-graders from disadvantaged circumstances. Students who have participated in the program have better reading skills and are less likely to be in special education classes than disadvantaged students who have not been involved in the program.

$\mathscr{D}$IVERSITY AND EDUCATION
The Valued Youth Program

In more than a hundred secondary schools across the country, the Valued Youth Program takes middle school and high school students who are not achieving well or are at risk for school-related problems and gives them the responsibility for tutoring elementary school children (Simons, Finlay, & Yang, 1991). The hope is that the tutoring experience will improve not only the achievement of the students being tutored but also the achievement of the tutors.

In one school's Valued Youth Program, 4 days a week participants walk or ride a bus to tutor for one class period at a nearby elementary school. Each tutor works with three children on subjects such as math or reading, and tutors work with the same children for the entire school year. On the fifth day of the week, the tutors work with their teacher at their own school, discussing tutoring skills, reflecting on how the week has gone, and brushing up on their own literacy skills. For their work, the tutors receive course credit and minimum-wage pay.

One of the Valued Youth Program tutors said, "Tutoring makes me want to come to school because I have to come and teach the younger kids." He also said that he did not miss many days of school, like he used to, because when he has been absent the elementary school children always ask him where he was and tell him that they missed him. He says that he really likes the kids he teaches and that if he had not been a tutor he probably would have dropped out of school by now.

In one analysis, fewer than 1 percent of the Valued Youth Program tutors had dropped out of school, compared with a 14 percent national dropout rate (Intercultural Development Research Association, 1996).

The boy on the left is a tutor in the Valued Youth Program, which takes at risk middle and high school students and gives them the responsibility of tutoring elementary school children.

Peer Tutoring

Peer Tutors   Fellow students also can be effective tutors. In peer tutoring, one student teaches another. In *cross-age peer tutoring,* the peer is older. In *same-age peer tutoring,* the peer is from the same class. Cross-age peer tutoring usually works better than same-age peer tutoring. An older peer is more likely to be more skilled than a same-age peer, and being tutored by a same-age classmate is more likely to embarrass a student and create negative social comparison. The Diversity and Education box describes a cross-age peer tutoring program that has merit.

Researchers have found that peer tutoring often benefits students' achievement (Mathes & others, 1998; Simmons & others, 1995). And in some instances, the tutoring benefits the tutor as well as the tutee, especially when the older tutor is a low-achieving student. Teaching something to someone else is one of the best ways to learn.

In one study that won the American Educational Research Association's award for best research study, the effectiveness of a classwide peer tutoring program in reading was evaluated for three learner types: low-achieving students with and without disabilities and average-achieving students (Fuchs & others, 1997). Twelve schools were randomly assigned to experimental (peer tutoring carried out) and control (no peer tutoring) groups. The peer tutoring program was conducted during regularly scheduled reading instruction 3 days a week for 35 minutes each of these days and lasted for 15 weeks. The training of peer tutors emphasized helping students get practice in reading aloud from narrative text, reviewing and sequencing information read, summarizing large chunks of connected texts, stating main ideas, predicting and checking story outcomes, as well as other reading strategies. Pre- and

TEACHING STRATEGIES
For Using Peer Tutoring in the Classroom

Following are some suggestions for how to use peer tutoring (Goodlad & Hirst, 1989; Jenkins & Jenkins, 1987):

1. *Use cross-age tutoring rather than same-age tutoring when possible.* Set aside specific times of the day for peer tutoring and communicate the learning assignment clearly and precisely to the peer tutor. For example, "Today from 9 to 9:30 I would like you to work with Jimmy on the following math problem-solving exercises: _____, _____, and _____."
2. *Let students participate in both tutor and tutee roles.* This helps students learn that they can both help and be helped. Pairing of best friends often is not a good strategy because they have trouble staying focused on the learning assignment.
3. *Don't let tutors give tests to tutees because it can undermine cooperation between the students.*
4. *For peer tutoring to be successful, you will have to spend some time training the tutors.* To get peer tutors started off right, discuss competent peer-tutoring strategies. Demonstrate how scaffolding works. Give the tutors clear, organized instructions and invite them to ask questions about their assignments. Divide the group of peer tutors into pairs and let them practice what you have just demonstrated. Let them alternately be tutor and tutee.
5. *Don't overuse peer tutoring.* It is easy to fall into the trap of using high-achieving students as peer tutors too often. Be sure that these students get ample opportunities to participate in challenging intellectual tasks themselves.
6. *Communicate with parents that their child will be involved in peer tutoring.* Explain to them the advantages of this learning strategy and invite them to visit the classroom to observe how the peer tutoring works. Let them know that their child will be both a tutor and a tutee.

posttreatment reading achievement data were collected. Irrespective of the type of learner, students in the peer tutoring classrooms showed greater reading progress over the 15 weeks than their counterparts who did not receive peer tutoring.

Cooperative Learning

Cooperative learning *occurs when students work in small groups to help each other learn.* Cooperative learning groups vary in size, although a typical group will have about four students. In some cases, cooperative learning is done in dyads (two students). When students are assigned to work in a cooperative group, the group usually stays together for weeks or months, but cooperative groups usually occupy only a portion of the student's school day or year.

Research on Cooperative Learning

Researchers have found that cooperative learning can be an effective strategy for improving achievement, especially when two conditions are met (Slavin, 1995):

1. *Group rewards are generated.* Some type of recognition or reward is given to the group so that the group members can sense that it is in their best interest to help each other learn.
2. *Individuals are held accountable.* Some method of evaluating a student's individual contribution, such

THROUGH THE EYES OF TEACHERS
Buddy Readers

A peer-tutoring strategy that I use is buddy reading. My students buddy-read in a variety of situations, such as stories read in language arts and math word problems. A few difficulties can arise, as when one student does all of the reading, students don't focus on the task, and the noise level gets out of hand. To avoid these problems, I explain the expectations to the students before they leave their seat to go to buddy reading. For example, I tell them that the only person who should hear them read is the buddy they are sitting beside.

Once I give directions, I usually ask one student at a time to choose a buddy. As buddies are chosen, they spread out around the edges of the room and face the wall so sound won't carry across the room. It's a good idea to walk around the room and monitor this and to make informal observations. Because students often read/work at different rates, it helps to give them a related assignment to complete independently when they finish with their buddies.

Vicky Stone
Language Arts Teacher
Cammack Middle School
Huntington, West Virginia

Cooperative Learning Research
Cooperative Learning Links
Cooperative Learning Abstracts

*M*an is a knot, a web, a mesh into which relationships are tied.

Antoine de Saint-Exupéry
French Novelist and Essayist, 20th Century

as an individual quiz, is used. Without this individual accountability, some students might do some "social loafing" (let other students do their work) and some might be left out because it is believed that they have little to contribute.

When the conditions of group rewards and individual accountability are met, cooperative learning improves achievement across different grades and in tasks that range from basic skills to problem solving (Johnson & Johnson, 1999; Qin, Johnson, & Johnson, 1995).

Motivation   Increased motivation to learn is common in cooperative groups (Sapon-Shevin, 1999). In one study, fifth- and sixth-grade Israeli students were given a choice of continuing to do schoolwork or going out to play (Sharan & Shaulov, 1990). Only when students were in cooperative groups were they likely to forego going out to play. Positive peer interaction and student decision making likely were at work in the students' choice to stay in the cooperative groups. In another study, middle-class American high school students made greater gains and expressed more intrinsic motivation to learn algebraic concepts when they were in cooperative rather than individualistic learning contexts (Nichols & Miller, 1994).

Interdependence and Teaching One's Peers   Cooperative learning also promotes increased interdependence and connection with other students (Johnson & Johnson, 1999). In one study, fifth-graders were more likely to move to a correct strategy for solving decimal problems if the partners clearly explained their ideas and considered each other's proposals (Ellis, Klahr, & Siegler, 1994).

In a cooperative learning group, students typically learn a part of a larger unit and then have to teach that part to the group. When students teach something to others, they tend to learn it more deeply, as we noted in our earlier discussion of peer tutoring.

Cooperative Learning Approaches   A number of cooperative learning approaches have been developed. They include: STAD (Student-Teams-Achievement Divisions), the jigsaw classroom, learning together, group investigation, and cooperative scripting. To read about these approaches, see figure 9.1.

Structuring Small-Group Work

When you structure students' work in small groups, you will have a number of decisions to make. These include composing the group, building team skills, and structuring group interaction (Webb & Palincsar, 1996).

Composing the Group   Teachers often ask how they should assign students to small groups in their class. The cooperative learning approaches featured in figure 9.1 generally recommend heterogeneous groups with diversity in ability, ethnic background, socioeconomic status, and gender (Johnson & Johnson, 2000). The reasoning behind heterogeneous grouping is that it maximizes opportunities for peer tutoring and support, improves cross-gender and cross-ethnic relations, and ensures that each group has at least one student who can do the work (Kagan, 1992).

Heterogeneous Ability   One of the main reasons for using heterogeneous ability groups is that they benefit low-ability students, who can learn from higher-ability students. However, some critics argue that such heterogeneous groupings hold back high-ability students. In most studies, though, high-achieving students perform equally well on achievement tests after working in heterogeneous groups or homogeneous groups (Hooper & others, 1989). In heterogeneous groups, high-ability students often assume the role of "teacher" and explain concepts to other students. In homogeneous groups, high-ability students are less likely to assume this teaching role.

STAD (STUDENT–TEAMS–ACHIEVEMENT DIVISIONS)

STAD involves team recognition and group responsibility for learning in mixed-ability groups (Slavin, 1994). Rewards are given to teams whose members improve the most over their past performances. Students are assigned to teams of four to five members. The teacher presents a lesson, usually over one or two class periods. Next, students study worksheets based on material presented by the teacher. Students monitor their team members' performance to ensure that all members have mastered their material. Teams practice working on problems together and study together, but the members take quizzes individually. The resulting individual scores contribute to the team's overall score. An individual's contribution to the team score is based on that individual's improvement, not on an absolute score, which motivates students to work hard because each contribution counts. In some STAD classrooms, a weekly class newsletter is published that recognizes both team and individual performances.

The STAD approach has been used in a variety of subjects (including math, reading, and social studies) and with students at different grade levels. It is most effective for learning situations that involve well-defined objectives or problems with specific answers or solutions. These include math computation, language use, geography skills, and science facts.

THE JIGSAW CLASSROOM

In chapter 5, "Sociocultural Diversity," we described the jigsaw classroom, which involves having students from different cultural backgrounds cooperate by doing different parts of a project to reach a common goal. Here we elaborate on the concept.

Developed by Eliot Aronson and his colleagues (1978), *Jigsaw I* is a cooperative learning approach in which six-member teams work on material that has been broken down into parts. Each team member is responsible for a part. Members of different teams who have studied the same part convene, discuss their part, and then return to their teams, where they take turns teaching their part to other team members.

Robert Slavin (1994) created *Jigsaw II,* a modified version of *Jigsaw I.* Whereas *Jigsaw I* consists of teams of six, *Jigsaw II* usually has teams of four or five. All team members study the entire lesson rather than one part, and individual scores are combined to form an overall team score, as in STAD. After they have studied the entire lesson, students become expert on one aspect of the lesson, then students with the same topics meet in expert groups to discuss them. Subsequently, they return to their teams and help other members of the team learn the material.

LEARNING TOGETHER

Created by David and Roger Johnson (1994), this approach has four components: (1) face-to-face interaction, (2) positive interdependence, (3) individual accountability, and (4) development of interpersonal group skills. Thus, in addition to Slavin's interest in achievement, the Johnsons' cooperative learning approach also focuses on socio-emotional development and group interaction. In learning together, students work in four- or five-member heterogeneous groups on tasks with an emphasis on discussion and team building (Johnson & Johnson, 2000).

GROUP INVESTIGATION

Developed by Shlomo Sharan (1990; Sharan & Sharan, 1992), this approach involves a combination of independent learning and group work in two- to six-member groups), as well as a group reward for individual achievement. The teacher chooses a problem for the class to study, but students decide what they want to study in exploring the problem. The work is divided among the group's members, who work individually. Then the group gets together, integrating, summarizing, and presenting the findings as a group project. The teacher's role is to facilitate investigation and maintain cooperative effort. Students collaborate with the teacher to evaluate their effort. In Sharan's view, this is the way many real-world problems are solved in communities around the world.

COOPERATIVE SCRIPTING

Students work in reciprocal pairs, taking turns summarizing information and orally presenting it to each other (Dansereau, 1988; McDonald & others, 1985). One member of the pair presents the material. The other member listens, monitors the presentation for any mistakes, and gives feedback. Then the partner becomes the teacher and presents the next set of material while the first member listens and evaluates it.

Figure **9.1**
Cooperative Learning Approaches

Small-Group Work

One problem with heterogeneous groups is that when high-ability, low-ability, and medium-ability students are included, the medium-ability students get left out to some extent; high-ability and low-ability students might form a teacher-student relationship in these groups, excluding medium-ability students from group interaction. Medium-ability students might perform better in groups where most or all of the students have medium abilities.

Ethnic, Socioeconomic, and Gender Heterogeneity   One of the initial reasons cooperative learning groups were formed was to improve interpersonal relations among students from different ethnic and socioeconomic backgrounds. The hope was that interaction under conditions of equal status in cooperative groups would reduce prejudice. However, getting students to interact on the basis of equal status has been more difficult than initially envisioned.

Some experts recommend that, when forming ethnically and socioeconomically heterogeneous groups, careful attention be given to a group's composition (Miller & Harrington, 1990). One recommendation is to not make the composition too obvious. Thus, you might vary different social characteristics (ethnicity, socioeconomic status, and gender) simultaneously, such as grouping together a middle-income African American female, a white male from a low-income family, and so on. Another recommendation is to not form groups that have only one minority student, if at all possible; this avoids calling attention to the student's "solo status."

In mixed-gender groups, males tend to be more active and dominant (Tannen, 1990). Thus, when mixing females and males, an important task for teachers is to encourage girls to speak up and boys to allow girls to express their opinions and contribute to the group's functioning. A general strategy is to have an equal number of girls and boys. In groups of five or six children in which only one member is a girl, the boys tend to ignore the girl (Webb, 1984).

Team-Building Skills   Good cooperative learning in the classroom requires that time be spent on team-building skills. This involves thinking about how to start team building at the beginning of the school year, helping students become better listeners, giving students practice in contributing to a team product, getting students to discuss the value of a team leader, and working with team leaders to help them deal with problem situations.

Structuring Group Interaction   One way to facilitate students working in small groups is to assign students different roles. For example, consider the following roles that students can assume in a group (Kagan, 1992):

- Encourager—brings out reluctant students and is a motivator
- Praiser—shows appreciation of other students' work
- Gatekeeper—equalizes participation of students in the group
- Coach—helps with academic content
- Question Commander—ensures that students ask questions and that the group answers them

THROUGH THE EYES OF TEACHERS

An Eye-Level Meeting of the Minds

Ninth-grade history teacher Jimmy Furlow believes that students learn best when they have to teach others. He has groups of students summarize textbook sections and put them on transparencies to help the entire class prepare for a test. Furlow lost both legs in Vietnam but he rarely stays in one place, moving his wheelchair around the room, communicating with students at eye level. When the class completes their discussion of all the points on the overhead, Furlow edits their work to demonstrate concise, clear writing and help students zero in on an important point (Marklein, 1998).

Ninth-grade history teacher Jimmy Furlow converses with a student in his class.

TEACHING STRATEGIES
For Developing Students' Team-Building Skills

Here are some guidelines for helping students improve their team-building skills: (Aronson & Patnoe, 1996):

1. *Don't begin the school year with cooperative learning on a difficult task.* Teachers report that academic cooperative learning often works best when students have previously worked together on team-building exercises. A short period each day for several weeks is usually adequate for this team building.

2. *Do team building at the level of the cooperative group (two to six students) rather than at the level of the entire class.* Some students on the team will be more assertive, others will be more passive. The team-building goal is to get all members some experience in being valuable team members, as well as to get them to learn that being cooperative works more effectively than being competitive.

3. *In team building, work with students to help them become better listeners.* Ask students to introduce themselves by name all at the same time to help them see that they have to take turns and listen to each other instead of hogging a conversation. You also can ask students to come up with behavioral descriptions of how they can show others that they are listening. These might include looking directly at the speaker, rephrasing what she just said, summarizing her statement, and so on.

4. *Give students some practice in contributing to a common product as part of team building.* Ask each student to participate in drawing a group picture by passing paper and pen from student to student. Each student's task is to add something to the picture as it circulates several times through the team. When the picture is finished, discuss each student's contribution to the team. Students will sense that the product is not complete unless each member's contribution is recognized. The group picture serves to illustrate how working together can be beneficial.

5. *During team building, you may want to discuss the value of having a group leader.* You can ask students to discuss the specific ways a leader should function in order to maximize the group's performance. Their brainstorming might come up with such characteristics as "helps get the group organized," "keeps the group on task," "serves as liaison between the teacher and the group," "shows enthusiasm," "is patient and polite," and "helps the group deal with disagreements and conflicts." The teacher may select the group leader or students may be asked to elect one.

6. *You likely will need to work with team leaders to help them deal with problem situations.* For example, some members might rarely talk, one member might dominate the group, members might call each other names, some members might refuse to work, one member might want to work alone, and everyone might talk at once. You can get group leaders together and get them to role-play such situations and discuss effective strategies for handling the problem situations.

- Checker—makes sure the group understands the material
- Taskmaster—keeps the group on task
- Recorder—writes down ideas and decisions
- Reflector—thinks about and evaluates the group's progress
- Quiet Captain—monitors the group's noise level
- Materials Monitor—obtains and returns supplies

Such roles help groups to function more smoothly and give all members of the group a sense of importance. Note that although we just described eleven different roles that can be played in groups, most experts, as we noted earlier, recommend that groups not exceed five or six members to function effectively. Some members can fill multiple roles, and all roles do not always have to be filled.

Another way roles can be specialized is to designate some students as "summarizers" and others as "listeners." Researchers have consistently found that summarizing benefits learning more than listening, so if these roles are used, all members should get opportunities to be summarizers (Dansereau, 1988).

At this point we have studied a number of ideas about social constructivist approaches and teachers and peers as joint contributors to students' learning. A review of these ideas is presented in summary table 9.1. Next, we will describe some programs that reflect a social constructivist approach to learning.

SUMMARY TABLE 9.1
Social Constructivist Approaches to Learning, and Teachers and Peers as Joint Contributors to Students' Learning

Concept	Processes/ Related Ideas	Characteristics/Description
Social Constructivist Approaches to Learning	Constructivist Variations	• Piaget's and Vygotsky's theories are constructivist. Piaget's theory is a cognitive constructivist theory, whereas Vygotsky's is social constructivist. • The implication of Vygotsky's model for teaching is to establish opportunities for students to learn with the teacher and peers in constructing knowledge and understanding. In both Piaget's and Vygotsky's models, teachers are facilitators, not directors. • Distinctions between cognitive and social constructivist approaches are not always clear-cut. All social constructivist approaches emphasize that social factors contribute to students' construction of knowledge and understanding.
	Situated Cognition	• This refers to the idea that thinking is located (situated) in social and physical contexts, not within an individual's mind.
Teachers and Peers as Joint Contributors to Students' Learning	Scaffolding	• This is the technique of providing changing levels of support over the course of a teaching session, with more-skilled individuals providing guidance to fit the student's current performance.
	Cognitive Apprenticeship	• This involves a novice and an expert, who stretches and supports the novice's understanding of and use of the culture's skills.
	Tutoring	• Tutoring involves a cognitive apprenticeship between an expert and a novice. Tutoring can take place between an adult and a child, or a more skilled-child and a less-skilled child. Individual tutoring is an effective learning strategy. • Classroom aides, volunteers, and mentors can serve as tutors to support teachers and classroom learning. • Reading Recovery and Success for All are examples of tutoring programs. • In many cases, students benefit more from cross-age tutoring than from same-age tutoring. • Tutoring can benefit not only the tutee but the tutor as well.
	Cooperative Learning	• This occurs when students work in small groups to help each other learn. • Researchers have found that cooperative learning can be an effective strategy for improving students' achievement, especially when group goals and individual accountability are instituted. • Cooperative learning often improves intrinsic motivation, encourages student interdependence, and promotes deep understanding. • Cooperative learning approaches include STAD (Student-Teams-Achievement Divisions), the jigsaw classroom (I and II), learning together, group investigation, and cooperative scripting.
	Structuring Small-Group Work	• Cooperative learning approaches generally recommend heterogeneous groupings with diversity in ability, ethnicity, socioeconomic status, and gender. However, in some cases less heterogeneity might work best, as when middle-ability students are involved. • Structuring small-group work also involves attention to team-building skills. • A good strategy is to spend several weeks at the beginning of the school year on building team skills. • Assigning one student in each small group to be a team leader can facilitate team building. • A group also can benefit when students are assigned different roles that are designed to help the group function more smoothly.

Examples of Social Constructivist Programs

Let's explore several programs that systematically incorporate social constructivist philosophies in their efforts to challenge students to solve real-world problems and develop a deeper understanding of concepts.

EXAMPLES OF
SOCIAL CONSTRUCTIVIST
PROGRAMS

Fostering a
Community
of Learners

Schools for
Thought

Fostering a Community of Learners

Ann Brown and Joe Campione (1996; Brown, 1997) have developed a program called **Fostering a Community of Learners (FCL),** *which focuses on literacy development and biology. As currently established, it is set in inner-city elementary schools and is appropriate for 6- to 12-year-old children.* Reflection and discussion are key dimensions of the program. Constructive commentary, questioning, querying, and criticism are the mode rather than the exception, and the program emphasizes three strategies that encourage reflection and discussion: (1) using adults as role models, (2) children teaching children, and (3) implementing online computer consultation.

Adults as Role Models   Visiting experts and classroom teachers introduce the big ideas and difficult principles at the beginning of a unit. The adult demonstrates how to think and self-reflect in the process of finding a topic or reasoning with given information. The adults continually ask students to justify their opinions and then support them with evidence, to think of counterexamples of rules, and so on.

One example of a teaching theme used in the FCL program is "Changing Populations." Outside experts or teachers introduce this lesson and ask students to generate as many questions about it as possible—it is not unusual for students to come up with more than a hundred questions. The teacher and the students categorize the questions into subtopics according to the type of population they refer to (usually about five categories), such as extinct, endangered, artificial, assisted, and urbanized populations. About six students make up a learning group and each group takes responsibility for one of the subtopics.

Children Teaching Children   Brown (1997) says that children as well as adults enrich the classroom learning experience by contributing their particular expertise. Cross-age teaching, in which older students teach younger students, is used. This occurs both face-to-face and via electronic mail (e-mail). Older students often serve as discussion leaders. Cross-age teaching provides students with invaluable opportunities to talk about learning, gives students responsibility and purpose, and fosters collaboration among peers.

Reciprocal teaching, *in which students take turns leading a small-group discussion,* is used in FCL. Reciprocal teaching requires students to discuss complex passages, collaborate, and share their individual expertise and perspectives on a particular topic. Later in this chapter you also will see that reciprocal teaching can involve a teacher and a student as well as interaction between students.

A modified version of the jigsaw classroom also is used. As students create preliminary drafts of reports, they participate in "crosstalk" sessions. These are whole-class activities in which groups periodically summarize where they are in their learning activity and get input from the

A "Fostering a Community of Learners" classroom. What is the nature of this approach to education?

other groups. "Mini-jigsaws" (small groups) also are used. At both the whole-class level and mini-jigsaw level, if group members can't understand what a student is saying or writing about, the student must revise their product and present it again later. Students are then grouped into reciprocal teaching seminars in which each student is an expert on one subtopic, teaches that part to the others, and also participates in constructing test questions based on the subunit.

Online Computer Consultation

Face-to-face communication is not the only way to build community and expertise. FCL classrooms also use electronic mail. Through e-mail, experts provide coaching and advice, as well as commentary about what it means to learn and understand. Online experts function as role models of thinking. They wonder, query, and make inferences based on incomplete knowledge.

A culture of learning, negotiating, sharing, and producing work that is displayed to others is at the heart of FCL. The educational experience involves an interpretive community that encourages active exchange and reciprocity. This approach has much in common with what Jerome Bruner (1996) recommended for improving the culture of education. Research evaluation of the Fostering a Community of Learners approach suggests that it benefits students' understanding and flexible use of content knowledge, resulting in improved achievement in reading, writing, and problem solving.

Schools for Thought

Schools for Thought is another formal program of social constructivist teaching. Too often students emerge from instruction with only a fragile understanding of the material (Segal, 1996). For example, students might be able to repeat various scientific principles they have been taught in science, but they run into difficulties when they have to explain everyday scientific phenomena. Similarly, in math, students might be good at plugging numbers into formulas but when confronted with variations of these problems be unable to solve them. Thus, many students acquire enough information to pass tests in school but gain no deep understanding of concepts.

In a recent effort, **Schools for Thought (SFT)** (Lamon & others, 1996) *has combined aspects of* the Jasper Project, *Fostering a Community of Learners (FCL), and Computer Supported Intentional Environments (CSILE) in a school learning environment.* The project is named after John Bruer's (1993) award-winning book. The Jasper Project, FCL, and CSILE share certain features that allow them to be combined in a school learning environment. We already have described the Jasper Project and FCL. To read about CSILE, see the Technology and Education box.

Schools for Thought

Curriculum

The three core programs of Schools for Thought stress the importance of getting students to think about real-world problems. Problem-based and project-based activities are at the heart of the curriculum. Extended in-depth inquiry in domains such as science, math, and social studies are emphasized. All three programs also incorporate cross-disciplinary inquiry across traditional boundaries. For example, exploring what it means for an animal to be endangered could mean examining problems related to estimating populations, sampling, and other issues usually restricted to mathematics. In the Schools for Thought project, curricula are being developed that integrate geography, geology, environmental and physical science, ancient and American history, and language arts and reading.

Instruction

All three programs involve a change in the classroom instructional climate. In a traditional classroom, students are receivers of information that is dispensed by teachers, textbooks, and other media; the teacher's role is to give information and mold students' learning. In many traditional schools, what students mainly do is listen, watch, and mimic what teachers and texts tell them to do (Greeno, 1993).

In contrast, all three programs provide students with many opportunities to plan and organize their own learning and problem solving. They also encourage students

TECHNOLOGY AND EDUCATION
Computer Supported Intentional Learning Environments (CSILE)

A CSILE site might include more than one classroom. A typical classroom has eight networked computers (Bereiter & Scardamalia, 1989; Scardamalia & Bereiter, 1994). CSILE classrooms are connected to form a communal base for the entire school. Students are encouraged to enter their views and questions, compare perspectives, and reflect on joint understanding of ideas. Students work both individually and collaboratively. Students can add a comment or attach a graphic note, such as a picture or diagram, to another student's entry. However, only the original author of the note can edit or delete the notes. Authors are informed when a comment has been attached to one of their notes.

Following is an example of work done within one combined fifth/sixth-grade CSILE classroom (Bruer, 1989). The focus was on ecology, with one group working on the topic of fossil fuels. The group began with a kitchen scene that one student had previously created as a CSILE note. The students took this as a learning challenge to identify the uses of fossil fuels in an ordinary kitchen. Different students examined different parts of the kitchen, exploring such topics as the generation of electricity and the origin of natural gas. This information led to posting of notes explaining how the fossil fuels were used. The notes were attached to pictures of the various kitchen objects. The computer system allowed notes to be posted hierarchically. For example, a student could begin with a kitchen scene and click on the refrigerator. This would open a picture of the refrigerator's interior. Clicking on various items in the refrigerator then would bring up pictures and text about the fossil fuels. This learning exercise unfolded in a museum-like way with every detail of daily life made interesting.

CSILE helps students understand how knowledge and understanding are socially constructed and gives students opportunities to reflect on, revise, and transform their thinking. Students learn that thinking is not a brief, cursory exercise. Rather it takes place over an extended time and often needs to be modified based on feedback from a community of learners. Research evaluations indicate that students in CSILE classrooms perform better on standardized achievement tests of language and math, give deeper explanations of concepts, are better at solving problems, and have a more positive attitude toward learning than students in conventional classrooms (Scardamalia, Bereiter, & Lamon, 1994).

For more information about CSILE classrooms, contact Dr. Carl Bereiter and Dr. Marlene Scardamalia at the University of Toronto.

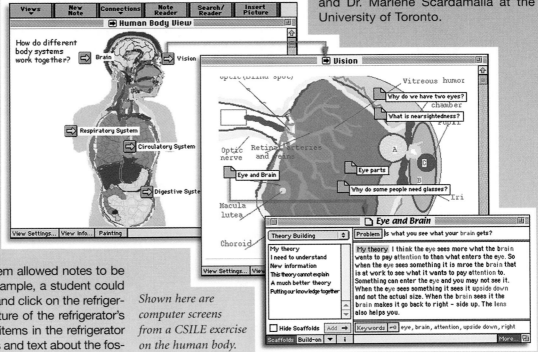

Shown here are computer screens from a CSILE exercise on the human body.

to work collaboratively as they learn and think. Students explore ideas, evaluate information, and consider others' ideas in an ongoing reciprocal interchange with peers, teachers, and experts.

The Schools for Thought environments are not simply free-wheeling discovery environments. They involve a considerable amount of structure. Teachers and community experts keep learning focused on key principles in the domains being studied,

CSILE

such as mathematics, science, or social science. They monitor and reframe students' self-generated questions and exploration to keep them within the perspective of the key principles. In this manner, they guide the direction of students' inquiry so that students discover the deep concepts of the domain. Still, there is considerable flexibility in how this understanding is achieved and the nature of the projects undertaken.

Community   In many schools, classrooms and teachers operate in isolation, not just from each other but from the outside community as well. The Jasper Project, FCL, and CSILE all emphasize the importance of giving students and teachers opportunities to see themselves as part of a team and as members of a larger community. Problems often have a community focus, to encourage students to think about how learning and problem solving can be used to better understand and improve the world in which we live.

Technology   The Jasper Project, FCL, and CSILE all use technology to break the isolation of the traditional classroom. They encourage students to communicate electronically with a community of learners beyond the classroom's walls.

Assessment   The goals in creating the Jasper Project, FCL, and CSILE were not to improve students' achievement test scores. Assessment in the three programs focuses on authentic performances (such as reading for the purpose of answering research questions, writing to build new knowledge), making assessment smoothly coordinate with learning and instruction, and encouraging students to engage in self-assessment. We will have much more to say about these types of assessment in chapter 14, "Assessing Students' Learning."

Further Exploration of the Schools for Thought Project
The Schools for Thought project is in the process of building and expanding its activities to make them easier for classroom teachers to implement. Two types of tools they are developing are (1) starter units and (2) performance support tools.

At this point we have discussed a number of ideas about Fostering a Community of Learners and Schools for Thought. A review of these ideas is presented in summary table 9.2.

**Schools For
Thought and Technology**

A Schools for Thought Science classroom at Compton-Drew School in St. Louis.

Summary Table 9.2
Examples of Social Constructivist Programs

Concept	Processes/ Related Ideas	Characteristics/Description
Fostering a Community of Learners	Its Nature	• This program, developed by Ann Brown and Joe Campione, is appropriate for 6- to 12-year-old students. Reflection and discussion are emphasized. • Three strategies that promote reflection and discussion are (1) using adults as role models, (2) children teach children (with a special emphasis on reciprocal teaching), and (3) implementing online computer consultation. Evaluations of the program have been positive.
Schools for Thought	Its Nature	• This project combines activities from three programs we discussed in chapter 8 and the current chapter: (1) The Jasper Project, (2) Fostering a Community of Learners, and (3) Computer Supported Intentional Learning Environments. • Extended in-depth inquiry in science, math, and social studies is fostered. Teachers guide students in becoming architects of their knowledge.

Domain-Specific Constructivist Approaches

From time to time in this chapter and the last, we have described constructivist approaches in specific domains, such as the Jasper Project in mathematics. Here we examine other constructivist approaches that have been developed for reading, writing, mathematics, and science.

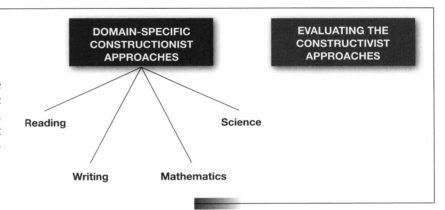

Reading

In chapter 2, "Physical and Cognitive Development," we described two main approaches to teaching reading: the basic-skills-and-phonetics approach, and the whole-language approach ◀‖‖ p. 70. You may wish to review that discussion at this time. The basic-skills-and-phonetics approach emphasizes decoding skills and therefore is more reflective of the cognitive constructivist view (Tierney & Readence, 2000). The whole-language approach focuses on becoming immersed in the world of print and therefore fits more within a social constructivist framework.

Cognitive Constructivist Approaches   Cognitive constructivist approaches to reading emphasize constructing meaning, decoding and comprehending words, and develop expert reader strategies.

Constructing Meaning   In the cognitive constructivist approach, text has meaning that a reader must discover. Readers actively construct this meaning by using their background knowledge and knowledge of words and how they are linked. For example, in one study, second-grade students were asked questions about their knowledge of spiders before they read about them (Pearson, Hansen, & Gordon, 1979). The students with more background knowledge about spiders understood the passage about spiders better than the other students did.

Reading Resources for Teachers

Cognition and Reading

Decoding and Comprehending Words   The cognitive constructivist approach also emphasizes the importance of discovering the cognitive processes involved in decoding and comprehending words. Important in this decoding process are some familiar processes metacognitive skills and general automaticity of information processing (see Chapter 8) ◀ⅢⅡ p. 277, 311.

Metacognition is involved in reading, in the sense that good readers develop control of their own reading skills and have an understanding of how reading works. For example, good readers know that it is important to comprehend the "gist" of what an author is saying.

With regard to automaticity of processing, when word recognition occurs rapidly, meaning also often follows in a rapid fashion (Stanovich, 1994). Many beginning or poor readers do not recognize words automatically. Their processing capacity is consumed by the demands of word recognition, so they have less capacity to devote to comprehension.

The cognitive constructivist approach also contributed to the discovery that phonemic awareness is present in children who learn to read and absent in those who do not (Hiebert & Raphael, 1996). As we noted in chapter 2, *phonemic awareness* refers to the ability to analyze words into phonemes (basic speech sounds) ◀ⅢⅡ p. 65. What makes phonics (the matching of words and sounds) work is the cognitive process of phonemic awareness, the ability to manipulate and think about sounds.

Developing Strategies   In the cognitive constructivist approach, researchers have tried to focus not so much on whether one teaching approach, such as whole language, is better than another, such as phonics. Rather, they have searched for the underlying processes that explain reading. This search had led to an interest in strategies, especially the strategies of expert readers compared with those of novice readers ◀ⅢⅡ p. 277. Researchers advise teachers to guide students in developing good reading strategies.

Michael Pressley and his colleagues (1992) developed the **transactional strategy instruction approach,** *a cognitive constructivist approach to reading that emphasizes instruction in strategies (especially metacognitive strategies).* In their view, strategies control students' abilities to remember what they read. It is especially important to teach students metacognitive strategies to monitor their reading progress. Summarizing is also thought to be an important reading strategy. In the strategy approach, designers of teachers' manuals are encouraged to include information about the importance of reading strategies, how and when to use particular strategies, and prompts to remind students about using strategies.

Social Constructivist Approaches   The social constructivist approaches bring the social dimensions of reading to the forefront (Hiebert & Raphael, 1996).

Basic Social Constructivist Assumptions About Reading   Two social constructivist assumptions about reading are that (1) the social context plays an important role in reading, and (2) knowledgeable readers in the culture assist less-knowledgeable readers in learning to read.

The contribution of the social context to reading includes such factors as how much emphasis the culture places on reading, the extent to which parents have exposed their children to books before they enter formal schooling, the teacher's communication skills, the extent to which teachers give students opportunities to discuss what they have read with the teacher and their peers, and the district-mandated reading curriculum. Whereas cognitive constructivists emphasize the student's construction of meaning, social constructivists stress that meaning is socially negotiated. What they mean by "socially negotiated" is that meaning involves not only the reader's contribution but also the context in which the text is read as well, as the purpose for reading. Social constructivist approaches emphasize the importance of giving students opportunities for engaging in meaningful dialogue about the books they have just read. One way of doing this is through reciprocal teaching.

Reciprocal Reading

Reciprocal Teaching In our discussion of the Fostering a Community of Learners program, we described *reciprocal teaching* in terms of students taking turns leading a small-group discussion. Reciprocal teaching also can involve a teacher and a student.

In reciprocal teaching, teachers initially explain the strategies and model how to use them in making sense of the text. Then they ask students to demonstrate the strategies, giving them support as they learn them. As in scaffolding, the teacher gradually assumes a less active role, letting the student assume more initiative. For example, Annamarie Palincsar and Ann Brown (1984) used reciprocal teaching to improve students' abilities to enact certain strategies to improve their reading comprehension. In this teacher-scaffolded instruction, teachers worked with students to help them generate questions about the text they had read, clarify what they did

To ask questions of a wise person is the beginning of wisdom.

German Proverb

not understand, summarize the text, and make predictions. Figure 9.2 portrays a teacher-student dialogue that reflects reciprocal teaching. Research on reciprocal teaching suggests that it is a very effective strategy for improving reading comprehension (Brown & Palincsar, 1989; Webb & Palincsar, 1996).

Book Clubs Book clubs *involve peer learning and consist of student-led discussions of literature* (McMahon, 1994; McMahon, Raphael, & Goatley, 1995). Teachers serve as guides but give students considerable responsibility for how text discussions evolve. Conducted in this manner, book clubs often involve a range of discussions, as children make connections to their own lives, clarify points of confusion in the texts, draw inferences to fill in gaps left by the text, and critique the quality of the texts.

Book clubs reflect the social constructivist principle that meaning is socially negotiated. And book clubs can help fill a void that exists in many classrooms: an absence of talk about text.

School/Family/Community Connections From the social constructivist perspective, schools are not the only sociocultural context that is important in reading. Families and communities are also important (McGhee & Richaels, 2000).

Of special concern are the language experiences of students from low-income families. In chapter 5, "Sociocultural Diversity," we discussed research findings that, on the average, young children in welfare homes hear about 600 words an

READING:
Cats also "talk" by making other sounds. Some scientists think cats may have as many as 100 different calls. Cats have calls for greeting people, for showing hunger, for making a threat to another cat, and even for scolding their kittens. When a cat is frightened or angry, it may growl, spit, hiss, or scream.

39.	T:	C_____, as a teacher, can you ask someone a question about this information? [pause] Sometimes it helps if you're having a hard time to summarize what I just told you. [pause] What was I telling you about, what kind of information?
40.	S2:	About different ways they talk.
41.	T:	You mean there are [*sic*] more than one way for them to communicate?
42.	S2:	A hundred ways.
43.	T:	I did talk about that. They communicate with a hundred different sounds. Why do they need all those different sounds?
44.	S2:	To tell people stuff.
45.	S6:	To see if their babies are okay.
46.	T:	Possibly. Now, with that information, C_____, knowing that they have all those different ways to talk and to communicate, can you think of a question to ask? You can start your question with the word what . . . or when . . . or why?
47.	S2:	Why do they purr?
48.	T:	Who is they?
49.	S2:	The cats.
50.	T:	Okay, let's have that information in your sentence. Why . . .
51.	S2:	Why do the cats purr?
52.	S5:	To tell them what they want.
53.	T:	Can you tell us a little bit more?
54.	S5:	[not audible]
55.	T:	Would it sound the same way for all those things?
56.	S5:	No.
57.	T:	So that's why it needs a hundred sounds. So, I might say, if I were going to ask a question, why do cats have so many different sounds or calls?
58.	S3:	Because they have so many different colors in their fur.
59.	T:	I said calls, not colors. Why do they have so many different calls, or sounds? [pause] Think of what R_____ told us. Do they always want the same thing?
60.	S3:	No.
61.	T:	Then why do they have so many different ones? Is it so they can communicate what they really want?

Figure **9.2**
Reciprocal Teaching and Reading

hour whereas young children in professional families hear about 2,100 words an hour (Hart & Risley, 1995) ◀▌▌▌ p. 162. In more recent studies, these researchers found that, on the average, children in welfare homes receive only half as much language experience in their early years as children in middle-income families (Hart & Risley, in press). They also revealed that children in high-income families have twice as much language experience as even children in middle-income families. At-risk students who do not engage in reading out of school fall farther behind as they go through the elementary school years (Rowe, 1994). Most students who are avid readers report that they have at least one other person to talk with about their reading and about what to read next (Fielding, Wilson, & Anderson, 1986). Many parents of at-risk students have their own reading difficulties as well as problems in obtaining books (Gunning, 2000; Jalongo, 2000; Robinson, McKenna, & Wedman, 2000).

In one strategy, parents' support of their children's literacy is emphasized by guiding parents to use books in their interactions with their children (Edwards, 1989). For instance, Project Family Literacy in Chicago's Latino community involves literacy training for children's English-deficient parents (Shanahan & Rodriguez-Brown, 1993). Parents attend twice-weekly English-as-a-second-language (ESL) classes, participate in Parents as Teacher classes twice a month, and attend a summer institute. In the ESL classes, activities include parents making books for their children or sharing books in English. From the larger group, several parent leaders are selected. Twice monthly they hold family literacy seminars at neighborhood schools. The parents' participation in the program over a 3-year period was linked with improved literacy in their children.

Next, we turn our attention to writing. In the whole-language approach, writing and reading instruction are often integrated (Ruddell, 1999). And innovations in technology are becoming available that help teachers in their effort not only to implement a whole-language approach, but also to improve students' decoding skills (Solley, 2000).

Writing

In chapter 2, "Physical and Cognitive Development," we discussed developmental changes in children's writing ◀▌▌▌ p. 74. Here, as with reading, we will explore cognitive and social constructivist approaches to writing.

Cognitive Constructivist Approaches

Cognitive constructivist approaches to writing emphasize many of the same themes that we discussed with regard to reading, such as constructing meaning and developing strategies (Kellogg, 2000). Problem-solving and metacognitive strategies are thought to be especially important in improving students' writing.

Writing can be viewed as a problem-solving process, constrained by the writer's need for integrated knowledge of the subject, general knowledge of how the language system works, and the writing problem itself, which involves the purpose of the paper, the audience, and the projected role of the writer in the piece to be produced (Flower & Hayes, 1981).

Emphasizing knowledge of writing strategies moves into the area of metacognition, which we discussed in chapter 8 ◀▌▌▌ p. 311. In one study, students 10 to 14 years of age were asked to write a paper that would be of interest to students in their own age range (Scardamalia, 1981). In carrying out this project, the students were hampered by a lack of planning, not recording ideas in notes for later use, and not monitoring their writing progress by rereading and rewriting. The results are indicative of the fact that many middle school students do not have good knowledge of the planning and organizational strategies required by good writing and need to be taught these skills.

Social Constructivist Approaches

As in reading, social constructivist approaches emphasize that writing is best understood as culturally embedded and socially constructed rather than internally generated. In the social

Cognition and Writing

A #2 pencil and a dream can take you anywhere.

Joyce Myers
American Businesswoman, 20th Century

constructivist approach to reading, the teacher's role shifts from transmitting knowledge to helping students restructure their knowledge. In this regard, both teachers and peers can serve as the more-knowledgeable reader. This social constructivist strategy also can be applied to writing.

The Social Context of Writing   The social constructivist perspective focuses on the social context in which writing is produced. It is important that students participate in a writing community to understand author/reader relationships and that they learn to recognize how their perspective might differ from that of other people (Hiebert & Raphael, 1996).

To see the importance of social context in writing, consider two students. One, Anthony, is a 9-year-old Latino student who has lived in the Manhattan area of New York City his entire life (McCarthey, 1994). He reads and writes extensively, keeps scientific journals, and participated in classrooms with a strong emphasis on writing in his earlier school years. He is enthusiastic about his writing topic, a tribute to his grandmother who had recently died. His teacher encourages Anthony to write about her death, discussing various writing possibilities on this topic with him during their student-teacher writing conference. She and Anthony talk about the best ways to structure and organize the paper. His final writing product is a moving account of his grandmother's life and death. Anthony's teacher believes that writing plays an important role in education, and she communicates this enthusiastically to her students.

Contrast Anthony's writing experience with that of another Latino student, Carlos, whose parents recently immigrated to the Bronx area of New York City. Although his English is good, Carlos has had few classroom experiences in which he has practiced writing about his personal experiences, and he has never done any writing on his own outside the classroom. He feels very uncomfortable when the teacher asks him to write about personal experiences. In the student-teacher writing conference, Carlos is reluctant to discuss his feelings. Carlos' teacher has been mandated by the district to include writing experiences in different subjects. She is not enthusiastic about this and spends little time working with Carlos to improve his writing.

As evidenced by Anthony's and Carlos' situations, the social context plays an important role in writing. Some students bring a rich background of writing to the classroom, others have little writing experience. In some classrooms the teacher places a high value on writing, in others the teacher treats writing as being less important.

THROUGH THE EYES OF CHILDREN
Writing Self-Evaluations

For their writing portfolios, San Francisco fifth-grade teacher Keren Abra periodically asks her students to evaluate their writing. Following are several of her students' comments toward the end of the school year:

I am in fifth grade right now and I love writing. Anytime that I get to write I will; as far as I can remember I have loved writing. I feel that my writing has developed since fourth grade and I am pleased with my writing. Some authors might not like their writing unlike me; I have *never* thrown away any of my writing. I love to share my writing and give and get ideas from other writers. . . . If I could describe myself as a writer I would say (not to brag) that I was a descriptive, imaginative, captivating writer.

Michelle

I think writing a story is easy because there is so much to write about and if I have to write about a certain thing there are also more things to do with the story. . . . If someone read my writing they would think I probably am a happy and energetic kid. They will think this because most of my stories are up beat.

Sarah

I feel that when I'm writing I could do better. I could do better especially on spelling. When I was in kindergarten we did not do a lot of writing. When I was in third grade I did not like writing. It was scary learning new things about writing. I'm in fifth grade and I love to write but sometimes it annoys me that I can't spell that well. One thing I like about my writing is the way I put action into all of my work because I love to get excited! I think that if someone were to read my writing uncorrected they would not be able to read it. If it was corrected I think the person would really like my story.

Janet

Writing "Real Texts" About Meaningful Experiences, and Student-Teacher Writing Conferences   In the social constructivist approach, students' writing should include opportunities to create "real" texts, in the sense of writing about personally meaningful situations. For example, Anthony, whose teacher frequently asks students to write about personal experiences, wrote about his grandmother's life and death and his teacher gave him considerable support for writing about this emotional experience. Student-teacher writing conferences play an important support role in helping students become better writers.

**Peer Collaboration
in Writing**

Peer Collaboration in Writing While working in groups, writers experience the processes of inquiry, clarification, and elaboration that are important in good writing (Webb & Palincsar, 1996). Students often bring diverse experiences to bear as they collaborate in writing text. Such rich, shared collaboration can produce new insights about what to write about and how (Daiute & Dalton, 1993).

Too often students write to meet the teacher's expectations, which results in writing that is constrained, imitative, and conforming. In peer writing groups, teacher expectations are often less apparent (Kearney, 1991).

School/Family/Community Connections In one effort, teachers were encouraged to recognize the existence and richness of the surrounding Latino community and then integrate this into school contexts (Moll & others, 1992; Moll, Tapia, & Whitmore, 1993). This included (1) an analysis of knowledge and how it is transmitted within households in the Latino community; (2) an after-school laboratory in which teachers and students used reading and writing more in line with the way it is used in their neighborhoods than the way it is used in school; and (3) classroom connections that integrated activities from the after-school laboratory. The goal was to integrate these three components. For example, students documented ways of writing in their community, such as letters to relatives in other countries and account books. Then, working with their peers, students created modules on topics that reflected the expertise of members of their communities, such as knowledge about mechanics and repair work. To obtain information for their module, students interviewed members of their communities. The students also communicated through e-mail with students who live in Latino communities in other parts of the United States.

Involve the writing community in your class. Look around your community and think about expert writers you could invite to your classroom to discuss their work. Most communities have such experts, such as journalists and other authors and editors. One of the four most successful middle schools in the United States identified by Joan Lipsitz (1984) built a special Author's Week into its curriculum. Based on students' interest, availability, and diversity, authors are invited to discuss their craft with students. Students sign up to meet individual authors. Before they meet the author, they are required to read at least one of the author's books. Students prepare questions for their author sessions. In some cases, authors come to the class for several days to work with students on their writing projects.

As can be seen, there are many ways that writing is constructed. Later, in chapter 14, "Assessing Students' Learning," we will have much more about the cognitive and social constructivist dimensions of writing.

In the course of our discussion of reading and writing, we have described a number of ideas that can be used in the classroom. To think about which reading and writing activities you will use with your students, complete Self-Assessment 9.1.

THROUGH THE EYES OF TEACHERS
Lamont Writes About His Dog

In celebration of Memorial Day, Joanne, the reading specialist, collaborated with me on a writing lesson based on the theme of heroes. Joanne started prewriting with my third graders by giving an example of a particular teacher who is a hero to her and explaining that a hero is someone who has qualities that we admire and would like to develop in ourselves. After giving her example, Joanne asked the students to create a word ladder with phrases describing their individual heroes. Both of us circulated around the room while helping the students develop their ideas and encouraging the use of "strong verbs."

At one point I stopped at Lamont's desk to see how he was coming along. He had just moved here recently and seemed to have a very unstable home life. He was on reading level but had extreme difficulty putting his thoughts down in writing, often writing only one sentence in a 30-minute period. When I looked at Lamont's word ladder, I noticed that he was writing about his dog. I was about to discourage him by saying that he needed to choose an actual person but I remembered that Joanne had been talking with him a few minutes earlier. She later explained that she encouraged Lamont to go ahead and write about his dog because there may not be an actual person in his life that he looks up to as a hero.

The next day, I was so thankful that I had not asked Lamont to change his topic. He had written his first full paragraph since he had moved here. By first paying attention to Lamont's emotional needs, Joanne also was able to help him improve his language skills.

Kristin Blankenship
Third-Grade Teacher
Salem Church Elementary School
Chesterfield Public Schools, Virginia

TEACHING STRATEGIES
For Incorporating Writing into the Curriculum

You will have many opportunities to incorporate writing into the curriculum. Here are some examples (Halonen, 1999):

1. *Writing to learn.* This can work in any subject area. For example, in biology, after students have studied the adaptation of different species, ask them to write a summary of the main ideas and generate examples not described in class or the text.
2. *Free-writing assignments.* In free writing, students write whatever they think about a subject. Such assignments are usually unstructured but have time limits. For example, one free-writing assignment in American history might be "Write about the American Revolution for five minutes." Free writing helps students discover new ideas, connections, and questions they might not have generated if they had not had this free-wheeling opportunity.
3. *Creative writing assignments.* These assignments give students opportunities to explore themselves and their world in creative, insightful ways. They include poetry, short stories, and personal essays involving real-world experiences.
4. *Formal writing assignments.* These involve giving students opportunities to express themselves using an objective point of view, precise writing style, and evidence to support their conclusions. Formal writing helps students learn how to make formal arguments. For example, high school students might construct a major paper on a topic like "Global Warming: Real Fears or Hype?" "An In-Depth Examination of Faulkner's Writing Style," or "Why People Are Prejudiced." Such writing projects stimulate students to think analytically, learn how to use resources, and cite references. Work with students on generating topics for a paper, structuring the paper, using planning and time management skills for completing the paper in a timely manner, drafting and revising, and turning in a paper that is free of spelling and grammatical errors.

Reprinted by permission of United Features Syndicate, Inc.

Mathematics

What is children's mathematical thinking like? What is children's understanding of numbers when they enter first grade?

Mathematical Thinking Children already have a substantial understanding of numbers before they enter first grade. Most middle-socioeconomic-status kindergartners can count past 20, and many can count as high as 100 or more; most can accurately count the number of objects in a set, can solve small-number addition and subtraction problems (such as 3 + 2), and know the relative magnitudes of single-digit numbers (such as, Which is bigger, 8 or 6?) (Siegler & Robinson, 1982).

When they go to school, children learn many more-advanced kinds of numerical skills (Ginsburg, Klein, & Starkey, 1997). People often think that children just either learn or fail to learn what they are taught. In fact, what they learn often reflects

SELF-ASSESSMENT 9.1

How I Plan to Incorporate Reading and Writing into My Classroom

Regardless of the subject matter you teach, giving students adequate opportunities for developing their reading and writing skills will be an important agenda for you. This chapter has discussed many ways you can do this. In the following self-assessment, place a checkmark next to each activity that you plan to use in your teaching.

_____ Computer technology, such as Computer Supported Intentional Learning Environments or IBM's Writing to Read program

_____ Whole-language opportunities such as using newspapers, magazines, and fiction and nonfiction books, as well as trying to integrate subject areas

_____ Phonological awareness and word-sound decoding skill activities

_____ Reciprocal teaching

_____ Reading strategies, such as monitoring and summarizing

_____ Book clubs

_____ Involving parents in students' reading and writing activities

_____ Working with students on writing as a problem-solving activity

_____ Emphasizing the social context in writing

_____ Having students write "real texts" about meaningful experiences

_____ Having regular student-teacher writing conferences

_____ Setting up writing projects on which students collaborate with each other

_____ Bringing in expert writers, such as authors and newspaper editors or writers, to talk with students

_____ Giving students "writing to learn" opportunities

_____ Giving students free writing assignments

_____ Giving students creative writing assignments

_____ Giving students formal writing opportunities

By incorporating many of these reading and writing activities in your classroom, you will significantly improve your students' literacy and enhance their opportunities for success in a world that places a high value on reading and writing skills. Thus, regardless of the subject(s) you teach, working with your students to help them improve their reading and writing skills will make an important contribution to their lives.

their own thinking as much as anything they are taught. This is true even in the case of basic addition and subtraction, which might be thought to involve only the simplest of learning procedures, memorization.

Arithmetic   In most instruction aimed at helping children learn basic arithmetic facts (such as, How much is 3 plus 9?), the goal is to teach children how to retrieve the answer from memory. For a period of several years after they enter school, however, children use a mix of strategies, including ones that no one ever taught them. Thus, on a problem such as 3 + 9, some first-, second-, and third-graders will retrieve the answer from memory, some will count from 1, some will count from 9, and some will reason that 9 is 1 less than 10, that 3 + 10 is 13, and therefore 3 + 9 must be 12. These last two strategies are rarely taught by teachers or parents, yet children frequently use them anyway.

The fact that first-, second-, and third-graders use all of these arithmetic strategies to solve single-digit problems does not mean that no development occurs over the period. Children become both much faster and more accurate, in part because they increasingly use the faster and more accurate strategies, such as retrieval, and in part because they execute each of the strategies more quickly and accurately. Eventually, they solve all of these problems consistently, correctly, and very quickly.

As they move toward the end of the elementary school period, children learn to solve multidigit arithmetic problems and problems involving fractions. Much of what's involved in learning these more advanced arithmetic skills is overcoming misconceptions. For example, in learning multidigit subtraction, children need to overcome "buggy" rules (named for the "bugs" that appear in faulty computer programs). Suppose a third-grader is given the following four problems and generates the answers shown here:

306	453	204	370
−43	−274	−177	−89
343	179	177	281

Can you figure out what the student was doing wrong?

Analysis of the problems indicates that the child was following a "buggy" rule, similar to the partially correct balance scale rules discussed earlier. The difficulty with these subtraction problems arose only when the problem involved borrowing across a zero; the child answered correctly on the problem that did not involve a zero and on the problem in which the zero was in the rightmost column. When it was necessary to borrow across a zero, the child proceeded in a consistent, but wrong, way that involved subtracting the zero from the number beneath it, rather than the reverse, and then not decrementing the number next to the zero (presumably because nothing had been borrowed from it). Such buggy algorithms are quite common in third-, fourth-, and fifth-graders' subtraction (VanLehn, 1986).

Making teachers aware of the bugs that interfere with their students' learning can lead to better mathematics instruction. For example, in one study a group of student teachers were taught how to design problems that would tell them the precise nature of the bugs in each student's performance (since different children show different bugs) (Brown & Burton, 1978). The precise assessment of children's difficulties promises to allow us to go well beyond standard written comments (such as "60 percent correct—You can do better!") to allow teaching geared to the needs of individual children.

Algebra   Children develop far more powerful mathematical reasoning when they learn algebra. A single equation can represent an infinite variety of situations. Even many students who get A's and B's in algebra classes, however, do so without understanding what they are learning—they simply memorize the equations. This approach might work well in the classroom, but it limits these students' ability to use algebra in real-world contexts.

This difficulty does not affect just junior high and high school students getting their first exposure to algebra—it also extends to the college level. Fewer than 30 percent of engineering students at a high-quality state university correctly solved the following problem:

> Write an equation using the variables C and S to represent the following statement: "At Mindy's restaurant, for every four people who order cheesecake, there are five people who order strudel." Let C represent the number of cheesecakes and S the number of strudels. (Clement, Lockhead, & Soloway, 1979, p. 46)

Most of the students represented this problem as $4C = 5S$. Although this might initially seem logical, this equation says that multiplying two smaller quantities (4 and the number of people ordering cheesecake) yields a result equal to multiplying two larger quantities (5 and the number of people ordering strudel). The underlying difficulty is that even college students at fine universities often do not connect their mathematical equations to what the equations mean. Without such connections, algebra becomes a meaningless exercise in symbol manipulation. Clearly, successful instruction in algebra, as in other areas of mathematics, requires not only teaching students how to solve problems, but also leading students to a deeper understanding of how the solution procedures yield the solutions.

The Math Forum
Math and Science Clearinghouse
Psychology and Math/Science Education

Controversy in Math Education   Mathematics education is currently swirled in controversy over whether a cognitive approach or a practice approach should be followed (Batcheldar, 2000; Stevenson, 2000; Stevenson, Hofer, & Randel, 1999). Some proponents of the cognitive approach argue against memorization and practice in teaching mathematics. They emphasize a constructivist approach to mathematical problem solving. Others assume that speed and automaticity are fundamental to effective mathematics achievement and emphasize that such skills can only be acquired through practice. In recent years, the constructivist approach has become increasingly popular. In this approach, effective instruction focuses on involving children in solving a problem or developing a concept and in exploring the efficiency of alternative solutions.

The field of mathematics education is undergoing dramatic change (Riedsel & Schwartz, 1999). In the low-tech past, shopkeeper paper-and-pencil math might have worked, but that no longer is the case in the high-tech age of computers and other electronic challenges that require new ways of understanding math. To meet these new challenges, the guide *Curriculum and Evaluation Standards for School Mathematics* (National Council of Teachers of Mathematics [NCTM], 1989) was developed. These standards emphasize that teaching math should involve giving students opportunities to

- solve meaningful math problems,
- develop critical reasoning skills,
- make connections to prior knowledge, and
- discuss math concepts with each other.

In general, these standards emphasize that teachers should guide students in making sense of math problems rather than directing them to just do math computational drills.

The guide *Professional Standards for Teaching Mathematics* (NCTM, 1991) was developed to help teachers implement the standards in the NCTM's *Curriculum and Evaluation Standards for School Mathematics*. Among the recommendations are a major shift in teaching practice away from the traditional lecture-drill format to a format in which individuals work together to solve meaningful math problems.

Some Constructivist Principles   From a constructivist perspective, the following principles should be followed when teaching math (Middleton & Goepfert, 1996).

Make Math Realistic and Interesting   Build your teaching of math around realistic and interesting problems. These problems might involve some kind of conflict, suspense, or crisis that motivates students' interest. The math problem-solving activities might center on the student, community issues, scientific discoveries, or historical events. Math game-playing provides a motivating context for learning math. Questions that teachers use during game playing, such as "What do you need to roll on the dice to move your piece to number 10 on the board?" are more meaningful than decontextualized problems. Math games also encourage students to discuss math strategies with others, including their peers and parents (Carpenter & others, 1983). Connecting math with other subject areas, such as science, geography, reading, and writing, also is recommended.

Consider the Prior Knowledge of the Student   Evaluate what knowledge the students bring to the unit and the context in which instruction takes place. Make enough information available for students to be able to come up with a method for solving math problems but withhold enough information so that students have to stretch their minds to solve the problems.

Make the Math Curricula Socially Interactive   Develop math projects that require students to work together to come up with a solution. Build into the math curriculum opportunities for students to use and improve their communication skills. Generate math projects that engender discussion, argument, and compromise.

Innovative Math Projects   The interest in making math instruction more constructivist has spawned a number of innovative programs (Middleton & Goepfert, 1996). These include programs for elementary school, middle school, and high school. We will describe a program at each level.

Elementary School   Everyday Mathematics is the elementary school component of the University of Chicago School Mathematics Project. A special feature is the high interest level of the math activities. Most activities are done with partners or in small groups with an emphasis on discussion, exploration, and projects. For more information about Everyday Mathematics, contact: Everyday Learning Corporation at (800) 382-7670.

Middle School   The Connected Mathematics Project is funded by the National Science Foundation. The program focuses on five themes: (1) understanding, (2) connections, (3) investigations, (4) representations, and (5) technology. Connections with other disciplines such as science, social science, and business are emphasized. Many math problems focus on the everyday experiences and interests of middle school students. Each unit uses problem solving as defined by the NCTM's *Curriculum and Evaluation Standards* to develop a major concept in these areas: number, geometry, probability, statistics, measurement, and algebra.

High School   The Interactive Mathematics Program (IMP) is a 4-year, problem-based high school math curriculum that meets the needs of both college-bound and non-college-bound students. IMP emphasizes solving math problems in context; large, complex problems; communication and writing skills; and technology. Over the course of 4 years, students revisit problems in a spiraling sequence, giving them opportunities to develop more sophisticated mathematical understanding. Students make oral and written presentations that help to clarify their math thinking.

Technology and Math Instruction   The NCTM's *Curriculum and Evaluation Standards* recommends that calculators be used at all levels of mathematics instruction. And some access to computers is also necessary, if students are to be adequately educated for future careers. In many school systems, adequate funds for computers is a major issue. One recommendation by math curriculum experts James Middleton and Polly Goepfert (1996) is that instead of purchasing a lab full of low-end computers, schools should purchase one really good, top-of-the-line computer for each math classroom, along with a projection device or large-screen monitor. This allows students to participate in using significant technology every day.

Connecting with Parents   In chapter 8, we described Family Math, a program that helps parents experience math with their children in a positive, supportive way ◀ p. 303. In addition to telling parents about Family Math, consider having family math nights. Especially have one at the beginning of the school year to let parents see how their students will be learning math and resolve any major concerns. At the family math night, offer resources that parents can use at home to help their children learn math more effectively.

THROUGH THE EYES OF TEACHERS
Math and Technology

Technology is an important part of my classroom. My math students are expected to be fluent users of the scientific calculator. I use the graphing calculator for specific topics, but the scientific calculator is a daily tool that we use. I use spreadsheets and graphing programs very frequently. The spreadsheets assist my teaching of formulas, estimation, and also encourages students to explore the world of mathematics. The graphics program allows them to show pictorial representation of their math data. I use the Internet for students to collect data for math projects. We can use those data for graphs, charts, tables, probability, statistics, or purely for researching a specific topic. Computers are also used to help students develop a professional looking résumé. In today's world, all students need to be computer literate in order to be employable.

Lou Aronson
Mathematics Teacher
Devils Lake High School
Devils Lake, North Dakota

Connected Mathematics
Interactive Mathematics

Continue to Be an Active Learner Yourself   If you teach math, one good active step is to join the National Council of Teachers of Mathematics (NCTM) and use its resources. NCTM has annual conferences, publishes an annual yearbook with stimulating chapters on recent developments in math education, and publishes journals such as *Mathematics Teacher*. For more information about NCTM call (703) 620-9840.

Science

Let's explore the extent to which children engage in scientific thinking and the nature of science education.

Scientific Thinking   Children's problem solving is often compared to that of scientists. Both children and scientists ask fundamental questions about the nature of reality. Both also seek answers to problems that seem utterly trivial or unanswerable to other people (such as, Why is the sky blue?). Both also are granted by society the time and freedom to pursue answers to the problems they find interesting. This "child as scientist" metaphor has led researchers to ask whether children generate hypotheses, perform experiments, and reach conclusions concerning the meaning of their data in ways resembling those of scientists (Clinchy, Mansfield, & Schott, 1995).

Scientific reasoning often is aimed at identifying causal relations. In some ways, children's causal inferences are similar to those of scientists. For example, like scientists, they place a great deal of emphasis on causal mechanisms (Frye & others, 1996). Their understanding of how events are caused weighs more heavily in their causal inferences than do even such strong influences as whether the cause happened immediately before the effect (Shultz & others, 1986).

There also are important differences between the reasoning of children and the reasoning of scientists, however. This is true even of preadolescents who have had some instruction in school regarding the scientific method. One difference comes in the preadolescents' much greater difficulty in separating their prior theories from the evidence that they have obtained. Often, when they try to learn about new phenomena, they maintain their old theories regardless of the evidence (Kuhn, Schauble, & Garcia-Mila, 1992).

Another difference is that they are more influenced by happenstance events than by the overall pattern of occurrences (Kuhn, Amsel, & O'Laughlin, 1988). They also have difficulty designing new experiments that can distinguish conclusively among alternative causes. Instead, they tend to bias the experiments in favor of whichever hypothesis they began with, and sometimes they will see the results as supporting their original hypothesis even when the results directly contradict it (Schauble, 1990). Thus, although there are important similarities between children and scientists, in their basic curiosity and in the kinds of questions they ask, there are also important differences in their ability to design conclusive experiments and in the degree to which they can separate theory and evidence (Schauble, 1996).

**Science Resources for Teachers
Science Learning Network**

Science Education   With an emphasis on discovery and hands-on laboratory investigation, many science teachers now help their students construct their knowledge of science (Abruscato, 2000; Tolman & Hardy, 1999). Constructivist teaching emphasizes that children have to build their own scientific knowledge and understanding. At each step in science learning, they need to interpret new knowledge in the context of what they already understand. Rather than putting fully formed knowledge into children's minds, in the constructivist approach teachers help children construct scientifically valid interpretations of the world and guide them in altering their scientific misconceptions (Martin, Sexton, & Gerlovich, 1999; Resnick & Chi, 1988).

Constructivist Teaching Strategies   Some contemporary constructivist approaches to teaching science include exploring everyday science problems, activities that help students think about how science works, and the social contexts of science (Linn, Songer, & Eylon, 1996).

Exploring Everyday Science Problems

Most students are far more interested in science that addresses problems relevant to their lives than they are in discussing abstract theories. One elementary school program that reflects this emphasis is the project funded by the National Science Foundation called Science for Life and Living (SLL) (Biological Sciences Curriculum Study, 1989). It emphasizes inquiry, structured groups, and technology.

Some critics of this and other constructivist approaches argue that too much attention is given to inquiry skills and not enough is given to discipline-specific information (American Association for the Advancement of Science, 1993).

Activities That Help Students Learn How Science Works

Some projects help students think about and visualize how science works. For example, Project STAR (Science Teaching through Astronomical Roots) uses astronomy as a foundation to teach complex physics principles to high school students (Schneps & Sadler, 1989). Computer simulations can be especially effective in helping students visualize and think about how science works.

The Social Contexts of Science

The Fostering a Community of Learners project (Brown, 1997; Brown & Campione, 1996), discussed earlier in the chapter, reflects an emphasis on the social contexts of science. Teacher-student and student-student collaborative interaction are stressed. Students investigate environmental science problems, create group or individual reports, and support each other as part of a community of science learners.

Another program that captures the social contexts of science theme is the Kids as Global Scientists Project (Songer, 1993). This project focuses on networked communication, incorporating students' perspectives from different countries on issues involving climate change.

An Innovative Middle School Life-Sciences Curriculum   In chapter 2, "Physical and Cognitive Development," we discussed the importance of revising middle school curricula. Especially lacking in middle school education have been courses that provide the information, skills, and motivation for young adolescents to learn about themselves and their widening world.

The **Human Biology Middle Grades Curriculum (HUMBIO)** *was developed by Stanford University scientists in collaboration with middle school teachers across the United States* (Heller, 1993; Carnegie Council on Adolescent Development, 1995). *It integrates the study of ecology, evolution, genetics, physiology, human development, culture, health, and safety.* It might seem ironic that we end this section on domain-specific constructivist approaches by emphasizing integration and connection across the school curriculum. However, such cross-curricular integration and connection is an important theme in many disciplines.

THROUGH THE EYES OF TEACHERS

Math and Science Getting Wet and Muddy

Sandra Eidson, a biology teacher, and Lela Whelchel, a mathematics teacher, recently won a $12,000 GTE grant to integrate biology and geometry at West Hall High School in Oakwood, Georgia. For example, students are using graphing calculators to monitor a creek behind the high school. The teachers describe this exercise as "math and science getting wet and muddy." Students also use triangles to calculate the height of trees. Lela Whelchel says that her dream is to see all math and science classes paired together.

Sandra Eidson and Lela Whelchel

HUMBIO not only is appropriate for teaching science to middle school students with a wide range of abilities, it simultaneously promotes healthy decision making. HUMBIO is a 2-year curriculum that consists of 24 units. Schools choose which units they want to teach. Initial units are "The Changing Body, Reproduction, and Sexuality," "Genetics," "The Nervous System," and "The Life of Cells." Next comes "From Cells to Organisms: Human Development." Finally, "The Circulatory System," "Breathing," and "Digestion and Nutrition" round out the curriculum.

In using HUMBIO, teachers work cooperatively from the perspectives of their individual disciplines toward imparting a central lesson. For example, a science class discussion of the impact of food and drugs on circulation is coordinated with a physical education class discussion of linkages between food intake, drugs, circulation, and breathing. The study of health includes decisions regarding smoking, analysis of different ways of planning menus, facts behind eating disorders, and ways to reduce stress. One lesson helps students understand how drugs affect their bodies. One bodily change that cocaine produces is increased production of adrenaline. In the HUMBIO curriculum at Egan Intermediate School in Los Altos, California, seventh-grade students explore the effects of adrenaline on metabolism by observing brine shrimp react to a single drop through a microscope. Students have an opportunity to discuss the ideas in the demonstration with the teacher and with each other. They ask questions and offer solutions.

Some English teachers who are involved in the HUMBIO program encourage students to read books related to what they have observed in science class. Some social studies teachers focus on the impact of scientific experiments on society and changing views of biology at different points in history.

HUMBIO has been extensively field-tested at schools selected for the diversity of their populations and geographic locations. Training for teaching the HUMBIO is available through summer institutes at Stanford University, and information about HUMBIO is available from Addison-Wesley-Longman Publishers.

In this HUMBIO classroom, students at Central Park East Secondary School in New York City investigate an important function of the human digestive system by performing the peristalsis activity. The group shown here is moving rice through long flexible plastic tubing representing the small intestine.

Science in High Schools   In most high schools, science is taught in this sequence: biology, chemistry, physics. Many students only take the biology course or the biology–chemistry sequence and don't go on to physics. An increasing number of scientists argue that science courses should be taught in the opposite sequence and that the science subjects also should be taught in a more integrated fashion (Siegfried, 1998). They believe that to understand biology, students need to know a lot of chemistry. Life is made of molecules and survives by such processes as photosynthesis and respiration. Teaching biology first and chemistry second, in their view, is like watching *The Empire Strikes Back* before the prior episode of *Star Wars*. Likewise, understanding chemistry without knowing something about physics is difficult. Chemistry is based on energy changes and the forces between atoms, which are the subject matter of physics. The science curriculum also should include real-world problems that tie physics, chemistry, and biology together. And it should explore these aspects of scientific thinking: theory, prediction, skepticism, and methods for assessing evidence.

**National Science
Teachers Association**

Evaluating the Constructivist Approaches

Many contemporary educational psychologists are enthusiastic about the constructivist approaches that portray the child as an active constructor of meaning (Anderson & others, 1996; Marshall, 1997). At many points in this book we have chronicled constructivist approaches to children's learning. This has included William James and John Dewey's initial infusion of constructivism into educational psychology early in the twentieth century (chapter 1) ◀||| p. 4, Piaget's cognitive constructivism and Vygotsky's social constructivism (chapter 2) ◀||| p. 49, constructivist emphases in moral education (values education, cognitive moral education in chapter 3) ◀||| p. 109, constructivist teaching strategies for improving children's creative thinking (chapter 4) ◀||| p. 142, constructivist aspects of critical thinking and solving problems (chapter 8) ◀||| p. 298, as well as the social constructivist dimensions of collaborative learning and cognitive and social constructivist strategies in domain-specific areas such as reading, writing, math, and science (this chapter). In later chapters, where appropriate, constructivist teaching strategies will continue to be presented. For example, in the next chapter we will describe a number of learner-centered principles that the Board of Educational Affairs of the American Psychological Association recommends teachers incorporate in their instruction. Many of these principles have constructivist leanings.

Though constructivism has taken on an increasingly popular role in educational reform, not all educational psychologists and teachers embrace it. As we saw earlier in our discussion of science, some critics argue that too much attention is given to inquiry skills and not enough to the content of the discipline. This criticism also has been leveled at whole-language approaches to teaching reading, which are constructivist. Critics also say that many constructivist approaches are too relativistic and vague. And critics argue that constructivism is a general approach and theory that has not yet been proven to be the best approach to teaching children.

In sum, controversy still surrounds constructivism in education. In the next chapter, we will continue to explore this controversy in our discussion of direct instruction, much of which runs counter to a constructivist philosophy of teaching.

At this point we have examined a number of ideas about domain-specific constructivist approaches and evaluating the constructivist approaches. A review of these ideas is presented in summary table 9.3. In the next chapter, we will explore the roles of planning, instruction, and technology in teaching and learning.

*M*eaning *is not given to us but by us.*

Eleanor Duckworth
Contemporary American Educator

Summary Table 9.3
Domain-Specific Constructivist Approaches, and Evaluating the Constructivist Approaches

Concept	Processes/ Related Ideas	Characteristics/Description
Domain-Specific Approaches	Reading	• Cognitive approaches to reading emphasize meaning, decoding and comprehending words, and developing strategies. Text has meaning that the reader must actively construct. Metacognitive strategies and both automatic and effortful processes are involved in decoding and comprehending words. The ability to manipulate and think about sounds also is important. Transactional strategy instruction is one approach to helping students learn to read. • Social constructivist approaches to reading stress that (1) the social context plays an important part in reading and (2) knowledgeable readers in the culture teach less-knowledgeable ones. Meaning is socially negotiated. Reciprocal teaching is a valuable technique in helping students improve their reading. Book clubs and school/family/community connections also reflect the social constructivist perspective.
	Writing	• Cognitive constructivist approaches to writing emphasize many of the same themes as for reading, such as constructing meaning and developing strategies. Problem-solving and metacognitive strategies are thought to be especially important. • Social constructivist approaches to writing focus on the social context in which writing is produced. This social context includes the importance of students participating in a writing community to understand author/reader relationships and taking perspectives of others. Social constructivist approaches to writing include writing "real texts" about meaningful experiences, teacher-student writing conferences, peer collaboration in writing, and school/family/community connections.
	Mathematics	• Children have a substantial understanding of numerical concepts before they enter first grade. When they go to school, children learn many more advanced kinds of numerical skills.
	Controversy in Math Education	• Currently, there is controversy in math education about whether it should be more cognitive or more practical.
	Some Constructivist Principles	• Reforms focus on making math education more meaningful, making connections to prior knowledge, and discussing math concepts with others.
	Innovative Math Projects	• We discussed innovative math curriculum projects, technology, connecting with parents, and continuing to be a learner yourself.
	Science	• Children's thinking skills share certain characteristics with those of scientists, but also differ in some ways. • With an emphasis on hands-on laboratory investigations and discovery learning, many science classrooms have a constructivist orientation. We discussed the Human Biology Middle Grades Curriculum (HUMBIO), and controversy about the sequence of science courses in high school.
Evaluating the Constructivist Approaches	The Controversy	• Many contemporary educational psychologists are enthusiastic about the constructivist approaches that portray the child as an active constructor of meaning. However, some critics say the constructivist approaches do not adequately teach content, are relativistic, and are vague.

Chapter Review

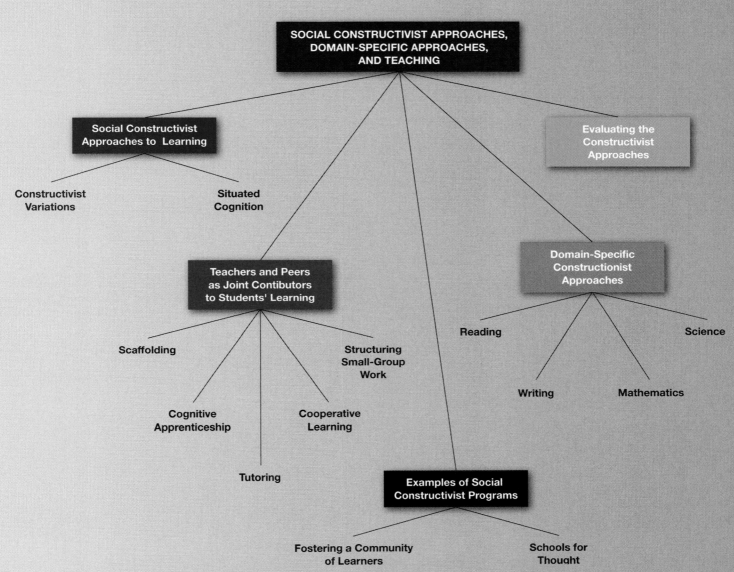

TO OBTAIN A DETAILED REVIEW OF THIS CHAPTER, STUDY THESE THREE SUMMARY TABLES:

Key Terms

Educational Psychology Checklist
SOCIAL CONSTRUCTIVIST APPROACHES, DOMAIN-SPECIFIC APPROACHES, AND TEACHING

How much have you learned since the beginning of this chapter? Use the following statements to help you review your knowledge and understanding of the chapter material. First, read the statement and mentally or briefly demonstrate on paper that you understand and can discuss the relevant information.

_____ I can define the social constructivist approaches in education and know what situated cognition means.
_____ I am aware of the different ways teachers and peers can both contribute to students' learning.
_____ I can explain how to structure small-group work for students.
_____ I can describe examples of social constructivist programs in education.
_____ I can discuss some constructivist approaches to teaching reading.

_____ I can profile the main components of constructivist approaches to writing.
_____ I know some constructivist approaches to teaching math.
_____ I can describe the strategies involved in teaching science from a constructivist perspective.
_____ I can evaluate the constructivist approaches and understand their strengths and weaknesses.

For any items that you did not check off, go back and locate the relevant material in the chapter. Review the material until you feel that you can check off the item. You may want to use this checklist later in preparing for an exam.

Adventures for the Mind

Now that you have good knowledge and understanding of the chapter, complete the following exercises to expand your thinking about the chapter's contents.

Kindergarten
Elementary school
Middle school
High school

• How much have you experienced various social constructivist approaches in your education? Think about your different levels of schooling (early childhood, elementary, middle, high school, and college) and evaluate your experience (or lack of experience) with scaffolding, cognitive apprenticeship, tutoring, and cooperative learning.
• How effectively do you think social constructivist strategies (scaffolding, cognitive apprenticeship, tutoring, and cooperative learning) can be used at each of these grades?

• With four or five other students in the class, discuss how much of the curriculum should include group activities and how much should involve individual activities at the levels of schooling listed above.
   Also discuss whether some subject areas might lend themselves better than others to group activities. Evaluate whether some children might benefit more than others from group work.
• We listed several phone numbers for constructivist math programs. Call one of these numbers to find out more about the particular math program or log on to the Internet and try to find information about other innovative math programs.

Taking It to the Net

1. Can you learn how to teach by taking classes in a college or university setting? Or, must one be in the classroom in order to learn how to teach? Why, or why not?
2. Examine the basic tenets of constructivism. How should one teach if one accepts the premises of constructivism?

3. Constructivism, while embraced by many teachers and theorists, is not supported by all. Can you think of two arguments against constructivism? What would they be?

   Connect to http://www.mhhe.com/socscience/psychology/santedu/ttnet.htm to find the answers!

Case Studies

Case 1   *Frank Oakley:* Frank finds that it can be a little complicated to use pairing as a collaborative technique in science class.

Case 2   *Elizabeth Rhodes:* Elizabeth is frustrated by her advanced-placement students, who want to work only for solutions to problems and do not want to apply higher-order reasoning skills. The students resist cooperative learning groups and problem-solving activities.

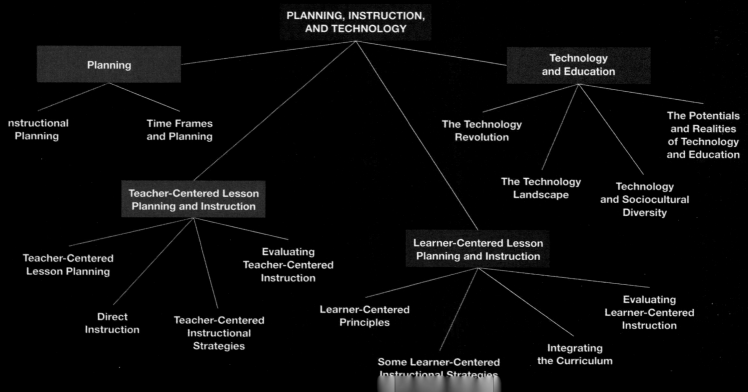

PLANNING, INSTRUCTION, AND TECHNOLOGY

Planning

nstructional Planning

Time Frames and Planning

Teacher-Centered Lesson Planning and Instruction

Teacher-Centered Lesson Planning

Evaluating Teacher-Centered Instruction

Direct Instruction

Teacher-Centered Instructional Strategies

Learner-Centered Lesson Planning and Instruction

Learner-Centered Principles

Evaluating Learner-Centered Instruction

Some Learner-Centered Instructional Strategies

Integrating the Curriculum

Technology and Education

The Technology Revolution

The Potentials and Realities of Technology and Education

The Technology Landscape

Technology and Sociocultural Diversity

Planning, Instruction, and Technology

"*Education* is the transmission of civilization."

Ariel and Will Durant
American Authors and Philosophers, 20th Century

Preview

In this chapter, we will examine teaching and learning primarily at the level of the overall lesson or unit, often making use of the various learning principles discussed in chapters 7 to 9. We especially will focus on teacher-centered lesson planning and learner-centered lesson planning. We also will study many dimensions of incorporating technology into lesson planning and instruction. Some central questions we will examine in this chapter are these:

- What are the most effective ways to plan for the school year, term, unit, week, and day?
- What objectives should you keep in mind when planning lessons?
- What are the best strategies for posing questions to students?
- How should homework be handled at different grade levels?
- What strategies should be followed in learner-centered planning and instruction?
- How can the curriculum be integrated?
- What are some guidelines for choosing and using technology?

Teaching Stories
Sandy Agle

Sandy Agle is an elementary school teacher and media specialist at Franklin Park Magnet School in Fort Myers, Florida. She talks about how her school is incorporating technology into classrooms:

> It has long been recognized in elementary education that a hands-on, multisensory approach is the best way to teach the broadest range of students. To this end, we attempted to create a multimedia experience for students in a classroom setting.

Each teacher is provided with an electronic teaching center, or workstation. The computer workstation is comprised of an overhead projector and LCD (liquid crystal display) projection panel, which allows full classroom orientation. Individual stand-alone student computer stations also have been distributed to each classroom. One room in the school also has been designated as a computer lab and it has 30 computers. Students are given weekly individualized instruction here. Electronic mail (e-Mail) is provided throughout the school, giving staff and students immediate access to shared information and communication.

FPM News is broadcast live each morning from the school's TV studio. Teams of fifth-grade students rotate each week among the jobs of sound technician, camcorder personnel, or news anchors. Recently, a new feature on the program called "Mystery Staff Baby Photo" was implemented. Students took still-video shots of faculty baby photos and aired them daily on the news show. Clues were given as to the identity of the faculty member and a prize was awarded at the end of the week to the student who had the most correct guesses.

Telecommunication through modems is another example of how technology is used at the school. Fifth-graders have computer pen pals in Russia and recently shipped out a videotape of Franklin Park Magnet School to their "unseen communicators." The tape was produced by students on the school grounds.

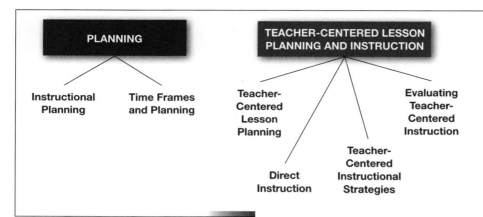

Planning

It has been said that when people fail to plan, they plan to fail. Many successful people attribute their accomplishments to effective planning. For example, Lee Iacocca (1984), former chairman of Chrysler Corporation, credits his success to his weekly planner. Our introduction to planning describes what instructional planning is and time frames of planning.

Instructional Planning

Planning is a critical aspect of being a competent teacher (Parkay & Mass, 2000). **Instructional planning** *involves developing a systematic, organized strategy for planning lessons.* Teachers need to decide what and how they are going to teach before they do it (Freiberg & Driscoll, 2000). Although some wonderful instructional moments are spontaneous, lessons still should be carefully planned.

It might seem tedious to spend so much time writing out lesson plans. However, they will give you confidence, guide you in covering the most important topics, and keep you from wasting precious class time.

Instructional planning might be mandated by the school in which you teach. Many principals and instructional supervisors require teachers to keep written plans, and in some cases you might be asked to submit lesson plans several weeks in advance. When observing classroom teachers, supervisors may refer to the plan to see if the teacher is following it. If a teacher is absent but has created a plan, a substitute teacher can follow the plan.

Time Frames and Planning

Developing systematic time plans involves knowing what needs to be done and when to do it, or focusing on "task" and "time." Here is one helpful six-part task and time plan (Douglass & Douglass, 1993):

What Needs to Be Done

1. *Set instructional goals* (What do I expect to accomplish?)
2. *Plan activities* (What do I have to do to reach the goals?)
3. *Set priorities* (Which tasks are more important than others?)

The Time to Do It

4. *Make time estimates* (How much time will each activity take?)
5. *Create schedules* (When will we do each activity?)
6. *Be flexible* (How will I handle unexpected occurrences?)

You will need to plan for different time spans, ranging from yearly to daily planning (Arends, 1998). If schoolwide planning or your own career planning are involved, the time frame likely will be a number of years.

Robert Yinger (1980) identified five time frames of teacher planning: yearly planning, term planning, unit planning, weekly planning, and daily planning. Figure 10.1 illustrates these time frames and shows planning for them. Yinger also

If you plan the day's transactions and follow that plan, you carry the thread that will guide you through the maze of the busiest life. But if you make no plan, chaos will reign.

Victor Hugo
French Novelist and Playwright, 19th Century

Planning Lessons
Topics for Planning

recommends that teachers attend to four areas when planning: goals, sources of information, form of the plan, and criteria for the effectiveness of the planning. Figure 10.2 shows what is involved in these areas across the five different time frames.

Although planning is a key dimension of successful teaching, don't overplan to the point of becoming an automaton. Develop organized plans and try to carry them out, but be flexible; as a year, month, week, or day unfolds, adapt to changing circumstances. A controversial current event or necessary topic might emerge that you did not originally include. Monitor and rework your plans as the school year goes by to suit these changing circumstances.

If you plan effectively, you won't have to keep all of the details of a lesson in mind all of the time (Middleton & Goepfert, 1996). Your plan lets you focus on the immediate dialogue you are having with students and guides the interactive aspect of your instruction.

Many teachers rely heavily on published teachers' guides or textbook structures to direct their instructional planning. This can have positive benefits because, with activities or lessons developed for the entire time, you can focus more on the day-to-day aspects of teaching. However, you might want to go into greater depth about some topics and develop larger projects for the entire term than are included in the teachers' guides.

Planning and instruction should be closely linked (Burden & Byrd, 1999). Next, we will explore teacher-centered planning and instruction, followed by learner-centered planning and instruction.

THROUGH THE EYES OF TEACHERS
Preventing Panic

The one thing that has helped me to become a better planner is learning to think ahead. Begin the year by coming up with general long-term plans for each subject area. This strategy will help you decide how much time to spend on certain things. Knowing what is coming next helps to provide structure and focus within your plans. It also helps to prevent the "panic" of deciding at the last minute what you have to teach. I have found that the earlier I have made my plans and gathered my materials, the more relaxed and confident I feel during the week.

Vicky Stone
Reading Teacher
Cammack Middle School
Huntington, West Virginia

You've got to be careful if you don't know where you are going because you might not get there.

Yogi Berra
American Baseball Star, 20th Century

Lesson Plans in
Different Subject Areas

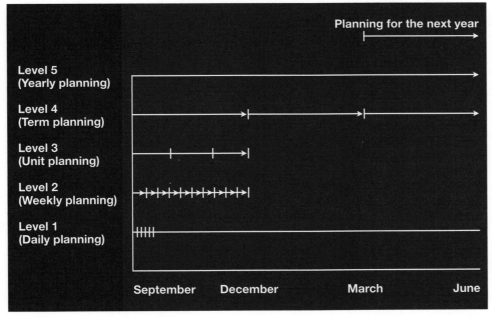

Figure 10.1
Five Time Spans of Teacher Planning and Their Occurrence over the School Year

	GOALS OF PLANNING	SOURCES OF INFORMATION	FORM OF THE PLAN	CRITERIA FOR JUDGING THE EFFECTIVENESS OF PLANNING
Yearly planning	1. Establishing general content (fairly general and framed by district curriculum objectives) 2. Establishing basic curriculum sequence 3. Ordering and reserving materials	1. Students (general information about numbers and returning students) 2. Resources available 3. Curriculum guidelines (district objectives) 4. Experience with specific curricula and materials	General outlines listing basic content and possible ideas in each subject matter area (spiral notebook used for each subject)	1. Comprehensiveness of plans 2. Fit with own goals and district objectives
Term planning	1. Detailing of content to be covered in next 3 months 2. Establishing a weekly schedule for term that conforms to teacher's goals and emphases for the term	1. Direct contact with students 2. Time constraints set by school schedule 3. Resources available	1. Elaboration of outlines constructed for yearly planning 2. A weekly schedule outline specifying activities and times	1. Outlines—comprehensiveness, completeness, and specificity of elaborations 2. Schedule—comprehensiveness and fit with goals for term, balance 3. Fit with goals for term
Unit planning	1. Developing a sequence of well-organized learning experiences 2. Presenting comprehensive, integrated, and meaningful content at an appropriate level	1. Students' abilities, interests, etc. 2. Materials, length of lessons, set-up time, demand, format 3. District objectives 4. Facilities available for activities	1. Lists of outlines of activities and content 2. Lists of sequenced activities 3. Notes in plan book	1. Organization, sequence, balance, and flow of outlines 2. Fit with yearly and term goals 3. Fit with anticipated student interest and involvement
Weekly planning	1. Laying out the week's activities within the framework of the weekly schedule 2. Adjusting schedule for interruptions and special needs 3. Maintaining continuity and regularity of activities	1. Students' performance in preceding days and weeks 2. Scheduled school interruptions (for example, assemblies, holidays) 3. Materials, aides, and other resources	1. Names and times of activities in plan book 2. Day divided into four instructional blocks punctuated by A.M. recess, lunch, and P.M. recess	1. Completeness of plans 2. Degree to which weekly schedule had been followed 3. Flexibility of plans to allow for special time constraints or interruptions 4. Fit with goals
Daily planning	1. Setting up and arranging classroom for next day 2. Specifying activity components not yet decided upon 3. Fitting daily schedule to last-minute intrusions 4. Preparing students for day's activities	1. Instructions in materials to be used 2. Set-up time required for activities 3. Assessment of class "disposition" at start of day 4. Continued interest, involvement, and enthusiasm	1. Schedule for day written on the chalkboard and discussed with students 2. Preparation and arrangement of materials and facilities in the room	1. Completion of last-minute preparations and decisions about content, materials, etc. 2. Involvement, enthusiasm, and interest communicated by students

Figure **10.2**

Five Time Spans of Teacher Planning and the Activities Involved

Teacher-Centered Lesson Planning and Instruction

Traditionally, the focus in schools has been on teacher-centered lesson planning and instruction. In this approach, planning and instruction are highly structured and the teacher directs students' learning.

Teacher-Centered Lesson Planning

Teacher-centered planning includes creating behavioral objectives, analyzing tasks, and developing instructional taxonomies (classifications).

Resources for Teacher Planning

Creating Behavioral Objectives   **Behavioral objectives** *are statements that communicate proposed changes in students' behavior to reach desired levels of performance.* In Robert Mager's (1962) view, behavioral objectives should be very specific and clearly communicated. Mager believes that behavioral objectives should have three parts:

- *Student's behavior.* Focus on what the student will learn or do. Describe activities as observable behaviors.
- *Conditions under which the behavior will occur.* State how the behaviors will be evaluated or tested.
- *Performance criteria.* Determine what level of performance will be acceptable.

For example, a behavioral objective of describing five causes of the decline of the British Empire might be developed (student's behavior). The teacher gives the student an essay test on this topic (conditions under which the behavior will occur). And explaining four or five causes is considered to be acceptable performance (performance criterion).

Task Analysis   Another key aspect of teacher-centered planning is **task analysis,** *which focuses on breaking down a complex task that students are to learn into its component parts* (Alberto & Troutman, 1996). A basic framework for analyzing tasks involves these steps (Moyer & Dardig, 1978):

1. Determine what skills or concepts the student needs to have to learn the task. For example, in teaching students the basic strategies for solving multiplication problems, ask yourself what skills or concepts students need to know to successfully solve the problems.
2. List any materials that will be required to perform the task, such as paper, pencil, calculator, and so on.
3. List all of the components of the task in the order in which they must be performed.

Instructional Taxonomies   Teacher-centered approaches have involved the development of instructional taxonomies. A **taxonomy** *is a classification system.* **Bloom's taxonomy** *was developed by Benjamin Bloom and his colleagues (1956). It consists of educational objectives in three domains: cognitive, affective, and psychomotor.*

The Cognitive Domain   Bloom's cognitive taxonomy has six objectives (Bloom & others, 1956):

- *Knowledge.* Students have the ability to remember information. For example, an objective might be to *list* or *describe* four main advantages of using a computer for word processing.

- *Comprehension.* Students understand the information and can explain it in their own words. For example, an objective might be to *explain* or *discuss* how a computer can effectively be used for word processing.
- *Application.* Students use knowledge to solve real-life problems. For example, an objective might be to *apply* what has been learned about using a computer for word processing to how this could be used in various careers.
- *Analysis.* Students break down complex information into smaller parts and relate information to other information. For example, an objective might be to *compare* one type of word-processing program with another for doing term papers.
- *Synthesis.* Students combine elements and create new information. For example, an objective might be to *organize* all that has been learned about the use of computers for writing.
- *Evaluation.* Students make good judgments and decisions. For example, an objective might be to *critique* different word-processing programs or to *judge* the strengths and weaknesses of a particular word-processing program.

When Bloom originally presented his taxonomy, he described these six cognitive objectives as hierarchically arranged from *lower-level* (knowledge, comprehension) to *higher-level* (application, analysis, synthesis, evaluation), with higher-level objectives building on the lower ones. However, educators often strip the objectives of their level and simply use them as a comprehensive way of considering different cognitive goals.

Bloom's cognitive objectives can be used when planning assessment. True/false, matching, multiple-choice, and short-answer items are often used to assess knowledge and comprehension. Essay questions, class discussions, projects, and portfolios are especially good for assessing application, analysis, synthesis, and evaluation.

The Affective Domain   The affective taxonomy consists of five objectives related to emotional responses to tasks (Krathwohl, Bloom, & Masia, 1964). Each of the five objectives requires the student to show some degree of commitment or emotional intensity:

- *Receiving.* Students become aware of or attend to something in the environment. For example, a guest comes to class to talk with students about reading. An objective might be for students to listen carefully to the speaker.
- *Responding.* Students become motivated to learn and display a new behavior as a result of an experience. An objective might be for students to become motivated to become better readers as a result of the guest speaker's appearance.
- *Valuing.* Students become involved in or committed to some experience. An objective might be for students to value reading as an important skill.
- *Organizing.* Students integrate a new value into an already existing set of values and give it proper priority. An objective might be to have students participate in a book club.
- *Value characterizing.* Students act in accordance with the value and are firmly committed to it. An objective might be that over the course of the school year, students increasingly value reading.

The Psychomotor Domain   Most of us link motor activity with physical education and athletics, but many other subjects, such as handwriting and word processing, also involve movement. In the sciences, students have to manipulate complex equipment; the visual and manual arts require good hand-eye coordination. Bloom's psychomotor objectives include these:

- *Reflex movements.* Students respond involuntarily without conscious thought to a stimulus. For example, students blink when an object unexpectedly hurtles their way.
- *Basic fundamentals.* Students make basic voluntary movements that are directed toward a particular purpose. For example, students grasp a microscope knob and correctly turn it.

- *Perceptual abilities.* Students use their senses, such as seeing, hearing, or touching, to guide their skill efforts. For example, students watch how to hold an instrument in science, such as a microscope, and listen to instructions on how to use it.
- *Physical abilities.* Students develop general skills of endurance, strength, flexibility, and agility. For example, students demonstrate an ability to run long distances or hit a softball.
- *Skilled movements.* Students perform complex physical skills with some degree of proficiency. For example, students effectively sketch a drawing.
- *Nondiscussive.* Students communicate feelings and emotions through bodily actions. For example, students do pantomimes or dance to communicate a musical piece.

Bloom's taxonomies for the cognitive, affective, and psychomotor domains can be used by teachers to plan instruction. In the past, instructional planning has generally focused on cognitive or behavioral objectives. Bloom's taxonomy provides for a more expansive consideration of skills by also including affective and psychomotor domains. Figure 10.3 presents Bloom's domains and lists associated action verbs you can use for creating objectives during instructional planning.

Direct Instruction

Direct instruction *is a structured, teacher-centered approach that is characterized by teacher direction and control, high teacher expectations for students' progress, maximizing the time students spend on academic tasks, and efforts by the teacher to keep negative affect to a minimum* (Joyce & Weil, 1996). The focus of direct instruction is academic activity; nonacademic materials (such as toys, games, and puzzles) tend not to be used; also deemphasized is nonacademically oriented teacher-student interaction (such as questions about self or personal concerns).

Teacher direction and control take place when the teacher chooses students' learning tasks, directs students' learning of the tasks, and minimizes the amount of nonacademic talk. The teacher sets high standards for performance and expects students to reach these levels of excellence.

An important goal in the direct instruction approach is maximizing student learning time (Stevenson, 2000). Learning takes time. The more time students spend on learning tasks, the more likely they are to learn the material and achieve high standards. The direct instruction

Bloom's Taxonomy

COGNITIVE DOMAIN	
Category	**Associated Verbs**
Knowledge	*List, read, identify, define, indicate, describe, name, quote, underline*
Comprehension	*Translate, transform, summarize, paraphrase, illustrate, interpret, estimate, interpolate, extrapolate, classify, categorize, re-organize, explain, predict*
Application	*Apply, generalize, relate, use, employ, transfer, graph, exemplify, illustrate, tabulate, calculate, compute, derive, calibrate*
Analysis	*Analyze, contrast, compare, distinguish, detect, edit, discriminate*
Synthesis	*Produce, constitute, modify, originate, propose, plan, design, combine, organize, synthesize, develop, formulate*
Evaluation	*Judge, argue, validate, predict, assess, decide, appraise, conclude, evaluate, explain, criticize*
AFFECTIVE DOMAIN	
Category	**Associated Verbs**
Receiving Responding	*Accept, differentiate, listen, separate, select, share, agree*
Valuing	*Approve, applaud, comply, follow, discuss, volunteer, practice, spend time with, paraphrase*
Organizing	*Argue, debate, deny, help, support, protest, participate, subsidize, praise*
Value Characterizing	*Discuss, compare, balance, define, abstract, formulate, theorize, organize*
	Change, avoid, complete, manage, resolve, revise, resist, require
PSYCHOMOTOR DOMAIN	
Category	**Associated Verbs**
Reflex Movements	*Blink, stretch, relax, jerk, straighten up*
Basic Fundamentals Perceptual Abilities	*Walk, run, jump, push, pull, manipulate, catch, grasp, stand*
Physical Abilities	*Follow, dodge, maintain, identify, read, write, list, balance, trace, brush, print, pronounce*
Skilled Movements	*Hop, skip, jump, run, touch, lift, push, pull, tap, float, hit, throw, toss, strum*
Nondiscussive	*Draw, dance, ski, skate, paint, build, volley, race, whistle, march, somersault, hammer, sculpt, sketch*
	Pantomime, mimic, direct, perform, communicate, gesture, use body movement

Figure **10.3**

Action Verbs for Writing Objectives in the Cognitive, Affective, and Psychomotor Domains

DIVERSITY AND EDUCATION
Cross-Cultural Comparisons in Learning Math and Math Instruction

The University of Michigan's Harold Stevenson is one of the leading experts on children's learning and has been conducting research on this topic for five decades. In the 1980s and 1990s, he has turned his attention to discovering ways to improve children's learning by conducting cross-cultural comparisons of children in the United States with children in Asian countries, especially Japan, China, and Taiwan (Stevenson, 1992, 1995, 2000; Stevenson & Hofer, 1999; Stevenson & others, 1990). In Stevenson's research, Asian students consistently outperform American students in mathematics. Also, the longer students are in school, the wider the gap becomes—the lowest difference is in first grade, the highest in eleventh grade (the highest grade studied).

To learn more about the reasons for these cross-cultural differences, Stevenson and his colleagues spent thousands of hours observing in classrooms, as well as interviewing and surveying teachers, students, and parents. They found that Asian teachers spent more of their time teaching math than American teachers did. For example, in Japan more than one-fourth of the total classroom time in first grade was spent on math instruction, compared with only one-tenth of the time in U.S. first-grade classrooms. Also, Asian students were in school an average of 240 days a year, compared to 178 days in the United States.

In addition to the substantially greater time spent on math instruction in Asian schools than in American schools, differences were found between Asian and American parents. American parents had much lower expectations for their children's education and achievement than Asian parents did. Also, American parents were more likely to believe that their children's math ability is due to innate ability, whereas Asian parents were more likely to say that their children's math achievement is the consequence of effort and training. Asian students were more likely than American students to do math homework, and Asian parents were far more likely to help their children with their math homework than American parents were (Chen & Stevenson, 1989).

In another cross-cultural comparison of math education, videotapes of eighth-grade teachers' instruction in the United States, Japan, and Germany were analyzed (Stigler & Hiebert, 1997, 1999). Differences among the countries included these: (1) Japanese students spent less time solving routine math problems and more time inventing, analyzing, and proving, than American or German students did; (2) Japanese teachers engaged in more direct lecturing than American or German teachers did; and (3) Japanese teachers were more likely to emphasize math thinking, whereas American and German teachers were more likely to stress math skills (solving a specific problem or using a specific formula). Also noticeable was how much emphasis there is on collaborative planning with other teachers in Japanese math education. We will have much more to say about cross-cultural comparisons in math and other subject areas in chapter 13, "Standardized Tests and Teaching." We will examine other research studies, explore the concept of "world-class standards" in education, and evaluate criticisms of cross-cultural studies of achievement.

Asian students score considerably higher than U.S. students on math achievement tests. What are some possible explanations for these findings?

Mathematics Learning in Asian and American Students

premise is that the best way to maximize time on academic tasks is to create a highly structured, academically oriented learning environment. Time spent by students on academic tasks in the classroom is called *academic learning time.* The Diversity and Education box describes cross-cultural research about the amount of time students spend on math in different countries, as well as other comparisons across countries.

Yet another emphasis in the direct instruction approach is to keep negative affect to a minimum. Researchers have found that negative affect interferes with learning (Rosenshine, 1971). Advocates of direct instruction underscore the importance of keeping an academic focus and avoiding negative affect, such as the negative affect that can give rise to and be aroused by a teacher's criticism of student performance.

Teacher-Centered Instructional Strategies

Teacher-centered strategies that reflect direct instruction include orienting students to new material; lecturing, explaining, and demonstrating; questioning, reciting, and discussing; mastery learning; seatwork; and homework.

Orienting   Before presenting and explaining new material, establish a framework for the lesson and orient students to the new material (Joyce & Weil, 1996): (1) Review the previous day's activities, (2) discuss the lesson's objective, (3) provide clear, explicit instructions about the work to be done, and (4) give an overview of today's lesson. Such orientation and structuring at the beginning of a lesson are linked with improved student achievement (Fisher & others, 1980).

Advance organizers *are teaching activities and techniques that establish a framework and orient students to material before it is presented* (Ausubel, 1960). You can use advance organizers when you begin a lesson to help students see the "big picture" of what is to come and how information is meaningfully connected.

Advance organizers come in two forms: expository and comparative (Mayer, 1984). **Expository advance organizers** *provide students with new knowledge that will orient them to the upcoming lesson.* The chapter-opening and within-chapter cognitive maps in this book are expository advance organizers. They provide you with new information about what you will study in the chapter and its main sections, and they are analogous to providing an overall outline of what a lesson will be about. Another way to provide an expository advance organizer is to describe the lesson's theme and why it is important to study this topic. For example, in orienting students to the topic of exploring the Aztec civilization in a history class, the teacher says that they are going to study the Spanish invasion of Mexico, who the Aztecs were, what their lives were like, and their artifacts. To heighten student interest, she also says that they will study worlds in collision as Spain's conquistadors were filled with an awe at sights of a spectacular Western civilization. There are Mexican American students in her class, and the teacher emphasizes how this information can help everyone in the class understand these students' personal and cultural identity.

Comparative advance organizers *introduce new material by connecting it with what students already know.* For example, in the history class just mentioned, the teacher says that the Spanish invasion of Mexico continues the transatlantic traffic that changed two worlds: Europe and the Americas. She asks students to think about how this discussion of the Aztecs connects with Columbus' journey, which they examined last week.

Lecturing, Explaining, and Demonstrating   Lecturing, explaining, and demonstrating are common teacher activities in the direct instruction approach. Researchers have found that effective teachers spend more time explaining and demonstrating new material than their less-effective counterparts do (Rosenshine, 1985).

On some occasions we sit through boring lectures, yet on other occasions we have been captivated by a lecturer and learned a great deal from the presentation.

Questioning and Discussing   It is necessary but challenging to integrate questions and discussion in teacher-centered instruction (Weinstein, 1997). In using these strategies, it is important to respond to each student's learning needs while maintaining the group's interest and attention. It also is important to distribute

TEACHING STRATEGIES
For Lecturing

Let's explore some guidelines for when lecturing is a good choice and some strategies for delivering an effective lecture. Following are some goals that lecturing can accomplish (Henson, 1988):

1. *Present information and motivate students' interest in a subject.*
2. *Introduce a topic before students read about it on their own, or give instructions on how to perform a task.*
3. *Summarize or synthesize information after a discussion or inquiry.*
4. *Provide alternative points of view or clarify issues in preparation for discussion.*
5. *Explain materials that students are having difficulty learning on their own.*

These are some good strategies to use when lecturing:

1. *Be prepared.* Don't just "wing" a lecture. Spend time preparing and organizing what you will present.
2. *Keep lectures short and intersperse them with questions and activities.* For example, a teacher might lecture for 10 or 15 minutes to provide the background information and framework for a topic, then place students in small discussion groups.
3. *Make the lecture interesting and exciting.* Think about what you can say that will motivate students' interest in a topic. Vary the pace of the lecture by interlacing it with related video clips, demonstrations, handouts, and/or activities for students.
4. *Follow a designed sequence and include certain key components:*
   a. Begin with advance organizers or previews of the topic.
   b. Verbally and visually highlight any key concepts or new ideas (like the boldfaced key terms in this book). Use the blackboard, an overhead projector, or other large-display device.
   c. Present new information in relation to what students already know about the topic.
   d. Periodically elicit student responses to ensure that they understand the information up to that point and to encourage active learning.
   e. At the end of the lecture, provide a summary or overview of the main ideas.
   f. Make connections to future lectures or activities.

I keep six honest serving people. They taught me everything I know. Their names are: What and Why and When and How and Where and Who.

Rudyard Kipling
English Novelist, 20th Century

participation widely while also retaining the enthusiasm of eager volunteers. An additional challenge is allowing students to contribute while still maintaining the focus on the lesson.

A special concern is that male students are more likely than female students to dominate the discussion. In one study of 10 high school geometry classes, males called out answers to the teacher twice as frequently as females did (Becker, 1981). Similar results were found in a study of 60 physical science and chemistry classes (Jones & Wheatley, 1990). Be sensitive to gender patterns and ensure that girls get equal discussion time.

Mastery Learning
Mastery learning *involves learning one concept or topic thoroughly before moving on to a more difficult one.* A successful mastery learning approach involves these procedures (Bloom, 1971; Carroll, 1963):

- Specify the learning task or lesson. Develop precise instructional objectives. Establish mastery standards (this typically is where "A" students perform).
- Break the course into learning units that are aligned with instructional objectives.
- Plan instructional procedures to include corrective feedback to students if they fail to master the material at an acceptable level, such as 90 percent correct. The corrective feedback might take place through supplemental materials, tutoring, or small-group instruction.
- Give an end-of-unit or end-of-course test that evaluates whether the student has mastered all of the material at an acceptable level.

TEACHING STRATEGIES

For the Effective Use of Questions

In chapter 8, we distinguished between fact-based questioning and thinking-based questioning (Sternberg & Spear-Swirling, 1996). Here we focus on effective strategies for using questions in the classroom.

1. *Use fact-based questions as entrées into thinking-based questions.* For example, in teaching a lesson on environmental pollution, the teacher might ask the fact-based question "What are three types of environmental pollution?" Then she could follow with this thinking-based question: "What strategies can you think of for reducing one of these types of environmental pollution?" Don't overuse fact-based questions, because they tend to produce rote learning rather than learning for understanding.

2. *Avoid yes/no and leading questions.* A yes/no question should be used only as a segue into a more probing question. For example, it is not a good strategy to ask a lot of questions like "Was environmental pollution responsible for the dead fish in the lake?" Keep these questions to a minimum, only occasionally using them as a warm-up for questions like these: "How did the pollution kill the fish?" "Why do you think companies polluted the lake?" "What can be done to clean up environmental pollution?"

   Asking leading questions such as "Don't you agree?" or other rhetorical questions such as "You do want to read more about environmental pollution, don't you?" is not a good strategy. These types of questions don't produce meaningful responses and simply hand the initiative back to the teacher (Grossier, 1964).

3. *Leave enough time for students to think about answers.* Too often when teachers ask questions, they don't give students enough time to think. In one study, teachers waited less than one second, on the average, before calling on a student to respond (Rowe, 1986)! In the same study, teachers waited only about one second, on the average, for the student to respond before supplying the answer themselves. Such intrusions don't give students adequate time to construct answers. In the study just mentioned, teachers were subsequently instructed to wait 3 to 5 seconds to allow students to respond to questions. The increased wait time led to considerable improvements in responses, including better inferences about the materials and more student-initiated questions. Waiting 3 to 5 seconds or more for students to respond is not as easy as it might seem; it takes practice. But your students will benefit considerably from having to think and construct responses.

4. *Ask clear, purposeful, brief, and sequenced questions.* Avoid being vague. Focus the questions on the lesson at hand. Plan ahead so that your questions are meaningfully tied to the topic. If your questions are long-winded, you run the risk that they will not be understood, so briefer is better. Also plan questions so that they follow a logical sequence, integrating them with previously discussed material before moving to the next topic (Grossier, 1964).

5. *Monitor how you respond to students' answers.* What should you do next after a student responds to your question? Many teachers just say "Okay" or "Uh-huh" (Sadker & Sadker, 1986). Usually it is wise to do more. You can use the student's response as a basis for follow-up questions and engage the student or other students in a dialogue. Provide feedback that is tailored to the student's existing level of knowledge and understanding.

6. *Be aware of when it is best to pose a question to the entire class or to a particular student.* Asking the entire class a question makes all students in the class responsible for responding. Asking a specific student a question can make other students less likely to answer it. Some reasons to ask a question to a particular student are (Grossier, 1964) (1) to draw an inattentive student into the lesson, (2) to ask a follow-up question of someone who has just responded, and (3) to call on someone who rarely responds when questions are asked to the class as a whole. Don't let a small group of assertive students dominate the responses. Talk with them independently about continuing their positive responses without monopolizing class time. One strategy for giving students an equal chance to respond is to pull names from a cookie jar or check names off a class list as students respond (Weinstein & Mignano, 1997).

7. *Encourage students to ask questions.* Praise them for good questions. Ask them "How?" and "Why?" and encourage them to ask "How?" and "Why?"

Mastery learning gets mixed reviews. Some researchers indicate that mastery learning is effective in increasing the time that students spend on learning tasks (Kulik & others, 1990), but others find less support for mastery learning (Bangert, Kulik, & Kulik, 1983). Outcomes of mastery learning depend on the teacher's skill in planning and executing the strategy. One context in which mastery learning might be

Mastery Learning

TEACHING STRATEGIES
For Using Seatwork

Following are some good guidelines for minimizing the problems that seatwork poses (Weinstein & Mignano, 1997):

1. *Check students' seatwork for clarity, meaningfulness, and appropriateness.* Seatwork often involves worksheets. Their layout should be attractive and functional. At least some of the worksheets should be fun to do.

2. *Describe seatwork assignments clearly.* Give students an introductory explanation of the seatwork and describe its purpose.

3. *Monitor students' behavior and comprehension.* Students can become bored and easily distracted during seatwork, especially if it goes on for a lengthy period. Thus, monitoring behavior during seatwork is crucial to its learning contribution. And it's not just enough for students to be busy and on-task, they also need to be actively engaged in learning something. One strategy is to spend the first 5 minutes circulating around the room. Once you feel confident that students understand what to do, convene the first small group. Then, after spending time with that group, you circulate some more, form a second group if desired, and so on.

4. *Teach students what to do if they get stuck.* Students need to know how and when they can ask for your help. Effective teachers often tell students not to disrupt them while they are working with a small group but rather to ask for help while the teacher circulates between small-group sessions. Some teachers develop special systems for help, such as a small red flag for students to keep on their desk and raise if they need assistance. You can tell students to skip the tasks that are troublesome and work on other tasks until you are available. You also need to make it clear to students whether it is okay to ask peers for assistance. Many teachers not only allow peer help, they actively encourage it.

5. *Tell students what to do when they are finished.* Provide enjoyable educational activities for students to engage in if they finish before the time allotted for seatwork is up. These activities might include working on a computer, doing free reading or journal writing, solving brainteasers and puzzles, or resuming work on long-term, ongoing projects.

6. *Search for alternatives to workbook pages.* Relying too much on commercially prepared workbook pages can induce boredom and off-task behavior. Spend some time creating seatwork that challenges your students to think reflectively, deeply, and creatively; don't bore them with trivial tasks. Alternatives to such common worksheet activities (such as fill-in-the-blanks) include reading, writing, doing ongoing projects, spending time in learning centers, working on a computer, and cross-age tutoring.

---

especially beneficial is remedial reading (Schunk, 1996). A well-organized mastery learning program for remedial reading allows students to progress at their own rates based on their skills, their motivation, and the time they have to learn.

Seatwork   *Seatwork* refers to the practice of having all or a majority of students work independently at their seats. Teachers vary in how much they use seatwork as part of their instruction. Some teachers use it every day, others rarely use it. Figure 10.4 summarizes the challenges of seatwork for the teacher and the student.

Learning centers are especially good alternatives to paper-and-pencil seatwork. Figure 10.5 provides some suggestions for learning centers. A computer station can be an excellent learning center. For example, in one classroom a teacher uses computer work rather than paper-and-pencil seatwork. Students identify acid rain patterns around the world with a National Geographic Society computer network, practice navigation and rescue whales with *Voyage of the Mimi* (Bank Street College, 1984), and learn about marine environments with *A Field Trip into the Sea* (In View, 1990). Two or three students work at each computer, which encourages collaborative learning.

Research on Homework

Homework   Another important instructional decision involves how much and what type of homework to give students. In the cross-cultural research discussed earlier in the chapter that focused on Asian and American students, the time students spent on homework also was examined (Chen & Stevenson, 1989). Asian students spent

FOR THE TEACHER	FOR THE STUDENT
1. Keeping track of what the rest of the class is doing	1. Completing assigned work on their own
2. Keeping students on task	2. Understanding how and when to obtain the teacher's help
3. Dealing with the varying paces at which students work ("ragged" endings)	3. Understanding the norms for assisting peers
4. Selecting or creating seatwork that is clear and meaningful	4. Learning how to be effective in obtaining help from peers
5. Matching seatwork to students' varying levels of achievement	
6. Collecting, correcting, recording, and returning seatwork assignments	

Figure **10.4**

Challenges of Seatwork for Teachers and Students

more time doing homework than American students did. For example, on weekends Japanese first-graders did an average of 66 minutes of homework, and American first-graders did only 18 minutes. Also, Asian students had a much more positive attitude about homework than American students did. And Asian parents were far more likely to help their children with their homework than American parents were.

Harris Cooper (1998; Cooper & others, 1998) recently analyzed more than a hundred research studies on homework in American schools and concluded that for elementary school students, the effects of homework on achievement are trivial, if they exist at all. In a recent study, Cooper (1998) collected data on 709 students in grades 2 through 4 and 6 through 12. In the lower grades, there was a significant negative relation between the amount of homework assigned and students' attitudes, suggesting that elementary school children resent having to do homework. But in grades 6 and higher, the more homework students completed, the higher their achievement. It is not clear what is cause and effect, though. Were really good students finishing more assignments because they were motivated and competent in academic subjects, or was completing homework assignments causing students to achieve more?

A key aspect of the debate about whether elementary school children should be assigned homework is the type of homework assigned (Begley, 1998). What is good homework? Especially for younger children, the emphasis should be on homework that fosters a love of learning and hones study skills. Short assignments that can be quickly completed should be the goal. With young children, long assignments that go uncompleted or completed assignments that bring a great deal of stress, tears, and tantrums should be avoided. Too often teachers assign homework that duplicates without reinforcing material that is covered in class. Homework should be an opportunity for students to engage in creative,

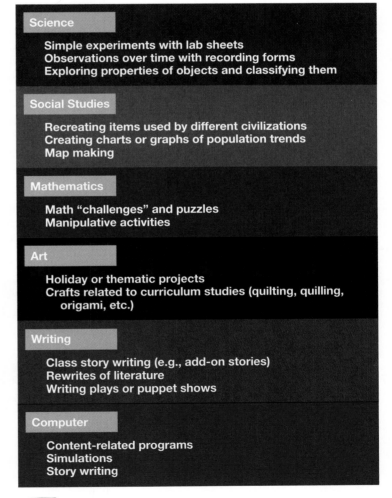

Science
Simple experiments with lab sheets
Observations over time with recording forms
Exploring properties of objects and classifying them

Social Studies
Recreating items used by different civilizations
Creating charts or graphs of population trends
Map making

Mathematics
Math "challenges" and puzzles
Manipulative activities

Art
Holiday or thematic projects
Crafts related to curriculum studies (quilting, quilling, origami, etc.)

Writing
Class story writing (e.g., add-on stories)
Rewrites of literature
Writing plays or puppet shows

Computer
Content-related programs
Simulations
Story writing

Figure **10.5**

Suggestions for Learning Centers

"I don't have my homework because my little brother put a Pop-Tart® in my disk drive!"

exploratory activities, such as doing an oral history of one's family or determining the ecological effects of neighborhood business. Instead of memorizing names, dates, and battles of the Civil War as a homework assignment, students might write fictional letters from a Northerner to a Southerner, expressing their feelings about the issues dividing the nation. The homework assignments should be linked to the next day's class activities to emphasize to students that homework has meaning and is not just a plot to make them miserable. Homework also should have a focus. Don't ask students to write an open-ended theme from a novel the class is reading. Rather, ask them to select a character and explain why she or he behaved in a particular way.

In Cooper's analysis of more than a hundred studies of homework, in middle school homework began to have a payoff. How can homework have little or no effect in elementary school, yet be so beneficial in middle and high school? In the higher grades, it is easier to assign imagined, focused, substantive homework that requires students to integrate and apply knowledge—the type of homework that promotes learning (Corno, 1998). Also, by high school, students have resigned themselves to the routine of homework. Working hard after school and having good study skills are more accepted by middle and high school students.

Some educational psychologists believe that the main reason homework has not been effective in elementary school is that it has focused too much on subject matter and not enough on developing attitudes toward school, persistence, and responsible completion of assignments (Corno, 1998). They believe that it is not homework per se that benefits students, but rather homework that provides opportunities and demands for the student to take responsibility. They think that teachers need to inform parents about guiding their children in these aspects of doing their homework: setting goals, managing their time, controlling their emotions, and checking their work, rather than playing avoidance games or leaving hard work for last. Teachers and parents can use homework in the early grades to help children wrestle with goal setting and follow-through.

Cooper (1989) also has found the following, about homework:

- Homework has more positive effects when it is distributed over a period of time rather than done all at once. For example, doing 10 math problems each night for five nights is recommended rather than doing 50 over the weekend.
- Homework effects are greater for math, reading, and English than for science and social studies.
- For middle school students, 1 or 2 hours of homework a night is optimal. High school students benefit from even more hours of homework, but it is unclear what a maximum number of hours ought to be.

Homework can be a valuable tool for increasing learning, especially in middle and high school. However, it is important to make homework meaningful, monitor it and give students feedback about it, and involve parents in helping their child with it. In chapter 3, "Social Contexts and Socioemotional Development," we described the importance of students doing "interactive homework" (Epstein, 1996, 1998)—homework that requires students to go to their parents for help 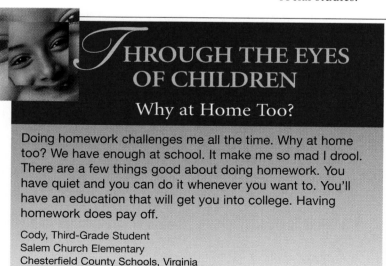 p. 93. In one elementary school, a weekly teacher's letter informs parents about the objectives of each homework assignment, gives them directions, and asks for comments. Think about setting up tutoring sessions for parents to help them interact effectively with their children in homework sessions.

THROUGH THE EYES OF CHILDREN

Why at Home Too?

Doing homework challenges me all the time. Why at home too? We have enough at school. It make me so mad I drool. There are a few things good about doing homework. You have quiet and you can do it whenever you want to. You'll have an education that will get you into college. Having homework does pay off.

Cody, Third-Grade Student
Salem Church Elementary
Chesterfield County Schools, Virginia

Evaluating Teacher-Centered Instruction

Research on teacher-centered instruction has contributed many valuable suggestions for teaching, including these:

- Be an organized planner and create instructional objectives.
- Have high expectations for students' progress and ensure that students have adequate academic learning time.
- Spend initial time orienting students to a lesson.
- Use lecturing, explaining, and demonstrating to benefit certain aspects of students' learning.
- Engage students in learning by developing good question-asking skills and getting them involved in class discussion.
- Have students do meaningful seatwork or alternative work to allow individualized instruction with a particular student or a small group.
- Give students meaningful homework to increase their academic learning time and involve parents in students' learning.

Advocates of the teacher-centered approach especially believe that it is the best strategy for teaching basic skills, which involve clearly structured knowledge and skills (such as those needed in English, reading, math, and science). Thus, in teaching basic skills, the teacher-centered approach might consist of a teacher explicitly or directly teaching grammar rules, reading vocabulary, math computations, and science facts (Rosenshine, 1986).

Teacher-centered instruction has not been without criticism. Critics say that teacher-centered instruction often leads to passive, rote learning and inadequate opportunities to construct knowledge and understanding, overly structured and rigid classrooms, inadequate attention to students' socioemotional development, external rather than internal motivation to learn, too much reliance on paper-and-pencil tasks, few opportunities for real-world learning, and too little collaborative learning in small groups. Such criticisms often are leveled by advocates of learner-centered planning and instruction, which we will turn to next.

At this point we have discussed a number of ideas about planning and teacher-centered lesson planning and instruction. A review of these ideas is presented in summary table 10.1.

What are some guidelines for assigning homework to students?

Learner-Centered Lesson Planning and Instruction

Just as the behavioral approaches described in chapter 7 provide the conceptual underpinnings for teacher-centered lesson planning and instruction, the cognitive information-processing and constructivist approaches, discussed in chapters 2, 8, and 9, form the theoretical backdrop for learner-centered lesson planning and instruction ◀▥ p. 59, 276, 320.

Learner-Centered Principles

Learner-centered lesson planning and instruction move the focus away from the teacher and toward the student. The increased interest in learner-centered principles of lesson planning and instruction resulted in the creation of the guidelines in *Learner-Centered Psychological Principles: A Framework for School Reform and Redesign*

SUMMARY TABLE 10.1
Planning, and Teacher-Centered Lesson Planning and Instruction

Concept	Processes/ Related Ideas	Characteristics/Description
Planning	Instructional Planning	• This involves developing a systematic, organized strategy of instruction that benefits students' learning.
	Time Frames and Planning	• Good planning addresses both task (setting instructional goals, planning activities, and setting priorities) and time (making time estimates, creating schedules, and being flexible). • You will need to make plans for different time frames, ranging from yearly planning to daily planning.
Teacher-Centered Lesson Planning and Instruction	Teacher-Centered Lesson Planning	• This includes creating behavioral objectives, analyzing tasks, and developing instructional taxonomies (classifications). • Behavioral objectives are statements that propose changes in students' behavior to reach desired performance levels. • Task analysis focuses on breaking down a complex task into its component parts. • Bloom's taxonomy consists of cognitive, affective, and psychomotor domains.
	Direct Instruction	• This approach is a structured, teacher-centered approach that involves teacher directions and control, high expectations for students' progress, maximizing the time students spend on academic tasks, and keeping negative affect to a minimum. • The use of nonacademic materials is deemphasized, as is nonacademically oriented teacher-student interaction.
	Teacher-Centered Instructional Strategies	• These include orienting students; lecturing, explaining, and demonstrating; questioning and discussion; mastery learning; seatwork; and homework. • Prior to presenting and explaining new material, establish a framework for the lesson. Advance organizers (expository or comparative) are a good way to do this. • Effective teachers spend more time explaining and demonstrating new material than their less-effective counterparts do. • Effective lectures have a number of features, including advance organizers, periodic elicitation of student responses, and summarizing. • Mastery learning refers to the idea of learning one concept or topic thoroughly before moving on to a more difficult one. • Teachers vary in how much they use seatwork as part of their instruction. • Researchers have found that the effects of homework on achievement are trivial, if they exist at all in American elementary schools. Homework has more positive effects in American middle school and high school. When homework is given, it is important to make it meaningful, monitor it, and give students feedback about it.
	Evaluating Teacher-Centered Instruction	• Teacher-centered instruction includes useful techniques and its advocates especially believe it is effective in improving children's basic skills. • Critics of teacher-centered instruction say that by itself it tends to lead to passive, rote learning, overly rigid and structured classrooms, inadequate attention to socioemotional development, external motivation, excess use of paper-and-pencil tasks, too few opportunities for real-world learning, and too little collaborative learning in small groups.

(Presidential Task Force on Psychology in Education, 1992; Work Group of the American Psychological Association's Board of Affairs, 1995; Learner-Centered Principles Work Group, 1997). They have been constructed and periodically revised by a prestigious group of scientists and educators from a wide range of disciplines and interests. These principles have important implications for the way teachers plan and instruct, as they are based on research on the most effective ways children learn.

The Learner-Centered Principles Work Group (1997) believes that research in psychology relevant to education has been especially informative in the last decade. Advances in our understanding of cognitive, motivational, and contextual aspects of learning can inform educators about the best ways to help children learn. The work group states that the learner-centered psychological principles they propose are widely shared and recognized in many excellent programs in today's schools. The learner-centered psychological principles provide a framework for developing and incorporating the components into new designs for schooling. The principles emphasize the active, reflective nature of learning and learners. From this perspective, education will benefit when the primary focus is on the learner.

The scope of the fourteen learner-centered principles involves cognitive and metacognitive factors (the nature of the learning process, goals of the learning process, the construction of knowledge, strategic thinking, thinking about thinking, and the context of learning), motivational and affective factors (motivational and emotional influences on learning, intrinsic motivation to learn, and effects of motivation on effort), developmental and social factors (developmental influences on learning and social influences on learning), and individual differences factors (individual differences in learning, learning and diversity, and standards and assessment). More in-depth information about each of the fourteen learner-centered psychological principles is presented in Figure 10.6.

**Learner-Centered
Psychological Principles**

Some Learner-Centered Instructional Strategies

We have already discussed a number of strategies that teachers can consider in developing learner-centered lesson plans. These especially include the teaching strategies based on the theories of Piaget and Vygotsky (chapter 2), constructivist aspects of thinking (chapter 8), and cognitive and social cognitive approaches (chapter 9). To provide you with a further sense of learner-centered strategies that you can incorporate into your lesson planning, we will elaborate here on the topic of problem-based learning (which was initially described in chapter 8), and examine two other strategies: essential questions and discovery learning.

Problem-Based Learning   *Problem-based learning* emphasizes real-life problem solving. A problem-based curriculum exposes students to authentic problems like those that crop up in everyday life (Jones, Rasmussen, & Moffitt, 1997).

Problem-based learning is a learner-centered approach. The content and nature of planning and instruction in problem-based learning is very different from that in the teacher-centered approach. In problem-based learning, planning and instruction focus on a problem to be solved through small-group discussion (rather than lecture, or after a short lecture or presentation). Students identify issues that they wish to explore, proceeding to locate materials and resources they need to solve the problem. Teachers act as guides, helping students to monitor their own problem-solving efforts.

One example of problem-based learning involves a project developed by Delamie Thompson, Paul Gilvary, and Mary Moffitt of Gladstone Elementary School, an inner-city school in Chicago (Jones, Rasmussen, & Moffitt, 1997). The purpose of the project is to involve the sixth-grade students in an authentic problem-solving context in which they explore the causes, incidence, and treatment of a health problem in the local community: asthma and its related conditions. Students learn how environmental conditions affect their health and share this understanding with others. The project integrates information from many subject areas, including health, science, math, and the social sciences.

Cognitive and Metacognitive Factors

1.   The Nature of the Learning Process

The learning of complex subject matter is most effective when it is an intentional process of constructing meaning from information and experience.

There are many different types of learning processes, such as habit formation in motor learning, learning that involves the generation of knowledge or cognitive skills. Earlier in this chapter, this was apparent in our exploration of Bloom's taxonomy, which focused on the cognitive domain, the affective domain, and the psychomotor domain. Strategies are especially important in the development of cognitive skills. We examined strategies in chapter 8, "The Cognitive Information-Processing Approach and Teaching" ◀lll p. 277. Learning in schools should emphasize the use of intentional processes that students can use to construct meaning from information, experiences, and their own thoughts and beliefs. Successful learners are active, goal-directed, and self-regulating, and they assume personal responsibility for contributing to their own learning. These are themes that we emphasized in a number of chapters in the book so far and will continue to emphasize in the remaining chapters. The following principles focus on this type of learning.

2.   Goals of the Learning Process

Successful learners, over time and with support and instructional guidance, can create meaningful, coherent representations of knowledge.

The strategic nature of learning means that students need to be goal-directed. To construct useful representations of knowledge and to acquire the learning and thinking strategies needed for continued learning throughout the life span, students need to generate and pursue personally relevant goals. Initially, students' short-term goals and learning might be sketchy in an area, but over time their understanding can be refined by filling gaps, resolving inconsistencies, and deepening their understanding of the subject matter so that they can reach longer-term goals. Educators can help learners create meaningful learning goals that are consistent with both personal and educational aspirations and interests. We will discuss goal setting and planning further in chapter 11, "Motivating Students to Learn."

3.   The Construction of Knowledge

Successful learners can link new information with existing knowledge in meaningful ways.

Knowledge widens and deepens as students continue to build links between new information and experiences in their existing knowledge base. These links can take a variety of forms, such as adding to, modifying, or reorganizing existing knowledge or skills. How these links are made or develop can vary in different subject areas, and among students with varying talents, interests, and abilities. However, unless new knowledge becomes integrated with the learner's prior knowledge and understanding, this new knowledge remains isolated, cannot be used most effectively in new tasks, and does not transfer readily to new situations. Recall our discussion of transfer in chapter 8 ◀lll p. 305. Educators can help learners acquire and integrate knowledge by a number of strategies that have been shown to be effective with learners of varying abilities, such as concept mapping, thematic organization, and categorizing. In chapter 8 we also discussed these aspects of successful learners.

4.   Strategic Thinking

Successful learners can create and use a repertoire of thinking and reasoning strategies to achieve complex learning goals.

Successful learners use strategic thinking in their approach to learning, reasoning, problem solving, and concept learning. They understand and can use a variety of strategies to help them reach learning and performance goals, and to apply their knowledge in novel situations. They also continue to expand their repertoire of strategies by reflecting on the methods they use to see which work well for them, by receiving guided instruction and feedback, and by observing or interacting with appropriate models. Learning outcomes can be improved if educators help learners develop, apply, and assess their strategic learning skills. We explored strategies in chapter 8 and the importance of observing competent models in chapter 7, "Behavioral Approaches, Social Cognitive Approaches, and Teaching" ◀lll p. 257, 277.

Figure **10.6**
Learner-Centered Psychological Principles

5. **Thinking About Thinking**

   Higher-order strategies for selecting and monitoring mental operations facilitate creative and critical thinking.

   Successful learners can reflect on how they learn and think, set reasonable learning or performance goals, select potentially appropriate learning strategies or methods, and monitor their progress toward these goals. In addition, successful learners know what to do if a problem occurs or if they are not making sufficient or timely progress toward a goal. They can generate alternative methods to reach their goal (or reassess the appropriateness and utility of the goal). Instructional methods that focus on helping learners develop these higher-order (metacognitive) strategies can enhance student learning and personal responsibility for learning. We examined metacognition in chapter 8 and self-regulatory skills in chapter 7. ◀⫶⫶ p. 265, 311.

6. **The Context of Learning**

   Learning is influenced by environmental factors, including culture, technology, and instructional practices.

   Learning does not occur in a vacuum. Teachers play a major interactive role with both the learner and the learning environment. Cultural or group influences on students can impact many educationally relevant variables, such as motivation, orientation toward learning, and ways of thinking. Technologies and instructional practices must be appropriate for learners' level of prior knowledge, cognitive abilities, and their learning and thinking strategies. The classroom environment, especially the degree to which it is nurturing or not, also can have a significant impact on student learning. We have discussed cultural influences throughout the book. For example, earlier in this chapter you read about Harold Stevenson's cross-cultural research on math achievement ◀⫶⫶ p. 360. In chapter 9, "Social Constructivist Approaches, Domain-Specific Approaches, and Teaching," we examined the concept of situated cognition. Vygotsky's theory (also discussed in chapter 2), and group influences ◀⫶⫶ p. 320, 321, 326. Throughout the book and more intensely later in this chapter, we will study technology and learning.

Motivational and Affective Factors

7. **Motivational and Emotional Influences on Learning**

   What and how much is learned is influenced by the learner's motivation. Motivation to learn, in turn, is influenced by the learner's emotional states, beliefs, interests, goals, and habits of thinking.

   The rich internal world of thoughts, beliefs, goals, and expectations for success and failure can enhance or interfere with the learner's quality of thinking and information processing. Students' beliefs have a marked influence on their motivation. Motivational and emotional factors also influence the quality of thinking and information processing as well as an individual's motivation to learn. Positive emotions, such as curiosity, generally improve motivation and facilitate learning and performance. Mild anxiety also can improve learning and performance by focusing the learner's attention on a particular task. However, intense negative emotions (such as anxiety, panic, rage, insecurity) and related thoughts (such as worrying about competence, ruminating about failure, fearing punishment, ridicule, or stigmatizing labels) generally detract from motivation, interfere with learning, and contribute to low performance. We will discuss motivation in considerable detail in chapter 11. We explored the nature of emotion in chapter 3, "Social Contexts and Socioemotional Development," and examined anxiety and depression in chapter 6, "Learners Who Are Exceptional" ◀⫶⫶ p. 112, 214.

8. **Intrinsic Motivation to Learn**

   The learner's creativity, higher-order thinking, and natural curiosity all contribute to motivation to learn. Intrinsic motivation is stimulated by tasks of optimal novelty and difficulty, tasks that are relevant to personal interests, and when learners are provided personal choice and control.

   Curiosity, flexible and insightful thinking, and creativity are major indicators of the learner's intrinsic motivation to learn, which is in large part a function of meeting basic needs to be competent and to exercise personal control. Intrinsic motivation is facilitated on tasks that

Figure **10.6**
Learner-Centered Psychological Principles *(continued)*

learners perceive as interesting, personally relevant, and meaningful, and appropriate in complexity and difficulty in terms of the learner's abilities, and on which they believe they can succeed. Intrinsic motivation also is facilitated on tasks that are comparable to real-world situations and meet needs for choice and control. Educators can encourage and support learners' natural curiosity and motivation to learn by being sensitive to individual differences in learners' perceptions of optimal novelty and difficulty, relevance, and personal choice and control. We will have much more to say about intrinsic motivation in chapter 11, "Motivating Students to Learn." We explored creativity and individual differences in chapter 4, "Individual Variations" ◀||| p. 141.

9. Effects of Motivation on Effort

Acquisition of complex knowledge and skills requires extended learner effort and guided practice. Without learners' motivation to learn, the willingness to exert this effort is unlikely without coercion.

Effort is another important indicator of motivation to learn. Acquiring complex knowledge and skills demands the investment of considerable energy and strategic effort, along with persistence over time. Educators need to be concerned with facilitating motivation by strategies that improve students' effort and commitment to learning and to achieving high standards of comprehension and understanding. Effective strategies include purposeful learning activities, guided by practices that enhance positive emotions and intrinsic motivation to learn, and methods that increase learners' perceptions that a task is interesting and personally relevant. We also will examine effort in chapter 11, "Motivating Students to Learn."

Developmental and Social Factors

10. Developmental Influences on Learning

As individuals develop, there are different opportunities and constraints for learning. Learning is most effective when differential development within and across physical, intellectual, social, and emotional domains is taken into account.

Individuals learn best when material is appropriate to their developmental level and is presented in an enjoyable and interesting way. Because individual development varies across physical, cognitive, social, and emotional domains, achievement in different instructional domains also can vary. Overemphasis on one type of developmental readiness—such as reading readiness—can keep learners from demonstrating that they are more capable in other domains. The cognitive, social, and emotional development of learners and how they interpret life experiences are influenced by prior schooling, family, cultural, and community factors. Early and continuing parental involvement in schooling, as well as effective communication between adults and children, can have a positive impact on children's learning. Awareness and understanding of developmental differences among children with and without physical, intellectual, or emotional disabilities, can facilitate the creation of optimal learning contexts. We extensively discussed children's physical, cognitive, and socioemotional development in chapters 2 and 3 ◀||| p. 36, 80.

11. Social Influences on Learning

Learning is influenced by social interactions, interpersonal relations, and communication with others.

Learning is enhanced when learners have an opportunity to interact and collaborate with others on instructional tasks. Learning settings that allow for social interactions and respect diversity encourage flexible thinking and social competence. In interactive and collaborative instructional contexts, individuals have an opportunity for perspective taking and reflective thinking that can lead to higher levels of cognitive, social, and moral development, as well as self-esteem. Quality personal relationships that provide stability, trust, and caring can increase learners' sense of belonging, self-respect, and self-acceptance, and produce a positive climate for learning. Family influences, positive interpersonal support and instruction in self-motivation strategies can offset factors that interfere with

Figure 10.6
Learner-Centered Psychological Principles *(continued)*

optimal learning such as negative beliefs about competence in a particular subject, high levels of text anxiety, negative gender role expectations, and undue pressure to perform well. Positive learning climates also can help to establish the context for healthier levels of thinking, feeling, and behaving. Such contexts help learners become motivated to share ideas, actively participate in the learning process, and create a learning community. We explored the importance of collaborative learning in chapter 9, "Social Constructivist Approaches, Domain-Specific Approaches, and Teaching," and examined family influences and other aspects of social relationships in chapter 3, "Social Contexts and Socioemotional Development" ◀‖‖ p. 86, 325.

Individual Differences Factors

12. Individual Differences in Learning

Learners have different strategies, approaches, and capabilities for learning that are a function of prior experience and heredity.

Individuals are born with and develop their own capabilities and talents. In addition, through learning and social acculturation, they have acquired their own preferences for how they like to learn and the pace at which they learn. However, these preferences are not always useful in helping students reach their learning goals. Educators need to help students examine their learning preferences and expand or modify them, if necessary. The interaction between learner differences and curricular and environmental conditions is another key factor that affects learning outcomes. Educators need to be sensitive to students' individual differences. They also need to attend to learner perceptions of the degree to which these differences are accepted and adapted to by varying instructional methods and materials. In chapter 4, "Individual Variations," we extensively explored individual differences in intelligence, learning and thinking styles, and personality ◀‖‖ p. 124.

13. Learning and Diversity

Learning is most effective when differences in learners' linguistic, cultural, and social backgrounds are taken into account.

The same basic principles of learning, motivation, and effective instruction apply to all learners. However, language, ethnicity, beliefs, and socioeconomic status all can influence learning. Careful attention to these factors in the instructional setting improves the likelihood that appropriate learning environments will be designed and implemented. When learners perceive that their individual differences in abilities, backgrounds, cultures, and experiences are valued, respected, and accommodated in learning tasks and contexts, levels of motivation and achievement are enhanced. We examined many aspects of diversity in chapter 5, "Sociocultural Diversity" ◀‖‖ p. 158.

14. Standards and Assessments

Setting appropriately high and challenging standards and assessing the learner as well as learning progress—including diagnostic, process, and outcome assessment—are integral parts of the learning process.

Assessment provides important information to both the learner and teacher at all stages of the learning process. Effective learning takes place when learners feel challenged to work toward appropriately high goals. Thus, appraisal of learners' cognitive strengths and weaknesses, as well as current knowledge and skills, is important for the selection of instructional materials of an optimal degree of difficulty. Ongoing assessment of learners' understanding of the curricular material can provide valuable feedback to both learners and teachers about progress toward learning goals. Standardized assessment of learners' progress and outcomes assessment yields one type of information about achievement levels both within and across individuals that can inform various types of instructional decisions. Performance assessments can generate other sources of information about the attainment of learning outcomes. Self-assessments of learning progress also can improve students self-appraisal skills and increase motivation and self-directed learning. We will extensively explore standards and assessments in chapters 13 and 14.

Figure 10.6
Learner-Centered Psychological Principles *(concluded)*

The students use a simple syringe air pump to assess air quality and determine its link to the incidence of asthma. The air pump was developed by Technical Education Research Centers (TERC), which also provides Gladstone students with shared databases of information gathered by students around the world. Gladstone students learn to think like scientists by working with data and addressing problems that need to be solved, collaborate with peers and mentors to plan and carry out a study, communicate and debate their findings, and evaluate their own work and the work of others.

The project's flow is organized around a number of student research groups, each group dealing with a separate problem related to the question of why there is so much asthma in the community and what can be done about it. All groups use the scientific method in their research.

Essential Questions

Essential questions *are questions that reflect the heart of the curriculum, the most important things that you believe students should explore and learn* (Jacobs, 1997). For example, in one lesson the essential question was "What flies?" (Jacobs, 1989). Students explored the question by examining everything from birds, bees, fish and space shuttles to the notion that time flies and ideas fly. Other questions can be used to follow the initial question ("What flies?"), such as these: "How and why do things fly in nature?" "How does flight impact humans?" "What is the future of flight?"

Essential questions like this perplex students, cause them to think, and motivate their curiosity. Essential questions are creative choices. With just a slight change, a lackluster question like "What was the effect of the Civil War?" can become the thought-provoking question "Is the Civil War still going on?"

Advocates of using essential questions argue that too often lesson planning and instruction become rigid and stiff. For example, a history teacher in high school might come up with this as one of the objectives for a year-long course on Western civilization: "Students will recognize personal responsibility to the community." Consider how much more enthusiastic students might be about studying Western civilization if they are asked to reflect on the question "How does my community affect my life?"

Discovery Learning

Discovery learning *is learning in which students construct an understanding on their own.* Discovery learning stands in contrast to the direct instruction approach discussed earlier, in which the teacher directly explains information to students. In discovery learning, students have to figure out things for themselves. Discovery learning meshes with the ideas of Piaget, who once commented that every time you teach a child something you keep the child from learning.

Educator John Dewey (1933) and cognitive psychologist Jerome Bruner (1966) promoted the concept of discovery learning by encouraging teachers to give students more opportunities to learn on their own ◀▥ p. 4. In their view, discovery learning encourages students to think for themselves and discover how knowledge is constructed. It also feeds their natural curiosity and inquiry.

Teachers facilitate discovery learning by providing students with stimulating activities that activate their natural curiosity. After you present such activities, your role becomes one of answering student-generated questions. You also promote discovery learning on the part of students by being naturally curious yourself and having a strong interest in uncovering solutions to problems.

Discovery learning is especially effective in science classes. Researchers have found that students in activity-based, discovery-learning science classes score higher on science achievement tests than students in traditional direct-instruction science classes (Bredderman, 1982; Glasson, 1989). These findings hold at the elementary, middle school, and secondary school levels.

However, most discovery learning approaches used in schools today do not involve "pure" discovery learning. In "pure" discovery learning, students are encouraged to learn on their own and instruction is minimal to nonexistent. Working completely on

Yes, children have to be educated, but they also have to educate themselves.
Ernest Dimnet
American Author, 20th century

their own doesn't benefit many students. For example, given materials and left to their own devices to learn, some students end up with the wrong solutions and use inefficient strategies to discover information. Others never discover what it is they are trying to find out or why. And in many cases, such as initially learning how to add and subtract, direct instruction can get the job done much more quickly (van Lehn, 1990).

As teachers began to use discovery learning, they soon found that for it to be effective as a systematic instruction approach it needed to be modified. This led to the development of **guided discovery learning,** *in which students are still encouraged to construct their understanding, but with the assistance of teacher-guided questions and directions.*

How might an elementary school science teacher use guided discovery to help students learn to classify animal groups? Initially, the teacher briefly lectures to convey the essential question students will be exploring. Instead of continuing to lecture students on the names of the animal groups and giving examples of each, she could ask students to generate the names of the animals, then guide students in classifying the animals by exploring their similarities and differences (Schunk, 1996).

Integrating the Curriculum

Integrating the curriculum is a theme in learner-based approaches to planning and instruction. By connecting and integrating information across different subject areas, students construct an understanding that ideas are linked, not isolated islands of information (Clarke & Agne, 1997; Mallery, 2000).

In *The Mindful School: How to Integrate the Curriculum,* Robyn Fogarty (1991) described a number of ways the curriculum can be integrated. Figure 10.7 shows three ways the curriculum can be integrated within a discipline and five ways it can be integrated across disciplines. Traditionally, in most schools, the curriculum has been planned according to the *fragmented model,* which involves little or no integration. Learners essentially are left to their own devices to make connections or integrate concepts, in this model.

There are five important models for integrating the curriculum across disciplines:

1. *Sequenced model:* Rearranging the sequence of topics to coincide with a parallel topic in another subject
2. *Shared model:* Integrating one subject with another through the learner's conceptual framework
3. *Webbed model:* Selecting an overall theme (such as "persistence" or "transportation") and using a thematic umbrella across disciplines
4. *Threaded model:* Integrating the content of what is taught with cognitive tools and cooperative strategies that cross disciplines and represent real-life circumstances
5. *Integrated model:* Integrating the curricula through inter-disciplinary team planning in which conceptual overlaps become the common focus across departments

Evaluating Learner-Centered Instruction

The learner-centered approach to lesson planning and instruction has many positive characteristics. The learner-centered principles developed by the American Psychological Association task force proved extremely helpful guides that can benefit student learning. These include thinking of ways to help students actively construct their understanding, set goals and plan, think deeply and creatively,

In an attempt to combine sports and academics, officials at Culver High devised aerobic algebra.

Close to Home © John McPherson/Dist. of Universal Press Syndicate.

FRAGMENTED
Periscope—one direction;
one sighting; narrow focus
on single discipline

Description
The traditional model of
separate and distinct
disciplines, which fragments
the subject areas.

Example
Teacher applies this view in
Math, Science, Social
Studies, Language Arts OR
Sciences, Humanities, Fine
and Practical Arts.

CONNECTED
Opera glass—details
of one discipline; focus
on subtleties and
interconnections

Description
Within each subject area,
course content is connected
topic to topic, concept to
concept, one year's work to
the next, and relates idea(s)
explicitly.

Example
Teacher relates the concept
of fractions to decimals,
which in turn relates to
money, grades, etc.

NESTED
3-D glasses—multiple
dimensions to one scene,
topic, or unit

Description
Within each subject area,
the teacher targets multiple
skills; a social skill, a
thinking skill, and a
content-specific skill.

Example
Teacher designs the unit
on photosynthesis to
simultaneously target
consensus seeking (social
skill), sequencing (thinking
skill), and plant life cycle
(science content).

SEQUENCED
Eyeglasses—varied
internal content framed by
broad, related concepts

Description
Topics or units of study are
rearranged and sequenced
to coincide with one another.
Similar ideas are taught in
concert while remaining
separate subjects.

Example
English teacher presents an
historical novel depicting a
particular period while the
History teacher teaches that
same historical period.

SHARED
Binoculars—two
disciplines that share
overlapping concepts
and skills

Description
Shared planning and
teaching take place in two
disciplines in which
overlapping concepts or
ideas emerge as organizing
elements.

Example
Science and Math teachers
use data collection, charting,
and graphing as shared
concepts that can be team-
taught.

WEBBED
Telescope—broad view of
an entire constellation as
one theme, webbed to the
various elements

Description
A fertile theme is webbed
to curriculum contents and
disciplines; subjects use the
theme to sift out appropriate
concepts, topics, and ideas.

Example
Teacher presents a simple
topical theme, such as the
circus, and webs it to the
subject areas. A conceptual
theme, such as conflict, can
be webbed for more depth
in the theme approach.

THREADED
Magnifying glass—big
ideas that magnify all
content through a
metacurricular approach

Description
The metacurricular approach
threads thinking skills, social
skills, multiple intelligences,
technology, and study skills
through the various
disciplines.

Example
Teaching staff targets
prediction in Reading, Math,
and Science lab experiments
while Social Studies teacher
targets forecasting current
events, and thus threads the
skill (prediction) across
disciplines.

INTEGRATED
Kaleidoscope—new
patterns and designs that
use the basic elements of
each discipline

Description
This interdisciplinary
approach matches subjects
for overlaps in topics and
concepts with some team
teaching in an authentic
integrated model.

Example
In Math, Science, Social
Studies, Fine Arts, Language
Arts, and Practical Arts,
teachers look for patterning
models and approach
content through these
patterns.

 **10.7**

Integrating the Curriculum
The first three strategies represent within-discipline integration. The last five strategies involve integration across disciplines.

monitor their learning, solve real-world problems, develop more positive self-esteem and control their emotions, be internally motivated, learn in a developmentally appropriate way, collaborate effectively with others (including diverse others), evaluate their learner preferences, and meet challenging standards.

Critics of learner-centered instruction argue that it gives too much attention to the process of learning (such as learning creatively and collaboratively) and not enough to academic content (such as the facts of history) (Hirsch, 1996). Some critics stress that learner-centered instruction works better in some subjects than in others (Feng, 1996). They say that in areas with many ill-defined problems, such as the social sciences and humanities, learner-centered instruction can be effective. However, they believe that in well-structured knowledge domains like math and science, teacher-centered structure works better. Critics also say that learner-centered instruction is less effective at the beginning level of instruction in a field because students do not have the knowledge to make decisions about what and how they should learn. And critics stress that there is a gap between the theoretical level of student-centered learning and its actual application (Airasian & Walsh, 1997). The consequences of implementing learner-centered strategies in the classroom are often more challenging than might be anticipated.

Although we have presented teacher-centered and learner-centered planning and instruction in separate sections, don't think of them as always being either/or approaches. Most teachers use some of both in making the classroom a positive learning experience for children.

At this point we have discussed many ideas about learner-centered lesson planning and instruction. A review of these ideas is presented in summary table 10.2.

THROUGH THE EYES OF TEACHERS

Look at What Children Can Do

Don't look at what children can't do. Look at what they can do and take them from there. Develop their full potential in a child-centered curriculum.

My students are active all day. They are on the floor reading with a partner or on their own. They are working on projects or experiments. I model and then give support as they are reading, writing, and learning. I also integrate language arts, social studies, and science whenever I can.

Marlene Wendler
Language Arts Teacher, Fourth Grade
St. Paul's Lutheran School
New Ulm, Minnesota

Technology and Education

Technology is such an important theme in education that it is woven throughout this book. In each chapter you read a Technology and Education box related to the chapter's contents. For example, you already have studied such topics as "Technology Resources for Improving Phonological Awareness and Decoding Skills" (chapter 2), "The Global Lab and Other Technology Connections with Students Around the World" (chapter 5), "Scientists in Action and Young Children's Literacy" (chapter 8), and "Computer Supported Intentional Learning Environments (CSILE)" (chapter 9) ◀ᶩᶩᶩ p. 72, 174, 331. You also read about the videodisc-based Jasper Project, which is designed to improve students' mathematical thinking (chapter 8) ◀ᶩᶩᶩ p. 300. Every chapter includes icons in the margins that direct you to relevant Internet sites. Here, we will explore the technology revolution, the technology landscape, technology and sociocultural diversity, and the potentials and realities of technology and education.

TECHNOLOGY AND EDUCATION

- The Technology Revolution
- The Technology Landscape
- Technology and Sociocultural Diversity
- The Potentials and Realities of Technology and Education

The Technology Revolution

Students today are growing up in a world that is far different technologically from the world in which their parents and grandparents were students. If students are to be adequately prepared for tomorrow's jobs, technology must become an integral part

Teaching
with Technology

page 378 Santrock Educational Psychology

Summary Table 10.2
Learner-Centered Lesson Planning and Instruction

Concept	Processes/ Related Ideas	Characteristics/Description
Learner-Centered Principles	Their Nature	• Learner-centered planning and instruction moves the focus away from the teacher and toward the student. • The APA's learner-centered psychological principles involve cognitive and metacognitive factors (the nature of the learning process, goals of the learning process, the construction of knowledge, strategic thinking, thinking about thinking, and the context of learning), motivational and affective factors (motivational and emotional influences on learning, intrinsic motivation to learn, and effects of motivation on effort), developmental and social factors (developmental influences on learning and social influences on learning), and individual differences factors (individual differences in learning, learning and diversity, and standards and assessment).
Some Learner-Centered Instructional Strategies	Problem-Based Learning	• This emphasizes real-world learning. • A problem-based curriculum exposes students to authentic problems. • Problem-based learning focuses on small-group discussion rather than lecture. Students identify issues they wish to explore, and teachers act as guides, helping students monitor their problem-solving efforts.
	Essential Questions	• These are questions that engagingly reflect the heart of the curriculum.
	Discovery Learning	• This is learning in which students construct an understanding on their own. Discovery learning is designed to get students to think for themselves, to discover how knowledge is constructed, to stimulate their curiosity, and to motivate their inquiry. • Most discovery learning approaches today involve guided discovery, in which students are encouraged to construct their understanding with the assistance of teacher-guided questions and directions.
Integrating the Curriculum	Its Nature	• When the curriculum is integrated, students learn that information is connected, not isolated. • Traditionally, schools have used a fragmented model that involves little or no integration. • Five models that integrate information across disciplines are the sequenced model, the shared model, the webbed model, the threaded model, and the integrated model.
Evaluating Learner-Centered Instruction	Strengths and Criticisms	• The learner-centered model of planning and instruction has many positive features. • The fourteen APA learner-centered principles are guidelines that can help teachers develop strategies that benefit student learning (such as encouraging students to actively construct knowledge, think deeply and creatively, be internally motivated, solve real-world problems, and collaboratively learn). • Critics argue that learner-centered planning and instruction focuses too much on process and not enough on content, is more appropriate for social sciences and humanities than science and math, is not appropriate for beginning instruction when students have little or no knowledge about the topic, and is more challenging to implement than most teachers envision. • Keep in mind that although we presented teacher-centered and learner-centered approaches separately, many teachers use aspects of both approaches.

of schools and classrooms (Geisert & Futrell, 2000; Sharp, 1999). In a recent poll of seventh- to twelfth-graders conducted jointly by CNN and the National Science Foundation (1997), 82 percent predicted that they will not be able to make a good living unless they have computer skills and understand other technology.

The technology revolution is part of the information society in which we now live. People are using computers to communicate today the way people used to use pens, postage stamps, and telephones. The new information society still relies on some basic nontechnological competencies: good communication skills, the ability to solve problems, thinking deeply, thinking creatively, and having positive attitudes. However, in today's technology-oriented world, how people pursue these competencies is being challenged and extended in ways and at a speed that few people had to cope with in previous eras (Bitter & Pierson, 1999; Collis & Sakamoto, 1996; Nickerson, 2000).

Technology has been a part of schooling for many decades, but until recently the technologies being used were rather simple and changed slowly. To underscore how technology in schools has changed dramatically, in 1983 there were fewer than 50,000 computers in America's schools. Today, there are more than 6 million! Hardly a school in America today is without at least one computer. Nearly every week, a school board approves the purchase of ten to twenty computers for improving students' writing skills, another school board approves a high school's use of Channel One (a 10-minute daily recap of news that has become controversial because it also includes 2 minutes of advertising), and another sets aside funds for a telecomputing network system that connects classrooms within a school and different schools. And more colleges are making it mandatory that first-year students purchase laptop computers (Young, 1997).

Toward the end of our discussion of technology and education, we will return to the topic of how extensive the technological revolution is in our nation's schools. First, we will explore the different types of technology being used in today's schools.

"I see what's wrong with your calculator—it's the remote control to your TV."

Integrating Technology and Education
Educational Technology Journal

The Technology Landscape

The technology landscape in schools is expanding dramatically. It includes computer-assisted instruction; word processing; computer programming as a learning tool; games, simulations, and microworlds; CD-ROMs and videodiscs; hypertext and hypermedia; and computer-mediated communication.

Computer-Assisted Instruction

Computer-assisted instruction (CAI) *is the term given to instruction that is provided by a computer. Computer-assisted instruction is closely linked with the concept of mastery learning,* which was discussed earlier in this chapter under direct instruction approaches. CAI includes drill-and-practice, as well as tutorials. **Drill-and-practice programs** *give students opportunities to learn and practice various academic skills, such as mathematics, science, and reading.* **Tutorials** *attempt to mimic a competent, patient human tutor in guiding a student's learning. Tutorial programs adapt their content and pace according to the way the student responds.* In a typical tutorial, students will be asked a number of questions and then the computer program will branch off in directions that are most likely to benefit the student's learning.

Critics of computer-assisted instruction, especially drill-and-practice programs, argue that the programs encourage rote learning but little thinking. They also say that CAI places too much emphasis on external rather than internal motivation. For example, CAI gives students considerable corrective feedback as they attempt to master a topic. CAI originated with Skinner's programmed instruction, based on the behavioral concept of operant conditioning (described in chapter 7) ◀▥ p. 243. Some recent versions of CAI embody more cognitive principles of learning by capturing

**Educational
Technology Journal**

and holding the student's attention, considering the student's prior level of knowledge, and improving long-term memory and positive transfer of information (Merrill & others, 1996).

Word Processing

Earlier in the twentieth century it was thought that learning how to type on a typewriter was indispensable for creating written documents. It also was believed to be important for college preparation and an indispensable career skill. Today, becoming competent at using computer software for word processing is rapidly becoming indispensable. Students benefit by learning how to use computer software to create their written compositions (Maddux, Johnson, & Willis, 1997). Word processing is especially valuable in providing a tool for students to revise their writing. Researchers have found that word processing improves students' writing skills and attitudes toward writing (Bangert-Drowns, 1993).

QUILL is an educational language-building strategy that involves word processing (Bruce & Rubin, 1993). QUILL emphasizes the integration of reading and writing, making writing public to increase meaningful communication with an audience, and revision (Cognition and Technology Group at Vanderbilt, 1996). QUILL consists of four interrelated programs: (1) Writer's Assistant (word processing), (2) Planner (to support brainstorming), (3) Library (for sharing written work with other students, and (4) Mailbag (an e-mail system). Other word-processing programs that have been developed to improve students' writing skills include Salomon's Writing Partner (Salomon, 1993) and Rubin's Story Maker (Rubin, 1983).

Computer Programming as a Learning Tool

In the book *Mindstorms,* Seymour Papert (1980) argued that by learning computer programming, students learn how to think and learn for themselves. Papert created the computer language LOGO, which is appropriate for even young children. Children use a small "turtle" graphic that moves around the screen in response to their programming efforts.

Early evaluations of LOGO were negative, but subsequent studies have found benefits, such as improved planning skills (Mayer, 1988). However, for LOGO to be effective in improving students' learning skills, students have to effectively learn the LOGO programming language and teachers need to use LOGO as a means to other ends, such as the development of planning skills or the acquisition of geometry skills (Cognition and Technology Group at Vanderbilt, 1996). When teachers use LOGO as part of a constructivist approach that involves guidance and scaffolding, LOGO's skills transfer positively to other learning contexts (Lehrer, Lee, & Jeong, 1994).

Games, Simulation, and Microworlds

Instructional games *are computer-based activities that capitalize on the increased motivation and interest that come from encasing learning in an animated, visually displayed game.* Recognizing that many children grow up on a steady menu of videogames, a number of software manufacturers have created learning activities that have a game format. The widely used educational game Where in the World Is Carmen Sandiego? places a student in the role of a detective whose job is to track down criminals in a number of countries (see figure 10.8).

Computer simulations *immerse the student in computer learning environments that model real-world situations.* Many simulations are vivid portrayals of environmental worlds that students cannot directly participate in. Students might be placed on a distant planet and challenged to create a society, or in an Amazon rain forest and given a series of learning experiences about deforestation and global climate. ScienceVision and Science 2000 are computer simulation programs that currently are being used to teach science.

Microworlds *are scaled-down, computer-based simulations of real environments in which learners construct knowledge as they explore and design new worlds* (Papert, 1993). In one project, students used microworlds to learn the geometry of bridge

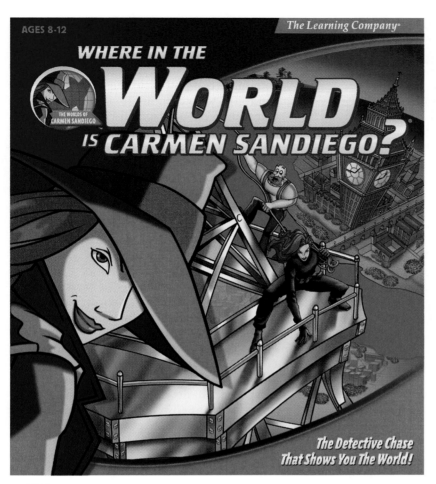

Figure **10.8**
Where in the World Is Carmen Sandiego?

design and the social issues involved in deciding on the location of a new bridge in a large city (Salisbury, 1995). At Paige Academy in Boston, Gregory Gargarian created innovative microworlds that stimulate young children to explore musical events (Ackermann, 1996). Children design soundtracks for their own animations, put characters in motion and make them dance, and record their own sounds and arrange them in rhythmic or melodic sequences. ThinkerTools is a computer software program that provides students with opportunities to explore a series of microworlds that help them learn the principles of physics (White, 1993) (see figure 10.9).

CD-ROMs and Videodiscs   CD-ROM *stands for "compact disk read-only memory." CD-ROMs are small storage disks like those that are used in digital compact disc players for music* (Maddux, Johnson, & Willis, 1997). CD-ROMs can store words, images, sounds, and databases of information. So much information can be stored on CD-ROMs that encyclopedias are now available on a single disc (see figure 10.10). CD-ROMs are increasingly used to store information. For example, when you do a computer search for information at your college's library, the host computer likely is reading some of its information off a CD-ROM drive.

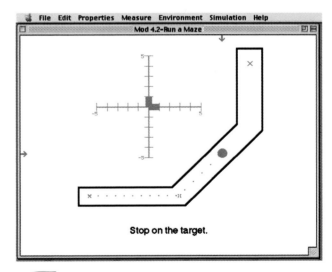

Figure **10.9**
The Microworlds of ThinkerTools

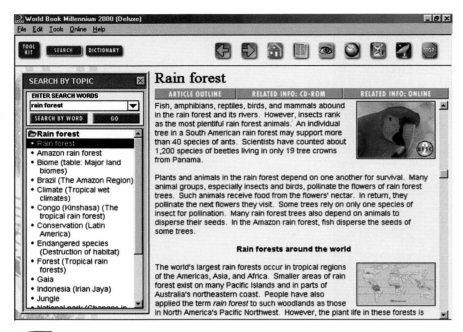

Figure 10.10
An Encyclopedia on CD-ROM

At this site on the World Book Millennium (2000 Edition), students can access extensive information about rain forests.

Hyperstudio

Videodiscs *are laser disks that are used to store visual images.* They are much larger than CD-ROMs and look like a silver version of an old 78 RPM record. Videodiscs can be used without a computer, although they often are connected to a computer to provide interactive video instruction. A special video monitor can display video and sound from the videodisc, as well as computer-generated texts and graphics (Maddux, Johnson, & Willis, 1997).

Videodisc technology allows information to be presented in more dynamic, visual, and spatial ways than ordinary textbooks can (Sharp & others, 1995). Videodiscs also allow teachers almost instant access to information for demonstration and discussion.

Recall that the Jasper Project, which we have discussed on a number of occasions, consists of twelve videodisc adventures to improve students' mathematical thinking skills (Cognition and Technology Group at Vanderbilt, 1997). Each videodisc contains a short (about 17-minute) video adventure that ends in a complex challenge. The adventures are designed like good detective novels in which the data necessary to solve the adventures are embedded in the stories. The videodisc episodes can be revisited as students need information to solve the adventures.

In the not-too-distant future, advances in CD-ROM technology that produce clearer images and greater memory capacity likely will mean that CD-ROMs will replace the need for videodiscs and will lower costs in the process (Maddux, Johnson, & Willis, 1997).

Hypertext and Hypermedia

Hypertext *consists of computer-based verbal content that lets the student read about one topic and then select related topics to explore.* Individual words, phrases, or images in the text are displayed as "hot links." Clicking on the word, phrase, or image with a mouse causes the software to transport the viewer to some other part of the document. The technology is similar to linking technology on a page of the World Wide Web. Hypertext is included in many CD-ROMs.

Hypermedia *are links of information that include verbal material as well as visual, auditory, and/or animated content.* Students choose which of the elements they want to explore. The links allow students to browse through introductory material or examine a particular topic in depth.

Beethoven's 5th is an example of hypermedia (Maddux, Johnson, & Willis, 1997). Figure 10.11 shows the opening screen of the program, where students select which of these options to examine: Beethoven's biography, listening to Beethoven's Fifth Symphony, the structure of the Fifth Symphony, musical instruments, games, and CD-player. Clicking on "Beethoven's Biography" produces a series of screens about the composer and his family.

The multimedia and self-selection aspects of hypermedia are very appealing to many students (MacGregor, 1999). Hypermedia such as Beethoven's 5th can make the composer's background and music come alive for students and stimulate them to study topics that they otherwise might perceive as boring. And the hypermedia presentation Treasures of the Smithsonian breathes life into American history (Hoekema, 1993).

Computer-Mediated Communication   Computer-mediated communication (CMC) *refers to communication through
electronic exchanges; it is sometimes referred to as telecommunications or
educational telecommunications.* Our exploration of computer-mediated
communication focuses on the Internet and cautions in using it.

The Internet   The **Internet** *is the core of computer-mediated communication. The Internet system is worldwide and connects thousands of
computer networks, providing an incredible array of information that students can access.* In many cases, the Internet has more current, up-to-date
information than textbooks. In 1996, President Clinton proposed that
every school in the United States should become wired for access to the
Internet because of how it has revolutionized access to information. By
1998, 89 percent of public schools had been connected to the Internet.

The **World Wide Web** (the **Web**) *is a hypermedia information retrieval
system that links a variety of Internet materials; it includes text and graphics.* The Web gives the Internet a much needed structure. Libraries, museums, universities, companies, organizations, and individuals display
information on the Web, all of which can be accessed by students with a
click on words or images presented on a computer screen. Web indexes
and search engines such as Infoseek, Lycos, Magellan, and Yahoo! can help
students find the information they are seeking by examining and collat-
ing a variety of sources. A **website** *is an individual's or an organization's
location on the Internet. Websites display information posted by the individual or organization.*

In every chapter, we have placed a number of Internet icons with a
label below them in the margins of the text. By going to the McGraw-Hill
Santrock *Educational Psychology* website, you can immediately connect
with the associated websites by scrolling to the appropriate chapter and label. For
example, the label in the margin for this discussion is "Tips for Using the Internet."
As the label indicates, this website will provide you with some good strategies for
using the Internet. Also, in the section on general Internet resources on the Santrock
Educational Psychology website, there are links to a number of websites with information about integrating technology into the classroom that you can access.

E-mail *stands for "electronic mail" and is another valuable way that the Internet can
be used. Messages can be sent to and received from individuals as well as large numbers
of people at once.* To read about some effective ways to use the Internet in classrooms,
see Technology and Education.

The Internet is an important learning tool in a technology-rich project called
Cooperative Networked Educational Community of Tomorrow (Co-NECT) (Jones,
Rasmussen, & Moffitt, 1997). Some Co-NECT schools become immersed in learning
about worldwide scientific expeditions like Earthwatch's Mystery of the Pipe Wreck
project in the Caribbean. In such investigations, students and teachers can download
data from project sites, conduct data analysis, and communicate electronically with
project participants and staff (Bolt, Beraneck, & Newman, 1993).

A Co-NECT student e-mailed a lawyer in Northern Ireland to request information about this question: Can there be lasting peace in Northern Ireland? The lawyer
responded with a two-page e-mail that included current news and perspectives on
the topic.

Internet Cautions   The Internet can be a valuable tool for helping students
learn (Roblyer & Edwards, 2000). However, it has some potential drawbacks (Gackenbach & Ellerman, 1999; Griffiths, 1999). To use it effectively with your students,
your access software will have to be competently installed in your computers. You will
have to know how to use it and feel comfortable with it. Concerns have been raised
about students accessing pornographic websites and about inaccuracy of information

Figure **10.11**

**An Example of Hypermedia:
Beethoven's 5th**

This screen is the opening menu of the hypermedia,
Beethoven's 5th. It includes text, graphics, and
CD-quality sound.

**Webliography
Tips for Using the Internet
Internet Pals**

TECHNOLOGY AND EDUCATION
Using the Internet in the Classroom

Following are some effective ways that the Internet can be used in classrooms.

- *To help students navigate and integrate knowledge.* The Internet has huge databases of information on a vast array of topics that are organized in different ways. As students explore Internet resources, they can place their own unique stamp on their research by constructing projects that integrate information from various sources that they otherwise cannot access (Cafolla, Kauffman, & Knee, 1997).
- *To foster collaborative learning.* One of the most effective ways to use the Internet in your classroom is through project-centered activities for small groups. The Internet is so huge and has so many resources that teamwork improves the outcome of most Internet searches. One collaborative learning use of the Internet is to have a group of students conduct a survey on a topic (Maddux, Johnson, & Willis, 1997). Students can construct the survey, put it out on the Internet, and expect to get responses back from many parts of the world in the matter of a few days. They can organize, analyze, and summarize the data from the survey and then share it with other classes around the world. Another type of collaborative learning project involves sending groups of students on Internet "scavenger hunts" to find out information and/or solve a problem.
- *To allow e-mail.* An increasing number of innovative educational projects include e-mail. In chapter 9, we examined Ann Brown and Joe Campione's program Fostering a Community of Learners (Brown, 1997; Brown & Campione, 1996). Students can communicate with experts by e-mail, which frees teachers from the burden of being the sole dispenser of knowledge, and gives students access to a wider circle of knowledgeable people. This is sometimes called "electronic mentoring." Students also can communicate with each other. In the Global Lab project, classrooms around the world are interconnected and students from the United States can communicate via e-mail with students in a number of other countries (Berenfeld, 1994). The Global Lab project is organized as a networked science laboratory.

  Students enjoy using e-mail to communicate with students in other schools, states, and countries. E-mail can especially be rewarding for shy students who get anxious and withdraw from communicating face-to-face with someone.
- *To improve the teacher's knowledge and understanding.* An excellent Internet resource for teachers is the ERIC Resource Information Center, which provides free information about a wide range of educational topics. You can send an e-mail inquiry to the AskERIC department (askeric@ericir.syr.edu), providing your keywords for the search and within 3 days they will e-mail you a list of citations. The AskERIC department also provides information about lesson plans and connections to other resources.

**Critical Analysis
of the Internet**

on personal websites. Equipment, installation, and training are expensive. To make the Internet work in a classroom, teachers need considerable instruction, ongoing workshops, and technical support.

However, when used effectively, the Internet expands access to a world of knowledge and people students cannot experience in any other way (Garner & Gillingham, 1999). If you do not know how to access the Internet, learn this skill as soon as possible on your own computer. You and your students will benefit from your ability to navigate the Internet. Two good sources for learning more about the Internet and how to bring it into your classroom are *Teaching and Learning in the Information Age* (Schrum & Berenfeld, 1997) and *World Wide Web for Teachers* (Cafolla, Kauffman, & Knee, 1997).

Technology and Sociocultural Diversity

Technology brings with it certain social issues. For example, will schools' increased use of technology, especially computers, widen the learning gap between rich and poor students, or between male and female students (Maddux, Johnson, & Willis,

1997; Spring, 2000)? Less than one-third of schools in which a majority of students are from low-income backgrounds have access to the Internet, compared to almost two-thirds of schools with mainly students from higher socioeconomic backgrounds (Schrum & Berenfeld, 1997). The problem of computer access and use also is compounded by the far greater presence of computers in the homes of middle- and upper-income families. There are gaps in computer availability across ethnic groups as well. In a study by the National Association of Education Progress, almost one-third of white high school students owned computers, compared with just over one-fifth of African American or Latino students (Sutton, 1991). And families with a male student are more likely to own a computer than families with a female student (DeVillar & Faltis, 1991).

Computers are often used for different activities in different sociocultural groups. Schools with high percentages of low-income ethnic minority students tend to use computers for drill-and-practice exercises (Maddux, Johnson, & Willis, 1997). In contrast, schools with high percentages of white, middle- and upper-income students are more likely to use computers for more active, constructivist learning activities. Boys are more likely to use computers for math and science applications, girls for word processing (Beal, 1994).

Here are some recommendations for preventing or reducing inequity in computer access and use (Gipson, 1997; Sheffield, 1997):

- Screen technology materials for ethnic, cultural, and gender bias.
- Use technology as a tool for providing active, constructive learning opportunities for all students, regardless of their cultural, ethnic, or gender background.
- Provide students with information about experts from diverse ethnic and gender backgrounds who use technology effectively in their work and lives. For example, invite an ethnic minority computer analyst to come to your classroom and talk with your students. Take your students on a field trip to an engineering firm and request that at least one of the available engineers be a female. Request that she demonstrate how she uses computer technology in her work.
- Talk with parents about providing their children with appropriate computer-based learning activities at home. Look for ways that government and community agencies may be able to help fund the purchase of a computer by low-income families with students in your classroom. Encourage parents to give their daughters positive feedback for using computers.

The Potentials and Realities of Technology and Education

Consider a teacher who is faced with instructing students about the ecology of the desert (Maddux, Johnson, & Willis, 1997). For schools not located in the desert, the traditional approach is to have students read about this topic in a textbook, perhaps observe some desert reptiles in a terrarium, lecture to students about it, and then ask if students have questions to ask. A very different choice is to incorporate a CD-ROM hypermedia package into the classroom exploration of desert ecology. Students explore the life cycles of desert plants and animals, "construct" a desert environment on the computer, populate it with plant and animal life, and then determine whether their selection of life forms and resources results in sustainable life. The inclusion of this technology in learning about life in the desert results in more exploratory and interactive learning for students than simply reading about deserts in a textbook.

As we indicated at the beginning of our inquiry about technology, the number of computers in schools has increased dramatically, yet despite its potential for improving student learning, schools continue to lag behind other segments of society, such as business, in the use of technology. A survey by the Office of Technology Assessment (1995) found that the majority of teachers do not feel comfortable with computers.

Critical Issues in Technology and Education

TEACHING STRATEGIES
For Choosing and Using Technology in the Classroom

Technology will be a part of your classroom. Following are some guidelines for choosing and using it:

1. *Choose technology with an eye toward how it can help students actively explore, construct, and restructure information* (Jonassen, 2000). Look for software that lets students directly manipulate the information. One review found that students' learning improved when information was presented in a multimedia fashion that stimulated them to actively select, organize, and integrate visual and verbal information (Mayer, 1997). You might want to consult with a school or district media specialist for the software that best reflects these characteristics. Software catalogs, education journals, and educational databases such as ERIC also can be good resources.

2. *Look for ways to use technology as part of collaborative and real-world learning.* In Ann Brown and Joe Campione's (1996) words, education should be about "fostering a community of learners." Students often learn better when they work together to solve challenging problems and construct innovative projects. Think of technologies like videodiscs, hypermedia, the Web, and e-mail as tools for providing students with opportunities to engage in collaborative learning, reaching outside the classroom to include the real world and the entire world, and communicating with people in locations that otherwise would be inaccessible to them.

3. *Choose technology that presents positive models for students.* When you invite someone from the community to talk with your class, you likely will consider the type of role model the person presents, what their values are. Keep in mind our earlier comments about monitoring technology for equity in ethnicity and culture. Be sure that the models that students associate with technology are diverse individuals who serve as positive role models.

4. *Your teaching skills are critical, regardless of the technology you use.* You don't have to worry that technology will replace you as a teacher. Technology becomes effective in the classroom only when you know how to use it, demonstrate it, guide and monitor its use, and incorporate it into a larger effort to develop students who are motivated to learn, actively learn, and communicate effectively. Even the most sophisticated hypermedia will not benefit students much unless you appropriately orient students to it, ask them good questions about the material, orchestrate its use, and tailor it to their needs.

5. *Continue to learn about technology yourself and increase your technological competence.* Digital technology is still changing at an amazing pace. Make it a personal goal to be open to new technology, keep up with technological advances by reading educational journals, and take courses in educational computing to increase your skills. You will be an important model for your students in terms of your attitude toward technology, your ability to use it effectively yourself, and your ability to communicate how to use it effectively to your students. In a recent study of computers and education in many countries, the main determinants of effective use of information technology in classrooms were the teachers' competence in using technology and the teacher's positive attitude toward technology (Collis & others, 1996). To evaluate your technology skills and attitudes, complete Self-Assessment 10.1.

Computers are still used too often for drill-and-practice activities rather than for active, constructive learning (Newby & others, 2000). In one survey, a majority of middle school and high school students reported using computers only minimally over a 30-week time frame (Becker, 1994). In this survey, only 1 student of 11 reported using school computers for an English class, 1 of 15 for a math class, and only 1 of 40 for a social science class.

Many teachers do not have adequate training in using computers, and many school districts have not provided the needed workshops. And with rapidly changing technology, the computers that many schools purchase become quickly outdated. Other computers break and sit in need of repair (Baines, Deluzain, & Stanley, 1999; Maney, 1999).

Such realities mean that learning in schools has not yet been technologically revolutionized. Only when schools have technologically trained teachers and current,

ꝼELF-ASSESSMENT 10.1
Evaluating My Technology Skills and Attitudes

How good are your technology skills? How positive are your attitudes about using technology and incorporating it into your classroom? Rate yourself from 1 to 5, with 1 = Not like me at all and 5 = Very much like me.

	1	2	3	4	5
1. I use computers for word processing and know how to incorporate word processing into the classroom.					
2. I understand computer simulations and know how to effectively use them in the classroom.					
3. I know what microworlds are and how to effectively use them in the classroom.					
4. I understand how CD-ROMs work and know how to effectively use them in the classroom.					
5. I know what laserdiscs are and know how to effectively use them in the classroom.					
6. I know what hypertext and hypermedia are, as well as how to effectively use them in the classroom.					
7. I use the Internet and know how to effectively incorporate it into the classroom.					
8. I use e-mail and know how it can be used effectively used in the classroom.					
9. I have participated in collaborative learning exercises that involve technology, such as hypermedia and the Internet.					
10. I am aware of the sociocultural issues involved in technology and education.					
11. I am excited about the increased use of technology in education and plan to use it in the classroom whenever possible.					
12. I recognize how important technological skills are for students because they need these skills for tomorrow's jobs.					

Scoring and Interpretation
Look at your scores for each item and evaluate your technology strengths and weaknesses. By the time you step into your classroom for your first day of teaching, make it a goal to be able to confidently rate yourself on each of these items at the level of 4 or 5. On items on which you rated yourself 1, 2, and 3, try to take technology courses at your college that will improve your knowledge and skills in those areas.

workable technologies will the technology revolution have an opportunity to truly transform classrooms (Howell & Dunnivant, 2000). To evaluate your technology skills and attitudes, see Self-Assessment 10.1.

At this point we have studied many ideas about technology and education. A review of these ideas is presented in summary table 10.3. In this chapter, we discussed several aspects of motivation in outlining the main themes of learner-based lesson planning and instruction. Motivation is a critical aspect of learning, and we will devote all of the next chapter to it.

SUMMARY TABLE 10.3
Technology and Education

Concept	Processes/ Related Ideas	Characteristics/Description
The Technology Revolution	Its Nature	• The technology revolution is part of the information society in which we now live, and students will increasingly need to have technological skills.
The Technology Landscape	Computer-Assisted Instruction (CAI)	• This is the term given to instruction that is given by a computer. CAI includes drill-and-practice programs as well as tutorials.
	Word Processing	• Becoming competent at using a computer for word processing is increasingly an indispensable skill.
	Computer Programming as a Learning Tool	• Papert argued that by learning computer programming, students learn how to think and learn for themselves. He created LOGO, a computer language that students can use to create computer programs.
	Games, Simulations, and Microworlds	• Instructional games are computer-based activities that capitalize on the increased motivation and interest that come from encasing learning in an animated, visually displayed game. • Computer simulations immerse the student in computer learning environments that model real-world situations. • Microworlds are scaled-down, computer-based simulations in which students construct knowledge as they explore and design new worlds.
	CD-ROMs and Videodiscs	• CD-ROM stands for "compact disk read-only memory." CD-ROMs are used for storing programs and data on discs. • Videodiscs are larger laser disks that are used to store visual images.
	Hypertext and Hypermedia	• Hypertext consists of computer-based verbal content that lets students read about one topic and then select related topics to explore. • Hypermedia are links of information that include verbal material as well as visual, auditory, and/or animated content.
	Computer-Mediated Communication (CMC)	• Computer-mediated communication (CMC) refers to communication through electronic exchanges; it is sometimes referred to as telecommunications or educational telecommunications. • The Internet is the core of CMC; it is worldwide and connects thousands of computer networks. The World Wide Web (the Web) is a hypermedia information retrieval system that links a variety of Internet materials; it includes text and graphics. A website is an individual's or an organization's location on the Internet. E-mail is electronic mail; messages can be sent to and received from individuals as well as large numbers of people via e-mail. • These are some effective ways to use the Internet in classrooms: as a tool to help students navigate and integrate knowledge; to foster collaborative learning; for e-mail; and to improve your own knowledge and understanding.
Technology and Sociocultural Diversity	Its Nature	• A special concern is that students from low-income, ethnic backgrounds, as well as schools in low-income areas, are underserved. • Females also might have less access and be technologically underserved.
The Potentials and Realities of Technology and Education	Their Nature	• Today's technologies can be remarkable tools for motivating students and guiding their learning. • Many teachers have not been adequately trained to use computers and other technology, and too often the computers become quickly outdated or break down. • Only when schools have technologically trained teachers and current, workable technologies will the technology revolution truly have an opportunity to transform classrooms.

Chapter Review

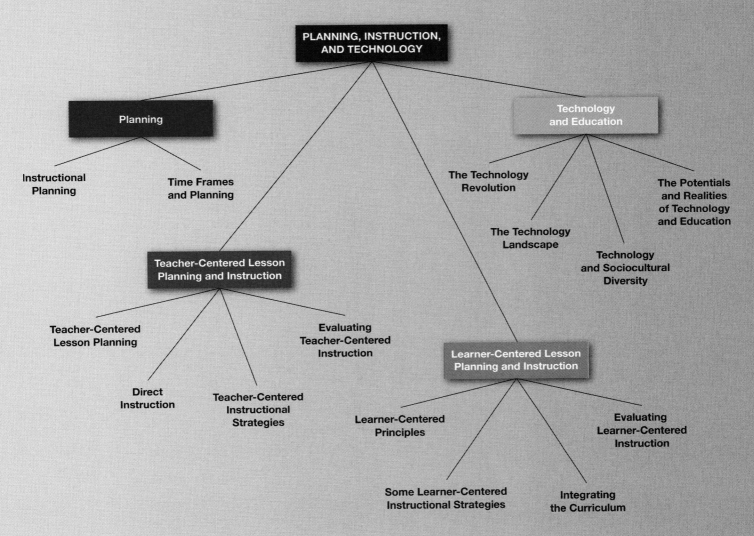

TO OBTAIN A DETAILED REVIEW OF THIS CHAPTER, STUDY THESE THREE SUMMARY TABLES:

Key Terms

instructional planning 354
behavorial objectives 357
task analysis 357
taxonomy 357
Bloom's taxonomy 357
direct instruction 359
advance organizers 361
expository advance
    organizers 361

comparative advance
    organizers 361
mastery learning 362
essential questions 374
discovery learning 374
guided discovery learning 375
computer-assisted instruction
    (CAI) 379

drill-and-practice
    programs 379
tutorials 379
instructional games 380
computer simulations 380
microworlds 380
CD-ROM 381
videodiscs 382

hypertext 382
hypermedia 382
computer-mediated
    communication (CMC) 383
Internet 383
World Wide Web
    (the Web) 383
Website 383
e-mail 383

Educational Psychology Checklist
PLANNING, INSTRUCTION, AND TECHNOLOGY

How much have you learned since the beginning of the chapter? Use the following items to help you review your knowledge and understanding of the chapter material. First, read the statement and mentally or briefly demonstrate on paper that you understand and can discuss the relevant information.

_____ I understand instructional planning.
_____ I can explain what teacher-centered lesson planning is.
_____ I know what direct instruction is.
_____ I can discuss a number of teacher-centered instructional strategies.
_____ I can describe teacher-centered lesson planning and instruction.
_____ I know what the APA learner-centered principles are and can describe them.

_____ I am aware of what problem-centered learning, essential questions, and discovery learning are.
_____ I can discuss a number of ways that the curriculum can be integrated.
_____ I can evaluate learner-centered lesson planning and instruction.
_____ I can discuss the nature of the technological revolution.
_____ I can describe many different ways technology can be used in classrooms.

For any items that you did not check off, go back and locate the relevant material in the chapter. Review the material until you feel you can check off the item. You also may want to use this checklist later in preparing for an exam.

Adventures for the Mind

Now that you have a good knowledge and understanding of the chapter, complete the following exercises to expand your thinking about the chapter's topics:

• Ask a teacher at the grade level you plan to teach to show you the materials she or he uses in planning lessons, units, the term, and the yearly curriculum for one or more subjects. Would you use the same system? How would you modify it to suit your own needs and style?

• With three or four other students in the class, discuss the grade level at which each of you plans to teach and the subject(s) you hope to teach, in terms of whether you think homework will benefit your students' learning and achievement. Also evaluate how much time each of you expects students to devote to homework each week and how the time is likely to vary across subjects.

• With three other students in the class, divide up the work of observing an early childhood, an elementary, a middle school, and a high school classroom. Reconvene after each of you has observed a classroom, and discuss the aspects of teacher-centered and learner-centered approaches the teachers were using. Evaluate how effective the approaches were.

• What has been your experience with computers in elementary, secondary, college, or home learning? Based on what you know about current and upcoming changes in technology, how might you improve on that experience for the students who will be in your classroom? Do you see one or more computers as an essential part of your classroom? What role are computers likely to play in your classroom?

Taking It to the Net

1. You have been asked to teach a class on clouds. What teaching methods or strategies might you use? What are some advantages and disadvantages to using those teaching methods or strategies?

2. There is currently an emphasis in teacher education on student-centered learning. What are the goals of a student-centered education? Why?

3. Consider again teaching a unit on clouds. How might you use technology to enhance learning and instruction? In general, how should technology be integrated with instruction?

Connect to http://www.mhhe.com/socscience/psychology/santedu/ttnet.htm to find the answers!

Case Studies

Case 1   *Alice Peterson:* Alice discovers that there might be a connection between room layout and behavior problems in a "pre-first-grade" classroom.

Case 2   *Julianne Bloom:* Julianne, an experienced teacher, tries to engage her students in writing activities during language arts. We observe her teaching and her frustrations when the lesson does not go as she had anticipated.

Case 3:   *Judith Kent:* Judith engages her students in whole-class discussion, and then the students work with partners on an assignment. Judith explains the planning process she went through to re-teach the lesson after it had not worked in the previous class.

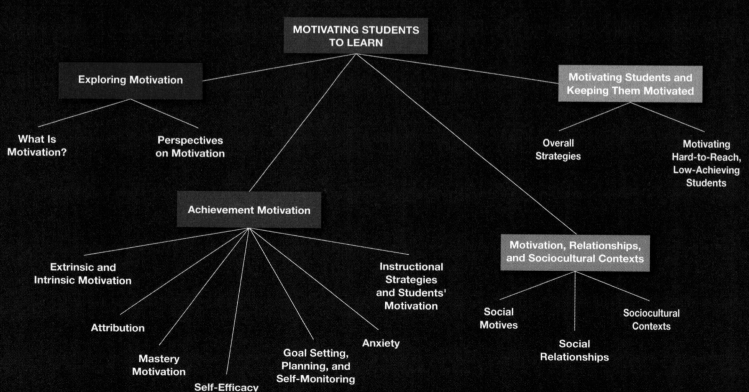

MOTIVATING STUDENTS
TO LEARN

Exploring Motivation

What Is
Motivation?

Perspectives
on Motivation

Achievement Motivation

Extrinsic and
Intrinsic Motivation

Attribution

Mastery
Motivation

Self-Efficacy

Goal Setting,
Planning, and
Self-Monitoring

Anxiety

Instructional
Strategies
and Students'
Motivation

Motivating Students and
Keeping Them Motivated

Overall
Strategies

Motivating
Hard-to-Reach,
Low-Achieving
Students

Motivation, Relationships,
and Sociocultural Contexts

Social
Motives

Social
Relationships

Sociocultural
Contexts

> " $\mathscr{T}$ he art of teaching is the art of awakening the curiosity of young minds. "
>
> Anatole France
> *French Novelist and Poet, 20th Century*

$\mathscr{P}$ review

In chapter 10, you learned that motivation is a key component of the American Psychological Association's learner-centered psychological principles. Indeed, motivation is a critical aspect of teaching and learning. Unmotivated students won't expend the necessary energy and effort to learn. Highly motivated students are eager to come to school and learn. These are some of the questions we will explore in this chapter:

- How can teachers get students to become more internally motivated?
- How can teachers get students to develop a better sense of mastering their environment?
- What are some good strategies to help students set goals and plan?
- How does anxiety interfere with students' achievement, and what can teachers do about it?
- How important is social motivation in students' lives?
- Once students are motivated, how can teachers keep them motivated?
- What are the best strategies for motivating hard-to-reach, low-achieving students?

Teaching Stories
Jaime Escalante

An immigrant from Bolivia, Jaime Escalante became a math teacher at Garfield High School in East Los Angeles in the 1970s. When he began teaching at Garfield, many of the students had little confidence in their math abilities and most of the teachers had low expectations for the students' success. Escalante took it as a special challenge to improve the students' math skills, even enable them to perform well on the Educational Testing Service Advanced Placement calculus exam.

The first year was difficult. Escalante's calculus class began at 8 A.M. He told the students the doors would be open at 7 A.M. and that instruction would begin at 7:30 A.M. He also worked with them after school and on weekends. He put together lots of handouts, told the students to take extensive notes, and required them to keep a folder. He gave them a 5-minute quiz each morning and a test every Friday. He started with 14 students, but in 2 weeks the number was cut in half. Only 5 students lasted through the spring. One of the boys who quit said, "I don't want to come at 7 o'clock. Why should I?"

On the five-point AP calculus test (with 5 highest, 1 lowest), a 3 or better means a student is performing at a level of being able to pass a college calculus class and will receive credit for it at most major universities. The AP calculus scores for Escalante's first five students were two 4s, two 2s, and one 1. This was better than the school had done in the past, but Escalante resolved to do better.

Three years later, the AP calculus test scores for Escalante's class of 15 students were one 5, four 4s, nine 3s, and one 2. Ten years after Escalante's first class, 151 students were taking calculus in the East Los Angeles high school, which is populated heavily by Latino students from low-income backgrounds.

Escalante's persistent, challenging, and inspiring teaching raised Garfield High, a school plagued by poor funding, violence, and inferior working conditions, to seventh place among U.S. schools in calculus. Escalante's commitment and motivation were transferred to his students, many of whom no one believed in before Escalante came along. Escalante's contributions were portrayed in the film *Stand and Deliver*. Escalante, his students, and celebrity guests also introduce basic math concepts for sixth- to twelfth-grade students on "Futures 1 and 2 with Jaime Escalante," a PBS series. Escalante has now retired from teaching but continues to work in a consulting role to help improve students' motivation to do well in math and improve their math skills. Escalante's story is testimony to how *one* teacher can make a major difference in students' motivation and achievement.

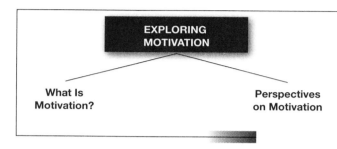

EXPLORING MOTIVATION

What Is Motivation?

Perspectives on Motivation

Exploring Motivation

A young Canadian, Terry Fox, completed one of the great long-distance runs in history (McNally, 1990). Averaging a marathon (26.2 miles) a day for 5 months, he ran 3,359 miles across Canada. What makes his feat truly remarkable is that Terry Fox lost one leg to cancer before the run. Fox completed his grueling run with the aid of a prosthetic limb. Terry Fox clearly was a motivated person. What does it mean to be motivated?

What Is Motivation?

A Teacher's View of Motivation

Motivation

Motivation *is the reasons why people behave the way they do. Motivated behavior is energized, directed, and sustained.* Why did Terry Fox complete his run? When Terry was hospitalized with cancer, he told himself that if he survived he would do something to help fund cancer research. Thus, the motivation for his run was to give purpose to his life by helping other people with cancer.

Terry Fox's behavior was energized, directed, and sustained. Running across Canada, he encountered unforeseen hurdles: severe headwinds, heavy rain, snow, and icy roads. Because of these conditions, he was averaging only 8 miles a day after the first month, far below what he had planned. But he kept going and picked up the pace in the second month until he was back on track to reach his goal. His example stands as a testimonial to how motivation can help each of us prevail.

Terry Fox's story is portrayed in a good classroom film, *The Power of Purpose*. One sixth-grade teacher showed the film to her class and then asked her students to write down what they learned from it. One student wrote, "I learned that even if something bad happens to you, you have to keep going, keep trying. Even if your body gets hurt, it can't take away your spirit."

As with Terry Fox's marathon run, a student's motivation in the classroom involves why the student is behaving in a particular way and the extent to which the student's behavior is energized, directed, and sustained. If a student doesn't complete an assignment because he is bored, lack of motivation is involved. If a student encounters challenges in researching and writing a paper, but persists and overcomes the hurdles, motivation is involved.

Perspectives on Motivation

Different psychological perspectives explain motivation in different ways. Let's explore three of these perspectives: behavioral, humanistic, and cognitive.

The Behavioral Perspective
The behavioral perspective emphasizes external rewards and punishments as keys in determining a student's motivation p. 240. **Incentives** *are positive or negative stimuli or events that can motivate a student's behavior.* Advocates of the use of incentives emphasize that they add interest or excitement to the class, and direct attention toward appropriate behavior and away from inappropriate behavior (Emmer & others, 1997).

Incentives that classroom teachers use include numerical scores and letter grades, which provide feedback about the quality of work the student has performed, and

Terry Fox, during his run across Canada to raise funds for cancer research.

Calvin & Hobbs, 1991, by United Press Syndicate.

checkmarks or stars for competently completing work. Other incentives include giving students recognition—for example, by displaying their work, giving them a certificate of achievement, placing them on the honor roll, or verbally mentioning their accomplishments. Another type of incentive focuses on allowing students to do something special, such as a desirable activity, as a reward for good work. This might include extra time at recess, playing computer games, a field trip, or even a party. Shortly, in our discussion of intrinsic and extrinsic motivation, we will look more closely at the issue of whether incentives are a good idea.

The Humanistic Perspective
The **humanistic perspective** *stresses students' capacity for personal growth, freedom to choose their destiny, and positive qualities.* This perspective is closely associated with Abraham Maslow's (1954, 1971) belief that certain basic needs must be satisfied before higher needs can be satisfied. According to Maslow's **hierarchy of needs,** *individuals' needs must be satisfied in the following sequence* (see figure 11.1):

Physiological: hunger, thirst, sleep
Safety: ensuring survival, such as protection from war and crime
Love and belongingness: security, affection, and attention from others
Esteem: feeling good about ourselves
Self-actualization: realization of one's potential

In Maslow's view, for example, students must satisfy their need for food before they can achieve.

Self-actualization, *the highest and most elusive of Maslow's needs, has been given special attention. It is the motivation to develop one's full potential as a human being.* In Maslow's view, self-actualization is possible only after the lower needs have been met. Maslow cautions that most people stop maturing after they have developed a high level of esteem and therefore never become self-actualized.

The idea that human needs are hierarchically arranged is appealing. Maslow's theory stimulates discussion about the

Maslow's Theory and Education
Self-Actualization

Figure 11.1
Maslow's Hierarchy of Needs
Abraham Maslow developed the hierarchy of human needs to show how we have to satisfy certain basic needs before we can satisfy higher needs. In the diagram, lower-level needs are shown toward the base of the pyramid, higher-level needs toward the peak.

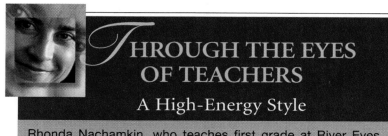

THROUGH THE EYES OF TEACHERS

A High-Energy Style

Rhonda Nachamkin, who teaches first grade at River Eves Elementary School in Roswell, Georgia, has a high-energy style and approaches each unit as if it is a Hollywood production. She turns the classroom into an Egyptian tomb, New York City, and Mount Olympus. She sends parents scurrying to learn who Anubis (Egyptian god) and Prometheus (Greek Titan who stole fire) were so they can converse about these topics with their six-year-olds. Rhonda likes to use multiple versions of fairy tales to teach reading, spelling, and analytical concepts.

Rhonda Nachamkin helps one of her students, Patrick Drones, with his work.

Always bear in mind that your own resolution to succeed is more important than any one thing.

Abraham Lincoln
President, 19th Century

ordering of motives in students' and teachers' lives. However, not everyone agrees with Maslow's ordering. For example, for some students cognitive needs might be more fundamental than esteem needs. Other students might meet their cognitive needs even though they have not experienced love and belongingness.

The Cognitive Perspective   According to the cognitive perspective on motivation, students' thoughts guide their motivation. In recent years there has been a tremendous surge of interest in the cognitive perspective on motivation (Pintrich, 2000; Winter, 2000) ◀▥ p. 241. This interest focuses on such ideas as students' internal motivation to achieve, their attributions about success or failure (especially the perception that effort is an important factor in achievement), and their beliefs that they can effectively control their environment, as well as the importance of goal setting, planning, and monitoring progress toward a goal (Pintrich, 2000; Schunk & Ertmer, 2000; Zimmerman, 2000).

Thus, whereas the behaviorist perspective sees the student's motivation as a consequence of external incentives, the cognitive perspective argues that external pressures should be deemphasized. The cognitive perspective recommends that students should be given more opportunities and responsibility for controlling their own achievement outcomes.

The cognitive perspective on motivation fits with the ideas of R. W. White (1959), who proposed the concept of **competence motivation,** *the idea that people are motivated to deal effectively with their environment, to master their world, and to process information efficiently.* White said that people do these things, not because they serve biological needs, but because people have an internal motivation to effectively interact with the environment.

A review of our discussion of perspectives on motivation is presented in summary table 11.1.

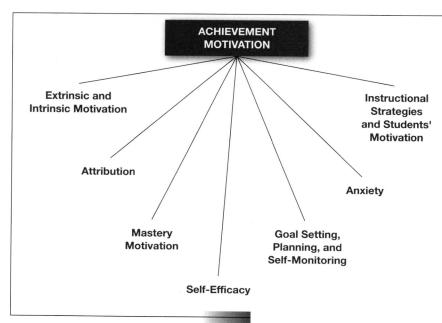

Achievement Motivation

The current interest in achievement motivation has been fueled by the cognitive perspective. We begin with the controversy over intrinsic versus extrinsic motivation, then discuss other aspects of achievement motivation, such as setting goals, planning, and monitoring progress toward goals. However, we begin with the topic in achievement motivation that has generated the most controversy and interest: extrinsic versus intrinsic motivation.

Extrinsic and Intrinsic Motivation

We begin our coverage of extrinsic and intrinsic motivation by examining what they are, then turn to a number of ideas about how they work best in learning and achievement.

$\mathcal{S}$UMMARY $\mathcal{T}$ABLE 11.1
Exploring Motivation

Concept	Processes/ Related Ideas	Characteristics/Description
What Is Motivation?	Its Nature	• The study of motivation focuses on why people behave the way they do. • Motivated behavior is energized, directed, and sustained.
Perspectives on Motivation	Behavioral	• The behavioral perspective on motivation emphasizes that external rewards and punishments are the key factors that determine a student's motivation. • Incentives are positive or negative stimuli or events that can motivate a student's behavior.
	Humanistic	• The humanistic perspective stresses our capacity for personal growth, freedom to choose our own destiny, and our positive qualities. • According to Maslow's humanistic perspective, there is a hierarchy of motives, and students' needs must be satisfied in a particular sequence. Self-actualization, the highest and most elusive of the needs Maslow describes, involves the motivation to develop one's full potential as a human being.
	Cognitive	• In the cognitive perspective on motivation, students' thoughts guide their motivation. • The cognitive perspective focuses on the internal motivation to achieve, attributions, students' beliefs that they can effectively control their environment, as well as goal setting, planning, and monitoring progress toward a goal. • The cognitive perspective meshes with R. W. White's concept of competence motivation.

What Are Intrinsic and Extrinsic Motivation?   The behavioral perspective emphasizes the importance of extrinsic motivation in achievement. **Extrinsic motivation** *involves external incentives such as rewards and punishments.* The humanistic and cognitive approaches stress the importance of intrinsic motivation in achievement. **Intrinsic motivation** *is based on internal factors such as self-determination, curiosity, challenge, and effort.* Some students study hard because they want to make good grades or avoid parental disapproval (extrinsic motivation). Other students study hard because they are internally motivated to achieve high standards in their work (intrinsic motivation).

Self-Determination and Personal Choice   One view of intrinsic motivation emphasizes self-determination (deCharms, 1984; Deci & Ryan, 1994). In this view, students want to believe that they are doing something because of their own will, not because of external success or rewards.

Researchers have found that students' internal motivation and intrinsic interest in school tasks increase when students have some choice and some opportunities to take personal responsibility for their learning (Stipek, 1996). For example, in one study, high school science students who were encouraged to organize their own experiments demonstrated more care and interest in laboratory work than did their counterparts who had to follow detailed instructions and directions (Rainey, 1965). In another study, which included mainly African American students from low-income backgrounds, teachers were encouraged to give the students more responsibility for their school programs (deCharms, 1976, 1984)—in particular, opportunities to set their own goals, plan how to reach the goals, and monitor their progress toward the goals.

Intrinsic Motivation

The reward of a thing well done is to have done it.

Ralph Waldo Emerson
American Poet and Essayist, 19th Century

TEACHING STRATEGIES
For Providing Students with Opportunities for Self-Determination and Choice

Some ways you can promote self-determination and choice in your classroom include (Brophy, 1998; Deci & Ryan, 1994):

1. *Take the time to talk with students and explain to them why a learning activity they are being asked to do is important.*
2. *Be attentive to students' feelings when they are being asked to do something they don't want to do.*
3. *Manage the classroom in a way that lets students make personal choices.* Let students select topics for book reports, writing assignments, and research projects. Give them the choice of how they want to report their work (for instance, to you or to the class as a whole, and individually or with a partner).
4. *Establish learning centers where students can work individually or collaboratively with other students on different projects.* These might include language arts, social studies, or computer centers where students can select the activities they want to engage in from a menu that you have developed.
5. *Divide students into self-selected interest groups and let them work on relevant research projects.*

These students were given an opportunity to write and perform their own play. These kinds of self-determining opportunities can enhance students' motivation to achieve.

"Your son has made a career choice, Mildred. He's going to win the lottery and travel a lot."

© 1986; Reprinted courtesy of Bunny Hoest and Parade Magazine.

Students were given some choice in the activities they wanted to engage in and when they would do them. They also were encouraged to take personal responsibility for their behavior, including reaching the goals that they had set. Compared to a control group, students in this intrinsic motivation/self-determination group had higher achievement gains and were more likely to graduate from high school.

Optimal Experiences and Flow   Mihaly Csikszentmihalyi (1990, 1993, 2000), whose work on creativity was discussed in chapter 4, also has developed ideas that are relevant to understanding motivation. He has studied the optimal experiences of people for more than two decades. People report that these optimal experiences involve feelings of deep enjoyment and happiness. Csikszentmihalyi uses the term **flow** *to describe optimal experiences in life. He has found that flow occurs most often when people develop a sense of mastery and are absorbed in a state of concentration while they engage in an activity.* He argues that flow occurs when individuals are engaged in challenges they find neither too difficult nor too easy.

Perceived levels of challenge and skill can result in different outcomes (see figure 11.2) (Brophy, 1998). Flow is most likely to occur in areas in which students are challenged and perceive themselves as having a high degree of skill. When students' skills are high but the activity provides little challenge, the result is boredom. When both the challenge and skill levels are low, students feel apathy. And when students face a challenging task that they don't believe they have adequate skills to master, they experience anxiety.

TEACHING STRATEGIES
For Encouraging Students to Achieve Flow

How can you encourage students to achieve flow? Some strategies are (Csikszentmihalyi, Rathunde, & Whalen, 1993):

1. *Be knowledgeable about the subject matter, show enthusiasm when you teach, and present yourself as a model who is intrinsically motivated.*
2. *Maintain an optimal match between what you challenge students to do and what their skills are.* That is, encourage students to achieve challenging but reasonable goals.
3. *Provide students with both instructional and emotional support that encourages them to tackle learning with confidence and a minimum of anxiety.*

Our discussions of self-determination and flow emphasized increasing students' intrinsic motivation. Next we examine the role that extrinsic rewards play in either undermining or promoting intrinsic motivation.

Effects of Rewards   In some situations, rewards can undermine learning. In one study, students who already had a strong interest in art and did not expect a reward spent more time drawing than did students who also had a strong interest in art but knew they would be rewarded for drawing (Lepper, Greene, & Nisbett, 1973). Other researchers have found similar effects (Morgan, 1984).

However, classroom rewards can be useful (Eisenberger & Cameron, 1998). Two uses are (Bandura, 1982; Deci, 1975) (1) as an incentive to engage in tasks, in which case the goal is to control the student's behavior, and (2) to convey information about mastery. When rewards convey information about mastery, they are more likely to promote student feelings of competence. However, rewards used as incentives lead to perceptions that the student's behavior was caused by the external reward, and not by the student's own motivation to be competent.

To better understand the difference between using rewards to control students' behavior and using them to provide information about mastery, consider this example (Schunk, 1996): A teacher puts a reward system in place in which the more work students accomplish, the more points they will earn. Students will be motivated to work to earn points because the points can be exchanged for privileges, but the points also provide information about their capabilities. That is, the more points students earn, the more work they have accomplished. As they accumulate points, students are more likely to feel competent. In contrast, if points are provided simply for spending time on a task, the task might be perceived as a means to an end. In this case, because the points don't convey anything about capabilities, students are likely to perceive the rewards as controlling their behavior.

Thus, rewards that convey information about students' mastery can increase intrinsic motivation by increasing their sense of competence. However, negative feedback, such as criticism, that carries information that students are *in*competent can undermine intrinsic motivation, especially if students doubt their ability to become competent (Stipek, 1996).

Judy Cameron and W. David Pierce (1996) argue that there is too strong a prevailing belief in education that rewards always decrease a student's intrinsic motivation. In their analysis of approximately a hundred studies, they found that verbal rewards (praise and positive feedback) can be used to enhance

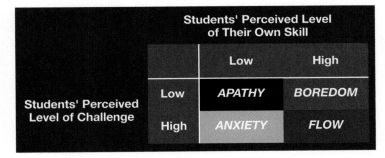

Figure **11.2**

Outcomes of Perceived Levels of Challenge and Skill

students' intrinsic motivation. They also concluded that when tangible rewards (such as gold stars and money) were offered contingent on task performance or given unexpectedly, intrinsic motivation was maintained. Some critics believe that Cameron and Pierce's analysis is flawed—for instance, that it does not adequately detect some of the negative effects of rewards on motivation (Kohn, 1996; Ryan & Deci, 1996).

Developmental Changes Many psychologists and educators believe that an important goal of parenting and teaching should be to have children develop greater internalization and intrinsic motivation as they grow older. However, researchers have found that as students move from the early elementary school years to the high school years, their intrinsic motivation decreases (Harter, 1996). In one research study, the biggest drop in intrinsic motivation and increase in extrinsic motivation was between sixth grade and seventh grade (Harter, 1981). In another study, as students moved from sixth through eighth grade, they increasingly said school is boring and irrelevant (Harter, 1996). In this study, however, students who were intrinsically motivated were doing much better academically than those who were extrinsically motivated.

Why the shift toward extrinsic motivation as children move to higher grades? One explanation is that school grading practices reinforces an external motivation orientation. That is, as students get older, they lock into the increasing emphasis on grades and their internal motivation drops.

Jacquelynne Eccles and her colleagues (Eccles, 2000; Eccles & Midgley, 1989; Eccles, Midgley, & Adler, 1984; Wigfield, Eccles, & Pintrich, 1996) identified some specific changes in the school context that help to explain the decline in intrinsic motivation. Middle and junior high schools are more impersonal, more formal, more evaluative, and more competitive than elementary schools ◀▥ p. 99. Students compare themselves more with other students because they increasingly are graded in terms of their relative performance on assignments and standardized tests.

Proposing the concept of **person-environment fit,** *Eccles and her colleagues (1993) argue that a lack of fit between the middle school/junior high environment and the needs of young adolescents produces increasingly negative self-evaluations and attitudes toward school.* Their study of more than 1,500 students found that teachers became more controlling just at the time when adolescents were seeking more autonomy, and the teacher-student relationship became more impersonal at a time when students were

According to Jacquelynne Eccles and her colleagues, too many middle and junior high schools do not reflect an adequate person-environment fit. What does this mean?

seeking more independence from their parents and needed more support from other adults. At a time when adolescents were becoming more self-conscious, an increased emphasis on grades and other competitive comparisons only made things worse.

Although there is less research on the transition to high school, the existing research suggests that, like the transition to middle school, it can produce similar problems (Eccles, Wigfield, & Schiefele, 1998; Wehlage, 1989). High schools often are even larger and more bureaucratic than middle schools. In such schools, a sense of community usually is undermined, with little opportunity for students and teachers to get to know each other (Bryk, Lee, & Smith, 1989). As a consequence, distrust between students and teachers develops easily and there is little communication about students' goals and values. Such contexts can especially harm the motivation of students who are not doing well academically.

Evaluating Intrinsic and Extrinsic Motivation   Evidence is very strongly in favor of establishing a classroom climate in which students are intrinsically motivated to learn (Eccles, 2000; Hennessey & Amabile, 1998; Lepper, 1998). Students are more motivated to learn when they are given choices, become absorbed in challenges that match their skills, and receive rewards that have informational value but are not used for control. Praise also can enhance students' intrinsic motivation. Middle school and junior high school teachers can benefit students by thinking of ways to make these school settings more personal, less formal, and more intrinsically challenging.

In the next section, our attention shifts to attribution. As you read about attribution, you will see that intrinsic and extrinsic motivation are often one set of causes that students look to as they attempt to explain their behavior.

Attribution

Attribution theory *states that in their effort to make sense of their own behavior or performance, individuals are motivated to discover its underlying causes.* Attributions are perceived causes of outcomes. In a way, attribution theorists say, students are like intuitive scientists, seeking to explain the cause behind what happens (Weary, 2000; Weiner, 2000). For example, a secondary school student asks, "Why am I not doing well in this class?" or "Did I get a good grade because I studied hard or the teacher made up an easy test, or both?" The search for a cause or explanation is most likely to be initiated when unexpected and important events end in failure, such as when a good student gets a low grade (Graham & Weiner, 1996). Some of the most frequently inferred causes of success and failure are ability, effort, task ease or difficulty, luck, mood, and help or hindrance from others.

Bernard Weiner (1986, 1992) identified three dimensions of causal attributions: (1) *locus,* whether the cause is internal or external to the actor; (2) *stability,* the extent to which the cause remains the same or changes; and (3) *controllability,* the extent to which the individual can control the cause. For example, a student might perceive his aptitude as located internally, stable, and uncontrollable. The student also might perceive chance or luck as external to himself, variable, and uncontrollable. Figure 11.3 lists eight possible combinations of locus, stability, and controllability and how they match up with various common explanations of failure.

A student's perception of success or failure as due to internal or external factors influences the student's self-esteem. Students who perceive their success as being due to internal reasons, such as effort, are more likely to have higher self-esteem following success than students who believe that their success was due to external reasons, such as luck. In the aftermath of failure, internal attributions lead to decreased self-esteem.

A student's perception of the stability of a cause influences her expectation of success. If she ascribes a positive outcome to a stable cause, such as aptitude, she expects future success. Similarly, if she attributes a negative outcome to a stable cause, she expects future failure. When students attribute failure to unstable causes such as

Attribution
Effort, Expectations,
and Motivation

Combination of Causal Attributions	Reason Students Give for Failure
Internal-Stable-Uncontrollable	Low aptitude
Internal-Stable-Controllable	Never study
Internal-Unstable-Uncontrollable	Sick the day of the test
Internal-Unstable-Controllable	Did not study for this particular test
External-Stable-Uncontrollable	School has tough requirements
External-Stable-Controllable	The instructor is biased
External-Unstable-Uncontrollable	Bad luck
External-Unstable-Controllable	Friends failed to help

Figure **11.3**

Combinations of Causal Attributions and Explanations for Failure

When students fail or do poorly on a test or assignment, they often generate causal attributions in an attempt to explain their poor performance. The explanations reflect eight combinations of Weiner's three main categories of attributions: locus (internal-external), stability (stable-unstable), and controllability (controllable-uncontrollable).

bad luck or lack of effort, they might develop expectations that they will be able to succeed in the future, because they perceive the cause of their failure as changeable.

A student's perception of the controllability of a cause is related to a number of emotional outcomes such as anger, guilt, pity, and shame (Graham & Weiner, 1996). When students perceive that they are prevented from succeeding because of external factors that other people could have controlled (such as noise or bias), they often become angry. When students perceive that they have not done well because of internally controllable causes (such as not making enough effort or being negligent), they often feel guilty. When students perceive that others do not achieve their goals because of uncontrollable causes (such as lack of ability or a physical handicap), they feel pity or sympathy. And when students fail because of internally uncontrollable factors (such as low ability), they feel shame, humiliation, and embarrassment.

To see how attributions affect subsequent achievement strivings, consider these two students (Graham & Weiner, 1996):

1. Jane flunks her math test. She subsequently seeks tutoring and increases her study time.
2. Susan also fails her math test but decides to drop out of school.

Jane's negative outcome (failing the test) motivated her to search for the reasons behind her low grade. She attributes the failure to herself, not blaming her teacher or bad luck. She also attributes the failure to an unstable factor—lack of preparation and study time. Thus, she perceives that her failure is due to internal, unstable, and also controllable factors. Because the factors are unstable, Jane has a reasonable expectation that she can still succeed in the future. And because the factors are controllable, she also feels guilty. Her expectations for success enable her to overcome her deflated sense of self-esteem. Her hope for the future results in renewed goal-setting and increased motivation to do well on the next test.

Susan's negative outcome (also failing the test) led her to drop out of school rather than resolving to study harder. Her failure also stimulates her to make causal attributions. Susan ascribes failure to herself and attributes her poor performance to lack of ability, which is internal, unstable, and uncontrollable. Because the perceived cause is internal, her self-esteem suffers. Because it is stable, she sees failure in her future and has a helpless feeling that she can't do anything about it. And because it is uncontrollable, she feels ashamed and humiliated. In addition, her parents and teacher tell her they feel sorry for her but don't provide any recommendations or strategies for success, furthering her belief that she is incompetent. With low expectations for success, low self-esteem, and a depressed mood, Susan decides to drop out of school.

What are the best strategies for teachers to use in helping students like Susan change their attributions? Educational psychologists often recommend providing students with a planned series of experiences in achievement contexts in which modeling, information about strategies, practice, and feedback are used to help them (1) concentrate on the task at hand rather than worrying about failing, (2) cope with failures by retracing their steps to discover their mistake or analyzing the problem to discover another approach, and (3) attribute their failures to a lack of effort rather than lack of ability (Brophy, 1998; Dweck & Elliott, 1983).

The current strategy is that rather than be exposed to models who handle tasks with ease and demonstrate success, students should be presented with models who struggle to overcome mistakes before finally succeeding (Brophy, 1998). In this way, students learn how to deal with frustration, persist in the face of difficulties, and constructively cope with failure.

Approaches to Attribution
Mastery Motivation
Mastery Motivation
and Sports

Mastery Motivation

Closely related to intrinsic motivation and attribution is mastery motivation. Researchers have identified mastery as one of three types of achievement orientation: mastery, helpless, and performance.

Carol Dweck and her colleagues (Henderson & Dweck, 1990; Dweck & Leggett, 1988) have found that children show two distinct responses to challenging or difficult circumstances: a mastery orientation or a helpless orientation. Children with a **mastery orientation** *focus on the task rather than on their ability, have positive affect (suggesting they enjoy the challenge), and generate solution-oriented strategies that improve their performance.* Mastery-oriented students often instruct themselves to pay attention, to think carefully, and to remember strategies that worked for them in the past (Anderman, Maehr, & Midgley, 1996). In contrast, children with a **helpless orientation** *focus on their personal inadequacies, often attribute their difficulty to a lack of ability, and display negative affect (including boredom and anxiety). This orientation undermines their performance.*

Mastery- and helpless-oriented students do not differ in general ability. However, they have different theories about their abilities. Mastery-oriented students believe their ability can be changed and improved. They endorse such statements as "Smartness is something you can increase as much as you want to." In contrast, helpless-oriented students believe that ability is basically fixed and cannot be changed. They endorse such statements as "You can learn new things, but how smart you are pretty much stays the same." The mastery orientation is much like the attributional combination of internal-unstable-controllable. The helpless orientation is much like the attributional combination of internal-stable-uncontrollable.

A mastery orientation also can be contrasted with a **performance orientation,** *which involves being concerned with outcome rather than with process. For performance-oriented students, winning is what matters and happiness is thought to be a result of winning.* For mastery-oriented students, what matters is the sense that they are effectively interacting with their environment. Mastery-oriented students do like to win, but winning isn't as important to them as it is to performance-oriented students. Developing their skills is more important.

Mastery motivation has much in common with Csikszentmihalyi's concept of flow—being absorbed in a state of concentration during an activity. Mastery-oriented students immerse themselves in a task and focus their concentration on developing

May you live all the days of your life.

Jonathan Swift
English Writer, 18th Century

their skills rather than worry about whether they are going to outperform others. In a state of flow, students become so attuned to what they are doing that they are oblivious to distractions.

Performance-oriented students who are not confident of their success face a special problem (Stipek, 1996). If they try and fail, they often take their failure as evidence of low ability. By not trying at all, they can maintain an alternative, personally more acceptable explanation for their failure. This dilemma leads some students to engage in behavior that protects them from an image of incompetence in the short run but interferes with their learning and achievement in the long run (Covington, 1992). To avoid the attribution of low ability, some of these students simply don't try, or they cheat; others might resort to more subtle image-protecting strategies such as procrastinating, making excuses, working halfheartedly, or setting unrealistic goals.

Self-Efficacy

In chapter 7, "Behavioral Approaches, Social Cognitive Approaches, and Teaching," we introduced Albert Bandura's concept of **self-efficacy,** *the belief that one can master a situation and produce positive outcomes* ◀▥ p. 256. Bandura (1994, 1997, 1998, 2000) believes that self-efficacy is a critical factor in whether or not students achieve. Self-efficacy has much in common with mastery motivation and intrinsic motivation. Self-efficacy is the belief that "I can"; helplessness is the belief that "I cannot" (Stipek, 1996). Students with high self-efficacy endorse such statements as "I know that I will be able to learn the material in this class" and "I expect to be able to do well at this activity."

Dale Schunk (1989, 1991, 1999) has applied the concept of self-efficacy to many aspects of students' achievement. In his view, self-efficacy influences a student's choice of activities. Students with low self-efficacy for learning might avoid many learning tasks, especially those that are challenging, whereas students with high self-efficacy eagerly work at learning tasks. Students with high self-efficacy are more likely to expend effort and persist at a learning task than are students with low self-efficacy.

Your self-efficacy as a teacher will have a major impact on the quality of learning that your students experience. Teachers with low self-efficacy often become mired in classroom problems. Low-self-efficacy teachers don't have confidence in their ability to manage their classrooms, become stressed and angered at students' misbehavior, are pessimistic about students' ability to improve, take a custodial view of their job, often resort to restrictive and punitive modes of discipline, and say that if they had it to do all over again they would not choose teaching as a profession (Melby, 1995).

In one study, teachers' instructional self-efficacy was linked with their students' mathematical and language achievement over the course of an academic year (Ashton & Webb, 1986). Students learned much more from teachers with a sense of efficacy than from those beset by self-doubts. Teachers with high self-efficacy tend to view difficult students as reachable and teachable. They regard learning problems as surmountable with extra effort and ingenious strategies to help struggling students. Low-self-efficacy teachers are inclined to say that low student ability is the reason their students are not learning.

The ability to transmit subject matter is one aspect of instructional self-efficacy, but instructional self-efficacy also includes the belief that one can maintain an orderly classroom that is an exciting place to learn and the belief that it is possible to enlist resources and get parents positively involved in children's learning (Bandura, 1997).

Bandura (1997) also addressed the characteristics of efficacious schools. School leaders seek ways to improve instruction. They figure out ways to work around stifling policies and regulations that impede academic innovations. Masterful academic leadership by the principal builds teachers' sense of instructional efficacy; in low-achieving schools, principals function more as administrators and disciplinarians (Coladarci, 1992).

*O*nly with confidence do we advance boldly in the direction of our dreams.

*O*nly with confidence do we tackle life's challenges with the belief that we can handle them.

David McNally
American Author, 20th Century

Self-Efficacy
Self-Efficacy Resources

TEACHING STRATEGIES
For Improving Students' Self-Efficacy

Following are some good strategies for improving students' self-efficacy (Stipek, 1996):

1. *Teach students specific strategies, such as outlining and summarizing, that can improve their ability to focus on their tasks.*
2. *Guide students in setting goals, especially in creating short-term goals after they have made long-term goals.* Short-term goals especially help students to judge their progress.
3. *Give students performance-contingent rewards, which are more likely to signal mastery, rather than rewards for merely engaging in a task.*
4. *Combine strategy training with an emphasis on goals, and give feedback to students on how their learning strategies relate to their performance.* Schunk and his colleagues (Schunk, 1996; Schunk & Rice, 1989; Schunk & Swartz, 1993) have found that this combination can enhance students' self-efficacy and skill development.
5. *Provide students with support.* Positive support can come from teachers, parents, and peers. So can statements from teachers like "You can do this."
6. *Make sure that students are not overly aroused and anxious.* When students worry and agonize about their achievement, their self-efficacy diminishes.
7. *Provide students with positive adult and peer models.* Certain characteristics of these models can improve students' self-efficacy. For example, students who observe teachers and peers cope effectively and master challenges often adopt the models' behaviors. Modeling is especially effective in promoting self-efficacy when students observe success by peers who are similar in ability to themselves. One positive way for teachers to use peer modeling to improve students' self-efficacy is to have each student work on some aspect of a task and then have the students explain their part to other group members after they have mastered it (Schunk & Zimmerman, 1996). This type of peer modeling, discussed earlier in the book as collaborative and cooperative learning, teaches skills and raises others' self-efficacy.

High expectations and standards for achievement pervade efficacious schools. Teachers regard their students as capable of high academic achievement, set challenging academic standards for them, and provide support to help them reach these high standards. In contrast, in low-achieving schools not much is expected academically of students, teachers spend less time actively teaching and monitoring students' academic progress, and tend to write off a high percentage of students as unteachable (Brookover & others, 1979). Not surprisingly, students in such schools have low self-efficacy and a sense of academic futility.

At this point we have studied a number of ideas about extrinsic and intrinsic motivation, attribution, mastery motivation, and self-efficacy. A review of these ideas is presented in summary table 11.2. Next, we will continue our coverage of achievement motivation by studying goal setting, planning, and self-monitoring.

Goal Setting, Planning, and Self-Monitoring

In chapter 7, "Behavioral Approaches, Social Cognitive Approaches, and Teaching," we discussed a number of ideas about self-regulatory learning, which consists of the self-generation of thoughts, feelings, and behaviors to reach a goal ◀||| p. 265. Here we expand on those ideas and focus on the importance of goal setting, planning, and self-monitoring in achievement.

Goal Setting

Researchers have found that self-efficacy and achievement improve when students set goals that are specific, proximal, and challenging (Bandura, 1997; Schunk, 1996; Schunk & Ertmer, 2000). A nonspecific, fuzzy goal is: "I want to be successful." A more concrete, specific goal is: "I want to make the honor roll by the end of the semester."

*S*UMMARY *T*ABLE 11.2
Extrinsic and Intrinsic Motivation, Attribution, Mastery Motivation, and Self-Efficacy

Concept	Processes/ Related Ideas	Characteristics/Description
Extrinsic and Intrinsic Motivation	What Are Intrinsic and Extrinsic Motivation?	• Extrinsic motivation involves external incentives such as rewards and punishment. • Intrinsic motivation is based on internal factors such as self-determination, curiosity, challenge, and effort.
	Self-Determination and Personal Choice	• One view of intrinsic motivation emphasizes its self-determining characteristics. • Giving students some choice and providing opportunities for personal responsibility increase intrinsic motivation.
	Optimal Experiences and Flow	• Csikszentmihalyi uses the term *flow* to describe life's optimal experiences, which involve a sense of mastery and absorbed concentration in an activity. • Flow is most likely to occur in areas in which students are challenged and perceive themselves as having a high degree of skill.
	Effects of Rewards	• In some situations, rewards can actually undermine performance. • When rewards are used, they should convey information about task mastery rather than external control.
	Developmental Changes	• Researchers have found that as students move from the early elementary school years to high school, their intrinsic motivation drops, especially during the middle school years. • The concept of person-environment fit calls attention to the lack of fit between adolescents' increasing interest in autonomy and schools' increasing control, which results in students' negative self-evaluations and attitudes toward school.
	Evaluating Intrinsic and Extrinsic Motivation	• Overall, most experts recommend that teachers create a classroom atmosphere in which students are intrinsically motivated to learn.
Attribution	Its Nature	• Attribution theory states that individuals are motivated to discover the underlying causes of behavior in an effort to make sense of the behavior. • Weiner identified three dimensions of causal attributions: (1) locus, (2) stability, and (3) controllability. Combinations of these dimensions produce different explanations of failure and success.
Mastery Motivation	Its Nature	• A mastery orientation focuses on the task rather than ability, involves positive affect, and includes solution-oriented strategies. • A helpless orientation focuses on personal inadequacies, attributing difficulty to lack of ability, and displaying negative affect (such as boredom or anxiety). • A performance orientation involves being concerned with the achievement outcome rather than the achievement process.
Self-Efficacy	Its Nature	• Self-efficacy is the belief that one can master a situation and produce positive outcomes. • Bandura believes that self-efficacy is a critical factor in whether students will achieve. • Schunk argues that self-efficacy influences a student's choice of tasks, and that low-efficacy students avoid many learning tasks, especially those that are challenging. • Instructional strategies that emphasize "I can do it" benefit students. • Low self-efficacy teachers become mired in classroom problems.

Students can set both long-term (distal) and short-term (proximal) goals. It is okay to let students set some long-term goals, such as "I want to graduate from high school" or "I want to go to college," but if you do, make sure that they also create short-term goals, which are steps along the way. "Getting an A on the next math test" is an example of a short-term, proximal goal. So is "Doing all of my homework by 4 P.M. Sunday." As mentioned earlier, attention should focus mainly on short-term goals, which help students judge their progress better than do long-term goals. David McNally (1990), author of *Even Eagles Need a Push,* advises that when students set goals and plan, they should be reminded to live their lives one day at a time. Have them make their commitments in bite-size chunks. A house is built one brick at a time, a cathedral one stone at a time. The artist paints one stroke at a time. The student should also work in small increments.

Another good strategy is to encourage students to set challenging goals. A challenging goal is a commitment to self-improvement. Strong interest and involvement in activities is sparked by challenges. Goals that are easy to reach generate little interest or effort. However, goals should be optimally matched to the student's skill level. If goals are unrealistically high, the result will be repeated failures that lower the student's self-efficacy.

Carol Dweck (1996; Dweck & Leggett, 1988), John Nicholls (1979; Nicholls & others, 1990), and their colleagues define goals in terms of immediate achievement-related focus and definition of success. For example, Nicholls distinguishes between ego-involved goals, task-involved goals, and work-avoidant goals. Students who have ego-involved goals strive to maximize favorable evaluations and minimize unfavorable ones. Thus, ego-involved students might focus on how smart they will look and how effectively they can outperform other students. In contrast, students who have task-involved goals focus on mastering tasks. They concentrate on how they can do the task and what they will learn. Students with work-avoidant goals try to exert as little effort as possible on a task. Encourage students to develop task-involved, mastery goals rather than ego-involved or work-avoidant goals.

Unfortunately, many of the changes involved in the transition to middle schools (such as a drop in grades, a lack of support for autonomy, whole-class task organization and between-class ability groupings that likely increase social comparison, concerns about evaluation, and competitiveness) are likely to increase students' motivation to achieve performance goals rather than mastery goals (Eccles, Wigfield, & Schiefele, 1998). In one research study, both teachers and students reported that performance-focused goals were more common and task-focused goals less common in middle school than in elementary school classrooms (Midgley, Anderman, & Hicks, 1995). In addition, the elementary-school teachers reported using task-focused goals more than middle school teachers did. At both grades, the extent to which the teachers were task-focused was linked with the students' and the teachers' sense of personal efficacy. Not unexpectedly, personal efficacy was lower for the middle school than elementary school participants. Thus, middle school teachers especially need to increasingly include task-focused goals in their instruction.

It is not enough just to get students to set goals. It also is important to encourage them to plan how they will reach their goals (Elliot, McGregor, & Gable, 1999; Randi & Corno, 2000). Being a good planner means managing time effectively, setting priorities, and being organized.

THROUGH THE EYES OF TEACHERS

The Taxman Cometh

Middle graders for the most part cannot see beyond the 3:30 bell. Their planning abilities are almost nil. I have a big calendar on my wall next to the pencil sharpener with not only my upcoming assignments but the other teacher's as well. Further, the kids are required to keep assignment notebooks with their assignments in them for each subject. I follow up, especially in the beginning of the year, by ensuring each individual student makes entries on their calendar. The whole idea is to make them conscious of time. Elementary and middle graders' concept of time is very different from adults, in that their frame of reference and focus is far narrower. Next week to them is like next month to us; therefore, a project that is due next month is in their eyes a lifetime away—hardly a blip on their radar. Hence the need for constant reminding, to reinforce the concept that time really does pass, and therefore progress has to be made. It's definitely an uphill battle, though, which frequently is never won—witness the lines at the post office on April 14th.

Chuck Rawls
Language Arts Teacher
Appling Middle School
Macon, Georgia

*T*he highest wisdom I know is that success is conquered by those who conquer it each day anew.

Johann Wolfgang von Goethe
German Poet and Playwright, 19th Century

Goal Setting Worksheet

THROUGH THE EYES OF TEACHERS

Helping Students Set Goals

Each quarter I have my students set goals for themselves and keep a copy of them. At the end of the quarter, they evaluate their work based on how fully they have accomplished those goals. They may want to finish three pieces of writing, explore two new authors, or improve their persuasion skills. Setting goals and monitoring progress toward them are vital life skills that all students should be given opportunities to practice.

Kathy Fuchser
English Teacher
St. Francis High School
Humphrey, Nebraska

Managing Time

In chapter 10, we described the importance of planning for teachers ◀▥ p. 354. Planning is also important for students. Give students, especially at the middle school and high school levels, practice at managing their time, setting priorities, and being organized.

You might start by giving them a calendar for the term on which they can write down when their important exam dates, papers, homework assignments, and other tasks and activities are going to occur. Ask them to think about how many days or weeks they will need to study for major exams and write major papers. Have them mark the necessary days or weeks in which these tasks will be their main priorities. Tell them that their term calendar is not etched in stone. Encourage them to monitor it regularly and evaluate whether they need to modify it. For example, you might add another assignment or two, change a test date, and so on. Students might find that they need more study time than they originally predicted for a particular course.

After they have made out their term calendar, photocopy a blank weekly plan form and give it to your students. The form should have the days of the week across the top, with headings of "Planned" and "Actual" under each day. The 24 hours of the day should be listed vertically on the left side of the paper in a column. Have students fill in their class hours, leisure activities (like sports, music practice, watching TV), and other routine activities like sleeping and eating. A good strategy is to have students create this plan at the end of the preceding week. Then have them monitor it the next week to see how effectively they carried out their plan.

After students have created term and weekly plans, give them practice in setting priorities for the next day. A critical skill for a good time manager is figuring out what the most important things are to get done and when to do them—in other words, *setting priorities.* An effective way to get students to do this is to have them create manageable daily "to do" lists. Their goal should be to make up the list in the evening and then complete all of the items on the list the next day. Get them to identify the top-priority tasks on the list and make sure that they get done. Have them examine their "to do" list toward the end of the day and evaluate what they have accomplished. Encourage students to challenge themselves to finish the few remaining tasks.

You might be surprised at what students discover from their time-use plans. Some students will be totally unaware of how much time they waste, underestimate how much time they need to study, and be far less effective at using time than they imagined. Other students will learn that proper time management requires planning, organization, and self-discipline, but that the results are worth it.

Most successful adults are good time managers, yet schools have not given students adequate opportunities to practice time management skills. If you are going to be a middle school or secondary teacher, make a commitment to working with students to help them improve their time management skills. This strategy not only should improve their achievement in your class but will help them develop critical skills for success in work and life beyond school.

Older students not only should plan their next week's activities but also monitor how well they are sticking to their plan. Once students engage in a task, they need to monitor their progress, judge how well they are doing on the task, and evaluate the outcomes to regulate what they do in the future (Eccles, Wigfield, & Schiefele, 1998). Researchers have found that high-achieving students often are self-regulatory learners (Pressley & others, 1995; Schunk & Zimmerman, 1994). For example, high-achieving students self-monitor their learning more and systematically evaluate their progress

TEACHING STRATEGIES
For Helping Students Manage Their Time

Following are some good strategies teachers can teach students to help them manage their time more effectively and increase their achievement (Zimmerman, Bonner, & Kovach, 1996):

1. *Be proactive, not reactive.* Students rarely plan or manage their available time for studying; instead, most tend to complete their assignments on a reactive basis at the last moment. Encourage them to be more proactive and develop term plans, weekly plans, and daily "to do" lists from the middle-school grades on.
2. *Set regular study times.*
3. *Use a regular study area that is well lighted and free from noise.*
4. *Learn to say no to distractions.* When friends, siblings, and others try to talk them out of studying, help them be prepared to say no in a polite but firm way.
5. *Reward yourself for your success.* Encourage students to delay desirable activities and use them as rewards for completing their studying. This can include food treats, watching TV, or spending time with friends.

toward a goal more than low-achieving students do. Encouraging students to self-monitor their learning conveys the message that students are responsible for their own behavior and that learning requires active dedicated participation by the student.

One developmental model of self-regulated learning consists of these four steps (Zimmerman, Bonner, & Kovach, 1996): First, children learn effective strategies by observing successful models. Second, children imitate these strategies, behaving like they've observed the models behave. Third, they learn to use the strategies apart from the models ("self-controlled learning"). And fourth, children begin to use the strategies in different situations and tailor them to meet their own needs and goals. As yet, research has not been conducted to determine whether this four-step developmental sequence models how self-regulated learning actually develops.

Anxiety
College Board Tips
for Reducing Anxiety

Anxiety

Anxiety *is a vague, highly unpleasant feeling of fear and apprehension.* It is normal for students to be concerned or worried when they face school challenges, such as doing well on a test. Indeed, researchers have found that many successful students have moderate levels of anxiety (Bandura, 1997). However, some students have high levels of anxiety and worry constantly, which can significantly impair their ability to achieve. For example, test anxiety is estimated to undermine the achievement of as many as 10 million children and adolescents (Wigfield & Eccles, 1989).

Some children's high anxiety levels are the result of parents' unrealistic achievement expectations and pressure. Many children have increasing anxiety as they reach higher grade levels, where they face more frequent evaluation, social comparison, and for some, experiences of failure (Eccles, Wigfield, & Schiefele, 1998). When schools create such circumstances, they likely increase students' anxiety.

A number of programs have been created to reduce an individual child's high anxiety level (Wigfield & Eccles, 1989). Some intervention programs emphasize relaxation

THROUGH THE EYES OF TEACHERS
Helping Students Feel Capable

When I began teaching, I did not understand why some students did not apply themselves or acted out at times. My teaching mentor helped me to see that some of the students did not know how to work on a project or assignment, did not know how to ask for help in an appropriate way, or had a high level of anxiety that was impeding their learning.

Experience and advice from educators has helped me to realize that nearly all students will apply themselves if they feel capable. As a teacher, I try to decrease students' anxiety by making projects compelling and creating an atmosphere in which students feel their questions and contributions are welcome. I also am explicit about guidelines and expectations.

Robynne Kirkpatrick
Math and Science Teacher
Northwest Middle School,
Salt Lake City, Utah

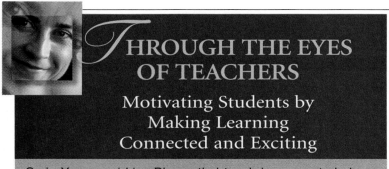

THROUGH THE EYES OF TEACHERS

Motivating Students by Making Learning Connected and Exciting

Craig Yager and Lise Blumenthal teach in connected classrooms at Whittier Elementary School in Boulder, Colorado. They begin and end the year with a ceremony in which students light a candle for each of these golden goals: scholarship, leadership, service, community, and character. They visit each student's home during the summer and again during the school year to increase school/family connections. They have a steady stream of parent and grandparent volunteers each school day. They also have set up an extensive "mini-society" in which students hold jobs, run businesses, and pay taxes in currencies with exchange rates for each class. Students keep extensive journals of learning activities. A yearly highlight is "Ellis Island," in which students simulate a journey across the ocean, eat meager fare, and at immigration are talked to in a language they cannot understand.

Craig Yager (as Dolly Madison) and Lise Blumenthal (as Patrick Henry) like to turn the classroom into a theater to help students learn.

Expectations
Teacher Expectations and Students' Motivation

techniques. These programs often are effective at reducing anxiety but they do not always lead to improved achievement. Anxiety intervention programs linked to the worry aspect of anxiety emphasize changing the negative, self-damaging thoughts of anxious students and replacing them with positive, task-focused thoughts (Meichenbaum & Butler, 1980). These programs have been more effective than the relaxation programs in improving students' achievement.

Instructional Strategies and Students' Motivation

In a review of instructional strategies and achievement motivation, Carol Ames (1992) examined how the various tasks used in instruction (such as meaningful aspects of learning activities), teacher-student relations (such as helping students participate in decision making), and the nature of evaluation and recognition (such as focusing on mastery motivation) can influence students' motivational patterns in such areas as intrinsic motivation, attributions involving effort-based strategies, and active engagement. Figure 11.4 summarizes her conclusions based on her review of the research in these areas. Notice that the motivational concepts in figure 11.4 reflect many of the ideas on achievement motivation we have discussed so far in this chapter.

The direction of causality in figure 11.4 goes from teacher to student, implying that the teacher influences the student's motivation rather than the student influencing the teacher or the student engaging in self-generated achievement beliefs and behaviors (Eccles, Wigfield, & Schiefele, 1998). However, students' own beliefs about effective instructional and motivational strategies also should be considered. For example, one study found that students and teachers often had different perspectives on motivational practices (Nolen & Nicholls, 1994). Students thought that extrinsic rewards like stars and money were more effective in motivating them than praise, which teachers believed was more effective.

An important aspect of instructional strategies not described in Ames' model is teacher expectancies. Students' motivation, and likely their performance, might be influenced by teachers' expectations. Teachers often have more positive expectations for high-ability than for low-ability students, and these expectations are likely to influence their behavior toward them. For example, teachers require high-ability students to work harder, wait longer for them to respond to questions, respond to them with more information and in a more elaborate fashion, criticize them less often, praise them more often, are more friendly to them, call on them more often, seat them closer to the teachers' desks, and are more likely to give them the benefit of the doubt on close calls in grading than they are for students with low ability (Brophy, 1985, 1998; Brophy & Good, 1974). An important teaching strategy is to monitor your expectations and be sure to have positive expectations for students with low abilities. Fortunately, researchers have found that with support teachers can adapt and raise their expectations for students with low abilities (Weinstein, Madison, & Kuklinski, 1995).

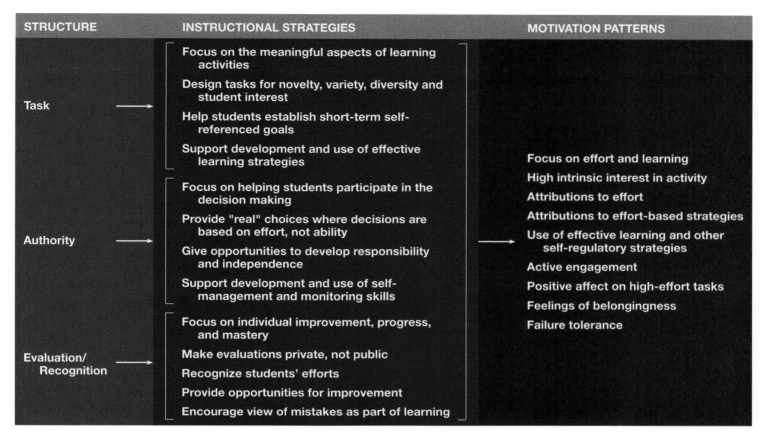

STRUCTURE	INSTRUCTIONAL STRATEGIES	MOTIVATION PATTERNS
Task	Focus on the meaningful aspects of learning activities Design tasks for novelty, variety, diversity and student interest Help students establish short-term self-referenced goals Support development and use of effective learning strategies	Focus on effort and learning High intrinsic interest in activity Attributions to effort Attributions to effort-based strategies Use of effective learning and other self-regulatory strategies Active engagement Positive affect on high-effort tasks Feelings of belongingness Failure tolerance
Authority	Focus on helping students participate in the decision making Provide "real" choices where decisions are based on effort, not ability Give opportunities to develop responsibility and independence Support development and use of self-management and monitoring skills	
Evaluation/ Recognition	Focus on individual improvement, progress, and mastery Make evaluations private, not public Recognize students' efforts Provide opportunities for improvement Encourage view of mistakes as part of learning	

Figure 11.4
Links Between Instructional Strategies and Students' Motivation

At this point we have studied a number of ideas about goal setting, planning, and self-monitoring, anxiety, and instructional strategies and student motivation. A review of these ideas is presented in summary table 11.3. Next, we will explore the nature of social motives, relationships, and sociocultural contexts, as we continue to examine various aspects of achievement.

Motivation, Relationships, and Sociocultural Contexts

Motivation has a social component. Students not only have achievement motives, they also have social motives. Our coverage of the social dimensions of motivation focus on students' social motives, relationships, and sociocultural contexts.

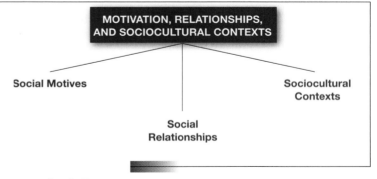

Social Motives

The social worlds of children are influential aspects of their lives at school. Every school day students work at establishing and maintaining social relationships. Researchers have found that students who display socially competent behavior are more likely to excel academically than those who do not (Wentzel, 1996). Overall, though, researchers have given too little attention to how students' social worlds are related to their motivation in the classroom.

Contextual Supports for Motivation

SUMMARY TABLE 11.3
Goal Setting, Planning, and Self-Monitoring; Anxiety; and Instructional Strategies and Students' Motivation

Concept	Processes/ Related Ideas	Characteristics/Description
Goal Setting, Planning, and Self-Monitoring	Their Nature	• Setting specific, proximal (short-term), and challenging goals benefits students' self-efficacy and achievement. • Dweck and Nicholls define goals in terms of immediate achievement-related focus and definition of success. • Being a good planner means managing time effectively, setting priorities, and being organized. • Giving students opportunities to develop their time management skills likely will benefit their learning and achievement. • Self-monitoring is a key aspect of learning and achievement.
Anxiety	Its Nature	• Anxiety is a vague, highly unpleasant feeling of fear and apprehension. • High anxiety can result from unrealistic parental expectations. • Students' anxiety increases as they get older and face more evaluation, social comparison, and failure (for some students). • Cognitive programs that replace students' self-damaging thoughts with positive, constructive thoughts have been more effective than relaxation programs in benefiting student achievement.
Instructional Strategies and Students' Motivation	Links	• Ames developed a model that examined how the various tasks used in instruction (such as meaningful learning opportunities), teacher-student relations (such as giving students opportunities for responsibility and independence), and evaluation/recognition (such as recognizing students' efforts) can influence students' motivation in areas like intrinsic motivation, attributions based on effort, and active engagement. • It also is important to consider the student's self-generated motivational beliefs and performance, as well as the teacher's expectations.

Social motives *are needs and desires that are learned through experiences with the social world.* Interest in social motives stems from Henry Murray's (1938) long catalog of needs (or motives), which included the **need for affiliation,** *which is the motive to be with other people. This involves establishing, maintaining, and restoring warm, close, personal relationships.* Students' social needs are reflected in their desires to be popular with peers and have one or more close friends, and the powerful attraction they feel to someone they love. Though each student has a need for affiliation, some students have a stronger need than others (O'Conner & Rosenblood, 1996). Some students like to be surrounded by lots of friends. In middle and high school, some students feel something is drastically missing from their lives if they don't have a girlfriend or boyfriend to date regularly. Other students don't have such strong needs for affiliation. They don't fall apart if they don't have several close friends around all day and don't sit in class in an anxious state if they don't have a romantic partner.

Both teacher approval and peer approval are important social motives for most students. In the elementary school years students are motivated to please their parents more than their peers (Berndt, 1979). By the end of elementary school, parent approval and peer approval are about equal in most students' motive systems. By eighth or ninth grade, peer conformity outstrips conformity to parents. By twelfth grade, conformity to peers drops off somewhat as students become more autonomous and make more decisions on their own.

Adolescence can be an especially important juncture in achievement motivation and social motivation (Henderson & Dweck, 1990) ◀▥ p. 99. New academic and social pressures force adolescents toward new roles that involve more responsibility. As adolescents experience more intense achievement demands, their social interests might cut into the time they need for academic matters. Or ambitions in one area can undermine the attainment of goals in another area, as when academic achievement leads to social disapproval. In early adolescence, students face a choice between whether they will spend more of their time pursuing social goals or academic goals. The results of this decision have long-term consequences in terms of how far adolescents will go in their education and the careers they will pursue.

Social Relationships

Students' relationships with parents, peers, friends, teachers, mentors, and others can have profound effects on their achievement and social motivation.

Parents   Research has been done on links between parenting and students' motivation. Studies have examined family demographic characteristics, child-rearing practices, and provision of specific experiences at home (Eccles, Wigfield, & Schiefele, 1998).

Demographic Characteristics   Parents with more education are more likely than less educated parents to believe that their involvement in their child's education is important, to be active participants in their child's education, and to have intellectually stimulating materials at home (Schneider & Coleman, 1993). When parents' time and energy are largely consumed by attention to parents' other concerns or people other than the child, the child's motivation can suffer. Living in a single-parent family, having parents who are consumed by their work, and living in a large family can undercut children's achievement.

Adolescence is a critical juncture in the achievement orientation of many students. Why is it such a critical juncture?

Child-Rearing Practices   Even though demographic factors can affect students' motivation, more important are the parents' child-rearing practices (Eccles, 1993; Eccles, Wigfield, & Schiefele, 1998).

The following are some positive parenting practices that result in improved motivation and achievement:

• Knowing enough about the child to provide the right amount of challenge and the right amount of support
• Providing a positive emotional climate, which motivates children to internalize their parents' values and goals
• Modeling motivated achievement behavior: working hard and persisting with effort at challenging tasks

Provision of Specific Experiences at Home   In addition to general child-rearing practices, parents can influence students' achievement motivation by providing specific experiences at home. Reading to one's preschool children and providing reading materials in the home are positively related to students' later reading achievement and motivation (Wigfield & Asher, 1984). Indeed, researchers have documented that children's skills and work habits when they enter kindergarten are among the best predictors of academic motivation and performance throughout the elementary and secondary school years (Entwisle & Alexander, 1993).

Peers   Peers can affect a student's motivation through social comparison, social competence and motivation, peer co-learning, and peer group influences (Eccles, Wigfield, & Schiefele, 1998) ◀⫴ p. 92.

Students can compare themselves with their peers on where they stand academically and socially (Ruble, 1983). Adolescents are more likely than younger children to engage in social comparison, although adolescents are prone to deny that they ever compare themselves with others (Harter, 1990). Positive social comparisons usually result in higher self-esteem, negative comparisons in lower self-esteem. Students are most likely to compare themselves with the students who are most similar to them in age, ability, and interests.

Students who are more accepted by their peers and who have good social skills often do better in school and have positive academic achievement motivation (Asher & Coie, 1990; Wentzel, 1996). In contrast, rejected students, especially those who are highly aggressive, are at risk for a number of achievement problems, including low grades and dropping out of school.

In chapter 9, "Social Constructivist Approaches, Domain-Specific Approaches, and Teaching," we highlighted the role of peers in collaborative and cooperative learning, as well as peer tutoring. Peers can help each other learn material through discussion in small groups. And peer tutoring often brings achievement gains to the tutor as well as the student being tutored.

Early work on the role of the peer group in students' achievement focused on its negative role in distracting adolescents from a commitment to academic learning (Goodlad, 1984). More recently, the peer group has been viewed as a positive or negative influence depending on its motivational orientation. If the peer group has high achievement standards, it will support the student's academic achievement. But, if a low-achieving student joins a low-achieving peer group or clique, the student's academic work can deteriorate even further (Kinderman, McCollam, & Gibson, 1996).

Teachers   Early studies of the teacher's role in student motivation focused on the importance of the teacher's warmth and supportiveness. More recently, researchers have expanded their interests to also include teacher instruction and managerial style. In research conducted by Malcolm Moos (1979), student motivation was maximized only when teacher warmth/supportiveness was accompanied by efficient organization, an emphasis on academics, and goal-oriented lessons. These practices are more common among teachers who believe they can improve their students' achievement (Brookover & others, 1979).

Students' motivation is optimized when teachers provide them with challenging tasks in a mastery-oriented environment that includes good emotional and cognitive support, meaningful and interesting material to learn and master, and sufficient support for autonomy and initiative (Eccles, Wigfield, & Schiefele, 1998).

As we saw in our earlier discussion of Bandura's ideas on self-efficacy, the motivation and achievement climate of the entire school makes a difference in how motivated students are. Schools with high expectations and academic standards, as well as academic and emotional support for students, often have students who are motivated to achieve. In the next chapter, we will have more to say about how school policies and classroom management affect achievement.

Teachers and Parents   In chapter 3, we highlighted the important role that parents play in children's development, as well as strategies that teachers can use to increasingly involve parents in their children's education ◀⫴ p. 91. In the past, schools have given little attention to how teachers can enlist parents as partners with them in improving students' achievement. Currently there is considerable interest in how to accomplish this partnership. When teachers systematically and frequently inform parents of their children's progress and help them get involved in their children's learning activities, children often achieve more (Epstein, 1996).

Sociocultural Contexts

In this section we will focus on how socioeconomic status, ethnicity, and gender can influence motivation and achievement.

Socioeconomic Status and Ethnicity   The diversity among
ethnic minority students that we discussed in chapter 5 also is evident in their achievement ◀◀‖ p. 164. For example, many Asian American students have a strong academic achievement orientation, but some do not.

In addition to recognizing the diversity that exists within every cultural group in terms of their achievement, it also is important to distinguish between difference and deficiency. Too often, the achievements of ethnic minority students—especially African American, Latino, and Native American—have been interpreted in terms of middle-class white standards as *deficits* when they simply are *culturally different and distinct* (Jones, 1994).

At the same time, many investigations overlook the socioeconomic status of ethnic minority students. In many instances, when ethnicity *and* socioeconomic status are investigated in the same study, socioeconomic status predicts achievement better than ethnicity. Students from middle- and upper-income families fare better than their counterparts from low-income backgrounds in a host of achievement situations—expectations for success, achievement aspirations, and recognition of the importance of effort, for example (Gibbs, 1989).

Sandra Graham (1986, 1990) has conducted a number of studies that reveal not only a stronger role of socioeconomic status than of ethnicity in achievement but also the importance of studying ethnic minority student motivation in the context of general motivational theory. Her inquiries fall within the framework of attribution theory and focus on the causes African American students identify for their achievement orientation, such as why they succeed or fail. Graham is struck by how consistently middle-income African American students do not fit the stereotype of being unmotivated. Like their White middle-income counterparts, they have high achievement expectations and understand that failure is usually due to a lack of effort rather than bad luck.

A special challenge for many ethnic minority students, especially those living in poverty, is dealing with racial prejudice, conflict between the values of their group and the majority group, and a lack of high-achieving adults in their cultural group who can serve as positive role models (McLoyd, 2000; Spencer & Markstrom-Adams, 1990). The lack of high-achieving role models relates to our discussion in chapter 7, "Behavioral Approaches, Social Cognitive Approaches, and Teaching" in which we described the importance of increasing the number of mentors in these students' lives. To read about one individual who has become an important role model for African American students, see the Diversity and Education box.

It also is important to consider the nature of the schools that primarily serve ethnic minority students (Eccles, Wigfield, & Schiefele, 1998). More than one-third of African American and almost one-third of Latino students attend schools in the 47 largest city school districts in the United States, compared with only 5 percent of White and 22 percent of Asian American students. Many of these ethnic minority students come from low-income families (more than one-half are eligible for free

UCLA educational psychologist Sandra Graham is shown talking with adolescent boys about motivation. She had conducted a number of studies which reveal that middle socioeconomic status African American students—like their White counterparts—have high achievement expectations and attribute success to internal factors such as effort rather than external factors such as luck.

DIVERSITY AND EDUCATION
Henry Gaskins

A special concern is to find ways to support the achievement efforts of ethnic minority students, many of whom come from low-income backgrounds. In the Teaching Stories segment that opened this chapter, you read about Jaime Escalante, who made a major difference in the motivation of Latino students to learn and excel at math in East Los Angeles. Another individual has been exceptional in supporting the motivation of African American students in Washington, D.C.

Henry Gaskins, a physician, began an after-school tutoring program for ethnic minority students. For 4 hours every weeknight and all day on Saturdays, 80 students receive study assistance from Gaskins, his wife, two adult volunteers, and academically talented peers. Those who can afford it contribute $5 to cover the cost of school supplies. In addition to tutoring in various school subjects, Gaskins helps the tutees learn how to set academic goals and plan how to achieve these goals. Gaskins also encourages students to self-monitor their progress toward the goals. Many of the students being tutored have parents who are high school dropouts and either can't or are not motivated to help their sons and daughters achieve.

Every community has people like Henry Gaskins who can help provide much-needed mentoring and tutoring for students from low socioeconomic backgrounds whose parents do not have the skills or are not motivated to help them achieve academically. Many of these potential mentors and tutors from the community have not been contacted by school personnel. If the need exists among your students, make a commitment to scour the community for talented, motivated, and concerned adults, like Gaskins, who might only need to be asked to provide mentoring and tutoring support for disadvantaged students.

Dr. Henry Gaskins, here talking with three high school students, began an after-school tutorial program for ethnic minority students in 1983 in Washington, D.C. Volunteers like Dr. Gaskins can be especially helpful in developing a stronger sense of the importance of education in ethnic minority adolescents.

or reduced cost lunches). These inner-city schools are less likely than other schools to serve more advantaged populations or to offer high-quality academic support services, advanced courses, and courses that challenge students' active thinking skills. Even students who are motivated to learn and achieve can find it difficult to perform effectively in such contexts.

Gender   Our discussion of gender and motivation focuses on attributions, beliefs, and values. Female and male students' competence-related beliefs vary by achievement context. For example, boys have higher competence beliefs than girls for math and sports, and girls have higher competence beliefs for English, reading, and social activities. These differences increase after puberty (Eccles & others, 1993). Thus, how competently female and male students expect to perform is consistent with gender-role stereotypes.

With regard to achievement values, beginning in high school, girls do not value math achievement as highly as boys do (Eccles & others, 1993). Gifted girls often experience conflicts between gender roles and achievement. One study of gifted girls showed them feeling caught between achieving and appearing either feminine or caring (Bell, 1989).

SUMMARY TABLE 11.4
Motivation, Relationships, and Sociocultural Contexts

Concept	Processes/Related Ideas	Characteristics/Description
Social Motives	Their Nature	• These are needs and desires that are learned through experience with the social world. • The need for affiliation involves the motive to be with other people, which consists of establishing, maintaining, and restoring warm, close personal relationships. • In terms of social approval, both teacher and peer approval are important. • Peer conformity peaks in early adolescence, a time of important decisions about whether to pursue academic or social motives.
Social Relationships	Parents	• Understanding the parent's role in students' motivation focuses on demographic characteristics (such as education level, time spent at work, and family structure), child-rearing practices (such as providing the right amount of challenge and support), and provision of specific experiences at home (such as providing reading materials).
	Peers	• Peers can affect students' motivation through social comparison, social competence, peer co-learning, and peer-group influences.
	Teachers	• Research on the teacher's role in motivation has shown the effects of instructional and managerial style. • A teacher's support can play a powerful role in motivating students to learn. • An important aspect of student motivation is enlisting parents as partners with you in educating the student.
Sociocultural Contexts	Socioeconomic Status and Ethnicity	• Special concerns focus on valuing diversity in any cultural group, as well as teasing apart socioeconomic status and ethnicity. • The quality of schools for many socioeconomically impoverished students is lower than for their middle-income counterparts.
	Gender	• Gender differences in achievement involve attributions, beliefs, and values. • Special concerns are gender differences in teacher-student interaction, curriculum and content, sexual harassment, and gender bias.

In chapter 5, "Sociocultural Diversity," we charted many other aspects of gender and school, such as gender differences in teacher-student interaction, curriculum and content; sexual harassment; and reducing gender bias ◀▥ p. 181. Because those differences are so important in students' achievement, we briefly summarize them here: Girls are more compliant, boys more rambunctious. Teachers give boys more attention and instruction than girls, yet boys get lower grades than girls. By middle school, girls have lower self-esteem. Boys list more career options than girls do.

Schools have made considerable progress in reducing sexism and sex stereotyping in books and curriculum materials, but sexism still exists. Sexual harassment is a special concern in schools and is more pervasive than once envisioned. Every student deserves an education free from gender bias. You might want to return to chapter 5 and read again the section on gender and schools, thinking about how such gender differences might affect students' achievement.

At this point we have discussed many ideas about social motives, relationships, and sociocultural contexts. A review of these ideas is presented in summary table 11.4.

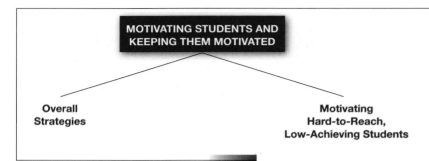

Motivating Students and Keeping Them Motivated

Throughout this chapter we have discussed many strategies for helping students become motivated to learn. In this section we revisit those strategies, provide further examples, and add some final thoughts on motivating students. We also will discuss some specific strategies for reaching hard-to-reach, low-achieving students.

Overall Strategies

Among the best overall strategies for improving students' motivation are being a competent achievement model as a teacher; creating an atmosphere of challenge and high expectations; communicating expectations that your students will achieve and providing them with the necessary support; encouraging intrinsic motivation, guiding students in setting goals, planning, and self-monitoring; selecting learning tasks that stimulate interest and curiosity; using technology effectively; and involving the community.

Always keep in mind that you and your classroom are not the only sources of motivation for your students. Parents are especially important in this regard. Involve them as partners with you in motivating students to learn. Tell them how much you value their providing an atmosphere to help their children learn and achieve. If a student is not achieving, meet with the parents and develop a strategy for helping the student. When parents are uncooperative or do not have the ability to work with you in helping their child, try to find a mentor who will share responsibility for helping the student succeed.

One program that attempts to involve the community in student achievement is the School of the Future Project, based in Austin, Texas (Donnelly, 1997). Through school and family collaboration and partnership, a number of resources have been established at Widen Elementary School and Mendez Middle School. These schools are located in low-income communities that are about 60 percent Latino. Following are some features of the project:

- *Peer Mediation.* This program was developed when a local attorney volunteered his services to discuss mediation and negotiation strategies with students.
- *Roving Leader.* This program was established through the support of local churches. The two roving leaders, one a social worker and the other a college graduate with a degree in criminal justice, use recreational activities as a context for guiding, counseling, and supporting students.
- *Cara y Corazon.* This is an education and support program for Spanish-speaking parents.
- *Harambe.* This family support program guides African American parents in identifying the strengths of their culture and using those strengths to help their children solve problems and make decisions.
- *Legal Aid.* This is a free, school-based service for anyone who needs legal advice and guidance.

Motivating Hard-to-Reach, Low-Achieving Students

Jere Brophy (1998) recently described strategies for improving the motivation of two main types of hard-to-reach and low-achieving students: (1) discouraged students who lack the confidence and motivation to learn, and (2) uninterested or alienated students.

Life is a gift . . . Accept it.

Life is an adventure . . . Dare it.

Life is a mystery . . . Unfold it.

Life is a struggle . . . Face it.

Life is a puzzle . . . Solve it.

Life is an opportunity . . . Take it.

Life is a mission . . . Fulfill it.

Life is a goal . . . Achieve it.

—Author Unknown

Curiosity has its own reason for existing.

Albert Einstein
German-Born American Scientist, 20th Century

*T*EACHING STRATEGIES
For Motivating Students

Some strategies for motivating your students are:

1. *Be a competent model who is motivated to learn.* The attitudes you convey about learning, effort, and achievement will be important factors in whether your students develop positive attitudes about these things. How curious and enthused you are will rub off on your students. Your excitement about a lesson will be contagious. Display an attitude that learning is an important goal in itself. Talk with students about how much you enjoy learning about various topics. Convey to them circumstances in which you established goals for yourself, planned how to reach the goals, faced hurdles along the way, struggled, but then persisted with considerable effort to succeed. These kinds of real-world stories about yourself help to personalize achievement and let students see you as a real person with whom they can identify and whom they will want to emulate.

   Much of what we have said in this chapter focuses on motivating students and keeping them motivated. However, it also is important to consider your own motivation as a teacher and how to sustain it. The principles of motivation that you have read about in this chapter can also be applied to your own motivation. To evaluate your own motivational makeup, complete self-assessment 11.1.

2. *Create an atmosphere of challenge and high expectations.* High achievement expectations and standards pervade successful classrooms. Don't accept low-quality work and minimal effort by students. Challenge every student to do their best, and accept nothing less. Tell them that it is their responsibility in life to take the talents they have and use them to reach the highest achievement levels possible. Place inspiring quotations in visible locations around your classroom. Create a menu of books that reflect achievement-related themes from which students can select the ones that interest them the most. Have achievement as a theme for one unit of a book club.

3. *Communicate your expectations that your students will achieve and provide the necessary academic and emotional support.* Carefully monitor your students' progress and communicate to them your confidence in their ability to handle academic challenges. When you detect that students are struggling, support them with comments like "I know you can do it. Keep going. You will get there." However, know your students well enough individually to understand how much skill support they need. Get them to stretch their talents realistically. Recognize when a student needs to learn specific academic skills, such as reading and math skills. Also recognize when students' emotions are hindering their achievement. Especially be sensitive to highly anxious students and give them some strategies (such as those based on the cognitive approaches that we discussed earlier in the chapter) to help them improve their confidence and reduce their anxiety. When students succeed, say how proud you are of them and how prideful they should feel about themselves.

4. *Encourage students' intrinsic motivation to learn.* When you get students to resolve that they are going to succeed and make a commitment to that success, they are on the right intrinsic motivation path to achievement. Help them understand that success comes from effort and determination in the face of challenges. Fuel their intrinsic motivation by giving them a menu of choices of topics to study and projects to do. You know that intrinsic motivation is at work when they are absorbed in a state of concentration while they are engaging in activities. Use rewards, not to control, but to convey information about mastery.

5. *Work with students to help them set goals, plan, and monitor their progress.* I don't remember a teacher ever working with me or my classmates when I was in elementary school, secondary school, or college on setting goals, planning, and monitoring progress toward those goals. Yet many successful people report that these are some of the most important reasons for their success. Make a commitment to include goal setting, planning, and self-monitoring in students' classroom experiences. Especially have students set short-term goals, give them experience in setting priorities, and have them do time management exercises.

6. *Select learning tasks that stimulate interest and curiosity.* The learning tasks you select for students, or the menu of tasks from which you let students choose, will have an impact on their motivation. One analysis of highly successful schools for young adolescents found that all of the schools had teachers who chose learning tasks that stimulated student interest and curiosity (Lipsitz, 1984).

7. *Use technology effectively.* In chapter 10, "Planning, Instruction, and Technology," as well as in the Technology and Education boxes in each chapter, we have described many ways technology can be used to motivate learning. Educational technology games are highly motivating to students and help you vary the format of instruction, which in itself often increases motivation. More about technology and motivation appears in the Technology and Education box.

SELF-ASSESSMENT 11.1
Evaluating My Motivation

Following are 16 statements you can use to analyze your motivational makeup. Rate yourself from 1 (Not like me at all) to 5 (Very much like me) on each of the statements.

	1	2	3	4	5
1. I am aware of the hierarchy of motives in my life and which ones are the most important for me.					
2. I am intrinsically motivated.					
3. I have high expectations and standards for success.					
4. My life has many moments of flow.					
5. I am aware of the people in my life who have motivated me the most and what it is they did that motivated me.					
6. I make achievement-related attributions that emphasize effort.					
7. I have a mastery motivation orientation rather than a helpless or performance orientation.					
8. I am motivated to learn and succeed because of my success aspirations, not because I want to protect my self-worth or avoid failure.					
9. I have high self-efficacy in general.					
10. I have high instructional self-efficacy in terms of my ability as a teacher and to manage my classroom effectively.					
11. I regularly set goals, plan how to reach those goals, and systematically monitor my progress toward the goals.					
12. I set specific, proximal, and challenging goals.					
13. I am a good time manager, regularly doing weekly plans, monitoring my use of time, and doing "to do" lists.					
14. I am good at learning from my mistakes to improve my future success.					
15. I don't let anxiety or other emotions get in the way of my motivation.					
16. I have a good support system for my motivation and have positive close relationships with people who can help me sustain my motivation.					

Scoring and Interpretation

Examine the pattern of your responses. If you rated yourself 4 or 5 on each of the items, you likely are getting your motivation to work to your advantage, and you likely will be a positive motivational model for your students. However, for any items on which you rated yourself 3 or below, spend some time thinking about how you can improve those aspects of your motivational life.

Rebuilding Discouraged Students' Confidence and Motivation to Learn   Discouraged students include (1) low achievers with low ability who have difficulty keeping up and have developed low achievement expectations, (2) students with failure syndrome, and (3) students obsessed with protecting their self-worth by avoiding failure.

Low-Ability, Low-Achieving Students with Low Expectations for Success   These students need to be consistently reassured that they can meet the goals and challenges you have set for them and that you will give them the help and support they need to succeed. However, they need to be reminded that you will accept their progress only as long as they make a real effort. They might require individualized instruction materials or activities to provide an optimal challenge for their skill

TECHNOLOGY AND EDUCATION
Technological Self-Efficacy, Authentic Tasks, Curiosity, and Interest

Albert Bandura (1997) underscored that teachers' beliefs in their technological efficacy influence their receptivity to, and adoption of, educational technologies. You yourself have to be motivated to use technology and have technological self-efficacy if your students are to benefit from the tools of the electronic age.

Authentic tasks spark students' interest and curiosity. Students often perceive technology-based learning experiences as real-world activities (Cognition and Technology Group at Vanderbilt, 1997). One example of computer-based authentic learning is the use of a commercial movie, *The Young Sherlock Holmes,* for social studies and humanities classes. Researchers have found that even when authentic computer-based tasks require considerable work, students often display considerable effort in pursuing solutions to the problems that they pose (Goldman & others, 1996).

Software that requires active thinking and has personal applications is likely to increase students' motivation. For example, you can use writing and publishing software as tools to help students create their own class newspaper.

Technology that is aimed at stimulating students' interest, curiosity, and creativity is likely to increase their motivation far more than technology that involves drill and practice. For example, an increasing number of computer simulations, such as SimCity, SimTown, and SimEarth, stir students' curiosity by letting them create and manage environments (Maddux, Johnson, & Willis, 1997).

A SimCity 3000 computer simulation of the downtown area of a city. SimCity is designed to increase students' motivation by letting them create and manage environments.

level. Help them set learning goals and provide them support for reaching these goals. Require these students to put forth considerable effort and make progress, even though they might not have the ability to perform at the level of the class as a whole.

Students with Failure Syndrome   **Failure syndrome** *refers to having low expectations for success and giving up at the first sign of difficulty.* Failure syndrome students are different from low-achieving students, who fail despite putting forth their best effort. Failure syndrome students don't put forth enough effort, often beginning tasks in a halfhearted manner and giving up quickly at the first hint of a challenge. Failure syndrome students often have low self-efficacy or attribution problems, ascribing their failures to internal, stable, and uncontrollable causes, such as low ability.

A number of strategies can be used to increase the motivation of students who display failure syndrome. Especially beneficial are cognitive retraining methods, such as efficacy retraining, attribution retraining, and strategy training, which are described in figure 11.5.

THROUGH THE EYES OF CHILDREN
"You Always Manage to Cheer Us Up"

I know our science class sometimes is obnoxious and negative but we really appreciate you. You always manage to cheer us up and treat us like your own kids. That shows how much you care about us. If you hadn't been there for me like you were, I probably wouldn't be where I am now. Good luck with all of your other students and I hope they learn as much as I have. I'll miss you next year. Hope to see you around.

Letter from Jennifer to William Williford, her Perry, Georgia, middle school science teacher

TRAINING METHOD	PRIMARY EMPHASIS	MAIN GOALS
Efficacy Training	Improve students' self-efficacy perceptions	Teach students to set and strive to reach specific, proximal, and challenging goals. Monitor students' progress and frequently support students by saying things like "I know you can do it." Use adult and peer modeling effectively. Individualize instruction and tailor it to the student's knowledge and skills. Keep social comparison to a minimum. Be an efficacious teacher and have confidence in your abilities. View students with a failure syndrome as challenges rather than losers.
Attribution and Achievement Orientation Retraining	Change students' attributions and achievement orientation	Teach students to attribute failures to factors that can be changed, such as insufficient knowledge or effort and ineffective strategies. Work with students to develop a mastery orientation rather than a performance orientation by helping them focus on the achievement process (learning the task) rather than the achievement product (winning or losing).
Strategy Training	Improve students' domain- and task-specific skills and strategies	Help students to acquire and self-regulate their use of effective learning and problem-solving strategies. Teach students what to do, how to do it, and when and why to do it.

Figure **11.5**

Cognitive Retraining Methods for Increasing the Motivation of Students Who Display a Failure Syndrome

THROUGH THE EYES OF TEACHERS

No More Whining

Susan was a real whiner. She always saw herself as a victim. "No one likes me," and they didn't because she whined and blamed. Small issues became mountains. Her social relationships were incendiary. Her mother reinforced it all. So we embarked on a praising-Susan campaign. We would counter a whine with "That's tough. What went well?" When she did something correctly, we'd say "You're smart." A couple of times, when she'd been particularly responsive and insightful in discussion, I held her back after class, praised specifically what she had said and done, and asked her to tell her Mom.

During annual testing she was very careful: afterwards I described exactly what she had done, checked her intentions ("Yes, I wanted to work slowly and check my work."), praised this approach, and asked her to tell her Mom. Susan began to tell good stories about herself, and by the end of the year was a much happier child with improving grades.

Keren Abra
Fifth-Grade Teacher
Schools of the Sacred Heart
San Francisco, California

Students Motivated to Protect Their Self-Worth by Avoiding Failure   As we indicated earlier in the chapter, some students are so interested in protecting their self-worth and avoiding failure that they become distracted from pursuing learning goals and engage in ineffective learning strategies. Following are some of their strategies for protecting self-esteem and avoiding failure (Covington & Teel, 1996):

- *Nonperformance.* The most obvious strategy for avoiding failure is to not try. Students' nonperformance tactics include these: appearing eager to answer a teacher's question but hoping the teacher will call on another student, sliding down in the seat to avoid being seen by the teacher, and avoiding eye contact. These might seem like minor deceptions, but they can portend other more chronic forms of noninvolvement such as dropping out and excessive absences.

- *Sham effort.* To avoid being criticized for not trying, some students appear to participate but do so more to avoid punishment than to succeed. Some student behaviors that reflect a sham effort are these: asking a question even though they already know the answer, adopting a pensive, quizzical expression, and feigning focused attention during a class discussion.

Here are some ways you might be able to reach students who are uninterested or alienated (Brophy, 1998):

1. *Work on developing a positive relationship with the student.* If the uninterested or alienated student doesn't like you, it is hard to get the student to work toward any achievement goals. Show patience, but be determined to help the student and push for steady progress in spite of setbacks or resistance.
2. *To make school more intrinsically interesting for this type of student, find out the student's interests and if possible include those interests in assignments that you make.*
3. *Teach them strategies for making academic work more enjoyable.* Help them understand that they are causing their own problems, and find ways to guide them in taking pride in their work.
4. *Consider enlisting the aid of a mentor in the community or an older student whom you believe the uninterested or alienated student will respect.*

- *Procrastination.* Students who postpone studying for a test until the last minute can blame their failure on poor time management, thus deflecting attention away from the possibility that they are incompetent. A variation on this theme involves students who take on so many activities and responsibilities that they have an excuse for not doing any one of them in a highly competent manner.
- *Setting unreachable goals.* By setting goals so high that success is virtually impossible, students can avoid the implication that they are incompetent, because virtually all students will fail to reach this goal.
- *The academic wooden leg.* In this strategy, students admit to a minor personal weakness to avoid acknowledging the greater feared weakness of being incompetent. For example, the student might blame a failing test score on anxiety. Having test anxiety is not as devastating to a personal sense of self-worth as lack of ability.

Martin Covington and his colleagues (Covington, 1992, 1998; Covington & Teel, 1996; Covington, Teel, & Parecki, 1994) proposed a number of strategies to help students reduce their preoccupation with protecting their self-worth and avoiding failure:

- Give these students assignments that are inherently interesting and stimulate their curiosity. The assignments should challenge but not overwhelm their skills. Allow them some choice of which learning activities to pursue. As their expertise increases, increase the level of challenge correspondingly.
- Establish a reward system so that all students—not just the brightest, highest-achieving students—can attain rewards if they put forth enough effort. Make sure that rewards reinforce students for setting meaningful goals. Also, try to make the act of learning itself a desirable goal.
- Help students set challenging but realistic goals, and provide them with the academic and emotional support to reach those goals.

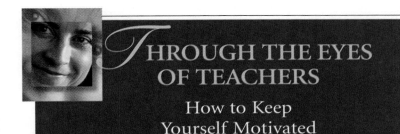

Improve your own professional portfolio. Reflect. Go to conferences. Take advantage of other opportunities to improve your competence, both for personal and professional growth.

Take your successes where you can get them. Don't dwell on your failures. Just figure out what went wrong and go on.

Find a need and try to fill it.

Stay connected to the whole community.

Exercise.

Stay open to change. Re-evaluate your goals and priorities.

Try the spiritual discipline of doing nothing related to school on Saturday.

Sing Tuesday nights in a choir.

Hang out with other teachers.

Hang out with other adults who don't teach.

Be a joy monger! Young children are and have the shortest route to joyful expression.

SUMMARY TABLE 11.5
Motivating Students and Keeping Them Motivated

Concept	Processes/ Related Ideas	Characteristics/Description
Overall Strategies	Their Nature	• These strategies include being a competent model who is motivated to learn; enveloping your classroom in an atmosphere of challenging expectations for learning and achievement; communicating expectations that students can achieve and providing them with the necessary academic and emotional support; encouraging students' intrinsic motivation to learn; working with students to help them set goals, plan, and monitor their progress; selecting learning tasks that stimulate curiosity and interest; using technology effectively; and involving the community.
Motivating Hard-to-Reach, Low-Achieving Students	Rebuilding Discouraged Students' Confidence and Motivation	• The discouraged student lacks the confidence and motivation to learn. This might be a student with low ability and low expectations for success who needs reassurance and support, but who also needs to be reminded that progress will be acceptable only when considerable effort is put forth; a student with failure syndrome (who has low expectations for success and gives up easily), who likely will benefit from cognitive retraining methods such as efficacy training, attribution retraining, and strategy training; and a student motivated to protect self-worth and avoid failure, who likely will benefit from inherently interesting activities, setting challenging but achievable goals, strengthening the link between self-worth and effort, having positive beliefs about their own ability, and a positive student-teacher relationship.
	Motivating Uninterested or Alienated Students	• Strategies for helping an uninterested or alienated student include establishing a positive relationship with the student, making school more intrinsically interesting, teaching strategies for making academic work more enjoyable, and considering a mentor in the community or an older student as a support person for the student.

• Strengthen the student's association between effort and self-worth. Encourage students to take pride in their effort and minimize social comparison.
• Encourage students to have positive beliefs about their abilities.
• Improve teacher-student relationships by emphasizing your role as a resource person who will guide and support student learning efforts rather than an authority figure who controls student behavior.

Motivating Uninterested or Alienated Students   Brophy (1998) believes that the most difficult motivation problem involves students who are apathetic, uninterested in learning, or alienated from school learning. Achieving in school is not an important value for them. To reach apathetic students requires sustained efforts to resocialize their attitudes toward school achievement (Murdock, 1999).

At this point we have explored a number of ideas about motivating students and keeping them motivated. A review of these ideas is presented in summary table 11.5. Motivating students to learn is an important dimension of classroom life. So is managing the classroom effectively, the topic of the next chapter.

Chapter Review

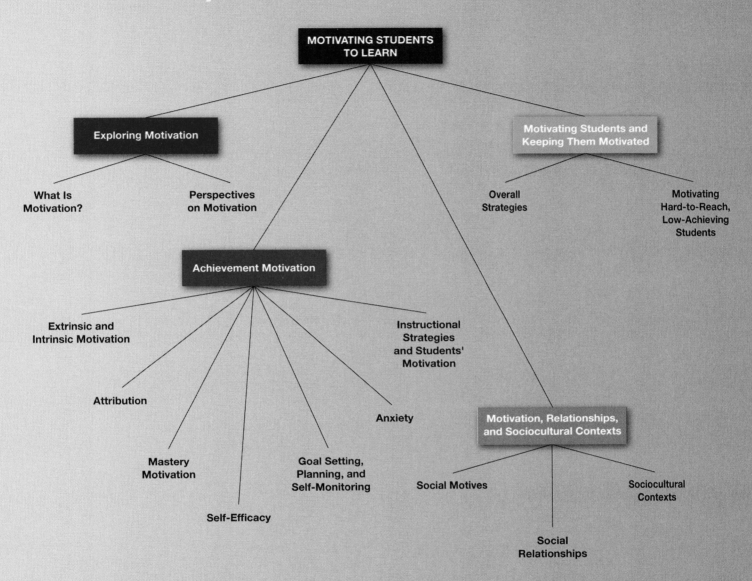

TO OBTAIN A DETAILED REVIEW OF THIS CHAPTER, STUDY THESE FIVE SUMMARY TABLES:

Key Terms

motivation 394	competence motivation 396	attribution theory 401	anxiety 409
incentives 394	extrinsic motivation 397	mastery orientation 403	social motives 412
humanistic perspective 395	intrinsic motivation 397	helpless orientation 403	need for affiliation 412
hierarchy of needs 395	flow 398	performance orientation 403	failure syndrome 421
self-actualization 395	person-environment fit 400	self-efficacy 404	

Educational Psychology Checklist
MOTIVATING STUDENTS TO LEARN

How much have you learned since the beginning of the chapter? Use the following statements to help you review your knowledge and understanding of the chapter material. First, read the statement and mentally or briefly on paper demonstrate that you understand and can discuss the relevant information.

_____ I know what it means to be motivated.

_____ I can describe different perspectives on motivation.

_____ I understand extrinsic and intrinsic motivation, including strategies for encouraging self-determination and personal choice.

_____ I can discuss optimal experiences and flow.

_____ I know what attribution is and how it influences students' achievement.

_____ I can describe what mastery motivation and why it is a good achievement strategy.

_____ I am aware of what self-efficacy is and educational strategies to promote it.

_____ I understand why goal-setting, planning, and self-monitoring are so important in achievement.

_____ I know how anxiety can interfere with achievement.

_____ I can describe links between instructional strategies and students' achievement.

_____ I can describe the roles of social motives, relationships, and sociocultural contexts in motivation and achievement.

_____ I know some good strategies for motivating students and keeping them motivated.

_____ I can discuss the best strategies for motivating hard-to-reach, low-achieving students.

For any items that you did not check off, go back and locate the relevant material in the chapter. Review the material until you can check off the item. You also may want to use this checklist later in preparing for an exam.

Adventures for the Mind

Now that you have a good knowledge and understanding of the chapter, complete the following exercises to expand your thinking about the chapter's topics.

- Design a motivationally rich classroom. What would it include? How would teaching proceed? What types of activities would go on?
- Create a plan to improve the motivation of the following students:
  - 7-year-old Tanya, who has low ability and low expectations for success
  - 10-year-old Samuel, who works overtime to keep his self-worth at a high level but has a strong fear of failure
  - 13-year-old Sandra, who is quiet in the classroom and underestimates her skills
  - 16-year-old Robert, who shows little interest in school. He currently lives with his aunt and you have been unable to contact his parents.
- At different points in the chapter, we have included a number of quotations about motivation, such as "The art of teaching is the art

of awakening the curiosity of young minds" and "The reward of a thing well done is to have done it." Craft your own quotation or slogan for motivation, one that has personal meaning for you. Put the quotation on the bulletin board in your classroom when you teach.
- In helping students plan, you likely will need to guide them in making vague plans more specific. To get some practice at this, make the following vague plans more specific:

Vague: I'm going to start getting to school on time.
Precise: _____
_____

Vague: I plan to watch TV less.
Precise: _____
_____

Vague: I plan to get good grades.
Precise: _____
_____

Taking It to the Net

1. The students in your class differ in their levels of motivation and self-direction. Would you teach these students differently? Why and how?
2. A student tells you that she lacks the ability to succeed in history. How do you respond? How do your locus of control and attribution style affect the way you interact with students? What are your locus of control and attribution style?

3. Self-efficacy is a student's belief in their ability to achieve. Attribution is the kinds of reasons a person gives to explain their success or failure. What's the relationship between a student's self-efficacy and that student's attributions?

Connect to http://www.mhhe.com/socscience/psychology/santedu/ttnet.htm to find the answers!

Case Studies

Case 1 *Rich Thorpe:* Rich discovers near the end of the school year that two students in different classes are giving up rather than trying to pass the course.

Case 2 *Emily Smith:* Emily, an energetic student teacher, requests and is assigned to student-teach social studies in an inner-city high school. Her cooperating teacher gradually lets her assume control of the most difficult survey class, and Emily succeeds in reaching them until they find out that her student-teaching assignment with them will soon end.

Chapter 12

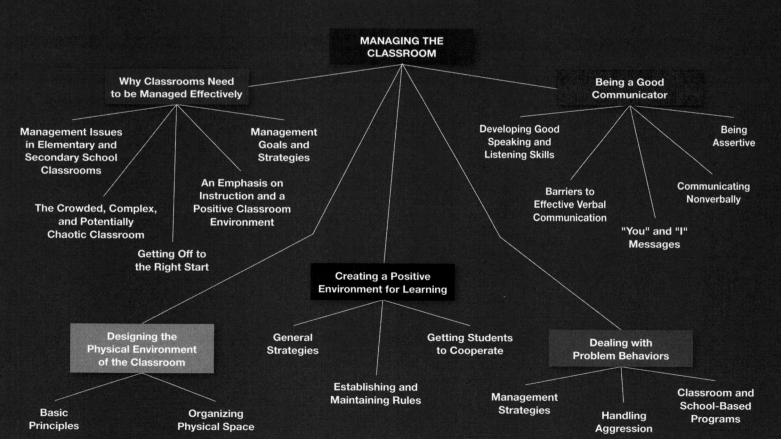

MANAGING THE CLASSROOM

Why Classrooms Need to be Managed Effectively

Management Issues in Elementary and Secondary School Classrooms

The Crowded, Complex, and Potentially Chaotic Classroom

Getting Off to the Right Start

Management Goals and Strategies

An Emphasis on Instruction and a Positive Classroom Environment

Being a Good Communicator

Developing Good Speaking and Listening Skills

Barriers to Effective Verbal Communication

"You" and "I" Messages

Communicating Nonverbally

Being Assertive

Creating a Positive Environment for Learning

General Strategies

Establishing and Maintaining Rules

Getting Students to Cooperate

Designing the Physical Environment of the Classroom

Basic Principles

Organizing Physical Space

Dealing with Problem Behaviors

Management Strategies

Handling Aggression

Classroom and School-Based Programs

Preview

In educational circles, it is commonly said that no one pays any attention to good classroom management until it is missing. When classrooms are effectively managed, they run smoothly and students are actively engaged in learning. When they are poorly managed, they can become chaotic settings in which learning is a foreign activity. These are some of the questions we will explore in this chapter:

- What are the essential challenges of managing a classroom?
- How can the classroom be physically designed to make it more manageable?
- What are some good strategies for establishing and maintaining classroom rules?
- How can teachers effectively deal with fighting and student hostility?
- What are some good teaching strategies for improving communication skills?
- How can teachers improve students' communication skills?

Teaching Stories
Adriane Lonzarich

Adriane Lonzarich owns and operates Heartwood, a small preschool in San Mateo, California. In the afternoons she also holds art classes for 5- to 12-year-old children. She talks about her ideas for managing the classroom:

The most valuable advice I ever received for managing the classroom is to approach a problem or area of difficulty with three questions in this order:

1. Is it the environment?
2. Is it the teacher?
3. Is it the child?

For example, if the issue of concern is unfocused energy of the group, I would first ask myself, Is it the environment? Is it overstimulating? Is there not enough to do? Do I need to rearrange the classroom and create more intimate spaces for quiet activity or do I need to let them have more time outside, and so on? In many cases, I don't need to go on to the next two questions.

Is it the teacher? Am I tired? nervous? uninspiring? Have I not taken the time to demonstrate the activities? Have I not been consistent in presenting, monitoring, and enforcing basic classroom rules? Have I not paid enough attention to their needs that day?

Is it the child? If I've addressed all the other possibilities and I'm convinced that the problem is the child's problem, not the environment's or the teacher's, I explore what might be going on. Is anything happening in the child's home that might be causing his or her problems? Is it time for a parent conference? Does the child need help in bonding with a friend? Is the child afraid of failure and avoiding meaningful learning for that reason?

This approach is empowering because it is much easier to change the environment or oneself than to change someone else's behavior. It also is effective because it does not zero in on the problem as the child's until all other avenues have been explored.

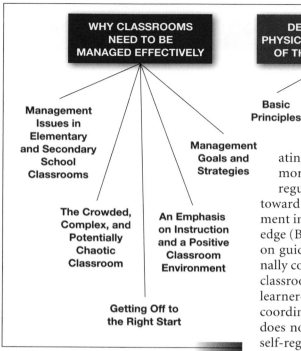

Why Classrooms Need to Be Managed Effectively

Effective classroom management maximizes children's learning opportunities (Levin & Nolan, 2000). Experts in classroom management report that there has been a change in thinking about the best way to manage classrooms. The older view emphasized creating and applying rules to control students' behavior. The newer view focuses more on students' needs for nurturing relationships and opportunities for self-regulation (Weinstein, 1999). Classroom management that orients students toward passivity and compliance with rigid rules can undermine students' engagement in active learning, higher-order thinking, and the social construction of knowledge (Brophy, 1999). The new trend in classroom management places more emphasis on guiding students to become more proficient at self-discipline and less on externally controlling the student (Freiberg, 1999; Skiba & Peterson, 1999). Historically in classroom management, the teacher was thought of as a director. In the current learner-centered trend in classroom management, the teacher is more of a guide, coordinator, and facilitator (Freiberg, 1999). The new classroom management model does not mean slipping into a permissive mode. Emphasizing caring and students' self-regulation does not mean that the teacher abdicates responsibility for what happens in the classroom (Weinstein, 1999).

As you explore various aspects of managing the classroom, realize the importance of consulting and working with other staff members on management issues (Evertson & Harris, 1999). Also recognize that your class is part of the broader context of school culture, and that in such areas as discipline and conflict management your policies will need to reflect and be consistent with the policies of the school and other teachers in the school. We will begin our tour of effective classroom management by exploring how management issues sometimes differ in elementary and secondary classrooms.

Management Issues in Elementary and Secondary School Classrooms

Elementary and secondary school classrooms involve many similar management issues. At all levels of education, good classroom managers design the physical environment of the classroom for optimal learning, create positive environments for learning, establish and maintain rules, get students to cooperate, effectively deal with problems, and use good communication strategies.

However, some differences in elementary and secondary schools have meaning for the way classrooms need to be managed. In many elementary schools, teachers face the challenge of managing the same 20 to 25 children for the entire day. In middle and high schools, teachers face the challenge of managing five or six different groups of 20 to 25 adolescents for about 50 minutes each day. Compared to secondary school students, elementary school students spend much more time with the same students in the small space of a single classroom, and having to interact with the same people all day can breed feelings of confinement and boredom and other problems. However, with 100 to 125 students, secondary school teachers are more likely to be confronted with a wider range of problems than elementary school teachers. Also, because secondary school teachers spend less time seeing students in the classroom, it can be more difficult for them to establish personal relationships with students. And secondary school teachers especially have to get the classroom lesson moving quickly and manage time effectively, because class periods are so short.

Secondary school students' problems can be more long-standing and more deeply ingrained, and therefore more difficult to modify, than those of elementary school students. Also in secondary schools, discipline problems are frequently more severe, the students being potentially more unruly and even dangerous. Because most secondary school students have more advanced reasoning skills than elementary school students, they might demand more elaborate and logical explanations of rules and discipline. And in secondary schools, hallway socializing can carry into the classroom. Every hour there is another "settling down" process. Keep in mind these differences between elementary and secondary schools as we further explore how to effectively manage the classroom. As we see next, at both elementary and secondary school levels, classrooms can be crowded, complex, and potentially chaotic.

The Crowded, Complex, and Potentially Chaotic Classroom

In analyzing the classroom environment, Walter Doyle (1986) described six characteristics that reflect its complexity and potential for problems:

- *Classrooms are multidimensional.* Classrooms are the setting for many activities, ranging from academic activities such as reading, writing, and math, to social activities, such as playing games, communicating with friends, and arguing. Teachers have to keep records and keep students on a schedule. Work has to be assigned, monitored, collected, and evaluated. Students have individual needs that benefit when the teacher takes them into account.
- *Activities occur simultaneously.* Many classroom activities occur simultaneously. One cluster of students might be writing at their desks, another might be discussing a story with the teacher, one student might be picking on another, others might be talking about what they are going to do after school, and so on.
- *Things happen quickly.* Events often occur rapidly in classrooms and frequently require an immediate response. Such events include two students arguing about the ownership of a notebook, a student complaining that another student is copying her answers, a student speaking out of turn, a student marking on another student's arm with a felt-tip pen, two students bullying another student, and a student being openly rude to you.
- *Events are often unpredictable.* Even though you might carefully plan the day's activities and be highly organized, events will occur that you never expect: A fire alarm goes off; a student gets sick; two students get into a fight; a computer won't work; a previously unannounced assembly takes place; the heat goes off in the middle of the winter; and so on.
- *There is little privacy.* Classrooms are public places where students observe how the teacher handles discipline problems, unexpected events, and frustrating circumstances. Some teachers report that they feel like they are in a "fishbowl" or constantly on stage. Much of what happens to one student is observed by other students, and students make attributions about what is occurring. In one case, they might perceive that the teacher is being unfair in the way she disciplines a student. In another, they might appreciate her sensitivity to a student's feelings.
- *Classrooms have histories.* Students have memories of what happened earlier in their classroom. They remember how the teacher handled a discipline problem earlier in the year, which students have gotten more privileges than others, and whether the teacher abides by her promises. Because the past affects the future, it is important for teachers to manage the classroom today in a way that will support rather than undermine learning tomorrow. This means that the first several weeks of the school year are critical for establishing effective management principles.

The crowded, complex nature of the classroom can lead to chaos and problems if the classroom is not managed effectively ◀ⅢⅢ p. 6. Indeed, such problems are a major public concern about schools. Year after year, the Gallup Poll has asked the public what they perceive to be the main problem schools face (Gallup Organization, 1996). The reply has consistently been "A lack of discipline."

TEACHING STRATEGIES
For a Good Beginning of the School Year

Some good teaching strategies for the beginning of the year are (Emmer, Evertson, & Worsham, 2000):

1. *Establish expectations for behavior and resolve student uncertainties.* At the beginning of the school year, students will not be sure what to expect in your classroom. They might have expectations, based on their experiences with other teachers, that are different from what your classroom will be like. On the first few days of school, lay out your expectations for students' work and behavior. Don't focus just on course content in the first few days and weeks of school. Be sure to take the time to clearly and concretely spell out class rules, procedures, and requirements so that students know what to expect in your class.
2. *Make sure that students experience success.* In the first week of school, content activities and assignments should be designed to ensure that students can do them successfully. This helps students develop a positive attitude and provides them with confidence to tackle more difficult tasks later.
3. *Be available and visible.* Show your students that you are someone who can be approached when they need information. During seatwork or groupwork, make yourself available instead of going to your desk and completing paperwork. Move around the room, monitor students' progress, and provide assistance when needed.
4. *Be in charge.* Even if you have stated your class rules and expectations clearly, some students will forget and others will try to test you to see if you are willing to enforce the rules, especially in the first several weeks of school. Continue to consistently establish the boundaries between what is acceptable and what is not acceptable in your classroom.

Alternatives to Control and Compliance

Getting Off to the Right Start

The first few days and weeks of school are important for classroom management. You will want to use this time to (1) communicate your rules and procedures to the class and get student cooperation in following them, and (2) get students to effectively engage in all learning activities.

Taking the time in the first week of school to establish these expectations, rules, and routines will help your class run smoothly and set the tone for developing a positive classroom environment.

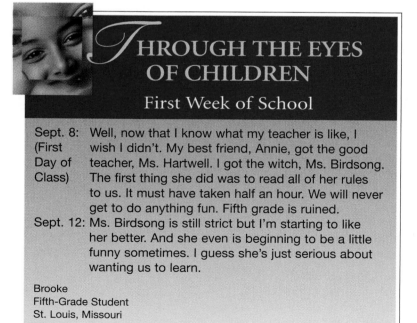

THROUGH THE EYES OF CHILDREN
First Week of School

Sept. 8: (First Day of Class) Well, now that I know what my teacher is like, I wish I didn't. My best friend, Annie, got the good teacher, Ms. Hartwell. I got the witch, Ms. Birdsong. The first thing she did was to read all of her rules to us. It must have taken half an hour. We will never get to do anything fun. Fifth grade is ruined.

Sept. 12: Ms. Birdsong is still strict but I'm starting to like her better. And she even is beginning to be a little funny sometimes. I guess she's just serious about wanting us to learn.

Brooke
Fifth-Grade Student
St. Louis, Missouri

An Emphasis on Instruction and a Positive Classroom Environment

Despite the public's belief that lack of discipline is the number one problem in schools, educational psychology has changed its focus. Formerly it emphasized discipline; today it emphasizes ways to develop and maintain a positive classroom environment that supports learning (Evertson, Emmer, & Worsham, 2000). This involves using preventive *proactive* strategies rather than becoming immersed in *reactive* disciplinary tactics (Paintal, 1999). In a classic study, Jacob Kounin (1970) was interested in discovering how teachers responded to student misbehaviors. Kounin was surprised to find that effective and ineffective classroom managers responded in very similar ways to students' misbehaviors. What the effective managers did far better than the ineffective managers was manage the group's activities. Researchers in educational psychology consistently find that teachers who competently guide and structure classroom activities are more effective than teachers who emphasize their disciplinary role (Brophy, 1996).

Throughout this book we emphasize a vision of students as active learners engaged in meaningful tasks, who think reflectively and critically and often interact with other students in collaborative learning experiences. Historically, the effectively managed classroom has been described as a "well-oiled machine," but a more appropriate metaphor for today's effectively managed classroom is "beehive of activity" (see figure 12.1 on p. 434) (Randolph & Evertson, 1995). This does not imply that classrooms should be wildly noisy and chaotic. Rather, students should be actively learning and busily engaged in tasks that they are motivated to do rather than quietly and passively sitting in their seats. Often they will be interacting with each other and the teacher as they construct their knowledge and understanding.

Management Goals and Strategies

Effective classroom management has two main goals: to help students spend more time on learning and less time on non-goal-directed activity, and to prevent students from developing academic and emotional problems.

Help Students Spend More Time on Learning and Less Time on Non-Goal-Directed Behavior
In chapters 10 and 11, we discussed the importance, for both teachers and students, of being a good time manager. Effective classroom management will help you maximize your instructional time and your students' learning time. Carol Weinstein (1997) described the amount of time available for various classroom activities in a typical 42-minute secondary school class over the course of a school year. Actual yearly learning time is only about 62 hours, which is approximately half of the mandated school time for a typical class. Although her time figures are only estimates, they suggest that the hours available for learning are far less than would appear. And as we underscored in chapter 10, "Planning, Instruction, and Technology," learning takes time.

Prevent Students from Developing Problems
A well-managed classroom not only fosters meaningful learning but also helps prevent academic and emotional problems from developing. Well-managed classrooms keep students busy with active, appropriately challenging tasks. Well-managed classrooms have activities in which students become absorbed and motivated to learn and clear rules and regulations students must abide by. In such classrooms, students are less likely to develop academic and emotional problems. By contrast, in poorly managed classrooms, students' academic and emotional problems are more likely to fester. The academically unmotivated student becomes even less motivated. The shy student becomes more reclusive. The bully becomes meaner.

THROUGH THE EYES OF TEACHERS
Creating Juvenile Video Court TV

Carmella Williams Scott, a middle school English and Law teacher at Fairmont Alternative School in Newnan, Georgia, created Juvenile Video Court TV, a student-run judicial system, so that students could experience the "other side of the bench" as a judge, lawyer, bailiff, and camera operator. She especially targeted gang leaders for inclusion in the system because they ran the school. Carmella likes to use meaningful questions to guide students' critical thinking. She believes that mutual respect is a key factor in her success as a teacher and the lack of discipline problems she has in her classes.

Carmella Williams Scott

Educational Time Factors

Designing the Physical Environment of the Classroom

When thinking about effectively managing the classroom, inexperienced teachers sometimes overlook the physical environment. As you will see in this section, designing the physical environment of the classroom involves far more than arranging a few items on a bulletin board.

Figure **12.1**

The Effectively Managed Classroom

"Well-Oiled Machine" or "Beehive of Activity"?

Basic Principles

Following are four basic principles that you can use when arranging your classroom (Evertson, Emmer, & Worsham, 2000):

- *Reduce congestion in high-traffic areas.* Distraction and disruption can often occur in high-traffic areas. These include group work areas, students' desks, the teacher's desk, the pencil sharpener, bookshelves, computer stations, and storage locations. Separate these areas from each other as much as possible and make sure they are easily accessible.
- *Make sure that you can easily see all students.* An important management task is to carefully monitor students. To do this, you will need to be able to see all students at all times. Make sure there is a clear line of sight between your desk, instructional locations, students' desks, and all student work areas. Stand in different parts of the room to check for blind spots.
- *Make often-used teaching materials and student supplies easily accessible.* This minimizes preparation and cleanup time, as well as slowdowns and breaks in activity flow.
- *Make sure that students can easily observe whole-class presentations.* Establish where you and your students will be located when whole-class presentations take place. For these activities, students should not have to move their chairs or stretch their necks. To find out how well your students can see from their locations, sit in their seats in different parts of the room.

Organizing Physical Space

In thinking about how you will organize the classroom's physical space, you should ask yourself what the main type of instructional activity students will be engaged in (whole-class, small-group, individual assignments, etc.). Consider the physical arrangements that will best support that type of activity.

Classroom Arrangement Styles

Figure 12.2 on p. 436 shows a number of classroom arrangement styles: auditorium, face-to-face, off-set, seminar, and cluster (Renne, 1997). In traditional **auditorium style,** *all students face the teacher* (see figure 12.2A). This arrangement inhibits face-to-face student contacts in a natural way, and the teacher is free to move anywhere in the room. Auditorium style often is used when the teacher lectures or someone is making a presentation to the entire class.

In **face-to-face style,** *students sit facing each other* (see figure 12.2B). Distraction from other students is higher in this arrangement than in the auditorium style.

In **off-set style,** *small numbers of students (usually 3 or 4) sit at tables but do not sit directly across from one another* (see figure 12.2C). This produces less distraction than face-to-face style and can be effective for cooperative learning activities.

In **seminar style,** *larger numbers of students (10 or more) sit in circular, square, or U-shaped arrangements* (see figure 12.2D). This is especially effective when you want students to talk with each other or to converse with you.

In **cluster style,** *small numbers of students (usually 4 to 8) work in small, closely bunched groups* (see figure 12.2E). This arrangement is especially effective for collaborative learning activities.

Clustering desks encourages social interaction among students. In contrast, rows of desks reduce social interaction among students and direct

TEACHING STRATEGIES
For Increasing Academic Learning Time

Strategies for increasing academic learning time include maintaining activity flow, minimizing transition time, and holding students accountable (Weinstein, 1997):

1. *Maintain activity flow.* In an analysis of classrooms, Jacob Kounin (1970) studied teachers' ability to initiate and maintain the flow of activity. Then he searched for links between activity flow and students' engagement and misbehavior. He found that some ineffective managers engaged in "flip-flopping"—terminating an activity, starting another, and then returning to the first one. Other ineffective managers were distracted from an ongoing activity by a small event that really did not need attention. For example, in one situation a teacher who was explaining a math problem at the board noticed a student leaning on his left elbow while working on the problem. The teacher went over to the student and told him to sit up straight, interrupting the flow of the class. Some ineffective managers "overdwell" on something that students already understand or go on at length about appropriate behavior. All of these situations—flip-flopping, responding to distractions, and overdwelling—can interrupt the classroom's flow.

2. *Minimize transition times.* In transitions from one activity to another, there is more room for disruptive behavior to occur. In one study of 50 classes, disruptions such as hitting, yelling, and using obscene gestures occurred twice as often during transitions between activities than during activities (Arlin, 1979). Teachers can decrease the potential for disruption during transitions by preparing students for forthcoming transitions, establishing transition routines, and clearly defining the boundaries of lessons.

3. *Hold students accountable.* If students know they will be held accountable for their work, they are more likely to make good use of class time. Clearly communicating assignments and requirements encourages student accountability. Explain to students what they will be doing and why, how long they will be working on the activity, how to obtain help if they need it, and what to do when they are finished. Helping students establish goals, plan, and monitor their progress also increases students' accountability. And maintaining good records can help you hold students accountable for their performance.

students' attention toward the teacher. Arranging desks in rows can benefit students when they are working on individual assignments, whereas clustered desks facilitate cooperative learning. In classrooms in which seats are organized in rows, the teacher is most likely to interact with students seated in the front and center of the classroom (Adams & Biddle, 1970) (see figure 12.3 on p. 437). This area has been called the "action zone" because students in the front and center locations interact the most with the teacher, are the students that most often ask questions, and are most likely to initiate discussion. If you use a row arrangement, move around the room when possible, establish eye contact with students seated outside the "action zone," direct comments to students in the peripheral seats, and periodically have students change seats so that all students have an equal opportunity of being in the front and center seats.

Figures 12.4 and 12.5 on p. 438–439 show two workable classroom arrangements, one in an elementary school and the other in a secondary school. Figure 12.4 portrays the arrangement created by a teacher who was assigned to a classroom with less space than he had in previous years. His classroom also had been moved from the periphery of the school to its center, which meant that it did not have windows or permanent walls. Given the

THROUGH THE EYES OF TEACHERS
Hissing Cockroaches and Mini-Cams

My classroom is set up with tables with about four students per table. This allows for individual or group activities without a lot of transition time or movement. Since my current subject is science, there is an aquarium with fish, a terrarium with a lizard or praying mantis, and a cage with Madagascar hissing cockroaches. There is a table with gadgets and mini-experiments. A mini-cam may be focused on an earthworm or a spider with the image on the TV as students enter the classroom. The idea is to arrange the classroom so that it promotes inquiry, questioning, and thinking about science.

William Williford
Science Teacher
Perry Middle School
Perry, Georgia

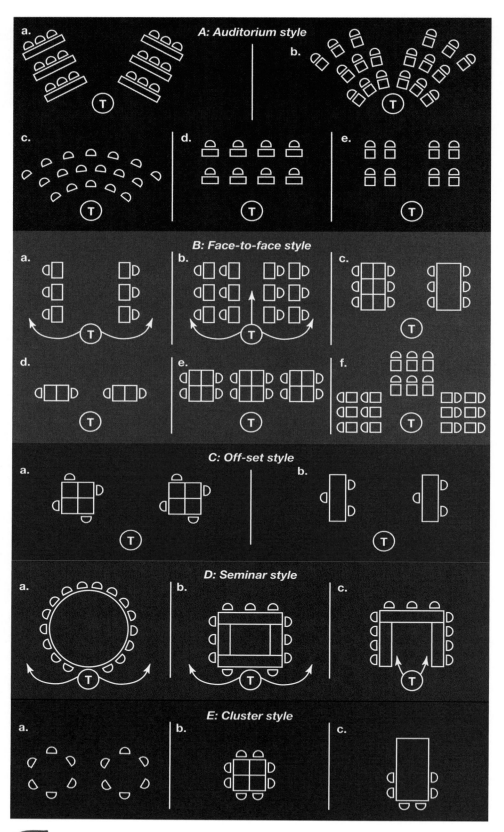

Figure 12.2

Variations of Classroom Seating Arrangements

cramped space, the teacher decided to place students' desks in clusters. This arrangement is compatible with his emphasis on cooperative learning activities.

A secondary school teacher's classroom arrangement is shown in figure 12.5. She even allows the students to move their tables into other configurations with which they feel more comfortable. The way she has arranged the tables facilitates small-group work. She has only two bulletin boards, but tries to make them reflect her students' activities and accomplishments. As we see next, this "personalization" of the classroom is especially important.

Personalizing the Classroom   According to classroom management experts Carol Weinstein and Andrew Mignano (1997), classrooms too often resemble motel rooms—pleasant but impersonal, revealing nothing about the people who use the space. Such anonymity is especially true of secondary school classrooms, where six or seven different classes might use the space in a single day. To personalize classrooms, post students' photographs, artwork, written projects, charts that list birthdays (early childhood and elementary school), and other positive expressions of students' identities. A bulletin board can be set aside for the "student of the week," or be used to display each student's best work of the week, personally chosen by each student.

None of the classrooms we have described will exactly match yours. However, keeping in mind the basic principles we have described should help you create an optimal classroom arrangement for learning.

At this point, we have studied many ideas about why classroom management is important and designing the classroom's physical environment. A review of these ideas is presented in summary table 12.1. Now that we have studied ways to effectively manage the physical environment of the classroom, let's turn our attention to strategies for managing its psychological dimensions.

THROUGH THE EYES OF TEACHERS
Tips on Classroom Arrangement

- Make areas of the classroom well defined.
- Arrange good traffic flow and storage.
- Safe, clean furniture is a must.
- It can be refreshing to rearrange the classroom during the year. Looking at the environment from a different angle puts a new perspective on people and things.
- Materials should be kept in the same places throughout the school year.
- A classroom should be bright and colorful with lots of posters, materials, and school memorabilia for students to read and look at.
- "My desk is always at the rear of the classroom. I keep a podium in one corner of the front and teach from there most of the time." (High school teacher)
- "My desk is in an open space that is easily accessible to students." (Middle school teacher)
- "I never stand in front of the classroom and speak. I constantly walk around the class, making contact with each and every student. I always make sure I am on the child's eye level when asking a question. Sometimes we sit in a circle so that I can be on their level." (Early childhood teacher)
- "I have one area where everyone can sit in one group for class lessons. I also like smaller areas where small groups can meet. Having students move about from one area to another gives students a chance to stretch. Small areas can also be set up to encourage learning about a specific subject area." (Special education high school teacher)
- See what other teachers do.
- Locate computers where they will not distract other students.

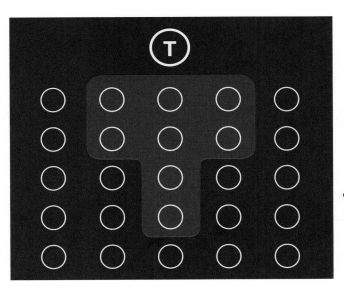

Figure 12.3
The Action Zone

"Action zone" refers to the seats in the front and center of row arrangement. Students in these seats are more likely to interact with the teacher, ask questions, and initiate discussion than students seated in more peripheral locations.

TEACHING STRATEGIES
For Designing a Classroom Arrangement

Follow these steps in designing a classroom arrangement (Weinstein, 1997; Weinstein & Mignano, 1997):

1. *Consider what activities students will be engaging in.* If you will be teaching kindergarten or elementary school students, you might need to create settings for reading aloud, small-group reading instruction, sharing time, group math instruction, and arts and crafts. A secondary school science teacher might have to accommodate whole-group instruction, "hands-on" lab activities, and media presentations. On the left-hand side of a sheet of paper, list the activities your students will perform. Next to each activity, list any special arrangements that need to be taken into account; for instance, art and science areas need to be near a sink, and computers need to be near an electrical outlet.

2. *Draw up a floor plan.* Before you actually move any furniture, draw several floor plans and then choose the one that you think will work the best.

3. *Involve students in planning the classroom layout.* You can do most of your environmental planning before school starts, but once it begins, ask students how they like your arrangement. If they suggest improvements that are reasonable, try them out. Students often report that they want adequate room and a place of their own where they can keep their things.

4. *Try out the arrangement and be flexible in redesigning it.* Several weeks into the school year, evaluate how effective your arrangement is. Be alert for problems that the arrangement might be generating. For example, one study found that when kindergarten students crowded around a teacher who was reading a story to them, they often misbehaved (Krantz & Risley, 1972). Just spreading the children apart in a semicircle significantly decreased the misbehaviors.

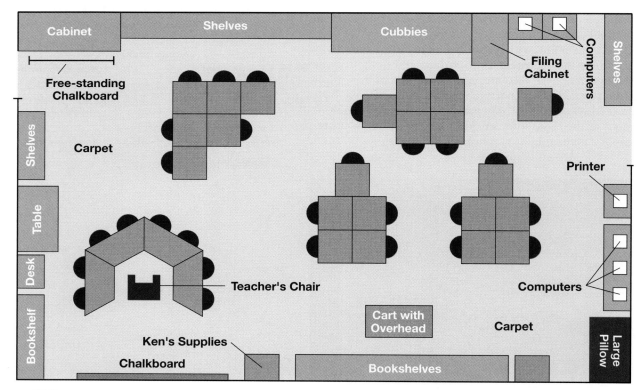

Figure **12.4**

An Example of an Effective Elementary School Classroom Arrangement

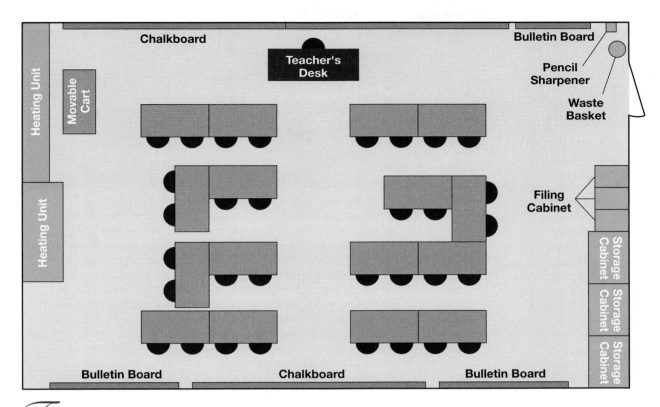

Figure **12.5**

An Example of an Effective Secondary School Classroom Arrangement

Creating a Positive Environment for Learning

Students need a positive environment for learning. We will discuss some general classroom management strategies for providing this environment, how to effectively establish and maintain rules, and positive strategies for getting students to cooperate.

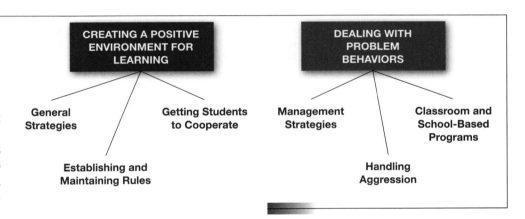

General Strategies

General strategies include using an authoritative strategy and effectively managing the group's activities.

Using an Authoritative Strategy   The authoritative classroom management strategy is derived from Diana Baumrind's (1971, 1996) parenting styles that were discussed in chapter 3, "Social Contexts and Socioemotional Development" ◀‖‖ p. 87. Like authoritative parents, authoritative teachers have students who tend to be self-reliant, delay gratification, get along well with their peers, and show high self-esteem. An **authoritative strategy of classroom management** *encourages students*

Your Classroom Management Profile

ᏚUMMARY ᎢABLE 12.1
Why Classrooms Need to Be Managed Effectively, and Designing the Physical Environment of the Classroom

Concept	Processes/ Related Ideas	Characteristics/Description
Why Classrooms Need to Be Managed Effectively	Management Issues in Elementary and Secondary School Classrooms	• Many management issues are similar across these classrooms. • However, these differences in elementary and secondary classrooms have meaning for the way classrooms need to be managed: Elementary school teachers often see 20 to 25 students all day long, secondary school teachers see 100 to 125 students about 50 minutes a day. Confinement, boredom, and having to interact with the same people all day in elementary school can create problems. Secondary school teachers have to get the lesson moving quickly. They also might see a greater range of problems and their students can have more longstanding problems that are more difficult to modify. These problems can be more severe than those of elementary school students. Secondary school students might demand more elaborate and logical explanations of rules and discipline.
	The Crowded, Complex, and Potentially Chaotic Classroom	• Doyle described six characteristics that reflect the classroom's complexity and potential for problems: (1) multidimensionality, (2) simultaneous activities going on, (3) events occurring at a rapid pace, (4) often unpredictable events, (5) lack of privacy, and (6) classroom histories.
	Getting Off to the Right Start	• Good strategies include these: (1) Establish expectations for behavior and resolve student uncertainties, (2) make sure that students experience success, (3) be available and visible, and (4) be in charge.
	An Emphasis on Instruction and a Positive Classroom Environment	• The focus in educational psychology used to be on discipline. • Today it is on developing and maintaining a positive classroom environment that supports learning. This involves using proactive management strategies rather than being immersed in reactive discipline tactics. • Historically, the well-managed classroom was conceptualized as a "well-oiled machine," but today it is more often viewed as a "beehive of activity."
	Management Goals and Strategies	• Goals and strategies include these: (1) Help students spend more time on learning and less time on non-goal-directed activity (maintain activity flow, minimize transition times, and hold students accountable), and (2) prevent students from developing problems.
Designing the Physical Environment of the Classroom	Basic Principles	• These include (1) reducing congestion in high-traffic areas, (2) making sure that you can easily see all students, (3) making often-used teaching materials and student supplies easily accessible, and (4) making sure that all students can see whole-class presentations.
	Organizing Physical Space	• This involves considering the best classroom arrangement style (auditorium, face-to-face, off-set, seminar, or cluster), personalizing the classroom, and becoming an environmental designer who considers what activities students will be engaging in, drawing up a floor plan, involving students in classroom design, and trying out the arrangement and being flexible in redesigning it.

to be independent thinkers and doers but still involves effective monitoring. Authoritative teachers engage students in considerable verbal give-and-take and show a caring attitude toward them. However, they still declare limits when necessary. Authoritative teachers clarify rules and regulations, establishing these standards with input from students.

The authoritative strategy contrasts with two ineffective strategies: authoritarian and permissive. The **authoritarian strategy of classroom management** *is restrictive and punitive. The focus is mainly on keeping order in the classroom rather than on instruction and learning. Authoritarian teachers place firm limits and controls on students and have little verbal exchange with them. Students in authoritarian classrooms tend to be passive learners,* fail to initiate activities, express anxiety about social comparison, and have poor communication skills.

The **permissive strategy of classroom management** *offers students considerable autonomy but provides them with little support for developing learning skills or managing their behavior. Not surprisingly, students in permissive classrooms tend to have inadequate academic skills and low self-control.*

Overall, an authoritative strategy will benefit your students more than authoritarian or permissive strategies. An authoritative strategy will help your students become active, self-regulated learners.

Effectively Managing the Group's Activities

We described some aspects of Jacob Kounin's (1970) work on classroom management earlier in the chapter. Kounin concluded that effective teachers differ from ineffective teachers not in the way they respond to students' misbehaviors but instead in how competently they manage the group's activities. Here we focus on some of the differences between effective and ineffective classroom managers. Effective classroom managers do the following:

- *Have "withitness."* Kounin used the term **"withitness"** *to describe a management strategy in which teachers show students that they are aware of what is happening. These teachers closely monitor students on a regular basis. This allows them to detect inappropriate behavior early before it gets out of hand.* Teachers who are not "with it" are likely to not notice such misbehaviors until they gain momentum and spread.

- *Cope effectively with overlapping situations.* Kounin observed that some teachers seem to have one-track minds, dealing with only one thing at a time. This ineffective strategy often led to frequent interruptions in the flow of the class. For example, one teacher was working with a reading group when she observed two boys on the other side of the room hitting each other. She immediately got up, went over to the other side of the room, harshly criticized them, and then returned to the reading group. However, by the time she returned to the reading group, the students in the reading group had become bored and were starting to misbehave themselves. In contrast, effective managers were able to deal with overlapping situations in less disruptive ways. For example, in the reading group situation they quickly responded to students from outside the group who came to ask questions but not in a way that significantly altered the flow of the reading group's activity. When moving around the room and checking each students' seatwork, they kept a roving eye on the rest of the class.

- *Maintain smoothness and continuity in lessons.* Effective managers keep the flow of a lesson moving smoothly, maintaining students' interest and not giving them opportunities to be easily distracted. Earlier in the chapter when we discussed strategies for increasing academic learning time, we mentioned some ineffective activities of teachers that can disrupt the flow of a lesson. These included flip-flopping, unnecessarily pulling away from an ongoing event, and dwelling too long on something that students already understand. Another teacher action that disrupts the lesson's flow is called "fragmentation," in which the teacher breaks an activity into components even though the activity could be performed as an entire unit. For example, a teacher might individually ask six students to do something, such as get out their art supplies, when all six could be asked to do this as a group. In another fragmented teaching situation, a teacher who was making the transition from spelling to math told students to close their spelling books, then put away their red pencils, then close their spelling books (again), next put their spelling books on their desks but keep them out of the way. Then the teacher told the students to take out their math books and put them on their desks but keep everything off their desks but the math books. Next, the students were told to get out their black pencils. Clearly, this segmented teaching disrupted the flow of the transition from spelling to math.

- *Engage students in a variety of challenging activities.* Kounin also found that effective classroom managers engage students in a variety of challenging but not overly hard activities. The students frequently worked independently rather than being directly supervised by a teacher who hovered over them.

Establishing and Maintaining Rules

**Classroom
Management Resources**

To function smoothly, classrooms need clearly defined rules. Students need to know specifically how you want them to behave. Without clearly defined classroom rules, the misunderstandings that can breed chaos are inevitable. For example, when students enter the classroom, are they supposed to go directly to their seats or can they socialize for a few minutes until you tell them to be seated? When students want to go to the library, do they need a pass? When students are working at their seats, can they help each other or are they required to work individually?

Getting Students to Cooperate

You want your students to cooperate with you and abide by classroom rules without always having to resort to discipline to maintain order. How can you get your students to cooperate? There are three main strategies: Develop a positive relationship with students, get students to share and assume responsibility, and reward appropriate behavior.

Develop a Positive Relationship with Students   When most of us think of our favorite teacher, we think of someone who cared about whether we learned or not. Showing that you genuinely care about students as individuals apart from their academic work helps to gain their cooperation. It is easy

---

THROUGH THE EYES OF TEACHERS
"Put Out the Fire with as Little Water as Possible"

Following are some strategies that several successful teachers use to create a positive classroom environment and get students to cooperate with them:

Teacher No. 1

"One of the ways I create a positive classroom environment involves when a student has not followed directions. I basically remind the student with the usual, 'What's the rule?' If the student continues to disobey my rules, I try to follow the maxim, 'Try to put out the fire with the least amount of water possible.' Sure, it's a generality, but it does prevent a lot of pointless power struggles that often escalate into a contest, in which everyone loses."

Teacher No. 2

"I believe that students learn best when they feel comfortable. I make it a practice to greet students as they enter the room and find out how they are feeling so I can understand their behavior better. My students understand that they are free to move around but also know the situations in which it may not be appropriate to do so. During class time, rather than tell students they are wrong, I try to guide them to an accurate answer. This keeps a positive flow in the classroom and lets students feel successful. Outside the classroom, I also try to listen to students when they want to talk. Sometimes this happens in the lunchroom, where students feel free to approach me if they want to talk about something."

TEACHING STRATEGIES
For Establishing Rules in the Classroom

Carol Weinstein (1997) described four principles to keep in mind when you establish rules for your classroom:

1. *Rules should be reasonable and necessary.* Ask yourself if the rules you are establishing are appropriate for this grade level. Also ask yourself if there is a good reason for the rule. For example, one secondary school teacher has a rule that students must come to class on time. Students are clearly told that if they are late, they will get a detention even on the first violation. She explains the rule to the students at the beginning of the school year and tells them the reason for the rule: If they are late, they might miss important material.
2. *Rules should be clear and comprehensible.* If you have general rules, make sure that you clearly specify what they mean. For example, one teacher has the rule "Be Prepared." Instead of leaving the rule at this general level, the teacher specifies what it means to be prepared: having your homework, notebook, pen or pencil, and textbook with you every day.

   One issue that crops up when establishing classroom rules is whether to let students participate in making them. Involving students in generating classroom rules can increase students' sense of responsibility to abide by them, especially in secondary schools. Some students will suggest ridiculous rules, which you can simply veto. Some teachers will establish general rules and then ask students to generate specific examples of the rules.
3. *Rules should be consistent with instructional and learning goals.* Make sure that rules do not interfere with learning. Some teachers become so concerned about having an orderly, quiet classroom that they restrict students from interacting with each other and from engaging in collaborative learning activities.
4. *Classroom rules should be consistent with school rules.* Know what the school's rules are, such as whether particular behaviors are required in the halls, in the cafeteria, and so on. Many schools have a handbook that spells out what is acceptable and what is not. Familiarize yourself with the handbook. Some teachers go over the handbook with students at the beginning of the school year so that students clearly understand the school's rules regarding absenteeism, truancy, fighting, smoking, substance abuse, abusive language, and so on.

to get caught up in the pressing demands of academic achievement and classroom business, and ignore the socioemotional needs of students.

One study found that, in addition to having effective rules and procedures, successful classroom managers also showed a caring attitude toward students (Emmer, Evertson, & Anderson, 1980). This caring was evidenced in part by a classroom environment in which students felt safe and secure and were treated fairly. The teachers were sensitive to their needs and anxieties (for example, they created enjoyable activities the first several days of the school year rather than giving them diagnostic tests) and also had good communication skills (including listening skills), and effectively expressed their feelings to students. The classroom atmosphere was relaxed and pleasant. For example, the focus was on academic work but teachers gave students breaks and let them play tapes and CDs.

The Child Development Project (CDP) is a comprehensive elementary school program in which teachers and administrators build supportive relationships with students and encourage students to develop similarly warm relationships with each other (Battistich & others, in press; Battistich & Solomon, 1995). Five instructional practices form the core of this project: (1) cooperative learning activities that facilitate teamwork; (2) a literature-based, values-rich, multicultural language arts program that encourages students to think critically about relevant social and ethical issues; (3) classroom management techniques that emphasize prevention and responsibility; (4) classroom and schoolwide community-building projects that involve students, teachers, parents, and extended family members; and (5) "homeside" activities that improve communication between students and parents, build bridges between schools and families, and encourage students' understanding of their family's heritage. Research evaluations of CDP in a large number of geographically diverse elementary

1. Give a student a friendly "hello" at the door.

2. Have a brief-one-on-one conversation about things that are happening in the student's life.

3. Write a brief note of encouragement to the student.

4. Use students' names in class more.

5. Show enthusiasm about being with students (even late in the day, week, or year).

6. Risk more personal self-disclosures, which help students see you as a real person. However, don't cross the line and go too far. Always take into account children's level of understanding and emotional vulnerability in disclosing information about yourself to them.

7. Be an active listener who carefully attends to what the student is saying, even if it is something trivial.

8. Let students know that you are there to support and help them.

9. Keep in mind that developing positive, trusting relationships take time. This especially is the case for students from high-risk environments who might not initially trust your motives.

Figure **12.6**

Guidelines for Establishing Positive Relationships with Students

Managing
Inappropriate Behavior

schools revealed that students who participated in the project were more cooperative, had better social understanding, possessed more positive values, were more likely to help others, and had better conflict resolution skills than their counterparts who did not participate in the project (Battistich & others, 1989; Battistich & others, in press). Figure 12.6 presents some teaching guidelines for developing a positive relationship with students.

Get Students to Share and Assume Responsibility Earlier in this chapter, we discussed the importance of developing an authoritative atmosphere in the classroom and the issue of whether students should be allowed to participate in establishing class rules. Some experts on classroom management believe that sharing responsibility with students for making classroom decisions increases the students' commitment to the decisions (Risley & Walther, 1995).

Reward Appropriate Behavior We have discussed rewards elsewhere, most extensively in chapter 7, "Behavioral Approaches, Social Cognitive Approaches, and Teaching" ◀◀||| p. 248. You might want to read the discussion of rewards in that chapter again, especially the section "Applied Behavior Analysis in Education," and think about how rewards can be used in effectively managing the classroom. The discussion of rewards in chapter 11, "Motivating Students to Learn," also is relevant to classroom management, especially the information about rewards and intrinsic motivation ◀◀||| p. 397. Following are some guidelines for using rewards in managing the classroom.

Choose Effective Reinforcers Find out which reinforcers work best with which students, and individualize reinforcement. For one student, the most effective reward might be praise; for another, it might be getting to do a favorite activity. Remember that pleasurable activities often are especially valuable in gaining students' cooperation. You might tell a student, "When you complete your math problems, you can go to the media area and play a computer game."

Use Prompts and Shaping Effectively Remember that if you wait for students to perform perfectly, it might never happen. A good strategy is to use prompts and shape students' behavior by rewarding improvement. Some prompts come in the form of hints or reminders, such as "Remember the rule about lining up." Recall from chapter 7 that shaping involves rewarding a student for successive approximations to a specified target behavior. Thus, you might initially reward a student for getting 60 percent of her math problems right, then for 70 percent the next time, and so on.

Use Rewards to Provide Information About Mastery, Not to Control Students' Behavior Rewards that impart information about students' mastery can increase their intrinsic motivation and sense of responsibility. However, rewards that are used to control students' behavior are less likely to promote self-regulation and responsibility. For example, a student's learning might benefit from the student's being selected as student of the week because the student engaged in a number of highly productive, competent activities. However, the student likely will not benefit from being given a reward for sitting still at a desk; such a reward is an effort by the teacher to control the student, and students in heavily controlled learning environments tend to act like "pawns."

TEACHING STRATEGIES
For Getting Students to Share and Assume Responsibility

Following are some guidelines for getting students to share and assume responsibility in the classroom (Fitzpatrick, 1993):

1. *Involve students in the planning and implementation of school and classroom initiatives.* This participation helps to satisfy students' needs for self-confidence and belonging.
2. *Encourage students to judge their own behavior.* Rather than pass judgment on students' behavior, ask questions that motivate students to evaluate their own behavior. These might include "Does your behavior reflect the class rules?" and "What's the rule?" Such questions place responsibility on the shoulders of the student. Initially, some students try to blame others or change the subject. In such situations, stay focused and guide the student toward accepting responsibility.
3. *Don't accept excuses.* Excuses just pass on or avoid responsibility. Don't even entertain a discussion about excuses. Rather, ask students what they can do the next time a similar situation develops.
4. *Give the self-responsibility strategy time to work.* Students don't develop responsibility overnight. Many student misbehaviors are ingrained habits that take a long time to break. One strategy is to be patient one more time than the student expects—difficult to do, but good advice.
5. *Let students participate in decision making by holding class meetings.* In his book *Schools Without Failure,* William Glasser (1969) argued that class meetings can be used to deal with student behavior problems or virtually any issue that is of concern to teachers and students.

Dealing with Problem Behaviors

No matter how well you have planned and created a positive classroom environment, problem behaviors will emerge. It is important that you deal with them in a timely, effective manner.

**Exploring Techniques
That Work and Don't Work**

Management Strategies

Classroom management expert Carolyn Evertson and her colleagues (Evertson, Emmer, & Worsham, 2000) distinguish between minor and moderate interventions for problem behaviors.

Minor Interventions   Some problems only require minor interventions. These problems involve behaviors that, if infrequent, usually don't disrupt class activities and learning. For example, students might call out to the teacher out of turn, leave their seats without permission, engage in social talk when it is not allowed, eat candy in class, and so on. When only minor interventions are needed for problem behaviors, the following strategies can be effective (Evertson, Emmer, & Worsham, 2000):

- *Use nonverbal cues.* Establish eye contact with the student. Then signal the student by placing your finger on your lips, shaking your head, or using a hand signal to stop the behavior.
- *Keep the activity moving.* Sometimes transitions between activities take too long or a break in activity occurs when students have nothing to do. In these situations, students might leave their seats, socialize, crack jokes, and begin to get out of control. A good strategy is not to correct students' minor misbehaviors in these situations, but

"How come when you say we have a problem, I'm always the one who has the problem?"

THROUGH THE EYES OF TEACHERS

Tips on Classroom Management and Discipline

- Make sure students know your expectations—academic and behavioral—from the first day of school.
- Exude confidence, even if you don't feel it. Have high but realistic expectations for your students and yourself.
- Teach "bell-to-bell."
- Observe and talk with teachers who seem to have a teaching style and values regarding teaching that are similar to your own; they are often helpful in suggesting strategies that will fit your style.
- Avoid power struggles. Yelling and condescending remarks usually make things worse.
- Students love knowing what to expect next. List on your board the agenda for the day. Set priorities for what needs to be done before free time.
- Set guidelines and see that they are followed. Change them if necessary.
- Having students help create classroom rules and procedures often assures more buy-in.
- Be clear with your students about what you expect. Let them see it in writing as well as hear it.
- Be consistent.
- A master teacher can provide you with encouragement and alternative approaches to curriculum frustrations or student struggles.
- Listen to your students. Immediate care is necessary if a student expresses fear for his or her safety at school or at home.

Handling Diffucult Situations

rather start the next activity in a more timely fashion. By effectively planning the day, you should be able to eliminate these long transitions and gaps in activity.

- *Move closer to students.* When a student starts misbehaving, simply moving near the student will often cause the misbehavior to stop.
- *Redirect the behavior.* If students get off-task, remind them of what they are supposed to be doing. You might say, "Okay, remember, everybody is supposed to be working on their math problems."
- *Give needed instruction.* Sometimes students engage in minor misbehaviors when they haven't comprehended how to do the task they have been assigned. Unable to effectively do the activity, they fill the time by engaging in misbehaviors. Solving this problem involves careful monitoring of students' work and providing guidance when needed.
- *Directly and assertively tell the student to stop.* Establish direct eye contact with the student, be assertive, and tell the student to stop the behavior. Make your statement brief, and monitor the situation until the student complies. This strategy can be combined with redirecting the student's behavior.
- *Give the student a choice.* Place responsibility in the student's hands by saying that he or she has a choice of either behaving appropriately or receiving a negative consequence. Be sure to tell the student what the appropriate behavior is and what the consequence is for not performing it. For example, an elementary school teacher might say, "Remember, appropriate behavior in this class means not eating candy in class. If you choose to do that, you won't be allowed to play games on the computer."

Moderate Interventions   Some misbehaviors require a stronger intervention than those described above—for example, when students abuse privileges, disrupt an activity, goof off, or interfere with your instruction or other students' work. Following are some moderate interventions for dealing with these types of problems (Evertson, Emmer, & Worsham, 2000):

- *Withhold a privilege or desired activity.* Inevitably, you will have students who abuse privileges they have been given, such as freedom to move around the classroom or to work on a project with friends. In these cases, you can revoke the privilege.
- *Create a behavioral contract.* In chapter 7, we described the concept of *contracting,* which involves putting reinforcement contingencies into writing. If problems arise and students don't uphold their end of the bargain, the teacher can refer to the contract the students agreed to. The contract should reflect input from both the teacher and the student. In some cases, teachers enlist a third party, such as another student, to sign the contract as a witness to the agreement.
- *Isolate or remove students.* In chapter 7, we also discussed the *time-out,* which involves removing a student from positive reinforcement ◀▥ p. 252. If you choose to use a time-out, you have several options. You can (a) keep the student in the classroom, but deny the student access to positive reinforcement; (b) take the student outside the activity area or out of the classroom; or (c) place the student in a time-out room designated by the school. If you use a time-out, be sure

to clearly identify the student's behavior that resulted in the time-out, such as, "You are being placed in time-out for 30 minutes because you punched Derrick." If the misbehavior occurs again, reidentify it and place the student in time-out again. After the time-out, don't comment on how well the student behaved during the time-out, just return the student to the activity that was interrupted.

• *Impose a penalty or detention.* A small amount of repetitious work can be used as a penalty for misbehavior. In writing, a student might have to write an extra page; in math, a student might have to do extra problems; in physical education, a student might have to run an extra lap. The problem with penalties is that they can harm the student's attitude toward the subject matter.

Students also can be made to serve a detention for their misbehaviors, either at lunch, during recess, before school, or after school. Problem behaviors that teachers commonly assign detentions for include goofing off, wasting time, repeated rule violations, not completing assignments, and disrupting the class. Some detentions are served in the classroom; some schools have a detention hall where students can be sent. If the detention occurs in your classroom, you will have to supervise it. The length of the detention should initially be short, on the order of 10 to 15 minutes, if the misbehavior is not severe. As when using the time-out, you will need to keep a record of the detention.

Use Others as Resources   Among the people who can help you get students to engage in more appropriate behavior are peers, parents, the principal or counselor, and mentors.

Peer Mediation   Peers sometimes can be very effective at getting students to behave more appropriately. Peer mediators can be trained to help students resolve quarrels between students and change undesirable behaviors. For example, if two students have started to argue with each other, an assigned peer mediator can help to mediate the dispute, as described later in the chapter when we discuss conflict resolution.

Parent-Teacher Conference   You also can telephone the student's parents or confer with them in a face-to-face conference. Just informing them can sometimes get the student to improve behavior. Don't put the parents on the defensive or suggest that you are blaming them for their child's misbehavior in school. Just briefly describe the problem and say that you would appreciate any support that they can give you.

**Handling
Peer Conflicts**

**Gangs and
Victimization at School**

Enlist the Help of the Principal or Counselor   Many schools have prescribed consequences for particular problem behaviors. If you have tried unsuccessfully to deal with the behavior, consider asking the school's administration for help. This might involve referring the student to the principal or a counselor, which might result in a detention or warning to the student, as well as a parent conference with the principal. Letting the principal or counselor handle the problem can save you time. However, such help is not always practical on a regular basis in many schools.

Find a Mentor   Earlier we have underscored the importance of students having at least one person in their life who cares about them and supports their development. Some students, especially those from high-risk impoverished backgrounds, do not have that one person. A mentor can provide such students with the guidance they need to reduce problem behaviors. Look around the community for potential mentors for students in high-risk, low-income circumstances.

Handling Aggression

Violence in schools is a major, escalating concern. In many schools it now is common for students to fight, bully other students, or threaten each other and teachers verbally or with a weapon. These behaviors can arouse your anxiety and anger, but it

School-Based
Crime Prevention

Gaining Control of Violence

Strategies for
Dealing with Bullies

*". . . and suddenly there were teachers
all over the place!"*

is important to be prepared for their occurrence and handle them calmly. Avoiding an argument or emotional confrontation will help you to solve the conflict.

Fighting

Classroom management expert Carolyn Evertson and her colleagues (Evertson, Emmer, & Worsham, 2000): give the following recommendations for dealing with students who are fighting. In elementary school, you can usually stop a fight without risking injury to yourself. If for some reason you cannot intervene, immediately get help from other teachers or administrators. When you intervene, give a loud verbal command: "Stop!" Separate the fighters, and as you keep them separated, tell other students to leave or return to what they are doing. If you intervene in a fight that involves secondary school students, you will probably need the help of one or two other adults. Your school likely will have a policy regarding fighting. If so, you should carry it out and involve the principal and/or parents if necessary.

Generally, it is best to let the fighters have a cooling-off period so that they will calm down. Then meet with the fighters and get their points of view on what precipitated the fight. Question witnesses if necessary. Have a conference with the fighters, emphasizing the inappropriateness of fighting, the importance of taking each other's perspective, and the importance of cooperation.

Bullying

Significant numbers of students are victimized by bullies. In one recent survey of bullying in South Carolina middle schools, 1 of every 4 students reported that they had been bullied several times in a 3-month period; 1 in 10 said they were chronically bullied (at least once a week) (Institute for Families in Society, 1997).

Students who are victimized by bullies can suffer both short-term and long-term effects of being tormented (Limber, 1997). Short-term, they can become depressed, lose interest in schoolwork, or even avoid going to school. The effects of bullying can persist into adulthood. A recent longitudinal study of male victims who were bullied during childhood found that in their twenties they were more depressed and had lower self-esteem than their counterparts who had not been bullied in childhood (Olweus, in press). Bullying also can indicate a serious problem for the bully as well as the victim. In the study just mentioned, about 60 percent of the boys who were identified as bullies in middle school had at least one criminal conviction (and about one-third had three or more convictions) in their twenties, a far higher rate than for non-bullies.

Defiance or Hostility toward the Teacher

Edmund Emmer and his colleagues (Emmer, Evertson, & Worsham, 2000) discussed the following strategies for dealing with students who defy you or are hostile toward you. If students get away with this type of behavior, it likely will continue and even spread. Try to defuse the event by keeping it private and handling the student individually, if possible. If the defiance or hostility is not extreme and occurs during a lesson, try to depersonalize it and say that you will deal with it in a few minutes to avoid a power struggle. At an appropriate later time, meet with the student and spell out any consequence the misbehavior might merit. If the student presses the confrontation further, tell the student to leave the room and go out in the hall. Let the student cool down for a few minutes while you give the class an activity to do, then go out and talk with the student.

In extreme and rare cases, students will be completely uncooperative, in which case you should send another student to the office for help. In most instances, though, if you stay calm and don't get into a power struggle with the student, the student will calm down and you can talk with the student about the problem.

Classroom and School-Based Programs

A number of classroom and school-based programs for dealing with problem behaviors involve social competence enhancement and conflict resolution (Coie & Dodge, 1998).

TEACHING STRATEGIES
For Reducing Bullying

To reduce bullying (Limber, 1997; Olweus, 1984):

1. *Develop school-wide rules and sanctions against bullying and post them throughout the school.*
2. *Form friendship groups for children who are regularly bullied by their peers.*
3. *Hold regular class meetings to discuss bullying among students.*
4. *Develop a schoolwide reinforcement program to "catch students being good."*
5. *Incorporate the message of the anti-bullying program into church, school, and other community activities in which children are involved.*
6. *Get older peers to serve as monitors for bullying and to intervene when they see it taking place.*

Social Competence Enhancement Programs

Some educational experts argue that coordinated school-based planning, high-quality curriculum and instruction, and a supportive school environment might be needed to deal with students' problem behaviors (Weissberg & Greenberg, 1998). These types of programs often try to improve the student's social competence by enhancing life skills, providing health education, and developing socioemotional skills.

Researchers have found that information-only or knowledge-only programs have minimal effects on decreasing students' problem behaviors (Kirby, 1992). In contrast, programs that teach broadly applicable personal and social competencies, such as self-control, stress management, problem solving, decision making, communication, peer resistance, and assertiveness, have been found to reduce students' aggressive behavior and improve their adjustment (Greenberg, 1996; Weissberg & others, 1981). Following are some examples of effective social competence enhancement programs.

The Improving Social Awareness–Social Problem Solving Project

This program is designed for elementary school students (Elias & others, 1991). During the instructional phase, teachers use scripted lessons to introduce classroom activities. The lessons follow this format: (1) group sharing of interpersonal successes, problem situations, and feelings that students wish to share with the teacher and other students; (2) a brief overview of cognitive, emotional, or behavioral skills to be taught during the lesson; (3) written and video presentations of situations that call for and model skill application; (4) discussion of the situations and ways to use the new skills; (5) role-playing that encourages behavioral rehearsal of skills; and (6) summary and review. Teachers also integrate problem-solving and social-awareness activities into the regular classroom routine and their daily instruction. Evaluations indicate that the program has been positive in helping students cope with everyday problem situations and reduce their violent behaviors (Elias & others, 1986).

The Social Competence Promotion Program for Young Adolescents

This 45-session program for middle school students provides classroom-based instruction and establishes environmental supports designed to (1) promote social competence by increasing self-control, managing stress, engaging in responsible decision making, solving social problems, and improving communication skills; (2) improve communication between school personnel and students; and (3) prevent antisocial and aggressive behavior, substance abuse, and high-risk sexual behaviors (Weissberg & Caplan, 1994). Evaluations of the social competence program have been

Humanity without constraint will dig its own grave.

Marya Mannes
American Author, 20th Century

Consistency Management and Cooperative Discipline

$\mathcal{D}$IVERSITY AND EDUCATION

Cultural Sensitivity, Social Development, and Collaboration with the Community

In an ideal world, the combined efforts of responsible parents, quality child care, health care services, and family-centered communities would provide the necessary foundations so that all children would come to school ready to learn (Weissberg & Greenberg, 1998). But in the real world of your classroom, children will bring varying propensities to learn. Some will be highly motivated, others listless. Some will require little management, others will test your patience and coping skills.

The growing diversity of students makes classroom management more challenging. You must be prepared to know and demonstrate sensitivity to the cultural and socioeconomic variations in your students (McLoyd, 1998). It is equally important to recognize the existence of differences within groups of students from ethnic minority and impoverished backgrounds. Without this knowledge and sensitivity, a trusting and mutually respectful relationship is difficult to establish.

An increasing number of programs reveal that showing greater cultural sensitivity to socioculturally diverse students benefits these students when they are at risk for academic and emotional problems (Weissberg & Greenberg, 1998). One type of successful intervention program for at-risk youth from poor rural or inner-city minority settings involves ethnically and culturally compatible adults from the community who develop culturally relevant activities for students that include ethnically relevant theater, music, and dance productions (Botvin, Schinke, & Orlandi, 1995; Hudley & Graham, 1995).

As we indicated in chapter 2, "Physical and Cognitive Development," effectively intervening in the lives of high-risk students often consists of providing not only individualized attention but also community-wide collaboration for support and guidance. The New Haven Social Development Project is one community-wide collaboration that involves a high percentage of students from low-income, ethnic minority backgrounds (Kasprow & others, 1993; Schwab-Stone & others, 1995). Problem behaviors such as drug use, poor sexual decision making, delinquency, and truancy seriously jeopardized the students' academic performance, health, and future. Many of the problem behaviors had common roots, such as poor problem-solving and communication skills and a lack of monitoring and guidance by positive adult role models.

The superintendent and board of education for the New Haven schools established a comprehensive K–12 social development curriculum. The project's mission was to help students (1) develop a sense of self-worth and feel effective as they deal with daily responsibilities and challenges; (2) engage in positive, safe, health-protective behaviors; (3) develop social skills and have positive relationships with peers and adults; (4) feel motivated to contribute responsibly to the peer group, family, school, and community; and (5) acquire a set of basic skills, work habits, and values to form a foundation for a lifetime of meaningful learning and work.

The program consists of 25 to 50 hours of classroom-based instruction at each grade level. The curriculum emphasizes self-monitoring, problem solving, conflict resolution, and communication skills; values such as personal responsibility and respect for self and others; and content about health, culture, interpersonal relationships, and careers. The program also involves educational, recreational, and health-promotion opportunities at the school and community levels to support classroom-based instruction. These activities include mentoring, peer mediation, and leadership groups, an Extended Day Academy with after-school clubs, health center services, and an outdoor adventure class. In addition, a school-based mental health planning team focuses attention on developing a positive climate for learning in the school. Teachers say they are very pleased with the program and report that it improved the social skills and frustration tolerance of more than 80 percent of the students in grades K–3. Also, secondary school students decreased their participation in fights, felt safer at school and in the neighborhood, and felt more positive about the future as the program progressed.

positive. Students involved in the program show fewer aggressive behaviors, more consideration of alternative solutions to problems, improved stress-management strategies, and more prosocial values than control groups (Weissberg, Barton, & Shriver, 1997). Teachers who have participated in the program indicate that it addresses important issues that are important for their students and helps them communicate better with students. A program that emphasizes cultural sensitivity as part of social competence enhancement is described in the Diversity and Education box.

TEACHING STRATEGIES
For Conflict Resolution

Following are some good strategies for conflict resolution in the classroom (Johnson & Johnson, 1995):

1. *Don't attempt to eliminate all conflicts.* Eliminating all violence does not mean getting rid of all conflict (Curwin & Mendler, 1999). For example, moderate conflicts can sometimes increase students' achievement, motivation to learn, and ability to solve problems. What is important is not eliminating conflict, but helping students to learn how to manage it more effectively.

2. *Create a supportive context.* The most effective conflict resolution programs attempt to do more than just change individual students. Rather, the goal is to transform the school environment into a learning setting in which students live in accord with a standard of nonviolence. Creating a supportive context involves placing students in situations in which they are more likely to cooperate than to compete. In a cooperative context, conflicts tend to be resolved in constructive rather than destructive ways. Students are more likely to communicate effectively with each other, trust each other, and define conflicts as mutual rather than individual problems.

3. *Decrease in-school risk factors.* Factors that place students at risk for violent behavior include academic failure and alienation from classmates. Thus, aspects of the school that can support students' academic success and sense of belongingness should be monitored and improved in an effort to reduce violence.

4. *Teach all students how to resolve conflicts constructively.* Two types of conflict resolution programs are the cadre approach and the total student body approach. In the **cadre approach,** *a small number of students are trained to serve as peer mediators for the entire school.* Johnson and Johnson (1995) believe this approach is not as effective as the **total student body approach,** *in which every student learns how to manage conflicts constructively by negotiating agreements and mediating schoolmates' conflicts.* A disadvantage of the total student body approach is the time and commitment required from school personnel. However, the more students who are trained in conflict resolution, the more constructively conflicts will be managed.

    One example of the total student body approach was developed by Johnson and Johnson (1991). Their Teaching Students to Be Peacemakers program involves both negotiation and mediation strategies. Students learn these negotiation steps: (1) Define what they want, (2) describe their feelings, (3) explain the reasons underlying the wants and feelings, (4) take the perspective of the other student to see the conflict from both sides, (5) generate at least three optional agreements that benefit both parties, and (6) come to an agreement about the best course of action.

    Students learn these mediation steps: (1) stop the hostilities, (2) ensure that the disputants are committed to the mediation, (3) facilitate negotiations between the disputants, and (4) formalize the agreement.

    When students have completed negotiation and mediation training, the school or teacher implements the Peacemakers program by choosing two student mediators for each day. Being a mediator helps students learn how to negotiate and resolve conflicts. Evaluations of the Peacemakers program have been positive, with participants showing more constructive conflict resolution than nonparticipants (Johnson & Johnson, 1994).

The Three Cs of School and Classroom Management

David and Roger Johnson (1999) created a classroom management program to deal with problems that cause disruptions and undermine learning. Their program emphasizes the importance of guiding students in learning how to self-regulate their behavior. These are the three Cs:

- *Cooperative community.* Learning communities benefit when the participants have a positive interdependence on each other. They work toward attaining mutual goals by engaging in cooperatively structured learning activities ◀▥ p. 324.
- *Constructive conflict resolution.* When conflicts arise, they can be resolved constructively through conflict resolution training for all participants in the learning community.
- *Civic values.* There can be cooperative communities and constructive conflict resolution only if the learning community shares common civic values, values that guide decision making. These values include believing that success depends on joint efforts to achieve mutual goals and valuing others.

COMP

Carolyn Evertson (center in red) in a COMP classroom with Arlene Harris. She created a classroom management framework that emphasizes problem prevention. What are other features of COMP classrooms?

Support for Managing Learning-Centered Classrooms: The Classroom Organization and Management Program (COMP)   The COMP program, developed by Carolyn Evertson and Alene Harris (1999), advocates a classroom management framework that emphasizes supporting students' learning and that guides students in taking responsibility for their own decisions, behavior, and learning. COMP emphasizes problem prevention, management and instruction integration, student involvement, and professional collaboration among teachers. The program is implemented through training workshops, classroom application, and collaborative reflection. Research has revealed that COMP results in positive changes in teacher and student behavior (Evertson & Harris, 1999).

At this point, we have discussed many ideas about creating a positive learning environment for learning and dealing with problem behaviors. A review of these ideas is presented in summary table 12.2.

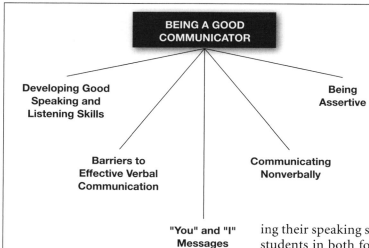

Being a Good Communicator

Managing classrooms and constructively resolving conflicts require good communication skills.

Developing Good Speaking and Listening Skills

Good communicators speak and listen effectively.

Speaking and Listening Skills

Becoming an Effective Speaker   You and your students will benefit considerably if you have effective speaking skills and you work with your students on developing their speaking skills. Not only will you be speaking in your class every day to your students in both formal and informal ways, but you also will have opportunities to give talks at educational meetings. As most of us reflect on our education, we can remember few opportunities to give talks in class unless we took a specific class in speech. But not only can students be given speaking opportunities through formal presentations, they also can participate in panel discussions and debates. All these activities give students opportunities to improve their speaking, organizational, and thinking skills.

Following are some helpful guidelines for delivering a good speech (Alverno College, 1995):

- *Connect with the audience.* Talk directly to the audience; don't just read your notes or recite a memorized script.
- *State your purpose.* Keep this focus throughout the talk.
- *Effectively deliver the speech.* Use eye contact, supportive gestures, and effective voice control.
- *Follow appropriate conventions.* This includes using correct grammar.
- *Effectively organize the speech.* Include an introduction, main body, and conclusion.
- *Include evidence that supports and develops your ideas.*
- *Use media effectively.* This can help the audience grasp key ideas and varies the pace of the talk.

Creating a Positive Environment for Learning, and Dealing with Problem Behaviors

Concept	Processes/ Related Ideas	Characteristics/Description
Creating a Positive Environment for Learning	General Strategies	• Use an authoritative style of classroom management rather than an authoritarian or permissive style. The authoritative style involves considerable verbal give-and-take with students, a caring attitude toward students, and placing limits on student behavior when necessary. Authoritative teaching is linked with competent student behavior. • Kounin's work revealed other characteristics that were associated with effective classroom management: "withitness," coping with overlapping situations, maintaining smoothness and continuity in lessons, and engaging students in a variety of challenging activities.
	Establishing and Maintaining Rules	• Classroom rules should be (1) reasonable and necessary, (2) clear and comprehensible, (3) consistent with instructional and learning goals, and (4) compatible with school rules.
	Getting Students to Cooperate	• This involves (1) developing a positive relationship with students, (2) getting students to share and assume responsibility (involve students in the planning and implementation of school and classroom initiatives, encourage students to judge their own behavior, don't accept excuses, and give the self-responsibility strategy time to work), and (3) rewarding appropriate behavior (choose effective reinforcers, use prompts and shaping effectively, and use rewards to provide information about mastery).
Dealing with Problem Behaviors	Management Strategies	• Interventions can be characterized as minor or moderate. • Minor interventions involve using nonverbal cues, keeping the activity moving, moving closer to students, redirecting the behavior, giving needed instruction, directly and assertively telling the student to stop the behavior, and giving the student a choice. • Moderate interventions include withholding a privilege or a desired activity, creating a behavioral contract, isolating or removing students, and imposing a penalty or detention. • A good management strategy is to have supportive resources. These include using peers as mediators, calling on parents for support, enlisting the help of a principal or counselor, and finding a mentor for the student.
	Handling Aggression	• Violence is a major, escalating concern in schools. • Be prepared for aggressive actions on the part of students so that you can calmly cope with them. • Try to avoid an argument or emotional confrontation. • We described some helpful guidelines for dealing with fighting, bullying, and defiance or hostility toward the teacher.
	Classroom and School-Based Programs	• These include social competence enhancement programs, the three Cs of school and classroom management, and support for managing learner-centered classrooms (the Classroom Organization and Management Program [COMP]). • Successful conflict resolution programs in schools can be based on several principles: (1) Go beyond violence prevention to eliminate all conflict, (2) create a supportive context, (3) decrease in-school risk factors (such as academic failure and alienation from peers), and (4) teach all students how to resolve conflicts constructively.

Improving Speaking Skills

Improving Listening Skills

People often list fear of public speaking as their single greatest fear. If we give students more opportunities to practice public speaking, this fear likely would diminish. To help your students overcome this fear, give them plenty of opportunities to talk in front of a group and provide them with supportive advice (Santrock & Halonen, 1999). When they prepare for their talk, get them to rehearse the talk a number of times until they are confident they know the material. Tell them that most people fear talking in front of groups, but that once they do it, their fear subsides. And get them to imagine how successful their talks are going to be.

Working with students on their speaking skills provides an excellent opportunity to invite someone from the community to come talk with your class. If a local college or university has a communications department, contact the department and ask one of their faculty to talk with your students about speaking skills or other aspects of communication. You also might have heard someone give a speech that you thought was outstanding; you might invite the speaker to come to your class and give students tips on how to give a great talk.

Developing Good Listening Skills

Effectively managing your classroom will be easier if you and your students have good listening skills. Listening is a critical skill for making and keeping relationships. If you are a good listener, students, parents, other teachers, and administrators will be drawn to you. If your students are good listeners, they will benefit more from your instruction and will have better social relationships. Bad listeners "hog" conversations. They talk "to" rather than "with" someone. Good listeners *actively* listen. They don't just passively absorb information. **Active listening** *means giving full attention to the speaker, focusing on both the intellectual and the emotional content of the message.*

Following are some good strategies for developing active listening skills (Santrock & Halonen, 1999). Incorporate these skills into your style of interacting with students and work with students to help them develop these skills:

- *Pay careful attention to the person who is talking.* This shows the person that you are interested in what she or he is saying. Maintain good eye contact and lean forward slightly when another person is speaking to you.
- *Paraphrase.* State in your own words what the other person has just said. You can start your paraphrase with words like "Let me see, what I hear you saying is . . ." or "Do you mean . . . ?" Use paraphrasing when someone says something that is important.
- *Synthesize themes and patterns.* The conversation landscape can become strewn with bits and pieces of information that are not tied together in meaningful ways. A good active listener puts together a summary of the main themes and feelings the speaker has expressed over a reasonably long conversation. The following sentence stems can help you and your students get started in synthesizing the themes of a conversation:

"One theme you keep coming back to is . . ."
"Let's go over what we have been covering so far . . ."

TECHNOLOGY AND EDUCATION
Mission Impossible, Listening Skills, Speaking Skills, and Decoding Messages

Communication expert Michael Cronin (1993) says that students get the least amount of instruction in the form of communication they do most. They get considerable instruction in reading and writing, but little or none in listening. As a result, a lot of students are poor listeners. Two days after listening to a 10-minute presentation, most individuals retain only 25 percent of what they heard.

To help remedy this problem, Michael Cronin (1993) developed the interactive videodisc "Mission Impossible: Listening Skills for Better Communication," which can be used to improve the listening skills of secondary school students. The videodisc provides instruction in identifying bad listening habits and improving active listening skills. A gamelike format teaches students how to develop active listening skills. Each activity involves a detective mission, and high scores are awarded "Super Spy" status. Humor also is built into the learning exercises to improve interest. Additional interactive media materials are available from the Oral Communications Program at Radford University in Radford, Virginia, where Cronin is a professor. These include:

- *"Coping with Speech Fright."* This software provides tutorial and simulation exercises to help students effectively manage their fear of public speaking. A student workbook also is included.
- *"Constructing and Using Speaking Outlines."* Outlining exercises and techniques for using speaking notes in simulated rehearsals for a speech are included in this software, as well as methods for effectively practicing a speech with speaking notes and an analysis of examples of speech outlines.
- *"Developing Key Ideas."* Students learn to identify the key aspects of messages. These exercises include a worksheet.

- *Give feedback in a competent manner.* Verbal or nonverbal feedback gives the speaker an idea of how much progress the speaker is making in getting a point across. Good listeners give feedback quickly, honestly, clearly, and informatively. To read further about improving students' listening and speaking skills, see Technology and Education.

Barriers to Effective Verbal Communication

Barriers to effective communication include these (Gordon, 1970):

- *Criticizing.* Harsh, negative evaluations of another person generally reduce communication. An example of criticizing is telling a student, "It's your fault you flunked the test; you should have studied." Instead of criticizing, you can ask students to evaluate why they did not do well on a test and try to get them to arrive at an attribution that reflects lack of effort as the reason for the poor grade.
- *Name calling and labeling.* These are ways of putting down the other person. Students engage in a lot of name calling and labeling. They might say to another student, "You are a loser" or "You are stupid." Monitor students' use of such name calling and labeling. When you hear this type of statement, intervene and talk with them about considering other students' feelings.
- *Advising.* By this we mean talking down to others while giving them a solution to a problem. For example, a teacher might say, "That's so easy to solve. I can't understand why . . ."
- *Ordering.* Commanding another person to do what you want is often not effective because it creates resistance. For example, a teacher might yell at a student, "Clean up this space, right now!" Instead, a calm, firm reminder like "Remember the rule of cleaning things up when we are finished" works better.
- *Threatening.* Threats are intended to control the other person by verbal force. For example, a teacher might say, "If you don't listen to me, I'm going to make your

life miserable here." A better strategy is to approach the student more calmly and talk *with* the student about listening better rather than *to* the student in a demeaning way.

- *Moralizing.* This means preaching to the other person about what he or she should do. For example, a teacher might say, "You know you should have turned your homework in on time. You *ought* to feel bad about this." Moralizing increases students' guilt and anxiety. A better strategy in this case is not to use words like *should* and *ought,* but instead to talk with the student in a less condemning way about why the homework was not turned in on time.

"You" and "I" Messages

How often have you been involved in a conversation in which someone says something like this:

"Why are you being so negative?"
"You did not do what you said you were going to do."
"You are not very considerate."

These are examples of what communication experts call **"you" messages,** *an undesirable style in which speakers appear to judge people and place them in a defensive position.* "You" communication does not always literally include the word *you.* "You" is implied when someone says:

"That was a really stupid thing to say" (which means, "What *you* said was really stupid.")
"Stay out of my life" (which means, "*You* are intruding in my life.")

It is easy for you and your students to fall into the trap of using too many "you" messages and not enough **"I" messages,** *which are less provocative.* "I" *messages reflect the speaker's true feelings better than judgmental "you" statements.*

Communication experts recommend replacing "you" messages with "I" messages:

"I'm angry that this has gotten so negative."
"I don't like it when promises get broken."
"I'm hurt when my feelings aren't taken into account."

"You" messages bog down conversation with judgments of the other person. "I" messages help to move the conversation in a more constructive direction by expressing your feelings without judging the other person. Monitor your own conversation from time to time to make sure you are using "I" messages rather than "you" messages. Also monitor your students' conversations and guide them toward using more "I" messages.

Communicating Nonverbally

In addition to what you say, you also communicate by how you fold your arms, cast your eyes, move your mouth, cross your legs, or touch another person. Here are some examples of some common behaviors by which individuals communicate nonverbally:

- Lift an eyebrow in disbelief
- Clasp their arms to isolate or protect themselves
- Shrug their shoulders when they are indifferent
- Wink one eye to show warmth and approval
- Tap their fingers when they are impatient
- Slap their forehead when they forget something

Indeed, many communication experts believe that most interpersonal communication is nonverbal. Even a person sitting in a corner silently reading is nonverbally communicating something, perhaps that they want to be left alone. And when you notice your students blankly staring out the window, it likely indicates that they are bored. It is hard to mask nonverbal communication and better to recognize that it can tell you how you and others really feel.

Facial Expressions and Eye Communication   Peoples' faces disclose emotions and telegraph what really matters to them. A smile, a frown, a puzzled look all communicate. Most Americans use more eye contact, the more they like the other person. They avoid eye contact with people they dislike. However, ethnic variations in eye contact exist, with African Americans, Latinos, and Native Americans avoiding eye contact more than Anglo-Americans. In general, smiling and maintaining eye contact with your students indicates that you like them.

Touch   Touch can be a powerful form of communication. Touch especially can be used when consoling someone who has undergone a stressful or unfortunate experience. For example, if a student's parent has become seriously ill or died, a student's parents recently became divorced, or a student has lost a pet, gently touching the student's hand while consoling the student can add warmth to the communication. Because of concerns about sexual harassment and potential lawsuits, many teachers have refrained from touching students at all. Tiffany Field (1995), director of the Touch Research Institute at the University of Miami (Florida) and a leading expert in developmental psychology, believes that teachers should use touch appropriately and courteously in their interaction with students.

Space   Each of us has a personal space that at times we don't want others to invade. Not surprisingly, given the crowdedness of the classroom, students report that having their own space where they can put their materials and belongings is important to them. Make sure that students all have their own desks or spaces. Tell students that they are entitled to have this individual space and that they should courteously respect other students' space.

Silence   In our fast-paced, modern culture we often act as if there is something wrong with anyone who remains silent for more than a second or two after something is said to them. In chapter 10 we indicated that after asking a question of students, many teachers rarely remain silent long enough for students to think reflectively before giving an answer.

By being silent, a good listener can:

- Observe the speaker's eyes, facial expressions, posture, and gestures for communication
- Think about what the other person is communicating
- Wonder what the other person is feeling
- Consider what the most appropriate response is

Of course, silence can be overdone and is sometimes inappropriate. It is rarely wise to listen for an excessive length of time without making some verbal response. Interpersonal communication should be a dialogue, not a monologue.

Being Assertive

There are four main styles in which people deal with conflict in their lives: aggressive, manipulative, passive, or assertive. People who use an **aggressive style** *run roughshod over others. They demand, are abrasive, and act in hostile ways.* Aggressive individuals are often insensitive to others' rights and feelings. People who use a **manipulative style** *try to get what they want by making people feel guilty or sorry for them.* Rather than take responsibility for meeting their own needs, they play the role of the victim or the martyr to get people to do things for them. People who use a **passive style** *are*

What you are speaks so loudly I cannot hear what you say.

Ralph Waldo Emerson
American Poet and Essayist, 19th Century

TEACHING STRATEGIES
For Communicating Effectively with Parents

Much of what we have discussed so far about communication has focused on teacher-student communication. However, the strategies we have described for improving teacher-student communication also will benefit you when you need to talk with parents. When you talk with parents, keep these ideas in mind:

1. *Be an active listener.* Talk *with* them, not *to* them. Treat them as an equal partner with you in educating their child. Ask them for input about ways to help their child learn and behave appropriately.
2. *Avoid barriers to effective communication.* Don't criticize, label, advise, order, threaten, or moralize when discussing the student's behavior. For example, don't say "Robert is mean" or "Heather is lazy." Instead of using such labels, clearly describe their behavior.
3. *Use "I" messages rather than "you" messages.*
4. *Use effective nonverbal communication.* When you talk with parents, maintain eye contact with them. When you ask them a question, be silent long enough to give them an opportunity to express themselves. Smile when it is appropriate.
5. *Be assertive rather than aggressive, manipulative, or passive.* When you need to communicate with parents about their child's problem behavior in school, express your view openly and underscore your belief in the importance of helping the student learn more appropriate behavior.

**Assertive
Communication**

nonassertive and submissive. They let others run roughshod over them. Passive individuals don't express their feelings and don't let others know what they want.

In contrast, people with an **assertive style** *express their feelings, ask for what they want, and say no to things they don't want.* When people act assertively, they act in their own best interests. They stand up for their legitimate rights and express their views openly. Assertive individuals insist that misbehavior be corrected, and they resist being coerced or manipulated (Evertson & others, 1997). In the view of assertiveness experts Robert Alberti and Michael Emmons (1995), assertiveness builds positive, constructive relationships.

Of the four styles of dealing with conflict, acting assertively is by far the best choice. Following are some strategies for becoming a more assertive individual (Bourne, 1995):

- *Evaluate your rights.* Determine your rights in the situation at hand. For example, you have the right to make mistakes and to change your mind.
- *State the problem to the person involved in terms of its consequences for you.* Clearly outline your point of view, even if it seems obvious to you. This allows the other person to get a better sense of your position. Describe the problem as objectively as you can without blaming or judging. For example, you might tell a student:

  "I'm having a problem with your humming in class. It is bothering me so please don't do it anymore."
  "When you come in late, it disrupts the class and you miss important information."
  "Saying that to another student hurts his feelings."

- *Express your feelings about the particular situation.* When you express your feelings, even others who completely disagree with you can tell how strongly you feel about the situation. Remember to use "I" messages rather than "you" messages.
- *Make your request.* This is an important aspect of being assertive. Simply ask for what you want (or don't want) in a straightforward manner.

SELF-ASSESSMENT 12.1
Evaluating My Communication Skills

Good communication skills are critical for effectively managing a classroom. Read each of the statements and rate them on a scale from 1 (Very much unlike me) to 5 (Very much like me).

	1	2	3	4	5
1. I am good at public speaking.					
2. I do not tend to dominate conversations.					
3. I'm good at giving my full attention to someone when they are talking with me.					
4. I talk "with" people, not "to" people.					
5. I don't criticize people very much.					
6. I don't talk down to people or put them down.					
7. I don't moralize when I talk with people.					
8. I use "I" messages rather than "you" messages.					
9. I maintain eye contact when I talk with people.					
10. I smile a lot when I interact with people.					
11. I know the value of silence in communication and how to practice it effectively.					
12. I do not have an aggressive style.					
13. I do not have a manipulative style.					
14. I do not have a passive style.					
15. I do not have an assertive style.					

Look over your self-ratings. For any items on which you did not give yourself a 4 or 5, work on improving these aspects of your communication skills. Both you and your students will benefit.

Following are some guidelines for making assertive requests:

- *Use assertive nonverbal behavior.* For example, establish eye contact, square your shoulders, remain calm, and be self-confident.
- *Keep your request simple.* One or two easy-to-understand sentences is adequate. For example, you might tell a student, "We need to go to the principal to get this straightened out."
- *Avoid asking for more than one thing at a time.* For example, don't ask the principal for a new computer *and* a new projector.
- *Don't apologize for your request.* Request directly, as in "I want you to . . ." Don't say "I know this is an imposition on you, but . . ." What if the other person responds with criticism, tries to make you feel guilty, or makes sarcastic remarks? Simply repeat your assertive request directly, strongly, and confidently.
- *Describe the benefits of the request.* Describing the benefits of cooperating with the request can be an honest offer of mutual give-and-take rather than manipulation.

If you feel that you are too aggressive, manipulative, or passive, work on being more assertive. An excellent book to read that can help you become more assertive is *Your Perfect Right,* by Robert Alberti and Michal Emmons (1995). When you are assertive and you help your students become more assertive rather than aggressive, manipulative, or passive, your class will run more smoothly.

Be fair with others, but then keep after them until they are fair with you.

Alan Alda
American Actor, 20th Century

$\mathcal{S}$UMMARY $\mathcal{T}$ABLE 12.3
Being a Good Communicator

Concept	Processes/ Related Ideas	Characteristics/Description
Developing Good Speaking and Listening Skills	Becoming an Effective Speaker	• You and your students will benefit considerably if you have effective speaking skills and you work with your students on improving their speaking skills. • Speaking opportunities can include formal presentations, panel discussions, and debates. • We discussed a number of guidelines for delivering a good speech and helping students overcome their fear of public speaking.
	Developing Good Listening Skills	• Be an active listener. Active listening occurs when a person gives full attention to the speaker, focusing on both the intellectual and the emotional content of the message. • Some good active listening strategies are to (1) pay careful attention to the person who is talking, including maintaining eye contact; (2) paraphrase; (3) synthesize themes and patterns; and (4) give feedback in a competent manner.
Barriers to Effective Verbal Communication	Their Nature	• Barriers include criticizing, name calling and labeling, advising, ordering, threatening, and moralizing.
"You" and "I" Messages	Their Nature	• "You" messages imply judgments of people and place them in a defensive position. • "I" messages are less provocative, better reflecting the speaker's true feelings.
Communicating Nonverbally	Its Nature	• A number of communication experts believe that the majority of communication is nonverbal rather than verbal. • It is hard to mask nonverbal communication, so a good strategy is to recognize that nonverbal communication usually reflects how a person really feels. • Nonverbal communication involves facial expressions and eye communication, touch, space, and silence.
Being Assertive	Its Nature	• Four main styles people use to deal with conflict are (1) aggressive (running roughshod over others, demanding, being abrasive, and acting hostile); (2) manipulative (trying to get what you want by making people feel sorry for them or guilty); (3) passive (being nonassertive and submissive); and (4) assertive (expressing feelings, asking for what they want, and saying no to things they don't want). • The assertive style is the best strategy for dealing with conflict. Assertive individuals act in their own best interests, insist that misbehavior be corrected, and resist being coerced or manipulated. Assertiveness builds positive, constructive relationships.

We have discussed a number of communication skills that will help you manage your classroom effectively. To evaluate your communication skills, complete Self-Assessment 12.1.

To learn more about communicating effectively with parents, consult the book *Parents as Partners in Education* (Berger, 1995).

At this point we have discussed a number of ideas about being a good communicator. A review of these ideas is presented in summary table 12.3. In the next chapter we will turn our attention to assessing children's learning and the role of standardized tests in teaching.

Chapter Review

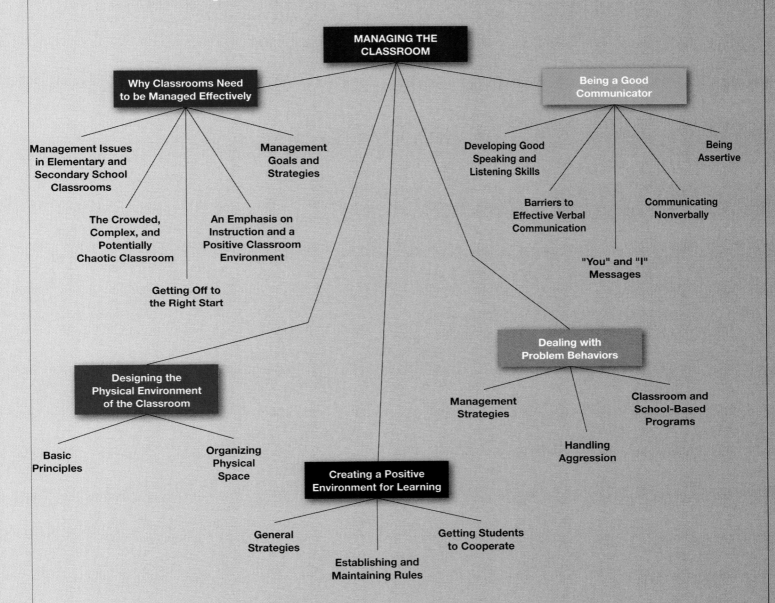

MANAGING THE CLASSROOM

Why Classrooms Need to be Managed Effectively

- Management Issues in Elementary and Secondary School Classrooms
- The Crowded, Complex, and Potentially Chaotic Classroom
- Getting Off to the Right Start
- An Emphasis on Instruction and a Positive Classroom Environment
- Management Goals and Strategies

Designing the Physical Environment of the Classroom

- Basic Principles
- Organizing Physical Space

Creating a Positive Environment for Learning

- General Strategies
- Establishing and Maintaining Rules
- Getting Students to Cooperate

Being a Good Communicator

- Developing Good Speaking and Listening Skills
- Barriers to Effective Verbal Communication
- "You" and "I" Messages
- Communicating Nonverbally
- Being Assertive

Dealing with Problem Behaviors

- Management Strategies
- Handling Aggression
- Classroom and School-Based Programs

TO OBTAIN A DETAILED REVIEW OF THIS CHAPTER, STUDY THESE THREE SUMMARY TABLES:

Key Terms

Educational Psychology Checklist
MANAGING THE CLASSROOM

How much have you learned since the beginning of the chapter? Use the following statements to help you review your knowledge and understanding of the chapter material. First, read the statement and mentally or briefly on paper demonstrate that you can discuss the relevant information.

_____ I can describe why classroom management is so important.
_____ I have some good ideas for how to physically design a classroom.
_____ I can outline some good strategies for creating a positive learning environment.
_____ I know how to establish and maintain classroom rules.

_____ I am aware of the best ways to get students to cooperate.
_____ I can describe a number of effective strategies for dealing with problem behaviors.
_____ I can discuss some effective ways to deal with aggression.
_____ I know some good strategies to help students with their communication skills.

For any items that you did not check off, go back and locate the relevant material in the chapter. Review the material until you feel you can check off the item. You also might want to use this checklist later in preparing for an exam.

Adventures for the Mind

Now that you have a good knowledge and understanding of the chapter, complete the following exercises to expand your thinking about the chapter's
topics.

- Write down what you think are the most important classroom rules
  for your students to abide by. Also write down how you will handle
  the situation when students break the rules. Then get together with
  3 or 4 other students in this class and react to each other's rules and
  ways of handling situations in which students break the rules.
- Imagine that the following incidents take place in your classroom.
  Describe how you would handle each one.
  - In second grade, a girl yells out to you when you are working with
    another student.
  - In fifth grade, a small boy comes up to you and tells you that two
    much larger boys are bullying him.
  - In ninth grade, you are on one side of the room when a fight
    breaks out between two boys on the other side of the room.
  - In eleventh grade, a girl openly defies you in front of the class and
    refuses to cooperate.
- Interview school counselors at an elementary, middle, or high
  school. Ask them to describe the discipline policies at their schools
  and how well they work. Also ask them to describe the most difficult student problem they have ever dealt with and how it was
  handled.
- How self-disclosing and open should teachers be with students? It
  is important for teachers to develop positive relationships with students, but is there a point at which teachers can develop a relationship that is too close with a student? Describe what this might
  involve.

Taking It to the Net

1. A classroom management program should be
   comprehensive, coherent, and based on a well-
   defined conceptual framework. What would a
   well-defined conceptual framework look like? On what will you
   base your management program?
2. You are in a fourth-grade classroom when you overhear two children arguing. Each child during the argument uses a racial slur.
   How do you handle these types of prejudicial remarks?

3. A student continually is noisy during your class. Which are you
   most likely to do: yell at him, ignore him, discuss with him, or
   write his name on the board? Why?

   Connect to http://www.mhhe.com/socscience/psychology/santedu/
   ttnet.htm to find the answers!

Case Studies

Case 1   *Maggie Lindberg:* Maggie is a new
teacher who struggles to manage class behavior.

Case 2   *Michael Watson:* Michael, a new teacher, receives a negative evaluation for focusing more on how students feel about him
than on what they're supposed to be learning.

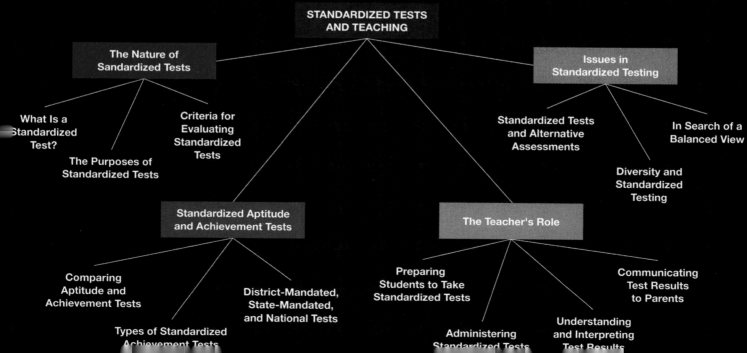

STANDARDIZED TESTS AND TEACHING

The Nature of Sandardized Tests

What Is a Standardized Test?

The Purposes of Standardized Tests

Criteria for Evaluating Standardized Tests

Standardized Aptitude and Achievement Tests

Comparing Aptitude and Achievement Tests

Types of Standardized Achievement Tests

District-Mandated, State-Mandated, and National Tests

Issues in Standardized Testing

Standardized Tests and Alternative Assessments

In Search of a Balanced View

Diversity and Standardized Testing

The Teacher's Role

Preparing Students to Take Standardized Tests

Administering Standardized Tests

Understanding and Interpreting Test Results

Communicating Test Results to Parents

Standardized Tests and Teaching

*"**K**nowledge is a treasure, but good judgment is the treasure of a wise person."*

William Penn
English Quaker Leader and Founder of Pennsylvania

Preview

Standardized tests are widely used to evaluate students' learning and achievement. Although they are increasingly used to compare students' performance in different schools, districts, states, and countries, they are not without controversy. These are some of the questions we will explore in this chapter:

- **What is the teacher's role in preparing students for and administering standardized tests?**
- **What criteria are used to evaluate standardized tests?**
- **What is involved in district-mandated, state-mandated, and national tests?**
- **What are some good strategies for interpreting test results?**
- **What are some guidelines for communicating test results to parents?**
- **What are some issues and controversies involving standardized tests?**

Teaching Stories
Barbara Berry

Barbara Berry teaches French and humanities at Ypsilanti High School in Ypsilanti, Michigan, where she also is chairperson of the foreign languages department. She offers the following story related to standardized tests:

> I had a fourth-year French student who was a wonderful student and clearly had a gift for languages. A minority student, she had been recruited by a major state university and offered a "full-ride" scholarship, provided she met certain requirements on the Scholastic Assessment Test (SAT). She took the test and did well on the verbal part but not well enough on the math part to meet the scholarship requirements. She was taking her fourth year of math classes and receiving above average grades but said she just didn't like math and didn't understand it.
>
> Although I was teaching French at the time, I knew that I enjoyed math and had done well in school and on standardized tests. I knew that the SAT math section includes a lot of algebra. I offered to tutor her before she retook the SAT. She accepted the offer. I obtained some algebra materials from the math department to help work with her. Mostly, though, she worked on her own, reading the book and doing problems, only coming to me when she encountered problems. We met about once a week. About six weeks later, she retook the test and improved her math SAT score by 110 points. She got the scholarship.
>
> I did not teach this student much math, although I did help her work through some of the more difficult problems. What I did most to help her were two things: (1) I communicated my own enthusiasm for math and expressed confidence in her ability to do it, and (2) I focused her efforts on the material that the test assesses. Since we related so well with each other in my French class, I felt that I could help her feel better about her ability to do math.

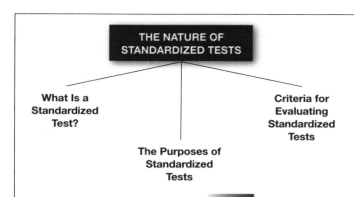

THE NATURE OF STANDARDIZED TESTS

What Is a Standardized Test?

The Purposes of Standardized Tests

Criteria for Evaluating Standardized Tests

ERIC Clearinghouse on Assessment and Evaluation

The Nature of Standardized Tests

Chances are, you have taken a number of standardized tests. In kindergarten, you may have taken a school readiness test, in elementary school some basic skills or achievement tests, and in high school the SAT or ACT test for college admission. Let's explore the concept of standardized testing.

What Is a Standardized Test?

A **standardized test** *is a commercially-prepared test that assesses students' performance under uniform conditions. A standardized test often allows a student's performance to be compared with the performance of other students at the same age or grade level, in many cases on a national basis.* How are such standardized tests different from the tests you will construct as a teacher to assess your students' achievement? Teacher-made tests tend to focus on instructional objectives for a particular classroom. Standardized tests attempt to include material that is common across most classrooms (Gay & Airasian, 2000; Airasian, 1997). Some other ways standardized tests from teacher-made tests are that standardized tests have norms, have more extensive assessments of the test's validity, and have more extensive evaluations of the test's reliability. We will explore these aspects of standardized tests shortly, but first let's examine the purposes of standardized tests.

The Purposes of Standardized Tests

Standardized tests can serve a number of purposes:

- *Provide information about students' progress.* Standardized tests are another source of information about how well students are performing. Students in one class might get A's but perform at a mediocre level on a nationally standardized test, and students in another class might get B's and do extremely well on the same nationally standardized test. Without an external, objective marker like a standardized test, individual classroom teachers have difficulty knowing how well their students are performing compared to students elsewhere in the state or nation.
- *Diagnose students' strengths and weaknesses.* Standardized tests also can provide information about a student's learning strengths or weaknesses (Cascio, 2000; Popham, 2000). For example, a student who is not doing well in reading might be given one or more standardized tests to pinpoint where the students' learning weaknesses are. When standardized tests are given for diagnostic purposes, they usually are given individually rather than to a group of students.
- *Provide evidence for placement of students in specific programs.* Standardized tests can be used to make decisions about whether a student should be allowed to enter a specific program. In elementary school, a standardized test might be used to provide information for placing students in different reading groups. In high school, a standardized test might be used to determine which math classes a student should take. In some cases, standardized tests are used along with other information to evaluate whether a student might be allowed to skip a grade or to graduate. Students also might take standardized tests to determine their suitability for particular careers.
- *Help administrators evaluate programs.* If a school changes to a new educational program, the school administration will want to know how effective the new program is. One way to determine this is to give students relevant standardized tests to see how they are performing under the new program. For example, a school might change from a direct-instruction approach to a social constructivist approach. Students' scores on a relevant standardized test can be used along with other evidence to determine the effectiveness of the change.

- *Contribute to accountability.* Schools and teachers are increasingly being held accountable for students' learning. Although this is controversial, standardized tests are being used to determine how effectively schools are using tax dollars (Bushweller, 1997). In Texas, principals can lose their job if their school's standardized test scores don't measure up. In Maryland, schools that don't do well forfeit thousands of dollars in reward money. Interest in accountability has led to the creation of **minimum competency tests,** *which assess skills that students are expected to have mastered before they can be promoted to the next grade or permitted to graduate.* Schools that use minimum competency tests often require students who do not pass the tests to attend special programs in the summer that will help them reach the minimum level of competency required by the school system (Jones, 1997).

High-stakes testing *is using tests in a way that will have important consequences for the student, affecting decisions such as whether the student will be promoted a grade, graduate, or get a scholarship.* Later in the chapter we will discuss district-mandated, state-mandated, and national tests, which are increasingly being used to make such "high-stakes" decisions.

For now, though, note that an important theme throughout this chapter is that a standardized test should not be the only method for evaluating a student's learning. Nor should standardized tests by themselves be considered sufficient information in holding schools accountable for students' learning (Popham, 2000).

Criteria for Evaluating Standardized Tests

Among the most important criteria for evaluating standardized tests are norms, reliability, and validity.

Norms   To understand an individual student's performance on a test, it needs to be compared with the performance of the **norm group,** *a group of similar individuals who previously had been given the test by the test maker.* The test is said to be based on **national norms** *when the norm group consists of a nationally representative group of students.* For example, a standardized test for fourth-grade science knowledge and skills might be given to a national sample of fourth-grade students in the United States. The scores of the representative sample of thousands of fourth-grade students become the basis for comparison. This norm group should include students from urban, suburban, and rural areas; different geographical regions; private and public schools; boys and girls; and different ethnic groups. Based on the student's score on the standardized science test, the teacher can determine whether a student is performing above, on level with, or below a national norm (Aiken, 2000). The teacher also can see how the class as a whole is performing in relation to the general population of students.

In addition to national norms, standardized tests also can have special group norms and local norms. **Special group norms** *consist of test scores for subgroups from the national sample.* For example, special group norms might be available for students from low, middle, and high socioeconomic groups, for inner-city, suburban, and rural schools, for public and private schools, for female and male students, and for students from different ethnic groups. **Local norms** *are sometimes available for standardized tests. These allow comparison of a student's performance to that of students in the same class, school, or district.* Thus, evaluations of a student's test performance might differ depending on what norm group is used.

Reliability   **Reliability** *means the extent to which a test produces a consistent, reproducible measure of performance.* Reliable measures are stable, dependable, and relatively free from errors of measurement (Fekken, 2000; Popham, 2000). Reliability can be measured in several ways, including test-retest reliability, alternate forms reliability, and split-half reliability.

Test-retest reliability *is the extent to which a test yields the same performance when a student is given the same test on two different occasions.* Thus, if the standardized fourth-grade science test is given to a group of students today and then given to them again a month later, the test would be considered reliable if the students' scores were consistent across the two testings. There are two negative features of test-retest reliability: Students sometimes do better the second time they take the test because of their familiarity with it, and some students may have learned information in the time between the first test and the second test that changes their performance.

Alternate forms reliability *consists of giving different forms of the same test on two different occasions to the same group of students to determine how consistent the scores are.* The test items on the two forms are similar but not identical. This strategy eliminates the likelihood that students will perform better on the second test administration due to their familiarity with the items, but it does not eliminate a student's increase in knowledge and familiarity with the procedures and strategies in testing.

Split-half reliability *involves dividing the test items into two halves, such as the odd-numbered and even-numbered items. The scores on the two sets of items are compared to determine how consistently the students performed across each set.* When split-half reliability is high, we say that the test is *internally consistent.* For example, on the standardized fourth-grade science test, the students' scores on the odd-numbered and even-numbered items could be compared. If they scored similarly on the two sets of items, we could conclude that the science test had high split-half reliability.

Reliability is influenced by a number of errors in measurement. A student can have adequate knowledge and skill yet still not perform consistently across several tests because of a number of internal and external factors. Internal factors include health, motivation, and anxiety. External factors include inadequate directions given by the examiner, ambiguously created items, poor sampling of information, and inefficient scoring. When students perform inconsistently across the same or similar tests of their knowledge and skill, careful analysis should be made of internal and external factors that may have contributed to the inconsistency.

Validity

Validity *is the extent to which a test measures what it is intended to measure.* Three important types of validity are content validity, criterion validity, and construct validity.

A valid standardized test should have good **content validity,** *which refers to the test's ability to sample the content that is to be measured.* This concept is similar to "content-related evidence." For example, if a standardized fourth-grade science test purports to assess both knowledge and problem-solving skills, then the test should include both items that measure content information about science and items that measure problem-solving skills.

Another form of validity is **criterion validity,** *which is the test's ability to predict a student's performance as measured by other assessments or criteria.* How might criterion validity be assessed for the standardized science test? One method is to get a representative sample of fourth-grade teachers to evaluate the competence of the students in their science classes and then compare those competence ratings with the students' scores on the standardized tests. Another method is to compare the scores of students on the standardized test with the scores of the same students on a different test that was designed to test the same material.

Criterion validity can be either concurrent and predictive (Gregory, 2000; Krueger, 2000). **Concurrent validity** *refers to the relation between the test's scores and other criteria that are currently (concurrently) available.* For example, does the standardized fourth-grade science test correspond to students' grades in science this semester? If it does, we say that test has high concurrent validity.

Predictive validity *refers to the relation between test scores and the student's future performance.* For example, scores on the fourth-grade science test might be used to predict how many science classes different students will take in high school, whether middle school girls say they are interested in pursuing a science career, or whether students will win an award in science at some point in the future. Another example of predictive validity is how accurately students' scores on the SAT test predict their later grades in college and occupational success thereafter.

A third type of validity is **construct validity.** *A construct is an unobservable trait or characteristic of a person, such as intelligence, creativity, learning style, personality, or anxiety. Construct validity consists of the extent to which there is evidence that a test measures a particular construct.* Construct validity is the broadest of the three types of validity we have discussed and can include evidence from concurrent and predictive validity (Gronlund, 1998). Construct validity also might include a description of the development of the test, the pattern of the relations between the test and other significant factors (such as high correlations with similar tests and low correlations with tests measuring different constructs), and any other type of evidence that contributes to understanding the meaning of test scores. Because a construct typically involves abstract qualities, obtaining these various forms of evidence can help us determine whether the construct is valid.

Validity and reliability are related. A test that is valid is reliable, but a test that is reliable is not necessarily valid. People can respond consistently on a test but the test might not be measuring what it purports to measure. To understand this, imagine that you have three darts to throw. If all three fall close together, you have reliability. However, you have validity only if all three hit the bull's-eye (see figure 13.1).

At this point we have studied a number of ideas about the nature of standardized tests. A review of these ideas is presented in summary table 13.1.

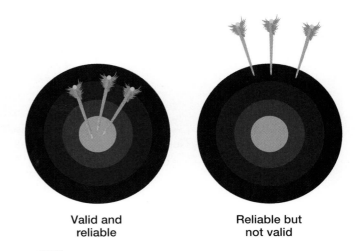

Valid and reliable   Reliable but not valid

Figure **13.1**
Links Between Reliability and Validity

A test that is valid is reliable, but a test that is reliable is not necessarily valid. This is illustrated by the dart-throwing analogy. All three darts may land far away from the bull's-eye but land in about the same place. To be valid, though, all three darts have to hit the bull's-eye or be very close to it, which also means they have to be reliable.

Standardized Aptitude and Achievement Tests

There are two main types of standardized tests: aptitude tests and achievement tests. We will first define these types of tests and compare them, then consider some different types of achievement tests, and finally describe district-mandated, state-mandated, and national tests.

Comparing Aptitude and Achievement Tests

An **aptitude test** *is used to predict a student's ability to learn a skill or accomplish something with further education and training.* Aptitude tests include general mental ability tests like the intelligence tests (Stanford-Binet, Wechsler Scales, and so on) that we described in chapter 4, "Individual Variations," and specific aptitude tests used to predict success in an academic subject or occupational area ◀||| p. 127. For example, one aptitude test might be given to students to predict their future success in math, another might be given to predict whether an individual is likely to do well in sales or medicine.

An **achievement test** *measures what the student has learned or what skills the student has mastered.* However, the distinction between the two types of standardized tests is sometimes blurred. Both types of tests assess a student's current status, both include similar types of questions, and the results of the two kinds of tests usually are highly correlated.

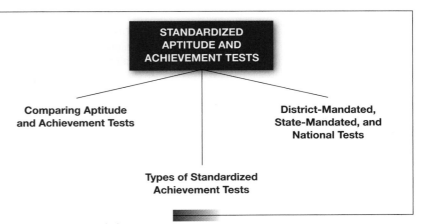

STANDARDIZED APTITUDE AND ACHIEVEMENT TESTS

Comparing Aptitude and Achievement Tests

Types of Standardized Achievement Tests

District-Mandated, State-Mandated, and National Tests

A sobering thought: What if, right at this moment,
I am living up to my full potential?

Jane Wagner
American Humorist and Writer, 20th Century

SUMMARY TABLE 13.1
The Nature of Standardized Tests

Concept	Processes/ Related Ideas	Characteristics/Description
What Is a Standardized Test?	Its Nature	• It is a test that is prepared by test specialists to assess performance under uniform conditions. • Many standardized tests allow a student's performance to be compared with the performance of other students at the same age or grade level, in many cases on a national basis.
The Purposes of Standardized Tests	Their Nature	• These include providing information about students' progress, diagnosing students' strengths and weaknesses, providing evidence for placement of students in specific programs, helping administrators evaluate programs, and contributing to accountability. • Interest in accountability has led to the creation of minimal competency tests and high-stakes testing. • Important decisions about students should be made not on the basis of a single standardized test but rather on the basis of information from a variety of assessments.
Criteria for Evaluating Standardized Tests	Norms	• Among the most important criteria are norms, reliability, and validity. • To understand an individual's performance on a test, it needs to be compared with the performance of a group of individuals who previously have been given the test by the test maker. This is the norm group. • National norms are based on a nationally representative group of students. • Standardized tests also can have special group and local norms.
	Reliability	• Reliability means the extent to which a test produces a consistent, reproducible measure of performance. • Reliable measures are stable, dependable, and relatively free from errors of measurement. • Reliability can be measured in several ways, including test-retest reliability, alternate forms reliability, and split-half reliability.
	Validity	• Validity is the extent to which a test measures what it is intended to measure. • Three important types of validity are content validity, criterion validity (which can be either concurrent or predictive), and construct validity.

The Scholastic Assessment Test (SAT) that many of you likely took as part of your admission to college is usually described as an aptitude test (*SAT* used to stand for "Scholastic Aptitude Test"). Actually, the SAT can be an aptitude test or an achievement test depending on the purpose for which it is used. If it is used to predict your success in college, it is an aptitude test. If it is used to determine what you have learned (such as vocabulary, reading comprehension, and math skills), it is an achievement test.

College Board
Test Publishers

Types of Standardized Achievement Tests

There are numerous types of standardized achievement tests. One common way to classify them is as survey batteries, specific subject tests, or diagnostic tests (Payne, 1997).

Survey Batteries A **survey battery** *is a group of individual subject-matter tests that is designed for a particular level of students.* Survey batteries are widely used in school testing programs. Some common batteries are the Stanford Achievement Test

Series, the Iowa Tests of Basic Skills, the Comprehensive Test of Basic Skills, the Metropolitan Achievement Tests, and the Science Research Associates Achievement Series.

The Stanford Achievement Test Series has tests for three different levels: kindergarten to grade 1.5, grades 1.5 to 9.9, and grades 9 to 13.0. The battery can be customized to fit the needs of a particular district or school. The Stanford battery includes a number of subject-matter tests at each level. For example, at the sixth-grade level, there are subject-matter tests for reading, mathematics, language, listening, spelling, study skills, science, social studies, using information, and thinking skills.

Many survey batteries also contain a number of subtests within a subject area. For example, the Metropolitan Achievement Tests include reading as one of the subject areas at each level. The reading subtests on the Metropolitan Tests include vocabulary, word recognition, and reading comprehension.

In their early years, survey batteries consisted of multiple-choice items to assess the student's content knowledge. However, recent editions have increasingly included more open-ended items that evaluate the student's thinking and reasoning skills (see figure 13.2).

Achievement Tests
Test Locator

Tests for Specific Subjects   Some standardized achievement tests assess skills in a particular area such as reading or mathematics. Because they focus on a specific area, they usually assess the skill in a more detailed, extensive way than a survey battery. Two examples of specific area tests that involve reading are the Woodcock Reading Mastery Tests and the Gates-McKillop-Horowitz Reading Diagnostic Test. Some standardized subject area tests cover topics such as chemistry, psychology, or computer science that are not included in survey batteries.

Diagnostic Tests   As we said earlier, diagnosis is an important function of standardized testing. **Diagnostic testing** *consists of a relatively in-depth evaluation of a specific area of learning. Its purpose is to determine the specific learning needs of a student so that those needs can be met through regular or remedial instruction* (ERIC Digest, 1989). In many cases, diagnostic testing is done after considerable instruction already has taken place. An achievement test is sometimes used for diagnostic purposes (such as one of the reading tests mentioned above). In many circumstances, though, a combination of observations and achievement tests will be used. A typical diagnostic sequence might involve (Payne, 1997) (1) informal observations by the teacher, (2) a survey battery, (3) a group diagnostic test, and (4) an individual diagnostic test. Note that in this sequence, diagnostic tests can often be given in a group format or individual format. Reading and mathematics are the two areas in which standardized tests are most often used for diagnosis.

District-Mandated, State-Mandated, and National Tests

As the public and government have demanded increased accountability of how effectively schools are educating our nation's children, district-mandated, state-mandated, and national tests have taken on a more powerful role (Roeber, 1999).

THROUGH THE EYES OF TEACHERS

Standardized Tests as a Tool for Planning

The Stanford Achievement Test is administered in our school system. Here is a procedure based on it that I have found most effective for my students:

1. Before the beginning of the new school year, I obtain the individual test record for each of my students.
2. Language arts being my teaching area, I highlight those areas for the language arts in which the individual has scored low or average.
3. I use the low and average scores as signals about what I will need to reinforce for the student throughout the school year.
4. Parental support is also vital to the success of my strategy. I hold parent conferences to inform and enable parents to be partners in the student's educational program for the year. We discuss the student's strengths and weaknesses.
5. Based on the SAT and the parental input, my lesson plans take into account the students' weaknesses, including outcome for correction.

Vicky Stone
Language Arts Teacher
Cammack Middle School
Huntington, West Virginia

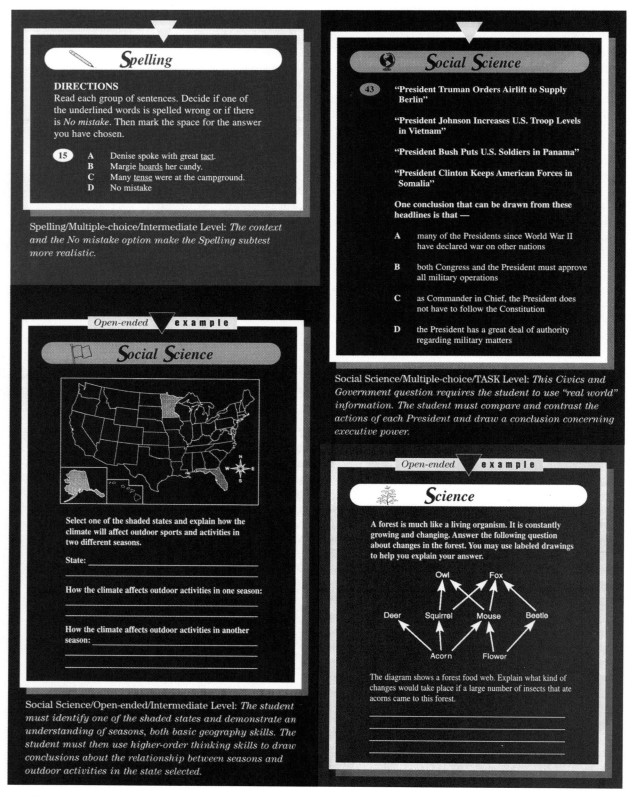

Spelling

DIRECTIONS

Read each group of sentences. Decide if one of the underlined words is spelled wrong or if there is *No mistake*. Then mark the space for the answer you have chosen.

15   A   Denise spoke with great <u>tact</u>.
     B   Margie <u>hoards</u> her candy.
     C   Many <u>tense</u> were at the campground.
     D   No mistake

Spelling/Multiple-choice/Intermediate Level: The context and the No mistake option make the Spelling subtest more realistic.

Open-ended ▼ **example**

Social Science

Select one of the shaded states and explain how the climate will affect outdoor sports and activities in two different seasons.

State: _____
_____

How the climate affects outdoor activities in one season:
_____
_____

How the climate affects outdoor activities in another season: _____
_____
_____

Social Science/Open-ended/Intermediate Level: The student must identify one of the shaded states and demonstrate an understanding of seasons, both basic geography skills. The student must then use higher-order thinking skills to draw conclusions about the relationship between seasons and outdoor activities in the state selected.

Social Science

43   "President Truman Orders Airlift to Supply Berlin"

"President Johnson Increases U.S. Troop Levels in Vietnam"

"President Bush Puts U.S. Soldiers in Panama"

"President Clinton Keeps American Forces in Somalia"

One conclusion that can be drawn from these headlines is that —

A   many of the Presidents since World War II have declared war on other nations

B   both Congress and the President must approve all military operations

C   as Commander in Chief, the President does not have to follow the Constitution

D   the President has a great deal of authority regarding military matters

Social Science/Multiple-choice/TASK Level: This Civics and Government question requires the student to use "real world" information. The student must compare and contrast the actions of each President and draw a conclusion concerning executive power.

Open-ended ▼ **example**

Science

A forest is much like a living organism. It is constantly growing and changing. Answer the following question about changes in the forest. You may use labeled drawings to help you explain your answer.

The diagram shows a forest food web. Explain what kind of changes would take place if a large number of insects that ate acorns came to this forest.

_____
_____
_____
_____

Figure 13.2

Examples of Items from the Stanford Achievement Test Series

District-Mandated Achievement Tests   In addition to state-mandated tests, a particular district might have standardized tests that it requires students to take. For example, in Spencerport, New York, the school district collects information about student performance with the following tests: the Stanford Achievement Test in Reading (grades 2–8) and Math (grades 1–8); the New York State Pupil Evaluation Test in Reading (grades 3–6), Written Expression (grade 5), and Mathematics (grades 3 and 6); the New York State Program Evaluation Test, which assesses programs in science and social studies; the New York Preliminary Competency Test, which is used to predict future success in reading, writing, and math (given in any grade); the New York States Regents Competency Test, which assesses competency in math, science, global studies, and U.S. history and government (given in high school to students who do not take the Regents Test); the Scholastic Assessment Test (SAT) and American College Test (ACT), given to students who plan to apply to college; and Advanced Placement tests in U.S. history, biology, chemistry, English literature and composition, French, Spanish, calculus, and music theory, which can be taken by students to place out of certain classes because of the knowledge and skill levels they have attained. In 1999, Spencerport also began assessing students' ability to apply knowledge and problem-solving skills in a number of subject areas.

Types of standardized tests vary across school districts. However, as in the Spencerport school district, the overall number is typically large.

State-Mandated Achievement Tests   Peter Airasian (1997, 2001) reviewed the use of state-mandated achievement tests. States have mandated tests for many years but their emphasis has recently changed. Prior to the 1990s, their content was not closely linked with what was actually taught and learned in the classroom. The early state-mandated assessments simply provided an overall view of how students in a state were performing in certain subject areas, especially reading and mathematics.

In the 1990s, state-mandated testing changed as part of an effort to connect state-endorsed educational objectives with instruction and testing. Most states already have or are in the process of identifying objectives that every student in the state is expected to achieve. These objectives form the basis not only for state-mandated tests but also for guiding such activities as teacher education and curriculum decisions (Whitford & Jones, 2000). Teachers are strongly encouraged to incorporate these objectives into their classroom planning and instruction. In many states, the objectives are reflected in achievement tests that are given to every student in the state.

Students' performance on the tests can have important consequences for students, teachers, and schools. In some states, how well a student does on the state-mandated tests determines whether the student will be allowed to move on to the next grade or to graduate from high school. In some states, teachers and schools are rated on how well their students perform on the tests. When students perform very poorly, teachers and schools might be placed on probation.

The format of the items on the state-mandated tests typically is mixed, including multiple-choice items as well as construction-based items, such as essays, and performance assessments (oral reading, cooperative problem solving, or science experiments). An increasing number of states also require a student portfolio as part of their assessment mandate (Educational Testing Service, 1995). Figure 13.3 profiles state-based testing in five states.

State Standards

THROUGH THE EYES OF CHILDREN

"High-Stakes" Tests

Samuel still does not have his high school diploma even though the 18-year-old has completed all of his senior-year course work. His grades were better than average, and he showed up every day for class. But he can't yet master two of the four proficiency tests required by the state of Ohio—so-called high-stakes tests—which must be passed to graduate. He has taken these nearly a dozen times over the past 4 years.

Samuel says, "I don't think it's fair. If you go to school for all 12 years and then they throw a test in your face and say you have to pass it to graduate."

State	Name of Standards	Assessment
Florida	*Curriculum*	Students must reach a number of performance standards to get a high school diploma. A new statewide assessment is being developed. A major initiative is under way to create authentic assessments to evaluate performance standards.
Kentucky	*Academic*	Statewide assessment takes place in grades 4, 8, and 11. The assessments include open-response items, portfolio, and performance assessments. Kentucky has returned multiple-choice items to the assessment and reduced the number of essay items.
Louisiana	*State Curriculum Guides*	Standards apply to grades K–12, with most organized into elementary, secondary, and high-school levels. The state curriculum guides are mandatory. Students in grades 3, 5, and 7 take criterion-referenced tests based on the curriculum standards. Students in grades 10–12 take exit exams. Students in tenth grade take math, language arts, and writing exams: in eleventh grade, they take science and social studies exams. Students who do not pass particular tests can retake them in twelfth grade, but they must pass all exit exams to graduate from high school.
Minnesota	*Basic Requirements and Required Profile of Learning*	Standards are geared toward high school graduation. Benchmarks for learning at grades 3, 5, and 8 are used to evaluate whether students are on track to meet the high school graduation requirements. The standards are mandatory, and students who do not meet them won't graduate. Students have to pass a basic requirements test and apply their knowledge to a variety of situated and real-life situations. A package of assessments is being developed to examine these aspects of learning.
Nevada	*Courses of Study*	These determine what students are supposed to learn in grades K, 3, 6, and 8 through 12. These standards are mandatory. Assessment includes a writing exam and a norm-referenced commercial test. A graduation test includes assessment of reading, writing, and mathematics.
Texas	*Essential Elements*	Districts are responsible for teaching the "essential elements." A state assessment system consists of a criterion-referenced test that measures whether students have mastered the essential elements. Assessment results are the main factor in determining whether the state reconstitutes or takes over a school.

Figure **13.3**

State Standards and Assessment

**Exploring
State Standards**

Most state-mandated tests have criterion-referenced scoring, which means that the student's score is evaluated against predetermined standards. Most states have a cut-off score (such as correct answers to 70 percent of the items) that the student has to reach to pass the test. Such tests also provide comparative scores.

Evaluating District- and State-Mandated Achievement Tests   The use of district- and state-mandated achievement tests is very controversial (Linn, 2000). Supporters of the tests argue that they are the best way to hold schools accountable for students' learning (Cibulka, 1999). Without the tests, say their supporters, schools and teachers are more likely to slack off and not put as much effort into educating students. Supporters also believe that the tests provide valuable feedback about which areas of learning need more attention.

Critics of the state- and district-mandated tests argue that they encourage teachers to teach for the test (Gallagher, 2000; O'Neil & Tell, 1999). That is, because teachers know that their students will be tested and they want their class to do well, they narrow their instruction to match the content of the tests. Many teachers say that the state-based tests, as well as some district-mandated standardized tests, infringe on their ability to teach what they think is best for their students and divert valuable class time from instruction and learning.

The National Assessment of Educational Progress The federal government also is involved in standardized testing through the National Assessment of Educational Progress (NAEP). States are not required to participate in the national assessment, although many do (for example, more than forty states have their students take the reading portion of the test). The NAEP is a census-like examination of young Americans' knowledge, skills, understanding, and attitudes (Bourque, 1999; Payne, 1997). The subject areas include reading, writing, literature, mathematics, science, social studies, art, citizenship, and career and occupational development. NAEP assessments began in 1969 for science, writing, and citizenship. Care is taken not to identify any student, school, city, or state, although states can choose to have scores identified by state. Any student who takes the NAEP responds only to a portion of the entire assessment.

Results from the NAEP are disseminated in the form of "report cards" that reveal the percentages of particular groups that perform at certain levels. Report cards are given for these categories: age (9, 13, and 17); type of community (impoverished inner city; affluent suburb; rural area); sex; and ethnic group.

Recent report cards suggest that American students are showing continued gradual improvement in math and science (Reese & others, 1997; O'Sullivan, Reese, & Mazzeo, 1977; Riley, 1997). For example, in 1978, 20 percent of 9-year-olds were proficient in adding, subtracting, multiplying, and dividing whole numbers. In 1996, the figure increased to 30 percent. For the same years, the figure for 13-year-olds increased from 65 percent to 79 percent. However, improvement in reading proficiency was minimal. For example, from 1984 to 1996, the reading proficiency of 9-year-olds increased only from 16 percent to 18 percent, and the reading proficiency of 13-year-olds increased from 83 percent to 89 percent. Also, students continue to show deficient writing skills on the national evaluation, especially at the secondary school level. Another disturbing result is that the achievement gap between Whites and students of color, which was narrowing at one time, has not decreased in recent years. And on items that require higher-level thinking skills (such as reasoning) and applications of knowledge, America's students do not fare well.

The federal government recently proposed a voluntary national test of fourth- and eighth-grade students' reading (Applebome, 1997). The hope is that it will become so widely used that it will become America's first truly national assessment of students' achievement. The national test would be similar to the NAEP reading and math tests and the math component of the Third International Mathematics and Science Study (figure 13.4 shows some types of items that would be used on the national test). However, currently tests are given only to a sample of students to compute national averages. The new tests would assess a much greater number of students and evaluate individual students.

However, the proposed standardized national test has been criticized by both liberals and conservatives. Many individuals who are politically liberal are suspicious of standardized tests

---

MATH

In 1995, most eighth-graders in the United States scored below the international average in math of students in the 41 countries involved in the Third International Mathematics and Science Study (TIMSS). Students at the international average can solve single-step problems and understand the basics of algebra and geometric terms. The following questions show what a student at or above the international average should know:

(1) A rubber ball rebounds to half the height it drops. If the ball is dropped from a rooftop 18 feet above the ground, what is the total distance traveled by the time it hits the ground the third time?

  A. 31.5 feet
  B. **40.5 feet**
  C. 45 feet
  D. 63 feet

(2) The table shows the values of x and y, where x is proportional to y. What are the values of P and Q?

TABLE	
x	y
3	7
6	Q
P	35

Answers
A. P=14 and Q=31
B. **P=10 and Q=14**
C. P=10 and Q=31
D. P=14 and Q=15
E. P=15 and Q=14

(Correct math answers are indicated in bold.)

READING

Results from the National Assessment of Education Progress (NAEP) are reported by three levels of fourth-grade reading: basic, proficient and advanced. These levels help to explain what it means to read well in the fourth grade. The following passage selected by the Department of Education from *Charlotte's Web,* by E. B. White, helps illustrate the kinds of skills expected of students at each level:

Having promised Wilbur that she would save his life, she was determined to keep her promise. Charlotte was naturally patient. She knew from experience that if she waited long enough, a fly would come to her web; and she felt sure that if she thought long enough about Wilbur's problem, an idea would come to her mind.

Finally, one morning toward the middle of July, the idea came. "Why how perfectly simple!" she said to herself. "The way to save Wilbur's life is to play a trick on Zuckerman. If I can fool a bug," thought Charlotte, "I can surely fool a man. People are not as smart as bugs."

• Students at the basic level are able to read the passage and then tell what Charlotte promised Wilbur.
• Students at the proficient level are able to describe why Charlotte thought she could fool Zuckerman.
• Students at the advanced level recognize that Charlotte compares waiting for ideas to entrapping a fly.

Figure **13.4**
Examples of Items on National Assessments

**National Assessment
of Education Progress
First in the World**

and believe they are culturally biased. Political conservatives are wary of expanding the federal government's role in education. At the time I am writing this book, the proposed national test has not been approved by Congress.

World-Class Standards   National assessment of students is part of an effort to get American students to measure up to, and eventually set the standard for, world-class achievement in education. In a recent analysis of national testing in twelve major countries, the United States and Canada were the only countries without a standardized national test (for example, most Asian countries, such as Japan, Thailand, and Singapore, have national tests) (Haynes & Chalker, 1997). In reading, American students do well against students from other countries during the elementary school years, but by the end of high school they have fallen behind students in many other countries. Among the reasons given for the poor performance of U.S. students are inadequate time spent on academic schoolwork, larger class sizes, too much time spent on television and nonacademic media, too little time spent doing homework, and inadequate spending on education (Ravitch, 1995).

Critics of the cross-national comparisons argue that in many comparisons virtually all U.S. children are being compared with a "select" group of children from other countries, especially in the secondary school comparisons. Therefore, they conclude, it is no wonder that American students don't fare so well. That criticism holds for some international comparisons. However, even when the top 25 percent of students in different countries were recently compared, U.S. students did not rank much higher (Mullis & others, 1999). For example, in a recent comparison of the top 25 percent of high school seniors (in terms of math and science knowledge and skills) in different countries, Sweden, the Netherlands, Norway, and Switzerland ranked highest. The United States was still below the international average in math and science knowledge and skills, even when their best students were compared with other countries' best students.

An analysis of national standardized tests found that, compared with American standardized tests, other countries' tests (1) included more short answer, open-ended, and essay questions and (2) were more closely linked with the curriculum and textbooks so that foreign students know what they need to study (Jacobson, 1996). Recently, publishers of commercial standardized tests in America have begun to include more constructed-item and performance assessments in their tests.

One of the dilemmas in pursuing internationally competitive standards involves deciding on what they are and determining who sets them (Tanner, 1997). Should they be based on the standards of other countries whose students achieve the highest scores on tests? What roles do the federal and state governments play in developing these standards? Which educators should participate in their creation? Should instruction be tied to the standards? Consensus on these questions has not yet been reached.

At this point we have discussed many ideas about standardized aptitude and achievement tests. A review of these ideas is presented in summary table 13.2.

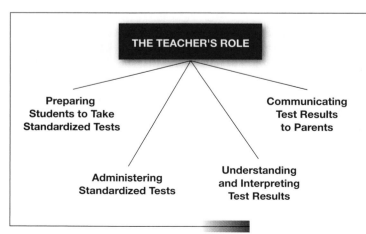

The Teacher's Role

The teacher's role in standardized testing involves preparing students for the test, administering the test, understanding and interpreting test results, and communicating test results to parents.

Preparing Students to Take Standardized Tests

James McMillan (1997) recently described the teacher's role in preparing students to take standardized tests. It is important for all students to have an opportunity to do their best. One way to do this is to make sure that students have good test-taking skills.

SUMMARY TABLE 13.2
Standardized Aptitude and Achievement Tests

Concept	Processes/ Related Ideas	Characteristics/Description
Comparing Aptitude and Achievement Tests	The Basic Difference	• An aptitude test predicts a student's ability to learn, or what the student can accomplish with further education and training. • An achievement test measures what the student has learned, or the skills the student has mastered. • Aptitude tests include general ability tests like intelligence tests or specific aptitude tests used to predict success in an academic subject or occupational area. • The SAT test is typically used as an aptitude test although it can be used as an achievement test.
Types of Standardized Achievement Tests	Survey Batteries	• These consist of a group of individual subject-matter tests that are designed for a particular level of students.
	Tests for Specific Subjects	• These assess a skill in a more detailed, extensive way than a survey battery.
	Diagnostic Tests	• These are given to students to pinpoint weaknesses, often after instruction has taken place.
District-Mandated, State-Mandated, and National Tests	District-Mandated Tests	• In addition to state-mandated tests, a particular school district might have standardized tests that its students must take.
	State-Mandated Achievement Tests	• In the 1990s, state-mandated tests became more closely connected with state-endorsed educational objectives and instruction. • In many states, students' performance has important consequences for students. For example, students who do poorly on a state-mandated test might be held back a grade or not allowed to graduate from high school. • Performance-based assessments and portfolios increasingly are being used in state-mandated testing. • Scoring and interpretation of state-mandated tests usually are criterion-referenced.
	Evaluating District- and State-Mandated Achievement Tests	• There is no controversy about the use of district- and state-mandated tests. • Supporters cite the importance of the tests in accountability and the feedback the tests provide about which aspects of students' learning need attention. • Critics argue that the tests encourage teachers to teach to the test, narrowing their instruction. They also say that the tests restrict their ability to teach what they think is most important and take up valuable classroom time that could be used for instruction and learning.
	The National Assessment of Educational Progress	• The NAEP is the federal government's census-like examination of young Americans' knowledge, skills, understanding, and attitudes. • Results from the NAEP are disseminated in the form of "report cards" that reveal the percentages of particular groups that perform above certain levels.
	World-Class Standards	• National assessment of students is part of an effort to get American students to measure up to, and eventually set, world-class standards. • On many comparisons with students in other countries, American students do not fare well. • Many issues are involved in the concept of world-class standards.

TEACHING STRATEGIES
For Improving Students' Test-Taking Skills

Following are some important test-taking skills that you might want to discuss with your students (Linn & Gronlund, 1998):

1. *Read the instructions carefully.*
2. *Read the items carefully.*
3. *Work quickly enough to complete the test.*
4. *Skip difficult items and return to them later.*
5. *Make informed guesses instead of omitting items, if scoring favors doing so.*
6. *Eliminate as many alternatives as possible on multiple-choice items.*
7. *Follow directions carefully in marking the answer (such as darkening the entire space).*
8. *Check to be sure that the appropriate response was marked on the answer sheet.*
9. *Go back and check answers if time permits.*

Teacher Competence in Educational Assessment

It also is important for you to communicate a positive attitude about the test to students. Explain the nature and purpose of the test. Describe the test as an opportunity and a challenge rather than an ordeal. Avoid saying anything that can cause students to get nervous about the test. If you observe that some students are so anxious that their performance on the test will be hindered, consider having a counselor talk with them about ways to reduce their test anxiety.

In this era of high-stakes testing in which scores on standardized tests can have serious consequences for students, teachers, and schools, many schools are establishing programs designed to improve students' test-taking skills (Payne, 1997). Researchers have found that "coaching" or training students to do well on a test, such as the SAT, gives only a slight boost to scores. For example, 20-hour coaching classes increase math and verbal scores on the SAT by only about 15 and 10 points, respectively, on the 200–800 point scale, contrary to the exaggerated claims made by SAT coaching programs (Bond, 1989; ETS, 1994). The Educational Testing Service, which publishes the SAT, says that the best way for students to do well on the SAT is to take rigorous courses, work hard in them, brush up on their algebra and geometry, familiarize themselves with the test, and get a good night's sleep the night before the test. Taking a practice test or two is a wise strategy in preparing for any standardized test.

Administering Standardized Tests

Most standardized tests spell out in considerable detail how the test should be administered (Airasian, 1997; Gay & Airasian, 2000). This includes how to set up the testing room, what to do when students take the test, how to distribute the test and answer sheets, and how to time the tests.

The physical testing environment should be well lighted and well ventilated. Students should have adequate work space. Seat students in a manner that will avoid distractions or cheating. Hang a sign on the door to the room that says something like "Testing in Progress—Do Not Disturb" (McMillan, 1997).

THROUGH THE EYES OF TEACHERS
Get Full-Animation 3-D

Standardized tests are just one very small, isolated picture of a child. A much fuller "video" comes from daily observations. Do not unfairly label a child based on a test.

Rarely or never during the school year do my students encounter fill-in-the-oval items like those on standardized tests. Therefore, to be fair, before standardized testing I give them examples similar to the format of the test. If adults take a test with a special format, they prepare themselves by practicing in that format. Why should it be any different for children?

Marlene Wendler
Fourth-Grade Teacher
St. Paul's Lutheran School
New Ulm, Minnesota

In administering the test, the teacher should follow word for word the script that is included in the test manual, to ensure that the test is being given under standardized conditions (Gay & Airasian, 2000). If this script is not followed exactly, comparisons of the students' performance with the population of students on which the norms for the test were established could be invalid (Airasian, 1997). Be sure to write the start and finish times for the test on the chalkboard. At start time, tell students clearly to begin. Make sure students stop when the time has expired.

After your students have completed the test, count the booklets and answer sheets. Also record any incidents that you observed that might invalidate students' scores.

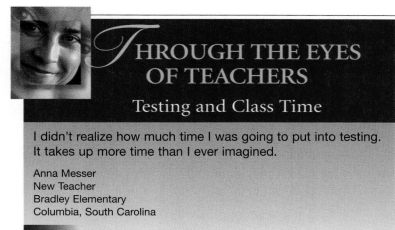

THROUGH THE EYES OF TEACHERS
Testing and Class Time

I didn't realize how much time I was going to put into testing. It takes up more time than I ever imagined.

Anna Messer
New Teacher
Bradley Elementary
Columbia, South Carolina

Understanding and Interpreting Test Results

Knowledge of some basic descriptive statistics will help you interpret standardized tests. We will discuss these basic statistics as well as some ways that test results are commonly reported.

Understanding Descriptive Statistics Although we are discussing statistics here to help you understand standardized tests, the information about statistics also can help you with many other aspects of classroom assessment, such as interpreting a student's scores on tests you have created and administered, as well as calculating a student's grade point average. Our primary focus here is on **descriptive statistics,** *which are mathematical procedures that are used to describe and summarize data (information) in a meaningful way* (Hockenbury, 1997). We will study frequency distributions, measures of central tendency, measures of variability, and the normal distribution.

*S*tatistical thinking will one day be as necessary for efficient citizenship as the ability to read and write.

H. G. Wells
English Novelist, 20th Century

Statistical Analysis

Frequency Distributions The first step in organizing data involves creating a **frequency distribution,** *a listing of scores, usually from highest to lowest, along with the number of times each score appears.* Imagine that a test was given and 21 students received the following scores on the test: 96, 95, 94, 92, 88, 88, 86, 86, 86, 86, 84, 83, 82, 82, 82, 78, 75, 75, 72, 68, and 62. Figure 13.5a shows a frequency distribution for these scores. Frequency distributions often are presented graphically. For example, a **histogram** *is a frequency distribution in the form of a graph. Vertical bars represent the frequency of scores per category.* Figure 13.5b shows a histogram for the 21 scores. A histogram often is called a *bar graph.* Notice in the histogram that the horizontal axis (*x*-axis) indicates the obtained scores and the vertical axis (the *y*-axis) presents how often each score occurs.

Although representing a group of scores *graphically* can provide insight about students' performance, so can some statistical techniques that represent scores *numerically.* These techniques involve the concepts of central tendency and variability, each of which we will discuss.

Measures of Central Tendency A **measure of central tendency** *is a number that provides information about the average or typical score in a set of data. There are three measures of central tendency: mean, median, and mode. The **mean** *is the numerical average of a group of scores, commonly labeled as M (Mn) of X (mean of X) by statisticians.* The mean is computed

"Tonight, we're going to let the statistics speak for themselves."

Drawing by Koren: © 1974 The New Yorker Magazine, Inc.

(a) Frequency Distribution

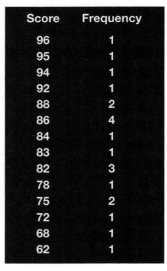

Score	Frequency
96	1
95	1
94	1
92	1
88	2
86	4
84	1
83	1
82	3
78	1
75	2
72	1
68	1
62	1

(b) Histogram

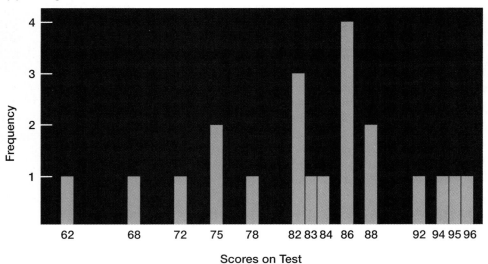

Figure 13.5
A Frequency Distribution and Histogram

by adding all the scores and then dividing by the number of scores. Thus, the mean for the 21 students' test scores above is 1740/21 = 82.86. The mean often is a good indicator of the central tendency of a group of scores.

The **median** *is the score that falls exactly in the middle of a distribution of scores after they have been arranged (or ranked) from highest to lowest.* In our example of 21 test scores, the 11th ranked score (10 above, 10 below it) is 84.

The **mode** *is the score that occurs most often.* The mode can be determined easily by looking at the frequency distribution or histogram. In our example of 21 scores, the mode is 86 (the score occurring most often—4 times). The mode is most revealing when its value is much more frequent than the other values or scores. For example, in the 21 scores in our example, if 15 of the 21 scores had been the same, then the mode probably would be the best measure of central tendency for the data. In this case, the mean and median would be less meaningful.

There can be two or more modes. For example, in our example of 21 students taking a test, if four students had scored 86 and four students had scored 75 (instead of the 2), then the set of scores would have had two modes (86 and 75). A set of scores with two modes is called a *bimodal distribution.* It is possible for a set of scores to have more than two modes, in which case it is called a *multimodal distribution.*

Measures of Variability   In addition to obtaining information about the central tendency of a set of scores, it also is important to know about their variability. **Measures of variability** *tell us how much the scores vary from one another.* Two measures of variability are range and standard deviation.

The **range** *is the distance between the highest and lowest scores.* The range of the 21 students' test scores in our example is 34 points ($96 - 62 = 34$). The range is a rather simple measure of variability and it is not used often. The most commonly used measure of variability is the standard deviation.

The **standard deviation** *is a measure of how much a set of scores varies on the average around the mean of the scores. Stated another way, it reveals how closely scores cluster around the mean. The smaller the standard deviation, the less the scores tend to vary from the mean.* The greater the standard deviation, the more the scores tend to spread out from the mean. Calculating a standard deviation is not very difficult, especially if you have a calculator that is capable of computing square roots. To calculate a standard deviation, follow these four steps:

1. Compute the mean of the scores.
2. From each score, subtract the mean and then square the difference between the score and the mean. (Squaring the scores will eliminate any minus signs that result from subtracting the mean.)
3. Add the squares and then divide that sum by the number of scores.
4. Compute the square root of the value obtained in step 3. This is the standard deviation.

The formula for these four steps is

$$\sqrt{\frac{\Sigma(\chi-\overline{\chi})^2}{N}}$$

where χ = the individual score minus the mean, represented by $\overline{\chi}$, N = the number of scores, and Σ means "the sum of."

Applying this formula to the test scores of the 21 students:

1. We already computed the mean of the scores and found that it was 82.86.
2. Subtract 82.86 from the first score: $96 - 82.86 = 13.14$. Square 13.14 to get 172.66. Save the value and go on to do the same for the second score, the third score, and so on.
3. Add the 21 squares to get 1543.28. Divide the sum by 21: $1543.28/21 = 73.49$.
4. Find the square root of 73.49. The result is 8.57, the standard deviation.

$$\sqrt{\frac{1543.28}{21}} = \sqrt{73.49} = 8.57$$

Calculators are very helpful in computing a standard deviation. To read further about using calculators effectively, see Technology and Education. And to evaluate your knowledge of and skills in computing the various measures of central tendency and variability we have described, complete Self-Assessment 13.1. Mastering these kinds of descriptive statistics is useful not only for classroom work but also for understanding research results.

The standard deviation is a better measure of variability than the range because the range represents information about only two bits of data (the highest and lowest scores), whereas the standard deviation represents combined information about all the data. It also usually is more helpful to know how much test scores are spread out or clustered together than to know the highest and lowest scores. If a teacher gives a test and the standard deviation turns out to be very low, it means the scores tend to cluster around the same value. That could mean that everyone in the class learned the material equally well, but it more likely suggests that the test was too easy and is not discriminating very effectively between students who mastered the material and those who did not.

TECHNOLOGY AND EDUCATION

Using Calculators Effectively

Gilbert Sax (1997) described various types of calculators and how teachers can use them effectively.

Four- or five-function calculators. These are the simplest calculators. They can add, subtract, multiply, and divide. Most also can compute square roots, which can be especially helpful if you need to calculate a standard deviation, *z*-score, or *T*-score. These calculators are inexpensive and they can compute all of the statistics described in this chapter. However, they are somewhat inconvenient when numerous steps are required to solve a problem.

More specialized calculators. More specialized calculators also are available. For example, they automatically accumulate score values, count the number of cases entered, square each entered value, and then sum the squares. In addition, such calculators are capable of computing internal reliability statistics. Such features save time and can reduce computational errors.

If you do not have a calculator, seriously consider purchasing one to use when you become a classroom teacher.

It can save you time and make your computations more accurate when you need to calculate various aspects of central tendency and variation in your students' test scores. Sax recommends that when you purchase a calculator, you have a salesperson take the time to show you how to compute the kinds of statistics you need.

What are some good strategies for using calculators effectively?

SELF-ASSESSMENT 13.1

Evaluating My Knowledge of and Skill in Computing Measures of Central Tendency and Variability

Examine each of the following statements and place a checkmark next to the statement if you feel confident of your knowledge of the concept and your skill in computing the measure or using the instrument.

_____   I know what a frequency distribution is.

_____   I can describe what a histogram is and know how to create one.

_____   I understand what a mean is and know how to compute it.

_____   I understand what a median is and know how to calculate it.

_____   I know what a mode is and I am aware of how to compute it.

_____   I know what a range is and how to arrive at it.

_____   I can discuss what a standard deviation is and know how to compute it.

_____   I have a good calculator and know how to use it to compute basic descriptive statistics.

For any items that you did not check off, go back and study the concept again. If you are still not confident about computing the various measures, keep practicing. For example, sometimes students need to compute a number of standard deviations before they get a sense of the concept and what it means.

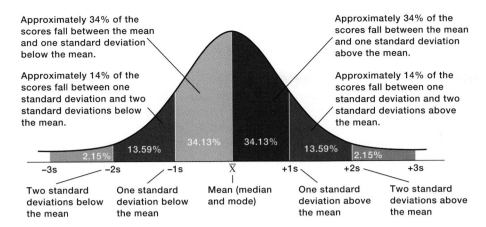

Approximately 34% of the scores fall between the mean and one standard deviation below the mean.

Approximately 14% of the scores fall between one standard deviation and two standard deviations below the mean.

Approximately 34% of the scores fall between the mean and one standard deviation above the mean.

Approximately 14% of the scores fall between one standard deviation and two standard deviations above the mean.

2.15%   13.59%   34.13%   34.13%   13.59%   2.15%

−3s   −2s   −1s   X̄   +1s   +2s   +3s

Two standard deviations below the mean

One standard deviation below the mean

Mean (median and mode)

One standard deviation above the mean

Two standard deviations above the mean

Figure **13.6**
The Normal Distribution

The Normal Distribution   In a **normal distribution,** *most of the scores cluster around the mean. The farther above or below the mean we travel, the less frequently each score occurs. A normal distribution also is called a "bell-shaped curve" or "bell curve."* Many characteristics, such as human intelligence measured by intelligence tests, athletic ability, weight, and height, follow or approximate a normal distribution. We presented the normal distribution for intelligence in chapter 4, "Individual Variations" ◀▥ p. 127. We show it again here to illustrate what a normal distribution, or "bell-shaped curve," looks like and focus more on its statistical properties (see figure 13.6).

Figure 13.6 illustrates several important characteristics of a normal distribution. First, it is symmetrical. Because of this symmetry, the mean, median, and mode are identical in a normal distribution. Second, its bell shape shows that the most common scores are near the middle. The scores become less frequent the farther away from the middle they appear (that is, as they become more extreme). Third, the normal distribution incorporates information about both the mean and the standard deviation, as indicated in figure 13.6. The area on the normal curve that is one standard deviation above the mean and one standard deviation below it represents 68.26 percent of the scores. At two standard deviations above and below the mean, 95.42 percent of the scores are represented. Finally, at three standard deviations above and below the mean, 99.74 percent of the scores are included. If we apply this information to figure 13.6, which shows the normal distribution of IQ scores in the population, we can see that 68 percent of the population has an IQ between 85 and 115, 95 percent an IQ between 70 and 130, and 99 percent between 55 and 145.

Interpreting Test Results   Understanding descriptive statistics provides the foundation for effectively interpreting test results. About 4 to 8 weeks after a standardized test has been administered, test results are returned to the school. A **raw score** *is the number of items the student answered correctly on the test.* Raw scores, by themselves, are not very useful because they don't provide information about how easy or difficult the test was or how the student fared compared with other students. Test publishers usually provide teachers with many different kinds of scores that go beyond raw scores. These include percentile rank scores, stanine scores, grade equivalent scores, and standard scores.

Percentile Rank Scores   A **percentile rank score** *reveals the percentage of the distribution that lies at or below the score. It also provides information about the score's position in relation to the rest of the scores. Percentile ranks range from 1 to 99.*

Stanine Score	Percentile Rank Score
9	96 or Higher
8	89–95
7	77–88
6	60–76
5	40–59
4	23–39
3	11–22
2	4–10
1	Below 4

Figure **13.7**

The Relation Between Stanine Score and Percentile Rank Score

If a student has a percentile rank of 81 on a test, it means that the student performed as well as or higher on the test than 81 percent of the sample who made up the norm group. Note that percentiles do not refer to percentages of items answered correctly on the test.

Stanine Scores   A **stanine score** *describes a student's test performance on a nine-point scale ranging from 1 to 9.* Scores of 1, 2, and 3 are usually considered to be below average; 4, 5, and 6 average; and 7, 8, and 9 above average. As in the case of a student's percentile rank score, a stanine score in one subject area (such as science) can be compared with the student's stanine score in other areas (such as math, reading, and social studies).

A stanine refers to a specific percentage of the normal curve's area. The correspondence between a stanine score and a percentile rank is shown in figure 13.7. A stanine score provides a more general index of a student's performance while a percentile rank score yields a more precise estimation.

Grade-Equivalent Scores   A **grade-equivalent score** *is expressed in terms of the grade level of students who are actually in a given grade level.* This often is represented in year and month, such as 4.5, which stands for fourth grade, fifth month in school. A grade equivalent of 6.0 stands for the beginning of the sixth grade. In some test reports, a decimal is omitted so that 45 is the same as 4.5 or 60 is the same as 6.0.

Grade-equivalent scores should be used only to interpret a student's progress, not for grade placement. Many educators believe that because grade-equivalent scores are often misleading and misinterpreted, other types of scores, such as standard scores are more appropriate to use.

Standard Scores   A **standard score** *is expressed as a deviation from the mean, which involves the concept of standard deviation that we discussed earlier.* The term *standard* as used in "standard score" does not refer to a specific level of performance or expectation but rather to the standard normal curve (McMillan, 1997). Actually, the stanine scores and grade-equivalent scores we already have profiled are standard scores. Two additional standard scores we will evaluate here are *z*-scores and *T*-scores.

A **z-score** *provides information about how many standard deviations a raw score is above or below the mean.* Calculation of a *z*-score is done using this formula:

$$z\text{-score} = \frac{X - \overline{X}}{SD}$$

where X = any raw score, $\overline{X}$ = mean of the raw scores, and *SD* equals the standard deviation of the raw score distribution.

Consider again our example of 21 students taking a test. What would a student's *z*-score be if the student's raw score were 86? Using the formula above it would be

$$\frac{86 - 82.86}{8.57} = .37$$

Thus, the raw score of 86 is .37 of a standard deviation above the mean. The *z*-score mean is 0 and the standard deviation is 1.

A **T-score** *is a standard score in which the mean is set at 50 and the standard deviation is set at 10.* The following formula can be used to compute a *T*-score:

$$T\text{-score} = 50 + 10(z)$$

For example, a *T*-score of 70 is the same as a *z*-score of 2, and a *T*-score of 40 is the same as a *z*-score of −1. For the raw score of 86, the corresponding *T*-score is, therefore, 54.

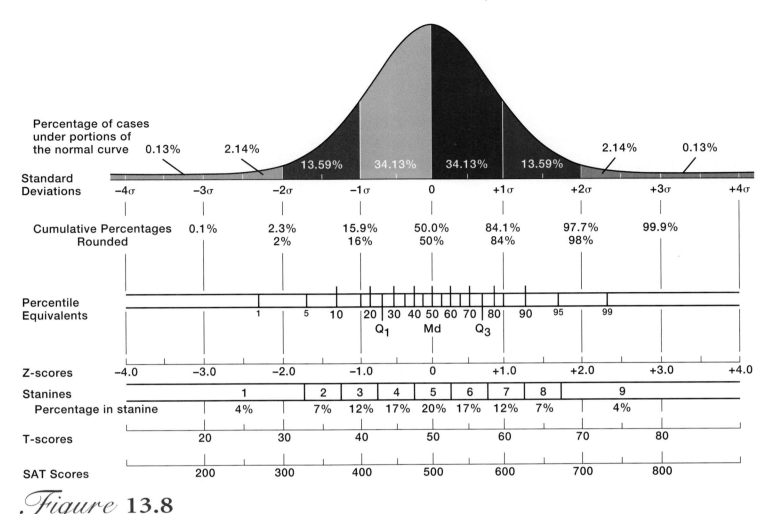

Figure 13.8
Some Commonly Reported Test Scores Based on the Normal Curve

The college entrance SAT is based on a similar scoring strategy. Its mean is 500 and its standard deviation is 100. The lowest possible score of 200 on the SAT is calibrated to occur at three standard deviations below the mean and the maximum score of 800 is designated to occur at three standard deviations above the mean. Thus, only a very small percentage of students (about 1/10th of one percent) score at these extremes.

Figure 13.8 presents an overall comparison of many of the types of standardized scores you will see on test reports. Most raw standardized test scores are forced into a normal curve representation. Figure 13.9 shows a report of one student's test scores on a national standardized survey test battery. Included in the report are the student's percentile rank score, stanine score, grade-equivalent score, and normal curve equivalent.

Don't Overinterpret Test Results   Use caution in interpreting small differences in test scores, especially percentile rank and grade-equivalent test scores (Airasian, 1997). All tests have some degree of error.

A good strategy is to think of a score not as a single number but as a location in a band or general range. Small differences in test scores are usually not meaningful.

Reporting Test Results

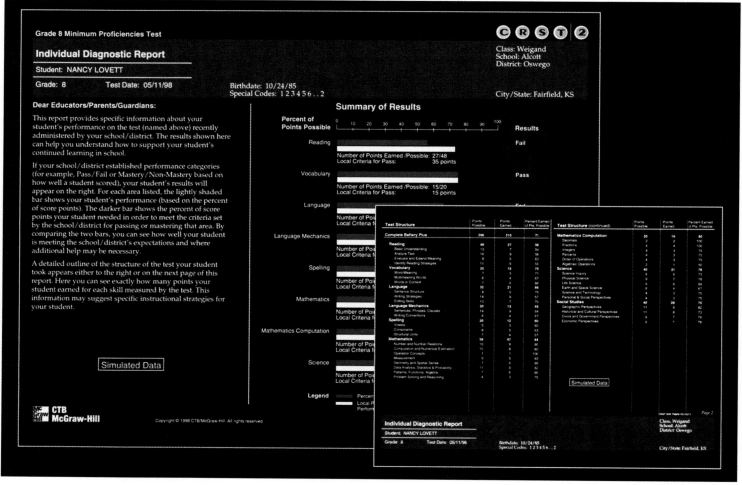

Figure 13.9

Example of a Student's Test Report

"How are her scores?"

Drawing by Koren: © 1987 The New Yorker Magazine, Inc.

Some test reports include **percentile bands,** *a range of scores (rather than a single score) around a mean value expressed in percentiles, such as 75th to 85th percentile.* The Metropolitan Achievement Tests use percentile bands in reporting scores. A percentile rank of 6 to 8 points or a 2- to 5-month grade-equivalence difference between two students rarely indicates any meaningful difference in achievement.

When considering information from a standardized test, don't evaluate it in isolation. Evaluate it in conjunction with other information you know about the student and your classroom instruction (Airasian, 1997). Most manuals that accompany standardized tests warn against overinterpretation.

Communicating Test Results to Parents

Teachers often present and interpret students' scores on standardized tests during a parent-teacher conference.

At this point, we have discussed a number of ideas about the teacher's role in standardized testing. A review of these ideas is presented in summary table 13.3.

TEACHING STRATEGIES
For Communicating Test Results to Parents

Here are some good strategies for communicating test results to parents (McMillan, 1997):

1. *Don't report the test scores in isolation.* Report the scores in the context of the student's overall work and performance on other classroom assessments. This will help keep parents from placing too much importance on a score from a single standardized test. Show them other examples of the student's work to support your conclusions about the student's strengths and weaknesses.
2. *Try to use easy-to-understand language when you describe the student's test results to parents.* Don't get caught up in using obscure test language. Be able to report the information in your own words.
3. *Let parents know that the scores are approximate rather than absolute.* You might say something about how various internal and external factors can affect students' test scores.
4. *Percentile scores or bands are the easiest set of scores for parents to understand.*
5. *Prior to the conference, spend some time familiarizing yourself with the student's test report.* Make sure you know how to interpret each score you report to parents. It is not a good idea just to show parents the numbers on a test report. You will need to summarize what the scores mean.
6. *Be ready to answer questions parents might have about their child's strengths, weaknesses, and progress.*
7. *Instead of talking "to" or lecturing parents, talk "with" them in a discussion format.* After you have described a test result, invite them to ask questions that will help you to further clarify for them what the test results mean.

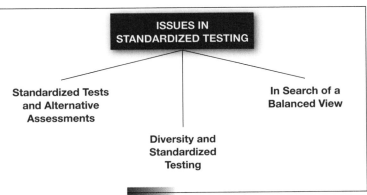

What are some good strategies that teachers can use to communicate test results to parents?

Issues in Standardized Testing

As we have already mentioned, standardized testing is controversial. One debate concerns how standardized tests stack up against alternative methods of assessment. Another is about whether standardized tests discriminate against ethnic minority students and students from low-income backgrounds.

Standardized Tests and Alternative Assessments

Alternative assessments include various performance assessments, such as oral presentations, real-world problems, projects, and portfolios (systematic and organized collections of the student's work that demonstrate the student's skills and accomplishments). Which is the best way to assess student performance—standardized tests that mainly rely on multiple-choice questions or alternative assessments? Grant Wiggins (1992) has argued that performance tests should be used instead of standardized tests that mainly include multiple-choice questions or at least be used as part of the student's total assessment. He concluded that performance assessment is

SUMMARY TABLE 13.3
The Teacher's Role

Concept	Processes/Related Ideas	Characteristics/Description
Preparing Students to Take Standardized Tests	Strategies	• Make sure that students have good test-taking skills. • Also communicate a positive attitude about the test to students. • Coaching programs to improve students' test scores have had minimal effects.
Administering Standardized Tests	Its Nature	• Most standardized testing manuals spell out how to set up the testing room, what to do when students take the test, how to distribute the test and answer sheets, and how to time the tests. • In administering the test, it is important to follow the script word for word.
Understanding and Interpreting Test Results	Understanding Descriptive Statistics	• Descriptive statistics are math procedures used to describe and summarize data in a meaningful way. • A frequency distribution is a listing of scores from highest to lowest along with the number of times each score appears. • A histogram is one way that frequency distribution information can be presented. • Measures of central tendency include the mean, median, and mode. • Measures of variability include the range and standard deviation. • The normal curve is a bell-shaped curve in which most scores cluster around the mean. A normal curve is symmetrical and incorporates information about both the mean and the standard deviation.
	Interpreting Test Results	• A raw score is the number of items a student gets right on a test, which typically is not as useful as many other types of scores. • Percentile-rank scores reveal the percentage of the distribution that lies at or below the score. • Stanine scores describe a student's performance on a 9-point scale ranging from 1 to 9. • Grade-equivalent scores are expressed in terms of the grade level of students who perform at that level. • Standard scores are expressed as a deviation from the mean and involve the concept of standard deviation (z-scores and T-scores are examples of standard scores). • Avoid overinterpreting test results. A good strategy is to think of a score not as a single score but as being located in a band or general range. Don't evaluate standardized test results in isolation from other information about the student, such as classroom performance and the nature of instruction.
Communicating Test Results to Parents	Its Nature	• This often occurs during a parent-teacher conference. • Some good strategies include not reporting scores in isolation from other information about the student, using easy-to-understand language, communicating that test scores are approximate rather than absolute, studying the test results and preparing for the conference, being ready to answer parents' questions, and talking "with" rather than "to" them.

more meaningful, involves higher-level thinking skills, and fits better with current educational reform that emphasizes constructivist and social constructivist learning.

As we indicated earlier in the chapter, an increasing number of states recognize the importance of using more than just a traditional standardized test that relies on multiple-choice items. More states are including performance and portfolio assessment in their evaluation of students' progress, even though these are more time-

DIVERSITY AND EDUCATION

Mirror, Mirror on the Wall, Which is the Fairest Test of All?

The title for this box recently was used to introduce a discussion of whether portfolio assessment is more equitable than standardized tests for ethnic minority students, students from impoverished backgrounds, and females (Supovitz & Brennan, 1997). Supovitz and Brennan (1997) compared the traditional standardized test results and portfolio assessment performance of first- and second-grade students in a medium-size urban setting. They analyzed the relative contribution of students' background characteristics to their performance. If the portfolio assessments are more equitable than standardized tests, the gap in scores between high-income White students and low-income minority students should be reduced.

At both grade levels, the gap in performance between African American and White students was reduced by about one-half in portfolio assessment when compared with scores on standardized tests. Thus, portfolio assessment significantly reduced the gap between African American and White students' performance but did not eliminate it. Interestingly, a gender gap appeared, with girls outperforming boys by a larger margin on portfolio assessment than on assessment with standardized tests. Portfolio assessment had no detectable impact, on the average, on the relative performance of students from low-income backgrounds or students in the English language learning program. These students performed consistently worse than their counterparts on both portfolio assessment and standardized tests.

In sum, although portfolio assessment holds considerable promise by focusing instruction on higher-level thinking skills, providing useful feedback to teachers about students' thinking skills, and emphasizing real-world problem solving, in this study portfolio assessment had mixed effects on equalizing the differences in performance of students with different backgrounds and experience.

consuming and costly. When alternative assessments are used, it is important that they meet acceptable standards for validity, reliability, administration, and scoring.

Ronald Hambleton (1996) concluded that multiple-choice standardized testing is not likely to be completely abandoned in the foreseeable future, but he predicts that we will see more of a balance in assessment with inclusion of writing tasks, performance tests, computer simulation exercises, hands-on projects, and portfolios of work. We will say much more about alternative assessments in the next chapter.

Diversity and Standardized Testing

In chapter 4, "Individual Variations," we discussed issues related to diversity and assessment ◀‖‖ p. 136. For example, we indicated that African American and Latino students score, on the average, about 15 points below White students on standardized intelligence tests. This gap was attributed to environmental rather than heredity factors. In addition, African American, Latino, and Native American students show the lowest proficiency levels, on the average, of all ethnic groups on mathematics, science, reading, writing, history, geography, and literature on the report cards based on the National Assessment of Educational Progress (Riley, 1997).

A special concern that we discussed in earlier chapters is cultural bias in tests and the importance of creating culturally responsive tests for diagnostic and instructional purposes (Bigelow, 1999; Gay, 1997; Sandoval & others, 1999). Because of the potential for cultural bias in standardized tests, it is important to assess students using a variety of methods. As we indicated earlier, many assessment experts believe that performance and portfolio assessments reduce some of the inequity that characterizes standardized tests for ethnic minority students and students from low-income backgrounds. To read further about whether portfolio assessment is more equitable for students from ethnic minority and other backgrounds, see the Diversity and Education box.

People do not have equal talents. But all individuals should have an equal opportunity to develop their talents.

John F. Kennedy
U.S. President, 20th Century

ᏚUMMARY ᏟABLE 13.4
Issues in Standardized Testing

Concept	Processes/Related Ideas	Characteristics/Description
Standardized Tests and Alternative Assessments	The Controversy	• When used correctly, standardized tests have value. However, they are only part of the assessment picture and they do have limits. • They are helpful in providing comparability information from a "big picture" perspective. • It is important for teachers to scrupulously avoid any misuses of tests or test results and to educate themselves about tests so they understand their capabilities and limitations. • Multiple-choice standardized testing is not likely to completely go away, but we are likely to see an increased balance in assessment that includes more writing tasks, performance assessments, computer simulation exercises, hands-on projects, and portfolios of work.
Diversity and Standardized Testing	Its Nature	• African American, Latino, and Native American students perform more poorly than White students on many standardized tests. • Cultural bias is of special concern in standardized testing. • Many assessment experts believe that performance assessments have the potential to reduce inequities in testing.
In Search of a Balanced View	Its Nature	• Controversy swirls about which assessments are best—standardized tests or alternative assessments such as performance and portfolio assessments. • Some experts argue that performance assessments are more meaningful, involve higher-level thinking skills, and fit better with current educational reform that emphasizes constructivist and social constructivist learning. • An increasing number of states include alternative assessments in their standardized assessment of students. • When alternative assessments are used, they should meet acceptable standards of validity, reliability, administration, and scoring.

In Search of a Balanced View

Blaine Worthen and Vicki Spandel (1991) offered a helpful perspective on the standardized test debate. They argued that when used correctly, standardized tests do have value but provide only part of the assessment picture and do have limits. Worthen and Spandel believe that standardized tests are especially helpful in providing information about comparability from a "big picture" perspective. Teachers cannot reliably compare their students' performance with that of students in another classroom down the hall and then make decisions about instruction based on that limited local comparison. Standardized tests can provide better information about "big picture" questions: Are my fourth-grade students learning basic math? Can my seventh-grade students read at a predefined level of competency?

Worthen and Spandel urge teachers to scrupulously avoid any misuses of tests or test results and to educate themselves about tests so that they understand their capabilities and limitations, not asking tests to do more than they can or are intended to do. They also say a standardized test should be only one of a number of assessments used to evaluate students.

At this point we have explored many ideas about issues in standardized testing. A review of these ideas is presented in summary table 13.4. In the next chapter, we will examine a broader range of strategies for assessing student's learning.

Equity and Excellence in Standards and Assessments

Chapter Review

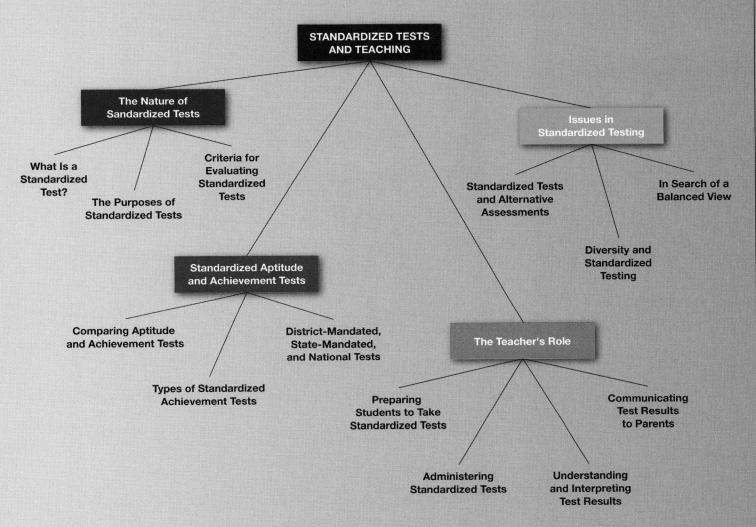

TO OBTAIN A DETAILED REVIEW OF THIS CHAPTER, STUDY THESE FOUR SUMMARY TABLES:

Key Terms

standardized test 466
minimum competency
   tests 467
high-stakes testing 467
norm group 467
national norms 467
special group norms 467
local norms 467
reliability 467
test-retest reliability 468
alternate forms reliability 468

split-half reliability 468
validity 468
content validity 468
criterion validity 468
concurrent validity 468
predictive validity 468
construct validity 469
aptitude test 469
achievement test 469
survey battery 470
diagnostic testing 471

descriptive statistics 479
frequency distribution 479
histogram 479
measure of central
   tendency 479
mean 479
median 480
mode 480
measures of variability 481
range 481

standard deviation 481
normal distribution 483
raw score 483
percentile rank score 483
stanine score 484
grade-equivalent score 484
standard score 484
z-score 484
T-score 484
percentile bands 486

Educational Psychology Checklist
STANDARDIZED TESTS AND TEACHING

How much have you learned since the beginning of the chapter? Use the following statements to help you review your knowledge and understanding of the chapter material. First, read the statement and mentally or briefly on paper demonstrate that you can outline and discuss the relevant information.

_____ I know what a standardized test is and can describe the purposes of standardized testing.
_____ I can describe the criteria that are used to evaluate standardized tests.
_____ I can discuss aptitude and achievement tests.
_____ I know about various aspects of district-mandated, state-mandated, and national tests.
_____ I can describe a teacher's role in preparing students for taking standardized tests and the teacher's role in administering them.

_____ I understand measures of central tendency.
_____ I can discuss measures of variability.
_____ I know what a normal curve is.
_____ I feel confident in interpreting test results.
_____ I am aware of some good strategies for reporting test scores to parents.
_____ I know about the nature of diversity and standardized testing.
_____ I can describe what is involved in taking a balanced view of standardized testing.

For any items that you did not check off, go back and locate the relevant material in the chapter. Review the material until you feel you can check off the item. You also may want to use this checklist later in preparing for an exam.

Adventures for the Mind

Now that you have a good knowledge and under-standing of the chapter, complete the following exercises to expand your thinking about the chapter's topics.

- Following are criticisms that have been leveled at state-mandated and national standardized tests in recent years. Evaluate each criticism by stating whether you agree with it, then explain your reasoning:
  a. High-stakes multiple-choice tests will lead to a dumbing-down of teaching and learning.
  b. Establishing national tests will undermine new educational programs at the state and local levels that focus on improving learning and developing more effective assessments.
  c. State and national tests won't tell teachers anything they don't already know.
- Create a frequency distribution and histogram for the following scores: 98, 96, 94, 94, 92, 90, 90, 88, 86, 86, 86, 82, 80, 80, 80, 80, 80, 78, 76, 72, 70, 68, 64
- Using the set of 23 scores above, calculate the mean, median, and mode of the scores. Again using the 23 scores above, compute the range and standard deviation for the scores.
- Draw a normal curve in which the standard deviation is small and one in which the standard deviation is large.

Taking It to the Net

1. The results of the Third International Mathematics and Science Study (TIMSS) (http://timssonline.cse.ucla.edu/) indicated that U.S. children scored lower than children in many other nations. Are U.S. students less educated? Could there be a problem with the TIMSS data?
2. Standardized tests that were designed to measure student achievement are now being used to assess the quality of a student's education, including the teacher, principal, school, and school system. Is this use of standardized achievement test scores valid? Why, or why not?
3. You have a student with a disability who is preparing to take a standardized college entrance exam. What type of modifications is she allowed? Who should she contact?

   Connect to http://www.mhhe.com/socscience/psychology/santedu/ttnet.htm to find the answers!

Case Studies

Case 1 *Elaine Adams:* Elaine, a student teacher near the end of her assignment, observes her cooperating teacher give the students help while administering the district-mandated standardized tests. Elaine is not sure how to deal with the situation.

Case 2 *Melinda Grant:* Melissa has developed an innovative curriculum, and she is concerned because another teacher continually warns her that she will be held responsible if her students have inadequate end-of-year standardized test scores.

Chapter 14

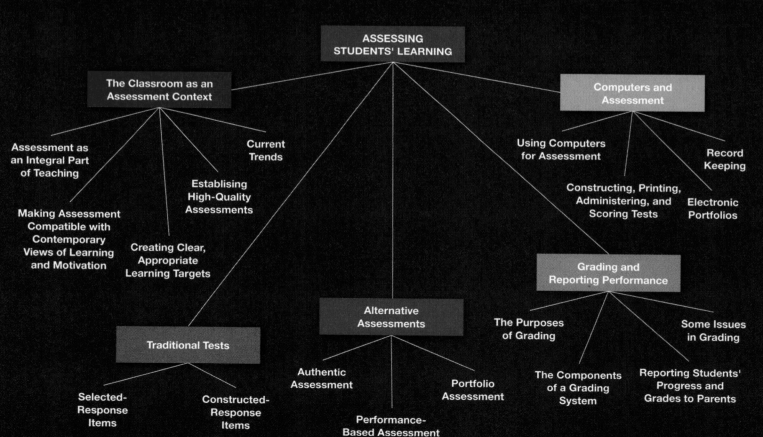

ASSESSING STUDENTS' LEARNING

The Classroom as an Assessment Context

Assessment as an Integral Part of Teaching

Making Assessment Compatible with Contemporary Views of Learning and Motivation

Creating Clear, Appropriate Learning Targets

Current Trends

Establising High-Quality Assessments

Traditional Tests

Selected-Response Items

Constructed-Response Items

Alternative Assessments

Authentic Assessment

Performance-Based Assessment

Portfolio Assessment

Computers and Assessment

Using Computers for Assessment

Constructing, Printing, Administering, and Scoring Tests

Record Keeping

Electronic Portfolios

Grading and Reporting Performance

The Purposes of Grading

The Components of a Grading System

Some Issues in Grading

Reporting Students' Progress and Grades to Parents

Preview

Assessment of students' learning has recently generated considerable interest in educational circles. This interest has focused on such issues as the extent to which teachers should incorporate national and state development of "standards" in their teaching and assessment, as well as the degree to which teachers should use traditional tests or alternative assessments such as performance assessments. These are some of the questions we will explore in this chapter:

- How can assessment be made an integral part of teaching?
- What does it take to construct high-quality assessments?
- What are traditional tests like?
- What is authentic assessment?
- What is performance assessment?
- What is portfolio assessment?
- What are some good strategies for grading and reporting students' performance?
- How can computers be used in assessment and grading?

Teaching Stories
Vicky Farrow

Vicky Farrow is a former high school teacher who currently teaches educational psychology at Lamar University in Beaumont, Texas. She reflects on the ongoing process of assessment in the classroom and what to do and what not to do in constructing tests:

Assessment is an ongoing process. It is more than giving tests or assigning grades. It is everything a teacher does to determine if his or her students are learning. It may be asking students questions, monitoring their understanding as you circulate through the room during an activity, and noticing the frown on the face of a student who is confused or the smile of a student who has grasped the concept. Without this ongoing assessment, a teacher can never know if instruction is effective or needs to be modified. Done effectively, assessment provides a teacher with valuable information for providing an optimal learning experience for every child.

When you do give tests, every item on a test should relate back to the objectives. This helps the teacher avoid "gotcha" questions—those questions that may be trivial or unimportant to the intended learning outcomes. If it is not important enough to spend valuable class time on, it probably is not important enough to test the student over.

Be careful that test items are written at an appropriate level. The test should be testing a student's understanding of the unit content, not their reading skills (unless, of course, it is reading skills that are being tested). I remember as a student taking an analogies test that was intended to assess my ability to identify relationships between concepts. However, the vocabulary was so difficult that I missed some items because the words were too difficult for that level of schooling.

If an essay question is on an examination, write a model answer *before* grading the exam. Would you make your answer key for a multiple-choice test from a student's paper, wrong answers and all? Of course not! It does not make any more sense to do that with an essay item. If an essay item is well written and a model answer is constructed in advance, the grade a student receives will more accurately reflect the level of that student's understanding of the material being tested.

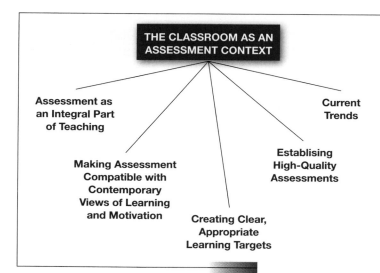

THE CLASSROOM AS AN ASSESSMENT CONTEXT

Assessment as an Integral Part of Teaching

Making Assessment Compatible with Contemporary Views of Learning and Motivation

Creating Clear, Appropriate Learning Targets

Establising High-Quality Assessments

Current Trends

Integrating Assessment and Learning

The Classroom as an Assessment Context

When you think of assessment, what comes to mind? Probably tests. However, as we discuss the classroom as an assessment context, you will discover that contemporary views of assessment involve far more than tests.

Assessment as an Integral Part of Teaching

Teachers spend more time in assessment than you might imagine. In one analysis, they spend 20 to 30 percent of their professional time dealing with assessment matters (Stiggins, 1987). With so much time spent on assessment, it is important that it be done well. Assessment expert James McMillan (1997, 2000) believes that competent teachers frequently evaluate their students in relation to learning goals and adapt their instruction accordingly. Assessment not only documents what students know and can do, but also affects their learning and motivation. These ideas represent a change in the way assessment is viewed, away from the concept that assessment is an isolated outcome done only after instruction is finished and toward the concept of integrating assessment with instruction.

Think of integrating instruction and assessment in terms of three time frames: pre-instruction, during instruction, and post-instruction. The Standards for Teacher Competence in Educational Assessment, developed jointly in the early 1990s by the American Federation of Teachers, National Council on Measurement in Education, and National Education Association, describe the teacher's responsibility for student assessment in these three time frames (see figure 14.1).

Pre-Instruction Assessment   Imagine that you want to know how well your students can solve a certain level of math problem before you begin formal instruction on a more advanced level. You might look at your students' prior grades and their scores on standardized math tests, and also observe your students for several days to see how well they perform. These assessments are designed to answer this question: "What math skills are my students able to demonstrate?" If the results of your assessment indicate that students lack prerequisite knowledge and skills, you will decide to begin with materials that are less difficult for them. If they do extremely well on your pre-instruction assessment, you will move your level of instruction to a higher plane. Without this pre-instructional assessment, you run the risk of having a class that is overwhelmed (your instruction level will be too advanced) or bored (your instruction level will be too low).

Much of pre-instructional assessment is informal observation. In the first several weeks of school, you will have numerous opportunities to observe students' characteristics and behavior. Be sensitive to whether a student is shy or outgoing, has a good or weak vocabulary, speaks and listens effectively, is considerate of others or is egocentric, engages in appropriate or inappropriate behavior, and so on. Also focus on the student's nonverbal behavior for cues that might reveal nervousness, boredom, frustration, or a lack of understanding. For example, a student might say that things are fine but come into class every day with a downturned head and sad look.

After you have made informal observations, you will need to interpret them. That is, what does the student's behavior mean? Are a downturned head and saddened look clues to a lack of self-esteem regarding academic skills or possibly stressful circumstances at home? Are the student's poor listening skills due to a lack of motivation?

Another type of pre-instructional assessment involves structured exercises for observing students in a specific context. On the first day of class I always take 5 or 10 minutes to tell students about myself and my interests. After I have finished giving students an idea of who I am, I ask each of them to state their name and tell several things about themselves. This gives me an opportunity to find out which students are shy and which ones are extraverted, how effectively they can speak, how nervous they get when speaking to the class, as well as to learn about their identity, which might include how large their family is and what their interests are. An alternative strategy is to get students to write this information on index cards, which can also provide information about their writing skills. A good strategy is to keep such pre-instructional assessments as nonthreatening as possible and not assign grades to them.

In pre-instructional assessments, guard against developing expectations that will distort your perception of a student. It is virtually impossible not to have expectations about students. Because teacher expectations are potentially powerful influences on student learning, some teachers don't even want to look at a student's prior grades or standardized test scores. Whether you do or do not examine such assessment information, work on making your expectations realistic. If you err, err in the direction of having overly positive expectations for students.

A good strategy is to treat your initial impressions of students as hypotheses to be confirmed or modified by subsequent observation and information. Some of your initial observations will be accurate, others will need to be revised. As you try to get a sense of what your students are like, refrain from believing hearsay information, from making enduring judgments based on only one or two observations, and from labeling the student (Airasian, 1997).

Some teachers also administer textbook review or diagnostic pretests in subject areas to examine a student's level of knowledge and skill. And many schools are increasingly collecting samples of students' work in portfolios, which can accompany a student from grade to grade. The portfolios provide teachers with a far more concrete, less biased set of information to evaluate than other teachers' hearsay comments. We will describe portfolios in much greater depth later in the chapter.

Activities Before Instruction

Understand students' cultural backgrounds, interests, skills, and abilities as they apply across a range of learning domains and/or subject areas

Understand students' motivation and interests in specific class content

Clarify and articulate the performance outcomes expected of students

Plan instruction for individuals or groups of students

Activities During Instruction

Monitor students' progress toward instructional goals

Identify gains and difficulties students are experiencing

Adjust instruction

Give specific and appropriate feedback

Motivate students to learn

Judge the extent to which students are attaining instructional outcomes

Activities After Instruction
(Lesson, Class, Semester, Grade)

Describe the extent to which each student has reached both short-term and long-term instructional goals

Communicate strengths and weaknesses, based on assessment results, to parents or guardians

Record and report assessment results for school-level analysis, evaluation, and decision making

Evaluate the effectiveness of instruction

Examine the effectiveness of the curriculum and materials

Figure **14.1**

A Teacher's Responsibility for Assessment Before, During, and After Instruction

Assessment During Instruction **Formative assessment** *is assessment during the course of instruction rather than after it is completed.* Your ongoing observation and monitoring of students' learning while you teach provides you with information about what to do next. Assessment during instruction helps you set your teaching at a level that challenges students and stretches their thinking. It also helps you to detect which students need your individual attention.

Assessment during instruction takes place at the same time as you make many other decisions about what to do, say, or ask next to keep the classroom running smoothly and help students actively learn (Airasian, 1997). It requires listening to student answers, observing other students for indications of understanding or confusion, framing the next question, and scanning the class for possible misbehavior (Doyle, 1986). At the same time, the teacher must be aware of the pace of the activity, the sequence of choosing students to answer, the relevance and quality of the answers, and the logical development of the content. When the class is divided into small groups, the teacher might need to monitor and regulate several different activities simultaneously.

Oral questions are an especially important aspect of assessment during instruction. Some teachers ask as many as 300 to 400 questions a day, not only to stimulate students' thinking and inquiry but also to assess their knowledge and skill level (Christensen, 1991; Morgan & Saxton, 1991). You might recall from our discussion of using questions in chapter 10, "Planning, Instruction, and Technology," that it is important to include thinking-based questioning in your instruction. Thinking-based questions follow from Bloom's Cognitive Taxonomy of Instructional Objectives, which was discussed in chapter 10. Such questions can elicit the following sorts of thinking from students:

- Application (for example, ask students to give a real-world example of a principle)
- Analysis (for example, ask a student to analyze which statements are true and which are false)
- Synthesis (for example, ask a student to support a conclusion with facts)
- Evaluation (for example, ask a student to judge what the main things are that need to be changed in the classroom)

Remember, when you ask questions, to avoid overly broad, general questions, involve the whole class in questioning instead of calling on the same students all of the time, allow sufficient "wait time" after asking a question, probe students' responses with follow-up questions, and highly value students' own questions (Airasian, 1997).

Post-Instruction Assessment   **Summative assessment** *is assessment after instruction is finished.* Assessment after instruction provides information about how well your students have mastered the material, whether students are ready for the next unit, what grades students should be given, what comments you should make to parents, and how you should adapt your instruction (McMillan, 1997, 2000). It is after instruction that more formal types of assessment are often used.

Making Assessment Compatible with Contemporary Views of Learning and Motivation

Rethinking Assessment and Educational Reform

Throughout this book, when talking about how to teach, we have emphasized the importance of considering students' learning and motivation. We have encouraged you to view students as active learners who discover and construct meaning; set goals, plan, and reach goals; associate and link new information with existing knowledge in meaningful ways; think reflectively, critically, and creatively; develop self-monitoring skills; have positive expectations for learning and confidence in their skills; are enthusiastically and internally motivated to learn; apply what they learn to real-world situations; and communicate effectively.

Assessment plays an important role in effort, engagement, and performance. Your informal observations can provide information about how motivated students are to study different subjects. If you have a good relationship with the student, direct oral questioning in a private conversation can often produce valuable insight about the student's motivation. In thinking about how assessment and motivation are linked, ask yourself if your assessments will encourage students to become more meaningfully involved in the subject matter and more intrinsically motivated to study the topic. Assessments that are challenging but fair should increase students' enthusiasm for learning. Assessments that are too difficult will lower students' self-esteem and self-efficacy, as well as raise their anxiety. Assessing students with measures that are too easy will bore them and not motivate them to study hard enough.

Susan Brookhart (1997) recently developed a model of how classroom assessment helps motivate students. She argues that every classroom environment hosts a series of repeated assessment events. In each assessment event, the teacher communicates with the students through assignments, activities, and feedback about performance. Students respond according to their perceptions of these learning opportunities and their perceived efficacy of accomplishing the tasks. Brookhart believes that this view of classroom assessment suggests that teachers should evaluate students using a variety of performances, especially performances that are meaningful to students.

Similarly, many other classroom assessment experts argue that if you believe that motivated, active learning is an important goal of instruction, you should create alternative assessments that are quite different from traditional tests, which don't evaluate how students construct knowledge and understanding, set and reach goals, and think critically and creatively (Brookhart, 1997; McMillan, 1997; Stiggins, 1997). Later in the chapter we will explore how alternative assessments can be used to examine these aspects of students' learning and motivation.

Integrating Assessment and Instruction

Creating Clear, Appropriate Learning Targets

Tying assessment to current views on learning and motivation also involves developing clear, appropriate learning goals or targets. A **learning target** *consists of what students should know and be able to do.* It is important to establish criteria for judging whether students have attained the learning target (McMillan, 1997). Figure 14.2 provides some examples of learning targets. The establishment of learning targets is compatible with the emphasis on instructional objectives that was discussed in chapter 10.

Among the types of learning targets that you can weave through instruction and assessment are these (Stiggins & Conklin, 1992):

- *Knowledge.* This involves what students need to know to solve problems and perform skills. Knowledge gives students the ability to master substantive subject matter.
- *Reasoning/thinking.* An important learning goal is not just for students to acquire knowledge, but to be able to think about the knowledge. For example, in chapter 8, "The Cognitive Information-Processing Approach and Teaching," we discussed

---

Students will be able to explain how various cultures are different and how cultures influence people's beliefs and lives by answering orally a comprehensive set of questions about cultural differences and their effects.

Students will demonstrate their knowledge of the parts of a plant by filling in words or a diagram for all parts studied.

Students will demonstrate their understanding of citizenship by correctly identifying whether previously unread statements about citizenship are true or false. A large number of items is used to sample most of the content learned.

Students will be able to explain why the American Constitution is important by writing an essay that indicates what would happen if we abolished our Constitution. The papers would be graded holistically, looking for evidence of reasons, knowledge of the Constitution, and organization.

Students will show that they know the difference between components of sentences by correctly identifying verbs, adverbs, adjectives, nouns, and pronouns in seven of eight long, complex sentences.

Students will be able to multiply fractions by correctly computing eight of ten fraction problems. The problems are new to the students; some are similar to "challenge" questions in the book.

Students will be able to use their knowledge of addition, subtraction, division, and multiplication to solve word problems that are similar to those used in the sixth-grade standardized test.

Students will demonstrate their understanding of how visual art conveys ideas and feelings by correctly indicating, orally, how examples of art communicate ideas and feelings.

Figure **14.2**
Examples of Unit Learning Targets

such aspects of thinking as problem solving, inductive and deductive reasoning, strategies, and critical thinking.

- *Products.* Products are samples of students' work. Essays, term papers, oral reports, and science reports reflect students' ability to use knowledge and reasoning.
- *Affect.* Affective targets are students' emotions, feelings, and values. For example, recall our discussion of emotional intelligence in chapter 4, "Individual Variations," in which we described the importance of helping students develop emotional self-awareness (such as understanding the causes of their feelings), managing emotions (such as managing anger), reading emotions (such as being good at listening to what other people say), and handling relationships (such as being competent at solving relationship problems). However, including affective goals in assessment is controversial.

Assessment Resources

Establishing High-Quality Assessments

Another important goal for the classroom as an assessment context is achieving high-quality assessment (Lester, Lambdin, & Preston, 1997; Phye, 1997). Assessment reaches a high level of quality when it yields reliable, valid, and useful information about students' performance. High-quality assessments also are fair (McMillan, 1997). Reliability and validity are concerned with the consistency and accuracy of the inferences teachers make about students from assessment information (Payne, 1997).

Reliability   Remember from chapter 13 that **reliability** *is the extent to which an assessment produces a consistent, reproducible measure of performance. Reliable measures are stable, dependable, and relatively free from errors of measurement* ◀‖‖ p. 467. An important point about reliability is that it does not involve the appropriateness of the assessment information. The role of reliability is to determine how consistently an assessment measures what it is measuring. If a teacher gives students three tests in a history class over a period of several months and the students perform in a consistent manner on the tests, this indicates that the assessments were reliable. However, the consistency in students' performance (with high scorers being high across all three tests, middle scorers performing similarly across the tests, and low scorers doing poorly on all three tests) says nothing about whether the tests actually measured what they were designed to measure (for example, being an accurate, representative sample of questions that measured the history content that had been taught). Thus, reliable assessments are not necessarily valid.

Reliability is reduced by errors in measurement. A student can have adequate knowledge and skill and still not perform consistently across several tests because of a number of factors. Internal factors can include health, motivation, and anxiety. External factors can include inadequate directions given by the teacher, ambiguously created items, poor sampling of information, and inefficient scoring of the student's responses. For example, a student might perform extremely well on the first test a teacher gives to assess the student's reading comprehension, but considerably lower on the second test in this domain. The student's lack of knowledge and skill could be the reason for the low reliability across the two assessments, but the low reliability also could be due to any number of measurement errors.

Validity   As we learned in chapter 13, **validity** *refers to the extent to which an assessment measures what it is intended to measure* ◀‖‖ p. 468. That traditional definition of validity focuses solely on whether an assessment, such as a test, measures what it is intended to measure. Does a test of intelligence really measure intelligence? Does a test on the American Revolution truly measure students' knowledge of that event?

In the context of classroom assessment, validity also includes how accurate and useful a teacher's inferences are about the assessment. **Inferences** *are conclusions that individuals draw from information.* You might infer that a test given to students on the American Revolution did a good job of assessing their *knowledge* of the American

Revolution but did a poor job of evaluating their ability to think critically about issues involved in the Revolution. Validity requires using the right kind of information to make a decision about a student, as well as judging whether the assessment was representative and fair.

You can't obtain information about everything a student learns. Thus, your assessment of a student will necessarily be a sample of the student's learning (Gredler, 1999; Weber, 1999). The most important source of information for validity in your classroom will be **content-related evidence,** *the extent to which the assessment reflects what you have been teaching* (McMillan, 1997).

If a test you give does a balanced job of sampling the full range of content that has been taught, and a student gets 80 percent of the answers right, it is reasonable to conclude that the student probably has learned about 80 percent of the content. On the other hand, if the test you give samples only part of the material and a student gets 80 percent right, the test results give no clear indication of how much of the overall content the student actually has learned.

Adequately sampling content is clearly an important goal of valid assessment (Mehrens, 1997; Trice, 2000). Use your best professional judgment when sampling content. Thus, you wouldn't want to use just one multiple-choice question to assess a student's knowledge of a chapter on geography. An increasing trend is to use multiple methods of assessment, which can provide a more comprehensive sampling of content. Thus, the teacher might assess students' knowledge of the geography chapter with some multiple-choice questions, several essay questions, and a project to complete. Always ask yourself whether your assessments of students are adequate samples of their performance. For example, is the completed science project all that you will use to grade the student, or will you include information about the student's effort and class participation in your grading?

Linking instruction and assessment leads to consideration of an important type of validity in the classroom called **instructional validity,** *the extent to which the assessment is a reasonable sample of what actually went on in the classroom* (Payne, 1997). For example, a classroom assessment should measure what the teacher taught and whether students had an adequate opportunity to learn the material. Consider a math class in which the teacher gives students a test on their ability to solve multiplication problems. For instructional validity, it is important that the teacher competently instructed students in how to solve the problems and gave students adequate opportunities to practice this skill.

An important strategy for validity in classroom assessment is to systematically link learning targets, content, instruction, and assessment (McMillan, 1997). Imagine that you are a science teacher and that one of your learning targets is to get students to think more critically and creatively in designing science projects. Ask yourself what content is important to achieve this learning target. For instance, will it help students to read biographies of famous scientists that include information about how they came up with their ideas? Also ask yourself what learning targets you will emphasize in instruction. For your target regarding students' science projects, it will be important for you to carry through in your instruction on the theme of helping students to think critically and creatively about science.

Fairness   High-quality classroom assessment is not only valid and reliable, but also fair (McMillan, 1997). Assessment is fair when all students have an equal opportunity to learn and demonstrate their knowledge and skill. Assessment is fair when teachers have developed appropriate learning targets, provided competent content and instruction to match those targets, and chosen assessments that reflect the targets, content, and instruction.

Fair assessments are unbiased and do not discriminate against certain students because of their ethnic background, gender, or disability. David Payne (1997) believes it is important to create a philosophy of **pluralistic assessment,** *which includes being responsive to cultural diversity in the classroom and at school.* This usually includes performance assessments during instruction and after instruction. Performance

DIVERSITY AND EDUCATION
Culturally Responsive Strategies
for Assessing Students

Geneva Gay (1997) recently evaluated the role of ethnicity and culture in assessment and recommended a number of culturally responsive strategies in assessing students. She advocates modifying (1) the Eurocentric nature of current U.S. instruction and achievement assessments, (2) using a wider variety of assessment methods that take into account the cultural styles of students of color, (3) evaluating students against their own records, and (4) assessing students in ways that serve culturally appropriate diagnostic and developmental functions.

Achievement assessments are designed to assess what students know, and presumably they reflect what has been taught in the classroom. Gay believes that although progress has been made in the last three decades to make school curricula more inclusive of ethnic and cultural diversity, most of the knowledge that is taught, and consequently the achievement assessments, continue to be Eurocentric. She points out that even mastery of skills tends to be transmitted through Eurocentric contexts. For example, achievement assessments might embed skills in contexts that are beyond the cultural backgrounds and life experiences of students from other parts of the world, as when a teacher asks immigrant students from the Caribbean who have never experienced snow to engage in problem solving by evaluating the challenges and dilemmas presented by a blizzard—the students might have the problem-solving skill to respond to this request, but their unfamiliarity with cold winters can interfere with their ability to perform the task effectively.

This does not mean that students of color should not be assessed or that they should not be expected to meet high achievement standards. They should. However, to avoid perpetuating educational inequality in assessment, these students should not be expected to demonstrate knowledge and skills in terms of contexts they are not familiar with. A good strategy is to use a variety of assessment methods to ensure that no single method gives an advantage to one ethnic group or another. These methods should include socioemotional measures as well as measures of academic content. Teachers also should carefully observe and monitor students' performance for verbal and nonverbal information in the assessment context.

Gay further argues that norm-referenced traditional assessments should be used only in conjunction with performance assessments. More emphasis should be given to evaluating students against their own records, with the focus being on improvement.

Gay also believes that assessment should always serve diagnostic and developmental functions that are culturally responsible. Narrative reports, developmental profiles, student-teacher-parent conferences, and anecdotal records should always be included in reporting students' progress.

assessments that can be used as part of pluralistic assessment include portfolios, projects, demonstrations, interviews, and oral presentations. This does not mean abandoning objective measurement in the form of multiple-choice exams and essay questions, but rather making sure that a variety of methods are used including at least some performance assessments. To read further about culturally responsive strategies in assessing students, see the Diversity and Education box.

Accomplishments have no color.

Leontyne Price
American Opera Star, 20th Century

Current Trends

Following are some current trends in classroom assessment (Hambleton, 1996):

- *Using at least some performance-based assessment.* Historically, classroom assessment has emphasized the use of **objective tests,** *such as multiple-choice, which have relatively clear, unambiguous scoring criteria.* In contrast, **performance assessments** *require students to write an essay, conduct an experiment, carry out a project, solve a real-world problem, create a portfolio, or perform some other task.* Performance assessments require students to create answers or products that demonstrate their knowledge or skill.
- *Examining higher-level cognitive skills.* Rather than assess only content knowledge as many objective tests do, a current trend is to evaluate a student's higher-level

cognitive skills, such as problem solving, critical thinking, decision making, drawing inferences, and strategic thinking.

- *Using multiple assessment methods.* In the past, assessment meant using a test—often a multiple-choice test—as the sole means of assessing a student. A current trend is to use multiple methods to assess students. Thus, a teacher might use any number of these methods: a multiple-choice test, an essay, an interview, a project, a portfolio, or even having students evaluate themselves. Multiple assessments provide a broader view of the child's learning and achievement than a single measure.

- *Having high performance standards.* Another trend is the demand for high performance standards, even "world-class" performance standards, for interpreting educational results. Some experts say that world-class performance standards are driving contemporary classroom assessment by providing goals or targets to attain (Taylor, 1994). However, as we saw in chapter 13, questions arise about who should set these standards and whether they should be set at all ◀▥ p. 474.

- *Using computers as part of assessment.* Traditionally, computers have been used to score tests, analyze test results, and report scores. Today, computers increasingly are being used to construct and administer tests, as well as to present different assessment formats to students in a multimedia environment. With coming advances in technology, expect assessment practices in the twenty-first century to be very different from our traditional paper-and-pencil tests (van der Linden, 1995).

Assessment and Issues in School Reform

Exploring Issues in Assessment

Trends in assessment also include emphasizing integrated rather than isolated skills, giving students more feedback, and making standards and criteria public rather than private and secretive. We will revisit many of these current trends later in this chapter.

At this point we have studied many ideas about the classroom as an assessment context. A review of these ideas is presented in summary table 14.1.

Traditional Tests

Traditional tests are typically paper-and-pencil tests in which students select from choices, calculate numbers, construct short responses, or write essays. Our coverage of traditional tests focuses on two main types of item formats in assessment: (1) selected-response items and (2) constructed-response items.

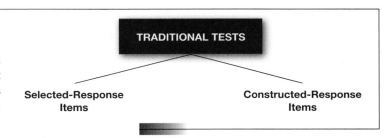

Selected-Response Items

Selected-response items *have an objective item format in which students' responses can be scored on quick inspection. A scoring key for correct responses is created and can be applied by an examiner or by a computer.* True/false, multiple-choice, and matching items are the most widely used types of items in selected-response tests. We also will describe several other recently developed objective-item formats.

Constructing Tests

True/False Items   A true/false item asks a student to mark whether a statement is *true or false*. For example:

Montpelier is the capital of Vermont.   True   False

The ease with which true/false items can be constructed has a potential drawback. Teachers sometimes take statements directly from a text or modify them slightly when making up true/false items. Avoid this practice, because it tends to encourage rote memorization with little understanding of the material.

The strengths and limitations of true/false items are described in figure 14.3.

SUMMARY TABLE 14.1
The Classroom as an Assessment Context

Concept	Processes/ Related Ideas	Characteristics/Description
Assessment as an Integral Part of Teaching	Pre-Instruction Assessment	• Much of this involves informal observations, which require interpretation. In informal observations, be sure to watch for nonverbal cues that will give you insight about the student. Structured exercises also can be used. • Guard against expectations that will distort your perception of a student. • Treat your initial perceptions as hypotheses to be confirmed or modified by subsequent observation and information. • Some teachers also administer pretests in subject areas. • An increasing trend is to examine students' learning portfolios from previous grades.
	Assessment During Instruction	• Formative assessment is assessment during instruction. This occurs at a fast pace and consists of ongoing observation and monitoring.
	Post-Instruction Assessment	• Summative assessment is assessment after instruction is finished. This usually involves more formal types of assessment, such as tests.
Making Assessment Compatible with Contemporary Views of Learning and Motivation	Its Nature	• This involves including these areas in assessment: active learning and constructing meaning; setting goals, planning, and reaching goals; thinking reflectively, critically, and creatively; having positive expectations for learning and confidence in skills; being motivated; applying what is learned to real-world situations; and communicating effectively. • Especially consider the role that assessment plays in effort, engagement, and performance. • Assessing such characteristics means using alternative assessments.
Creating Clear, Appropriate Learning Targets	Its Nature	• A learning target, much like an instructional objective, consists of what students should know and be able to do. • Learning targets might focus on knowledge, reasoning/thinking, products, or affect.
Establishing High-Quality Assessments	Defining Quality	• High quality in assessment means using assessments that are valid, reliable, useful, and fair.
	Reliability	• Reliability is the extent to which an assessment produces a consistent, reproducible measure of performance.
	Validity	• Validity is the extent to which an assessment measures what it is intended to measure, as well as how accurate and useful a teacher's inferences are. • The most important source of validity in the classroom is content-related evidence, the extent an assessment reflects what has been taught. • Adequately sampling content is an important aspect of validity. • Instructional validity is the extent to which an assessment is a reasonable sample of what went on in the classroom. • Validity is enhanced by the systematic linkage of learning targets, content, instruction, and assessment.
	Fairness	• Assessment is fair when all students have an equal opportunity to learn and demonstrate their knowledge and skills. • A pluralistic assessment philosophy also contributes to fairness.
Current Trends	Their Nature	• These include using at least some performance-based assessments, examining higher-level skills, using multiple assessment methods, having high performance standards, and using computers as a part of assessment. • Other trends focus on assessing an integration of skills, giving students considerable feedback, and making standards and criteria public.

TEACHING STRATEGIES
For Writing True/False Questions

Some good strategies for writing true/false items are (Gronlund, 1998):

1. *Include only one central idea in each statement.* Incorporating several ideas in a true/false statement usually should be avoided because it tends to confuse the student and the answer is likely to be influenced more by reading ability than learning.
   Example: The first item is better than the second.
   Montpelier is the capital of Vermont.
   Montpelier is the capital of Vermont, is a New England state, and has less than 50,000 inhabitants.
2. *Keep the statement short, and use simple vocabulary and sentence structure.*
   Example: The first item is better than the second.
   Montpelier is the capital of Vermont.
   The capital city of the state of Vermont is a small metropolis known as Montpelier.
3. *Word the statement so precisely that is can clearly be judged as true or false.* True statements should be true under all circumstances and yet free of qualifiers, such as *might* and *possible.* Vague terms such as *seldom, frequently,* and *often* should be avoided.
   Example: The first item is better than the second.
   Polls at the end of 1989 showed that a majority of Americans supported sending U.S. troops to Kuwait.
   A lot of people believed that the Gulf War might have been justified.
4. *Use negatives sparingly and avoid double negatives.*
   Example: The first item is better than the second.
   In the presence of high heat, oxygen bonds readily with hydrogen.
   In the presence of high heat, oxygen is not unlikely to bond with hydrogen.
5. *Avoid extraneous clues to the answer.* Statements that include absolutes such as *always, never, all, none,* and *only* tend to be false. Statements with qualifiers such as *usually, might,* and *sometimes* tend to be true. Either eliminate these verbal clues to correct answers or balance them between true and false items.
   Example: The first item is better than the second.
   Martin Luther King made important civil rights speeches.
   Martin Luther King never made an unimportant speech.

Strengths

1. The item is useful for outcomes where there are only two possible alternatives (e.g., fact or opinion, valid or invalid).
2. Less demand is placed on reading ability than in multiple-choice items.
3. A relatively large number of items can be answered in a typical testing period.
4. Scoring is easy, objective, and reliable.

Limitations

1. It is difficult to write items at a high level of knowledge and thinking that are free from ambiguity.
2. When a statement indicates correctly that a statement is false, that response provides no evidence that the student knows what is correct.
3. No diagnostic information is provided by the incorrect answers.
4. Scores are more influenced by guessing than with any other item type.

Figure 14.3
Strengths and Limitations of True/False Items

TEACHING STRATEGIES
For Writing Multiple-Choice Items

Some good strategies for writing high-quality multiple-choice items include (Gronlund, 1998; Haladyna, 1997; Linden, 1996; Sax & Newton, 1997):

1. *Write the stem as a question.*
2. *Give three or four possible alternatives from which to choose.*
3. *Construct stems and options that are stated positively when possible.* Elementary school students especially find negatives confusing. If you use the word *not* in the stem, *italicize* or <u>underline</u> it. For example,

   Which of the following cities is <u>not</u> in New England?
   a. Boston   b. Chicago   c. Montpelier   d. Providence

4. *Include as much of the item as possible in the stem, thus making the stem relatively long and the alternatives relatively short.* For example,

   Which U.S. president wrote the Gettysburg Address?
   a. Thomas Jefferson   b. Abraham Lincoln   c. James Madison   d. Woodrow Wilson

5. *Alternatives should grammatically match the stem so that no answers are grammatically wrong.* For example, the first item is better than the second:

   Orville and Wilbur Wright became famous because of which type of transportation?
   a. airplane   b. automobile   c. boat   d. train

   Orville and Wilbur Wright became famous because of an:
   a. airplane   b. automobile   c. boat   d. train

6. *Write items that have a defensible or correct or best option.* Unless you give alternative directions, students will assume that there is only one correct or best answer to an item.
7. *Vary the placement of the correct option.* Students who are unsure of an answer tend to select the middle options and avoid the extreme options. Alphabetizing response choices helps to avoid this writing flaw.
8. *Beware of cues from length of the options.* Correct answers tend to be longer than incorrect ones because of the need to include specifications and qualifications that make it true. Lengthen the distractors (incorrect responses) to approximately the same length as the correct answer.
9. *Don't expect students to make narrow distinctions among answer choices.* For example, the first item is better than the second:

   The freezing point of water is:
   a. 25°F   b. 32°F   c. 39°F   d. 46°F

   The freezing point of water is:
   a. 30°F   b. 31°F   c. 32°F   d. 33°F

10. *Do not overuse "None of the Above" and "All of the Above."* Also avoid using variations of "A and B," or "C and D but not A."
11. *Don't use the exact wording in a textbook when writing a question.* Weak students might recognize the correct answer but not really understand its meaning.

Multiple-Choice Items   A **multiple-choice item** *consists of two parts: the stem, plus a set of possible responses.* The stem is a question or statement, and it is followed by a set of possible answers from which to choose. Incorrect alternatives are called *distractors*. The student's task is to select the correct choice from among the distractors. Example:

What is the capital of Vermont?   (Stem)
  a. Portland   (Distractor)
  b. Montpelier   (Answer)
  c. Boston   (Distractor)
  d. Weston   (Distractor)

Writing Multiple-Choice Items

Scoring Multiple-Choice Items   Students below the fourth grade probably should answer questions on the test page rather than on a separate answer sheet. Young elementary school students tend to respond slowly and lose their place easily when they have to use a separate answer sheet (Sax & Newton, 1997). Using a separate answer sheet with older students often reduces scoring time because the answers usually can fit on only one page. Many school districts have commercially printed answer sheets that teachers can order for their classes. If you hand-score multiple-choice tests, consider preparing a scoring stencil by cutting or punching holes in the answer sheet in the locations of the correct answers.

For most classroom requirements, simply count the number of answers marked correctly. Some teachers penalize students for guessing by deducting for wrong answers, but assessment experts say that this probably is not worth the extra bother and frequently leads to mistakes in scoring (Sax & Newton, 1997).

Strengths and limitations of multiple-choice items are listed in figure 14.4.

Matching Items   Used by many teachers with younger students, matching requires students to connect one group of stimuli correctly with a second group of stimuli (Hambleton, 1996). Matching is especially well suited for assessing associations or links between two sets of information. In a typical matching format, a teacher places a list of terms on the left side of the page and a description or definition of the terms on the right side of the page. The student's task is to draw lines between the columns that correctly link terms with their definitions or descriptions. In another format, a space is left blank next to each term and the student writes in the correct number or letter of the description/definition. When using matching, limit the number of items to be matched to no more than 8 or 10. Many experts recommend using no more than 5 or 6 items per set (Linden, 1996).

Criticisms of matching-items assessments include these (Sax & Newton, 1997): (1) They tend to ask students to connect trivial information, and (2) most matching tasks require students to connect information they have memorized, although items can be constructed that measure more complex cognitive skills.

Other Objective Assessment Formats
Other objective or selected-response formats include audiovisuals and problem sets (Hambleton, 1996).

Using Audiovisuals to Set the Context   The audiovisual format takes advantage of the ease with which we now can create and show slides and videotapes. Students are presented with a problem in an audiovisual format and asked to make decisions about what is going on or how to solve the problem. The student selects answers from sets of options, just like in a paper-and-pencil multiple-choice test. The main advantages of this audiovisual format are that it can depict the real world and can be used to evaluate higher-level cognitive skills. The main drawbacks are the costs in time and money.

Problem Sets   **Problem sets** *involve writing two or more multiple-choice or objective short-answer items that are related to the same stimulus, such as an illustration, graph, or passage.*

Strengths

1. Both simple and complex learning outcomes can be measured.
2. The task is high structured and clear.
3. A broad sample of achievement can be measured.
4. Incorrect alternatives provide diagnostic information.
5. Scores are less influenced by guessing than true-false items.
6. Scoring is easy, objective, and reliable.

Limitations

1. Constructing good items is time consuming.
2. It is frequently difficult to find plausible distractors.
3. The multiple choice format is ineffective for measuring some types of problem solving and the ability to organize and express ideas.
4. Score can be influenced by reading ability.

Figure **14.4**
Strengths and Limitations of Multiple-Choice Items

To arrive at correct answers, students have to apply their knowledge and skills. For example, in math class, a graph might be displayed together with a series of multiple-choice items. In history or social studies, a map might be the stimulus. Some students report that the problem-set format seems more realistic than a set of discrete, independent items.

How Good Are Your Test Items?

One way to evaluate the quality of your test items is to conduct an item analysis of them. Two methods for doing this involve computing the difficulty level of the items and determining how well they discriminate among students who scored high and those who scored low on the entire test (Gronlund, 1998; Linn & Gronlund, 1999; Linden, 1996).

The **item difficulty index** *is the percentage of students who obtain the correct answer on an item.* To compute the difficulty index for each item, go through the following steps:

1. Rank-order the scores on the test from highest to lowest.
2. Identify the high-scoring group and the low-scoring group. With 30 students you might choose the 10 students who scored the highest on the test and the 10 students who scored the lowest. A good strategy is to select the top-scoring one-third of students and the bottom-scoring one-third of students.
3. Determine the percentage of high scorers and low scorers passing an item by adding a zero. In one example, 8 of 10 students in the high-scoring group correctly answered the item, which equals 80 percent; 4 of 10 students in the low-scoring group answered it correctly, which equals 40 percent.
4. To obtain the item difficulty index, add the percentage correct in the high and low groups and then divide by 2. Add a percent sign to the answer. Thus, in our example,

$$\frac{80 + 40}{2} = 60\%$$

When the item difficulty index is 75 percent or higher, the item is usually interpreted as easy in terms of difficulty level; when the index is 25 percent or less, the item is usually interpreted as hard, or low, in difficulty level. All other percentages—including the 60 percent in our example—are usually interpreted as average in difficulty level. Assessment experts recommend that most of the items be in the 40 to 60 percent range with only a few hard items (0 to 25 percent) or easy (75 to 100 percent) items.

The **item discrimination index** *reflects the item's ability to discriminate between individuals who scored high and those who scored low on the entire test.* Obtain the item discrimination index by subtracting the percentage correct in the low-scoring group from the percentage correct in the high-scoring group. Then, add a decimal point to the answer. Thus, in our example:

$$80 - 40 = .40$$

This item discrimination index has a decimal point, and its value ranges from 0 to 1.00. If the index is 0 to .19, there was little or no difference between the high- and low-scoring groups on the item; if the index is .20 to .39, the item discriminated moderately well between the high- and low-scoring groups; if the index is .40 or greater, the item strongly discriminated between the high- and low-scoring groups (which was the case for the item in our example: .40). If the item discrimination index is below .20, you likely will want to improve the item or eliminate it; if it is .20 to .39, you might want to keep the item but improve it; and if the index is .40 or above, you likely will want to keep the item as it is.

The first time you compute item difficulty and item discrimination indexes, they might seem more complicated than they really are. After you have done several of these, the computations should be easy for you to do.

Items Analysis

Constructed-Response Items

Constructed-response items *require students to write out information rather than select a response from a menu. Short-answer and essay items are the most commonly used forms of constructed-response items. In scoring, many constructed-response items require judgment on the part of the examiner.*

Short-Answer Items   A **short-answer item** *is a constructed-response format in which students are required to write a word, short phrase, or several sentences in response to a task.* For example, a student might be asked

> Who discovered penicillin?

The short-answer format allows recall and could provide a problem-solving assessment of a wide range of material. The disadvantages of short-answer questions are that they can require judgment to be scored and typically measure rote learning.

Sentence completion is a variation of the short-answer item, in which students express their knowledge and skill by completing a sentence. For example, a student might be asked to complete this sentence stem: *The name of the person who discovered penicillin is* _____.

Essays   **Essay items** *allow students more freedom of response to questions but require more writing than other formats. Essay items are especially good for assessing students' understanding of material, higher-level thinking skills, ability to organize information, and writing skills.* Here are some examples of high school essay questions:

> What are the strengths and weaknesses of a democratic approach to government?
> Describe the main themes of the novel you just read.
> Argue that the United States is a gender-biased nation.

Essay items can require students to write anything from a few sentences to much more extended responses. In some cases, teachers ask all students to answer the same essay question(s). In others, teachers let students select from a group of items the item(s) they want to write about, a strategy that makes it more difficult to compare students' responses across essays.

Suggestions for writing good essay items include these (Sax, 1997):

- *Specify limitations.* Be sure to inform students about the length of the desired answer and the weight that will be given to each item in determining scores or judgments.
- *Structure and clarify the task.* Make clear what they are supposed to write about. A poorly worded item is "Who was George Washington?" This could be answered in six words: "First president of the United States." In cases like this, ask yourself what more you want the student to tell. The following more-structured essay items would require more thinking on the part of the student:

  > Discuss several events in the life of George Washington that confirm or disprove the claim that "he never told a lie." Use the events to support a claim of your own about how truthful Washington was.
  > Describe two major accomplishments of Susan B. Anthony's political life. What was important about each accomplishment?

- *Ask questions in a direct way.* Don't get too tricky.

You might hear the term *rubric* used in regard to scoring students' responses on essays and other tests. *Rubric* is simply an alternative term for *scoring system*. Figure 14.5 lists some strengths and limitations of essay questions.

At this point we have discussed a number of ideas about traditional tests. A review of these ideas is presented in summary table 14.2.

Do not on any account attempt to write on both sides of the paper at once.

W. C. Sellar
English Author, 20th Century

Research and Assessment

TEACHING STRATEGIES
For Scoring Essays

Here are some good strategies for scoring essays (Sax & Newton, 1997):

1. *Devise a method by which you can score the essays without knowing which students wrote them.* You might do this by having students write their name beside a number on a separate sheet, then write only their number on the test. When you record the grade you can match up the student's number and name. This reduces the chance that your positive or negative expectations for the student will enter into your evaluation of the responses.

2. *Evaluate all answers to the same question together.* Read and score each student's response to one item before moving on to the next item. It is easier for you to remember the criteria for evaluating an answer to a single essay item than to remember the criteria for all essay items. Also, if you read all of one student's responses together, your evaluation of the first few items will tend to influence your evaluation of the remaining items.

3. *Decide on a policy for handling irrelevant or incorrect responses.* Some students try to bluff their way through essays. Other students write everything they know about a topic without taking the time to zero in on specifically what the item is asking for. Still other students might use poor grammar, misspell words, or write illegibly. Decide ahead of time whether and how much you will penalize such responses.

4. *If possible, reread papers before handing them back to students.* This helps you guard against any flaws or oversights in your scoring.

5. *Write comments on the paper.* An essay, especially a long one, with only a number or letter grade on it does not give adequate feedback to a student. And if you only circle or correct spelling errors and grammar, you are not giving students insight about the content of their essay responses. A good strategy is to write a number of brief comments at appropriate places throughout the essay, such as "Expand this idea more," "Unclear," or "Needs an example," in addition to making overall comments about the essay at its beginning or end. It is better to write comments throughout the essay than to make one or two minor comments in one part of the essay.

6. *Outline a plan for what constitutes a good or acceptable answer prior to administering or scoring students' responses* (McMillan, 1997). Essays can be scored holistically or analytically. **Holistic scoring** *means making an overall judgment about the student's answer and giving it a single number or letter.* You might make this judgment based on your overall impression of the essay or base it on several criteria that you have generated. Holistic scoring is often used when essays are long. **Analytic scoring** *means scoring various criteria separately, then, in most cases, adding up the points to produce an overall score for the essay.* Analytic scoring can be time consuming, so avoid having more than three or four criteria for an essay.

Strengths

1. **The highest level of learning outcomes (analysis, synthesis, evaluation) can be measured.**
2. **The integration and application of ideas can be emphasized.**
3. **Preparation time is usually less than for selection-type formats.**

Limitations

1. **Achievement may not be adequately sampled due to the time needed to answer each question.**
2. **It can be difficult to relate essay responses to intended learning outcomes because of freedom to select, organize, and express ideas.**
3. **Scores are raised by writing skill and bluffing, and lowered by poor handwriting, misspelling, and grammatical errors.**
4. **Scoring is time consuming, subjective, and may be unreliable.**

Figure 14.5
Strengths and Limitations of Essay Questions

SUMMARY TABLE 14.2
Traditional Tests

Concept	Processes/ Related Ideas	Characteristics/Description
Selected-Response Items	Their Nature	• Selected responses are usually objective and can be scored on quick inspection. • A scoring key is created and can be used by an examiner or a computer. • True/false, multiple-choice, and matching items are the most widely used items in selected-response tests.
	True/False Items	• These ask a student to mark whether a statement is *true* or *false*. • A special caution for true/false items involves the ease with which they are constructed, which can lead to the creation of items that encourage memorization. • Strategies for constructing true/false items, as well as their strengths and limitations, were discussed.
	Multiple-Choice Items	• A multiple-choice item has two parts: a stem and a number of options or alternatives. • Incorrect alternatives are called distractors. • Strategies for constructing multiple-choice items, as well as their strengths and limitations, were described.
	Matching Items	• These often are used by teachers with younger students. • They have been criticized for often asking children about trivial information.
	Other Objective Assessment Formats	• These include audiovisuals and problem sets.
	How Good Are Your Test Items?	• Two ways to compute the quality of test items involve the item difficulty index, which describes the percentage of students who obtain the correct answer, and the item discrimination index, which reflects the item's ability to discriminate between students who scored high on the entire test and those who scored low on it.
Constructed-Response Items	Their Nature	• These items require students to write out information rather than select it from a menu. • Short-answer and essay items are the most commonly used constructed-response items.
	Short-Answer Items	• These require students to write a word, a short phrase, or several sentences in response to a task. • Sentence completion is a variation of a short-answer item. • One criticism of short-answer items is that often encourages rote memorization.
	Essays	• Essay questions allow students considerably more freedom of response than the other item formats. • Essay questions are especially good for assessing students' understanding, higher-level thinking skills, organizational skills, and writing skills. • We discussed how to construct and score essay questions, and their strengths and limitations.

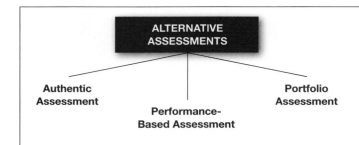

Authentic
Assessment

Performance-
Based Assessment

Portfolio
Assessment

Alternative Assessments

Alternative Assessments

There are alternatives to the traditional assessments that we just discussed. One current trend is to include performance assessments that require students to perform a task such as carry out a project, solve a real-world problem, or create a learning portfolio (Gronlund, Linn, & Davis, 2000; Popham, 2000). Alternative assessments are needed to make instruction compatible with contemporary views of learning and motivation.

Consider several alternative assessments that a middle school language arts teacher devised (Combs, 1997). She gave students a menu of options to choose from that included such formats as book reports, artwork, videos, and creating models. For example, in a unit on Mystery, students might choose to write a report on an author of mystery stories, write an original mystery, make a children's mystery book, or conduct an interview with a private investigator. Each of these options comes with a detailed set of instructions and a scoring guide for quality control. Figure 14.6 shows the directions and scoring guide for alternative assessments that focus on the Middle Ages and Family History.

Middle Ages Option
Model

Directions:
Make a model of a creature or character from the middle ages. Write a one-half to one page description of your character (tell who or what it is and its importance in the middle ages). Your model must portray the creature or character through the use of appropriate costume, props, or other attributes.

Scoring Guide
25   Model Portrays the character or creature and time period through the use of attire, props, and other attributes
10   Artistic quality
15   The model shows evidence of effort
50   A 1/2 to 1 page written description of the character is included

Family Unit Option
Family Tree Poster

Directions:
Make a poster of your family tree, you must go back at least 3 generations. Provide as much information about family member as possible, including but not limited to birthdate, death date (if not living), occupation, place of birth, accomplishments, etc. In addition, provide at least two anecdotes about your family's history (how they came to live in our town, special notoriety, honors, awards, medals, etc.). You must *write out* your family tree! (You may not make a copy of a commercially prepared family tree and paste it on the poster.) Make your poster attractive and neat!

Scoring Guide
25   Family tree includes at least three generations prior to you
25   In addition to names, most entries include information such as birth, death, and place of birth
25   Poster includes at least two anecdotes about interesting or well-known family members
15   Poster is neatly and attractively typed or written by you
10   Mechanics, spelling, usage

Figure **14.6**

Examples of Alternative Assessment in a Middle School Language Arts Class

Authentic Assessment

Traditional assessment has involved the use of paper-and-pencil tests that are far removed from real-world contexts. An increasing trend is to assess students with items that more closely reflect reality (Palomba & Bantai, 1999). **Authentic assessment** *means evaluating a student's knowledge or skill in a context that approximates the real world or real life as closely as possible.*

In some circles, the terms *performance-based assessment* and *authentic assessment* have been used interchangeably. However, not all performance-based assessments are authentic (McMillan, 1997). Performance assessments include what is commonly thought of as students' actual performances (such as in dance, music, art, and physical education), as well as papers, projects, oral presentations, experiments, and portfolios.

Critics of authentic assessment argue that such assessments are not necessarily superior to more conventional assessments, such as multiple-choice and essay tests (Terwilliger, 1997). They say that the proponents of authentic assessment rarely present data in support of the validity of authentic assessments. They also believe that authentic assessments don't adequately examine knowledge and basic skills.

Performance-Based Assessment

Moving from traditional assessment with objective tests to performance-based assessment has been described as going from "knowing" to "showing" (Burz & Marshall, 1996). Figure 14.7 shows an example of a performance-based assessment in science (Solano-Flores & Shavelson, 1997). We will cover the main features of performance-based assessments, guidelines for using them, and their strengths and weaknesses.

Authentic Assessments
Oral Communication
Assessments

Features   Features common to many performance-based assessments include an emphasis on "doing," direct assessment, realism, activities for which there is no correct, objective answer, assessment of group performance as well as individual performance, assessment that takes place over an extended period of time, self-assessment, and open-ended tasks that assess higher-level thinking (Hambleton, 1996).

An Emphasis on "Doing"   Traditional tests emphasize what students know. Performance-based assessments are designed to evaluate what students know *and* can do.

Direct Assessment   Performance-based assessments use direct methods of evaluation, such as writing samples to assess writing skills and oral presentations to assess speaking skills. Observing a student give an oral presentation is a more direct assessment than asking the student a series of questions about speaking skills on a paper-and-pencil test.

Realism   Many performance-based assessments are authentic, although, as we indicated earlier, some are not. Allowing students to use calculators or computers in solving math problems on tests reflects closer ties to the real world than requiring students to do them only with paper and pencil. When students have to solve math problems in the real world, they likely will use calculators and computers.

Activities for Which There Is No Correct, Objective Answer   In many performance-based activities, there is no correct, objective answer. For example, there is no correct answer to be scored when a student gives a talk in class, creates a painting, performs a gymnastic routine, or designs a science project.

Assessing Group Performance as Well as Individual Performance
Some performance-based assessments evaluate how effectively a group of students perform, not just how the students perform individually. This emphasis ties in with our discussion of cooperative learning and other group activities in chapter 9, "Social

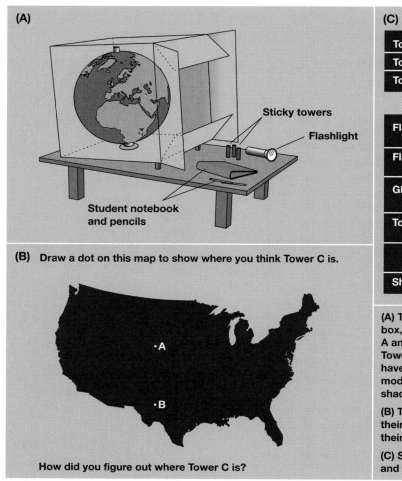

(A)

Sticky towers

Flashlight

Student notebook
and pencils

(B) Draw a dot on this map to show where you think Tower C is.

•A

•B

How did you figure out where Tower C is?

(C)   *Observations/Results*

Tower C is in Eastern US	1
Tower C is in North Eastern US	1
Tower C is somewhere between Pennsylvania and Maine	1

Data Gathering/Modeling

Flashlight Position	Points flashlight at Equator	2
Flashlight motion	Moves flashlight from E to W	2
Globe Rotation	Rotates globe	1
	Rotates globe from W to E	2
Towers	Moves tower C around on the map/globe until shadow is matched	1
	Moves tower C around on the map/globe only in the E/NE region until shadow is matched	2
Shadows	Uses shadows of towers A and B as reference	1

(A) The equipment consists of a spinning Earth globe inside a carton box, three sticky towers, and a flashlight; the students stick Towers A and B at two specific U.S. locations on the globe and are told what Tower C's shadow looks like when it is noon for Towers A and B. They have to find out where in the U.S. Tower C is. The solution requires modeling the sunlight by using the flashlight to project the towers' shadows onto the globe.

(B) The response format involves having students record in notebooks their solutions, the actions they carried out, and the reasoning behind their actions.

(C) Students' performances are scored for the accuracy of their results and the accuracy of their modeling, reasoning, and observations.

Figure **14.7**
A Performance-Based Assessment in Science: Daytime Astronomy

Constructivist Approaches, Domain-Specific Approaches, and Teaching." Thus, a group of students might be assigned to create a science project rather than having each student do a project individually. Evaluation of the student can include both the individual's contribution and the group's product. Group projects are often complex and allow for the assessment of cooperative skills, communication skills, and leadership skills.

Assessment That Takes Place over an Extended Period of Time   In traditional assessment, assessment occurs in a single time frame. For example, a teacher gives a multiple-choice test and students are allowed an hour to take it. However, it is not unusual for performance assessments to involve sustained work over days, weeks, and even months (Bracken, 2000). For example, a student might be evaluated once each month on the progress the student is making on a science project, and then receive a final evaluation when the project is completed.

Self-Assessment   Some performance assessments involve having students evaluate their own performances. This emphasis shifts responsibility away from teachers and places it more squarely on the student's shoulders. For example, students might be asked to judge the quality of their own dance performance, oral presentation, or dramatic acting.

Open-Ended Tasks That Assess Higher-Level Thinking Skills   Many performance-based assessments give students considerable freedom to construct their own responses rather than narrowing their range of answers. Although this makes scoring more difficult, it provides a context for evaluating students' higher-level thinking skills, such as the ability to think deeply about an issue or a topic (Wiggins, 1993).

Guidelines for Using Performance-Based Assessment

Guidelines for using performance-based assessments cover four general issues (Airasian, 1997): (1) establishing a clear purpose, (2) identifying observable criteria, (3) providing an appropriate setting, and (4) judging or scoring the performance.

Make sure that any performance-based assessment has a clear purpose and that a clear decision can be made from the assessment (McKinley, Boulet, & Hambleton, 2000). The purposes can be diverse: to assign a grade, to evaluate a student's progress, to recognize the important steps in a performance, to generate products to be included in a learning portfolio, to provide concrete examples of students' work for admission to college or other programs, and so forth.

Performance criteria *are specific behaviors that students need to perform effectively as part of the assessment.* Establishing performance criteria helps you to go beyond general descriptions (such as "Do an oral presentation" or "Complete a science project") of what students need to do. Performance criteria help you make your observations more systematic and focused. As guidelines, they direct your observations. Without such criteria, your observations can be unsystematic and haphazard. Communicating these performance criteria to students at the beginning of instruction lets students know how to focus their learning. Figure 14.8 contrasts examples of weak and effective criteria.

Once you have clearly defined the performance criteria, it is important to specify the setting in which you will observe the performance or product. You may want to observe behaviors directly in the regular flow of classroom activity, in a special context you create in the classroom, or in a context outside the classroom. As a rule of thumb it is a good idea to observe the student on more than one occasion, because a single performance might not fairly represent the student's knowledge or skill.

Finally, you will need to score or rate the performance, either holistically or analytically. The performance criteria you established earlier provide the key dimensions for scoring. Some teachers use scales to rate students' performance. For example, a teacher could rate each of the criteria listed in figure 14.8 on a four-point scale of how the student performs the behavior: 1 = never, 2 = seldom, 3 = usually, and 4 = always.

Evaluating Performance-Based Assessments

Many educational psychologists endorse the increased use of performance-based assessment (Eisner, 1999; Neil, 1997; Stiggins, 1997). They believe performance-based assessments involve students more in their learning, often encourage higher-level thinking skills, can measure what is really important in the curriculum, and can tie assessment more to real-world, real life experiences.

Some states, such as Kentucky and Vermont, now attempt to measure students with performance assessments. The Kentucky Instructional Results Information System includes a number of domains (such as science and social science), each of which is organized in terms of four components: learner outcomes, the tasks themselves, scoring guides, and examples of student papers (called "anchor papers").

Ensuring Equity with
Performance-Based Assessment

Criteria That Are Too General and Not Well Organized

Speaks clearly and slowly
Pronounces correctly
Makes eye contact
Exhibits good posture when presenting
Shows good effort
Presents with feeling
Understands the topic
Has an enthusiastic attitude
Organizes effectively

Criteria That Are More Specific and Better Organized

I. PHYSICAL EXPRESSION
   Stands straight and faces audience
   Changes facial expression with changes in the tone of the report
   Maintains eye contact with audience

II. VOCAL EXPRESSION
   Speaks in a steady, clear voice
   Varies tone to emphasize points
   Speaks loudly enough to be heard by audience
   Paces words in an even flow
   Enunciates each word

III. VERBAL EXPRESSION
   Chooses precise words to convey meaning
   Avoids unnecessary repetition
   States sentences with complete thoughts or ideas
   Organizes information logically
   Summarizes main points at conclusion

Figure **14.8**
Examples of Performance Criteria for Oral Presentations

**The State of
Performance Assessment**

Although support for performance-based assessment is high in many areas of the United States and Canada, effective implementation faces several hurdles (Hambleton, 1996). Performance assessment often takes considerably more time to construct, administer, and score than objective tests. Also, many performance tests do not meet the standards of validity and reliability outlined by such education groups as the American Educational Research Association, American Psychological Association, and National Council on Measurement in Education. Moreover, the research base for performance-based tests is not well established.

Still, even the strongest supporters of traditional tests acknowledge that they do not measure all of what schools expect students to learn (Hambleton, 1996). Although planning, constructing, and scoring performance tests is challenging, teachers should make every effort to include performance assessments as an important aspect of their teaching (Mabry, 1999).

Portfolio Assessment

Interest in portfolio assessment has mushroomed in recent years. Portfolios represent a significant departure from traditional tests of learning. Figure 14.9 summarizes the contrast between portfolios and traditional testing.

What Is a Portfolio?

A **portfolio** *consists of a systematic and organized collection of a student's work that demonstrates the student's skills and accomplishments* (Lankes, 1995). A portfolio is a purposeful collection of work that tells the story of the student's progress and achievements (Arter, 1995). It is much more than a compilation of student papers stuffed into a manila folder or a collection of memorabilia pasted into a scrapbook (Barton & Collins, 1997; Hatch, 2000). To qualify for inclusion in a portfolio, each piece of work should be created and organized in a way that demonstrates progress and purpose. Portfolios can include many different types of work, such as writing samples, journal entries, videotapes, art, teacher comments, posters, interviews, poetry, test results, problem solutions, recordings of foreign language communication, self-assessments, and any other expression of the student that the teacher believes demonstrates the student's skills and accomplishments. Portfolios can be collected on paper, in photographs, and on audiotape, videotape, computer disk, or CD-ROM. Assessment expert Joan Herman (1996) says that portfolio assessment has become increasingly popular because it is a natural way to integrate instruction and assessment.

Four classes of evidence that can be placed in students' portfolios are artifacts, reproductions, attestations, and productions (Barton & Collins, 1997). **Artifacts** *are documents or products, such as student papers and homework, that are produced during normal academic work in the classroom.* **Reproductions** *consist of documentation of a student's work outside the classroom, such as special projects and interviews.* For example, a student's description of an interview with a local scientist in the community about the scientist's work is a reproduction. **Attestations** *represent the teacher's or other responsible persons' documentation of the student's progress.* For example, a teacher might write evaluative notes about a student's oral presentation and place them in the student's portfolio. **Productions** *are documents the student prepares especially for the portfolio.* Productions consist of three types of materials: goal statements, reflections, and captions. Students generate goal statements about what they want to accomplish with their portfolio, write down their reflections about their work and describe their progress, and create captions that describe each piece of work in the portfolio and its importance.

Using Portfolios Effectively

Effective use of portfolios for assessment requires six things: (1) establishing the portfolio's purpose, (2) involving the student in decisions about it, (3) effectively implementing the use of portfolios in the classroom, (4) reviewing the portfolio with the student, (5) setting criteria for evaluation, and (6) scoring and judging.

Traditional Tests	Portfolios
• Separate learning, testing, and teaching	• Link assessment and teaching to learning
• Fail to assess the impact of prior knowledge on learning by using short passages that are often isolated and unfamiliar	• Address the importance of student's prior knowledge as a critical determinant to learning by using authentic assessment activities
• Rely on materials requesting only literal information	• Provide opportunities to demonstrate inferential and critical thinking that are essential for constructing meaning
• Prohibit collaboration during the assessment process	• Represent a collaborative approach to assessment involving both students and teachers
• Often treat skills in isolated contexts to determine achievement for reporting purposes	• Use multi-faceted activities while recognizing that learning requires integration and coordination of communication skills
• Assess students across a limited range of assignments that may not match what students do in classrooms	• Represent the full range of instructional activities that students are doing in their classrooms
• Assess students in a predetermined situation where the content is fixed	• Can measure the student's ability to perform appropriately in unanticipated situations
• Assess all students on the same dimensions	• Measure each student's achievements while allowing individual differences
• Address only achievement	• Address improvement, effort, and achievement
• Seldom provide vehicles for assessing students' abilities to monitor their own learning	• Implements self-assessment by having students monitor their learning
• Are mechanically scored or scored by teachers who have little input into the assessment	• Engage students in assessing their progress and/or accomplishments and establishing on-going learning goals
• Rarely include items that assess emotional responses to learning	• Provide opportunities to reflect upon feelings about learning

Figure 14.9
Contrasting Traditional Tests and Portfolios

Establishing Purpose   Portfolios can be used for different purposes (Lyons, 1999). Two broad types of purpose are to document growth and to show best work. A **growth portfolio** *consists of the student's work over an extended time frame (throughout the school year or even longer) to reveal the student's progress in meeting learning targets.* Growth portfolios also are sometimes referred to as "developmental portfolios." Growth portfolios are especially helpful in providing concrete evidence of how much a student has changed or learned over time. As students examine their portfolios, they can see for themselves how much they have improved. One example of a growth portfolio is the Integrated Language Arts Portfolio used in the elementary school grades in Juneau, Alaska (Arter, 1995). It is designed to replace report cards and grades as a way to demonstrate growth and accomplishments. Growth is tracked along a developmental continuum for levels of skills in reading, writing, speaking, and listening. A student's status on the continuum is marked at several designated times during the year. Samples of the students' work are used as the basis for judgments about the student's developmental level.

A **best-work portfolio** *showcases the student's most outstanding work.* Sometimes it even is called a "showcase portfolio." Best-work portfolios are more selective than developmental portfolios and often include the student's latest product. Best-work portfolios are especially useful for parent-teacher conferences, students' future teachers, and admission to higher education levels.

"Passportfolios" or "proficiency portfolios" are sometimes used to demonstrate competence and readiness to move on to new level of work (Arter, 1995; Lankes, 1995). For example, the Science Portfolio is an optional aspect of the Golden State Evaluation in California (California State Department of Education, 1994). It is produced during a year of science and contains a problem-solving investigation, a creative expression (presenting a scientific idea in a unique and original manner), a "growth through writing" section that demonstrates progress over time in understanding a concept, and self-reflection. The Central Park East Secondary School in New York City uses portfolios to determine graduation eligibility. Students are required to complete 14 portfolios that demonstrate their competence in areas such as science and technology, ethics and social issues, community service, and history (Gold & Lanzoni, 1993).

Involving Students in Selecting Portfolio Materials   Many teachers let students make at least some of the decisions about the portfolio's contents (Shaklee & others, 1997). Throughout Vermont, students in the fourth through eighth grades select five to seven items to be placed in their portfolio to demonstrate their competence in math problem solving. Student-led parent conferences allow students to demonstrate to parents what they have learned (Little & Allan, 1988). When students are allowed to choose the contents for their own portfolios, a good strategy is to encourage self-reflection by having them write a brief description of why they chose each piece of work (Airasian, 1997).

Reviewing with Students   It is important to explain to students at the beginning of the year what portfolios are and how they will be used. You also should have a number of student-teacher conferences throughout the year to review the student's progress and help the student to plan future work for the portfolio (McMillan, 1997; Weldin & Tumarkin, 1999).

Setting Criteria for Evaluation   Clear and systematic performance criteria are essential for effectively using portfolios (Linn & Gronlund, 2000; Ruiz-Primo, Li, Ayala, & Shavelson, 2000). Clear learning targets for students makes developing performance criteria much easier. Ask yourself what knowledge and skills you want your students to have. This should be the focus of your teaching and your performance criteria.

Scoring and Judging   Scoring and judging portfolios is time consuming (Airasian, 1997). Teachers must evaluate not only each individual item but also the portfolio as a whole. When the portfolio's purpose is to provide descriptive information about the student for the teacher at the next grade level, no scoring or summarizing of the portfolio might be necessary. However, when its purpose is to diagnose, reflect improvement, provide evidence for effective instruction, motivate students to reflect on their work, or give grades to students, summary scoring and judgments need to be made. Checklists and rating scales are commonly used for this purpose. As with other aspects of portfolio assessment, some teachers give students the opportunity to evaluate and critique their own work.

Evaluating the Role of Portfolios in Assessment

Learning portfolios have several strengths: Their comprehensive nature captures the complexity and completeness of the student's work and accomplishments. They provide opportunities for encouraging student decision-making and self-reflection. They motivate students to think critically and deeply. And they provide an excellent mechanism for evaluating student progress and improvement.

Learning portfolios also have several weaknesses: They take considerable time to coordinate and evaluate. Their complexity and uniqueness have meant that they are difficult to evaluate, and their reliability is often much lower than for traditional tests. And their use in large-scale assessments (such as statewide evaluation) is expensive.

SELF-ASSESSMENT 14.1
Planning My Classroom Assessment Philosophy

With the subject matter and grade level at which you plan to teach in mind, examine the list of assessments below that we have discussed in this chapter. Rate each of the assessments on this scale: 1 = I don't plan to use this at all, 2 = I plan to use this occasionally, 3 = I plan to use this moderately, 4 = I plan to use this often, and 5 = This will be one of the most important assessments I will use.

	1	2	3	4	5
1. Informal observations in pre-instructional assessment					
2. Structured exercises in pre-instructional assessment					
3. Observation during instruction					
4. Questions during instruction					
5. Assessments of students' affect					
6. True/false tests					
7. Multiple-choice tests					
8. Matching					
9. Audiovisual context setting					
10. Problem sets					
11. Figural responses					
12. Short-answer items					
13. Essays					
14. Authentic assessment					
15. Experiments					
16. Projects					
17. Oral presentations					
18. Interviews					
19. Performances					
20. Exhibitions					
21. Portfolios					

Look back through your responses and then use this information to help you formulate your classroom assessment in the space below. If you need more space, do this outside the book.

SUMMARY TABLE 14.3
Alternative Assessments

Concept	Processes/ Related Ideas	Characteristics/Description
Authentic Assessment	Its Nature	• It means evaluating a student's knowledge or skill in a context that approximates the real world or real life as closely as possible. • Many, but not all, performance-based assessments are authentic. • Critics argue that authentic assessments are not necessarily better than more conventional assessments, that there are few data to support their validity, and that they don't adequately examine knowledge and basic skills.
Performance-Based Assessment	Features	• These include an emphasis on "doing," direct assessment, realism, activities for which there is no correct, objective answer, assessing groups as well as individuals, assessment that takes place over an extended period of time, self-assessment, and open-ended tasks that assess higher-order thinking skills.
	Guidelines for Using Performance-Based Assessment	• There are four main issues: (1) identifying a clear purpose, (2) identifying observable criteria, (3) providing an appropriate setting, and (4) judging or scoring the performance. • Performance criteria are specific behaviors that students need to effectively perform as part of the assessment. • The performance can be scored or rated holistically or analytically.
	Evaluating Performance-Based Assessments	• Many educational psychologists endorse the increased use of performance-based assessment. • These assessments have both strengths and limitations.
Portfolio Assessment	What Is a Portfolio?	• It is a systematic and organized collection of a student's work that demonstrates the student's skills and accomplishments. • Four classes of evidence can be placed in students' portfolios: artifacts, reproductions, attestations, and productions.
	Using Portfolios Effectively	• This requires six things: (1) establishing the portfolio's purpose, (2) involving students in decisions about it, (3) effectively implementing its use in the classroom, (4) reviewing it with students, (5) setting criteria for evaluating it, and (6) scoring and judging it. • Two broad types of purposes are to document growth through a growth portfolio and showcase the student's most outstanding work through a best-work portfolio.
	Evaluating the Role of Portfolios in Assessment	• Learning portfolios have both strengths (such as capturing the complexity and completeness of the student's work and accomplishments, and encouraging student decision making and self-reflection) and weaknesses (such as the time required to coordinate and evaluate them, and the difficulty in evaluating them).

Even with these weaknesses in mind, most educational psychology experts and educational organizations, such as the National Education Association, support the use of portfolios (Coffin, 1996).

We have discussed many types of assessment, and this is a good time to think about what your classroom assessment philosophy will be. Self-Assessment 14.1 on page 519 gives you this opportunity.

At this point we have studied a number of ideas about alternative assessments. A review of these ideas is presented in summary table 14.3.

Grading and Reporting Performance

Grading *means translating descriptive assessment information into letters, numbers, or other marks that indicate the quality of a student's learning or performance.*

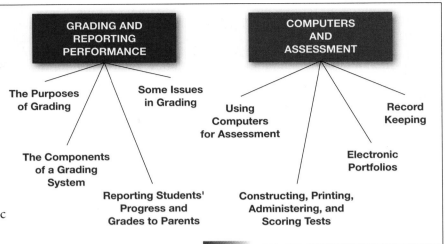

The Purposes of Grading

Grading is carried out to communicate meaningful information about a student's learning and achievement. In this process, grades serve four basic purposes (Airasian, 1997):

- *Administrative.* Grades help determine students' class rank, credits for graduation, and whether a student should be promoted to the next grade.
- *Informational.* Grades can be used to inform students, parents, and others (such as admissions officers for subsequent schooling) about a student's work. A grade represents the teacher's summary judgment of how well a student has met instructional objectives and learning targets.
- *Motivational.* As we saw in chapter 11, "Motivating Students to Learn," a good strategy is to help students become intrinsically motivated. Nonetheless, in an educational world in which grades are given, many students work harder because they are motivated to achieve high grades and they fear low grades (extrinsic motivation).
- *Guidance.* Grades help students, parents, and counselors to select appropriate courses and levels of work for students. They provide information about which students might need special services and what levels of future education students will likely be able to handle.

Exploring
Grading Issues

The Components of a Grading System

Grades reflect teachers' judgments. Three main types of teacher judgments underlie a teacher's grading system (Airasian, 1997): (1) What standard of comparison will I use for grading? (2) What aspects of students' performance will I use to establish grades? and (3) How will I weight different kinds of evidence in giving grades?

Standards of Comparison   A student's performance can be graded by comparing it to the performance of other students or to predefined standards of performance.

Comparing Performance Across Students
Norm-referenced grading *is a grading system based on comparison of a student's performance with that of other students in the class or of other classes and other students.* Students who get high grades performed better than most of their classmates, students who get low grades performed worse than most of their classmates. Norm-referenced grading is commonly referred to as *grading on the curve.* In norm-referenced grading, the grading scale determines what percentages get particular grades. In most instances, the scale is created so that the largest percentage of students get C's.

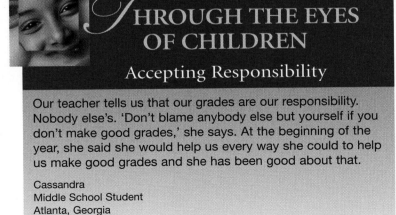

THROUGH THE EYES OF CHILDREN
Accepting Responsibility

Our teacher tells us that our grades are our responsibility. Nobody else's. 'Don't blame anybody else but yourself if you don't make good grades,' she says. At the beginning of the year, she said she would help us every way she could to help us make good grades and she has been good about that.

Cassandra
Middle School Student
Atlanta, Georgia

"Your grading curve and my learning curve don't intersect."

This is a typical breakdown of grades: 15 percent A's, 25 percent B's, 40 percent C's, 15 percent D's, and 5 percent F's. In assigning grades, instructors often look for gaps in the range of scores. If six students score 92 to 100 and 10 students score 81 to 88, and there are no scores between 88 and 92, the teacher would assign a grade of A to the 92–100 scores and a B to the 81–88 scores. Norm-referenced grading has been criticized for reducing students' motivation, increasing their anxiety, increasing negative interactions among students, and hindering learning.

Comparing Performance with a Predetermined Standard   *Criterion-referenced grading is a grading system based on comparison with predetermined standards.* All students who reach a particular level get the same grade. Sometimes criterion-referenced grading is called *absolute grading.* Typically, criterion-referenced grading is based on the proportion of points attained on a test or the level of mastery reached in a performance skill, such as giving an oral presentation and meeting all the predetermined criteria. Criterion-referenced grading is recommended over norm-referenced grading.

In theory, the standard established is supposed to be absolute, but in practice it doesn't always work out that way (McMillan, 1997). For example, a school system often develops a grading system that goes something like this: A = 94–100 percent correct, B = 87–93, C = 77–86, D = 70–76, F = Below 70. Although this system is absolute in the sense that every student must get 94 points to get an A and every student who does not get at least 70 points gets an F, teachers and classrooms vary enormously in what constitutes mastery of material to get a 94, an 87, a 77, or a 70. One teacher might give very hard tests, another very easy tests.

Many teachers use different cutoff scores than the ones just mentioned. Some teachers argue that low grades discourage student motivation and refuse to give D's or F's; others won't fail students unless their scores fall below 50.

Aspects of Performance   Over the course of a grading period, students will likely have created many products that can be evaluated and used to formulate their grades. These can include test and quiz results, as well as various alternative assessments such as oral reports, projects, interviews, and homework. Increasingly, portfolios are used as the complete collection of materials to be graded or a portion of the work on which an overall grade is based. Grades should be based mainly on academic performance, but teacher ratings of motivation and effort can be factored in as well.

Many teachers use tests as the main, or even sole, basis for assigning grades. A good strategy is to base an overall grade on a series of tests and other types of assessments. Thus, a semester grade in geography might be based on two major tests and a final, eight quizzes, homework, two oral reports, and a project. Basing a grade on a series of tests and different types of assessment helps to balance out students' strengths and weaknesses, as well as compensate for a poor performance or two because of internal and external sources of measurement errors.

Some educators advocate factoring affective characteristics such as motivation and effort into grades, especially by giving borderline students a plus or minus. Thus, a teacher might convert a student's B to a B+ if the student was highly motivated, put forth considerable effort, and actively participated in the class—or to a B– if the student was poorly motivated, made little effort, and did not actively participate. However, some educators believe that grades should be based only on academic performance. One of the problems with including factors such as effort in grades is the difficulty in determining the reliability and validity of effort.

Weighting Different Kinds of Evidence   You will need to determine how much weight to give the different components used in determining a student's grade. Thus, in the earlier example of a geography class, the teacher will have to decide how much weight to give the major tests, final test, quizzes, homework, oral report, and project. The teacher might arrive at a weighting system that looks something like this:

Major tests (2)	20%
Final test	25%
Quizzes	20%
Homework	5%
Oral report	10%
Project	20%

Many teachers don't use homework as a component for a grade. However, if a student fails to turn in a certain number of homework assignments, some teachers lower the student's grade. Also, when a student's grade depends heavily on homework or other work outside class, parents might be tempted to do their child's work to ensure a good grade. Including homework as a component of grading also favors students who have better home environments. As with other aspects of classroom assessment, your judgment is involved in how you synthesize information to arrive at a student's grade.

"How much to shred a report card?"

Reporting Students' Progress and Grades to Parents

Grades are the most common method of informing students about their progress and performance in the classroom (Airasian, 1997). However, grades by themselves provide limited information, are usually given infrequently, communicate little in the way of specific information about how the student is learning, and rarely include information about the student's motivation, cooperation, and classroom behavior. Because of these limitations, more than grades are needed to give parents a full portrait of the student.

The Report Card   The report card is a standard method of reporting students' progress and grades to parents. The form of judgments on report cards varies from one school system to another, and, in many cases, from one grade level to another. Some report cards convey letter grades (typically A, B, C, D, and F, sometimes also allowing pluses and minuses). Some report cards convey numerical scores (such as 91 in math, 85 in English, and so on). Other report cards have a pass/fail category in one or more subjects. Yet other report cards have checklists indicating skills or objectives the student has attained. Some report cards have categories for affective characteristics, such as effort, cooperation, and other appropriate and inappropriate behaviors. Many report cards also have space for a teacher's written, summative comments.

In the higher elementary school grade levels and secondary schools, letter grades are mainly used, although these might be accompanied by other information such as written comments. Checklists of skills and objectives are mainly used in elementary schools or kindergartens. In many school districts, there is spirited debate about what form of grading should be used and what should be included on report cards.

*T*HROUGH THE EYES OF TEACHERS
Some Grading Strategies

I think it is extremely important that parents and students clearly know what is expected of students if they are to succeed in my class. I try to help students understand that they are in control of the grade they get. If students think a grading system is capricious or unknowable, it creates frustration, anxiety, and is of little use in motivating students. By getting them to see that their grades are in their own hands, I move to the position of 'facilitator' in the classroom. The students see me as someone who is there to *help* them achieve rather than someone who sits in judgment of their work and gives them a grade.

I now use the computer in grading and use it to generate an individual report on each student. I print these reports every two weeks. I give a copy to each student so that he or she is clear about a particular grade and what can be done about it. I also make sure these grades get home to parents. I also print out a copy of what I call a "grade sheet" for long assignments, which indicates how I intend to grade the assignments. I give it to my students before they do the assignment and then use it to score the assignment when it is submitted.

Lynn Ayres
English and Drama Teacher
East Middle School
Ypsilanti, Michigan

TEACHING STRATEGIES
For Parent-Teacher Conferences

Here are some good strategies for meeting with parents about their child's progress and grades (Payne, 1997):

1. *Be prepared.* Review the student's performance prior to the meeting with parents. Think about what you are going to say to the parents.
2. *Be positive.* Even if the student has performed poorly, try to find at least some areas to discuss in which the student has performed well. This does not mean glossing over and ignoring a student's lack of achievement, it means including positive areas in addition to the negative ones.
3. *Be objective.* Even though you want to look for positive aspects of the student's record to communicate to parents, be objective and honest. Don't give parents false hopes if the student has low ability in a particular subject area.
4. *Practice good communication skills.* As we noted in chapter 12, "Managing the Classroom," this means being an active listener and giving parents adequate opportunities to contribute to the conversation.
5. *Don't talk about other students.* The focus of the parent-teacher conference should be on the parent's child. Don't compare their child with other students.

Written Progress Reports   Another reporting strategy is to provide parents with a weekly, biweekly, or monthly report of the student's progress and achievement (McMillan, 1997). These written reports can include the student's performance on tests and quizzes, projects, oral reports, and so on. They also can include information about the student's motivation, cooperation, and behavior, as well as suggestions for how parents can help students improve their performance. If you have enough information to form a grade for the student at that time, you also might consider including it in the written communication.

Parent-Teacher Conferences   Parent-teacher conferences are another way to communicate information about grades and assessment. Such conferences are both a responsibility and an opportunity (Payne, 1997). Parents have a right to know how their child is doing in school and how their child might improve. Conferences provide an opportunity for giving parents helpful information about how they can be partners with you in helping the child learn more effectively.

Some Issues in Grading

Should grading be abolished? Is there too much grade inflation?

Should Grading Be Abolished?   Occasionally there are calls to abandon grades, usually based on the belief that evaluation of students is necessary but that competitive grading deemphasizes learning in favor of judging. Critics argue that grading discourages the vast majority of students, especially those who receive below-average grades. The critics often call for more-constructive evaluation that encourages students to engage in maximum effort by underscoring their strengths, identifying concrete ways to improve, and providing positive feedback (Culbertson & Jalongo, 1999). Critics also point out that grading often motivates students to study only the material that will be on the test.

Even with these criticisms in mind, it is difficult to imagine schools in which judgments about students' performance would not be made and communicated to students, parents, and others, although the basis on

"I don't know why you're so surprised by his poor grades. Every day you asked him what he did at school, and every day he answered, 'Nothing.'"

which judgments are made might change, the format of grades might be modified, and the judgments might no longer be called "grades" at some point in the future. For example, in some K–5 elementary schools there are no formal grades, only narrative evaluations from each teacher. A judgment of whether the student is ready to go on to the next grade is made at the end of the school year.

As classroom assessment expert Peter Airasian (1997) concluded, grades are powerful symbols in our society that are taken seriously by students, teachers, and the public. Regardless of whether you like the way grading is currently conducted or think it should be drastically changed, in the foreseeable future it is important for you to take grading your students seriously and do it in a way that is fair to your students. Never use grades to reward or punish students because you like them or don't like them. Always base students' grades on how well they have learned the subject matter, based on objective evidence of learning (Colby, 1999).

Is There Too Much Grade Inflation?   Some teachers do not like to give low grades because they believe they diminish the student's motivation to learn. However, some critics believe that grade inflation, especially in the form of giving high grades for mediocre performance, provides students a false belief that they are learning and achieving more than they actually are. The result is that many students discover that they can perform well below their ability and still achieve high grades. A rising tide of grade inflation was recently noted by College Board president Donald Stewart (1997). For example, from 1987 to 1997, among students taking the SAT test, the proportion of students with an A average rose from 28 to 37 percent. However, over the same period the combined verbal and math scores of those A students dropped 14 points.

Computers and Assessment

Earlier in the chapter we described the use of audiovisuals for creating realistic contexts for assessment. Here we continue our exploration of the use of computers in assessment.

Using Computers for Assessment

Computers can be used to construct, print, administer, and score tests, provide a medium for portfolios, and maintain student records (Gronlund, 1998). Concerns about the validity and reliability of assessment using a computer are no different than for paper-and-pencil measures. Be aware that just because validity and reliability have been established for a paper-and-pencil assessment does not mean that the validity and reliability will automatically hold when the student is assessed with the same measure on a computer.

Although the assessment data can be analyzed by a computer, computers are not capable of including common sense, intuition, and judgment of effort in their analysis. Much of what is involved in making decisions about assessment scores relies on the teacher's interpretation and judgment, just as with paper-and-pencil measures (Jones, 1999).

Constructing, Printing, Administering, and Scoring Tests

One way computers can aid test construction is through *item banking*. This consists of maintaining test item files that can be retrieved for preparing a test. Items typically are coded by subject area, instructional level, instructional objective measured, and item difficulty.

Software for
Educational Assessment

Computers can be used to print tests from the item bank. The coded information about each item makes it possible to create different forms of tests, such as a test arranged by instructional objective or increasing difficulty.

Computers also can be used directly in the administration of tests. The student is presented with test items on a computer screen and answers the items accordingly.

After the test is administered, the computer can be used to score the test and arrange the scores in different ways. Computer scoring especially can be helpful in relieving teachers from the time-consuming task of scoring test item responses.

Electronic Portfolios

Electronic Portfolios

As we saw earlier in the chapter, portfolio assessment is increasingly common. The terms *electronic portfolio* and *computer-based portfolio* are used to describe portfolio work that is saved in an electronic format (Lankes, 1995). The record can include text, graphics, sound, and video (Barrett, 1994). Thus, students can save writing samples, math solutions, samples of art work, depictions of science projects, and multimedia presentations in an electronic portfolio. A single computer with a large storage capacity can store portfolios for all the students in a class. If a number of students store multimedia material, a floppy or hard disk might not have sufficient storage. An alternative is to store students' portfolios on a "rewritable" compact disk (CD-RW, a compact disk that stores text, sound, graphics, and video). A computer-based portfolio allows for easy transfer of information from teacher to teacher or school to school.

Several electronic portfolio programs are available. The most widely used is Aurbach's Cirady Profile, in which both teachers and students can enter work samples. The electronic portfolio programs can include writing samples, standardized test scores, oral communication skills, and math assessments. Other software programs (such as Hyperstudio by Roger Wagner [1993] and Filemaker Pro by Claris) let teachers create their own template for portfolio assessment. Teachers can adapt these programs to the needs of their classes. For example, one high school English portfolio might consist of the outlines and drafts for each writing assignment; another might include only the finished product along with the student's reflections and self-evaluation of the product. Figure 14.10 shows a computer screen of a lab report that was included in one student's portfolio.

One school that uses electronic portfolios is East Syracuse–Minoa High School in Syracuse, New York. Its students create electronic portfolios that can be sent to colleges as part of an admissions application and to potential employers as part of their job application. The electronic portfolios are created using Hyperstudio software. They contain information about the student (such as transcripts, letters of recommendation, and work history) and student-selected work (such as writing samples, multimedia projects, artwork, and video clips from a school play). The students are responsible for updating and selecting the work samples in their portfolios. Students begin creating these portfolios in their sophomore year and continue updating and revising them through their senior year. The portfolios can be distributed in computer disk, CD-RW, videotape, or print versions.

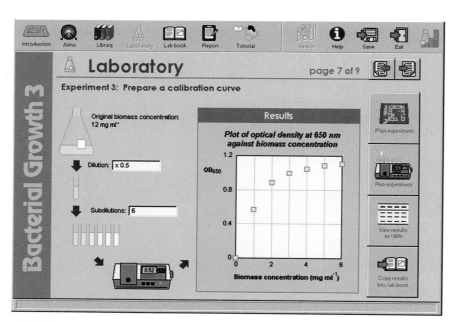

Figure **14.10**

Computer Screen of One Student's Lab Report in an Electronic Portfolio

TECHNOLOGY AND EDUCATION
The Features of an Electronic Portfolio

David Niguidula (1997) designs and customizes computer software that includes electronic portfolios. He believes it is important to integrate the following considerations into any plan for student electronic portfolios.

Vision

The main menu of an electronic portfolio should contain a set of goals that reflect the vision of what the student should know and be able to do. For example, at one high school, the domains students are expected to master include communicating, crafting, reflecting, knowing, respecting oneself, and respecting others. At others, they might include such goals as content knowledge about subject matter, ability to think critically, effective communication, and cooperative skills. As students and teachers enter work into their portfolios, they consider how the activities in the classroom correspond to the learning goals.

Assessment

Assessment involves answering such questions as "How can students demonstrate that they have reached the learning goals?" "How will the portfolio be evaluated and scored?" and "What audiences are the portfolios intended for?"

Technology

Technology involves making decisions about what hardware, software, and networking will be needed. At one school where students and teachers spend most of their day together as a team (about eighty students and three teachers), each team shares a set of six computers, at least one of which has multimedia input capabilities, a scanner, and a laser printer. In other schools, five to fifteen computers are designated as electronic portfolio stations. Ideally, a school will have a technical coordinator who can help teachers set up electronic portfolios. At one high school, the school's technical coordinator prepares a class of twenty students to become the electronic portfolio support team for the rest of the school.

Logistics

Decisions will need to be made about when the information will be placed in the electronic portfolios, who will do it, who will select the work, and who will reflect on the work. Putting together portfolios requires teacher and student time. Two middle school teachers at Pierre van Cortlandt Middle School in Croton-Harmon, New York, described the logistics of electronic portfolios as "collecting, selecting, reflecting, and presenting." Students need to think about what entries they will *collect,* how to *select* the ones that best represent their abilities, how to *reflect* on what their portfolio means, and how to *present* what they have learned. Similarly, teachers need to be involved in these steps as well.

The School's Culture

The school's culture is an important aspect of whether electronic portfolios will become innovative, meaningful aspects of a student's learning or merely a technological version of a file cabinet. Several school administrators and teachers that Niguidula worked with presented their vision statement to others to get feedback, which helped them fine-tune their learning goals. When the school community encourages teachers, students, and others to reflect on their learning goals and effectively integrate technology in the classroom, electronic portfolios can become far more than file cabinets. They can represent an important, meaningful dimension of a student's learning.

Electronic portfolios are mandated by the 1996 Jobs Through Education Act, which is intended to get public schools to focus more on preparing students for the workplace (Kabler, 1997). The vision is that student transcripts will eventually be replaced with electronic portfolios that include a full history of the student's classroom performances, work samples, and activities. To read further about electronic portfolios, see the Technology and Education box.

Record Keeping

Record keeping is a burden for many teachers. Assessment information represents a considerable chunk of this record keeping. Computer technology can help to reduce the burden of record keeping (Maddux, Johnson, & Willis, 1997). For example, electronic grade books can keep track of students' grades in a course. Excelsior's Grade 2 program can store many types of student information, including test scores, project

Technology and Alternative Assessment

SUMMARY TABLE 14.4
Grading and Reporting Performance, and Computers and Assessment

Concept	Processes/Related Ideas	Characteristics/Description
Grading and Reporting Performance	The Purposes of Grading	• There are administrative, informational, motivational, and guidance purposes for grading.
	The Components of a Grading System	• Three main types of teacher judgments underlie a grading system: (1) standard of comparison to use for grading (norm-referenced or criterion-referenced); (2) aspects of performance (a good strategy is to base an overall grade on a series of assessments, including tests and other assessments); and (3) weighting different kinds of evidence (judgment is involved in how teachers synthesize information to arrive at a student's grade).
	Reporting Students' Progress and Grades to Parents	• Report cards are the standard method of reporting. • Letter grades are mainly used in the higher elementary grades and secondary schools. • Checklists of skills and objectives might be used in kindergarten and elementary school. • Reporting also includes written progress reports and parent-teacher conferences.
	Some Issues in Grading	• These include (1) whether grading should be abolished (although the form of grading might change in the future, judgments about students' performance will still be made and communicated to students, parents, and others); and (2) whether grade inflation is a problem.
Computers and Assessment	Using Computers for Assessment	• There are the same concerns about validity and reliability for electronic assessment as for paper-and-pencil assessment.
	Constructing, Printing, Administering, and Scoring Tests	• Computers can be used for all of these functions.
	Electronic Portfolios	• The terms *electronic portfolio* and *computer-based portfolio* are used to describe portfolios that are saved in an electronic format. • Several electronic portfolio programs are available.
	Record Keeping	• Computer technology can help to reduce the burden of record keeping for teachers. For example, electronic grade books can keep track of a student's grades in a course.

grades, homework assignments, semester averages, and teacher judgments. Each component of your assessment system can be weighted, and the program will compute the student's overall performance based on the formula you create. This can take less time than tediously computing grades by hand. Some electronic grade book programs have parent access options. Parents or students who have an appropriate computer and modem can connect with the school computer, enter a personal identification number, and access the student's grades and teacher's comments.

At this point we have studied a number of ideas about grading and performance, as well as computers and assessment. A review of these ideas is presented in summary table 14.4.

Chapter Review

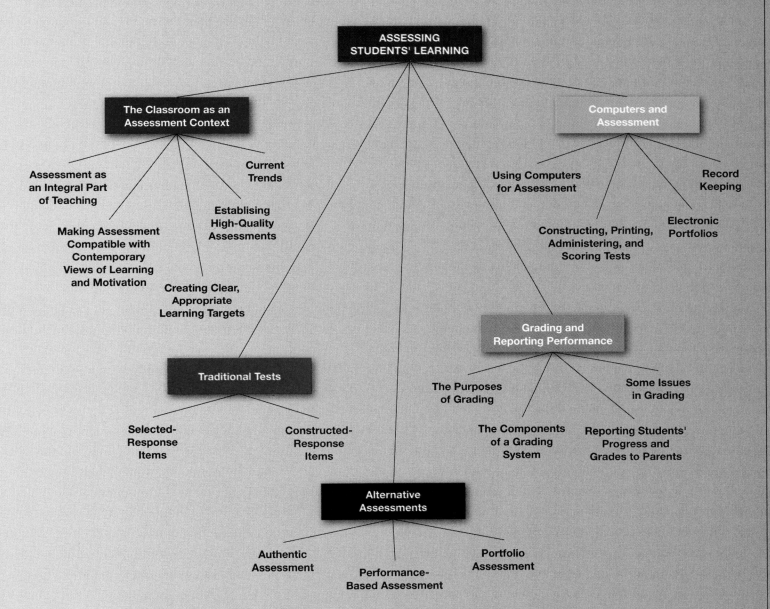

ASSESSING STUDENTS' LEARNING

The Classroom as an Assessment Context
- Assessment as an Integral Part of Teaching
- Making Assessment Compatible with Contemporary Views of Learning and Motivation
- Creating Clear, Appropriate Learning Targets
- Establising High-Quality Assessments
- Current Trends

Traditional Tests
- Selected-Response Items
- Constructed-Response Items

Alternative Assessments
- Authentic Assessment
- Performance-Based Assessment
- Portfolio Assessment

Grading and Reporting Performance
- The Purposes of Grading
- The Components of a Grading System
- Reporting Students' Progress and Grades to Parents
- Some Issues in Grading

Computers and Assessment
- Using Computers for Assessment
- Constructing, Printing, Administering, and Scoring Tests
- Electronic Portfolios
- Record Keeping

TO OBTAIN A DETAILED REVIEW OF THIS CHAPTER, STUDY THESE FOUR SUMMARY TABLES:

Key Terms

formative assessment 497
summative assessment 498
learning target 499
reliability 500
validity 500
inferences 500
content-related evidence 501
instructional validity 501
pluralistic assessment 501

objective tests 502
performance assessments 502
selected-response items 503
multiple-choice item 506
problem sets 507
item difficulty index 508
item discrimination index 508
constructed-response
   item 509

short-answer item 509
essay items 509
holistic scoring 510
analytic scoring 510
authentic assessment 513
performance criteria 515
portfolio 516
artifacts 516
reproductions 516

attestations 516
productions 516
growth portfolio 517
best-work portfolio 517
grading 521
norm-referenced
   grading 521
criterion-referenced
   grading 522

Educational Psychology Checklist
ASSESSING STUDENTS' LEARNING

How much have you learned since the beginning of the chapter? Use the following statements to help you review your knowledge and understanding of the chapter material. First, read the statement and mentally or briefly demonstrate on paper that you understand and can discuss the relevant information.

_____ 1. I can describe how to make assessment an integral part of teaching.
_____ 2. I know how to make assessment compatible with contemporary views of learning and motivation.
_____ 3. I know how to create clear, appropriate learning targets.
_____ 4. I can discuss what it takes to construct high-quality assessments.
_____ 5. I am aware of current trends in assessing students' learning.

_____ 6. I can evaluate the various types of traditional tests, including those that have selected-response and constructed-response items.
_____ 7. I know what authentic assessment is.
_____ 8. I can describe what performance assessment is.
_____ 9. I am aware of what portfolio assessment is.
_____ 10. I know about many aspects of grading and reporting students' performances.
_____ 11. I can discuss the use of computers in assessment.

For any items that you did not check off, go back and locate the relevant material in the chapter. Review the material until you feel you can check off the item. You may want to use this checklist later in preparing for an exam.

Adventures for the Mind

Now that you have a good knowledge and understanding of the chapter, complete the following exercises to expand your thinking about the chapter's topics.

• Consider a course you took in grade school or high school that you remember fairly well and that was assessed traditionally. Explore how students could have been evaluated with alternative assessments or some combination of traditional and alternative assessments. What would have been gained (or lost) by using alternative assessments?

• Think about the following statements and decide whether you agree or disagree with each. Explain your stance.
  – Multiple-choice tests should not be used to assess students' learning.

  – A teacher should never use a single measure to assess learning.
  – Performance-based assessment is too subjective.

• We have discussed numerous issues related to grading. Decide whether you agree or disagree with the following statements. Explain your decisions.
  – A teacher should not look at a student's record from the previous year because it creates too many expectations.
  – Affective information should not be used in assigning grades.
  – An absolute score, such as 70, should not be used as a cutoff for giving students an "F."

• Think about the subject(s) and grade level that you plan to teach. Select a subject and describe what you plan to use as a basis for a student's final grade in the subject.

Taking It to the Net

1. Currently there is an emphasis on raising the quality of students' educational achievement through the use of standardized tests. In your classroom, how might you use assessment to raise the level of your students' educational achievement?

2. You've just finished a unit that includes a section on Christopher Columbus and his journey to the Americas in 1492. How might you assess your students' knowledge of this topic? Can you construct both a recall assessment and a critical thinking assessment? How?

3. In a parent-teacher conference, the parents tell you that their daughter usually earns A's but is currently earning C's in your class. The parents then accuse you of writing tests that are biased against girls. How do you respond? How does a teacher guard against writing or using biased assessments?

    Connect to http://www.mhhe.com/socscience/psychology/santedu/ttnet.htm to find the answers!

Case Studies

Case 1 *Joan Marin, Marilyn Coe, & Warren Groves:* A classroom teacher, a special education teacher, and a principal hold different views about mainstreaming a boy with poor reading skills. The dilemma comes to a head over the method of grading him at the end of the marking period.

Case 2 *Sarah Hanover:.* Sarah has given an outstanding student a lower grade than he expected because he never turned in any homework. The student's angry parents challenge Sarah's grading system.

Epilogue
*L*OOKING BACK, LOOKING FORWARD

I hope that you can look back and say that you learned a lot in this course about teaching and learning. The insightful words of nineteenth-century Danish philosopher Soren Kierkegaard capture the importance of looking back to increase our understanding: "Life is lived forward but understood backwards." As we come to the end of this book, I leave you with the following montage of thoughts and words that convey the wonderful opportunities that lie ahead for you in shaping future generations of children.

Teaching and learning are educational psychology's heart and soul. By teaching, you will touch the future because children are the future of any society. Teaching is complex, fast-paced, multidimensional, sometimes unpredictable, and involves a diverse mosaic of students. Teaching is art and teaching is science. When you teach, be challenged to awaken the curiosity of young minds. It is no small thing in life to enjoy the sun, live light in the spring, think, feel, and *teach*. Good teachers care for their students and are dedicated to helping them learn.

Becoming an effective teacher involves understanding how children develop—their individual variations and diversity, how they learn and think—being an effective planner, using technology effectively, motivating students to learn, managing the classroom, and assessing children's learning.

Children's Development

Children are on a different plane. They grow and change physically, cognitively, and socioemotionally. It is the wisdom of human development that children thirst to know and understand. Poet Noah Perry asked, "Who knows the thoughts of a child?" Possibly more than anyone else, Piaget and Vygotsky knew, describing them as active, constructivist thinkers and teachers as guides and facilitators rather than directors and controllers. In language, children gradually develop from stammering a first word to constructing infinitely complex sentences. In learning to read, they develop phonological awareness and decoding skills. When both parents and teachers immerse children in a world of print and talk, their literacy skills benefit.

Note: Portions of the Epilogue are derived from quotations and material that were referenced in the main portion of the text.

Parents might look back and think that if they had their child to raise all over again, they would do less correcting and more connecting, take more hikes and fly more kites, build the child's self-esteem first and the house later. Children benefit when their parents are affectionate, involved, and firm, and when linkages between families and schools are forged. Parents cradle children's lives, but children's development is shaped by successive choirs of peers, friends, and teachers. Children's small worlds widen when they go to school, where they spend many years as members of a society in which they are socialized and socialize others. As children move into adolescence, they try on one face after another, seeking to find a face of their own.

Individual Variations and Diversity

No two students are exactly alike. An important task for you as a teacher is to provide students with an education that allows them to play out their lives differently. Intelligence, learning and thinking styles, creativity, and personality and temperament are areas where individual variations are prominent. Children have multiple intelligences, and they benefit when teachers discover and appreciate what children do best. Children also have multiple learning and thinking styles. You can help children who are impulsive by getting them to think more reflectively, and you can help surface learners to think more deeply. To improve children's creative thinking, provide students with environments that stimulate creativity, don't overcontrol, encourage internal motivation, foster playful and flexible thinking, introduce students to creative people, and be a creative role model for students. Monitor students' personality traits and temperament, seeking ways to help children who are emotionally unstable, shy, not open to new experiences, uncooperative, or undisciplined.

Be conscious not only of children's individual variations but also of the diverse, multicultural world in which they live. We need every human gift and cannot afford to neglect any gift because of artificial barriers of culture, ethnicity, or gender. Of special concern are students who grow up in poverty and whose dreams become deferred or dry up. Encourage students to think deeply and productively about diverse others and to be emotionally intelligent about ethnic issues. Be aware of how gender pervades the classroom and seek ways to reduce gender bias. Think of the curriculum as an inclusive quilt that is colorful and diverse. No two patches are the same. A good curriculum is like a poem that follows a particular pattern but allows students to bring their own experiences to the construction of its meaning.

For many years, public schools did little to educate children with disabilities. In recent decades, federal legislation has mandated that these children receive a free, appropriate education. Increasingly, children with disabilities are educated in the regular classroom. You are likely to face challenges in educating these children but will be deeply rewarded for your efforts. You can give these children wonderful gifts by effectively teaching them. All children benefit when they are not underchallenged.

Learning and Thinking

Learning is an important function of schools. For children, learning should be a natural pleasure, not strained and constrained. Applied behavior analysis provides teachers with strategies for increasing desirable behaviors and decreasing undesirable ones. As a teacher, you are an important model in children's lives, and children need models more than critics. Think critically about what type of model you will present to students and ways that you can increase the positive models and mentors your students will encounter. Students benefit when they engage in self-regulatory learning by generating and monitoring their thoughts, feelings, and behaviors to reach a goal.

The child's mind is an enchanting thing. Don't look at it as an empty vessel to be filled with information. Look at it as an active, constructivist system that can effectively process information with the right guidance. Good teachers help children use knowledge and develop strategies to adapt their responses to new learning situations. Children remember better when they understand what they are remembering rather than rotely memorizing something. Encourage students to process information deeply, elaborate on the information, construct images, and organize the information. When teaching concepts, make them as clear as possible and give concrete examples. Help students relate new concepts to what they already know. Many competent teachers believe the call to teach involves the call to help children become better thinkers. They believe that students should do less reciting, defining, describing, stating, and listing and do more analyzing, inferring, connecting, synthesizing, criticizing, creating, evaluating, thinking, and rethinking. An important educational goal for students is to be able to take what they learn and apply it to new situations. To help students accomplish this transfer, think about what your students will need to know for success in life, give them opportunities for real-world learning, root concepts in applications, and teach strategies that will generalize. Guide students in developing their metacognitive skills, helping them know about knowing.

Children do some of their thinking by themselves, but as social beings their cognition is often collaborative. Because of our American emphasis on the individual rather than the group, collaborative thinking only recently has emerged as an important theme in education. In the social constructivist approach, knowledge is mutually built and constructed. Through scaffolding, cognitive apprenticeships, tutoring, cooperative learning, and reciprocal teaching, teachers and peers can jointly contribute to children's learning. In structuring students' small-group work, pay attention to team-building skills. Many experts on children's thinking believe that critical thinking should mainly be emphasized in the context of rich subject matter in domains such as reading, writing, mathematics, science, and social studies.

Instruction, Motivation, and Management

Planning is a critical aspect of being a competent teacher. Develop a systematic, organized strategy of planning lessons. Set instructional goals, plan activities, set priorities, make time estimates, and create schedules, but build some flexibility into these. When thinking about planning, consider educational objectives in the cognitive, affective, and psychomotor domains. Remember that learning takes time and that students learn best when they spend more time on-task in the classroom. When giving homework, find ways to make it meaningful and interesting. Increasingly, educational psychologists recommend that teachers infuse their classrooms with learner-centered principles. Students are growing up in a world that is far different technologically than when their parents and grandparents were students. If your students are to be adequately prepared for tomorrow's jobs, technology needs to be an integral part of your classroom. Commit to becoming more technologically competent but keep in mind that technology alone does not ensure the best learning. Choose technology with an eye toward how it can help students actively explore, construct, and restructure information. Look for ways to use technology as part of collaborative and real world learning.

Motivation is a key aspect of learner-centered principles of teaching. Unmotivated, students don't expend the energy and effort to learn. Highly motivated, they are eager to come to school and learn. Many educational psychologists believe that children learn best when they are internally motivated—stimulated by tasks that pique their curiosity, are optimally challenging, are relevant to their personal interests—and when they are afforded personal choice and control. Present yourself as a model who is internally motivated, and provide students with support that encourages them to tackle learning with confidence and a minimum of anxiety. Guide students to develop a mastery orientation in which they focus more on the strategies necessary to solve a problem rather than on their ability or how well they are doing in relation to other students. Give students opportunities to create goals, plan how to reach these goals, and monitor their progress toward the goals. Have high expectations for students but provide the support and guidance necessary for them to reach these expectations.

When classrooms are effectively managed, they run smoothly and students are actively engaged in learning. When they are poorly managed, they become chaotic and learning is a foreign activity. Classrooms need to be managed effectively to maximize students' learning. The contemporary trend in managing classrooms is away from controlling students and toward supportive, nurturing relationships and opportunities for self-regulation. Good teaching strategies for beginning the school year are to be in charge, establish expectations for behavior, and resolve student uncertainties. In managing your classroom, keep the focus on instruction and a positive classroom environment. Use an authoritative strategy rather than authoritarian or permissive strategies. Establish rules but make sure they are necessary, reasonable, clear, and consistent with instructional and learning goals. No matter how well you have planned and created a positive environment, problem behaviors will emerge. It is critical that you deal with them in a timely, effective manner. Be a good communicator with students by developing effective speaking and listening skills. Work with students to help them become better speakers and listeners.

Assessment

As a teacher, you will need to know about the nature of standardized tests. Your role as a teacher in standardized tests might involve preparing students to take the tests, administering the tests, understanding and interpreting them, and communicating test results to parents. One debate focuses on how standardized tests stack up against alternative assessments. All tests—whether standardized or alternative—should meet acceptable standards of validity and reliability. Another issue concerns whether standardized tests discriminate against ethnic minority students and students from low-income backgrounds.

Assessment is an important aspect of teaching and learning. Think of integrating instruction and assessment in terms of three time frames: pre-instruction, during instruction, and post-instruction. Make assessment compatible with contemporary views of learning and motivation that emphasize children as active, constructive learners who are internally motivated. Current trends in assessment focus on using at least some performance-based assessments (such as portfolios), examining higher-level cognitive skills such as critical thinking, using multiple assessment methods, and having high performance standards for students. Among the issues in grading are whether it should be abolished and whether grade inflation is a problem.

Some Final Words

By choosing to become a teacher, you have answered one of America's highest callings, because you will have an opportunity to make a difference—a big difference—in children's lives. Take the calling seriously and pour your heart and mind into challenging children to actively construct their learning.

John W. Santrock

Bloom's taxonomy   Educational objectives in three domains: cognitive, affective, and psychomotor; developed by Benjamin Bloom and his colleagues.   357

book clubs   A small group that meets to discuss books that all members of the group have read; a useful tool for peer learning and for giving students experience in leading small-group discussions.   335

brainstorming   A technique in which individuals in a group come up with creative ideas, play off each others' ideas, and say practically whatever comes to mind relevant to a particular issue.   144

cadre approach   A conflict resolution strategy in which a small number of students are trained to serve as peer mediators for the entire school.   451

care perspective   A moral perspective that views people in terms of their connectedness, emphasizing relationships and concerns for others. Gilligan believes this approach should be incorporated more in understanding moral development.   109

case studies   In-depth looks at individuals.   22

CD-ROM   Compact disk read-only memory. Small storage disks similar to laser digital compact discs for music.   381

centration   In preoperational thought, focusing (or centering) attention on one characteristic to the exclusion of all others.   52

cerebral palsy   A disorder that involves a lack of muscular coordination, shaking, or unclear speech.   200

character education   A direct approach to moral education that involves teaching students basic moral literacy to prevent them from engaging in immoral behavior and doing harm to themselves and others.   110

children who are gifted   Children with above-average intelligence (usually defined as an IQ of 120 or higher) and/or superior talent in some domain such as art, music, or mathematics.   217

chronosystem   In Bronfenbrenner's ecological theory, the sociohistorical contexts of development.   82

chunking   A beneficial organizational memory strategy that involves grouping or "packing" information into "higher-order" units that can be remembered as single units.   279

classical conditioning   A type of learning in which an organism learns to connect or associate stimuli. A neutral stimulus becomes associated with a meaningful stimulus and acquires the capacity to elicit a similar response.   240

cluster style   A classroom arrangement style in which small numbers of students (usually 4 to 8) work in small, closely bunched groups.   434

cognitive apprenticeship   A learning relationship between a novice and an expert who stretches and supports the novice's understanding of and use of the culture's skills.   320

cognitive behavior approaches   Approaches to learning that emphasize getting students to monitor, manage, and regulate their own behavior rather than let it be controlled by external factors.   258

cognitive developmental theory of gender   Kohlberg's theory that children's gender typing occurs after they have developed a concept of gender.   180

cognitive moral education   An approach to moral education based on the belief that students should learn to value things like democracy and justice as their moral reasoning develops. Kohlberg's theory has been the basis for a number of cognitive moral education programs.   111

cognitive processes   Changes in thinking, intelligence, and language.   39

collaborative consultation   An educational strategy in which people with diverse expertise interact to establish competent services for children; increasingly used in the education of children with disabilities.   229

collectivism   A set of values that give priority to the group rather than the individual.   160

comparative advance organizers   Advance organizers that introduce new material by connecting it with what students already know.   361

competence motivation   R. W. White's concept that people are motivated to deal effectively with their environment, to master their world, and to process information efficiently.   396

computer simulations   Computer learning environments that model real-world situations.   380

computer-assisted instruction (CAI)   Instruction that is provided by a computer; closely linked with mastery learning.   379

computer-mediated communication (CMC)   Communication through electronic exchanges; sometimes referred to as telecommunications or educational telecommunications; includes the Internet and e-mail.   383

concept map   A visual presentation of a concept's connections and hierarchical organization.   293

concepts   Categories used to group objects, events, and characteristics on the basis of common properties.   291

concrete operational stage   Piaget's third stage, lasting from about 7 to 11 years of age. Involves using operations, logical reasoning instead of intuitive reasoning (but only in concrete situations), and classification.   53

concurrent validity   A form of criterion validity that refers to the relation between a test score and other criteria that are currently (concurrently) available.   468

conditioned response (CR)   A learned response to a conditioned stimulus that occurs after a US-CS pairing.   242

conditioned stimulus (CS)   A previously neutral stimulus that eventually elicits a conditioned response after being associated with the US.   241

confirmation bias   The tendency to search for and use information that supports our ideas rather than refutes them.   300

conservation   The idea that some characteristic of an object stays the same even though the object might change in appearance.   52

construct validity   A broad form of validity that can include concurrent and predictive validity, as well as other evidence regarding the extent to which a test measures a particular construct (an unobservable trait or characteristic of a person, such as intelligence).   469

constructed-response item   Assessment items that require students to write out answers rather than select a response from a menu; they usually do not allow objective scoring but require judgment on the part of the examiner. Short-answer and essay items are the most common examples.   509

constructivism   An approach to learning that emphasizes the individuals actively construct and knowledge and understanding. Children are encouraged to explore their world, discover knowledge, reflect, and think critically.   10

constructivism   An educational approach that emphasizes that individuals learn best when they actively construct knowledge and understanding.   318

content validity   A test's ability to sample the content that is to be measured.   468

content-related evidence   The extent to which assessment reflects the material that has been taught.   501

continuity in development   Gradual, cumulative developmental change.   41

contracting   Putting reinforcement contingencies into a written agreement.   250

control group   A comparison group in an experiment that is treated in every way like the experimental group except for the manipulated factor.   24

controversial children   Children frequently nominated both as someone's best friend and as being disliked by peers.   95

conventional reasoning   In Kohlberg's theory, the second level of moral development. At this level, internalization is intermediate. Individuals abide internally by certain standards, but these essentially are the standards imposed by other people.   108

convergent thinking   A pattern of thinking in which individuals produce one correct answer, characteristic of the kind of thinking required on conventional intelligence tests; a term coined by Guilford.   141

cooperative learning   Learning that occurs when students work in small groups to help each other learn.   323

correlational research   Research whose goals is to describe the strength of the relation between two or more events or characteristics.   22

creativity   The ability to think about something in novel and unusual ways and come up with unique solutions to problems.   141

criterion validity   A test's ability to predict a student's performance as measured by other assessments or criteria.   468

criterion-referenced grading   A grading system based on comparison with predetermined standards.   522

critical thinking   Thinking reflectively and productively, and evaluating the evidence.   297

cross-cultural studies   Studies that compare what happens in one culture with what happens in other cultures, providing information about the degree to which people are similar and to what degree certain behaviors are specific to certain cultures.   160

cross-sectional research   Research that studies groups of people all at one time.   25

cue-dependent forgetting   Memory retrieval failure caused by a lack of effective retrieval cues.   288

culture   The behavior patterns, beliefs, and all other products of a particular group of people that are passed down from generation to generation.   160

culture-fair tests   Tests of intelligence that are intended to be free of cultural bias.   137

curriculum compacting   A variation of acceleration in which teachers skip over aspects of the curriculum that they believe are not needed by children who are gifted.   219

decay theory   The theory that new learning involves the creation of a neurochemical "memory trace," which will eventually disintegrate. Thus, decay theory suggests that the passage of time is responsible for forgetting.   289

declarative memory   The conscious recollection of information, such as specific facts or events that can be verbally communicated.   282

deductive reasoning   Reasoning from the general to the specific.   296

deep/surface styles   A dichotomy reflecting the extent to which students approach learning in a way that helps them understand the meaning of the materials (deep style) or as simply what needs to be learned (surface style).   147

dependent variable   The factor that is measured as the result of an experiment.   24

depression   A type of mood disorder in which the individual feels worthless, believes that things are not likely to get better, and behaves in a lethargic manner for a prolonged period of time.   214

descriptive statistics   Mathematical procedures that are used to describe and summarize data (information) in a meaningful way.   479

development   The pattern of biological, cognitive, and socioemotional changes that begins at conception and continues through the life span.   38

developmentally appropriate education   Education based on knowledge of the typical development of children within an age span (age appropriateness) as well as the uniqueness of the child (individual appropriateness).   98

diagnostic testing   A relatively in-depth evaluation of a specific area of learning; its purpose is to determine the specific learning needs of a student so those needs can be met through regular or remedial instruction.   471

difficult child   A child who tends to react negatively, has aggressive tendencies, lacks self-control, and is slow to accept new experiences.   153

direct instruction   A structured, teacher-centered approach to teaching that is characterized by teacher direction and control, high teacher expectations for students' progress, maximizing the time students spend on academic tasks, and keeping negative affect to a minimum.   359

disability   A limitation on a person's functioning that restricts the individual's abilities.   198

discontinuity in development   Distinctive, stage-like developmental change.   41

discovery learning   Learning in which students construct an understanding on their own.   374

discrimination (in classical conditioning)   The response of organism to certain stimuli and not others.   242

discrimination (in operant conditioning)   Differentiating among stimuli or environmental events.   246

divergent thinking   A pattern of thinking in which individuals produce many answers to the same question; more characteristic of creativity than convergent thinking; a term coined by Guilford.   141

Down syndrome   A genetically transmitted form of mental retardation in which children have an extra (47th) chromosome.   203

drill-and-practice programs   Computer programs that give students opportunities to learn and practice academic skills, such as mathematics, science, and reading.   379

dyslexia   A category of learning disabilities involving a severe impairment in the ability to read and spell.   208

early adulthood   The period beginning in the late teens or early twenties and stretching into the thirties.   39

early childhood   Sometimes called the preschool years, the period from infancy to about 5 or 6 years.   39

early-later experience issue   The degree to which early experiences (especially in infancy and/or early childhood) or later experiences are viewed as the key determinants of development.   41

easy child   A child who is generally in a good mood, quickly establishes regular routines, and easily adapts to new routines.   153

ecological theory   Bronfenbrenner's theory that analyzes the environment's influence on children's development in terms of five systems: microsystem, mesosystem, exosystem, macrosystem, and chronosystem.   82

educational psychology   The branch of psychology that specializes in understanding teaching and learning in educational settings.   6

educationally blind   An inability to use one's vision in learning; implies a need use hearing and touch to learn.   199

egocentrism   In preoperational thought, the inability to distinguish one's own perspective from someone else's perspective.   51

elaboration   The extensiveness of information processing involved in memory.   278

e-mail   Electronic mail; messages can be sent to and received from individuals as well as large numbers of people at once.   383

emotional and behavioral disorders   Serious, persistent problems that involve relationships, aggression, depression, fears associated with personal or school matters, as well as other inappropriate socioemotional characteristics.   213

emotional intelligence   Emotional self-awareness and the ability to manage emotions, read emotions, and handle relationships.   114

empowerment   Providing people with the intellectual and coping skills to succeed and make this a more just world.   172

encoding   The process by which information gets into memory.   275

encoding specificity principle   Associations formed at the time of encoding or learning tend to be effective retrieval cues.   288

enrichment program   A program for children who are gifted that provides opportunities for learning that usually are not present in the curriculum.   219

epilepsy   A nervous disorder characterized by recurring sensorimotor attacks or movement convulsions.   201

episodic memory   Declarative memory that involves the retention of information about the where and when of life's happenings.   283

essay items   Assessment items that require extensive writing. They allow more freedom of response than other item formats and can be especially good for assessing understanding, higher-level thinking skills, ability to organize information, and writing skills.   509

essential questions   Questions that reflect the heart of the curriculum, the most important things a teacher thinks students should explore and learn.   374

ethnic gloss   The use of an ethnic label such as *African American, Latino, Asian American,* or *Native American* in a superficial way that makes an ethnic group seem more homogeneous than it really is.   30

ethnicity   A shared pattern of characteristics such as cultural heritage, nationality, race, religion, and language.   164

exosystem   In Bronfenbrenner's ecological theory, other settings (in which the student does not play an active role) that influence what teachers and students experience in their immediate context.   82

experiment   A carefully regulated procedure in which one or more of the factors believed to influence the behavior being studied is manipulated and all other factors are held constant.   23

experimental group   A group whose experience is manipulated in an experiment.   24

experimental research   Research involving experiments that permit the determination of cause.   23

expository advance organizers   Advance organizers that provide students with new knowledge that will orient them to an upcoming lesson.   361

expressive language   The ability to express one's thoughts.   205

extinction (in classical conditioning) The weakening of a conditioned response in the absence of the unconditioned stimulus.   242

extinction (in operant conditioning) A decrease in the frequency of a response when it is no longer reinforced.   246

extrinsic motivation Response to external incentives such as rewards and punishments.   397

face-to-face style A classroom arrangement style in which students sit facing each other.   434

failure syndrome A pattern of having low expectations for success and a tendency to give up at the first sign of difficulty.   421

far transfer Transfer of learning to a situation that is very different from the one in which the initial learning took place.   307

fetal alcohol syndrome (FAS) A cluster of abnormalities (including mental retardation and facial abnormalities) that appear in the offspring of mothers who drink alcohol heavily during pregnancy; appears in about one-third of the offspring of pregnant alcoholic women.   203

field dependent/independent styles A dichotomy that involves the extent to which the surrounding field (environment) dominates the person's perception. When it dominates, the person is said to be field dependent; when it doesn't dominate, the person is said to be field independent.   145

fine motor skills Skills involving finely tuned movements, such as the finger dexterity required for writing and drawing.   42

fixation Using a prior strategy and failing to look at a problem from a fresh, new perspective.   299

fixed-interval schedule A reinforcement schedule in which the first appropriate response after a fixed amount of time is reinforced.   249

fixed-ratio schedule A reinforcement schedule in which a set number of responses elapses and then the first appropriate response is reinforced.   249

flow Csikszentmihalyi's concept that optimal life experiences occur most often when people develop a sense of mastery and are absorbed in a state of concentration when they are engaged in an activity.   398

fluency disorders Various disorders that involve what is commonly called "stuttering."   204

formal operational stage Piaget's fourth and final cognitive stage, which emerges at about 11 to 15 years of age. Individuals move beyond reasoning only about concrete experiences and think in more abstract, idealistic, and logical ways.   55

formative assessment Assessment during the course of instruction rather than after it is completed.   497

forward-reaching transfer Transfer of learning in which individuals think about how they can apply what they have learned to new situations in the future.   307

Fostering a Community of Learners (FCL) Developed by Ann Brown and Joe Campione, this social constructivist program focuses on literacy development and biology in 6- to 12-year-olds. It emphasizes adults as role models, children teaching children, and online computer consultation.   329

fragile X syndrome The second most commonly identified form of mental retardation; it is genetically transmitted by an abnormality on the X chromosome, resulting in severe retardation in males and less severe retardation in females.   203

frequency distribution A listing of scores, usually from highest to lowest, along with the number of times each score appears.   479

functional fixedness A type of fixation in which the individual fails to solve a problem because she or he views the elements involved solely in terms of their usual functions.   300

gender roles Expectations that prescribe how males and females should think, feel, and act.   178

gender schema theory The theory that the individual's attention and behavior are guided by an inner motivation to conform to gender-based sociocultural standards and stereotypes.   181

gender stereotypes Broad categories that reflect impressions and beliefs about what behavior is appropriate for females and males.   181

gender The sociocultural dimensions of being female or male.   178

gender-role transcendence The view that people's competence should be conceptualized independently of their masculinity, femininity, or androgyny.   187

generalization (in classical conditioning) The tendency of a new stimulus similar to an original conditioned stimulus to produce a similar response.   242

generalization (in operant conditioning) Giving the same response to similar stimuli.   246

generativity versus stagnation Erikson's seventh psychosocial stage (forties, fifties).   86

grade-equivalent score A score expressed in terms of the grade level of students who are actually in the given grade level. Because it often is misinterpreted, other types of scores, such as standard scores, are more appropriate to use.   484

grading Translating descriptive assessment information into numbers, letters, or other marks that indicate the quality of the student's learning or performance.   521

gross motor skills Skills involving large-muscle activities, such as running and playing sports.   42

growth portfolio A portfolio of the student's work over an extended time frame, which reveals how much the student has changed or learned over time.   517

guided discovery learning Learning in which students are encouraged to construct their understanding, but with the assistance of teacher-guided questions and directions.   375

handicap A condition imposed on a person who has a disability, which might come from society, the physical environment, or the person's own attitudes.   198

helpless orientation An outlook in which children focus on their personal inadequacies, often attribute their difficulty to a lack of ability, and display negative affect (including boredom and anxiety). This orientation undermines their performance.   403

heteronomous morality In Piaget's theory, the first stage of moral development (about 4 to 7 years of age), in which justice and rules are conceived of as unchangeable properties of the world, beyond the control of people.   107

heuristics Strategies or rules of thumb that can suggest a solution to a problem but do not guarantee a solution.   299

hidden curriculum According to Dewey, the pervasive moral atmosphere every school has even if it doesn't have a program of moral education.   110

hierarchy of needs Maslow's view that certain basic needs must be satisfied before higher needs can be satisfied. In this view, needs must be satisfied in this sequence: physiological, safety, love and belongingness, esteem, cognitive, aesthetic, and self-actualization.   395

high-road transfer Conscious and effortful transfer of learning to a new situation.   307

high-stakes testing Using test results in a way that has important consequences for the student, affecting decisions such as whether the student will be promoted to the next grade, graduate, or get a scholarship.   467

histogram A frequency distribution presented in the form of a graph, in which vertical bars represent the frequency of scores per category.   479

holistic scoring Making an overall judgment about the student's answer to an essay assessment item and giving it a single number or letter.   510

hostile environment sexual harassment The subjection of students to unwelcome sexual conduct that is so severe, persistent, or pervasive that it limits the students' ability to benefit from their education.   190

Human Biology Middle Grades Curriculum (HUMBIO) Developed by Stanford University scientists in collaboration with middle school teachers, HUMBIO integrates the study of ecology, evolution, genetics, physiology, human development, culture, health, and safety.   345

humanistic perspective A perspective that stresses our capacity for personal growth, our freedom to choose our destiny, and our positive qualities.   395

hypermedia Computer-based content that includes linked verbal, visual, auditory, and/or animated content.   382

hypertext Computer-based verbal content with embedded links that lets students read about one topic and then select related topics to explore.   382

hypotheses Assumptions that can be tested to determine their accuracy. A theory contains hypotheses.   20

hypothetical-deductive reasoning Developing hypotheses about ways to solve problems and systematically reaching conclusions, a form of reasoning Piaget believed adolescents become capable of as they become formal operational thinkers.   55

"I" messages   A desirable style of communication in which speakers reflect their own true feelings better than when they use "you" messages.   356

identification theory   The Freudian view that the preschool child develops a sexual attraction to the opposite-sex parent, then, by about 5 or 6 years of age, renounces this attraction because of anxious feelings, identifies with the same-sex parent, and unconsciously adopts the same-sex parent's characteristics.   180

identity achievement   The identity status in which individuals have adequately explored alternative courses of action and made a commitment.   106

identity diffusion   The identity status in which individuals have neither explored meaningful alternatives nor made a commitment.   106

identity foreclosure   The identity status in which individuals have made a commitment but have not explored meaningful alternative courses of action.   106

identity moratorium   The identity status in which individuals are in the midst of exploring alternative courses of action but have not yet made a commitment.   106

identity versus identity confusion   Erikson's fifth psychosocial stage (adolescence).   85

idiographic needs   The needs of the individual, not of the group.   31

immanent justice   The belief of the heteronomous thinker that if a rule is broken, punishment will be meted out immediately.   107

impulsive/reflective styles   Also referred to as conceptual tempo, a dichotomy reflecting a student's tendency to act quickly and impulsively or take more time to respond and reflect on the accuracy of an answer.   146

incentives   In the behavioral perspective, positive or negative stimuli that can motivate behavior.   394

inclusion   Educating a child with special educational needs full-time in the regular classroom.   224

independent variable   The manipulated, influential, experimental factor in an experiment.   23

individual differences   The stable, consistent ways in which people are different from one another.   126

individualism   A set of values that give priority to personal goals rather than to group goals.   160

individualized education plan (IEP)   A written statement that spells out a program specifically tailored for the child with a disability. The plan should be (1) related to the child's learning capacity, (2) specially constructed to meet the child's individual needs and not merely a copy of what is offered to other children, and (3) designed to provide educational benefits.   224

Individuals with Disabilities Education Act (IDEA)   The IDEA spells out broad mandates for services to all children with disabilities (IDEA is a renaming of *Public Law 94-142*); these include evaluation and eligibility determination, appropriate education and an individualized education plan (IEP), and education in the least restrictive environment (LRE).   221

inductive reasoning   Reasoning from the specific to the general.   295

indulgent parenting   A parenting style in which parents are highly involved with their children but place few limits or restrictions on their behaviors; associated with children's socially incompetent behavior, especially low self-control.   89

industry versus inferiority   Erikson's fourth psychosocial stage (elementary school years).   85

infancy   The period from birth to 18–24 months.   39

inferences   Conclusions that individuals draw from information.   500

infinite generativity   The ability to produce an endless number of meaningful sentences using a finite set of words and rules.   65

information-processing approach   An approach to learning that emphasizes that individuals manipulate information, monitor it, and strategize about it. Central to this approach are the processes of memory and thinking.   274

initiative versus guilt   Erikson's third psychosocial stage (early childhood years).   85

instructional games   Computer-based activities that capitalize on the increased motivation and interest that comes from encasing learning in an animated, visually displayed game.   380

instructional planning   A systematic, organized strategy for planning lessons.   354

instructional technology   Various types of hardware and software, combined with innovative teaching methods, to accommodate students' learning needs in the classroom.   230

instructional validity   The extent to which the assessment is a reasonable sample of what actually went on in the classroom.   501

integrity versus despair   Erikson's eighth psychosocial stage (sixties to death).   86

intelligence   Verbal and problem-solving skills, and the ability to adapt to and learn from life's everyday experiences. Not everyone agrees on what constitutes intelligence.   126

intelligence quotient (IQ)   A person's tested mental age divided by chronological age, multiplied by 100.   127

interference theory   The theory that we forget, not because we lose memories from storage, but because other information gets in the way of what we are trying to remember.   288

internalization   The developmental change from behavior that is externally controlled to behavior that is internally controlled.   108

Internet   A worldwide system that connects thousands of computer networks, providing an incredible array of information that students can access; the core of computer-mediated communication.   383

intimacy versus isolation   Erikson's sixth psychosocial stage (early adulthood).   86

intrinsic motivation   Internal motivational factors such as self-determination, curiosity, challenge, and effort.   397

intuitive thought substage   The second substage in preoperational thought, lasting from about 4 to 7 years of age. Children begin to use primitive reasoning, ask countless questions, and seem sure of their knowledge but are unaware of how they know what they know.   51

item difficulty index   The percentage of students who obtain the correct answer on an item.   508

item discrimination index   A numeric value, from 0 to 1.00, that reflects the item's ability to discriminate among individuals who scored high and those who scored low on the entire test.   508

jigsaw classroom   Having students from different cultural backgrounds cooperate by doing different parts of a project to reach a common goal.   173

Joplin plan   A standard nongraded program for instruction in reading.   139

justice perspective   A moral perspective that focuses on the rights of individuals; Kohlberg's theory is a justice perspective.   109

keyword method   A mnemonic device in which vivid imagery is attached to specific words.   286

laboratory   A controlled setting from which many of the complex factors of the real world have been removed.   20

language   A form of communication, whether spoken, written, or signed, that is based on a system of symbols.   65

language disorders   Disorders involving significant impairments in receptive and expressive language.   204

law of effect   Thorndike's concept that behaviors followed by positive outcomes are strengthened, and that behaviors followed by negative outcomes are weakened.   244

learning   A relatively permanent change in behavior that occurs through experience.   238

learning and thinking styles   People's individual preferences regarding how they use their abilities.   145

learning disability   Children with a learning disability (1) are of normal intelligence or above, (2) have difficulty in at least one academic area and usually several, and (3) have no other diagnosed problem or disorder, such as mental retardation, that can be determined as causing the difficulty.   207

learning target   A specific statement of what students should know or be able to do as a result of instruction; compatible with instructional objectives.   499

least restrictive environment (LRE)   An educational setting that is as similar as possible to the one in which children who do not have a disability are educated.   224

levels of processing theory   Craik and Lockhart's theory that the processing of memory occurs on a continuum from shallow to deep, with deeper processing producing better memory.   278

local norms   In standardized testing, the scores of a group that is more locally based than a national group; examples include scores of students in the same class, school, or district.   467

longitudinal research   Research that studies the same people over a period of time, usually several years or more.   25

long-term memory   The memory system that holds enormous amounts of information for a long period of time in a relatively permanent fashion.   280

low vision   Visual acuity between 20/70 and 20/200 with corrective lenses.   199

low-road transfer   The automatic, often unconscious, transfer of learning to another situation.   307

M

macrosystem   In Bronfenbrenner's ecological theory, the broader culture in which students and teachers live.   82

mainstreaming   Educating a child with special educational needs partially in a special education classroom and partially in a regular classroom.   224

manipulative style   A way of dealing with conflict in which individuals try to get others to feel sorry for them or to feel guilty.   457

manual approaches   Educational approaches to help children with hearing impairments; they involve sign language and finger spelling.   200

mastery learning   Learning one concept or topic thoroughly before moving on to a more difficult one.   362

mastery motivation   An outlook in which children focus on the task rather than on their ability, have positive affect, and generate solution-oriented strategies that improve their performance.   403

maturation   The orderly sequence of changes dictated by the child's genetic blueprint.   40

mean   A measure of central tendency that is the numerical average of a group of scores; commonly labeled M or Mn of X (mean of X) by statisticians.   479

means-end analysis   A heuristic in which one identifies the goal (end) of a problem, assesses the current situation, and evaluates what needs to be done (means) to decrease the difference between the two conditions.   299

measure of central tendency   A number that provides information about the average or typical score in a set of data; the three measures of central tendency are the mean, median, and mode.   479

measures of variability   Measures that show how much scores vary from one another; two measures of variability are range and standard deviation.   481

median   The score that falls exactly in the middle of a distribution of scores after they have been ranked from highest to lowest; a measure of central tendency.   480

memory   The retention of information over time, involving these main activities: encoding, storage, and retrieval.   275

memory span   The number of digits an individual can report back without error in a single presentation.   280

mental age (MA)   An individual's level of mental development relative to others, a concept developed by Binet.   127

mental processes   The thoughts, feelings, and motives that each of us experiences but that cannot be observed by others.   238

mental retardation   A condition with an onset before age 18 that involves low intelligence (usually below 70 on a traditional individually administered intelligence test) and difficulty in adapting to everyday life.   202

mental set   A type of fixation in which an individual tries to solve a problem in a particular way that has worked in the past.   300

mesosystem   In Bronfenbrenner's ecology theory, the system composed of linkages between microsystems.   82

metacognition   Cognition about cognition, "knowing about knowing."   275

metacognitive activity   The conscious adaptation and management of thinking strategies during purposeful thinking and problem solving.   309

metacognitive knowledge   Monitoring and reflecting on one's current or recent thoughts.   309

method of loci   A mnemonic device in which individuals develop images of items to be remembered and mentally store them in familiar locations.   286

microsystem   In Bronfenbrenner's ecological theory, a setting in which individuals spend considerable time. Examples of such contexts are the student's family, peers, schools, and neighborhoods. The student has direct interactions with others in these settings.   82

microworlds   Scaled-down, computer-based simulations of real environments in which learners construct knowledge as they explore and design new worlds.   380

middle and late childhood   Sometimes called the elementary school years, the period from about 6 to 11 years of age.   39

minimum competency tests   Tests that assess skills students are expected to have mastered before they can be promoted to the next grade or permitted to graduate.   467

mnemonics   Aids for remembering information.   286

mode   The score that occurs most often in a set of scores; a measure of central tendency.   480

moral development   Development with respect to the rules and conventions about just interactions between people.   106

morphology   The language system for combining morphemes, which are meaningful strings of sounds that contain no smaller meaningful parts.   65

motivation   Why people behave the way they do. Motivated behavior is energized, directed, and sustained.   394

multicultural education   An educational approach that values diversity and includes the perspectives of a variety of cultural groups on a regular basis.   171

multiple-choice item   A selected-response item that consists of two parts: a stem and number of options or alternatives.   506

myelination   A biological process in which many cells of the brain and nervous system are covered with an insulating layer of fat cells. This increases the speed at which information travels through the nervous system.   42

N

national norms   The scores on a standardized test of a nationally representative group of individuals; a student's score is evaluated in relation to this group's scores.   467

naturalistic observation   Observations that take place out in the real world instead of in a laboratory.   20

nature-nurture controversy   The debate about whether development is primarily influenced by maturation (biological inheritance, "nature") or primarily by experience (environment, "nurture").   40

near transfer   Transfer of learning when situations are very similar. For example, if the classroom learning situation is similar to the transfer situation, near transfer is involved.   307

need for affiliation   The motive to be with other people; involves establishing, maintaining, and restoring warm, close, personal relationships.   412

negative affectivity (NA)   The range of negative emotions, including anxiety, anger, guilt, and sadness.   114

negative reinforcement   The removal of an aversive (unpleasant) stimulus after the occurrence of a response, causing the response to increase in frequency.   245

neglected children   Children infrequently nominated as a best friend but not disliked by their peers.   95

neglectful parenting   A form of permissive parenting in which parents are uninvolved in their children's lives; associated with children's lack of social competence, especially low self-control.   89

neo-Piagetians   Developmental psychologists who believe that Piaget got some things right but that his theory needs revision. They give more emphasis to information processing.   58

network theories   Theories that describe how information in memory is organized and connected, with an emphasis on nodes in the memory network.   284

nomothetic research   Research conducted at the level of the group.   30

nongraded (cross-age) program   A variation of between-class ability grouping in which students are grouped by their ability in particular subjects, regardless of their age or grade level.   139

norm group   In standardized testing, the group of students previously given the test by the test maker for purposes of calibration; a student's score on a standardized test is evaluated in relation to this group's scores.   467

normal distribution   A distribution in which most of the scores cluster symmetrically around the mean. The farther above or below the mean a score is, the less frequently it occurs. A normal distribution also is called a "bell-shaped curve" or "bell curve."   127

normal distribution   A symmetrical distribution of values or scores, with a majority of scores falling in the middle of the possible range of scores and few scores appearing toward the extremes of the range; a distribution that yields what is called a "bell-shaped curve."   483

norm-referenced grading   A grading system based on comparison of a student's performance with that of other students in the class or of other classes and other students.   521

object permanence   An important infant accomplishment in Piaget's theory that involves understanding that objects and events continue to exist even when they cannot be seen, heard, or touched.   50

objective tests   Tests with clear, unambiguous scoring criteria; multiple-choice tests are objective tests.   502

observational learning   Learning that occurs when a person observes and imitates someone else's behavior; also called imitation or modeling.   256

off-set style   A classroom arrangement style in which a small number of students (usually 3 or 4) sit at tables but do not sit directly across from one another.   434

operant conditioning   A form of learning in which the consequences of behavior produce changes in the probability that the behavior will occur; also called instrumental conditioning.   243

operations   In Piaget's theory, mental representations that are reversible.   53

oral approaches   Educational approaches to help children with hearing impairments; they include lip reading, speech reading, and whatever hearing the child has.   200

orthopedic impairments   Restrictions in movement abilities due to muscle, bone, or joint problems.   200

participant observation   Research in which the observer-researcher is actively involved as a participant in the activity or setting.   27

passive style   A way of dealing with conflict in which individuals are nonassertive and submissive.   457

peers   Children of about the same age or maturity level.   92

percentile bands   A range of scores (rather than a single score) around a mean value expressed in percentiles, such as 75th to 85th percentile.   486

percentile rank score   A score that expresses the percentage of a distribution of scores that lie at or below a given raw score; percentile ranks range from 1 to 99.   483

performance assessments   Assessments that require students to perform a task, such as write an essay, conduct an experiment, carry out a project, solve a real-world problem, or create a portfolio.   502

performance criteria   Specific behaviors that students are expected to effectively perform as part of an assessment.   515

performance orientation   An outlook in which children are concerned with performance outcome rather than performance process. For performance-oriented students, winning is what matters.   403

permissive strategy of classroom management   A management style that offers students considerable autonomy but provides them with little support for developing skills or managing their behavior. Taught in this manner, students often do not develop adequate academic skills and do not learn self-control.   441

personality   The pattern of distinctive thoughts, emotions, and behaviors that characterize the way an individual adapts to the world.   151

person-environment fit   The fit between the needs of students (person) and the type of schooling (environment) they experience. Eccles and her colleagues argue that a lack of fit between the middle school/ junior high environment and the needs of young adolescents produces increasingly negative self-evaluations and attitudes toward school.   310

person-situation interaction   The view that the best way to conceptualize personality is not in terms of personal traits alone but also in terms of the situation involved.   152

phonology   The sound system of a language.   65

pluralistic assessment   Assessment that is responsive to cultural diversity in the classroom and at school.   501

popular children   Children frequently nominated as a best friend and rarely disliked by their peers.   95

portfolio   A systematic and organized collection of a student's work that demonstrates the student's skills and accomplishments.   516

positive affectivity (PA)   The range of positive emotions, whether high energy or low energy; joy and happiness are examples of PA.   114

positive reinforcement   A stimulus that follows a response and increases the frequency of the response.   244

postconventional reasoning   In Kohlberg's theory, the third and highest level of moral development. At this level, morality is completely internalized and not based on external standards.   108

pragmatics   The system of rules for the use of appropriate conversation.   66

preconventional reasoning   In Kohlberg's theory, the lowest level of moral development. At this level the child shows no internalization of moral values. Moral reasoning is controlled by external punishments and rewards.   108

predictive validity   A form of criterion validity that refers to the relation between a test score and the student's future performance.   468

prejudice   An unjustified negative attitude toward an individual because of the individual's membership in a group.   167

Premack principle   A high-probability activity can be used as a reinforcer for a low-probability activity.   248

preoperational stage   Piaget's second stage, lasting approximately from 2 to 7 years of age. It is more symbolic than sensorimotor thought, does not involve operational thought, is egocentric, and is intuitive rather than logical.   50

primacy effect   Items at the beginning of a list tend to be remembered.   285

problem sets   Two or more assessment items that are related to the same stimulus, such as an illustration, graph, or passage.   507

problem solving   Finding an appropriate way to attain a goal.   298

problem-based learning   An approach to learning that emphasizes solving authentic problems like those that occur in daily life.   300

procedural memory   Knowledge in the form of skills and cognitive operations about how to do something. This knowledge cannot be consciously recollected, at least not in the form of specific facts.   282

productions   Documents that a student prepares especially for a portfolio.   516

program evaluation research   Research that is designed to make decisions about the effectiveness of a particular program.   25

Project Head Start   A federal program designed to provide young children from low-income families opportunities to acquire the skills and experiences that are important for success in school.   99

prompt   An added stimulus or cue that is given just prior to a response and increases the likelihood that the response will occur.   250

prototype matching   Deciding whether an item is a member of a category by comparing it with the most typical item(s) of the category.   294

puberty   A maturational phase that occurs mainly in early adolescence, involving changes in height, weight, and sexual functions.   45

Public Law 94-142   The Education for All Handicapped Children Act, enacted in 1975, which requires that all children with disabilities be given a free, appropriate public education and provides the funding to help with the costs of implementing this education.   221

punishment   A consequence that decreases the probability a behavior will occur.   244

quid pro quo sexual harassment   Threatening to base an educational decision (such as a grade) or other reward or punishment on a student's submission to unwelcome sexual conduct.   190

R

random assignment   In experimental research, the assignment of participants to experimental and control groups by chance.   24

range   The distance between the highest and lowest scores in a set of scores; a measure of variability.   481

rapport talk   The language of conversation and a way of establishing connections and negotiating relationships; usually preferred by females more than by males.   185

raw score   The number of items a student gets correct on a test.   483

reading   The ability to understand written discourse.   70

recall   A memory task in which individuals must retrieve previously learned information, as for fill-in-the-blank or essay questions.   288

recency effect   Items at the end of a list tend to be remembered.   285

receptive language   Linguistic information that is received by the brain.   205

reciprocal determinism model   Bandura's social cognitive model in which three main factors—behavior, environment, and person (cognition)—interact to influence learning.   254

reciprocal teaching   A learning arrangement in which students take turns leading a small-group discussion.   329

recognition   A memory task in which individuals only have to identify ("recognize") learned information, as for multiple-choice items.   288

rehearsal   Conscious repetition of information over time to increase the length of time information stays in memory.   277

reinforcement (reward)   A consequence (either positive or negative) that increases the probability that a behavior will occur.   244

rejected children   Children infrequently nominated as a best friend and disliked by their peers.   95

reliability   The extent to which a test produces a consistent, reproducible measure of performance.   500

reliability   The extent to which an assessment produces a consistent, reproducible measure of performance; reliable measures are stable, dependable, and relatively free from errors of measurement.   467

report talk   Talk that gives information; usually preferred by males more than by females.   185

reproductions   Portfolio documentation of a student's work outside the classroom, such as special projects and interviews.   516

response cost   Taking a positive reinforcer away from the student, as when the student loses certain privileges.   252

retrieval   Taking information taken out of storage.   276

S

scaffolding   The technique of changing the level of support over the course of a teaching session; the more-skilled person adjusts the amount of guidance to fit the student's current performance level.   320

scaffolding   The technique of gradually changing the level of support over the course of a teaching session. The more-skilled person adjusts her or his guidance to fit the student's current performance level.   61

schedules of reinforcement   Partial reinforcement timetables that determine when a response will be reinforced.   249

schema   A concept or framework that exists in an individual's mind to organize and interpret information.   49

schema   Information—concepts, knowledge, information about events—that already exists in a person's mind.   284

schema theories   Theories that when people reconstruct information, they fit it into information that already exists in their minds.   284

Schools for Thought (SFT)   A social constructivist program that combines aspects of the Jasper Project, Fostering a Community of Learners (FCL), and Computer Supported Intentional Learning Environments (CSILE).   330

scientific method   A method for discovering accurate information that includes these steps: conceptualize the problem, collect data, draw conclusions, and revise research conclusions and theory.   19

scientific research   Objective, systematic, and testable research that aims at reducing the likelihood that conclusions will be based on personal beliefs, opinions, and feelings.   19

script   A schema for an event.   285

selected-response items   Assessment items with an objective format in which students select an answer from several given choices rather than construct the answer themselves. A scoring key is created and can be applied by an examiner or by a computer to score students' responses.   503

self-actualization   The highest and most elusive of Maslow's needs, involving the motivation to develop one's full potential as a human being.   395

self-efficacy   The belief that one can master a situation and produce positive outcomes; proposed by Bandura.   404

self-efficacy   The belief that one can master a situation and produce positive outcomes.   256

self-esteem   The global, evaluative dimension of the self, also referred to as self-worth or self-image, that reflects an individual's overall confidence and satisfaction in themself.   105

self-instructional methods   Cognitive behavior techniques aimed at teaching individuals to modify their own behavior.   261

self-regulatory learning   The self-generation and self-monitoring of thoughts, feelings, and behaviors in order to reach a goal.   265

semantic memory   Declarative memory of general knowledge about the world.   283

semantics   The language system that involves the meaning of words and sentences.   65

seminar style   A classroom arrangement style in which groups of about 10 or more students sit in circular, square, or U-shaped arrangements.   434

sensorimotor stage   Piaget's first stage, which lasts from birth to about 2 years of age. Infants construct an understanding of the world by coordinating their sensory experiences with their motor actions.   50

sensory memory   The memory system that holds information from the world in its original sensory form for only an instant.   280

serial position effect   Recall is better for items at the beginning and end of a list than for items in the middle.   285

seriation   The concrete operation that involves ordering stimuli along some quantitative dimension (such as length).   54

service learning   A form of education that promotes social responsibility and service to the community.   111

sex   The biological dimensions of being female or male.   178

sexism   Prejudice and discrimination against an individual because of the person's sex.   183

shaping   Teaching new behaviors by reinforcing successive approximations to a specified target behavior.   250

short-answer item   A constructed-response assessment item in which students are required to write a word, a short phrase, or several sentences in response to a task.   509

short-term (working) memory   The limited-capacity memory system in which information is retained for as long as 30 seconds, unless the information is rehearsed, in which case it can be retained longer.   280

situated cognition   An important assumption in social constructivist approaches that thinking is located (situated) in social and physical contexts, not within an individual's mind.   319

slow-to-warm-up child   A child who has a low activity level, is somewhat negative, shows low adaptability, and displays a low intensity of mood.   153

social cognitive theory   Bandura's view that social and cognitive factors, as well as behavior, play important roles in learning.   254

social constructivist approach   An emphasis on the social contexts of learning and knowledge as mutually built and constructed, characteristic of Vygotsky's theory.   318

social constructivist approaches   Approaches to teaching that emphasize the social contexts of learning and knowledge as mutually built and constructed.   63

social learning theory of gender   The theory that gender development occurs through observation and imitation of gender behavior, as well as reinforcement and punishment of gender behavior.   180

social motives   Needs and desires that are learned through experiences with the social world.   412

socioeconomic status (SES)   The categorization of people according to their economic, educational, and occupational characteristics.   161

socioemotional processes   Changes in the child's relationships with other people, emotion, and personality.   39

special group norms   In standardized testing, scores of subgroups from a national sample. Such a subgroup might be students with low socioeconomic status, females, or Latinos.   467

speech and language disorders   A number of speech problems (such as articulation disorders, voice disorders, and fluency disorders) and language problems (which involve difficulties in receiving and expressing language).   203

split-half reliability   A method of checking the reliability of a test by dividing the test items into two halves, such as the odd-numbered and even-numbered items; the scores on the two sets are compared to determine how consistently students performed across the sets.   468

standard deviation   A measure of variability that reveals how much a set of scores varies on the average around the mean of the scores; that is, this measure shows how closely scores cluster around the mean. The smaller the standard deviation, the less variability from the mean, and vice versa.   481

standard score   A score expressed as a deviation from the mean.   484

standardized test   A test that is prepared by test specialists to assess performance under uniform conditions; allows a student's performance to be compared with other students' performance, often on a national basis.   466

standardized tests   Commercially prepared tests that assess students' performance in different domains.   22

stanine score   A score that describes a student's test performance on a nine-point scale ranging from 1 to 9.   484

storage   The retention of information in memory over time.   276

strategy construction   The discovery of a new procedure for processing information.   275

subgoaling   Setting intermediate goals that put one in a better position to reach a final goal or solution.   298

summative assessment   Assessment after instruction is finished.   498

survey battery   A group of individual subject-matter tests that is designed for a particular level of students.   470

symbolic function substage   In Piaget's theory, a substage of preoperational thought occurring roughly between 2 and 4 years of age. The young child gains the ability to represent mentally an object that is not present.   51

syntax   The language system that involves the way words are combined to form acceptable phrases and sentences.   65

systematic desensitization   A method based on classical conditioning that reduces anxiety by getting the individual to associate deep relaxation with successive visualizations of increasingly anxiety-producing situations.   243

task analysis   Breaking down a complex task into its component parts.   357

taxonomy   A classification system.   357

teacher-as-researcher   Also called "teacher-researcher," the idea that classroom teachers can conduct their own studies to improve their educational practices.   27

temperament   A person's behavioral style and characteristic ways of responding.   153

test-retest reliability   The extent to which a test yields the same performance when a student is given the same test on two different occasions.   468

theory   A coherent set of ideas that helps to explain and make predictions.   20

thinking   Manipulating and transforming information in memory; often done to form concepts, reason, think critically, and solve problems.   291

time-out   The extinction strategy most widely used by teachers to remove desirable stimuli. The student is taken away from positive reinforcement.   252

top-dog phenomenon   Moving from the top position to the lowest position in a transition from one level of schooling to another (such as elementary school to middle school).   102

total student body approach   A conflict resolution strategy in which every student learns how to manage conflicts constructively by negotiating agreements and mediating schoolmates' conflicts.   451

transactional strategy instruction approach   A cognitive constructivist approach to reading that emphasizes instruction in strategies (especially metacognitive strategies).   334

transfer   The process by which a person applies previous experiences and knowledge to learning or problem solving in a new situation.   275

transitivity   In concrete operational thought, a mental concept about the relations between classes that underlies the ability to logically combine relations to understand certain conclusions.   54

triarchic theory of intelligence   Sternberg's view that intelligence comes in three main forms: analytical, creative, and practical.   129

trust versus mistrust   Erikson's first psychosocial stage (first year of life).   84

T-score   A standard score in which the mean is set at 50 and the standard deviation is set at 10.   484

tutorials   Computer-based learning that attempts to mimic a competent, patient human tutor in guiding a student's learning. Tutorials adapt their content and pace according to the way the student responds.   379

unconditioned response (UR)   An unlearned response that is automatically elicited by the US.   241

unconditioned stimulus (US)   A stimulus that automatically produces a response without any prior learning.   241

validity   The extent to which a test measures what it is intended to measure.   468, 500

values clarification   An approach to moral education that emphasizes helping people clarify what their lives are for and what is worth working for. Students are encouraged to define their own values and understand the values of others.   110

variable-interval schedule   A reinforcement schedule in which a response is reinforced after a variable amount of time has elapsed.   249

variable-ratio schedule   A reinforcement schedule in which a behavior is reinforced after an average number of times, but on an unpredictable basis.   249

videodiscs   Large laser disks used to store visual images.   382

voice disorders   Disorders reflected in speech that is hoarse, harsh, too loud, too high-pitched, or too low-pitched.   204

website   An individual's or an organization's location on the Internet that displays information posted by the individual or the organization.   383

whole-language approach   An approach to reading instruction based on the idea that instruction should parallel children's natural language learning. Reading materials should be whole and meaningful.   71

within-class ability grouping   The placement of students in different groups within a class to take into account differences in students' abilities.   140

"withitness"   A management style described by Kounin in which teachers show students that they are aware of what is happening, closely monitoring students on a regular basis. This especially helps teachers detect inappropriate behavior before it gets out of hand.   441

working-memory model   Alan Baddeley's model in which working memory is a kind of mental "workbench" that lets individuals manipulate, assemble, and construct information when they make decisions, solve problems, and comprehend written and spoken language. The model consists of a general "executive" and two subsystems (articulatory loop and visuospatial scratchpad).   281

World Wide Web (the Web)   A hypermedia information retrieval system that links a variety of Internet materials; can include text, graphics, sound, and animation.   383

"you" messages   An undesirable form of communication that suggests the speaker is judging people and placing them in a defensive position.   456

zone of proximal development (ZPD)   In Vygotsky's theory, the term for the range of tasks that are too difficult for children to master alone but that can be learned with guidance and assistance from adults or more-skilled children.   60

z-score   A standard score that provides information about how many standard deviations a raw score lies above or below the mean.   484

A

Abruscato, J. (2000). *Teaching children science: A discovery approach* (5th ed.). Boston: Allyn & Bacon.

Academic Software. (1996). *Adaptive Device Locator System* [computer program]. Lexington, KY: Author.

Achenbach, T. M., Howell, C. T., Quay, H. C., & Conners, C. K. (1991). National survey of problems and competencies among four- to sixteen-year-olds. *Monographs of the Society for Research in Child Development,* Serial No. 225 (Vol. 56, No. 3).

Ackerman, E. (1996). Foreword to "The art of design" by Gregorary Gargarian. In Y. Kafai & M. Resnick (Eds.). *Constructionism in practice.* Mahwah, NJ: Erlbaum.

Adams, A., Carnine, D., & Gersten, R. (1982). Instructional strategies for studying content area texts in the intermediate grades. *Reading Research Quarterly, 18,* 27–53.

Adams, R., & Biddle, B. (1970). *Realities of teaching.* New York: Holt, Rinehart & Winston.

Aiken, L. R. (2000). *Psychological testing and assessment* (10th ed). Boston: Allyn & Bacon.

Airasian, P. W. (1997). *Classroom assessment* (3rd ed.). New York: McGraw-Hill.

Airasian, P. (2001), *Classroom assessment* (4th Ed.). New York: McGraw-Hill.

Airasian, P., & Walsh, M. E. (1997, February). Constructivist cautions. *Phi Delta Kappan,* pp. 444–450.

Albert, T. (1997, February 25). Common theme is behind new popularity: Service. *USA Today,* pp. A1–2.

Alberti, R., & Emmons, M. (1995). *Your perfect right* (7th ed.). San Luis Obispo, CA: Impact.

Alberti, R. E., & Emmons, M. L. (1995). *Your perfect right* (8th ed.). San Luis Obispo, CA: Impact.

Alberto, P., & Troutman, A. (1995). *Applied behavior analysis for teachers* (4th ed.). Upper Saddle River, NJ: Prentice Hall.

Alberto, P. A., & Troutman, A. C. (1995). *Applied behavior analysis for teachers* (4th ed.). Englewood Cliffs, NJ: Merrill.

Alberto, P. A., & Troutman, A. C. (1996). *AppliedbBehavior analysis for teachers* (4th ed.). New York: McGraw-Hill.

Alexander, A., Anderson, H., Heilman, P. C., & others. (1991). Phonological awareness training and remediation of analytic decoding deficits in a group of severe dyslexics. *Annals of Dyslexia, 41,* 193–206.

Alverno College. (1995). *Writing and speaking criteria.* Milwaukee, WI: Alverno Productions.

Amabile, T. (1993). [Commentary]. In D. Goleman, P. Kafman, & M. Ray, (Eds.), *The creative spirit.* New York: Plume.

Amabile, T. M., & Hennesey, B. A. (1992). The motivation for creativity in children. In A. K. Boggiano & T. S. Pittman (Eds.), *Achievement and motivation.* New York: Cambridge University Press.

American Association for the Advancement of Science. (1993). *Benchmarks for science literacy: Project 2061.* New York: Oxford University Press.

American Association of University Women. (1992). *How schools shortchange girls: A study of major findings on girls and education.* Washington, DC: Author.

American Association of University Women. (1993). *Hostile hallways.* Washington, DC: Author.

American Association on Mental Retardation, Ad Hoc Committee on Terminology and Classification. (1992). *Mental retardation* (9th ed.). Washington, DC: Author.

American Psychiatric Association. (1994). *Diagnostic and statistical manual of mental disorders* (4th ed.). Washington, DC: Author.

Ames, C. (1992). Classrooms: Goals, structures, and student motivation. *Journal of Educational Psychology, 84,* 261–271.

Anderman, E. M., Maehr, M. L., & Midgley, C. (1996). *Declining motivation after the transition to middle school: Schools can make a difference.* Unpublished manuscript, University of Kentucky, Lexington.

Anderson, J. R. (1993). Problem solving and learning. *American Psychologist, 48,* 35–44.

Anderson, L., Blumenfeld, P., Pintrich, P. R., Clark, C. M., Marx, R. W., & Peterson, P. (1996). Educational psychology for teachers: Reforming our courses, rethinking our roles. *Educational Psychologist, 30,* 143–157.

Anselmi, D. L. (1998). *Questions of gender.* New York: McGraw-Hill.

Applebome, P. (1997, September 3). Students' test scores show slow but steady gains at nation's schools. *New York Times,* Section B, p. 8.

Arends, R. I. (1998). *Learning to teach* (4th ed.). New York: McGraw-Hill.

Arends, R. I., Winitzky, N. E., & Tannenbaum, M. D. (1998). *Introduction to education: Exploring teaching.* New York: McGraw-Hill.

Arlin, M. (1979). Teacher transitions can disrupt time flow in classrooms. *American Educational Research Journal, 16,* 42–56.

Aronson, E. (1986, August). *Teaching students things they think they already know about: The case of prejudice and desegregation.* Paper presented at the meeting of the American Psychological Association, Washington, DC.

Aronson, E., & Patnoe, S. (1996). *The jigsaw classroom* (2nd ed.). Boston: Addison-Wesley.

Aronson, E. E., Blaney, N., Sephan, C., Sikes, J., & Snapp, M. (1978). *The jigsaw classroom.* Beverly Hills, CA: Sage.

Arter, J. (1995). *Portfolios for assessment and instruction.* ERIC Reproduction Service No. ED388890.

Asher, J., & Garcia, R. (1969). The optimal age to learn a foreign language. *Modern Language Journal, 53,* 334–341.

Asher, S. R., & Coie, J. D. (Eds.) (1990). *Peer rejection in childhood.* New York: Cambridge University Press.

Ashton, P. T., & Webb, R. B. (1986). *Making a difference: Teachers' sense of efficacy and student achievement.* White Plains, NY: Longman.

Atkinson, R. C., & Shiffrin, R. M. (1968). Human memory: A proposed system and its control processes. In K. W. Spence & J. T. Spence (Eds.), *The psychology of learning and motivation* (Vol. 2). San Diego: Academic Press.

Au, K., Carroll, J., & Scheu, J. (in press). *Balanced literacy instruction: A teacher's resource book.* Norwood, MA: Christopher-Gordon.

Ausubel, D. P. (1960). The use of advance organizers in the learning and retention of meaningful verbal material. *Journal of Educational Psychology, 51,* 267–272.

Axelrod, S. (1996). What's wrong with behavioral analysis? *Journal of Behavioral Education, 6,* 247–256.

B

Baber, C. R. (2000). Multicultural education. In A. Kazdin (Ed.), *Encyclopedia of psychology.* Washington, DC, and New York: American Psychological Association and Oxford U. Press.

Baddeley, A. (1990). *Human memory: Theory and practice.* Boston: Allyn & Bacon.

Baddeley, A. (1993). Working memory and conscious awareness. In A. F. Collins, S. E. Gathercole, M. A. Conway, & P. E. Morris (Eds.), *Theories of memory.* Mahwah, NJ: Erlbaum.

Baddeley, A. (1995). Applying the psychology of memory to clinical problems. In D. Hermann, C. McEvoy, C. Hertzog, P. Hertel, & M. Johnson (Eds.), *Basic and applied memory research* (Vol. 1). Mahwah, NJ: Erlbaum.

Baddeley, A. (1998). *Human memory: Theory and practice* (rev. ed.). Boston: Allyn & Bacon.

Baddeley, A. (1999). *Essentials of human memory.* Philadelphia: Psychology Press.

Baines, L. A., Deluzain, R. E., & Stanley, G. K. (1999). Computer technology in Florida and Georgia secondary schools: Propaganda and progress. *American Secondary Education, 27,* 33–38.

Baldwin, J. D., & Baldwin, J. L. (1998). *Behavior principles in everyday life.* Upper Saddle River, NJ: Prentice Hall.

Bandura, A. (1965). Influence of models' reinforcement contingencies on the acquisition of imitative responses. *Journal of Personality and Social Psychology, 1,* 589–596.

Bandura, A. (1982). Self-efficacy mechanism in human agency. *American Psychologist, 37,* 122–147.

Bandura, A. (1986). *Social foundations of thought and action.* Englewood Cliffs, NJ: Prentice Hall.

Bandura, A. (1994). *Self-efficacy: The exercise of control.* New York: W. H. Freeman.

Bandura, A. (1997). *Self-efficacy: The exercise of control.* New York: W. H. Freeman.

Bandura, A. (1998). Self-efficacy. In H. S. Friedman (Ed.), *Encyclopedia of mental health* (Vol. 3). San Diego: Academic Press.

Bandura, A. (2000). Self-efficacy. In A. Kazdin (Ed.), *Encyclopedia of psychology.* Washington, DC, & New York: American Psychological Association and Oxford U. Press.

Bandura, A. (2000). Social cognitive theory. In A. Kazdin (Ed.), *Encyclopedia of psychology.* Washington, DC, and New York: American Psychological Association and Oxford U. Press.

Bangert, R., Kulik, J., & Kulik, C. (1983). Individualized systems of instruction in secondary schools. *Review of Educational Research, 53,* 143–158.

Bangert-Drowns, R. L. (1993). The word processor as an instructional tool: A meta-analysis of word processing in writing instruction. *Review of Educational Psychology, 53,* 143–158.

Bank Street College of Education. (1984). *Voyage of the Mimi.* New York: Holt, Rinehart & Winston.

Banks, J. A. (1995). *Multicultural education: Its effects on students' racial and gender role attitudes.* In J. A. Banks & C. A. M. Banks (Eds.), *Handbook of research on multicultural education.* New York: Macmillan.

Banks, J. A. (1997a). Approaches to multicultural education reform. In J. A. Banks & C. A. M. Banks (Eds.), *Multicultural education.* Boston: Allyn & Bacon.

Banks, J. A. (1997b). *Teaching strategies for ethnic studies* (6th ed.). Boston: Allyn & Bacon.

Banks, J. A. (1998). The lives and values of researchers: Implications for Educating citizens in a multicultural society. *Educational Researcher, 27,* 4–17.

Banks, J. A., & Banks, C. A. (Eds.). (1997). *Multicultural education* (3rd ed.). Boston: Allyn & Bacon.

Barr, W. B. (2000). Epilepsy. In A. Kazdin (Ed.), *Encyclopedia of psychology.* Washington, DC, and New York: American Psychological Association and Oxford U. Press.

Barrett, H. C. (1994). Technology-supported assessment portfolios. *Computing Teacher, 21* (6), 9–12.

Barron, B. J., Mayfield-Stewart, C., Schwartz, D., & Dzarnik, C. (1996, April). *Students' use of tools for formative assessment.* Paper presented at the meeting of the American Educational Research Association, New York.

Barsalou, L. W. (2000). Concepts: Structure. In A. Kazdin (Ed.), *Encyclopedia of psychology.* Washington, DC, and New York: American Psychological Association and Oxford U. Press.

Bartlett, J. C. (1998, July). Personal communication. Program in Psychology, University of Texas at Dallas.

Barton, J., & Collins, A. (1997). Starting Out: Designing your portfolio. In J. Barton & A. Collins (Eds.), *Portfolio assessment: A handbook for educators.* Boston: Addison-Wesley.

Batchelder, W. (2000). Mathematical psychology. In A. Kazdin (Ed.), *Encyclopedia of psychology.* Washington, DC, and New York: American Psychological Association and Oxford U. Press.

Battistich, V., & Solomon, D. (1995, April). *Linking teacher change to student change.* Paper presented at the meeting of the American Educational Research Association, San Francisco.

Battistich, V., Schaps, E., Watson, M., & Solomon, D. (in press). Prevention effects of the Child Development Project: Early findings from an ongoing multi-site demonstration trial. *Journal of Adolescent Research.*

Battistich, V., Solomon, D., Watson, M., Solomon, J., & Schaps, E. (1989). Effects of an elementary school program to enhance prosocial behavior on children's cognitive social-problem solving skills and strategies. *Journal of Applied Developmental Psychology, 10,* 147–169.

Baumann, J. F., Hoffman, J. V., Moon, J., & Duffy-Hester, A. M. (1998). Where are teachers voices in the phonics/whole language debate? Results from a survey of U.S. Elementary classroom teachers. *Reading Teacher, 51,* 636–650.

Baumrind, D. (1971). Current patterns of parental authority. *Developmental Psychology Monographs, 4* (1, Part 2).

Baumrind, D. (1996, April). Unpublished review of J. W. Santrock's *Children,* 5th ed.) (New York: McGraw-Hill).

Beal, C. (1994). *Boys and girls: The development of gender roles.* New York: McGraw-Hill.

Beatty, B. (1998). From laws of learning to a science of values: Efficiency and morality in Thorndike's educational psychology. *American Psychologist, 53,* 1145–1152.

Becker, H. J. (1994). *Analysis of trends of school use of new information technology.* Irvine: University of California.

Becker, J. R. (1981). Differential treatment of females and males in mathematics classes. *Journal for Research in Mathematics Education, 12,* 40–53.

Beckham, E. E. (2000). Depression. In A. Kazdin (Ed.), *Encyclopedia of psychology.* Washington, DC, and New York: American Psychological Association and Oxford U. Press.

Bednar, R. L., Wells, M. G., & Peterson, S. R. (1995). *Self-esteem* (2nd ed.). Washington, DC: American Psychological Association.

Begley, S. (1998, March 30). Homework doesn't help. *Newsweek,* pp. 30–31.

Behrmann, M. M. (1994). Assistive technology for students with mild disabilities. *Intervention in School and Clinic, 30,* 70–83.

Bell, L. A. (1989). Something's wrong here and it's not me: Challenging the dilemmas that block girls' success. *Journal for the Education of the Gifted, 12,* 118–130.

Bem, S. L. (1977). On the utility of alternative procedures for assessing psychological androgyny. *Journal of Consulting and Clinical Psychology, 45,* 196–205.

Bender, W. (1998). *Learning disabilities* (3rd ed.). Boston: Allyn & Bacon.

Bennett, W. (1993). *The book of virtues.* New York: Simon & Schuster.

Benson, P. (1993). *The troubled journey.* Minneapolis: Search Institute.

Bereiter, C., & Scardamalia, M. (1989). Intentional learning as a goal of instruction. In L. B. Resnick (Ed.), *Knowing, learning, and instruction. Essays in honor of Robert Glaser.* Hillsdale, NJ: Erlbaum.

Bereiter, C., & Scardamalia, M. (1993). *Surpassing ourselves: An inquiry into the nature and implications of expertise.* Chicago: Open Court.

Berenfeld, B. (1994). Technology and the new model of science education. *Machine-Mediated Learning, 1,* 121–138.

Berger, E. H. (1995). *Parents as partners in education: Families and schools working together* (4th ed.). Englewood Cliffs, NJ: Prentice Hall.

Berger, E. H., & Pollman, M, J. (1996). Multiple intelligences: Enabling diverse learning. *Early Childhood Education Journal, 23* (No. 4), 249–253.

Berko-Gleason, J. (1958). The child's learning of English morphology. *Word, 14,* 150–177.

Berko-Gleason, J. (2000). Language. In M. H. Bornstein & M. E. Lamb (Eds.), *Developmental psychology* (4th ed.). Mahwah, NJ: Erlbaum.

Berliner, D. C. (1988, February). *The development of expertise in pedagogy.* Paper presented at the meeting of the American Association of Colleges for Teacher Education, New Orleans.

Berliner, D. C. (1997). Educational psychology meets the Christian right: Differing views of schooling, children, teaching, and learning. *Teachers College Record, 96,* 381–415.

Berndt, T. J. (1979). Developmental changes in conformity to peers and parents. *Developmental Psychology, 15,* 608–616.

Berndt, T. J. (1996). Transitions in friendship and friends' influence. In J. A. Graeber, J. Brooks-Gunn, & A. C. Petersen (Eds.), *Transitions through adolescence.* Mahwah, NJ: Erlbaum.

Berndt, T. J., & Keefe, K. (1996). Friends' influence on school adjustment: A motivational analysis. In J. Juvonen & K. R. Wentzel (Eds.), *Social motivation.* New York: Cambridge University Press.

Berry, J. W. (2000). Cultural foundations of behavior. In A. Kazdin (Ed.), *Encyclopedia of psychology.* Washington, DC, and New York: American Psychological Association and Oxford U. Press.

Bersoff, D. N. (1999) (Ed.). *Ethical conflicts in psychology* (2nd Ed.). Washington, DC: American Psychological Association.

Bertini, M. (2000). Field dependence and independence. In A. Kazdin (Ed.), *Encyclopedia of psychology.* Washington, DC, and New York: American Psychological Association and Oxford U. Press.

Bhavnagri, N. P., & Samuels, B. G. (1996, Summer). Making and keeping friends. *Childhood Education, 26,* 219–224.

Bialystock, E. (1997). Effects of bilingualism and biliteracy on children's emerging concepts of print. *Developmental Psychology, 33,* 429–440.

Bigelow, B. (1999, April). Why standardized tests threaten multiculturalism. *Educational Leadership, 56,* 37–40.

Bigler, R. S., Liben, L. S., & Yekel, C. A. (1992, August). *Developmental patterns of gender-related beliefs.* Paper presented at the meeting of the American Psychological Association, Washington, DC.

Billips, L. H., & Rauth, M. (1987). Teachers and research. In V. Richardson-Koeler (Ed.), *Educator's handbook.* White Plains, NY: Longman.

Biological Sciences Curriculum Study. (1989). *Science for life and living: Integrating science, technology, and health. Third Annual Progress Report.* Dubuque, IA: Kendall Hunt.

Bitter, G. C., & Pierson, M. E. (1999). *Using technology in the classroom* (4th ed.). Boston: Allyn & Bacon.

Bjorklund, D. F. (2000). Middle childhood: Cognitive development. In A. Kazdin (Ed.), *Encyclopedia of psychology.* Washington, DC, and New York: American Psychological Association and Oxford U. Press.

Blachman, B. A., Ball, E., Black, R., & Tangel, D. (1994). Kindergarten teachers develop phoneme awareness in low-income inner-city classrooms: Does it make a difference? In B. A. Blachman (Ed.), *Reading and writing.* Mahwah, NJ: Erlbaum.

Blackhurst, A. E. (1997, May/June). Perspectives on technology in special education. *Teaching Exceptional Children,* pp. 41–47.

Block, J. H., & Block, J. (1980). The role of ego-control and ego-resiliency in the organization of behavior. In W.A. Collins (Ed.), *Minnesota symposium on child psychology* (Vol. 13). Minneapolis: University of Minnesota Press.

Bloom, B. S. (Ed.). (1985). *Developing talent in young people.* New York: Ballantine Books.

Bloom, B. S. (1971). Mastering learning. In J. H. Block (Ed.), *Mastery learning.* New York: Holt, Rinehart & Winston.

Bloom, B. S., Engelhart, M. D., Frost, E. J., Hill, W. H., & Krathwohl, D. R. (1956). *Taxonomy of educational objectives.* New York: David McKay.

Bloom, L. (1998). Language acquisition in its developmental context. In W. Damon (Ed.), *Handbook of child psychology* (4th ed., Vol. 2). New York: Wiley.

Blumenfeld, P. C., Pintrich, P. R., Wessles, K., & Meece, J. (1981, August). *Age and sex differences in the impact of classroom experiences on self-perceptions.* Paper presented at the meeting of the Society for Research in Child Development, Boston.

Boekaerts, M., Pintrich, P., & Zeidner, M. (Eds.). (2000). *Handbook of self-regulation.* San Diego: Academic Press.

Bolt, Beraneck, & Newman, Inc. (1993). *The Co-NECT school: Design for a new generation of American schools.* Cambridge, MA: Author.

Bond, L. (1989). The effects of special preparation measures of scholastic ability. In R. Linn (Ed.), *Educational measurement* (3rd ed.). New York: Macmillan.

Borko, H., & Putnam, R. T. (1996). Learning to teach. In D. C. Berliner & R. C. Calfee (Eds.), *Handbook of educational psychology.* New York: Macmillan.

Bornstein, M. H. (1995). (Ed.). *Handbook of parenting* (Vols. 1–3). Mahwah, NJ: Erlbaum.

Botvin, G. J., Schinke, S., & Orlandi, M. A. (1995). School-based health promotion: Substance abuse and sexual behavior. *Applied and Preventive Psychology, 4,* 167–184.

Bourne, E. J. (1995). *The anxiety and phobia workbook.* Oakland, CA: New Harbinger.

Bourque, M. L. (1999). The role of national assessment of educational progress (NAEP) in setting, reflecting, and linking national policy to states' needs. In G. J. Cisek (Ed.), *Handbook of educational policy.* San Diego: Academic Press.

Bowe, F. G. (2000). *Physical, sensory, and health disabilities.* Upper Saddle River, NJ: Merrill.

Bower, G. H., Clark, M., Winzenz, D., & Lesgold, A. (1969). Hierarchical retrieval schemes in recall of categorized word lists. *Journal of Verbal Learning and Verbal Behavior, 3,* 323–343.

Bowlby, J. (1989). *Secure attachment.* New York: Basic Books.

Boyles, N. S., & Contadino, D. (1997). *The learning differences sourcebook.* Los Angeles: Lowell House.

Bracey, G. W. (1997, May). The culture of sexual harassment. *Phi Delta Kappan,* pp. 725–726.

Bracken, B. A. (2000) (Ed.), *Psychoeducational assessment of preschool children.* Boston: Allyn & Bacon.

Branch, M. N. (2000). Punishment. In A. Kazdin (Ed.), *Encyclopedia of psychology.* Washington, DC, and New York: American Psychological Association and Oxford U. Press.

Bransford, J. D., & Stein, B. S. (1993). *The IDEAL problem solver.* New York: W. H. Freeman.

Bransford, J. D., Brown, A. L., & Cocking, R. R. (Eds.). (1999). *How people learn.* Washington, DC: National Academy Press.

Bredderman, T. (1982). Activity science—The evidence shows it matters. *Science and Children, 20,* 39–41.

Bredekamp, S., & Copple, C. (1997). (Eds.) *Developmentally appropriate practice in early childhood programs* (rev. ed.). Washington, DC: National Association for the Education of Young Children.

Bredekamp, S., & Rosegrant, T. (1996). *Reaching potentials* (Vol. 2). Washington, DC: National Association for the Education of Young Children.

Brewer, D. J., Rees, D. I., & Argys, L. M. (1995). Detracking America's schools. *Phi Delta Kappan, 77,* 210–215.

Brewer, M. B. & Campbell, D. I. (1976). *Ethnocentrism and intergroup attitudes.* New York: Wiley.

Briggs, T. W. (1998, November 24). In the classroom with our All-USA teachers. *USA Today,* p. 9D.

Bronfenbrenner, U. (1986). Ecology of the family as a context for human development: Research perspectives. *Developmental Psychology, 22,* 723–742.

Bronfenbrenner, U., & Morris, P. A. (1998). The ecology of developmental processes. In W. Damon (Ed.), Handbook of child psychology (5th ed., Vol. 1). New York: Wiley.

Bronfenbrenner, U., McClelland, P., Wethington, E., Moen, P., & Ceci, S. J. (1996). *The state of Americans.* New York: Free Press.

Brookhart, S. M. (1997). A theoretical framework for the role of classroom assessment in motivating student effort and achievement. *Applied Measurement in Education, 10,* 161–180.

Brookover, W. B., Beady, C., Flood, P., Schweitzer, U., & Wisenbaker, J. (1979). *School social systems and student achievement: Schools make a difference.* New York: Praeger.

Brooks, J. G., & Brooks, M. G. (1993). *The case for constructivist classrooms.* Alexandria, VA: Association for Supervision and Curriculum Development.

Brooks-Gunn, J. (1996, March). *The uniqueness of the early adolescence transition.* Paper presented at the meeting of the Society for Research on Adolescence, Boston.

Brooks-Gunn, J., & Paikoff, R. (in press). Sexuality and developmental transitions during adolescence. In J. Schulenberg, J. Maggas, & K. Hurrelmann (Eds.), *Health risks and developmental transitions during adolescence.* New York: Cambridge University Press.

Brooks-Gunn, J., Klebanov, P. K., & Duncan, G. J. (1996). Ethnic differences in children's intelligence tests scores: Role of economic deprivation, home environment, and maternal characteristics. *Child Development, 67,* 396–408.

Brophy, J. (1985). Teacher-student interaction. In J. B. Duseck (Ed.), *Teacher expectancies.* Mahwah, NJ: Erlbaum.

Brophy, J. (1996). *Teaching problem students.* New York: Guilford.

Brophy, J. (1998). *Motivating students to learn.* New York: McGraw-Hill.

Brophy, J. (1999). Perspectives of classroom management: Yesterday, today, and tomorrow. In H. J. Freiberg (Ed.). *Beyond behaviorism: Changing the classroom management paradigm.* Boston: Allyn & Bacon.

Brophy, J., & Good, T. (1974). *Teacher-student relationships: Causes and consequences.* New York: Holt, Rinehart & Winston.

Brown, A. L. (1997). Transforming schools into communities of thinking and learning about serious matters. *American Psychologist, 52,* 399–413.

Brown, A. L., & Campione, J. C. (1996). Psychological learning theory and the design of innovative environments. In L. Schuable & R. Glaser (Eds.), *Contributions of instructional innovation to understanding learning.* Mahwah, NJ: Erlbaum.

Brown, A. L., & Day, J. D. (1983). Macrorules for summarizing texts: The development of expertise. *Journal of Verbal Learning and Verbal Behavior, 22,* 1–14.

Brown, A. L., & Palincsar, A. S. (1989). Guided, cooperative learning and individual knowledge acquisition. In L. B. Resnick (Ed.), *Knowing, learning, and instruction.* Mahwah, NJ: Erlbaum.

Brown, J. S., & Burton, R. B. (1978). Diagnostic models for procedural bugs in basic mathematical skills. *Cognitive Science, 2,* 155–192.

Brown, R. (1973). *A first language: The early stages.* Cambridge, MA: Harvard University Press.

Bruce, B. C., & Rubin, A. (1993). *Electronic quills: A situated evaluation of using computers for writing in classrooms.* Mahwah, NJ: Erlbaum.

Bruer, J. (1989). *1989 Report.* St. Louis: James S. McDonnell Foundation.

Bruer, J. (1993). *Schools for thoughy: A science of learning in the classroom.* Cambridge, MA: MIT Press.

Bruner, J. (1996). *Toward a theory of instruction.* Cambridge, MA: Harvard University Press.

Bruner, J. S. (1996). *The culture of education.* Cambridge, MA: Harvard University Press.

Bryant, B. R., & Seay, P. C. (1998). The technology-related assistance to individuals with learning disabilities and their advocates. *Journal of Learning Disabilities, 31,* 4–15.

Bryant, D. P., & Bryant, B. R. (1998). Using assistive technology adaptations to include students with learning disabilities in cooperative learning activities. *Journal of Learning Disabilities, 31,* 41–54.

Bryk, A. S., Lee, V. E., & Smith, J. B. (1989, May). *High school organization and its effects on teachers and students: An interpretive summary of the research.* Paper presented at the conference on Choice and Control in American Education, University of Wisconsin, Madison.

Buhrmester, D., & Furman, W. (1987). The development of companionship and intimacy. *Child Development, 61,* 1387–1398.

Burden, P. R., & Byrd, D. M. (1999). *Methods for effective teaching* (2nd ed.). Boston: Allyn & Bacon.

Burger, J. M. (2000). Personality (5th ed.). Belmont, CA: Wadsworth.

Burkham, D. T., Lee, V. E., & Smerdon, B. A. (1997). Gender and science learning early in high school: Subject matter and laboratory experiences. *American Educational Research Journal, 34,* 297–331.

Burz, H. L., & Marshall, K. (1996). *Performance-based curriculum for mathematics: From knowing to showing.* Eric Document Reproduction Service No. ED400194.

Bushweller, K. (1997, September). Teach to the test. *American School Board Journal,* pp. 20–25.

Cafolla, R., Kaufman, D., & Knee, R. (1997). *World Wide Web for Teachers.* Boston: Allyn & Bacon.

Calabrese, R. L., & Schumer, H. (1986). The effects of service activities on adolescent alienation. *Adolescence, 21,* 675–687.

Calderhead, J. (1996). Teachers: Beliefs and knowledge. In D. C. Berliner, & R. C. Calfee (Eds.), *Handbook of educational psychology.* New York: Macmillan.

Calfee, R. C. (1999). Educational Psychology. In A. Kazdin (Ed.), *Encyclopedia of psychology.* Washington, DC, and New York: American Psychological Association and Oxford U. Press.

Calhoun, E. M. (1994). *How to use research in the self-renewing school.* Alexandria, VA: Association for Supervision and Curriculum Development.

California State Department of Education. (1994). *Golden State examination science portfolio.* Sacramento: California State Department of Education.

Cameron, J., & Pierce, W. D. (1996). The debate about rewards and intrinsic motivation. *Review of Educational Research, 66,* 39–62.

Cameron, J. R., Hansen, R., & Rosen, D. (1989). Preventing behavioral problems in infancy through temperament assessment and parental support programs. In W. B. Carey & S. C. McDevitt (Eds.), *Clinical and educational applications of temperament research.* Amsterdam: Sets & Zeitlinger.

Campbell, C. Y. (1988, August 24). Group raps depection of teenagers. *Boston Globe,* p. 44.

Campbell, D. T., & LeVine, D. T. (1968). Ethnocentrism and intergroup relations. In R. Abelson & others (Eds.), *Theories of cognitive consistency.* Chicago: Rand McNally.

Campbell, F. A. & Ramey, C. T. (1994). Effects of early intervention on intellectual and academic achievement: A follow-up study of children from low-income families. *Child Development, 65,* 684–698.

Campbell, L., Campbell, B., & Dickinson, D. (1999). *Teaching and learning through multiple intelligences* (2nd ed.). Boston: Allyn & Bacon.

Cardelle-Elawar, M. (1992). Effects of teaching metacognitive skills to students with low mathematics ability. *Teaching and Teacher Education, 8,* 109–121.

Carnegie Council on Adolescent Development. (1989). *Turning points: Preparing American youth for the 21st century.* New York: Carnegie Foundation.

Carnegie Council on Adolescent Development. (1995). *Great transitions.* New York: Carnegie Foundation.

Carpenter, T. P., Ansell, E., Franke, M. L., Fennema, E., & Weisbeck, L. (1993). Models of problem-solving. *Journal of Research in Mathematics Education, 24,* 428–441.

Carpenter, T. P., Lindquist, M. M., Matthews, W., & Silver, E. A. (1983). Results of the Third NAEP Mathematics Assessment: Secondary school. *Mathematics Teachers, 76* (9), 652–659.

Carroll, J. B. (1963). A model of school learning. *Teachers College Record, 64,* 723–733.

Cascio, W. (2000). Test utility. In A. Kazdin (Ed.), *Encyclopedia of psychology.* Washington, DC, & New York: American Psychological Association and Oxford U. Press.

Case, R. (1987). Neo-Piagetian theory: Retrospect and prospect. *International Journal of Psychology, 22,* 773–791.

Case, R. (1997, April). *A dynamic model of general numerical understanding and its development in specific contexts.* Paper presented at the meeting of the Society for Research in Child Development, Washington, DC.

Case, R. (1998). The development of conceptual structures. In W. Damon (Ed.), *Handbook of child psychology* (5th ed., Vol. 2). New York: Wiley.

Case, R. (1999). Conceptual development in the child and the field: A personal view of the Piagetian legacy. In E. K. Skolnick, K. Nelson, S. A. Gelman, & P. H. Miller (Eds.), *Conceptual development.* Mahwah, NJ: Erlbaum.

Case, R. (2000). Conceptual structures. In M. Bennett (Ed.), *Developmental psychology.* Philadelphia: Psychology Press.

Caspi, A., Henry, B., McGee, R. O., Moffitt, T. E., & Silva, P. A. (1995). Temperamental origins of child and adolescent behavior problems: From age three to age fifteen. *Child Development, 66,* 55–68.

Ceci, S. J. (1990). *On intelligence . . . more or less: A bioecological treatise.* Upper Saddle River, NJ: Prentice Hall.

Ceci, S. J. (2000). Memory: Constructive processes. In A. Kazdin (Ed.), *Encyclopedia of psychology.* Washington, DC, and New York: American Psychological Association and Oxford U. Press.

Ceci, S. J., Rosenblum, T., de Bruyn, E., & Lee, D. Y. (1997). A bio-ecological model of intellectual development. In R. J. Sternberg & E. Grigorenko (Eds.), *Intelligence, heredity, and environment.* New York: Cambridge University Press.

Chall, J. S. (1979). The great debate: Ten years later with a modest proposal for reading stages. In L. B. Resnick & P. A. Weaver (Eds.), *Theory and practice of early reading.* Mahwah, NJ: Erlbaum.

Charles, C. M. (1997). *Introduction to educational psychology* (3rd ed.). New York: Longman.

Chen, C., & Stevenson, H. W. (1989). Homework: A cross-cultural comparison. *Child Development, 60,* 551–561.

Chess, S., & Thomas, A. (1977). Temperamental individuality from childhood to adolescence. *Journal of Child Psychiatry, 16,* 218–226.

Chi, M. T. H. (1978). Knowledge structures and memory development. In R. S. Siegler (Ed.), *Children's thinking.* Mahwah, NJ: Erlbaum.

Child Trends. (1997). *Facts at a glance.* Washington, DC: Author.

Children's Defense Fund. (1992). *The state of America's children.* Washington, DC: Author.

Chira, S. (1993, June 23). What do teachers want most? Help from parents. *New York Times,* sec. 1, p. 7.

Chmielewski, C. (1997, September). Sexual harassment meet Title IX. *NEA Today, 16* (No. 2), 24–25.

Chomsky, N. (1957). *Syntactic structures.* The Hague: Mouton.

Christensen, C. R. (1991). The discussion teacher in action: Questioning, listening, and response. In C. R. Christensen, D. A. Garvin, & A. Sweet (Eds.), *Education for judgment.* Boston: Harvard University Business School.

Cibulka, J. G. (1999). Moving toward an accountable system of K–12 education: Alternative approaches and challenges. In G. J. Cisek (Ed.), *Handbook of educational policy.* San Diego: Academic press.

Clark, K. B., & Clark, M. P. (1939). The development of the self and the emergence of racial identification in Negro preschool children. *Journal of Social Psychology, 10,* 591–599.

Clarke, J. H., & Agne, R. M. (1997). *Interdisciplinary high school teaching.* Boston: Allyn & Bacon.

Clay, M. M., & Cazden, C. B. (1990). A Vygotskian interpretation of Reading Recovery. In L. Moll (Ed.), *Vygotsky and education.* New York: Oxford University Press.

Clay, R. A. (1997, December). Are children being overmedicated? *APA Monitor,* pp. 1, 27.

Clement, J., Lockhead, J., & Soloway, E. (1979, March). *Translation between symbol systems: Isolating a common difficulty in solving algebra word problems.* COINS technical report No. 79-19. Amherst: University of Massachusetts, Department of Computer and Information Sciences.

Clinchy, B. M., Mansfield, A. F., & Schott, J. L. (1995, March). *Development of narrative and scientific modes of thought in middle childhood.* Paper presented at the meeting of the Society for Research in Child Development, Indianapolis.

CNN and the National Science Foundation. (1997). Poll on technology and education. Washington, DC: National Science Foundation.

Coben, S. S., Thomas, C. C., Sattler, R. O., & Morsink, C. V. (1997). Meeting the challenge of consultation and collaboration: Developing interactive teams. *Journal of Learning Disabilities, 30,* 427–432.

Cochran-Smith, M. (1995). Color blindness and basket making are not the answers: Confronting the dilemmas of race, culture, and language diversity in teacher education. *American Educational Research Journal, 32,* 493–522.

Cochran-Smith, M., & Lytle, S. (1990, March). Research on teaching and teacher research: The issue that divide. *Educational Researcher,* pp. 2–11.

Coffin, L. (1996). Commentary in "The latest on student portfolios." *NEA Today, 17,* 18.

Cognition and Technology Group at Vanderbilt. (1996). A framework for understanding technology and education research. In D. C. Berliner & R. C. Calfee (Eds.), *Handbook of educational psychology.* New York: Macmillan.

Cognition and Technology Group at Vanderbilt. (1997). *Designing environments to reveal, support, and expand our children's potentials.* Paper presented at the meeting of the Society for Research in Child Development, Washington, DC.

Cognition and Technology Group at Vanderbilt. (1997). *The Jasper Project.* Mahwah, NJ: Erlbaum.

Cohen, R. J., & Swerdlik, M. E. (1999). *Psychological testing and assessment* (4th ed.). Mountain View, CA: Mayfield.

Coie, J. D., & Dodge, K. A. (1998). Aggression and antisocial behavior. In W. Damon (Ed.), *Handbook of child psychology* (Vol. 3). New York: Wiley.

Coladarce, T. (1992). Teachers' sense of efficacy and commitment to teaching. *Journal of Experimental Education, 60,* 323–337.

Colby, A., Kohlberg, L., Gibbs, J., & Lieberman, M. (1973). A longitudinal study of moral judgment. *Monographs of the Society for Research in Child Development* (Serial No. 201).

Colby, S. A. (1999, March). Grading in a standard-based system. *Educational Leadership, 56,* 52–55.

Cole, M. (1999). Culture in development. In M. H. Bornstein & M. E. Lamb (Eds.), *Developmental psychology* (4th Ed.). Mahwah, NJ: Erlbaum.

Coleman, M. (1997). Families and schools: In search of common ground. *Young Children, 52,* 14–20.

College Board. (1996, August 22). *News from The College Board.* New York: College Entrance Examination Board.

Collins, M. (1996, Winter). The job outlook for '96 grads. *Journal of Career Planning,* pp. 51–54.

Collis, B. A., & Sakamoto, T. (1996). Children in the information age. In B. A. Collis & others (Eds.), *Children and computers in schools.* Mahwah, NJ: Erlbaum.

Collis, B. A., Knezek, G. A., Lai, K.-W., Miyashita, K. T., Pelgrum, W. J., Plomp, T., & Sakamoto, T. (1996). *Children and computers in school.* Mahwah, NJ: Erlbaum.

Combs, D. (1997, September). Using alternative assessment to provide options for student success. *Middle School Journal,* pp. 3–8.

Comer, J. P. (1988). Educating poor minority children. *Scienfic American, 259,* 42–48.

Comer, J. P., Haynes, N. M., Joyner, E. T., & Ben-Avie, M. (1996). *Rallying the whole village: The Comer process for reforming urban education.* New York: Teachers College Press.

Cone, J. (1999). Observational assessment. In P.C. Kendall, J. N., Butcher, & G. Holmbeck (Eds.), *Handbook of research methods in clinical psychology.* New York: Wiley.

Connell, D. (1998, April 6). Commentary, *Newsweek,* p. 24.

Connors, L. J., & Epstein, J. L. (1995). Parent and school partnerships. In M. Borstein (Ed.), *Handbook of parenting* (Vol. 2). Mahwah, NJ: Erlbaum.

Conti, R., & Amabile, T. (1999). Motivation/drive. In M. A. Runco & S. Pritzker (Eds.), *Encyclopedia of creativity.* San Diego: Academic Press.

Cooper, C. R. (1995, March). *Multiple selves, multiple worlds.* Paper presented at the meeting of the Society for Research in Child Development, Indianapolis.

Cooper, H. (1989). Synthesis of research on homework. *Educational Leadership, 47* (3), 85–91.

Cooper, H. (1998, April). *Family, student, and assignment characteristics of positive homework experiences.* Paper presented at the meeting of the American Educational Research Association, San Diego.

Cooper, H., Lindsay, J. J., Nye, B., & Greathouse, S. (1998). Relationships among attitudes about homework, amount of homework assigned and completed, and student achievement. *Journal of Educational Psychology, 90,* 70–83.

Corno, L. (1998, March 30). Commentary. *Newsweek,* p. 51.

Costa, P. (2000). NEO Personality Inventory. In A. Kazdin (Ed.), *Encyclopedia of psychology.* Washington, DC, and New York: American Psychological Association and Oxford U. Press.

Costa, P. T., & McRae, R. R. (1995). Solid ground on the wetlands of personality: A reply to Black. *Psychological Bulletin, 117,* 216–220.

Costa, P. T., & McRae, R. R. (1998). Personality assessment. In H. S. Friedman (Ed.). *Encyclopedia of mental health* (Vol. 3). San Diego: Academic Press.

Council for Exceptional Children. (1998). *CEC's comments on the proposed IDEA regulations.* Washington, DC: Author.

Covington, M. V. (1992). *Making the grade: A self-worth perspective on motivation and school reform.* New York: Cambridge University Press.

Covington, M. V. (1998, April). *Caring about learning: The nature and nurturing of subject-matter appreciation.* Paper presented at the meeting of the American Educational Research Association, San Diego.

Covington, M. V., & Teel, K. T. (1996). *Overcoming student failure.* Washington, DC: American Psychological Association.

Covington, M. V., Teel, K. M., & Parecki, A. D. (1994, April). *Motivation benefits of improved academic performance among middle-school African American students through an effort-based grading system.* Paper presented at the meeting of the American Educational Research Association, New Orleans.

Cowley, G. (1998, April 6). Why children turn violent. *Newsweek,* pp. 24–25.

Coyne, J. C. (2000). Mood disorders. In A. Kazdin (Ed.), *Encyclopedia of psychology.* Washington, DC, and New York: American Psychological Association and Oxford U. Press.

Craik, F. I. M. (2000). Memory: Coding processes. In A. Kazdin (Ed.), *Encyclopedia of psychology.* Washington, DC, and New York: American Psychological Association and Oxford U. Press.

Craik, F. I. M., & Lockhart, R. S. (1972). Levels of processing: A framework for memory research. *Journal of Verbal Learning and Verbal Behavior, 11,* 671–684.

Crawford, M., & Unger, R. (2000). *Women and gender* (3rd ed.). New York: McGraw-Hill.

Cronin, M. W. (1993). Teaching listening skills via interactive videodisc. *Technological Horizons in Education Journal, 21,* (5), 62–68.

Cruikshank, D. R., Bainer, D., & Metcalf, K. (1996). *The act of teaching.* New York: McGraw-Hill.

Csikszentmihalyi, M. (1990). *Flow.* New York: Harper & Row.

Csikszentmihalyi, M. (1993). *The evolving self.* New York: HarperCollins.

Csikszentmihalyi, M. (1995). *Creativity.* New York: HarperCollins.

Csikszentmihalyi, M. (2000). Creativity: An overview. In A. Kazdin (Ed.), *Encyclopedia of psychology.* Washington, DC, and New York: American Psychological Association and Oxford U. Press.

Csikszentmihlayi, M. (2000). Flow. In A. Kazdin (Ed.), *Encyclopedia of psychology.* Washington, DC, & New York: American Psychological Association and Oxford U. Press.

Csikszentmihalyi, M., Rathunde, K., & Whalen, S. (1993). *Talented teenagers: The roots of success and failure.* Cambridge, UK: Cambridge University Press.

Culbertson, F. M. (1997). Depression and gender. *American Psychologist, 52,* 25–31.

Culbertson, L. D., & Jalongo, M. R. (1999). "But what's wrong with letter grades?" Responding to parents' questions about alternative assessments. *Childhood Education, 75,* 130–135.

Curwin, R. L., & Mendler, A. N. (1999, October). Zero tolerance for zero tolerance. *Phi Delta Kappan, 81,* 119–120.

Cushner, K., McClelland, A., & Safford, P. (1996). *Human diversity and education* (2nd ed.). New York: McGraw-Hill.

Cushner, K. H., McClelland, A., & Safford, P. (2000). *Human diversity in education* (3rd ed.). Boston: Allyn & Bacon.

Daiute, C., & Dalton, B. (1993). Collaboration between children learning to write: Can novices be masters? *Cognition and Instruction, 10,* 281–333.

Damon, W. (1995). *Greater expectations.* New York: Free Press.

Damon, W. (2000). Moral development. In A. Kazdin (Ed.), *Encyclopedia of psychology.* Washington, DC, and New York: American Psychological Association and Oxford U. Press.

Dansereau, D. F. (1988). Cooperative learning strategies. In C. E. Weinstein, E. T. Goetz, & P. A. Alexander (Eds.), *Learning and study strategies.* Orlando, FL: Academic Press.

Das, J. P. (2000). Mental retardation. In A. Kazdin (Ed.), *Encyclopedia of psychology.* Washington, DC, and New York: American Psychological Association and Oxford U. Press.

Davidson. J. (2000). Giftedness. In A. Kazdin (Ed.), *Encyclopedia of psychology.* Washington, DC, and New York: American Psychological Association and Oxford U. Press.

Davidson, R. J. (1996). The effects of decision characteristics on children's selective search of predecisional information. *Acta Psychologica, 92,* 263–281.

Davila, R., Williams, & MacDonald, J. (1991). Memorandum of chief state school officers regarding clarification of policy to address the needs of students with attention deficit hyperactivity disorders. Washington, DC: U.S. Department of Education.

Davis, S. M., Lambert, L. C., Gomez, Y., & Skipper, B. (1995). Southwest Cardiovascular Curriculum Project: Study findings for American Indian elementary school students. *Journal of Health Education, 26,* S72–S81.

de Villers, J. (1996). Towards a rational empiricism: Why interactionism isn't behaviorism any more than biology is genetics. In M. E. Rice (Ed.), *Towards a genetics of language.* Mahwah, NJ: Erlbaum.

de Villiers, J. G., & de Villiers, P. A. (1999). Language development. In M. H. Bornstein & M. E. Lamb (Eds.), *Developmental psychology: An advanced textbook* (4th ed.). Mahwah, NJ: Erlbaum.

Deaux, K. (1999). Identity. In A. Kazdin (Ed.), *Encyclopedia of psychology.* Washington, DC, and New York: American Psychological Association and Oxford U. Press.

deCharms, R. (1976). *Enhancing motivation: Change in the classroom.* New York: Irvington.

deCharms, R. (1984). Motivation enhancement in educational settings. In R. Ames & C. Ames (Eds.), *Research on motivation in education* (Vol. 1). Orlando: Academic Press.

Deci, E. (1975). *Intrinsic motivation.* New York: Plenum Press.

Deci, E., & Ryan, R. (1994). Promoting self-determined education. *Scandinavian Journal of Educational Research, 38,* 3–14.

Delisle, J. R. (1984). *Gifted children speak out.* New York: Walker.

Dempster, F. N. (1981). Memory span: Sources of individual and developmental differences. *Psychological Bulletin, 89,* 63–100.

Deno, E. (1970). Special education as developmental capital. *Exceptional Children, 37,* 229–237.

Derlega, V., Winstead, B., & Jones, W. (1999). *Personality: Contemporary theory and research* (2nd ed.). Belmont, CA: Wadsworth.

Derman—Sparks, L., & the Anti-Bias Curriculum Task Force (1989). *Anti-bias curriculum.* Washington, DC: National Association for the Education of Young Children.

DeVillar, R. A., & Faltis, C. J. (1991). *Computers and cultural diversity: Restructuring for school success.* Albany: State University of New York Press.

Dewey, J. (1933). *How we think.* Lexington, MA: D. C. Heath.

Diaz, C. (1997). Unpublished review of J. W. Santrock's *Educational Psychology* (New York: McGraw-Hill).

Dishion, T. J., & Spracklen, K. M. (1996, March). *Childhood peer rejection in the development of adolescent substance abuse.* Paper presented at the meeting of the Society for Research on Adolescence. Boston.

Domino, G. (2000). *Psychological testing.* Upper Saddle River, NJ: Prentice Hall.

Domjan, M. (2000). Learning: An overview. In A. Kazdin (Ed.), *Encyclopedia of psychology.* Washington, DC, and New York: American Psychological Association and Oxford U. Press.

Donnelly, M. (1997). School of the Future Project. *Family Futures, 1,* 12–14.

Doolittle, P. (1997). Vygotsky's zone of proximal development as a theoretical foundation for cooperative learning. *Journal on Excellence in College Teaching, 8,* 81–101.

Douglass, M. E., & Douglass, D. N. (1993). *Manage your work yourself* (updated ed.). New York: American Management Association.

Doyle, J., & Paludi, M. (1997). *Sex and gender* (3rd ed.). New York: McGraw-Hill.

Doyle, J. A., & Paludi, M. A. (1998). *Sex and gender* (4th ed.). New York: McGraw-Hill.

Doyle, W. (1986). Classroom organization and management. In M. C. Wittrock (Ed.), *Handbook of research on teaching* (3rd ed.). New York: Macmillan.

Driscoll, M. (2000). *Psychology of learning for instruction* (2nd ed.). Boston: Allyn & Bacon.

Drummond, R. J. (2000). *Appraisal procedures for counselors and helping professionals* (4th ed.). Upper Saddle River, NJ: Merrill.

Dryfoos, J. G. (1990). *Adolescents at risk.* New York: Oxford University Press.

Dunn, L., & Kontos, S. (1997). What have we learned about developmentally appropriate practice? *Young Children, 52* (2), 4–13.

Dunphy, D. C. (1963). The social structure of urban adolescent peer groups. *Society, 26,* 230–246.

Dweck, C. (1996). Social motivation: Goals and social-cognitive processes. In J. Juvonen & K. R. Wentzel (Eds.), *Social motivation.* New York: Cambridge University Press.

Dweck, C., & Elliott, E. (1983). Achievement motivation. In P. Mussen (Ed.), *Handbook of child psychology* (4th ed., Vol. 4). New York: Wiley.

Dweck, C., & Leggett, E. (1988). A social cognitive approach to motivation and personality. *Psychological Review, 95,* 256–273.

Eagly, A. (1996). Differences between women and men. *American Psychologist, 51,* 158–159.

Eagly, A. (2000). Sex differences and gender differences. In A. Kazdin (Ed.), *Encyclopedia of psychology.* Washington, DC, and New York: American Psychological Association and Oxford U. Press.

Eagly, A. H., & Crowely, M. (1986). Gender and helping behavior. *Psychological Bulletin, 100,* 283–308.

Eagly, A. H., & Steffen, V. J. (1986). Gender and aggressive behavior: A meta-analytic review of the social psychological literature. *Psycnological Bulletin, 111,* 3–22.

Eaton, W. O., & Enns, L. R. (1986). Sex differences in human motor activity. *Psychological Bulletin, 10,* 309–330.

Eccles, J. (2000). Social patterns, achievements, and problems. In A. Kazdin (Ed.), *Encyclopedia of psychology.* Washington, DC, & New York: American Psychological Association and Oxford U. Press.

Eccles, J. S. (1993). School and family effects on the onto geny of children's interests, self-perceptions, and activity choice. In J. Jacobs (Ed.), *Nebraska Symposium on Motivation.* Lincoln: University of Nebraska Press.

Eccles, J. S., & Harold, R. D. (1996). Family involvement in children's and adolescents' schooling. In A. Booth & J. F. Dunn (Eds.), *Family-school links.* Mahway, NJ: Erlbaum.

Eccles, J. S., & Midgley, C. (1989). Stage-environment fit: Developmentally appropriate classrooms for young adolescents. In C. Ames & R. Ames (Eds.), *Research on motivation in education* (Vol. 3). Orlando: Academic Press.

Eccles, J. S., & Roeser, R. W. (1999). School and community influences on human development. In M. H. Bornstein & M. E. Lamb (Eds.), *Developmental psychology* (4th Ed.). Mahwah, NJ: Erlbaum.

Eccles, J. S., Jacobs, J., Harold, R., Yoon, K., Aberbach, A., & Dolan, C. F. (1991, August). *Expectancy effects are alive and well on the home front.* Paper presented at the meeting of the American Psychological Association, San Francisco.

Eccles, J. S., Lord, S., & Buchanan, C. M. (1996). School transitions in early adolescence: What are we doing to our young people? In J. A. Graeber, J. Brooks-Gunn, & A. C. Petersen (Eds.), *Transitions in adolescence.* Mahway, NJ: Erlbaum.

Eccles, J. S., Midgley, C., & Adler, T. E. (1984). Grade-related changes in the school environment: Effects on achievement motivation. In J. T. Nicholls (Ed.), *The development of achievement motivation.* Greenwich, CT: JAI Press.

Eccles, J. S., Wigfield, A., & Schiefele, U. (1998). Motivation to succeed. In W. Damon (Ed.), *Handbook of child psychology* (5th ed., Vol. 3). New York: Wiley.

Eccles, J. S., Wigfield, A., Harold, R., & Blumenfeld, P. B. (1993). Age and gender differences in children's self- and task perceptions during elementary school. *Child Development, 64,* 830–847.

Edelman, M. W. (1997, April). *Families, children, and social policy.* Invited address, Society for Research in Child Development, Washington, DC.

Educational Testing Service. (1994). *Taking the SAT I reasoning test.* Princeton, NJ: College Board SAT Program.

Educational Testing Service. (1995). *Performance assessment.* Princeton, NJ: Author.

Edwards, P. A. (1989). Supporting lower SES mothers' attempts to provide scaffolding for book reading. In J. Allen & J. M. Mason (Eds.), *Risk makers, risk takers: Reducing the risks for young literacy learners.* Portsmouth, NH: Heinemann Educational Books.

Efron, S., & Joseph, P. B. (1994). Reflections in the mirror: Teacher-generated metaphors for self and others. In P. B. Joseph & G. E. Burnaford (Eds.), *Images of schoolteachers in twentieth-century America.* New York: St. Martin's Press.

Eisenberg, N., & Fabes, R. A. (1998). Prosocial development. In W. Damon (Ed.), *Handbook of child psychology* (5th ed., Vol. 3). New York: Wiley.

Eisenberg, N., Martin, C. L., & Fabes, R. A. (1996). Gender development and gender effects. In D. C. Berliner & R. C. Calfee (Eds.), *Handbook of educational psychology.* New York: Macmillan.

Eisner, E. W. (1999, May). The uses and limits of performance assessment. *Phi Delta Kappan, 80,* 658–661.

Elias, M. J., Gara, M., Ubriaco, M., Rothbaum, P. A., Clabby, J. F., & Schuyler, T. (1986). The impact of a preventive social problem-solving intervention on children's coping with middle-school stressors. *American Journal of Community Psychology, 14,* 259–275.

Elias, M. J., Gara, M. A., Schuyler, T. F., Branden-Muller, L. R., & Sayette, M. A. (1991). The promotion of social competence: Longitudinal study of a preventive school-based program. *American Journal of Orthopsychiatry, 61,* 409–417.

Elicker, J. (1996). A knitting tale. Reflections on scaffolding. *Childhood Education, 72,* 29–32.

Elkind, D. (1976). *Child development and education.* New York: Oxford University Press.

Elkind, D. (1978). Understanding the young adolescent. *Adolescence, 13,* 127–134.

Elkind, J. I. (2000). Technology and disabilities. In A. Kazdin (Ed.), *Encyclopedia of psychology.* Washington, DC, and New York: American Psychological Association and Oxford U. Press.

Elliot, A. J., McGregor, H. A., & Gable, S. (1999). Achievement goals, study strategies, and exam performance: A mediational analysis. *Journal of Educational Psychology, 91,* 549–563.

Ellis, H. C. (1987). Recent developments in human memory. In V. P. Makosky (Ed.), *The G. Stanley Hall Lecture Series.* Washington, DC: American Psychological Association.

Ellis, S., Klahr, D., & Siegler, R. S. (1994, April). *The birth, life, and sometimes death of good ideas in collaborative problem-solving.* Paper presented at the meeting of the American Educational Research Association, New Orleans.

Emery, R. E. (1999). *Marriage, divorce, and children's adjustment* (2nd ed.). Thousand Oaks, CA: Sage.

Emmer, E. T., Evertson, C. M., & Anderson, L. M. (1980). Effective classroom management at the beginning of the school year. *Elementary School Journal, 80,* 219–231.

Emmer, E. T., Evertson, C. M., & Worsham, M. E. (2000). *Classroom management for secondary teachers* (5th ed.). Boston: Allyn & Bacon.

Emmer, E. T., Evertson, C. M., Clements, B. S., & Worsham, M. E. (1997). *Classroom management for successful teachers* (4th ed.). Boston: Allyn & Bacon.

Entwisle, D. R., & Alexander, K. L. (1993). Entry into the school: The beginning school transition and educational stratification in the United States. *Annual Review of Sociology, 19,* 401–423.

Epstein, J. L. (1983). Longitudinal effects of family-school-person interactions on student outcomes. *Research in Sociology and Education and Socialization, 4,* 101–127.

Epstein, J. L. (1996). Perspectives and previews on research and policy for school, family, and community partnerships. In A. Booth & J. F. Dunn (Eds.), *Family-school links.* Mahwah, NJ: Erlbaum.

Epstein, J. L. (1997, June 6). Commentary, *Wall Street Journal,* sec. 1, p. 1.

Epstein, J. L. (1998, April). *Interactive homework: Effective strategies to connect home and school.* Paper presented at the meeting of the American Educational Research Association, San Diego.

Epstein, J. L., Salinas, K. C., & Jackson, V. E. (1995). *Manual for teachers and prototype activities: Teachers involve parents in Schoolwork (TIPS)* (rev. ed.). Baltimore: Johns Hopkins University, Center on Families, Communities, Schools, and Children's Learning.

ERIC Digest. (1989). *A glossary of measurement terms.* ERIC Document Reproduction Service No. ED315430.

Erikson, E. H. (1968). *Identity: Youth and crisis.* New York: W. W. Norton.

Everbach, T. (1997, October 8). Bettering the odds: 3-to-1 mentoring program aims to surround each boy with support of three men. *Dallas Morning News,* pp. 27A, 29A.

Everston, C. M., Emmer, E. T., & Worsham, M. E. (2000). *Classroom management for elementary school teachers,* (5th ed.). Boston: Allyn & Bacon.

Evertson, C. M., & Harris, A. H. (1999). Support for managing learning-centered classrooms: The classroom organization and management program. In H. J. Freiberg (Ed.), *Beyond behaviorism: Changing the classroom management paradigm.* Boston: Allyn & Bacon.

Evertson, C. M., Emmer, E. T., Clements, B. S., & Worsham, M. E. (1997). *Classroom management for elementary teachers.* Boston: Allyn & Bacon.

Evertson, C.M., Emmer, E.T., & Worsham, M. E. (2000). *Classroom management for secondary teachers* (5th Ed.). Boston: Allyn & Bacon.

Farrington, D. P. (2000). Delinquency. In A. Kazdin (Ed.), *Encyclopedia of psychology.* Washington, DC, and New York: American Psychological Association and Oxford U. Press.

Fearn, L. (1972). *The maligned wolf.* San Diego: Kabyn Press.

Feirson, R. (1997). Creating a middle school culture of literacy. *Middle School Journal, 28,* 10–15.

Fekken, G. C. (2000). Reliability. In A. Kazdin (Ed.), *Encyclopedia of psychology.* Washington, DC, & New York: American Psychological Association and Oxford U. Press.

Felber, S. A. (1997, September/October). Strategies for parent partnerships. *Teaching Exceptional Children,* pp. 20–23.

Feldhusen, J. F. (1997). Secondary services, opportunities, and activities for talented youth. In N. Colangelo & G. A. Davis (Eds.), *Handbook of gifted education.* Boston: Allyn & Bacon.

Feng, Y. (1996). Some thoughts about applying constructivist theories to guide instruction. *Computers in the Schools, 12,* 71–84.

Fenzel, L. M., Blyth, D. A., & Simmons, R. G. (1991). School transitions, secondary. In R. M. Lerner, A. C. Petersen, & J. Brooks-Gunn (Eds.). *Encyclopedia of Adolescence* (Vol. 2). New York: Garland.

Ferrari, M., & Sternberg, R. J. (1998). *Self-awareness.* New York: Guilford.

Ferrari, M., & Sternberg, R. J. (1998). The development of mental abilities and styles. In W. Damon (Ed.), *Handbook of child psychology* (Vol. 2). New York: Wiley.

Field, T. (Ed.). (1995). *Touch in early development.* Mahwah, NJ: Erlbaum.

Fielding, L. G., Wilson, P. T. & Anderson, R. C. (1986). A new focus on free reading: The role of tradebooks in reading instruction. In T. Raphael (Ed.), *The contexts of school-based literacy.* New York: Random House.

Firlik, R. (1996). Can we adapt the philosophies and practices of Reggio Emilia, Italy, for use in American schools? *Young Children, 51,* 217–220.

Firpo-Triplett, R. (1997, July). *Is it flirting or sexual harassment?* Paper presented at the Working with America's Youth conference, Pittsburgh.

Fisher, C. W., Berliner, D. C., Filby, N. N., Marliave, R., Ghen, L. S., & Dishaw, M. M. (1980). Teaching behaviors, academic learning time, and student achievement: An overview. In C. Denham & A. Lieberman (Eds.), *Time to learn.* Washington, DC: National Institute of Education.

Fitzpatrick, J. (1993). *Developing responsible behavior in schools.* South Burlington, VT: Fitzpatrick Associates.

Flake, C., Kuhs, T., Donnelly, A., & Ebert, C. (1995). Teacher as researcher: Reinventing the role of teacher. *Phi Delta Kappan, 76,* 405–407.

Flavell, J. H. (1999). Cognitive development. *Annual Review of Psychology* (Vol. 50). Palo Alto, CA: Annual Reviews.

Flavell, J. H., & Miller, P. H. (1998). Social cognition. In W. Damon (Ed.), *Handbook of child psychology* (Vol. 2). New York: Wiley.

Flavell, J. H., Friedrichs, A., & Hoyt, J. (1970). Developmental changes in memorization processes. *Cognitive Psychology, 1,* 324–340.

Flavell, J. H., Miller, P. H., & Miller, S. A. (1993). *Cognitive development* (3rd ed.). Englewood Cliffs, NJ: Prentice Hall.

Flower, L. S., & Hayes, J. R. (1981). Problem-solving and the cognitive processes in writing. In C. Frederiksen & J. F. Dominic (Eds.), *Writing: The nature, development, and teaching of written communication.* Mahwah, NJ: Erlbaum.

Fogarty, R. (1991). *The mindful school.* Arlington Heights, IL: IRI/Skylight.

Fogarty, R. (Ed.) (1993). *The multiage classroom.* Palatine, IL: IRI/Skylight.

Ford, D. (1996). *Reversing underachievement among gifted Black students.* New York: Teachers College Press.

Forehand, R., Ragosta, J., & Rock, D. (1976). *Conditions and processes of effective school desegregation.* Princeton, NJ: Educational Testing Service.

Fox, B. A. (1993). *The Human Tutorial Dialogue Project.* Mahwah, NJ: Erlbaum.

Fraenkel, J. R., & Wallen, N. (2000). *How to design and evaluate research in education.* New York: McGraw-Hill.

Frasier, M., & Passaw, A. (1995). *A review of assessment issues in gifted education and their implications for identifying gifted minority students.* Storrs, CT: National Research Center for the Gifted and Talented.

Freedman, D. S., Dietz, W. H., Srinivasan, S. R., & Berensen, G. S. (in press). The relation of overweight to cardiovascular risks among children and adolescents: The Bogalusa Heart Study. *Pediatrics.*

Freiberg, H. J. (Ed.). (1999). *Beyond behaviorism: Changing the classroom management paradigm.* Boston: Allyn & Bacon.

Freiberg, H. J., & Driscoll, A. (2000). *Universal teaching strategies* (3rd ed.). Boston: Allyn & Bacon.

Freppon, P. A., & Dahl, K. L. (1998). Balanced instruction: Insights and considerations *Reading Research Quarterly, 33,* 240–251.

Frieberg, H. J. (1999). Sustaining the paradigm. In H.J. Frieberg (Ed.), *Beyond behaviorism: Changing the classroom management paradigm.* Boston: Allyn & Bacon.

Friend, M., & Bursuck, W. (1999). *Including students with special needs* (2nd ed.). Boston: Allyn & Bacon.

Frye, D., Zelazo, P. D., Brooks, P. J., & Samuels, M. C. (1996). Inference and action in early causal reasoning. *Developmental Psychology, 32,* 120–131.

Fuchs, D., Fuchs, L. S., Mathes, P. G., & Simmons, D. C. (1997). Peer-assisted learning strategies: Making classrooms more responsive to diversity. *American Educational Research Journal, 34,* 174–206.

Fuchs, L. S., Fuchs, D., Bentz, J., Phillips, N. B., & Hamlett, C. L. (1994). The nature of student interactions during peer tutoring with and without prior training and experience. *American Educational Research Journal, 31,* 75–103.

Furman, D., & Buhrmester, D. (in press). Age and sex differences in perceptions of networks of personal relationships. *Child Development.*

Furth, H. G., & Wachs, H. (1975). *Thinking goes to school.* New York: Oxford University Press.

Gackenbach, J., & Ellerman, E. (1999). Introduction to psychological aspects of Internet use. In J. Gackenbach (Ed.), *Psychology and the Internet.* San Diego: Academic Press.

Gage, N. L. (1978). *The scientific basis of the art of teaching.* New York: Teachers College Press.

Galambos, N. L., Petersen, A. C., Richards, M., & Gitleson, I. B. (1985). The Attitudes toward Women Scale for Adolescents (AWSA). *Sex Roles, 13,* 343–356.

Gallagher, C. (2000). A seat at the table: Teachers reclaiming assessment through rethinking accountability. *Phi Delta Kappan, 81,* 502–507.

Gallup and National Science Foundation Poll. (1997). Princeton, NJ: Gallup.

Gallup Organization. (1996). *Poll on problems in public education.* Princeton, NJ: Author.

Garbarino, J. (2000). The effects of community violence. In L. Balter & C. S. Tamis-LeMonda (Eds.), *Child psychology: A handbook of contemporary issues.* Philadelphia: Psychology Press.

Garcia, E. E. (1992). "Hispanic" children: Theoretical, empirical, and related policy issues. *Educational Psychology Review, 4,* 69–93.

Gardner, H. (1983). *Frames of mind.* New York: Basic Books.

Gardner, H. (1985). *The mind's new science.* New York: Basic Books.

Gardner, H. (1993). *Multiple intelligences.* New York: Basic Books.

Gardner, H. (1999). *The disciplined mind.* New York: Simon & Schuster.

Gardner, H., Feldman, D. H., & Krechevsky, M. (Eds.). (1998). *Project Spectrum.* New York: Teachers College Press.

Garmon, A., Nystrand, M., Berends, M., & LePore, P. C. (1995). An organizational analysis of the effects of ability grouping. *American Educational Research Journal, 32,* 687–715.

Garner, R., & Gillingham, M. G. (1999). New voices: The Internet connection of high school kids who (usually) won't write. *High School Journal, 82,* 172–181.

Garrod, A., Smulyan, L., Powers, S. I., & Kilenny, R. (1992). *Adolescent portraits.* Boston: Allyn & Bacon.

Gaskins, I. W. (1998). There's more to teaching at-risk and delayed readers than good reading instruction. *Reading Teacher, 51,* 534–547.

Gay, G. (1997). Educational equality for students of color. In J. A. Banks & C. M. Banks (Eds.), *Multicultural Education* (3rd ed.). Boston: Allyn & Bacon.

Gay, L. R., & Airasian, P. (2000). *Educational research* (6th ed.). Upper Saddle River, NJ: Merrill.

Gay, L. R., & Airasian, P. (2000). *Educational research.* Columbus, OH: Merrill.

Geisert, P. G., & Futrell, M. K. (2000). *Teachers, computers, and curriculum.* Boston: Allyn & Bacon.

Gelman, R. (1969). Conservation acquisition: A problem of learning to attend to relevant attributes. *Journal of Experimental Child Psychology, 7,* 67–87.

Gelman, R., & Brennerman, K. (1994). Domain specificity and cultural specificity are not inconsistent. In L. A. Hirschfeld & S. Gelman (Eds.), *Mapping out domain specificity in cognition and culture.* New York: Cambridge University Press.

Gelman, R., & Williams, E. M. (1998). Enabling constraints for cognitive development and learning. In W. Damon (Ed.), *Handbook of child psychology* (5th ed., Vol. 4). New York: Wiley.

Gentile, J. R. (2000). Learning, transfer of. In A. Kazdin (Ed.), *Encyclopedia of psychology.* Washington, DC, and New York: American Psychological Association and Oxford U. Press.

Gibbs, J. T. (1989). Black American adolescents. In J. T. Gibbs & L. N. Huang (Eds.), *Children of color.* San Francisco: Jossey-Bass.

Gill, J. (1997, July). Personal conversation. Richardson: University of Texas at Dallas.

Gilligan, C. (1982). *In a different voice.* Cambridge, MA: Harvard University Press.

Gilligan, C. (1996). The centrality of relationships in psychological development: A puzzle, some evidence, and a theory. In G. G. Noam & K. W. Fischer (Eds.), *Development and vulnerability.* Mahwah, NJ: Erlbaum.

Gilligan, C. (1998). *Minding women: Reshaping the education realm.* Cambridge, MA: Harvard University Press.

Ginsburg, H. P., Klein, A., & Starkey, P. (1997). The development of children's mathematical thinking. In I.E. Sigel & K. A. Renninger (Eds.), *Handbook of child psychology* (5th ed., Vol. 4). New York: Wiley.

Gipson, J. (1997, March/April). Girls and computer technology: Barrier or key? *Educational Technology,* pp. 41–43.

Glasser, W. (1969). *Schools without failure.* New York: Harper & Row.

Glasson, G. E. (1989). The effects of hands-on and teacher demonstration laboratory methods on science achievement in relation to reasoning ability and prior knowledge. *Journal of Research in Science Teaching, 26,* 121–131.

Gleason, J. B., & Ratner, N. (1998). *Psycholinguistics* (3rd ed.). Fort Worth: Harcourt Brace.

Gold, J., & Lanzoni, M. (Eds.). (1993). *Graduation by portfolio—Central Park East Secondary School.* Videotape. New York: Post Production, 29th St. Video, Inc.

Goldberg, M. (1997, March/April). Review of "The Julliard Music Adventure." *Electronic Learning,* p. 24.

Goldberg, M. F. (1997, March). Maintaining a focus on child development. *Phi Delta Kappan,* pp. 557–559.

Goldin-Meadow, S. (2000). Language development, syntax, and communication. In A. Kazdin (Ed.), *Encyclopedia of psychology.* Washington, DC, and New York: American Psychological Association and Oxford U. Press.

Goldman, S. (1998, October). Unpublished review of J. W. Santrock's *Educational Psychology* (New York: McGraw-Hill).

Goldman, S. R., Petrosino, A., Sherwood, R. D., Garrison, S., Hickey, D., Bransford, J. D., & Pellegrino, J. (1996). Anchoring science instruction in multimedia learning environments. In S. Vosniadou, E. De Corte, R. Glaser, & H. Mandl (Eds.), *International perspectives on the design of technology-supported learning environments.* Hillsdale, NJ: Erlbaum.

Goldstein, H., & Hockenberger, E. (1991). Significant progress in child language intervention: An 11-year retrospective. *Research in Developmental Disabilities, 12,* 401–424.

Goleman, D. (1995). *Emotional intelligence.* New York: Bantam.

Goleman, D., Kaufman, P., & Ray, M. (1993). *The creative spirit.* New York: Plume.

Goncu, A. (1999). *Children's engagement in the world.* New York: Cambridge University Press.

Goodlad, J. I. (1984). *A place called school.* New York: McGraw-Hill.

Goodlad, S., & Hirst, B. (1989). *Peer tutoring: A guide to learning by teaching.* New York: Nichols.

Gordon, T. (1970). *Parent effectiveness training.* New York: McGraw-Hill.

Gottman, J. M. (1996). *What predicts divorce.* New York: Milton H. Erickson Foundation.

Graham, S. (1986, August). *Can attribution theory tell us something about motivation in Blacks?* Paper presented at the meeting of the American Psychological Association, Washington, DC.

Graham, S. (1990). Motivation in African Americans. In G. L. Berry & J. K. Asamen (Eds.), *Black students.* Newbury Park, CA: Sage.

Graham, S. (1992). Most of the subjects were white and middle class. *American Psychologist, 47,* 629–637.

Graham, S. (1996). What's "emotional" about social motivation? A comment. In J. Juvonen & K. R. Wentzel (Eds.), *Social motivation.* New York: Cambridge University Press.

Graham, S., & Harris, K. R. (1994). The effects of whole language on children's writing: A review of the literature. *Educational Psychologist, 29,* 187–192.

Graham, S., & Weiner, B. (1996). Theories and principles of motivation. In D. C. Berliner & R. C. Calfee (Eds.), *Handbook of educational psychology.* New York: Macmillan.

Gratz, R. R., & Bouton, P. J. (1996). Erikson and early childhood educators. *Young Children, 51,* 74–78.

Graziano, A. M., & Raulin, M. L. (2000). *Research methods* (4th ed.). Boston: Allyn & Bacon.

Gredler, M. (1999). *Classroom assessment and learning.* Boston: Addison Wesley.

Greenberg, M. T. (1996). *The PATHS project.* Seattle: University of Washington.

Greene, B. (2000). Gender and culture. In A. Kazdin (Ed.), *Encyclopedia of psychology.* Washington, DC, and New York: American Psychological Association and Oxford U. Press.

Greenfield, P. M. (2000). Culture and development. In A. Kazdin (Ed.), *Encyclopedia of psychology.* Washington, DC, and New York: American Psychological Association and Oxford U. Press.

Greeno, J. G. (1993). For research to reform education and cognitive science. In L. A. Penner, G. M. Batche, H. M. Knoff, & D. L. Nelson (Eds.), *The challenge in mathematics and science education: Psychology's response.* Washington, DC: American Psychological Association.

Greeno, J. G., Collins, A. M., & Resnick, L. (1996). Cognition and learning. In D. C. Berliner & R. C. Calfee (Eds.), *Handbook of educational psychology.* New York: Macmillan.

Greenough, W. (1997, April 21). Commentary: *U.S. News & World Report.* p. 79.

Greenough, W. (2000). Brain development. In A. Kazdin (Ed.), *Encyclopedia of psychology.* Washington, DC, and New York: American Psychological Association and Oxford U. Press.

Gregory, R. J. (2000). *Psychological testing* (3rd ed.). Boston: Allyn & Bacon.

Griffiths, M. (1999). Internet addiction. In J. Gackenbach (Ed.), *Psychology and the Internet.* San Diego: Academic Press.

Gronlund, N. E. (1998). *Assessment of student achievement.* Boston: Allyn & Bacon.

Gronlund, N. E., Linn, R. L., & Davis, K. M. (2000). *Measurement and assessment in teaching.* Upper Saddle River, NJ: Prentice-Hall.

Grossier, P. (1964). *How to use the fine art of questioning.* New York: Teachers' Practical Press.

Grotevant, H. D. (1998). Adolescent development in family contexts. In W. Damon (Ed.), *Handbook of child psychology* (5th ed., Vol. 3). New York: Wiley.

Guilford, J. P. (1967). *The structure of intellect.* New York: McGraw-Hill.

Gunning, T. G. (2000). *Creating literacy instruction for all children* (3rd ed.). Boston: Allyn & Bacon.

Guttentag, M., & Bray, H. (1976). *Undoing sex stereotypes: Research and resources for educators.* New York: McGraw-Hill.

Guyer, B. (2000). *ADHD.* Boston: Allyn & Bacon.

H

Hackenberg, T. D. (2000). Schedules of reinforcement. In A. Kazdin (Ed.), *Encyclopedia of psychology.* Washington, DC, and New York: American Psychological Association and Oxford U. Press.

Haith, M. M., & Benson, J. B. (1998). Infant cognition. In W. Damon (Ed.), *Handbook of child psychology* (5th ed., Vol. 2). New York: Wiley.

Hakuta, K. (2000). Bilingualism. In A. Kazdin (Ed.), *Encyclopedia of psychology.* Washington, DC, and New York: American Psychological Association and Oxford U. Press.

Hakuta, K., & Garcia, E. E. (1989). Bilingualism and education. *American Psychologist, 44,* 374–379.

Hakuta, K., Ferdman, B. M., & Diaz, R. M. (1987). Bilingualism and cognitive development: Three perspectives. In S. Rosenberg (Ed.), *Advances in applied linguistics* (Vol. 2). New York: Cambridge University Press.

Haladyna, T. M. (1997). *Writing test items to evaluate higher-order thinking.* Boston: Allyn & Bacon.

Hall, R. V., & Hall, M. L. (1998). *How to select reinforcers* (2nd ed.). Austin: Pro-Ed.

Hall, W. (1998, February 24). I.Q. scores are up, and psychologists wonder why. *Wall Street Journal,* pp. B11–12.

Hallahan, D., Kaufman, J., & Lloyd, J. (1999). *Introduction to learning disabilities* (2nd ed.). Boston: Allyn & Bacon.

Hallahan, D. P., & Kaufmann, J. M. (2000). *Exceptional learners* (8th Ed.). Boston: Allyn & Bacon.

Halonen, J. A. (1999). Writing and speaking. In J. W. Santrock & J. A. Halonen, *Mastering the college experience.* Belmont, CA: Wadsworth.

Hambleton, R. K. (1996). Advances in assessment models, methods, and practices. In D. C. Berliner & R. C. Calfee (Eds.), *Handbook of educational psychology.* New York: Macmillan.

Hamburg, D. A. (1997). Meeting the essential requirements for healthy adolescent development in a transforming world. In R. Takanishi & D. Hamburg (Eds.), *Preparing adolescents for the 21st century.* New York: Cambridge University Press.

Hardman, M., Drew, C., & Egan, M. (1999). *Human exceptionality: Society, school, and family.* Boston: Allyn & Bacon.

Hart, B., & Risley, T. (in press). *Advantage and disadvantage.* Baltimore: Paul H. Brookes.

Hart, B., & Risley, T. R. (1995). *Meaningful differences.* Baltimore: Paul H. Brookes.

Hart, C. H., Charlesworth, R., Durland, M. A., Burts, D. C., DeWolf, M., & Fleege, P. O. (1996). *Developmentally appropriate practice in preschool classrooms.* Unpublished manuscript, Brigham Young University, Provo, Utah.

Harter, S. (1981). A new self-report scale of intrinsic versus extrinsic orientation in the classroom: Motivational and informational components. *Developmental Psychology, 17,* 300–312.

Harter, S. (1990). Processes underlying adolescent self-concept formation. In R. Montemayor, G. R. Adams, & T. P. Gulotta (Eds.), *From childhood to adolescence: A transitional period?* Newbury Park, CA: Sage.

Harter, S. (1990). Self and identity development. In S. S. Feldman & G. R. Elliott (Eds.), *At the threshold: The developing adolescent.* Cambridge, MA: Harvard University Press.

Harter, S. (1996). Teacher and classmate influences on scholastic motivation, self-esteem, and level of voice in adolescents. In J. Juvonen & K. R. Wentzel (Eds.), *Social motivation.* New York: Cambridge University Press.

Harter, S. (1998). The development of self-representations. In W. Damon (Ed.), *Handbook of child psychology* (5th ed., Vol. 3). New York: Wiley.

Harter, S. (1999). *The construction of the self.* New York: Guilford.

Harter, S., & Marold, D. B. (1992). Psychosocial risk factors contributing to suicide ideation. In G. Noam & S. Borst (Eds.), *Child and adolescent suicide.* San Francisco: Jossey-Bass.

Hartup, W. W. (1983). Peer relations. In P. H. Mussen (Ed.), *Handbook of child psychology* (4th ed., Vol 4). New York: Wiley.

Hartup, W. W. (2000). Socialization and social contexts. In A. Kazdin (Ed.), *Encyclopedia of psychology.* Washington, DC, and New York: American Psychological Association and Oxford U. Press.

Hartup, W. W., & Stevens, N. (1997). Freindships and adaptation in the life course. *Psychological Bulletin, 121,* 355–370.

Hatch, T. (2000, April). *Portfolios and the scholarship of teaching.* Paper presented at the meeting of the American Educational Research Association, New Orleans.

Hawkins, J. A., & Berndt, T. J. (1985). *Adjustment following the transition to junior high.* Paper presented at the meeting of the Society for Research in Child Development, Toronto.

Hayes, S. C. (2000). Applied behavior analysis. In A. Kazdin (Ed.), *Encyclopedia of psychology.* Washington, DC, and New York: American Psychological Association and Oxford U. Press.

Haynes, R. M., & Chalker, D. M. (1997, May). World class schools. *American School Board Journal,* pp. 20–25.

Heath, S. B. (1989). Oral and literate traditions among Black Americans living in poverty. *American Psychologist, 44,* 367–373.

Heatherington, E. M. (1999). *Coping with divorce, single parenting, and remarriage.* Mahwah, NJ: Erlbaum.

Heller, C., & Hawkins, J. (1994, Spring). Teaching tolerance. *Teachers College Record,* p. 2.

Heller, H. C. (1993). The need for a core, interdisciplinary, life-sciences curriculum in the middle grades. In R. Takanishi (Ed.), *Adolescence in the 1990s*. New York: Teachers College Press.

Henderson, V. L., & Dweck, C. S. (1990). Motivation and achievement. In S. S. Feldman & G. R. Elliott (Eds.), *At the threshold: The developing adolescent*. Cambridge, MA: Harvard University Press.

Henley, M., Ramsey, R., & Algozzine, R. (1999). *Characteristics and strategies for teaching students with mild disabilities* (3rd ed.). Boston: Allyn & Bacon.

Hennessey, B. A., & Amabile, T. M. (1998). Reward, intrinsic motivation, and creativity. *American Psychologist, 53*, 674–675.

Henry, T. (1997, September 30). Black graduates answering call. *USA Today*, pp. D1–2.

Henson, K. (1988). *Methods and strategies for teaching in secondary and middle schools*. New York: Longman.

Herman, J. (1996). Commentary in "The latest on student portfolios." NEA *Today, 15* (4), 17.

Herrnstein, R. J., & Murray, C. (1994) *The bell curve: Intelligence and class structure in modern life*. New York: Free Press.

Hertzog, N. B. (1998, January/February). Gifted education specialist. *Teaching Exceptional Children*, pp. 39–43.

Hess, D., Machosky, M. D., & Deal, N. (1997, June 18). Highlights of humor in the classroom. *USA Today*, p. 9D.

Hetherington, E. M. (1995, March). *The changing American family and the well-being of others*. Paper presented at the meeting of the Society for Research in Child Development, Indianapolis.

Hetherington, E. M. (1999). *Should we stay together for the sake of the children?* Unpublished manuscript, Department of Psychology, University of Virginia, Charlottesville.

Hetherington, E. M., Bridges, M., & Isabella, G. M. (1998). What matters? Five perspectives on the association between marital transitions and children's adjustment. *American Psychologist, 53*, 167–184.

Heuwinkel, M. K. (1996). Piagetian perspectives on understanding children's understanding. *Childhood Education, 72*, 258–259.

Heward, W. (1996). *Exceptional children* (5th ed.). Upper Saddle River, NJ: Prentice Hall.

Heward, W. L. (2000). *Introduction to special education* (6th ed.). Upper Saddle River, NJ: Merrill.

Hewitt, J. S., & Whittier, K. S. (1997). *Today's schools*. Boston: Allyn & Bacon.

Hiebert, E. H., & Raphael, T. E. (1996). Psychological perspectives on literacy and extensions to educational practice. In D. C. Berliner & R. C. Calfee (Eds.), *Handbook of educational psychology*. New York: Macmillan.

Higgins, A., Power, C., & Kohlberg, L. (1983, April). *Moral atmosphere and moral judgment*. Paper presented at the meeting of the Society for Research in Child Development, Detroit.

Higgins, E. T. (2000). Self-regulation. In A. Kazdin (Ed.), *Encyclopedia of psychology*. Washington, DC, and New York: American Psychological Association and Oxford U. Press.

Hightower, E. (1990). Adolescent interpersonal and familial precursors of positive mental health quality at midlife. *Journal of Youth and Adolescence, 19*, 257–275.

Himber, C. (1989). *How to survive hearing loss*. Washington, DC: Gallaudet University Press.

Hirsch, E. D. (1987). *Cultural literacy*. New York: Random House.

Hirsch, E. D. (1996). *The schools we need: And why we don't have them*. New York: Doubleday.

Hockenbury, D. (1997). Statistical appendix. In J. W. Santrock, *Psychology* (5th ed.). New York: McGraw-Hill.

Hocutt, A. M. (1996). Effectiveness of special education: Is placement the critical factor? *Future of Children, 6* (1), 77–102.

Hoekema, J. (1993). Hypercard and CD-I: The "Mutt and Jeff" of multimedia platforms. In D. M. Gayeski (Ed.), *Multimedia for learning*. Englewood Cliffs, NJ: Educational Technology.

Hoff-Ginsburg, E., & Tardif, T. (1995). Socioeconomic status and parenting. In M. H. Borstein (Ed.). *Children and parenting* (Vol. 2). Hillsdale, NJ: Erlbaum.

Hogan, D. M., & Tudge, J. (1999). Implications of Vygotsky's theory for peer learning. In A. M. O'Donnell & A. King (Eds.), *Cognitive perspectives on peer learning*. Mahwah, NJ: Erbaum.

Hogan, R. T. (1987, August). *Conceptions of personality and the prediction of job performance*. Paper presented at the meeting of the American Psychological Association, New York City.

Hollingworth, L. S. (1914). *Functional periodicity: An experimental study of the mental and motor abilities of women during menstruation*. New York: Columbia University, Teachers College.

Hollingworth, L. S. (1916). Sex differences in mental tests. *Psychological Bulletin, 13*, 377–383.

Holzberg, C. (1995). Technology in special education. *Technology and Learning, 14*, 18–21.

Holzberg, C. S. (1997, March/April). Software for home learning. *Electronic Learning*, p. 35.

Honig, A. S., & Wittmer, D. S. (1996). Helping children become more prosocial: Ideas for the classroom, families, schools, and communities. *Young Children, 51*, 62–70.

Hooper, S., Ward, T. J., Hannafin, M. J., & Clark, H. T. (1989). The effects of aptitude composition on achievement during small group learning. *Journal of Computer-Based Instruction, 16*, 102–109.

Howell, J., & Dunnivant, S. (2000). *Technology for teachers*. New York: McGraw-Hill.

Howes, C., & Tonyan, H. (2000). Peer relations. In L. Balter & C. S. Tamis-LeMonda (Eds.), *Child psychology: A handbook of contemporary issues*. Philadelphia: Psychology Press.

Hudley, C., & Graham, S. (1995). School-based interventions for aggressive African-American boys. *Applied and Preventive Psychology, 4*, 185–195.

Huitt, W. G. (1997). *A transaction model of the teaching/learning process*. Retrieved from the World Wide Web: http://www.valdosta.edu/~whuitt/psy702/mdltlp.html.

Hunt, R. R., & Ellis, H. C. (1999). *Fundamentals of cognitive psychology* (6th ed.). New York: McGraw-Hill.

Hunt, R. R., & Kelly, R. E. S. (1996). Accessing the particular from the general: The power of distinctiveness in the context of organization. *Memory and Cognition, 24*, 217–225.

Hyde, J. S., & Plant, E. A. (1995). Magnitude of psychological gender differences: Another side of the story. *Ameircan Psycholgist, 50*, 159–161.

Hyman, I. (1994). *Is spanking child abuse? Conceptualizations, research, and policy implications*. Paper presented at the meeting of the American Psychological Association, Los Angeles.

Iacocca, L. (1984). *Iacocca: An autobiography*. New York: Bantam.

Ickes, W., Snyder, M., & Garcia, S. (1997). Personality influences or the choice of situations. In R. Hogan, J. Johnson, & S. Briggs (Eds.), *Handbook of personality psychology*. San Diego: Academic Press.

Idol, L. (1997). Key questions related to building collaborative and inclusive schools. *Journal of Learning Disabilities, 30*, 384–394.

Idol, L., Nevin, A., & Paolucci-Whitcomb, P. (1994). *Collaborative consultation*. Austin, TX: PRO-ED.

In View. (1990). *A field trip into the sea* (software). Pleasantville, NY: Sunburst Communications.

Institute for Families in Society. (1997). *Program to combat bullying in schools*. Columbia: University of South Carolina.

Intercultural Development Research Association. (1996). *More at-risk students to tutor others*. Unpublished manuscript, Intercultural Development Research Association, San Antonio.

International Society for Technology in Education. (ISTE). (1999). *National educational technology standards for students document*. Eugene, OR: Author.

Irvin, J. L. (1997). Building sound literacy learning programs for young adolescents. *Middle School Journal, 28*, 4–9.

Irvin, J. L., & Conners, N. A. (1989). Reading instruction in middle level schools: Results of a U.S. survey. *Journal of Reading, 32*, 306–311.

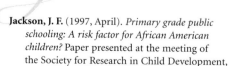

Jackson, J. F. (1997, April). *Primary grade public schooling: A risk factor for African American children?* Paper presented at the meeting of the Society for Research in Child Development, Washington, DC.

Jackson, N., & Butterfield, E. (1986). A conception of giftedness designed to promote research. In R. J. Sternberg & J. E. Davidson (Eds.), *Conceptions of giftedness*. New York: Cambridge University Press.

Jackson, P. W. (1968). *Life in classrooms*. New York: Holt, Rinehart & Winston.

Jacobs, H. H. (1989). *Interdisciplinary curriculum: Design and implementation*. Alexandria, VA: Association for Supervision and Curriculum Development.

Jacobs, H. H. (1997). *Mapping the big picture: Integrating curriculum and assessment K–12.* Alexandria, VA: Association for Supervision and Curriculum Development.

Jacobson, L. (1996, January). First in the world? *American School Board Journal,* pp. 21–23.

Jalongo, M. R. (2000). *Early childhood language arts: Meeting diverse literacy needs through collaboration with families and professionals* (2nd ed.). Boston: Allyn & Bacon.

James, W. (1890). Principles of psychology. New York: Dover.

James, W. (1899/1993) *Talks to teachers.* New York: W. W. Norton.

Jenkins, J., & Jenkins, L. (1987). Making peer tutoring work. *Educational Leadership, 44,* 64–68.

Jensen, A. R. (1969). How much can we boost IQ and academic achievement? *Harvard Educational Review, 39,* 1–123.

Johnson, B., & Christensen, L. (2000). *Educational research.* Boston: Allyn & Bacon.

Johnson, D. W., & Johnson, F. P. (2000). Joining together: Group theory and skills (7th Ed.). Boston: Allyn & Bacon.

Johnson, D. W., & Johnson, R. (1991). *Teaching students to be peacemakers.* Edina, MN: Interaction.

Johnson, D. W., & Johnson, R. T. (1989). *Cooperation and competition: Theory and research.* Edina, MN: Interaction.

Johnson, D. W., & Johnson, R. T. (1994). *Learning together and alone* (2nd ed.). Englewood Cliffs, NJ: Prentice Hall.

Johnson, D. W., & Johnson, R. T. (1994). *Learning together and alone* (4th ed.). Boston: Allyn & Bacon.

Johnson, D. W., & Johnson, R. T. (1995, February). Why violence prevention programs don't work— And what does. *Educational Leadership,* pp. 63–68.

Johnson, D. W., & Johnson, R. T. (1999). *Learning together and alone: Cooperative, competitive, and individualistic learning* (5th ed.). Boston: Allyn & Bacon.

Johnson, D. W., & Johnson, R. T. (1999). The three Cs of school and classroom management. In H. J. Frieberg (Ed.), *Beyond behaviorism: Changing the classroom management paradigm.* Boston: Allyn & Bacon.

Johnson, J. S., & Newport, E. L. (1989). Critical period effects in second language learning: The influence of maturational state on the acquisition of English as a second language. *Cognitive Psychology, 21,* 60–99.

Johnson, M. K., Beebe, T., Mortimer, J. T., & Snyder, M. (1998). Volunteerism in adolescence: A process perspective, *Journal of Research on Adolescence, 8,* 309–332.

Johnson, V. R. (1994). *Parent centers in urban schools.* (Center Report no. 23). Baltimore: Johns Hopkins University, Center on Families, Communities, Schools, and Children's Learning.

Johnson-Laird, P. (2000). Reasoning. In A. Kazdin (Ed.), *Encyclopedia of psychology.* Washington, DC, and New York: American Psychological Association and Oxford U. Press.

John-Steiner, V., & Mahn, H. (1996). Sociocultural approaches to learning and development: A Vygotskian framework. *Educational Psychologist, 31,* 191–206.

Jonassen, D. H. (2000). *Computers as mindtools for schools: Engaging critical thinking* (2nd ed.). Upper Saddle River, NJ: Prentice Hall.

Jonassen, D. H., & Grabowski, B. L. (1993). *Handbook of Individual differences, learning, and instruction.* Mahwah, NJ: Erlbaum.

Jones, B. D. (1999). Computer-rated essays in the English composition classroom. *Journal of Educational Computing Research, 20,* 169–188.

Jones, B. F., Rasmussen, C. M., & Moffitt, M. C. (1997). *Real-life problem solving.* Washington, DC: American Psychological Association.

Jones, C. (1993). Commentary in D. Goleman, P. Kaufman, & M. Ray, *The creative spirit.* New York: Plume.

Jones, J. M. (1994). The African American: A duality dilemma? In W. J. Lonner & R. Malpass (Eds.), *Psychology and culture.* Boston: Allyn & Bacon.

Jones, J.M. (1997). *Prejudice and racism* (2nd ed.). New York: McGraw-Hill.

Jones, L. V. (1984). White-black achievement differences: The narrowing gap. *American Psychologist, 39,* 1207–1213.

Jones, M. G., & Wheatley, J. (1990). Gender differences in teacher-student interactions in science classrooms. *Journal of Research in Science Teaching, 27,* 861–874.

Jones, R. (1997, July). Getting tough in Chicago. *American School Board Journal,* pp. 24–26.

Joyce, B., & Weil, M. (1996). *Models of teaching* (5th ed.). New York: McGraw-Hill.

K

Kabler, P. (1997, November 14). School officials work bugs out of computer act. *Charleston Gazette,* p. C1.

Kagan, J. (1965). Reflection-impulsivity and reading development in primary grade children. *Child Development, 36,* 609–628.

Kagan, J. (1992). Yesterday's promises, tomorrow's promises. *Developmental Psychology, 28,* 990–997.

Kagan, J. (1998). The biology of the child. In W. Damon (Ed.), *Handbook of child psychology* (5th ed., Vol. 3). New York: Wiley.

Kagan, J. (2000). Temperament. In A. Kazdin (Ed.), *Encyclopedia of psychology.* Washington, DC, and New York: American Psychological Association and Oxford U. Press.

Kagan, S. (1992). *Cooperative learning.* San Juan Capistrano, CA: Resources for Teachers.

Kagiticibasi, C. (1996). *Human development across cultures.* Mahway, NJ: Erlbaum.

Kahn, A. (1999). *The schools our children deserve.* Boston: Houghton Mifflin.

Kail, R., & Pellegrino, J. W. (1985). *Human intelligence.* New York: W. H. Freeman.

Kamii, C. (1985). *Young children reinvent arithmetic: Implications of Piaget's theory.* New York: Teachers College Press.

Kamii, C. (1989). *Young children continue to reinvent arithmetic.* New York: Teachers College Press.

Kamphaus, R. W. (2000). Learning disabilities. In A. Kazdin (Ed.), *Encyclopedia of psychology.* Washington, DC, and New York: American Psychological Association and Oxford U. Press.

Kasprow, W. J., & others. (1993). *New Haven Schools Social Development Project: 1992.* New Haven, CT: New Haven Public Schools.

Katx, L., & Chard, S. (1989). *Engaging the minds of young children: The project approach.* Norwood, NJ: Ablex.

Katz, P. A. (1987, August). *Children and social issues.* Paper presented at the meeting of the American Psychological Association, New York City.

Kearney, B. A. (1991, April). *The teacher as absent presence.* Paper presented at the meeting of the American Educational Research Association, Chicago.

Keil, F. (1999). Cognition. In M. Bennett (Ed.), *Developmental psychology: Achievements and prospects.* Philadelphia: Psychology Press.

Kelder, S. H., Perry, C. L., Peters, R. J., Lytle, L. L., & Klepp, K. (1995). Gender differences in the class of 1989 study: The school component of the Minnesota Heart Health Program. *Journal of Health Education, 26,* S36–S44.

Kellogg, R. T. (2000). Writing. In A. Kazdin (Ed.), *Encyclopedia of psychology.* Washington, DC, and New York: American Psychological Association and Oxford U. Press.

Kendall, P. (2000). Cognitive behavior therapy. In A. Kazdin (Ed.), *Encyclopedia of psychology.* Washington, DC, and New York: American Psychological Association and Oxford U. Press.

Kennedy, M. (1999). Infusing educational research with decision making. In G. J. Cizek (Ed.), *Handbook of educational policy.* San Diego: Academic Press.

Keogh, B. K., & MacMillan, D. L. (1996). Exceptionality. In D. Berliner & R. Calfee (Eds.), *Handbook of educational psychology.* New York: Macmillan.

Kiewra, K. A. (1989). A review of note-taking: The encoding-storage paradigm and beyond. *Educational Psychology Review, 1,* 147–172.

Kimmel, A. (1996). *Ethical issues in behavioral research.* Cambridge, MA: Blackwell.

Kinderman, T. A., McCollam, T. L., & Gibson, E. (1996). Peer networks and students' classroom engagement during childhood and adolescence. In J. Juvonen & K. R. Wentzel (Eds.), *Social motivation.* New York: Cambridge University Press.

King, A. (2000). Situated cognition. In A. Kazdin (Ed.), *Encyclopedia of psychology.* Washington, DC, and New York: American Psychological Association and Oxford U. Press.

Kirby, D. (1992). School-based programs to reduce sexual risk-taking behaviors. *Journal of School Health, 62,* 280–287.

Kivel, P. (1995). *Uprooting racism: How White people can work for racial justice.* Philadelphia: New Society.

Kohlberg, L. (1966). A cognitive-developmental analysis of children's sex role concepts and attitudes. In E. E. Maccoby (Ed.), *The development of sex differences.* Palo Alto, CA: Stanford University Press.

Kohlberg, L. (1976). Moral stages and moralization: The cognitive-developmental approach. In T. Lickona (Ed.), *Moral development and behavior.* New York: Holt, Rinehart & Winston.

Kohlberg, L. (1986). A current statement of some theoretical issues In S. Modgil & C. Modgil (Eds.), *Lawrence Kohlberg.* Philadelphia: Falmer.

Kohn, A. (1996). By all available means: Cameron and Pierce's defense of extrinsic motivators. *Review of Educational Research, 66,* 5–32.

Kotlowitz, A. (1991). *There are no children here.* New York: Anchor Books.

Kounin, J. S. (1970). *Discipline and management in classrooms.* New York: Holt, Rinehart & Winston.

Kowalski, R. M. (2000). Anxiety. In A. Kazdin (Ed.), *Encyclopedia of psychology.* Washington, DC, and New York: American Psychological Association and Oxford U. Press.

Koxulin, A. (2000). Vygotsky. In A. Kazdin (Ed.), *Encyclopedia of psychology.* Washington, DC, and New York: American Psychological Association and Oxford U. Press.

Kozol, J. (1991). *Savage inequalities.* New York: Crown.

Kozulin, A. (2000). Vygotsky, Lev. In A. Kazdin (Ed.), *Encyclopedia of psychology.* Washington, DC, and New York: American Psychological Association and Oxford U. Press.

Krantz, P. J., & Risley, T. R. (1972, September). *The organization of group care environments: Behavioral ecology in the classroom.* Paper presented at the meeting of the American Psychological Association, Honolulu.

Krathwohl, D. R., Bloom, B. S., & Masia, B. B. (1964). *Taxonomy of educational objectives. Handbook II: Affective domain.* New York: David McKay.

Kretuzer, L. C., & Flavell, J. H. (1975). An interview study of children's knowledge about memory. *Monographs of the Society for Research in Child Development, 40* (1, Serial No. 159).

Krueger, R. (2000). Validity. In A. Kazdin (Ed.), *Encyclopedia of psychology.* Washington, DC, & New York: American Psychological Association and Oxford U. Press.

Kuhn, D. (1999a). A developmental model of critical thinking. *Educational Researcher, 28,* 16–25.

Kuhn, D. (1999b). Metacognitive development. In L. Balter & S. Tamis-Lemonda (Eds.), *Child psychology: A handbook of contemporary issues.* Philadelphia: Psychology Press.

Kuhn, D., Amsel, E., & O'Laughlin, M. (1988). *The development of scientific thinking skills.* Orlando, FL: Academic Press.

Kuhn, D., Garcia-Mila, M., Zohar, Z., & Anderson, C. (1995). Strategies for knowledge acquisition. *Monographs of the Society for Research in Child Development, 60* (4, Serial No. 245), 1–127.

Kuhn, D., Schauble, L., & Garcia-Mila, M. (1992). Cross-domain development of scientific reasoning. *Cognition and Instruction, 9,* 285–327.

Kulik, C. L., Kulik, J. A., & Bangert-Drowns, R. L. (1990). Effectiveness of mastery learning programs: A meta-analysis. *Review of Educational Research, 60,* 265–299.

Kulik, J. A. (1992). An analysis of the research on ability grouping. *Monograph of the National Research Center on the Gifted and Talented* (No. 9204). Storrs: University of Connecticut.

Kupersmidt, J. B., & Coie, J. D. (1990). Preadolescent peer status, aggression, and school adjustment as predictors of externalizing problems in adolescence. *Child Development, 61,* 1350–1363.

Labinowicz, E. (1980). *The Piaget primer: Thinking, learning, teaching.* Reading, MA: Addison-Wesley.

Labov, W. (1973). The boundaries of words and their meanings. In C. N. Bailey & R. W. Shuy (Eds.), *New ways of analyzing variations in English.* Washington, DC: Georgetown University Press.

Lamon, M., Secules, T., Petrosino, A. J., Hackett, R., Bransford, J. D., & Goldman, S. R. (1996). Schools for Thought. In L. Schauble & R. Glaser (Eds.), *Innovations in learning.* Mahwah, NJ: Erlbaum.

Lankes, A. M. D. (1995). *Electronic portfolios: A new idea in assessment.* ERIC Reproduction Service No. ED390377.

Lareau, A. (1996). Assessing parent involvement in schooling: A critical analysis. In K. L. Alexander & D. R. Entwisle (Eds.), *Schools and children at risk.* Mahway, NJ: Erlbaum.

Larsen, L. (1997, June 18). Commentary in "Diagnosing learning problems can be difficult for parents and teachers." *USA Today,* p. D8.

Lazar, L., & others (1982). Lasting effects of early education. *Monographs of the Society for Research in Child Development, 47.*

Learner-Centered Principles Work Group (1997). *Learner-centered psychological principles: A framework for school reform and redesign.* Washington, DC: American Psychological Association.

Lee, D. L., & Belfiore, P. J. (1997). Enhancing classroom performance: A review of reinforcement schedules. *Journal of Behavioral Education, 7,* 205–217.

Lee, L. C. (1992, August). *In search of universals: What ever happened to race?* Paper presented at the meeting of the American Psychological Association, Washington, DC.

Lee, V. E., Croninger, R. G., Linn, E., & Chen, X. (1995, March). *The culture of sexual harassment in secondary schools.* Paper presented at the meeting of the Society for Research in Child Development, Indianapolis..

Lehrer, R., Lee, M., & Jeong, A. (1994). *Reflective teaching of LOGO.* Unpublished manuscript. Department of Educational Psychology, University of Wisconsin, Madison.

Leinhardt, G., & Greeno, J. G. (1986). The cognitive skill of teaching. *Journal of Educational Psychology, 78,* 75–95.

Lepper, M., Greene, D., & Nisbett, R. (1973). Undermining children's intrinsic interest with intrinsic rewards: A test of the overjustification hypothesis. *Journal of Personality and Social Psychology, 28,* 129–137.

Lepper, M. R. (1998). A whole much less than the sum of its parts. *American Psychologist, 53,* 675–676.

Lerner, J. (2000). *Learning disabilities* (8th ed.). Boston: Houghton Mifflin.

Lesser, G. (1972). Learning, teaching, and television production for children: The experience of Sesame Street. *Harvard Educational Review, 42,* 232–272.

Lester, F. K., Lambdin, D. V., & Preston, R. V. (1997). A new vision of the nature and purposes of assessment in the mathematics classroom. In G. D. Phye (Ed.), *Handbook of classroom assessment.* Orlando: Academic Press.

Levesque, J., & Prosser, T. (1996). Service learning connections. *Journal of Teacher Education, 47,* 325–334.

Levin, J. (1980). *The mnemonics '80s: Keywords in the classroom.* Theoretical paper No. 86. Wisconsin Research and Development Center for Individualized Schooling, Madison.

Levin, J., & Nolan, J. F. (2000). *Principles of classroom management: A professional decision-making model* (3rd Ed.). Boston: Allyn & Bacon.

Lewis, R. (1997). With a marble and telescope: Searching for play. *Childhood Education, 36,* 346.

Lewis, R. B. (1998). Assistive technology and learning disabilities: Today's realities and tomorrow's promises. *Journal of Learning Disabilities, 31,* 16–26.

Limber, S. P. (1997). Preventing violence among school children. *Family Futures, 1,* 27–28.

Linden, K. W. (1996). *Cooperative learning and problem solving.* Prospect Heights, IL: Waveland Press.

Linn, R. L. (2000). Assessments and accountability. *Educational Research, 29,* 4–15.

Linn, M., & Hyde, J. S. (1989). Gender, mathematics, and science. *Educational Researcher, 18,* 17–27.

Linn, M. C., Songer, N. B., & Eylon, B. (1996). Shifts and convergences in science learning and instruction. In D. C. Berliner & R. C. Calfee (Eds.), *Handbook of educational psychology.* New York: Macmillan.

Linn, R. L., & Gronlund, N. E. (1998). *Measurement and assessment in teaching* (8th ed.). Englewood Cliffs, NJ: Prentice Hall.

Linn, R. L., & Gronlund, N. E. (1999). *Measurement and assessment in teaching* (8th Ed.). Upper Saddle River, NJ: Prentice-Hall.

Linn, R. L., & Gronlund, N. E. (2000). *Measurement and assessment in teaching* (8th ed.). Upper Saddle River, NJ: Prentice Hall.

Lipsitz, J. (1984). *Successful schools for young adolescents.* New Brunswick, NJ: Transaction Books.

Little, N., & Allan, J. (1988). *Student-led parent conference.* Los Angeles: UCLA Graduate School of Education, RAND Institute on Education Training.

Logan, J. (1997). *Teaching stories.* New York: Kodansha International.

LoLordo, V. M. (2000). Classical conditioning. In A. Kazdin (Ed.), *Encyclopedia of psychology.* Washington, DC, and New York: American Psychological Association and Oxford U. Press.

Lonner, W. J. (1990). An overview of cross-cultural testing and assessment. In R. W. Brislin (Ed.), *Applies cross-cultural psychology.* Newbury Park, CA: Sage.

Louis Harris & Associates. (1995). *The Metropolitan life survey of the American teacher, 1984–1995.* New York: Author.

Louv, R. (1990). *Childhood's future.* Boston: Houghton Mifflin.

Lovett, S. B., & Pillow, B. H. (1996). Development of the ability to distinguish between comprehension and memory: Evidence from goal-state evaluation tasks. *Journal of Educational Psychology, 88,* 546–562.

Lowenstein, G. (1994). The psychology of curiosity: A review and reinterpretation. *Psychological Bulletin, 116*, 75–95.

Lubinski, D. (2000). Measures of intelligence: Intelligence tests. In A. Kazdin (Ed.), *Encyclopedia of psychology*. Washington, DC, and New York: American Psychological Association and Oxford U. Press.

Luria, A., & Herzog, E. (1985, April). *Gender segregation across and within settings*. Paper presented at the meeting of the Society for Research in Child Development, Toronto.

Lyon, G. R. (1996). Learning disabilities. *Future of Children, 6* (1), 54–76.

Lyon, G. R., & Moats, L. C. (1997). Critical conceptual and methodological considerations in reading intervention research. *Journal of Learning Disabilities, 30*, 578–588.

Lyon, T. D., & Flavell, J. H. (1993). Young children's understanding of forgetting over time. *Child Development, 64*, 789–800.

Lyons, N. (1999, May). How portfolios can shape emerging practice. *Educational Leadership, 56*, 63–67.

Mabry, L. (1999, May). Writing to the rubric: Lingering effects of traditional standardized testing on direct writing assessment. *Phi Delta Kappan, 80*, 673–679.

Maccoby, E. E. (1995). The two sexes and their social systems. In P. Moen, G. H. Elder, & K. Luscher (Eds.), *Examining lives in context*. Washington, DC: American Psychological Association.

Maccoby, E. E. (1997, April). Discussant, *Missing pieces in the puzzle: Biological contributions to gender development*. Symposium at the meeting of the Soceity for Research in Child Development, Washington, DC.

Maccoby, E. E., & Jacklin, C. N. (1974). *The psychology of sex differences*. Palo Alto, CA: Stanford University Press.

MacGregor, S. K. (1999). Hypermedia navigation profiles: Cognitive characteristics and information processing strategies. *Journal of Educational Computing Research, 20*, 189–206.

MacLean, W. E. (2000). Down syndrome. In A. Kazdin (Ed.), *Encyclopedia of psychology*. Washington, DC, and New York: American Psychological Association and Oxford U. Press.

MacWhinney, B. (Ed.). (1999). *The emergence of language*. Mahwah, NJ: Erlbaum.

Maddux, C. D., Johnson, D. L., & Willis, J. W. (1997). *Educational computing* (2nd ed.). Boston: Allyn & Bacon.

Mager, R. (1962). *Preparing instructional objectives* (2nd ed.). Palo Alto, CA: Fearon.

Maggio, R. (1987). *The non-sexist word finder: A dictionary of gender-free usage*. Phoenix: Oryx Press.

Magnusson, D. (1988). *Individual development from an interactional perspective*. Mahwah, NJ: Erlbaum.

Mahoney, M. (1991). *Human change processes*. New York: Basic Books.

Malik, N. M., & Furman, W. (1993). Practitioner review: Problems in children's peer relations: What can the clinician do? *Journal of Child Psychology and Psychiatry, 34*, 1303–1326.

Mallery, A. L. (2000). *Creating a catalyst for thinking: The integrated curriculum*. Boston: Allyn & Bacon.

Mandler, G. (1980). Recognizing: The judgment of previous occurrence. *Psychological Review, 87*, 252–271.

Maney, J. K. (1999). The role of technology in education: Reality, pitfalls, and potential. In G. J. Cizek (Ed.), *Handbook of educational policy*. San Diego: Academic Press.

Maratsos, M. (1998). The acquisition of grammar. In W. Damon (Ed.), *Handbook of child psychology* (4th ed., Vol. 2). New York: Wiley.

Marcia, J. E. (1980). Identity in adolescence. In J. Adelson (ed.), *Handbook of adolescent psychology*. New York: Wiley.

Marcia, J. E. (1998). Optimal development from an Eriksonian perspective. In H. S. Friedman (Ed.), *Encyclopedia of mental health* (Vol. 2). San Diego: Academic Press.

Marklein, M. B. (1998, November 24). An eye-level meeting of the minds. *USA Today*, p. 9D.

Marshall, H. H. (1996). Clarifying and implementing contemporary psychological perspectives. *Educational Psychologist, 31* (1), 29–34.

Marshall, H. H. (1996). Implications of differentiating and understanding constructivist approaches. *Educational Psychologist, 31*, 243–240.

Marshall, H. H. (1997). Clarifying and implementing contemporary psychological perspectives. *Educational Psychologist, 31* (1), 29–34.

Marshall, S. P., & Smith, J. D. (1987). Sex differences in learning mathematics: A longitudinal study with item and error analyses. *Journal of Educational Psychology, 79*, 372–383.

Martin, E. W., Martin, R., & Terman, D. L. (1996). The legislative and litigation history of special education. *Future of Children, 6* (1), 25–53.

Martin, R., Sexton, C., & Gerlovich, J. (1999). *Science for all children: Lessons for constructing understanding*. Boston: Allyn & Bacon.

Marton, F., Hounsell, D. J., & Entwistle, N. J. (1984). *The experience of learning*. Edinburgh: Scottish Academic Press.

Maslow, A. (1971). *The farther reaches of human nature*. New York: Viking Press.

Maslow, A. H. (1954). *Motivation and personality*. New York: Harper & Row.

Mathes, P. G., Howard, J. K., Allen, S. H., & Fuchs, D. (1998). Peer-assisted learning strategies for first-grade readers: Responding to the needs of diverse learners. *Reading Research Quarterly, 33*, 62–94.

Matsumoto, D. (1996). *Culture and psychology*. Pacific Grove, CA: Brooks/Cole.

Mayer, R. E. (1984). Twenty-five years of research on advance organizers. *Instructional Science, 8*, 133–169.

Mayer, R. E. (1996). Learners as information processors. *Educational Psychologist, 3*, 151–161.

Mayer, R. E. (1997). Multimedia learning: Are we asking the right questions? *Educational Psychologist, 32*, 1–19.

Mayer, R. E. (Ed.). (1998). *Teaching and learning computer programming: Multiple research perspectives*. Mahwah, NJ: Erlbaum.

Mayer, R. E. (1999). *The promise of educational psychology*. Upper Saddle River, NJ: Prentice-Hall.

Mayer, R. E., & Wittrock, M. C. (1996). Problem-solving transfer. In D. C. Berliner & R. C. Calfee (Eds.), *Handbook of educational psychology*. New York: Macmillan.

Mazurek, K., Winzer, M. A., & Majorek, C. (2000). *Education in a global society*. Boston: Allyn & Bacon.

McCarthey, S. (1994). Opportunities and risks of writing from personal experience. *Language Arts, 71*, 182–191.

McCormick, C. B., & Pressley, M. (1997). *Educational psychology*. New York: Longman.

McDonald, B. A., Larson, C. D., Dansereau, D. I., & Spurlin, J. E. (1985). Cooperative dyads: Impact on text learning and transfer. *Contemporary Educational Psychology, 10*, 369–377.

McKinley, D. W., Boulet, J. R., & Hambleton, R. K. (2000, August). *Standard-setting for performance-based assessment*. Paper presented at the meeting of the American Educational Research Association, New Orleans.

McLoyd, V. C. (1998). Children in poverty: Development, public policy, and practice. In W. Damon (Ed.), *Handbook of child psychology* (5th ed. Vol. 4). New York: Wiley.

McLoyd, V.C. (2000). Poverty. In A. Kazdin (Ed.), *Encyclopedia of psychology*. Washington, DC, & New York: American Psychological Association and Oxford U. Press.

McMahon, S. I. (1994). Student-led book clubs: Traversing a river of interpretation. *New Advocate, 7*, 109–125.

McMahon, S. I., Raphael, T. E., & Goatley, V. J. (1995). Changing the context for classroom reading instruction: The Book Club project. In J. Brophy (Ed.), *Advances in research on teaching*. Greenwich, CT: JAI Press.

McMillan, J. H. (1996). *Educational research* (2nd ed.). New York: HarperCollins.

McMillan, J. H. (1997). *Classroom assessment*. Boston: Allyn & Bacon.

McMillan, J. H. (2000). *Educational research* (3rd Ed.). Upper Saddle River, NJ: Merrill.

McNally, D. (1990). *Even eagles need a push*. New York: Dell.

McNeil, D. (2000). Systematic desensitization. In A. Kazdin (Ed.), *Encyclopedia of psychology*. Washington, DC, and New York: American Psychological Association and Oxford U. Press.

McNulty, J. (2000). Five-factor model of personality. In A. Kazdin (Ed.), *Encyclopedia of psychology*. Washington, DC, and New York: American Psychological Association and Oxford U. Press.

Medin, D. L. (2000). Concepts: An overview. In A. Kazdin (Ed.), *Encyclopedia of psychology*. Washington, DC, and New York: American Psychological Association and Oxford U. Press.

Mehrens, W. A. (1997, Summer). The consequences of consequential validity. *Educational Measurement, 16*, 16–18.

Meichenbaum, D. (1993). Cognitive behavior modification. In F. H. Kanfer & A. P. Goldstein (Eds.). *Helping people change: A handbook of methods*. New York: Pergamon Press.

Meichenbaum, D., & Butler, L. (1980). Toward a conceptual model of the treatment of test anxiety: Implications for research and treatment. In I. G. Sarason (Ed.), *Test Anxiety.* Mahwah, NJ: Erlbaum.

Meichenbaum, D., Turk, D., & Burstein, S. (1975). The nature of coping with stress. In I. Sarason & C. Spielberger (Eds.), *Stress and anxiety.* Washington, DC: Hemisphere.

Melby, L. C. (1995). *Teacher efficacy and classroom management: A study of teacher cognition, emotion, and strategy usage associated with externalizing student behavior.* Ph.D. dissertation, University of California at Los Angeles.

Merrill, P. F., Hammons, K., Vincent, B. R., & Reynolds, M. N. (1996). *Computers in education* (3rd ed.). Boston: Allyn & Bacon.

Mesibov, G. (2000). Autistic disorder. In A. Kazdin (Ed.), *Encyclopedia of psychology.* Washington, DC, and New York: American Psychological Association and Oxford U. Press.

Metzger, M. (1996, January). Maintaining a life. *Phi Delta Kappan, 77,* 346-351.

Michael, W. (1999). Guilford's view. In M. A. Runco & S. Pritzker (Eds.), *Encyclopedia of creativity.* San Diego: Academic Press.

Middleton, J., & Goepfert, P. (1996). *Inventive strategies for teaching mathematics.* Washington, DC: American Psychological Association.

Middleton, M. A., & Goepfert, P. (1996). *Inventive strategies for teaching mathematics.* Washington, DC: American Psychological Association.

Midgley, C., Anderman, E., & Hicks, L. (1995). Differences between elementary school and middle school teachers and students: A goal theory approach. *Journal of Early Adolescence, 15,* 90–113.

Miller, G. A. (1956). The magical number seven, plus or minus two: Some limits on our capacity for information processing. *Psychological Review, 48,* 337–442.

Miller, N., & Harrington, H. J. (1990). A situational identity perspective on cultural diversity and teamwork in the classroom. In S. Sharan (Ed.), *Cooperative learning: Theory and research.* New York: Praeger.

Miller-Jones, D. (1989). Culture and testing. *American Psychologist, 44,* 360–366.

Mills, G. E. (2000). *Action research: A guide for the teacher-researcher.* Columbus, OH: Merrill.

Minuchin, P. P., & Shapiro, E. K. (1983). The school as a context for social development. In P. H. Mussen (Ed.), *Handbook of child psychology* (4th ed., Vol. 4). New York: Wiley.

Mizelle, N. B., Irvin, J. L., & Ivey, G. (1997). Creating literature environments. *Middle School Journal, 28,* 3.

Moely, B. E., Santulli, K. A., & Obach, M. S. (1995). Strategy instruction, metacognition, and motivation in the elementary school classroom. In F. E. Weinert & W. Schneider (Eds.), *Memory performance and competencies.* Mahwah, NJ: Erlbaum.

Moldoveanu, M. C., & Langer, E. (1999). Mindfulness. In M. A. Runco & S. Pritzker (Eds.), *Encyclopedia of creativity.* San Diego: Academic Press.

Moll, L., Amanti, C., Neff, D., & Gonzalez, N. (1992). Funds of knowledge for teaching: Using a qualitative approach to connect homes and classrooms. *Theory into Practice, 31,* 132–141.

Moll, L., Tapia, J., & Whitmore, K. (1993). Living knowledge: The social distribution of cultural resources for thinking. In G. Salomon (Ed.), *Distributed cognitions: Psychological and educational considerations.* Cambridge: Cambridge University Press.

Monteith, M. (2000). Prejudice. In A. Kazdin (Ed.), *Encyclopedia of psychology.* Washington, DC, and New York: American Psychological Association and Oxford U. Press.

Moore, K. D. (1998). *Classroom teaching skills* (4th ed.). New York: McGraw-Hill.

Moos, M. (1979). *Evaluating educational environments.* San Francisco: Jossey-Bass.

Morgan, M. (1984). Reward-induced decrements and increments in intrinsic motivation. *Review of Educational Research, 54,* 5–30.

Morgan, N. & Saxton, J. (1991). *Teaching, questioning, and learning.* New York: Routledge.

Morrison, G. S. (2000). *Teaching in America* (2nd ed.). Boston: Allyn & Bacon.

Moyer, J. R., & Dardig, J. C. (1978). Practical task analysis for teachers. *Teaching Exceptional Children, 11,* 16–18.

Mullis, I. V. S. (1999, April). *Using TIMSS to gain new perspectives about different school organizations and policies.* Paper presented at the meeting of the American Educational Research Association, Montreal.

Murdock, T. B. (1999). The social context of risk: Status and motivational predictors of alienation in middle school. *Journal of Educational Psychology, 91,* 62–75.

Murphy, K., & Schneider, B. (1994). Coaching socially rejected adolescents regarding behaviors used by peers to infer liking: A dyad-specific intervention, *Journal of Early Adolescence, 14,* 83–95.

Murray, H. A. (1938). *Exploration in personality.* New York: Oxford University Press.

Murrell, A. J. (2000). Discrimination. In A. Kazdin (Ed.), *Encyclopedia of psychology.* Washington, DC, and New York: American Psychological Association and Oxford U. Press.

Myers, I. B. (1962). *The Myers-Briggs Type Indicator.* Palo Alto, CA: Consulting Psychologists Press.

N

NAASP. (1997, May/June). Students say: What makes a good teacher? *Schools in the Middle,* pp. 15–17.

Nairne, J. S. (2000). Forgetting. In A. Kazdin (Ed.), *Encyclopedia of psychology.* Washington, DC, and New York: American Psychological Association and Oxford U. Press.

Nash, J. M. (1997, February 3). Fertile minds. *Time,* pp. 50–54.

National Assessment of Educational Progress (1996). Gender differences in motivation and strategy use in science. *Journal of Research in Science Teaching, 33,* 393–406.

National Assessment of Educational Progress. (1997). *NAEP 1996 mathematics report card for the nation and the states.* Washington, DC: National Center for Education Statistics.

National Association for the Education of Young Children. (1996). *How to choose a good early childhood program.* Washington, DC: Author.

National Association for the Education of Young Children. (1996). NAEYC position statement: Responding to linguistic and cultural diversity —Recommendations for effective early childhood education. *Young Children, 51,* 4–12.

National Center for Education Statistics. (1997). *School-family linkages.* [Unpublished mansucript.] Washington, DC: U.S. Department of Education.

National Community Service Coalition. (1995). *Youth volunteerism.* Washington, DC: Author.

National Council of Teachers of Mathematics. (1989). *Curriculum and evaluation standards for school mathematics.* Reston, VA: Author.

National Council of Teachers of Mathematics. (1991). *Professional standards for teaching mathematics.* Reston, VA: Author.

Neil, D. M. (1997, September). Transforming student assessment. *Phi Delta Kappan,* pp. 34–40, 58.

Neisser, U., Boodoo, G., Bouchard, T. J., Boykin, A. W., Brody, N., Ceci, S. J., Halpern, D. F., Loehlin, J. C., Perloff, R., Sternberg, R. J., & Urbina, S. (1996). Intelligence: Knowns and unknowns. *American Psychologist, 51,* 77–101.

Neugarten, B. L. (1988, August). *Policy issues for an aging society.* Paper presented at the meeting of the American Psychological Association, Atlanta.

Newby, T. J., Stepich, D. A., Lehman, J. D., & Russell, J. D. (2000). *Instructional technology and learning* (2nd ed.). Upper Saddle River, NJ: Prentice Hall.

Nicholls, J. G. (1979). Development of perception of own attainment and causal attribution for success and failure in reading. *Journal of Educational Psychology, 71,* 94–99.

Nicholls, J. G., Cobb, P., Wood, T., Yackel, E., & Pataschnick, M. (1990). Assessing students' theories of success in mathematics: Individual and classroom differences. *Journal for Research in Mathematics Education, 21,* 109–122.

Nichols, J. D., & Miller, R. B. (1994). Cooperative learning and student motivation. *Contemporary Educational Psychology, 19,* 167–178.

Nickerson, R. S. (2000). *Technology and communiccation.* In A. Kazdin (Ed.), *Encyclopedia of psychology.* Washington, DC, & New York: American Psychological Association and Oxford U. Press.

Nicklas, T. A., Webber, L. S., Johnson, C. S., Srivivasan, S. R., & Bernesen, G. S. (1995). Foundations of health promotion with youth. *Journal of Health Education, 26,* S18–S26.

Nieto, S. (1992). *Affirming diversity: The sociopolitical context of multicultural education.* White Plains, NY: Longman.

Niguidula, D. (1997, November). Picturing performance with digital portfolios. *Educational Leadership,* pp. 26–29.

Nikola-Lisa, W., & Burnaford, G. E. (1994). A mosaic: Contemporary schoolchildren's images of teachers. In P. B. Joseph & G. E. Burnaford (Eds.), *Images of schoolteachers in twentieth century America.* New York: St. Martin's Press.

Noddings, N. (1992). Teaching themes of care. *Phi Delta Kappan, 76,* 675–679.

Nolen, S. B., & Nicholls, J. G. (1994). A place to begin (again) in research on student motivation: Teachers' beliefs. *Teaching and Teacher Education, 10,* 57–69.

Nolen-Hoeksema, S. (1990). *Sex differences in depression.* Stanford, CA: Stanford University Press.

O'Conner, S. C., & Rosenblood, L. K. (1996). Affiliation motivation in everyday experience: A theoretical comparison. *Journal of Personality and Social Psychology, 70,* 513–522.

O'Hara, L., & Sternberg, R. J. (1999). Learning styles. In M. A. Runco & S. Pritzker (Eds.), *Encylopedia of creativity.* San Diego: Academic Press.

O'Neil, J., & Tell, C. (1999, September). Why students lose when "tougher standards" win: A conversation with Alphi Kohn. *Educational Leadership, 57,* 18–23.

O'Shea, D. J., & O'Shea, L. J. (1997). What have we learned and where are we headed? Issues in collaboration and school reform. *Journal of Learning Disabilities, 30,* 376–377.

O'Sullivan, C. Y., Reese, C. M., & Mazzeo, J. (1997, May). NAEP science report card for the nation and states. *ERIC Digest,* pp. 1–6.

Office of Technology Assessment. (1995). *Teachers and technology: Making the connection.* Washington, DC: Author.

Ogbu, J. U. (1989, April). *Academic socialization of Black children: An inoculation against future failure?* Paper presented at the meeting of the Society for Research in Child Development, Kansas City.

Oldfather, P., West, J., White, J., & Wilmarth, J. (1999). *Learning through children's eyes: Social constructivism and the desire to learn.* Washington, DC: American Psychological Association.

Olson, D. R. (2000). Literacy. In A. Kazdin (Ed.), *Encyclopedia of psychology.* Washington, DC, and New York: American Psychological Association and Oxford U. Press.

Olweus, D. (1984). Development of stable aggressive reaction patterns in males. In *Advances in the study of aggression* (Vol. 1). Orlando: Academic Press.

Olweus, D. (in press). *Bullying at school: What we know and what we can do.* Oxford: Blackwell.

Ovando, C. J., & McLaren, P. (2000). *The politics of multiculturalism and bilingual education.* Boston: Allyn & Bacon.

Overton, T. (2000). *Assessment in special education* (3rd ed.). Upper Saddle River, NJ: Merrill.

Paintal, S. (1999). Banning corporal punishment of children. *Childhood Education, 76,* 36–40.

Paivio, A. (1971). *Imagery and verbal processes.* Fort Worth, TX: Harcourt Brace.

Paivio, A. (1986). *Mental representations: A dual coding approach.* New York: Oxford University Press.

Palincsar, A. S. (1986). The role of dialogue in providing scaffolding instruction. *Educational Psychologist, 21,* 73–98.

Palincsar, A. S., & Brown, A. L. (1984). Reciprocal teaching of comprehension-fostering and comprehension-monitoring activities. *Cognition and Instruction, 1,* 117–175.

Palomba, C., & Banta, T. W. (1999). *Assessment essentials.* San Francisco: Jossey Bass.

Panofsky, C. (1999, April). *What the zone of proximal development conceals.* Paper presented at the meeting of the Society for Research in Child Development, Montreal.

Papert, S. (1980). *Mindstorms: Children, computers, and powerful ideas.* New York: Basic Books.

Papert, S. (1993). *The children's machine: Rethinking school in the age of the computer.* New York: Basic Books.

Parcel, G. S., Simons-Morton, G. G., O'Hara, N. M., Baranowksi, T., Kolbe, L. J., & Bee, D. E. (1987). School promotion of healthful diet and exercise behavior. *Journal of School Health, 57,* 150–156.

Paris, S. G., & Ayres, L. R. (1994). *Becoming reflective students and teachers with portfolios and authentic assessment.* Washington, DC: American Psychological Association.

Paris, S. G., & Lindauer, B. K. (1982). The development of cognitive skills during childhood. In B. B. Wolman (Ed.), *Handbook of developmental psychology.* Englewood Cliffs, NJ: Prentice Hall.

Parkay, F. W., & Hass, C. G. (2000). *Curriculum planning: A contemporary approach* (7th ed.). Boston: Allyn & Bacon.

Parke, R. D., & Buriel, R. (1998). Socialization in the family: Ethnic and ecological perspectives. In W. Damon (Ed.), *Handbook of child psychology* (5th ed., Vol. 3). New York: Wiley.

Pashler, H. (Ed.) (1998). *Attention.* Philadelphia: Psychology Press.

Patterson, K., & Wright, A. E. (1990, Winter). The speech, language, or hearing-impaired child: At-risk academically. *Childhood Education,* pp. 91–95.

Pavlov, I. P. (1927). *Conditioned reflexes.* New York: Dover.

Payne, D. A. (1997). *Applied educational assessment.* Belmont, CA: Wadsworth.

Pearson, P. D., Hansen, J., & Gordon, C. (1979). The effect of background knowledge on young children's comprehension of explicit and implicit information. *Journal of Reading Behavior, 11,* 201–210.

Perkins, D. (1999). The many faces of constructivism. *Educational Leadership, 57,* No. 3, 6–11.

Perkins, D., & Tishman, S. (1997, March). Commentary in "Teaching today's pupils to think more critically." *APA Monitor,* p. 51.

Perry, C. (1999). *Creating health behavior change: How to develop community-wide programs for youth.* Thousand Oaks, CA: Sage.

Peskin, H. (1967). Pubertal onset and ego functioning. *Journal of Abnormal Psychology, 72,* 1–15.

Petersen, A. C. (2000). Puberty and biological maturation. In A. Kazdin (Ed.), *Encyclopedia of psychology.* Washington, DC, and New York: American Psychological Association and Oxford U. Press.

Peterson, K. S. (1998, July 14). Teens learn "I do" can last forever, *USA Today,* p. D1, D2.

Phillips, R. (1997, July). *Strengthening school and community partnerships.* Paper presented at the conference on Working with America's Youth, Pittsburgh.

Phye, G. D. (1990). Inductive problem solving: Schema induction and memory-based transfer. *Journal of Educational Psychology, 82,* 826–831.

Phye, G. D. (Ed.) (1997). *Handbook of classroom assessment.* Orlando: Academic Press.

Phye, G. D., & Sanders, C. E. (1994). Advice and feedback: Elements of practice for problem solving. *Contemporary Educational Psychology, 19,* 286–301.

Piaget, J. (1932). *The moral judgment of the child.* New York: Harcourt Brace Jovanovich.

Piaget, J. (1952). *The origins of intelligence in children.* New York: International Universities Press.

Piaget, J., & Inhelder, B. (1969). *The child's conception of space.* New York: Norton.

Pinnell, G. S., Lyons, C. A., DeFord, D. E., Bryk, A. S., & Seltzer, M. (1994). Comparing instructional models for the literacy education of high risk first graders. *Reading Research Quarterly, 29,* 8–38.

Pintrich, P R.. (2000). Learning and motivation. In A. Kazdin (Ed.), *Encyclopedia of psychology.* Washington, DC, & New York: American Psychological Association and Oxford U. Press.

Pintrich, P. R. (2000). The role of goal orientation in self-regulated learning. In M. Boekaerts, P. R. Pintrich & M. Zeidner (Eds.), *Handbook of self-regulation.* San Diego: Academic Press.

Pleck, J. H. (1983). The theory of male sex identity. In M. Lewin (Ed.), *In the shadow of the past: Psychology portrays the sexes.* New York: Columbia University Press.

Pleck, J. H. (1995). The gender-role strain paradigm. In R. F. Levant & W. S. Pollack (Eds.), *A new psychology of men.* New York: Basic Books.

Pleiss, M. K., & Feldhusen, J. F. (1995). Mentors, role models, and heroes in the lives of gifted children. *Educational Psychologist, 30,* 159–169.

Plomin, R. (2000). Behavior genetics. In M. Bennett (Ed.), *Developmental psychology: Achievements and prospects.* Philadelphia: Psychology Press.

Poest, C. A., Williams, J. R., Witt, D. D., & Atwood, M. E. (1990). Challenge me to move: Large muscle development in children. *Young Children, 45,* 4–10.

Pogue, L. (1997, March/April). Review of "Picture It!" *Electronic Learning,* p. 18.

Polloway, E. A., Patton, J. R., Smith, T. E. C., & Buck, G. H. (1997). Mental retardation and learning disabilities: Conceptual and applied issues. *Journal of Learning Disabilities, 30,* 297–308.

Poole, B. J. (1998). *Education for an information age* (2nd ed.). New York: McGraw-Hill.

Popham, W. J. (1999). *Classroom assessment* (2nd ed.). Boston: Allyn & Bacon.

Popham, W. J. (1999, March). Why standardized tests don't measure educational quality. *Educational Leadership, 56,* 8–16.

Popham, W. J. (2000). Classroom assessment (3rd ed.). Boston: Allyn & Bacon.

Popham, W. J. (2000). *Modern educational measurement* (3rd Ed.). Boston: Allyn & Bacon.

Presidential Task Force on Psychology and Education. (1992). *Learner-centered psychological principles: Guidelines for school redesign and reform* [Draft]. Washington, DC: American Psychological Association.

Pressley, J., Johnson, C. J., Symons, S., McGoldrick, J. A., & Kurita, J. A. (1989). Strategies that improve children's memory and comprehension of text. *Elementary School Journal, 90,* 3–32.

Pressley, M. (1983). Making meaningful materials easier to learn. In M. Pressley & J. R. Levin (Eds.), *Cognitive strategy research: Educational applications* (pp. 239–266). New York: Springer-Verlag.

Pressley, M. (1995). More about the development of self-regulation: Complex, long-term, and thoroughly social. *Educational Psychologist, 30,* 207–212.

Pressley, M. (1996, August). *Getting beyond whole language: Elementary reading instruction that makes sense in light of recent psychological research.* Paper presented at the meeting of the American Psychological Association, Toronto.

Pressley, M. (in press). *Effective reading instruction: The case for balanced teaching.* New York: Guilford Press.

Pressley, M., Borkowski, J. G., & Schneider, W. (1989). Good information processing: What it is and what education can do to promote it. *International Journal of Educational Research, 13,* 857–867.

Pressley, M., Schuder, T., SAIL Faculty and Administration, German, J., & El-Dinary, P. B. (1992). A researcher-educator collaborative interview study of transactional comprehension strategies instruction. *Journal of Educational Psychology, 84,* 231–246.

Pressley, M., Woloshyn, V., Burkell, J., Cariglia-Bull, T., Lysynchuk, L., McGoldrick, J. A., Schneider, B., Snyder, B. L., & Symons, S. (1995). *Cognitive strategy instruction that really improves children's academic performance* (2nd ed.). Cambridge, MA: Brookline Books.

Price, R. H. (2000). Prevention and intervention. In A. Kazdin (Ed.), *Encyclopedia of psychology.* Washington, DC, and New York: American Psychological Association and Oxford U. Press.

Prutzman, P., & Johnson, J. (1997). Bias awareness and multiple perspectives: Essential aspects of conflict resolution. *Theory into Practice, 36,* 27–31.

Pueschel, S. M., Scola, P. S., Weidenman, L. E., & Bernier, J. C. (1995). *The special child.* Baltimore: Paul H. Brookes.

Pugach, M. C., & Johnson, L. J. (1995). *Collaborative practitioners, collaborative schools.* Denver: Love.

Purcell-Gates, V. (1997, June 18). Commentary in "Diagnosing learning problems can be difficult for parents and teachers." *USA Today,* p. D8.

Qin, Z., Johnson, D. W., & Johnson, R. T. (1995). Cooperative versus competitive efforts and problem solving. *Review of Educational Research, 65,* 129–143.

Rainey, R. (1965). The effects of directed vs. non-directed laboratory work on high school chemistry achievement. *Journal of Research in Science Teaching, 3,* 286–292.

Ramey, C. T., Bryant, D. M., Campbell, F. A., Sparling, J. J., & Wasik, B. H. (1988). Early intervention for high-risk children. The Carolina Early Intervention Program. In R. H. Price, E. L. Cowen, R. P. Lorion, & J. Ramos-McKay (Eds.), *14 ounces of prevention.* Washington, DC: American Psychological Association.

Randi, J., & Corno, L. (2000). Teacher innovations in self-regulated learning. In M. Boekaerts, P. R. Pintrich, & M. Zeidner (Eds.), *Handbook of self-regulation.* Boston: American Psychological Association.

Randolph, C. H., & Evertson, C. M. (1995). Managing for learning: Rules, roles, and meanings in a writing class. *Journal of Classroom Instruction, 30,* 17–25.

Raschke, D. (1981). Designing reinforcement surveys: Let the student choose the reward. *Teaching Exceptional Children, 14,* 92–96.

Raver, C. C., & Zigler, E. F. (1997). Social competence: An untapped dimension in evaluating Head Start's success. *Early Childhood Research Quarterly, 13,* 365–385.

Ravitch, D. (1995). *National standards in American education: A citizen's guide.* Washington, DC: Brookings Institution.

Raymond, E. (2000). *Learners with mild disabilities.* Boston: Allyn & Bacon.

Rayner, K. (2000). Reading. In A. Kazdin (Ed.), *Encyclopedia of psychology.* Washington, DC, and New York: American Psychological Association and Oxford U. Press.

Read, L. (1995). Amos Bear gets hurt. *Young Children, 50,* 19–23.

Reed, A. J. S., Bergemann, V. E., & Olson, M. W. (1998). *A guide to observation and participation in the classroom.* New York: McGraw-Hill.

Reed, S. (2000). Problem solving. In A. Kazdin (Ed.), *Encyclopedia of psychology.* Washington, DC, and New York: American Psychological Association and Oxford U. Press.

Reese, C. M., Miller, K. E., Mazzeo, J., & Dossey, J. A. (1997, February). NAEP mathematics report card for the nation and the states. *ERIC Digest,* pp. 1–5.

Renne, C. H. (1997). Excellent classroom management. Belmont, CA: Wadsworth.

Renzulli, J. S., & Reis, S. M. (1997). The schoolwide enrichment model. In N. Colangelo & G. A. Davis (Eds.), *Handbook of gifted education.* Boston: Allyn & Bacon.

Reschly, D. (1996). Identification and assessment of students with disabilities. *Future of Children, 6* (1), 40–53.

Resnick, L. B., & Chi, M. T. H. (1988). Cognitive psychology and science learning. In M. Druger (Ed.), *Science for the fun of it: A guide to informal science education.* Washington, DC: National Science Teachers Association.

Rhodes, J. (2000). Mentoring programs. In A. Kazdin (Ed.), *Encyclopedia of psychology.* Washington, DC, and New York: American Psychological Association and Oxford U. Press.

Rickards, T. (1999). Brainstorming. In M. A. Runco & S. Pritzker (Eds.), *Encyclopedia of creativity.* San Diego: Academic Press.

Riedsel, C. A., & Schwartz, J. E. (1999). *Essentials of elementary mathematics* (2nd ed.). Boston: Allyn & Bacon.

Riley, R. W. (1997, August 31). Long-term trend assessment of American students finds significant progress in science and mathematics. *New York Times,* Section 1, p. 18.

Rinehart, S. D., Stahl, S. A., & Erickson, L. G. (1986). Some effects of summarization training on reading and studying. *Reading Research Quarterly, 21,* 422–438.

Risley, D. S., & Walther, B. (1995). *Creating responsible learners.* Washington, DC: American Psychological Association.

Robinson, N. S. (1995). Evaluating the nature of perceived support and its relationship to perceived self-worth in adolescents. *Journal of Research on Adolescence, 5,* 253–280.

Robinson, R. D., McKenna, M. C., & Wedman, J. M. (2000). *Issues and trends in literacy education* (2nd ed.). Boston: Allyn & Bacon.

Roblyer, M. D., & Edwards, J. (2000). *Integrating educational technology into teaching* (2nd ed.). Upper Saddle River, NJ: Prentice Hall.

Roblyer, M. D., Edwards, J., & Havriluk, M. A. (1997). *Integrating educational technology into education.* Upper Saddle River, NJ: Merrill/Prentice Hall.

Rock, E. A., Fessler, M. A., & Church, R. P. (1997). The concomitance of learning disabilities and emotional/behavioral disorders: A conceptual model. *Journal of Learning Disabilities, 30,* 245–263.

Rodgers, C. (2000). Gender schema. In A. Kazdin (Ed.), *Encyclopedia of psychology.* Washington, DC, and New York: American Psychological Association and Oxford U. Press.

Roeber, E. D. (1999). Standards initiatives and American educational reform. In G. J. Cizek (Ed.), *Handbook of educational policy.* San Diego: Academic Press.

Roediger, H. (2000). Learning: Cognitive approach for humans. In A. Kazdin (Ed.), *Encyclopedia of psychology.* Washington, DC, and New York: American Psychological Association and Oxford U. Press.

Roff, M., Sells, S. B., & Golden, M. W. (1972). *Social adjustment and personality development in children.* Minneapolis: University of Minnesota Press.

Rogers, C. R. (1961). *On becoming a person.* Boston: Houghton Mifflin.

Rogoff, B. (1990). *Apprenticeship in thinking.* New York: Oxford University Press.

Rogoff, B. (1998). Cognition as a collaborative process. In W. Damon, D. Kuhn, & R. S. Siegler (Eds.), *Handbook of child psychology* (5th ed., Vol. 2). New York: Wiley.

Rosch, E. H. (1973). On the internal structure of perceptual and semantic categories. In T. E. Moore (Ed.), *Cognition and the acquisition of language.* New York: Academic Press.

Rosenshine, B. (1971). *Teaching behaviors and student achievement.* London: National Foundation for Educational Research.

Rosenshine, B. (1985). Direct instruction. In T. Husen & T. N. Postlethwaite (Eds.), *Encyclopedia of education* (Vol. 3). New York: Pergamon.

Rosenshine, B. (1986). Synthesis of research on explicit teaching. *Educational Leadership, 43,* pp. 60–69.

Rosenthal, D. M., & Sawyers, J.Y. (1997). Building successful home/school partnerships. *Young Children, 52,* 194–200.

Ross, B. H. (2000). Concepts: Learning. In A. Kazdin (Ed.), *Encyclopedia of psychology.* Washington, DC, and New York: American Psychological Association and Oxford U. Press.

Rosselli, H. C. (1996, February/March). Gifted students. *National Association for Secondary School Principals,* pp. 12–17.

Rothbart, M. K., & Bates, J. E. (1998). Temperament. In W. Damon (Ed.), *Handbook of child psychology* (5th ed., Vol. 3). New York: Wiley.

Rothstein, R. (1997, March/April). Program of the month. *Electronic Learning,* p. 18.

Rothstein, R. (1998, May). Bilingual education: The controversy. *Phi Delta Kappan,* pp. 672–678.

Rowe, M. (1986). Wait time: Slowing down may be a way of speeding up! *Journal of Teacher Education, 37,* 43–50.

Rowe, R. J. (Ed.). (1994). *Preschoolers as authors: Literacy learning in the social world of the classroom.* Cresskill, NJ: Hampton Press.

Rubin, A. D. (1983). The computer confronts language arts: Cans and shoulds for education. In A. C. Wilkinson (Ed.), *Classroom computers and cognitive science.* New York: Academic Press.

Rubin, K. H. (2000). Peer relation. In A. Kazdin (Ed.), *Encyclopedia of psychology.* Washington, DC, and New York: American Psychological Association and Oxford U. Press.

Rubin, K. H., Bukowski, W., & Parker, J. G. (1998). Peer interactions, relationships, and groups. In W. Damon (Ed.), *Handbook of child psychology* (5th ed., Vol. 3). New York: Wiley.

Rubin, K. H., Coplan, R. J., Nelson, L. J., Dheah, C. S. L., & Lagace-Seguin, D. G. (2000). Peer relationships in childhood. In M. H. Bornstein & M. E. Lamb (Eds.), *Developmental psychology* (4th Ed.). Mahwah, NJ: Erlbaum.

Ruble, D. (1983). The development of social comparison processes and their role in achievement-related self-socialization. In E. T. Higgins, D. N. Ruble, & W. W. Hartup (Eds.), *Social cognition and development.* New York: Cambridge University Press.

Ruddell, R. B. (1999). *Teaching children to read and write* (2nd ed.). Boston: Allyn & Bacon.

Ruiz-Primo, M., Li, M., Ayala, C., & Shavelson, R. (2000, April). *Students' science journals as an assessment tool.* Paper presented at the meeting of the American Educational Research Association, New Orleans.

Runco, M. (1999). Critical thinking. In M. A. Runco & S. Pritzker (Eds.), *Encyclopedia of creativity.* San Diego: Academic Press.

Runco, M. (1999). Critical thinking. In M. Runco (Ed.)., *Handbook of creativity.* San Diego: Academic Press.

Runco, M. A., & Pritzker, S. (Eds.) (1999). *Encyclopedia of creativity.* San Diego: Academic Press.

Rutter, M., & Schopler, E. (1987). Autism and pervasive developmental disorders: Concepts and diagnostic issues. *Journal of Autism and Pervasive Developmental Disorders, 17,* 159–186.

Ryan, A. M., & Patrick, H. (1996, March). *Positive peer relationships and psychosocial adjustment during adolescence.* Paper presented at the meeting of the Society for Research on Adolescence, Boston.

Ryan, R. M., & Deci, E. L. (1996). When paradigms clash: Comments on Cameron and Pierce's claim that rewards do not undermine intrinsic motivation. *Review of Educational Research, 66,* 33–38.

Ryan-Finn, K. D., Cauce, A. M., & Grove, K. (1995, March). *Children and adolescents of color: Where are you? Selection, recruitment, and retention in developmental research.* Paper presented at the meeting of the Society for Research in Child Development, Indianapolis.

Rychman, R. M. (2000). *Theories of personality* (7th ed.). Belmont, CA: Wadsworth.

S

Sadker, D. M. P., & Sadker, D. M. (2000). *Teachers, schools, and society* (5th ed.). New York: McGraw-Hill.

Sadker, M. and Sadker, D. (1986). *PEPA (Princial Effectiveness, Pupil Achievement): A training program for principals and other educational leaders.* Washington, DC: American University.

Sadker, M., & Sadker, D. (1994). *Failing at fairness: How America's schools cheat girls.* New York: Scribners.

Sadker, M., Sadker, D., & Long, L. (1997). Gender and educational equality. In J. A. Banks & C. A. M. Banks (Eds.), *Multicultural education* (3rd ed.). Boston: Allyn & Bacon.

Sadker, M. P., & Sadker, D. M. (2000). *Schools in society* (5th ed.). New York: McGraw-Hill.

Salisbury, D. J. (1995, September). Does Cincinnati need another bridge? *Learning and Leading with Technology, 23,* 17–19.

Salomon, G. (1993). On the nature of pedagogic computer tools: The case of the Writing Partner. In S. P. Lajoie & S. J. Derry (Eds.), *Computers as cognitive tools.* New York: Cambridge University Press.

Salomon, G., & Perkins, D. (1989). Rocky roads to transfer: Rethinking mechanisms of a neglected phenomenon. *Educational Psychologist, 24,* 113–142.

Sandoval, J., Scheuneman, J. D., Ramos-Grenier, J., Geisinger, K. F., & Frisby, C. (Eds.) (1999). *Test interpretation and diversity: Achieving equity in assessment.* Washington, DC: American Psychological Association.

Sanford. A. J. (2000). Semantics. In A. Kazdin (Ed.), *Encyclopedia of psychology.* Washington, DC, and New York: American Psychological Association and Oxford U. Press.

Santrock, J. W. (1998). *Adolescence* (7th ed.). New York: McGraw-Hill.

Santrock, J. W., & Halonen, J. S. (1999). *The guide to college success.* Belmont, CA: Wadsworth.

Sapon-Shevin, M. (1999). *Because we can change the world: A practical guide to building cooperative, inclusive classroom communities.* Boston: Allyn & Bacon.

Sax, G. (1997). *Principles of educational and psychological measurement and evaluation* (4th ed.). Belmont, CA: Wadsworth.

Sax, L. (1996). *Principles of educational and psychological measurement* (4th ed.). Belmont, CA: Wadsworth.

Sax, L. J., Astin, K. W., Korn, W. S., & Mahoney, K. M. (1996). *The American freshman.* Los Angeles: UCLA, Higher Education Institute.

Scardamalia, M. (1981). How children cope with the cognitive demands of writing. In C. Frederiksen & J. F. Dominic (Eds.), *Writing: The nature, development, and teaching of written communication.* Mahwah, NJ: Erlbaum.

Scardamalia, M., & Bereiter, C. (1994). Computer support for knowledge-building communities. *Journal of the Learning Sciences, 3* (3), 265–283.

Scardamalia, M., Bereiter, C., & Lamon, M. (1994). The CSILE Project: Trying to bring the classroom into the world. In K. McGilly (Ed.), *Classroom lessons.* Cambridge, MA: MIT Press.

Scarr, S. (1996). Best of human genetics. *Contemporary Psychology, 41,* 149–150.

Scarr, S., & Weinberg, R. A. (1983). The Minnesota Adoption Studies: Genetic differences and malleability. *Child Development, 54,* 253–259.

Schacter, D. L. (2000). Memory systems. In A. Kazdin (Ed.), *Encyclopedia of psychology.* Washington, DC, and New York: American Psychological Association and Oxford U. Press.

Schauble, L. (1990). Belief revision in children: The role of prior knowledge and strategies for generating evidence. *Journal of Experimental Child Psychology, 49,* 31–57.

Schauble, L. (1996). The development of scientific reasoning in knowledge-rich contexts. *Developmental Psychology, 32,* 102–119.

Schauble, L., Beane, D. B., Coates, G. D., Martin, L. M. W., & Sterling, P. V. (1996). Outside classroom walls: Learning in informal environments. In L. Schauble & R. Glaser (Eds.), *Innovations in learning.* Mahwah, NJ: Erlbaum.

Schiever, S. W., & Maker, C. J. (1997). Enrichment and acceleration: An overview and new directions. In N. Colangelo & G. A. Davis (Eds.), *Handbook of gifted education.* Boston: Allyn & Bacon.

Schlesinger, A. M. (1991). *The disuniting of America.* Knoxville, TN: Whittle Direct Books.

Schneider, B., & Coleman, J. S. (1993). *Parents, their children, and schools.* Boulder, CO: Westview Press.

Schneider, W., & Bjorklund, D. F. (1998). Memory. In W. Damon (Gen. Ed.), and D. Kuhn, & R. S. Siegler (Vol. Eds.), *Handbook of child psychology: Vol. 2. Cognition, perception, and language.* New York: Wiley.

Schneider, W., & Pressley, M. (1997). *Memory development from 2 to 20* (2nd ed.). Mahwah, NJ: Erlbaum.

Schneps, M. H., & Sadler, P. M. (1989). *A private universe.* [Video.] Cambridge, MA: Harvard–Smithsonian Center for Astrophysics.

Schoenbrodt, L., Kumin, L., & Sloan, J. M. (1997). Learning disabilities existing concomitantly with communication disorder. *Journal of Learning Disabilities, 30,* 282–296.

Schrum, L., & Berenfeld, B. (1997). *Teaching and learning in the information age: A guide to telecommunications.* Boston: Allyn & Bacon.

Schuell, T. J. (1996). The role of educational psychology in the preparation of teachers. *Educational Psychologist, 3* (1), 5–14.

Schunk, D. H. (1989). Self-efficacy and cognitive skill learning. In C. Ames & R. Ames (Eds.), *Research on motivation and education* (Vol. 3). Orlando: Academic Press.

Schunk, D. H. (1991). Self-efficacy and academic motivation. *Educational Psychologist, 25,* 71–86.

Schunk, D. H. (1996). *Learning theories* (2nd ed.). Englewood Cliffs, NJ: Merrill.

Schunk, D. H. (1999). *Social-self interaction and achievement behavior.* Presidential address, Division 15, presented at the meeting of the American Psychological Association, Boston.

Schunk, D. H. (2000). *Theories of learning* (3rd Ed.). Upper Saddle River, NJ: Prentice-Hall.

Schunk, D. H., & Ertmer, P. A. (1999, August). *Sustaining effort through goal and self-efficacy self-regulation.* Paper presented at the meeting of the American Psychological Association, Boston.

Schunk, D. H., & Ertmer, P. A. (2000). Self-regulation and academic learning: Self-efficacy enhancing intervention. In M. Boekarts, P. Pintrich, & M. Zeidner (Eds.), *Handbook of self-regulation.* San Diego: Academic Press.

Schunk, D. H., & Rice, J. M. (1989). Learning goals and children's reading comprehension. *Journal of Reading Behavior, 23,* 351–364.

Schunk, D. H., & Swartz, C. W. (1993). Goals and progressive feedback: Effects on self-efficacy and writing achievement. *Contemporary Educational Psychology, 18,* 337–354.

Schunk, D. H., & Zimmerman, B. J. (1996). Modeling and self-efficacy influences on children's development of self-regulation. In J. Juvonen & K. R. Wentzel (Eds.), *Social motivation.* New York: Cambridge University Press.

Schunk, D. H., & Zimmerman, B. J. (1997). Social origins of self-regulatory competence. *Educational Psychologist, 32,* 195–208.

Schunk, D. H., & Zimmerman, B. J. (Ed.). (1994). *Self-regulation of learning and performance: Issues and educational applications.* Mahwah, NJ: Erlbaum.

Schwab-Stone, M., & others. (1995). *New Haven Public Schools Social Development Project: 1994.* New Haven, CT: New Haven Public Schools.

Schweinhart, L. J. (1999, April). *Generalizing from High/Scope longitudinal studies.* Paper presented at the meeting of the Society for Research in Child Development, Albuquerque.

Segal, J. W. (1996). Foreword. In L. Schauble & R. Glaser (Eds.), *Innovations in learning.* Mahwah, NJ: Erlbaum.

Seidman, E. (2000). School transitions. In A. Kazdin (Ed.), *Encyclopedia of psychology.* Washington, DC, and New York: American Psychological Association and Oxford U. Press.

Serow, R. C., Ciechalski, J., & Daye, C. (1990). Students as volunteers. *Urban Education, 25,* 157–168.

Serpell, R. (2000). Culture and intelligence. In A. Kazdin (Ed.), *Encyclopedia of psychology.* Washington, DC, and New York: American Psychological Association and Oxford U. Press.

Shade, S. C., Kelly, C., & Oberg, M. (1997). *Creating culturally-responsive schools.* Washington, DC: American Psychological Association.

Shaklee, B. D., Barbour, N. E., Ambrose, R., & Hansford, S. J. (1997). *Designing and using portfolios.* Boston: Allyn & Bacon.

Shanahan, T., & Rodriguez-Brown, F. V. (1993, April). *Project FLAME: The theory and structure of a family literacy program for the Latino community.* Paper presented at the meeting of the American Educational Research Association, Atlanta.

Sharan, S. (1990). Cooperative learning and helping behavior in the multi-ethnic classroom. In H. C. Foot, M. J. Morgan, & R. H. Shute (Eds.), *Children helping children.* New York: Wiley.

Sharan, S., & Sharan, S. (1992). *Expanding cooperative learning through group investigation.* New York: Teachers College Press.

Sharan, S., & Shaulov, A. (1990). Cooperative learning, motivation to learn, and academic achievement. In S. Sharan (Ed.), *Cooperative learning.* New York: Praeger.

Sharp, D. L. M., Bransford, J. D., Goldman, S. R., Risko, V. J., Kinser, C. K., & Vye, N. J. (1995). Dynamic visual support for story comprehension and mental model building by young, at-risk children. *Educational Technology Research and Development, 43,* 25–42.

Sharp, V. (1999). *Computer education for teachers* (3rd ed.). New York: McGraw-Hill.

Sheffield, C. J. (1997, March–April). Instructional technology for teachers: Preparation for classroom diversity. *Educational Technology,* pp. 16–18.

Sherman, C. W., & Mueller, D. P. (1996, June). *Developmentally appropriate practice and student achievement in inner-city elementary schools.* Paper presented at Head Start's Third National Research Conference, Washington, DC.

Shields, S. A. (1991). Gender in the psychology of emotion. In K. T. Strongman (Ed.), *International review of studies on emotion* (Vol. 1). New York: Wiley.

Shirts, R. G. (1997). *BAFA. BAFA, a cross-cultural simulation.* Del Mar, CA: SIMILE II.

Shonkoff, J. (1996). Mental retardation. In R. Behrman, R. Kliegman, & A. Arvin (Eds.), *Nelson textbook of pediatrics* (15th ed.). Philadelphia: W. B. Saunders.

Shultz, T. R., Fisher, G. W., Pratt, C. C., & Rulf, S. (1986). Selection of causal rules. *Child Development, 57,* 143–152.

Siegfried, T. (1998, July 13). In teaching scientific subjects, high schools are out of order. *Dallas Morning News,* p. 9D.

Siegler, R. S. (1998). *Children's thinking* (3rd ed.). Upper Saddle River, NJ: Erlbaum.

Siegler, R. S., & Robinson, M. (1982). The development of numerical understandings. In H. W. Reese & L. P. Litsitt (Eds.), *Advances in child development and behavior* (Vol. 12). New York: Academic Press.

Sigel, B. (1997, April). *Developmental and social policy issues and the practice of educational mainstreaming and full inclusion.* Paper presented at the meeting of the Society for Research in Child Development, Washington, DC.

Silverman, L. K. (1993). A developmental model for counseling the gifted. In L. K. Silverman (Ed.), *Counseling the gifted and the talented.* Denver: Love.

Simmons, D. C., Fuchs, L. S., Fuchs, P., Mathes, P., & Hodge, J. P. (1995). Effects of explicit teaching and peer tutoring on the reading achievement of learning-disabled and low-performing students in a regular classroom. *Elementary School Journal, 95,* 387–408.

Simons, J., Finlay, B., & Yang, A. (1991). *The adolescent and young adult fact book.* Washington, DC: Children's Defense Fund.

Simons, J. M., Finlay, B., & Yang, A. (1991). *The adolescent and young adult fact book.* Washington, DC: Children's Defense Fund.

Singer, D. G., & Singer, J. L. (1987). Practical suggestions for controlling television. *Journal of Early Adolescence, 7,* 365–369.

Skiba, R., & Peterson, R. (1999, January). The dark side of zero tolerance. *Phi Delta Kappan, 80,* 372–376.

Skinner, B. F. (1938). *The behavior of organisms.* New York: Appleton-Century-Crofts.

Skinner, B. F. (1953). *Science and human behavior.* New York: Macmillan.

Slavin, R. E. (1990). Achievement effects of ability grouping in secondary schools: A best-evidence synthesis. Review of *Educational Research, 60,* 471–500.

Slavin, R. E. (1995). *Cooperative learning: Theory, research, and practice* (2nd ed.). Boston: Allyn & Bacon.

Slavin, R. E. (1995). Detracking and the detractors. *Phi Delta Kappan, 77,* 220–221.

Slavin, R. E., Madden, N. A., Dolan, L., Wasik, B. A., Ross, S. M., Smith, L. J., & Diana, M. (1995, April). *Success for All: A summary of research.* Paper presented at the meeting of the American Educational Research Association, San Francisco.

Slavin, R. S. (1994). *Using team learning* (4th ed.). Baltimore: Johns Hopkins University, Center for Research on Elementary Schools.

Smith, T., Polooway, E., Patton, J., & Dowdy, C. (1998). *Teaching students with special needs in inclusive settings* (2nd ed.). Boston: Allyn & Bacon.

Smith-Maddox, R., & Wheelock, A. (1995). Untracking and students' futures. *Phi Delta Kappan, 77,* 222–228.

Smoll, F. L., & Schutz, R. W. (1990). Quantifying gender differences in physical performance: A developmental perspective. *Developmental Psychology, 26,* 360–369.

Snow, C. (1999). Social perspectives on the emergence of language. In B. MacWhinney (Ed.), *The emergence of language.* Malwah, NJ: Erlbaum.

Snow, D. E. (1998). *Preventing reading difficulties in young children.* Washington, DC: U.S. Department of Education.

Snow, R. E., Corno, L., & Jackson, D. (1996). Individual differences in affective and conative functions. In D. C. Berliner & R. C. Calfee (Eds.) *Handbook of educational psychology.* New York: Macmillan.

Soderman, A. K., Gregory, K. M., & O'Neill, L. T. (1999). *Scaffolding emerging literacy.* Boston: Allyn & Bacon.

Solano-Flores, G., & Shavelson, R. J. (1997, Fall). Development of performance assessments in science: conceptual, practical, and logistical issues. *Educational Measurement,* pp. 16–24.

Solley, B. A. (2000). *Writers' workshop: Reflections of elementary and middle school teachers.* Boston: Allyn & Bacon.

Songer, N. B. (1993). Learning science with a child-focused resource: A case study of Kids as Global Scientists. In *Proceedings of the 15th Annual Meeting of the Cognitive Science Society.* Mahwah, NJ: Erlbaum.

Spearman, C. E. (1927). *The abilities of man.* New York: Macmillan.

Spear-Swerling, L., & Sternberg, R. J. (1994). The road not taken: An integrative theoretical model of reading disability. *Journal of Learning Disabilities, 27,* 91–103.

Spence, J. T., & Helmreich, R. (1978). *Masculinity and femininity: Their psychological dimensions.* Austin: University of Texas Press.

Spencer, M. B. (2000). Ethnocentrism. In A. Kazdin (Ed.), *Encyclopedia of psychology.* Washington, DC, and New York: American Psychological Association and Oxford U. Press.

Spencer, M. B., & Dornbusch, S. (1990). Challenges in studying ethnic minority youth. In S. S. Feldman & G. R. Elliott (Eds.). *At the threshold: The developing adolescent.* Cam-bridge, MA: Harvard University Press.

Spencer, M. B., & Markstrom-Adams, C. (1990). Identity processes among racial and ethnic minority children in America. *Child Development, 61,* 290–310.

Spring, J. (1998). *American education* (8th ed.). New York: McGraw-Hill.

Spring, J. (1998). *The intersection of cultures.* New York: McGraw Hill.

Spring, J. (2000). *American education* (9th ed.). New York: McGraw-Hill.

Spring, J. (2000). *The intersection of cultures* (2nd ed.). New York: McGraw-Hill.

Squire, L. (1987). *Memory and brain.* New York: Oxford University Press.

St. Pierre, R., Layzer, J., & Barnes, H. (1996). *Regenerating two-generation programs.* Cambridge, MA: Abt Associates.

Stanovich, K. E. (1994). Romance and reality. *Reading Teacher, 47,* 280–291.

Steinberg, L. D., Catalano, R., & Dooley, D. (1981). Economic antecedents of child abuse and neglect. *Child Development, 52,* 975–985.

Sternberg, R. J. (1986). *Intelligence applied.* Fort Worth, TX: Harcourt Brace.

Sternberg, R. J. (1994, November). Allowing for thinking styles. *Educational Leadership,* pp. 36–40.

Sternberg, R. J. (1997a). Educating intelligence: Infusing the triarchic theory into instruction. In R. J. Sternberg & E. Grigorenko (Eds.), *Intelligence, heredity, and environment.* New York: Cambridge University Press.

Sternberg, R. J. (1997b). *Thinking styles.* New York: Cambridge University Press.

Sternberg, R. J. (1999). Looking back and looking forward on intelligence: Toward a theory of successful intelligence. In M. Bennett (Ed.), *Developmental psychology: Achievement and prospects.* Philadelphia: Psychology Press.

Sternberg, R. J. (2000). Looking back and looking forward on intelligence: Toward a theory of successful intelligence. In M. Bennett (Ed.), *Developmental psychology.* Philadelphia: Psychology Press.

Sternberg, R. J. (2000). Thinking: An overview. In A. Kazdin (Ed.), *Encyclopedia of psychology.* Washington, DC, and New York: American Psychological Association and Oxford U. Press.

Sternberg, R. J., & Clinkenbeard, P. R. (1995, May/June). The triarchic model applied to identifying, teaching, and assessing gifted children. *Roeper Review,* 255–260.

Sternberg, R. J., & Lubart, T. I. (1995). *Defying the crowd: Cultivating creativity in a culture of conformity.* New York: Free Press.

Sternberg, R. J., & Spear-Swerling, P. (1996). *Teaching for thinking.* Washington, DC: American Psychological Association.

Sternberg, R. J., Torff, B., & Grigorenko, E. (1998, May). Teaching for successful intelligence raises school achievement. *Phi Delta Kappan,* 667–669.

Stevenson, H. G. (1995, March). *Missing data: On the forgotten substance of race, ethnicity, and socioeconomic classifications.* Paper presented at the meeting of the Society for Research in Child Development, Indianapolis.

Stevenson, H. W. (1992, December). Learning from Asian schools. *Scientific American,* pp. 6, 70–76.

Stevenson, H. W. (1995). Mathematics achievement of American students: First in the world by 2000? In C.A. Nelson (Ed), *Basic and applied pespectives in learning, cognition, and development.* Minneapolis: University of Minnesota Press.

Stevenson, H. W. (2000). Middle childhood: Education and schooling. In A. Kazdin (Ed.), *Encyclopedia of psychology.* Washington, DC, & New York: American Psychological Association and Oxford U. Press.

Stevenson, H. W., & Hofer, B. K. (1999). Education policy in the United States and abroad: What we can learn from each other. In G. J. Cizek (Ed.), *Handbook of educational policy.* San Diego: Academic Press.

Stevenson, H. W., Hofer, B. K., & Randel, B. (1999). *Middle childhood: Education and schooling.* Unpublished manuscript, Dept. of Psychology, University of Michigan, Ann Arbor.

Stevenson, H. W., Lee, S., Chen, C., Stigler, J. W., Hsu, C., & Kitamura, S. (1990). Contexts of achievement. *Monographs of the Society for Research in Development, 55* (Serial No. 221).

Stewart, D. (1997, August 27). Commentary in "SAT scores up, but so is grade inflation." *USA Today,* p. A1.

Stiggins, R. J. (1987). Design and evaluation of performance assessments. *Educational Measurement: Issues and Practices, 6,* 33–42.

Stiggins, R. J. (1997). *Student-centered classroom management* (2nd ed.). Boston: Allyn & Bacon.

Stiggins, R. J., & Conklin, N. F. (1992). *In teachers' hands: Investigating the practices of classroom assessment.* Albany: State University of New York Press.

Stigler, J. W., & Hiebert, J. (1997, September). Understanding and improving classroom mathematics instruction. *Phi Delta Kappan, 79,* 14–21.

Stigler, J. W., & Hiebert, J. (1999). *The teaching gap.* New York: Free Press.

Stipek, D. J. (1996). Motivation and instruction. In D. C. Berliner & R. C. Calfee (Eds.), *Handbook of educational psychology.* New York: Macmillan.

Stipek, D. S., Feiler, R., Daniels, D., & Milburn, S. (1995). Effects of different instructional approaches on young children's achievement and motivation. *Child Development, 66,* 209–223.

Sullivan, H. S. (1953). *The interpersonal theory of psychiatry.* New York: Norton.

Sullivan, L. (1991, May 25). US secretary urges TV to restrict "irresponsible sex and reckless violence." *Boston Globe,* p. A1.

Sund, R. B. (1976). *Piaget for educators.* Columbus, OH: Merrill.

Supovitz, J. A., & Brennan, R. T. (1997, Fall). Mirror, mirror on the wall, which is the fairest test of all? An examination of the equality of portfolio assessment relative to standardized tests. *Harvard Educational Review, 67* (No. 3), 472–501.

Sutton, R. E. (1991). Equity and computers in the schools: A decade of research. *Review of Educational Research, 61,* 475–503.

Swanson, D. P. (1997, April). *Identity and coping styles among African-American females.* Paper presented at the meeting of the Society for Research in Child Development, Washington, DC.

Swanson, H. L., & Hoskyn, M. (1998). Experi-mental intervention research on students with learning disabilities: A meta-analysis of treat-ment outcomes. *Review of Educational Research, 68,* 277–321.

Swanson, J. M., McBrunett, K., Wigal, T., & others. (1993). The effect of stimulant medication on ADD children. *Exceptional Children, 60,* 154–162.

Tannen, D. (1990). *You just don't understand!* New York: Ballantine.

Tanner, D. (1997, Spring). Standards. *Educational Horizons,* pp. 115–120.

Tanner, J. M. (1978). *Fetus into man.* Cambridge, MA: Harvard University Press.

Tappan, M. B. (1998). Sociocultural psychology and caring psychology: Exploring Vygotsky's "hidden curriculum." *Educational Psychologist, 33,* 23–33.

Tavris, C., & Wade, C. (1984). *The longest war: Sex differences in perspective.* Fort Worth, TX: Harcourt Brace.

Taylor, C. (1994). Assessment of measurement or standards: The peril and the promise of large-scale assessment reform. *American Educational Research Journal, 32,* 231–262.

Temple, C., Nathan, R., Temple, F., & Burris, N. A. (1993). *The beginnings of writing* (3rd ed.). Boston: Allyn & Bacon.

Tennyson, R., & Cocchiarella, M. (1986). An empir-ically based instructional design theory for teaching concepts. *Review of Educational Research, 56,* 40–71.

Terman, D. L., Larner, M. B., Stevenson, C. S., & Behrman, R. E. (1996). Special education for students with disabilities: Analysis and recom-mendations. *Future of Children, 6* (1), 4–24.

Terman, L. (1925). *Genetic studies of genius. Vol. 1: Mental and physical traits of a thousand gifted children.* Stanford, CA: Stanford University Press.

Terman, L., & Oden, M. H. (1959). *Genetic studies of genius. Vol. 5: The gifted group at mid-life.* Stanford, CA: Stanford University Press.

Terwilliger, J. (1997). Semantics, psychometrics, and assessment reform: A close look at "authentic" assessments. *Educational Researcher, 26,* 24–27.

Tetreault, M. K. T. (1997). Classrooms for diversity: Rethinking curriculum and pedagogy. In J. A. Banks & C. A. Banks (Eds.), *Multicultural education* (3rd ed.). Boston: Allyn & Bacon.

Thomas, A., & Chess, S. (1991). Temperament in adolescence and its functional significance. In R. M. Lerner, A. C. Petersen, & J. Brooks-Gunn (Eds.), *Encyclopedia of adolescence* (Vol. 2). New York: Garland.

Thomas, C. C., Correa, V. I., & Morsink, C. V. (1995). *Interactive teaming: Consultation and collaboration in special programs* (2nd ed.). Upper Saddle River, NJ: Merrill/Prentice Hall.

Thomas, J. R., & Thomas, K. T. (1988). Developmental of gender differences in physical activity. *Quest, 40,* 219–229.

Thomas, R. M. (2000). *Human development theories: Windows on culture.* Thousand Oaks, CA: Sage.

Thorndike, E. L. (1906). *Principles of teaching.* New York: Seiler.

Thurstone, L. L. (1938). *Primary mental abilities.* Chicago: University of Chicago Press.

Tierney, R. J., & Readence, J. E. (2000). *Reading strategies and practices: A compendium* (5th ed.). Boston: Allyn & Bacon.

Tolman, M. N., & Hardy, G. R. (1999). *Discovering elementary science* (2nd ed.). Boston: Allyn & Bacon.

Tomlinson, C. A., Callahan, C. M., & Lelli, K. M. (1997). Challenging expectations: Case studies of high-potential, culturally diverse young children. *Gifted Child Quarterly, 41* (2), 5–17.

Tomlinson-Keasey, C. (1993, August). *Tracing the lives of gifted women.* Paper presented at the meeting of the American Psychological Association, Toronto.

Tomlinson-Keasey, C. (1997, April). *Gifted women: Themes in their lives.* Paper presented at the meeting of the Society for Research in Child Development, Washington, DC.

Tompkins, G. (1997). *Literacy for the 21st century: A balanced approach.* Upper Saddle River, NJ: Prentice Hall.

Torff, B. (2000). Multiple intelligences. In A. Kazdin (Ed.), *Encyclopedia of psychology.* Washington, DC, and New York: American Psychological Association and Oxford U. Press.

Torgesen, J. D. (1995, December). *Prevention and remediation of reading disabilities.* Progress Report (NICHD Grant HD 30988). Bethesda, MD: National Institute of Child Health and Human Development.

Tousignant, M. (1995, April 11). Children's cure or adults' crutch? Rise of Ritalin prompts debate over the reason. *Washington Post,* p. B1.

Triandis, H. C. (1994). *Culture and social behavior.* New York: McGraw-Hill.

Triandis, H .C. (1997). Cross-cultural perspectives on personality. In R. Hogan, J. Johnson, & S. Briggs (Eds.), *Handbook of personality psychology.* San Diego: Academic Press.

Triandis, H. C. (2000). Cross-cultural psychology: The history of the field. In A. Kazdin (Ed.), *Encyclopedia of psychology.* Washington, DC, and New York: American Psychological Association and Oxford U. Press.

Triandis, H. C., Brislin, R., & Hui, C. H. (1988). Cross-cultural training across the individualism divide. *International Journal of Intercultural Relations, 12,* 269–288.

Trice, A. D. (2000). *Handbook of classroom assessment.* Boston: Addison Wesley.

Trimble, J. E. (1989, August). *The enculturation of contemporary psychology.* Paper presented at the meeting of the American Psychological Association, New Orleans.

Tubman, J. G., & Windle, M. (1995). Continuity of difficult temperament in adolescence: Relations with depression, life events, family support, and substance abuse across a one-year period. *Journal of Youth and Adolescence, 24,* 133–152.

Tucker, L. A. (1987). Television, teenagers, and health. *Journal of Youth and Adolescence, 16,* 415–425.

Tuckman, B. W., & Hinkle, J. S. (1988). An experimental study of the physical and psychological effects of aerobic exercise on school children. In B. G. Melamed, K. A. Matthews, D. K. Routh, B. Stabler, & N. Schneiderman (Eds.), *Child health psychology.* Mahwah, NJ: Erlbaum.

Tulving, E. (1972). Episodic and semantic memory. In E. Tulving & W. Donaldson (Eds.), *Origins of memory.* San Diego: Academic Press.

Tulving, E. (2000). Memory: An overview. In A. Kazdin (Ed.), *Encyclopedia of psychology.* Washington, DC, and New York: American Psychological Association and Oxford U. Press.

Turecki, S., & Tonner, L. (1989). *The difficult child.* New York: Bantam Books.

Turiel, E. (1997). The development of morality. In W. Damon (Ed.), *Handbook of child psychology* (5th ed., Vol. 3). New York: Wiley.

U

U.S. Department of Education (1993). *Violence in schools.* Washington, DC: Author.

U.S. Department of Education. (1996). *Number and disabilities of children and youth served under IDEA.* Washington, DC: Office of Special Education Programs, Data Analysis System.

Unger, R., & Crawford, M. (1996). *Women and gender* (2nd ed.). New York: McGraw-Hill.

V

Valsiner, J. (2000). *Culture and human development.* Thousand Oaks, CA: Sage.

van der Linden, W. J. (1995). Advances in computer applications. In T. Oakland & R. K. Hambleton (Eds.), *International perspectives on academic assessment.* Boston: Kluwer Academic.

Van Houten, R., Nau, P., Mackenzie-Keating, S., Sameoto, D., & Colavecchia, B. (1982). An analysis of some variables influencing the effectiveness of reprimands. *Journal of Applied Behavior Analysis, 15,* 65–83.

van Lehn, K. (1990). *Mind bugs.* Cambridge, MA: MIT Press.

VanLehn, K. (1986). Arithmetic procedures are induced from examples. In J. Hiebert (Ed.), *Conceptual and procedural knowledge: The case of mathematics.* Hillsdale, NJ: Erlbaum.

Venn, J. J. (2000). *Assessing students with special needs* (2nd ed.). Upper Saddle River, NJ: Merrill.

Vidal, F. (2000). Piaget, Jean. In A. Kazdin (Ed.), *Encyclopedia of psychology.* Washington, DC, and New York: American Psychological Association and Oxford U. Press.

Vining, E. P. G. (1992). Down syndrome. In R. A. Hoekelman (Ed.), *Primary pediatric care* (2nd ed.). St. Louis: Mosby.

Vygotsky, L. S. (1962). *Thought and language.* Cambridge, MA: MIT Press.

Vygotsky, L. S. (1978). *Mind in society.* Cambridge, MA: Harvard University Press.

Vygotsky, L. S. (1987). Thinking and speech. In R. W. Rieber & A. S. Carton (Eds.), *The collected works of L. S. Vygotsky.* New York: Plenum.

W

Wadlington, E., Jacob, S., & Bailey, S. (1996, Fall). Teaching students with dyslexia in the regular classroom. *Childhood Education,* pp. 2–5.

Wagner, M. (1995). Outcomes for youths with serious emotional disturbance in secondary school and early adulthood. *Future of Children 5* (2), 90–112.

Wagner, M. W., & Blackorby, J. (1996). Transition from high school to work or college: How special education students fare. *Future of Children, 6* (1), 103–120.

Wagner, R. (1993). *Hyperstudio.* El Cajon, CA: Roger Wagner.

Wahlsten, D. (2000). Behavioral genetics. In A. Kazdin (Ed.), *Encyclopedia of psychology.* Washington, DC, and New York: American Psychological Association and Oxford U. Press.

Wakschlag, L. S., Chase-Lansdale, P. L., & Brooks-Gunn, J. (1996, March). *Not just "ghosts in the nursery": Contemporaneous intergenerational relationships and parenting in young African American families.* Paper presented at the meeting of the Society for Research on Adolescence, Boston.

Walther-Thomas, C., Korinek, L., McLaughlin, V. L., & Williams, B. T. (2000). *Collaboration for inclusive education.* Boston: Allyn & Bacon.

Waterman, A. S. (1997). An overview of service learning and the role of research and evaluation in service-learning programs. In A. S. Waterman (Ed.), *Service learning.* Mahwah, NJ: Erlbaum.

Weary, G. (2000). Attribution theories. In A. Kazdin (Ed.), *Encyclopedia of psychology.* Washington, DC, & New York: American Psychological Association and Oxford U. Press.

Weaver, C. (in press). *Reconsidering a balanced approach to reading.* Urbana, IL: National Council of Teachers of English.

Webb, L. D., Metha, A., & Jordan, K. F. (2000). *Foundations of American education* (3rd ed.). Boston: Allyn & Bacon.

Webb, N. M. (1984). Sex differences in interaction and achievement in cooperative small groups. *Journal of Educational Psychology, 76,* 33–34.

Webb, N. M., & Palincsar, A. S. (1996). Group processes in the classroom. In D. C. Berliner & R. C. Calfee (Eds.), *Handbook of educational psychology.* New York: Macmillan.

Weber, E. (1999). *Student assessment that works.* Boston: Allyn & Bacon.

Wehlage, G. (1989). Dropping out: Can schools be expected to prevent it? In L. Weis, E. Farrar, & H. Petrie (Eds.), *Dropouts from school.* Albany: State University of New York Press.

Weiner, B. (1986). *An attributional theory of motivation and emotion.* New York: Springer.

Weiner, B. (1992). *Human motivation: Metaphors, theories, and research.* Newbury Park, CA: Sage.

Weiner, B. (2000). Motivation: An overview. In A. Kazdin (Ed.), *Encyclopedia of psychology.* Washington, DC, & New York: American Psychological Association and Oxford U. Press.

Weinstein, C. E., Husman, J., & Dierking, D. R. (2000). Self-regulation interventions with a focus on learning strategies. In M. Moekaerts, P. R. Pintrich, & M. Zeidner (Eds.), *Handbook of self-regulation.* Boston: American Psychological Association.

Weinstein, C. S. (1997). *Secondary classroom management.* New York: McGraw-Hill.

Weinstein, C. S. (1999). Reflections on the best practices and promising programs: Beyond assertive classroom discipline. In H. J. Friedberg (Ed.), *Beyond behaviorism: Changing the classroom management paradigm.* Boston: Allyn & Bacon.

Weinstein, C. S., & Mignano, A. J., Jr. (1997). *Elementary classroom management.* New York: McGraw-Hill.

Weinstein, R. S., Madison, S. M., & Kuklinksi, M. R. (1995). Raising expectations in schooling: Obstacles and opportunities for change. *American Educational Research Journal, 32,* 121–159.

Weissberg, R. P., & Caplan, M. (1994). *Promoting social competence and preventing antisocial behavior in young urban adolescents.* Unpublished manuscript, University of Illinois, Chicago.

Weissberg, R. P., & Greenberg, M. T. (1998). School and community competence-enhancement prevention programs. In W. Damon (Ed.), *Handbook of child psychology* (Vol. 4). New York: Wiley.

Weissberg, R. P., Barton, H. A., & Shriver, T. P. (1997). The Social-Competence Promotion Program for young adolescents. In G. W. Albee & T. P. Gullotta (Eds.), *Primary prevention exemplars: The Lela Rowland Awards.* Thousand Oaks, CA: Sage.

Weissberg, R. P., Gesten, E. L., Rapkin, B. D., Cowen, E. L., Davidson, E., Flores de Apodaca, R., & McKim, B. J. (1981). The evaluation of a social problem-solving training program for suburban and inner-city third grade children. *Journal of Consulting and Clinical Psychology, 49,* 251–261.

Weldin, D. J., & Tumarkin, S. R. (1999). Parent involvement: More power in the portfolio process. *Childhood Education, 75,* 90–96.

Wellhousen, K. (1996, Fall). Do's and don'ts for eliminating hidden bias. *Childhood Education,* pp. 36–39.

Wentzel, K. R. (1996). Social goals and social relationships as motivators of school adjustment. In J. Juvonen & K. R. Wentzel (Eds.), *Social motivation.* New York: Cambridge University Press.

Wentzel, K. R., & Asher, S. R. (1995). The academic lives of neglected, rejected, popular, and controversial children. *Child Development, 66,* 754–763.

Wentzel, K. R., & Erdley, C. A. (1993). Strategies for making friends: Relations to social behavior and peer acceptance in early adolescence. *Developmental Psychology, 29,* 819–826.

Wertsch, J. (2000). Cognitive development. In M. Bennett (Ed.), *Developmental psychology: Achievements and prospects.* Philadelphia: Psychology Press.

Wertheimer, M. (1945). *Productive thinking.* New York: Harper.

West, K. R. (1998). Noticing and responding to learners: Literacy evaluation and instruction in the primary grades. *Reading Teacher, 51,* 550–556.

Whalen, C. (2000). Attention deficit hyperactivity disorder. In A. Kazdin (Ed.), *Encyclopedia of psychology.* Washington, DC, and New York: American Psychological Association and Oxford U. Press.

Wheelock, A. (1992). *Crossing the tracks: how "untracking" can save America's schools.* New York: New Press.

White, B. Y. (1993). ThinkerTools: Causal models, conceptual change, and science education. *Cognition and Instruction, 10,* 1–100.

White, R. W. (1959). Motivation reconsidered: The concept of confidence. *Psychological Review, 66,* 297–333.

Whitford, B. L., & Jones, K. (Eds.) (2000). *Accountability, assessment, and teacher commitment.* Albany: State University of New York Press.

Wigfield, A., & Asher, S. R. (1984). Social and motivational influences on reading. In P. D. Pearson, R. Barr, M. L. Kamil, & P. Mosenthal (Eds.), *Handbook of reading research.* New York: Longman.

Wigfield, A., & Eccles, J. S. (1989). Test anxiety in elementary and secondary school students. *Journal of Educational Psychology, 24,* 159–183.

Wigfield, A., & Gutherie, J. T. (1997). Motivation for reading: An overview. *Educational Psychologist, 32,* 57–58.

Wigfield, A., Eccles, J. S., & Pintrich, P. R. (1996). Development between the ages of 11 and 25. In D. C. Berliner & R. C. Calfee (Eds.), *Handbook of educational psychology.* New York: Macmillan.

Wiggins, G. (1992, May). Creating tests worth taking. *Educational Leadership,* pp. 26–33.

Wiggins, G. (1993, November). Assessment: Authenticity, context, and validity. *Phi Delta Kappan,* pp. 200–214.

Wigginton, E. (1985). *Sometimes a shining moment.* Garden City, NY: Anchor Books.

Williams, V. I., & Cartledge, G. (1997, September/October). Notes to parents. *Teaching Exceptional Children,* pp. 30–34.

Wilson, M. (1999). Cultural diversity. In A. Kazdin (Ed.), *Encyclopedia of psychology.* Washington, DC, and New York: American Psychological Association and Oxford U. Press.

Winne, P. H. (1995). Inherent details in self-regulated learning. *Educational Psychologist, 30,* 173–187.

Winne, P. H. (1997). Experimenting to bootstrap self-regulated learning. *Journal of Educational Psychology, 89,* 397–410.

Winner, E. (1986, August). Where pelicans kiss seals. *Psychology Today,* pp. 24–35.

Winner, E. (1996). *Gifted children: Myths and realities.* New York: Basic Books.

Winner, E. (1997). Exceptionally high intelligence and schooling. *American Psychologist, 52,* 1070–1081.

Winsler, A., Diaz, R. M., & Montero, I. (1997). The role of private speech in the transition from collaborative to independent task performance in young children. *Early Childhood Research Quarterly, 12,* 59–79.

Witkin, H. A. (1976). Cognitive style in academic performance and in teacher-student relations. In S. Messick (Ed.), *Individuality in learning.* San Francisco: Jossey-Bass.

Witkin, H. A., & Goodenough, D. R. (1976). *Field dependence and interpersonal behavior.* Princeton, NJ: Educational Testing Service.

Wittmer, D. S., & Honig, A. S. (1994). Encouraging positive social development in young children, *Young Children, 49,* 4–12.

Wolery, M. (2000). Special education. In A. Kazdin (Ed.), *Encyclopedia of psychology.* Washington, DC, and New York: American Psychological Association and Oxford U. Press.

Woodrich, D. L. (1994). *Attention-deficit hyperactivity disorder: What every parent should know.* Baltimore: Paul H. Brookes.

Work Group of the American Psychological Association's Board of Educational Affairs. (1995). *Learner-centered psychological principles: A framework for school redesign and reform* [Draft]. Washington, DC: American Psychological Association.

Workman, S. H., & Gage, J. A. (1997). Family-school partnerships: A family strengths approach. *Young Children, 52,* 10–14.

Worthen, B. R., & Spandel, V. (1991, February). Putting the standardized test debate in perspective. *Educational Leadership,* pp. 65–69.

Wroblewski, R., & Huston, A. C. (19987). Televised occupational stereotypes and their effects on early adolescents: Are they changing? *Journal of Early Adolescence, 7,* 283–297.

Y

Yates, M. (1995, March). *Community service and political-moral discussions among Black urban adolescents.* Paper presented at the meeting of the Society for Research in Child Development, Indianapolis.

Yinger, R. J. (1980). Study of teacher planning. *Elementary School Journal, 80,* 107–127.

Young, J. R. (1997). Invasion of the laptops: More colleges adopt mandatory computing programs. *Chronicle of Higher Education, 19,* A33–A35.

Zigler, E. F., & Finn-Stevenson, M. (1999). Applied developmental psychology. In M. H. Bornstein & M. E. Lamb (Eds.), *Developmental psychology* (4th ed.). Mahwah, NJ: Erlbaum.

Zigler, E. F., & Styfco, S. J. (1994). Head Start: Criticisms in a constructive context. *American Psychologist, 47,* 127–132.

Zimmerman, B. J. (1998, April). *Achieving academic excellence: The role of self-efficacy and self-regulatory skill.* Paper presented at the meeting of the American Psychological Association, San Diego.

Zimmerman, B. J. (2000). Attaining self-regulation: A social cognitive perspective. In M. Boekaerts, P. Pintrich, & M. Seidner (Eds.), *Self-regulation: Theory, research, and application.* Orlando, FL: Academic Press.

Zimmerman, B. J., Bonner, S., & Kovach, R. (1996). *Developing self-regulated learners.* Washington, DC: American Psychological Association.

Zimmerman, R. S., Khoury, E., Vega, W. A., Gil, A. G., & Warheit, G. J. (1995). Teacher and student perceptions of behavior problems among a sample of African American, Hispanic, and non-Hispanic White students. *American Journal of Community Psychology, 23,* 181–197.

Credits

LINE ART AND TEXT

CHAPTER 1

Page 3: From *Maintaining a Life* by Margaret Metzger. Copyright © 1996. Reprinted with permission of Phi Delta Kappa, Box 789, Bloomington, IN 47402-0789

Figure 1.1: From "Students say what makes a good teacher" in *Middle School Journal*, May/June 1997. Used with permission of the National Association of Secondary School Principals (NASSP) Copyright © 1997. All rights reserved.

Page 27: From *Maintaining a Life* by Margaret Metzger. Copyright © 1996. Reprinted with permission of Phi Delta Kappa, Box 789, Bloomington, IN 47402-0789

CHAPTER 2

Page 37: From "Sorry About Betty Teufel" by Jana Fowler Copyright © 1998. Reprinted with permission by the author.

Figure 2.1: From *Adolescence* by John Santrock. Copyright © 1998 by McGraw-Hill College Division. Reprinted with permission by The McGraw-Hill Companies.

Figure 2.2: From *Adolescence* by John Santrock. Copyright © 1998 by McGraw-Hill College Division. Reprinted with permission by The McGraw-Hill Companies.

Figure 2.3: From J.M. Tanner, R.H. Whitehouse, and M. Takaishi, "Standards from Birth to Maturity for Height, Weight, Height Velocity, and Weight Velocity: British Children, 1965" in *Archives of Diseases in Childhood*, 41. Copyright "1966 British Medical Association, London, England. Reprinted by permission.

Figure 2.6a: (left) Dennis Palmer Wolf/Project PACE

Figure 2.6b: (right) Courtesy of Dr. Ellen Winner, Project Zero

Figure 2.7: From *Child Development* by John Santrock. Copyright © 1998 by McGraw-Hill College Division. Reprinted with permission by The McGraw-Hill Companies.

Figure 2.8: From *Child Development* by John Santrock. Copyright © 1998 by McGraw-Hill College Division. Reprinted with permission by The McGraw-Hill Companies.

Figure 2.9: From *Child Development* by John Santrock. Copyright © 1998 by McGraw-Hill College Division. Reprinted with permission by The McGraw-Hill Companies.

Figure 2.10: From *Child Development* by John Santrock. Copyright © 1998 by McGraw-Hill College Division. Reprinted with permission by The McGraw-Hill Companies.

Figure 2.13: From Berko, Word, 14:361. Copyright "1958 International Linguistic Association, New York, NY. Reprinted by permission.

Page 74: "Through the Eyes of Children" From Dickinson, Wolf, and Stotsky, *The Development of Language*, 3d ed, Jean Berko Gleason (ed.). Copyright "1993 by Allyn and Bacon. Reprinted by permission.

Page 79: "Through the Eyes of Teachers" Source: Bauman & others, 1998

Page 75: "Through the Eyes of Teachers" From "Observing Young Children's Literacy" by K. R. West in *The Reading Teacher* 51 Copyright © 1998. Reprinted with permission by the author and the International Reading Association.

CHAPTER 3

Figure 3.1: CB Kopp/JB Krakow, *Child Development in the Social Context*, (page 648), ©1982 by Addison-Wesley Publishing Company, Inc. Reprinted by permission of Addison-Wesley Longman, Inc.

Figure 3.2: From *Adolescence* by John Santrock. Copyright © 1998 by McGraw-Hill College Division. Reprinted with permission by The McGraw-Hill Companies.

Page 89: "Quotation" "If I Had My Child to Raise Over Again," from the book Full Esteem Ahead " 1994 by Diane Loomans with Julia Loomans. Reprinted by permission of JH Kramer, PO Box 1082, Tiburon, CA. All rights reserved.

Figure 3.3: From *Life-Span Development* by John Santrock. Copyright © 1999 by McGraw-Hill College Division. Reprinted with permission by The McGraw-Hill Companies.

Figure 3.4: Excerpted from *Developmentally Appropriate Practice* (pp. 54-56), S. Bredekamp, ed., 1987, Washington, D.C.: the National Association for the Education of Young Children. Copyright " 1987 by NAEYC.

Page 102: "Through the Eyes of Teachers" From "Reflections of a Middle School Teacher" by J. Logan in *Teaching Stories* Copyright © 1997. Published by Koshansha International, New York

Figure 3.5: From *Child Development* by John Santrock. Copyright © 1998 by McGraw-Hill College Division. Reprinted with permission by The McGraw-Hill Companies.

Page 115: "Through the Eyes of Children" From *The Creative Spirit* by Dan Goleman, Paul Kaufman, & Michael Ray Copyright Copyright © 1992 by Alvin H. Perlmutter, Inc. Use by permission of Dutton, a division of Penguin Putnam Inc.

Figure 3.12: From *Life-Span Development* by John Santrock. Copyright © 1999 by McGraw-Hill College Division. Reprinted with permission by The McGraw-Hill Companies.

CHAPTER 4

Figure 4.1: From *Child Development* by John Santrock. Copyright © 1998 by McGraw-Hill College Division. Reprinted with permission by The McGraw-Hill Companies.

Figure 4.2: From *Child Development* by John Santrock. Copyright © 1998 by McGraw-Hill College Division. Reprinted with permission by The McGraw-Hill Companies.

Figure 4.3: "Increasing IQ Scores from 1932–1997" by Ulric Neisser Copyright © 1997. Reprinted with permission by the author.

Figure 4.4: Item A5 from Raven's *Standard Progressive Matrices*. Reprinted by permission of J. C. Raven Limited

Figure 4.5: From "A Successful Program of Teachers Assisting Teachers" by Kent, K in *Educational Leadership* 43, 3: 30-33. Used by permission of the Association for Supervision and Curriculum Development. Copyright Copyright © 1985 by ASCD. All rights reserved.

Figure 4.6: From "A Successful Program of Teachers Assisting Teachers" by Kent, K in *Educational Leadership* 43, 3: 30-33. Used by permission of the Association for Supervision and Curriculum Development. Copyright Copyright © 1985 by ASCD. All rights reserved.

CHAPTER 5

Figure 5.1: From "Gender Differences in Mathematics Performance" in *Psychological Bulletin*, 107: 139-155. Copyright 1990 by the American Psychological Association. Reprinted with permission.

Page 187: "Self-Assement 5.1" From *Adolescence* by John Santrock. Copyright © 1998 by McGraw-Hill College Division. Reprinted with permission by The McGraw-Hill Companies.

CHAPTER 6

Figure 6.1: Source: Data from the "The Diversity of Children Who Have a Disability," Copyright © 1996 by U.S. Department of Education Office of Special Education Program, Washington, D. C.

Page 201: "Through the Eyes of Children" From Newsweek, October 24 Copyright ©1994 Newsweek, Inc. All rights reserved. Reprinted by permission.

Figure 6.3: From "Mental Retardation Based on Levels of Support" Copyright © 1996 by the American Association for Mental Retardation. All rights reserved. Reprinted by permission.

Page 219: "Through the Eyes of Children" From *Gifted Children Speak Out*. Copyright © 1984 by James R. Delisle. Reprinted with permission from Walker and Company, 435 Hudson Street, New York, New York 10014. 1-800-289-2553. All Rights Reserved.

Figure 6.5: Source: "Individualized Education Program (IED)" from the State of Ohio Department of Education. Reprinted by permission

Figure 6.6: Source: Data from "Percentage of Special Education Services Provided in Various Settings" in *Implementation of the Individuals with Disabilities Education Act*. Copyright © 1994 by U.S. Department of Education Office of Special Education Program, Washington, D. C.

CHAPTER 7

Page 237: From *Elementary Classroom Management* by Weinstein, C. S. and Mignano, A. J. Copyright © 1997 by McGraw-Hill College Division. Reprinted with permission by The McGraw-Hill Companies.

Figure 7.5: From *Psychology, 6e* by John Santrock. Copyright © 2000 by McGraw-Hill College Division. Reprinted with permission by The McGraw-Hill Companies.

Figure 7.6: From *Life-Span Development, 7e* by John Santrock. Copyright © 1999 by McGraw-Hill College Division. Reprinted with permission by The McGraw-Hill Companies.

Figure 7.9: From *Self-Talk for Teachers and Students: Metacognitive Strategies for Personal and Classroom Use* by Manning, B. H. & Payne, B. D. Copyright © 1996 by Allyn & Bacon, a Pearson Education Company. Reprinted by permission.

Page 264: "Self-Assessment 7.2" From *Developing Self-Regulated Learners* by Zimmerman, B. J., Bonner, S. & Kovach, R. Copyright © 1996 by American Psychological Association, Washington, D. C. Reprinted by permission.

Figure 7.10: From *Developing Self-Regulated Learners* by Zimmerman, B. J., Bonner, S. & Kovach, R. Copyright © 1996 by American Psychological Association, Washington, D. C. Reprinted by permission.

Figure 7.11: From *Developing Self-Regulated Learners* by Zimmerman, B. J., Bonner, S. & Kovach, R. Copyright © 1996 by American Psychological Association, Washington, D. C. Reprinted by permission.

CHAPTER 8

Figure 8.2: From *Psychology, 5e* by John Santrock. Copyright © 1997 by McGraw-Hill College Division. Reprinted with permission by The McGraw-Hill Companies.

Figure 8.3: From *Psychology, 6e* by John Santrock. Copyright © 2000 by McGraw-Hill College Division. Reprinted with permission by The McGraw-Hill Companies.

Figure 8.5: From *The Universe Within.* Copyright „ 1982 by Morton Hunt. Reprinted by permission of Simon & Schuster.

Figure 8.6: From *Psychology* by John Santrock. Copyright © 1997 by McGraw-Hill College Division. Reprinted with permission by The McGraw-Hill Companies.

Figure 8.7: From Joel Levin, et al., "The Keyword Method in the Classroom" in *Elementary School Journal*, 80:4. Copyright © 1980 University of Chicago Press. Reprinted by permission.

Figure 8.9: From *Psychology* by John Santrock. Copyright © 1997 by McGraw-Hill College Division. Reprinted with permission by The McGraw-Hill Companies.

Figure 8.10: From *New Ways of Analyzing Variations in English* by W. Labov. Copyright © 1993. Reprinted by permission of Georgetown University Press. All rights reserved.

Figure 8.11: From Gordan H. Bower, "Organizational Factors in Memory" in *Cognitive Psychology,* 1:18-46. Copyright © 1970 Academic Press. Reprinted by permission.

CHAPTER 9

Figure 9.2: From *Educational Psychologist* by Palinscar, A. S. Copyright © 1986 by Lawrence Erlbaum Associates, Inc., Publishers. Reprinted by permission.

Page 317: From *Education for an Information Age: Teaching in the Computerized Classroom* by Poole, Bernard, J. Copyright © 1998 by McGraw-Hill College Division. Reprinted with permission by The McGraw-Hill Companies.

CHAPTER 10

Figure 10.1: From "A Study of Teacher Planning" by Yinger, R. J. *in The Elementary School Journal* Copyright © 1980. Reprinted by permission of the University of Chicago Press.

Figure 10.2: From "A Study of Teacher Planning" by Yinger, R. J. *in The Elementary School Journal* Copyright © 1980. Reprinted by permission of the University of Chicago Press.

Figure 10.3: Reprinted by permission of Waveland Press, Inc. from K. W. Linden in *Cooperative Learning and Problem Solving,* Second Edition. (Prospect Heights, IL: Waveland Press, Inc., 1996). All rights reserved.

Figure 10.4: From *Elementary Classroom Management* by Weinstein, C. S. and Mignano, A. J. Copyright © 1997 by McGraw-Hill College Division. Reprinted with permission by The McGraw-Hill Companies.

Figure 10.5: From *Elementary Classroom Management* by Weinstein, C. S. and Mignano, A. J. Copyright © 1997 by McGraw-Hill College Division. Reprinted with permission by The McGraw-Hill Companies.

Figure 10.6: From Learner-Centered Psychological Principles: A Frame up for School Reform and Design The Learner-Centered Principles Work Group and The Board of Educational Affairs Copyright © 1997 by American Psychological Association, Washington, D. C. Reprinted by permission.

Figure 10.7: Extrapolated from "Design Options for an Integrated Curriculum" by Heidi Hayes Jacobs in Interdisciplinary Curriculum: Design and Implementation published in 1990 by the Association of Supervision and Curriculum Development, Alexandria Virginia. Reprinted from The Mindful School: How to Integrate the Curricula by Robin Fogarty. Copyright © 1991 by IRI/SkyLight Training and Publishing, Inc. Reprinted by permission of SkyLight Professional Development, Arlington Heights, Illinois. http://skylightedu.com

Figure 11.2: From *Motivating Students to Learn* by Brophy, J. Copyright © 1998 by McGraw-Hill College Division. Reprinted with permission by The McGraw-Hill Companies.

Figure 11.3: From Weiner, B. in *Human Motivation: Metaphors, Theories and Research* Copyright © 1992 by Sage Publications, Inc. Reprinted by Permission of Sage Publications, Inc.

Figure 11.4: From "Classrooms : Goals, Structures, and Student Motivation" by Ames, C. Copyright © 1992 in *Journal of Educational Psychology* . Reprinted by permission of American Psychological Association, Washington, D. C.

Figure 11.5: From *Motivating Students to Learn* by Brophy, J. Copyright © 1998 by McGraw-Hill College Division. Reprinted with permission by The McGraw-Hill Companies.

CHAPTER 12

Figure 12.3: From *Excellent Classroom Management,* 1st edition, by C. L. Rinne. Copyright © 1997. Reprinted with permission of Wadsworth Publishing, a division of Thomson Learning. Fax 800 730-2215.

Figure 12.4: From *Realities of Teaching* by Adams, R., & Biddle, B. Copyright © 1970 by Holt, Rinehart & Winston. Reprinted by permission.

Figure 12.5: From *Elementary Classroom Management* by Weinstein, C. S. and Mignano, A. J. Copyright © 1997 by McGraw-Hill College Division. Reprinted with permission by The McGraw-Hill Companies.

Figure 12.6: From *Secondary Classroom Management* by Weinstein, C. S. Copyright © 1996 by McGraw-Hill College Division. Reprinted with permission by The McGraw-Hill Companies.

Page 442: "Through the Eyes of Teachers" From *Creating Responsible Learners* by Ridley, D. S. & Walther, B. Copyright © 1995 by American Psychological Association, Washington, D. C. Reprinted by permission.

Page 443: "Teaching Strategies" From *Elementary Classroom Management* by Weinstein, C. S. and Mignano, A. J. Copyright © 1997 by McGraw-Hill College Division. Reprinted with permission by The McGraw-Hill Companies.

Figure 12.7: From *Creating Responsible Learners* by Ridley, D. S. & Walther, B. Copyright © 1995 by American Psychological Association, Washington, D. C. Reprinted by permission.

CHAPTER 13

Figure 13.2: From *Stanford Achievement Test Series,* 9th ed. Reprinted by permission of Holt, Rinehart & Winston.

Figure 13.3: From "Setting the Standards from State to State" by Olson. Reprinted with permission from Education Week, April 12, 1995.

Figure 13.4: Source: Data "Examples of Items On National Assessments" Copyright © 1996 by U.S. Department of Education, Washington, D. C.

Figure 13.6: From *Psychology* by John Santrock. Copyright © 1997 by McGraw-Hill College Division. Reprinted with permission by The McGraw-Hill Companies.

Figure 13.8: Adapted from "The Psychological Corporation, Test Service Notebook, No. 148" by The Psychological Corporation. Reprinted by permission of Holt, Rinehart & Winston.

Figure 13.9: From The Comprehensive Test of Basic Skills Copyright © 1999 by CTB/McGraw-Hill. Reprinted with permission by The McGraw-Hill Companies.

CHAPTER 14

Figure 14.2: From *Classroom Assessment* by McMillan, James. Copyright © 1996 by Allyn & Bacon, a Pearson Education Company. Reprinted by permission.

Figure 14.3: From *Assessment of Student Achievement* by Gronlund. Copyright © 1998 by Allyn & Bacon, a Pearson Education Company. Reprinted by permission.

Figure 14.4: From *Assessment of Student Achievement* by Gronlund. Copyright © 1998 by Allyn & Bacon, a Pearson Education Company. Reprinted by permission.

Figure 14.5: From *Assessment of Student Achievement* by Gronlund. Copyright © 1998 by Allyn & Bacon, a Pearson Education Company. Reprinted by permission.

Figure 14.6: Source: "Using alternative assessment to provide options for student success" by Combs, D in *Middle School Journal*, 1997, Sept., p. 5, Fig. 1. Used by permission of National Middle School Association.

Figure 14.7: Source: "Development of Performance Assessments in Science" by Solano-Flores, G. & Shavelson, R. J. in *Educational Measurement*, 1997, Sept. Used by permission of National Council on Measurement in Education.

Figure 14.8: From *Classroom Assessment* by Airasian. Copyright © 1997 by McGraw-Hill College Division. Reprinted with permission by The McGraw-Hill Companies.

Figure 14.9: From Portfolios by Johnson, N. J. & Rose, L. M. Copyright © 1997 by Rowman & Littlefield Publishing Company. Reprinted by permission.

ICONS

Marginal web icon: Photodisc
Adventures of the Mind: Designer Tools Series, Vol. 3-Maps and Navigation
Taking It to the Net: Photodisc
Teaching Strategies: Object Series, Vol. 17-Doors and Windows
Through the Eyes of Teachers: Photodisc, Volume 41, Education 2
Through the Eyes of Children: Photodisc
Diversity and Education: Vol. 64, Global Communications
Self-Assessment Tables: Photodisc
Technology and Education: Vol. 64, Global Communications

PHOTOGRAPHS

PROLOGUE

1: Copyright © Paul Conklin/Photo Edit; **2.1** Copyright © Richard Howard; **3:** Copyright © Tony Freeman/Photo Edit; **4:** Copyright © Lawrence Migdale/Tony Stone Images; **5:** Copyright © David Young-Wolff/Tony Stone Images; **6:** Copyright © Frank Siteman/Photo Edit; **7:** Copyright © Elizabeth Crews; **8:** Copyright © Zigy Kaluzny/Tony Stone Images; **9:** Courtesy of Compton-Drew Investigative Learning Center Middle School, St. Louis, MO; **10:** Copyright © David Young-Wolff/Tony Stone Images; **11:** Copyright © Michael Newman/Photo Edit; **12:** Copyright © A. Ramey/Photo Edit; **13:** Copyright © Robert E. Daemmrich/Tony Stone Images; **14:** Copyright © David Young-Wolff/Photo Edit

CHAPTER 1

Opener: Copyright © Paul Conklin/Photo Edit; **p. 4** (left): Copyright © Brown Brothers; (right): Columbia University Archives and Columbiana

Library; **p. 5 (left):** Prints and Photographs Collection CN10383, Center for American History, University of Texas at Austin.; **(middle):** Courtesy of Kenneth Clark; **(right):** Copyright © Archives of the History of American Psychology, University of Akron; **(top):** Copyright © Alan Marler; **p. 12 (bottom):** Copyright © Tony Freeman/Photo Edit; **p. 22:** Courtesy of Steven and Cindi Binder; **p. 27:** Copyright © PhotoDisc; **p. 29 (left):** Copyright © Andy Sacks/Tony Stone Images; **(right):** Copyright © David Young-Wolff/Tony Stone Images

CHAPTER 2

Opener: Copyright © Richard Howard; **p. 43:** Copyright © Bob Daemmrich/The Image Works; **p. 49:** Copyright © Archives Jean Piaget; **p. 56:** Copyright © Paul Conklin; **2.11:** Copyright © Elizabeth Crews/The Image Works; **2.12 (left):** A.R. Lauria/Dr. Michael Cole, Laboratory of Human Cognition, University of California, San Diego; **(right):** Copyright © 1999 Yves deBraine/Black Star; **p. 72:** Courtesy of International Business Machines Corporation. Unauthorized use not permitted

CHAPTER 3

Opener: Copyright © Tony Freeman/Photo Edit; **p. 82:** Courtesy of Cornell University; **p. 86:** Copyright © Sarah Putnam/Index Stock; **p. 90:** Copyright © Elizabeth Crews; **p. 93:** Courtesy of Madeline Cartwright; **p. 95:** Copyright © Eric Anderson/Stock Boston; **p. 98:** Courtesy of Anita Marie Hitchcock; **3.4:** Copyright © Ken Fisher/Tony Stone Images; **p. 109:** Copyright © Keith Carter; **p. 111:** Copyright © Anthony Verde Photography; **p. 118 (left & right):** Copyright © AP/Wide World Photos

CHAPTER 4

Opener: Copyright © Lawrence Migdale/Tony Stone Images; **p. 129:** Courtesy of Robert Sternberg; **p. 130:** Copyright © Jay Gardner, 1998; **p. 132:** Copyright © Joe McNally; **p. 142 (left):** Copyright © James Wilson, 1990/Woodfin Camp & Associates; **(right):** Copyright © Tom Snyder Productions

CHAPTER 5

Opener: Copyright © David Young-Wolff/Tony Stone Images; **p. 162:** Copyright © The Courier-Journal, photographer Sam Upshaw, Jr.; **p. 163:** Copyright © Jonathan Kozal; **p. 165:** Copyright © Peter Byron/Photo Edit; **p. 166:** Copyright © Patty Wood; **p. 170:** Copyright © Elizabeth Crews; **p. 173:** Copyright © Ellis Herwig/Stock Boston; **p. 174:** Copyright © Mike Yamashita/Woodfin Camp & Associates; **p. 176:** Copyright © John S. Abbott; **p. 181:** Copyright © Suzanne Szasz/Photo Researchers; **p. 189:** Copyright © SuperStock, Inc.

CHAPTER 6

Opener: Copyright © Frank Siteman/Photo Edit; **p. 191:** Copyright © Judy Logan; **p. 199:** Copyright © Will & Deni McIntyre/Photo Researchers; **p. 201:** Courtesy of Angie Erickson; **6.4:** Copyright © Jill Canneax/EKM Nepenthe; **p. 207:** Copyright © Spencer Tirey; **p. 211:** Copyright © David Young-Wolff/Photo Edit; **p. 217:** Copyright © AFP/CORBIS; **p. 225:** Copyright © Richard Hutchings/Photo

Researchers; **6.7 (left):** Bob Daemmrich/Stock Boston; **(right):** Used by permission of Don Johnston Inc.

CHAPTER 7

Opener: Copyright © Elizabeth Crews; **p. 241:** Copyright © Sovfoto; **p. 242:** Copyright © Elizabeth Crews; **p. 244:** Nina Leen, Life Magazine. Copyright © Time, Inc.; **7.4 (top):** Copyright © Bob Daemmrich/Stock Boston; **(middle):** Copyright © Michael Newman/Photo Edit; **(bottom):** Copyright © David Young-Wolff/Photo Edit; **p. 252:** Copyright © B. Daemmrich/The Image Works; **p. 256:** Courtesy of Albert Bandura; **7.7 (left & right):** Courtesy of Albert Bandura; **7.8:** Copyright © Jeffry W. Myers/Corbis; **p. 260:** Copyright © Irvin Thompson/Dallas Morning News; **p. 261:** Copyright © 1999 Children's Television Workshop. Copyright © 1999 Jim Henson Company. Photograph by Richard Termine

CHAPTER 8

Opener: Copyright © Zigy Kaluzny/Tony Stone Images; **p. 283:** Copyright © Elizabeth Crews; **p. 297 (top):** Copyright © Elizabeth Crews; **(bottom):** Copyright © Copyright 1999, USA TODAY. Reprinted with permission; **8.12 (left & right):** Copyright © Cognition & Technology Group, LTC, Peabody College, Vanderbilt University; **8.13:** Copyright © Learning Technology Center, Vanderbilt University; **p. 307:** Copyright © James Kegley Photography; **p. 311:** Copyright © Suzanne Szasz/Photo Researchers

CHAPTER 9

Opener: Courtesy of Compton-Drew Investigative Learning Center Middle School, St. Louis, MO; **p. 319:** Copyright © Will Hart/Photo Edit; **p. 320:** Copyright © S.E. McKee; **p. 322:** Courtesy of Coca-Cola Valued Youth Program; **p. 326:** Copyright © Todd Hampton Lillard; **p. 329:** Courtesy of Joe Campione, University of Berkeley, School of Education.; **p. 331:** This screen shot is from a second-generation CSILE product, Knowledge Forum®. The authors of this work are Marlene Scardamalia and Carl Bereiter, directors of the CSILE research and development team at OISE/University of Toronto. The publisher is Learning in Motion (Marge Cappo, President).; **p. 332:** Courtesy of Compton-Drew Investigative Learning Center Middle School, St. Louis, MO; **p. 345:** Copyright © Michael A. Schwarz Photography, Inc.; **p. 346:** Courtesy of The Middle Grades Life Science Project, Program in Human Biology, Stanford University

CHAPTER 10

Opener: Copyright © David Young-Wolff/Tony Stone Images; **p. 360:** Copyright © Robert Isaacs/Photo Researchers; **p. 367:** Copyright © Anna Palma; **10.8:** Carmen Sandiego ™ Copyright © 1998, Broderbund Software, Inc. All rights reserved. Used with permission; **10.9:** Copyright © ThinkerTools; **10.10:** Screen shot from *World Book Millennium 2000.* Copyright © 1999 World Book, Inc. by permission of the publisher; **10.11:** Photo by The McGraw-Hill Companies, Inc./Bob Coyle, photographer

Subject Index